KU-770-916

HOME
MANAGEMENT

HOME MANAGEMENT

EDITED BY

Alison Barnes

Volume One

GEORGE NEWNES LIMITED

15–17 LONG ACRE, LONDON, W.C.2

c. 1961

PRINTED AND BOUND IN ENGLAND BY
HAZELL WATSON AND VINEY LTD
AYLESBURY AND SLOUGH

FOREWORD

Home is the most important place in the world. It may be a bachelor bed-sitting-room, a rather poky little flat, a part of someone else's house, an inconvenient cottage or a rambling barn of a place. Whatever it is, making it into a home brings its own unique brand of personal satisfaction.

A good home is a well-organised one and produces happy, well-balanced, tolerant human beings, able to give and take. It is in the badly managed homes that you find constant quarrelling, strain, distrust, emotional tension and spoilt, undisciplined children destined, if their parents only realised it, for untold unhappiness when they get out into a world where they can no longer have all their own way. For a child's earliest experience of adapting itself to others—and so into the pattern of a civilised community—begins in the home. Without the right home atmosphere, no child can ever really learn the true art of living.

Personal happiness and national welfare therefore depend very largely upon sound home management, which is the joint responsibility of all who live in the home.

Here let me add a word of warning: the house that runs as smoothly as well-oiled machinery (and just as soullessly) must never be confused with the real home that has a warm, friendly atmosphere because it is built on a sure foundation of affection and understanding.

On the other hand, a great deal of specialised knowledge and expert guidance are needed to help put these ideals into practice. That is why Newnes' Home Management came into existence—as the first and only practical guide to this vast new modern subject that embraces everything from the old "domestic science" to psychology, from the development of individual self-expression to the treatment of a feverish cold. . . .

When in doubt about some new domestic wonder, see what Home Management has to say about it. How, for instance, does one take the fullest advantage of all the exciting synthetic fabrics and materials, the cleverly packed foods from all over the world, press-button tins of paint, double-duty furniture and "build-it-yourself" kits? Which of the multitude of labour-saving devices *really* make life easier for the housewife and don't require complicated installation or maintenance? Our experts have weighed the pros and cons of such new methods and appliances, and so can give unbiased opinions.

You can't cook at all? Our basic cookery section really does tell you how to boil an egg, cook a potato and make good tea and coffee. You can go on from there to more exotic dishes.

For the best home-maker is always ready to try something new, ever anxious to master a new skill. To all those with this spirit and particularly those happy couples whose marriage is a true partnership in adventurous home-making, this book is dedicated.

Alison Barnes –

CONTENTS

Volume One

CONTENTS

CONTENTS

xi

CONTENTS

COLOUR ILLUSTRATIONS

Volume One

COLOUR ILLUSTRATIONS

VOLUME ONE

ACKNOWLEDGMENTS

We acknowledge with gratitude the kind co-operation of the Editor of "The Houseworker," the journal of the National Institute of Houseworkers, for permission to publish the chapters on "Food Storage without a Refrigerator," "Equipping a Kitchen," "Take Care of Your Household Equipment," "Household Pests," "Making and Mending" and "The Linen Cupboard."

The IMPORTANCE – and PLEASURE of FOOD

Showing how man has turned a necessity of life into an enjoyable social custom—with a glimpse into the future of our eating habits

Quite apart from the nutrition value of our food, the vitamins and calories, it is a human—and very pleasant—instinct to eat because we enjoy it. Primitive man had to hunt to feed his family—and much of what he found good is still enjoyed today, though more easily obtained

WHY do we eat? First of all, because it is a fundamental necessity, as instinctive as sleeping and moving; secondly, because it has gradually become an integral part of our social life; thirdly, and most human of all, because we like it.

Talking of food under these three divisions, it becomes an absorbing subject in theory, an apéritif perhaps before the mental and physical digestion becomes involved in practical cookery.

WE EAT TO LIVE

Ever since our earliest ancestors trapped wild animals for family meals, human beings have had the same instinct to supply themselves with food. The method of supply and the raw materials have altered and increased, through inventiveness and experiment kept needle-keen by the urge to survive. We have to thank our forefathers for trying out much of what we eat today —meat, fish, roots, fruits, cereals. What they then discovered to be edible has not changed except in kind: where they ate bison steaks long ago, we now eat cuts from the domesticated ox, and enjoy much more varied cereals, fruits, fish and so on. But without the gastronomic instincts of early man we should not exist today, as

we do, with a fabulous history of food development to account for our own physical development and progress.

Again, we have only improved on and expanded our forebears' methods of preparing food for eating. It was in the prehistoric days that they stumbled on the means of making fire by rubbing flints together. The potentialities of fire were quickly applied to raw foodstuffs. Cooked meats and bread-like cakes resulted, and probably the first step was taken then towards the present method of cooking by broiling—that is, in front of or over an open fire. And it is to the men and women of the Bronze Age that we owe the benefits of agriculture, for in that pre-Christian era they herded flocks and started wheat growing.

It is hard for us, who get what we want so easily, to realise the deep satisfaction that must have been felt by early man in

Fishing during the Stone Age was a strenuous and often dangerous business—but the methods were not so different from those used today

Photo's: "Picture Post".

continually raising his standard of food production, by his own efforts and without the aid of science or machinery. It is easier to imagine how our ancestors' culinary efforts must have been stimulated by the first coming of raw foods, spices and flavourings from other countries. As trade routes grew, so did appetites and variety in food.

FOOD AS A "SOCIAL GESTURE"

Eating as a social gesture is practically as fundamental as eating to keep alive. From very early times, hospitality has been built on the offering of victuals and drink to the visitor. Simple enough in the earliest days, gradually becoming more elaborate as resources grew, social life and culture expanded and the demands of hospitality changed accordingly.

But from time immemorial, one custom has astonishingly prevailed, that of giving the visitor better than the family. Whatever the underlying motive, and it would be difficult to pin it down, it would seem to be a prime—and excellent — excuse for continued experiment with different foods and combinations of foods, to produce new recipes and more varied menus.

It would take much delightful browsing through many books to decide definitely in which period of history the greatest culinary heights were scaled: perhaps in England when she was so closely allied to France, or when Henry VIII set such a lavish standard of entertainment, in the time of the Georges or the Victorian era. It is safe to say that we today have gained much from them all, and that the coming and going of more and more visitors, from monarchs and statesmen down, has kept the standard of entertainment and menu-planning ever stimulated.

It is particularly amusing to take a look at the comparatively recent Victorian entertaining and to find that in the 1890s a chicken cost around 2s., a whole salmon 15s. and the most expensive asparagus ran away with about 4s. 6d. for a generous bunch. Large families were usual, a dinner

The ancient Egyptians were good farmers and agriculturalists very early in their history—here the grain is seen being poured from baskets on to the threshing floor, where it was trodden out by cattle

party for eighteen was no trouble and the provision was lavish. Almost everything eatable put in an appearance: soups, a choice of fish, several entreés, a choice of meats, followed by two or three sweets, cheese and dessert, formed the kind of menu offered to Victorian dinner guests in the capacious dining rooms of well-to-do middle-class homes. And bearing out the point that down the years greater effort was always made for the guest, the same Victorian family would sit down themselves to a simple enough meal, probably soup, a choice of two meats and a sweet.

Now look to our own time. The custom of making rather more effort for guests still continues, but a certain change has come about. We are much better able now to offer the unexpected guest what we are having ourselves. It is not so long ago that the housewife, taken unawares, would go cold inside at the thought of "family-only" provisions in the larder, and a dropper-in in the sitting room. She would try either to "rig" the meal, becoming hot, harassed and fatally apologetic in the process or, when made of sterner stuff, would sit her visitor out. But today, with more elastic larders, and such things as television meals, impromptu picnics because a couple of cars are handy to go off at a moment's notice, and suchlike, taking potluck is hospitality given and received with no loss of social prestige.

we now know that certain quantities of protein, fats and carbohydrates, together with complementary quantities of mineral salts and water, are essential to keep us in good health.

About 1906 to 1912, English and German scientists added a further development; working on the pure protein, carbohydrate and fat requirements of animals for energy, new growth and replacement of waste tissue, they came to the conclusion that something more was necessary. "Ac-

By the sixteenth century entertaining had become a well-established social custom—though table manners as we know them were conspicuous by their absence from the banquets of the day

NEW LIGHT ON FOOD

Towards the end of the last century, and at the beginning of the present one, something akin to a revolution took place. The science of chemistry suddenly became involved in food and eating habits. Answers began to emerge to some of the many "whys?" involved in the choice and preparation of food. The relation between various foodstuffs and the growth and general development of those who ate them was investigated; so was the effect of heat on the cook's raw materials. From all this

cessory factors" known as Fat-soluble A and Water-soluble B resulted—what we now know as vitamins A and B. By 1915 three of these essential growth factors had been discovered; more than fifteen have been found since.

It would be interesting to witness the reactions of our forebears to the sciences of chemistry, dietetics and cookery, and the results which have come about through their own provisioning of the land in order to live.

3

In the 1890s hospitality was lavish; a dinner party like this for eighteen or twenty people was considered no trouble, and almost everything eatable appeared on the laden table

Scientific Eating

Since it became established scientifically and accepted publicly that a balanced diet was the eating standard to aim at for full health and vigour, we have run the gauntlet of diet worship, even to eating grass! Experts have written books galore, all countries have contributed dietetic formulæ, until the last war put us all on rations. But thanks to the findings of chemists, the co-operation of dietitians and enlightened cooks, we were fed to the best dietetic standard possible under the circumstances. Eating scientifically has become almost as instinctive to us, as just plain eating was instinctive to long-ago races.

A survey of food consumption was prepared in 1953 which showed that the average diet of families in Great Britain was then adequate over the year. It is interesting to note, from the same survey, however, that the vitamin C content of urban family diet remained fairly constant all the year, but that of rural families (who grow fruit and vegetables) was above the urban

average in summer and below it the rest of the year.

Income also is an influencing factor, vitamin intake dropping steadily between the highest and lowest income groups. Vitamin C showed the greatest variation, between 23 per cent. above the average figure in the highest income group, to 17 per cent. below in the lowest group.

Even so, nutritional standards all round have steadily improved since the war, through better living conditions, nutritional education, compulsory fortification of margarine, flour and bread, school meals and milk. Before the war, it was only the three highest income groups that showed an adequate daily supply of vitamins A and C.

Those Calories

To the layman, calories have proved an almost indigestible part of our more sensible modern eating habits; perhaps because there are so many figures involved, and the thought of paper and pencil calculations before preparing a meal is discouraging. However, this is not really neces-

4

sary. Calories are simply the name for the units of heat by which the energy value of our food is measured. Another comforting thought, going back to the instinctive aspect of eating again, is that we eat what we need under normal circumstances, and so make up the calories without paper and pencil.

The Oslo Meal

If we do not entirely replace them, hunger gives a warning that we need some more. But to be well and healthy, it is wise not to slack up on sensible, balanced eating, and Norway has a contribution to make here.

In Norway the one cooked meal of the

Different lands—different customs. When they visited Tonga, the Queen and the Duke of Edinburgh were entertained to a typical feast, like that shown below, with the food laid on stretchers and eaten with the fingers

day is taken between 3 and 5 p.m. Many children used to go to school without an adequate breakfast, and had either a few sandwiches or a hot school meal, followed shortly after by the hot meal at home; they had little else during the rest of the day. To counteract the effects of such ill-spaced eating, it was arranged in 1925 for schools to open earlier, and the Oslo Breakfast was devised to give the children a good meal before school. It consisted of measured quantities of milk, wholewheat bread, butter or margarine, cheese, one scraped raw carrot or half an orange, apple or banana.

In England this has been modified and served in place of a hot school meal, made up as follows: (a) milk and cheese; (b) herring or sardine; (c) wholemeal biscuit or brown bread with (d) butter or vitaminised margarine; (e) an orange and a carrot.

Such a meal provides animal protein, fats, minerals and vitamins A, B, C and D, "protective factors" which are sometimes missing from the child's diet.

This is a helpful and simple dietetic plan, and useful to keep in mind as a basis for one good, balanced meal.

Planning Balanced Meals

To repeat, normally we eat what we need and some more if we get hungry. Planning balanced meals can be practically, if not quite, as simple as this. Two things are important: (a) to keep in mind a workable list of foods under the three headings—proteins, carbohydrates and fats and their vitamin content, and (b) to plan as varied meals as possible with these components, well-cooked and attractive to the eye. Monotony reduces appetite, and food that is varied but served up anyhow and not properly cooked also has a bad effect on the appetite. There is plenty to come in the following chapters to promote good cookery and varied menus. Here let us take a brief look at the nutritional needs of various stages of growth and classes of person.

Young children are likely to lack iron and vitamins A, C and D, if milk is depended upon too much as a complete food. Orange juice (vitamin C), cod-liver oil (vitamins A and D), and sieved greens and eggs (iron) are necessary additions.

Schoolchildren in normal health usually have big appetites, not through greed, but because they burn up more energy than adults and are also growing. They need particularly: protein, calcium and vitamins A, C and D. Cheese, meat, eggs, fruit and green vegetables provide them, with bread and cake made with fat, sugar, milk and eggs to give concentrated sources of calories. For in-between-meals hunger, milk should be encouraged.

Adolescents need more nourishment than most other groups; more calcium than adults, almost as much protein, more iron and the same amount of vitamin A. Mothers who can instil in their adolescent sons and daughters a workable eating plan for when they leave school and start work or further study, can help them to know the difference between full and indifferent adult health.

Adults need balanced meals at all times, the amount of food eaten daily depending on whether occupation is sedentary, moderately active, active or very active. Women in all these groups need less calories than men, except during pregnancy and breast-feeding. For example, an active woman needs 3,000 calories daily and the same amount during breast-feeding, where an active man needs 3,500 calories a day.

Those confined to bed. Their needs are in general reduced through lack of action. Eggs, fish, milk, dairy produce, fruit and vegetables (for protein, calcium and vitamins A and C) are more vital to them than rich sources of calories, such as bread and butter or fatty cooked foods.

Eating at Odd Times

It is still a popular belief that eating between meals is "bad for the digestion," "bad for the figure," etc. Another common theory is that exercise before breakfast is more beneficial to health than exercise at other times. According to nutritional experts, muscle action is at its

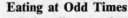

Now science has taken a hand in our diets; we know that all essentials are to be found in milk, cereals, cheese and fresh vegetables

lowest ebb before the first meal of the day. The best start to the day's work is therefore a cooked breakfast and time in which to eat it comfortably—and *then* your P.T.

The snack-between-meals habit is quite in order so long as it does not interfere with the total amount of nutrients that the individual needs each day. If, for instance, we overdo sweet-eating between meals and then have no appetite for the next meal, it means that we eat too much carbohydrate (in the sugar of the sweets), less vitamins and protein because we are disinclined for meat and vegetables. But the busy housewife who sits down to a cup of tea and a bun at 11 o'clock may simply be instinctively restoring energy by giving herself necessary calories.

Modern hostesses entertain on a more modest scale—but still providing "something special" for a guest. Usually it is not more than three courses and a party for six at most

WHAT OF THE FUTURE?

Two trends stand out at present; packeted and frozen foodstuffs.

It is obvious that in the future more and more food will come wrapped. This hygienic method is becoming universal. Cleaner-food campaigns agitate for more wrapping and protection generally, and it seems reasonable to suppose that these improvements will come.

The de-hydration of food is a further development with a future, a taste of which we had during the war. Publicity has already been given to a complete meal—soup, meat, vegetables and sweet—that could be packed in a matchbox before being transformed, very quickly, into an edible meal. Research is going forward, particularly into the nutritional value of this type of food.

Then there are ready-prepared cake mixes, pudding mixtures and prepared pastries, all of which need very little extra preparation before going into the oven or no cooking at all. The brains that have achieved them are not likely to stop there.

Deep freezing is another effective aid to simplified housekeeping. In country homes, particularly farms, the home freezer is gaining in popularity. All the good things of garden, orchard and dairy can be stored for a year if need be, as well as bread, fish, poultry, and so on. The urban housewife has two benefits from this rapidly developing form of refrigeration. She can buy deep-frozen delicacies as she needs them, for shops large and small are installing these freezing cabinets; secondly, she can buy the type of refrigerator with a freezing

7

compartment set lower in temperature than the main fridge, and in this keep a stock of frozen foods.

Our Shopping Habits

Here again we can look forward to changes for the better. Self-service shops are becoming complete shopping centres, personal needs and clothes as well as food, being displayed all on one floor. The housewife can take her basket-on-wheels (which may include a seat for the baby if need be) and buy a week's provisions, plus cigarettes and cosmetics if she wishes. And *everything* is wrapped.

It takes time and costs money for our food shopping methods to become entirely revolutionised. So the good housewife, in her own interest, should support with her custom the retailer who installs expensive air-conditioned chests for the efficient and hygienic display under glass of meat and fish. The retailing of meat in the U.K. has just come in for a number of long overdue improvements. In many shops it is now possible to choose a joint, which has been weighed and priced in advance, all nicely

packed in a cellophane bag. From Continental butchers in London and many of our big cities, it is possible to buy all the cuts of meat used by the French housewife and hitherto unavailable outside France.

Then there is America's most spectacular venture—the Cross-Country Centre—a community shopping centre *par excellence* in which the operative word is "automatic." It has vast car parks, cinemas, concerts and gardens above, with anything up to a mile of shops under cover. You can buy what you want from any shop and never carry a parcel. Each purchase is taken from a given point in each shop by conveyor belt to a collection point and from there to the purchaser's car.

There is everything to be said for quicker and better shopping methods. But it would be sad indeed if we lost the art of good home cooking by becoming too dependent on modern methods of preparing-a-meal-in-five-minutes. If food is to remain an interesting, absorbing and essential part of living, it will need the constant stimulation of experiment and original thought by individual cooks.

Shopping for food has undergone a radical change—we now buy nearly everything hygienically packed from the display shelves of the many self-service stores—and perhaps quite soon our purchases will be delivered to us by conveyor belt

ANYONE CAN BE A GOOD COOK

*The secret of success is chiefly attention
to detail—partly an adventurous spirit*

An ideal menu for a bride's first dinner party: Shrimp Cocktails followed by Baked Ham
with Pineapple, Brussels Sprouts, Chestnuts and Duchess Potatoes, Plum Meringue and Coffee

SOME people have naturally cool hands for pastry; a flair for making a sponge as light as a feather; the knack of turning out a perfect soufflé; or a way with sauces. So the idea arises that a good cook has some special faculty, like the born gardener's "green fingers" that make everything grow.

It is probably nothing more than that time-honoured definition of genius: "An infinite capacity for taking pains." And, since anyone can—if she will—take pains, it follows logically that everyone is *potentially* a good cook.

These simple rules will help you achieve your aim, whether you are a young bride or a busy mother with so many hungry mouths to feed that there is little time for experimenting.

1. Use a good recipe and follow it exactly, weighing or measuring the ingredients accurately. Even if you have made dozens of Yorkshire Puddings from memory, try making one by a new recipe just for once. The essence of good cooking is never to get set in your ways.

2. Be brave and original. Make the best of the wonderful variety of exciting and unusual foods now available. Perhaps you once enjoyed a Chinese meal at a restaurant or loved the food you had on a

9

Serve roast duck surrounded by orange slices and crisp lettuce leaves, and you will build a reputation as a hostess with ideas

A good cook never scorns the simple, cheap foods, but gives them a millionaire appearance, like these baked potatoes stuffed with cheese (below)

holiday in Spain? Well, then, try your hand at cooking the Chinese or the Spanish way. Never let anyone convince you that you have to be a professional chef to make choux pastry or ice a wedding cake. If you have the courage to try, you will almost certainly find what nonsense such warnings are.

3. Equip your kitchen with the basic necessities, add only the gadgets you are *sure* will really help you, as and when you can afford them, and do keep an open mind about new ideas and inventions. For instance, the quick mixing method for pastry and cakes, made possible by the introduction of the vegetable fat shortenings, has improved many people's cooking out of all recognition, particularly those who were apt to skimp on the creaming of cake mixtures and pastry mixing. Tomorrow's new idea may eliminate the weak spot in *your* cooking.

4. Do not scorn simple dishes or inexpensive ingredients. A really good cook can make the cheapest cuts look and taste delicious—and that must be your aim. Remember that the appearance of a dish is every bit as important as its vitamin content and its flavour, for it is the appeal to the eye that tempts the appetite.

The simplest garnish will transform an otherwise ordinary meal into a sumptuous repast; the way you present a dish can alter its whole value. What could be cheaper or easier to prepare for supper than potatoes baked in their jackets and stuffed with cheese? And what could be less inspiring to behold? But not if you do them this way:

Stuffed Potatoes with Eye Appeal

Split the skins of the nicely baked potatoes downwards from a central point to look like petals, scoop out the floury inside, mix it well with butter, plenty of grated cheese, salt, pepper and a little milk or cream, then put it back inside the potato shells and heat through. Garnish with sprigs of parsley and serve with whole un-cooked tomatoes, for a colourful and tasty meal.

When you dish up roast duck, surround it on the dish with slices of fresh, peeled orange and lettuce leaves; the contrast in flavour as well as colour is memorable, the kind of little detail that marks you out as a hostess of ideas.

Mince Tart en Surprise

Another little trick that never fails is to serve a well-known and popular dish with a surprise trimming. Mince Tart en Surprise is a good example. You make a flat mince tart, flavouring the mincemeat with rum or brandy, if possible. Leave it to cool and, just before serving, spoon a family brick of vanilla ice cream over the mincemeat. Make the meringue by whisk-ing 2 egg-whites until very stiff, then folding in 3 oz. castor sugar with a metal spoon. Pipe or spoon the meringue over the flan, making sure that the ice cream is entirely covered. " Flash" cook in a very hot oven for 2 to 3 minutes only, until the meringue is just tinged with golden brown. You can vary this with an apple or banana filling, but the mincemeat is particularly good.

5. Do not attempt too much in the early stages of training to be a good cook. If you do, you will only get flustered and wor-ried and things will go unexpectedly wrong.

It is a mistake to experiment with a lot of fancy, complicated dishes when entertain-ing. Always try them out on the family circle first, to make sure. The ideal meal for a bride entertaining her first guests would be a cold first course which can be put on the table in advance, a main course that can be dished up and kept hot ready to be brought to table without fuss, and a simple sweet. Here is a suggested menu:

Lobster Cocktails (see Hors d'œuvres and Appetisers)
Baked Ham with Pineapple (see Cookery in the United States)
Sprouts and Chestnuts (see Vegetables in the New England Manner)
Duchess Potatoes (see Vegetables)
Plum Meringue

For the **Plum Meringue,** put a large can of red plums, or 1½ lb. fresh South African plums, lightly stewed in a little water and 2 dessertspoonfuls sugar, into a fireproof glass dish. Bring ½ pint of plum juice to the boil. Mix 2 teaspoonfuls cornflour to a smooth paste with juice or water, blend with the heated juice, return to the pan and stir until it clears and thickens slightly. Pour over plums and cool. Beat 2 egg-whites until stiff, fold in 2 dessertspoonfuls castor sugar, pile meringue on top of cooled fruit, bake in a slow oven for 20 to 30 minutes until meringue is slightly browned.

There is nothing against the mere male learning to be a good cook too—and he need not look as scared as Danny Kaye

One sure way to cookery success is to make an old and tried favourite with a surprise trimming. This is Mince Tart en Surprise, with an ice cream and meringue top

ENTERTAINING

If you have no room for a formal sit-down dinner party, you can still invite your friends to a wine and cheese evening, a fork luncheon or just for tea

MODERN entertaining has become so adaptable that it can be made to fit any household or flatlet.

A golden rule for all hostesses should be: "The less help available, the simpler the meal." A worried, preoccupied hostess only communicates her feelings to her guests. In fact, it is far better to give your guests bread and cheese and beer or wine, plus your whole attention, than an elaborate meal which has obviously worried you to death in its planning.

The sort of entertaining which gives the hostess most work is, of course, the formal luncheon or dinner party. If the housewife has to prepare everything herself, or with very little help, it is best to choose dishes that can be cooked, as far as possible, beforehand. If there is a refrigerator, dishes made the day before can be kept fresh and sweet.

An electric hot plate in the dining room is very useful when one is single-handed. The first course can be put on the table before the guests come into the room, the second on the hot plate. Then, if the sweet is a cold one, the hostess need only put each course as it is finished on a trolley, which can be wheeled away when the meal is over.

Earthenware and fireproof dishes, in which the food can be served as well as cooked, save washing up and look very attractive.

Aim at simplicity in table decorations: shining glass, well-polished silver and a bowl of flowers (low enough to allow the guests to see each other's faces) are all that is required.

SUGGESTED MENUS FOR A FORMAL LUNCHEON OR DINNER PARTY

(A few recipes marked with an * are given after these menus, the others will be found in their respective chapters.)

Hors d'œuvres
Grilled steak maître d'hôtel
Chip potatoes and cauliflower
Fruit flan and cream
Cheese and biscuits
Coffee

Grapefruit
Blanquette of veal and mushrooms or
Fish à la Meunière*
Mashed potatoes and green peas
Pineapple fritters or fresh asparagus
Cheese and biscuits
Coffee

Eggs en cocotte with asparagus tips
(or chopped mushrooms or green peas)
Cutlets en casserole with carrots
Mashed potatoes and peas, beans, or
Brussels sprouts
Strawberries or raspberries (frozen, if out
of season) with cream
Cheese and biscuits
Coffee

Grapefruit or foie gras
Beef en daube with new potatoes, peas and
young carrots or baby marrows
Green salad
Lemon meringue pie
Cheese
Coffee

(*Hot weather meal*)
Melon or iced consommé
Sole Véronique with new potatoes and
French beans
Vanilla ice cream with hot chocolate sauce
Cheese
Coffee

Taramasalata (see Cookery in Greece) or
smoked cod's roe
Roast duck, roast potatoes, green peas
and apple sauce
Orange salad
Fresh pineapple and cream
Cheese
Coffee

12

An ideal cold buffet supper for Boxing Day. On the hot-plate is a bowl of creamy soup. Foods are: savoury biscuits topped with gherkin slices; French bread with slices of cheese; a fruit flan; sausage rolls; cheese straws; a fruit cup; pears with ice cream. Note the olives, cherries and cocktail sausages speared on sticks round the candles

Hors d'œuvres
Pheasant, partridge or grouse
(according to season)
Chip potatoes and salad
Pear or peach melba
Coffee

Melon
Tournedos of beef
Mashed potatoes and green peas
Vanilla soufflé
Coffee

Foie gras
(served with very thin, crisp, hot toast and
fresh butter)
Chicken Maryland*
Chip potatoes and cauliflower
Melon (or pineapple) en surprise*
Coffee

Do not forget to provide some form of packet crispbread, as well as ordinary bread, and have barley water, lemonade, orange squash or cider for those who do not drink wine.

Remember, too, that not only is fresh fruit appreciated inwardly; it is also a delight to the eye.

Asparagus, if in season, should be served after the poultry or meat course.

An excellent extra course to take its place can be made by mixing together almost any kind of fresh vegetables in a white sauce (such as tiny carrots, green peas and beans).

Informal Luncheons and Dinners

Informal meals can be as long or as short as you like, and can include the many delicious dishes which are not suitable for more formal occasions, such as steak and kidney pie, joints, or poultry; and for the sweet course the more substantial type of pudding. Serving and setting should be carefully thought out. Even the most informal meal should look attractive.

Recipes

Fish à la Meunière (suitable for small soles, whiting or trout or larger fish in slices)

Melt enough clarified butter in an earthenware dish (in which the fish can be served) to half cover the fish. Make small cuts in each side of the fish, dip into seasoned flour and brown well on one side before turning it over on to the other. Just before serving, add a very little finely chopped parsley and a squeeze of lemon juice.

A cantaloup melon is equally good served in this way. Pineapple or melon-flavoured ice cream can be used instead of ordinary cream.

BUFFET MEALS AND FORK LUNCHES

The "stand up and help yourself" meal is a popular form of modern entertaining particularly suitable for small premises. A wide variety of different foods should be attractively dis-

If you serve Stilton at the end of a meal, treat it with reverence—wrap it in a clean table napkin and accompany it with port and walnuts

For informal entertaining, there is nothing better than a cheese and beer or wine party. Beer and Cheddar are natural soul-mates—and throw in plenty of crusty bread and pickled onions for good measure

Chicken Maryland

Cut a young bird into joints, brush each piece over with melted butter, season, and roll in flour and breadcrumbs. Put into a well-buttered dish and bake in the oven for about $\frac{1}{2}$ hour, basting frequently with butter. Serve with a sauce made from the giblets. Fried bananas go excellently with this dish.

Pineapple (or Melon) en Surprise

Take a ripe pineapple, cut a slice off the bottom so that it stands firmly on a dish, then cut off the head low enough to enable the contents to be removed with a sharp knife. Put aside the head with the leaves intact.

Cut out the inside (keeping the juice carefully), chop it into neat pieces and mix with it any fresh fruit in season, as you would do for a fruit salad. Add the juice and put the mixture back into the pineapple. Just before serving, add plenty of fresh cream. Replace the top.

played on a long, narrow buffet table, with piles of clean plates and spoons and forks (no other cutlery should be necessary if the right foods are chosen) at intervals. The guests are then invited to help themselves. A big tureen of steaming soup, a bowl of hot risotto or a flat dish full of sizzling sausages on a hot-plate makes a pleasant change from an entirely cold buffet.

COCKTAIL AND SHERRY PARTIES

This is one of the easiest ways of entertaining people to whom one owes hospitality, because a large number of close friends and casual acquaintances can be asked together. Indeed, one of the first rules for a successful cocktail or sherry party seems to be that it should be as crowded as possible.

Though sherry is more popular and less extravagant than cocktails, the best plan is to provide both, plus lemonade, barley water, grapefruit, pineapple or tomato juice or iced coffee for those who prefer soft drinks.

Six o'clock is the usual time for such a party, and as many of your guests, if they happen to be going on to a theatre or cinema afterwards, will cut out dinner, provide plenty of "eats." (See chapter on Party Snacks and Sandwiches.)

The Drinks

Have a good supply of cocktails ready mixed in a large jug before your guests arrive. For an average party of twenty, a bottle of dry sherry together with one of a sweeter type will be enough, with a bottle of gin and one each of French and Italian vermouth for the cocktails. Recipes for making these will be found in the chapter on Mixed Drinks.

Sweet cocktails are generally served with a maraschino cherry on a stick in each glass, dry ones with green olives.

If the party is a very large one, it is some-times possible to arrange with your wine merchant that any unopened bottles of spirits can be returned.

INVITATION FOR TEA AND CARDS

Many women find that a Bridge or Canasta tea is an easy and pleasant way of entertaining their women friends. Start your party about three o'clock, play for an hour, then have tea, and there will probably be time for another hour's play afterwards.

Tea is a simple affair, but make it look as attractive as you possibly can. Have tiny hot scones in the winter and small, dainty sandwiches all the year round. There are many attractive fancy cutters to be bought which add very much to the appearance of sandwiches. Bridge rolls are easily filled and easy to handle. Choose small cakes, and provide China as well as Indian tea, with slices of lemon for those who prefer it to milk with China tea. Dishes of sweets or chocolates may be placed so that they can easily be reached during play, and there should be plenty of cigarettes and ashtrays.

Cocktails or sherry are often served just before the party breaks up.

Serve asparagus as a separate course, just after the meat or poultry, accompanied by melted butter, which is nicest if you keep it really hot over a spirit lamp or night-light hot-plate

15

HORS D'ŒUVRES AND APPETISERS

*Make your savoury delicacies interesting, dainty and good
to eat—or serve piquant fruit juice to start the meal*

HORS D'ŒUVRES—originally side dishes "outside the works" (so to say) of a formal dinner—have long been established as appetisers at the beginning of a meal, often taking the place of the soup course.

Their purpose is to whet the appetite, not to allay it; they should therefore be piquant in flavour and attractively served in small portions. All kinds of fish, meat, vegetables and fruit, well seasoned and dressed, go to the making of these savoury delicacies, generally served cold. Imagination has plenty of scope in the combination of ingredients and their decoration with colourful morsels. Canapés—choice bits mounted on bread sliced and cut into small squares or circles the size of a penny and then toasted or fried—are popular.

Fruit or fruit juices fairly tart in flavour are frequently served at the beginning of a meal in place of a variety of hors d'œuvres. Suggestions for these, rather a class apart, are given first.

FRUIT APPETISERS

Avocado Pear.—This is served raw, unskinned, cut in half lengthwise, the seeds removed and with a vinaigrette sauce sprinkled into the hollow. It looks its best on a cool lettuce leaf, but the avocado pear should not be put into a refrigerator.

Grapefruit.—This is often served halved in its skin. Cut the grapefruit in half and remove the seeds. Using a sharp knife, separate each section from its membrane, or remove the membrane between the sections altogether. Cut round and under the sections to detach them from the skin. Cut out the core. Sprinkle with sugar and chill before serving in grapefruit glasses or on plates. Decorate with a glacé cherry at the centre.

Grapefruit and Orange.—Mix equal quantities of grapefruit and orange pulp cut into small pieces. Sprinkle with lemon juice and sugar. Chill and serve in grapefruit glasses.

Melon (Cantaloup).—Allow a good thick segment for each person. Take out the seeds carefully, chill and serve with or without sugar, or with ground ginger.

Melon (Honeydew).—Serve in sections 2 or 3 in. wide, prepared as for Cantaloup.

Melon (Water).—Cut the pulp into small balls. Sprinkle with lemon juice and sugar; chill and serve in glasses, decorated with small sprigs of fresh mint.

Orange Juice (Iced).—Strain the juice and serve in small glasses set in cracked ice on plates.

Orange and Mint.—Choose small and preferably sour oranges. Remove the skin from the sections (using scissors) and chill. Serve in glasses, sprinkled liberally with lemon juice, icing sugar and finely chopped mint.

Pineapple and Strawberries. — Mix halved strawberries with an equal amount of diced pineapple in glasses; pour over a mixture of one-third lemon juice to two-thirds orange juice, sweetened.

Strawberry and Cherry Cocktail.—Combine strawberry juice with an equal quantity of icing sugar, sharpened to taste with lemon juice, and pour over stoned cherries and some chopped almonds. Serve very cold in cocktail glasses.

Tomato Juice Cocktail.—Mix together ½ pint of tomato juice, 1 tablespoonful each of lemon juice and vinegar, 2 teaspoonfuls of sugar, 1 teaspoonful of grated onion, ½ teaspoonful of Worcester sauce, a pinch of celery salt and a piece of bay leaf. Let it stand for a while, then strain through muslin, chill, and serve in small glasses.

HORS D'ŒUVRES VARIETIES

Fish

Anchovies.—Wash to remove the brine in which they have been preserved. Fillet,

16

Photo : Canned Foods Advisory Bureau

APPETISERS : **1. Rounds of beetroot on luncheon meat, carrot and luncheon meat on mashed pilchard. 2. Peas and an anchovy on mashed herring and onion, paprika and meat on scrambled egg. 3. Sieved hard-boiled egg on pilchard with beet. 4. Tomato and luncheon meat rounds; asparagus on cream cheese and onion.**

THREE-COURSE DINNER COOKED IN A PRESSURE COOKER

Tomato Soup, followed by Braised Pigeons with cauliflower and potatoes, with Steamed Canary Puddings as a sweet—all cooked quickly and well in a Presto 508B Pressure Cooker.

First prepare and cook the soup—pressure cooking time 3 minutes at 15 lb. pressure.

Then rinse cooker. Pre-heat base, add fat and brown pigeons well on all sides. Add water and pressure-cook birds for 9 minutes at 15 lb. pressure. Cool cooker and place cooking rack over birds. Add cauliflower and potatoes (halved lengthwise so that they take same time as cauliflower) in separators and cook for 6 minutes. Cool cooker. Dish up pigeons and vegetables and garnish as required.

Place 1 pint boiling water in cooker and put individual dariole moulds two-thirds full of sponge mixture on rack in cooker. Steam gently for 10 minutes, then cook at 15 lb. pressure for 10 minutes— while eating the first two courses. Let cooker cool and serve.

For full details and recipes, see chapter on Pressure Cooking, page 272.

SIMPLE BUT APPETISING—above, minced meat in a pastry flan case; below, fried lamb cutlets attractively served in a ring of creamed potatoes with green peas has eye appeal

Photo: Canned Foods Advisory Bureau

IN THE PARTY SPIRIT

It is a great art—and the secret of success as a hostess—to be able to produce at short notice a meal that looks as if it had taken hours of painstaking preparation and which positively invites the guests to stay and enjoy it. Imagination is the essential factor. Here is a tasty meal most attractively served, yet made from the supplies in any well-stocked store cupboard. The recipes for Cold Meat Mould, seen above garnished with a fresh salad, and Forgotten Dessert are to be found in the chapter on Emergency Meals, which begins on page 232

and arrange the fillets attractively, adding a little oil, alone or on lettuce. Garnish with chopped parsley, capers, hard-boiled egg. The fillets, which can be bought already prepared, are also a useful garnish for other dishes.

Anchovy Butter (see also French Cookery).—Pound six or seven anchovies with ¼ lb. of butter; season and put through a sieve. Serve very cold on small biscuits or rounds of prepared bread.

Anchovy Canapés.—Use anchovy butter, or pounded anchovies, or anchovy paste bought already prepared. Season with lemon juice and pile on the prepared bread. Decorate with hard-boiled egg slices.

Caviare.—This is the epicure's dish. Caviare, or salted sturgeon's roe, should be kept very cold. Serve it from the pot in which it is bought—placed on a folded napkin with shavings of ice—with Cayenne and quarters of lemon; or in halved hard-boiled eggs from which the yolks have been removed.

Caviare Canapés.—Cover one-half of the prepared pieces of bread with the caviare, topped by a ring of hard-boiled egg-white, and cover the remainder with minced raw onion, topped by a little sieved hard-boiled egg-yolk.

Fish Mayonnaise. — Arrange cooked white fish or salmon, flaked or cut into short lengths, on lettuce. Coat with mayonnaise and decorate with fillets of anchovy, sliced hard-boiled eggs, cold sliced potatoes, capers, parsley, etc.

Herrings (Salt).—Remove the excess salt by soaking in cold water for several hours. Fillet, and let the fillets, cut into narrow diagonal strips, stand for about 6 hours in vinegar with pepper and sliced onion.

Lobster in Aspic.—Set the lobster pieces in aspic with slices of hard-boiled egg, cooked peas, etc., using small moulds. Turn out when set and serve on lettuce, decorated with parsley.

Lobster or Crab Canapés. — Pile chopped cooked fish, seasoned with lemon juice and Worcester sauce, on small rounds of prepared bread or biscuits, and decorate with pieces of pickled beetroot and olives; or mix with cream, season with salt and Cayenne, and decorate with parsley.

Oysters.—These are served alone, with no other hors d'œuvres dishes offered.

Serve on the half-shell, allowing five or six oysters to each person, with a quarter-lemon and thin brown bread and butter.

Oyster Cocktail.—Put four or five oysters into each glass and pour over a dressing prepared (for six persons) from 3 tablespoonfuls tomato ketchup, 4 tablespoonfuls lemon juice, 2 tablespoonfuls vinegar, 2 teaspoonfuls horseradish, 1 teaspoonful salt and ¼ teaspoonful tabasco sauce.

Prawns or Shrimps.—Arrange round the edge of a wineglass containing crushed ice, or round half a cut lemon, cut side downwards, with their tails tucked underneath; or serve very cold, shelled, sprinkled with lemon juice, with brown bread and butter, or on a lettuce leaf coated with mayonnaise.

Prawn Canapés.—Pound shelled prawns in a mortar with lemon juice, oil and small chilli peppers, and pile on small rounds of prepared bread.

Prawn or Lobster Cocktail.—Place shredded lettuce in glasses and fill up with chopped or sliced prawns or lobster. Cover with whisked mayonnaise sauce with

Prawn or Lobster Cocktail, with its sharp dressing, is served in individual glasses

Mixed hors d'œuvres looks attractive in a special dish with separate compartments for olives, tomato salad, anchovy eggs, vegetable salad and cod's roe

tomato ketchup and a little Worcester sauce added and top with lettuce leaf and whole prawn or piece of lobster.

Rollmops.—These pickled rolled fillets of herrings can be bought in Continental stores ready to serve.

Smoked Salmon.—Slice very thinly and serve with lemon, Cayenne pepper and thin brown bread and butter.

Sardines.—Serve whole, sprinkled with lemon juice and a little oil, and decorated with parsley; or remove skin and backbones, add lemon juice, mash with a fork and mount on small rounds of prepared bread; or mix with an equal quantity of butter, adding lemon juice and Cayenne.

Shrimps (Potted).—Buy prepared; or put picked shrimps into a pot with salt, pepper and nutmeg to taste; cook in moderate oven for 10 minutes, cool, then seal with softened butter on top. Serve in tiny individual jars with hot toast and lots of butter.

Tunny Fish.—Slice the fish thinly. Dress with oil and lemon juice or vinegar; decorate with chopped parsley and capers.

Meat Pastes, Sausages

Meat pastes can be served straight from the pot or in small chunks, eaten with bread or toast, or are used, with garnishes, to make *canapés* or small sandwiches. French, German, Belgian and Dutch specialities can be bought—the most noted (and expensive) being the Strasbourg *pâté de foie gras* (pure goose liver). The French *pâté maison*, generally a goose liver mixed with some pork, varies, according to the maker.

Calf's Liver Paste.—Slowly cook $\frac{1}{4}$ lb. of chopped calf's liver with an equal amount of diced fat bacon in an ounce of butter, adding finely chopped parsley, salt, pepper and a teaspoonful of mixed spice. Drain off the fat, pound in a mortar, add a teaspoonful of anchovy essence, and sieve. Press into small pots and let them stand in a cool oven for $\frac{1}{2}$ hour. Then pour melted butter over the tops of the pots.

Chicken Liver Paste.—Mash together to a paste $\frac{1}{4}$ lb. of cooked chicken livers and 2 oz. of finely chopped onion, fried in butter or chicken fat. Season with pepper, salt and mustard.

Pâté de foie gras Canapés.—Thin the paste with cream, add Cayenne pepper and salt; pile on rounds of prepared bread; garnish with parsley.

Sausages.—Liver sausage, cold pork sausage, salami and other boiled or smoked Continental sausages are useful. Remove skin, cut into very thin slices, arrange in rows on a dish, garnish with parsley, radishes, gherkins, olives, or make into small decorated sandwiches. Tiny cooked sausages can be served on their own.

Eggs

Hard-boiled eggs may be served alone, with a dressing, or stuffed, or in aspic, or as a decoration. When used whole or halved cut a small piece off the end so that the egg will stand.

Halved Eggs.—Mask with mayonnaise or chaudfroid sauce. Decorate with chopped parsley.

Chopped Eggs.—Chop or slice, mix with dressing, and decorate.

Anchovy Eggs.—Halve hard-boiled eggs. Take out the yolks and pound with anchovies or anchovy sauce, butter and seasoning. Fill the egg-whites with the mixture, using a warm knife, and decorate with chopped parsley, capers, pieces of egg, small pieces of tomato, or green or red peppers.

Egg and Onion.—Remove the yolks from hard-boiled eggs; mix with a little oil, vinegar and seasoning; then add the egg-white, chopped, and chopped spring onions. Serve piled in little mounds or as canapés, with garnishes.

Devilled Eggs.—Mash the yolks from halved hard-boiled eggs with butter, vinegar, mustard and seasoning, and refill the egg-whites. Or pound the yolks with butter, anchovy essence, Cayenne and salt.

Egg with Anchovies.—Arrange anchovy fillets on small lettuce leaves, place pieces of hard-boiled egg on top (or chopped white and sieved yolk), with finely chopped parsley and seasoning. Moisten with oil.

Egg and Devilled Ham Canapés.—Mince ham with gherkin, Cayenne, salt,

Some hors-d'œuvre suggestions attractively presented on modern pottery plates with wooden accessories—Fresh Haddock Mayonnaise, Parsley Tomatoes, Asparagus, and, above, Shrimps and Dressed Cucumber

anchovy essence; mix with chopped hard-boiled egg, and place on rounds of prepared bread.

Plovers' Eggs (when in season).—Hardboil and shell the eggs. Group in a nest of watercress or chopped lettuce, dressed with oil and vinegar.

Vegetables and Fruit

Asparagus Tips.—Cook (see Chapter on Vegetables) and serve with French dressing.

Beans.—Mix cooked butter beans with oil and vinegar dressing while still warm. Sprinkle with chopped parsley or gherkins. Combine cooked French beans with chopped apple and mix with salad dressing.

Beetroot.—Slices of cooked beetroot are particularly useful for decorations, cut into rings, stars and other fancy shapes.

Beetroot and Onion.—Soak thin slices of cooked beetroot and raw onion in dressing, then arrange on dish, the onion on top. Sprinkle with chopped mint.

Beetroot (Stuffed).—Cut thick slices into small rounds and scoop out the centre. Stuff with chopped celery, onion, grated Brussels sprouts, or fish, etc., moistened with salad dressing. Garnish with parsley.

Cauliflower.—Arrange cooked sprigs dressed with mayonnaise in a dish and decorate with anchovy fillets curled round them.

Celery.—Shred it into matchstick lengths or cut into slices and serve with salad dressing or mayonnaise.

Celery with Cheese.—Mix cream cheese with cream and mayonnaise. Pepper well, and add chopped celery.

Cucumber.—Slice very thinly, sprinkle with salt and leave to stand for a while. Drain and dress with vinegar, sugar and pepper, or salad dressing. Sprinkle with chopped parsley.

Gherkins and Salted Nuts.—An attractive platter can be made up with salted almonds or peanuts; gherkins (sweet or sour) and perhaps pickled peaches.

Olives (Black or Green).—Drain off the pickle and serve them plain (whole or stoned), stuffed, or as a garnish.

Olive Canapés (1).—Mix finely chopped olives, watercress, lettuce, parsley with paprika and mayonnaise, and pile on small rounds of brown bread and butter. Or mix the chopped olives with chopped nuts, apples, cream cheese and mayonnaise. Or

place small slices of garlic sausage on rounds of fried bread. Pile chopped olives on top.

Olive Canapés (2).—Use Spanish olives, which are the larger kind. Stone them and stuff with various mixtures, allowing the stuffing to show at the top, e.g. cream some butter and flavour it with anchovy essence to use as a filling, or pound together hard-boiled egg-yolk, butter, *foie gras* and seasoning. Spread some of the mixture on small rounds of fried bread, or place a beetroot or egg-white ring on the prepared bread, and stand the stuffed olives on top.

Olive and Anchovy Sandwiches.—Make tiny sandwiches filled with finely chopped olives mixed with an equal amount of anchovy paste and some butter.

Peppers (Green and Red).—Slice green and red peppers finely and serve in alternate layers on a crisp lettuce leaf with French dressing or mayonnaise.

Potato Salad.—Cook small potatoes in their skins and peel and slice while still warm. Add finely chopped onion, salt and pepper. Mix with mayonnaise. Sprinkle with chopped parsley or mint.

Radishes.—Cut off the roots and scrape around the top, but leave a leaf or two by which the radish can be held. Serve while fresh, standing in a very little water. Or make radish "flowers" for decorations by cutting petal shapes from the root end to just below the stalk and placing in water (the "petals" will open out in about 1 hour).

Tomatoes.—Plunge into boiling water, then into cold, to remove skin easily. Slice, and serve with French dressing or with alternate thin slices of dressed onion. Sprinkle with chopped parsley. Or alternate with slices of hard-boiled egg and dress with mayonnaise. Garnish with chopped parsley and paprika.

Tomatoes (Stuffed).—Cut out the centre and drain. Cut a small piece off the base so that the tomato will stand. Fill with dressed chopped vegetables, or fish, prawns, etc., pounded butter, lemon juice and seasoning.

Tomato and Green Pepper.—Skin and slice the tomatoes, add small strips of green pepper (raw) and chopped onion. Dress with oil, vinegar and seasoning, and garnish with chopped parsley.

Consommé en-
riched by Quaker
Soup Drops

SOUPS

*The first course sets the tone of a meal—choose consommé to
stimulate appetite, a thick soup to satisfy it*

STOCK is the basis of most soups and
many sauces. Stock-making is a very
simple process, with

Six Stock-Making Rules
(1) Always use a large, strong, clean sauce-
    pan with a close-fitting lid and prefer-
    ably small handles so that it can be put
    into the oven.
(2) Ingredients for stock must be fresh, but
    meat and bones may be used again for
    a second stock. Cut meat into small
    pieces, chop bones up small, remove
    all fat. Peel and wash vegetables and
    cut into pieces.
(3) Start with cold water to extract the
    flavour from meat and bones, bring
    slowly to the boil, skimming off scum
    as it forms, then simmer slowly with
    the lid on.
(4) Vegetables, since they require only
    about half as long to cook as meat,
    should be put in half-way through the
    total cooking time.
(5) Strain stock while hot through a sieve
    into a basin and leave to cool. Do not
    remove the fat from the top until you
    are ready to use the stock, because a
    layer of fat keeps out the air and so
    acts as a preservative. To remove fat,

loosen it round the edge of the basin
with a knife, and lift off.
(6) Stock is best made the day before you
    want to use it. It should not be kept
    for long, particularly in hot weather.
    If it contains vegetables, it must be
    boiled up daily. Water in which
    vegetables have been boiled may be
    added to stock, but *not* thickened
    gravy.

There are six kinds of stock:
(1) *Brown Stock,* made from the bones
    and meat of beef.
(2) *White Stock,* made from meat and
    bones of chicken, veal, rabbit or turkey,
    with vegetables and seasoning.
(3) *Clear Brown Stock for Clear Soup,*
    made from shin of beef, with or with-
    out a knuckle of veal.
(4) *Fish Stock.*
(5) *Vegetable Stock.*
(6) *Second Stock,* made by boiling up
    meat a second time.

Brown Stock
  This should be made, if possible, the day
before it is required. Allow a quart of cold
water and half a teaspoonful of salt to a
pound of beef bones (cooked or uncooked),

adding any scraps of meat available, with the fat carefully removed. Bring slowly to the boil, skimming often, and simmer very slowly, with the lid on, for 4–5 hours. Half-way through cooking time, add a few slices of carrot, turnip, onion and a bouquet garni consisting of sprigs of thyme, parsley, mace, marjoram and a bay leaf tied up in a muslin bag (dried herbs will do if fresh are not available). Allow to cool. Strain into a basin, removing fat before use.

White Stock

Allow a quart of cold water to a pound of knuckle of veal. Cut up meat and bones, cover with water, add a teaspoonful of salt and bring slowly to the boil. Skim often and simmer very slowly for 5 hours. Half-way through cooking time, add a slice each of turnip and onion, a small stick of celery and a bunch of mixed herbs, 3 or 4 peppercorns, a bay leaf and 3 or 4 cloves tied up in a muslin bag. Be sparing with the vegetables or the stock will not be a good colour. Strain through a hair sieve or fine cloth into a bowl. Stand in a cool place and remove fat when cold and stock is required for use.

Clear Brown Stock for Clear Soup

Allow a quart of cold water and a teaspoonful of salt to a pound of shin of beef (meat and bones together, or a mixture of beef and knuckle of veal). Break up bones, slice the meat thinly, removing fat. Put into pan with the water and salt and bring slowly to the boil. Simmer very gently, skimming regularly, for 3 hours. Then add one small carrot, one small onion and a stick of celery all cut up small, and a bouquet garni (as for Brown Stock). Simmer for a further 2 hours, then strain through a fine cloth or hair sieve.

Fish Stock

Fish stock, unlike other kinds of stock, should be used the day it is made. Allow a quart of cold water and a teaspoonful of salt to a pound of white fish, bones and trimmings, which *must* be absolutely fresh. Mackerel, salmon, herring and other strongly flavoured fishes are not suitable. Wash fish well in cold salted water and bring to the boil. Skim thoroughly and simmer for 20 minutes, then add a sliced onion, a bay leaf, a stick of celery cut into pieces and a bouquet garni (see under Brown Stock). Cook very gently for $\frac{1}{2}$ hour, strain, and the stock is ready for immediate use.

Vegetable Stock

Allow a quart of cold water to a pound of mixed vegetables (turnips, onions, celery, parsley stalks, leeks, carrots, as available). Wash, peel and slice the vegetables and fry them lightly in 1 oz. melted fat for about 10 minutes, without browning them. Add water and bring to the boil, adding 2 or 3 peppercorns, 2 or 3 cloves and bouquet garni (see under Brown Stock). Simmer with the lid on for 2 or 3 hours, then strain.

NOTE: If vegetable stock is not available, the next best thing for soups or gravies is the water in which vegetables have been boiled.

Second Stock

This is made by returning to the stock-pot meat and/or bones already used for stock-making, together with the same quantity of cold water as previously used. Odd scraps of left-over meat (cooked or uncooked) may be added. Bring slowly to the boil and simmer for 3 or 4 hours, strain and use for sauces and purées.

Soup Quantities

Allow $\frac{1}{2}$ pint of soup per person; somewhat less (say 1–1$\frac{1}{2}$ gills) if soup forms one course of a substantial meal.

TO SERVE WITH SOUP

Squares of dry toast or fried dice of bread may be served with all vegetable and meat soups which have no individual garnish. Alternatives are Rice Krispies or Puffed Rice, warmed and crisped in the oven. A little sherry (about 2 tablespoonfuls to a quart) improves the flavour of most soups. Grated Parmesan cheese is another delicious addition.

Quaker Soup Drops

These make an excellent addition to clear soups. The following quantities make enough drops for 3 pints of soup.

1 oz. plain flour	1 teaspoonful melted
1 egg	butter or margarine
$\frac{1}{2}$ oz. One.Minute	1 teaspoonful minced
Quaker Oats	parsley
$\frac{1}{2}$ teaspoonful	$\frac{1}{4}$ teaspoonful baking
Worcester sauce	powder
$\frac{1}{4}$ gill tepid water	Salt and pepper

Sift flour into a basin with salt and pepper to taste. Hollow out centre and add melted fat and yolk of egg. Make into a batter with the water and stir in the Quaker Oats, parsley and Worcester sauce. Set aside for about ½ hour. Just before using, fold in the beaten egg-white and baking powder to make a mixture thin enough to drop easily from the spoon. Pour mixture gently through a coarse colander over the saucepan of gently simmering soup. Cover and simmer for about 5 minutes, then serve. (If less soup is used, reduce the quantity of drops accordingly.)

CLEAR SOUPS

Consommé (Clear Soup) (for 4–5)

1 *quart clear brown stock*	2 *tablespoonfuls sherry*
¼ *lb. gravy beef*	*Vegetables, according*
Whites and shells of 2 eggs	*to taste, to flavour Seasoning*

Remove all traces of fat from the stock, then, while still cold, pour on to the broken egg-shells, meat and vegetables cut up small, in a large saucepan. Add the beaten egg-whites and heat slowly, whisking till the scum rises. Then stop whisking and bring to the boil. When scum reaches nearly to the top of the pan, reduce heat and simmer gently for 30 minutes.

Strain through a clean cloth, season, add sherry and bring to required temperature for serving.

Consommé à la Jardinière

Make the consommé as above and garnish with tiny diced pieces of carrot and turnip, or green peas and little sprigs of cauliflower first cooked till tender.

Iced Consommé

Make consommé as above, chill, and serve in cups.

Consommé Julienne

Make consommé as above. Shred a carrot and a turnip into strips 1–1½ in. long and not more than ⅛ in. thick, cook in salted water till tender, then add to consommé just before serving.

Consommé au Riz

Make consommé as above. Boil 1 oz. rice in a pint of salted water till the grain feels soft when it is pressed between the finger and thumb. Strain and pour cold water over the rice. Add to consommé and bring to the boil before serving.

A good vegetable soup can be reinforced by the addition of extra rice and peas or beans boiled separately, flavoured with a little Cayenne pepper

Consommé Royal

This is a clear soup served with a garnish of savoury custard. For a quart of consommé, made as above, you need for the custard garnish:

1 *gill clear stock*   1 *egg*
          Seasoning

Beat the egg with the stock and season well. Put into a well-greased basin over a saucepan of slowly boiling water and steam gently until firm, but do *not* allow custard to boil. Cool, then turn out on to a plate and cut into fancy shapes. Put these in a hot tureen and pour the hot consommé over them. Serve promptly.

As a variation, ½ tablespoonful of grated Parmesan cheese may be added to the egg and stock before steaming.

Consommé Portugais

Make consommé as above. Garnish with a raw tomato diced small, 8 prunes stoned and cut into circles, and a leek cut into 1½ in. strips and cooked until tender in salted water.

Consommé Tomate

Add ½ lb. tomatoes cut into quarters when vegetables are added, then proceed as for consommé above.

Tomato Soup (Clear) (for 6–7)

2 *lb. ripe tomatoes*	1 *onion*
¼ *lb. lean beef*	1 *turnip*
3 *pints good stock*	6 *peppercorns*
Bouquet garni (see	*Whites and shells of*
Brown Stock)	*2 eggs*
Pepper, salt and sugar	½ *gill cold water*
to taste	

Cut the tomatoes, onion and turnip in quarters and put them into a saucepan with the bouquet garni, peppercorns and stock. Mince the beef finely and mix with it the cold water. Put this with the vegetables. Whip the egg-whites, crush the shells and add to the rest of the ingredients in the saucepan. Bring slowly to the boil, whisking all the time. Simmer for 30 minutes, strain through a cloth, then return to the saucepan, reheat, season and dissolve in it one lump of sugar. Serve with slightly whipped cream or grated Parmesan cheese, according to taste.

THICK VEGETABLE SOUPS

The basis of these soups is either Brown or White Stock. In the absence of stock, milk or the liquid in which vegetables have been boiled can be used as a substitute.

Artichoke Soup (for 6–7)

2 *lb. Jerusalem arti-*	1 *oz. butter*
chokes	1 *oz flour*
1 *onion*	½ *pint milk*
1 *stick celery*	*A few bacon rinds*
1 *quart white stock*	*Seasoning*
Lemon juice	¼ *pint cream*
	(optional)

Wash, peel and slice the vegetables, squeezing lemon juice over the artichokes to keep their colour. Melt the butter in a saucepan and toss the vegetables in it for about 5 minutes, with the lid on, shaking to prevent them from getting brown or sticking. Pour on cold stock, add bacon rinds cut small and seasoning, bring to the boil and simmer gently until all vegetables are soft and tender. Put through a hair sieve, return to the pan, adding the milk mixed to a smooth paste with the flour. Bring to the boil, stirring continually. Boil for 5 minutes.

A ¼ pint of cream, added after it has cooled slightly, lifts this soup right into the luxury class. Reheat, but do not allow to boil again.

Brown Vegetable Soup (for 4–5)

1 *small head of celery*	2 *oz. flour*
2 *small onions*	1 *quart brown or*
2 *small carrots*	*bone stock*
2 *small potatoes*	*Salt and pepper*
2 *small tomatoes*	*Bouquet garni (as for*
2 *oz. dripping*	*Brown Stock)*

Wash, peel and cut the vegetables up small. Fry the onions in the hot dripping until slightly browned. Add flour, stirring well into the fat, then stock, bouquet garni and all the vegetables and bring to the boil, stirring constantly. Simmer about 1½ hours until vegetables are quite tender. Sieve, reheat and season to taste. Serve with croûtons of fried bread.

Carrot Soup (for 4–5)

1 *lb. carrots*	1 *oz. butter*
1 *quart white or*	½ *pint milk*
vegetable stock	1 *dessertspoonful fine*
Sprig of parsley	*oatmeal or cornflour*
	Salt and pepper

Wash and scrape the carrots well, then grate them on a coarse grater. Wash, dry

24

White vegetable soup, thick and creamy, makes a welcoming first course on a cold night

and break the parsley into small pieces. Fry the parsley lightly in the butter, then add the grated carrot and "sweat" in the fat, shaking the pan frequently to prevent burning. Add the stock and simmer for about 45 minutes until the carrot is tender. Mix the oatmeal or cornflour to a paste with the milk, add to the soup with seasoning and cook for 5 minutes.

Celery Soup (for 4)

1 *head of celery*	1 *onion*
1 *oz. butter*	½ *pint milk*
1½ *pints white stock*	1 *oz. cornflour*
Bay leaf	*Pepper and salt*
Bacon rinds or ham	*Bouquet garni (as for*
bone	*Brown Stock)*

Wash and shred the celery. Melt the butter in a saucepan and cook the celery, sliced onion and bay leaf for about 15 minutes, with the lid on, shaking occasionally to prevent burning. Add the stock, chopped bacon rinds, seasoning and bouquet garni, bring to the boil and simmer gently until the celery is soft. Put through a sieve, return to the saucepan and reheat.

Make a smooth paste with the cornflour and milk, and stir it into the soup. Bring to the boil and serve.

Cucumber Soup (for 4–5)

2 *large cucum-*	½ *pint milk*
bers	1 *oz. butter*
1 *quart white stock*	2 *egg-yolks*
Pepper and salt	

Peel the cucumbers, take out seeds, cut into slices. Melt the butter and in it fry the sliced cucumbers lightly, without browning them. Add stock, bring to the boil and simmer until the cucumber is tender. Rub through a hair sieve and return to pan, season with salt and pepper. Beat the egg-yolks, stir them into the milk, then gradually add the milk and egg mixture to the cucumber purée, stirring. Reheat, but do not allow to boil.

Haricot Bean Soup (for 5–6)

8 *oz. haricot beans*	*A few bacon rinds*
1 *onion*	1 *gill milk*
1 *stick of celery*	½ *oz. butter*
1 *quart white stock*	*Blade of mace*
Pepper and salt	

Wash the beans thoroughly, soak in water overnight, then rinse well, put with blade of mace, cut up celery, bacon rinds and sliced onion into a pan with the butter and cook for a few minutes. Add the stock, cold, and bring to the boil. Simmer gently for about 2 hours, stirring now and again.

25

Rub through a sieve, then return to the pan, adding the milk and pepper and salt, stirring well all the time.

Tomato Soup (for 3–4)

1 lb. fresh or tinned tomatoes
2 oz. ham or bacon
3 shallots
1 pint white stock, or
  ¼ pint milk and
  ½ pint water
1 oz. butter or margarine
Bay leaf
Pepper and salt
½ oz. finest sago
2 lumps sugar

Put the chopped bacon or ham, the bay leaf and sliced shallots into a saucepan with the butter and simmer slowly for 5 minutes, stirring carefully. Add the tomatoes and cook slowly for about 20 minutes. Rub through a sieve and put back into the saucepan. Add the stock. Bring to the boil. Then add the sago and sugar and simmer for 5 minutes. Season and serve with croûtons.

THICK MEAT SOUPS AND BROTHS

Kidney Soup (for 5–6)

¼ lb. ox kidney
1 quart brown or bone stock
1 oz. flour
1 oz. dripping
Bouquet garni (see Brown Stock)
Small turnip and carrot
Large onion
Pepper and salt
Mushroom trimmings or 1 tablespoonful mushroom ketchup
Glass of sherry (optional)

Wash and cut the kidney into pieces, removing all fat. Wash and peel the vegetables, cut them up and fry them with the kidney in the hot fat until brown. Add the stock and bring to the boil. Skim well. Simmer very gently for two hours. Rub the kidney and vegetables through a sieve and put back in the saucepan. Make the flour into a paste with a very little water and pour into the stock, stirring well. Add bouquet garni and boil for a few minutes. Season, add mushroom trimmings or mushroom ketchup and, if liked, a glass of sherry just before serving.

Mulligatawny Soup (for 4–5)

1 quart brown stock
2 onions
1 carrot
1 turnip
1 oz. flour
1 apple
1 teaspoonful chut-
1 oz. dripping
1 teaspoonful lemon juice
1 tablespoonful curry powder
1 dessertspoonful shredded coconut

Cut the vegetables up into small pieces and fry quickly in the dripping until brown; stir in the flour and curry powder, fry for a few minutes, stirring all the time, then add the stock, the apple (peeled, cored and chopped small) and the coconut. Simmer for 1–2 hours, and sieve. Put back into the pan and heat. Add the chutney and lemon juice at the end.

A dish of boiled rice should be served with this soup.

Oxtail Soup (for 8–10)

1 oxtail
2 quarts brown stock
1 turnip
1 carrot
Salt and pepper
2 oz. dripping
1 oz. flour
Bouquet garni (see Brown Stock)
6 peppercorns
3 cloves
¼ teaspoonful celery salt

Wash the tail well, wipe, break up into pieces and fry with the vegetables, peeled and cut small, in dripping until brown. Add stock, celery salt, peppercorns, cloves and bouquet garni tied up in a muslin bag. Simmer gently for about 3–4 hours, season and strain, putting back the smaller pieces of the tail. Reheat and thicken with the flour made into a paste with warm water, adding a little browning if necessary. The larger pieces of meat from the tail can be served as a main dish with vegetables.

Pot-au-Feu (for 4–5)

1 lb. shin of beef
1 quart of water
1 leek
1 parsnip
1 carrot
Stick of celery (or a few celery seeds)
1 turnip
1 cabbage
2 oz. sago or tapioca
Bouquet garni (see Brown Stock)
Blade of mace
6 peppercorns
Salt to taste
A few cloves

Wipe the meat and tie it with tape so that it does not lose its shape. Put in a saucepan or casserole with the water. Bring to the boil, add salt to taste and skim well. Simmer for ½ hour.

Wash, peel and cut up the vegetables except the cabbage, and add, together with the bouqet garni, peppercorns, mace and cloves tied up in a muslin bag. Simmer gently for 1½ hours.

Clean the cabbage, cut it in half and tie together with a piece of tape. Add it to the liquid and simmer gently till tender. Take out the meat, untie it and put on a hot dish surrounded by the vegetables. The cabbage should be served separately.

Strain the liquid through a colander, using some for gravy. Leave the rest to get cold, and when it is required, take off the fat, bring it to the boil and throw in the sago or tapioca. Cook gently till transparent. Serve.

Chicken Broth (for 6)

Carcase of 1 chicken (and any available chicken left-overs)	1 oz. rice or pearl barley
1 small carrot	Bouquet garni (see Brown Stock)
1 small turnip	Salt and pepper
1 small onion	1 teaspoonful chopped parsley
1 stick of celery	
3 pints water	

Break the carcase into pieces, peel, wash and cut up the vegetables and put them all in a large pan with the water, the washed rice or barley and the bouquet garni. Bring slowly to the boil and simmer gently for 2 hours. Strain, reheat and add the chopped parsley and seasoning just before serving.

Mock Turtle Soup (for 7–8)

½ calf's head
2 oz. lean ham
Bouquet garni (see Brown Stock)
Juice of ½ lemon
1 carrot
1 turnip
2 onions
1 stick celery
2 quarts water
1 oz. cornflour
2 tablespoonfuls sherry
Salt and Cayenne pepper

Wash and blanch the head by covering it with cold water and bringing it to the boil, chop it in pieces and put into a pan with the bouquet garni, ham diced small, and water. Bring slowly to the boil, skim, and simmer gently for at least 2 hours. Then take out the head and simmer the peeled and cut-up vegetables in the stock for 2 hours. Strain, leave till cold to remove all fat from the top. Finally, reheat the stock, thicken it with the cornflour made into a paste with a little water. Add sherry, lemon juice, salt and Cayenne,

and serve garnished with little cubes of the meat from the head.

Rabbit Broth (for 4)

1 rabbit	Salt and pepper
1 large onion	1 oz. flour
1 quart boiling water	1 oz. dripping

Cut the rabbit into pieces and blanch. Wipe thoroughly. Sprinkle with flour and fry in the dripping until brown. Add the boiling water and the onion chopped fine. Season and simmer for 2 hours. Thicken with the flour mixed to a smooth paste with a little water, bring to the boil, stirring well, and cook for 2–3 minutes. Take out the rabbit, cutting off a few small pieces of the meat and adding them to the broth as a garnish. Serve the rest as a main dish.

CREAM SOUPS

Asparagus Soup (for 4–5)

30 heads of asparagus	¼ pint cream (optional)
1 quart vegetable stock or vegetable water	Seasoning

Cut the tips off the asparagus heads and keep them for garnishing. Clean and cut

Grated Parmesan cheese is a delicious addition to many soups

27

the stalks into pieces and bring to the boil with the stock. Simmer for 1 hour, then rub through a hair sieve and heat the purée once more to boiling point. Add seasoning to taste, and the asparagus tips, and cook slowly until the tips are tender—about 10 minutes. Just before serving, add cream, if liked, and reheat, but do not allow to boil. Serve with croûtons of fried bread.

Barley Cream Soup (for 4–5)

2 oz. pearl barley	1 onion
1 quart white stock	1 carrot
1 oz. butter or mar-	Stick of celery
garine	¼ pint cream or milk
Salt and pepper	Nutmeg

Wash and blanch the pearl barley by covering it with cold water and bringing it to the boil, then straining and rinsing it in cold water. Melt the butter in a pan and cook the washed, peeled and sliced vegetables in it for 2–3 minutes, with the lid on, shaking to prevent them sticking. Add the barley, stock, salt and pepper to taste, bring to the boil and simmer for 2 hours. Sieve. Add cream, a little grated nutmeg and reheat without boiling.

Brussels Sprouts Soup (1) (for 4–5)

1 lb. Brussels sprouts	½ pint milk
1 quart white stock	Pepper and salt
1 level dessertspoon-	Green colouring
ful finest sago	

Wash sprouts, taking off old leaves, and cook in boiling salted water until tender but not "mushy." Drain and rub through a sieve. Bring the stock, milk and sago to the boil. Add the sprout purée, pepper and salt, a few drops of colouring and whisk up. Serve hot, but do not boil again.

Brussels Sprouts Soup (2) (for 4–5)

1 lb. Brussels sprouts	2 oz. butter
1 quart stock	1 oz. flour
Pepper and salt	A little cream

Melt the butter in a saucepan, add the flour and mix well together, then add the stock. Boil Brussels sprouts in salted water till just tender, preserving the colour, and rub through a fine hair sieve. Add to the boiling stock and season. A dash of cream added just before serving is a great improvement.

Cabbage Soup (for 3–4)

1 small cabbage	½ pint milk
1 small onion	½ oz. cornflour
1 pint white stock	Chopped parsley
	Pepper and salt

Wash the cabbage, removing the stalk and all coarse outside leaves. Drain, chop finely, plunge into boiling salted water and boil for 5 minutes. Drain and add to the stock with the chopped onion, bring to the boil and simmer gently for 20 minutes. Make a paste with the cornflour and milk, and add, stirring all the time until soup boils. Season to taste and add the chopped parsley at the last moment before serving.

Cauliflower Soup (for 5–6)

1 good-sized cauli-	1 pint white stock
flower	1 oz. cornflour
1 pint milk	Chopped parsley
Pepper and salt	1 tablespoonful cream
	(optional)

Remove the outer leaves from the cauliflower, wash and cut into small pieces. Plunge into salted boiling water and boil hard until tender enough to rub through a hair sieve. Drain and sieve. Bring the stock to the boil. Make the cornflour into a smooth paste with a little of the milk and add to the stock, stirring well. Bring to the boil, add the cauliflower purée, the remainder of the milk, pepper and salt and, at the last minute, the chopped parsley. A tablespoonful of cream added before serving greatly improves this soup.

Chestnut Soup (for 3–4)

¼ lb. chestnuts	Pinch of celery salt
1 pint white stock	Cayenne pepper and
1 gill milk	salt
1 gill cream	1 oz. flour

Shell the chestnuts by scoring them with a cross, then roasting until the skins crack and come off easily. Take off inner brown skin—if necessary, by plunging shelled chestnuts into boiling water—then mash slightly and put into a pan with stock. Simmer until tender enough to rub through a sieve—about 1½ hours. Make a paste with the flour and milk, add with the seasoning, heat, but do not allow to boil. Add the cream just before serving.

Cream of Onion Soup (for 6–7)

1 quart milk	1 tablespoonful
6 large onions	brown or whole-
2 oz. butter	meal flour
A little salt	2 egg-yolks
	A little cream

Small squares of toast can be served
with vegetable or meat soups

Peel, scald and slice the onions, and cook them lightly in the melted butter for ½ hour. Heat the milk. Add the dry flour to the onions, stirring constantly for 3 minutes. Then turn the mixture into the milk and cook for 15 minutes. Strain, reheat and add salt. Beat the egg-yolks with the cream, then stir into the soup. Cook for a few minutes, stirring constantly and not allowing to boil. (If cream is not available, milk can be used instead, in which case add a tablespoonful of butter at the same time.)

Fish Soup (1) (for 6–7)

2 *pints fish stock*	1 *oz. butter or mar-*
1 *oz. cornflour*	*garine*
Pepper and salt	*Dessertspoonful*
¼ *pint milk*	*chopped parsley*

Melt the butter or margarine in a saucepan and add the cornflour, stirring to a smooth paste. Pour on the stock and bring to the boil, stirring all the time. Add the milk and boil again. Season with salt and pepper, and at the last moment add the chopped parsley.

Fish Soup (2) (for 5–6)

To vary the above soup, make a fish stock without vegetable flavouring, allowing 1 quart of water and a teaspoonful of salt to a pound of white fish bones and trimmings.

Make 1 oz. cornflour into a smooth paste with 1 gill milk, add to the stock, stirring all the time as it comes to the boil. Season to taste and simmer gently for 5 minutes. Beat 1 egg, pour it into a hot tureen, and at once add the soup, stirring well. Serve with fried dice of bread.

Leek and Potato Soup (for 5–6)

2 *leeks*	2 *or* 3 *potatoes*
1 *oz. flour*	1 *quart water*
½ *pint milk*	1 *onion*
Salt and pepper	1 *oz. butter*

Melt the butter in a saucepan, stir in the flour and cook for a few minutes, then gradually add the milk, stirring as it comes to the boil. Add the water, the potatoes, peeled and cut up, and the leeks and onion cut small. Bring to the boil and simmer gently for 20–30 minutes until the vegetables are tender. Put through a coarse sieve, pressing the vegetables through, return to the saucepan, reheat, season and serve. (If the soup is too thick, thin it with a little more milk.)

Lobster or Oyster Soup (for 4–5)

½ *pint can lobster or*	2 *oz. flour*
oysters	½ *gill milk*
1 *quart fish stock*	*Juice of* ½ *lemon*
	Seasoning

29

Strain the liquid from the can into the stock. Bring to the boil, add the flour blended to a smooth paste with the milk, boil for 5 minutes, stirring all the time. Then add lobster or oysters, lemon juice and seasoning.

If fresh oysters are used, remove the beards and stew for 5 minutes in a little water. Strain, and add to stock.

Mushroom Soup (for 4)

½ lb. mushrooms	2 oz. flour
2 oz. butter	½ pint milk
1 tablespoonful vinegar	Bouquet garni (see Brown Stock)
Salt and pepper	

Cover the washed but not peeled mushrooms with cold water and a tablespoonful of vinegar. Bring slowly to the boil and simmer gently until mushrooms are soft enough to be rubbed through a sieve. Return the resulting purée to the pan and keep hot. Now melt the butter, stir the flour into it and gradually add the milk, stirring all the time. Season with salt and pepper and a bouquet garni tied up in a muslin bag. Bring to the boil and boil for 3 minutes, then add the mushroom purée. Stir well and serve hot with fried croûtons.

Lentil or Split Pea Soup (for 3–4)

½ lb. split peas or lentils	1 oz. butter or margarine
1 onion	1½ pints water (or part water from ham or boiling bacon)
Small carrot	
Small turnip	
Bacon rinds to flavour	
A few outer leaves of celery	½ pint milk
	Salt and pepper

Wash and soak the dried peas or lentils overnight in the cold water. Next day, bring to the boil with the cut up bacon rinds and simmer for 1 hour. Wash, peel and slice the vegetables and add, cooking until they are soft. Put through a sieve, or mash with a wooden spoon. Replace in the saucepan with the milk, reheat, stirring all the time, put in the margarine or butter and pepper and salt and serve.

If water from ham or bacon boiling is used, omit salt.

Potage Maigre (for 4–5)

1 quart water	1 fairly large slice of bread
Medium-sized cabbage	
Pepper and salt	2 oz. butter
1 onion	½ lb. potatoes, sliced in thin rounds

Boil the water in a saucepan. Add the butter (not margarine) and let it melt. Put in the potatoes.

Shred the cabbage, chop the onion and cut up the bread in very small cubes and add them to the potatoes, with pepper and salt. Boil all together for ½ hour.

Potato Soup (for 5–6)

1 lb. potatoes	1 teaspoonful salt
1½ pints milk	Pinch of pepper
½ pint white stock	1 teaspoonful chopped parsley
1½ oz. butter, margarine or dripping	1 medium onion
1 oz. cornflour	

Boil the potatoes, strain and mash in the usual way. Scald the milk with the sliced onion in it. Add the stock, most of the milk and the butter to the mashed potatoes, and stir well. Mix the cornflour to a paste with a little of the milk and pour into the hot soup, stirring well. Simmer for 3 minutes, add the seasoning, and sprinkle chopped parsley on top at the last minute. Serve with fried dice of bread.

Spinach Soup (for 3–4)

1 lb. spinach	½ pint milk
1 pint white stock	1 teaspoonful cornflour
1 oz. butter or margarine	Pepper and salt

Wash the spinach in several lots of water, then cook in its own moisture and rub through a sieve. Bring the stock to the boil. Make the cornflour into a smooth paste with the milk, add it to the stock and again bring to the boil. Then add the butter or margarine and seasoning. At the last moment, add the purée of spinach and remove from the fire the moment it boils or the colour of the soup will be spoiled. Serve with Puffed Rice heated in the oven.

A little cream greatly improves the flavour.

White Vegetable Soup (for 4)

1 moderate-sized carrot, turnip and onion	Pinch of dried herbs
	1 oz. cornflour
	1½ pints white stock or vegetable water
1 parsnip or swede	
1 stick of celery	½ pint milk
1 leek	Pepper and salt

Wash, peel and cut the vegetables into small dice; bring to the boil with the stock or water, herbs, and a pinch of salt. Simmer gently for ½ hour. Then add the cornflour mixed to a smooth paste with the milk, and stir well while it thickens. Add seasoning.

FISH

There are more fish in the sea than many housewives have ever tried
—a wonderful chance for originality

FISH is not only a good and digestible item of diet, but one of the few remaining natural foods still available to us over-civilised human beings. Its food value is high, being a splendid source of protein. A pound of herrings more than equals a pound of red meat in food value and, though herrings are the most nutritious of all, other fish rank high in the estimation of the nutrition experts.

There are so many different kinds of fish —with infinitely varied flavours, textures and characteristics—yet in the choice of no other basic food are people inclined to be so conservative. Cod, haddock, plaice, sole and herring are not by any means the only delicacies to be found on the fishmonger's slab.

Whiting, so delicious cooked with their "tails in their mouths"; mackerel, King George V's favourite, with the distinctive flavour that is just as good whether eaten hot or "soused" in vinegar; brill, that looks rather like turbot but is always far cheaper and available most of the year round; the colourful red mullet—these are but a few of the lesser-known fish the adventurous housewife will want to introduce into her menus.

When Fish is in Season

(*a*) **Sea Fish.** All kinds can safely be eaten all the year round, but the following list shows those which are at their best in certain seasons:

Bream (Sea)	June to November
Brill	All the year
Coal Fish (Coley)	September to May
Cod	September to May
Conger Eel	June to March
Flounder	January to March
Gurnet	July to March
Haddock (Fresh)	May to January
Hake	July to January
Halibut	July to April
Herring	**June to February**

31

John Dory	January to March
Lemon Sole	December to April
Mackerel	April to November
Mullet, Grey	August to April
Mullet, Red	May to July
Plaice	May to January
Skate	October to May
Smelt	September to March
Sole	March to January
Sprat	November to February
Turbot	March to December
Whitebait	March to July
Whiting	December to March
Witch Sole	August to March

(b) **Freshwater Fish** must not be caught between March 14th and June 16th, the breeding season. These are the commonest varieties:

Barbel	Loach
Bleak	Minnow
Bream (Freshwater)	Perch
Carp	Pike
Chub	Rainbow Trout
Dace	Roach
Eel	Rudd
Grayling	Tench
Gudgeon	

NOTE: Fresh salmon (home-caught) has a close season from August 31st to February 1st, but imported salmon is available all the year round. Freshwater trout (home-caught) has a close season from September 30th to March 1st, but imported trout is available all the year round.

(c) **Shell Fish**

Crab is at its best from April to June.
Lobster (close season in Scotland June 1st to September 1st) is in best supply in the summer months.
Oysters—Natives and Deep Sea Oysters are in season from September 1st to June 14th. Foreign Oysters are available all the year round.
Prawns—all the year round, but most abundant in summer.
Escallop—best quality from November to March.
Mussel—in season from end of July to April; at their best August to November.

How to Shop for Fish

Fish in its prime should be stiff and firm, plentifully covered with fresh-looking scales and with bright, colourful eyes. There should be nothing dry or flabby about it. Colouring should be bright— such as the spots on plaice, the scales and fins of herring, cod or mackerel, the shell of a crab.

All sorts of factors, including the time of year, the weather, etc., affect the price of fish. Cod may therefore be cheapest one day, haddock another, and it pays to ask your fishmonger's advice. Herring is always good value, whether you buy it fresh, salted, smoked, pickled or canned.

If the fishmonger fillets a fish for you, ask him to give you the skin and bones. These are good for making a stock, which in turn will make a delicious sauce to go with the fish.

Keeping Fish Fresh

Never leave fish wrapped up in paper. When you get home, unwrap it promptly and put in the refrigerator in a covered container or polythene bag, or on a plate covered loosely but securely with muslin wrung out in vinegar and water. This is particularly important in hot weather and when there are flies about. Fresh fish should always be cooked the day it is bought.

Preparing Fish for Cooking

Even when fish is bought cleaned and filleted, it should be washed thoroughly under the cold tap and wiped inside and out with a clean damp cloth. The scales can be removed by scraping from the tail to the head with a sharp knife.

Sole, plaice, etc., to be cooked whole, should have their heads and fins cut off, and the belly, just behind the head, cleaned out thoroughly. Remember to keep the trimmings and use them for stock. Scraps of cooked fish should also be kept, as there are many ways of using them.

A fillet may be skinned by placing it on a board, skin downwards. Grasp the tail and, with a knife, roll the flesh back off the skin from tail-end to head.

Fried Fish

This is the most popular way of cooking fish, and the following method is one that cannot go wrong. First wash, dry and sprinkle fish with salt, then dip it in egg. Next, dip it into hard breadcrumbs (bought in packets or baked in the oven till crisp). Heat the frying pan slightly and *then* put in enough fat to cover the pan to a depth of ¼ in. When a faint blue smoke appears and *not* before, lay the fish gently into the fat. Turn it over when the bottom half is

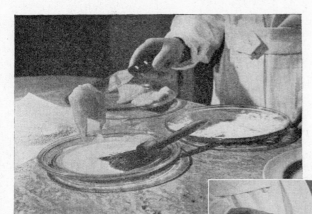

For perfect fried fish: Wash, dry, sprinkle with salt, then dip in egg (left)

Next, coat the fillets in seasoned flour, shaking off the surplus (below)

Put breadcrumbs on a sheet of kitchen paper, place fish on top and shake until well coated (below)

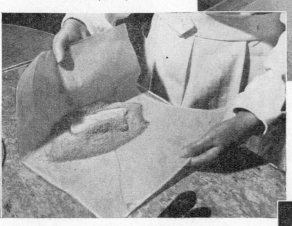

For deep frying always use a basket, have the fat really hot and do not cook too much at once (below)

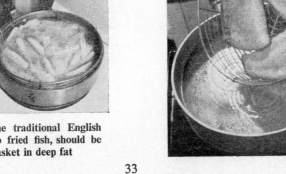

Chip potatoes, the traditional English accompaniment to fried fish, should be cooked in a basket in deep fat

brown and cook the other side. Lift on to crumpled kitchen paper and drain off the fat.

NOTE: Keep a special frying pan for fish and nothing else. If necessary, tie a label marked "Fish" on the handle to deter other members of the family from using it for anything else. Clean the fish frying pan out with a small handful of dry salt—no water or anything else is necessary. The salt will leave it clean and sweet for next time. Also start a deep-fat frier for fish and chips. Keep the fat well strained and you can use it over and over again.

The cooking time naturally varies enormously, thick fish steaks requiring much longer than thin fillets. For this reason, large fish and fish steaks should be fried in a little fat; fillets or small fish, such as whitebait, in deep fat.

Baked Fish

Most suitable way of cooking whole round white fish, such as haddock or whiting, or for thick cuts.

Wash and wipe the fish with a clean cloth, season well, squeeze a few drops of lemon juice over them, stuff if liked. Place the fish in a buttered baking tin or casserole, cover with greased paper and bake in a moderate oven. When cooked, the skin will crack or the flesh come away from the bones easily when tested with a skewer. Whole fish, the size of a herring, take between 10 and 15 minutes, others in proportion, according to size.

Boiled Fish

Boiling is advisable only when large fish or thick pieces are to be cooked. A fish kettle is the best for this purpose, as the drainer makes it easy for the fish to be lifted out without breaking. If you have no fish kettle, use an ordinary saucepan and tie up the fish in a pudding cloth.

Put into hot but not actually boiling water with 1 dessertspoonful of salt and 1 tablespoonful of vinegar or lemon juice to every quart of water and, if possible, a bouquet garni. The water should just cover the fish, no more.

Exceptions to this are: (1) salmon, which on account of its tough skin should be put into gently boiling water, and (2) mackerel, which should be put into tepid water because of its delicate skin.

Allow about 6 minutes to each pound of fish and 6 minutes over. Thick cuts of fish, such as salmon or cod, need 10 minutes to the pound and 10 minutes over. Fish is done when it comes away from the bone at the slightest pressure; fillets when a liquid like thick cream comes out of them.

Steamed Fish

Steaming is preferable to boiling because more of the flavour is retained, but it takes almost twice as long. Thin slices or fillets of fish should always be steamed, never boiled.

Rub whole flat fish or fish cut in large pieces with a cut lemon to preserve the colour.

Wash and wipe the fish well, season, squeeze a little lemon juice over, wrap in greased paper and put in a steamer over boiling water.

Fish can also be steamed between two greased plates over a saucepan of boiling water, or in a moderate oven. Allow 10–15 minutes. This way preserves all the delicate flavour.

Poached Fish

An excellent method for smoked haddock and small whole fresh fish.

Half fill a shallow pan (a frying pan will do very well) with water flavoured with salt and vinegar (proportions 1 dessertspoonful salt and 1 tablespoonful vinegar to each quart of water), bring to the boil, put in fish and cook gently (for times, see under Boiled Fish above).

Grilled Fish

Grilling is particularly suitable for fillets or slices of fish and is, incidentally, more digestible than frying. Wipe the fish thoroughly with a clean cloth, soak in a plate of olive oil or brush over with melted butter before putting under the hot grill. Slash the skin of small whole fish in several places. Baste white fish with melted fat.

Fish Stock (see Soup-making, p. 22)

Brill Supreme

Cut a small brill into fillets; skin them and sprinkle with chopped egg and breadcrumbs. Cook in margarine. Serve with grilled tomatoes and, if possible, croquettes of rice. A Béarnaise sauce is ideal, but tartare will do almost as well.

COD AND SIMILAR WHITE FISH RECIPES

American Cod

In a well-greased deep casserole, place alternate layers of buttered bread, seasoning, flaked cod, partly boiled onions and raw tomatoes. On the top layer place bread dotted with knobs of butter. Soak whole in milk (each ½ pint beaten with 1 egg). Cover dish well and cook in moderate oven until set (about 1 hour).

Baked Cod with Mushrooms (for 4)

1 lb. cold boiled flaked cod fillet	¾ pint seasoned white sauce
Juice of ½ lemon	2 oz. sliced cooked mushrooms
Breadcrumbs	
Mashed potatoes	Butter or margarine

Mix the fish with the white sauce, adding the lemon juice and mushrooms. Place the mixture in a well-buttered casserole, cover with breadcrumbs and dot with knobs of butter or margarine. Decorate the edges with a border of mashed potatoes, using a star tube. Cook in fast oven until browned.

Casserole of Cod, Haddock or Plaice (for 4)

1 lb. cod, haddock or plaice (whichever is cheapest and best)	Salt and pepper
	½ lb. parboiled potatoes
2 medium-sized onions, sliced	4 tomatoes
	2 oz. margarine
Chopped parsley	

Skin, bone and cut the fish into pieces about 1 in. square. Arrange in a shallow well-greased ovenproof dish and surround with quartered parboiled potatoes, whole skinned tomatoes and sliced onions. Season with salt and pepper, dot with margarine and bake in moderate oven until cooked, basting with melted margarine. Sprinkle with chopped parsley before serving.

Cod and Mushroom Scallops (for 4)

1 lb. fresh cod fillets	2 oz. mushrooms
1 gill milk	Salt, pepper and a little grated cheese
1 oz. margarine	
½ oz. flour	Breadcrumbs

Poach the cod gently in the milk and a little water. Separately cook the mushrooms, sliced, in half the margarine. When cooked, drain the fish and mushrooms, saving the fish liquor for sauce. Flake the fish, mix with mushrooms and pack fairly tightly into individual scallop shells. Make a roux with the flour and remaining margarine, gradually add the liquor from the fish, season, return to heat and cook until the sauce thickens. Spoon sparingly over the fish and mushroom mixture, scatter breadcrumbs and grated cheese on top, dot with margarine and heat in a fast oven.

Cod Fillets Portugaise

Cod fillets	1 Spanish onion
2 or 3 tomatoes	1 oz. butter
1 oz. grated cheese	Salt and pepper

Place fillets in a greased fireproof dish. Slice onion very thinly and place on top with sliced tomatoes. Sprinkle over salt and pepper and grated cheese, top with butter in small pieces. Bake 20–30 minutes.

Cod Fillets with Mushroom Stuffing (for 4)

4 cod fillets (middle cut about 1 in. thick)	
Salt and pepper	
1 egg-yolk	

4 oz. white bread (without crust)
1½ oz. margarine
1 tablespoonful chopped parsley
Finely grated rind of 1 lemon
A little milk   4 mushrooms

Crumble bread into bowl, pour over enough milk to moisten and leave to soak. Squeeze any surplus milk out of bread so that it is fairly dry, stir in chopped parsley, lemon rind and egg-yolk, season with salt and pepper. Wash mushrooms, keep tops on one side. Chop stalks finely and add to stuffing.

Wipe fish with damp cloth. Stuff the centres, wrapping the side pieces firmly round stuffing, tie with string. Put into fireproof dish or baking tin, sprinkle with pepper and salt. Brush over fillets and mushroom tops with melted margarine. Cover fish with greaseproof paper and bake in moderate oven for 20–30 minutes. After first 10 minutes, put the mushrooms in beside the fish. Serve hot with green peas.

COOK'S TIP

FOR GOOD LOOKING FISH

Before frying, dry the fish, dip in milk and roll in coating made from 1 heaped tablespoonful cornflour, ½ level teaspoonful salt and ¼ level teaspoonful pepper. (Tested in the experimental kitchen of Brown & Polson Ltd.)

Codfish in Golden Sauce (for 4)

1 lb. cooked cod fillet	1 oz. butter or mar-
½ pint milk	garine
1 tablespoonful made	1 oz. flour
or French mustard	1 tablespoonful
(thick consistency)	vinegar
3–4 medium, cooked,	½ level tablespoonful
diced potatoes	sugar
Croûtons	Salt and pepper

Flake the fish into small pieces. Melt butter or margarine in a saucepan; add flour and stir over low heat for a few seconds. Remove saucepan from heat. Gradually add the milk and stir well until smooth. Bring slowly to the boil, stirring all the time, and cook gently for 5 minutes. Remove from heat, stir in the mustard, vinegar and sugar. Mix well. Add the potatoes and flaked cod fillet; season with salt and pepper. Heat through. Serve garnished with croûtons of fried bread.

Cod Mornay (for 4)

4 cod fillets	2 oz. grated cheese
½ pint Mornay sauce (see Sauces chapter)	

Cover the bottom of a serving dish with some of the Mornay sauce, arrange on this the cod fillets, poached and well drained, cover with more of the sauce, sprinkle with grated cheese and brown quickly.

Cod Oriental (for 2)

¼ lb. fresh and firm	1 tablespoonful olive
cod	oil
Bay leaf	Squeeze of lemon
Salt and pepper	juice
Boiled rice	Chopped parsley

Wash and dry the cod and cut it into small chunks, about 1½ in. square. Put these into a basin containing the olive oil blended with the lemon juice, salt and pepper, and a bay leaf. Leave to marinade for ½ hour or so, then skewer the pieces and grill, under a hot grill, turning frequently, until they are lightly browned. Serve on a bed of rice, with sliced tomato and chopped parsley to garnish. Even better served with savoury rice—cooked rice tossed in hot fat with cooked strips of bacon and onion and a suspicion of garlic.

Cod Puffs (for 2–3)

8 oz. cooked flaked	1 oz. melted mar-
cod fillet	garine or butter
2 eggs	Onion or lemon juice
Salt and pepper	to taste
6 oz. mashed potatoes	

Mix fish with eggs, add potatoes, melted margarine or butter, salt and pepper. A teaspoonful of onion or lemon juice may be added to taste. Mix all the ingredients well and drop from a spoon into hot deep fat. Cook until browned and serve with egg or tomato sauce.

Cod with Cheese and Potatoes (for 3–4)

¾ lb. cod fillets	¾ lb. potatoes
3 oz. grated cheese	¾ pint well-seasoned
2 tomatoes	white sauce
2 tablespoonfuls	1 oz. margarine
breadcrumbs	

Partly cook the cod in a little salted water and parboil the potatoes. Grease a fireproof dish and arrange alternate layers of flaked cod, finely sliced potato and grated cheese in it. Pour over the white sauce, making certain all the crevices are filled up. Cover with sliced tomato, dot with margarine and sprinkle the breadcrumbs on top. Bake in a moderate oven for about 30 minutes.

Cod with Mushroom Sauce (for 4)

4 medium-sized cod	½ pint scalded milk
fillets	½ pint water
4 oz. chopped mush-	2 oz. butter
rooms	2 oz. flour
1 oz. chopped onion	Salt and pepper

Place the onion and mushrooms in the water and cook for 3 minutes. Add butter and flour, stirring continuously. Add the scalded milk and heat all to boiling point. Season to taste and pour over the fish in a well-greased baking dish. Bake in moderate oven for 30 minutes.

Cod with Spinach (for 3–4)

1 lb. flaked cod fillet	Few drops olive oil
½ lb. chopped cooked	2 sliced onions
spinach	⅔ pint milk
1 oz. flour	Breadcrumbs
Salt, pepper, nutmeg	Fat for frying

Gently fry onions until slightly browned. Add spinach, stirring constantly. Still stirring, slowly add the flour and warmed milk. Season with salt, pepper and nutmeg. Simmer for 15 minutes. Into a casserole dish put a layer of prepared spinach, covering this with a layer of fish, repeating the layers until spinach and fish are used up, and finishing with spinach. Sprinkle with breadcrumbs and a few drops of olive oil. Bake in a moderate oven for 30 minutes until golden brown.

Cod's Roe

This is often bought ready boiled, but to cook a whole fresh roe, place in enough boiling salted water to cover, with a tablespoonful of vinegar. Boil for 20–30 minutes, according to size. Cool, then cut into thick slices and fry in hot shallow fat.

Cold Fish Savoury (for 4)

½ lb. cooked cod fillets	Cayenne pepper
¼ pint milk	4 squares of buttered toast
Anchovy essence	Hard-boiled egg
Vinegar	Parsley

Flake the fish. Moisten with the milk. Season to individual taste with anchovy essence, vinegar and Cayenne pepper. Pile when cold on the squares of buttered toast. Sprinkle with the chopped hard-boiled egg and finely chopped parsley.

Coquilles au Colin (for 3–4)

½ lb. cooked boned fish	1 large dessertspoonful flour
2 oz. butter	2 dessertspoonfuls grated Gruyère cheese
2 oz. mushrooms	
Salt and pepper	A few shrimps
About ¼ pint milk	4 scallop shells

Make a white sauce with the butter and flour and the heated milk (see chapter on Sauces). Peel and cut up the mushrooms, and add them with salt and pepper to the sauce. Cook for 10 minutes, then add the shelled shrimps and at the last moment the grated cheese. Be sparing with the salt because of the shrimps.

Butter four scallop shells, half-fill them with fish, then pour over the sauce and sprinkle a little grated cheese over each shell. Top with a small piece of butter and put under a hot grill until brown.

Coquilles of Cod (for 4)

½ lb. flaked cooked cod	4 well-scrubbed and dried scallop shells (obtainable from fishmongers for a few pence)
Anchovy essence, if liked	
1 or 2 hard-boiled eggs	½ lb. macedoine of vegetables
A little mayonnaise	
Chopped parsley	

Coat the inside of the scallop shells with a little mayonnaise, flavoured, if liked, with anchovy. Put in a layer of seasoned macedoine of vegetables, then a layer of flaked cooked cod. Border with chopped hard-boiled egg and chopped parsley.

Fish fillets, deep-fried an appetising golden shade, are served with crisp potato balls

FISH

Cottage Crab (for 4)

1 lb. cod fillets	2 eggs
Lettuce	1 oz. margarine
Cucumber	Pepper
2 oz. shrimps	Made mustard
Sliced cucumber to garnish	

Steam the cod fillets, flake them and leave to cool. Wash and dry lettuce, slice cucumber and chop shrimps. Melt the margarine in a saucepan, add the beaten eggs, season with pepper and a little made mustard. Stir together over a gentle heat until the mixture thickens. Leave to cool. Arrange a ring of lettuce leaves around a dish. Pile the flaked fish inside them and top with the egg mixture. Garnish with a ring of sliced cucumber.

Fish and Bacon Casserole

In the bottom of individual casserole dishes sprinkle fried sliced onions and cooked bacon strips. Lay a slice of fresh cod fillet in each casserole, sprinkle with salt and pepper and cover with sliced cooked potatoes. Fill the casserole with fish stock. Cook gently in a slow oven.

Fish and Macaroni Pie (for 3–4)

1 filleted fresh haddock	1 tablespoonful grated cheese
2 oz. macaroni	½ oz. butter
1 teaspoonful made mustard	½ oz. flour
	¼ pint milk
Pepper and salt	

Break the macaroni into small pieces and boil it. Put a layer of macaroni into a well-greased pie dish, then a layer of flaked seasoned fish. Fill the pie dish with alternate layers until almost full. Then pour over it white sauce made from the butter, flour, mustard and milk.

Sprinkle grated cheese on top and bake in a moderate oven until brown on top (about ½ hour).

Fish and Potato Rolls

To each half-teacupful of cooked fish, add the same quantity of mashed potato, a small piece of butter, pepper, salt and just a flavouring of mace. Work the mixture into a stiff paste with a beaten egg, and make into little rolls 3 in. long, with flat ends. Flour well, egg-and-breadcrumb, and fry in deep fat until a golden brown. Garnish with parsley and lemon, and serve with melted butter.

Fishcakes

½ lb. cold boiled cod	¾ lb. mashed potatoes
1 egg	Streaky bacon
Seasoning	Browned breadcrumbs

Mash the fish, add mashed potatoes, season, bind with an egg and roll in crisp breadcrumbs. Shape into round flat cakes. Put a few strips of streaky bacon in a cold frying pan and cook gently till some of the fat is fried out. Then put in codfish cakes and brown in the bacon fat.

Fishcakes Creole

1 lb. cooked cod fillet	Parsley or crisp sprigs of watercress
1 tablespoonful melted margarine	1 large onion
6 oz. fine breadcrumbs	A small piece of garlic
½ teaspoonful dried thyme	3 sprigs of chopped parsley
Egg and breadcrumbs	

Flake the cod very finely. Mix into it the margarine and breadcrumbs. Chop the onion and garlic together very finely, add the chopped parsley and thyme, then mix well with the fish, adding a little milk if the mixture tends to fall apart. Shape into smallish, flat, round cakes and coat with egg and breadcrumbs. Fry in shallow fat. Garnish with parsley or watercress.

Fish Casserole (for 4)

A 3-oz. can of lobster	1 lb. fresh fillet of cod
4 oz. margarine	2 oz. raw chopped onion
A 16-oz. can lobster soup	4 oz. plain flour
¼ pint milk	Salt and pepper to taste
4 oz. grated cheese	

Cut the raw cod into pieces 1 in. square. Roll in the flour and lightly brown very quickly in the margarine in a frying pan. Put the partly cooked fish into a casserole, flake lobster, add all ingredients except cheese, and mix well. Finally, sprinkle cheese on top. Bake in a moderate oven for 40 minutes. Serve very hot with peas and mashed potatoes.

Fish Custard

Cold cooked fish	Pepper and salt
Shallot	Milk and eggs for custard
A few chopped capers	

Flake the fish, removing any bones, and put some into a buttered pie dish. Sprinkle pepper and salt over it, a little chopped caper and a very little chopped shallot. Add more layers of fish and seasoning until

Fried fillets garnished with mixed vegetables, sliced lemon, tomato and sprigs of parsley

all is used. Make a custard, allowing 3 eggs to a pint of milk. Pour it carefully over the fish and bake in a slow oven (standing the dish in a tin with a little water in it) until a delicate brown.

Fish Cutlets (for 3–4)

½ *lb. cooked fish*	1 *teaspoonful*
½ *oz. butter*	*chopped parsley*
½ *oz. flour*	1 *teaspoonful*
½ *gill milk or fish*	*anchovy essence*
stock	*Egg, breadcrumbs*
1 *egg-yolk*	*and fat for frying*
Pepper and salt	

Remove the skin and any bones from the fish and flake it up finely. Add the parsley, anchovy essence and pepper and salt. Melt the butter in a saucepan, stir in the flour and add the milk or fish stock, stirring until the mixture thickens and draws away from the side of the saucepan. Remove from the heat and put in the fish and the beaten egg-yolk. Turn the mixture out on to a plate to get cold, then make it into neat cutlets, using a little flour if necessary. Egg-and-breadcrumb them and fry in deep fat until golden brown. Drain well and garnish with fried parsley and slices of lemon.

Fish Hotpot (for 3–4)

1 *lb. cod fillets*	2 *oz. grated cheese*
Marrow (about 1 lb.)	2–3 *tablespoonfuls*
1 *lb. new potatoes*	*cider or milk*
2 *stalks celery (or*	*Garlic*
2 *peppers)*	*Browned bread-*
1 *oz. butter or mar-*	*crumbs (or corn-*
garine	*flakes)*
Salt and pepper	

Cut fillets into eight or ten even-sized pieces. Peel marrow, remove seeds and cut into sections. Cut potatoes into rounds ⅛ in. thick. Finely dice celery or peppers. Mix vegetables and divide into three portions.

Rub casserole with cut garlic and then grease with butter or margarine. Put a layer of marrow, potato and celery or peppers at the bottom, then *half* the fish. Add salt, pepper and 1 oz. grated cheese, another layer of vegetables, then remaining fish, seasoning and cider or milk. Add remaining cheese, then the vegetables and, finally, browned breadcrumbs or cornflakes. Dot on top with pats of butter or margarine. Bake in a moderate oven for 1 hour.

Fish Mousse (for 3–4)

1 lb. cooked whiting or fresh haddock	½ pint white sauce
1 teaspoonful powdered gelatine	2 egg-whites
	1 tablespoonful cream
	Pepper and salt

Make the white sauce with fish stock if possible and dissolve the gelatine in it. Pound the fish and add to the sauce, with seasoning to taste, the cream and, lastly, the well-whisked egg-whites. Beat lightly and put in a soufflé mould. Serve cold with salad and cold tomato sauce.

Fish Omelet

Flake finely about 2 oz. cooked fish. Season, add a little cream, work it into a paste, heat and put aside in a warm place. Make a plain omelet and fold the fish into it just before dishing it up.

Fish Patties or Vol-au-Vent

Make some patty cases (see Pastry chapter). Use any cooked fish, flaked into small pieces and moistened with some good fish sauce. Season well, add a squeeze of lemon juice or a little grated rind, a beaten egg-yolk and, if possible, a little cream. Heat the mixture and pile into the patty cases. Put on the lids and heat the patties in the oven for 2 or 3 minutes. If liked, a few shelled chopped shrimps may be added to the mixture.

Fish Pie (1) (for 3–4)

½ lb. cooked white fish (cold)	Grated lemon rind
1 gill anchovy sauce	1 tomato
1 teaspoonful chopped parsley	1 lb. potatoes (cooked)
1 hard-boiled egg	Pepper and salt
	Butter

Make anchovy sauce (see Sauces), stir in flaked fish, chopped parsley, cut-up egg, lemon rind, pepper and salt. Grease a pie dish, put in the mixture, then some slices of tomato and cover with mashed potato. Put a few pieces of butter on top and bake for ¾ hour.

NOTE: Uncooked fish should be steamed before being added to the sauce.

Fish Pie (2) (for 4)

¾ lb. cooked cod fillet	1 lb. cooked potatoes (mashed)
½ pint thick white sauce	¾ oz. butter or margarine
2 hard-boiled eggs (finely chopped)	A little hot milk
1 level dessertspoonful chopped capers	Salt and pepper
	Good pinch grated nutmeg

Skin and flake the cod. To the white sauce add the fish, eggs and capers. Season with salt and pepper. Put into a pie dish. Melt the butter in a saucepan and add the potatoes, salt, pepper, nutmeg and sufficient hot milk to give a fairly soft creamy consistency. Beat well and pile on top of the fish. Smooth the surface, "rough up" with a fork, brush with egg or milk and brown in a moderate oven for approximately 25 minutes.

Garnish with lemon wedges and parsley.

Fish Pie—Russian Style (for 4)

½ lb. flaky pastry	1 chopped hard-boiled egg
1 filleted haddock or codling	2 tablespoonfuls white sauce
Grated lemon rind	
Pepper and salt	

(This recipe is at its best when made with flaky pastry, but is almost as good made with short. Though haddock is its proper constituent, a codling makes a reasonable substitute.)

Cut the fish into small pieces and mix with the other ingredients for the filling. Roll the pastry into a square, trim and lay the filling in the centre. Fold the pastry to the centre, decorate with pastry leaves. Place on a greased baking sheet and bake in a hot oven for 30–40 minutes or until the pastry is golden brown.

Fish Pudding (for 3–4)

½ lb. cooked fish	1 gill milk
2 oz. breadcrumbs	Pepper and salt
1 egg	Chopped parsley
	Anchovy essence

Break up the fish into small pieces, add the breadcrumbs, pepper and salt, parsley, anchovy essence, the beaten egg and, lastly, the milk. Put the mixture into a greased basin, cover with greased paper and steam for 1 hour. Serve with anchovy or tomato sauce.

Fish Soufflé (for 3–4)

2 oz. butter	Pepper and salt
2 oz. flour	2 or 3 eggs (separated)
1 tablespoonful anchovy essence	About a gill of milk
5 oz. white fish	1 tablespoonful cream

Melt the butter and add the flour, anchovy essence and seasoning, stirring well. Then add the egg-yolks and milk. Continue stirring over the fire until the mixture is about to boil, then take it off. Stir in the finely pounded white fish and the cream. When well blended, stir in the well-beaten egg-whites lightly, pour into a buttered soufflé dish and bake for about ½ hour.

Fish Surprises (for 4)

¼ lb. uncooked cod fillet	Lemon wedges and parsley for garnish
2 level tablespoonfuls finely chopped parsley	Strained juice of 1 lemon
2 rounded tablespoonfuls flour	Grated rind of ½ lemon
Salt and pepper	4 level tablespoonfuls butter or margarine

Skin the fillet and reduce it to a fine, smooth consistency by mashing well with two forks. Add lemon rind, parsley and seasoning. Beat the butter or margarine to a smooth paste with the flour. Work in the fish and other ingredients. Add the lemon juice. Divide the now firm and pliable mixture into from six to eight pieces. Shape on a lightly floured board into fish balls or cakes. Fry in hot fat and serve garnished with lemon wedges and parsley.

Fish Timbales (for 3–4)

1 lb. cooked white fish	2 egg-whites
White sauce	Pepper and salt

Make some white sauce (see Sauces chapter), using fish stock and cornflour. Add seasoning and then put in the fish, pounded up. Lastly, fold in the well-beaten whites. Butter some timbale moulds, fill almost full with the mixture, twist a piece of buttered paper over the top, steam for 20 minutes, then turn out carefully.

Fresh Haddock (Stuffed)

Wash and dry the haddock. Make sufficient veal stuffing (see Poultry and Game chapter) to fill, and then sew up with a needle and thread. Put in a tin with some dripping or butter. Cover with a piece of buttered paper and then another tin, and bake for 30 minutes or according to size, basting well. Serve with brown sauce.

NOTE: Cod or hake can also be stuffed and baked.

Grilled Haddock Marinade

For each person, take half a large fillet of haddock. Prepare a marinade of olive oil (or melted margarine), a dash of lemon juice, salt and pepper, and a bay leaf, the quantity depending on the number of fillets. Leave the fillets to marinade for ½ hour or more, then grill, turning to ensure thorough cooking, until lightly browned. Serve on a hot dish, with maître d'hôtel butter (see Cookery in France), served separately.

Haddock baked with Egg Sauce

Cut fillets of haddock into pieces, season

Grilled or fried trout, are cooked whole in olive oil, brought to the table with lemon slices in their mouths and garnished with parsley

strongly with salt, pepper and paprika, and place in generously buttered baking dish with strips of fat bacon on top and between them. Cover with a piece of greaseproof paper and bake slowly for about 1 hour. Make white sauce with 1 oz. butter or margarine, 2 dessertspoonfuls flour and a breakfastcupful of milk. When thick and smooth, add chopped hard-boiled egg and a teaspoonful of capers and pour over fish. Sprinkle with freshly chopped parsley and serve in baking dish.

Haddock stuffed with Grapes (for 2–3)

1¼ lb. fresh haddock	½ lb. white grapes
1 oz. breadcrumbs	½ oz. melted butter
1 egg	8 squashed grapes
Browned bread-	½ tumbler of fish
crumbs	stock or water
Mixed herbs	Salt and pepper

Ask the fishmonger to cut off the head of the haddock, open fish on belly side and remove backbone. Peel grapes and remove pips. Make stuffing with breadcrumbs, herbs, seasoning, melted butter, squashed grapes and egg for binding to soft consistency. Spread out cleaned fish, run a double row of halved grapes along one side, cover with stuffing, top with halved grapes. Sew up the fish. Place in a well-greased fireproof dish, pour in fish stock or water and juice that has run out of the grapes. Season fish, break a walnut of margarine over it. Bake in a moderate oven for 25 minutes, keeping basted. Remove cotton, peel off top skin, sprinkle fish and bind cooking liquor with browned breadcrumbs, add remaining grapes to sauce.

Kedgeree (see Breakfast Dishes)

Miracle Fish Salad

1 lb. cod fillets	Lime juice (prefer-
3 tablespoonfuls	ably unsweetened)
olive oil	1 tablespoonful white
Salt, pepper, sugar	vinegar
Watercress	

Flake the fish and place it in lime juice (just enough to cover). Leave for about 8 hours in a cool place—not the refrigerator—when it will look and taste "cooked." Pour off the juice, make a French dressing with the oil, and a tablespoonful of vinegar to a teaspoonful of the lime juice. Season well. Dress the watercress with this and

pile the fish up in the middle of it. If preferred, mayonnaise can be used instead of the French dressing.

Quick Creamed Cod on Toast (for 4)

1 lb. smoked cod	1 oz. flour
fillets	1 oz. margarine
½ pint milk	4 slices buttered toast

Poach the cod gently for 15–20 minutes. Melt the margarine in a stout saucepan, add the flour and blend well. Gradually pour on milk, away from heat, stirring all the time, return to heat and bring to the boil, still stirring. Make four slices of buttered toast and, meanwhile, flake the cooked and drained fish into the sauce. Stir it gently to heat right through. Spoon this mixture on to the hot buttered slices of toast and serve at once. If liked, garnish with slices of hard-boiled egg or sieved hard-boiled yolk.

Robin Hood Curry (for 4)

(Named, not after the famous outlaw, whose staple diet was venison, but after the lovely little fishing village and holiday resort nestling below the Yorkshire cliffs.)

1 lb. flaked cod	1 oz. margarine
1 small onion, finely	2 level teaspoonfuls
chopped	curry powder
1 small apple, finely	1 rounded table-
chopped	spoonful plain flour
½ pint water or fish	1 teaspoonful salt
stock	1 tablespoonful
1 tablespoonful	chutney
sultanas	

Melt the fat and fry the apple and onion lightly. Add curry powder and flour and fry for a minute or two, stirring well, gradually stir in the liquid, then add salt, sultanas and chutney. Bring to the boil and simmer gently for 20–30 minutes. Add the flaked fish and simmer for another 10 minutes. Serve boiled rice separately.

Savoury Baked Fish (for 4)

1 lb. cod or haddock	½-pint tin tomato,
Breadcrumbs	mushroom or
2 oz. margarine	onion soup

Cut the fish up into four thick slices and put these into a fireproof dish. Pour the soup over the fish—it should just cover the fish; if it does not, add water. Sprinkle generously with breadcrumbs, add dabs of margarine and bake in a moderate oven for 20 minutes.

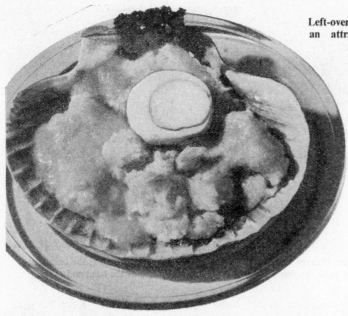

Left-over fish can be used to make an attractive dish, served in scallop shells

dish. Sprinkle pepper and salt over it. Put the butter in pieces on the top and bake in a moderately hot oven for 10 minutes, basting well. Take out, add the chopped mushrooms and cream, and cook for 10 minutes more. Finally, stir the beef extract into the liquor and finish in the oven, basting once or twice.

Halibut with Tomatoes (Baked) (for 3–4)

1 lb. halibut	3 tomatoes
1 oz. melted butter	1 very small onion
2 tablespoonfuls	Pinch of castor sugar
cream	Fat for frying
Pepper and salt	

Wipe the fish and skin it; put it in a buttered dish and sprinkle pepper and salt on top. Pour over the melted butter and cook in a moderately hot oven for about 20 minutes. Meanwhile, fry the onion, sliced very finely, in a little fat until it is golden brown, take out the fish, put slices of tomato on top with a pinch of sugar, then the onion, and lastly the cream. Put back in oven for 10 minutes.

HERRINGS, BLOATERS, KIPPERS AND MACKEREL

Baked Herrings and Tomatoes (for 4)

2 level teaspoonfuls dry mustard	2 teaspoonfuls vinegar
4 herrings cleaned and boned	8 oz. tomatoes skinned and sliced
1 small onion, very finely sliced	½–1 teaspoonful salt
¼ level teaspoonful pepper	1 tablespoonful stock or water

Mix the mustard and vinegar together. Open the herrings out flat and, if large, cut each into three pieces. Spread with the mustard mixture. Arrange the onion, herrings and tomatoes in alternate layers in an ovenproof dish, seasoning each layer. Add

Shattuck Haddock

Cut fish into fillets and lay them in a fireproof dish, lined with butter or margarine. Sprinkle with salt and pepper, and arrange on top of the fish five or six thick slices of peeled tomato. Bake in a hot oven for ½ hour, basting frequently with its own liquor.

Spiced Cod

2 lb. cod fillet	1 egg-white
1 pint water	Clove of garlic
3 tablespoonfuls vinegar	A few peppercorns
1 clove	Chopped parsley
1 onion (sliced)	Batter
	Salt and pepper
Fat for frying	

Flake cod and put into a large dish. In a separate dish mix water, vinegar, garlic, peppercorns, parsley, onion and clove, and pour over fish. Leave for 1½ hours, then remove fish, dry in a clean cloth, dip in well-seasoned batter and thinly whipped egg-white. Fry in very hot fat to a rich golden colour. Serve with egg sauce (see Sauces chapter).

HALIBUT

Halibut à la Suisse (for 3–4)

1 lb. halibut	2 oz. mushrooms
2 oz. butter	2 tablespoonfuls cream
½ teaspoonful beef extract	Pepper and salt

Wipe the fish and put it in a buttered

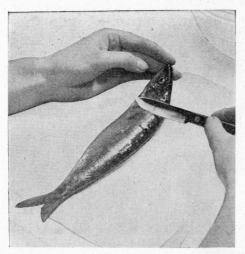 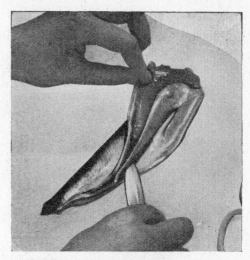

To prepare a herring: (1) With a sharp knife, cut off the head and tail and scale the fish

(2) Make a shallow cut along the backbone, beginning at the head end

the stock and bake in a moderate oven ¾ hour. Serve hot.

Baked Stuffed Herrings (for 4)

4 herrings
½ teacupful bread-
  crumbs
Salt and pepper
1 teaspoonful
  chopped parsley
1 small onion
½ teaspoonful butter

Clean and wash herrings and remove heads. Split open and remove backbones. To make the stuffing, chop the onion very finely and add breadcrumbs, parsley and seasoning. If the fish have roes, mix two with the stuffing and this will bind it, otherwise use a little beaten egg. Sprinkle the inside of each herring with salt and pepper and spread a portion of the stuffing down the centre. Roll up and tie with cotton or pierce with a small wooden skewer. Cook in a buttered fireproof dish covered with greaseproof paper for 15 minutes. Remove paper and allow to brown.

Goodwood Herrings (for 6)

6 fresh herrings
4 tablespoonfuls
  breadcrumbs
1 small minced onion
1 tablespoonful
  chopped parsley
Small wooden
  skewers
6 tomatoes
1 tablespoonful mar-
  garine or dripping
½ teaspoonful grated
  lemon rind
A pinch of dried
  thyme
Salt and pepper

Scale, clean and behead the herrings, but leave in the roes. Twist the fish head to tail and fasten with a tiny wooden skewer or cocktail stick. Slice the top off each tomato with a sharp knife. Keep the slice. Scoop out the inside of each, discard the hard core, keep the pulp. Put bread-crumbs, herbs, onion, lemon, salt and pepper into a basin and add enough tomato pulp to moisten. Fill each tomato with this mixture, put a tiny piece of mar-garine on top and replace the covers. Set a tomato in the centre of each curled herring. Put in a greased fireproof dish and cook for 20 minutes in a fairly hot oven. Serve in the dish in which they are cooked.

Grilled Bloaters

Bloaters
A little margarine or dripping for frying roes

Break off the heads of the fish, split open the backs and remove roes and backbone. Toss roes in a little hot margarine or drip-ping in a small pan until golden brown. Heat grill, grease the grid and place fish on it with insides to the heat. When browned, turn over and grill the backs. Serve very hot with the roes.

Grilled Herrings with Lemon

1 herring per person   Lemon juice
        A little butter

Scale and clean the fish, then wipe with a clean cloth. Skewer the heads and tails to-gether. Brush each with a very little butter and grill quickly under a very hot grill until brown. Squeeze on the lemon juice and serve at once.

44

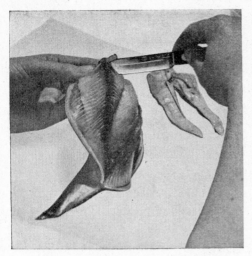

(3) Remove roe, if any, and insert knife under backbone

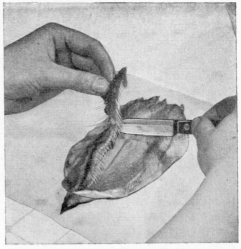

(4) Flatten out fish and lift backbone. Small bones should come away at the same time

Grilled Kippers

Kippers
Pepper
Lemon juice
Margarine or butter

Wipe each kipper with a damp cloth and cut off the head. Heat the grill and put the kippers on the hot grid, skin side uppermost, and grill for 1 minute. Turn kippers, place a pat of margarine or butter on top and cook for a further 5–6 minutes. Sprinkle with pepper and, if liked, a squeeze of lemon juice. Serve at once.

(5) Separate hard roes from soft, and handle as little as possible. Roes can be cooked with the herrings or kept for use as a separate dish

Herrings à la Maître d'Hôtel (for 4)

4 *large herrings*	1 *dessertspoonful*
2 *teaspoonfuls finely*	*olive oil*
chopped parsley	*Juice of ½ lemon*
Salt and pepper	*½ pint white sauce*
Cayenne	

Scale, clean and wash the herrings. Cut off the heads, split them down the back, and remove the backbone and as many small bones as possible. Put them on a flat dish and sprinkle with salt, pepper and the oil. Leave for 1 hour, basting frequently. Grill until golden brown. Prepare a good white sauce, not too thick (see Sauces chapter). Stir in the parsley and lemon juice, season well with salt and a few grains of Cayenne and serve cold.

Herrings fried in Oatmeal (see chapter on Cookery in Scotland).

Herrings, Lowestoft Style

Scale, clean and behead the fish. Make a strong brine by putting 2 handfuls of common salt into 1½ pints of water. Bring to the boil, put in the fish and let the water gallop for 6 minutes. The flesh will be firm and full of flavour and not at all mushy, because the heavy brine prevents the water from soaking into it. Can be eaten hot, or served cold with salad.

Herring Pie (for 4–5)

½ lb. grated raw potato	¼ teaspoonful nutmeg
½ lb. grated raw apple	1 onion (chopped)
2 teaspoonfuls lemon juice	Salt and pepper
	4 herrings, boned
	6 oz. pastry

Grease a shallow dish and arrange half the potato, apple and onion on it. Sprinkle on the nutmeg, seasoning and lemon juice. Lay the herrings on top. Cover with remainder of the potato, apple and onion mixture. Roll out pastry and cover dish. Bake in a hot oven for 30 minutes.

Herrings with Mustard Sauce

Wipe the fish with a clean cloth, split open, then egg-and-breadcrumb them. Fry in a little butter, cut side downwards first, for 7 to 8 minutes. Serve with mustard sauce (see chapter on Sauces).

Jugged Kippers

Roll up kippers, put them into a jug and pour on enough fast-boiling water to cover them. Cover the jug and let it stand in a warm place for 5 minutes, then take out fish, drain and serve with a pat of butter. NOTE: This method avoids cooking smells.

Kipper Creams (for 3)

2 large kippers	Pinch of nutmeg
Pepper	2 egg-yolks
3 or 4 tablespoonfuls top of milk	1 egg-white
	Lemon juice

Cover kippers with boiling water and leave for a few minutes. Drain, remove skin and bones, and mash. Beat up the yolks and white of egg, add fish, pepper, nutmeg, a squeeze of lemon juice and, lastly, the milk. Put into lightly buttered individual fireproof dishes and cook in a cool oven for 20–25 minutes, until golden brown and set.

Mackerel (Fried)

Wipe the fish well with a clean cloth, split open and egg-and-breadcrumb them. Fry in a little butter, cut-side down first, for 7–8 minutes. Serve with maître d'hôtel butter (see Cookery in France).

Mackerel with Apple or Gooseberry Sauce

Wash the fish, cut off the heads and wipe with a clean cloth. (Do not wash after the heads are cut off as the flavour will be spoilt.) Score in two or three places and put small pieces of butter on the fish. Put under a hot grill and cook for 15 minutes, turning half-way. (The fish can be split open if preferred.) Serve with apple or gooseberry sauce or with pats of maître d'hôtel butter (see Cookery in France).

Marinated Herrings

Soak salt herrings in water for 24 hours, changing the water several times. Clean, bone and skin the herrings and dry them with a cloth. Roll fillets in flour and fry quickly in margarine. Put into glazed or ovenproof dish, add bay leaves, spices and pepper. Cover with cold boiled vinegar and leave for 2–3 days.

Marinated Mackerel or Herrings (for 3–4)

3 or 4 fish	12 peppercorns
¼ pint vinegar	Bay leaf
¼ pint water	Pepper and salt

Wash and clean the fish, put into a deep dish, head to tail. Pour over them the vinegar and water; then add the peppercorns, bay leaf and seasoning. Bake in a slow oven for about 1 hour, allow to cool, and serve cold.

Pickled Herrings (see chapter on Cookery in Scotland)

Savoury Herrings (for 4)

4 herrings	Juice of 1 lemon
1 tablespoonful chutney	Salt and pepper
	¼ oz. margarine

Scale, clean and bone the herrings and open them out flat. Sprinkle with salt and pepper, spread with a little chutney and fold together again. Place in a well-greased baking dish, sprinkle with the lemon juice and cover with a greased paper. Bake in a moderate oven for 10 minutes, then remove the paper and cook for a further 5 minutes until brown. NOTE: There is no fishy smell when herrings are cooked by this method.

Summer Kippers

Wrap kippers in greaseproof paper or put in a covered casserole and bake for 10 minutes.

PILCHARDS

Paprika Pilchards (for 4)

4 *pilchards*	*Potatoes*
Porridge oats	*About ½ pint milk*
½ oz. margarine	*1 tablespoonful*
1 dessertspoonful	*paprika*
flour	*Salt and pepper*
1 dessertspoonful	*1 tablespoonful*
tomato purée	*evaporated milk*

Butter a baking dish and cover the bottom with very thin slices of peeled potatoes. Dust with pepper and salt, then put on another layer of potatoes. Salt and pepper these, and sprinkle a few raw porridge oats over them. Heat a small cup of milk with margarine and pour over the potatoes. Cover the dish and bake for at least 1 hour, basting twice. Remove cover, place the cleaned and decapitated pilchards on the potatoes. Blend the paprika, flour, salt, pepper, tomato purée and evaporated milk, add ¼ pint milk and any liquid in the dish and bring to the boil, stirring carefully. Pour the sauce over the fish, replace in the oven and cook for a further ½ hour, basting at frequent intervals.

PLAICE

Fried Fillets of Plaice, Whiting, Haddock, etc.

See p. 32 for instructions on how to fry fish.

Fillets of Plaice (Grilled)

Heat the grill thoroughly and brush the fillets of plaice (two for each person) with oil to which has been added some chopped herbs, preferably fennel or thyme. Sprinkle the fillets with lemon juice and grill them slowly, first on one side and then on the other, brushing them occasionally with the herb - flavoured oil. Serve alone or with mornay or tartare sauce (see Sauces), or maître d'hôtel butter.

Fish in Batter

1 lb. fish
1 large egg
½ pint milk
¼ lb. flour
A dash of pepper and nutmeg
1 oz. dripping
Pinch of salt

Place dripping in a pie dish or meat tin. Wash and dry fish, cut into about eight pieces an darrange in dish. Cover with greaseproof paper and put into the oven for fat to get hot. Make the rest of the ingredients into a Yorkshire pudding batter (see Puddings and Sweets) and, when the fat is really hot, remove greaseproof paper, pour the batter into the tin and bake for about 40 minutes.

Fillets of Plaice (Steamed)

Wipe the fillets, season them and fold them over once. Then put them in a well-buttered tin with a very little milk. Cover with a piece of greased paper, put another tin on top and steam in a slow oven for about 10 minutes.

Make some white sauce, add to it the liquor from the fish and serve separately.

Fillets of Plaice with Shrimp Sauce (for 2–3)

Medium-sized plaice	*1 tablespoonful salt*
(filleted)	*Shrimp sauce (see*
Juice of a lemon	*Sauces chapter)*

Have the plaice cut into four fillets, roll each one up and pass a wooden skewer through them all. Put them in a deep pie dish, cover with cold water, squeeze in the juice of a lemon, add the salt, put the dish in the oven with a plate on top and bake until the fish is quite done.

Drain, remove the skewers and arrange the fillets neatly in an upright position. Pour the hot sauce over them and serve at once.

RED MULLET

Red Mullet (Grilled)

Cut off fins and tails of fish, scrape lightly, wash well and wipe with a cloth.

Score the sides of the fish, season with plenty of salt and pepper and a generous sprinkling of lemon juice. Smear with olive oil and put on a very hot grill. The fish should be accompanied by steamed potatoes (new, if possible) and by melted or anchovy butter.

COOK'S TIP

FISHY SMELLS quickly disappear from utensils used for cooking and eating fish if wiped with soft paper, then rinsed in cold water. A little mustard in the washing-up water also removes odour

Red Mullet à la Crème (for 4)

4 *small red mullet*	1 *teaspoonful olive*
1 *teaspoonful corn-*	*oil*
flour	1 *teaspoonful*
1 *tablespoonful butter*	*butter*
6 *tablespoonfuls*	3 *tablespoonfuls*
cream or top of	*sherry*
milk	

Salt, pepper and lemon juice

Cut off the fins and tails, scrape lightly and wipe with a cloth. Season through the gills with salt, pepper and lemon juice. Melt the tablespoonful of butter and olive oil and, when hot, fry the fish in it for 5 or 6 minutes on each side. Remove and keep warm. Add the extra butter to what is left in the pan and blend in the cornflour. Add the cream, season with salt, pepper and lemon juice, and stir in the sherry. Cook for a few minutes till smooth and serve over the fish.

Red Mullet au Gratin (for 2–3)

2 *red mullet*	½ *teaspoonful*
4 *button mushrooms*	*chopped onion*
1 *tablespoonful*	*Grated rind of ½ a*
sherry	*lemon*
1 *teaspoonful mush-*	1 *tablespoonful*
room ketchup	*browned bread-*
2 *oz. butter*	*crumbs*
1 *teaspoonful*	*Parsley and lemon*
chopped parsley	*slices to garnish*

Pepper and salt

Wash the fish, cut off their heads and fins, then dry with a clean cloth. Grease a dish with some of the butter, sprinkle over it half the onion, mushrooms, lemon rind and chopped parsley. Score the fish across once or twice and put them on top. Season, and add the rest of the chopped ingredients. Add sherry and ketchup, sprinkle on breadcrumbs, cut the remainder of the butter into small pieces and place on top, and bake in a moderate oven for about 20 minutes. Garnish with parsley and slices of lemon.

Red Mullet in Paper Cases (for 4)

4 *small red mullet*	*Salt, pepper, lemon*
3 *tablespoonfuls*	*juice*
butter	1 *tablespoonful*
1 *tablespoonful*	*chopped parsley*
finely minced	1 *teaspoonful*
shallot	*chopped fennel (if*
	available)

Cut off the fins and tails with kitchen scissors, but do not empty the fish as the liver is considered a delicacy. Scrape lightly, and wipe with a clean cloth. Season through the gills with salt, pepper and lemon juice. Work the parsley and shallot —and fennel if used—into the butter and spread the creamed mixture on the fish. Wrap each fish loosely but securely in a square of oiled greaseproof paper and cook in a fairly hot oven for about 15 minutes until tender. Serve the fish in their wrappers, but accompany with anchovy butter or a home-made tomato sauce or simply with cut lemon. (Chopped shrimps or anchovy fillets can be creamed into the butter with which the mullet are spread before baking, with excellent results).

Red Mullet Meunière (for 4)

4 *small red mullet*	1 *tablespoonful*
½ *teaspoonful olive*	*butter*
oil	*Good squeeze of*
1 *dessertspoonful*	*lemon juice*
chopped parsley	*Parsley and lemon*
Flour	*slices to garnish*

Salt and pepper

Trim and wipe the fish, and season well. Roll lightly in a little flour. Heat the butter and oil together and, when hot, fry the fish in it for about 10 minutes, turning once. Add the lemon juice and parsley to the pan, and another tablespoonful of butter; pour over the fish and serve simply garnished with sprigs of parsley and slices of lemon.

For a more elaborate dish, pound 4 anchovy fillets (previously soaked for several hours in water to remove the salt) with 1 sardine and 2 tablespoonfuls of butter, a tablespoonful of chopped parsley and a squeeze of lemon juice, and add this to the butter in the pan.

Red Mullet Venetian

Fry the mullet in oil. Serve surrounded by button mushrooms and stuffed olives with Sauce Venitienne: Reduce 8 tablespoonfuls of Tarragon vinegar and a good dessertspoonful of finely chopped shallot or chives by a good half and add it to ¾ pint of good white sauce.

SALMON

Salmon (Boiled)

Clean the fish and carefully scrape off the scales, then poach it *very* gently in salted water or court bouillon over a low heat so that it never quite boils. Allow 10 minutes per pound of fish plus an extra 10 minutes, at the end of which it should be a good even pink shade right through and

A special occasion fish dish: lightly poached trout, served cold, covered with green mayonnaise and decorated with red pimento to give a bizarre effect

will flake easily. If using frozen salmon, add a tablespoonful of olive oil to the cooking water; this eliminates any danger of excessive dryness.

Boiled salmon to be served cold should be left to cool in the water in which it was cooked and served with mayonnaise (see Salads chapter) or tartare sauce (see Sauces) and a cucumber salad.

Salmon (Baked)

Brush the piece of salmon well all over with melted butter or olive oil, season with salt and pepper, wrap up in greased paper and bake in a fairly hot oven, allowing about 1 hour for a piece of fish weighing about 1½ lb.

Salmon (Steamed)

Clean and scale the fish, then dip in boiling water for a few seconds to seal in the flavour and preserve the colour. Cook very gently over boiling water in a fish kettle, allowing about 20 minutes to the pound and 20 minutes over. Serve as for Boiled Salmon.

Salmon Steaks (Grilled)

Scrape off the scales with a very sharp knife and either marinade the steaks in olive oil for ½ hour or spread them well with butter on both sides. Grill them until both sides are golden. Serve with sliced lemon, pats of maître d'hôtel butter (see Cookery in France) or tartare sauce, fresh green peas or cucumber salad.

Salmon Steaks (Steamed)

Scrape off scales with a very sharp knife. Put the steaks in a casserole with a tablespoonful of water, a pinch of salt and a few lumps of butter. Cover first with greaseproof paper and then with the lid of the casserole, and cook in a moderate oven until the fish comes easily away from the bone.

Salmon Mousse (see p. 40)

SARDINES

Sardines Fried in Batter

Drain the sardines well on paper to remove the oil, skin them, remove heads and tails. Make fritter batter (see p. 123), dip the sardines in, one at a time, and fry in deep fat until brown. Serve with lemon and bread and butter.

SHELL FISH

Cockles and Mussels

Wash several times in clean water, sprinkle with salt and boil for about 10 minutes or until the shells open. Remove black weed from mussels. Steam off liquid. Serve with vinegar.

Dressed Crab (for 4)

1 cooked crab	1 tablespoonful
Chopped parsley	mayonnaise or
Green salad	French dressing
1 oz. breadcrumbs	(see Salads chapter)
Pepper and salt	

Remove the flesh from the large claws and the meat from the shell (being careful to discard the fingers or gills stuck to the sides of the shell, the bag or sac near the head and the green intestines). Mix the ingredients together, wash and dry the shell and fill with the mixture. Serve on a bed of green salad garnished with parsley and the small claws.

Lobster

Lobster is nearly always sold cooked. A good lobster is heavy in proportion to its size.

If uncooked, tie up the claws, wash, and plunge head down into boiling water. Cook for 35–45 minutes.

To prepare for table, break off the big claws and crack them carefully. Cut down the back with a sharp knife from head to tail, and remove the inside and the spongy-looking gills. Arrange the pieces of the body and the large claws on a dish and garnish with the small claws and salad. Serve with tartare sauce (see Sauces chapter), mayonnaise or French dressing (see Salads chapter).

Lobster au Gratin (for 4–5)

1 good-sized lobster	Breadcrumbs
1 teaspoonful	1 tablespoonful flour
chopped shallot	½ pint milk
1 oz. butter	Cayenne pepper
Chopped parsley	Anchovy essence
1 tablespoonful	1 egg-yolk
cream	Butter

Cut the lobster in half, dividing the head from the body, and take out all the meat, saving the shells. Cut the meat in slices.

Put a teaspoonful of chopped shallot in a saucepan with the butter and cook for a few minutes, add the flour, mixing well, and the milk, stir continually and let it boil gently for 5 minutes.

Add the lobster, seasoned with Cayenne pepper, chopped parsley and anchovy essence, put the saucepan back on the fire and stir until it boils. Remove from fire and stir in the egg-yolk and the cream. Fill the shells with the mixture, sprinkle breadcrumbs on top, dot with butter and bake in the oven for 20 minutes.

Lobster in the American Style (Homard à l'américaine) (see chapter on Cookery in France)

Lobster Mornay (as served at the Ivy Restaurant, London)

Take the cooked lobster off the shell and steep in white cream sauce (Béchamel) with grated Parmesan cheese. Replace lobster in shell and cover with sauce, sprinkle grated cheese over the top and place in a moderate oven or under the grill until golden brown.

Lobster Neuberg (see chapter on Cookery in the U.S.A.)

Lobster Thermidor (see chapter on Cookery in the U.S.A.)

Oyster Patties

Make puff pastry patties (see Pastry).

Beard and scald the oysters, cut them up into three or four pieces, put into a sauce made with cornflour, Cayenne pepper and salt, lemon juice and cream, and heat through. If the patties are to be served hot, put some of the mixture into each patty, put on the lids, and heat for 2 or 3 minutes in the oven. If they are to be served cold, let the mixture get cold before filling the patties.

Scalloped Oysters

Scald the oysters in their own liquor. Take them out, beard them and strain. Put in scallop shells and between each layer of oysters sprinkle a few breadcrumbs seasoned with pepper, salt and a little nutmeg. Top with small pieces of butter and enough breadcrumbs to make a smooth surface to cover the oysters. Bake in a quick oven for 5 minutes.

Scalloped Scallops

Wash the scallops, wipe them, remove the beards and black part, then cut up into three or four pieces. Stew in a little milk with pepper and salt, remove the scallops, thicken the liquor with flour made into a smooth paste, replace the scallops and re-heat. Butter the shells, scatter bread-crumbs over them and put in enough of the mixture just to cover. Scatter some more breadcrumbs over each, put a small piece of butter on top and brown in the oven.

Scallops (for 2–3)

6 scallops	Fat for frying
Pepper and salt	Flour
Egg and breadcrumbs	

Scallops must be absolutely fresh to be wholesome. Open the shells and remove the beards and any black parts, leaving only the yellow and white part to be eaten. Wash, dry and scatter seasoned flour over them, then egg-and-breadcrumb and fry in deep fat for 3–4 minutes. Drain well and serve in shells, garnished with parsley and cut lemon.

Scampis (Dublin Bay Prawns) Frits (as served at the Ivy Restaurant, London)

(1) Pass the prawns in milk and flour and fry in deep fat until golden. May be served with Tartare or Tomato Sauce or lemon.

(2) Pass the prawns in flour, milk and breadcrumbs and fry in deep fat until golden. Serve with sauces as above.

(3) *Meunière.* Pass the prawns in flour. Pour oil into frying pan, cook the scampis in it until a golden colour. Serve with lemon juice, golden (melted) butter to which parsley is added, and season to taste.

SKATE

Skate (for 3–4)

1 lb. skate	1½ oz. grated cheese
4 oz. breadcrumbs	1 gill white sauce

Boil the fish in salted water until it comes away easily from the bones, drain well and flake up. Put a layer of fish into a greased fireproof dish, cover with breadcrumbs and a good sprinkling of cheese. Continue these layers until all are used up, then pour over the well-seasoned sauce and bake in a fairly hot oven until brown on top—about 30 minutes.

SMELTS

Smelts (for 2)

6 smelts	Butter
Seasoning	1 dessertspoonful
Egg and breadcrumbs	chopped parsley

Wipe the fish, split them open and season

Red Mullet, cooked in greaseproof paper, are served in their wrappers

them. Then egg-and-breadcrumb them and fry in a little butter until a golden brown. Sprinkle chopped parsley over them and serve with anchovy sauce, black butter or melted butter (see Sauces).

SOLE

Sole au Parmesan

Fillets of sole	Cheese sauce
Pepper, salt and	Grated cheese
Cayenne	

Wipe the fillets, roll up and put in a well-buttered tin with a little pepper and salt, and bake for 15 minutes. Make cheese sauce (see Sauces and use fish stock instead of milk) and add a little Cayenne. Pour the sauce over the fish and sprinkle grated cheese over the top. Finish either under a hot grill or in the oven.

NOTE: Fillets of any other white fish can be cooked in the same way.

Sole Béchamel

Cook in the same way as for Sole au Parmesan (see previous recipe), but serve with Béchamel sauce) (see Sauces) in place of cheese sauce. Use fish stock, if possible, for the sauce instead of milk.

Sole Duglère (as served at the Ivy Restaurant, London)

Place sole in a casserole and smother with chopped shallots, parsley and tomatoes, a little white wine or lemon juice and cook in the oven. When cooked, take fish up. To make sauce, bring what remains in the dish to the boil (adding a little fish stock if too thick), reduce slightly, then add a little cream or top of the milk, butter and seasoning.

Sole Véronique (for 4)

4 large fillets of sole (lemon will do)	2 oz. butter
1 shallot	4 tablespoonfuls white wine or dry
2 tablespoonfuls white sauce	cider
	½ lb. white grapes
Salt and pepper	

Peel the grapes and take out the pips. Lay the fillets of sole flat in a frying pan, dot with half the butter, sprinkle with salt and pepper and finely chopped shallot and pour over them the wine or cider. Cover and poach very gently for about 10 minutes. Dish up and keep hot while you stir the white sauce and rest of the butter into the liquor in the pan. Stir over a low heat until piping hot and creamy. At the last minute stir in the prepared grapes and pour over the fish, serving immediately.

SPRATS

Salt Fried Sprats

Wash sprats. Heat a heavy iron frying pan. Sprinkle fairly generously with salt and put the sprats in over a moderate heat. When brown on one side, turn and brown on the other. Serve immediately on really hot plates with sliced lemon.

TROUT

Trout

This fish may be grilled, fried, baked or boiled. Freshwater trout should be thoroughly washed in salted water to get rid of the muddy taste.

Trout (Boiled)

Poach very gently over a low heat in salted water or a court bouillon containing white wine. When cooked, drain thoroughly, then arrange the fish on a hot dish. Garnish with Hollandaise or gooseberry sauce (see Sauces) and serve boiled potatoes with it.

Trout in Court Bouillon

In a court bouillon made from white wine, seasoned with onion, parsley, thyme, bay leaf, salt and pepper, simmer the trout very gently. When done, remove from liquid and leave to cool. Serve cold, preferably quite plain but, if desired, with a sauce made from a little of the liquor in which the fish were cooked, blended with butter and flour and reduced by half.

Trout (Baked)

Drain and dry the fish after cleansing, then put in a greased fireproof dish and sprinkle with pepper and salt, chopped parsley and shallot. Pour over plenty of melted butter and lemon juice, and bake in a moderate oven for 20–25 minutes, according to size of fish. Serve with black butter sauce (see Sauces).

Trout (Fried)

Clean, wash and dry some small trout and fry in olive oil. Sprinkle with lemon juice and serve with slices of lemon.

Trout (Grilled)

Score the prepared trout on both sides, brush them liberally with olive oil and grill for 3 or 4 minutes on each side. Serve hot with tartare sauce (see Sauces chapter).

TURBOT

Turbot

The delicate flavour of this fish is best preserved by either boiling or, better still, steaming. It should be rubbed over with lemon to preserve its colour, and on no account should it be overcooked. Garnish with parsley and lemon and serve a good sauce with it.

NOTE: An excellent way to steam turbot is to put it between two dishes with a little milk and butter and cook it slowly in the oven.

(Brill can be cooked in the same way as turbot.)

WHITEBAIT

Whitebait (Fried)

Wash the whitebait, drain in a colander, then put on a cloth and turn over and over until the fish are quite dry. Put some seasoned flour on a piece of paper and toss the fish in it. Put them in a strainer and shake off any surplus flour. Have some deep fat ready, put a few fish at a time in the frying basket and plunge the basket into the boiling fat for about 2 minutes. Take out, put on paper and keep hot. Reheat the fat between each frying. When all are cooked, put the whole lot back in the basket and plunge them back in the fat for 1 minute. They should be a very light brown and quite crisp. Drain well on paper, and serve with lemon slices and brown bread and butter.

WHITING

Whiting au Parmesan

Wipe the fillets and put them on a greased tin in the oven with some pepper and salt and a tablespoonful of milk. Cover with greased paper and put another tin on top. Cook for a few minutes. Make cheese sauce (see Sauces chapter) with grated Parmesan cheese and pour it over the fillets. They can either be put under the grill to finish or back into the oven.

Whiting Bercy

Butter a dish, sprinkle it with chopped shallot and parsley, and lay the fish on this. Season with salt and pepper, moisten with cider and cook in the oven with frequent bastings. Dish up the whiting, reduce the cooking liquor by half, thicken it, pour it over the fish and boil quickly.

Whiting Colbert

Open the fish down the centre of the back and remove the backbone after breaking it near the head and tail. Season, egg-and-breadcrumb, and fry in deep fat. Serve covered with maître d'hôtel butter (see Cookery in France).

Whiting with Caper Sauce

Wipe the fish with a dry cloth, put the tails into the mouths and fasten with skewers, egg-and-breadcrumb them and fry a rich brown. Drain well and serve with caper sauce.

NOTE: Whiting can also be steamed or put between two dishes in the oven with a little milk or butter.

Most luxurious of all fish dishes is steamed salmon, here seen decorated with endive and slices of lemon colourfully topped with beetroot and cucumber

MEAT

Choose it with skill, cook it with loving care and serve it elegantly—
for it is the basis of most main meals

IT is a well known fact that tough meat is not always the butcher's fault and that wrong cooking can ruin the choicest cuts. It is equally true that the best cooking in the world can do little to help if the meat itself is at fault. For that reason it is essential that every housewife who wants her meat course to be successful should know something about how to choose meat wisely. Here are the guiding principles.

CHOOSING MEAT
General

Meat, one of the most valuable sources of protein in our diet, consists mainly of fibres bound together by a tough substance known as connective tissue. The parts of the animal which are in most active use during its lifetime—such as the legs and neck—have more connective tissue and are therefore tougher than cuts from less active portions of its anatomy. They therefore need longer, slower cooking.

Too recently killed—and therefore too fresh—meat always tends to be tough. The best way to make it tender is to steep it in a marinade of vinegar (with or without olive oil), flavoured with spices and herbs, or to add lemon juice, vinegar, wine or cider during cooking. There are also several good proprietary meat tenderisers on the market which achieve the same result.

Imported meat which is still frozen must be carefully thawed, preferably in a warm kitchen. During this process it will change colour: this is only the effect of defrosting and does not mean the meat is not good. There is very little difference—except in price—between home-killed and good imported meat. When well cooked, imported joints have the same flavour, tenderness and nourishment.

Beef should be bright red in colour, well covered with firm, white fat and the flesh firm to the touch. If it is to be tender, it should be well hung before cooking and, whether kept in a cool larder or in a refrigerator, should always stand at room temperature for an hour or more before cooking. There is as much food value in the cheaper cuts as the expensive ones, but the cheaper ones need longer, more careful cooking. The diagram facing p. 64 shows from which parts of the animal the main cuts of beef come; here is a guide to cooking them.

Roasting Joints of Beef.—Sirloin, rib, aitchbone, sometimes silverside, brisket, topside, flank (thick end), baron of beef (2 sirloins together).

Grill or Fry.—Fillet or rump steak.

Salt and Boil.—Silverside, brisket.

Braise/Stew. — Aitchbone or top rib, silverside, flank, hock, brisket, shin, oxtail, blade and chuck.

For Soups and Gravies.—Hock, neck, shin, oxtail.

Mutton should be a dull red, firm and fine in grain. The fat should be white and hard. It is more easily digested than beef and should also be hung well before it is cooked.

Lamb is pink rather than red, the fat being firm and of a clear whitish colour, the bone at the joint in chops being reddish. It is also more digestible than beef, but should not be hung for long.

Turn to the diagram facing p. 64 to see where the joints of mutton and lamb are located on the animal. Now to cook them:

Roasting Joints of Mutton and Lamb.—Leg, loin, saddle of mutton, shoulder, best end of neck.

Fry, Grill or Bake.—Loin chops and cutlets, lamb's kidneys and liver.

Boil.—Leg.

Stew.—Scrag, breast, loin, lamb's tongue, lamb's kidneys, lamb's liver, sweetbreads.

Veal, the flesh of a calf, should be pinkish

54

With roast mutton, either hot or cold, the perfect contrast in flavour is a tart red currant jelly

white, not so firm as beef and the fat slightly pink. The flesh should on no account feel clammy to the touch or be flabby. Unlike the pinkish veal known in Britain, Continental veal is almost pure white—being the flesh of milk-fed calves. Veal requires longer cooking than other meats and is less easily digested.

See diagram facing p. 65 for the joints of veal, which are best cooked as follows:

Roasting Joints.—Fillet or loin, leg, shoulder, best end.

Stew.—Breast, knuckle, calf's tongue.

Grill or Fry.—Chops or cutlets, fillet, calf's liver, calf's kidneys.

Pork fat should be white but the lean varies in colour according to the age of the animal. In a young pig it is practically white, while in an older one it is pink. The flesh should be finely grained and firm to touch. When cooked, the pork fat should be white, *never* pink. It is important that pork should be absolutely fresh and cooked very thoroughly—and slowly. If cooked too quickly, it will be tough and indigestible, and it is not in any case as easily digested as beef or mutton.

Turn to illustration facing p. 65 for diagrams showing where joints of both pork and bacon are cut from the pig. Here is the general cooking guide:

Roasting Joints of Pork.—Leg, spare rib, chine, loin, blade.

Salt and Boil.—Chine, pig's head.

Boil.—Belly, hand, tongue, pig's feet.

Grill or Fry.—Chops.

Stew.—Pig's fry.

Pickle.—Pig's cheeks (bath chaps).

Bacon and Ham

Bacon is the name for the back and sides and ham for the hind legs of a pig when they have been salted, cured and, perhaps, also smoked. Bacon that is salted and dried only is known as green bacon.

The fat should be a clear white and the lean firm, with a thick rind. The best way to test the condition of a whole uncooked ham is to run a long thin carving knife right in as far as the bone; if the blade point smells fresh and pleasant when withdrawn, the ham is nice and fresh. Most hams require soaking overnight before they are boiled.

The diagram facing p. 65 shows from

which part of the pig the various pieces of bacon come. This is the cooking guide:

Boiling Joints of Bacon.—Gammon, hock, loin, collar.

Grill or Fry (Rashers).—Gammon, streaky, back, collar, long loin.

Venison, the flesh of the deer, must be kept for some time to attain its proper game flavour and must therefore be chosen with great care to make certain it is fresh. The safest test is that suggested for ham— to plunge a long thin-bladed knife into the joint close to the bone. If the tip of the blade smells sweet when withdrawn, the venison is in good condition.

Roasting Joints of Venison.—Leg and loin (separately or together as the haunch), fillet.

Grill or Fry.—Chops.

Stew or Broil.—Steak, best end of neck, breast.

For Pie or Pasty.—Neck or breast.

TO PREPARE MEAT FOR COOKING

All meat should be thoroughly wiped with a damp cloth before cooking. Salted meats should first be soaked in cold water for about 4 hours. If in hot weather meat develops a slight smell, wipe it with a cloth dipped in vinegar and wrung out.

COOKING MEAT

Meat may be boiled, braised, pot roasted, stewed, grilled, fried or roasted.

Boiling

Fresh meat should be put into boiling water, cooked rapidly for about 5 minutes, then simmered gently. Salted meat should be covered with cold or tepid water, brought slowly to the boil and simmered. The minimum of water—just enough to cover—ensures the best flavour, and a bouquet garni, some peppercorns and/or an onion stuck with half a dozen cloves should be included. When the water has boiled, skim, put a lid on the pan and cook until it is possible to run a fine skewer easily through the meat. Cooking times are difficult to give in general terms, as so much depends on the meat and the dish to be made. An average of 20 minutes to the pound plus 20 minutes over is a good rough

guide for beef and mutton; 25-30 minutes per pound for pork, bacon and ham (minimum 45 minutes), 30 minutes per pound and 30 minutes over for salt beef.

Small joints do not lend themselves so well to boiling as larger ones and easily get overcooked and tough. The water must never be allowed to boil fast or the meat will be tasteless as well as hard. For a tender joint with a full rich flavour, simmer gently. Keep the liquid for soups and gravies.

Braising

This is an excellent way of cooking cheaper and less tender cuts. First brown the meat in enough melted fat to cover the bottom of the pan; then brown some mixed diced vegetables—carrots, onions, parsnips, turnips and potatoes—and drain off all surplus fat. Season to taste, add a bouquet garni, put the meat on top of the vegetables in the saucepan or casserole, pour in about half a pint of stock or water, cover with a tight-fitting lid and simmer very gently, either in the oven or over a low heat until the meat is tender. This method is ideal for small joints, kidneys, cutlets, fillets, sweetbreads, etc.

Pot Roasting

This is a very similar method to braising except that no liquid is used, the meat being cooked in a saucepan in fat only. A very strong saucepan is necessary or it will burn. Brown the meat—and the vegetables, if these are to be cooked with the joint— exactly as for braising. Leave the surplus liquid fat in the saucepan with the meat, put on a tight-fitting lid and cook very slowly till tender, allowing 40-45 minutes per pound, according to the thickness of the meat.

Stewing

This is often the busy housewife's refuge when she has little time to spare and a meal to cook for the family. Once a stew is prepared, it needs little or no attention—except to see that it never actually boils. This is all-important—to keep it simmering gently only. A stew cooks equally well on the top of the stove in a saucepan with a well-fitting lid or in a covered fireproof dish or casserole in the oven. The cheaper cuts of meat can be cooked slowly in this way until they are tender, preferably with not too much liquid and plenty of vegetables and seasonings. Allow between 2 and 3 hours. When done, the gravy should be thick and rich.

Grilling

One of the most delicious ways of cooking meat, it is also one of the quickest. For this reason it is suitable only for the best thin cuts, such as lamb or pork chops, fillets of beef, steaks, kidneys, sausages, bacon and ham. First, make sure that the grill is red hot when you start cooking the meat. Next, grease and warm the grid. Spread the meat lightly on both sides with butter or let it stand for a few minutes on a plate in olive oil. Season it, put it on the heated and greased grid, and let it sizzle gently until one side is cooked. Turn it with two knives or plastic meat tongs, but never with a fork because, if the meat is punctured, the juices will run out and much of the goodness and flavour be lost. Cook the other side, basting with the liquid fat.

The time required varies according to the thickness of the meat but, roughly, steak should take 8–20 minutes (depending on thickness and also on whether it is preferred well- or under-done); cutlets 7–10 minutes, kidneys about 8 minutes, bacon rashers between 3 and 5 minutes (according to thickness), sausages about 10 minutes.

Frying

This is a tasty way of cooking meat, whether it is deep- or shallow-fried, but much less digestible than grilling. Oil, lard, vegetable fat or clarified dripping may be used and should be heated until a faint blue smoke rises from the pan. (Beyond this point it will smoke and burn, and the fat become unsuitable for further use. The test of a high-quality frying fat or oil is that it can be heated to at least 360° F. before it begins to smoke or burn.)

For deep-fat frying, a deep but not too wide and very solid saucepan is needed and a frying basket that will fit into it easily. Meat to be fried is usually covered either with flour and egg and breadcrumbs, or batter. If in flour and egg and breadcrumbs, it should be put into the basket

For crisp crackling like this, get your butcher to score the pork, then baste it frequently while roasting. And don't forget the apple sauce !

57

MEAT

and lowered into the hot fat, which should nearly half-fill the pan. Meat coated in batter should be lowered straight into the pan and not put into a frying basket because the batter tends to stick to the wires; as it cooks, it rises to the top and can be easily taken out with a fish slice or ladle.

Do not try to fry too much at a time, as this reduces the temperature of the fat. Remember to heat up the fat again to the point where the faint blue haze appears before putting in another batch for cooking. When the meat is cooked, drain well on kitchen paper and keep hot.

Shallow-frying is the method used for food not encased in batter or flour, egg and breadcrumbs. A frying pan is used and only just enough clean, moisture-free fat (vegetable oil or fat, lard or clarified dripping) to cover the bottom. Heat until the faint blue haze appears, then put in the meat, brown it on one side and turn it for the other side to brown. Allow the same times as for grilling. When shallow-frying fat bacon, heat the pan well but do not use any fat; just put in the rashers and cook them in their own fat.

Of the two methods, deep-fat frying, though it needs far more fat to begin with, is the more economical since the same fat can be used again and again, provided it is kept in good condition. After use and when it has cooled a little, it should be run through a strainer into a jar.

To clarify fat.—Fat that has become brown and discoloured or contains particles of food can be clarified for future use. Put the fat into a saucepan and cover it with water. Bring to the boil, stir in a pinch of bicarbonate of soda and pour into a clean basin and leave to cool. When cold, the fat will rise and form a cake on top. Lift this off, scrape away any sediment from underneath, wipe the fat and put aside for future use. If required for frying, melt the fat again in a saucepan and heat until it stops bubbling—an indication that no more water remains in it. Cool and store for frying.

To render fat.—Any scraps of fat from beef, mutton, pork or veal may be used. Remove skin, flesh and discoloured parts, then cut the fat up small, put into a strong saucepan and cover with cold water. Simmer, without a lid on the pan, for several hours, stirring from time to time, until the remaining liquid is clear yellow. Cool, strain through a cloth and use for all frying.

Roasting

(1) Put the joint on a rack in a baking tin with the fat side upwards and some pieces of dripping on top. Stand this tin in a larger tin and put a little water in the lower one, filling it up when necessary. The steam from the water helps to keep the joint moist and prevents it from shrinking. Cover the meat with greased paper—partly to prevent it from getting scorched and partly to keep the oven clean. The oven should be very hot for the first 10 minutes, moderate for the rest of the cooking time. Allow roughly 20 minutes for each pound of meat and 20 minutes over for beef and mutton; say, 25 minutes to the pound and 25 minutes over for veal and pork. Baste frequently, particularly if the joint is lean, or to provide good crackling on a joint of pork. Basting is not so necessary when the joint is cooked in a covered roasting tin.

(2) Large joints are better cooked at a moderate temperature throughout and the cheaper cuts should always be roasted slowly at low temperature.

To Make Gravy

Drain off the fat from the baking tin, leaving only the sediment, and put the tin over a low heat, add a little pepper and salt and some stock or vegetable water, and stir well. Serve it clear with beef and mutton.

To thicken the gravy, leave a tablespoonful of the liquid fat with the sediment, stir in a tablespoonful of flour and cook for 5 minutes until brown, stirring frequently, then add stock or vegetable water and seasoning, together with a little browning if liked.

BEEF

Beef à la Mode (for 4)

2 lb. lean beef	3 oz. butter or dripping
Stock	ping
Bouquet garni	Pepper and salt to
A few button onions	taste
and mushrooms	6 small carrots

Wash and peel vegetables and halve mushrooms and carrots. Fry the meat

When grilling steak, always turn it between two knives—or with plastic tongs—
so that the meat is not punctured

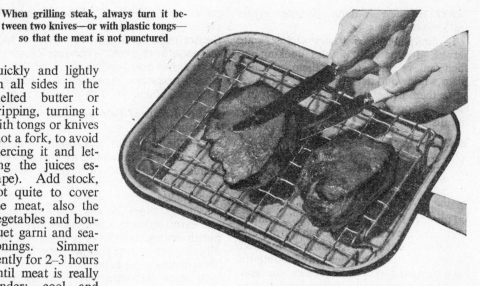

quickly and lightly on all sides in the melted butter or dripping, turning it with tongs or knives (not a fork, to avoid piercing it and letting the juices escape). Add stock, not quite to cover the meat, also the vegetables and bouquet garni and seasonings. Simmer gently for 2–3 hours until meat is really tender; cool and skim fat from gravy; reheat and serve hot from casserole.

Beef Olives (for 4–5)

1 lb. lean beefsteak cut very thin in small slices	1 oz. butter or dripping
½ pint stock	Pepper and salt
1 dessertspoonful mushroom ketchup	1 oz. flour
	Veal stuffing (see Poultry chapter)
1 onion	

Make some veal stuffing. Put the slices of meat on a board and spread them with stuffing, keeping it well away from the edges. Roll them and put them four deep on a skewer or tie them up separately with cotton. Shake a little flour over them. Melt the butter and, when hot, fry the sliced onion until brown. Put the onion into a casserole, then fry the meat until brown and add it to the onion.

Make some thick gravy in the frying pan with the flour and stock, season and strain it over the olives. Put the casserole either in a moderate oven or over a slow flame and cook for 2 hours or more until the meat is tender. Add the mushroom ketchup just before serving. Garnish with shredded cooked carrot and turnip in little heaps, sprinkling chopped parsley over them.

NOTE: Cold under-done beef can also be made into olives, but in this case fry the onions only, add the olives to the gravy and cook over a low heat or in the oven for 30 minutes, then serve.

Beef Roll (for 4–5)

1 lb. fresh minced beef	1 dessertspoonful flour
2 bacon rashers, chopped	1 gill stock
2 oz. breadcrumbs	Pepper and salt
	Pinch of dried herbs
1 egg	

Mix the dry ingredients together in a basin and add the stock and beaten egg. Bind the mixture together and form into a roll on a floured board, pressing the edges well together. Scald a pudding cloth, flour it and put the roll in it, tying it securely. Steam for 1½ hours and serve cold.

A hot beef roll can be baked or steamed. If baked, cover with greased paper and baste well. Serve with brown or tomato sauce.

Beef Stew (Economical) (for 4–5)

1 lb. shin or thick flank of beef or oxtail or oxcheek	1 level tablespoonful flour
¾ pint water or brown stock	Pinch of herbs, if desired
Seasoned flour	Onion, carrot and turnip
Fat for frying	

Wipe the meat, cut it into small pieces, roll it in seasoned flour and fry quickly in a saucepan or casserole in just enough fat to prevent it burning. Then add the water or stock and the cut-up vegetables and herbs, bring to the boil and simmer very gently for about 2 hours.

Make a smooth paste with the flour and a little water, and add, stirring well, just before the stew is done. Simmer gently for 5 minutes.

If dumplings (see Pastry chapter) are served, give them 20 minutes' cooking and then remove them, putting them on a hot-plate while you stir in the flour. Then replace them if the stew is to be served in a casserole, or put them with the stew on a hot dish.

Boiled Beef and Dumplings

Silverside, thick flank, brisket, aitch-bone or round of beef	Carrots, turnips and onions

Weigh the meat and rinse it well. Allow 20 minutes for each pound and 20 minutes over. Put the meat into enough warm water to cover it and bring it slowly to the boil. Skim, then simmer very gently, adding the sliced vegetables ½ hour before the end. Suet dumplings (see Pastry chapter) may be added, and these will take 20 minutes to cook. Serve a little of the liquid in a sauce boat.

Braised Beef (for 5–6)

2 lb. round, shin, thick flank or rib of beef (boned, rolled and skewered) or oxtail or oxcheek	2 oz. butter or dripping Onion, carrot, turnip, parsnip, celery, as desired Pepper and salt
About 1 gill water	

Wipe the meat and tie it into shape. Melt the fat in a deep casserole or saucepan. Peel and cut up the vegetables and put them in with the seasoning. When they are hot, add the meat and the water. Put a piece of greased paper under the lid and cook in a slow oven for at least 2 hours.

Casserole of Beef (for 4–5)

1 lb. lean beefsteak	¾ pint stock (or water with a little Marmite)
1 large onion	
1 carrot	
1 turnip	Seasoning
Small head of celery	1 oz. butter or dripping
1 tablespoonful flour	

Cut the steak into fair-sized pieces and dip in the seasoned flour. Heat the butter in a frying pan, slice the onion and fry it quickly until brown. Put it into a casserole, then fry the meat quickly until brown and place it on top of the onion. Slice the other vegetables and put them on the meat. Pour in the stock. Brown the flour in the remaining fat in the frying pan, add enough water or stock to make it into a paste and

cook until it thickens. Strain it into the casserole and cook in a slow oven, or on the hot-plate, for at least 1½ hours. A half-teaspoonful of anchovy essence or two or three cloves add very much to the flavour. Boiled macaroni, separately cooked, may be placed round the dish when serving.

Grilled Fillets of Beef or Steak
(Tournedos)

Cut the meat into neat rounds about 1½ in. thick, season and grill for about 8 minutes, using plenty of butter or olive oil and turning once. (For grilling see p. 57.) The fillets can be served on a bed of mashed potatoes, or any green vegetable, and garnished with a little shredded horseradish on each fillet, or a pat of maître d'hôtel butter (see chapter on Sauces). Serve with a good gravy.

A more elaborate way is to fry some croûtes of bread exactly the size of the fillets and serve the fillets on these, topped with a mushroom and a little butter. A scrape of horseradish may also be added.

Grilled Steak

Always beat steaks hard on both sides with a rolling pin or large wooden spoon before cooking. Then grill as described earlier in this chapter, adapting the time according to whether it is liked under- or well-done. Steak may be slashed three or four times across the top and a piece of butter inserted in each. Serve with vegetables according to taste, and garnish with grilled tomatoes, mushrooms and fresh watercress.

Jugged Beef (for 7–8)

2 lb. thick lean beef-steak	Port, claret or marsala
2 rashers of fat bacon	2 tablespoonfuls flour
1 large onion, peeled and sliced	Rind of half a lemon, 4 cloves, bay leaf,
1 pint stock or water	bunch of herbs
2 oz. butter or dripping	(in muslin bag)
1 carrot	1 tablespoonful red currant jelly
Forcemeat balls (see chapter on Poultry)	

Cut the meat into 1-in. cubes and roll in flour. Cut the bacon into cubes. Melt the butter or dripping in a frying pan and, when hot, fry the onion until brown. Put it into a deep casserole or saucepan. Then fry the meat and bacon until brown and add them to the casserole with the stock, the carrot (cut in half), and the lemon rind, cloves, etc., tied up in a muslin bag.

Specially cooked and photographed in the Creda kitchens

An appetising way of serving Haricot Mutton, garnished with small whole onions and rosettes of mashed potato. With it go chicory and young carrots in white sauce and green peas

Make some thick gravy in the frying pan with a little stock or water and flour and strain it into the casserole. Simmer gently for 2 hours, or cook in a moderate oven.

Make forcemeat balls, roll them in breadcrumbs and fry until brown. Put them in the casserole 10 minutes before serving. At the last moment, add the wine as desired and the red currant jelly. Serve with red currant jelly.

Oxtail

Wash the tail well, divide into pieces, then dry. Proceed as for Casserole of Beef (see previous page), but allow a quart of stock or water instead of three-quarters of a pint and cook slowly for 3–4 hours

or longer, if necessary, until the tail is quite tender and the meat comes easily off the bones.

Ox Tongue

Ox tongue
1 large onion
1 large carrot
    Salt
1 turnip
Bunch of herbs in a
   muslin bag

Trim the tongue, cleaning the root thoroughly, and let it soak in cold water for 1 hour, or up to 24 hours if the tongue has been smoked and hung for some time. Then put it on its side in a saucepan in tepid water, with the herbs, and bring slowly to the boil. Skim well, and simmer gently for 3 hours, or until tender. Cut up the vegetables and put them in with the tongue for the last $\frac{3}{4}$ hour. Take out the tongue and skin it, then place it on a warm dish and use the vegetables as a garnish.

Serve with caper, Cumberland or parsley sauce (see chapter on Sauces). If to be served cold, press tightly into a round tin only just big enough to take it. Leave to get quite cold, then turn out of tin.

Pressed Beef

4 lb. brisket	A few peppercorns,
1 dessertspoonful salt	2 bay leaves, blade
A pinch of mixed	of mace, a few all-
spice	spice, $\frac{1}{2}$ teaspoonful
Large onion	mixed herbs (tied
Carrot	up in a muslin bag)
Turnip	

For the glaze

1 teacupful stock	1 teaspoonful
Browning	powdered gelatine

Wipe the meat well, rub in the salt and the mixed spice, and leave it in a bowl for 12 hours, turning it once during that time. Put it into a saucepan, just cover with tepid water, add the vegetables, cut up, and the herbs in muslin bag, and bring to the boil. Simmer very slowly for about 2 hours or until the bones can be easily removed. Take out the meat, remove the bones and turn the meat on to a dish. Put another dish on top and heavy weights on this. Leave to get cold. Strain off a cupful of the liquor, add a teaspoonful of powdered gelatine and a little browning to colour it. Stir it well until the gelatine is dissolved. Allow to cool, then pour it over the meat. Before the glaze hardens, garnish the beef either with hard-boiled eggs cut into patterns, or with sprinkles of heaped chopped parsley, or with the remains of the gelatine made darker and cut into fancy shapes.

Roast Beef

Sirloin or ribs of beef are the best joints for roasting, but round of beef, aitchbone or thick flank can also be cooked in this way. They should, however, have longer cooking and frequent basting (see Roasting, p. 58).

Serve with Yorkshire pudding (see Puddings chapter) and horseradish sauce.

Vienna Steaks (for 3–4)

1 lb. lean beefsteak	Very small pinch of
1 rasher of bacon	spice
1 very small onion	1 level tablespoonful
Egg or milk to bind	flour
Pepper and salt	Fat for frying

Mince the beef, bacon and onion, and mix with the spice, seasoning and enough egg or milk to bind. Make into small cakes about 1 in. thick, flour lightly and fry in a very little hot fat, browning quickly on both sides. Then cover the pan and cook very slowly for $\frac{1}{4}$ hour. Serve with thick brown gravy or tomato sauce and either chip or cone potatoes and small tomatoes baked whole.

MUTTON AND LAMB

Boiled Lamb or Mutton

Leg or middle neck can be boiled (see p. 56). Serve either with caper or onion sauce.

Braised Shoulder of Mutton

Shoulder of mutton	1 pint hot water
Onion, carrot,	Pepper and salt
parsnip, turnip,	Bunch of herbs
celery	2 oz. butter or drip-
1 tablespoonful flour	ping

Remove the bone from the meat, or get the butcher to do this. Wipe the meat and tie it into shape. Melt the fat in a deep baking tin or very large casserole and put in the cut-up vegetables, herbs, and pepper and salt. Cook for a few minutes. Put the mutton in a quick oven for 10 minutes, then place it on top of the vegetables, pour over the water and put a piece of greased paper over the meat. Cover with lid or another tin and cook in a slow oven for at least 3 hours, removing the lid for the last $\frac{1}{2}$ hour. Take out the meat, strain off the gravy and put the vegetables round the meat. Then thicken the gravy with the flour and serve separately. Red currant jelly or cranberry sauce should also be served with this dish.

Cutlets—Mutton or Lamb (Fried)

Best end of neck	Dripping or butter
Pepper and salt	Egg and breadcrumbs

Get the butcher to saw off the chine bone; it is then quite easy to separate the cutlets. Wipe the meat and divide up the cutlets, cutting off the end bones. Trim away any superfluous fat and make them as good a shape and as much of a size as possible. Season, brush over with beaten egg, dip in fine breadcrumbs and stand for a few minutes on a piece of paper in a dish or tin. Melt the fat until the blue smoke rises, then put in the cutlets and cook for about 10 minutes, or until they are a nice brown on both sides. Drain well before serving.

The usual way of serving is to prop them up round a heap of mashed potatoes or green vegetables with the bones all the same side, or arrange them in the middle and put a ring of mashed potatoes round. Garnish with green peas, baked tomatoes or mushrooms, and serve with brown onion, piquant or tomato sauce (see chapter on Sauces).

Cutlets—Mutton or Lamb (Grilled)

Prepare as for frying, but instead of egg and breadcrumbs, either spread with butter on both sides or stand in olive oil on a plate for a few minutes, turning them over once (for grilling, see p. 57).

Haricot Mutton (for 4–5)

1 lb. best end of neck or middle neck	2 oz. haricot beans
1 oz. flour	1 onion
1 oz. butter or dripping	1 small carrot
	Pepper and salt
	¾ pint stock (or water)

Soak the beans overnight, put them into cold water and boil gently until soft. Keep them hot. Prepare the meat by cutting off the fat and dividing into small pieces. Melt the butter in a saucepan or casserole and fry the sliced onion until pale brown. Take it out and keep hot, then fry the meat and, when brown, remove. Put the flour in the pan and brown it, then add the stock and seasoning and bring to the boil, skimming well. Put the meat and onion back, and the sliced carrot, and simmer gently for 1½ hours. To serve, put the meat on a hot dish, season the sauce and pour over it, and add the beans either in small heaps or at either end. Sprinkle them with parsley. Garnish with any seasonable vegetables.

Hotpot (for 5–6)

1½ lb. best end or middle neck of mutton	1 onion
	2 sheep's kidneys
	1 oz. flour
1½ lb. potatoes	Pepper and salt
½ pint warm stock or water	1 tablespoonful mushroom ketchup
1 oz. dripping	

Cut meat into neat pieces and brown in the hot dripping; then put in a casserole or deep fireproof dish, and sprinkle with salt

For a really substantial and very appetising meal, serve a poached egg on top of a grilled steak, with fresh green peas and beans and new potatoes

and pepper. Brown the sliced onion in the dripping, add it to the casserole, and season. Next, brown the cut-up kidneys, season and add them. Cut half the potatoes into thick slices and the other half into quarters, and put the sliced ones on top of the kidneys. Make a thick gravy with the stock and flour in the frying pan; add the ketchup and strain over the potatoes. Then add the potato quarters and a few pieces of dripping on top. Put on the lid and cook in a moderate oven for 2 hours, removing the lid for the last ½ hour so that the potatoes may brown. Serve in the dish in which it is cooked. Mushrooms may be added if desired.

Irish Stew (for 5–6)

2 lb. middle neck or scrag end of mutton	1 lb. onions
2 lb. potatoes	About ½ pint water
	Pepper and salt

Wipe the meat and cut it up. Peel and cut up the potatoes and onions. Put into a saucepan alternate layers of potatoes, meat, onions and, lastly, potatoes. Add the water and pepper and salt, and simmer very gently for 2 hours.

Ragoût of Mutton (for 5–6)

1½ lb. middle neck	1 bay leaf
Onion, parsnip, turnip	2 oz. dripping or butter
1 pint water	1 tablespoonful mushroom ketchup or a few mushrooms
1 tablespoonful pearl barley soaked overnight	
Pepper and salt	

Wipe and cut up the meat. Brown it in the dripping in a frying pan, then put into a casserole. Dice the vegetables, fry them and put into the casserole with the water, bay leaf, pearl barley, pepper and salt, and ketchup or mushrooms. Bring to simmering point. Cover with a well-fitting lid and cook in a slow oven or on the hot-plate for 2 hours.

Roast Mutton or Lamb

Leg, loin, neck (best end), shoulder or stuffed breast can all be roasted (for roasting, see p. 58).

Serve with mint sauce or red currant jelly.

NOTE: Be careful to serve a shoulder the right way for carving. If you are not certain, put a fork in to find which is the fleshy part, allowing for a deep cut; this part should be farthest away from the carver.

Stuffed Roast Shoulder of Mutton

Take out the bone, wipe the meat well and season. Make some veal stuffing (see Poultry chapter) and put it in the middle of the mutton. Then tie it into shape with a piece of string, or sew it up. Weigh the meat, and roast in the usual way. When about to serve, take off the string or remove stitches.

NOTE: Leg of mutton or breast can also be stuffed and roasted.

PORK, BACON AND HAM

Boiled Bacon

Cover the bacon, in a saucepan, with cold water and bring slowly to the boil. Remove scum as it rises and simmer gently until skin comes off easily. Leave to cool in the cooking water (which, if not too salt, may be used for soups and gravies), remove skin, cover with browned breadcrumbs and serve either reheated or cold.

Boiled Ham

Soak the ham overnight, then put in a saucepan of warm water and bring slowly to the boil, letting it simmer very gently until it is tender. Allow 25 minutes to the pound and 25 minutes over. Test with a skewer or by seeing if the rind comes away easily. If overcooked, the meat will shrink away from the bone. Leave in cooking water until nearly cold, then take out and skin. Sprinkle with baked breadcrumbs and a little moist brown sugar.

To Bake.—Boil as above, but remove from heat just before the ham is cooked, stand in water until nearly cold, then skin and stick with cloves, cover with brown sugar and breadcrumbs, and bake in a moderate oven for 1 hour.

Brawn (for 5–6)

Half a pig's head (pickled)	1 teaspoonful dried herbs, 12 peppercorns (in a muslin bag)
2 onions	
1 tablespoonful chopped parsley	

Put the head in warm salted water for a few hours, and then clean thoroughly with a brush. Put it into enough warm water to cover, with the onions (whole) and the herbs in a bag, and bring to the boil. Sim-

HOW TO BUY MEAT

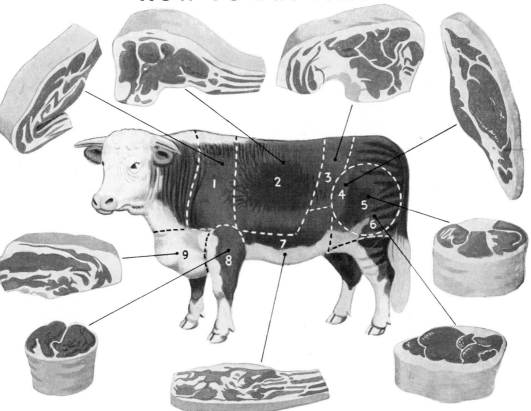

Choose **BEEF** with the help of the diagram above ; the flesh should be rich red and the fat white and firm.
1. Chuck, a cheap cut, needs slow cooking.   2. Ribs are good for roasting.   3. Sirloin is a fine but expensive joint.   4. Rump—steak for grilling or frying.   5. Silverside will roast, is perfect for traditional boiled beef.
6. Topside; pot roast or cook in casserole.   7. Flank, a cheap cut, for pies and stews.   8. Shin is cheap; use for beef tea.   9. Brisket is good salted and boiled.

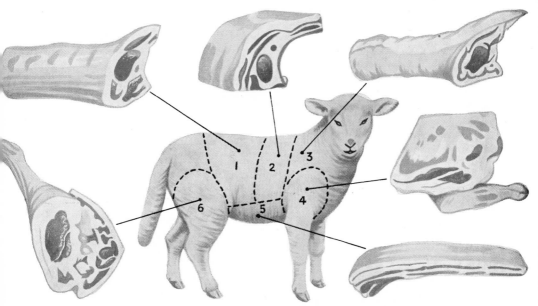

LAMB comes in the following joints, shown above; its flesh should be pink, the fat creamy white and firm.
1. Loin roasts well.   2. Best end of neck, a good roasting joint.   3. Neck makes excellent stews.   4. Shoulder is a fat but very tasty joint to roast.   5. Breast, the cheapest cut, is good for stewing; can also be boned, stuffed and roasted.   6. Leg may be roast or boiled.

HOW TO CARVE
MEAT AND POULTR[Y]

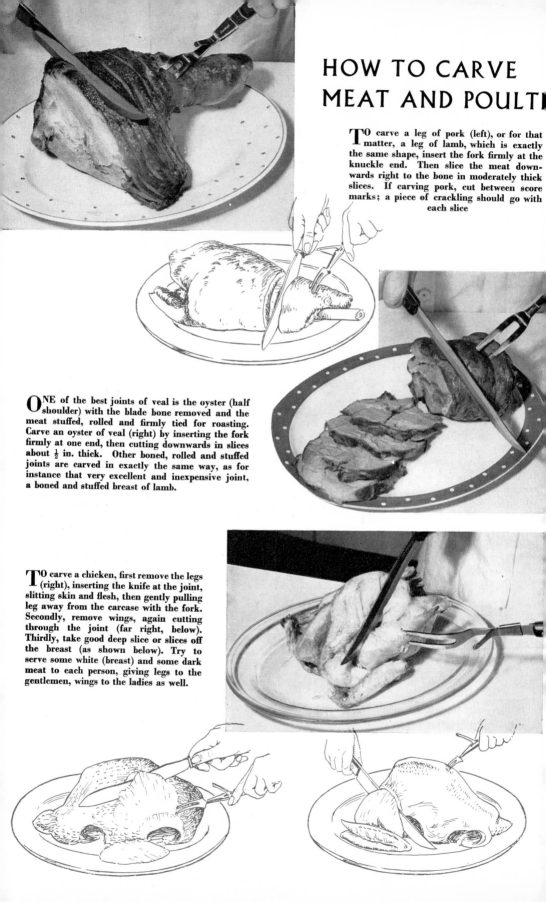

TO carve a leg of pork (left), or for that matter, a leg of lamb, which is exactly the same shape, insert the fork firmly at the knuckle end. Then slice the meat downwards right to the bone in moderately thick slices. If carving pork, cut between score marks; a piece of crackling should go with each slice

ONE of the best joints of veal is the oyster (half shoulder) with the blade bone removed and the meat stuffed, rolled and firmly tied for roasting. Carve an oyster of veal (right) by inserting the fork firmly at one end, then cutting downwards in slices about $\frac{1}{2}$ in. thick. Other boned, rolled and stuffed joints are carved in exactly the same way, as for instance that very excellent and inexpensive joint, a boned and stuffed breast of lamb.

TO carve a chicken, first remove the legs (right), inserting the knife at the joint, slitting skin and flesh, then gently pulling leg away from the carcase with the fork. Secondly, remove wings, again cutting through the joint (far right, below). Thirdly, take good deep slice or slices off the breast (as shown below). Try to serve some white (breast) and some dark meat to each person, giving legs to the gentlemen, wings to the ladies as well.

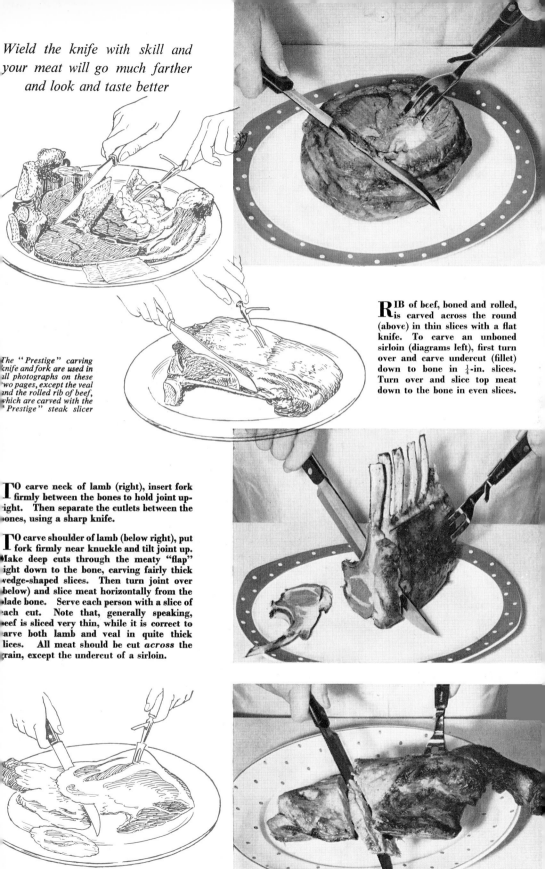

Wield the knife with skill and your meat will go much farther and look and taste better

The "Prestige" carving knife and fork are used in all photographs on these two pages, except the veal and the rolled rib of beef, which are carved with the "Prestige" steak slicer

RIB of beef, boned and rolled, is carved across the round (above) in thin slices with a flat knife. To carve an unboned sirloin (diagrams left), first turn over and carve undercut (fillet) down to bone in $\frac{1}{4}$-in. slices. Turn over and slice top meat down to the bone in even slices.

TO carve neck of lamb (right), insert fork firmly between the bones to hold joint upright. Then separate the cutlets between the bones, using a sharp knife.

TO carve shoulder of lamb (below right), put fork firmly near knuckle and tilt joint up. Make deep cuts through the meaty "flap" right down to the bone, carving fairly thick wedge-shaped slices. Then turn joint over (below) and slice meat horizontally from the blade bone. Serve each person with a slice of each cut. Note that, generally speaking, beef is sliced very thin, while it is correct to carve both lamb and veal in quite thick slices. All meat should be cut *across* the grain, except the undercut of a sirloin.

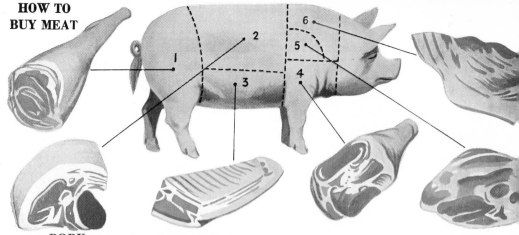

HOW TO BUY MEAT

The **PORK** joints to choose from (above) are:
1. Leg, roast or boil.   2. Loin, roast whole or divide into chops and grill.   3. Belly, boil or braise.   4. Hand, salt, boil and serve cold.   5. Blade bone is best braised.   6. Spare rib, either roast whole or cut into chops and grill or fry.   Note—ask the butcher to score all pork for roasting.

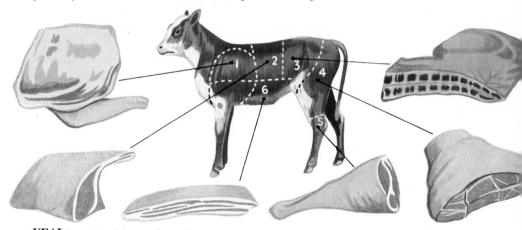

VEAL is cut into joints as shown above:
1. Shoulder, roast either whole or cut in half.   2. Best end of neck, roast or cut into cutlets and fry.   3. Loin provides thin slices for escallops, chops for frying; or stuff and roast.   4. Fillet, good but expensive, is usually fried in slices.   5. Knuckle is cheaper; stew or braise.   6. Breast, a cheap cut, for stewing.

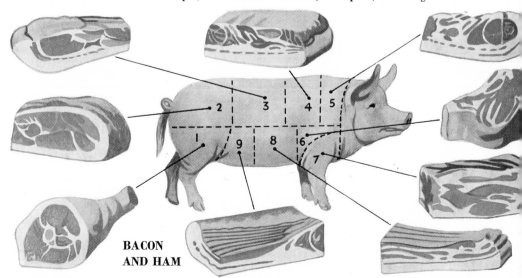

BACON AND HAM

1. Gammon hock, boil and/or bake. 2. Gammon, fry, or boil whole. 3. Long back, best rashers. 4. Prime collar, boil. 5. End of collar, inexpensive; boils well. 6. Slipper, lean; good for boiling. 7. Fore hock, cheaper; good for boiling. 8. Thick streaky, cheaper rashers. 9. Flank, cheaper, with a lot of fat.

mer very gently until the bones can be removed. Take out the meat and, when cool enough, remove the bones. Let the liquor boil rather fast meanwhile, and put in the bones when removed from the head. Cut up the meat into small squares and take out any gristle or skin. Put the squares together with the chopped parsley into a mould (it should be three parts full), then pour in enough strained scalding liquor to fill it to the top. Leave until cold to set. It should be a firm jelly.

Curried Sausages (for 4–5)

1 lb. pork sausages	1 apple
1 oz. butter	1 onion
Curry powder to taste	Squeeze of lemon juice
½ oz. rice flour	Salt
Breadcrumbs	1 teaspoonful chopped chutney
Boiled rice	
1 pint stock	

Skin the sausages and cut them in half, then roll in breadcrumbs and fry until brown. Peel and slice the onion and apple. Melt the butter and, when hot, fry the apple and onion, then add the rice flour, curry powder and salt, stirring well, and cook gently for 5 minutes. Add the stock slowly and bring to the boil. Put the sausages and chopped chutney in the sauce and reheat, adding a squeeze of lemon juice right at the end. Serve the sausages on a hot dish surrounded by boiled rice and pour the sauce over them.

Mock Goose (for 3–4)

1 lb. pork sausages, skinned	Sage
1 onion	1 lb. mashed potatoes
	Pepper and salt

Break up the sausages with a fork and put alternate layers of sausage and potatoes, seasoned with chopped onion, sage, pepper and salt into a fireproof dish. Bake until brown and serve with apple sauce.

Pig's Feet

Cover the feet with water, put in a small handful of salt and simmer gently for 6–8 hours. Leave to cool but, while still warm, press out the bones gently with the hand and leave until the following day. Dip in egg and breadcrumbs and fry until a good brown.

Pork Chops

Fried.—Trim each chop into a neat shape, removing nearly all the fat, season and sprinkle a little flour over them. The fat trimmings can be used to fry them in (for frying, see p. 57). Serve with apple or gooseberry sauce or fry sliced apples and serve round them.

Baked or Grilled.—They may also be baked in a moderate oven and should take about ½ hour; or they can be grilled (see p 57).

Roast Pork

Either leg, loin or spare rib is best for roasting. Get the butcher to score the rind well (for roasting, see p. 57). Serve with apple or gooseberry sauce.

Roast Pork (Stuffed)

Bone the pork. Make sage and onion stuffing (see Poultry chapter), put it in, roll the meat up and tie it firmly. Serve with apple or gooseberry sauce.

Sausages

Fried.—Put the sausages in a tin and pour over them enough almost boiling water to cover them; let them remain in it for 3 minutes. Then take them out, wipe and dry thoroughly, and puncture the skins with a fork. Fry them in a very little fat until they are a good brown, turning frequently. Do not cook them too quickly. Drain well and serve on a bed of mashed potatoes.

Grilled.—Sausages to be grilled should be brushed with fat in the usual way and put under a hot griller. Pork sausages are excellent served with apple sauce, sliced fried apples or bananas.

Toad-in-the-Hole

Make a Yorkshire pudding batter mixture (see Puddings chapter) and leave to stand for at least ½ hour. Melt a little fat in a baking tin and get it really hot in the oven, pour in the batter and then put in the sausages, or skin sausages, put them into the hot fat and pour batter on top. Bake in a moderate oven for 30 minutes.

VEAL

Blanquette of Veal (for 3–4)

1 lb. fillet of veal	1 gill of stock
2 oz. butter	2 or 3 cloves
Pepper and salt	Button mushrooms or small whole tomatoes
1 bay leaf	
1 tablespoonful flour	

Coat the fillet with flour. Melt the butter

in a frying pan and fry the veal until golden brown on both sides. Put the meat and butter into a casserole, add the stock, cloves, bay leaf and seasoning. Put on the lid and simmer for 1½ hours. Add the mushrooms or tomatoes a quarter of an hour before the end. Take out the meat and the mushrooms or tomatoes. Strain the liquor and pour it over the meat. If it is too thick, add a little water and heat it.

Fricassée of Veal (for 3–4)

1 lb. fillet of veal	Half a lemon
1 onion, sliced	Pepper and salt
1 egg-yolk	1 oz. butter
6 peppercorns	1 tablespoonful flour
Pinch of dried herbs	1 gill milk
½ pint water	

Cut the meat into neat pieces and put in a saucepan, with the warm water, and bring it to the boil. Add the herbs, onion, peppercorns, lemon peel and seasoning, and simmer very gently for about 1½ hours. Take up the veal, strain off the stock and make it into a creamy white sauce with the butter, flour and milk (see Sauces chapter). Bring to the boil and cook for 5 minutes. Take off the fire and stir in the beaten egg-yolk and a teaspoonful of lemon juice. Put the meat in the sauce and reheat without boiling. Garnish with rolls of bacon (grilled on a skewer) or grilled rashers, or with fried diamonds or crescents of bread, segments of lemon and small, whole, fried or grilled mushrooms.

Ragoût of Veal (or Rabbit) (for 3–4)

1 lb. lean meat	1 oz. butter
(breast or fillet)	½ pint stock
1 tablespoonful flour	Salt and pepper
Pinch of mixed spice	1 bay leaf
1 large onion	Thyme
Garlic, if desired	Parsley
4 or 5 carrots	Grate of nutmeg

Wipe the meat and cut it into neat pieces. Melt the butter and fry the meat until golden brown, being careful it does not burn. Take it out of the saucepan and keep hot. Make a thick sauce with the flour and stock. Add salt, pepper, mixed spice, herbs, onion (whole), garlic, carrots cut in rounds, and a grate of nutmeg. Put the meat back in the saucepan and cook slowly for 1½ hours, keeping the lid on. Take out the onion and garlic, put the meat on a hot dish with the carrots and strain the sauce over it. Rabbit may be substituted for the meat.

Stewed Knuckle of Veal (for 4–5)

2 or 3 lb. knuckle of	1 turnip
veal	Hot water
¼ lb. rice	1 tablespoonful
2 onions	chopped parsley
1 carrot	Pepper and salt
Squeeze of lemon	Small dumplings
juice	(see Pastry chapter)

Wipe the meat with a damp cloth. Put it into a saucepan with enough hot water to cover, bring to the boil and skim. Put in the chopped onions, carrot and turnip, and seasoning, and simmer slowly for 1½ hours. Add the rice (well washed) for the last ½ hour of the cooking. Small dumplings should be added during the last 10 minutes. Add a squeeze of lemon juice right at the end. Put the meat on a hot dish, surrounded by the rice and vegetables, and sprinkle with chopped parsley, or serve with parsley sauce.

Stuffed Veal

Boned breast (or fillet	Lemon juice
or loin) of veal	Veal stuffing (see
Pepper and salt	Poultry chapter)

Put the meat flat on a board, the skin side underneath, and rub with a little lemon juice. Then season, spread the stuffing over it, roll it up, skewer and tie securely. Trim the ends if necessary. Put in a baking tin and roast in the usual way.

NOTE: It is quite simple to bone the meat if you cannot get the butcher to do it. Simply spread it flat on the table and, with a short, sharp knife, prise out the bones, taking excess fat too. These can be used separately for a stew, casserole or soup.

Veal Cutlets (for 3–4)

1 lb. fillet of veal	½ pint brown, mush-
1 egg	room or tomato
Breadcrumbs	sauce (see Sauces
A little lemon juice	chapter)
and rind	2 oz. dripping
Chopped parsley	Rolls of bacon
Boiled potatoes	Pepper and salt

Cut the veal into neat rounds or ovals and, if necessary, beat them until they are a good shape. Squeeze a little lemon juice over them. Break the egg on a plate, beat it and add the chopped parsley, seasoning, lemon juice and rind. Dip the cutlets into this mixture and then roll them in the breadcrumbs, pressing them on well. Leave to stand until dry. Meanwhile, make whichever sauce is preferred and mash

Toad-in-the-Hole consists of a Yorkshire pudding batter poured over sausages, which are nicer if skinned; or you can make it with small chops instead of sausages

some freshly cooked potatoes. Put a few small rolls of thin slices of bacon on a skewer and cook in the oven. Melt the dripping in a frying pan and, when hot, fry the cutlets until they are brown on both sides. Cook fairly slowly and allow between 10 and 12 minutes. Drain well. To serve, pile them on a heap of mashed potatoes, peas or spinach and garnish with lemon and bacon rolls. Serve the sauce separately.

Veal Galantine (for 6 or more)

1 *lb. veal* (*breast or shoulder*)	4 *oz. breadcrumbs*
½ *lb. ham or bacon*	2 *hard-boiled eggs*
Rind of half a lemon, grated	1 *tablespoonful chopped parsley*
	Egg to bind

For the glaze

1 *cupful stock*	*Meat extract*
1 *teaspoonful powdered gelatine*	

Mince the veal and ham, and make it into a firm dough with the breadcrumbs, parsley, lemon rind and egg to bind. Put it on a wet board and press it out flat, then lay the hard-boiled eggs, cut in thick slices, down the centre and fold over, pressing the edges well together. Scald a pudding cloth, flour it and put the roll in, tying it loosely. Steam for 1½ hours.

For the glaze.—Make a cupful of stock with any meat extract and add a teaspoonful of powdered gelatine. Stir it well until the gelatine is dissolved. Cool, and put it over the galantine.

Veal in Tomato Sauce (for 3–4)

1 *lb. lean veal*	2 *oz. sausage or chopped ham*
1 *oz. butter or some olive oil*	*Salt and pepper*
1 *onion*	3 *tablespoonfuls tomato purée*
1 *small carrot*	*Flour*
Stick of celery	

Put the butter or oil into a saucepan and add the meat (whole), the vegetables (cut up), the sausage (cut in small pieces) and the seasoning. Cook until brown, being careful not to burn. Pour in the tomato purée and sprinkle in a little flour. Stir in some hot water now and again, and simmer the mixture gently until the veal is tender. Serve meat separately with potatoes or other vegetables, the sauce being served with macaroni and grated Parmesan cheese as a first course.

Veal Marengo (for 3-4)

1 *lb. lean veal (breast* *or fillet)*	1 *dessertspoonful* *tomato ketchup*
1 *dessertspoonful oil*	*Pinch of dried herbs*
1 *oz. butter*	1 *dessertspoonful*
1 *onion*	*flour*
1 *shallot*	½ *pint stock or water*
Little garlic, if *desired*	*Salt and pepper* *2 or 3 cloves*
Mushrooms, small onion, dessertspoonful of *sherry, if desired*	

Wipe and cut the meat into pieces, put in a saucepan and fry quickly in the oil and butter, moving it about to prevent burning. Take out the meat and keep hot; then fry the onion and add to the meat. Make a thick sauce with the flour and the stock in the saucepan. Replace the meat and onion, and add salt, pepper, herbs, minced shallot, garlic, tomato ketchup and cloves, cover and simmer gently for 1½ hours. If liked, mushrooms may be added ¼ hour before the cooking is finished.

Arrange the meat on a dish, surrounded by the mushrooms. Strain the sauce and pour over the dish, or serve with small onions put in ½ hour before the end of the cooking. A dessertspoonful of sherry added to the sauce improves the flavour.

OFFAL

Brains

Baked.—Soak the brains well in warm salted water until they are quite clean, then drop in boiling water and boil for 2 minutes. Drain well. Next coat them with egg and breadcrumbs and put in a greased baking tin with some fat bacon on top and bake in the oven until a pale brown. They should take about 20 minutes. Serve with grilled tomatoes or tomato sauce.

Braised.—Soak the brains well in warm salted water until they are quite clean. Slice an onion and put it in a saucepan. Put the brains on the onion, with a little pepper and salt, and a gill of milk. Put a piece of greased paper under the lid and simmer very slowly for about 20 minutes. Take out the brains and put on a warm dish. Thicken the liquor with a little cornflour and simmer for 5 minutes. Remove the onion, add some chopped parsley and pour the sauce over the brains.

Fried.—Soak the brains well in warm salted water until they are quite clean, then drop them in boiling salted water and boil for 2 minutes. Take up carefully and drain well. When cool, flour, egg-and-breadcrumb them, and fry in deep fat until brown. Drain and serve with gravy. Grilled tomatoes are an excellent addition.

Calf's Liver

Fried.—Wash and dry the liver, and cut into slices. Remove the rinds from a few rashers of bacon and fry the rashers. Keep the bacon hot while you fry the liver in the bacon fat for 10–15 minutes, according to the thickness of the slices. Put on a hot dish with the rashers on top. Brown a little flour in the fat, add water and cook for 5 minutes, then season well and pour round the liver.

Grilled.—Wash the liver, dry and cut into slices, put on a plate with a little olive oil and seasoning, and leave for 10 minutes or so, turning the slices over after about 5 minutes. Then put under the hot grill and cook for about 7 minutes.

Fried brains make a delicious and nourishing dish. Serve with grilled tomatoes and garnish with parsley

Fricasée of Veal in a creamy white sauce, colourfully garnished with bacon rolls, mushrooms, parsley, lemon butterflies and diamond-shaped croûtons

Casserole of Liver

Wash and dry the sliced liver and coat it lightly with seasoned flour. Cut the rinds off some thin bacon rashers. Peel and slice one or two onions thinly. Cover the bottom of a casserole with a layer of bacon, then put in layers of onions and liver, continuing alternately until all are used up, ending with bacon. Just cover with hot stock or water, cover and cook in a slow oven for about an hour or until liver is tender.

Kidneys (Devilled) (for 2–3)

4 kidneys	Pinch of salt
1 oz. butter or dripping	Pinch of sugar
	1 teaspoonful Harvey's or Worcester
1 teaspoonful dry mustard	sauce and 1 of mushroom ketchup

Put the kidneys in very hot water for 2 or 3 minutes, then drop them into cold water. Remove the skins; cut them almost through and lay open. Fry in a little butter or dripping (or brush over with melted butter, season and grill). Take out the kidneys and put on a hot dish. Make a sauce with the mustard, salt, sugar, Harvey's sauce and mushroom ketchup, and put a little in each kidney's centre and shut it up, or else add a little stock and make a thinner sauce to serve separately. Serve with little rolls of grilled bacon on croûtons, or on grilled sliced tomatoes.

Kidneys (Grilled)

Put the kidneys into very hot water for 2 or 3 minutes, then drop them into cold water. This prevents them from curling during cooking. Remove the skin, cut almost through and lay open. Brush over with melted butter, season and grill. Serve each on a croûton of bread with a small pat of maître d'hôtel butter (see French Cookery), closing the kidney on the butter. Sprinkle with a little chopped parsley. They can also be served with grilled tomatoes, bacon or flat mushrooms on the bread, and the kidney on top.

Kidneys and Onions (for 4)

4 large onions	4 kidneys
Stock	1 glass of rum

Carefully peel the onions and scoop out enough of the centres to take a kidney each. Cut a slice off the top of each for a lid. Wash the kidneys and stuff each onion with a kidney, top with the lid, put into a casserole, and half cover with stock. Simmer, with the lid on, for 2 hours, until the kidney is tender and, about 3 minutes before it is cooked, add a glass of rum.

Mock Turtle (for 4–5)

Half a calf's head	Forcemeat balls (see
Small piece of veal	Poultry chapter)
Vegetables	Flour
Mixed herbs	Butter
½ pint mixed sherry and port	Seasoning

Wash the head thoroughly and leave to soak. Then boil it with the vegetables, herbs and veal. Take the head out when done and strain off the stock. Next day, cut the meat into square pieces. Put the stock on to boil. Fry some flour in a little butter. When brown, put it into a basin and gradually mix with some of the boiling stock. Then put all back in the pan and bring to the boil. Season with Cayenne, salt and a little Harvey's sauce. Put in the meat and forcemeat balls and re-heat. Remove from fire and add mixed sherry and port. Do not let it boil after the wine is added.

Stuffed Heart (Sheep's or Lamb's)

Soak the heart in warm salted water until thoroughly clean. Then take away the pipes from the top and cut through the division in the middle. Stuff with veal stuffing (see Poultry chapter). Tie a piece of greased paper over the stuffing and bake in a very slow oven, either in a casserole with the lid on or in a covered baking tin, for 1–1½ hours. Put plenty of dripping over the heart and baste occasionally. Serve with red currant jelly.

NOTE: Ox heart can also be cooked in the same way, but takes 2 hours. It should be partly steamed first to get the best results.

Sweetbreads

Baked.—Soak in warm salted water for ½ hour, then drop into fast-boiling salted water for 2 minutes. Take out and dry well. Dip in egg and breadcrumbs, or flour them. Put some fat bacon on top, cover with a piece of greased paper and bake in a slow oven for 30 minutes, or according to size.

NOTE: Calves' or lambs' sweetbreads may be cooked in this way, but lambs' sweetbreads take less time.

Braised.—Clean the sweetbreads as above. Slice an onion and a carrot, and put them in a saucepan with the sweetbreads on top, a little pepper and salt, and a gill of milk. Put a piece of greased paper under the lid and simmer very slowly for 40 minutes. Take out the sweetbreads and put on a warm dish. Thicken the liquor with a little cornflour and let it simmer for 5 minutes, put in some button mushrooms, cooked separately in a little stock. Take out the mushrooms and put them round the sweetbreads. Remove the onion and carrot. At the last moment, add a little cream and a beaten egg-yolk to the sauce. Stir well and add a little chopped parsley. Pour the sauce over the sweetbreads and serve.

Tripe and Onions (for 4–5) (see also chapter on English Counties)

1 lb. dressed tripe	1 oz. butter
2 onions	1 tablespoonful flour
1 gill milk	1 pint milk (or milk
Chopped parsley	and water)
Pepper and salt	

Wash the tripe well. Put into cold water and bring to the boil, drain and cut into neat pieces. Put in a saucepan with the pint of milk and simmer for 1½ hours, adding the onions, sliced, for the last ½ hour. Take out the tripe and keep it hot. Make the flour into a paste with the remaining milk added to the liquor, stirring well. Bring to the boil, add the seasoning and butter, and cook for 5 minutes. Pour the sauce over the tripe, and sprinkle with a little chopped parsley before serving.

Tripe with Bacon (for 4–5)

1 lb. cooked tripe	Grated rind of half a
4 rashers of bacon	lemon
1 onion, chopped	1 gill of milk
Chopped parsley	1 dessertspoonful
Pepper and salt	cornflour
Milk to cover	Mashed potato

Cut the tripe into strips and put a piece of bacon, some chopped onion, parsley, lemon rind and seasoning on each. Roll up and tie firmly. Put in a saucepan with enough cold milk just to cover, bring to the boil and simmer gently for 20 minutes. Take out the tripe and keep hot. Make a sauce with the liquor and the cornflour made into a paste with the milk. Let it simmer gently for 5 minutes. Put the mashed potato on a dish, arrange the rolls on it and pour over the sauce. Sprinkle with chopped parsley and serve.

POULTRY AND GAME

How to choose, cook and serve the Christmas turkey, a boiling fowl or
one of the many delicious game birds, with their stuffings and garnishes

IT is most important when choosing poultry to be able to tell whether a bird is young or old. One method of cooking may be excellent for a little poussin. An older bird will only be satisfactory if cooked in quite a different way. Here, therefore, are the points to bear in mind when choosing and buying poultry.

Chickens are roughly of three kinds:
(1) *Poussins*, weighing 1–2 lb. each, aged 7–12 weeks, usually roasted and served whole; or cut into quarters and fried or grilled.
(2) *Spring Chickens, Fowls and Cockerels* —the larger type (from 3 lb. upwards) suitable for roasting. A fowl (hen weighing up to about 8 lb.) is also excellent for fricassée or casseroles.
(3) *Boiling Hens*—for fricassée, casserole or boiling.

No chicken, whatever its age, should have a gamy smell, however slight. The flesh should be firm, with enough fat to make the bird nice and plump. Wings and

breast bone should be pliable, feet soft and rather moist. The older a chicken is, the harder and dryer its feet and the stiffer its breast bone.

Duck (or Duckling) can sometimes weigh as much as 7 lb., but is liable to be tough if more than 12 months old. A young bird can be recognised by its bright yellow feet and bill, which get darker as the bird grows older. The bill should also be pliable, the flesh white and the breast feel nicely meaty.

Wild Duck (or Mallard) is distinguished by its red bill.

Goose must be under 2 years old at the very most. Choose for the table a bird with some down on its legs and with soft and pliable feet and bill.

Green Goose is a young bird, not more than 6 months old, and is served roast, but unstuffed.

Turkey should have black legs, white flesh, pliable cartilage at the end of the breast bone, and a broad plump breast. Though a cock may weigh as much as

71

20 lb. at only 9 months, the best turkey to choose is a hen of about 7–9 months old. As a general rule, the hens are tenderer and more economical than the cocks, which have heavy bones.

Pigeons.—Both tame pigeons and the larger wild variety should, when young and good for the table, have pinkish legs and claws, well-covered limbs and breasts, and not too dark-coloured skin. They should be eaten fresh.

Game Birds are usually sold unplucked and it is therefore more difficult to judge their condition. Points to look for are soft feet and smooth, pliable legs. In young birds the feathers under the wing and on the breast are soft and downy and the spurs rounded. The breast should be hard and plump.

It is impossible to lay down hard and fast rules as to the length of time game should be hung, because tastes vary so much, and what strikes some as unpleasantly high will prove almost tasteless to others. The birds should always be hung from the neck, unplucked and undrawn, in a cool larder with a good current of air circulating round them. When a feather can be pulled easily from the tail, the birds have hung long enough.

It is also important to know the times of year when it is permissible to shoot the various game birds.

Grouse is in season from August 12th to December 10th.

Hare is in season from August 1st to end of February.

Partridge is in season from September 1st to January 31st.

Pheasant is in season from October 1st to January 31st.

Plover is in season from September 1st to March 1st.

Ptarmigan is in season from August 20th to December 20th.

Snipe is in season from August 12th to January 31st.

Wild Duck is in season from August 12th to January 31st.

Wild Goose is in season from August 1st to March 15th.

Woodcock is in season from August 12th to January 31st.

Quail and *Wood Pigeon* are in season all the year round.

Guinea Fowl is in season when game is not. The flesh tends to dryness, but it can be cooked in any way suitable for a chicken: well larded and roasted, or stewed being the two favourite methods.

Hare and *Rabbit*.—Hares should be hung (not paunched) in a cool place in a good current of air for at least a week, according to the weather. They must be very well cooked and the flesh should not be reddish in colour.

Tame rabbits have a more delicate flavour and are much tenderer than wild ones, have an almost white flesh and take less time to cook. Many people, however, favour the stronger flavour of the wild variety. But wild or tame, the flesh of a rabbit suitable for the table should be quite stiff and without any discoloration. If young, the teeth are small and white and the claws long and pointed. In an older rabbit, the teeth are long and yellow and the claws round and rough. Rabbits should be cooked and eaten fresh.

Preparing Poultry and Game

Poultry and game are now nearly always purchased ready for the table. In the country, however, there may be occasions when the housewife is required to pluck, draw and truss a bird herself, so here are instructions on how to do it.

To Pluck and Singe.—Holding the bird firmly with its neck facing your right, pull out the feathers one at a time, grasping them firmly between the finger and thumb, taking care not to damage the skin. Singe the bird all over with a lighted taper to remove stubs of old feathers.

To Draw.—Cut off the head and neck close to the body but leaving the skin loose. Remove the crop and windpipe, bend and snap off legs just below the joint, then pull out, one at a time, the eight tendons in each leg (if not removed, these will make the bird tough). Put the forefinger inside the bird and loosen the heart, etc., inside the breast, working the finger from left to right. Then lay the bird on its back and make a crossways slit just above the tail. You should then have an opening large enough to allow the insides to be first loosened with the fingers and then drawn away in one mass. Cut the gall bladder away from the liver, being very careful not to break the gall bladder, as this would give a bitter taste to the flesh;

slit the gizzard and remove inner skin and contents. Wash the gizzard, liver and neck well and put aside to make gravy. Wash a fowl under the cold tap and then in cold salted water; wipe out game with a damp cloth.

To Truss for Roasting.—For a roasting fowl, break the long bones above the spur, twist and draw out the sinews. Stuff the bird at the neck end and fold the skin over. Then press the legs forward at the knee joints to the breast bone, turn the wings in and under, and put a trussing needle threaded with string through the wing joint, the leg and the body, drawing it out at the other side through leg and wing. Cross the string on the back, wind round the legs and tail and tie firmly.

To Truss a Fowl for Boiling.—First cut the skin at the knee joints, twist off feet and legs, draw out sinews from the thighs; then, with a finger in the neck end and a thumb against the knee joint, push the legs upwards inside the loosened skin and fold in the lower end of the bird to make a compact shape. Truss with needle and string as for roast fowl.

To Joint.—Any large bird, such as a chicken, can conveniently be divided into twelve pieces as follows:

First cut off legs at thigh joints, then cut each leg into two portions at knee joints, making *four pieces.*

Repeat the process with the wings, making another *four pieces.*

Remove the breast whole, by cutting through the ribs with a pair of scissors, and divide this lengthwise into *two pieces.*

The underneath of the bird can also be divided down the middle lengthwise and gives another *two pieces.*

To Stuff.—After the contents of the bird's inside have been removed and it has been well washed out, stuffing may be put in at either or both ends, and then stitched in with thread, which is, of course, removed before serving.

To Cook Poultry and Game

Larding.—To improve the flavour and overcome the tendency of many birds to dryness, they are often larded. Long thin strips of very hard fat bacon (lardoons) are inserted into the flesh, with the ends sticking out.

A less satisfactory but quicker alternative is to put rashers of fat bacon on the breast of a bird before roasting. A knob of margarine or butter may also be inserted right inside a small bird or fowl to prevent the flesh from becoming too dry during cooking.

Chicken (Boiled)

1 *boiling fowl*	Salt, pepper, pepper-
Cloves, *if liked*	corns, parsley,
1 *onion*	thyme
1 *bay leaf*	

Place a trussed fowl, with a small onion and a bay leaf inside it, in a large saucepan with a tight-fitting lid, add other ingredients and cover with boiling water. Simmer, with the lid on, but do *not* boil, until the chicken is tender (1½ hours or more, according to size and age of bird). Serve with rice moistened with the chicken liquor and garnish with chopped parsley.

Chicken (Fried)

1 *spring chicken*	1½ *gills milk*
divided into	4 *oz. flour*
quarters	1 *egg*
Salt and pepper	

First steam the chicken until very nearly but not quite tender. Meanwhile, make the other ingredients into a batter. Stand for ½ hour, then dip the pieces of chicken in it and deep-fry them (see Meat chapter) till golden brown (about 10–12 minutes).

Chicken (Roast)

Put the trussed bird on a rack in a baking tin, with some slices of fat bacon, or pieces of dripping, over the breast, cover it with greased paper and put into a hot oven for a few minutes, then lower the heat and cook until tender. A

COOK'S TIP

TO MAKE BREADCRUMBS

Brown some bread slices in the oven, then crush with rolling pin to fine crumbs and store in an airtight jar. Good for crisp toppings to many dishes, coating food, frying and garnishing game.

73

small chicken should take about ¾ hour, a heavier one 1 hour, whereas an older bird may take up to 1½ hours. Baste occasionally. Remove the paper just before the bird is cooked, baste well and brown. Sausages or rolls of bacon may be served with the chicken, which should be garnished with watercress and accompanied by bread sauce.

Put the giblets in a little water, with an onion and a pinch of salt, simmer gently while the chicken is cooking, and use the liquor to make the gravy. Before serving, take out the skewers and remove the string.

NOTE: If the bird is over a year old, it is better to steam it for about 1 hour and then roast it slowly, basting frequently.

Chicken (Steamed)

Put the chicken in a piece of greased paper and place it in a steamer over boiling water. Cook until tender. Allow 1–2½ hours according to age and size. The giblets should be put in the boiling water, as they will make excellent stock which can be used in making thick Béchamel, egg, lemon or parsley sauce to serve with the chicken.

NOTE: In the absence of a steamer, a fowl can be steamed in a colander with a lid on top over a saucepan.

Chicken en Casserole (for 5–6)

1 chicken (4–5 lb.)	1 oz. butter
2½ pints of water	1 tablespoonful flour
3 rashers of bacon	1 or 2 hard-boiled
1 lb. raw sausage	eggs, broken up
meat	Pinch of dried thyme
Pepper and salt	Boiled rice
Breadcrumbs	

Joint a fowl and cook very slowly in 2½ pints of water for about 2 hours, until it is quite tender and easily separated from the bone. Line a 3-pint casserole with well-boiled rice. Put in the chicken, cut into small pieces, the rashers of bacon cut up small and fried, the sausage meat in bits, and the hard-boiled eggs cut up. Thicken the stock, which should measure 1–1½ pints, with the flour, season, and add a tiny pinch of dried thyme. Strain into the casserole and bake for 1 hour. Take off the lid of the casserole, put some browned breadcrumbs and a few dabs of butter on the top, and return to the oven without the lid for 5 minutes or so. Then serve. A very little onion can be added if liked.

Chicken Fricassée (for 4–5)

A young chicken	2 oz. butter
1 onion	1 dessertspoonful
1 egg-yolk	cornflour
6 peppercorns, pinch	1 pint white stock, or
of dried herbs (in	milk and water
muslin bag)	A squeeze of lemon
Pepper and salt	juice
A little milk	

Cut the chicken into joints and remove as much of the skin as possible. Put in a saucepan with the stock, onion, herbs, peppercorns and seasoning, and simmer very gently for ¾ hour. Remove the chicken and keep it hot. Strain off the liquor. Put the stock back into the pan, make a paste with the cornflour and a little milk, and add it to the stock, stirring all the time. Bring to the boil and simmer for 5 minutes. Remove from the heat and add the beaten yolk, butter and a squeeze of lemon juice. Reheat without boiling. Pour the sauce over the chicken and serve with grilled rolls of bacon, or decorate with slices of lemon. If liked, fried bread cut into fancy shapes can be served with it.

NOTE: If cooked chicken is used, simmer the stock, onion, herbs, peppercorns and seasoning together for about 20 minutes, then strain the liquor and make the sauce. Add the chicken and reheat without letting it boil.

Duck (Roast)

Stuff with sage and onion (see p. 76) and roast in the same way as chicken, allowing ¾–1 hour. Serve with apple sauce.

Game (Grouse, Pheasant, Partridge, Snipe, Plover, Ptarmigan, Wild Goose) (Roast)

Cook exactly as for chicken, the time varying with the size and variety:

Grouse and pheasant, 40–50 minutes.
Partridge, ptarmigan, 25–35 minutes.
Snipe, plover, 15–20 minutes.
Wild goose, 15 minutes per lb.

Serve with fried crumbs and bread sauce and garnish with watercress.

To fry crumbs.—Fry 4 oz. fresh breadcrumbs in ½ oz. clarified butter over a gentle heat until brown. Drain and serve.

Goose (Roast)

Stuff with sage and onion (see p. 76) and cook in the same way as chicken, allowing 2–2½ hours. Serve with brown gravy and either apple or cranberry sauce.

Specially cooked and photographed in the Creda kitchens

A piquant Orange Salad is the perfect accompaniment to wild duck, served with peas, creamed potatoes, apple sauce and gravy

Guinea Fowl (Roast)

Roast as for chicken.

Turkey (Roast)

Cook in the same way as chicken, but stuff with chestnut or veal stuffing or sausage meat (see p. 76), and serve with brown gravy and bread or cranberry sauce. Allow 15 minutes to the pound and 15 minutes over.

Salmi of Pheasant (or any Cold Game)

Cut a roast pheasant into neat pieces (see Jointing, p. 73). Make thick brown sauce with trimmings of the bird and some vegetables. Put the pieces of pheasant into the sauce and reheat without letting it boil. A few stewed prunes and a tablespoonful of sherry or marsala add greatly to the flavour. Serve with red-currant jelly.

Jugged Hare (for 10–12)

A hare	*1 tablespoonful red-*
Bacon rinds or bone	*currant jelly*
1 large onion	*1 stick of celery*
1½ pints water	*2 tablespoonfuls flour*
2 oz. butter or drip-	*Rind of half a lemon,*
ping	*4 cloves, 1 bay leaf,*
1 carrot	*bunch of herbs (tied*
Port, claret or	*up in muslin bag)*
marsala	*Veal stuffing*

Wash and cut up the hare, and flour the pieces. Melt the butter in a frying pan and when hot, fry the sliced onion until brown. Put into a deep casserole or saucepan. Then fry the meat until brown, add to the casserole with the carrot, cut in half, the celery, cut up, and the lemon rind, cloves, etc., in a muslin bag, add the bacon rinds and, lastly, the water. Make some thick gravy in the frying pan with a little stock or water and flour, and strain it into the casserole. Simmer gently for 2 hours on the hot plate, or in a moderate oven. Make forcemeat balls (see below), roll in breadcrumbs and fry until brown, then put into the casserole 10 minutes before dishing up. Just before serving, remove the carrot, celery, bacon rinds and herbs, add the wine as desired and a tablespoonful of red-currant jelly. Serve with red-currant jelly.

Stewed Rabbit (for 4–5)

1 rabbit	Pepper and salt
2 large onions, sliced	1 tablespoonful flour
2 fresh, streaky pork rashers	1 oz. butter
	½ pint milk
½ pint water	

Wash, dry and cut the rabbit into neat pieces. Put first the rabbit, then the pork and lastly the onions into the saucepan, add the milk, water and seasoning. Bring to the boil and simmer gently for 1¼ hours.

Take up the meat and onions and put them on a hot dish. Strain off the liquor and make it into a sauce with the flour, butter and a little milk. Bring to the boil and cook for 5 minutes. Pour the sauce over the rabbit and serve. A few button mushrooms put in ¼ hour before the rabbit is cooked add greatly to the flavour.

STUFFINGS AND GARNISHES

Chestnut Stuffing (sufficient for medium-sized turkey)

2 lb. chestnuts, par-boiled	1 rasher of bacon
Liver of turkey, par-boiled	2 oz. butter
	Pepper and salt

To parboil the chestnuts, cut a slit in the skins, plunge into boiling water and leave to soak for 20 minutes. Then put them in the oven to crisp the skins, after which they should peel easily. Mince the chestnuts, liver and bacon. Add the butter,

warmed, and the seasoning, and mix well together.

Liver Forcemeat

½ lb. liver (cooked)	A little stock
2 oz. fat bacon	2 oz. breadcrumbs
1 small onion	Salt and pepper
A grate of nutmeg	

Mince the liver and bacon, add the finely chopped onion, the breadcrumbs soaked in a little stock, seasoning and nutmeg. Add more stock, if necessary, to moisten the mixture so that it will bind.

This forcemeat can be used to stuff game or chicken.

Sage and Onion (sufficient for 2 ducks or a goose)

4 onions	4 oz. breadcrumbs
1 dessertspoonful powdered sage or 6 leaves of fresh sage	1 oz. butter
	Egg to bind
	Pepper and salt
	Stock or water

Peel the onions, chop finely and simmer in a little water or stock until tender. Add the sage (chopped or powdered), breadcrumbs, butter, pepper and salt, and stir well. Then add enough beaten egg to bind. If preferred, this can be served in a sauce boat instead of as a stuffing, in which case omit the egg and add instead enough stock to make it into a purée.

Sausage Stuffing (sufficient for medium turkey)

1 lb. sausage meat	2 oz. breadcrumbs
½ teaspoonful mixed herbs	1 teaspoonful chopped parsley
1 egg	

Break up the sausage meat with a fork, mix in other ingredients and bind with egg.

Veal (or Forcemeat) Stuffing (sufficient for 2 chickens or rabbits or a turkey)

4 oz. breadcrumbs	1 dessertspoonful chopped parsley
1 oz. chopped suet	Milk or egg to bind
Grated rind of ½ lemon	Chopped ham as desired
Pepper and salt	
Pinch of dried herbs	

Put all the dry ingredients in a basin, mix them well, and then add enough milk or beaten egg to make into a stiff paste which will bind together very firmly.

NOTE: May be used for fish as well as meat and poultry.

Aspic Jelly

1½ *pints water*
¼ *pint mixed vinegars*
    (Tarragon and
    French wine)
Small carrot, onion
    and turnip
A few peppercorns
Small piece of celery
Rind and juice of half a lemon
2½ *oz. sheet gelatine*
Egg-white and egg-shell

Cut the vegetables into small pieces. Put all the ingredients, except the egg, into a stewpan and stir until the gelatine is dissolved. Add the egg-shell and the egg-white and whisk well until it forms thick scum on the top. Boil well and then draw to side for 20 minutes. Pour gently through a jelly bag or cloth.

Aspic jelly is used to make cold savoury dishes containing meat, game, poultry, fish, vegetables and/or hard-boiled eggs in moulds. Line a mould (or small individual ones) with aspic jelly, add chopped cooked meats, etc., fill up with jelly and put in cool place to set. It should be firm enough to turn out for serving.

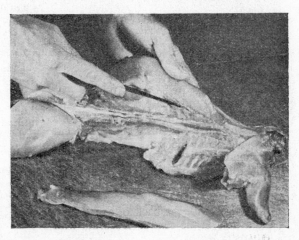

To bone a rabbit: (1) Slit along each side of backbone from neck end and remove meat

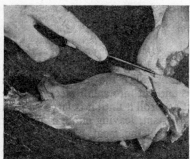

(2) Remove saddle portions, keeping knife close to bone, and sever backbone where back legs join body (above)

(3) Cut away leg portions, removing as much meat as possible with each (above)

(4) Ease out leg bones, starting at point nearest body, scraping meat from bone as you pull it (right)

Aspic Jelly (Quick Method)

1 *teaspoonful*
    Marmite
½ *pint water*
2 *level teaspoonfuls*
    powdered gelatine
Seasoning
1 *teaspoonful lemon*
    juice
1 *dessertspoonful*
    Tarragon vinegar

Heat the water, add the Marmite, seasoning and gelatine, and stir well until the gelatine is dissolved and the mixture clear. Then remove from the fire, add the lemon juice and vinegar, and stir well.

SAVOURY PIES
AND PUDDINGS

*Combined with a pastry or suet crust, either meat or
poultry makes a substantial and tasty main course*

Beef or Mutton Patties (for 5–6)

8 oz. rough puff   *Beaten egg*
or puff pastry

Filling for Beef Patties

6 oz. fresh meat (minced) ⎫
A little chopped kidney   ⎬ *To be mixed*
Pepper and salt   ⎪ *together*
Stock to moisten   ⎭

Filling for Mutton Patties

6 oz. fresh mutton (cut very   ⎫
small)   ⎪
1 teaspoonful chopped onion   ⎪
1 teaspoonful chopped parsley ⎬ *To be mixed*
Pinch of mixed herbs   ⎪ *together*
Pepper and salt   ⎪
Chopped mushroom   ⎪
Stock to moisten   ⎭

Make a rough puff or puff pastry (see
Pastry chapter) and grease patty pans. Roll
out to about $\frac{1}{4}$ in. thick and leave for 5
minutes to allow for shrinking. Then cut
out rounds to fit the patty pans, allowing
two rounds for each. Put one into the
bottom of each pan, and fill with meat
mixture. Moisten the edges and put on the
tops, pressing them firmly together. Nick
up the edges with the back of a fork and
make a hole in the centre. Decorate with
small pastry leaves.

Bake the patties for about 45 minutes,
lowering the heat after the pastry has risen
well. Brush with beaten egg 10 minutes
before they are to come out. Test with a
skewer before removing them from the
oven.

Chicken or Veal Patties (for 4–5)

8 oz. rough puff or puff pastry
Filling for Chicken Patties

4 oz. cooked chicken, cut very fine ⎫
1 oz. ham or bacon, cut very fine   ⎬ *pounded*
Squeeze of lemon juice   ⎪ *together*
A little cream to moisten   ⎭

Filling for Veal Patties

4 oz. cooked veal, cut into small dice ⎫
A little grated lemon rind   ⎪
1 oz. ham or bacon, cut into small dice ⎬ *well*
1 hard-boiled egg, if liked (chopped)   ⎪ *mixed*
Pepper and salt   ⎪ *together*
White stock   ⎭

Make patty cases as for Beef or Mutton
Patties. Mix together either the chicken or
veal filling, heat it and then pile it into the
patty cases. Put on the lids and put the
patties into the oven for 2 or 3 minutes to
heat through.

Cornish Pasty (see Recipes from English
Counties)

Egg and Bacon Pie (for 4)

8 oz. potato or short-   4 large or 6 small
crust pastry (see   rashers bacon
Pastry chapter)   2 eggs
2 tablespoonfuls milk   Salt and pepper

Line a pie plate with half the potato or
shortcrust pastry. Cut the bacon rashers
into slices and scatter over the pastry. Then
pour on the eggs lightly beaten with the
milk and seasoning, cover with a pastry lid
and bake in a hot oven for 25–30 minutes.
Serve hot or cold.

Mutton Pudding (for 6–8)

2 lb. best end or   Chopped parsley
middle neck   Pepper and salt
mutton   Stock or water
Onion $\frac{1}{2}$ lb. suet crust
        A few mushrooms

Grease a pudding basin and get ready a
pudding cloth. Slice the meat away from
the bones and cut into small pieces. Make
suet crust and roll it until it is large enough
to line the basin, leaving enough to cover
the top. Put in the meat, chopped onion
and parsley in layers, and season. Then
add a few mushrooms and fill with white
stock or water. Moisten the edge of the
suet crust and put on the top, pressing the
edges well together. Put a piece of greased
paper over it, then the pudding cloth, and
steam over boiling water for about $2\frac{1}{2}$
hours.

Pork Pie (for 4–5)

$\frac{3}{4}$ lb. lean pork   Salt and pepper
2 tablespoonfuls hot   Hard-boiled egg
stock or water   Egg for coating
        Pinch of sage
$\frac{1}{2}$ lb. hot-water pastry (see Pastry chapter)

Raised Pork Pie, the top ornamented with pastry whirls, makes a delicious cold main dish—so do Beef or Mutton, Chicken or Veal patties

Cut meat into small pieces and season it. Line a tin with the pastry while it is warm, leaving enough for the top. Fill the tin with the pork and hard-boiled egg cut in slices, and sprinkle in the sage. Pour in 2 tablespoonfuls of hot water or stock. Moisten the edge of the pie and put on the cover, making a hole in the centre. Decorate with pastry leaves. Brush the pie with egg-yolk and bake in hot oven for $1\frac{1}{2}$ hours.

Add some good stock flavoured with onion (if there are any bones, put them in a stewpan and let them simmer for this) while the pie is cooling.

NOTE: The most suitable tin for making pork pies is a collar tin, the sides of which open on a hinge kept in place by a skewer, thus enabling one to take out the pie very easily. Failing this, use a cake tin with a movable bottom.

79

Rabbit Pie (for 6–8)

1 rabbit	Grated lemon rind
1 hard-boiled egg	Pepper and salt
Rolls of bacon	Rough puff or short-
Chopped parsley	crust pastry
Stock or water	

Wash the rabbit thoroughly, dry and cut up Put layers of rabbit, bacon and slices of hard-boiled egg into a pie dish with a pie funnel, and sprinkle each layer with parsley, lemon rind and seasoning. Half fill the dish with stock or water.

Roll out rough puff or shortcrust pastry (see Pastry chapter) to the size of the pie dish (it should be about $\frac{1}{2}$ in. thick). Cut a strip wide enough to fit the edge of the dish; wet the edge and put the strip on. Then moisten the strip and put on the top. Trim round the edge and decorate as desired. Cut a hole in the centre so that the steam can escape, and decorate round the hole. Bake in a very hot oven until the pastry has risen (about 20 minutes), then lower the heat and give it another hour, covering the pie with greased paper. Paint the crust with egg just before the end, raising the heat enough to brown it. Unless the rabbit is a young one, it is advisable to stew and cool it first.

Sausage and Bacon Pudding (for 5–6)

1 lb. sausages	1 dessertspoonful
3 rashers lean bacon	flour
1 onion	White stock or water
1 apple	$\frac{1}{2}$ lb. suet crust
Pinch of dried herbs	(see Pastry chapter)
Pepper and salt	

Grease a pudding basin and get ready a pudding cloth. Cut up the sausages into short pieces and roll the bacon. Make suet crust and roll it out until it is large enough to line the basin, keeping back enough to cover the top. Put in the sausages, bacon, thinly sliced onion and apple, and dried herbs in layers, sprinkling a little flour and seasoning in between each. Fill the basin three parts full with stock or water. Moisten the edge of the suet crust and put on the top, pressing the edges well together. Put a piece of greased paper over it, then the pudding cloth and steam over boiling water for $2\frac{1}{2}$–3 hours.

Sausage Rolls

Sausages	Flaky pastry
Egg-yolk	(see Pastry chapter)

Dip the sausages in boiling water and remove skins with a knife. Cut each in half and roll into shape, using a little flour. Roll out the pastry to $\frac{1}{4}$ in. thick. Cut into squares about 5 in. wide. Place a roll of sausage in the centre of each. Damp all round the edges with beaten egg. Fold the pastry round the sausage and press the edges well together. Trim the edges with a sharp knife. Brush with egg-yolk. Cut three slashes on the top of each sausage roll. Place on a floured baking sheet and bake in a hot oven for 20 minutes.

Savoury Suet Roll

Roll suet crust (see Pastry chapter) into an oblong on a floured board. Make one end slightly wider than the other. Put some chopped bacon, a little chopped parsley, a very small onion, chopped finely, and seasoning on the crust, spreading it to within an inch of the edge. Moisten the edges all round and then roll it up, the narrow end towards the wider one, pressing it firmly as you roll. Put the roll into a scalded, floured pudding cloth, steam for $2\frac{1}{2}$ hours and serve with a good gravy.

Steak and Kidney Pie (for 5–6)

1 lb. rump or beef	Flour
steak	Seasoning
1 kidney (calf's or	8 oz. rough puff or
sheep's)	shortcrust pastry
1 gill water or stock	Egg

Wipe the meat, skin the kidney and cut into small pieces; then dip them into the flour and seasoning. Put the pieces into a pie dish with a pie funnel in the middle and add water or stock. Make rough puff or shortcrust pastry (see Pastry chapter) and proceed as for rabbit pie. Put a piece of greased paper over the pie, bake in a very hot oven until the pastry has risen (about 20 minutes), then lower the heat and cook slowly for about 2 hours, reducing the heat gradually all the time.

NOTE: If beefsteak is used, it is advisable to cook the meat partly first, simmering it very slowly, and then allow it to cool before putting on the pastry. Add the kidney just before you put the crust on, and cook the pie for 1 hour.

Beat an egg and paint the surface of the pie about 10 minutes before you take it out of the oven, increasing the heat to brown. Before serving, add a little hot stock or water. If the pie is to be served cold, add a very little gelatine to the liquid before putting it through the funnel.

For supper or buffet parties, outdoor picnics or TV evenings, sausage rolls are always popular—and they are quick and easy to make, too

Steak and Kidney Pudding (for 4–5)

1 lb. beefsteak	½ lb. suet crust
1 kidney (ox, calf's or sheep's)	A little water or unsalted stock
A little flour	Seasoning

Grease a pudding basin and get ready a pudding cloth. Wipe the meat and skin the kidney, and cut into small pieces. Dip into the flour and seasoning. Roll out suet crust (see Pastry chapter) until large enough to line the basin, leaving enough to cover the top. Put in the meat, adding a very little water or unsalted stock. Moisten the edge of the suet crust and put on the top, pressing the edges well together. Put a piece of greased paper over it, then the pudding cloth, and steam it over boiling water for 3 hours. Either turn on to a hot dish or serve in the basin with a napkin tied round it. Before serving, cut a small hole in the crust and add a little hot stock or water through a paper funnel, replacing the piece of crust.

Veal and Ham Pie (for 7–8)

1½ lb. fillet of veal	2 eggs
4 oz. bacon or ham	1 gill white stock or water
Grated rind of half a lemon	¾ lb. rough puff pastry or shortcrust
Teaspoonful chopped parsley	Salt and pepper

Hard-boil the eggs. Cut the meat into small pieces; put the salt and pepper, chopped parsley and lemon rind on a plate and dip the pieces in. Put alternate layers of veal, ham and eggs into a pie dish and add the stock or water.

Make the pastry (see Pastry chapter) and proceed as for rabbit pie, but cook for 1½ hours only. If preferred, the veal can be partly cooked first and then allowed to cool, in which case ½ hour's baking will be enough.

Vol-au-Vent of Chicken, Meat or Game

Make some patty or Vol-au-Vent cases from puff pastry (see Pastry chapter). For the filling any cooked chicken, game or well-flavoured meat may be used. Flake it into small pieces and moisten with a rich white sauce. Season well, add a squeeze of lemon juice or a little grated lemon rind, a beaten egg-yolk and, if possible, a little cream. Heat the mixture, then pile into the scooped-out patty cases. Put on the lids of the cases and heat the patties through in the oven for 2 or 3 minutes. If liked, a little chopped parsley or chives or other savoury flavourings may be added to the mixture.

COLD MEAT AND
MADE-UP DISHES

There are many tasty ways of using up the remains of a joint

COLD joints are sometimes not very appetising to look at, especially if they have suffered at the hands of an unskilled carver. If they are to be served as they are, it is a good plan to cut the meat into neat slices beforehand, and arrange them on a dish with little bunches of watercress, slices of tomato, celery tops, endive, etc., according to the season. Serve with potatoes baked in their jackets, an attractive salad and a home-made chutney.

Twice-cooked meat loses much of its nutritive value, so when you come to warm up the remnants of joints, remember that the less they are cooked the better. They merely need heating.

Corned Beef Hash (for 5–6)

1 lb. can of corned beef	1½ lb. cold boiled potatoes
Milk or cream	Pepper and salt

Mix well together the beef and potatoes, chopped small, then season. Put the mixture into a hot, buttered frying pan, moisten with milk or cream, stir well, then spread evenly over the pan and cook very slowly over low heat for 40–45 minutes. (It is safer to use an asbestos mat if the pan is on a direct flame.) Then turn the hash and fold on to a hot dish. Garnish with parsley.

Croquettes

Cold cooked beef, veal or mutton	Flour and egg and breadcrumbs
Equal quantity of cold mashed potatoes	Milk, egg or gravy to bind
	1 or 2 onions
Fat for frying	Chopped parsley
Pepper and salt	

Mince the meat and add it to the mashed potatoes. Cut the onion into slices and fry until brown. Then add them to the mixture with a little chopped parsley, pepper and salt, and enough egg, milk or gravy to make a firm dough. Shape into rounds, ovals or rolls, and sprinkle well with flour,

then roll in egg and breadcrumbs. Fry in deep fat until brown, and serve with brown or piquant sauce (see Sauces Chapter).

Curried Beef, Chicken, Mutton or Veal (for 5–6)

1 lb. cooked chicken, beef, mutton or veal	Boiled rice
	1 teaspoonful chutney
1 oz. butter or dripping	½ pint cold stock or water
1 onion	1 tablespoonful flour
Curry powder to taste	Juice of half a lemon
Pinch of spice	1 dessertspoonful tomato ketchup
1 small apple	Salt

Cut the meat into small pieces. Melt the butter in a saucepan, add the sliced onion and apple, and fry until brown. Stir in the sieved curry powder, flour and spice, and cook for a few minutes. Then add the stock, salt and ketchup, bring to the boil and skim. Simmer for 20 minutes. Add the chopped meat, lemon juice and chutney, and reheat without boiling. A few slices of banana, or some chopped sultanas, or a little grated orange peel can be added according to taste. Serve with boiled rice.

NOTE: If uncooked meat is used, fry the meat first, and after it is added to the curry simmer slowly for 1–1½ hours in a double saucepan.

Ghiac (for 3–4)

1 lb. cooked meat	1 large round of bread
1 large egg	
Sauce to flavour	Pepper and salt
Breadcrumbs	Gravy, stock or soup

Mince the meat, a quarter of which should be fat. Put the bread in a basin, pour hot gravy, stock or soup over it, soak, then beat smooth. Beat the egg and add to the meat with a little sauce to flavour, and seasoning. Mix with the bread. Put the mixture into a greased oblong tin and bake in a moderate oven for 1 hour. Leave to settle for a few minutes, turn on

Left-overs can be turned into tasty dishes, like these made in the Creda kitchens. Top: Roman Pie filled with peas and carrots, Fish Pie and a Sweet Mould made from left-over fruit and custard. Centre: Duchesse Flan—asparagus and egg in cheese sauce. Left: Shepherd's Pie. Right: Meat Rissoles

to a hot dish, sprinkle with breadcrumbs and brown under the grill. Serve with hot gravy.

Ham Cake (for 5–6)

This is an excellent way of using up the remains of a ham.

1½ lb. ham, fat and lean	1 large slice of bread
	½ pint milk
1 egg	

Pound the ham in a mortar or mince it as finely as possible. Boil the bread in the milk, and beat it and the ham well together. Lastly, add the beaten egg. Put the mixture into a mould and bake until it is a rich brown.

Ham Mousse (for 4–5)

½ lb. lean ham	1 gill cream
About ½ pint savoury stock	(unsweetened condensed milk can be used)
2 small teaspoonfuls powdered gelatine	
Aspic jelly to garnish	Pinch of Cayenne pepper

Put the ham through the mincer twice.

Melt the gelatine in a little stock. Strain the rest of the stock on to the minced ham and add the seasoning. Pour in the gelatine and cream and whip together until smooth and frothy. Put the purée into a plain soufflé mould and smooth it down very lightly. Garnish with aspic jelly.

If the mousse is to be turned out of the mould, add another teaspoonful of powdered gelatine and put some slices of hard-boiled egg at the bottom of the mould. When turned out, garnish with aspic jelly.

Chicken, pheasant or veal mousse can be made in the same way, garnished with green peas or baby carrots, and mayonnaise sauce served as a dressing.

Hasty Pie (for 4–5)

1 lb. minced cold meat	1 onion
	1 lb. hot potatoes
Cooked parsnips, carrots, leek, celery, etc.	Pepper and salt
	Gravy
	1 oz. butter
Dripping	

83

Fry the sliced onion in the butter. Line a greased pie dish with mashed potato and then put alternate layers, well seasoned, of onion, minced meat and chopped vegetables. Add some gravy to moisten. Top with a layer of mashed or quartered potatoes and a little oiled dripping, and bake in a moderate oven for ¾ hour.

Jombalayah (for 3–4)

4 oz. Patna rice	Cayenne pepper and
4 oz. cooked ham	salt
1 lettuce	

Wash the rice and put it into a large pan of quickly boiling salted water. Boil until tender, steam and dry well. Chop the ham into small pieces, season it, and add it to the rice when cold. Serve on lettuce leaves, as cold as possible.

Rissoles (for 4–5)

1 lb. cold beef, mutton or veal, chopped small or minced	Flour, egg and breadcrumbs for coating
½ teaspoonful pounded onion	2 oz. breadcrumbs
Salt and pepper	1 oz. melted butter
Worcester sauce	1 egg-yolk
	Egg, milk or gravy to bind
	Fat for frying

Season the meat with the salt and pepper, Worcester sauce and pounded onion; add the breadcrumbs, melted butter, and enough egg, milk or gravy to bind, and form into rounds. Flour them, roll in egg and breadcrumbs, and fry in deep fat until brown. Drain well and serve with tomato sauce.

Savoury Cake (for 3–4)

1½ lb. boiled potatoes	1 egg
½ lb. minced mutton	½ pint stock
1½ oz. butter	½ oz. flour
1 teaspoonful mushroom ketchup	1 tablespoonful browned breadcrumbs
Salt and pepper	

Put the potatoes through a sieve. Add ½ oz. melted butter, salt and egg-yolk, and mix well. Butter the inside of a deep cake tin. Put in the breadcrumbs and cover the sides and bottom with potato, pressing it well in. Brush the inside and edge of potato lining with beaten egg-white and bake until a nice brown.

Turn out, then carefully turn over on to a dish so that the opening faces upwards. Keep hot. Melt the remainder of the butter in a pan; add the flour and brown well. Add stock, seasoning and ketchup, and bring to the boil. Add meat and heat through; then pour it into the potato cake. Serve with gravy.

Croquettes are always a family favourite. They can be shaped into rolls, rounds or ovals, according to taste

Savoury Mince (for 5–6)

1½ lb. cold mutton
½ oz. gelatine
1 teacupful of water
¾ pint brown stock
A few button mush-
    rooms
Pepper and salt
2 or 3 tomatoes (or
    a small can of
    tomato purée)
2 lb. potatoes
1 egg
1 oz. butter
Flour

Mince the meat. Dissolve the gelatine in the warm water. Put a few mushrooms into the stock and cook until tender. Boil the tomatoes to pulp in another saucepan, sieve, and add the juice and the pulp (or the purée if fresh tomatoes are not used) to the stock. Add the mince and the dissolved gelatine, and season with pepper and salt. Stand the pan on the side of the stove where it will keep hot without boiling. Boil the potatoes, drain and mash well with a fork; whisk in the butter, the beaten egg and add a sprinkling of flour. Beat the mixture well and arrange it as a border round a dish and bake in a moderate oven. When golden brown, pour in the mince and serve.

Minced cold chicken or turkey makes a good filling for little open patties—excellent for cold supper on Boxing Day

Shepherd's Pie (for 5–6)

1 lb. cold meat   Dripping
1 lb. hot potatoes   Pinch of dried herbs
Gravy   Salt and pepper
            Small onion, minced

Grease a pie dish, and put in the meat (minced or chopped very fine), the minced onion, dried herbs, pepper and salt, and some good rich gravy. Spread the mashed potatoes over the top, put slices of tomato on top, dot with dripping and heat well in a hot oven until brown.

A layer of sliced tomatoes can be added between the meat and the potatoes.

Taffy Sole (1) (for 3–4)

½ lb. any kind of cold   2 eggs
    meat, chopped fine   Pepper, salt, and a
2 oz. butter   little chopped
Gravy or cream   parsley

Mix all together with a cupful of gravy or cream. Butter a small tin, put the mixture in it and bake for ½ hour. Turn out and serve with or without gravy.

Taffy Sole (2) (for 5–6)

½ lb. rice stewed in   ½ lb. minced meat,
    brown gravy   seasoned with salt
1 egg   and pepper

Mix all together and bake for 1 hour in a mould. Serve with brown gravy. A little grated ham improves.

Stew the rice in white stock—using veal, stewed rabbit or chicken.

SAUCES

These finishing touches are the art of cookery—they will brighten up a homely dish or add distinction to an elaborate one

SAUCES are, as it were, the finishing touches to the dish they accompany and, therefore, a very important part of the menu. It is no exaggeration to say that they can either make or mar a meal. A well-made appetising sauce will brighten up many a homely dish and add piquancy to more elaborate ones.

A perfect sauce proves its creator a true artist, so extra time devoted to this branch of cooking is well spent.

This chapter contains simple and inexpensive recipes for sauces likely to be used in the ordinary household from day to day. In many cases we also suggest how and with what to serve them.

But for the truly ambitious cook there are many more sauces, both more exotic and sometimes considerably more extravagant, to be found in the chapters on Cookery at Home and Abroad.

Sauces may be sweet or savoury, made with milk or stock; thickened with flour, cornflour, arrowroot or eggs; and served thick or thin, hot or cold. But infinite as the variety is, there are certain basic principles of sauce-making.

(1) Smoothness is essential, so always stir well; continuously when making and blending a roux.

(2) Flour, if used in sauce, must be cooked for 2 or 3 minutes to avoid a pasty taste. When using cornflour instead of flour, remember it is bulkier, so a little less is needed.

(3) If using stock for sauces, first skim off fat and strain it thoroughly: a sauce may be rich but never greasy.

(4) Rich sauces are slowly simmered for a long time, then strained through a tammy cloth, which should be boiled after use and kept scrupulously clean.

Roux

Basis of many sauces is a roux, made by stirring equal quantities of flour or cornflour and butter together over a moderate heat until thoroughly blended. This is called a *White Roux* when cooked without being coloured; a *Blond Roux* when cooked to a pale fawn shade, and a *Brown Roux* when allowed to turn slightly brown.

Reducing

To "reduce" a sauce, strain it, bring to the boil and boil hard over a quick heat in a shallow pan till the required quantity of liquid has "boiled away," leaving what remains very much richer and better.

White Sauce

1 oz. butter or mar-	Pepper and salt
garine	½ pint milk or white
1 oz. flour or corn-	stock
flour	

Melt the butter, add sieved flour very slowly, stirring all the time, and cook over moderate heat for a few minutes till smooth, without colouring. Remove from the fire, beat in the milk or stock gradually with a whisk or wooden spoon. Put it back on the fire and bring to the boil, stirring all the time. Season and cook for 5 minutes.

NOTE. If you want a thick coating sauce, allow a little more flour and an equal quantity of fat. For a thin sauce, double the liquid. If your sauce has a tendency to be lumpy, use cornflour instead of flour.

This foundation can be used for the following sauces for which you will find recipes in this chapter:

Anchovy, Béarnaise, brain, caper, cheese, egg, horseradish, mustard, onion, oyster, parsley, shrimp and Velouté.

SAUCES—SAVOURY

Admiral's Sauce (for 4) (Served with boiled fish)

½ pint melted butter	2 pounded anchovies
1 teaspoonful chopped	Some fine slices of
capers	lemon peel
3 chopped shallots or	Salt and pepper
chives	

Simmer all ingredients over a low heat till the anchovies disintegrate. Remove

A good sauce can make or mar a dish. Sole Caprice is only baked fillets served in a thick, creamy white sauce, garnished with grapes and almonds

lemon peel and add salt and pepper as required.

Anchovy Sauce (for 4)

½ pint white sauce	1 teaspoonful an-
Pepper and salt	chovy essence (or more according to taste)

Make a white sauce (see p. 86), omitting seasoning, and, when cooked, add anchovy essence and pepper and salt to taste.

Apple Sauce (for 4) (Served with pork)

1 lb. apples (sharp cookers are best)	Grated rind of half a lemon
½ oz. butter	1 tablespoonful brown sugar
½ gill water	

Wash and slice, but do not peel the apples, and cook with the water, lemon rind and sugar till they become pulp, stirring from time to time. Put through a sieve, reheat, and add the butter.

Béarnaise Sauce (for 4) (Served with grilled steak)

2 egg-yolks	1 dessertspoonful Tarragon vinegar
3 tablespoonfuls chopped shallots or onions	1 gill malt vinegar
1 tablespoonful cream or a little butter	1 gill white sauce (see p. 86)
	Salt and pepper

Boil the shallots or onions in the malt vinegar, and strain. Stir the onion-flavoured vinegar into the white sauce, bring to boiling point, then remove pan from heat and add the beaten yolks. Season, and add the Tarragon vinegar and cream or butter last thing before serving.

Béchamel Sauce (for 4) (see also French Cookery)

½ pint milk	1 clove
1 small onion or shal-lot	5 peppercorns
Small piece of carrot	1 oz. flour
Piece of celery	1 oz. butter
1 bay leaf	¼ gill of cream
	Salt

Bring the milk to the boil with the vegetables, bay leaf, clove and peppercorns, and leave to stand for 5 minutes with the lid on, then strain. Make a white sauce in the usual way (see p. 86) with the flour, butter and flavoured milk. Bring to the boil and simmer for 10–15 minutes. Finally, add the salt and cream.

Black Butter Sauce (for 3–4)

This can be served with grilled fish or baked skate or trout. It is also very good with French beans or with old broad beans which have to be skinned.

> 2 oz. fresh butter   Salt and pepper
> Vinegar to taste

Melt the butter and heat till it is a good brown, but not burned. Add the vinegar and seasoning and reheat, stirring well, but do not allow to boil.

Bolognese Sauce (see Italian Cookery)

Brain Sauce (for 3–4) (Served with calf's or sheep's head)

> ½ pint white sauce   1 teaspoonful lemon
> (see p. 86)   juice
> Sheep's brains   Chopped parsley

Wash the brains thoroughly and simmer in a little salted water for 10 minutes. Strain, rub through a hair sieve and stir with the lemon juice and chopped parsley into the white sauce.

Bread Sauce (for 3–4) (Served with roast poultry)

> Small onion   1 oz. butter
> ½ pint milk   Salt and pepper
> 2 oz. breadcrumbs   2 peppercorns
> 2 cloves

Simmer the onion, cut in half and stuck with the cloves, with the peppercorns and a pinch of salt in the milk for about 30 minutes. Strain, and put the milk back into the saucepan. Bring to the boil, stir in the breadcrumbs slowly and heat to boiling point again. Add butter and seasoning.

Brown Sauce (for 6)

> 1 carrot   Lemon juice
> 2 oz. butter   1 pint stock
> 1½ oz. flour   1 onion
> 1 tomato   2 mushrooms
> Salt and pepper

Peel and slice vegetables, and fry onion and carrot in melted butter until brown. Stir in flour, cook to a pale brown colour, then add mushrooms, tomato, lemon juice and stock and bring to the boil, stirring continuously. Simmer for 10 minutes, skim off fat, season and strain.

Caper Sauce (for 4) (Served with boiled mutton or fish)

> ½ pint white sauce   1 tablespoonful
> (see p. 86)   capers
> 1 teaspoonful of the caper vinegar or lemon
> juice

Make the white sauce and, when cooked, add the capers, chopped; remove from fire and stir in the vinegar or lemon juice.

Celery Sauce (for 4)

> 1 small head white   ½ pint milk
> celery   1 oz. butter or 1 table-
> 1 small onion   spoonful cream
> 1 oz. flour   Seasoning to taste

Mix the flour to a paste with a little of the milk. Peel the onion. Wash and cut the celery, including leaves, into small pieces and cook both in the rest of the milk until tender. Remove onion and rub celery through a sieve. Put the purée back into the pan and add the flour paste, stirring well. Bring to the boil and cook for 5 minutes. Add seasoning and cream or butter.

Cheese Sauce (for 4)

> ½ pint white sauce   2 tablespoonfuls grated
> (see p. 86)   cheese (either good
> Made mustard to   dry Cheddar and a
> taste   little Parmesan or all
> A little butter   Parmesan)

Make a thin white sauce, using only about half the usual quantity of flour. Put in the grated cheese, mustard and butter. Stir till the cheese is dissolved.

Cranberry Sauce (for 4)

An American favourite served with turkey, roast pork, ragoût of mutton, veal cutlets, or salmi of pheasant. (See also Cookery in the United States.)

> ½ pint water   4 oz. brown sugar
> 1 lb. cranberries

Wash the cranberries and stew in the water till they turn to pulp, stirring frequently. Add brown sugar, stir till dissolved, then beat up well with a metal whisk.

Cumberland Sauce

> 2 tablespoonfuls red   2 tablespoonfuls
> currant jelly   vinegar
> ½ teaspoonful   A few chopped glacé
> mustard   cherries
> 1 lemon and 1 orange   Salt and pepper
> ½ gill water   ½ gill port wine

Peel lemon and orange carefully, shred the skins and boil for 5 minutes in the water. Cool and strain. Add the juice of the lemon and orange and other ingredients. Let the sauce stand from morning to evening, on ice if possible. If bottled and tied down, it will keep for several days. Do not strain.

Curry Sauce (for 3–4)

½ pint vegetable stock	1 carrot
1 small onion	1 apple
1 tomato	1 teaspoonful curry
1 oz. flour	powder
Pepper and salt	A few drops of
1½ oz. dripping	lemon juice

Heat the dripping and fry the sliced onion and carrot lightly in it, then stir in the sieved flour and curry powder, with the lemon juice, and cook gently for a few minutes, stirring all the time. Add the stock slowly, then the sliced tomato and the apple, peeled and sliced, and seasoning to taste. Bring to the boil and simmer gently for about 10 minutes. Strain and reheat.

Demi Glacé Sauce

½ pint Espagnole	1 teaspoonful meat
sauce (see below)	glaze (see French
¼ pint meat gravy	Cookery)

Boil sauce, gravy, and glaze together for about 15 minutes to reduce. Strain and serve.

Egg Sauce (for 4) (Served with steamed fish)

½ pint white sauce	2 hard-boiled eggs
(see p. 86)	

(see p. 86)

Make ½ pint white sauce and add the eggs, chopped finely; or put eggs through a coarse sieve before adding.

Espagnole Sauce

2 oz. lean ham or	2 oz. flour
bacon	Bouquet garni
1 small onion	Salt and pepper
1 carrot	2 oz. butter
1 pint brown stock	

Photographs taken in the Experimental Kitchen of Brown & Polson Ltd.

How to make a white sauce, step by step: (1) Melt 1 oz. butter in a small saucepan over a low heat. (2) Add 1 level tablespoonful cornflour and stir until well blended. (3) Pour on ½ pint of milk gradually, stirring all the time, bring gently to the boil and boil for 3 minutes. (4) When the sauce is thick and smooth, add seasonings or flavouring as required

Melt butter and lightly fry it in the onion, carrot and ham, and cut into small pieces. Stir in flour and cook till light brown on low heat. Add bouquet garni and then the stock gradually, bring to boil and simmer very gently for about 1½ hours, skimming at intervals. Strain through tammy and either serve with 2 tablespoonfuls of sherry added at the last minute or use as basis for other sauces, such as Poivrade.

Gooseberry Sauce (for 4) (Serve with roast pork, mackerel, or white fish)

½ pint green goose-berries	Pepper and salt
1 oz. butter	½ gill cold water
1 dessertspoonful granulated sugar	½ teaspoonful arrow-root
	A little water

Top and tail and wash the gooseberries and put them with the sugar into the water. Simmer till they are soft enough to rub through a fine sieve. Mix the arrowroot with a very little cold water into a smooth paste and add, stirring well, to the boiling pulp. Cook for 3 minutes. Season, and lastly beat in the butter.

Green Sauce

Leaves of parsley, Tarragon and fennel	Mayonnaise (see Salads)

Wash, dry and mince the herbs, add a little cold water and pass through a hair sieve or tammy. Add to a well-seasoned mayonnaise.

Hollandaise Sauce (see also French Cookery)

2 egg-yolks	Juice of ½ lemon (or 1 tablespoonful Tarragon vinegar)
Salt and pepper	
2 oz. butter	

Melt half the butter, either in the top of a double boiler or in a basin over boiling water. Beat egg-yolks well and add to butter with lemon juice and seasoning. Keep water boiling gently and stir until sauce thickens, being careful it does not curdle, and adding the rest of the butter at the last minute.

Horseradish Sauce (for 3–4)

1 tablespoonful grated horseradish	½ pint white sauce (see p. 86)
1 teaspoonful granulated sugar	1 tablespoonful cream (if liked)
Pinch of salt and pepper	A very little made mustard
1 tablespoonful vinegar	

Put all the ingredients into a bowl and beat well with a fork. This sauce keeps for some time if put into a corked bottle.

Marmite Sauce (for 4)

Excellent for children; serve with vegetables or poached eggs.

½ pint vegetable water	1 tablespoonful flour
	Teaspoonful Marmite
1 oz. butter	Pepper and salt to taste

Make the flour into a smooth paste with a little water, and pour it slowly into the hot vegetable water. Add the Marmite, butter and seasoning, bring to the boil, and cook for 5 minutes.

Mayonnaise (see Salads and French Cookery)

Green Mayonnaise: Add a little parsley or spinach juice.

Red Mayonnaise: Add a little beetroot juice.

Melted Butter (for 4–5) (Serve with asparagus)

2 oz. butter	Squeeze of lemon juice

Melt the butter very slowly, so that it does not lose its creamy appearance. Add a squeeze of lemon juice if liked.

Mint Sauce (for 4–5) (Serve with roast lamb)

2 tablespoonfuls chopped mint	A little boiling water
2 dessertspoonfuls sugar (or to taste)	1 gill vinegar (or half vinegar and half lemon juice)

Wash and strip mint leaves from stalks and chop finely. Pour boiling water over mint and sugar, barely enough to cover. Leave to stand till cold. Add the vinegar, or vinegar and lemon juice.

Mornay Sauce

Add grated Parmesan or other hard cheese to Béchamel sauce (see p. 87).

Mushroom Sauce

½ pint Béchamel sauce (see p. 87)	1 oz. butter
	½ lb. mushrooms

Wash, peel and slice mushrooms and cook them lightly in the butter. Add to the Béchamel sauce the mushrooms and, strained, the butter in which they were cooked.

SAUCES

Mustard Sauce (Served with grilled herrings)

Make a white sauce (see p. 86), adding 1 teaspoonful dry mustard at the same time as the flour.

Onion Sauce (for 3–4) (Serve with boiled mutton)

2 or 3 onions   ½ pint white sauce
Cream   (see p. 86)

Cook the onions in salted boiling water till tender, drain and chop finely. Add to the white sauce and reheat, adding a dash of cream just before serving.

Oyster Sauce (for 5–6)

¼ pint white sauce (see p. 86)
Pinch of Cayenne
1 doz. oysters
Squeeze of lemon juice

Beard the oysters and cut each up into three or four pieces, being careful to save the liquor in the shells. Blanch them in the liquor. Add the oysters, the liquor, a pinch of Cayenne and a squeeze of lemon juice to the white sauce. Reheat, without allowing to boil.

Parsley Sauce (for 4)

½ pint white sauce   1 dessertspoonful
(see p. 86)   chopped parsley

When the white sauce is cooked and still boiling, stir in the parsley.

Piquant Sauce

To brown sauce (see p. 88) add a tablespoonful of vinegar and, if liked, some chopped gherkins and capers.

Poivrade Sauce (for 4)

½ pint brown   1 oz. lean ham
sauce (see p. 88)   6 peppercorns
1 oz. butter   Herbs (parsley,
1 carrot   thyme, etc.)
    1 small onion

Gently fry the sliced carrot and onion with the diced ham and herbs in butter, add crushed peppercorns, pour on the sauce, bring to the boil and simmer for 10 minutes. Skim well, season, add sherry, if liked, and strain through tammy.

Poulette Sauce (for 5–6)

2 oz. butter   Salt and pepper
2 oz. flour   Bouquet garni
1 pint white stock   2 egg-yolks
   Cream and lemon juice, if liked
    2 or 3 mushrooms (optional)

Make as for a thick white sauce. Remove from heat, beat in the egg-yolks and flavourings. 2 or 3 chopped mushrooms are also delightful cooked in this sauce.

Shrimp Sauce (for 3–4) (Served with turbot or halibut)

1 oz. butter or margarine
A few drops of lemon juice
1 blade of mace and 1 bay leaf
1 oz. flour
2 or 3 drops anchovy essence
1 gill picked shrimps
½ pint milk and water
Salt and pepper

Cook the shrimp shells in milk and water with a blade of mace and a bay leaf, and use the liquor to make a white sauce with the flour and butter. Season well, then add the picked shrimps, anchovy essence and lemon juice stir thoroughly and reheat.

Soubise Sauce (for 3–4)

½ pint Béchamel   1½ lb. onions
sauce (see p. 87)   1 tablespoonful cream
½ pint milk   or butter
2 cloves   Salt and pepper

Peel and cut onions into pieces and simmer till soft in milk with salt, pepper and cloves. Meanwhile, gently simmer Béchamel sauce till reduced to half. Sieve onions, mix with the Béchamel, and add cream or butter just before serving.

Supreme Sauce (for 4)

½ pint Velouté sauce   Juice of ½ lemon
(see next page)   ½ oz. butter
    2 well-beaten egg-yolks

Add egg-yolks, lemon juice and butter

COOK'S TIP

MAKE RICHER GRAVY

To 1 tablespoonful of fat add 1 dessertspoonful 'Patent' Cornflour. Cook for a few minutes, add ½ pint stock, boil for 1 minute, season

cut up in small pieces to the sauce before serving.

Sweet and Sour Sauce

1 *tablespoonful corn-flour*	1 *tablespoonful sugar*
1 *tablespoonful malt vinegar*	1 *tablespoonful soy sauce (dark)*
1½ *cups water*	1 *tablespoonful tomato sauce*

Place all the ingredients except the tomato sauce in a pan and cook over a slow heat, stirring all the time, until it has the consistency of treacle; add the tomato sauce. This sauce can be made in advance and re-heated when needed and is excellent with Belly of Pork.

Tartare Sauce (for 4)

1 *pint mayonnaise (see Salads chapter)*	1 *tablespoonful chopped gherkins*
1 *tablespoonful chopped parsley*	1 *tablespoonful chopped capers*

Mix all ingredients well together and serve cold.

Tomato Sauce (1) (for 4–5)

1 *lb. tomatoes (fresh or canned)*	2 *small lumps of sugar*
Bacon bone or rinds	1 *oz. butter*
1 *small onion*	*Seasoning*
¼ *pint milk or white stock*	

Melt the butter in a saucepan and add the sliced tomatoes, bacon rinds or bone, sugar and onion, peeled and cut up. Cook very slowly till tender, stirring well. Rub through a sieve and thin with milk or stock. Season and serve.

Tomato Sauce (2) (for 4) (Serve with boiled macaroni or rice)

6 *large tomatoes*	1 *tablespoonful flour*
3 *oz. butter*	*Large pinch of salt*
2 *tablespoonfuls grated Parmesan cheese*	1 *tablespoonful chopped onion*

Stew and rub the tomatoes through a sieve. Cook the chopped onion in the butter for a few minutes, then add the cheese, flour and salt. Mix well together and, when the mixture boils, add the tomato purée. Bring it to the boil again.

Velouté Sauce (1) (for 4)

The classical French recipe for this sauce, including a fowl, is given in the chapter on French Cookery. For a small family it can be made from the following ingredients:

2 *oz. butter*	1 *pint water*
2 *medium carrots*	2 *onions*
3 *or 4 peeled mush-rooms*	½ *pint white sauce (see p. 86)*
Bouquet garni	*Salt and pepper*

Fry sliced carrots and onions lightly over low heat without browning, gradually adding water, seasoning and mushrooms. Simmer gently for 30 minutes, skimming carefully. Strain through tammy, bring to boiling point again and stir in white sauce.

Velouté Sauce (2)

A very simple Velouté sauce can be made by adding 1 teaspoonful lemon juice to ½ pint white sauce (see page 86) made from white stock (see Soup chapter).

Vinaigrette Sauce (for 4) (Served with asparagus or calf's head)

3 *tablespoonfuls olive oil*	*Chopped capers, gherkins, parsley, shallots, Tarragon, chervil and chives, according to taste*
1 *tablespoonful wine vinegar*	
Salt and pepper	

Mix herbs and seasoning with vinegar, then gradually blend in the oil, beating thoroughly.

BUTTERS

Anchovy Butter (see also French Cookery chapter)

2 *oz. butter*	2 *or 3 anchovy fillets (or dessertspoonful anchovy essence)*
Lemon juice	
Pepper	

Warm and beat the butter with a wooden spoon till it is the consistency of thick cream, drop in the anchovies or essence, beating all the time. A squeeze of lemon juice and some pepper greatly improves the flavour.

Brandy or Rum Butter (Hard Sauce) (Served with Christmas pudding)

2 *oz. butter*	2 *oz. castor sugar*
Brandy or rum to taste	

Slightly warm the butter and beat to a cream with the sugar. Add brandy or rum to taste and put in a cool place till required.

Honey Butter (Served on steamed puddings)

1 *oz. honey*	4 *oz. butter*

Beat the butter to a cream, then add the honey (melted) and mix thoroughly.

Maître d'hôtel Butter (see French Cookery chapter)

SAUCES—SWEET

Exactly the same principles apply to sweet sauces, the seasoning being omitted and sugar and the desired flavouring added instead. For instance, lemon or orange sauce can be made by adding a little juice to sweetened white sauce.

If you want something a little richer than the ordinary white sauce, use a little more butter or beat in the yolk of an egg, being careful first to remove your sauce from the fire, as it will curdle if it boils. Cream or unsweetened condensed milk may also be added.

If flavouring with brandy, rum or sherry, put it in right at the end, sherry particularly being very liable to curdle sauce.

Apricot Sauce (for 4)

12 *fresh apricots*
1 *glass Madeira*
Demerara sugar to
taste

Halve apricots, remove and break stones, peel and pound kernels and stew together in a little water till fruit is really soft. Then add Madeira and sugar, and stir well over moderate heat until sauce is reduced to syrup. Pass through a sieve before serving.

Brandy Sauce (for 4) (Served with plum pudding)

1 *dessertspoonful*   1 *egg-yolk*
cornflour   1 *oz. butter*
½ *pint milk*   *A wineglassful of*
Sugar to taste   *brandy*

Make the cornflour into a smooth paste with a little of the milk. Heat the rest of the milk with the sugar and, when boiling, pour it over the cornflour. Return to saucepan, bring to the boil, and cook for 5 minutes. Remove from the heat and, when it is no longer boiling, add the beaten egg-yolk, butter and brandy. Stir con-

Caper Sauce, with its characteristically sharp taste, gives piquancy to boiled mutton or fish

tinuously over a low heat, or, better still, in a double boiler, until it thickens, not letting it boil or it will curdle.

Rum or sherry can be used instead of brandy.

Chocolate Sauce (Plain) (for 4–5)

½ *pint milk*   3 *teaspoonfuls cocoa*
1 *level teaspoonful*   *Vanilla essence*
cornflour or cus-   *A little butter*
tard powder

Mix the cocoa and the cornflour or custard powder into a smooth paste with a little of the milk. Bring the rest of the milk to the boil, then stir in the paste. Bring to the boil again, simmer for 5 minutes, stirring well, add a few drops of vanilla essence and, lastly, the butter.

Chocolate Sauce (Rich) (for 4–5)

½ pint milk	¼ lb. chocolate
¼ level teaspoonful cornflour or custard powder	Vanilla essence or vanilla stick
	A little cream or butter

Stir the chocolate with 2 tablespoonfuls of the milk and the stick of vanilla until it boils. Add the rest of the milk (keeping back just enough to make the cornflour or custard powder into a paste) and bring to the boil. Add the paste, stirring all the time, and bring to the boil again. Cook for 5 minutes. Remove from heat and, if a stick of vanilla was not used, add a few drops of vanilla essence.

If desired, a little cream or butter can be added to make it richer.

Coffee Sauce (for 4)

¼ pint black coffee	1 dessertspoonful arrowroot or cornflour
1 oz. Demerara sugar	
1 tablespoonful cream	
1 egg-yolk	Pinch of salt

Mix the arrowroot or cornflour to a smooth paste with a very little water. Heat the coffee, sugar and salt to boiling point, and pour on to the paste, stirring well. Put back into the saucepan, bring to the boil and cook for 3 minutes. Just before serving, stir in the cream and beaten egg-yolk. Serve hot, but do not allow to boil or the egg may curdle.

Custard Sauce (1) (for 3–4) (May be served hot or cold)

2 or 3 egg-yolks	Rind of a lemon, or stick of vanilla, or sherry to flavour, according to taste
½ pint milk	
¾ oz. castor sugar	

Bring milk and lemon rind or vanilla nearly to the boil and pour into well-beaten egg-yolks. Strain back into pan (top of double boiler for preference), add sugar and stir until it thickens, then remove quickly from heat. If liked, stiffly beaten egg-white may be whisked into the sauce when it is cool. If flavoured with sherry, put this in at the last minute when cooked.

Custard Sauce (2) (for 3–4)

1 egg	1 level teaspoonful cornflour
½ pint of milk	
1 oz. castor sugar	Flavouring

Put the milk and sugar on to boil, keeping back enough milk to mix the cornflour to a smooth paste. Add the beaten egg to cornflour paste, then pour the milk slowly in, stirring well. Put back in the saucepan and bring almost to boiling point. Add flavouring as desired.

German Sauce (for 3–4)

¼ pint sherry	1 oz. castor sugar
3 egg-yolks	

Whisk all the ingredients together over a moderate heat until the mixture turns frothy, without curdling.

Ginger Sauce (for 3–4)

½ small teaspoonful ground ginger	1 tablespoonful Golden Syrup
½ pint water	1 oz. butter
Lemon juice	Crystallised ginger, chopped
1 dessertspoonful cornflour	

Mix the cornflour and ground ginger together into a paste with a little of the water. Bring the rest of the water to the boil with the syrup, then stir in the paste. Cook for 5 minutes, adding the butter towards the end, and add a little chopped crystallised ginger and a squeeze of lemon juice just before serving.

Hard Sauce (see Brandy Butter, p. 92)

Jam Sauce (for 3–4) (Served with sponge puddings)

3 tablespoonfuls of any jam	1 teaspoonful cornflour
½ pint water	1 teaspoonful lemon juice

Make the cornflour into a smooth paste with a little of the water. Boil the jam with the rest of the water and pour it on to the paste. Return to the saucepan and boil for 5 minutes, add lemon juice and strain through a coarse sieve.

Lemon or Orange Sauce (for 3–4)

½ pint white sauce, unseasoned (see p. 86)	1 lemon or orange
	4 oz. granulated sugar

Make some white unseasoned sauce, putting the rind of the fruit into the milk to flavour. Add sugar, bring to the boil, remove from the fire and, after a minute or two, add the lemon or orange juice.

Marmalade Sauce (for 3–4)

1 tablespoonful marmalade	1 dessertspoonful lemon juice
1 teaspoonful cornflour	1 tablespoonful Golden Syrup
1 gill water	

Bring marmalade, syrup, lemon juice and most of the water to the boil. Mix the cornflour to a smooth paste with a little water and stir into the mixture, cook for 5 minutes, stirring all the time, then serve.

Melba or Raspberry Sauce (for 5–6)
(Served with ice cream)

½ lb. fresh, canned or	½ oz. cornflour
frozen raspberries	½ pint water

2 oz. castor sugar

(Raspberry jam may be substituted for the fruit, the sugar then being omitted)

Stew the fruit till soft, pass through a fine sieve, then simmer the pulp with the sugar for 10 minutes very slowly. Mix cornflour to a smooth paste with a little water, stir in and boil for 2 or 3 minutes.

Moussaline Sauce (Sweet) (for 3–4)

3 egg-yolks
2 egg-whites
½ gill cream
Lemon juice
1 oz. sugar
A few drops vanilla

Whisk egg-yolks, cream, sugar and flavourings together in a double boiler over gently boiling water until mixture becomes thick and frothy. Mix in the stiffly beaten egg-whites and serve.

Rum Sauce (for 4)

1 egg-yolk
2 dessertspoonfuls Jamaica rum
2 dessertspoonfuls icing sugar
1 egg-white, stiffly beaten
1 small bottle double cream, whipped
Grated lemon rind

Beat egg-yolk with rum and sugar. Add beaten egg-white, whipped cream and lemon rind.

Sabayon Sauce (for 3–4)

3 egg-yolks
1 oz. castor sugar
1 gill Madeira or Marsala wine

Whisk egg-yolks and sugar in upper part of a double boiler over gently boiling water till frothy. Add wine gradually, stirring all the time, and strain.

Treacle Sauce (for 5–6)

1 gill water	1 level dessertspoon-
8 oz. treacle or syrup	ful arrowroot
1 oz. butter	Lemon juice

Mix the arrowroot into a paste with a little of the water, bring the rest of the water, syrup (or treacle) and butter to the boil. Add the paste and cook for 3 minutes. Add a squeeze of lemon juice.

Wine Foam Sauce (for 3–4)

1 egg	¼ pint sherry or Mar-
1 dessertspoonful	sala
sugar	A strip of lemon peel

Put all the ingredients into a double boiler over gently boiling water, warming the sherry or Marsala slightly first. Whisk well until frothy. Remove peel and serve.

Christmas dinner would be incomplete without Hard Sauce, known in some parts of the country as Brandy Butter, but just right to bring out the flavour of a good rich plum pudding

VEGETABLES

*How to cook and serve these important foods as tastily as they do
on the Continent—and introducing some that may be new to you*

THE French and, indeed, most Continental peoples are far better vegetable cooks than the British. The reason is not difficult to find. In France, Holland, Belgium and other Continental countries vegetables are regarded as important foods, quite often worthy of being served as a separate dish and always chosen for their absolute freshness. See chapters on Cookery at Home and Abroad.

There really is no excuse to-day for watery cabbage, sad, tasteless carrots and soapy potatoes. These are three of the cheapest vegetables on the market. They are full of valuable vitamins and, when properly cooked, taste absolutely delicious.

Yet, according to the dieticians, most families would do better if, instead of serving up the vegetables and throwing away the water in which they were cooked, they reversed the process, drinking the water and letting the vegetables go. For there is no sense in eating food after all the goodness has been boiled out of it—which is what happens to many vegetables in the hands of over-zealous cooks. Therefore:

Never overcook vegetables.—When boiling them, use no more water than is absolutely necessary, cover the pan (unless otherwise instructed) and do not let them go off the boil. As a general rule, vegetables grown *above* the ground should be plunged into water that is already boiling and cooked fast; those from *below* ground put into cold water and cooked slowly. Cooking time depends chiefly upon the age of the vegetables, very young ones taking the least time.

Do not use soda to preserve colour.—A pinch of sugar does just as well and neither destroys the vitamins nor makes the vegetables indigestible.

Cook vegetables in their skins to get the best—and the nicest flavour—out of them. Either serve them like that or peel them after cooking. If you must peel vegetables before cooking, do it as thinly as possible, because the best part lies just below the skin.

Save the vegetable water for soups, stews and sauces.

Always serve vegetables as soon as they are cooked. If they are kept hot or reheated the vitamins are destroyed.

Boiling vegetables is the quickest method of cooking them. Very little of their value or flavour will be lost if you remember to choose a small pan with a close-fitting lid, to use the very minimum of water and to avoid overcooking. Just before serving, drain well and put them back in the pan or into a warmed casserole with a little butter or margarine and return to the stove for a few minutes, shaking the pan to prevent them sticking. Alternatively, drain the vegetables just *before* they are completely cooked and finish them in a casserole in the oven with a lump of butter.

Stewing or Steaming are ideal methods for getting the full value from vegetables. Both methods naturally take longer than boiling—allow about twice as long—but the result is delicious and not extravagant if you choose days when you have the oven on or are using a saucepan on top of which a steamer can be put.

Put the vegetables into salted boiling water for a few seconds only. Drain them well and, while still hot, put them with a little butter or margarine and salt into a warmed casserole or fireproof dish with a well-fitting lid. Put the casserole either into the oven or in a steamer over a saucepan, whichever fits in with your other cooking.

Vegetables stewed or steamed are particularly useful as a separate course, an economical catering idea which is not nearly as popular as it deserves to be. A meal beginning with a substantial soup, followed by at least two well cooked and tasty vegetables and ending with a satisfying sweet course makes a welcome change from the ordinary lunch or dinner menu.

When fresh vegetables are both scarce

and *expensive*, you can get a variety of frozen or canned vegetables, both of which taste excellent and also retain their valuable vitamins, provided they are cooked according to the instructions on the package (see chapter on Emergency Meals).

Left-over vegetables, as well as the water in which they have been cooked, are well worth keeping. They can be used to garnish soups or, cut up small, are useful in salads.

Artichokes (Green or Globe)

Allow one per person. Cut off the stalks close to the leaves and take off outer leaves; trim the points if discoloured. Wash well and soak in cold water for at least ½ hour. Drop, head downwards, into plenty of salted boiling water to which a little lemon juice has been added and boil for 40–45 minutes. When cooked, the leaves should come out easily. Drain and serve hot with melted butter or white sauce or cold with salad dressing. The leaves are pulled out one at a time, dipped in the sauce or dressing and eaten.

Artichokes (Jerusalem)

Boiled.—(1) Wash, peel and put the artichokes for a few minutes into cold water to which a little lemon juice has been added, to preserve their colour. Drain and put them into boiling salted water with a squeeze of lemon juice and cook for 30–35 minutes. Drain when tender, and serve with white or parsley sauce.

(2) Prepare as for the first method, then put the artichokes into a *very* little boiling salted water with a squeeze of lemon juice and cook for a few minutes, then add an equal quantity of boiled milk. Simmer until the artichokes are tender. Drain and either serve with a sauce made from the milk and water in which they were cooked and a little cornflour and butter, or pour some warmed and well mixed cream and butter over them

A basket of freshly gathered vegetables is transformed into a delicious cooked dish. A small marrow is served whole, surrounded by young green peas, cauliflower, new potatoes, tomatoes, broad beans, carrots, asparagus and onions

and sprinkle with chopped parsley.

Fried.—Wash, pare and slice the artichokes thinly. Fry immediately in very hot fat. Drain, and serve piping hot.

Asparagus

Cut the white skin off the lower end of the stalks, wash well and trim the stalks to an even length. Tie into a bundle and stand upright, tips upwards, in well-salted boiling water. Cook until tender (between 25 and 40 minutes, according to size of stalks). If liked, a sprig of fresh mint may be added to the cooking water. Drain, untie bundle and lay flat on dish with stems parallel. Serve hot with melted butter or Béchamel sauce. Cold cooked asparagus may also be served with a French dressing of olive oil and lemon juice or vinegar (see Salads).

Aubergine (Egg-plant)

Fried.—Peel off the deep violet-coloured skin, slice across about ½ in. thick, dip in seasoned flour and brown for about 20 minutes in a little fat. Serve hot—excellent with fried or grilled bacon.

Baked.—Wash, but do not peel. Slice the aubergines in half lengthwise, making a few incisions in the skin with a sharp knife and put them, outside downwards, into a well greased casserole. Dot with fat and bake in a hot oven for 20–25 minutes.

Stuffed.—See Greek Cookery chapter.

Bananas

Baked.—Choose firm but ripe bananas, peel and put either whole or halved lengthwise in a buttered casserole, dot with butter or dripping and bake in a moderate oven for 10–15 minutes until soft.

Scalloped.—See page 105.

Beetroot

To boil, wash well, being careful not to damage the outside skin (the beet would then lose its colour). Boil gently until soft —the time varies considerably. Young beets take from 30 to 45 minutes, old ones anything from 2 to 3 hours.

To serve hot, peel immediately, slice thinly, sprinkle with lemon juice or dress with parsley sauce, melted butter or white sauce.

To serve cold, remove the outer skin when cooked and cooled, cut into convenient slices, serve with lemon juice, vinegar or French dressing (see Salads).

Broad Beans

Shell and drop the beans into enough salted, fast-boiling water to cover them. Boil gently until soft (15–30 minutes, according to age), drain, add a knob of butter and some chopped parsley or serve with parsley sauce.

Broccoli

Cut off the stalks and coarse outside leaves, wash thoroughly, then cook in boiling salted water until just tender (about 15 minutes). Drain well and serve with melted butter (with or without lemon juice) or white sauce.

Brussels Sprouts

Remove outer leaves and wash well. Drop into boiling salted water and cook fast until tender but *not* mushy (10–15 minutes), then drain thoroughly and serve hot. Properly cooked sprouts should be whole and just crisp. Alternatively, drain and dry the sprouts just *before* they are completely cooked, then either return them to the saucepan or put them into a warmed casserole with a little butter or margarine, salt and pepper. Either toss them gently in the pan over a moderate flame until they are quite hot, but without allowing them to fry, or heat them through in the casserole in the oven.

Cabbage

Choose the freshest possible cabbage and cook it with care just before serving. Trim off hard stalk and discoloured and damaged leaves, but remember the outside green leaves contain more food value—and are far tastier—than the heart, so don't throw them away. Wash thoroughly and leave, head downwards, in salted cold water for 15–20 minutes to remove insects; but do *not* soak for any longer than that. Cut cabbage into four or more pieces, according to its size, and plunge into boiling salted water (just enough to cover it). Cook without the lid on until tender but *not* mushy (about 10–15 minutes). Drain well, pressing out all the moisture, add a piece of butter or margarine when putting into the serving dish and serve immediately.

Another method is to shred the cabbage finely; just cover the bottom of a saucepan with boiling salted water, put in cabbage and cover with a tight-fitting lid. Cook for 3–5 minutes, shaking the pan once or twice, by which time the water should have boiled away. Add a lump of butter or margarine and toss over heat until melted. Grate a little nutmeg on top before serving.

Cabbage cooked in this way keeps its colour, and there are no cooking smells.

Carrots

Wash well and scrape. Cook whole if young; slice old ones lengthwise or dice them small. Cook in boiling salted water with a lump of sugar in it. Young carrots take from 15 to 20 minutes, old ones from ¾ to 1 hour. Drain and put back into the pan or into a warmed casserole with a good knob of butter or margarine, salt and pepper. Serve hot, garnished with parsley.

If you are using the oven, you can cook carrots in a covered casserole with a good knob of butter or margarine, salt and pepper—and just enough water to prevent them from sticking.

Cold cooked carrots may be reheated by frying lightly in butter, or used cold in salads.

Cauliflower

Remove the outer leaves, cut off stalk, wash well and soak in cold, well salted water for $\frac{1}{2}$ hour to eliminate insects. Then plunge head downwards into salted boiling water and cook until soft. It should take about 20 minutes if young, up to 30 minutes for older ones. Drain well and serve whole, garnished with white sauce, or divide into individual flowerets and cover with breadcrumbs fried brown in butter. Alternatively, sprigs of cooked cauliflower may be covered with white sauce, breadcrumbs and (if liked) grated cheese, dotted with butter or margarine and browned under the grill; or they may be dipped in batter and fried.

Celeriac

Peel the roots and cut in pieces. Cook in boiling salted water until tender, drain and serve hot with melted butter or cold with oil and vinegar.

Celery

Boiled. — Wash a head of celery and scrape the outside sticks well. Cut into 3- or 4-in. pieces. Cover with salted boiling water or milk and water and simmer until just tender (about 1 hour). Drain well and serve with a white or cheese sauce made from the liquid.

Braised.—Wash and scrape the sticks and cut into 3-in. pieces. Dry well. Cook slowly in butter, either in a frying pan or a casserole in the oven, until the celery is tender and a nice brown. Remove and keep hot. Add either a very little water or some stock to the cooking liquid, season and pour over the celery.

To serve raw.—Wash the celery, cut off very rough outside sticks (and keep for cooking) then cut either into quarters lengthwise or separate into individual sticks. The green tops as well as the heart are eaten raw and are excellent in salads. Celery is also served raw with cheese. To keep it fresh and crisp, stand in cold water.

Chestnuts

Roasted.—Slit the chestnuts with a pointed knife, then roast until done, peel while hot and serve promptly with butter.

Boiled.—Slit the chestnuts, cover with cold water and bring to the boil. Drain and peel while still hot. Then simmer the peeled chestnuts until tender in salted water or milk and water. Serve hot with butter.

Chicory

Wash, but do not leave in water longer than necessary. If chicory has to be kept, wrap it in a moist cloth to prevent the light and air from turning its leaves brown. Cook

A sprinkling of finely chopped parsley or chives and a dab of butter make all the difference to a dish of tiny new potatoes, green peas and young broad beans

the heads whole. Grease the bottom of the pan with butter or margarine or good-quality fat and put the chicory in. Dissolve 1 teaspoonful of salt in 2 tablespoonfuls of water, add the juice of 1 lemon and pour over the chicory. Put a saucer or small plate on the chicory to press it down, put on the lid and bring to the boil. Boil for about $\frac{1}{2}$ hour, drain well and serve hot with a few knobs of butter.

Chicory is also excellent eaten raw, either alone or as part of a salad.

NOTE: The lemon juice is essential to keep chicory a good colour.

Corn on the Cob (or Indian Corn)

Remove husk and silk, and drop the cobs into a pan of fast-boiling salted water, preferably with a teaspoonful of sugar in it. Cook for about 6 minutes and serve, just as it is, with lots of butter and salt and pepper. Alternatively, scrape the seeds from the cobs and gently warm them in a pan with a little butter and seasoning, shaking to prevent them sticking.

Cucumber

Boiled.—Peel thinly and cut lengthwise, removing seeds. Cook in enough boiling salted water to cover until soft (about 10 minutes). Drain, keeping the liquid to make a sauce.

Fried.—Peel and wipe, cut into small slices. Dry in a cloth, season and dip in egg and breadcrumbs. Fry till brown, and drain.

French Beans

French beans should be young and tender enough to be cooked whole. Simply nip off the ends and peel off the string right round the pod. Wash and plunge them into boiling salted water with a teaspoonful of sugar to bring out the flavour. When young, they should not need more than 12–15 minutes to cook. As soon as they are tender, drain, then put them back in the hot pan or a warmed casserole with a good knob of butter or margarine, pepper and salt. Serve hot. Older ones must be sliced before cooking, boiled for about 20 minutes, and may be served with a tomato or Hollandaise sauce (see Sauces chapter).

Kale or Turnip Tops

Remove tough leaves and thick stalks,

To make Stuffed Cabbage: Wash and trim cabbage, cut off stalk and remove outside leaves. Line a basin with a clean cloth and arrange leaves inside. Cut cabbage in four, slice finely, place in a saucepan with 2 oz. margarine and cook slowly for about $\frac{1}{2}$ hour, stirring often

wash well and cook in boiling salted water for 15–20 minutes. Drain and serve with butter, salt and pepper.

Kohl Rabi

Peel, wash and cut into cubes. Simmer in a little boiling salted water until tender (about 20 minutes). Drain and serve with white sauce.

Leeks

Boiled.—Cut off the roots, remove coarse outer leaves and wash very thoroughly under running water, splitting if necessary to get out the earth and mud. Put into boiling salted water and cook gently until tender (about 20–25 minutes). Drain well and pour over them either melted butter, seasoned with salt and pepper, or white sauce.

Cooked in Milk.—Proceed as above, but take the leeks out of the boiling water after a few minutes and cook them slowly in milk. When tender, drain and use the milk to make a sauce with a little butter and flour, flavouring with cheese if liked.

Lettuce

Boiled.—Wash well, removing damaged leaves and stalk. Plunge into enough salted boiling water to cover, and cook for 12–18

When the cabbage is soft and golden, add 2 teaspoonfuls chopped parsley, 1 onion chopped fine, and seasoning. Continue cooking for 10 minutes. Add 2 tablespoonfuls fresh breadcrumbs, 1 egg, and place in cabbage leaves

Tie up the cloth and cook in a pan of boiling salted water for 1 hour. Serve on a hot dish sprinkled with crumbs fried golden brown in a little margarine, with tomato sauce, small browned onions and sauté potatoes as a garnish

minutes, according to size and age. When tender, drain, chop, season well and add a small piece of butter. Serve either alone or on slices of fried bread.

Marrow

Baby marrows and courgettes have the most delicate flavour and hardly any seeds. They should be cooked whole, unpeeled, in a pan with a tightly fitting lid containing a very little salted water, a knob of butter or margarine, salt and pepper. Bring to the boil and simmer gently till tender (about 10–15 minutes). Serve with the liquor poured over them or with melted butter.

Larger marrows must be peeled, have their seeds removed and be cut into slices. Then boil gently for about 20 minutes, drain and serve with white or cheese sauce made from the water in which the marrow was cooked.

Mushrooms

Fried.—Remove stalks, peel and, if large, cut into pieces. Melt a little butter in a frying pan. Dredge mushrooms with flour and cook for about 5 minutes or until tender, with a little salt and pepper. Serve on toast or with crisp bacon rashers.

Stewed.—Peel, wash and remove stalks

from mushrooms. If large, cut into pieces. Put about 2 oz. butter into a casserole or saucepan and fry the mushrooms in it for a few minutes. Add seasoning and a few drops of lemon juice. Put on the lid and simmer very slowly for about 10 minutes or until tender, stirring now and again. Make a smooth paste with 1 teaspoonful of cornflour and 1 gill of stock or milk; add this, stirring gently, bring to the boil and cook slowly for a few minutes. Sprinkle with parsley and serve hot.

Nettles

Only young nettles should be used. Wash them thoroughly in several changes of water, then cook as for spinach, without any additional water, stirring occasionally to prevent them sticking. Either rub through a sieve or chop finely. Reheat, season well and add a small piece of butter.

Onions

Always peel onions under cold water and wash the knife and your hands in *cold* water afterwards to get rid of the smell.

Boiled.—Peel and cover with cold salted water and boil until tender. Drain well and serve either with a good knob of butter or with white sauce.

Fried.—Slice finely and fry gently until

golden brown. Drain on paper and serve hot.

Baked.—Place the onions (whole) in a well greased baking tin and cook in a moderate oven for about 1 hour or until tender.

Casseroled.—Small whole onions should be used. Peel them and put into a covered casserole with some butter or dripping and seasoning. Cook gently for about 2 hours.

Parsnips

Boiled.—Wash and scrape, cut lengthwise in quarters, then across into ½-in. thick slices. Boil in enough salted water to cover until soft but firm (about 10–15 minutes). Drain and put into a casserole or back into the pan with a little butter or margarine and seasoning, and sauté a light brown. Sprinkle with chopped parsley before serving.

Baked.—Wash, peel and cut lengthwise into quarters, removing the hard core from the centre. Then either steam for 45 minutes or 1 hour and finish off in a baking tin with a little dripping and seasoning until nicely brown, or roast in the tin with meat or poultry, basting from time to time with seasoned dripping.

Mashed.—Wash, peel, cut into small pieces and boil in salted water until soft. Drain, rub through a sieve, then put the purée back in the pan with a little butter and heat through gently, stirring in a little cream or top of the milk and seasoning just before serving.

Peas (Green)

Shell and rinse in cold water. Put the peas into just enough salted boiling water to cover them, add a few leaves of mint and a pinch of sugar. Boil, uncovered, slowly until soft when tested between the finger and thumb (about 10 minutes for young peas, 20–25 minutes for older ones). Drain thoroughly and return to the pan or a warmed casserole with a little butter or margarine and seasoning. Serve.

Peppers

These are known as Spanish Peppers (or Pimento), Long, Green or Red Peppers (or Capsicum) according to their shape and colour.

Fried.—Split the peppers lengthwise down the middle and take out seeds. Plunge into boiling salted water, leave for 5 minutes, drain, then toss in butter and seasoning for about 5 minutes. Alternatively, the slices of peppers may be dipped in egg and breadcrumbs and fried crisp and golden in deep fat.

Stuffed.—Cut tops off the peppers and remove seeds. Boil for 2 minutes, then pour cold water over them, stuff with a mixture of minced meat and seasoning or macaroni and cheese. Put back the tops and bake in a moderate oven in a well-greased casserole, basting from time to time with the liquor.

Potatoes

Baked.—Thoroughly wash and dry some good large potatoes, prick the skins with a fork and bake them in a moderate oven for between 40 and 80 minutes, according to size, or until they feel soft when gently squeezed. Serve at once or the potatoes will get hard and shrivelled—and keep them hot, if necessary, by wrapping them in a hot cloth, never in the oven. Split them open along one side with a fork, put a knob of butter or margarine and a sprinkling of salt and pepper (preferably Cayenne) inside, and serve at once.

Baked and Stuffed.—Wash and dry thoroughly, prick the skins with a fork and bake in a moderately hot oven until soft, time depending on age and size of potatoes. When done, split skins lengthwise, scoop out the contents, add butter, seasoning and a little milk or cream, flavoured, if liked, with grated cheese, chopped parsley or diced fried bacon and onion. Put the mixture back into the skins and return to a hot oven or brown under a hot grill for 5–10 minutes.

Boiled (old).—Either scrub clean, if to be cooked in their skins, or, if not, peel as thinly as possible (the best flavour is to be found just below the skin), put into a saucepan of cold salted water, bring to the boil and cook gently until very nearly soft, taking care not to break them. Drain, peel if cooked in their skins, then stand them in the dry saucepan on one side of the stove for a few minutes with the lid on. A few seconds before serving, remove the lid to allow the steam to escape, leaving them dry and floury. Cooking time varies tremendously, according to the variety, age and size, but 20–30 minutes is about average. Choose potatoes of uniform size, or cut up the large ones.

Boiled (*new*).—Wash well and rub with a rough cloth to remove skin, or scrape with a sharp knife. Put into boiling salted water with a sprig of mint and simmer gently until done (about 20 minutes), drain and then replace for a few minutes in the pan at the side of the stove to dry. Put with a small piece of butter or margarine into a casserole or hot vegetable dish, and serve. A little chopped parsley scattered over new potatoes glistening with golden butter makes them look and taste delicious.

Fried.—Wash, peel and cut the potatoes in slices, straws or any shapes you like, throwing them into cold water until you are ready to use them. Then drain and dry thoroughly with a clean cloth. Put them into hot deep fat (butter, fat or oil may be used), preferably in a frying basket, and fry till they are a rich brown. Cook only a few at a time and do them slowly, tossing them about to prevent them from sticking. Drain well and put in a warm place on soft paper. When all are ready, put them back in the basket, boil up the fat and plunge them in for about 2 minutes. Drain and season.

Mashed.—Boil old potatoes (see oppo-site) till tender, drain and peel or, if peeled first, cook till just tender and drain. Either rub through a coarse sieve or beat well with a fork, then put back in the pan over the heat, add a good knob of butter or margarine, salt and pepper, and beat well with a wooden spoon, thin to the right creamy consistency with a little hot milk. Serve garnished with a sprinkling of chopped parsley.

New Potatoes with Orange.—Slice some large new potatoes, put them in layers in a casserole and between each layer grate a little orange peel. Add plenty of salt to give the dish sharpness, just cover with milk and cook for half an hour in a fairly hot oven till the top is brown like Lancashire Hot Pot. If liked, you can chop a little garlic into the dish low down between layers.

Puffed.—Cut the potatoes into slices about $\frac{1}{8}$ in. thick and fry, preferably in a frying basket, in hot deep fat, removing them just *before* they brown. Cook a few at a time and toss to prevent them from sticking. When all are done, return them to

Mushrooms, always a favourite among vegetables, will go much farther if they are stuffed with a savoury mixture bound with an egg

the basket, boil up the fat again and plunge the basket into it. Repeat this process twice. Drain well and serve.

Roast.—Peel large potatoes thinly and cut into halves or quarters. Put into the baking tin with meat, either under or around the joint. Baste well with dripping. Turn when brown on one side and season with pepper and salt. Allow about 1–1½ hours for potatoes to roast a nice rich brown.

Sauté.—Wash, peel, cut in slices and parboil some old potatoes. Drain well, then toss them in a frying pan with a little butter until a pale brown. Turn and cook the other side, keeping the pan moving constantly to prevent burning. Season and garnish with chopped parsley before serving.

Steamed (old).—Wash and put the potatoes, preferably unpeeled, into the steamer over a saucepan of fast boiling water. Just before they are tender, peel and put them back in the steamer, pour away the boiling water from underneath, cover the potatoes with a cloth and the steamer lid, and leave them to finish cooking on the side of the stove in their own steam.

Potatoes Anna.—Wash, peel and slice the potatoes into thin rings, toss them into cold water for 10 minutes, then drain and dry them thoroughly. Into a round, deep, well buttered casserole put a layer of the potato rings, season well with salt and pepper, dot with butter, then put in another layer of potatoes, season and dot with butter, and so on until the dish is nearly full. Bake in a hot oven for 1 hour, after which the potatoes should be a nice pale brown and able to be turned out of the mould.

Potato Cakes.—Mix some mashed potatoes (see p. 103) into a thick paste with a little flour and a pinch of salt. Roll the paste out on a pastry board, cut into rounds or triangles and fry in butter until brown on both sides. Drain well and serve hot. May be eaten with a meat dish or as a sweet, sprinkled with sugar.

Potato Cones.—Put some hot mashed potatoes (see p. 103) into a saucepan with a little butter, salt and pepper. Then add a beaten egg-yolk and, if possible, a little cream. Stir the mixture well. Beat in the egg-white after removing from the fire. Flour a board, shape the mixture into cones and brown in a quick oven.

Potato Croquettes.—Mash some hot potatoes (see previous page). When cool, season and add an egg-white, well beaten, and just enough flour to make the mixture hold together. Form into balls, roll in flour, coat with egg and breadcrumbs, and fry in deep fat to a light brown. Drain well and serve hot.

This mixture can also be made into cottage loaves or little rolls and baked in a quick oven. In this case, pour a little oiled butter over them before putting in to bake, to glaze surface.

Duchess Potatoes.—Cook and mash 1 lb. of potatoes. Add one or two egg-yolks, 1 oz. of butter, about a tablespoonful of cream, salt, pepper and a little nutmeg, if liked. Pipe this creamy mixture into the shape of rosettes on a greased baking tin, brush with egg and bake in a hot oven until well browned.

Runner Beans

Cut off the ends and remove the strings, then slice the beans diagonally into long thin strips, using a sharp knife. Put them straight into a saucepan of cold water. Bring to the boil and cook fast, uncovered, for about 15 minutes, or until the beans are tender. Drain and put into a hot dish with a piece of butter or margarine and seasoning and serve hot.

Salsify

Wash and scrape well, adding a little lemon juice to the water to preserve the colour. Cook in boiling salted water with a little lemon juice until tender (about 30–40 minutes). Drain and serve hot with white sauce or tossed in butter in a frying pan until nicely browned, then seasoned with pepper, salt and a squeeze of lemon. Salsify can also be served cold with a good French dressing (see Salads chapter).

Sea Kale

Wash well, separating the stalks, and tie in bundles or break into small pieces and place in sufficient salted boiling water with a squeeze of lemon juice just to cover. Simmer gently until soft (about 30 minutes) with the lid off. Drain well and serve with melted butter or white sauce.

Sorrel

Remove the stalks, wash in several changes of water till absolutely clean, then

MEET A NEW VEGETABLE DISH

BANANA SCALLOPS

Here's a new and exciting way of serving bananas— cooked, hot and crisply fried—instead of potatoes, to go with a meat, fish or vegetarian dish. Delicious with boiled cauliflower

Banana Scallops (for 4)

4 firm bananas
Melted fat or salad oil
1½ teaspoonfuls salt
1 egg, slightly beaten, or ¼ cupful
 undiluted evaporated milk
½ cupful cornflake crumbs, bread or biscuit
 crumbs

Salt egg or milk slightly. Peel bananas and slice crosswise into pieces ¾–1 in. thick. Dip into egg or milk. Drain. Roll in crumbs, and fry in the hot fat for about 1½–2 minutes, or until brown and tender. To deep-fry, have deep frying saucepan ½–⅔ full of melted fat or oil. To shallow-fry, have 1 in. of melted fat or oil in frying pan. Heat fat until a 1-in. cube of bread will brown in about 40 seconds. Drain well and serve hot as a vegetable.

cook in just sufficient water to cover the bottom of the pan, with salt sprinkled over, until tender (about 10–15 minutes). Stir frequently. Drain and chop finely.

Spinach

Wash carefully in several different waters, discarding the coarse and discoloured leaves. Put into a saucepan and cook in the moisture adhering to it, without adding any other liquid, stirring to prevent sticking, for about 15 minutes or until nice and soft. Drain very thoroughly, squeezing the excess moisture out, then chop. Put back into the pan or into a warmed casserole with a good knob of butter or margarine and seasoning, and reheat.

Spinach Purée.—Cook as above, then rub through a sieve. Reheat, adding a little butter, pepper and salt.

Creamed Spinach.—Proceed as for Spinach Purée (above), then stir in a little cream till it is the desired consistency.

Swedes

Peel, slice and cook in salted boiling water until tender. Drain and mash with butter and seasoning.

Tomatoes

Baked or Grilled: Cut the tomatoes in half, sprinkle with salt and pepper, put a little oiled butter or a dab of margarine, bacon fat or dripping on each, and either grill or bake in a moderate oven for about 10–15 minutes.

Turnips

Peel and dice, then cook in salted boiling water until tender (young ones will need about 15 minutes, old 45 minutes or even more). Drain and mash or rub through a sieve with a wooden spoon—or keep in dice if small and young—and return to the saucepan or a warmed casserole with a little butter or margarine, seasoning and milk. Reheat and serve.

Turnip Tops (see Kale)

SALADS

The most useful dish on the menu, a salad is at home with most foods, hot or cold—or by itself

AT any time of the year, from January to December, you can serve a delicious, tempting, health-giving salad every day— and it need not be expensive either. The Victorian conception of a little wilted lettuce, a few slices of tomato and cucumber, and some beetroot soaked in vinegar was a depressing dish at any time and, fortunately, only made its appearance on hot summer days, as an accompaniment to cold meat. Now salads provide the most wonderful opportunity for the imaginative housewife to introduce variety—in flavours and colour—into her family's meals.

We know from the dieticians that we get the *full* flavour and value out of fruit and vegetables only if we eat them raw. Once you put those theories into practice, your palate proves how right the experts are. Raw vegetable salads are appetising and a sure way of getting sufficient vitamin C into the daily diet, for all green leaves and, to a lesser extent, edible roots and blanched stems, supply this vitamin in abundance. They are also richly endowed with such important alkaline elements as potassium, calcium, iron, magnesium and sodium, all of which are essential to health —and very conducive to beauty.

Getting a salad into the menu every day need not present any problems. There is no nicer start to a meal than crisp green lettuce, sliced raw tomato, grated raw vegetables or fruits, served with an appetising dressing. As an accompaniment to a main dish, or to follow it; as a course on its own or a garnish with fish, meat or poultry— salad is at home anywhere in the meal.

It is fun to make almost as much of a ritual of the salad bowl as Victorian menfolk used to make out of passing the port. Prepare the green ingredients beforehand and bring them to the table, beautifully crisp and dry, in a big wooden bowl, then mix your dressing to your liking and toss the salad thoroughly and lovingly with a wooden spoon and fork.

Practically every vegetable that is more often cooked can just as well be eaten raw if it is properly prepared—and preferably when young and tender. When the more conventional salad ingredients are scarce, expensive or unobtainable, there is always an alternative. Lettuce can be replaced by that favourite of Continental housewives, cornsalad, or, cheaper still, by the crisp heart of a white or red cabbage finely chopped, or the tender inside leaves of raw spinach. Nearly all the culinary herbs— chives, mint, parsley, marjoram, thyme, etc.—are delicious in salads, and so are nasturtium and dandelion leaves. You can put all kinds of fruit—fresh, tinned, dried or cooked—into salads, and so make a dish that is a meal in itself.

WINTER INGREDIENTS

Here are just a few of the amazing variety of vegetables usually obtainable in the U.K. between November and March (the most difficult time for salads), all of which are excellent raw:

Jerusalem artichokes, cabbage, beetroot, carrots, cornsalad (or lamb's lettuce), garlic, leeks, onions, parsnips, winter radishes, shallots, swedes, watercress, beet-spinach, celery, celeriac, dandelion, endive, land-cress, chives, turnips, Brussels sprouts, chicory, seakale.

These and many other ingredients can be combined in innumerable different ways, though a salad should contain a well-blended mixture of a few things, rather than too many at once.

The chief rules for good salad-making are:

(1) Everything must be crisp, cool, dry. Don't dress a green salad until the last minute before serving; green leaves wilt quickly under oil. The exceptions are the salads you marinate in a French dressing—Potato, Russian, Fish, for example.

(2) If you cut up vegetables, make them small enough to eat easily, but large enough to keep their identity.

Dressing the salad with oil and vinegar, perfectly blended, should be done slowly, carefully, lovingly—preferably at the table, as a ritual

(3) Choose the ingredients with an eye to contrast in flavour, colour and texture —and arrange attractively.

Green vegetables, such as lettuce, watercress, endive, etc., should be very carefully handled or they will lose their crispness. If they are inclined to be limp, plunge them into fresh cold water for 20 minutes before using, but never soak them for longer. A tablespoonful of Milton should be added to a quart of water to cleanse thoroughly, and will not make the greens taste if washed off in clean water. Salad greens not required for immediate use should be put, unwashed, into a tightly covered receptacle, such as a saucepan, or wrapped in a damp cloth or put into a polythene bag in a cold place (but not near the freezing compartment of the refrigerator).

Lettuce and Batavia Endive.—Remove discoloured outside leaves and cut off root stump. Plunge into cold water, separating the leaves and opening up the heart. Wash thoroughly at least twice in fresh cold water, then shake well in a salad basket or colander to remove excess moisture, and finally toss lightly in a clean dry cloth.

Curly Endive.—Prepare as for lettuce, but remember the dark green outer leaves have a characteristic bitter taste not liked by everyone. If in doubt, remove these.

Watercress is now mostly grown in running water under perfectly hygienic conditions and sold in bundles with the grower's name attached. Even so, it sometimes has little quite harmless insects, so wash it in several waters, the first containing a tablespoonful of Milton to the quart, remove decayed leaves and all fibrous matter or straggly roots. Dry well.

Cornsalad.—Remove roots and rinse in cold water. Dry.

Mustard and Cress.—To remove all the black seeds and wash properly, hold a handful of the cress in one hand under a running tap so that the seeds get washed away. Or put the cress into a bowl of cold water and swish the water round and round, so that the seeds travel out, leaving the cress free.

Radishes.—Wash in cold water, do not peel or scrape, and dry with a cloth. Young ones may be served with their green tops on, larger ones are better sliced, some of

107

the smaller leaves being used separately.

Spring Onions.—Cut away root fibres, peel off outside skin and remove a little of the green tops. Wash in cold water and serve either whole or sliced.

Celery.—Wash carefully, cutting away discoloured and coarse parts but keeping these for use cooked or for soup. Use both the crisp white stalks and the tender green leaves in salad. To make a very attractive garnish, take a stick of celery and with a sharp knife cut about five or six parallel slits downwards one-third of its length. Put into water and leave for an hour or two, when the ends will all curl back. Both ends may be curled in this way.

Cucumber should be rinsed in cold water and cut, unpeeled, into chunks. This is less likely to cause indigestion than when it is eaten peeled and sliced very thin so that the valuable vitamins, etc., in the skin are lost, and it is often not properly masticated.

Cabbage.—Choose a firm white or red cabbage, cut away the outer leaves, which can be cooked, and use the heart only for salad. Cut out the hard core, wash well in cold water, leave for 10 or 15 minutes (but not more) in salted cold water to remove insects, then shake off surplus moisture and slice thinly or shred with a sharp knife.

Brussels Sprouts.—Prepare as for cabbage.

Spinach, Nasturtium Leaves and Herbs. —Wash well in cold salted water, shaking dry afterwards.

Root Vegetables (artichokes, carrots, young turnips, parsnips, etc.) should be scrubbed, scraped rather than peeled, and either grated or cut into very thin strips. NOTE: They must be grated at the last minute, just before serving, or they will lose their attractive colour and much of their vitamin content.

Cooked Vegetables (carrots, peas, potatoes, for instance) are a pleasant addition to many salads. They must be very firm so that they can be diced or cut into fancy shapes. Potatoes intended for salad should be boiled in their skins and peeled afterwards.

SERVING SALADS

Salads may be served in a glass, china or wooden bowl, in small individual dishes or on dinner plates. The arrangement is most important. No dish has more "eye-appeal" than a good salad. Avoid overcrowding and never let leaves project over the edge of the plate.

You can make an attractive effect by arranging the top layer of a salad in different coloured quarters. Hard-boiled egg-whites and yolks chopped very fine, green peas, diced beetroot, sprigs of parsley, celery tops, diced cucumber, capers, grated raw carrot, nuts, segments of apple, orange or grapefruit, fluted slices of bananas, a few black or green grapes or olives, some dates, can all be used to make a fascinating colour scheme as well as a tasty and nourishing salad. But remember—it's contrast that makes a good effect.

DRESSINGS

Light French dressing (or Vinaigrette) is best with green salads. Heavier dressings, such as cream salad dressing or a rich mayonnaise, are good with more substantial salad dishes. But the question of which dressing for which salad is very much a matter of taste.

Remember, whichever you choose, never to mix the dressing with a green salad until just before serving—or the greens will wilt —and always use a wooden spoon for mixing.

For recipes for dressings see end of chapter.

FRUIT AND VEGETABLE SALADS

Apple, Cabbage and Celery Salad

Shred the heart of a white cabbage finely, cut up some celery, peel and dice one or two apples. Mix with cream salad dressing.

Banana and Nut Salad

Peel bananas and cut them in three. Then cut each piece in half lengthways and roll in chopped walnuts (or any other nuts). Arrange the banana pieces on lettuce and pour over some French dressing.

Banana Vegetable Salad

Wash and dry one or more varieties of fresh crisp greens and arrange in a bowl previously rubbed with garlic (if liked). Add long strips of ripe banana, garnish with celery curls, onion, radish roses, wedges of tomato or strips of carrot. Serve with French dressing.

Beetroot and Egg Salad

| Lettuce | Radishes |
| Beetroot or tomato | Hard-boiled egg |

Arrange some whole inner leaves of lettuce on a dish. Put a few slices of beetroot or tomato on each and a slice of hard-boiled egg on top. Garnish with radish flowers.

Celery and Nut Salad

Chop some walnuts and dice some celery and mix well together. Serve with French dressing.

Celery, Cabbage and Nut Salad

| Head of celery | Small cabbage or |
| Chopped walnuts | lettuce |

Clean the celery and dice it. Shred the lettuce or cabbage finely, using only the inside. Mix together, sprinkle with the chopped nuts and serve with cream salad dressing.

Celery and Potato Salad

4 medium-sized
   potatoes cooked in
   their skins, peeled
   and cut in cubes
Celery tips
Stick of celery cut
   into small pieces
Apple, peeled, cored
   and sliced
French dressing

Mix the potato, apple and celery together with French dressing. Garnish with celery tips.

Cream Cheese Salad

Work together salad dressing and enough cream cheese to bind the mixture. Make into small balls on a wet board with a wet knife and roll in chopped nuts. Serve on lettuce or mustard and cress, and decorate with grated raw carrot, chopped parsley or slices of tomato.

Cream Cheese and Pineapple Salad

Pineapple rings
Cream cheese
Salad dressing
Lettuce
Cress

Make cream cheese balls by working enough cream cheese into salad dressing for the mixture to bind, and then rolling it on a wet board with a wet knife. Put some lettuce leaves on a dish with pineapple rings on top and put a cream cheese ball into the centre of each. Arrange the cress in between the rings.

Cucumber and Sour Cream Salad

Into a cup of sour cream stir 6 finely chopped spring onions or chives. Slice the cucumber and toss in the dressing.

Date Salad

Dates	Lettuce
Chopped stoned	Cream cheese
raisins	Chopped almonds

Stone the dates and stuff them with a mixture of raisins, cream cheese and

Star Salad has slices of hard-boiled egg and beetroot on a bed of grated cheese and lettuce

chopped almonds. Serve on lettuce or any green salad with French dressing.

Egg and Green Pea Salad

Hard-boiled eggs	Mayonnaise
Green peas	Lettuce
(cooked)	Cream cheese balls

Wash the lettuce and arrange the leaves whole in a dish. Cut the eggs in half lengthwise, scoop out the yolks and fill the eggs with green peas mixed with mayonnaise. Arrange the eggs on the lettuce. Mix the yolks with a little cream cheese and enough mayonnaise to bind and roll into balls. Garnish with these.

English Salad

Tomatoes	Lettuce
Cucumber	Watercress
Spring onions	Hard-boiled egg
Beetroot	Radishes

Prepare the lettuce and watercress and place some of it in a salad bowl. Add alternate layers of tomato, cucumber, spring onion and beetroot, cut into thin slices. Garnish with radishes and quarters of hard-boiled egg. Serve with French dressing or cream salad dressing.

Fluted Banana Fruit Salad (for 1)

½ peach, apricot or	1 ripe banana
pear (fresh or	Salad greens
canned)	Berries

Place half a peach, apricot or pear in a lettuce cup (made by cutting out the stem from a small lettuce, then letting the water from the cold tap run inside, forcing open the leaves) on a plate. Arrange a half-circle of fluted banana slices (see picture opposite), garnish with berries and sprigs of greens. Serve with French or cream dressing.

Frozen Salad (for 10–12)

1 tablespoonful	6 oz. cream cheese
lemon juice	2 tablespoonfuls
2 tablespoonfuls	crushed pineapple
mayonnaise	½ cupful chopped
1 teaspoonful salt	walnuts
½ cupful maraschino	3 ripe bananas,
cherries (quartered)	cubed
1 cupful whipped	Salad greens
cream	

Add lemon juice and salt to mayonnaise and stir into cheese. Add pineapple, cherries, nuts and fold in cream. Then add bananas. Turn into refrigerator tray and freeze until firm. Garnish with salad greens.

Green Salad

A green salad is best served by itself. It may consist of lettuce, cress, endive or chicory, well washed and dried. Serve with a dressing made from 3 tablespoonfuls of olive oil, 1 tablespoonful vinegar, salt and pepper, and a little finely chopped parsley, chives, tarragon or a hint of garlic, according to taste. Excellent to follow a hot meat or poultry dish.

Melon Ball Salad (for 1)

1 ripe banana	Melon balls
	Salad greens

Peel and cut banana lengthwise into halves. Place the halves cut side up, side by side, in centre of plate. Place a few melon balls at each end, garnish with crisp salad greens and serve with mayonnaise.

Mixed Fruit and Vegetable Salad

2 bananas	Nuts
Orange	A small cucumber
Lettuce	2 tomatoes
	Watercress

Arrange some whole inner leaves of lettuce on a dish. Peel the bananas and slice them and the cucumber. Peel the orange and remove the pith. Slice it thinly and remove the pips. Slice the tomatoes. Arrange these four ingredients in quarters and garnish with a little watercress and a few walnuts.

Orange Salad

Peel and quarter the oranges, removing the white pith and the pips. Season with salt, pepper and a little lemon juice mixed together with a little olive oil. Garnish with watercress. Serve with guinea fowl or wild duck.

Orange Tomato Aspic Salad

1 dessertspoonful	¼ cupful canned
gelatine	tomato soup
1 breakfastcupful	Lettuce
orange juice	½ cupful chopped
Dash of Cayenne	celery
	¼ teaspoonful salt

Soak gelatine in ½ cupful orange juice for 5 minutes. Dissolve over hot water. Add rest of orange juice and mix well. Add soup and seasoning. Chill. When mixture thickens, add celery, pour into small greased cups and leave to set. Serve on a couple of crisp lettuce leaves on small individual plates.

Delicious with beef pot roast, jugged

Fluted bananas add a professional touch—you do it by running the prongs of a fork down the banana

hare or stew with a rich dark gravy. An orange salad also makes rich meat dishes easier to digest as well as more enjoyable to eat.

Pineapple and Banana Salad (for 1)

> 2 *slices canned pineapple*
> *Salad greens*
> 1 *ripe banana*

Place a ring of pineapple round each end of a peeled banana. Garnish with crisp salad greens and, if liked, strawberries. Serve with mayonnaise.

Potato Salad (Cold)

Cut freshly cooked, peeled cold potatoes (cooked in their skins) into cubes and add some chopped parsley or chives. Mix the potato cubes well with vinaigrette. Sprinkle with a little chopped parsley.

Potato Salad (Hot)

Peel and slice some freshly cooked cold potatoes into a fireproof dish. Season with salt and pepper, a little chopped parsley and some chives. Carefully blend 2 tablespoonfuls wine vinegar with 4 tablespoonfuls olive oil, add the juice of a lemon and heat this dressing to boiling point. Pour over the potatoes, cover, and gently heat in the oven. Serve hot.

Russian Salad

> *Cooked peas, beans, carrots, potatoes*
> *Mayonnaise*

Cut vegetables into small dice and mix well with mayonnaise. To decorate the top, divide into squares and garnish each section differently: one with chopped egg-yolk, one with chopped white, one with peas and one with beans.

Stuffed Tomato Salad

Cut off a thin slice from the top of each tomato. Remove the seeds and pulp, and put a little salt in each. Allow them to stand for a time upside down. Then fill and serve on lettuce.

Tomatoes prepared in this way can be stuffed with all kinds of fillings, including the following:

Pineapple Banana Salad—a whole banana slipped through two pineapple rings garnished with fruit or green salad

Cucumber cut in cubes, and mixed with mayonnaise.

Chopped apple and celery mixed with mayonnaise.

Sardines, boned and cut up, mixed with tomato and mayonnaise.

Cream cheese and French dressing worked together.

Tomato and Pineapple Salad

Tomatoes	*Lettuce*
Crushed pineapple	*Mayonnaise*

Put some lettuce in a shallow bowl. Cut the tomatoes into quarters without quite cutting through. Remove the pips and fill the centres with crushed pineapple (or pineapple cubes chopped very finely) mixed with mayonnaise, and place them on the lettuce.

Tomato Salad

4 *tomatoes*	*Chopped chives or*
1 *tablespoonful wine*	*spring onion*
vinegar	*Pinch of salt and*
2 *tablespoonfuls*	*pepper*
olive oil	*Parsley and shredded*
	celery

Scald the tomatoes to remove the skins. Peel and slice thinly and arrange them in a dish with the chopped chives or onion sprinkled over. Blend the oil and vinegar, and season. Garnish with parsley and celery shredded finely.

Vegetarian Salad Lunch

Arrange on individual plates freshly grated raw carrot, swede, beetroot, white turnip, grated cheese or cream cheese, milled nuts, shredded fresh herbs (mint, parsley, marjoram). Serve with French dressing and wholemeal bread, butter and Marmite.

Waldorf Banana Salad (for 4–6)

1 *diced unpeeled red*	*Crisp lettuce or other*
apple	*salad greens*
½ *cupful mayonnaise*	½ *cupful diced celery*
or salad dressing	2 *sliced ripe bananas*
	Walnut halves

Mix together apple, celery, mayonnaise or salad dressing, and lightly add banana slices. Arrange on lettuce. Garnish with greens and nuts.

CHICKEN AND FISH SALADS

Chicken Salad

Cooked chicken	*Beetroot*
Lettuce	*Capers*
Cress	*Mayonnaise*

Slice the meat and put it in the centre of

For a summer main dish, prawns and hard-boiled eggs in aspic, served with salad

Salmon Salad Tropical is an exotic dish combining fruit, fish and green salad. You can ring the changes by using chicken or tuna fish instead of salmon

the dish and cover with mayonnaise. Arrange the lettuce and cress round the chicken. Cut the beetroot into small dice and place in groups on top of the sauce, and garnish with capers in between.

Fish Salad

Any cold cooked fish   *Mayonnaise*
Cooked potatoes   *Cress*
      Cucumber

Flake the fish and put it in a dish with slices of potato and cucumber. Pour some mayonnaise over and surround with cress.

Lobster (or Crab) Salad

Lobster (canned or   *French dressing or*
   freshly boiled)   *mayonnaise*
Lettuce   *Beetroot*
      Seasoning

Shred the lobster finely. Wash the lettuce and arrange it in a dish with the lobster. Season well with pepper and salt. Arrange slices of beetroot round and cover with either French dressing or mayonnaise.

Salmon Salad

Cooked salmon (fresh   *Radishes*
   or canned)   *Pepper and salt*
New potatoes   *French dressing*

Flake and season the salmon, then pile it in a dish and pour over it a little French dressing. Slice the potatoes thinly, pour dressing over them, season, and arrange them round the salmon with an outer ring of small radishes with a little of their green left on.

Salmon Salad Tropical (for 4–6)

1 cupful diced ripe   *1 tablespoonful pre-*
   banana   *pared mustard*
1 cupful diced pine-   *1½ cupfuls flaked*
   apple   *salmon*
2 tablespoonfuls   *1½ teaspoonfuls salt*
   chopped sweet   *1 tablespoonful*
   pickle   *mayonnaise*
½ cupful diced celery   *Lettuce*

Mix together lightly and arrange on the lettuce. Garnish with sprigs of parsley, etc.

QUICK MAIN COURSE SALADS

Avocado Pear and Cottage Cheese Salad

1 *large ripe avocado*   1 *small onion,*
   pear   *chopped fine*
1 *lb. firm tomatoes*   ¼ *lb. cottage cheese*

Peel avocado, remove seed and chop up finely. Skin and cut the tomatoes up small and put in salad bowl with the avocado, the cheese and onion. Serve with a dressing made by mixing thoroughly together:

3 *dessertspoonfuls*   1 *dessertspoonful*
   olive oil   *lemon juice or*
1 *teaspoonful white*   *white wine*
   pepper   *vinegar*
      A speck of Cayenne

This is a slightly exotic salad that can be served equally well by itself or with such meats as a pot roast, escallop of veal or boiled ham.

Ham and Tomato Salad

Cut some cold boiled ham or boiled bacon off the bone and put it through a mincer. Mix with enough good mayonnaise to make into a thick paste. Add roughly chopped cucumber. Scoop out large firm tomatoes with a teaspoon and stuff them with the ham mixture. Place on a bed of watercress and serve with half a hard-boiled egg, a few radishes and a freshly sliced banana with a squeeze of lemon juice.

Hot Weather Salad Cooler

This is a dish very popular in many parts of the world for its refreshing flavour and because it is nourishing and healthful, as well as very quick and easy to prepare.

All you need are a few inches per person of fresh cucumber, pared and roughly cut into ½-in. cubes, one or two firm, ripe tomatoes cut into quarters and then across, and a bottle of yoghourt scooped out on to the plate with the salad. Serve either with a few young spring onions or just a fine grating of freshly ground black pepper.

10-Minute Tomato Salad

Hard-boil one or two eggs per person for 10 minutes in just boiling water. Cool quickly in cold water. Skin one or two tomatoes per person. Thinly slice a cucumber. Prepare the salads on individual plates, starting with a wide border of cucumber slices with black pepper grated over them. Cover the centre of the plate with thick slices of tomato sprinkled with chopped parsley or chives, top with the hard-boiled egg cut lengthwise into four quarters and arranged to look like flower petals. In the centre put rolled anchovy fillets, boned and mashed sardines, or a few olives or capers (for a contrast in flavour and colour). Squeeze fresh lemon juice over the salad and serve with a good mayonnaise and plenty of fresh crusty bread and butter.

SALAD DRESSINGS

Cream Salad Dressing

1 *tablespoonful*   1 *teaspoonful salt*
   mustard   1 *cupful whipped*
2 *tablespoonfuls*   *cream*
   lemon juice

Put the mustard and salt in a basin, add the lemon juice and 2 tablespoonfuls of cream. Beat the rest of the cream stiffly and then add the mixture, beating well until it is quite stiff.

French Dressing (1)

½ *gill vinegar*   *Salt and pepper*
     1 *gill olive oil*

Mix the vinegar, oil, and salt and pepper together. Beat well, or shake in a covered container till thoroughly mixed. Chill. Shake before using.

To vary French dressing.—Use lemon juice instead of vinegar; or add a little dry mustard; or a little finely chopped shallot.

French dressing is used for plain green salads. It can be made at the last moment and should be mixed with the salad just before serving.

French Dressing (2)

Make some French dressing with olive oil and lemon juice and add to it a little Worcester sauce, dry mustard and a very little onion juice. Shake the ingredients well together before using.

Mayonnaise (see also Cookery in France)

The thought of making mayonnaise often frightens busy people because of the idea still prevailing that it is such a slow process. Certainly the oil must be poured in in a very thin stream, but it is not necessary to put it in drop by drop after the first few minutes. The mixture should be stirred smoothly and quickly the whole time with a wooden spoon or a wire whisk until so stiff that it can only be stirred with difficulty. Vinegar is then added to thin it.

Mayonnaise Sauce (1)

1 egg-yolk	1–2 tablespoonfuls
Salt and pepper	vinegar or lemon
½ teaspoonful made	juice
mustard	½ pint best salad oil

Put the egg-yolk into a bowl with the mustard and seasoning. Pour the oil in drop by drop at first, then in a very thin stream, stirring smoothly and quickly all the time. Add sufficient vinegar to make the sauce of the required consistency.

Mayonnaise sauce keeps for a short time. It should be added just before serving.

Mayonnaise Sauce (2)

2½ teaspoonfuls plain	2 tablespoonfuls
flour	dried egg (dry)
1 teaspoonful salt	½ pint vinegar
4 dessertspoonfuls	4 teaspoonfuls
salad oil	mustard
½ teaspoonful pepper	½ teacupful sugar
1 pint fresh milk	

Mix the flour and seasonings with oil, add sugar, dried egg, milk and vinegar. Bring gently to the boil, stirring all the time. This mayonnaise keeps well for some time if bottled.

Piquant Dressing

1 cupful thick or	¼ teaspoonful paprika
sour cream	(optional)
⅛ teaspoonful pepper	¼ teaspoonful grated
1 tablespoonful	lemon rind
bottled horseradish	2 teaspoonfuls sugar
4 teaspoonfuls lemon	½ teaspoonful pre-
juice	pared mustard, or
¾ teaspoonful salt	⅛ teaspoonful dry
	mustard

Whip cream until fluffy but not stiff. Fold in salt, pepper, paprika, horseradish, lemon rind, lemon juice, sugar and mustard. If sour cream is used, the lemon juice should be reduced to 3 teaspoonfuls.

Salad Dressing

Pinch of salt and	1 tablespoonful flour
pepper	1½ tablespoonfuls
1 teaspoonful dry	melted butter
mustard	1 egg
1½ tablespoonfuls	1 teacupful boiling
sugar	milk
¼ teacupful vinegar	

Mix the dry ingredients together and then add the egg, slightly beaten. Next, add the melted butter and then the hot milk. Stir well over boiling water until it thickens without boiling. Take off and add the vinegar slowly. When cold, store in well-corked jar. It will keep for weeks.

The secret of a good mayonnaise is to be lavish with the olive oil and sparing with the vinegar. For extra piquancy, add chopped home-grown chives or other flavourings, according to individual taste

PUDDINGS AND SWEETS

*The sweet course is most important—particularly
if there are children or men in the family*

A WIDE repertoire of sweet dishes is a necessity in any household where there are children. The sweet course is very often a favourite with the men, too. Fortunately, the variety of ways in which the chief pudding ingredients can be used to produce different results is almost unlimited.

Here, first of all, are a few general hints on pudding making.

Boiled and Steamed Puddings

A steamed pudding is always lighter than a boiled one. Whichever you are making, be sure to have the water boiling at the right moment. A scalded floured pudding cloth should be put over the top of the basin when cooking a boiled pudding; for a steamed one, a double piece of greased paper.

Soufflés

Moulds for steamed or baked soufflés should be well buttered first, and then a double band of paper, wide enough to come above the tin and to reach half-way down it, should be buttered and tied round the outside of the tin, the single edge being at the top and the double edge below. A round of greased paper should be cut to cover the top.

Baked soufflés are served in the dish they are baked in, the paper being removed. They *must* be served the moment they leave the oven, or they will "flop." Steamed soufflés are turned out.

Cold Puddings

Moulds for cold puddings should be rinsed under the tap before they are used. When the mixture is to be turned out, put the mould into hot water for a minute or two to loosen it.

INGREDIENTS

In these recipes, plain flour is used unless otherwise stated, and the necessary amount of baking powder, or bicarbonate of soda, given. If self-raising flour is substituted, the baking powder must be omitted. Where bicarbonate of soda is to be used, it is best to use plain flour.

Sultanas and currants should be thoroughly cleaned before use. The quickest way to do this is to put them on a wire sieve, sprinkle them with flour, and rub them well over the sieve with your hand. Look them over carefully and remove any stalks that remain. Raisins, unless already prepared, should always be stoned.

HOT PUDDINGS

American Banana Fritters

Melted fat or oil	3 or 4 firm bananas
¼ cupful flour	Fritter batter (p. 123)

Peel bananas, cut into three or four diagonal pieces and roll in flour. Dip in batter, completely coating each banana piece. Fry in hot fat for 4–6 minutes, turning frequently to brown evenly. Serve very hot with fruit sauce.

Apple and Raisin Pudding (for 5–6)

8 oz. rice	Sugar
1 pint water	Butter
Pinch of salt	1½ lb. apples
	4 oz. raisins

Boil the rice in the water until nearly done but not too soft, strain, and add a pinch of salt and a small piece of butter while the rice is hot, stirring well. Peel and core the apples and cut into slices; clean and stone raisins and mix with the apples. Butter a pie dish, put in alternate layers of rice and apple and raisin mixture, sprinkling each fruit layer with sugar, and finishing with a layer of apples on top. Put the butter in small pieces on the top and bake in a moderate oven for ¾ hour.

Apple Cake with Lemon Sauce (for 4)

½ lb. self-raising flour	1 egg
½ teaspoonful salt	About ⅓ pint milk
1½ oz. butter or margarine	4 cooking apples
	Cinnamon
2 dessertspoonfuls sugar	Lemon juice

Mix and sift dry ingredients. Work in butter or margarine with tips of fingers,

116

or two knives, add milk with well-beaten egg and mix quickly with knife. Dough must be soft enough to spread in tin. Put into buttered shallow baking tin—square, oblong or 9-in. flan tin. Have the apples ready—pared, cored and cut in quarters—and when dough has spread, press apples into dough in parallel rows. Sprinkle with sugar and cinnamon and a few drops of lemon juice. Bake in hot oven for ½ hour. Serve hot or cold with lemon sauce.

Lemon sauce

1 *pint boiling water*	*Rind and juice of*
½ *lb. sugar*	1 *lemon*
1 *oz. butter*	2 *dessertspoonfuls*
	cornflour

Mix the sugar and cornflour. Add boiling water gradually, stirring all the time. Cook for 8–10 minutes. Add lemon juice, rind and butter. Serve hot.

Apple Charlotte (1) (for 4–6)

4 *oz. breadcrumbs*	*Juice and rind of* 1
2 *lb. cooking apples*	*lemon*
2 *oz. brown sugar*	2 *tablespoonfuls*
Butter	*syrup*
1 *tablespoonful water*	

Stew the apples, peeled, cored and sliced, gently in a little water with the sugar. Grease a pie dish and sprinkle some breadcrumbs over the bottom. Then add alternate layers of apples and breadcrumbs, finishing with breadcrumbs.

Heat the lemon juice, syrup, water and lemon rind, and pour over the mixture. Put a few pieces of butter on top and bake in a moderate oven for about ½ hour.

Apple Charlotte (2) (for 4–6)

Slices of stale bread	3 *oz. clarified butter*
2 *lb. cooking apples*	1 *oz. margarine*
Juice and rind of half	2 *oz. brown sugar*
a lemon	

Cut up the apples but do not core or peel them; stew with the lemon juice, rind, sugar, margarine and a *very* little water, then rub through a sieve. Take a soufflé tin or round fireproof dish and cut two rounds of bread to fit the top and bottom, and fingers of bread to fit round the sides. Dip the bread into clarified butter and line the tin with it. (To clarify butter, melt it in a pan over a gentle heat, remove any scum that rises, pour off the clear liquid and throw away the sediment.)

Apple Meringues—the apples are baked, filled with mincemeat, topped with meringue and served with chocolate sauce

Pour in the apple purée, put on the bread lid, cover with a piece of buttered paper, put a plate on top to weight it down and bake in a moderate oven till the bread is crisp and brown (about 45 minutes). Either turn out on to a dish or serve in the casserole sprinkled with castor sugar.

Apple Dumplings with Suet Crust

Peel some good baking apples thinly, core them and fill the centres with castor sugar.

Make suet crust (see Pastry section) and roll it out on a floured board. Cut into rounds large enough to cover the apples. Put an apple on each round, moisten the edges of the pastry and bring them together, covering the apple completely. Turn over on to a greased tin and bake in a moderate oven for 30–40 minutes.

Apple Meringue (for 4–5)

1 lb. apples, peeled and cored	2 eggs
	Sugar to taste

For the shortbread

6 oz. butter	8 oz. flour
	1 oz. sugar

Rub the butter into the sieved flour, add the sugar, and work into a dough. Roll into a round, press up the edges with the fingers, prick the centre and bake in a moderate oven for 25–30 minutes. Put the apples, peeled and cored, into a saucepan with a very little water and boil to a pulp. Add sugar and 2 egg-yolks. Put the apple mixture on the shortbread, beat the egg-whites stiff and pile on top. Brown in a cool oven.

Apple Meringues with Chocolate Sauce (for 4)

4 apples	Mincemeat
1 egg-white	2 oz. castor sugar

Peel and core apples. Place in a fire-proof dish and fill centres with mincemeat. Bake in a moderate oven until soft. Whisk egg-white until stiff, fold in sugar, pile on top of each apple and brown lightly in a cool oven.

For the chocolate sauce

2 oz. block chocolate	2 oz. sugar
1 teaspoonful cocoa	¼ pint water
1 egg-yolk	1 teaspoonful strong
½ teaspoonful vanilla	black coffee

Put chocolate, cocoa, sugar and water into a pan and bring to the boil. When dissolved, simmer until consistency of thin cream (about 15–20 minutes). Fold in vanilla, coffee and, finally, the egg-yolk, gradually. Beat thoroughly, but do not re-heat before serving.

Apple Soufflé (for 4–5)

1½ pints milk	1 oz. butter
1 oz. castor sugar	1 lb. apples
1 teacupful rice	2 eggs

Boil the rice in the milk until tender, then add the butter and the egg-yolks, without allowing to boil. Stew the apples with sugar to taste and put them at the bottom of a buttered pie dish with the rice on top. Bake in a cool oven until set. Beat the egg-whites to a stiff froth, fold in the sugar, pile on top of the soufflé and bake till golden brown. This may be eaten hot or cold.

Apricot Upside-down Cake (for 4–5)

1½ lb. fresh apricots	½ lb. soft light brown
1 oz. butter	sugar (pieces)
	Sponge cake batter

Wash apricots in colander and remove stems. Drain, and cut in half, removing stones. Butter large, thick, iron frying pan very generously and sprinkle with the brown sugar. Place apricots closely all over the sugared pan, keeping the cut side up. Now make sponge cake batter:

2 eggs, separated	4 oz. flour
¼ lb. sugar (less 1 tablespoonful)	1½ level teaspoonfuls baking powder (or
3 tablespoonfuls boiling water	½ teaspoonful if self-raising flour is
¼ teaspoonful lemon juice	used)
	¼ teaspoonful salt

Beat yolks until thick and light. Gradually add half the sugar, the boiling water and lemon juice, and beat. Whip egg-whites until stiff but not dry, and add the rest of the sugar gradually. Combine with yolks. Fold in flour, mixed and sifted with baking powder and salt. Spread batter over the apricots and bake in moderate oven for about ½ hour. When done, turn on to large plate upside down and serve with sweetened whipped cream handed separately. Can also be served plain.

Australian Pudding (for 8–10)

1 lb. flour	4 oz. raisins
8 oz. suet	8 oz. sugar
4 oz. currants	Salt
Pinch of mixed spice	A little grated lemon
2 oz. candied peel	rind
1 teaspoonful bicar-bonate of soda	½ pint milk and water

Sift the flour, add the suet, fruit, peel chopped finely, lemon rind, sugar, salt and spice. Mix well together. Warm the milk and water and pour on to the soda so that it froths up well. Pour at once into the dry ingredients and stir thoroughly. Put into a greased basin (it should come only two-thirds of the way up because it rises), cover with a double piece of greased paper and steam for 3 hours, or bake for 1½ hours in a moderate oven.

Baked Alaska (see Soufflé Omelets, p. 129)

Baked Bananas

Peel bananas. Place in a well-greased baking tray. Sprinkle with brown sugar. Bake in a moderate oven for 15–18 minutes or until tender. Serve with fruit sauce. (Baked bananas may also be served as a vegetable if sprinkled with salt instead of sugar before baking.)

Baked Banana Custard (for 4)

3 *eggs*	*Nutmeg or cinnamon*
3 *bananas*	1 *oz. castor sugar*
	1 *pint milk*

Break eggs separately into a basin, add sugar and beat thoroughly, then add the pulp of the bananas and the milk. Pour this into one large or two small buttered pie dishes, grate over a little nutmeg or powdered cinnamon and bake in a moderately heated oven (in a tin containing water) for about 35 minutes. Dish up and serve hot.

Baked Bread Pudding (for 3–4)

4 *oz. baked bread-*	1 *pint milk*
crumbs	3 *oz. currants*
1 *tablespoonful sugar*	½ *oz. chopped lemon*
1 *tablespoonful*	*peel*
Golden Syrup	½ *teaspoonful mixed*
Pinch of salt	*spice*
	1 *egg*

Heat the milk and pour it over the bread-crumbs. Add all the other ingredients, except the syrup, which must be mixed in last. Stir the mixture well. Put into a greased pie dish and bake in a hot oven for 1 hour.

Baked Custard (for 3–4)

1 *pint milk*	*Flavouring (vanilla*
Sugar to taste	*essence, lemon,*
2 *eggs*	*orange or almond)*

Beat the eggs, milk and sugar together,

Chocolate Crumble Pudding, with a crisp top, is very easy to make

and add flavouring as desired. Pour the mixture into a buttered pie dish and stand it in a tin of water in a moderate oven to prevent curdling. Add a cupful of cold water to the tin in about 20 minutes. Cook in a very slow oven for 30–40 minutes.

Banana Apple Betty (for 6)

2 *tart apples, pared*	½ *cupful sugar*
and cored	3 *firm bananas, peeled*
½ *teaspoonful cinna-*	3 *cupfuls soft bread-*
mon	*crumbs*
	¼ *teaspoonful salt*

Slice apples and cut bananas crosswise into ½-in. pieces. Mix sugar, cinnamon and salt with crumbs. Place alternate layers of crumbs and fruit in a well buttered baking dish, using crumbs for top and bottom layers. Cover baking dish and bake in a moderate oven about 40 minutes. Uncover. Bake 5 minutes longer or until crumbs are browned. Serve hot, with cream, custard or fruit sauce.

Banana Stuffed Pancakes (for 4)

These are made with the usual pancake batter (p. 126), but are folded in three round a spoonful of banana filling, and served either with a smooth vanilla sauce or a hot jam sauce.

For the banana filling

2 *large ripe bananas*   1 *dessertspoonful*
A *good squeeze of*   *sugar*
   lemon juice

Mash bananas, mix in sugar and lemon juice to taste. Put 2 or 3 teaspoonfuls in centre of each pancake and fold ends over.

For the vanilla sauce

½ *oz. butter*   ¾ *pint boiling water*
1 *tablespoonful flour*   ¼ *cupful sugar*
1 *teaspoonful vanilla*

Melt butter, add flour and stir over low heat until it bubbles. Do not brown. Add boiling water with sugar and cook until smooth and thick. Add vanilla, strain and serve hot.

Banana Pancakes Flambées

Roll pancakes round banana filling as for Banana Stuffed Pancakes and place side by side on silver entrée dish or decorative shallow fireproof dish. Heat 3 tablespoonfuls dark Jamaica rum in saucepan and pour over filled pancakes to moisten thoroughly and flavour. Set light to rum and serve.

Batter Pudding (Steamed) (for 4)

4 *oz. flour*   ½ *pint milk*
2 *eggs*   *Pinch of salt*

Sieve the flour and salt into a basin. Make a well in the centre and break the eggs into it; add a little of the milk and mix it in well. When half the milk is in, beat well for 10 minutes, then add the rest, still beating. Leave for 1 hour. Grease a mould, pour the mixture in, cover with a double piece of greased paper and steam for 1½ hours. Serve with Golden Syrup or jam.

Bread and Butter Pudding (for 4)

3 *oz. stale bread*   *Grated lemon rind*
Butter   1 *pint milk*
Sultanas   2 *eggs*
     Sugar to taste

Cut some thin slices of stale bread, remove the crusts, cut into neat squares and butter. Put about half the bread and butter into a buttered pie dish, then a handful of sultanas and a little grated lemon rind, then the rest of the bread, with a few sultanas on top. Beat the eggs, add them to the milk, with sugar to taste, and pour this mixture into the pie dish. Leave to soak for ½ hour, then put into a tin of water and bake in moderate oven for 30 minutes

Bread Pudding

Stale bread   *Currants*
Suet or dripping   *Brown sugar*
Sultanas   *Pinch of spice*
     Chopped peel

Put some stale bread in a basin and pour boiling water over it. Let it stand for a few minutes, then squeeze dry. Beat some dripping or suet into the bread, add sultanas, currants, sugar, spice and peel to taste, and mix well. Grease a pie dish, sprinkle the sides and bottom with brown sugar, and put in the mixture. Bake in moderate oven till brown (about 45 minutes), then turn out on to a dish. If liked, this pudding can be steamed instead, but in this case an egg should be added.

Cabinet Pudding (for 6–7)

5 *oz. sponge fingers* 2 *oz. glacé cherries*
   or cakes   1 *pint milk*
3 *oz. sugar*   *Rum or Madeira*
4 *oz. sultanas*   3 *eggs*

Soak the sultanas and cherries in a little rum or Madeira, stirring well with a fork. Butter and sugar a pudding basin, then line it with sponge fingers cut in pieces. Arrange the remainder in alternate layers with the cherries and sultanas and sugar. Make a custard with the milk and eggs (see Caramel Custard below) and pour in slowly so that the fingers get well soaked. Steam for 1 hour and serve with custard or any sweet sauce.

Caramel Custard (for 3–4)

2 *oz. loaf sugar*   2 *whole eggs and 2*
½ *gill cold water*   *egg-yolks*
Squeeze of lemon   ½ *pint milk*
   juice   *Flavouring*
     Sugar

To make the caramel: Cook the loaf sugar, water and lemon juice until golden brown, shaking the pan now and again. Pour quickly into a dry hot soufflé tin and tilt the tin so that the caramel runs over the bottom and sides. Leave to cool. *For the custard:* Beat the eggs with the sugar and add the milk, warmed to blood heat, and flavouring to taste, then strain it into the

Chocolate Rainbow Pudding—pink, brown and yellow—topped with custard is popular with children of all ages

soufflé tin. Cover with a double piece of greased paper and steam *very* slowly for about 50 minutes or till the custard is set and firm; or bake in a moderate oven, standing the tin in another tin containing water. Turn out on to a hot dish. Caramel custard can also be served cold, and should then be left to cool before turning out.

Castle Puddings (for 4–5)

2 oz. butter	1 egg
2 oz. sugar	Pinch of baking
2 oz. flour	powder

Beat the butter and sugar to a cream, add the egg and then the flour and baking powder, sieved together. Mix well. Grease and half fill some small moulds and steam for about 30 minutes, or bake in a quick oven for 15–20 minutes. Serve with ginger, jam or treacle sauce.

Chocolate Pudding (for 3–4)

2 oz. chocolate	Pinch of salt
powder	2 eggs
½ pint milk	2 oz. butter
2 oz. breadcrumbs	2 oz. sugar
2 oz. ground rice	Vanilla essence

Beat the butter and sugar together until creamy. Separate the whites and yolks of the eggs and add the well beaten yolks to

the mixture. Sieve the dry ingredients together and stir lightly into the mixture. Then add the milk and, lastly, the stiffly beaten egg-whites and vanilla essence. Put into a greased mould, cover with a double piece of greased paper and steam for 1½ hours. Serve with custard.

Chocolate Almond Pudding with Orange Sauce (for 4–5)

4 oz. castor sugar	4 oz. flour
3 oz. margarine	1 teaspoonful almond
3 eggs	essence
2 oz. ground rice	1 teaspoonful baking
4 oz. drinking choco-	powder
late	Pinch of salt

Cream margarine and sugar, and beat in egg-yolks. Blend chocolate with a little water and add with dry ingredients and flavouring. Fold in stiffly-whipped egg-whites. Turn into a greased basin, and steam for 1½–1¾ hours.

For the orange sauce

Juice and rind of 1	1 level teaspoonful
large orange	arrowroot or corn-
¼ pint water	flour
1 oz. sugar	

Blend arrowroot or cornflour with a little cold water. Boil sugar, juice and grated rind with remaining water and pour over

121

arrowroot. Return to pan, bring to boil, stirring until it thickens.

Chocolate Crumble Pudding (for 6)

For the chocolate pudding

1 *pint milk*	2 *oz. sugar*
1½ *oz. cornflour*	1 *oz. cocoa*

For the crumble top

4 *oz. plain flour*	1 *oz. sugar*
2 *oz. margarine*	*Pinch of salt*

Blend cocoa, cornflour and sugar together with a little of the cold milk. Boil remainder of the milk and pour over blended mixture. Return to pan and cook until thickened. Pour into pie dish and allow skin to form.

To make crumble.—Rub fat into flour and stir in sugar and pinch of salt. Spread on top of the chocolate pudding and bake in moderate oven until golden brown.

Chocolate Rainbow Pudding (for 4)

5½ *oz. flour*	1½ *teaspoonfuls baking powder*
¼ *oz. custard powder*	
Pinch of salt	¼ *teaspoonful vanilla essence*
3 *oz. sugar*	
3 *oz. margarine*	¼ *pint milk*
1 *teaspoonful cocoa*	*Carmine*

Cream the fat and sugar, add the sifted flour, salt, baking powder and custard powder, and mix with milk to a soft, dropping consistency. Add vanilla essence. Divide into three. With carmine, colour one-third pink, add cocoa to another third. Put the three mixtures into a greased pudding basin in scattered spoonfuls. Cover with greased paper and steam for 2 hours. Serve with custard.

Chocolate Meringue Pudding (for 4)

2 *oz. breadcrumbs*	1 *or* 2 *eggs*
½ *pint milk*	1 *oz. drinking chocolate*
1 *oz. sugar*	
1 *oz. margarine*	
(2 *oz. castor sugar to each egg-white for meringue*)	

Bring sugar, chocolate and margarine to the boil with the milk, pour on to the breadcrumbs in a basin. Cool slightly and add egg-yolks. Place in greased pie dish and bake in moderate oven until set.

For meringue.—Whisk egg-whites until stiff and fold in castor sugar lightly. Pile on top of pudding. Place on low shelf in slow oven and bake until golden brown.

Christmas Pudding (for about 20)

2 *lb. raisins*	2 *lb. chopped suet*
2 *lb. currants*	2 *oz. chopped*
2 *lb. sultanas*	*almonds*
1 *lb. breadcrumbs*	½ *teaspoonful salt*
1 *lb. flour*	½ *gill sherry*
¼ *lb. mixed peel*	½ *gill brandy*
1 *lb. brown sugar*	*A little milk*
2 *teaspoonfuls bak-*	*Juice of 2 lemons*
ing powder	*Grated nutmeg*
6 *eggs*	½ *teaspoonful ginger*

Clean fruit, removing all stalks. Sift and mix all dry ingredients together. Stir in the beaten eggs, the sherry, brandy and lemon juice. Add enough milk to make the mixture a fairly stiff consistency. Put into greased basins with a piece of greased paper on the top and then a scalded pudding-cloth. Steam for 8 hours, or according to size. Reboil for several hours when the pudding is to be eaten.

NOTE: This quantity makes about 12 lb. The time required for cooking the puddings naturally depends on their size. Puddings of 1–2 lb. would not require so long.

Coffee Crumble (for 4–6)

¾ *oz. cornflour*	1 *oz. margarine*
1 *teaspoonful cocoa*	2 *tablespoonfuls*
1 *tablespoonful coffee*	*quick porridge oats*
essence or black	2 *tablespoonfuls*
coffee	*breadcrumbs or*
½ *pint milk*	*biscuit crumbs*
2 *oz. sugar*	

Blend cornflour and cocoa with a little of the milk. Heat remainder of the milk and coffee together. Pour on to the cornflour mixture. Return to the pan and boil for 3 minutes, stirring all the time. Add 1½ oz. sugar and pour into a fireproof dish. Cream margarine with the remainder of the sugar. Add porridge oats and breadcrumbs. Mix well and spread on top of the coffee cream. Put into hot oven for about 10 minutes.

Cottage Pudding (for 3–4)

4 *oz. cooked potatoes*	2 *eggs*
1 *pint of milk*	2 *oz. sugar*

Mash the potatoes, add the sugar, eggs and, lastly, the milk. Mix well together. Grease a pie dish, pour in the mixture and bake in a moderate oven for ¾ hour.

Curate's Pudding (for 3–4)

6 *tablespoonfuls*	2 *or* 3 *tablespoonfuls*
mashed potatoes	*milk*
4 *oz. sugar*	2 *eggs*
2 *oz. butter*	1 *lemon*
1 *saltspoonful salt*	

Cream the butter and sugar together until thick and smooth, add the eggs and beat well. Add the juice and grated rind of the lemon, then the salt and milk, and mix in the potato. Pour into a greased pie dish and bake for 30–35 minutes in a moderate oven.

Date Pudding (for 3–4)

8 oz. stoned dates	2 oz. flour
4 oz. brown bread-	3 oz. shredded suet
crumbs	1 tablespoonful
½ teaspoonful baking	Golden Syrup
powder	Milk

Cut up the dates and mix with the dry ingredients and the Golden Syrup. Add enough milk to make into a fairly stiff mixture and put into a greased basin; cover with a double piece of greased paper and steam for 2–2½ hours.

Fig Pudding (for 4–6)

8 oz. breadcrumbs	2 eggs
8 oz. figs	Scrape of nutmeg
6 oz. shredded suet	½ pint milk
	6 oz. sugar

Chop the figs very finely and mix with the breadcrumbs, sugar, suet and nutmeg. Add the beaten eggs and the milk. Put the mixture into a greased basin, cover with a double piece of greased paper and steam for 3 hours. Serve with wine foam sauce.

French Pancakes (for 4–6)

2 oz. flour	2 oz. sugar
2 oz. butter	2 eggs
Pinch of baking	1 gill milk
powder	Jam

Grease some flat, round tins. Cream the butter and sugar, add the beaten egg-yolks, then the flour, baking powder and milk, and lastly fold in the whipped whites. Pour the mixture into the tins and bake in a moderate oven for about 10 minutes, when the pancakes should be well risen and brown. Turn out on to a hot dish, sandwich the pancakes together with hot jam and sprinkle with castor sugar.

Fritter Batter (for 6–7)

4 oz. flour	Pinch of salt
1 gill tepid water	1 egg

Separate the egg-white from yolk. Sieve the flour and salt into a basin, make a well in the centre and drop in the yolk. Add the water, mixing it in gradually with a wooden spoon. Work in the flour well and leave to stand. Lastly, whip the egg-white to a stiff froth and fold it in. This batter can be used for either sweet or savoury fritters. Sprinkle sugar over sweet fritters, and add a pinch of Cayenne pepper and salt to savoury ones.

Chocolate Meringue Pudding—the base is mainly breadcrumbs, milk, chocolate and egg-yolk, very quickly prepared

Fruit Fritters

Apples, bananas, oranges, pineapple, apricots, etc., all make excellent fritters. Canned fruit can also be used, but it should be well drained first. For batter recipe, see previous page.

Sprinkle the slices, sections or chunks of fruit with castor sugar and dip them in the batter. Have some hot fat ready (it should be at least 2 in. deep), and drop in a few fritters. Leave enough room for them to swell. Brown one side, then turn and brown the other, lowering the heat a little. When they puff out and become crisp, lift them out and let the fat drain away. Then put them on kitchen paper to finish draining and sprinkle with plenty of castor sugar. Arrange in a neat pile on a d'oyley and eat at once.

Frying Batter (for 6–7)

4 oz. flour	1 oz. oiled butter or
1 gill tepid water	salad oil
Pinch of salt	

Sieve the flour and salt into a bowl, make a well in the centre, add the butter or oil and warm water gradually, beating well with a wooden spoon. Leave for at least 1 hour before using. A stiffly beaten white of egg can be folded into the mixture just before using.

Ginger Pudding (for 3–4)

2 oz. flour	2 tablespoonfuls
4 oz. breadcrumbs	Golden Syrup
3 oz. shredded suet	1 teaspoonful ground
½ teaspoonful baking	ginger (or more,
powder	according to taste)
Chopped ginger, if	Milk
available	

Mix the dry ingredients in a basin, add the Golden Syrup, and, lastly, enough milk to make a fairly firm mixture. Put into a greased basin, cover with a double piece of greased paper and steam for 2–2½ hours.

NOTE: A little chopped ginger adds greatly to the flavour of this pudding.

Grainger Pudding (for 6)

2 oz. ground rice	1 egg
1 pint milk	1 teaspoonful almond
2 oz. margarine	essence
2 oz. sugar	Apricot jam
2 oz. drinking choco-	Coconut or blanched
late	almonds

Sprinkle ground rice and chocolate on to warm milk in saucepan, bring to the boil and cook until thick. Add sugar, margarine and almond essence and, finally, beaten egg. Pour into greased pie dish and cover with apricot jam. Coat with coconut or blanched almonds and bake in moderate oven for 15–20 minutes.

Half-pay Pudding (for 4–5)

3 oz. shredded suet	½ teaspoonful baking
3 oz. breadcrumbs	powder
3 oz. flour	3 oz. sultanas
1 tablespoonful	3 oz. currants
Golden Syrup	1½ gill milk
Pinch of mixed spice	

Mix all the dry ingredients together, stir in the syrup and, lastly, the milk. Beat well and put the mixture into a buttered basin. Cover with a double piece of greased paper and steam for 3 hours.

Hasty Pudding (for 3–4)

1 pint milk	1 oz. butter
4 tablespoonfuls flour	Sugar to taste

Bring the milk to the boil. Mix the flour to a thick paste with cold water, and add it gradually to the milk, stirring the whole time. Add the butter and sugar, and continue stirring till the mixture thickens (about 10–15 minutes). Serve with Golden Syrup, jam or brown sugar.

Jubilee Pudding (for 3–4)

4 oz. flour	1 whole egg and 1
3 oz. butter and mar-	white
garine mixed	4 oz. currants
2 tablespoonfuls sugar	A little peel, if liked
¼ teaspoonful bicar-	Milk
bonate of soda	

Cream the butter and sugar together, add the beaten eggs, then the dry ingredients mixed together, and enough milk to make a thickish batter. Put the mixture into a greased basin with a double piece of greased paper on top, and steam for 1½ hours. Serve with treacle or wine foam sauce.

Kitchen Pudding (for 7–8)

1 lb. flour	1 teaspoonful bak-
8 oz. dripping	ing powder
4 oz. stoned raisins	A little milk
A little moist sugar	

Sieve the flour and the baking powder, and rub in the dripping. Add the moist sugar and the raisins, and stir well. Mix with a little milk until fairly stiff, sprinkle a little Demerara sugar on top and bake in a moderate oven until brown (about 45 minutes). It should be very light and crisp.

Almond flavoured Lafayette Puddings are cooked in dariole moulds. Hot chocolate custard is poured on top

Lafayette Puddings (for 4)

3 oz. ground almonds
4 oz. flour
2 oz. breadcrumbs
2 eggs
4 oz. margarine
4 oz. castor sugar
1 teaspoonful baking powder
2 oz. glacé cherries
Milk to mix

Grease 8 dariole moulds. Sieve flour and baking powder together. Add ground almonds and breadcrumbs. Cream margarine and sugar together. Beat in the eggs. Add the dry ingredients and milk if necessary. Lastly, add the glacé cherries, quartered, and mix well. Fill the moulds three-quarters full. Cover with greased paper. Steam for 40 minutes to 1 hour. Serve with chocolate custard sauce:

For the chocolate sauce

½ pint milk
½ oz. drinking chocolate
1 egg
2 teaspoonfuls sugar

Put the milk and sugar on to boil, sprinkle in the drinking chocolate and stir until dissolved. Beat the egg lightly with a fork. When the milk is almost boiling, pour on to the beaten egg and whisk for a few minutes. Pour mixture into a jug and stand in a saucepan of boiling water, or cook in a double saucepan, until the custard thickens.

Lemon Pudding (for 3–4)

4 oz. breadcrumbs
1 oz. flour
½ teaspoonful baking powder
2 oz. shredded suet
2 oz. moist sugar
Grated rind of 1 lemon
1 egg
¾ gill milk

Mix all the dry ingredients together with the lemon rind. Add the beaten egg and milk, and stir the mixture well. Put into a greased mould, cover with a double piece of greased paper and steam for 2 hours. Serve with lemon sauce, using the juice of the lemon.

Marmalade Pudding (for 3–4)

2 oz. breadcrumbs
2 oz. flour
2 oz. shredded suet
Grated rind of 1 lemon
2 tablespoonfuls marmalade
2 oz. castor sugar
1 egg
¼ teaspoonful baking powder
½ gill milk
Sauce

Mix all the dry ingredients together, sieving the flour and baking powder. Add the marmalade, egg and milk. If the mixture is too stiff, add a little more milk. Put mixture into a greased basin, cover with a double piece of greased paper and steam for 2½ hours.

To make the sauce.—Peel a lemon very

thinly and cut the peel into short strips. Boil these in water until soft, then add 2 tablespoonfuls of sugar and 2 teaspoonfuls of cornflour made into a paste with a little water. Stir well and simmer for about 3 minutes. Remove from fire and add 2 teaspoonfuls of lemon juice. Dish up the pudding and serve with the sauce.

Milk Pudding (for 2–4)

2 oz. rice, sago or tapioca	½ oz. butter
	1 pint milk
1 tablespoonful sugar	Pinch of salt

Just cover the cereal with water and let it stand for 5 minutes. Strain off water, and put the cereal in a greased pie dish with the sugar, butter, salt and milk. Let it soak for about 1 hour. Then stir it well and cook slowly in a cool oven for 2 hours, stirring well after ½ hour.

The above recipe makes a pudding of medium thickness; more or less cereal should be used to vary the consistency according to taste. An egg can be added if desired, in which case the cereal should be boiled in the milk first and the egg added when cool. Then bake in the oven for 20 minutes.

Mysterious Pudding (for 4–5)

2 eggs and their weight in flour, fresh butter and moist sugar	1 teaspoonful marmalade
	A level teaspoonful bicarbonate of soda

Separate the egg-whites from the yolks. Cream the butter and sugar, add the yolks, then the flour, soda and marmalade. Fold in the beaten whites. Pour into a basin or mould, which the mixture should only half fill since it rises very much. Steam for 1¼ hours.

Nuremberg Pudding (for 6–7)

¼ pint Golden Syrup	½ teaspoonful bicarbonate of soda
8 oz. flour	
4 oz. shredded suet	1 oz. candied peel
1 gill milk	1 egg

Mix the milk and the syrup together. Add the suet to the sieved flour and chopped peel. Then beat in the egg and, lastly, add the milk, syrup and soda. Put either into small greased moulds or into a large one and steam for ½ hour or 2½ hours as the case may be. Serve with Golden Syrup.

Oatmeal Pudding (for 3–4)

4 oz. coarse oatmeal	2 oz. shredded suet
½ pint milk	Nutmeg
2 oz. currants	Sugar to taste
Small egg	

Boil the milk and pour it on the oatmeal. Let it stand till the next day. Then add the other ingredients and bake in a slow oven for 2 hours.

Orange Pudding (for 4–5)

3 oranges	1 oz. butter
1¼ pints milk	3 oz. sugar
1½ oz. cornflour	2 eggs
Pinch of salt	

Peel the oranges, cut in pieces and place in a buttered dish. Mix cornflour with a little of the milk. Boil remainder of milk, add to the cornflour paste and cook for 10 minutes, stirring constantly. Add the butter and a pinch of salt. Sprinkle a little sugar over the oranges. Mix the rest of the sugar with the yolks of the eggs, and add to the milk and cornflour mixture. Stir for a minute or two longer over the fire without boiling. Pour over the oranges and bake for 10 minutes. Beat the egg-whites stiffly, fold in a little castor sugar, pile on top and return to cool oven for about 10 minutes, to set and tinge a very pale brown.

Pancakes (for 7–8)

8 oz. flour	2 eggs
Butter or lard for frying	1 pint milk
	Pinch of salt

Sift the flour and salt into a basin, make a well in the centre and pour into it the beaten eggs. Mix with a wooden spoon, adding half the milk a little at a time and stirring in the flour from the sides gradually to keep the mixture a smooth creamy consistency. When all the flour is mixed in, beat well for 10 minutes and stir in the remaining milk. Pour the batter into a jug. It can be used at once, or may be left to stand uncovered, but not for more than 1½–2 hours.

In a thick-based frying pan (preferably an omelet pan), heat the butter or lard and pour it off into a cup, leaving just enough to coat the pan thinly. Heat until a thin film of blue smoke can be seen, then pour in a little batter, tilting the pan so that an even coating is obtained. Cook until the surface of the batter is dry—which

should be in a few seconds. Slide the pancake to the side of the pan and either toss, with a quick sharp upward jerk of the pan, or turn with a palette knife or slice. Cook the second side for about $\frac{1}{2}$ minute, until slightly browned. Invert pancake on to sugared paper and sprinkle with lemon juice and castor sugar. Fold in three and keep warm while making the other pancakes. Serve with castor sugar and quarters of lemon.

Pancakes may also be served with hot jam or fruit inside, or flat with hot jam or fruit spread on them, the pancakes then being placed one on top of the other.

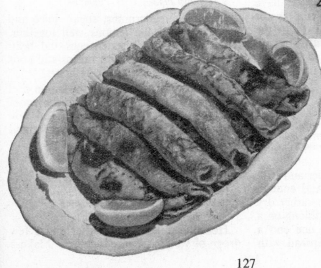

Pancake-making step by step. 1. **Pour in just enough batter to cover the pan. 2. When underside is cooked, tilt pan, shaking it gently. 3. Turn over—or toss—pancake and cook other side. 4. Turn out on to sugared greaseproof paper. Fold in three and serve hot**

Pudding à la Margot (for 3-4)

3 slices of bread ⅛ in.   Butter
   thick   Jam
       Whisky or brandy

For the sauce

2 oz. butter   3 tablespoonfuls
1 tablespoonful corn-   sugar
   flour   1 pint water

Spread the slices of bread lightly with butter and thickly with jam. Put them on top of one another in a pudding dish and pour over them a glass of brandy or whisky. When it has soaked in, fill up with melted butter sauce made as follows:

Make a paste with the cornflour, the sugar and a little water. Boil the rest of the water with the butter and pour it over the paste, stirring well. Pour this sauce over the slices of bread and bake in a moderate oven till the pudding is a nice brown.

Queen's Pudding (for 3-4)

½ pint milk   2 egg-yolks
2 oz. breadcrumbs   2 oz. sugar
Rind of ½ lemon   1 oz. butter
     3 tablespoonfuls jam

For the meringue

2 oz. castor sugar and 2 egg-whites

Heat the milk with the lemon rind, remove the peel and pour milk over the breadcrumbs. Add the sugar and the butter, and leave to soak for about 30 minutes. Then add the beaten yolks. Butter a pie dish, pour in the mixture and bake in a moderate oven for ½ hour, or until set. Take out the pudding, spread the top with jam and pile on the stiffly beaten egg-whites into which 2 oz. sugar have been folded. Sprinkle the top with castor sugar and put the pudding back into the oven until the meringue is slightly brown.

NOTE: This pudding can also be made with any dry biscuit or cake crumbs.

Roly-poly Pudding, with Jam, Treacle or Mincemeat (for 4)

8 oz. flour   ½ teaspoonful baking
3 or 4 oz. shredded   powder
   suet   Water or milk
     Pinch of salt

Sieve the flour, baking powder and salt, add the suet and mix well. Add enough water or milk to make a firm rather dry dough. Roll the crust into an oblong on a floured pastry board, making one end a little wider than the other. Spread with jam, Golden Syrup or mincemeat to within 1 in. of the edge (if syrup is used, scatter a tablespoonful of breadcrumbs over it). Moisten the edges of the crust and roll up from the narrow end, pressing it down as you roll. Scald and flour a pudding-cloth and put the roly-poly, wrapped in greased paper, in it. Fold over the cloth and tie the ends firmly, or bring them together in the middle and pin with a safety-pin. Boil for 1½ hours.

Roly-poly Pudding with Sultanas and Currants

Proceed as above, but add to the dry ingredients 3 oz. sultanas, 3 oz. currants, 2 oz. sugar and 1 oz. chopped peel. Omit the jam, treacle or mincemeat.

St. Cross Pudding (for 3-4)

6 oz. flour   2 eggs
4 oz. sugar   1 teaspoonful baking
2 oz. lard   powder
2 tablespoonfuls milk   Jam

Rub 1 oz. lard into the flour, add the sugar and baking powder, then the eggs well beaten and, lastly, the milk. Melt the other ounce of lard in the pie dish and add a thick layer of jam; then pour in the mixture and bake in a moderate oven for ¾-1 hour.

Snowdon Pudding (for 5-6)

12 oz. breadcrumbs   Raisins
8 oz. moist sugar   1½ small lemons
       3 eggs

For the sauce

½ pint water   Rind and juice of 1½
8 oz. lump sugar   lemons

Mix the breadcrumbs, sugar, juice and grated rind of the lemons well together. Then add the well-beaten eggs and beat. Line a greased basin with raisins and pour in the mixture. Steam for 2½ hours.

To make the sauce.—Cut the lemon rind into very thin strips and boil in the water until soft; add the lump sugar and boil until quite clear. Add the lemon juice and pour over the pudding.

Soufflé à la Vanille (for 3-4)

4 oz. sugar   5 egg-yolks
1½ oz. flour   4 egg-whites
1½ oz. butter   ½ pint milk
     Vanilla essence

Heat the milk, sugar, butter and a few drops of vanilla essence together. Make a smooth paste with the flour and a little milk, add this to the hot milk, stirring well. Cook for 2 minutes, then cool. Beat in the egg-yolks and, when quite cool, fold in the stiffly beaten whites. Pour the soufflé into a buttered, sugared dish which should not be more than three-quarters full. Cook in a moderate oven for 20–25 minutes and serve immediately.

Soufflé Omelet (for 1–2)

2 eggs	½ oz. butter
Pinch of salt	Flavouring

Separate the egg-yolks from the whites. Get ready a buttered pan. Whisk the yolks and add desired flavouring (vanilla, lemon, etc.). Then whisk the whites very stiffly, adding a pinch of salt, fold into the yolks and pour the mixture into the hot buttered pan and let it cook for about 4 minutes over a moderate flame. Do not stir. Take it off and put it under the hot grill for 2 or 3 minutes until slightly firm. Cut a slit almost across and put in your filling (hot jam, hot fruit purée, etc.); then fold over carefully and slide on to a hot dish. Sprinkle with a little castor sugar and serve *at once*.

This omelet can also be served unfilled, in which case it should be accompanied by a chocolate, ginger or treacle sauce.

Vanilla ice cream is the foundation of this
Chocolate Sundae

Soufflé Omelet (Baked) (for 3–4)

5 eggs	2 or 3 oz. sugar
	Vanilla

Separate the egg-yolks from the whites. Beat the yolks with sugar for 20 minutes. Beat the whites separately for 10 minutes (just before serving). When the time to serve has arrived, stir the yolks and whites lightly together and put the mixture on to a flat dish and into a *very* hot oven for 3–5 minutes, when the soufflé should have risen at least 5 in. and be well browned. Sprinkle with castor sugar and serve immediately.

NOTE: This soufflé mixture can be poured over a block of ice-cream to make a **Baked Alaska**. The oven must be *very* hot to cook the soufflé before the ice melts and the ice must be completely covered with the soufflé mixture.

Sponge Pudding (for 3–4)

4 oz. flour	¼ teaspoonful baking
3 oz. butter and mar-	powder
garine mixed	A little milk
2 oz. sugar	1 tablespoonful
1 whole egg and 1	Golden Syrup
egg-white	Fruit

Cream the fat and sugar together, add the beaten eggs, the flour and the baking

Chocolate Mousse makes a delicious cold
sweet for summer meals

powder. Then add sufficient milk to make a thickish batter. Lastly, add the Golden Syrup. Put the mixture into a greased basin with a double piece of greased paper on top and steam for 1½ hours. Serve with treacle sauce.

NOTE: Chocolate powder or ground ginger can be used as a flavouring for this pudding if liked. If chocolate is used, add a few drops of vanilla and omit the syrup.

Suet Pudding with Fresh or Bottled Fruit (for 4–5)

½ lb. flour	½ teaspoonful baking
4 oz. shredded suet	powder
Water or milk	Fruit
Pinch of salt	Sugar to taste

Sieve flour, baking powder and salt, and add suet, mixing well together. Add enough water or milk to make a firm dough, roll out the crust on a floured board, keeping back enough for the lid, and line a greased basin with it. Put in the fruit and sugar. Moisten the edges of the crust and put on the lid, pressing it firmly. Cover with a double piece of greased paper and steam for 2½ hours.

Ten-minute Dumplings (for 4–5)

4 oz. breadcrumbs	2 oz. sugar
4 oz. shredded suet	2 eggs
4 oz. currants	Salt and nutmeg
Milk (if required)	

Mix the dry ingredients together, add the beaten eggs and a little milk (if required), and make into about ten firm dumplings. Boil for 10 minutes, and serve with lemon sauce.

Toffee Pudding (for 4–5)

12 oz. bread, cut in	8 oz. Demerara sugar
squares	8 oz. Golden Syrup
4 oz. butter	Milk

Put the sugar, butter and syrup into a frying pan, and boil until golden brown. Dip the squares of bread in milk, then put into pan and let them get really hot. Pile them up on a hot dish and serve, if possible, with whipped cream.

Treacle Layer Pudding (for 5–6)

8 oz. flour	Water or milk
½ teaspoonful baking	Pinch of salt
powder	Treacle
3–4 oz. shredded suet	Breadcrumbs
Rind of ½ lemon	

Sieve the flour, baking powder and salt, add the suet and mix well. Add enough water or milk to make a firm, rather dry dough. Divide the crust in half and roll out one half to line the basin. Cut off enough from the remaining half to make the lid, then roll out the rest thinly. Put in some treacle, with a sprinkling of breadcrumbs and grated lemon rind. Cut out a round of crust large enough to cover the treacle, moisten the edge and join on to the paste lining. Continue until the basin is full, finishing with the lid.

Cover with double greased paper and then the pudding cloth. Steam for 2½–3 hours.

Treacle Sponge (for 5–6)

8 oz. flour	½ teaspoonful bicar-
4 oz. shredded suet	bonate of soda
1 egg	1 teacupful milk
1 teaspoonful ground	1 teacupful Golden
ginger	Syrup

Sieve the flour and the ginger, and add the shredded suet. Beat in the egg, add the syrup and most of the milk, leaving just enough to dissolve the bicarbonate of soda. Mix thoroughly, and at the last moment stir in the soda in the warmed milk. Put into a greased basin and cover with a double piece of greased paper. Steam for 2½ hours.

Victoria Pudding (for 4–5)

3 egg-yolks and 2 egg-	4 oz. butter
whites	4 oz. powdered
4 oz. castor sugar	biscuits
Jam	

Beat the egg-yolks, add the sugar, the melted butter and powdered biscuit. Mix well together. Beat the egg-whites very stiffly and fold into the mixture. Put some jam in the bottom of small buttered moulds and fill with the mixture. Bake in a moderate oven for 30 minutes, then turn out carefully.

Yorkshire Pudding (for 4–6)

8 oz. flour	1 pint milk
2 eggs	Pinch of salt

Sieve the flour and salt into a basin. Make a well in the centre and break the eggs into it; add a little of the milk and mix it in well. When half the milk is in, beat well for 10 minutes, then add the rest of the milk, still beating. The batter should stand for at least 1 hour before it is used. Add about a tablespoonful of cold water at the last minute for a really light pudding. Get a little fat really hot before pouring in the batter, then bake in a moderate oven for 30 minutes, raising the heat just enough to brown it at the end.

COLD PUDDINGS

Apple Snow (for 3–4)

1½ lb. apples
2 tablespoonfuls castor sugar
2 egg-whites

Strip of lemon rind
Whipped cream and red currant jelly

Cut the apples up, without either peeling or coring, and stew with the lemon rind in a very little water (just enough to prevent them sticking to the pan) on moderate heat until soft. Rub through a sieve and leave to cool, then beat in the sugar and fold in the stiffly beaten whites. Arrange in a dish and decorate with whipped cream and red currant jelly. A few chopped pistachio nuts are an excellent addition.

Australian Jelly (for 3–4)

2 oz. sago
½ pint milk
Lemon essence

½ pint water
1 tablespoonful Golden Syrup
Cochineal

Soak the sago in the water for 1 hour, then boil until transparent, add the milk and syrup, and cook for 2 or 3 minutes. Add flavouring and colouring. Pour into a wetted mould and leave till cold before turning out.

Charlotte Russe (for 4–5)

Sponge finger biscuits
Cherries

Angelica
Jelly

For the vanilla cream

½ pint cream
1 gill milk
½ oz. powdered gelatine

½ gill water
Castor sugar to taste
Vanilla essence

Line the sides of a soufflé mould closely with the biscuits so that no spaces are left between. Pour in a thin layer of coloured jelly and, when almost set, arrange some cherries and angelica in it. Next make the vanilla cream as follows: Slightly whip the cream, add the sugar, milk and vanilla. Dissolve the gelatine in the water (warmed), and when cool, add it to the mixture. Stir till it begins to set, then pour into the mould. Leave to get quite cold and set firm. Turn out carefully and serve with apricot jam sauce poured round the pudding.

For a hot day—Fruit Chocolate Marshmallow served in parfait glasses

Chestnut Surprise

Wash some chestnuts, cut a slit in the skins and boil till they are soft enough to peel. If they are put in the oven for a minute or two, the skins will come off more easily. Flavour a small quantity of milk with vanilla, add a little sugar and boil the chestnuts in it until they are perfectly soft. Pass through a sieve, after which they should look like vermicelli. Serve topped or surrounded with custard or whipped cream.

Chestnut Cream (for 4)

1 lb. peeled chestnuts (about 1½ lb. unpeeled)
2 tablespoonfuls cream

2 oz. sugar
¼ lb. chocolate
2 oz. butter
1 orange

Cook chestnuts slowly and pass them through a sieve to make purée (see recipe above). Melt chocolate in a little water and add to it the butter and sugar, stirring until well mixed. While the purée is still warm, stir the two mixtures together. Pour into glasses and leave for 24 hours in a cold place. Decorate with orange segments and whipped cream.

Chocolate Blancmange (for 3–4)

1 tablespoonful cocoa	Butter
or grated chocolate	Vanilla essence
1½ tablespoonfuls	1½ tablespoonfuls
castor sugar	cornflour
1 pint milk	

Mix the cocoa, sugar and cornflour into a smooth paste with some of the milk. Boil the rest of the milk and pour it on to the paste, stirring well, then return to the saucepan and bring to the boil. Simmer gently for 6 minutes, stirring well all the time. Add vanilla essence to taste and a little butter. Pour into a mould and turn out when set.

Chocolate Cream (for 4–5)

1 quart milk	2 tablespoonfuls
½ lb. grated choco-	potato flour (or
late	3 or 4 egg-yolks)
5 or 6 lumps of sugar	

Dissolve the chocolate in a small quantity of milk, stirring the whole time, till it is a smooth paste. Then add the potato flour, which has been mixed with a little cold water (or the beaten yolks), and the sugar. Add the rest of the milk and bring to the boil. If eggs are used, reheat without boiling. Turn into glass dish or custard glasses.

Chocolate Jelly (for 4–5)

1 quart milk	¼ oz. powdered gela-
1 oz. castor sugar	tine
6 tablespoonfuls	Vanilla essence
grated chocolate	

Dissolve the gelatine in the milk, then add the grated chocolate and the sugar and cook for 10 minutes, stirring all the time. Allow to cool, beat well with a whisk and add the vanilla essence. Pour into a wetted mould and leave to set. Turn out carefully.

Chocolate Mayonnaise (for 5–6)

4 small sponge cakes	4 eggs
½ lb. chocolate	A little sherry

Flake the chocolate into a basin and dissolve over hot water. Cut the sponge cakes in half across, put them at the bottom of a soufflé dish and pour a little sherry over them. When the chocolate has melted, move from the hot water and stir in the beaten egg-yolks. Whip the whites stiffly and fold them into the chocolate, then pour the mixture over the sponge cakes and leave to stand for 12 hours.

Chocolate Mousse (1) (for 4)

1 pint milk	Sugar to taste
1 oz. cornflour or	Vanilla essence
custard powder	3 tablespoonfuls hot
¼ pint evaporated milk	water
or cream	¼ oz. gelatine
1 oz. cocoa	

Wet a mould or individual cups. Dissolve the gelatine in the hot water. Blend the cornflour and cocoa with a little milk. Put the remainder on to boil. When boiling, pour on to the cornflour mixture, return to saucepan to cook for 2–3 minutes, stirring continuously. Sweeten and add the essence. Cool slightly. Pour the evaporated milk into a basin and whisk until thick, then fold immediately into the chocolate mixture. Pour into wetted mould and leave to set.

NOTE: Evaporated milk will thicken more easily and quickly when whisked if it is previously boiled in its tin for about 20 minutes, then thoroughly chilled for an hour or two, preferably in the refrigerator, before being opened.

Chocolate Mousse (2) (for 4)

¼ lb. plain chocolate	4 eggs

Melt the chocolate gently over hot water. Separate the egg-whites from the yolks and stir yolks into melted chocolate. Beat the whites until stiff and fold into the mixture. Pour into wetted moulds and leave to set.

Decorate with whipped cream.

Chocolate Soufflé (for 4–5)

1½ gills cream	2 eggs
1 oz. castor sugar	1½ oz. grated choco-
¼ oz. powdered gela-	late
tine	Warm water and milk

Separate the egg-whites from the yolks. Whisk the yolks with the sugar over hot water until the consistency of thick cream is reached. Dissolve the gelatine in a little warm water, the grated chocolate in a little milk and strain both into the beaten yolks. Whip the cream and add. Lastly, beat the egg-whites to a stiff froth and fold lightly into the mixture. Pour into a soufflé dish and stand in a cold place.

Chocolate Sundae

Vanilla ice cream	Chocolate sauce
Apricot jam syrup	Bananas or pears
Chopped nuts	Cream

Place ice cream in glasses and coat with

To prepare a soufflé mould, cut a double band of paper 1 in. deeper than the mould and tie or pin in place (right). When the soufflé is cooked, remove paper with knife (below)

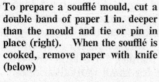

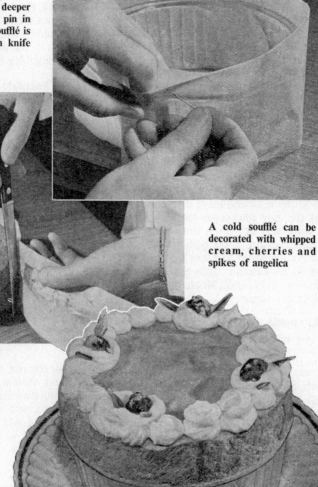

A cold soufflé can be decorated with whipped cream, cherries and spikes of angelica

syrup made by warming apricot jam with a little water. Sprinkle with chopped nuts. Coat with chocolate sauce. Add sliced fruit and top with cream. Decorate with crystallised fruit, preserved ginger, etc.

Chocolate Trifle (for 4)

Small sponge fingers
Chopped nuts
Fruit in season
½ pint chocolate sauce
½ pint whipped cream
Juice from fruit

Arrange sponge fingers around the bottom and sides of either individual sundae glasses, waxed cases or a large glass bowl and moisten thoroughly with fruit juice. Leave to soak for 30 minutes in the juice. Then sprinkle on the chopped nuts and arrange fruit on top. Pour on chocolate sauce as evenly as possible and put in a refrigerator or other cold place to set. When cold, decorate with cream.

Cider Jelly (for 3–4)

½ pint cider   *½ pint water*
½ oz. powdered gela-   *2 tablespoonfuls*
· tine   *sugar*

Put the gelatine into a saucepan with the water and the sugar and heat sufficiently to dissolve the gelatine, then strain into the cider and pour into a wetted mould. Turn out when set.

Coffee Cream (for 3–4)

½ pint milk	2 oz. sugar
2 eggs	¼ oz. powdered gela-
½ pint coffee (strained)	tine

Separate the egg-whites from the yolks. Soak the gelatine with the milk, coffee and sugar for 15 minutes. Then heat slowly, without boiling. Stir until the gelatine is dissolved, take off the fire and cool a little, then pour gradually on to the egg-yolks and beat well. Beat the whites to a stiff froth and fold into the mixture. Pour into a soufflé dish and leave to set.

Coffee Pudding (for 4–5)

1 gill strong coffee	4 eggs
5 oz. sugar	1 pint milk
Small pinch of salt	

Boil the milk and leave it to cool a little. Beat the eggs and sugar together and add the milk and salt, then the coffee. Strain the mixture into a pie dish, stand in a tin with boiling water half way up the dish and cook in a moderate oven until quite firm. Leave to cool and, when cold, sprinkle with castor sugar.

Cold Soufflé (for 3–4)

1 pint milk	½ oz. powdered gela-
Thinly peeled rind of	tine
1 lemon	1 oz. sugar
2 eggs	Cream

Stir the milk, lemon rind, gelatine and sugar over the fire until the gelatine is dissolved and the flavour extracted from the lemon. Leave to cool a little, then strain over the beaten egg-yolks and put back in the saucepan. Cook for 5 minutes, stirring all the time, without boiling. Stand in cold water to cool, fold in a little whipped cream and the stiffly beaten egg-whites and pour the mixture into a prepared soufflé dish to set. Decorate with whipped cream.

Cream Cheese (Petit Gervais)

Stand a pint of milk in a temperature of about 70° F. overnight or till solid. Drain through muslin for about 4–6 hours, and turn into a dish. This can be eaten as a sweet with fresh cream or strawberries, or as a cheese with salt and pepper, on biscuits or bread.

Custard

2 eggs	½ pint milk
	½ oz. sugar

Beat together the eggs, sugar and milk and pour the mixture into a well-buttered basin or individual moulds and cover with greaseproof paper. Stand on a folded cloth in a saucepan containing enough water to come not more than half way up the basin or moulds. Simmer gently over a low heat for 30–35 minutes for a large custard, 15–20 minutes for small individual ones.

Date Chocolate Flan (for 4)

2 oz. margarine	6 oz. stale cake
3 teaspoonfuls sugar	crumbs
3 teaspoonfuls	6 oz. dates
Golden Syrup	2 bananas
3 teaspoonfuls cocoa	Cream
powder	

Cream margarine, sugar and syrup. Add cocoa and cake crumbs, knead well together. Press mixture into a flan ring, place upside down on the plate to be used for serving. Remove ring when mixture is set. Arrange stoned dates and sliced bananas alternately and decorate with whipped cream.

Empress Rice Pudding (for 4)

3 oz. rice	1 pint milk
3 oz. sugar	1 oz. butter
Stick of vanilla	4 leaves of gelatine
1½ oz. fruit preserve	1 gill whipped cream
A little Kirsch	

Boil the rice in the milk with sugar, butter and vanilla. When well cooked and creamy, dissolve gelatine leaves in a little milk, mix with the fruit preserve steeped in Kirsch and add the whipped cream. Pour into mould and chill in refrigerator for about 2 hours. Turn out and serve with a Sabayon sauce.

Fruit Blancmange (for 3–4)

1 lb. juicy fruit	2 tablespoonfuls
Water	cornflour
Sugar to taste	

Stew the fruit with a little water and put through a sieve. Add water to bring the pulp to ¾ pint and sweeten to taste. Mix cornflour with ¼ pint of cold water, and add it to the fruit. Boil for 3 minutes, stirring all the time. Pour into a wetted mould and turn out when cold.

Fruit Chocolate Marshmallow

3 oz. marshmallows	1 level teaspoonful
¼ pint hot drinking	gelatine
chocolate made	Pineapple
with water	Pineapple jelly
¼ pint evaporated milk	Cream

Dissolve marshmallows in hot chocolate. Add gelatine and stir well until dissolved. Whip milk and add to chocolate. When cool and beginning to set, whisk well again. Place pineapple in base of parfait glasses. Fill nearly to the top with chocolate marshmallow. Finish with chopped pineapple jelly, cream and pineapple pieces. (For quick method of whipping evaporated milk, see Chocolate Mousse recipe.)

Fruit Mousse

1 *packet lemon or orange jelly*	*¼ pint nearly boiling water*
Grated peel and juice of 1 orange	*¼ pint evaporated milk*

Melt the jelly in the hot water. Add the orange juice and grated peel, and leave to cool. Whisk the evaporated milk until it becomes thick and doubles its quantity. (For quick method see Chocolate Mousse recipe.) Fold in the jelly mixture and whisk well. Leave to cool, but when it begins to set whisk well again, then turn into a mould and leave for several hours to set firm.

NOTE: There are many variations of this recipe. It can be made with orange jelly and a fresh orange or with all lemon, with black currant jelly or, for a very special one, with a tin of black currant purée and 1 oz. gelatine instead of packet jelly. It can be made equally well with ¼ pint strong black coffee and 1 oz. gelatine.

Fruit Mould (Danish) (for 4–5)

1 *lb. raspberries*	2 *tablespoonfuls*
1 *lb. red currants*	*potato flour*
Sugar to taste	

Cover the fruit with water and simmer gently until soft. Strain, and put the juice in a pan on the fire with sugar to taste. Mash up the potato flour with a little cold juice, add this and simmer until the mixture stiffens. Pour into a wetted mould. Serve cold with cream and sugar.

Fruit Russe

Make a Genoese Cake (see Cakes) and when cold, scoop out a large circle in the middle and fill with alternate layers of any sweetened stewed fruit (fresh or canned) and cream, keeping back the juice. The fruit should be stewed with very little water. Decorate with angelica, cherries or any crystallised fruit and whipped cream.

Garden Fancies will appeal to children. The fern-decorated orange cases are filled with blancmange and topped with fresh fruit

Garden Fancies (for 4)

4 large oranges	*1 oz. cornflour*
1 egg-yolk	*¼ oz. butter*
1 oz. sugar	*A pinch of salt*
½ oz. chopped glacé cherries	*Grated rind of 1 orange*
1 pint milk	

Cut a slice off the top of each orange and, using stainless steel scissors, remove insides (which can be kept for fruit salad). Scrub outsides of oranges and with cement glue arrange foliage on the outsides. Leave to dry. Make a blancmange with the milk, cornflour and sugar and, when thickened and still hot, add the butter and beaten egg-yolk. Reheat, without boiling, for 2 minutes, add grated rind of an orange, salt and glacé cherries and pour immediately into the orange cases. Allow to cool and, just before serving, decorate the tops with any fruit available, or, if preferred, with piped cream. Arrange on a bed of leaves for serving. Keep the orange cases—they can be used again.

Gâteau de Pommes (for 3–4)

¾ lb. loaf sugar	*½ pint water*
Grated rind of small lemon	*1 lb. apples, peeled and cored*

Boil the sugar and water until it becomes sugary again. Then add the apples and the lemon rind and boil again until quite stiff, stirring carefully. Put into a mould and, when cold, turn out and serve with custard or cream.

Ginger Cream (for 3–4)

½ oz. powdered gelatine	*2 tablespoonfuls ginger syrup*
1 gill hot water	*¾ pint cream*
2 oz. castor sugar	*3 oz. preserved ginger*

Dissolve the gelatine in the hot water. Whip the cream and the sugar together till stiff, then add the gelatine and water (just warm), the ginger syrup and preserved ginger cut small. Stir gently until it begins to set, then pour into a mould. It must be stirred until it is poured into the mould, or the gelatine and sugar will sink to the bottom and spoil the appearance.

Gooseberry Fool (for 6–7)

2 lb. gooseberries	*½ pint custard or cream*
8 oz. sugar	

1 gill water

Stew the gooseberries in the water with the sugar until soft, then put through a fine sieve. Cool, add the custard or cream and beat together well. Serve with cream, either in custard glasses or in a dish.

NOTE: Any fresh, soft fruit can be used instead of gooseberries.

Gottespeiss (for 4)

4 oz. stale bread-crumbs	*4 oz. cup chocolate*
4 oz. Demerara sugar	*1 oz. chopped nuts (for decoration)*

¼ pint cream

Place breadcrumbs, cream, sugar and made cup chocolate in that order in layers in glass bowl or individual dishes, finishing with a layer of cream. Decorate with chopped nuts and a circle of dry cup chocolate.

Honeycomb Pudding (for 4–5)

1 quart milk	*2 oz. loaf sugar*
3 eggs	*1 teaspoonful vanilla essence*
½ oz. powdered gelatine	

Separate the egg-whites from the yolks. Dissolve the gelatine in a little warm milk, add the sugar, the rest of the milk and the beaten yolks and stir over a gentle heat until it thickens like a custard. Then take the saucepan off the fire, leave to cool, fold in the stiffly beaten whites. Add the vanilla essence and pour into a wetted mould. Turn out when set.

Hungarian Soufflé (for 4–5)

5 eggs	*3 tablespoonfuls cold water*
14 lumps of sugar	

5 sheets gelatine

Cook the sugar in the water until it browns, to form caramel. Whip the whites of the eggs well. Then pour in the gelatine dissolved in a little water, stirring gently, and add the boiling sugar. Keep whisking well all the time. Pour into a well-wetted mould and leave to set.

For the sauce, boil some more caramel, as above, add it to the egg-yolks with a little cold milk, whisking all the time until it thickens and is free of lumps. When the mould is cold, turn out and pour this sauce over.

Jamaica Rum Sponge

Sponge fingers	*3 dessertspoonfuls Jamaica rum*
1 lemon jelly and a little extra	*4 oz. pink marshmallows*
¼ pint evaporated milk	*Glacé cherries*
Just under ½ pint hot water.	*Hazel nuts*

Sponge cakes with chocolate cream make this nut-coated Party
Dessert which tastes as nice as it looks

Dissolve the jelly in a little less than half a pint of hot water and leave to cool but not to set. Make a little extra jelly and dip the sponge fingers into it, arranging them round a wetted mould. Whisk milk until it thickens (for method, see Chocolate Mousse recipe), add jelly a little at a time. Gradually add the rum. Whisk until beginning to set, then stir in cherries, nuts and marshmallows (cut in four). Fill up mould and leave to set.

For a simpler variation of this sweet, use quarter slices of bananas alternately with sponge fingers and thin slices of banana instead of the nuts, marshmallows and cherries.

Lemon Jelly (for 4–5)

½ pint cold water	1-in. stick cinnamon
½ pint boiling water	and 2 cloves
1 oz. powdered gela-tine	12 oz. loaf sugar
	Whites and shells of 2
Rind and juice of 4 lemons	eggs
	Sherry (optional)

Put the gelatine in the cold water, add the rind of the lemons, the cinnamon and cloves. Stand for a few minutes, then pour on the boiling water and stir until the gelatine is dissolved. Add the juice of the lemons, the sugar and the slightly beaten whites. Then add the egg-shells washed and crushed, and bring the mixture to the boil, whisking all the time. Simmer very gently for 3 minutes, then remove from the heat and stand for 5 minutes. Scald a jelly bag and pour the jelly mixture slowly through it When nearly cold, put into a wetted mould. A little sherry can be added if desired.

Orange jelly can be made in the same way, substituting orange juice and rind for the lemons and omitting the cinnamon and cloves.

Wine jelly can be made in the same way, using ½ pint wine instead of the ½ pint cold water.

Lemon Pudding (for 5)

2 eggs	6 oz. sugar
Juice and rind of 1 lemon	2 dessertspoonfuls flour
½ pint hot milk	¼ teaspoonful salt

Beat egg-yolks, beat in sugar, lemon juice and flour, and add scalded milk. Fold in stiffly beaten egg-whites, lemon rind and salt. Pour into buttered custard cups. Stand these in hot water in dripping-pan and bake in moderate oven for 45 minutes. Serve cold.

Lemon Sponge (for 3-4)

½ pint boiling water	2 egg-whites
½ oz. powdered gelatine	Juice and rind of 2 lemons
2 oz. sugar	

Put the lemon rind in the boiling water and leave for 5 minutes. Strain, dissolve the gelatine in the water and add the lemon juice and sugar. Stand until cold. Whisk well and fold in the stiffly beaten egg-whites, whisking until the mixture is firm enough for a spoon to stand upright in it. Pour into a glass dish. Serve cold with custard.

Maraschino Prunes (for 4-5)

8 oz. stewed prunes	1 pint custard
½ wineglassful maraschino	2 oz. loaf sugar
	A little water
Cream	

Stone the prunes and soak them in a soufflé dish with the maraschino. Cover with the custard. Boil the sugar and a little water until pale brown, then pour over the custard and prunes and leave to set. Crack the caramel and cover with whipped cream just before serving.

Meringues

6 egg-whites	9 oz. castor sugar
Whipped cream for filling	3 oz. granulated sugar

NOTE: for every egg-white used allow 1½ oz. castor sugar and ½ oz. granulated sugar. Meringues can be coloured by adding cochineal, coffee essence or cocoa.

Grease a flat baking tin. Line with greaseproof paper and brush this lightly with olive oil. Add another layer of paper and oil this too. Mix the sugars. Beat the egg-whites until stiff so that when the basin is turned upside down they will not move. Add one quarter of the sugar and whisk again. Fold in remainder of sugar with a metal spoon. Put the mixture into an icing pump or forcing bag with plain nozzle and pipe on to the tin in rounds. Alternatively, shape with a dessertspoon, smooth surface with a palette knife and slip out with the help of a second dessertspoon. Dust well with castor sugar and bake in a *very* cool oven for 2-3 hours until crisp. Remove

meringues, turn upside down and press centres gently. Return to oven until quite dry.

An alternative method is to leave the meringues in a warm airing cupboard overnight. This ensures that they remain white and obviates the use of the oven.

Mocha Cream (for 4-5)

6 small sponge cakes	3 egg-yolks
½ teacupful strong coffee	4 oz. butter
	3 oz. castor sugar

Cream the butter and sugar together, then add the coffee and the beaten yolks, slowly. Line a plain mould with the sponge cakes cut in slices, pour in some of the mixture, then add more sponge cakes. Continue until the mould is full. Put a saucer on top, with a heavy weight on it. Stand until next day, then turn out and serve with whipped cream.

Orange Baskets

Make and cool an orange jelly. Cut oranges in half, scoop out the insides and keep for orangeade or fruit salad. Fill skins with jelly and leave to set. Cover the jelly with whipped cream and decorate with thin slices of crystallised orange or glacé cherries. Make handles of thin strips of angelica.

Overturned Chocolate Cream (for 4)

1 pint milk	5 oz. chocolate powder
2 oz. castor sugar	
6 eggs	

Bring the milk to the boil and add chocolate powder. In a basin, beat the sugar energetically with the whole eggs, and pour in the milk and chocolate. Turn into a mould, cook in a slow oven in a bain-marie (or stand the mould in a tin containing water) until well set. Leave to cool, and turn out.

Party Dessert

Sponge cakes	Angelica
Chocolate butter cream	Cream
	Nuts
Warm drinking chocolate	Cherries

Split the sponge cakes and sandwich them together with the chocolate cream (for recipe, see Regency Gâteau). Cut into slices, dip in warm chocolate and pack into a dish or basin. Stand for ½ hour, turn out and coat with cream and nuts, decorate with halved glacé cherries and spikes of angelica.

Pudding à la Royal (for 4–5)

½ pint whipped cream
½ pint milk
3 eggs
7 sheets of gelatine
3 oz. brown bread-crumbs
Sugar and vanilla to taste

Make a custard with the milk, sugar, vanilla and eggs and, when cold, add the whipped cream. Add the dissolved gelatine and breadcrumbs. Stir lightly and pour into a wetted mould. When cold, turn out and serve with whipped cream or custard and fruit.

Prune Caramel (for 3–4)

½ lb. prunes
¼ lb. brown sugar
Piece of stick cinnamon
½ cupful milk or thin cream
2 eggs
1 pint cold water

Soak the prunes overnight in the cold water, then cook them gently with the sugar and cinnamon for 2 hours. Put through a hair sieve, take out the cinnamon, add the eggs, well beaten, and the milk or cream, and pour the mixture into a mould previously lined with burnt sugar (see Caramel Custard recipe). Steam for ½ hour. When cold, turn out and serve with whipped cream.

Prune Mould (for 3–4)

1 lb. prunes
R ind and juice of a lemon
Powdered gelatine
1 pint water
2 oz. brown sugar

Wash the prunes and soak with the lemon rind in the water overnight. Cook them with the sugar until soft. Put through a sieve. Allow ½ oz. gelatine to a pint of prune purée. Dissolve the gelatine in a little water and add, together with the lemon juice, to the purée. Stir until it begins to thicken, then pour into a wetted mould. When set, turn out and decorate with blanched almonds and whipped cream.

Raspberry Sponge (for 5–6)

1 oz. powdered gelatine
½ pint water
8 oz. sugar
8 oz. raspberry syrup (or jam)
1 pint boiling water
Juice of a lemon
2 egg-whites

Dissolve the gelatine in ½ pint of water, then add the pint of boiling water. When

Regency Gâteau, a delicious party sweet, in which the flavours of coffee and chocolate are combined

cool, add the sugar and raspberry syrup (or jam), the juice of the lemon and the beaten egg-whites. Whisk until stiff. Serve cold with cream.

Regency Gâteau

Marie biscuits	Chocolate butter
Cold coffee	cream
Whipped cream (for decoration)	Nuts

Use the plate on which the sweet will be served. Fill a piping bag, using a vegetable pipe, with chocolate butter cream or chocolate flavoured cream or custard. Dip several biscuits into the coffee, just long enough to take off the crispness. Place about six biscuits close together on the plate. Cover with cream from the piping bag. Repeat layers of biscuits and cream alternately. Decorate with whipped cream, nuts and piping of chocolate cream.

Butter Cream.—This is a simple filling which can be flavoured to suit many recipes.

3 oz. butter or mar-garine	6 oz. sieved icing sugar
1–2 teaspoonfuls milk or water	

Cream margarine and sugar until soft and light. Beat in liquid gradually. Add flavouring to taste. Chocolate flavour—1 oz. drinking chocolate, a few drops of vanilla essence. Other flavours: Peppermint—a few drops of peppermint essence and green colouring. Walnut—½ oz. chopped walnuts and a teaspoonful coffee essence or strong black coffee.

Russian Cream (for 5–6)

2 oz. sugar	½ oz. powdered gela-tine
1 pint milk	
½ pint whipped cream	Chopped glacé cherries
2 oz. ground rice	
Flavouring	

Wet the ground rice with a little milk. Put the rest of the milk and the sugar on to boil, then stir in the ground rice, gradually, and continue stirring for about 8 minutes. Then draw the saucepan to one side. Dissolve the gelatine in a little warm milk and pour it into the rice, stirring well. When sufficiently cool, add the whipped cream and mix lightly together. Flavour with vanilla or a liqueur, and pour into a mould which has already been decorated with preserved cherries chopped small. Leave to set and serve cold.

NOTE: If liked, omit the cherries in the mould, colour the mixture with cochineal and decorate with chopped pistachio nuts.

Strawberry or Raspberry Cream (for 5–6)

1 pint strawberries (or raspberries)	3 oz. castor sugar
1 gill water	½ oz. powdered gela-tine
½ pint double cream	

Prepare the fruit and put it into a basin, sprinkle with the sugar and stand for 1 hour, then rub through a sieve. Dissolve the gelatine in the warm water, and add the fruit purée. Whip the cream until quite stiff, then add the fruit and gelatine, stirring well together. Pour the mixture into a wetted mould to set.

Summer Pudding

This pudding can be made with any soft, fresh fruit, such as raspberries, black currants, etc., or with canned, quick-frozen or bottled fruit. Fresh or quick-frozen fruit must first be stewed with a little water and sugar to taste. Cut some stale bread in slices to fit the top and bottom of a pudding basin and then pieces to go round the sides. Dip the bread in the fruit juice and line the basin with it. Pour in the hot fruit and put a round of bread on top as a lid. Put a plate on top with a weight on it and let the pudding stand for the night. Turn out and serve with custard or cream.

NOTE: Summer Pudding can also be made with sponge cakes instead of bread.

Sweet Chestnut Mousse

25 chestnuts	3 oz. vanilla sugar
1 pint cream	1 egg-white

Cook and peel the chestnuts and put through a sieve to make a purée. Stir over moderate heat with the sugar until very smooth. Add the whipped cream and the egg-white. Pour into a mould, chill for about 3 hours. Turn out on to a folded napkin.

Tapioca Cream (for 3–4)

¼ oz. gelatine	1 tablespoonful tapioca
1 pint milk	
1 tablespoonful sugar	1 tablespoonful cream

Dissolve the gelatine in a little milk. Bring the rest of the milk to the boil and, while boiling, stir in the tapioca. Boil for 5–10 minutes. Add the sugar and cream, then stir in the gelatine. When nearly cold, put into wetted mould to set.

Tonito Pudding (for 4-5)

8 oz. castor sugar
¼ oz. gelatine
1 pint water
4 eggs
Rind and juice of a
    lemon
Cream

Separate the egg-whites from the yolks. Melt the gelatine in the warmed water and boil. Cool a little, then pour on to the sugar, lemon and yolks. Stir well. When nearly cold, whip the whites stiffly, fold them into the mixture and put into a glass dish with whipped cream on top.

Trifle

Cut some sponge cakes in half lengthwise and sandwich them together again with jam, arranging them neatly in a glass dish. Put some ratafia biscuits on top and stick blanched split almonds into the sponge cakes. Pour over them a wineglassful of sherry or fruit syrup made either with fresh fruit stewed and strained, or jam diluted with hot water and strained or from a can of fruit. Cover with a good cold custard and stand overnight. Before serving, decorate with almonds, angelica, "hundreds and thousands," glacé cherries or crystallised fruit, according to taste, and small piles of whipped cream.

Winter Sport

1 pint milk
2 oz. sugar
2 bananas
2 oz. rice
1 oz. sultanas
1 oz. chopped walnuts

¼ level teaspoonful
    salt
1 tablespoonful
    Jamaica rum or a
    few drops vanilla
    flavouring

Rice cooked in milk and flavoured with either rum or vanilla is the basis of Winter Sport. It can be served in individual dishes and decorated either with sliced bananas and Maltesers, or with grated chocolate and almond rolls

Wash rice. Cook gently in a double saucepan with the sugar, milk and salt for approximately 1½ hours. Cool thoroughly, stir in diced bananas, walnuts and sultanas. Add the rum or vanilla flavouring, and mix well. Turn into individual dishes and decorate with sliced bananas and Maltesers, or with grated cup chocolate and almond rolls. Serve with cream or custard.

Puddings and sweets requiring pastry will be found in the Pastry chapter immediately following.

All photographs in Puddings and Sweets Chapter by Cadbury Bros., except those on pages 127, 133, 135 and 141.

PASTRY

*The secret of a light hand
with pastry is very simple
—"Keep Cool"*

Making Flaky Pastry: dab small pieces
of fat on the rolled-out dough—

SUCCESS in pastry making depends on two essentials: the minimum of handling, and keeping everything as cool as possible at all stages. If you observe these two basic rules, you will soon gain a reputation for "a light hand with pastry."

You will need a mixing bowl big enough to get both hands into; kitchen scales; a flour sifter (failing that, the flour may be passed through a fine sieve); a kitchen knife; a rolling pin, and either a pastry board or a large cool surface on which to roll the pastry.

Ingredients, as well as your hands and the utensils you use, should be as cool as possible. Use really cold water for mixing, keep flour and fat in a very cool place (the fat preferably in the refrigerator), roll the pastry out on a cold surface, such as an enamel topped table or a marble slab, and choose one of the modern rolling pins made of cool glass or china. (In an emergency, a pint milk bottle, well washed and rinsed in cold water, makes an excellent rolling pin.)

The only handling necessary is when you rub the fat into the flour, and this should be done with a light touch and hands freshly washed, rinsed in cold water and thoroughly dried, using the tips of the fingers only. Remember, the more air there is in the pastry, the lighter it will be, so don't press or roll it hard.

Butter, lard, vegetable fat, clarified dripping and margarine are all suitable for different kinds of pastry. Lard and vegetable fat make the shortest pastry; half lard, half vegetable fat is a good general-purpose mixture. Baking powder is not necessary,

and plain flour should be used in preference to self-raising.

The amount of water required varies according to what flour is used. The lighter and finer the flour, the more water it will take. If you use too much water, the pastry may be tough.

Flour the board and the rolling pin so that the pastry does not stick. Be very sparing with the flour you sprinkle over the pastry, as too much dry flour spoils its appearance and toughens it.

The cooking of pastry is as important as the making. The oven must be hot enough to prevent the fat melting and running out before the starch grains in the flour have had time to burst and absorb it. It should be cooked quickly and the oven door must not be opened until it is very nearly done.

There are several different kinds of pastry:

(1) *Short Pastry* is the quickest and easiest, and should be used at once.

(2) *Flaky Pastry* can be kept for several days provided the weather is cold. In any case it should be made at least an hour before you intend to use it.

(3) *Puff Pastry* requires more time in the making. It can be used the day it is made, or, if the weather is cold or if put in a refrigerator, it will keep, wrapped in well-greased paper.

(4) *Rough Puff Pastry* should be left for at least ½ hour before it is used or, if

Spry Cookery Centre photographs

Then, having folded the dough in three, seal the edges with the rolling pin

wrapped in well-greased paper, it will keep for several days in cold weather.

(5) *Potato Pastry* is economical and excellent for jam puffs, tarts or pies.

(6) *Choux Pastry*, which is made in an entirely different way from the other kinds, is used for continental pastries such as éclairs, cream buns, etc.

(7) *Biscuit Pastry*, often used as an alternative to short pastry for flans.

(8) *Hot Water Pastry* for raised meat pies.

(9) *Suet Crust* for steamed and boiled puddings.

Short Pastry (Used for flans, tarts and pies)

8 oz. flour   *¼ teaspoonful salt*
4 oz. lard or 3½ oz. *Cold water for mixing*
 vegetable fat

Sift flour and salt. Cut fat into small pieces and rub it lightly into the flour with the fingertips until the mixture looks like fine breadcrumbs. Then add just sufficient very cold water to make a dry dough, mixing it in with a knife. Lightly flour the board and rolling pin and roll out the pastry, being careful not to put any weight on the rolling pin, neither kneading nor handling the pastry more than is absolutely necessary, and always rolling in the same direction. The thickness is a matter of taste, but pastry should never be more than ¼ in. thick or there is a danger of the outside getting brown before the inside is properly cooked. Trimmings left over can be gathered together in layers, without kneading or pressure, and lightly rolled out again.

For a Fruit or Jam Tart on a Plate.—Line the greased pie-plate with short pastry, trimming round the edges. Put in fruit or jam cold, damp edges of the pastry and cover with another layer of pastry. Brush with milk and sprinkle lightly with sugar.

For a Flan Case.—Grease the flan tin or ring and sprinkle it lightly with flour, then line with the short pastry. Trim edges. Put a piece of greaseproof paper inside the flan with a little rice or a few breadcrumbs on it (this is known as "baking blind") and cook in a moderate oven (400° F.) until the pastry begins to brown, then remove rice and paper and return to oven for a few minutes. Flan case is then ready for filling.

Flaky Pastry (Used for pies, tarts, sausage rolls, patties, etc.)

8 oz. flour   *6 oz. lard or 5 oz.*
½ teaspoonful salt *vegetable fat*
  Cold water for mixing

Put the flour and salt in a basin and rub in one-third of the fat until it has the appearance of fine breadcrumbs. Mix to a stiff dough with a little cold water, using a knife for mixing. Roll out on a floured board into an oblong piece. Cut half the remainder of the fat into small pieces and scatter them over two-thirds of the paste. Flour well and fold the paste in three, sealing the edges neatly with the rolling pin. Leave for 10 minutes. Turn the paste round so that the sides become the ends and roll out again, then add the rest of the fat in the same way as before. Flour, fold in three, turn and roll out again. Leave for 10 minutes. Fold in three once more and, if possible, put away in a cool place in a covered basin for 1 hour or more. Roll out before using and bake in a hot oven.

NOTE: When using up trimmings of this pastry, always put them one on top of the other and beat together with a rolling pin before rolling out, to preserve the flaky effect.

Puff Pastry (Used for patty and vol-au-vent cases, etc.)

Equal quantities of *Cold water for mixing*
 best quality flour *Pinch of salt*
 and butter

Sieve the flour and salt, and mix to a springy dough with the water. Roll out on a floured board and leave for 15 minutes. Squeeze the butter in a floured cloth or beat

PASTRY

it with a butter pat on a slab to get out the moisture, and flatten it to about 1 in. thickness. Put the butter in one piece in the middle of the pastry, then fold the pastry up over it, first at the two ends, then at the sides, pressing the edges with the rolling-pin to seal in the air. Leave for 15 minutes or more, then roll into a long, narrow strip, fold in four again and leave for another 15 minutes. Repeat four times, allowing the pastry to rest—covered with a clean cloth—for 15 minutes between each turn. Finally, roll into the required shape.

Rough Puff Pastry (Used for meat pies which have to be in the oven for a long time, also fruit pies and patties)

8 oz. flour	3 oz. lard or vegetable
½ teaspoonful salt	fat
Cold water to mix	(Use less fat in hot
3 oz. butter or	weather)
margarine	

Chop the fats into the sieved flour, using two knives and keeping it in fairly large pieces. Add the salt and enough water to bind the dough, the pieces of fat still remaining whole. Do not use the hands at all, but mix the water in with a knife. Turn on to a floured board and roll out four times, folding in three and leaving to rest for 15 minutes each time. Put away in a cool place for at least ½ hour before rolling out for use.

Potato Pastry (May be used for meat pies, jam puffs, tarts and pies)

9 oz. flour	1 teaspoonful baking
2 oz fat	powder
2 oz. cooked mashed	Cold water to mix
potato	Pinch of salt

Sieve the flour, salt and baking powder, and rub in the fat finely; then work in the mashed potato. When smooth, mix to a stiff dough with a very little cold water. Roll out and bake in a hot oven.

Choux Pastry (Used for éclairs, cream buns and continental pastries)

1 gill water	3 eggs
Pinch of salt and	2¼ oz. flour
sugar	1¼ oz. butter

Bring the butter and water to the boil, with the pinch of salt and sugar. Sieve the flour and shoot it into the pan. Stir over a low heat until the mixture leaves the bottom of the pan quite clean. Remove from

heat and allow to cool, then gradually mix in the beaten eggs, one at a time. Beat well and flavour as required.

Biscuit Crust (Used for fruit flans)

4½ oz. flour	2 oz. butter or
1 egg-yolk	margarine
1 oz. castor sugar	Pinch of salt

Beat the butter and sugar to a cream, add the egg-yolk and work in the sieved flour and salt. Place flan ring on a baking sheet. Roll out pastry and line the ring with it. Cover the pastry with a piece of grease-proof paper and spread beans or rice on it to keep the pastry in shape. Bake blind in a hot oven for 20 minutes. Remove the paper and beans or rice. Allow the pastry to dry off in the oven for 2 or 3 minutes, then put to cool.

Hot Water Pastry (For raised meat pies)

½ lb. flour	2 oz. lard or vegetable
½ gill milk	fat
½ gill water	Pinch of salt

Put the sieved flour and salt into a basin. Boil the lard, water and milk together, and pour it into the middle of the flour. Mix well with a knife. Knead the dough until it is smooth. Use while warm and line a basin, using the hands to mould it.

Suet Crust (Used for steamed or boiled meat or sweet puddings and dumplings) (for 4–5)

8 oz. flour	3 or 4 oz. shredded
Pinch of salt	suet
Water or milk	½ teaspoonful baking
	powder

Sieve the flour, baking powder and salt, add the suet with enough water or milk to make a firm but rather dry dough.

NOTE: If desired, 6 oz. flour and 2 oz. breadcrumbs can be used instead of 8 oz. flour for sweet puddings.

PASTRY SWEET DISHES

Almond Cheese Cakes (for 5–6)

8 oz. flaky pastry	Grated rind of quar-
2 oz. ground almonds	ter of lemon
2 oz. butter	1 drop almond
2 oz. castor sugar	essence
1 whole egg and	1 drop maraschino
1 egg-yolk	(or sherry or
Raspberry jam	brandy)

Line patty pans with the pastry and put a drop of raspberry jam in the bottom of each. Cream the butter and sugar, add the

A sure favourite with children and grown-ups alike—Chocolate Meringue Pie is easy to make but looks most professional

egg and yolk, unbeaten. Add the rest of the ingredients and beat well. Put a spoonful of the mixture into each tartlet. Cook in a hot oven until risen and brown. Finish off in a cooler oven until the pastry is cooked through (about 25 minutes altogether).

Apple Dumplings (for 4–5)

8 oz. short pastry   6 medium-sized
Castor sugar   apples

Peel the apples and cut out the cores. Fill the centres with castor sugar. Roll the pastry ⅛ in. thick and cut out six circles large enough to cover the apples. Put an apple on each and work the dough over the apple, pressing the edges (slightly moistened) together. Brush with cold water and sprinkle with castor sugar, or paint with a little milk. Bake in a moderately hot oven until the apples are tender and the pastry crisp.

Apple Tart (Open) (for 3–4)

6 oz. short pastry   Apples and brown
Raspberry jam   sugar

Grease a deep pie plate and line it with pastry, then spread a thin layer of raspberry jam, a layer of thinly sliced apples sprinkled with brown sugar, and bake until the apples are cooked and the pastry just brown.

Apricot Flan (for 4–5)

For the crust

½ oz. butter   ½ teaspoonful baking
4 oz. flour   powder (unless self-
1 egg   raising flour is
1 tablespoonful milk used)
     1½ teaspoonfuls sugar

For the filling

1½–2 lb. fresh apricots ½ teaspoonful cinna-
¼–½ lb. sugar (accord- mon or grated nut-
  ing to taste)   meg
3 dessertspoonfuls top 1 egg-yolk
  of milk, or cream

Sieve flour and mix in dry ingredients.

Blend in butter with finger-tips. Add egg and milk, and mix. Toss on slightly floured board and pat or roll $\frac{1}{4}$ in. thick. Cover a large, well-greased flan tin (round or oblong) with the pastry, and place on it stoned, halved apricots (hollow side up) in neat rows. Sprinkle thickly with sugar and spice. Beat egg-yolk, mix with top of milk or cream, and drip over fruit. Bake in a hot oven until fruit is soft and crust well browned underneath.

Banana and Golden Syrup Tart (for 4–5)

8 oz. short pastry	1 tablespoonful
2 bananas	Golden Syrup
1 oz. grated breadcrumbs	

Line a deep sandwich tin with some of the pastry. Pour on Golden Syrup and spread all over. Cut bananas into thin rounds and cover the syrup with them, and top with breadcrumbs. Roll out the remaining pastry thinly and cover the whole with it, pressing the edges together after trimming round the tin. Bake in a moderate oven for 15 minutes. Serve hot or cold.

Chocolate Amber Pudding (for 6–8)

6 oz. short pastry	2 oz. drinking chocolate
1 lb. apples	
3 oz. sugar	2 egg-yolks
1 oz. margarine	2 tablespoonfuls water
For the meringue	
4 oz. castor sugar	2 egg-whites

Line a pie plate with pastry. Peel, core and slice apples, and stew until soft with sugar and water. Add the margarine, drinking chocolate and egg-yolks. Beat well. Put apple mixture into pastry case and bake in moderate oven for 20–25 minutes until pastry is done. About 10 minutes before pudding is cooked, whisk egg-whites until stiff, fold in sugar lightly and pile on to the pudding. Bake in slow oven until meringue is set.

Chocolate Flan (for 6–8)

6 oz. short pastry or	1 oz. cornflour
biscuit crust	1 oz. sugar
$\frac{1}{2}$ oz. cocoa	$\frac{3}{4}$ pint milk

Line a 7-in. flan tin with the pastry and bake blind. Mix cocoa and cornflour to a paste with a little of the milk. Bring remainder of milk to the boil with sugar, pour on to paste, then return to saucepan and bring to the boil again, stirring all the time. Cook for 2 minutes, then pour into cooked flan case and leave to cool. Decorate with piped cream or mock cream.

Chocolate Meringue Pie (for 6–8)

6 oz. short pastry	$\frac{1}{2}$ pint milk
$\frac{1}{2}$ oz. cocoa	2 oz. cornflour
2 egg-yolks	1 tablespoonful sugar
$\frac{1}{2}$ oz. margarine	
For the meringue	
3 oz. castor sugar	2 egg-whites

Line an 8-in. flan ring with the pastry and bake blind. Blend the cornflour and cocoa to a smooth paste with a little of the milk, bring remainder of milk to the boil and pour on, with the sugar. Allow to cool, then add margarine and egg-yolks and pour into cooked flan case. Bake in moderate oven for 20–25 minutes until firm. Whip egg-whites until stiff, fold in sugar and pile on chocolate. Bake in a cool oven until set, and serve hot or cold

Cornish Treacle Tart

Short pastry	Golden Syrup
Breadcrumbs	Grated lemon rind

Line a greased enamel pie plate with pastry and cut out another round to go on top. Sprinkle breadcrumbs over pastry, pour Golden Syrup over, then more breadcrumbs and a little grated lemon rind. Moisten pastry edges and put on the top, pressing it down gently. Nick the edges with the back of a fork. Bake in a moderately hot oven for about 40 minutes. Be careful that the tart is not too full or the mixture will ooze out.

Custard Tarts (for 5–6)

8 oz. short pastry	1 pint milk
3 eggs	Sugar to taste
Grated nutmeg	

Line small fireproof dishes with the pastry, prick at the bottom and bake lightly, then take out of the oven. Make a custard with the milk and eggs, add sugar to taste and fill the tarts. Grate a little nutmeg on each. Put back in oven and bake slowly until the custard is set.

Eccles Cakes (for 6–7)

8 oz. flaky or rough	1 oz. castor sugar
puff pastry	1 oz. butter
4 oz. currants	$\frac{1}{2}$ oz. chopped peel

Melt the butter in a pan and add the sugar, currants and peel. Roll out the pastry and cut into rounds. Place a little of the mixture on each round. Moisten the edges of the pastry and draw it all together

146

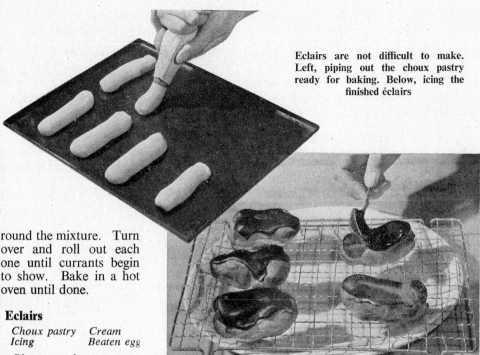

Eclairs are not difficult to make. Left, piping out the choux pastry ready for baking. Below, icing the finished éclairs

round the mixture. Turn over and roll out each one until currants begin to show. Bake in a hot oven until done.

Eclairs

Choux pastry   Cream
Icing   Beaten egg

Pipe out choux pastry into an éclair tin or on to a baking tin, making éclairs the required size, brush with beaten egg and bake in a quick oven for about 30 minutes. Be very careful of draughts while they are cooking. When cooked, leave to cool, then make an incision in the side, near the bottom, take out the soft part of the centre and fill with whipped cream, sweetened and flavoured with vanilla if liked. Spread chocolate or coffee glacé icing on top.

NOTE: For the piping, use either a forcing bag or a metal syringe. The éclairs before going into the oven should be about $\frac{3}{4}$ in. wide and 3–4 in. long. Put them into an oven of about 400° F. for the first 10 minutes, then reduce the heat to 350° F.

Eclair Delights

Make éclairs as above, but fill with a mixture of whipped cream and chopped fruit (cherries, grapes, orange, etc.). Coat with chocolate icing made from a 2-oz. block of plain chocolate, 4 oz. icing sugar, 2 tablespoonfuls milk and water, and a few drops of vanilla essence; decorate with piped whipped cream and fruit.

Fruit Flan

Canned or fresh   Biscuit crust
* stewed fruit*
For the syrup
$\frac{1}{4}$ oz. arrowroot $\frac{1}{4}$ pint juice
1 tablespoonful sugar

Boil the sugar and juice. Put the arrowroot in a basin and mix with a little liquid. Pour the hot syrup on to it and bring the whole mixture to the boil, stirring until it thickens. Colour the mixture, according to what fruit is used, arrange the fruit, cut in slices if large, in the bottom of the flan. When the syrup is cool, pour it evenly over the fruit.

NOTE: If canned fruit is used, its own syrup will provide the liquid and no sugar is needed. If oranges are used, make syrup with orange juice and water.

Fruit Pie (for 4–5)

8 oz. short pastry   4 oz. sugar (or to
2 lb. fruit   taste)
Water

Prepare the fruit and put in a quart sized pie dish with sugar, a little water and a pie funnel or inverted egg cup in the middle. Roll out the pastry a little larger than the pie dish. Cut off a strip to line the edge of the dish. Moisten the edge and put on the strip. Then moisten the pastry and put on the top, pressing well together and nicking the edges with the back of a fork. Make a ½-in. slit in the centre of the pastry to let the steam out. Bake in a moderately hot oven for 35–45 minutes, lowering the heat once the pastry has risen.

NOTE: Do not stretch the pastry when putting it on or it will shrink away from the edge as it cooks. The dish should be well filled with fruit or the pastry will collapse.

The cooking time varies according to what fruit is used.

Fruit pies can also be made on an enamel plate with the fruit between two rounds of pastry (see Cornish Treacle Tart).

Gâteau Saint Honoré aux Oranges (for 5–6)

Short pastry made from 3 oz. flour, 1½ oz. fat, pinch of salt and water to mix

Choux pastry made from 2 oz. flour, 1 oz. margarine, ½ gill water, 1 egg, pinch of salt

For the filling and decoration

Mandarin oranges   Cream
Pistachio nuts

For the chocolate icing

3 oz. icing sugar   1 dessertspoonful
¼ oz. margarine   cocoa
1 tablespoonful water

Roll short crust pastry into a large, round, place on a greased tin and prick well. Using a star pipe, pipe a ring of choux pastry round the short pastry to form a border, and pipe about nine separate stars on to the tin. Bake in a fairly hot oven for about 30 minutes. Leave until cold.

To make the chocolate icing.—Boil margarine, water and cocoa together and stir to a smooth paste. Remove from heat, stir in icing sugar, and beat until smooth.

Ice the separate choux stars, decorate with pistachio nuts and fix into position with cream round the ring of pastry. Mix oranges and cream together and fill the centre of the case with this mixture, building up with stars of cream and the choux stars. Decorate with sections of mandarin orange.

Grape Boats (for 6)

6 oz. plain flour
Pinch of salt
1 small egg-yolk
¼ lb. white grapes

3 oz. margarine
1 teaspoonful castor sugar
A little water for mixing

For the glaze

3 tablespoonfuls sieved apricot jam   3 tablespoonfuls castor sugar
3 tablespoonfuls water

Sieve flour and salt together, rub in fat with the finger-tips. Mix to a stiff paste with the egg-yolk and a little cold water, add sugar, knead very lightly and roll out thinly. Line twelve boat-shaped tartlet tins (4½-in. size) with the pastry, pricking at the bottom with a fork. Stand tins on a baking sheet, bake in a hot oven for 12–15 minutes. Remove from tins and, when cold, put three grapes in each. Coat grapes with apricot glaze and leave to set.

To make the glaze.—Boil together for a few minutes the jam, sugar and water until the syrup is of the consistency to thicken lightly when tested on a plate.

Grape and Apple Sauce Pie (for 4–5)

2 cups washed grapes
2 cups apple sauce
2 tablespoonfuls quick-cooking tapioca
Whipped cream for topping

8 oz. sugar
¼ pint water
9-in. pastry flan shell, made with short pastry or biscuit crust

Cook grapes for about 10 minutes in a little water in a covered saucepan over moderate heat. Rub through strainer, add sugar, apple sauce, water and return to heat. Stir in tapioca and cook until clear. Leave to cool, then turn into the pastry shell. Top with whipped cream just before serving.

Grape Chiffon Pie (for 4–5)

1 packet raspberry or strawberry jelly
¼ pint whipped cream
1½ teacupfuls washed grapes (peeled and stoned)
Just under 1 pint water

1 egg-white
4 oz. castor sugar
1 egg-yolk
9-in. pastry case, made from short pastry or biscuit crust

Make the jelly, using just under 1 pint hot water, leave to cool and, when almost set, whisk until light. Beat the egg-white until stiff and fold into the whipped cream. Combine the jelly and cream mixtures by stirring lightly together; add sugar to the grapes and fold into jelly and cream mixture. Brush over the pastry case with egg-yolk, to prevent it becoming soggy, and put the mixture into it. Decorate the top with whole grapes and chill until firm.

Gâteau Saint Honoré aux Oranges is a delicious party sweet made of choux pastry, cream and mandarin oranges

Jalousie (Venetian Blind)

Puff pastry
Beaten egg
Chopped apples and sugar

Roll out the pastry to the length of the baking tin and cut into two strips, 3 or 4 in. wide. Place one strip on the tin and paint all round the edge with beaten egg. Put the apple and sugar down the middle of the pastry, piling it fairly high but keeping it $\frac{1}{2}$ in. away from the edges. Fold the other strip of pastry in half sideways and cut the folded side evenly with a knife to within $\frac{1}{2}$ in. of the other side; cuts should be about 1 in. apart. Unfold the strip, which will now resemble a Venetian blind, and place it over the strip on the tin, pressing the sides down well together. Paint all over with egg. Decorate the edges by nicking with the blunt side of a knife. Bake in a hot oven. When cooked, scatter sugar all over and return to the oven for 1 minute to glaze.

Jam, Lemon Curd or Treacle Tart

Short pastry
Jam, lemon curd, or Golden Syrup and breadcrumbs

Grease an enamel plate and line it with pastry. Fill the centre with jam or lemon curd, or Golden Syrup mixed with breadcrumbs. Decorate with narrow strips of pastry twisted and stretched across the tart. Nick the edge with the back of a fork and bake in a fairly hot oven for about 15 minutes, taking care that the filling does not burn or get too dark.

Jam Puffs

Flaky pastry
Raspberry jam

Roll out the pastry and cut it into 4- or 5-in. squares. Put a little jam in the centre of each square. Wet round the edges with beaten egg. Fold each square diagonally and press down the edges. Brush the tops with cold water and sprinkle with sugar. Bake in a hot oven until light brown (about 20 minutes).

Jam Roly-poly

Roll short pastry into an oblong, making one end slightly wider than the other. Spread jam evenly over it, leaving 1 in. all round, moisten the edges and roll up, starting at the narrower end. Press gently as you do so. Bake in a moderately hot oven for about 45 minutes.

Jam Tartlets

Short pastry   *Jam or lemon curd*

Roll out the pastry, cut into rounds with a crinkly cutter and line patty pans with it. Put a small teaspoonful of jam or lemon curd in each. Cook in a hot oven for 10 minutes.

Mille Feuilles

Puff pastry   *Browned almonds*
Apricot jam   *Pistachio nuts*
Whipped cream   *(chopped)*
Glacé icing

Roll out the pastry fairly thin and divide into four strips about 4 in. wide. Leave for $\frac{1}{4}$ or $\frac{1}{2}$ hour. Prick very well all over with a fork. Bake on a baking sheet in a hot oven until brown. When cold, trim into shape and spread one strip with apricot jam, place another strip on top and spread with whipped cream; add another strip and spread with jam. Place the fourth strip on the top, cut into fingers, and ice. Decorate with pipings of cream, pistachio nuts and almonds.

Mince Pies

Flaky or short pastry   Mincemeat

Roll out pastry and cut into rounds. Grease patty pans and line with half the rounds of pastry. Put 1 or $1\frac{1}{2}$ teaspoonfuls mincemeat in each, damp edges all round with cold water, put remaining rounds of pastry on top, press down well together all round the edges. Paint tops of mince pies with cold water and sprinkle with sugar. With a skewer, prick a hole through the pastry in the centre of each mince pie. Bake in a hot oven for 20 minutes.

Pastry Fingers

Take any flaky or short pastry left over, roll it out and spread jam over half of it. Moisten the edges of the lower half, fold over top half, brush over with cold water and sprinkle with castor sugar. Bake in a moderate oven. When cooked, cut into squares or fingers. Eat either hot or cold.

Patty Cases

Roll out puff pastry to a little more than $\frac{1}{4}$ in. in thickness. Let it stand in a cold place for a few minutes. Then cut rounds with either a plain or crinkly cutter about $2\frac{1}{2}$ in. across. Take a smaller cutter ($1\frac{1}{2}$ in. across) and cut a round in the centre of half the large rounds for the lids. Damp the edges of the larger rounds with cold water or beaten egg and put the rings on top. Put the patties on a baking tin and prick the middles with a fork to prevent them rising. Brush with beaten egg and bake for 20–25 minutes in a hot oven. Scoop out a little of the soft part from the centre when they are cooked.

The small rings, or lids, should be put on another tin, brushed over with egg and baked for 10–12 minutes. If the patties are to be served hot, fill them with the warm filling, put on the lids and then heat in the oven for 2 or 3 minutes.

Patty Cases for Vol au Vent

Proceed as for patty cases above, but roll out the pastry to about $\frac{3}{4}$ in. thick, keeping it very even. Bake the cases for about 30 minutes in a hot oven (400° F.) until the sides are firm but the pastry not turning brown. About 10 minutes before cooking is complete, brush the lids with egg. For suitable vol-au-vent fillings see Fish, Meat and Poultry sections.

Viennese Grape Tart (for 6–8)

8 oz. plain flour   *Water for mixing*
1 dessertspoonful   5 oz. margarine
    castor sugar   *Most of 1 egg-yolk*

For the filling

5 oz. castor sugar $\frac{1}{2}$ lb. white grapes
Grated rind of half a $2\frac{1}{2}$ oz. ground
    lemon   almonds
            2 egg-whites

Rub fat into flour with fingertips, mix to a stiff paste with the egg-yolk and a very little cold water. Add sugar, knead lightly and roll out thinly, using rather more than half to line a deep 8-in. sandwich tin.

Mix sugar, ground almonds, lemon rind and egg-whites into a softish paste, beating for a minute. Fill pastry case with this, then press into it at intervals the grapes, previously washed and stoned. Cover with a trellis of pastry strips, brush with egg-yolk diluted with water. Bake in a slow oven for 1 hour. When cool, remove from tin, serve cold, dredged with sifted icing sugar.

Alternatively, desiccated coconut and a little almond essence may be used instead of ground almonds.

FRUIT

Cooked or raw, tropical or home-grown, there is a fruit for every occasion and every taste

At any time of the year a bowl of fresh fruit makes a perfect table decoration

AS with everything else, there is an art in preparing and serving fruit, whether raw or cooked. Nothing looks more appetising than half a grapefruit, nicely chilled, with a cherry in the centre. A simple dish of stewed or baked apples can be delicious if perfectly cooked and attractively presented.

Preparing Fruit

Whether the fruit is bought from a greengrocer or—far better—picked from your own trees or bushes, discard quite ruthlessly any that is damaged or over-ripe. Examine fruit carefully to see that the skins are unbroken—and soft fruits (the berries, for example) particularly for grubs and insects. The best way to clean soft fruits is to put them in a colander and then plunge it into a bowl of cold water. Drain thoroughly and remove damaged or unsound fruit.

The quickest and easiest way to prepare currants is to run a fork down the stalks so that the berries fall off into a bowl. Gooseberries need to be topped and tailed, and this can be done quite quickly with an old pair of small scissors.

Stewed Fruit

Calculate ½ pint of water to each pint of fruit, adding sugar according to taste.

Freshly peeled fruits (such as apples, soft pears, grapefruit, oranges, rhubarb) and soft fruits (such as raspberries, logan-

berries, blackberries, gooseberries, cherries, white and red currants) should be stewed in syrup. Allowing ½ pint of water for each pound of fruit, boil the water with 2–4 oz. sugar per ½ pint (according to sweetness of fruit and to personal taste), cook for 3 or 4 minutes, then add the washed and prepared fruit. Simmer gently until cooked, the time varying according to the type of fruit. Rhubarb, for example, needs only a minute or two in the hot syrup.

Incidentally, those who find rhubarb too acid should try cooking it this way. Wash and cut the sticks of rhubarb into 1-in. lengths, discarding the leaves but keeping as much of the red part as possible. Put into a saucepan and just cover with cold water. Bring quickly to the boil, remove immediately from the heat and drain off all

151

the water. Return the rhubarb to the pan, add cold water and sugar to taste (or syrup made as above) in the correct proportions and cook in the usual way.

Hard pears and black currants, which have hard skins, should be put into cold water with the sugar, brought to the boil and simmered very gently until done.

Apples retain their flavour best if cooked in their skins this way: Wash the apples well, then cut them up quite roughly into chunks, removing any bruised or damaged parts but leaving the skins and cores. Put them into a saucepan with a *very* little cold water (only just enough to cover the bottom and prevent them from sticking) and bring gently to the boil. Simmer until they become frothy and feel quite soft when tried with a fork. Remove from the heat and rub through a fine sieve. The resulting apple purée has all the flavour from the skins and is often quite sweet enough without any additional sugar. It is delicious served hot, with a tiny pat of butter stirred in with a little brown sugar, honey or Golden Syrup; or cold as a sweet with cream or as the basis of Apple Snow.

Baked Fruit

Apples, pears, bananas and grapefruit can be baked whole, with excellent results. The apples should be cooked whole, cored but not peeled, and may then have the space filled with brown sugar, dates, or a mixture of stoneless raisins and sugar. Cut round the skin with a sharp knife to prevent bursting. Place them in a buttered fireproof dish with about a tablespoonful of water and a small knob of butter, and bake until just soft to the touch but not bursting through their skins. Grapefruit and pears are better cut in half before they are baked in the same way.

Halved grapefruit are also delicious grilled and served hot.

Baked bananas are appetising as a vegetable (particularly with bacon) or as a dessert with cream or a hot fruit sauce. Peel the bananas, place them in a well-buttered baking pan, brush well with butter and sprinkle with salt. Bake in a moderate oven for 15–18 minutes or until tender (that is, easily pierced with a fork).

Dried Fruit

Dried fruit, such as apple rings, apricots, peaches, prunes, pears and figs, should be well washed and soaked overnight. Then bring to the boil in the water in which they have been soaked, with sugar to taste. They need very little cooking once they have come to the boil.

Out-of-Season Fruits

Frozen and canned fruits in great variety are now available at reasonable prices and are extremely useful for fruit salads, flans and tarts. South African apricots, peaches and grapes coming in the English winter are also a great boon.

Apple Porcupines (for 3–4)

4 apples	Sugar
Jelly or jam	Water
Whipped cream	Almonds

Wipe, core and peel the apples (whole). Boil together enough sugar and water (in the proportion of 4 oz. sugar to $\frac{1}{2}$ pint water) to cover the apples and a little over. Cook the syrup for 7 minutes, then put in the whole apples and simmer them until soft. Skim occasionally. Take out and cool the apples. Then fill with either jelly or apricot jam, and stick with blanched split almonds. Serve in the syrup and decorate with whipped cream.

Apple Salad (for 2–3)

1 lb. ripe eating apples	2 oz. preserved ginger
	4 oz. red currant jelly
Whipped cream	

Peel and core the apples and slice them finely. Put them in a dish and cover with the preserved ginger, cut into very thin shavings. Warm the red currant jelly until it runs. Cool it a little, then pour over the apples and ginger. Just before serving, whip some cream and decorate with it.

Baked Bananas (1) (for 4–5)

6 bananas	3 oz. brown sugar
2 tablespoonfuls melted butter	2 tablespoonfuls lemon juice

Peel the bananas, cut them in half lengthwise and put them in a fireproof dish. Brush well with butter, sprinkle with sugar and lemon juice, and bake slowly for about 20 minutes, basting occasionally.

Or, instead of the sugar, pour $\frac{3}{8}$ cupful of molasses or maple syrup over the bananas before baking. Cook in the same way and serve hot, garnished with hot toasted almonds.

Baked Bananas (2) (for 4–5)

6 bananas   3 oz. sugar
Sherry to cover   Arrowroot

Peel the bananas and cut them in half lengthwise. Let them soak in a little sherry for $\frac{1}{2}$ hour, then put them into a fireproof dish, sprinkle 2 oz. sugar over them, add a little water and bake

Prepare bananas for baking by brushing with melted butter (above). They can be served as a sweet or vegetable (left)

in a moderate oven for about 20 minutes. Put the sherry into a saucepan, add the rest of the sugar and a little arrowroot mixed to a paste with cold water, and simmer until it thickens. Pour over the bananas and serve.

Banana Ambrosia (for 6–8)

2 oranges   1½ cupfuls shredded
3 bananas   coconut
¼ cupful icing sugar

Peel oranges and cut crosswise into thin slices. Peel and slice bananas. Arrange alternate layers of oranges and bananas in a serving dish on a bed of coconut and sugar. Repeat the layers until all ingredients are used. Chill.

Banana Creams (The Quick Sweet)

A spoonful of jam   Grated chocolate
Slices of banana   Whipped cream
Cherries and angelica

Fill champagne or sundae glasses with the following layers: a spoonful of jam,

some whipped cream, slices of banana covered with grated chocolate, then some whipped cream and more jam. Finish with cream and decorate with cherries and angelica.

Banana Cream Whip (for 4–6)

2 to 3 bananas   ½ cupful whipped
1 tablespoonful   cream
lemon juice   ¼ cupful sugar
⅛ teaspoonful salt

Mash the peeled bananas and mix in the lemon juice, sugar and salt. Fold in whipped cream. Chill and serve within 1 hour, garnished with sliced bananas.

Banana Custard

Peel some bananas and cut them in half lengthwise. Spread the halves with raspberry jam and put together again. Put them in a dish and pour custard over them.

Black-eyed Susan

1 large orange per   Blackberries or
  person   chopped dates to
Fruit salad dressing   garnish

Peel one large sweet orange for each serving. Remove as much as possible of the white pith and separate into segments.

153

Arrange in a circle like marguerite petals on a small plate for individual service. Put a small mound of fresh blackberries or chopped dates in the centre and pour over dressing made as follows: Stir well, or shake thoroughly in a tightly screwed glass jar, the juice of one orange, the juice of half a lemon and honey to taste. (This is excellent on any fresh fruit salad.)

Combination Fruit Plate (for 1)

1 *sweet red-skinned apple (unpeeled)*	1 *ripe banana*
1 *orange*	2 or 3 *strawberries (optional)*

Cut unpeeled apple lengthwise into four thin wedges and remove core. Peel orange and slice crosswise. Cut two slices into halves. Peel and slice banana. Arrange three rows of fruit on a plate with strawberries on top as shown below.

Compôte of Apples (for 2–3)

1 *lb. apples*	4 *oz. loaf sugar*
½ *pint water*	*Lemon juice*

Put the sugar, water and a few drops of lemon juice into a casserole and boil quickly for 10 minutes. Peel, core and quarter the apples, put into boiling syrup and cook slowly in the oven until tender, being careful they do not break. Take out the apples, boil the syrup a little longer to reduce it, and then pour it over the apples. Serve with cream.

NOTE: A little white wine, sherry or kirsch is a great improvement to this compôte.

Fruit Jelly

Make lemon, orange or wine jelly and pour into a mould into which have been put slices of banana, strawberries, raspberries, grapes, apricots, peaches, stoned raisins, etc.

An even more delicious fruit jelly can be made with the syrup from a can or bottle of fruit. Dissolve either gelatine or a packet jelly (of the same flavour as the fruit) in ¼ to ½ pint of hot water and make up to a pint with the fruit syrup. Particularly suitable fruits are gooseberries, currants, plums or cherries.

Apple, orange, banana, decorated with strawberries, make this individual serving of Combination Fruit Plate

Orange, grapes and banana "trimmed" with walnuts make a colourful sweet

Fruit Salad

All fruit used in the making of fruit salads should be ripe, but never over-ripe, and absolutely sound. Oranges should have all the white pith removed and, of course, the pips. Plums should be well wiped, cut in half and stoned. If the skin is coarse, they should be peeled. Other fruit, such as bananas, apples, etc., should be peeled and cut in neat small pieces.

When canned fruit is used, the syrup is excellent as a dressing. A little sherry, Madeira, brandy or liqueur may be added as desired.

To make a syrup, allow 4 oz. sugar to $\frac{1}{2}$ pint of water (this should be enough to cover 1 lb. of fruit) and boil together for 10 minutes. Let the syrup cool and then pour it over the salad and mix well. Always let a salad stand for some hours, if possible, to allow the syrup to soak in well, but do not add raw apple until the last moment, as it turns brown. Serve chilled, or as cold as possible.

A few shredded almonds, chopped walnuts or a little shredded coconut can also be added. Small meringue cases filled with cream are very good served with fruit salads, or a handful of ratafia biscuits put over the top just before serving is an excellent addition.

Fruit Salad for a Party (for 30)

6 *oranges*	*Chopped walnuts*
1 *grapefruit*	3 *bananas*
1-*lb. can peaches*	$\frac{1}{2}$ *lb. grapes*
1 *small bottle or can*	2 *oz. Golden Syrup*
gooseberries	$\frac{1}{2}$-*lb. can pineapple*

Simmer the finely cut rinds of 3 oranges in a very little water with the Golden Syrup for quite $\frac{1}{2}$ hour. Cut up all the fruit (except the grapes and gooseberries) into small pieces and pour the syrup over them, together with that from the canned fruit. Let the whole remain covered for 6 hours before serving. Serve very cold with cream.

NOTE: This is a most delicious salad and suitable for children's parties, wedding receptions, etc.

Suggestions for other Fruit Salads:
Oranges, bananas, pineapple cubes, maraschino cherries.

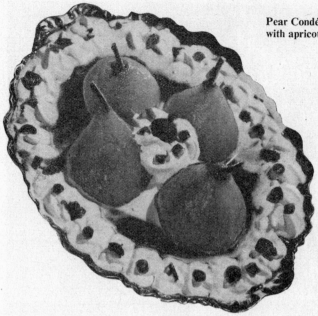

Pear Condé is a famous sweet. The fruit, covered with apricot jam sauce, stand on a bed of rice and whipped cream

Bake for ½ hour or longer, basting frequently. Serve in the dish in which they are cooked.

Orange Fantasy (for 4)

(Recipe by Luigi of the Savoy Hotel Grill Room, London)

4 oranges (large "navel" ones)
1 cupful sugar
2 tablespoonfuls Grand Marnier
1 cupful water

Peel oranges carefully, removing as much of the white pith as possible. Cut peel of 1 orange (with white pith removed) into very fine longish strips. Soak in a little Grand Marnier liqueur while you prepare syrup by boiling 1 cupful of water with 1 cupful of sugar for 5 minutes. Now cook peel in syrup over low flame till fairly tender. Cool. Slice oranges in quarters and add juice to syrup. Stir well and add the rest of the Grand Marnier. Put sliced oranges in a glass bowl and pour over the peel and syrup. Serve very cold.

Orange Mousse (for 10)

2 cupfuls double cream
¼ lb. confectioner's sugar
⅛ teaspoonful salt

2 cupfuls orange pulp cut in small pieces and drained
1 teaspoonful vanilla essence

Whip cream, sugar and salt together until stiff. Add fruit and vanilla and mix well. Chill, and then freeze in ice-cube compartment, turning refrigerator on to very cold so as to freeze as fast as possible. Serve with whipped cream and wafers or petit-fours.

Oranges with Coconut

Oranges
Sugar

Finely grated coconut

Peel some oranges, taking away all the pith, and cut them into slices on a plate so that none of the juice is wasted. Put some in a deep bowl and sprinkle with

---

Oranges, stoned dates, stoned raisins and chopped nuts.

Cubes of avocado pear and fresh pineapple, and grapefruit segments, in pineapple syrup (made from the pineapple juice, sweetened with honey and a dash of lemon juice).

Pineapple chunks and seedless grapes in pineapple juice.

Fresh pineapple slices and fresh strawberries.

Diced cantaloup melon, strawberries, sliced pears.

Bananas, peaches and raspberries.

Apples, pears and loganberries.

Halved plums and loganberries.

New Baked Apples

Apples
Slices of bread ½-in. thick

Brown sugar
Marmalade
Butter

Core, but do not peel, the apples and cut round with a very sharp knife under the skin to allow them to expand. Fill with butter, marmalade and brown sugar. Spread the bread with butter, marmalade and brown sugar, and put an apple on each slice. Put them in a buttered fireproof dish not too close together and add lumps of butter and a few dessertspoonfuls of marmalade. Pour in a little water and sprinkle the apples well with brown sugar.

finely grated coconut and sugar; put in more layers until the bowl is full, the top layer being coconut and sugar. Stand for 1–2 hours so that the orange and coconut get well blended. Serve with cream if liked.

Oranges, Whole

Soak oranges for 24 hours, then boil until tender. Cut a hole in the top and take out all the pulp and pips. Make a syrup, allowing 1 oz. sugar for each orange, put the pulp in the syrup and fill the oranges with it. Decorate with glacé cherries, angelica or split almonds.

Pear Condé (for 4–6)

4–6 pears	Double cream
1 cupful sugar	1 cupful rice (boiled)
Apricot jam	1½ cupfuls water
Rum or rum essence	

Rinse cooked rice thoroughly by placing in strainer and pouring plenty of hot water through it. Allow to cool in strainer or colander. Peel the pears thinly and cook until tender, but still firm, in syrup made by boiling the sugar and water for 5 minutes. Prepare apricot sauce by heating the jam with just enough water to make a thin, smoothly flowing sauce, and add a drop or two of rum or rum essence. Whip the cream and mix about half of it with the cold rice. Place rice in serving dish, stand cooked cold pears on top, stalks up, pour sauce over and pipe the remainder of the whipped cream round the edge of the dish.

Pears à la Alexandra (for 3–4)

Canned Bartlett pears	½ pint lemon jelly
Whipped cream	1 pint thick custard

Make a thick custard, allowing 4 eggs to a pint of milk, and adding sugar to taste. Pour it into the bottom of a glass dish. Make the jelly and, when cool but still liquid, pour over the custard. Arrange the pears in quarters on top and pipe the whipped cream over them. Decorate with glacé cherries and angelica.

Stewed Pears

Hard stewing pears	Sugar to taste
Water to cover	Strip of lemon peel
2 or 3 cloves	

Peel, quarter and core the pears, and put them in a saucepan with enough cold water to cover them. Add the lemon, sugar and cloves, bring to the boil and simmer gently until soft. When they turn pink, boil more rapidly, to deepen the colour.

Chilled melon cut in half and filled with mixed fruit salad looks gay on a summer dinner party table

ICES

Summer or winter, for lunch, dinner, tea or supper, an ice-cold sweet always goes down well

Four mouth-watering sundaes—you can make them all from home-made ice cream, combined with whipped cream and various fruits

ICES are always a popular item on the menu, especially with the children and at parties. They are really very simple to make at home and are also nutritious.

When making ices it is important to remember that freezing takes away from the sweetness of the mixture, so more sugar is required. Too little sugar will make the mixture freeze too hard and too much will prevent it freezing properly.

Colouring should be used sparingly, as crude colours make ices look unattractive.

To avoid ices that have ice splinters in them and are coarse in texture, take them out of the freezing tray when half-frozen, turn into a chilled basin and beat well, adding some lightly whipped cream, egg-white or evaporated milk.

Generally speaking, the best results are obtained by switching the freezing control to the coldest freezing-point to start with, allowing the mixture from 1–1½ hours'

freezing before taking it from the tray and beating it with cream, egg-white or evaporated milk until light and frothy. If the mixture is a rich one, it should be put back in the tray with the control left at freezing; a less rich and thinner mixture should have the control at half-freeze. In either case, when the ice is frozen to the right consistency the switch should be turned back to normal.

When using evaporated milk as a substitute for cream, measure the amount you need, put it in the top of a double saucepan over boiling water (or in to tin in a saucepan of boiling water) and heat to scalding point, then turn into a basin and chill quickly. Whip and add to the ice cream.

WATER ICES

Water ices need a syrup made of sugar and water as a foundation. To this syrup either fruit purée or fruit juice can be added. A little wine or liqueur added to a water ice is a great improvement.

Syrup for Water Ices

1 *pint water*	½ *lb. sugar*
Juice of half a lemon	

Put the water and sugar into a saucepan, bring to the boil and boil for 10 minutes, skimming when necessary. Add the lemon juice and strain through a jelly bag.

158

Lemon or Orange Water Ice

½ pint syrup (as opposite)
½ pint lemon or orange juice

1 egg-white
Rinds of 2 lemons or oranges

Pour the syrup, while still hot, over the thinly peeled fruit rinds, leave to cool and then add the fruit juice. Strain through a jelly bag. When half-frozen, whip in the stiffly beaten egg-white and freeze until ready for the table.

Raspberry or Strawberry Water Ice

1 pint raspberries or strawberries
Lemon juice

4 oz. sugar
1 gill water

Sprinkle the sugar over the raspberries or strawberries, let them stand for 2 hours, then mash them, squeeze through muslin, add the water and a squeeze of lemon juice and freeze.

Ice Lollies

These prime favourites with the children can be made at home in special "lolly"-shaped containers. Use any of the above recipes for water ices or, alternatively, make a strong, sweet lemon or orangeade, pour it into the containers, put a cocktail stick in each—and when you take them out of the freezing compartment of the refrigerator you will have most professional lollies.

ICE CREAMS

Though they are generally known as ice *creams*, cream need not form part of the foundation. Custard made with eggs and milk or cornflour is generally used. If a richer ice is desired, a little cream can be added, or if a very rich ice is wanted half cream and half custard makes a delicious mixture. Remember that if cream is used, the same proportion of sugar must be used as if only custard were employed—i.e. 3 oz. to 1 pint.

Basic Ice Cream (1)

1 pint milk
3 oz. sugar

2 egg-yolks

Bring the milk and sugar almost to the boil. Beat the egg-yolks well and add to the milk, stirring all the time. Put the mixture in the top of a double saucepan over hot water and stir until it thickens. Leave to get quite cold before freezing.

Basic Ice Cream (2)

1 pint milk
1 oz. cornflour
¼ pint thick cream (or evaporated milk)

3 oz. sugar
2 eggs
Vanilla flavouring as liked

Pineapple water ice, above, is delightfully refreshing, a pleasant change from the more usual ice cream

Hot chocolate sauce makes a wonderful contrast served with vanilla ice cream

Mix the cornflour with a little of the milk, heat the remainder of the milk with the sugar in a double saucepan, then add to the cornflour and stir in double saucepan until the mixture thickens. Cook gently for about 8 minutes, then remove from heat and leave to cool. Beat the eggs, then gradually stir in the mixture, add flavouring and cream, cool thoroughly, then freeze.

Chocolate Ice Cream (1)

1 *pint custard*	1 *gill cream, if liked*
Vanilla essence	3 *oz. grated chocolate*
A little water	

Make a custard and let it cool. Dissolve the chocolate in a little water and add it to the custard. Then add a few drops of vanilla essence and mix well. Add the cream, which should be lightly whipped, and freeze.

Chocolate Ice Cream (2)

Boil together 1 gill evaporated milk, 1 gill water and 4 oz. castor sugar. Put 1½ dessertspoonfuls powdered gelatine to soak in 1 tablespoonful of cold water. Then dissolve it in the hot syrup. Stir in 4 oz. grated chocolate until dissolved. When cool, add ½ teaspoonful vanilla essence, 1 gill chilled evaporated milk and the same quantity whipped enough to hold its shape, and stir thoroughly. Freeze until of the right consistency, stirring now and again in the tray.

Coffee Ice Cream

Make a custard as for Chocolate Ice Cream (1), but use equal parts of milk and strong black coffee. Cream can be added if desired.

Fruit Ice Cream

1 *pint vanilla ice cream (see next page, or buy in block)*	2 *oz. each glacé cherries, angelica or any crystallised fruit, according to taste*

Cut the fruit up small and beat it into the vanilla ice cream, then turn into freezing-tray and freeze.

Maraschino Ice Cream

1 *wineglassful Maraschino*	1 *pint vanilla ice cream*
1 *oz. castor sugar*	

Beat the cream until stiff, stir in sugar and Maraschino and freeze.

Neapolitan Ice Cream

This consists of three or more different coloured and flavoured ice creams frozen together in layers—pink (strawberry), white (vanilla), green (Maraschino or peppermint) and chocolate being the most popular combination.

Peach Melba

Make vanilla ice cream (see next page) and put a spoonful each into the necessary number of sundae glasses. Peel fresh peaches, quarter them and put two quarters into each glass. Pour over them either raspberry purée or raspberry jam (sieved if liked) and cover the top with whipped cream.

NOTE: When fresh peaches are not available, canned ones may be used instead.

Pear Melba

Make as for Peach Melba, but use fresh ripe or canned pears instead.

Peppermint Ice Cream

2 *tablespoonfuls crème de menthe*	1 *pint ice cream*

Before freezing the plain ice cream, stir in the crème de menthe, mixing thoroughly. This is a wonderfully refreshing hot weather dish.

Raspberry Ice Cream

Put ½ lb. raspberry jam into a gravy strainer and pour on to it ¾ pint milk. Press the jam against the sides of the strainer with the back of a wooden spoon until only the seeds of the jam remain. Stir the mixture well, then freeze hard. Half an hour before serving, turn into a chilled basin and beat well; return to the refrigerator until needed.

Strawberry or Raspberry Ice Cream

½ *pint strawberry or raspberry pulp*	1 *egg-white*
	10–12 *oz. sugar*
1 *pint milk*	½ *pint cream*
Juice of a lemon	

To make the pulp, clean and stalk about 1 lb. fruit, sprinkle with sugar and leave to stand for about 2 hours, then rub through a hair sieve.

Boil the milk, add the rest of the sugar and let it get nearly cold. Then add the fruit pulp, the lemon juice and, lastly, the stiffly

Photos by Electrolux

The perfect "important occasion" sweet—an Ice Pudding made in a special mould from any kind of home-made ice cream, preferably in a variety of flavours and colours

whipped cream. Partially freeze the mixture, then beat in the stiffly whipped egg-white and continue to freeze.

NOTE: If canned fruit is used, put it through a sieve and use a little of the syrup, but reduce the quantity of sugar.

Vanilla Ice Cream (1)

3 gills milk	1 whole egg and 2
1 gill cream or	yolks
evaporated milk	1 tablespoonful
½ teaspoonful vanilla	sherry (optional)
essence	2 oz. castor sugar

Heat the milk and sugar without boiling. Beat the egg and yolks, stir in the milk, mix well and put back in the saucepan. Then cook over a gentle heat until the mixture thickens without letting it boil. Stir all the time. Pour into a basin and leave until cool. When cold, put into the freezing tray and, when half frozen, turn into a chilled basin and add the sherry, vanilla, cream or evaporated milk whipped just enough to hold its shape. Beat well, return to the tray and continue freezing until ready, then turn the control back to

normal. Excellent served with hot chocolate sauce (see Sauces).

Vanilla Ice Cream (2)

1 pint custard	1 gill cream if desired
	Vanilla essence

Make custard and let it cool, add vanilla essence to taste and the whipped cream, and freeze.

NOTE: If cream is used, a little more sugar is needed when making the custard.

ICE PUDDINGS

Special moulds with lids are required for these. The mould should be placed in the freezing compartment for 15 minutes before it is used. Cut a piece of greaseproof paper ½ in. larger than the lid of the mould, grease it on both sides, fill the mould with half-frozen ice cream, cover with greased paper, put on lid and freeze until firm. When ready, dip mould in cold water, take off lid and paper, turn pudding on to a chilled dish and decorate as liked.

Any kind of ice cream may be used for puddings.

Tomato Cheese Surprises make savoury mouthfuls. Serve them on crisp chicory leaves, garnished with watercress and sliced hard-boiled egg

SAVOURIES

Round off a good dinner with a tasty dish that is well seasoned and piping hot—and serve it in small quantities

Fry quickly on both sides in hot fat, or grill, and serve on the croûtes.

Buck Rarebit

Make Welsh Rarebit (see p. 164) and put a poached egg on top of each serving.

SAVOURIES, coming as they do, at the end of a meal, must be particularly appetising to be appreciated. Two things are essential: (1) definite and distinctive flavour, so be generous with the seasoning; and (2) they should be served really piping hot, if possible straight from the grill or oven. This is not always possible, but savouries suffer more than other dishes from being kept hot, especially those served on croûtes. **Croûtes**, that is, fingers or rounds of fried or toasted bread, form the basis of many savouries.

In addition to the recipes in this chapter, see also those under the heading "Lunch and Supper Dishes" for slightly more substantial savouries which could be served after a light main course.

Anchovy Toast

Fry some croûtes, spread with anchovy paste and garnish with a little chopped parsley.

Angels on Horseback

Oysters	*Squeeze of lemon*
Rolls of fat bacon	*juice*
Anchovy essence	*Cayenne pepper*
Croûtes	*Anchovy paste*

Get ready some fried croûtes, spread them with anchovy paste and keep them hot. Beard the oysters and lay them on slices of fat bacon with a dash of anchovy essence, a squeeze of lemon juice and a sprinkling of Cayenne. Roll up the bacon and fasten with a skewer or cocktail stick.

Cheese Aigrettes (for 6–7)

1 gill water	*2 eggs*
1 oz. butter or mar-	*2 oz. flour*
garine	*2 oz. grated cheese*
	Pepper and salt

Put the water and the butter into a saucepan and bring to the boil. Shake in the flour and stir all the time until the mixture comes away from the sides. Then stir in the cheese, still beating, until the mixture is smooth. Add a pinch of pepper and salt. Cool a little, then beat in the eggs one at a time and continue beating until smooth. Break the mixture into little rocky lumps and drop into deep boiling fat, cook slowly at first, increasing the heat towards the end. Allow 10–15 minutes. Drain well on paper and sprinkle with a little grated cheese before serving.

Cheese d'Artois (for 5–6)

6 oz. flaky or short	*1 egg-white*
pastry	*3 oz. grated cheese*
1 oz. butter or mar-	*Cayenne pepper*
garine	*Salt and pepper*
2 egg-yolks	*A little made mustard*

Make pastry (see Pastry chapter). Put the cheese into a basin, add yolks and melted butter, then seasoning, and stir in the stiffly beaten egg-white. Roll out the pastry thinly. Spread the mixture on half the pastry. Moisten the edges with beaten egg and fold over the other half of the pastry. Mark across in squares or strips. Brush with beaten egg and sprinkle with cheese. Bake in a hot oven for 10–15 minutes and cut where marked.

Cheese Savouries (for 6–7)

2 oz. flour	2 oz. grated Parmesan
2 oz. butter or mar-	cheese
garine	Salt and Cayenne
	A little water

For the filling

½ teacupful cream	1 tablespoonful
Cayenne	Parmesan cheese

Sift the flour and seasoning together and rub in the butter. Add the grated cheese and mix well. Mix to a stiff dough with a little water. Put the mixture on a floured board and roll out. Line some small greased boat-shaped tins and bake "blind" in the oven until a golden brown. Allow to cool.

For the filling.—Whip the cream and fold in the Parmesan cheese; add a pinch of Cayenne, pile the mixture into the shapes and garnish with green salad. Serve cold.

Chicken Liver on Toast

Uncooked chicken	Fat for frying
liver	Pepper
Rashers of fat bacon	Croûtes

Get ready some fried croûtes and keep them hot. Cut uncooked chicken liver into neat pieces, roll them in slices of fat bacon with a pinch of pepper and fasten each with a skewer or cocktail stick. Fry quickly on both sides in hot fat and serve on croûtes.

Cod's Roe

Smoked cod's roe	Capers
Egg-yolk	Butter
A little milk	Pepper
Fried croûtes	

Fry the croûtes, drain and keep hot. Soak the roe in water for 1 hour to soften it, then dry and slice. Warm it in a little butter, add the beaten yolk, a little milk and pepper. Reheat without boiling. Serve on the croûtes and garnish with a few capers.

Cod's Roe on Potato Cakes

Cold, cooked, fresh	A little cream
cod's roe	Pepper and salt
Potato cakes	Capers

Cut up the roe and mix it with the cream and a pinch of pepper and salt, and heat in a saucepan. Make flat potato cakes (see chapter on Vegetables), fry them until brown and put some of the cod's roe on each. Garnish with a few capers.

Devilled Biscuits

Water biscuits	A very little dry
Grated cheese	mustard
Butter	A pinch of Cayenne

Mix some butter and a very little dry mustard together and spread the biscuits thickly with it, adding a pinch of Cayenne. Cover thickly with grated cheese and put under the griller or in the oven for a few minutes until brown.

Haddock Croûtes (for 3–4)

2 tablespoonfuls cold,	Chopped parsley
cooked smoked	Chopped gherkins
haddock, flaked	1 dessertspoonful
½ oz. butter	cream
Cayenne	1 egg-yolk
	Croûtes

Prepare some fried croûtes and keep them hot. Melt the butter and add the haddock, cream, Cayenne and gherkins. Stir in the yolk and heat, without boiling. Pile neatly on the croûtes and sprinkle with chopped parsley.

Herring Roes on Toast

Herring roes	Butter
Flour	Pepper
	Croûtes

Two savoury flavours combine to make Sardine Welsh Rarebit Fingers specially tasty for the last course of a meal

Put the roes in salt water to clean them, then drain and pour boiling water over them to make them curl up. Drain again. Put a pinch of pepper in some flour and sprinkle the flour lightly over the roes. Prepare croûtes and keep them hot. Fry the roes in a little butter for 3 or 4 minutes, then put them on the croûtes and garnish with chopped parsley or chopped hard-boiled egg-yolk.

Sardines on Toast

Sardines	1 tablespoonful milk
Croûtes	or cream
1 egg-yolk	3 drops Tarragon
½ oz. butter	vinegar
Pepper	

Bone the sardines, fold together again and put in the oven to warm. Fry croûtes and keep hot. Mix the egg-yolk, butter, vinegar, pepper and milk or cream in a saucepan, stirring to a smooth batter, without boiling. Put the sardines on the croûtes and pour the mixture over them. Garnish with a little chopped parsley or a small piece of tomato.

Sardine Welsh Rarebit Fingers (for 6)

4 whole slices of toast	12 sardines
covered with Welsh	Sprigs of parsley or
Rarebit (see recipe	watercress
(1) next column)	Paprika pepper

Lay 3 sardines side by side on each slice of Welsh Rarebit and heat through under the grill. Cut into fingers and sprinkle decoratively with the paprika pepper. Serve hot, garnished with parsley or watercress

Scotch Woodcock

Croûtes	½ oz. butter
Anchovy paste	1 tablespoonful milk
1 egg-yolk	or cream
Pepper	

Fry croûtes, make a dent in the middle of each, spread with anchovy paste and keep hot. Mix the egg-yolk, butter, pepper and milk or cream in a saucepan and stir to a smooth batter without boiling. With a teaspoon, fill the hollows in the croûtes with the mixture and sprinkle with chopped parsley or put a curled anchovy on each.

Stuffed Mushrooms

Cup mushrooms	Chopped parsley
Chopped ham or liver	Butter
Breadcrumbs	Pepper and salt
A very little chopped	A little milk or stock
onion	Croûtes

Wash the mushrooms and remove the skin and stalks. Mix together the ham, breadcrumbs, onion, parsley and seasoning, and bind with a little milk or stock. Fill the mushrooms with the mixture and put a small piece of butter on top of each. Put the mushrooms on a buttered tin in a moderate oven and bake for 15-20 minutes. Prepare fried croûtes and serve the mushrooms, hot, on these.

Tomato Cheese Surprises (for 4)

8 small firm tomatoes	Seasoned flour
2 oz. grated cheese	Brown breadcrumbs
Salt	Vegetable fat for
Cayenne pepper	frying
1 egg	

Skin the tomatoes and remove the cores. Stuff tightly with the grated cheese seasoned well with salt and Cayenne. Roll in seasoned flour. Dip in egg and coat well with breadcrumbs. Fry in hot vegetable fat for 2-3 minutes until a golden brown. Serve cold garnished with chicory or watercress.

Venetian Toasts (for 3-4)

1 egg-yolk	Pinch of dried herbs
2 tablespoonfuls	Butter
minced ham	Pepper
Croûtes	

Mince the ham very finely, add a pinch of herbs and pepper. Heat in a saucepan with a little butter and the egg-yolk. Pile it on croûtes and serve at once. A little minced chicken liver can be added.

Welsh Rarebit (1) (for 5-6)

12 oz. grated Cheddar	Cayenne and salt
cheese	2 oz. margarine
Made mustard to	4 tablespoonfuls milk
taste	Buttered toast

Put the cheese and margarine into a basin and mix well. Add milk and seasoning and mix to a stiff paste. Spread the mixture smoothly on buttered toast and place under the griller until light brown.

Welsh Rarebit (2) (for 5-6)

4 oz. grated cheese	1 oz. melted butter
Made mustard to	1 tablespoonful milk
taste	Buttered toast
Cayenne and salt	

Stir the butter, milk, cheese, mustard and seasoning in a saucepan until it thickens, then pour smoothly over the toast and put under the griller for a few minutes until brown.

NOTE: The cheese should not be allowed to go stringy. If it does, add 2 teaspoonfuls of fine breadcrumbs and stir well.

CHEESE

Among the finest home-produced English cheeses are Cheddar, Wensleydale, Stilton, Leicester and Caerphilly

The delight of the gourmet, cheese completes a perfect meal—and is one of the most nutritive and concentrated of foods

CHEESE has a history going back for more than twenty centuries—it formed part of the diet of Greek athletes in classical times, and poets from Homer onwards have sung its praises. In our day there is such a variety available, especially from the Continent, that selection becomes a fascinating occupation in itself.

Cheese is one of the most nutritive and concentrated forms of food: the fat and protein content of about a gallon of milk is found in one pound of cheese, and an ounce of cheese has nearly twice the amount of body-building protein of an ounce of meat. For those needing a high percentage of protein and calcium in their diet, such as children and old people, cheese is an invaluable and easily digested food. It is also economical because, being so highly concentrated, it is best eaten in small quantities.

A piece of cheese, with bread, biscuit or fruit, is the perfect last or next to the last course of a meal.

The simplest cheese is made by draining the whey from the curds of naturally soured milk (pasteurised milk, by the way, will not sour correctly), and this soft cream cheese must be eaten fresh, not more than three or four days after it is made. In general, cheese is made from the curd of milk formed as the result of the addition of rennet. The curds are sometimes scalded, sometimes not. The whey is drained off and, in hard or semi-hard cheeses, the curds are pressed into traditional and characteristic shapes. The cheeses are then set aside to ripen, the ripening period varying from a few days to many months. In a large number of varieties moulds are introduced into the cheese to produce, during the ripening process, blue-veining or other characteristics. Some cheeses are flavoured with herbs.

The varieties arise from differences in the quality of the milk used—from skimmed milk to full cream—and in the cheese-making processes.

Buying and Keeping

For domestic use, it is best to buy cheese in small quantities, and, when buying, to ask the supplier whether it is ready for immediate eating, as it may be displayed for sale not quite ripe. A cheese reaches a definite peak of maturity, and after that has been passed, deterioration may begin, in some cheeses, within two days; others will keep for months.

A cut piece of cheese must be kept moist unless you wish to dry it for grating; it should be wrapped in a damp cloth and kept in a covered dish, or it can be kept in a polythene bag. If you wish to store a whole cheese, the rind should be left exposed to the air and turned over frequently. Any mould on it should be scraped off, the cheese rubbed dry and then rubbed with oil or melted fat. Once it is cut, the cut surface should be protected with greaseproof paper.

CHEESE

Varieties

Over a hundred varieties of cheese are available in the U.K. Of these, only a tenth are home produced. The greatest number of cheeses imported from the Continent come from France; others come from Italy, Switzerland, Holland, Denmark, and there are cheeses, too, from Norway, Sweden and Germany. A great deal of cheese, mostly Cheddar in type, comes from the Commonwealth. In addition, there are the popular processed cheeses, attractively packed in tinfoil and easy to keep.

Cheeses, like wines, bear the names of their places of origin, where they have been made for centuries on the local farms. There is still considerable small-scale production of regional cheeses, particularly in France, but in all countries production of the well-known cheeses is now mostly large-scale.

In the U.K., "farmhouse" cheese, which used to be sold in the ancient local "Cheese Fairs," is often sought nostalgically. Although still available, the supply is steadily declining. There are fewer than 120 farmhouse cheese producers to-day; in 1939 there were 1,120. The shift to large-scale production is partly due to planned milk marketing and the attendant development of cheese factories; partly to the fact that farmers' daughters are no longer content with their traditional tasks in the dairy. (In the old days a Cheshire farmer looking out for a wife would ask a girl to lift the heavy lid of the parish chest. If she could do this, she was considered strong enough for the cheese-making.) The cheeses made by the women of the farmer's family were taken for sale to the local Cheese Fairs.

Nevertheless, the characteristics of a regional cheese are retained in large-scale production, which has the advantages of modern machinery; and the cheeses are carefully tested and graded.

The following are some of the well-known cheeses of different countries. Most are generally obtainable, but in case of difficulty write direct to Thomas Marsh (Leadenhall) Ltd., Leadenhall Market, London, E.C.3, who import cheeses from all parts of the world and who supplied the cheeses shown in the photographs on pages 168 and 169.

U.K. CHEESES

Caerphilly

Though Welsh in origin, Caerphilly now comes from the West Country, chiefly Somerset. It has a mild tangy flavour, is rather flaky in texture, not hard, though firm in body. It ripens quickly and is ready for consumption in 10 to 14 days after manufacture. After 3 or 4 weeks it begins to deteriorate.

Cheddar

The best known of all English cheeses. Half the cheese made in the U.K. is Cheddar (some of it actually made in its place of origin), and so is most of the cheese imported from Canada, Australia and New Zealand. It is a firm, smooth cheese, close in texture and clean and mellow in flavour, of high nutritive value. Its colour should be uniform and the rind unbroken. Among its virtues are its good keeping qualities It is a cheese used most commonly for cooking; buy it for the table but harden it by exposure to air for grating.

The largest cheese ever made was among Queen Victoria's wedding presents: a Cheddar weighing 11 cwt. and standing more than 9 ft. high.

Cheshire

The most ancient of English cheeses. Though Cheshire-type cheese comes from as far afield as Holland and New Zealand, the main centre of production is still in or near Cheshire, where the salty soil is responsible for its distinctive piquant flavour. The body is firm, not hard, and flaky in texture. A Cheshire cheese has the same height as diameter, with square edges.

Derby

A flat-shaped cheese, uniformly white and of close, smooth texture; clean and mild in flavour.

Dunlop

A Scottish cheese from Ayrshire; flattish in shape, flaky in texture.

Gloucester and Double Gloucester

The single Gloucester is good for toasting. The Double Gloucester is better known—an enriched Cheshire kind of cheese, with a mellow, distinctive flavour.

Lancashire

A little-known cheese, differing from other hard-pressed varieties in that, when three years old, it can be spread like butter. It is notably good for toasting when ripe.

Leicestershire

Not well known outside the Midlands, and formerly an exclusive farmhouse product. It is red-brown in colour inside and rather crumbly. It keeps well. Recommended to be eaten with apple pie.

Stilton

The "King of Cheeses," and world famous. A semi-hard, double-cream, blue-veined cheese, which, though now produced on a large scale in the Midlands, still retains its character and is made by highly skilled enthusiasts—it is a difficult cheese to produce. Its fame spread in the old days when travellers staying at the Bell Inn, Stilton, on the Leicestershire border, took away pieces of this admirable cheese. A fully matured Stilton has a clean, mild flavour and is velvety—or of a flaky open texture. The body should be uniformly creamy white, apart from the blue-grey mould radiating from the centre. The coat should be thin, moist, slightly wrinkled and drab coloured. It takes six months or even more to ripen, and should be eaten when fully ripe. There is also a quick-ripening *White Stilton*, without blueing.

Stilton cheeses used to be put under a wine tap to absorb a few drops every day, and port is sometimes added now if the cheese has become too dry.

Wensleydale

A rich, creamy soft cheese, delicately blue-veined, and sweet. The ripe cheese should have a greyish-white skin, clearly showing the pressure marks of its bandage. There is also a creamy *White Wensleydale*, with no blue-veining, which is eaten fresh and sold in cheeses from $\frac{1}{2}$ lb. to 14 lb. in weight. It was formerly little known outside the Yorkshire dales, where the formula was first introduced by the Abbots of the Abbey of Jervaulx, but it now has a wide reputation.

English Cream Cheeses

These unheated and unpressed cheeses, which spread like butter, must be eaten within four days of manufacture, as they deteriorate quickly.

FRENCH CHEESES

The following are the most celebrated and most easily obtainable of more than 400 varieties of French regional cheeses.

Throughout Scandinavia cheese is eaten at almost every meal. Above, a selection from Denmark includes Danish Blue, Samsoe, Esrom, and other types

Bleu d'Auvergne

A fine quality whole milk blue-mould cheese, uncooked and unpressed, either crustless, or with a very light crust.

Brie

A famous whole milk, inoculated, soft cheese, flat and round in shape, named after La Brie province east of Paris, but now made in other parts also. It is uncooked and unpressed, and is best bought in small quantities as deterioration begins within 48 hours after it has passed its peak of maturity. Sections can be bought in light wooden boxes. There are three varieties: *Brie de Coulommiers* (or simply *Coulommiers*), *Brie de Melun* and *Brie de Meaux*, the last being one of the most celebrated French cheeses.

Camembert

The French cheese best known in England is made mainly in Normandy, but

From Switzerland come Emmenthal, Petit Gruyère (in sections) and Geska. Norway provides Gjetost and Germany Limburger

elsewhere also on a considerable scale, and even in other countries. It is rich and soft, uncooked and unpressed, with a dark rind and pale yellow inside. Like Brie, it begins to deteriorate within 48 hours of reaching maturity. It is best eaten when beginning to go soft; later the mould with which it is inoculated decomposes the casein further, and an exceedingly strong smell is produced. It is usually exported in small boxes.

Cantal

A hard whole milk cheese, somewhat sharp in flavour; red or white. It is similar to the English Cheddar.

Carré de l'Est

A soft cheese, similar to Camembert.

Demi-Sel

A whole milk soft cheese sold in quarter pounds. Made mostly in Normandy.

Demi-Suisse

A highly perishable soft cheese made from pure double cream, which should be eaten within three days of arrival by air from Normandy.

Le Port du Salut (or Port-Salut)

The "veritable fromage" is made by the Trappist monks in the Abbey of that name at Entrammes (Mayenne), though production goes on now in a much wider field. It is medium solid, round and flat, mild in flavour, and of great repute. The factory-produced Port-Salut is heavier and thicker than the hand-made Abbey production.

Munster

A semi-hard whole milk cheese with a dark red rind, made in the Munster valley in Alsace and in other parts of that area.

Pont l'Evêque

This yellow, semi-hard, fermented cheese is still produced exclusively on farms of the Pont l'Evêque district of Normandy, where its production is more than a thousand years old.

France produces (left to right, top row): Carré de l'Est, Port Salut, Tome de Savoie, Demi-Sel. Centre: Pont l'Evêque, Bleu d'Auvergne, Demi-Suisse, Brie and Roquefort. Bottom row: Camembert, Saint Paulin, Coulommiers

Roquefort

French law lays it down that Roquefort Cheese can be made only from ewe's milk, and the genuine Roquefort, with a world-wide reputation, bears a label of a red sheep in an oval. The cheeses are matured in the natural limestone caves at Roquefort in the Cevennes, where the unique atmospheric conditions produce a flavour which, it is claimed, cannot be reproduced in the many Roquefort imitations made elsewhere. As sheep's milk is extremely rich, Roquefort cheese has a great nutritive value. If kept covered in a refrigerator, it will remain unspoiled for a long time.

Saint Paulin

A mild and creamy "Le Port du Salut"-type cheese, round and flat in shape.

Tome de Savoie au Raisin

This cheese from Haute Savoie is fermented in vats in which the local wine is made, so acquiring its characteristic flavour. It is a round, flat cheese, its rind coated with the skins and stones of black grapes, and consequently a dark purple colour.

ITALIAN CHEESES

Bel Paese

A well-known cheese, 4 lb. in weight, soft, creamy and mild in flavour, with very small holes, from the plains of North Lombardy.

Burrini

Gourd-shaped and rich in fats, as it is filled with a kind of butter. It is served cut into small portions.

Caciocavelli

A pear-shaped hard cheese of strong flavour, with a glazed rind. It will keep indefinitely. Used grated in cooking.

Gorgonzola

This celebrated semi-hard, blue-veined cheese takes its name from a village near Milan, and its principal place of production is still in that region. It is made, however, elsewhere on a considerable scale, and there is a Danish "Gorgonzola." There are two types: the conventional 20-lb. cheese, and a small "mountain Gorgonzola" which is not mass-produced and is of better quality.

Parmesan

A very hard cheese of fine flavour from Parma, used chiefly for grating. (It can be bought in tins already grated or, more economically, in a piece for grating at home.)

Sardo

A black, very hard cheese from Sardinia, used grated for culinary purposes.

SWISS CHEESES

Emmenthal (Emmentaler)

A hard cheese very similar to the famous Gruyère but with bigger "eyes" or holes, milder and somewhat softer. Most of the Emmenthal in the U.K. is sold under the name of Gruyère. It is made near

Berne and elsewhere, not only in Switzerland.

Gruyère

The premier Swiss cheese and world famous. A cooked hard cheese, pale yellow, smooth and firm, distinguished by the large "eyes" with which it is honeycombed and by its characteristic and agreeable odour and flavour. It comes from the Canton of Friburg, but is made also in many other parts. (There is a French Gruyère.)

Petit Gruyère

Processed Gruyère sold in tin-foil-wrapped sections.

Schabzieger (Geska)

A very hard and highly flavoured cheese, green in colour, used chiefly for grating, and sold in small cones. It is made from skimmed milk, cooked with herbs and matured for several months.

DUTCH CHEESES

There is a long-standing Government control on the genuineness and composition of Dutch cheeses, and every cheese for export bears a Government mark as a guarantee.

Edam

A globe-shaped cheese about 4 lb. in weight, with a polished red rind and a smooth, deep yellow interior; mild in flavour.

Gouda

A famous cheese, round and flat with a polished yellow rind; about 10 lb. in weight. There is also a small size. Genuine Gouda is rich in fat, made from whole milk on about 5,000 farms in the provinces of southern Holland and Utrecht.

GERMAN CHEESE

Limburger

The most famous of all German cheeses; a semi-hard, whole milk cheese, highly flavoured and strong smelling, from the Hartz mountains.

SCANDINAVIAN CHEESES

Crême Chantilly (Hablé)

A national speciality of Sweden made from pasteurised cream. It is sold in wedge-shaped boxes, wrapped in tin-foil and should be kept under mild refrigeration.

Danish Blue

The speciality cheese of Denmark; a smooth, creamy cheese with a network of blue-green veins and a mellow aromatic flavour.

Danish Fynbo

A semi-hard cheese made from whole milk, similar to Samsoe (see below) but milder.

Esrom (Danish Port-Salut)

An imitation of the French Port-Salut and less expensive. Mild and creamy.

Samsoe

A firm, pressed cheese, taking its name from the Danish island of Samsoe, made from whole milk; mild and creamy with a nutty flavour. It keeps well.

Gjetost

A national speciality of Norway; a semi-hard cheese with a delicate caramel flavour, sold in oblong blocks; made from mixed goat's and cow's milk. It should be served cut wafer thin.

PROCESSED CHEESES

These cooked cheeses are comparatively new to the U.K. market, but their development has been rapid. They are extremely popular and there are many varieties. Wrapped in tin-foil in small portions, they are attractively boxed and can be kept for long periods. Both English and Continental processed cheeses are obtainable everywhere.

SERVING CHEESE

Cheese is usually served at the end of the meal. Some people, however, prefer to have it before the sweet. This has one big advantage: the cheese comes to table while there is still red wine left from the meat course, and this goes excellently with it. If it is taken after the sweet (which is served with a white wine), port should be handed with the cheese.

Serve cheeses on a wooden board, with a wooden-handled cheese knife. Those in the photograph of Swiss cheeses are obtainable from the Civil Service Stores, London.

BREAKFAST DISHES

Start the day well with a nourishing meal, well cooked and nicely served

A cheerful breakfast cloth and matching napkins, in fine Irish linen, with checks of scarlet, green and white.

A GOOD breakfast is essential for anyone with a day's work to do. Children at play or school, who burn up a tremendous amount of energy running about, the breadwinner who goes off to office or factory—*and* the housewife herself—will all feel fitter and get less tired if a good foundation is laid at the breakfast table. It need not be the traditional eggs and bacon necessarily. Fish, porridge and cereals are all suitable.

Here are a few suggestions. Other recipes for breakfast foods come under Egg Dishes (see p. 174) and Fish (see p. 31).

Bacon for Boiling

Good bacon has red lean and white firm fat. Thick streaky is the best cut, but for small pieces the flank is excellent and cheaper. Since bacon is often salt, it is a good plan to soak it in warm water for 1 or 2 hours before cooking. Then remove the rusty parts and scrape the rind and underside with a sharp knife to get it as clean as possible. Put into a saucepan of cold water and bring slowly to the boil, skimming as the scum rises to the surface. Simmer gently until thoroughly cooked (allow 45 minutes per pound). When cooked, the rind should strip off quite easily. Cover the top with bread-raspings.

Bacon, Baked

Remove the rinds and put the rashers into a tin so that they overlap each other; cook in a moderate oven until the fat is transparent—about 10–15 minutes, according to the thickness of the rashers.

Bacon, Fried

Cut off the rinds with kitchen scissors or a sharp knife and put with the rashers into a frying pan, warm slowly, and then fry until the fat is transparent and as crisp as liked. (If the lean looks very dry and there is only a little fat, add a teaspoonful of dripping to the pan (when frying.)

Bacon, Grilled

Remove rinds with kitchen scissors and put the rashers on previously warmed griller under hot grill. Cook until as crisp as desired.

Bacon and Apple

Allow a moderate-sized apple to 2 rashers of bacon. Wipe and core the apples without peeling them, cut into slices ¾ in. thick. Grill or fry the bacon first, remove from the pan and keep hot, then fry or grill the sliced apple in the bacon fat. Put on to a hot dish, sprinkle the apple lightly with sugar and add a scrape of nutmeg, then arrange the rashers on top.

Bacon and Bananas

Allow 1 banana to 2 rashers of bacon. Peel and cut in half lengthwise. Grill or fry the bacon, keep hot, and grill or fry the bananas in the bacon fat. Serve hot.

Bacon and Kidneys

Fry or grill the bacon and put aside to keep hot. Fry or grill the kidneys, previously washed and cored, in the bacon fat, turning them over once; when the red gravy flows freely, arrange on the bacon. Brown a teaspoonful of sieved flour in the fat, stir in a very little stock and bring to the boil. Season well and pour over the kidneys.

Bacon and Macaroni (for 2–3)

2 oz. macaroni	2 oz. bacon rashers
Pepper and salt	½ pint stock
Scrape of nutmeg	½ oz. butter

Break the macaroni into small pieces, put into quickly boiling salted water and boil for 5 minutes, then drain. Put the macaroni into the boiling stock and simmer gently until tender. Cut the bacon into small pieces and fry, then add the drained macaroni, the butter, nutmeg and seasoning. Mix over a gentle heat until the macaroni is brown, turn on to a hot dish.

Bacon and Tomatoes

Fry or grill the bacon, remove and keep hot. Slice the tomatoes, skinned if liked, and cook in the bacon fat until thoroughly hot, then arrange round the bacon, sprinkle with salt and pepper and serve.

Bacon may also be served with sausages, fried or grilled, with eggs, fried, scrambled or boiled, and fried bread.

Eggs (see chapter on Egg Dishes, p. 174)

Finnan Haddock

Put smoked haddock into cold water and soak for some hours. When required, simmer very gently in milk and water until quite tender; drain and cut into neat squares. Put on to a hot dish with a small piece of butter on each, sprinkle with pepper and keep hot while you lightly poach some eggs. Slide an egg on to each square and serve at once.

Haddock à la Reine (for 4)

4 oz. boiled rice	Smoked haddock
3 hard-boiled eggs	(cooked)
Seasoning	1 oz. butter
Fried bread	

Fry half the well drained dry rice in the hot butter. When thoroughly hot, add 2 chopped egg-whites, seasoning and the flaked-up haddock. Stir until thoroughly heated through, then pile up on a hot dish, put the rest of the rice (heated) round, and garnish with the remaining hard-boiled egg cut in slices and 2 egg-yolks sprinkled over the fish, etc. Arrange fried bread round

and put the fish in the oven for a few minutes to make sure it is thoroughly hot.

Herrings (see Scottish and Fish chapters)

Kedgeree (for 4–5)

6 oz. cooked fish	2 hard-boiled eggs
(any fish will do,	1 egg
but smoked	2 oz. butter
haddock is best)	2 chillies or pinch of
4 oz. boiled rice	Cayenne pepper
Seasoning	

Flake the fish smoothly. Chop the hard-boiled eggs and chillies. Melt the butter in a pan and, when hot, add the fish, rice, eggs and chillies (or Cayenne), and heat thoroughly. Beat the egg, stir it in, adding seasoning if necessary, reheat and serve.

Kippers (see also chapter on Fish Dishes)

Put the kippers into boiling water for a minute or two, remove and dry. Heat a small quantity of fat in a frying pan, put in the kippers, cover with a lid and cook until tender; or grill on a warmed griller.

Porridge (see also Scottish section)

This may be made of any of the varieties of flaked oats which cook quickly, or with oatmeal, coarse, medium or fine. Allow 2 tablespoonfuls to a pint of salted water, bring the water to the boil, sprinkle in the oatmeal, stirring so that it does not form lumps, boil and stir for 5 minutes.

Coarse oatmeal needs at least 2 hours' cooking in a double saucepan—the longer it is cooked the more digestible it will be. Medium oatmeal should simmer for at least 1 hour. When using fine oatmeal it is advisable to mix it to a smooth paste with cold water and then add it to the boiling water, otherwise it is apt to go lumpy. Add more boiling water, if necessary, during the cooking process. Porridge should be of a pouring consistency.

Salmon Cakes (for 4–5)

8 oz. tinned salmon	Anchovy sauce
Salt and pepper	Lemon juice
3 tablespoonfuls	6 oz. mashed potato
breadcrumbs	1 egg
Fat for frying	

Flake the salmon, removing any skin or bones, and mix with the potato. Add a few drops of lemon juice, seasoning to taste and moisten with anchovy sauce. Form into balls, flatten them slightly, brush over with beaten egg and toss in the breadcrumbs. Fry in hot deep fat.

Specially cooked and photographed in the Creda kitchens

A cooked breakfast will ensure a good day's work and play. This tempting array provides a suggestion for every day of the week : grilled herrings; fish rissoles on tomatoes; scrambled eggs; bacon and tomato on sausage meat; kidney, sausage, tomato and mushrooms; sausage, bacon, eggs and tomato; and sausages wrapped in pancakes. Grapefruit, hot or cold, can be served as a first course

173

EGG DISHES

Tasty and nourishing, they are a stand-by for any meal, from break-fast to supper

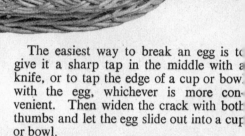

EGG dishes have three great points in their favour. They are quick to prepare, they are very nourishing, and they often save the situation in an emergency. A golden rule in every household should be: Never be short of eggs.

As everyone knows, there are all sorts and conditions of eggs, from new-laid to cooking eggs. Nothing but really new-laid eggs should be used for boiling, poaching, scrambling or frying, as the slightest suggestion of staleness is very disagreeable.

A simple test to find out whether an egg is new-laid or not is to put it into a pint of water containing 1 oz. salt. If it sinks to the bottom, it is absolutely fresh. If it is more than 3 days old, it floats. If 2 or 3 days old, it neither sinks to the bottom nor floats, but hovers in between.

Here are a few more facts about eggs.

The yolk of an egg is rich in vitamins and salts, the white is nourishing and very easily digested.

The colour of the shell makes no difference to the food value of the egg. An egg with a white shell is just as good as one with a brown shell.

Eggs between 2 and 4 days old are best for beating. Put in a pinch of salt and beat them in a draught.

Ducks' eggs are stronger flavoured and richer than hens', but less digestible. They must always be cooked for 10 minutes.

Eggs put down in waterglass will keep for a year. If eggs are plentiful in the spring and the price therefore low, it is undoubtedly an economy to preserve them for the winter, but the eggs must be *fresh*, not more than 24 hours old and infertile. They should be wiped over before being put into the waterglass.

The easiest way to break an egg is to give it a sharp tap in the middle with a knife, or to tap the edge of a cup or bowl with the egg, whichever is more convenient. Then widen the crack with both thumbs and let the egg slide out into a cup or bowl.

When using several eggs, break them separately into a cup or bason. Otherwise a stale one may spoil them all.

To separate white from yolk, crack the egg as described above, hold half of the shell in each hand over a basin and pour the egg gently from one to the other so that the white runs into the basin. Be careful not to break the egg-yolk, and when the white has been separated put it into another cup or bowl.

The commonest ways of cooking eggs are:

Soft-boiled (1)

Plunge the egg into a pan of fast-boiling water and cook according to taste: 3 minutes (very soft); 3½ minutes (average light); 4 minutes (medium-hard) or 4½ minutes (firm).

Soft-boiled (2)

Cover the egg with cold water and bring slowly to the boil. The moment the water boils, remove from the heat.

Hard-boiled

Put the egg into boiling water and boil for 10 minutes—not more or the egg will be discoloured. Put immediately into cold water to cool.

Coddled

Put the egg into a pan of boiling water, cover the pan and reduce the heat so that the water does not boil again. Leave eggs 4 minutes for soft; 6–7 minutes for medium; 15–20 for hard.

Poached

Break the egg carefully into a cup. Unless a special poacher is used, put a teaspoonful of vinegar and a pinch of salt into a frying pan half-full of water, slide in the egg, keeping the white together with a spoon. Simmer gently until the egg is set and the white opaque, spooning water over the egg. Remove with a slice, drain and serve on hot buttered toast.

Fried

Use as small a pan as possible. Heat some lard or butter, and when the blue smoke rises, slide in the egg and draw off heat for a minute. Then replace over a very low heat and fry until set, shaking the pan to prevent the egg sticking. A plate put over the frying pan helps the top to set. Remove with a slice and drain well.

Steamed

Grease an individual fireproof dish and break an egg into it. Stir the yolk and white together, add a pinch of salt, put the dish in a saucepan with enough boiling water to come half-way up, and steam until set.

Scrambled

Allow to each egg $\frac{1}{2}$ oz. butter or margarine and 1 tablespoonful milk. Melt the butter in a saucepan and add the slightly beaten eggs, milk and a little pepper and salt. Stir until nearly set. Remove from the heat and serve on hot buttered toast.

Anchovy Eggs

Hard-boil the eggs, shell them and cut in half. Take out the yolk and mix it with anchovy essence and cream or oiled butter. Mash with a fork on a plate, then put the mixture back in the whites, garnish with mustard and cress or watercress, and put a few capers on top of each half. Serve with brown bread and butter.

Eggs in Bread Sauce look attractive served in the dish in which they are cooked. A border of green peas adds a pleasing note of colour contrast

Curried Eggs (for 3–4)

4 hard-boiled eggs	Squeeze of lemon
1 oz. butter	juice
Curry powder to taste	1 teaspoonful
½ oz. rice flour	chopped chutney
Boiled rice	Salt
1 apple and 1 onion	½ pint stock

Melt the butter and, when hot, fry the sliced apple and onion, then add the rice flour, curry powder and salt, and cook for 5 minutes, stirring well. Stir in the stock and bring to the boil. Cut the eggs into halves or quarters and put them in the sauce with the chopped chutney and re-heat. Add a squeeze of lemon juice right at the end. Serve on a dish, surrounded by the rice, and pour the sauce over.

Devilled Eggs (for 4–5)

6 eggs	2 tablespoonfuls
Pinch of castor sugar	cream
A little mustard	1 tablespoonful
Cayenne and salt	vinegar
Parsley and thyme	

Hard-boil the eggs, cut them in half and take out the yolks. Pound until very fine and add to them the sugar, mustard, Cayenne, salt, cream and vinegar. Mix well together with a little chopped parsley and thyme, and fill the whites. Serve cold, garnished with mustard and cress or water-cress.

Eggs à la Béchamel

Poach eggs in good white or brown stock and serve in Béchamel sauce (see Sauces chapter). Garnish with chopped gherkins, capers or parsley.

Egg and Bacon Fritters

Poach the required number of eggs and leave to get cold. Drain and roll each in a thin slice of bacon. Dip in batter and fry. Serve with fried parsley.

Eggs and Cheese

Hard-boil the eggs and chop them. Pour cheese sauce into a greased fireproof dish, put in the eggs and sprinkle Parmesan cheese over them. Then put the dish under the griller or in the oven until brown on top.

Egg Cutlets (for 3–4)

3 hard-boiled eggs	1 teaspoonful
1 oz. butter	chopped parsley
1 tablespoonful flour	Pepper and salt
1 gill milk	½ teaspoonful
2 oz. breadcrumbs	anchovy essence
Egg and breadcrumbs	Fat for frying
for coating	

Make a thin paste with a little of the milk and the flour. Heat the rest of the milk and pour in the paste, stirring well, and add the butter. Boil gently for 5 minutes. Then add the eggs, chopped finely, the breadcrumbs, seasoning, chopped parsley and anchovy essence, and mix well. Put the mixture on a plate and, when cool enough, make into cutlets. Flour, roll in egg and breadcrumbs, and fry in deep fat until a good brown. Drain well and serve with anchovy sauce (see Sauces chapter).

NOTE: Tomato ketchup can be used instead of anchovy. In this case serve the cutlets with tomato sauce; alternatively, add 2 oz. chopped ham and serve with brown or tomato sauce.

Eggs en Cocotte

Eggs	Pepper and salt
Butter	A little cream

Butter the required number of small fire-proof cocotte dishes, break eggs into them, put a little cream on each egg, and a sprinkle of pepper and salt. Bake in a moderate oven for 6–8 minutes, according to taste. A little grated cheese can be sprinkled over the top, or some chopped ham or tomato purée placed at the bottom.

Eggs in Bread Sauce

Put hot bread sauce (for recipe see Sauces chapter) into a fireproof dish. Break eggs into a cup and slide them one at a time into the bread sauce, being careful the yolks do not break. Sprinkle a little grated cheese over the eggs and bake for about 10 minutes.

Eggs in Mustard Sauce

Hard-boiled eggs	Grated cheese
(hot)	Mustard sauce (see
Cream	Sauces chapter)

Make mustard sauce, and add a little cream to it. Cut hard-boiled eggs into slices and put them in a fireproof dish. Sprinkle half the cheese over them and then pour in the mustard sauce. Sprinkle the rest of the cheese over it and brown under the griller or in the oven.

Egg Mayonnaise (1)

Hard-boiled eggs	Ham, crab or
Mayonnaise	lobster

Cut the eggs lengthwise. Take out the yolks and mash with a fork on a plate.

For a mushroom-filled omelet, place the cooked mushrooms across the centre of the omelet when it has just set

Then tilt the pan and, with a fork or palette knife, fold the omelet carefully in half without breaking it

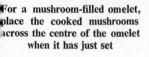

Fill the whites with chopped ham, crab or lobster. Pour mayonnaise sauce over them and sprinkle the yolk on the top. Garnish with strips of cucumber cut very small, or beetroot or peas, and serve surrounded by mustard and cress.

Have a warm plate ready, slide the omelet on to it, serve—and eat it—immediately

Egg Mayonnaise (2)

As an alternative to hard-boiled eggs, which some people find indigestible, poach the eggs and let them get cold. Serve on a bed of lettuce with mayonnaise on top.

Eggs on Spinach

Cook spinach (see Vegetable chapter) and make it into a purée. Hard-boil eggs, cut them into quarters and arrange on the spinach. Serve with fried croûtons of bread.

NOTE: Hot poached eggs can also be served on a bed of spinach purée; quick-frozen or canned spinach may be used instead of fresh.

Eggs stuffed with Cheese (for 3–4)

4 hard-boiled eggs	White sauce
2 tablespoonfuls Parmesan cheese (grated)	A very little made mustard
1 teaspoonful vinegar	Salt and pepper
	Melted butter

Cut the eggs in half. Scoop out the yolk, and add to it the cheese, vinegar, mustard, seasoning and enough melted butter to make a firm mixture. Roll it into balls to fit into the whites. Serve either hot or cold. If served hot, make white sauce, place the eggs in it and reheat in a casserole in the oven.

Eggs stuffed with Chicken or Veal (for 3–4)

4 hard-boiled eggs	Chopped chicken or veal (cooked)
Salt and pepper	Peas, beetroot and carrot (cooked)
Mayonnaise sauce	
Salad	

Cut the eggs in half. Scoop out the yolk and add to it the chopped dice of chicken or veal, green peas, dice of beetroot and carrot, and seasoning. Make mayonnaise sauce (see Salad chapter) and toss the yolk, etc., lightly in it. Fill the whites with the mixture and serve on a bed of salad.

Eggs with Cheese and Breadcrumbs
(for 3–4)

4 eggs	½ oz. butter
1 gill thin cream	1 teaspoonful
Breadcrumbs	chopped parsley
2 oz. grated cheese	Salt and pepper

Break the eggs carefully and put them into a well-buttered fireproof dish. Whip the cream slightly and season it with salt and pepper, then pour it over the eggs and sprinkle over it the chopped parsley, grated cheese, breadcrumbs and small pieces of butter. Cook in a moderate oven until the eggs are just set and serve at once.

Fricasséed Eggs (for 3–4)

1 tablespoonful chopped onion	Squeeze of lemon juice
1 oz. butter	1 teacupful of milk
Pinch of ground ginger	A little flour
Fried bacon	Pepper and salt
	4 eggs

Fry the onion in the butter until golden brown, sprinkle in a little flour, pinch of ginger, pepper and salt, and cook for 3 minutes, stirring all the time. Add the milk slowly and bring to the boil. Remove from fire, and add a squeeze of lemon juice. Hard-boil and slice eggs, pour sauce over them and serve with fried bacon.

Omelets

Making an omelet is not really difficult —provided the rules are carefully followed.

(1) Keep a special pan (preferably not an aluminium one) for omelets and never use it for anything else. Instead of washing the pan after use, wipe it clean with kitchen paper.

(2) Always fry in *butter*.

(3) Serve *immediately* the omelet is cooked, before it falls flat.

French Omelet (for 2–3)

3 eggs	1 tablespoonful
Pepper and salt	cold water
	1 oz. butter

Beat the eggs well with the water and a pinch of pepper and salt, using a rotary beater if possible—the more it is beaten the lighter the omelet will be. Well butter the pan and, when very hot but not quite smoking, pour in the mixture and reduce the heat. Run a knife round the edge and underneath so that the mixture does not stick, and tilt the pan to allow the still-liquid part to run under and get evenly cooked. When just set, fold over quickly with a knife and slide on to a hot dish. *Serve at once.*

Omelets with the same Foundation but with Different Flavours

Mixed Herbs.—Add a good pinch of mixed herbs and a teaspoonful of very finely chopped onion to the mixture before pouring it into the pan.

Cheese.—Add 2 tablespoonfuls of grated Parmesan cheese to the mixture before pouring it into the pan.

Ham.—Add 2 tablespoonfuls of finely chopped ham to the mixture before pouring it into the pan.

Mushroom.—Either add 2 tablespoonfuls of very finely chopped cooked mushrooms to the mixture before pouring it into the pan, or cook shredded mushrooms in a little butter, cream or white sauce and put across centre of omelet just before folding over.

Kidney.—Fry minced kidney and add to the omelet just before it is turned over.

Soufflé Omelet

3 eggs (separated)	1 tablespoonful
Pepper and salt	cold water
(if savoury)	1 oz. butter

Beat egg-yolks, and add water and seasoning. Beat whites until very stiff and fold into yolks. Either fry as for French omelet until outer surface begins to crisp and then finish in a very hot oven or under hot grill, or cook entirely in a very hot oven, in a buttered pan, for 10 minutes. Serve instantly.

Varieties of Flavouring for Soufflé Omelet

Jam.—Make soufflé omelet without salt and pepper and fold in hot jam, sprinkle with sugar and put under hot grill for 1 or 2 minutes to melt sugar.

Rum.—Fill soufflé omelet with hot apricot jam, pour warm rum over and set it alight. Serve with ice-cold cream.

Poached Eggs with Mushrooms

Make toast and cut it into rounds. Fry flat mushrooms, put them on the buttered toast and keep hot. Put a poached egg on each and place in a fireproof dish. Make cheese or mushroom sauce (see Sauces chapter) and pour on the eggs, sprinkle with cheese and brown under the grill.

Savoury Custards (for 2–3)

3 eggs	½ gill cream
1 gill strong well-flavoured white stock	Chopped chive
	Shallot
	Grated ham or tongue

Beat the eggs well. Add the cream and the stock. Season with a finely chopped chive, shallot, and chopped, grated or shredded ham or tongue. Mix well. Pour the mixture into small buttered moulds. Steam for 10 minutes. Turn out on to a dish and serve with or without gravy as preferred. Garnish with little heaps of French beans or carrots.

Scotch Eggs (for 5–6)

1 lb. sausage meat	Breadcrumbs and flour
4 hard-boiled eggs	1 egg (for coating)
Fat for frying	

Hard-boil the eggs, shell and dry them. Sprinkle with flour and cover with sausage meat. Roll in egg and breadcrumbs, and fry in deep fat until golden brown. Drain well, cut in half and serve hot with brown gravy or tomato sauce, or cold with salad.

Scrambled Eggs with Bacon or Ham

Allow 1 egg, ½ oz. butter or margarine, and 1 tablespoonful of milk for each person. Heat the diced bacon or ham in a saucepan with the butter, add the slightly beaten egg and milk, and stir until nearly set. Remove from the fire and serve on hot buttered toast.

Scrambled Eggs with Cheese (for 4)

2 oz. butter	1 teaspoonful chopped parsley chives and shallots
6 oz. Gruyère cheese, grated	
1 wineglassful dry white wine	A little grated nutmeg
4 eggs	

Melt the butter and cheese slowly over a moderate flame, then add the wine, herbs and nutmeg. Bring slowly to the boil, stir in the egg-yolks separately and finally the well-beaten whites. Stir until the mixture thickens like scrambled egg and serve on toast.

Scrambled Eggs with Tomato

Allow 1 egg per person. Skin tomatoes, cut them up and cook in a little butter and add them to the lightly beaten eggs. Melt a little butter or margarine in the saucepan, add the egg and tomato mixture with a little pepper and salt. Stir until nearly set. Remove from the fire and serve on hot buttered toast.

Scotch Eggs, covered with sausage meat and fried till crisp and golden, are equally tasty hot or cold

LUNCH AND SUPPER DISHES

Some ideas to provide enough nourishment for the
family at the lighter of the two main meals in the day

IN addition to the following recipes, consult also the chapters on Egg Dishes and Vegetarian Cookery.

Cauliflower au Gratin

1 cauliflower	White sauce
3 oz. grated cheese	Browned bread-
A little margarine	crumbs

Wash the cauliflower well, cutting away most of the stalk, and soak in cold water. Cook until tender, drain well (keeping the water for the sauce), break up the flowers into fair-sized pieces and put them in a fire-proof dish. Make the sauce (see Sauces chapter), using half milk and half cauli-flower water, add half the cheese and stir well. Pour sauce over cauliflower, sprinkle remainder of cheese on top, cover with browned breadcrumbs, dot with margarine and brown under grill.

Cheese Fondue (for 6)

1½ cupfuls fresh	2 eggs (separated)
breadcrumbs	1½ cupfuls milk
1½ cupfuls grated	1 tablespoonful
cheese	butter, melted
¼ teaspoonful salt	

Soak breadcrumbs in milk. Add cheese, beaten egg-yolks, salt and melted butter. Fold in stiffly beaten egg-whites. Pour into a greased baking dish, place in a pan of hot water and oven-poach in a moderate oven for about 40 minutes.

Cheese Pudding (for 3–4)

1 oz. butter	Pinch of mustard and
2 oz. breadcrumbs	salt
¼ pint milk	2 oz. grated cheese
1 egg (separated)	

Heat the milk, stir in the butter, bread-crumbs, mustard and salt, and add the cheese and beaten egg-yolk. Whip the egg-white to a stiff froth and fold in lightly. Pour the mixture into a well-greased pie dish and bake for 15–20 minutes.

Cheese Puffit (for 6–8)

12 ½-in. slices stale	½ lb. cheese, sliced
bread	¼ pint milk
4 eggs	Dash of pepper and
¼ teaspoonful salt	paprika

Arrange slices of bread and cheese in alternate layers in a greased baking dish. Beat eggs slightly, add milk and seasonings, and pour over the bread and cheese. Cover and keep in the refrigerator until ready to bake. Place in a pan of hot water and oven-poach in a moderate oven until set (about 45 minutes). If thoroughly chilled before baking, the puffit will puff up like a soufflé.

Cheese Soufflé (for 4–6)

1 oz. butter	2 eggs
1 gill milk	2 oz. Parmesan
1 dessertspoonful	cheese
cornflour	Cayenne and salt

Melt the butter in a pan. Add corn-flour and seasoning and then the milk. Boil for 3 minutes, stirring well. Cool slightly. Separate the egg-whites from the yolks and beat in the yolks and the cheese. Whip the whites until they are very stiff and fold into the sauce. Put into a prepared and well-buttered soufflé dish, and bake in a moder-ate oven for 20–25 minutes until risen and light brown. Serve at once.

Cheese Vegetable Rarebit (for 6)

1 cupful tomato juice	Toast
1½ teaspoonfuls dry	1 tablespoonful fat
mustard	2 teaspoonfuls
Salt and pepper to	Worcester sauce
taste	2 cupfuls cooked
3 cupfuls grated	vegetables or
cheese	spaghetti
1 egg	

Heat tomato juice, fat, mustard, Worces-ter sauce, salt and pepper in top of double boiler. Add well-beaten egg and cook until mixture thickens (about 3 minutes). Add grated cheese and stir until melted. Arrange hot vegetables on toast, pour sauce on top and serve at once.

Galette au Nouilles (for 3–4)

6 oz. macaroni	2 oz. grated Gruyère
2 eggs	cheese
A little minced ham	2 oz. butter

Cook the macaroni in boiling, salted water for about ¼ hour, drain well, add half the butter while the macaroni is hot, mixing well, and finally add the Gruyère and minced ham. Beat the eggs and add them to the macaroni. Melt the rest of the butter in a saucepan, put in the mixture and brown the galette on one side. Turn it on to a plate for a moment, put a small piece of butter in the saucepan, replace the galette and brown the other side. Serve alone or with tomato sauce (see Sauces chapter).

Gnocchi of Semolina
(for 4–5)

1 pint milk
6 oz. semolina
1½ oz. butter
1½ oz. grated Parmesan cheese
2 eggs
Salt

Grilled tomatoes on toast, topped with melted Cheddar cheese or cheese sauce and a crisp bacon rasher, are a perfect light meal

Cook the semolina in the milk, take it off the fire, add seasoning, half the butter, half the cheese, and then the eggs. Mix well. Spread about 1 in. thick on a plate. When firm, cut into almond-shaped pieces. Pile the gnocchi on a dish, sprinkling the layers with the rest of the cheese and the butter in tiny pieces, but not putting any on the top layer. Lastly, brown in the oven and serve hot, either alone or as an accompaniment to meat.

Macaroni à la Forge

Cook macaroni until tender in a good stock made the day before. Drain and put into a fireproof dish with plenty of grated Gruyère and Parmesan cheese, a good piece of butter and some grated breadcrumbs. Bake in the oven until brown.

Celery cut in 1-in. lengths and cooked till tender in salted water can be used instead of macaroni.

Macaroni Cheese (for 3–4)

4 oz. macaroni	4 oz. grated Cheddar
Pepper, salt and, if	cheese
liked, paprika	1 oz. butter or fat
1 teacupful of milk	bacon

Put the macaroni into boiling, salted water and cook until just tender (about 10 minutes). Drain well and put in a fireproof dish with layers of grated cheese, seasoning each layer. Add a teacupful of milk, sprinkle grated cheese on top and dot either with lumps of butter or with sliced bacon or garnish with Cheese Balls. To make them, combine 1½ oz. Cheddar cheese with 3 teaspoonfuls browned breadcrumbs and a little Cayenne; form into balls. Bake in a moderate oven until slightly brown (20–30 minutes).

Rice Croquettes (for 4–5)

4 oz. rice	1 tablespoonful
4 oz. grated cheese	tomato purée
Breadcrumbs	Pepper and salt
1 egg	Fat for frying

Wash the rice well, boil in a very little water (adding more if necessary) until soft. Put the rice, the grated cheese, tomato purée, pepper and salt into a basin and add enough egg to bind. When cool, make into croquettes. Roll them in breadcrumbs and fry in deep fat for 5 minutes. Serve with cheese or tomato sauce. (For recipes see Sauces chapter).

Rice, Macaroni or Spaghetti with Tomato Sauce (for 6–7)

1 lb. rice	Small onion
1½ oz. butter	A little stock
2 tablespoonfuls grated cheese	Pinch of nutmeg Tomato sauce
1 egg-yolk	(see Sauces chapter)
Large pinch of salt	

Put the rice, butter and onion, finely chopped, into a saucepan with enough stock to make the rice swell. Simmer for 25 minutes, stirring and adding more stock as needed. When the rice is well filled out and quite soft, stir in the cheese, nutmeg and salt. Just before taking it off the fire, add the egg-yolk. The tomato sauce may be stirred into the rice or served separately.

NOTE: If macaroni or spaghetti is used, it should be cooked in boiling salted water until quite soft (between 15 and 20 minutes—the time varies with the quality).

Risotto (see Italian Cookery chapter)

Savoury Pie (for 4–5)

1 breakfastcupful brown breadcrumbs	2 oz. melted margarine
2 cooked potatoes	1 teacupful vegetable
1 tomato, sliced	stock
Spanish onion, par-boiled and sliced finely	Pinch of salt
1 teaspoonful mixed herbs	1 tablespoonful soaked tapioca
¼ lb. cooked rice	1 oz. ground nuts or grated cheese
	Butter

Grease a pie dish and line it with half the breadcrumbs, keeping the rest for the top. Mix together all the other ingredients except the stock and butter and put into the pie dish. Pour the stock over them and then sprinkle over the breadcrumbs. Put small pieces of butter on the top and bake in the oven for ½ hour.

Savoury Rice

Cook rice slowly in stock until very tender, then put it into a shallow fireproof dish and cover with a good layer of grated cooking cheese. Bake until the top is a nice golden brown. If liked, the rice can be flavoured all through with layers of cheese, finishing with a sprinkling of cheese on the top.

Savoury Rice with Onion

Cook rice in good stock until tender. Melt a little butter, slice up a large onion and fry it until brown. Put the rice and onion in layers in a greased fireproof dish, with a pinch of mixed herbs and a little pepper and salt. Put lumps of butter or margarine on top and bake in the oven until brown (about ½ hour).

Sole Ribbons (for 2)

1 medium filleted sole	1 dessertspoonful
Beaten egg	seasoned flour
Browned bread-crumbs	Vegetable fat shorten-ing for frying
A little Cayenne pepper	

Wash and dry the fillets and skin. Cut lengthways into ¼–½-in. ribbons. Roll in seasoned flour, dip in beaten egg and coat with breadcrumbs. Fry in hot vegetable fat shortening for 3–4 minutes. Sprinkle with Cayenne and serve with potato chips.

Spaghetti with Tomatoes (for 3–4)

1 small onion	4 oz. spaghetti
1 lb. fresh cooked or canned tomatoes	Bacon bone or rinds
Tomato purée	2 oz. butter
	Salt and pepper

Put the spaghetti, bacon bone or rinds and onion into boiling water and cook for 15–20 minutes. Drain well and remove the rinds or bone and onion. Then add the tomatoes (sieved), the purée and the seasoning. Reheat in the saucepan with the butter. Serve, preferably with grated Parmesan cheese.

Stuffed Potatoes

1 large potato per person	Pepper and salt
	Grated cheese
Butter	A little milk

Wash the potatoes thoroughly, but do not peel them; dry, prick with a fork and bake in a hot oven until soft. Slit each one in half lengthwise and, with a fork, scoop out the floury part. Add to it the butter, pepper and salt, a little milk, some grated cheese and mash together. Return the mixture to the shells, sprinkle a little cheese on top and put in a hot oven or under the grill for 5–10 minutes.

NOTE: As alternative stuffings, instead of cheese, try hot green peas with a little butter; finely chopped fried onion, minced meat or bacon. Tomato purée may be used instead of the milk.

Stuffed Vegetable Marrow

1 medium-sized marrow	Sausage meat or minced meat or
Pepper and salt	veal stuffing
A little milk	Chopped parsley
Gravy	

Stand the tomatoes in a basin of boiling water for 1 or 2 minutes, remove the skins, dry, and cut in half. Put some of the tomatoes into a greased fireproof dish, then put in half the butter, a pinch of pepper and salt, and sprinkle in half the breadcrumbs and cheese. Add the rest of the tomatoes, butter, breadcrumbs and cheese, and bake in a quick oven for about 15 minutes.

(Above) Sole Ribbons—a new variation on the fried fish theme—are tasty with lemon and parsley garnish

(Right) An old and tried favourite — Macaroni Cheese, with cheese balls on the top—goes well with fairy toast

Photographs in this chapter taken at the Spry Cookery Centre

Wash and peel the marrow. If young, cut off one end and with a long-handled spoon scoop out the pips and the pulpy part. If not so young, cut lengthwise, peel and remove the seeds. Put the meat into a basin with the parsley and a little pepper and salt. Stir it together and bind with a little milk. Then put the stuffing into the marrow and either put the top on again, cover with greased paper and tie securely, or put the halves together and tie firmly in several places. Place the marrow in a tin greased with dripping or butter. Cover it with a piece of greased paper and put a tin over it. Bake in a moderate oven until the marrow is quite tender; it will take 1–1½ hours, according to the size and age of the marrow. Baste it occasionally. Serve with gravy.

Tomatoes au Gratin (for 3–4)

1 lb. tomatoes	2 heaped tablespoonfuls grated cheese
2 oz. breadcrumbs	
1 oz. butter	Pepper and salt

Vegetable Marrow au Gratin (for 3–4)

8 oz. marrow (when prepared)	1 gill water
	2 oz. butter
3 oz. grated cheese	3 oz. breadcrumbs

Wash and peel the marrow and cut it up. Simmer with 1 oz. butter and the water until tender. Put alternate layers of marrow with the liquid and cheese and breadcrumbs into a greased fireproof dish, finishing with a layer of breadcrumbs, etc. Dot with butter. Bake for about 10 minutes.

Vegetable Pie (for 4–5)

1 lb. mashed potatoes	1 lb. cooked turnips, carrots, parsnips and onion
1 oz. butter	
2 tomatoes	
¼ pint gravy or stock	Pepper and salt

Put the vegetables (except potatoes) in a greased fireproof dish in layers, pour over the gravy; season. Top with the potatoes and dot with butter. Bake for 30 minutes.

CAKES

For special parties or tea after school there's nothing quite so
popular as home-made cake—and it's nourishing too

CAKE-MAKING is one of the pleasantest forms of cookery, and nothing gives a cook a greater feeling of satisfaction than a perfectly made and perfectly baked cake.

There are three main methods used in cake-mixing:

(1) Beating the sugar and eggs together with an egg whisk until the mixture is thick and creamy, and then folding in the flour lightly. This method is used for sponge cakes and usually no shortening is needed.

(2) Beating the sugar and butter (or other fat) together until the mixture is light in colour and creamy. The longer they are beaten, the better the cake. Scrape the sides of the basin with a palette knife at intervals to ensure that all the mixture is well beaten.

   In cold weather, when the fat is very hard, the basin may be stood in warm water for a minute or two, but the butter must never be allowed to melt or become oily.

   The eggs (or the yolks only) should be beaten and added separately, the mixture being beaten hard the whole time. Add them slowly, with a little flour in between, to prevent curdling.

   The main bulk of the flour and the baking powder are added last. In some recipes the egg-whites are kept until the end, when they must be whisked stiffly enough to stay in the bowl when it is turned upside down, then folded in. This makes cakes very light.

   This method is used for all rich cakes.

(3) Rubbing the butter (or other fat) lightly into the flour with the tips of the fingers and thumb until the mixture is like fine breadcrumbs. In hot weather, rinse the hands in cold water first. The eggs and any other liquid are added at the end.

   This method is used for plain cakes, pastry and scones.

Shortening

Good margarine and/or one of the branded vegetable shortenings can be substituted for butter when necessary, with excellent results. Lard or cooking fat often successfully combine with butter or margarine.

Eggs

Preserved eggs can be used for all cakes except where the whites have to be beaten stiffly, when new-laid eggs must be used. Remember to break each egg into a cup and not straight into the mixture when one "doubtful" egg may spoil all the ingredients.

Sugar

Castor sugar should be used for biscuits and sponges, granulated for other cakes. Soft brown sugar gives fruit cakes a very good dark colour.

Flour

Never mix new flour with the old in the bin. It is best to use plain flour and add the necessary baking powder or soda. Always sieve flour and baking powder before use; the more air it contains, the lighter the cake will be.

Baking Powder

Whether bought or home-made, baking powder must be kept in a tin with a tight-fitting lid. To make it at home, put equal parts of bicarbonate of soda, cream of tartar and ground rice through a sieve seven times to get them well mixed. Put away in a tin, and stir well before using.

Dried Fruit

All dried fruit should be well cleaned before use. Put on a sieve, sprinkle with flour and rub well. This will remove many of the stalks; the fruit should then be carefully looked over. Washed fruit must be thoroughly dried before use. Raisins and dates should be stoned if necessary, and glacé cherries cut in halves or quarters.

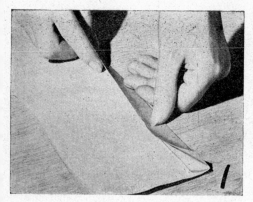

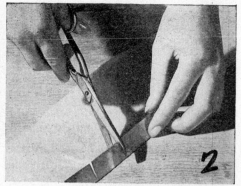

THE SECRET OF LIGHT CAKES

Give them the Air

Whether a cake is delightfully light—or sad and heavy—depends more than anything upon the amount of air and carbon dioxide it contains. Though these are not listed in the ingredients in cake recipes, you introduce air when you sieve the flour (and the more you sieve it, the more air you get into it), when you beat the eggs and, finally, when you beat the mixture (hence the need to beat really thoroughly). The equally important carbon dioxide is produced when you add either (a) baking powder, which contains a balanced mixture of alkali and acid, or (b) bicarbonate of soda combined with something acid, such as cream of tartar, treacle, sour milk, etc.

So when you make a sponge cake, which should be the lightest, airiest of all cakes, be sure to aerate the mixture as much as you possibly can—by beating the eggs well before you lightly fold in, first the

Preparing a cake tin. Cut a strip of greaseproof paper long enough to go round tin and 2 in. deeper. Fold up $\frac{1}{2}$ in. along bottom edge (1); nick with scissors (2); place in tin, pressing well against sides (3); cut a circle to fit bottom and grease them both (4); pour in cake mixture and make a well in centre before baking (5)

(A) Incorrect recipe balance gives insufficient aeration; (B) correct balance gives perfect cake

sugar and then the flour (well-sieved, of course).

Recipe Balance

Another secret of successful cake making is to follow a good recipe accurately and always watch carefully that the various ingredients are in the right proportions.

For instance, you won't make your cake lighter simply by increasing the quantity of baking powder, but only by getting the exact amount in relation to the other ingredients. The richer the cake and the more fruit it contains, the less baking powder it needs. In the case of a really rich Christmas cake, for instance, no baking powder at all should be used, since the ingredients themselves are sufficient to form the structure of the cake. For this reason, plain flour should always be used for rich cakes so that the amount of the raising agent can be varied.

The research scientists of Messrs. George Borwick & Sons, Ltd., the baking powder manufacturers, have prepared the following table showing how the quantities of baking powder should be varied **per pound of flour** with the amount of fruit in semi-rich and rich cakes:

	Semi-rich
No fruit	2½ level teaspoonfuls
8 oz. fruit	1½ level teaspoonfuls
12 oz. fruit	1¼ level teaspoonfuls
16 oz. fruit	1 level teaspoonful

	Rich
No fruit	2 level teaspoonfuls
8 oz. fruit	1¼ level teaspoonfuls
12 oz. fruit	¾ level teaspoonful
16 oz. fruit	No baking powder

Provided you keep the balance of the ingredients the same, you can adapt and improve standard recipes to please yourself.

Chief points of recipe balance that must be remembered are these: an egg is a toughening agent and fat a shortening one, so they must stay in step. Increase eggs and fat, remember to reduce baking powder. If you reduce the egg content, you must also reduce the quantity of fat, or the cake may collapse. If you increase the fat to make the cake richer, you must also increase the egg content and reduce the baking powder.

When about to Make a Cake

(1) Light the oven in good time so that it is hot enough when the cake is ready to go in. Until you get to know your own oven, allow about 10 minutes for a gas oven, 15 minutes for electric.

(2) Prepare your cake tin. To do this, melt a little lard or olive oil and paint the sides and bottom of the tin well (keep a pastry brush for the purpose); cut a strip of greaseproof paper to go round the side and about 2 in. deeper so that it will stick up above the top of the tin; fold up ½ in. at the bottom edge and nick all round with scissors (this will make it lie flat at the bottom of the tin); cut greaseproof paper to fit the bottom of the tin, grease all the paper, and press down well. The cake will not be a good shape unless the paper fits neatly. Fill tins no more than two-thirds full to allow for rising.

For rich fruit cakes, which have to be in the oven a long time, put a double layer of paper, greasing the first one well.

Small crinkly paper cases or well-greased tins can be used for little cakes.

Alternatively, you can put the tin or tins, unlined and ungreased, into the oven to get hot. Take out when the cake mixture is quite ready. Turn it

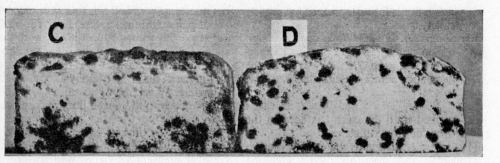

(C) Incorrect balance gives coarse texture, flat top and fallen fruit; (D) the cake as it should be

into the hot tin and return imediately to the oven.

(3) Next, weigh the ingredients carefully. Then make your cake.

Cake-baking

To the inexperienced cook, this is the most difficult part of cake-making. If the oven is too hot, a hard crust forms on the cake and the inside cannot rise properly; if it is too slow, the cake becomes dry and does not rise properly.

As a general guide, here is a chart of the required heats:

Bread, scones and pastry . . .	450° F.
Small cakes and Swiss roll . . .	400° F.
Genoese, Madeira, sponges . . .	370° F.
Small fruit cakes	340° F.
Large, rich, fruit cakes . . .	320° F.
Biscuits	330° F.

In the recipes for sandwiches, small cakes, etc., that follow in this section, the time has been given. In the case of larger cakes, however, this varies so much according to the size of the tin used that it is not possible to be precise. Remember that the thicker the cake, the longer it will take to cook. When a large cake has risen and begun to set on the top, the heat can be lowered a little, but cakes should never be moved once in the oven and the door should be closed gently. Sponge cakes are best left alone.

Some ovens are apt to burn cakes at the top or bottom, even when the heat is correct. If this happens, put some kitchen salt or silver sand on a baking sheet under the cakes. Water in the bottom of a gas oven will help to prevent burning and prevent the cake getting too dry.

To test whether a cake is cooked, touch the top lightly with the tip of the finger. If the cake is done, the surface should spring back once the finger is removed. If you hear a little crunch as you touch the cake, it is not quite done. To test a large, rich, fruit cake, it is best to put a heated fine-steel knitting needle right through the middle. Then draw it out carefully. If the cake is done, the needle will be quite clean.

When the cake is done, lift it out of the tin by the paper, or turn it gently on to the hand and put it on a rack or sieve, out of the draught, to cool. If it sticks, stand the tin on a damp cloth for 10 minutes and it will come out easily. When quite cold, put it in a tin until wanted.

Cake Failings and How to Avoid Them

Everybody makes occasional mistakes and nobody achieves perfection without a good deal of practice, so there is no need to be disheartened if your first attempts at cake-making are not absolutely up to your own self-imposed standards. Try again—and again—carefully following the basic rules already given. And here are some of the misfortunes that beset the cake-maker, with their probable causes:

(1) *Fruit sinking* to the bottom is nearly always due to too much baking powder, occasionally to too much liquid making the batter too slack to support the fruit. Use plain (not self-raising) flour, and measure the baking powder very carefully according to the richness of the cake and the amount of fruit it contains (see table of baking powder quantities opposite). If you use an electric mixer, over-creaming of the fat and sugar is a possible contributory cause, but not if you cream by hand.

(2) *Heavy cake* is usually the result of too

187

much flour, fat or liquid, or baking too slowly.

(3) *Sinking in the middle* is usually a sign of too much raising agent in the mixture, too hot an oven, or slamming the oven door before the cake has had time to set.

NOTE: The door should never be opened until the cake has been in the oven for 15 minutes.

(4) *Coarse texture* may be due to the fat, sugar and eggs not being creamed enough at the beginning, too much baking powder, or too slow an oven.

(5) *Excessive dryness* is often the result of too stiff a mixture or baking at too low a temperature or for too long.

Icing Cakes: For recipes and instructions see separate chapter.

PLAIN CAKES

Chocolate Cake

6 oz. plain flour	Vanilla essence
1 oz. cocoa	4 oz. sugar
1 teaspoonful baking powder	2 eggs
	Milk or water to mix
4 oz. margarine	Pinch of salt

Grease a 6-in. cake tin. Cream the margarine and sugar until white and fluffy. Beat in the eggs gradually. Stir in the sieved flour, cocoa, baking powder and pinch of salt with enough liquid to make a soft dropping consistency. Add a few drops of vanilla essence to flavour. Bake in a moderate oven for ¾–1 hour.

Chocolate Coconut Cake

1½ oz. desiccated coconut	4 oz. plain flour
¼ pint milk	1 level dessertspoonful cocoa
4 oz. margarine	Pinch of salt
6 oz. sugar	1 teaspoonful baking powder
2 eggs	

Soak the coconut in the milk for ½ hour. Cream fat and sugar, add the lightly beaten eggs and then the coconut and milk. Stir in the well-sieved dry ingredients, mix well and turn into a greased lined tin 10 in. by 8 in. Bake in a moderate oven for 30–40 minutes. When cold, decorate the top as desired, or cut into fingers.

Chocolate Swiss Roll

2 eggs	1 tablespoonful warm water
1½ oz. flour	
2 oz. castor sugar	1 oz. grated sweetened chocolate
1 teaspoonful baking powder	

Grease a Swiss roll tin, line with greaseproof paper and then grease the paper well. Separate the whites from the yolks of the eggs. Beat the yolks and the sugar together until the mixture is creamy. Then add the warm water, and immediately after that the chocolate. Whisk the whites stiffly, and add alternately with the sieved flour and baking powder, folding them in lightly. Put the mixture in the tin and bake in a hot oven for about 12 minutes. Turn out on to a piece of greaseproof paper well sprinkled with icing sugar, trim the edges and roll it up. Then put it on a rack to cool.

When quite cold, unroll and fill with whipped cream or vanilla butter icing.

Coconut Cake

6 oz. flour	3 oz. desiccated coconut
3 oz. butter	nut
4 oz. castor sugar	1 small teaspoonful baking powder
A little milk	
2 small eggs	

Cream the butter and sugar, and add the beaten eggs gradually. Then add the flour, baking powder and the coconut and lastly, a little milk. Put the mixture into a prepared cake tin and bake in a moderate oven for about 1¼ hours.

Cornflour Cake

4 oz. cornflour	1 teaspoonful baking powder
1 oz. flour	
2 oz. castor sugar	1 egg
2 oz. butter	A little milk

Cream the butter and sugar, and add the egg beaten with a little milk. Then add the sieved cornflour, flour and baking powder. Put into a prepared cake tin and bake in a moderate oven for about 1 hour.

Eggless Cake

8 oz. plain flour	3 oz. sugar
3 oz. margarine	1 teaspoonful vanilla essence
Pinch of salt	
4 teaspoonfuls baking powder	About ¼ pint milk and water

Mix flour, baking powder and salt. Rub in the fat, add the sugar and vanilla and mix to a dropping consistency with the milk and water. Turn into a greased 7-in. tin and bake in a moderate oven for ¾ to 1 hour.

Honey Cake

8 oz. flour	3 oz. sugar
4 oz. honey	1 teaspoonful baking powder
2 eggs	
3 oz. butter	

Cream the butter and sugar, and add the beaten eggs gradually. Beat in the honey and, lastly, add the sieved flour and baking powder. Put into a prepared shallow cake tin and bake in a moderate oven for about 45 minutes.

Madeira Cake

8 oz. flour	1 teaspoonful baking
5 oz. butter	powder
5 oz. sugar	Grated rind of a
4 eggs	lemon or orange

Cream the butter and sugar until white and fluffy, and add the beaten eggs gradually, alternating with the flour, baking powder and fruit rind all sieved together. If the mixture is too dry, moisten to dropping consistency with a little milk. Put into a prepared cake tin and bake in a moderate oven for about 1¼ hours. After about 25 minutes put two pieces of lemon peel on top.

Marble Cake

6 oz. self-raising flour	Pinch of baking
4 oz. margarine	powder
4 oz. sugar	Pinch of salt
2 eggs	Vanilla essence
¼ oz. cocoa	Green colouring
Milk or water to mix	

Grease a 6-in. cake tin. Cream the margarine and sugar until light and fluffy. Beat in the eggs gradually, then stir in the sieved flour and salt, add vanilla essence to flavour and enough milk or water to make a soft dropping consistency. Take out one-third of the mixture, place on a saucer and colour green. Take out half of remaining mixture, place on saucer. Add cocoa and pinch of baking powder, together with liquid. Using teaspoons, place alternate colours in cake tin. Bake in a moderate oven for ¾–1 hour.

Sponge Cake

3 eggs	½ teaspoonful baking
4 oz. castor sugar	powder
4 oz. flour	

Prepare a tin by first brushing it over thoroughly with melted butter. Then mix equal small quantities of sieved flour and castor sugar; put it into the tin and shake the tin well until both sides and bottom are well coated. Then shake out any superfluous flour and sugar. Beat the eggs and sugar together until the mixture is thick and creamy (quite ½ hour). Then fold in the sieved flour and baking powder very lightly, using a metal spoon.

Put the mixture into the tin and bake *at once* in a hot oven for 20 minutes. Do not touch the mixture once it is in the tin.

Chocolate Madeleines are coated with melted jam, desiccated coconut and grated chocolate

Swiss Roll

3 *eggs*	*Small pinch of baking*
2½ *oz. flour*	*powder*
3½ *oz. castor sugar*	*Icing sugar and jam*

Grease a Swiss roll tin, line with grease-proof paper and then grease the paper well. Beat the eggs and sugar together until the mixture is thick and creamy, then lightly fold in the flour and the baking powder, sieved well together, using a metal spoon. Pour the mixture into the tin and bake in a hot oven for about 10 minutes. While it is cooking, get ready a piece of greaseproof paper a little larger than the tin and sprinkle it well with icing sugar. Also heat some jam. Turn the cake on to the paper, trim the edges and spread rather thinly with the hot jam. Roll up quickly.

Vanilla Cake

4 *oz. butter*	½ *teacupful milk*
2 *eggs*	6 *oz. sugar*
1 *teaspoonful baking*	12 *oz. flour*
powder	*Vanilla essence*

Separate the yolks and whites of the eggs. Beat the butter to a cream, then stir in the sugar and the well-beaten egg-yolks. Beat the mixture well, then fold in the egg-whites whisked stiff. Sift flour and baking powder together and stir gradually into the mixture, adding the milk and a few drops of vanilla essence. Bake in a well-greased tin in a moderate oven for about 1 hour.

Victoria Sandwich

2 *eggs, their weight in*	¼ *teaspoonful baking*
butter, sugar and	*powder*
flour	*Jam for filling*

Cream the butter, add sugar and cream well again. Add the beaten eggs gradually and then the flour and baking powder, well sieved together. Put the mixture into two greased sandwich tins and bake in a fairly quick oven for 20 minutes. When cold, spread with raspberry jam and put together.

SMALL CAKES

Chocolate Buns

4 *oz. butter*	*Pinch of baking*
2 *oz. grated chocolate*	*powder*
2 *tablespoonfuls milk*	4 *oz. castor sugar*
2 *eggs*	3 *oz. flour*
	Pinch of salt

Cream the butter and sugar, and add the grated chocolate dissolved in the warmed milk. Beat in the eggs slowly, then add the flour, baking powder and salt sieved together. Put the mixture into greased bun tins and bake in a hot oven for 15–20 minutes. Either leave plain, or ice with chocolate glacé icing, and decorate with cherries and angelica or desiccated coconut.

Chocolate Cream Crunchies

6 *oz. self-raising flour*	*Vanilla essence*
2 *oz. cornflour*	6 *oz. margarine*
2 *oz. cornflakes*	3 *oz. sugar*
1 *oz. drinking choco-*	1 *egg*
late	*Pinch of salt*

Cream the margarine and sugar, then gradually beat in the egg. Stir in sieved dry ingredients, vanilla, and the cornflakes. If soft, leave to become firm. Mould into balls the size of walnuts, place on a greased tin and bake in a moderate oven for about 15 minutes. When cold, sandwich together with suitable filling, such as peppermint butter cream.

Chocolate Lemon Buns

7 *oz. flour*	*Lemon curd*
1 *teaspoonful baking*	1 *oz. cocoa*
powder	3 *oz. margarine*
4 *oz. sugar*	*Milk to mix*

Rub the fat into the sieved flour. Add the cocoa, sugar and baking powder. Mix to a stiff dough with milk. Turn on to floured board and shape into a sausage of 2-in. diameter. Cut into rounds ½ in. thick and neaten with a knife. Place on greased baking sheet and make hole in centre of each with thumb. Fill each hole with lemon curd, sprinkle with sugar and bake in a hot oven for 15–20 minutes. (These quantities make about 14 buns.)

Chocolate Macaroon Tartlets

Short pastry	3 *oz. ground almonds*
1 *oz. grated chocolate*	4 *oz. castor sugar*
1 *egg*	*Vanilla essence*

Roll out pastry, cut into rounds with a crinkly cutter and line greased patty pans with it. Mix together the ground almonds and the castor sugar. Beat the egg and add it to the mixture. Melt the chocolate and add with a few drops of vanilla essence. Put some of the mixture into each of the patty pans and bake in a fairly quick oven for 15–20 minutes.

Cream or butter icing can be used to sandwich together these dainty Chocolate Shells

Chocolate Madeleines

2 eggs
2 oz. castor sugar
2 oz. self-raising flour
Vanilla essence
¼ oz. cocoa

1½ oz. margarine
Pinch of salt
Desiccated coconut,
grated chocolate
and jam

Grease about nine dariole moulds. Melt the fat. Whisk eggs and sugar until thick, add vanilla. Lightly fold in sieved flour, cocoa and salt alternately with the melted fat. Quickly half-fill the moulds and bake in a hot oven for approximately 11 minutes. Turn on to a wire tray to cool. Decorate by coating with a little melted jam and rolling in desiccated coconut and grated chocolate.

Chocolate Melting Moments

2 oz. margarine
1 egg
3½ oz. self-raising
flour

2 oz. sugar
½ oz. cocoa
Rolled oats

Cream the fat and the sugar until light and fluffy. Gradually beat in the egg. Stir in cocoa and flour. Damp hands and roll mixture into walnut-sized balls. Toss in the oats. Place on greased tray, flatten slightly and bake in a moderate oven for 15–20 minutes. (These quantities make about 9 cakes.)

Chocolate Shells

3 oz. fat
1 small egg
1 oz. cocoa

3 oz. castor sugar
4 oz. self-raising flour
Whipped cream

Cream fat and sugar until light and fluffy. Gradually add the lightly beaten egg, then stir in the sieved flour and cocoa. Using a forcing bag with a star nozzle, pipe small shell shapes on to a greased baking sheet. Bake in a moderately hot oven for 10–15 minutes. Cool on a wire tray and sandwich together with cream. (These quantities make about 6 cakes.)

Chocolate Swiss Tarts

4 oz. margarine
3 oz. self-raising flour
Vanilla essence
1 oz. icing sugar

1 oz. cocoa
Whole nuts for
decoration

Cream the fat and sugar until light and fluffy. Add the essence and mix in the sieved flour and cocoa until thoroughly blended. Using a large star pipe, force into baking cases with a spiral motion. Place nut in centre of each and bake on a baking sheet in a moderate oven for about 30 minutes. (These quantities make about 6 tarts.)

Coconut Buns

6 oz. flour	2 oz. desiccated coco-
1 egg	nut
2 oz. castor sugar	¼ teaspoonful baking
1½ oz. butter	powder

Rub the butter into the sieved flour and baking powder, add the sugar and then the coconut. Beat the egg and add it gradually. Take two forks and put the mixture in rocky drops on a greased baking sheet. Bake for 10 minutes in a fairly hot oven.

Gingerbread Slab

12 oz. self-raising flour	8 oz. treacle
	3 oz. chopped peel
4 oz. butter	4 oz. sugar
3½ oz. preserved ginger	½ gill milk
	1 teaspoonful bicar-
2 eggs	bonate of soda
½ oz. ground ginger	

Sieve the flour and mix with sugar and ginger. Rub in the butter, then add the peel and preserved ginger cut in small pieces. Beat the eggs into the treacle and add to the mixture. Dissolve the soda in the warmed milk and add. Then mix all well together. Put the mixture in a flat tin and bake in a moderate oven for about 45 minutes. Cut up when cold.

Orange Buns

4 oz. butter	½ teaspoonful baking
4 oz. sugar	powder
4½ oz. flour	Grated rind of an
2 eggs	orange

Beat the butter and sugar to a cream, add the orange rind, then the beaten eggs gradually, and lastly the flour and baking powder. Put the mixture into small, round, greased tins and bake for about 12 minutes in a fairly hot oven. Either leave plain or ice with orange glacé icing and decorate with crystallised orange slices, or strips of angelica and crystallised flower petals.

Queen Cakes

2 oz. butter	1 oz. sultanas
2 oz. sugar	1 egg
3 oz. flour	Pinch of baking
1 oz. cherries (or peel)	powder

Cream the butter and sugar until light and fluffy, add the beaten egg and then the dry ingredients. Bake in a hot oven, in well-greased small fancy tins or in crinkly paper cases, for 10 minutes.

NOTE: Finish off either by scattering a few chopped almonds on the top or putting half a cherry on each before baking; or, when cold, ice with white glacé icing and decorate with a cherry and a little angelica.

Ring Doughnuts (see also Bread chapter)

4 oz. flour	1 teaspoonful baking
1 oz. castor sugar	powder
1 oz. butter	Pinch of spice
1 egg	A little milk

Rub the butter into the flour, then sieve in the sugar, baking powder and spice. Beat the egg and add it with enough milk to make a light stiff dough. Put the dough on a floured board and roll it out to about ½ in. in thickness. Cut into rounds and remove the centres with a smaller cutter, leaving the ring about ½ in. in width. Fry in deep fat until a good brown and dredge with castor sugar.

Rock Cakes

12 oz. flour	Milk (if required)
1 teaspoonful baking	4 oz. currants
powder	1 oz. chopped peel
3 oz. butter	3 oz. sugar
1 egg	Good pinch of spice
Nutmeg	

Rub the butter into the sieved flour. Add all the dry ingredients. Beat the egg and add it and a little milk if necessary, but the mixture must be dry. Stir with a spoon, keeping it rough. Put little heaps on a floured tin and bake in a moderate oven for 15 minutes.

Yorkshire Parkin

8 oz. self-raising flour	1 oz. chopped peel
8 oz. oatmeal	4 oz. butter
8 oz. treacle	1 teaspoonful ground
4 oz. sugar	ginger
1 egg	2 teaspoonfuls bicar-
1 gill milk	bonate of soda
Pinch of salt	

Rub the butter into the sieved flour, then add the rest of the dry ingredients, the treacle, milk and beaten egg. Mix well together. Put the mixture in a prepared shallow tin and cook in a slow oven for about 2 hours. When cool, cut into squares.

NOTE: Parkin will keep for some time in an airtight tin.

ICED CAKES

For icing recipes, see separate chapter.

Battenberg Cake

6 oz. margarine	½ teaspoonful baking
6 oz. sugar	powder
6 oz. plain flour	Pinch of salt
3 eggs	1 oz. cocoa
Vanilla essence	Milk to mix
Lemon curd or jam	

Grease and line two 4 in. × 8 in. loaf tins. Cream margarine and sugar until light and frothy, then beat in the eggs, a little at a time. Add the dry ingredients, except cocoa, and enough milk to make a soft dropping consistency. Divide the mixture in half, adding cocoa to one and vanilla essence to the other. Bake in separate tins in a moderate oven for about 20–25 minutes.

When cool, cut each cake in half, lengthways. Sandwich a vanilla strip to a chocolate strip, using lemon curd or jam, put a thin layer of lemon curd or jam on top and then the remaining two strips, so that the vanilla strip is on top of the chocolate and the chocolate on top of the vanilla. Cover all over with almond paste, mark out a trellis pattern on the top and, if liked, decorate with glacé cherries and small pieces of angelica.

NOTE: A few drops of cochineal can be used instead of the cocoa to give an alternative colour scheme, or a vegetable colouring chosen according to taste.

Caramel Gâteau

2 eggs	2 teaspoonfuls cocoa
3 oz. sugar	2½ oz. plain flour
Pinch of salt	

For the filling

2 oz. butter or margarine	3 oz. icing sugar
	Vanilla essence
1 level tablespoonful cocoa	1–2 teaspoonfuls milk or water

For the icing

4 oz. brown sugar	Pinch of cream of
2 tablespoonfuls water	tartar
	1 small egg-white

Grease and line three 6-in. sandwich tins. Whisk eggs and sugar together until foamy, then lightly fold in the sieved flour and salt. Divide the mixture into three equal parts and add cocoa to one part. Bake in hot oven for 10 minutes. Cool on a wire tray and sandwich the cakes together, the chocolate one in the middle, with butter icing made by mixing the above ingredients.

To make the caramel icing, put the sugar and water into a strong saucepan with a pinch of cream of tartar and boil for 4 minutes, then pour gradually on to the lightly whisked egg-white and continue to whisk until thick. Pour over the cake and allow to set. Decorate with chocolate drops or as desired.

Battenberg Cake, in two colours and coated with almond paste, is a long-established favourite

Cherry Trellis Cake

3 eggs   3 oz. plain flour
3 oz. castor sugar   Pinch of salt
    1 oz. cocoa

For the butter cream

3 oz. margarine   2 oz. glacé cherries
4½ oz. icing sugar 2 teaspoonfuls milk
    Vanilla essence

Grease and line three 6-in. sandwich tins. Whisk eggs and sugar together until thick and foamy. Lightly fold in sieved flour, cocoa and salt. Divide equally between the three tins and bake in a hot oven for 10 minutes. Cool on a wire tray, then sandwich the cakes together with cherry butter cream, made by creaming the margarine and adding the other ingredients. Coat the sides with plain butter cream and roll in sugar. Decorate the top in trellis design and add halved cherries.

Chocolate Cake (Rich)

6 oz. flour   Vanilla essence
6 oz. sugar   Pinch of salt
6 oz. margarine 1 teaspoonful baking
3 eggs   powder
    1½ oz. cocoa

Grease and line a 7-in. cake tin. Separate egg-yolks from whites. Cream the fat and sugar until light and fluffy, add the egg-yolks gradually, stir in the sieved dry ingredients and add flavouring. Then, quickly, add stiffly beaten egg-whites. Bake in a moderate oven (middle shelf) for 1¼ hours. Cool, and decorate with chocolate icing.

Chocolate Cakes

3 oz. sugar   5 oz. self-raising flour
2½ oz. margarine ½ oz. cocoa
1 egg   Pinch of salt
A few drops of vanilla 3 tablespoonfuls milk
  essence

Grease and line a Swiss roll tin 9½ in. × 7 in. Cream the margarine and sugar until light and fluffy, then beat in the egg gradually. Add dry ingredients, milk to mix to a smooth dropping consistency, and vanilla. Bake in a moderate oven for 20–25 minutes. Cool before icing, then cut into slices.

Chocolate Gâteau

2 eggs   ¾ oz. cocoa
2 oz. sugar   1½ oz. melted butter
2 oz. plain flour   or margarine
Pinch of salt   Cream and jam

Grease and line a Swiss roll tin 11 in. × 7 in. Whisk the eggs and sugar together un-

til light and foamy, then lightly fold in the sieved flour, cocoa and salt alternately, with the melted fat. Pour quickly into the tin and bake in hot oven for about 8 minutes. Turn on to a wire tray to cool. When cool, cut into four and sandwich the pieces together with cream. Coat the sides with cream or jam and nuts or chocolate vermicelli. Ice the top with chocolate icing and decorate as desired.

Chocolate Japs

2 egg-whites   Small pinch of cream
8 oz. castor sugar   of tartar
   4 oz. ground almonds

Whisk egg-whites and cream of tartar until very thick, then whisk in 4 oz. sugar. Mix in the remaining sugar and ground almonds, blending thoroughly. Using a plain ½-in. nozzle, pipe rounds on to a greased, floured baking sheet and bake in a moderate oven for about 25 minutes. Allow to cool, then, using a 2-in. plain cutter, cut into circles. Sandwich together with chocolate butter icing, spread the sides with butter icing and coat with chocolate vermicelli or crumbs made from the cake trimmings. Cover the tops with icing and decorate as desired.

Chocolate Log

2 oz. plain flour   2 eggs
2 oz. sugar   1 oz. cocoa
   Pinch of salt

Grease and line a Swiss roll tin. Whisk the eggs and sugar together until thick and foamy, then lightly fold in the sieved flour, cocoa and salt. Bake in hot oven for about 7–8 minutes. Turn on to sugared paper over a damp cloth and roll up. When cold, unroll, spread with butter icing and roll up again. Cover the outside of the cake with chocolate butter icing and mark with a fork so that it looks like a log.

Chocolate Macaroon Fancies

4 oz. ground almonds 4 oz. castor sugar
1 oz. margarine   2 egg-whites
 (melted)   Blanched almonds
   2½ oz. cocoa

Grease a baking sheet, or line it with rice paper. Whip the egg-whites until stiff, then fold in the dry ingredients and the margarine. Place in small heaps, or pipe, on baking sheet, and bake in a slow to moderate oven until firm (about 15 minutes). Cool on wire tray, then sandwich together in

Caramel Gâteau is a three-layer sponge—the middle layer chocolate-flavoured
—filled with butter icing

twos with butter cream and coat tops with chocolate glacé icing. Put a split blanched almond on top of each. (These quantities make 14 macaroons.)

Chocolate Mushroom Cake

2 oz. margarine	Milk to mix
2 oz. sugar	3 oz. self-raising flour
1 egg	½ oz. cocoa
Pinch of salt	Apricot jam

Grease and line a 6-in. sandwich-tin, preferably one with sloping sides. Cream fat and sugar together until white and fluffy, then add beaten egg gradually, beating well in between each addition. Stir in the sieved dry ingredients, keeping the mixture a soft dropping consistency by adding milk as necessary. Bake in a moderate oven for 20–25 minutes, turn out and cool on a wire tray. When cold, brush the bottom and sides with a little melted apricot jam. Make almond icing, set aside a small piece for the "stalk," then roll the remainder into a circle to fit the bottom and sides of cake and press into place. Spread the top with chocolate butter icing, mark with a fork to look like mushroom gills, and place "stalk" in position.

Chocolate Sandwich Cake

Proceed as for Chocolate Cake (see Plain Cakes) but bake, in two 6-in. greased sandwich tins, in a moderate oven for 20 minutes. When cool, sandwich together with chocolate butter icing, spread butter icing smoothly over the top and decorate with a piped border, or as desired.

Alternative Flavours

(1) Mocha Cake—add 1 tablespoonful coffee essence or strong black coffee.
(2) Chocolate Date Cake—add 3 oz. chopped dates.
(3) Chocolate Coconut Cake—add 1 oz. desiccated coconut.

Chocolate Walnut Cake

4 oz. margarine	4 oz. self-raising flour
4 oz. sugar	2 eggs
2 oz. cup chocolate	Pinch of salt
	Milk to mix

Grease and line a 7-in. cake tin. Heat oven to moderate and use middle shelf. Cream the margarine and sugar until white and fluffy, then add well-beaten eggs gradually. Fold in sieved flour and salt and, lastly, add the chocolate. If necessary, add a little milk to make a soft dropping consistency. Bake for 35–40 minutes, until well risen and firm to the touch, and turn on to a wire tray to cool. Cover the top with chocolate glacé icing and decorate with walnuts.

Coffee Cake

2 oz. butter	1¼ teaspoonfuls bak-
3 oz. brown sugar	ing powder
6 oz. flour	1 dessertspoonful
1 egg and 1 egg-yolk	coffee essence

For the sauce

¼ pint milk	3 oz. castor or granu-
	lated sugar

Put the milk and white sugar in a pan, heat until the sugar is dissolved, and leave to cool.

Cream the butter and brown sugar, add the beaten eggs gradually, and beat in well. Fold in the flour and baking powder, add the sauce and, lastly, the coffee essence. Bake in a fairly quick oven for about 1 hour.

Ice on top with coffee glacé icing or coffee butter icing; or cut the cake across once or twice and fill with coffee butter icing and ice all over with coffee glacé icing. Decorate with walnuts. If coffee butter icing is used for the top, put a little in a forcing bag with a rose squeezer and pipe designs on the top.

Coffee Nougatine

Make a coffee cake as above and, when it is cold, cut it open and fill with coffee butter icing. Spread the butter icing all over the cake as smoothly as possible and scatter chopped browned almonds over it.

Genoese Cake

4 oz. butter	¼ teaspoonful baking
4 oz. sugar	powder
2 eggs	4½ oz. flour
½ oz. ground rice	Jam

Cream the butter and sugar until light and fluffy. Then add the beaten eggs gradually and beat well. Put in the flour, ground rice and baking powder and, when it is well mixed, turn into a prepared tin and bake in a fairly quick oven for about 1 hour. When cold, cut in half and put a layer of either apricot, raspberry or strawberry jam in the middle and ice the top with meringue icing flavoured with a little sieved jam and coloured to match the jam.

Genoese Slab for Small Iced Cakes

4 eggs	3 oz. flour
4 oz. castor sugar	Pinch of baking
2 oz. melted butter	powder

Beat the eggs and sugar with a whisk over hot water until the mixture is thick and creamy. Then whisk until cold. Add the sieved flour, baking powder and melted butter. Put the mixture into a greased, lined flat tin and smooth down. The mixture should not be more than ½ in. deep before it is cooked. Bake in a hot oven for 15–20 minutes.

When the slab is cold, turn it upside-down and trim the edges. Beat up meringue icing, flavour and colour as desired, and spread it smoothly over the slab. With a sharp knife, cut into strips of suitable size and cut each strip into different shapes— diamonds, triangles, squares and fingers. Do this as quickly as possible or the icing will begin to set and will crack. Decorate according to taste.

Alternatively, cut the cake into strips before icing, and ice the strips in different colours.

If liked, some of the slab can be cut through and filled with jam. Scatter icing sugar on the top and cut into squares.

Another alternative is to flavour the slab with orange rind and ice it with orange glacé icing.

Hungarian Cake

6 oz. self-raising flour	3 eggs
5 oz. castor sugar	2 teaspoonfuls strong
4 oz. margarine	black coffee
Pinch of salt	A little milk

Grease and line an 8-in. cake tin. Cream the margarine and sugar until light and fluffy, and beat in the eggs gradually. Stir in dry ingredients and the coffee, with a little milk if necessary to make a dropping consistency. Bake in a moderate oven for 1¼ hours. When cool, split across and sandwich together with chocolate butter. Ice with chocolate glacé icing.

Neapolitan Cake

5 oz. margarine	A little milk if
5 oz. sugar	necessary
2 eggs	Glacé and butter
8 oz. plain flour	icings
1 teaspoonful baking	Nuts
powder	Cherries
	Angelica

Hungarian Cake, right, is a coffee-flavoured sponge with chocolate icing

For Christmas, a Chocolate Log made like a Swiss Roll looks seasonable and attractive

For colouring

1 *dessertspoonful cocoa*	*Cochineal*

Cream margarine and sugar until light and fluffy, beat in eggs and fold in sieved flour and baking powder. Mix with milk to a soft dropping consistency. Divide into three portions and colour one with the cocoa and another with the cochineal. Put into three well-greased sandwich tins and bake in a moderate oven for 15–20 minutes. Turn out on to a wire tray and, when cool, sandwich together with butter icing and coat with glacé icing. Decorate as desired with nuts, cherries and angelica.

Orange Cake

5 oz. butter	$\frac{1}{2}$ teaspoonful baking
6 oz. sugar	powder
6 oz. flour	3 eggs
	1 orange

Beat the sugar and butter to a cream and add the beaten eggs, then the grated orange rind. Fold in the flour and baking powder, sieved together. Put into a prepared cake tin and bake in a fairly quick oven for about 1 hour.

When cool, ice with orange glacé icing. One or two fillings of orange curd can be put in if desired. Decorate with crystallised orange slices.

Orange Sandwich

2 *eggs and their weight in butter, sugar and flour*	$\frac{1}{4}$ *teaspoonful baking powder*
	Grated rind of $\frac{1}{2}$ orange

Beat the butter and sugar to a cream, add the beaten eggs, then the orange rind and, lastly, the sieved flour and baking powder. Put into two greased sandwich tins and bake in a fairly quick oven for 20 minutes. When cool, but not cold, spread orange glacé icing on both pieces of sandwich and put them together. When the sandwich is completely cold and the icing has set, ice the top with orange glacé icing and decorate with crystallised orange slices and angelica.

197

Queen Mary's Birthday Cake

6 egg-yolks   2 oz. melted butter
4 oz. castor sugar   2 egg-whites
3 oz. flour

For the chocolate ganache filling
½ pint cream   8 oz. grated choco-
6 oz. sugar   late

Whisk together the egg-yolks, whites and sugar in a bowl over hot water until light and thick. Lightly stir in the melted butter and sieved flour, pour the mixture into two prepared round cake tins and bake in a moderate oven for about 30 minutes. Turn out and leave on a wire tray to cool.

To make the filling.—Cook the cream, sugar and chocolate together in a heavy saucepan. Leave for 1 hour to cool, then cut each of the cakes across in half and spread with the ganache so that you have a four-layer sandwich. Coat the cake with the remainder of the ganache, which by this stage has almost set.

Tiger Cakes

4 oz. flour   4 oz. margarine
½ oz. castor sugar   A little water

For the decorations
Caramel
4 oz. loaf sugar   ¼ gill water

Mocha icing
Coffee flavoured   Chopped nuts
butter cream

Rub the fat into the flour and add sugar. Mix to a stiff paste with a little water, then roll out ¼ in. thick and cut into small rounds. Place on a greased tray and bake in a moderate oven until pale brown. When cool, sandwich together with mocha icing, coat sides also with mocha icing and roll in chopped nuts. Pipe icing round the top edge of each cake. Make caramel by dissolving sugar slowly in water and when clear boiling until golden colour. Put a little caramel on top of each cake. (Quantities given make about 9 cakes.)

Walnut or Hazelnut Cake

4½ oz. butter   3 eggs
6 oz. sugar   ¾ teaspoonful baking
7½ oz. flour   powder
2¼ oz. chopped wal-   ¾ teaspoonful salt
nuts (or hazelnuts)   Milk

Cream the butter and sugar until light and fluffy, and gradually add the beaten eggs. Put all the dry ingredients together and add them to the mixture. Lastly, add the milk. Put into a prepared cake tin and bake in a fairly quick oven for about 1¼ hours. Ice all over, or just on top, with white meringue icing.

CAKES THAT CAN BE ICED OR PLAIN

Cherry Cake

8 oz. flour   1 teaspoonful baking
4 oz. sugar   powder
4 oz. butter   4 oz. cherries
2 eggs   1 oz. chopped
A little milk   almonds

Cream the butter and sugar, and add the beaten eggs gradually. Cut the cherries in half and add them with the almonds. Then put in the flour and baking powder sieved together and, lastly, a little milk. Put the mixture into a prepared tin and bake in a moderate oven for about 1¼ hours. If desired, ice with white meringue icing and decorate with cherries and angelica.

Golden Cake

3 oz. butter or mar-   6 oz. self-raising flour
garine   ½ gill milk
3 egg-yolks   ¼ teaspoonful vanilla
Pinch of salt   essence or grated
6 oz. castor sugar   rind of orange

Cream fat and sugar until fluffy. Beat in egg-yolks, one at a time. Sift dry ingredients and mix in alternately with the milk and essence. Bake for 1 hour in a moderate oven. This cake is equally good eaten as it is or iced with American frosting or orange icing, according to the flavouring used.

Pineapple Cake

6 oz. flour   1 oz. glacé pineapple
2 oz. butter   cubes
3 oz. sugar   ½ teaspoonful baking
1 egg   powder
A little milk

Cream the butter and sugar, and add the beaten egg. Then mix in the sieved flour and baking powder, a little milk and, lastly, the pineapple cut in small pieces. Put the mixture into a prepared cake tin and bake in a fairly quick oven for about 1 hour. If desired, ice with pineapple glacé icing and put in a pineapple filling.

Preserved Ginger Cake

6 oz. butter	4 eggs
6 oz. sugar	4 oz. preserved ginger
10 oz. flour	4 oz. mixed peel
1 teaspoonful baking powder	½ teaspoonful ground ginger
Rind of ½ lemon	

Cream the butter and sugar, and add the beaten eggs gradually. Sieve the flour and baking powder, and add the peel and ginger chopped small, the grated lemon rind and the ground ginger. Then add all these to the mixture and mix them in well. Put into a prepared cake tin and bake in a fairly quick oven for about 1¼ hours. If desired, ice with white meringue icing and decorate with preserved ginger and angelica.

PARTY GATEAUX

Banana Shortcake

Plain round sponge cake	2–3 teaspoonfuls sugar
Small carton of double cream	2 or 3 ripe bananas
	1 egg-white (optional)
A little grated orange peel	

Whip the cream with the sugar and orange peel and, if desired, add a stiffly beaten egg-white (this makes the cream fluffier, and also makes it go further). Cut the sponge cake right across (as for a sandwich) and, just before serving, fill with sliced bananas and cream. Top with remainder of cream.

Chocolate Banana Gâteau

2 oz. plain flour	1 oz. cocoa
2 oz. sugar	Pinch of salt
2 eggs	1 oz. melted margarine
Whipped cream and sliced bananas	

For the jam glaze

2 tablespoonfuls apricot jam	1 tablespoonful water
1 tablespoonful sugar	1 teaspoonful lemon juice

Grease a flan tin and heat up oven to hot. Whisk the eggs and sugar until thick and foamy, then fold in lightly the sieved flour, cocoa and salt. Add melted fat, folding in quickly. Pour into prepared tin and bake for 8–9 minutes. Leave to cool, then fill with sliced bananas and pour glaze over. The glaze is made by boiling all the ingredients together until reduced. Then

Tiger Cakes are coated with mocha icing and nuts, and topped with caramel

remove from heat, sieve, and leave to cool a little before using. When set, pipe a decoration of whipped cream round the edge.

Chocolate Pear Gâteau

Canned or fresh ripe pears cut in quarters	1 pint orange jelly ½ pint whipped cream Chopped nuts
Angelica	

For the sponge base

2 eggs	2 oz. plain flour
2 oz. sugar	1 oz. cocoa
Pinch of salt	

Grease and sugar a sponge flan tin. Whisk eggs and sugar together until thick and frothy, fold in sieved flour, cocoa and salt. Pour immediately into tin and bake in moderate oven for 10–15 minutes. When cooked, turn out and leave to cool. Make orange jelly and pour slowly over sponge until sponge is moist, then leave to set. Prepare pears either by simmering in a pink syrup until faintly pink, or by painting on pink colouring with a small brush. Mix a little of the cream with a little chopped pear and pile on to the sponge base. Arrange remaining pears in quarters on top and pipe cream round the edge. Decorate with chopped nuts and angelica.

Fruit Basket

3 eggs	3 oz. plain flour
3 oz. castor sugar	Pinch of salt
¼ oz. cocoa	Cherries and cream
Chocolate icing	for filling

Grease and line three 6-in. sponge sandwich tins. Heat up oven to hot. Whisk eggs and sugar together until thick and foamy, then lightly fold in the sieved flour, cocoa and salt. Divide equally between the three tins and bake for 10 minutes. Cool on a wire tray, then sandwich two of the cakes together with a little fruit and cream. Coat the sides of the cake with cream and sprinkle with chocolate vermicelli or cup chocolate. Cut a circle out of the third cake, to make the lid, and cover with chocolate icing. Put the third cake on top of the other two, coating the sides as before, and fill with fruit and cream. Place the lid on top and decorate with stars of cream and cherries.

Gâteau Suprême

3 eggs	½ oz. cocoa
3 oz. castor sugar	3 oz. plain flour
Pinch of salt	

For the butter cream

3 oz. margarine	2 teaspoonfuls milk or
4½ oz. icing sugar	water
Vanilla essence	

For the praline

3 oz. castor sugar	3 oz. whole almonds

Proceed as for Fruit Basket (previous recipe) making three sponge cakes.

To make the praline.—Put ingredients into a thick saucepan and melt on a low heat. Stir frequently when sugar has melted and is turning colour until it caramels well and the almonds appear to be roasted. Turn out on to a greased tin and leave until cold and set. Break into pieces and grind or pound to a powder. Keep in an airtight tin until wanted.

Add 3 tablespoonfuls of praline to half the butter cream and sandwich the cakes together with this mixture. Coat the sides with plain butter cream and roll in praline. Decorate the top with cream and marzipan fruits, or as desired.

FRUIT AND RICHER CAKES

Cherry Cake (Rich)

8 oz. plain flour	1½ level teaspoonfuls
6 oz. castor sugar	baking powder
Pinch of salt	6 oz. margarine
1 tablespoonful	3 eggs
lemon juice	4 oz. glacé cherries

Heat the oven to very moderate, and grease and line a 7-in. cake tin. Wash and dry the cherries thoroughly, then cut into quarters and toss in a little flour. Sieve together the flour, baking powder and salt. Cream the fat and sugar thoroughly, until soft and pale cream in colour. Add the eggs one at a time, with a little of the sieved flour mixture after each one, and beat well. Fold in the remaining flour mixture, together with the lemon juice, using a metal spoon. Fold in the quartered cherries, mix thoroughly, but do not beat. Turn into the prepared tin and smooth the top. Bake for 2 hours. Remove from oven and, after 5 minutes, remove from tin and cool on a wire tray.

Dundee Cake

4½ oz. butter	½ teaspoonful baking
6 oz. brown sugar	powder
6 oz. flour	Pinch of salt
6 oz. sultanas	Pinch of spice
3 oz. currants	3 eggs
3 oz. mixed peel (chopped)	Almonds for top

Fruit Basket, for a special party, can be served either as a cake or sweet

Cream the butter and sugar until light and fluffy, add the beaten eggs gradually, and then the dry ingredients, sifted and mixed together. Stir in the fruit, previously prepared and cleaned, put the mixture into a cake tin, doubly lined with ungreased greaseproof paper, scatter the almonds on the top and bake in a moderate oven for about 1¼ hours.

Empire Cake

6 oz. flour	2 oz. chopped peel
4 oz. butter	3 eggs
4 oz. sugar	Small ½ teaspoonful
4 oz. sultanas	baking powder and
2 oz. currants	mixed spice
1 oz. chopped	Grated lemon rind
almonds	

Sift dry ingredients, with exception of the sugar, and clean and prepare fruit. Cream the butter and sugar together until light and fluffy, gradually add the beaten eggs, then the other ingredients. Put the mixture in a cake tin lined with 2 layers of ungreased greaseproof paper and bake in a moderate oven for about 1¼ hours. This cake may be iced with almond paste and royal icing.

Family Cake (Eggless and inexpensive)

8 oz. flour	1 oz. chopped lemon
4 oz. soft brown sugar	peel, if liked
4 oz. sultanas	½ teaspoonful bicar-
4 oz. margarine	bonate of soda
½ teaspoonful mixed	1 teaspoonful vinegar
spice or nutmeg	½ gill milk

Rub the margarine into the flour and add the sugar, fruit and spice or nutmeg. Mix together the milk, soda and vinegar, and stir immediately into the mixture. Put into a prepared cake tin and bake in a quick oven, lowering the heat when the cake has risen (about 1½ hours altogether).

Gingerbread (1)

6 oz. flour	1 egg
1 dessertspoonful	2 oz. Golden Syrup
ground ginger	2 oz. black treacle
Pinch of salt	1 tablespoonful mar-
2 oz. butter	malade
2 oz. moist brown	½ teaspoonful bicar-
sugar	bonate of soda
A little milk	

Sieve the flour, salt and ginger into a basin. Put the butter, sugar, syrup, treacle and marmalade into a saucepan and stir over a gentle heat until liquid. Then pour into the dry ingredients and beat well. Add the well-beaten egg and then the soda dissolved in a little hot milk. Beat well and pour into a greased, shallow cake tin. Bake for about 1 hour in a slow oven.

Gingerbread (2) (Eggless)

9 oz. flour	1 teaspoonful baking
½ teaspoonful salt	powder
¼ lb. treacle or syrup	1 teaspoonful ground
2 tablespoonfuls	ginger
margarine	1 gill sour milk

Sift the flour thoroughly with the baking powder, salt and ginger. Melt the margarine until it has the consistency of oil. Stir the treacle and sour milk together until well mixed, then beat them into the flour mixture until really smooth. Add the melted fat and turn into a well-greased shallow tin. Bake in a moderate oven for about 1 hour. Can be eaten cold as a cake, but is best served hot with plenty of butter.

Honey Fruit Cake

8 oz. flour	1 teaspoonful cinna-
3½ oz. margarine or	mon
fat	2 oz. sugar
4 oz. dried fruit	1 teaspoonful bicar-
(currants, sultanas,	bonate of soda
etc.)	2 tablespoonfuls
¼ pint milk	honey

Sieve the flour and cinnamon and rub in the fat, then add the sugar and dried fruit, cleaned and prepared. Dissolve the bicarbonate of soda in the milk, stir in the honey and gradually pour this mixture into the dry ingredients, stirring thoroughly. Put into a well-greased tin and bake in a moderate oven for 15 minutes, reduce the heat when the cake begins to brown and cook for a further 50–60 minutes. It should be firm when pressed in the centre and golden brown in colour.

Housekeeper's Cake

8 oz. flour	1 teaspoonful baking
4 oz. granulated sugar	powder
4 oz. currants	2 oz. chopped mixed
4 oz. lard and mar-	peel
garine, mixed	A little spice
2 small eggs	A little milk

Sieve together the flour, baking powder and spice, and rub in the lard and margarine. Then add the currants, sugar and peel. Beat the eggs and add them to the mixture. Lastly, add a little milk. Put into a prepared cake tin, sprinkle some castor sugar on top and bake in a moderate oven for about 1 hour.

Lunch Cake

12 oz. flour	2 oz. lard
2 oz. butter	2 oz. chopped peel
3 eggs	8 oz. currants
1 teaspoonful ground	6 oz. sugar
ginger	2 teaspoonfuls
½ oz. caraway seeds	baking powder
	A little milk

Rub the butter and lard into the well-sieved flour and baking powder. Add all the dry ingredients. Separate the egg-yolks from the whites, add a little milk to the yolks, then stir into the mixture. Beat the whites to a stiff froth and fold them in lightly. Put the mixture in a prepared cake tin and bake in a slow oven for about 1½ hours.

Marmalade Cake

8 oz. self-raising flour	Vanilla essence
2 eggs	1 oz. lard or vege-
1 tablespoonful	table fat
Golden Syrup	3 oz. margarine
1 tablespoonful	3 oz. sugar
marmalade	Mixed fruit as liked
Pinch of salt	

Cream the sugar and fats very thoroughly together, add the salt, syrup and marmalade. Beat the eggs. Sift the flour and add to the mixture alternately with the eggs, beating well. Stir in the fruit (sultanas, raisins, currants, chopped dates, glacé cherries, mixed peel, according to taste and availability) and flavouring. Bake in a well-greased, unlined tin in a moderate oven for about 1 hour 20 minutes.

Nut and Chocolate Lump Cake

4 oz. margarine	2 eggs
4 oz. sugar	2 oz. drinking choco-
4 oz. flour	late
2 oz. chopped nuts	1 teaspoonful baking
4 oz. plain or milk	powder
block chocolate	1 dessertspoonful
broken into pea-	coffee essence
sized pieces	

Cream the margarine and sugar together until frothy. Beat the eggs in gradually. Stir in the well-sieved dry ingredients with sufficient liquid to make a dropping consistency. Finally, fold in the nuts and broken chocolate. Turn into a prepared cake tin and bake in a moderate oven for 50–60 minutes.

CAKES

Plum Cake

12 oz. flour	4 oz. treacle
6 oz. butter	8 oz. raisins
4 eggs	8 oz. currants
1 teaspoonful bicar- bonate of soda	4 oz. chopped mixed peel
A little milk	4 oz. brown sugar

Cream the butter and sugar together until frothy, then add the treacle and, after that, the beaten eggs gradually, then the sieved flour and cleaned and prepared fruit. Dissolve the soda in a little warm milk and add to the mixture at once. Stir well. Put the mixture into a prepared cake tin and bake in a moderate oven for 1½–1¾ hours.

Raisin Cake

8 oz. brown sugar	1 lb. flour
4 eggs	8 oz. stoned raisins
8 oz. currants	¼ teacupful milk
1 teaspoonful bicar- bonate of soda	1 teaspoonful mixed spice
8 oz. butter	

Rub the butter into the sieved flour and add the rest of the dry ingredients. Then add the beaten eggs and, lastly, the milk. Bake in a moderate oven for about 1¾ hours.

Seed Cake

3 eggs	4 oz. flour
3 oz. butter	4 oz. sugar
2 teaspoonfuls cara- way seeds	Small ¼ teaspoonful baking powder

Separate the egg-yolks from the whites.

Beat the butter and sugar to a cream, then add one egg-yolk and a third of the flour and baking powder sieved together. Add another yolk and more flour, and so on until all the flour is in. Lastly, add the cara-way seeds. Whisk up the egg-whites to a stiff froth and fold them in at the end. Put the mixture into a prepared cake tin and bake in a moderate oven for about 1 hour.

Spicy Topped Fruit Cake

8 oz. plain flour	2 eggs
4 oz. lard and mar- garine mixed	4 oz. sugar
4 oz. dried fruit	Grated rind of 1 lemon
1½ teaspoonfuls baking powder	½ teaspoonful vanilla essence
Water for mixing	

For spicy top

3 oz. flour	1 teaspoonful mixed
1½ oz. sugar	spice
1½ oz. margarine	

Rub the fats into the well sieved flour and baking powder till it looks like fine breadcrumbs. Add sugar, lemon rind and fruit, then beaten eggs, vanilla and enough water to make a soft dropping consistency. Put into a well greased cake tin. For the spicy top, mix flour, spice and sugar, rub in fat and sprinkle on top of cake before baking. Bake in moderate oven for about 1½ hours.

Photographs of cakes on pages 189, 191, 193, 195, 197, 199 201 and 203 by Cadbury Bros.

Gâteau Suprème is coated in butter icing, then rolled in praline

HOW TO MIX A
CAKE
IN THREE MINUTES

1. Sieve flour, baking powder and sugar into a large mixing bowl

2. Add fat in a lump, unbeaten eggs and water

WITH the vegetable fat shortenings now on the market, an entirely new method of quick cake-mixing has revolutionised cooking. Speed is the keynote of this new technique—and you really can mix the ingredients, add liquid, pour into the baking tin and put the cake in the oven all inside three minutes.

The method shown here is the one specially devised in the Spry Cookery Centre to be used with Spry and is called "Lightning Mix." The Trex method is somewhat similar, except that the manufacturers advocate cutting the fat into small pieces before mixing, and there are minor variations in recipe proportions.

These quick-mix methods are equally suitable for large and small cakes and baked puddings. The great advantage is that the busy housewife can prepare a cake or pudding in a fraction of the time normally required.

3. Beat for 1 minute with wooden spoon till ingredients are well mixed

4. Turn into a greased sandwich tin lined with greaseproof paper on the bottom

5. The baked sandwich, after 30 to 35 minutes in a moderate oven

CAKES FOR SPECIAL OCCASIONS

Weddings, Christenings, Easter and Christmas—they all call for celebration cakes of their own

INSTRUCTIONS for making the various kinds of icing mentioned in this chapter will be found in the following chapter on "Icings and Fillings."

Birthday Cake

10 *oz. butter*	4 *oz. chopped peel*
10 *oz. sugar*	4 *oz. ground almonds*
10 *oz. flour*	1 *eggcupful rum*
6 *eggs*	½ *teaspoonful baking*
8 *oz. sultanas*	*powder*
	4 *oz. currants*

Beat the butter and sugar to a cream, then add the beaten eggs one by one, beating well. Add a little flour with the last two or three eggs if the mixture shows any signs of curdling. Put all the other dry ingredients together and add them to the mixture gradually; half-way through, add the rum. Stir the mixture thoroughly so that everything is well blended. Put the mixture into a cake tin, greased and doubly lined with greaseproof paper, and bake in a slow oven until thoroughly cooked through (about 1½ hours). When cold, cover with almond paste, and when this is thoroughly dry and firm (after a day or two), ice either with American icing, decorating at once, or with royal icing. When the icing is set, suitable wording such as "A Happy Birthday," or a child's name, can be written on top in coloured royal icing. Sugar roseholders in different colours and tiny candles to match can be bought from any good confectioner or grocer.

NOTE: Birthday cakes need not necessarily be fruit cakes. It is entirely a matter of taste. A large chocolate or orange cake is popular with children, and in this case use chocolate or orange glacé icing.

Christening Cake

8 *oz. butter*	½ *gill brandy*
8 *oz. castor sugar*	¼ *teaspoonful almond*
12 *oz. sultanas*	*essence*
12 *oz. currants*	8 *oz. chopped peel*

"The key of the door" is the theme of this gay 21st birthday cake iced in two colours

12 *oz. flour*	½ *teaspoonful baking*
5 *eggs*	*powder*
2 *oz. chopped*	1 *dessertspoonful*
almonds	*black treacle*

Cream the butter and sugar. Beat the eggs and add them slowly, beating well. Add a little flour towards the end, if the mixture shows any signs of curdling. Mix all the dry ingredients together and add them to the mixture, putting in the almond essence, treacle and brandy alternately with the sifted flour. Stir well, so that all the ingredients are well blended. Put the mixture into a well greased, doubly lined cake tin and bake in a slow oven until thoroughly cooked (about 3 hours).

Christening cakes should be iced with royal icing and decorated with formal pipings. A sugar cradle with a tiny doll inside or a sugar stork holding a cradle can be bought from any good confectioner and should be placed in the centre of the cake.

Christmas Cake

8 *oz. flour*	4 *oz. glacé cherries*
8 *oz. butter*	*A little rum or*
8 *oz. dark sugar*	*brandy*
8 *oz. currants*	½ *teaspoonful baking*
8 *oz. sultanas*	*powder*

4 *oz. orange peel (chopped fine)*
4 *oz. lemon peel (chopped fine)*
1 *oz. ground almonds*
½ *teaspoonful cinnamon*
¼ *teaspoonful mixed spice*
4 *eggs*

Cream the butter and sugar. Add the beaten eggs one at a time, beating well. Add a little flour with the last egg or two, if the mixture shows any signs of curdling. Put all the other dry ingredients together, and add

The traditional white Royal Icing, with lettering and decorations piped on, always looks right on a Christmas Cake

them to the mixture. Put in the rum half-way through. Stir the mixture well so that all the ingredients are well blended. Put the mixture into a well greased doubly lined cake tin and bake in a slow oven until thoroughly cooked (about 3 hours).

NOTE: **This cake should be made at least 3 weeks before Christmas as it improves with keeping.**

A Christmas cake can be iced in several different ways.

First put on a layer of almond paste, then ice with royal icing in one of the following ways:

(1) Coat with royal icing and, when set, decorate with formal pipings and finish off with marzipan berries, silver balls, angelica leaves, etc., etc.; or with a Father Christmas, Esquimaux, Polar bears, etc.

(2) Coat the top and decorate in the same way as above. Put a paper frilling of whatever colour is desired round the sides; white and gold or white and silver look very attractive.

(3) Beat up the royal icing extra stiff (double the ordinary amount will be required)

Even a beautiful three-tiered Wedding Cake can be made and iced at home—or you can compromise by making your own cake and having it professionally iced

For an Easter Sunday tea party, the traditional Simnel Cake, topped and sandwiched together with almond paste, has spring chicks and coloured eggs as decoration

and lay it thickly and roughly all over the cake. Do not smooth it down. Instead, take a fork and with it rough up the icing all over the cake until it resembles a wind-blown snowdrift. Make the points of icing all go in the same direction to make it look more realistic. Put red marzipan berries unevenly between the points of icing and finish off with tiny diamond shapes of angelica, two to each berry. This is a very attractive decoration and makes a change from the usual extremely formal icing.

Simnel or Easter Cake

8 oz. butter	½ teaspoonful baking
8 oz. sugar	powder
12 oz. flour	1 dessertspoonful
6 oz. sultanas	black treacle
6 oz. currants	Almond paste
4 eggs	6 oz. chopped peel

207

Beat the butter and sugar to a cream. Beat the eggs and add them gradually to the mixture, beating well. Put all the dry ingredients together and add them to the mixture, stirring thoroughly. Add the treacle half-way through. Cut a round of almond paste the size of the cake tin. Put half the cake mixture into the tin. Then put in the round of almond paste and press down well. Put in the rest of the cake mixture and bake in a moderate oven until thoroughly cooked (about $1\frac{3}{4}$ hours). (If a plainer cake is required, omit the almond paste filling.)

When cold, put another round of almond paste on the top, sticking it on with a little melted Golden Syrup. Cut a strip about 1 in. wide, or according to the size of the cake, and put it round the edge, first painting it with a little beaten egg-yolk to make it stick. Mark the strip with a fork. Then paint the whole top lightly with egg-yolk and put the cake in a very hot oven until the almond paste is a golden brown. Take out of the oven and cool on a rack.

When quite cold, place Easter decorations in the centre—small sugar eggs, fondant sweets, chickens, etc.

Wedding Cake (Three-tiered)

1 lb. 3 oz. butter	12 eggs
1 lb. 3 oz. castor sugar	9½ oz. chopped almonds
2 lb. 6 oz. currants	1¼ gills rum
2 lb. 6 oz. sultanas	1 lb. 3 oz. chopped peel
9½ oz. glacé cherries	
9½ oz. raisins	1½ tablespoonfuls black treacle
½ teaspoonful almond essence	¼ teaspoonful mixed spice
2 teaspoonfuls baking powder	½ teaspoonful cinnamon
1 lb. 12½ oz. flour	

Cream the butter and sugar. Add the beaten eggs gradually, beating well, and adding flour towards the end if the mixture shows any signs of curdling. Put all the dry ingredients together and add them slowly to the mixture, stirring well. Put in the almond essence, the treacle and the rum alternately with the flour. Mix well so that all the ingredients are well blended. Put the mixture into well greased, doubly lined cake tins (10-in., 8-in. and 6-in.) and bake in a slow oven until thoroughly cooked.

NOTE: **Wedding cake should be made at least a month before it is needed as it improves greatly with keeping.**

To Ice a Wedding Cake.—Wedding cakes are usually made in two or three tiers. First, cover each cake thickly with almond paste, then coat smoothly with royal icing and put each cake on a thick silver board a little wider than the cake.

When the coating is absolutely hard, decorate with formal pipings rather more elaborately than for other cakes, and ornament with wedding favours which can be bought from any good confectioner—sugar doves, little silver shoes, silver horseshoes, small sprays of orange blossom, etc.—arranging them round the edge only of the tops of the cakes and round the sides. Leave the centres of the cakes bare.

For a wedding cake in tiers, small sugar pillars are necessary. Put them towards the centre of the cake and then build it up. The small cake on top should be finished off with a central ornament such as a small silver vase filled with sprays of orange blossom.

Centrepiece of a **Valentine's Day** party is this sponge sandwich, with lemon curd inside and a fluffy pink icing trimmed with a heart in button sweets

CACTUS CAKES—a chocolate macaroon mixture decorated with green marzipan

MARBLE CAKE in three colours, topped with decorative feather icing

Photographs by Cadbury Bros.

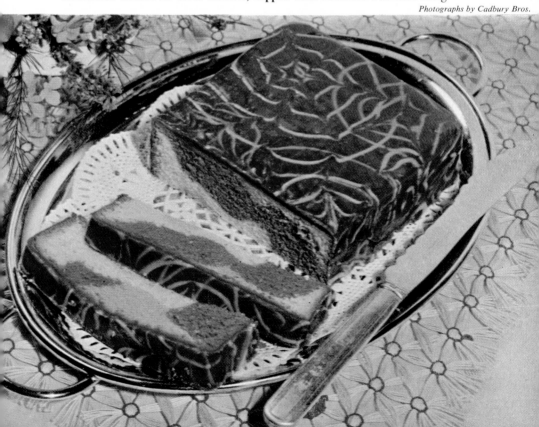

ICINGS AND FILLINGS

How to put all sorts of trimmings, simple or elaborate, on your cakes

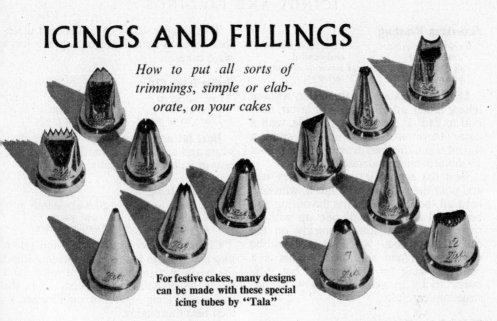

For festive cakes, many designs can be made with these special icing tubes by "Tala"

ICING and decorating is the most fascinating part of cake-making, providing ample scope for originality in appearance and flavours.

Much practice is needed to become expert at icing, but some kinds are much easier than others. Butter icing is, perhaps, the easiest to begin on, as it is soft and does not set quickly. Glacé and meringue icing are also within the scope of the beginner.

Royal icing is in a class by itself, as it is used only for Christmas, wedding and such special occasion cakes. This will set into any shape and therefore lends itself to elaborate designs.

Almond Paste

10 *oz. sugar (half icing and half castor)*	8 *oz. ground almonds*
	1 *teaspoonful sherry (optional)*
1 *teaspoonful vanilla essence*	1 *teaspoonful lemon juice*
1 *teaspoonful rum (optional)*	8 *drops of almond essence*
Egg to mix (about 1)	

Sieve the two sugars well and mix with the almonds and flavourings and enough egg to bind thoroughly. Knead with the hands, adding the moisture very gradually, as the oil in the almonds comes out with working. Knead till it forms a dough. When rolling, sprinkle icing sugar on board.

Almond paste is used chiefly on rich fruit cakes and also for Simnel cakes.

Trim the cake neatly before putting on the almond paste and brush it lightly with a little warm apricot jam or Golden Syrup.

Make whatever quantity of almond paste you require. Roll it out to the required thickness and mark it in a circle with the edge of the tin in which the cake was baked. Cut round this mark with a sharp knife and apply paste to the top of the cake, smoothing with a palette knife or ordinary knife dipped into hot water. Press it down well and roll it flat with the rolling pin.

If desired, the sides of the cake can also be coated with almond paste. Roll it out and cut it into strips of the depth of the cake and stick them to the sides of the cake with a little melted Golden Syrup. Flatten and smooth with a rolling pin or knife, particularly where the strips join.

If the cake is also to have a white icing, the almond paste must be really smooth and the cake a good shape. Leave for 2 or 3 days in a warm, dry place for the almond paste to dry out and harden.

When making a Simnel cake, which has no white icing on top, the almond paste should be scored with a fork to form a pattern, brushed with egg-yolk and lightly browned under the grill or in a quick oven.

Colour Page opposite:

Chocolate Swiss Roll, Dundee Cake, Scones, Madeleines, Marble Cake, Preserved Ginger Cake

American Frosting

8 oz. loaf or granu-	A little lemon juice
lated sugar	and vanilla
1 egg-white	A pinch of cream of
1 gill water	tartar

Dissolve the sugar in the water, without letting it boil, add the cream of tartar, then boil to 240° F., testing, if possible, with a sugar thermometer—or until it spins a thread when dropped from a spoon (about 10 minutes on a moderate flame).

Beat the egg-white until it is very stiff and pour the syrup slowly into it, whisking hard all the time. Add the flavouring and beat until the icing will pile up without spreading. Then spread quickly on the cake before it sets. When set, it should be crisp outside and soft inside. This is a delicious icing for fruit cakes, but it is rather tricky to make, so follow the instructions carefully.

Butter Icing (1)

| 6 oz. sieved icing | 4 oz. fresh butter |
| sugar | |

Beat the butter with a wooden spoon until it has the consistency of thick cream, then gradually mix in the sugar until thick and creamy.

For Chocolate Butter Icing.—Grate some unsweetened chocolate (about a tablespoonful) into a saucer and stand it in a warm place, but away from direct heat, until the chocolate is quite dissolved. Pour it into the butter icing and beat it in well.

For Coffee Butter Icing.—Add a tablespoonful of strong black coffee or, if liked, coffee essence to the butter icing and beat well.

For Orange or Lemon Butter Icing—Grate the rind of an orange or lemon and mix with the sieved sugar before adding it to the butter.

For Vanilla Butter Icing.—Flavour the butter icing with a little vanilla essence.

Butter icing must be really cold and hard when used and should be spread as smoothly as possible over the cake with a small palette knife.

If used for decorating purposes, put some into a forcing bag or syringe, using whichever icing head you like (a rose squeezer is always effective), and pipe little roses or a border or whatever you please, working quickly, as the warmth of the hand tends to soften the icing.

This icing is very rich and should therefore be used as a filling or topping for a *plain* cake.

Butter Icing (2)

2 oz. butter or	1–2 teaspoonfuls milk
margarine	A few drops of
3 oz. icing sugar	vanilla essence

Beat fat and sieved sugar together until white and creamy, add vanilla essence and beat in milk very gradually.

Chocolate Icing

2-oz. block of plain	2 tablespoonfuls milk
chocolate	and water
4 oz. icing sugar	Vanilla essence

Chop the chocolate coarsely and put it into a basin with the milk and water. Stand the basin in a saucepan of hot water, and when the chocolate has melted, stir in the well sieved icing sugar and vanilla essence, then beat thoroughly.

Glacé Icing

| 1 lb. icing sugar | 3½ tablespoonfuls |
| | warm water |

Sieve the sugar to eliminate all lumps. Put the warm water in a basin and add the icing sugar gradually, beating all the time with a wooden spoon. The basin should be placed over warm water, but the icing should not be allowed to get more than lukewarm or it may be lumpy and dull. When ready for use it should be of the consistency of thick sauce that will flow over and coat the back of the spoon.

This icing is inclined to be transparent, but a second coat can always be put on if necessary. If it is too soft, add a little more sugar.

Spread evenly over the cake with a small palette knife as soon as it is made. Add decorations while the icing is soft. The cake should then not be moved until the icing is quite set or it will crack.

For Chocolate Glacé Icing.—Warm the icing a little and add a few drops of vanilla essence and grated unsweetened chocolate until the icing is well flavoured and a good colour. If too thick, add a *very* little water.

For Coffee Glacé Icing.—Use strong black coffee instead of warm water when mixing the icing.

For Orange or Lemon Glacé Icing.—Make the icing with orange or lemon juice instead of water and colour it with a few

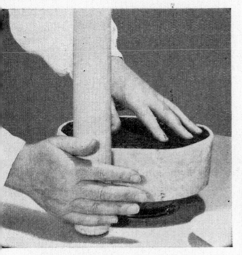

Applying Almond Icing to the side of the cake. Joins are neatened with a rolling pin

To flatten the top when putting on Royal Icing, hold a metal rule or palette knife straight, with both hands, and draw the edge of the blade right across

drops of orange or lemon vegetable colouring.

For Pineapple Glacé Icing.—Take a small can of crushed pineapple, strain off the juice and use it instead of water for making the icing. Use the pineapple pulp, mixed well with castor sugar, for pineapple filling.

For Raspberry or Strawberry Glacé Icing.—Strain off the syrup from a small can of fruit and use it instead of water for making the icing. Keep fruit for raspberry or strawberry filling.

Meringue Icing

Slightly beat an egg-white and gradually add to it sieved icing sugar. When fairly stiff, add a tablespoonful of water and put the basin over warm water. Beat the icing hard and add more icing sugar until it is of the same consistency as thick sauce. Continue beating for about 10 minutes, when it should be thick and creamy. Never let it get more than lukewarm.

This is the best icing for a slab cake which is to be cut up into small iced cakes because it sets slowly. It can be coloured or flavoured as desired.

Royal Icing

2 egg-whites   1 teaspoonful lemon
1 lb. icing sugar   juice

(These quantities will make sufficient icing to coat and decorate a moderate-sized

Smooth Royal Icing round the side of the cake with a damp palette knife. Stand the cake on a turntable, if possible

cake, up to about 8 in. in diameter and 3 in. deep. For larger cakes, increase the quantities in the proportions of 8 oz. icing sugar for each egg-white.)

Sieve the icing sugar at least three times and put two-thirds of it into a bowl, keeping the remainder to be added later. Whisk the egg-whites very lightly and add, a little at a time, to the sugar, beating hard with a wooden spoon. Add the lemon juice, a few drops at a time, and continue beating.

211

working in the remaining sugar by degrees. The icing should be beaten really hard for about 10 minutes, until it is so stiff that the wooden spoon will stand up in it without falling.

Royal icing sets harder and keeps better than any other and is therefore used for large, rich, fruit cakes for special occasions such as Christmas, birthdays, christenings and weddings.

Always keep the basin of royal icing covered with a damp cloth and in a cool place.

How to Use Royal Icing

(1) *Coating.*—Beat up the quantity of royal icing required and make sure the cake is smooth and even on top. Place the cake, preferably covered with almond paste, on an upturned plate or inverted cake tin and spread the icing evenly all over the cake. Smooth it over the top and round and round the sides until it is quite even. A good way to get it smooth is to dip a palette knife in hot water, shake off the drops and give a last sweep all over the icing with the hot wet knife. A turning board can be used to stand the cake on if available.

Now leave the cake all night or until the icing is absolutely set and hard. (This takes longer in wet weather.) Before the icing hardens, trim it round the bottom with a knife. It is a good plan to put the cake on a silver board, as it looks nice and is much easier to handle. For a wedding cake, two coats are usually put on in this way and each coat *must* dry thoroughly before the next one is put on.

(2) *Decorating.*—Beat up some royal icing as stiffly as possible. Choose the icing head you wish to use. (A rose squeezer is very popular and is most effective. A shell squeezer is also attractive and not difficult to use.) Put it in the end of an icing syringe or forcing bag and fill up the bag or syringe with icing.

Now squeeze any patterns you choose all over the cake in any design you fancy. It is best for a beginner to practise on the back of a plate until even patterns can be produced.

If desired, the icing can be coloured. Pink piping on a white-coated cake is very effective. By using a head with a small plain hole at the end, any wording can be written on the top of the cake.

The pipings must be ornamented before they set. Silver balls are always an attractive addition.

If the cake is on a silver board, squeeze a pattern of icing all round the bottom of the cake where it joins the board, to finish it off.

For a simpler form of trimming, use coloured edible cake decorations, glacé cherries, angelica, crystallised fruits, coloured fondants, crystallised rose or violet petals, nuts, coloured coffee sugar, real or artificial flowers.

FILLINGS

The simplest sponge or other plain cake can be raised to the party class with the addition of a good filling. The butter icing recipes given under Icings can be used equally well as fillings, and here are some alternative suggestions.

Apple Filling

2 good-sized eating apples	1 lemon
	8 oz. granulated sugar
Sherry (optional)	

Wash, peel and core the apples and grate them into a saucepan, add the strained lemon juice and grated rind, and then the sugar. Bring slowly to the boil, stirring well, then cook gently for 5 minutes, stirring all the time. Add a very little sherry if liked. Leave the mixture to get cold, then spread it on one half of the cake and press the other half on top.

Banana Filling

2 or 3 bananas	2 tablespoonfuls
Cream	apricot jam

Put the bananas through a hair sieve and mix the apricot jam with the purée. Whip up a little cream and fold into the mixture. Spread on one half of the cake and put the other half on top, pressing together well.

Chocolate Filling

4 oz. plain chocolate	2 oz. butter
8 oz. icing sugar	2 oz. carton of cream

Melt the chocolate and the butter together in the top of a double boiler or in a basin over a saucepan of boiling water. Sift the icing sugar well, then stir it into the mixture, together with about half the cream. Leave over the hot water for 10 minutes, then beat in as much more cream as required to make it the right consistency.

Coffee Candy Filling

Make butter icing, using 3 oz. icing sugar and 2 oz. butter and flavour with coffee essence. Spread on half the cake, then sprinkle crushed sugar candy on top. Spread the other half of the cake very lightly with coffee icing and put the halves together, pressing well.

Confectioners' Cream

½ teacupful cold milk
1 dessertspoonful cornflour
1 teaspoonful lemon juice
1 egg-yolk
3 oz. castor sugar

Make the cornflour into a

To ice a birthday cake, pipe decorative borders on with a star tube (above), then write the owner's name with a thread tube (left). Note the right way to hold the icing syringe

smooth paste with the milk and add the sugar. Put into a saucepan and stir over a gentle heat till it thickens. Allow to cool, then add the beaten yolk and, lastly, the strained lemon juice. Stir well and put aside to get quite cold. Then spread on one half of the cake and press the other half on top.

Prune and Almond Filling

8 oz. granulated sugar
2–3 oz. chopped almonds
4 oz. prunes
½ gill prune liquid
2 egg-whites
1 tablespoonful sherry

Wash the prunes and put to soak overnight in cold water, then cook in the same water until tender. Take ½ gill of the juice and put into a saucepan with the sugar, heating slowly while the sugar dissolves. Then boil to 245° F. (or until a drop or two tested in cold water forms a soft ball between the finger and thumb). Have ready the egg-whites beaten to a stiff froth and slowly add the boiling syrup to them, beating all the time. Lastly, add the stoned chopped prunes and the chopped almonds, together with the sherry. Spread on each half of the cake and press lightly together.

Raspberry Filling

Whip some cream and spread each half of the cake with it. Crush some fresh raspberries in a basin with a little castor sugar and spread over one half, put the other half on top and press gently together. This filling can also be made with frozen or, if necessary, canned strawberries. As a variation, raspberries may be substituted for the strawberries.

BISCUITS

So quick to make, and they go perfectly with coffee or tea at any time of the day

Afghans

8 oz. flour	1 tablespoonful cocoa
7 oz. butter	1 tablespoonful coco-
3 oz. sugar	nut
2 oz. cornflakes	

Cream butter and sugar thoroughly together. Add well-sifted flour, cocoa and coconut, then the cornflakes. Mix thoroughly, then put spoonfuls of the mixture on to a well-greased baking tray—at a good distance apart as they spread surprisingly—and bake in a moderate oven for 15–20 minutes. When cold, ice with chocolate icing (see Cake Icings chapter).

Almond Fingers

Short pastry	Macaroon paste
Raspberry jam	Chopped almonds

Roll the pastry out fairly thin and cut it into long rectangles. Spread each very thinly with raspberry jam, keeping it well away from the edge. Then put on a layer of macaroon paste and sprinkle with chopped almonds.

Bake on a baking sheet in a moderate oven until the pastry is cooked and the macaroon paste firm and set. Cool; then, with a sharp knife, cut into fingers.

Australian Shortbread

8 oz. rolled oats	2 oz. white sugar
4 oz. butter	A little salt

Cream the butter and sugar, and add the oats and salt. Put the mixture into a greased flat tin and flatten it down well. Bake in a moderate oven for 20 minutes. Stand until almost cold, and then cut into rather broad fingers.

Banana Oatmeal Biscuits

1½ cupfuls flour	3 oz. margarine
½ teaspoonful baking powder	1 cupful sugar
1 teaspoonful salt	1 egg
¾ teaspoonful cinnamon	1 cupful mashed ripe bananas
½ cupful chopped nuts	1¼ cupfuls rolled oats

Sift together the flour, baking powder, salt and cinnamon. Beat the margarine until creamy, add the sugar gradually and continue beating until the mixture is light and fluffy. Add the egg and beat well, then add bananas, rolled oats and nuts, and mix thoroughly. Add the flour mixture and blend well. Drop by teaspoonfuls on to a greased baking tray, keeping the spoonfuls about 1½ in. apart. Bake in a moderate oven for about 15 minutes. (These quantities make about 3½ dozen biscuits.)

Bourbon Biscuits

2 oz. plain flour	1 oz. cocoa
2 oz. margarine	1 egg
2 oz. sugar	A few drops of
2 oz. semolina	vanilla essence

For the filling

½ oz. margarine	1 heaped tablespoon-
1 teaspoonful cocoa	ful icing sugar

Cream the fat and sugar together and beat in the egg a little at a time. Sieve the flour and cocoa, and mix with the semolina. Lightly knead the dry ingredients into the creamed mixture, then add vanilla essence and a little water, if necessary, to make a firm dough. Roll out and with a knife cut into fingers (about 24). Prick, and sprinkle with granulated sugar before baking. Place on a greased tin and bake in a moderate oven for about 20 minutes until crisp. Turn on to a cake rack and leave until cold.

To make the filling.—Melt the margarine, and sieve the sugar and cocoa together. Mix the cocoa and sugar with the melted margarine a little at a time and use at once to sandwich the biscuits together.

Brandy Snaps (see also Scottish Cookery chapter)

2 oz. flour	2 oz. butter
2 oz. castor sugar	Pinch of ground
2 oz. Golden Syrup	ginger

Melt the butter in a saucepan, add the sugar, syrup, sieved flour and ginger, stirring well over the heat until smooth. Have ready a greased tin and put teaspoonfuls of the mixture on it, far apart. Bake in a moderate oven for 6–8 minutes until golden brown and lacey in appearance. Then take out quickly, leave for a minute to cool a little, take up each in turn on a palette knife and put round a greased rolling-pin for a few seconds until it starts to set, then

Bourbon Biscuits, one of the nicest of the chocolate varieties, are easily
made and sandwiched together with butter icing

A vegetable star pipe is used to give these Chocolate Cream Fingers this professional appearance

quickly take off and curl round the finger. Store in an airtight tin until needed, otherwise they will get very sticky. When quite cold, fill with whipped cream.

Butterscotch Cookies

12 oz. plain flour	8 oz. brown sugar
4 oz. margarine or fat	1 teaspoonful vanilla
½ teaspoonful salt	essence
1 egg	Chopped nuts
4 teaspoonfuls baking powder	(optional)

Beat the egg, then mix with it the sugar, vanilla and fat melted to an oily consistency. Mix thoroughly. Sift the dry ingredients together, stir into the sugar and egg mixture, and knead into a stiff, rather dry dough (no additional moisture must be used). Shape into a roll about 1½ in. in diameter. Leave for at least 1 hour, then cut into slices about ½ in. thick and bake on a greased tray in a moderate oven for about 20 minutes. Space well out on the baking tray, as they tend to spread.

Cheese Biscuits

3 oz. butter	Pinch of salt and
2 oz. grated cheese	pepper
About 4 oz. flour	

Cream the butter and cheese, add the salt, pepper and flour. Work in sufficient flour to make a firm dough. Then roll out on a floured board and cut into rounds. Prick before putting them in the oven. Bake on a baking sheet until pale brown (about 15 minutes).

Chocolate Biscuits

8 oz. flour	1½ dessertspoonfuls
4 oz. castor sugar	chocolate powder
4 oz. butter	1 small egg

Rub the butter into the flour, chocolate powder and sugar. Beat the egg, add to the mixture and knead it into a dough. Roll out on a board and cut into small rounds just under ¼ in. thick. Put the rounds on a baking sheet and bake in a moderate oven for about 20 minutes until quite firm. When cold, put them together in pairs with vanilla butter icing and ice with chocolate glacé icing (see Cake Icings chapter).

Chocolate Cream Fingers

5 oz. flour	1 egg
3 oz. margarine	A few drops vanilla
3 oz. sugar	essence
1 oz. cocoa	Pinch of salt
Milk or water to mix	

Cream the fat and sugar until light and fluffy. Beat in the egg. Sieve dry ingredients into this and mix to a very stiff dropping consistency with liquid and vanilla essence. Using a vegetable star pipe in a forcing bag, pipe in lengths on to a greased baking sheet. Bake in a hot oven for 10–15 minutes. Leave to cool, then sandwich together with pink or white butter cream, dust with icing sugar or dip the ends in chocolate icing (see chapter on Icings).

Chocolate Drops

2 eggs	1 oz. cocoa
2 oz. castor sugar	A few drops vanilla
Pinch of salt	essence
2 oz. plain flour	1 teaspoonful milk

Heat the oven to moderate; grease and lightly flour a baking sheet. Whisk the eggs and sugar until thick and creamy; add milk and vanilla, then fold in the sieved dry ingredients. Drop in small teaspoonfuls well apart on to the tin. Bake until firm. Cool on a wire tray and, when cold, sandwich together in twos with whipped cream or butter cream (see Icings). Dust the tops icing sugar and decorate as desired.

Chocolate Macaroons

4 oz. ground almonds	2½ oz. drinking
1 oz. margarine	chocolate
4 oz. castor sugar	2 egg-whites
Blanched almonds	

Grease a baking sheet or line with rice paper. Whip the egg-whites until stiff, then fold in the dry ingredients and melted margarine. Place in small heaps on baking sheet, putting a blanched almond on each. Bake in a slow to moderate oven until firm (about 20 minutes). (These quantities make about 10 macaroons.)

Chocolate Shortbread Biscuits

4 oz. flour	3 oz. sugar
4 oz. butter or margarine	1 oz. ground rice
	1 tablespoonful cocoa

Rub the fat into the flour and add dry ingredients. Knead all together to a smooth dough then roll into a round ½ in. thick. Crimp the edges with fingers and thumb. Place on a baking sheet, prick well and mark into nine triangular sections. Bake in a moderate oven until firm (about 1 hour).

Chocolate Whirls

4 oz. flour	1 egg-yolk
2 oz. margarine	Pinch of salt
2 oz. sugar	1 tablespoonful milk
1 dessertspoonful cocoa	to mix

Grease a baking sheet. Rub the margarine into the sieved flour and salt, then

Macaroons are not difficult to make. These are a change because they are flavoured with chocolate

add the sugar. Divide the mixture in half, and to one half add the cocoa and sufficient beaten egg-yolk and milk to form a stiff dough. Roll out both pieces and place one on top of the other. Roll up as for Swiss roll, then cut into slices. Place slices on a greased tray and bake in a hot oven for 15 minutes.

Coconut Pyramids

8 oz. desiccated coco-nut	3 egg-whites
	4 oz. castor sugar

Mix the sugar and coconut together, then fold them into the stiffly beaten egg-whites until the mixture is dry and crumbly. Colour half the mixture pink. Using a fork, pile into pyramids on a greased tin and bake in a fairly slow oven until set (about 30–40 minutes).

Easter Biscuits

6 oz. flour	Pinch of mixed spice
3 oz. butter	½ oz. chopped peel
1½ oz. currants	3 oz. castor sugar
Half an egg	Small pinch of salt

Cream the butter and sugar, and add the beaten egg; then add the other ingredients and knead into a dough. Put on a floured

board and roll out to about ¼ in. thick. Cut into rounds with a crinkly cutter and put on a baking sheet. Brush with egg-white, dredge with sugar and bake in a moderate oven until pale brown (about 15 minutes).

Fancy Biscuits

8 oz. flour	4 oz. butter
4 oz. sugar	Half an egg

Rub the butter into the flour and sugar, and add the beaten egg. Knead the mixture into a firm dough, roll it on a floured board and cut into small rounds just under ¼ in. thick. Put on a baking sheet and bake in a moderate oven for about 20 minutes until quite firm. When cold, put together in pairs with lemon curd or raspberry jam and ice the tops with pink or yellow glacé icing or meringue icing (see Icings chapter).

Ginger Biscuits

8 oz. flour	1 dessertspoonful ground ginger
3 oz. butter	
4 oz. castor sugar	1 dessertspoonful black treacle
Small pinch of soda	
Half an egg	

Beat the butter and sugar to a cream and add the beaten egg. Next, add the dry ingredients, adding the treacle half-way.

Knead the mixture into a dough, roll out as thinly as possible on a floured board and cut into rounds with a plain large cutter. Bake in a moderate oven until brown and set (about 10 minutes).

Golliwogs (Shrewsbury biscuit mixture)

2 oz. fat
2 oz. sugar
4 oz. plain flour
Egg-yolk to mix
Vanilla essence

Cream fat and sugar, and beat in egg. Add vanilla essence and gradually fold in the flour. Knead lightly to a stiff consistency, roll thinly on a floured board and cut out rounds with a 3-in. plain cutter. On half the circles, cut out "faces." Bake in a moderate oven for 7–10 minutes until firm and pale yellow, but *not* brown.

Make white glacé icing, take out 1 teaspoonful (to be used for the eyes), take out another teaspoonful and colour pink (to be used for mouths), and to the remainder add cocoa and a little water to make a coating consistency. Cover the top biscuits with the chocolate-coloured icing, and sandwich to plain biscuits with butter cream or apricot jam. Fill in the eyes with white icing and the mouths with pink, and add tiny dollops of chocolate to the eyes. (For icings see Icings chapter.)

Hungarian Chocolate Biscuits

4 oz. margarine
2 oz. castor sugar
½ teaspoonful vanilla essence
4 oz. self-raising flour
1 oz. cocoa
Pinch of salt

For the filling
Chocolate butter cream, rum flavoured
(see Icings)

Cream the margarine, sugar and vanilla essence. Sieve the flour, cocoa and salt into the mixture, then roll into balls the size of a walnut and place on a greased baking sheet. Flatten with a fork dipped in water and bake in a moderate oven for 12 minutes. Cool, sandwich together in pairs with the filling and dust tops with icing sugar.

Macaroons

2 oz. ground almonds
½ oz. ground rice
4 oz. castor sugar
Almonds for tops
1½ egg-whites (not whipped)
Rice paper
Almond essence, if liked

Line a tin with rice paper. Mix all the ingredients together, put the mixture in a

Golliwog faces are fun for a children's party. The foundation is a Shrewsbury Biscuit mixture

These fancy biscuit cutters from the Bex range of kitchen equipment are in gay colours and cannot rust. With a set of six different shapes you can make most attractive biscuits

forcing bag and squeeze out on to the rice paper in small heaps far apart. Put an almond on the top of each and bake in a moderate oven for 20 minutes.

Nut Biscuits

8 oz. flour	Small pinch of salt
4 oz. castor sugar	2 oz. chopped hazel-
4 oz. butter	nuts or walnuts
Half an egg	

Rub the butter into the flour, add the rest of the dry ingredients and then the beaten egg. Knead the mixture into a firm dough and roll it out on a floured board until it is about ¼ in. thick. Cut into rounds with a crinkly cutter. Put on a baking sheet and bake in a moderate oven until pale brown (about 15 minutes).

Oatcakes (see also Scottish Cookery)

4 oz. fine oatmeal	1 teaspoonful salt
4 oz. coarse oatmeal	Pinch of bicarbonate
8 oz. white flour	of soda
2½ oz. lard	Hot water

Rub the lard into the flour and oatmeals. Add the soda and salt, and mix to a dough with hot water. Roll out very thin, cut into triangles and bake on a floured baking sheet in a moderate oven for about 20 minutes, turning them over half-way through.

Oatmeal Biscuits

4 oz. flour	2 oz. fine oatmeal
2 oz. butter	1 oz. castor sugar
	1 egg

Mix the dry ingredients. Add the melted butter and the beaten egg with a little milk if the mixture is too dry. Roll out and cut into rounds, and bake on a floured baking sheet in a moderate oven until pale brown (about 15 minutes).

Orange and Chocolate Biscuits

4 oz. margarine	1 oz. rice flour
4 oz. castor sugar	1 egg
6 oz. flour	1 teaspoonful grated
1 oz. drinking	orange rind
chocolate	Pinch of salt
	Pinch of cinnamon

Cream margarine and sugar, beat in egg gradually. Stir in flour and salt. Divide into two portions. Into one, stir rice flour and orange rind, and into the other, drinking chocolate and a pinch of cinnamon. Roll out each piece of dough ⅛ in. thick on a floured board. Cut into shapes and place on a greased baking sheet. Bake in a moderately hot oven for about 12 minutes. When cold, sandwich together with orange butter cream (see Icings chapter) or orange curd.

Parkin Biscuits

4 oz. flour	1 teaspoonful ground
4 oz. oatmeal	ginger
1 oz. butter	½ teaspoonful
4 oz. black treacle	bicarbonate of soda

Mix all the dry ingredients in a basin, melt the butter and treacle together, and stir in. Knead the mixture well, put on a floured board and roll out. Cut into rounds with a crinkly cutter. Bake on a baking sheet in a fairly slow oven until firm and set (about 20 minutes).

Shortbread Biscuits (see also Scottish Cookery)

8 oz. flour	6 oz. butter
4 oz. sugar	2 oz. ground rice

Beat the butter and sugar to a cream, add the flour and ground rice. Knead into a firm dough, roll on a floured board and cut into shapes with fancy cutters. Prick with a fork. Bake in a moderate oven for about 20 minutes, then take out and sprinkle with castor sugar.

Shrewsbury Biscuits

3 oz. butter	1 egg
3 oz. castor sugar	6 oz. flour
	1 lemon

Cream the butter and sugar, and add the beaten egg. Then add the flour, the grated lemon rind and 6 drops of the juice. Knead the mixture well and roll out thinly. Cut into rounds and bake for 10 minutes until they are a pale lemon colour.

Spice Biscuits (1)

3 oz. butter	1 tablespoonful
2 oz. sugar	treacle
6 oz. flour	1 teaspoonful ground
1 teaspoonful	ginger
cinnamon	¼ teaspoonful
1 tablespoonful syrup	bicarbonate of soda

Beat the sugar and butter to a cream, warm the treacle and syrup, and mix together. Then add the flour, ginger, cinnamon and soda, and knead into a dough. Roll out on a well-floured board and cut into rounds. Bake in a fairly slow oven until firm and set (about 20 minutes).

Spice Biscuits (2)

2 oz. fat	2 oz. margarine
1 dessertspoonful	2 teaspoonfuls mixed
Golden Syrup	spice
2 oz. sugar	6 oz. flour

Bring fats and syrup to boiling point in a saucepan. Mix the dry ingredients together, pour in the hot fat and syrup, and mix well. Take a teaspoonful at a time and put well apart on to a greased baking sheet, flattening at the top with a fork. Bake in a moderate oven until nicely brown (about 20 minutes).

Biscuit pho o aphs
in this chapter by
Cadbury Bros.

Orange and Chocolate Biscuits cut into fancy shapes and sandwiched together with orange butter cream or orange curd

HOME-MADE SWEETS

*Let the children help to make—
as well as eat—these wholesome
luxuries*

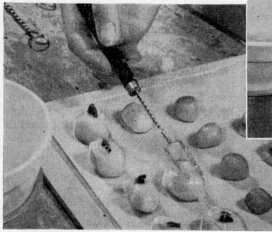

For Nut Fondants, just dip the shelled
nuts in fondant mixture (above), put
them on a slab, decorate the tops
(left) and leave to set

SWEET-MAKING is an attractive hobby, and home-made sweets, if well made, are far nicer and more original than bought ones. If going in for sweet-making at all seriously, it is as well to buy the proper equipment: a sweet thermometer, a set of steel bars and a marble slab. These are particularly useful for toffee, fudge and caramel. The thermometer can be put into the mixture while it is boiling. Fudge should boil to 240° F., caramel to 255° F. and toffee to 300° F.

The steel bars are for setting the candy. They should be arranged on the slab to enclose a square or an oblong of the size required. The inner side of the bars and the enclosed part of the slab should be well greased with olive oil; a pastry brush is best for the purpose. When ready, the hot candy should be poured between the bars. When cool, the bars can be removed and the candy cut up.

If, however, sweets are only to be made occasionally, the following test can be used. Drop a little of the candy into some cold water and then roll it between the fingers; fudge will form a soft ball when done, caramel a hard ball and toffee will crack

when tested. Instead of steel bars, well-oiled tins or dishes can be used.

Everything used for sweet-making must be scrupulously clean, and it is a good plan to keep a special aluminium saucepan for the purpose. Enamel should not be used as it is inclined to chip. An upturned enamel tray or an enamel slab can be used instead of the marble slab.

Boiling sweets should be stirred occasionally to prevent them sticking to the bottom of the pan and burning, but the stirring must be as gentle as possible or the mixture will go sugary. If a thermometer is used, the mixture can be stirred by gently dragging it across the bottom of the pan.

In the following pages you will find recipes for different kinds of sweets. After having practised on these, you can try to invent original ones of your own.

Caramel

1 lb. castor sugar	4 tablespoonfuls
½ pint cream	glucose
½ pint milk	4 oz. unsweetened
2 oz. butter	cooking chocolate

Grate the chocolate. Put the butter, sugar, cream, milk and glucose into a pan,

221

After cooling, fondants can de dipped in melted coating chocolate to make chocolate creams

Flake the chocolate and melt it over hot water. Add fruit (stoned and chopped fine), cinnamon and lemon juice. Remove from heat and beat with a wooden spoon until it thickens. Take out in spoonfuls, roll in balls in a mixture of grated chocolate and castor sugar.

Chocolate Krispies

7 tablespoonfuls Rice Krispies	1 oz. vegetable fat shortening
1 tablespoonful syrup	1 heaped tablespoonful drinking chocolate

Melt fat and syrup slowly in a saucepan, add chocolate and heat thoroughly. Remove from heat and, using a metal spoon, fold in Rice Krispies, making sure that they are well coated. Place in small spoonfuls on a lightly greased baking sheet and leave until cold.

Chocolate Krackolates

7 tablespoonfuls Corn Flakes	1 level tablespoonful cocoa
1 tablespoonful icing or castor sugar	1 tablespoonful syrup
1 oz. vegetable fat shortening	2 tablespoonfuls coconut or 1 tablespoonful grated orange peel

Melt fat and syrup slowly in a saucepan, but do not boil. Add cocoa, remove from heat and stir in sugar. With a metal spoon, quickly fold in the Corn Flakes and coconut (or orange peel), until well coated. Place in small spoonfuls on a lightly greased baking sheet and leave to cool.

heat and stir them until the sugar is dissolved, then simmer gently for 10 minutes. Add the grated chocolate and boil quite hard, stirring gently all the time, until the temperature is 255° F. (or until the caramel will form a hard ball when tested in cold water). Take off the fire and, when the bubbles have settled, pour at once into an oiled tin (or on to an oiled slab between bars). As soon as it is cold, cut into neat squares with a sharp knife.

Chocolate Coconut Truffles

4 tablespoonfuls castor sugar	2 tablespoonfuls milk
1 tablespoonful cocoa or drinking chocolate	5 oz. coconut
	2 oz. margarine
	Vanilla or coffee essence

Put the sugar, milk and margarine in a pan and dissolve over a gentle heat. Remove from heat, add cocoa, essence and coconut, and mix well. Form into balls and roll in dry coconut. Leave to harden. (These quantities make 12 truffles.)

Chocolate Drops

4 oz. plain chocolate	6 oz. dates
2 oz. raisins	¼ teaspoonful cinnamon
A few drops of lemon juice	

Coconut Ice

1 lb. granulated sugar	½ gill cold water and milk mixed
6 oz. desiccated coconut	Cochineal

Using a large pan, dissolve the sugar in the milk and water, then boil fast to 240° F. (or until the mixture will form a soft ball when tested in cold water). Take if off the fire, add the coconut and stir until the mixture thickens.

Pour half into an oiled tin (or on to an oiled slab between bars). Colour the remainder pink and pour it on top of the white ice. When cool, cut into fingers.

NOTE: For Chocolate Coconut Ice add 1 dessertspoonful cocoa and a little vanilla essence instead of pink colouring.

Coconut Ice always comes in two colours—chocolate and
vanilla here make a change from the usual pink and white

Porcupines are baked sweetmeats containing dates, nuts and coconut
and are substantial enough to appear on the tea table

Date Truffles

1 *box of dates*	4 *oz. plain chocolate*
Marzipan (*see*	*Chocolate vermicelli*
opposite page)	

Remove stones from dates and replace with rolls of marzipan. Dip dates in melted chocolate, then roll in chocolate vermicelli and place in paper sweet cases.

Fondants

2 *lb. sugar*	1 *dessertspoonful*
¼ *pint water*	*glucose*

Soak sugar and water for 1 hour and bring gently to the boil, adding glucose and boil to 237° F., then leave until bubbles disappear. Pour on to a damped slab to cool; work with spatula until smooth, then put into a pan with a little water and flavouring and warm gently, without boiling, until liquid. Pour into a cool tin or, preferably, into dry, ribbed moulds and leave to set. Or dip shelled hazel nuts in the liquid mixture and leave to set.

Fudge (Chocolate)

1 *gill milk*	1 *lb. granulated sugar*
1 *gill cream*	2 *oz. grated, un-*
2 *oz. butter*	*sweetened chocolate*

Put the milk, cream, butter and sugar into a pan and bring to the boil. Add the chocolate and boil for 15–20 minutes until it is 240° F. (or will form a soft ball when tested in cold water). Stir gently at intervals to prevent burning.

Take off the fire and let the bubbles settle. Beat against the sides with a spatula until the mixture granulates. Then pour it quickly into an oiled tin (or on to an oiled slab between bars). When cold, cut into squares.

Fudge (Coffee)

1 *lb. granulated sugar*	1 *dessertspoonful*
1 *gill milk*	*coffee essence or*
1½ *oz. butter*	*strong black coffee*

Make in exactly the same way as chocolate fudge, adding the coffee flavouring after taking the mixture off the fire and before beating it. It will need rather more beating than chocolate fudge to make it granulate, owing to the extra liquid.

Fudge (Walnut)

2 *lb. granulated sugar*	2 *oz. butter*
3 *oz. grated, unsweet-*	½ *pint chopped*
ened chocolate	*walnuts*
Pinch of cream of	1 *teaspoonful vanilla*
tartar	*essence*
	½ *pint milk*

Make in exactly the same way as chocolate fudge, adding the walnuts, cream of tartar and vanilla after taking the mixture off the fire and before beating it.

Glacé Fruits

For the syrup

½ *lb. granulated*	¼ *level teaspoonful*
sugar	*cream of tartar*
	¼ *pint water*

Stir sugar and water together until sugar is dissolved. Add cream of tartar. Boil to 290° F. (or until it cracks when tested in cold water). Dip each separate fruit—or, in the case of grapes, small bunch—into the hot syrup so that it is completely coated. Place on an oiled slab and leave until dry and quite cold. If the syrup begins to set hard, it can be brought back to the right consistency if stood over hot water.

Suitable fruits are cherries, figs, segments or peel of grapefruit, lemons and oranges, prunes. They should be firm and not too ripe, and must first have stalks and stones removed.

Lemon Creams

1 *egg-white*	*Icing sugar*
1 *lemon*	*Yellow vegetable*
A little crystallised	*colouring*
lemon peel	

Sieve plenty of icing sugar on to a piece of paper. Slightly beat the egg-white in a basin and gradually stir in the icing sugar. When thick and creamy, add the lemon juice and grated lemon rind and continue stirring in icing sugar until the mixture forms a dough. (Just before this, add the colouring until the mixture is pale lemon colour.) Roll out the dough on a sugared board and cut into rounds with a small cutter. Line a rack with greaseproof paper, scatter some sieved icing sugar on it and put the creams on the rack. Press down a small square of crystallised lemon peel on the top of each and leave them to set.

Marrons Glacés

2 *lb. chestnuts*

For the syrup

½ *pint water*	3 *tablespoonfuls*
1 *lb. sugar*	*vanilla essence*

Make slits in the chestnuts with a sharp knife and plunge them into boiling water and boil for 10 minutes. Cool and peel

LIGHT AND COLOUR ON THE DINNER TABLE

LIGHT and colour are important and closely related factors in the artistic preparation and serving of food. A soft mellow light from two candles on the table, augmented by more candles or shaded wall lamps in the room, creates a leisured atmosphere of gracious living. This soft lighting combines with a beautiful traditional table setting to suggest an intimate dinner-party for four. Some people, however, insist on being able to "see what they are eating." The clear bright light from a hanging chandelier or from lightly shaded wall lamps shows up to full advantage a strongly contrasted colour scheme, like the modern table setting photographed below. Here the keynote is freshness, and clear bright colours invite one to linger and enjoy the meal to come.

Above: a fine Iris linen damask cloth in th chrysanthemum design York Street, which h been popular for over hundred years, makes lovely setting for fi china, gleaming silve good food and wine

It's a modern idea mix and match your tab linen. Left: table clot and napkins are Hunt Green Irish linen sca loped in white, the plac mats in terra-cotta edge with white, from Warin & Gillow. Try vivi colours with white, do grey, pale blue or prim rose yellow

Sweets you can make even when you're short of sugar! Chocolate Krispies are sweetened with syrup

being careful to remove the inside skin as well. Boil sugar, vanilla and water until it is white and roughens round the edge of the pan. Put the chestnuts in the syrup and simmer very gently for about 15 minutes, not letting it boil. Leave the chestnuts to soak in the syrup for 24 hours, then take them out and drain. Add more sugar to syrup and boil until really thick. Return chestnuts to hot syrup, simmer for 5 minutes at most and leave to cool. Take chestnuts out of syrup and stand to dry on a cake tray.

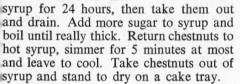

Marzipan

1 lb. loaf sugar	12 oz. ground
1 gill water	almonds
3 oz. icing sugar	2 egg-whites

Dissolve the loaf sugar in the water and boil to 240° F. (or until it forms a soft ball when tested in cold water). Draw the pan aside and, when slightly cooled, add the ground almonds and egg-whites. Stir by the side of the fire for a few minutes. Then turn on to a sugared slab and add the icing sugar, working it in with a spatula until the mixture is cool enough to handle. Knead until quite smooth. When cold, wrap up the marzipan in greaseproof paper and store in a tin until required.

Marzipan (Uncooked)

½ lb. ground almonds	¼ lb. castor sugar
¼ lb. icing sugar	Almond essence
	2 egg-whites

Mix the almonds with the carefully crushed and sifted icing sugar and the castor sugar. Add essence and the well-beaten egg-whites, a little at a time, using as much as is needed to make a firm dough. Use in the same way as cooked marzipan.

Marzipan Potatoes and Fruits

Model some marzipan into shapes like new potatoes. Prick them with a skewer to resemble eyes and roll them in fine chocolate powder.

NOTE: Marzipan can be coloured as desired by dabbing it with vegetable colouring or essence, and kneading it on a board sprinkled with icing sugar. (Little oranges, apples and lemons can be made in this way.)

Marzipan Stuffed Fruits

Glacé cherries, cut in half, may be filled with uncoloured, stoned prunes and dates with coloured marzipan.

Mint Cake

1 lb. granulated sugar	2 teaspoonfuls
1 gill milk	peppermint essence
	(or a few drops oil
	of peppermint)

Boil the sugar and milk to 240° F. (or until a soft ball is formed when tested in cold water). Take off the fire and add the peppermint. Beat hard until the mixture thickens. Pour into an oiled tin (or on to an oiled slab between bars). When cold, cut into squares with a sharp knife. For brown mint cake, use Demerara sugar.

Neapolitan Bars

Using half the quantity of marzipan made above, divide into three, colouring one green and one pink with vegetable colourings. Roll out into three strips. On the pink one spread some chocolate filling; put the plain marzipan on top; spread some vanilla filling on that and finish with green marzipan. Cut into slabs and leave to cool. (For chocolate and vanilla fillings, see chapter on Icings.)

Nougat

9 oz. granulated sugar
1½ oz. glucose
½ gill water
½ teaspoonful vanilla essence
½ teaspoonful brandy or rum
½ oz. angelica (cut up small)
1 egg-white
1 oz. chopped walnuts
1 oz. chopped glacé cherries
1 oz. chopped blanched almonds
½ teaspoonful lemon juice
Rice paper

Line a tin, or bars and slab, with rice paper. Dissolve the sugar and glucose in the water in a pan and boil to 240° F. (or until the mixture forms a soft ball when tested in cold water). Meantime, beat the egg-white very stiff in a basin. Pour half the syrup gradually on to it, whisking all the time.

Boil the rest of the syrup to 270° F. (or to a very hard ball) and then add to it the beaten mixture and all the other ingredients. Stir for a few minutes until the mixture is firm and white, and then put it in the prepared tin. Put a piece of rice paper on the top and press down until it sticks to the nougat. When cold, cut into bars.

Peppermint Creams

2 egg-whites
1 teaspoonful water
Icing sugar
Oil of peppermint (or peppermint essence)

Sieve plenty of icing sugar. Slightly beat the egg-whites and gradually add the icing sugar, beating hard. When fairly thick, add the water and a few drops of oil of peppermint (or 2 teaspoonfuls of essence). Continue adding sugar until the mixture will knead on a sugared board. Roll out and cut into rounds. Place on sugared paper to set.

Porcupines

6 oz. chopped dates
3 oz. chopped nuts
2 oz. sugar
1 oz. margarine
1½ oz. cocoa
Egg
Desiccated coconut

Cream margarine and sugar. Stir in dry ingredients and bind with egg. Roll into balls the size of a walnut. Coat with coconut. Bake in a slow oven for 10 minutes.

Toffee (Plain)

1 lb. granulated sugar
4 oz. butter
1 large dessertspoonful glucose
1 gill water

Put the sugar, water and glucose into a pan and heat until completely dissolved. Boil for about 10 minutes. Add the butter and boil to 300° F. (or until it will crack when tested in cold water). Let the bubbles settle. Then pour out at once into an oiled tin (or on to an oiled slab between bars). When cold, cut into squares.

Treacle Toffee

12 oz. Demerara sugar
4 oz. butter
Pinch of cream of tartar
8 oz. black treacle
¾ gill water

Dissolve the sugar, butter and treacle in the water and bring to the boil. Add the cream of tartar and boil to 260° F. (or until a hard ball is formed when tested in cold water). Pour into an oiled tin (or on to an oiled slab between bars) and cut up as soon as it is cool. Put into an airtight tin.

Turkish Delight

1 lb. loaf sugar
Icing sugar
1 oz. gelatine
2 oz. almonds
1½ gills water

Put the gelatine to soak in ½ gill cold water. Blanch the almonds and chop them rather coarsely. Dissolve the sugar in 1 gill water and then boil to 240° F. (or until it will make a soft ball when tested in cold water). Meanwhile, bring the gelatine to the boil, add it to the mixture with the nuts and pour into an oiled tin. When cold, cut into squares and roll in icing sugar.

Date Truffles are stuffed with marzipan and coated with chocolate—a delicious mixture of flavours

BREAD, BUNS AND SCONES

*Even the staff of life is not too hard to make at home
—and scones are really quick bakes*

BREAD making at home is thought by some to take more time than a modern housewife has to spare, while kneading is believed to be unduly hard work. But it is, in fact, no more tiring than beating a batch of cakes, and while the dough is rising one can get on with other work. It is necessary to bake only once a week, as home-made bread keeps well for a week.

YEAST RECIPES

Compressed yeast can be bought from bakers and should be ordered as required. If kept moist and at blood heat, its cells multiply and let off gases which give bread its light, porous consistency. Too much heat kills the yeast, while too little prevents its action. It should be kept in a cool place until wanted, then creamed with a little sugar, to start it working, before the warmed liquid is added to it.

The basins used for mixing bread, the flour and the milk or water should always be warmed to blood heat. While the dough is rising, it should be covered with a cloth and put in a warm place (but away from direct heat), either in front of or over the oven. It should be left until it has risen to twice its original size.

The kneading is extremely important, as it distributes the yeast and its gases evenly through the bread.

Bread (White)

3½ lb. flour
2 teaspoonfuls salt
1 tablespoonful sugar
1 oz. yeast
3 oz. lard
1½ pints milk and water (half and half)

Rub the lard into the sifted flour. Cream the yeast with the sugar and add to it the milk and water heated to blood heat. Make a hole in the centre of the warmed flour and pour in the milk and yeast. Scatter a little flour over the top and sprinkle the salt round the edge away from the yeast and milk. Stand to rise in a warm place for 20 minutes. Mix the flour by hand to a dough till there is no dry flour left. Clean the hand with flour and knead for 5 minutes. Stand to rise in a warm place, covered with a cloth, for 1½–2 hours, when the dough should have doubled itself. Knead for 15 minutes. Then form into loaves and put in warm well-greased bread tins, or make into desired shape and put on a warm baking tin. (For a Coburg loaf mark the top with a cross just before baking.) Put in a warm place for 10 minutes. Bake in a hot oven for 30 minutes and reduce the heat gradually until done. Bread is ready when it feels firm and sounds hollow if tapped.

Bread (Brown)

This can be made in exactly the same way, using wholemeal instead of white flour.

Fruit Bread

To each 1 lb. of dough made as above, knead in 1 oz. sugar and 2 oz. currants. Put into greased tins and leave in a warm place until doubled in size. Then bake at

Doughnuts—either the ring or the round variety—are fried in deep fat, then well drained before rolling in sugar

400° F. for 10 minutes, reducing to 300° F. for 35–40 minutes.

Bread Rolls

1¼ lb. flour	1 oz. sugar
1 oz. yeast	1 teaspoonful salt
½ pint milk	3 oz. fat

Warm the milk, and melt the fat in it, then add sugar and salt, and leave to cool. When lukewarm, stir in the yeast and flour, mix well, turn into greased pan and leave to double itself. Knead, leave to rise, form into shapes required (round balls, knots, twists or crescents) and bake on a floured baking sheet at 425° F. for 15–20 minutes.

Bridge Rolls

1 lb. flour	½ pint water
2 oz. lard	1 egg
½ oz. yeast	Salt
1 teaspoonful sugar	

Rub the fat into the flour and make a well in the middle. Cream the yeast with the sugar and pour lukewarm water over it. Then add the mixture to the flour. Set to rise for 30 minutes in a warm place. Then add the egg and a little salt, and mix well. Stand to rise again for 1½ hours. Put on a saucepan of water to boil. Knead the dough and cut it in half. Cut up and form into oval rolls. Put them on a baking sheet and stand over the steam from the boiling water for ½ hour. Bake in a very hot oven for 10–15 minutes.

NOTE: Be careful of draughts while the rolls are rising.

Doughnuts

1 lb. flour	½ pint milk
2 oz. butter	2 eggs
½ oz. yeast	Jam
½ teaspoonful salt	½ teaspoonful sugar

Rub the butter into the flour, add the salt, then warm. Cream the yeast with the sugar. Make a hole in the centre of the flour, pour in the warm milk and well beaten eggs. Then add the yeast. Mix to a light dough and leave to rise in a warm place for 1 hour. Roll out on a floured board and cut into rounds ¼ in. thick. Put a little jam on alternate rounds. Moisten the edges, cover with another round and press the edges together. Put in tart tins in a warm place for 20–30 minutes. Fry in deep fat, drain well and roll in castor sugar.

Lardy Cake (Buckinghamshire recipe)

1 lb. dough (which has just finished rising)	3 oz. currants
	Pinch of spice
	3 oz. sugar
6 oz. lard	

Knead the dough and flatten it out with a rolling pin. Then spread it with lard, sprinkle the currants and sugar over it, and a pinch of spice. Roll the dough up, flatten it out again and slash it on the top with a knife. Put in a greased tin and let it stand in a warm place for 10 minutes. Then bake in a fairly quick oven for about 45 minutes, lowering the heat well towards the end.

NOTE: Lardy Cake should be eaten the day it is made.

Spiced Loaf

1 lb. flour	A little chopped peel, if liked
3 oz. lard	
3 oz. sugar	½ teaspoonful mixed spice
½ oz. yeast	
6 oz. sultanas	Not quite ½ pint milk

Dissolve the fat in the milk and heat to blood heat. Cream the yeast with a little sugar and add it to the milk. Pour this mixture into the warmed flour, sugar, sultanas, chopped peel and spice, and mix well. It should be a very soft dough. Set it in a warm place for 1½ hours, then knead well, keeping the hands dry with a little flour. Put into a bread tin and set it in a warm place again until it is well risen.

What could possibly be more appetising than a batch of freshly baked loaves of all shapes and sizes, served with lots of fresh butter? These were specially baked and photographed in the Creda kitchens

Bake in a moderate oven for 40 minutes. Mix together a dessertspoonful of milk and a teaspoonful of castor sugar, take out the loaf, brush it over with this mixture and put it back in the oven for a few minutes.

Tea Cakes

8 oz. flour	½ oz. yeast
½ teaspoonful salt	About a gill of milk
1 teaspoonful sugar	or milk and water
1 oz. lard or butter	

Rub the lard into the sifted flour and warm slightly. Then add the sugar. Cream the yeast with a little extra sugar and pour some of the warm milk into it. Then pour this mixture into the centre of the flour. Add the salt round the edge away from the yeast. Scatter flour over the yeast lightly. Let it stand in a warm place for 10 minutes. Add the rest of the milk and mix to a light dough and knead well. Put in a warm place to rise, covering the bowl over with a cloth. Leave until risen to double its size. Knead again, divide into three, roll and shape into round tea cakes. Prick each one with a fork. Put them on a warmed, greased tin, covered with a cloth, and stand in a warm place to rise, for 10 minutes. Then bake in a quick oven for about 12 minutes. Brush with butter and put back in the oven for 1 minute.

NOTE: To test if they are done, tap them. If cooked, this should make a hollow sound.

Tea Cakes (with Currants)

Make in the same way as tea cakes (above). When the dough has risen to double its size, knead in 1 oz. currants and ½ oz. sugar and work in well. Allow to rise again. Then cut into three and roll into rounds. Stand the rounds on a warm tin, covered with a cloth, to rise (about 20 minutes). Then bake in a quick oven for about 12 minutes. Brush with butter and put back in the oven for 1 minute.

Currant Buns or Bun Men

¼ lb. flour	2 oz. margarine
Pinch of salt	1 egg
½ oz. yeast	⅛ pint tepid water
1 oz. sugar	2 oz. currants
½ teaspoonful mixed spice	

Rub fat into well sifted flour and salt. Make a well in the centre and stir in the egg. Add the yeast and sugar mixed together with the water. Knead well and leave to rise till it has doubled in quantity. Then knead the currants and spice very lightly into the dough on a floured board. Shape into eight round balls or bun men, put on to a greased baking tray, allow to prove for about 10 minutes, then bake in a hot oven for 5 minutes, reducing temperature to moderate for another 5 minutes.

While the buns are baking, put a tablespoonful of sugar into a little water, add ½ pint milk, boil hard for 2 or 3 minutes, then cool. While the buns are still hot, paint them lightly with this glaze.

SODA BREAD

Soda bread makes a change from yeast bread and is very quick to make as it can be baked at once. Soda scones should be eaten fresh, but if any are left over, they can be toasted and served hot the next day.

Soda Bread (Brown) (1)

8 oz. flour	About ½ pint sour
8 oz. wholemeal flour	milk or buttermilk
1 teaspoonful salt	1 level teaspoonful
2 teaspoonfuls sugar	bicarbonate of soda

Sieve all the dry ingredients together and mix with milk or buttermilk. Knead to a dough, then roll out and cut into two large loaves or four smaller ones. Put on a floured baking sheet and bake in a very hot oven for about 20 minutes.

Soda Bread (Brown) (2)

Use the same quantities as for Soda Bread (Brown) (1). Rub 3 oz. butter, lard or dripping into the flour, then sieve in the other dry ingredients and mix with buttermilk or milk. Instead of rolling out the dough, make it moister by adding a little more sour milk or buttermilk, put in a greased cake or bread tin and bake in a very hot oven.

Soda Bread (White)

Make in the same way as Brown Soda Bread (1) or (2) above, but use all white flour.

Steamed Bread

1 lb. wholemeal flour	1 dessertspoonful
1 tablespoonful	cream of tartar
brown sugar	1 teaspoonful bicar-
½ teaspoonful salt	bonate of soda
½ pint milk	

Sieve together all the dry ingredients, then add the milk. Put the dough into a greased 4-lb. stone jam jar, with a piece of greased paper on top. Steam for 2 hours.

Fruit Tea Bread

1¼ cupfuls sifted flour	1 cupful mashed ripe
2 teaspoonfuls baking	bananas (2 to 3
powder	bananas)
¼ teaspoonful bicar-	⅔ cupful sugar
bonate of soda	2 eggs, well beaten
⅓ cupful vegetable fat	½ teaspoonful salt

Sift together the flour, baking powder, bicarbonate of soda and salt. Beat the fat in a mixing bowl until creamy, then gradually add the sugar and continue beating until light and fluffy. Add eggs and beat well, then add the flour mixture alternately with bananas, a small amount at a time, mixing after each addition only enough to moisten the dry ingredients. Turn into a greased loaf pan ($8\frac{1}{2} \times 4\frac{1}{2} \times 2\frac{1}{2}$ in.) and bake in a moderate oven for about 1 hour 10 minutes or until bread is done.

Variations can be made by adding to the egg mixture:

(1) 1 cupful finely chopped dried apricots. (If the apricots are very dry, soak them in warm water until soft. Drain and dry well before using.)
(2) ½ cupful coarsely chopped nuts.
(3) 1 cupful finely chopped dried prunes (if very dry, treat as apricots above).
(4) 1 cupful seedless raisins.
(5) 1 cupful mixed candied fruit, ¼ cupful raisins and ½ cupful chopped nuts.

SCONES

Drop Scones (see also Scottish cookery)

4 oz. flour	½ teaspoonful cream
Half an egg	of tartar
1 dessertspoonful	½ teaspoonful bicar-
Golden Syrup	bonate of soda
Milk to mix	Pinch of salt

Sieve together the flour, cream of tartar, soda and salt. Make a hole in the middle, drop in the beaten egg and the Golden Syrup. Mix to a stiff batter with milk, added gradually. Grease and heat a girdle.

Drop the mixture on it in tablespoonfuls. Brown on one side, then turn over and cook on the other side. Keep hot in a soft cloth. Butter and serve hot.

Plain Scones (1)

8 oz. flour	½ teaspoonful cream
1½ oz. butter	of tartar
1 teaspoonful castor	Buttermilk or sour
sugar	milk to mix
½ teaspoonful bicar-	Pinch of salt
bonate of soda	

Sieve the dry ingredients and rub in the butter. Add enough buttermilk to make a spongy dough. Turn on to a floured board, knead lightly and roll out. Cut in rounds and put them on a hot girdle. Cook steadily until well risen and a very pale brown. Then turn over and cook the other side.

NOTE: These scones may be baked in a quick oven for 10–15 minutes.

Plain Scones (2)

8 oz. flour	Pinch of salt
1 teaspoonful baking	1 oz. butter or lard
powder	Half an egg
½ gill milk	

Rub the butter into the flour, then add the baking powder and salt. Beat the egg,

Just an ordinary currant bun mixture, but they win all hearts at tea if shaped into little men

add it, and then the milk. Knead the mixture into a dough and put on a floured board. Roll out 1 in. thick, cut into rounds and bake in a hot oven for 10–15 minutes.

Potato Scones

Boil some potatoes and, when cooked, drain off the water, and put the potatoes through a masher on to a floured board. Add a pinch of salt, and work in as much sifted flour as will make the mixture into a stiff dough. Roll out, sprinkle with flour and cut into rounds or triangles. Grease and heat a girdle and put the rounds on it. Brown on one side, turn over with a palette knife and brown the other side. Serve hot.

Sultana Scones

8 oz. flour	Milk to bind
2 oz. granulated sugar	2 oz. sultanas
1 oz. butter	Small egg
½ teaspoonful cream	½ teaspoonful bicar-
of tartar	bonate of soda

Rub the butter into the flour and add the rest of the dry ingredients. Then add the beaten egg and enough milk to make the mixture into a dough. Roll out on a floured board and cut into large rounds. Then cut each round in half. Paint with a little beaten egg and bake in a hot oven for about 15–20 minutes.

You can make a fascinating variety of fruit-flavoured tea breads, combining banana with nuts, raisins, prunes, etc.

EMERGENCY MEALS

*When unexpected guests arrive, the clever housewife
turns to her store cupboard to save the situation*

THESE days no practical housewife need be stumped by the arrival of unexpected guests for Sunday dinner—or unduly put out when her husband telephones on early closing day to say he is bringing the boss home for dinner. You really can buy—and safely store for long periods in quite a small space in your emergency cupboard—the necessary ingredients for a banquet or a simple picnic meal, all in cans, jars, tubes and packets.

If you can manage the initial outlay, you can always invest in a jar of chicken breasts, a tin of whole chicken, some cans of pâté de foie gras, perhaps something really exotic like a jar of grapes in wine.

But without being as extravagant as that, you can call an emergency cupboard excellently stocked if it contains the following:

Soups.—Several cans and packets in different flavours—excellent to flavour dull meat and fish dishes.

Meat.—Cans of luncheon meat, chicken, stewed steak, kidneys, tongue; Ravioli.

Fish.—Cans of herrings, tuna, salmon.

Vegetables.—Canned peas, corn, tomatoes, mixed vegetables, beans, asparagus tips, carrots, celery, beetroot. Packets of "Swel" prepared (dried) vegetables.

Fruits.—Canned strawberries, peaches, fruit salad, pineapple, apple purée.

Oddments for Trimmings.—Carton of Parmesan cheese. Small can tomato juice. Cans of evaporated (unsweetened) and condensed (sweetened) milk and cream. Jar of horseradish cream. Tubes of French mustard and tomato purée.

You can supplement these emergency rations with some of the excellent quick-frozen foods now on the market which are easy and quick to cook or heat.

SOUPS

With some canned and packet soups in the store cupboard you can always start a meal off well. The obvious thing is to serve canned soup "neat"; but you can make more subtle flavours by adroit mixing.

Remember that canned soups are best turned out of the can before heating, as they are nearly always concentrated and need diluting. Milk added to a thick soup increases its nutritive value and improves the creamy texture and flavour. Never heat canned soups more than is necessary.

Here are some ideas for flavour experiments. Once you start, you will no doubt think out many of your own:

(1) Combine a can of Scotch broth with an equal quantity of milk or milk and water. Season and sprinkle liberally with chopped parsley.

(2) Combine a can of consommé with the same quantity of water or clear stock. After heating, add a dessertspoonful of sherry and some shredded carrots, and sprinkle with sieved hard-boiled egg-yolk.

(3) Mix a can of chicken soup with a can of asparagus or onion soup and a can measure of milk. Season and add a half-teaspoonful of fresh thyme and simmer for a few minutes. Add fresh chopped chives just before serving.

(4) Add a can measure of milk to a can of tomato soup. Season as desired. Heat through and, on serving, add some very thinly sliced raw onion and a tablespoonful of fried croûtons to each portion.

(5) Mix a can of kidney soup with an equal quantity of bone stock and a cupful of cooked spaghetti. Season as desired and serve very hot.

(6) Combine a can of mushroom soup with a can of onion soup and a can measure of milk or water. Season and heat. Serve sprinkled with grated Parmesan cheese.

Another use for canned soups.—When you want to give a dish a distinctive and exciting flavour and have not the time—or the raw ingredients—to make a special sauce, try using canned chicken, celery, onion or mushroom soups in place of cream sauces.

This hors d'œuvre doesn't look like a last-minute concoction, but it could not be quicker or easier to prepare from a can of smoked herring fillets

HORS D'ŒUVRES

Herring and Horseradish

Flake up the flesh of some canned herring. Mix with horseradish sauce to taste and spread in sandwiches or on tiny pieces of toast (see Sauces chapter for horseradish sauce, or it can be bought in jars).

Herring Fillets as Hors d'œuvres

1 can smoked herring fillets
1 hard-boiled egg
1 very small onion or shallot
Chopped parsley

Remove the fillets carefully from the tin and drain them. Arrange in an hors d'œuvres dish or on plates. Scatter with a few very fine rings of onion. Chop white and yolk of egg separately and arrange in lines between the fillets. Garnish with chopped parsley.

Hot Savoury Bouchées

6 oz. rough puff or flaky pastry (see Pastry chapter)
1 tablespoonful cream or top of milk
1 teaspoonful chopped parsley
1 small can soft herring roes
Lemon rind and juice
Salt and pepper

Bake some small puff pastry cases. Drain all liquid from the roes, mash them lightly with a fork and mix with the cream or top of milk. Put into a small pan and heat very gently, stirring all the time. Add chopped parsley, the grated rind of half a lemon and a teaspoonful of lemon juice. Season well and, when quite hot, fill the pastry cases and serve at once.

Marine Puffs

6 oz. rough puff pastry (see Pastry chapter)
½ teaspoonful lemon juice
Salt and pepper
1 small can fresh herrings in tomato sauce

A little milk or beaten egg

Roll the pastry into an oblong ¼ in. thick and cut in half. Remove bones and tails from the herrings, flake them and add salt and pepper and lemon juice to taste. Spread the fish on one piece of pastry and cover with the other. Brush top with milk or beaten egg and cut into fingers. Bake in a very hot oven for 25 minutes. (These quantities make about 12 puffs.)

A tasty dish made from your "iron rations"—Herring and Corn Fritters are both satisfying and appetising

FISH DISHES

Friday Dish (for 2)

1 *small can herrings*	1 *small can tomato or*
2 *oz. cooked rice*	*mushroom soup*
1 *tablespoonful*	1 *oz. grated cheese*
breadcrumbs	*Salt and pepper*

If the herrings are packed in tomato sauce, use tomato soup. If they are packed in their own juice, use mushroom soup.

Remove the skin and backbones from the fish and flake them. Mix with the cooked rice and add salt and pepper to taste. Pour over sufficient soup to make a moist consistency. Turn into a fireproof dish and sprinkle with cheese and breadcrumbs. Bake in a hot oven for 20–25 minutes.

Herring and Corn Fritters (for 3–4)

1 *small can herrings*	1 *small can whole*
in tomato sauce	*kernel corn*
2 *tablespoonfuls flour*	*Fat for frying*
1 *egg*	*Salt and pepper*

Sift the flour into a bowl and make into a batter with the egg. Remove tails and centre bones from the fish and flake it. Add fish, tomato sauce and drained corn to the batter. Season with salt and pepper and

drop tablespoonfuls of the mixture into smoking hot fat. Fry golden brown and serve at once.

Herring Milanaise (for 4)

1 *can herring in*	¼ *lb. macaroni or*
tomato sauce	*spaghetti*
1 *oz. butter or mar-*	2 *oz. grated or thinly*
garine	*sliced cheese*

Cook the macaroni in salted water, drain well, add the butter or margarine and stir gently. Drain the herring, make it very hot and place on a hot dish. Add the tomato sauce to the macaroni at the last moment, add the cheese and garnish round the herring.

NOTE: Rice may be used in place of macaroni or spaghetti if preferred.

Herring Roll (for 4)

6 *oz. short crust*	1 *can herrings*
pastry (see Pastry	*Salt and pepper*
chapter)	*Lemon juice*
	Milk or egg

Remove tails and centre bones and flake the fish. Add salt, pepper and lemon juice to taste. Roll the pastry into an oblong shape, spread the fish over it, bringing it

234

ell to the edges. Damp the edges, roll up
nd seal the ends. Brush the top with milk
r beaten egg. Bake in a hot oven for 30
ninutes.

Herring Tyrolienne (for 3)

1 egg-yolk	½ teaspoonful salt
2 tablespoonfuls salad oil	½ teaspoonful French mustard
1 tablespoonful vinegar or lemon juice	1 small teaspoonful each Tarragon, finely chopped spring onion and chervil
1 can herring in tomato	
Pepper	

Put the egg-yolk into a basin with the
salt, pepper and mustard. Using a small
whisk, mix well and stir in, very gradually,
he salad oil. Add the tomato sauce from
he herring and the Tarragon, onion and
chervil. If too rich, stir in vinegar or lemon
uice. Pour this sauce over the herring and
erve with sliced or diced beetroot.

Mock Oyster Pie (for 3)

1 large can soft herring roes	2 oz. breadcrumbs
1 egg	½ pint milk
Salt and pepper	1 oz. melted margarine

Mash the herring roes and mix them with
the breadcrumbs. Place in a greased pie
dish. Beat the egg and add the milk,
melted margarine, ¼ teaspoonful salt and
pepper to taste. Pour this custard over the
fish mixture. Allow to stand 20 minutes.
Bake in a moderate oven for 25 minutes or
until the custard is set.

Scalloped Herring Mornay

1 can herring in tomato	White sauce (see Sauces chapter.)
Grated cheese	Cold mashed potato

Remove backbone from the herring and
break up the fish with a fork in the tomato
sauce. Add a small quantity of white
sauce to bind, and pile the mixture into
scallop shells. Surround with a border of
mashed potatoes, sprinkle with grated
cheese and heat under the grill until golden
brown.

Soft Roes and Bacon (for 4)

16 oz. can soft roes	2 tablespoonfuls plain flour (approx.)
4 oz. bacon rashers	
1 lb. mashed potatoes	Parsley

Fry the bacon and keep hot. Roll the
roes in the flour and fry in the bacon fat.
Meanwhile, make a bed of the mashed

You can whip these up between the warning 'phone call and the guests' arrival—Supper Cakes served with grilled tomatoes

potatoes and arrange the roes and bacon on top. Garnish with parsley. Serve with canned baked beans.

Spiced Pilchards (for 4)

1 *large can pilchards*	4 *tablespoonfuls*
2 *tablespoonfuls*	*vinegar*
water	*Liquor from canned*
2 *oz. finely*	*fish*
chopped onion	½ *teaspoonful mixed*
½ *oz. chopped parsley*	*herbs*

Drain the liquor from the can and, if the dish is to be served hot, warm the fish in the oven while making the sauce. To make the sauce, simmer the onion, herbs, vinegar, water and fish liquor together for 3–5 minutes, then add chopped parsley and pour the sauce over the fish. Serve hot with canned tomatoes and mashed potatoes or cold with salad and mashed potatoes.

Stuffed Herring (for 4)

1 *large can herring in*	*Parsley*
tomato	1 *dozen capers*
1 *onion*	1 *egg*
3 *tablespoonfuls*	1 *oz. melted butter or*
breadcrumbs	*margarine*
Pinch of salt	*Pinch of pepper*
Made mustard	

Mix the breadcrumbs and melted butter or margarine with the chopped capers, parsley and onion. Add seasoning and about ½ teaspoonful made mustard and mix in the beaten egg. Remove fish carefully from the tin, fill with stuffing and bake.

Supper Cakes (for 4)

1 *small can fresh*	1 *teaspoonful*
herrings	*chopped parsley*
Salt and pepper	*Browned bread-*
1 *small egg*	*crumbs*
1 *lb. cooked potatoes*	*Fat for frying*

Remove tails and centre bones, and flake the fish. Mash the potato and mix it lightly with the fish, parsley, pepper and a very little salt. Turn on to a floured board and form into flat cakes. Coat with beaten egg and crumbs. Fry in hot shallow fat until golden brown on both sides.

Tuna Moulds (for 3–4)

7 *oz. can tuna fish*	1½ *tablespoonfuls*
8 *oz. can peas*	*gelatine*
½ *pint liquor from the*	1 *teaspoonful salt*
peas and water	2 *teaspoonfuls*
1 *dessertspoonful*	*chopped parsley*
anchovy essence	¼ *teaspoonful pepper*
Colouring, if desired	

Dissolve the gelatine in the hot water and vegetable liquor. Roughly chop the tuna fish and mix it with the rest of the ingredients. Add colouring, if desired. Rinse out 8 dariole moulds with cold water and fill them with the mixture. Allow to set then turn out. Serve with salad.

MEAT DISHES

Bacon and Bean Pie (for 4)

16 *oz. can baked*	½ *teaspoonful pepper*
beans	4 *oz. streaky bacon*
1 *oz. chopped onion*	1 *teaspoonful salt*
1 *lb. potatoes*	*Milk*

Cook and mash potatoes with a little milk and seasoning. Cut bacon into strips, fry it and the onion until lightly browned, then mix with the beans, add seasoning, pour into a casserole and cover with the mashed potatoes. Bake in a fairly hot oven for 20–30 minutes. Serve hot, with canned spinach.

Casserole of Pork (for 4)

1 *can pork luncheon*	¼ *lb. each cooked*
meat	*carrot, turnip, and*
2 *small onions*	*macaroni*
Vegetable stock	1 *bay leaf*
Fat for frying	

Chop the onions and fry in fat until brown. Place in bottom of casserole, then add layers of vegetables, macaroni and diced meat. Add bay leaf. Moisten well with vegetable stock or gravy made with vegetable extract. Cook slowly until well heated through.

Chicken Soufflé (for 3–4)

10 *oz. can chicken*	½ *pint milk*
(or other canned	1 *teaspoonful salt*
meat)	2 *oz. plain flour*
2 *oz. margarine*	2 *eggs (separated)*
1 *tablespoonful*	1 *tablespoonful*
chopped onion	*chopped parsley*
¼ *teaspoonful pepper*	

Melt the margarine in a saucepan, add flour, then milk mixed with any chicken liquor from the can and cook until smooth. Remove from heat, add beaten egg-yolks, seasoning, onion, parsley, chopped chicken and, finally, fold in the stiffly whipped egg whites. Pour mixture into a greased casserole dish. Bake in a moderate oven for approximately 45 minutes. Serve immediately, with canned garden peas and new potatoes tossed in butter.

A delicious cold buffet made entirely from canned goods. The main dish is vegetables in aspic, followed by Gâteau St. Honoré à la Crême and Cheese Dreams

Cold Meat Mould (for 4)

8 oz. can luncheon meat	1 teaspoonful sherry
12 oz. can diced carrots	Pepper and salt
	8 oz. can peas
¾ pint vegetable liquor	¼ oz. aspic jelly crystals
Lettuce leaves	1 hard-boiled egg
	Mayonnaise

Mix the liquor from peas and carrots together and, if it is not quite ¾ pint, make up with water. Heat the liquor and dissolve aspic crystals in it. Cut meat into small cubes and dice hard-boiled egg. Rinse out mould in cold water, pour in a little aspic jelly and arrange some of the peas in a pattern. Allow to set. Mix meat, egg, peas, a third of the carrots, sherry and seasoning with the remainder of the jelly, and when it begins to "jell" pour into the mould and allow to set. To serve, turn out on to lettuce leaves and mix remainder of the diced carrots with 3 tablespoonfuls mayonnaise and arrange as a garnish round the mould.

Corned Beef Cakes (for 4)

8 oz. canned corned beef	1 oz. raw onion (chopped)
Pepper and salt	Flour, egg, bread-crumbs and fat for frying
8 oz. cooked mashed potato	

Mix all ingredients together and shape into cakes. Roll them in flour and then in egg and, finally, breadcrumbs. Fry in hot, shallow fat. Serve with tomato sauce (see Sauces chapter).

Kidney Omelet (for 4)

2 oz. butter or margarine	6 eggs
	Salt and pepper to taste
2 tablespoonfuls cold water	

For the filling
8 oz. can stewed kidneys

Beat the eggs well together, add the cold water and season to taste. Melt a knob of butter in the frying pan and, when fairly hot, pour in a quarter of the egg mixture. Tilt the pan backwards and forwards, allowing the uncooked egg to run to the sides of the pan and at the same time keeping the omelet moving until just set. The kidneys, which should have been seasoned and heated in a separate pan, are then placed on one half of the omelet. Fold

237

over the other half and turn on to a hot dish. Make three more omelets in the same way. Serve immediately with canned broad beans and duchesse potatoes.

Netherlands Puffs (for 3–4)

2 cupfuls finely chopped Dutch luncheon meat

For the batter

2 oz. flour	*½ pint milk*
1 egg	*Salt*

Make a Yorkshire pudding batter (see Puddings chapter), add the meat, divide the mixture into well-greased patty pans and bake for about 15 minutes in a hot oven.

Quick Salad Platter (for 4)

8 oz. can mixed vege-	*8 oz. can garden peas*
tables in mayon-	*8 oz. can diced carrots*
naise	*8 oz. can sliced beet-*
8 oz. can pork	*root*
luncheon meat	*2 hard-boiled eggs*
2 large tomatoes	*Chopped parsley*

Cut the tomatoes in half, hollow out the centres and fill with the diced vegetables in mayonnaise. Arrange down the centre of the dish. Cut the luncheon meat in slices and the eggs in halves, and arrange at opposite ends of the dish. Place the rest of the canned foods in rows on the dish. Cover the eggs with a little mayonnaise and garnish the whole with chopped parsley.

Risotto (for 4)

2 oz. margarine	*Salt and pepper to*
2 oz. chopped onion	*taste*
6–8 oz. canned lun-	*Pinch of mixed herbs*
cheon meat (diced)	*1 pint meat stock or*
6 oz. Patna rice	*water*

Heat margarine in a saucepan, add onion, rice and mixed herbs, cook until lightly browned, then add salt and pepper and about a quarter of the stock. Cook for about 20 minutes, adding remainder of liquid at intervals as it is absorbed. When rice is tender, add diced meat and cook for a further 5 minutes. Serve very hot.

Spaghetti with Bolognaise or Napolitaine Sauce (for 4)

1 lb. spaghetti	*Grated Parmesan*
Knobs of butter	*cheese*
	Salt

Make the sauce first because it takes longer.

Boil spaghetti in plenty of fast-boiling water for 18–20 minutes, stirring with a fork occasionally. Keep on the firm side but do not overcook. Drain very well, and place on a dish. Add knobs of butter and grated Parmesan cheese. Toss and mix well together; season. Serve at once with one of the following sauces separately:

Bolognaise Sauce

4 oz. finely chopped	*Salt and pepper*
meat	*Chopped parsley*
1 capsule tomato	*½ chopped onion*
purée	*Olive oil*

Heat a little olive oil in a saucepan, add the chopped onion, fry briskly until golden. Add meat and fry briskly for 2 or 3 minutes. Empty tomato purée into a cup, dilute with warm water and stir until dissolved, then pour into the saucepan. Season; cook slowly for 1 hour. Add chopped parsley.

Napolitaine Sauce

Prepared in the same way as the Bolognaise Sauce, but without the meat.

Steak and Mushroom Pie (for 4)

8 oz. flaky pastry	*16 oz. can stewed*
(see Pastry chapter)	*steak*
2 oz. chopped onion	*4 oz. sliced mush-*
1 tablespoonful plain	*rooms*
flour	*4 tablespoonfuls cold*
Salt and pepper to	*water*
taste	

Empty the can of stewed steak into a pie dish, add remainder of ingredients, place pie funnel in centre of mixture and cover with flaky pastry. Bake in a hot oven until pastry is cooked (about 30–40 minutes). Serve with canned celery hearts and new potatoes.

VEGETABLES AND VEGETARIAN DISHES

Carrots au Gratin (for 4)

½ pint white sauce	*3 or 4 tablespoonfuls*
(see Sauces chapter)	*grated cheese*
Salt and pepper	*4 teacupfuls of*
2 oz. "Swel" carrots	*boiling water*
	Breadcrumbs

Soak the carrots in boiling water for 1 hour. Bring to the boil and cook until tender (about 15–20 minutes). Strain and keep hot in a baking dish, while making the white sauce with the liquid in which the carrots were cooked. Season the sauce well, add half the grated cheese, pour over carrots, sprinkle remaining cheese and the breadcrumbs on top, and brown under the grill or in a hot oven. Serve hot.

A real party dish—Charlotte Russe, one of the most luxurious of all sweets, yet made from "emergency stores"

Cheese Dreams (for 2–3)

8 oz. can asparagus	8 oz. processed
Fingers of toast	cheese
A little butter	Cayenne pepper

Butter the toast, place asparagus on each piece and cover with a thin slice of cheese. Place under the grill and leave until the cheese just starts to melt. Sprinkle with Cayenne pepper and serve very hot.

Creamed Beetroot (for 4)

½ pint white sauce	2 oz. "Swel" beet-
(see Sauces chapter)	root dice
Salt and pepper	1 tablespoonful
Small pinch of	vinegar
ground cloves or	Chopped parsley to
grated nutmeg	garnish
4 teacupfuls of boiling water	

Soak the beetroot in water and vinegar for 4 hours (or overnight). Bring to the boil in the soaking water and cook until tender (about 20–30 minutes). Make white sauce, season and add ground cloves or nutmeg and vinegar, then add the cooked beetroot. Serve hot, garnished with chopped parsley.

Mixed Vegetable Fritters (for 4)

2 oz. "Swel" mixed	4 teacupfuls boiling
vegetables	water
Seasoning	Fat for frying

For the batter

4 oz. flour	½ teacupful milk
	1 egg

Pour the water on to the vegetables and leave to soak for 1 hour. Bring to the boil and cook for 5 minutes, season and strain.

239

Make batter (see Pudding chapter) and add vegetables. Drop in dessertspoonfuls into hot fat and fry until golden brown. Drain, serve hot with fried bacon. This quantity makes about 18 fritters.

Onion Savoury (for 4)

2 oz. "Swel" onion	White sauce (made
3 teacupfuls milk and	with 2 oz. flour and
water	2 oz. margarine)
2 tablespoonfuls	½ oz. "Swel" carrots
chopped nuts or	2 tablespoonfuls
grated cheese	white breadcrumbs
Salt	

Soak the carrots in 1 teacupful boiling water. After 1 hour add the onion, 2 teacupfuls milk and water, and salt to taste. Bring to the boil and simmer for 15 minutes or until tender. Strain, and use the liquid to make the white sauce. Put the vegetables into a pie dish, cover with sauce, sprinkle the top with breadcrumbs and the chopped nuts or grated cheese. Heat thoroughly in a hot oven until crisp and brown, or brown under the grill. Serve with fried potatoes.

Spaghetti and Egg Croquettes (for 4)

16 oz. can spaghetti	Browned bread-
in tomato	crumbs
2 oz. plain flour	2 oz. chopped raw
1 tablespoonful	onion
chopped parsley	2 hard-boiled eggs
1 beaten raw egg	Fat for frying

Empty the spaghetti into a saucepan, add onion and flour, and cook until the mixture thickens, then add diced egg and chopped parsley. Turn out on to a plate to cool. When nearly cold, divide mixture into equal-sized sections and shape into croquettes on a floured board; then dip each one into beaten egg, then breadcrumbs. Fry in very hot deep fat for a few seconds only. (If not removed quickly, the croquettes will split.) Serve hot with canned carrots tossed in melted butter or margarine and new potatoes.

Vegetable Cheese Flan (for 3–4)

8 oz. short pastry	12-oz. can mixed
6 oz. grated cheese	vegetables
¼ pint vegetable liquor	2 oz. margarine
and milk mixed	2 oz. plain flour
2 teaspoonfuls salt	½ teaspoonful pepper

Make a sauce with the margarine and flour, adding strained vegetable liquor and milk, salt, pepper, half the cheese and vegetables. Pour this mixture into uncooked

pastry case, sprinkle remainder of cheese on top. Bake in a hot oven for 30–40 minutes.

Vegetable Patties (for 4)

1 oz. "Swel" mixed	Browned bread-
vegetables	crumbs
4 oz. cooked mashed	2 teacupfuls boiling
potatoes	water
Beaten egg	Fat for frying

Pour the water on to the vegetables and leave to soak for 1 hour. Bring to the boil and cook until tender, then strain. Mix the vegetables with the potato and bind with half the beaten egg. When cool enough to handle, form into patties, coat with egg and breadcrumbs, and fry in hot fat until golden brown. Drain, and serve hot.

SWEETS

Apple Charlotte (for 4)

16 oz. can of sweet-	½ lemon (grated rind
ened apple purée	and juice)
or slices	2 oz. castor sugar
½ teaspoonful cinna-	4–6 oz. thinly sliced
mon	bread (without
2 oz. margarine	crust)

Melt the margarine and use a pastry brush to brush it lightly over each side of the sliced bread. Line a dish with some of the prepared bread, pour in the apple with the other ingredients added, cover the top of the mixture with remaining slices of bread. Bake in a moderate oven for about 1 hour or until bread is brown and crisp. Serve hot or cold.

Charlotte Russe (for 4)

8 oz. can peaches or	8 oz. can evaporated
apricots	milk
¼ pint lemon jelly	2 tablespoonfuls
2 tablespoonfuls hot	gelatine
water	¼ pint fresh milk
1½ oz. sugar	2 tablespoonfuls
1 tablespoonful rum	sherry
1 doz. (approx.)	½ teaspoonful vanilla
sponge fingers	essence

Rinse out a charlotte russe mould with cold water. Pour in the lemon jelly about ¼ in. deep and arrange the drained fruit in a pattern on it and allow the jelly to set. Then place sponge fingers all round the inside of the mould. Dissolve gelatine in the hot water. Heat fresh milk and sugar together and add dissolved gelatine, vanilla essence, sherry and rum. Allow this mixture to stand until just beginning to set. Fold in the whipped evaporated milk and pour the mixture into the mould and allow t to set in a very cool place. To serve, turn out and garnish with any left-over jelly or fruit.

Forgotten Dessert (for 4)

16 oz. can straw- berries	½ teaspoonful vanilla essence
6 oz. castor sugar	6 oz. can evaporated
¼ oz. gelatine	milk
3 egg-whites	

Whip egg-whites until they are very stiff, fold in castor sugar and vanilla essence. Grease a plate with olive oil and spread the meringue about ¼ in. thick over the bottom but pile it high around the sides. Heat the oven to approx. 400° F., place meringue in the oven and turn off the heat. Leave for at least 6 hours. Drain juice from the strawberries, heat and dissolve gelatine in it, cool, then just as it begins to set, fold in the stiffly whipped evaporated milk. Allow to set, then pile it into the meringue "plate." Garnish on top with the strawberries.

Jelly Fluff (for 4)

1 pint packet jelly	1 pint canned fruit
8 oz. can fruit	juice
2 egg-whites	

Dissolve the jelly in the heated fruit juice, which can be a mixture of juice from the can of fruit together with any left over from another can of fruit. When beginning to set, fold in the stiffly beaten egg-white and fruit, pour into a jelly mould and leave to set. To serve, turn out of the mould.

Rhubarb Ring (for 4–5)

2 16-oz. cans rhubarb (drained)	8 oz. short pastry (see Pastry chapter)

For the sauce

2 teaspoonfuls red jam	2 teaspoonfuls corn- flour
½ pint fruit juice	

Roll out the pastry into an oblong about 15 in. by 6 in. Cover with the rhubarb and roll up, having moistened the edges of the pastry to secure the roll firmly. Form into a ring, moisten each end again and secure firmly. Slash the roll at 1-in. intervals around outer edge. Place on a tin and bake in a moderate oven for about 40 minutes.

For the sauce.—Mix the cornflour with a little juice. Boil remainder with jam, add to the cornflour mixture, boil and pour over ring.

Rhubarb Ring is an unusual dessert. If you have no rhubarb in the cupboard, make a Cherry Ring instead—it's just as good

Introduced by Ronald Lightowler, Secretary, London Vegetarian Society

VEGETARIAN CATERING

Proving for those who still have doubts that there are many tasty alternatives to fish, flesh and fowl

SOME clarification appears to be necessary concerning the meaning of the term "vegetarian," since some people seem to believe that vegetarians eat fish, though they do not eat flesh foods. Some even believe that poultry can be classified as a vegetarian food. Others, going to the opposite extreme, think that a strict vegetarian not only refuses flesh, fish and fowl but all dairy produce as well, i.e. milk, cheese, butter, eggs, etc.

The definition of the word, as used by the Vegetarian Societies, has always implied the exclusion of flesh, fish and fowl from the diet, with or without the addition of dairy produce. The majority of vegetarians in the U.K. to-day do include dairy produce in their diet, which is sometimes called "lacto-vegetarian." The few strict vegetarians who do not take dairy produce now use the term "vegan" to differentiate their dietary from that of ordinary vegetarians.

As there are certain dangers involved in adopting a "vegan" diet unless the subject is very carefully studied and applied, the material here presented concerns itself only with the diet in which dairy produce is included.

Newcomers to the vegetarian way of living are frequently anxious to know how to balance their diet correctly so that their health may not suffer as a result of the change. Such concern is natural in view of the fact that, until recently, orthodox medical and scientific opinion has frowned upon the fleshless diet.

Circumstances affecting food supplies in recent years—namely the two world wars and the tremendous increase in world population—have brought such a degree of pressure to bear on this aspect of life that traditional beliefs have had to be reconsidered and are now shown to be incorrect in the light of recent scientific research. Over a century of organised vegetarianism in the U.K. has brought with it concrete evidence, not only that one can remain healthy, but that with reasonable care one's health, if it has previously been impaired, can often be improved by such a diet.

The majority of vegetarians favour a diet consisting of 50 per cent. raw salads and fruit with 50 per cent. conservatively cooked vegetables—both accompanied by an adequate portion of carbohydrate (energy-giving) foods and protein (body-building) foods.

CARBOHYDRATES

There is a tendency to overdo the consumption of carbohydrates, especially in the early days of changing over to vegetarianism, because of a false belief that larger quantities are needed to take the place of the foods eliminated from the diet. The carbohydrates consist of starchy foods and sugars, many of which suffer from the modern tendency to "process" them. If genuine wholewheat bread is obtainable or made at home, this provides an excellent foundation food which is very satisfying and is claimed by some to be the most nearly perfect human food, containing carbohydrates, protein, fat, mineral salts and certain vitamins.

The sugar to be preferred is the natural Barbados or genuine Demerara, both of which are usually obtainable at Health Food Stores. Honey is an excellent food

PROTEINS

While, as indicated above, there are certain vegetarians who do not use dairy produce such as milk, cheese and eggs, it is usually inadvisable to make too sweeping a change in one's diet. The normal alternatives to take the place of flesh, fish and fowl will therefore be cheese, eggs, nut kernels and pulse foods (beans, peas and lentils).

There is frequently anxiety about suitable *quantities* of foods, even among those

To appeal to the eye as well as the palate, cauliflower attractively arranged
with green peas and spaghetti

who have never worried about the amount of meat and other protein foods formerly taken. The requirements of individuals will always vary considerably, according to temperament and such circumstances as occupation, etc. It cannot be emphasised too strongly, however, that it is very dangerous just to eliminate fish, flesh and fowl from the diet. Adequate amounts of alternative protein foods, of good quality, must be included if health and vigour are to be maintained, and part of these should be in the form of dairy produce. **As a rough guide, at least 2–4 ounces of protein should be included in each day's diet —a proportion at each main meal.**

The growing child requires the larger amount of body-building (protein) food, and this is, of course, seen to be reasonable when its specific purpose is understood. The adult body requires protein mainly for purposes of *renewal* of tissue. Vegetarians believe that more harm may well be done by excessive anxiety about the quantities required than is likely to result from too much or too little being taken. The human organism is amazingly adaptable, so do not fear to experiment within reasonable limits, as the normally healthy body has numerous devices which safeguard it.

Of the alternative foods, **cheese** contains a good proportion of protein (quite equal to good-quality meat) and has a considerable fat content. It can be used just as it is, or it can form the basis of many very palatable cooked dishes.

Eggs are handy for a quick meal and also add appreciably to the protein content of cooked dishes in which the other ingredients may be somewhat deficient, as in the case of some of the pulse foods.

Most **nut kernels** provide a good balance of protein, carbohydrate and fat, and have the advantage that they can be used as purchased, either whole or milled, with salads or fruit. They also form a good basis for innumerable fried, baked or steamed savouries, which can be very appetising when served with seasonable, conservatively cooked fresh vegetables, or cold with salads.

The pulse foods, with the exception of the soya bean, provide only a small amount of protein in relation to their bulk *when cooked*. Analysis of the raw beans, peas or lentils shows a good percentage of protein but, because they absorb a large amount of water in cooking, the protein content after cooking is relatively small. The addition of eggs or cheese to such dishes increases their value as protein foods.

Soya flour, although not possessing an outstanding flavour, is rich in excellent protein and can therefore be used with advantage in conjunction with other tastier foods.

Dried milk powder is also a valuable addition to dishes requiring more protein.

FATS

The vegetarian need experience no difficulty over the fat content of the diet. The nut and pure vegetable fats available in place of the ordinary cooking fats are excellent, and are so rich in pure oils that rather less of them should be used when making pastry or cakes. The vegetarian margarines are also excellent and contain no whale oil, being manufactured exclusively from vegetable and nut oils.

All the nuts contain appreciable quantities of readily assimilable oils and, if more is required, olive oil or nut oil is easily obtainable.

FLAVOURINGS

Herbs, either dried or, preferably, fresh, can be used with advantage in the making of savoury dishes. Sprigs of freshly picked herbs also add considerably to the attractiveness of raw salads. When using dried herbs, the flavour is greatly improved if they are steeped in a small quantity of boiling water for a little while before use.

MENTAL ATTITUDE TO FOOD

This matters a great deal and affects the body's assimilation. At times of emotional stress or strain, it is advisable not to eat until the body and mind can be relaxed.

The vegetarian should truly be able to enjoy his food, for he takes it as fresh and full of vitality as it is possible to get it, and he has the happy knowledge that no human being has been engaged in slaughtering animals for food on his behalf. Vegetarian foods are in themselves attractive, full of colour, fragrance and variety of flavour.

ALTERNATIVES TO MEAT EXTRACTS

There are several well-known yeast extracts on the market which can be used in place of meat extracts in making gravies, soups and stews, as well as in other ways. Among the better known are Marmite and Yeastrel.

A useful tip for improving the flavour of gravies is to cook the yeast extract slightly in the fat before adding thickening and stock or water. This gives a fuller and better flavour to the gravy.

SOUPS

Almost any ordinary soup recipe can be easily adapted to fit the requirement of vegetarian catering. Vegetable stock can take the place of meat stock and yeast extracts, such as Marmite and Yeastrel, that of meat extracts as flavouring agents, at the same time adding appreciable amounts of vitamin B. A further excellent flavouring agent, of entirely vegetable origin, is Vesop, which is in liquid form.

The flavour of most vegetable soups is considerably enhanced if the vegetables are cut up small and "sweated" for about 15–20 minutes in vegetarian margarine before adding liquids. The lid of the saucepan should be kept on and the heat low during this part of the process.

SAVOURIES

These provide the main protein contribution to vegetarian menus and are therefore of supreme importance. They must not merely appeal to the palate or to the eye—although they should do both of these things—but must contain adequate protein foods. If there is any doubt as to the sufficiency of proteins in a meal, add either an egg or, where suitable, some grated cheese.

A selection of dishes based on nut

kernels, pulses, cheese and eggs follows. The chapter on Egg Dishes provides further variations, the only necessary alterations being that the fat used should be vegetarian and the "filling" of the omelets, for example, be in harmony with vegetarian requirements.

VEGETARIAN SWEETS

Most recipes for the sweet course can be readily adapted for vegetarians by the substitution of vegetarian fats in place of lard, etc. Also wholemeal flour can be used in place of white flour for those who prefer it.

In place of gelatine, agar-agar (which is a form of seaweed) can be used for making jellies and for thickening purposes. This not only serves a ultilitarian purpose, but also adds organic iodine and other mineral elements to the diet.

In general, vegetarians prefer fresh fruit.

Raw Fruit Porridge (Bircher muesli)

Raw fruit porridge is a whole-year-round dish. It can be made from nearly all fruits and is very good with apples grated with core and peel.

During spring when no fresh fruit is available, the dish should be made from dried fruit (prunes, apple rings, pears, apricots) or from grated raw carrots. During summer and autumn a large choice of soft and stone fruit gives ample variety.

The Basic Mixture per person is the same for every fruit.

1 dessertspoonful medium oatmeal, 1 tablespoonful sweetened condensed milk or milk (top of the milk) or 1 teaspoonful nut cream (diluted with water to a whitish consistency). Sweeten with honey or brown sugar to taste. Juice of half fresh lemon.

Soak oats, covered with water, for 12–24 hours. Mix condensed milk (or nut cream or sweetened milk) with lemon juice, add to the oats and stir well. Then add fruit pulp and stir well again. Serve at once with sprinkled milled nuts if available. If it has to be kept for some time before serving, cover it well.

Fruit Pulp—per person

Dried Fruit. 3½ oz. dried fruit soaked for 12–24 hours or more until the stones come easily from the prunes; stone and

Tomatoes stuffed with a mixture of grated cheese, breadcrumbs and beaten egg, and topped with parsley

either chop finely or pass through a mincer or emulsifier

Carrot. 3 oz. raw carrots peeled and grated into the basic mixture. Mix quickly to prevent loss of colour. Carrot muesli has to be prepared with special care as carrots have not the flavour of fruit. It requires more sweetening and lemon flavour. If available, add 2 oz. raw rhubarb juice. (Raw rhubarb juice can be made in a juice extractor or by grating washed and wiped unpeeled rhubarb on a two-way grater into a bowl, covered with a piece of butter muslin. Then squeeze butter muslin and add juice to the mixture. This gives a better flavour and is a rich source of vitamin C, so necessary in spring.

Soft Fruit. 5 oz. soft fruit, selected, washed and mashed with a plated fork or wooden masher—e.g. strawberries, raspberries, loganberries, bilberries, red and blackcurrants, blackberries, etc.

Stone Fruit. 5 oz. stone fruit, washed, stoned and chopped or passed through a mincer or emulsifier — e.g. cherries, peaches, apricots, plums, greengages, damsons, etc.

Apple. One big or two small apples, washed and wiped: take off stalks, tops and brown spots, and then grate with core and peel into bowl with the mixture. Mix quickly and well to prevent browning.

Protein Stock

2 oz. haricot beans	2 oz. split peas
1 onion	1 carrot
½ teaspoonful celery salt	Some parsley, herbs, pepper and salt
3 cloves	A blade of mace

Soak the dried vegetables overnight, and in the morning add the other ingredients. Cover with 4 pints of water, bring to the boil and then simmer for 4 hours. Strain into a bowl and use as required. The yield is about 2¾–3 pints and the stock will keep very well.

Savoury Sandwich Spread

½ pint haricot beans	2 oz. fine wholewheat breadcrumbs
2 oz. grated cheese	
Pepper and salt	2 oz. vegetarian margarine
Nutmeg	
Paprika	Protein stock

Soak the beans overnight, and the next morning drain and wash them and put them into a fireproof casserole with enough protein stock to cover them. Cover and cook gently in a slow oven until soft, then pass the beans through a mincer and, while they are still hot, beat in the cheese, margarine and breadcrumbs. Season with pepper, salt and nutmeg, adding, if liked, a little paprika. Press the mixture into scrupulously clean dry pots and run a little melted margarine over the top to seal.

Store until needed. This should keep for a reasonable time, but should be watched for signs of mould.

VARIOUS MAIN DISHES

Almond and Potato Croquettes

6 oz. milled almonds	1 egg
3 cupfuls mashed potatoes	2 tablespoonfuls grated raw onion
2 dried and crushed shredded wheat sections	1 teaspoonful mixed dried herbs
	Pepper and salt
½ cupful finely minced parsley	Grated cheese for sprinkling

Mix all the ingredients except the cheese, shape the mixture into large egg-size balls, arrange these on a well-greased baking dish, sprinkle a little grated cheese over each, bake for 30 minutes in a moderate oven.

Cheese Delight (for 4–6)

2 eggs, well beaten	2 oz. wholemeal flour
2 oz. vegetarian margarine	1 breakfastcupful cold water
2 oz. grated cheese	Salt and pepper

Season the flour with salt and pepper, and add the cold water very gradually, mixing to a smooth cream. Melt the margarine in a saucepan and add the flour mixture. Stir and boil for 5 minutes. Stir in the grated cheese and remove from the heat. Add the well-beaten eggs and pour into a well-greased baking dish.

Bake for 30 minutes.

Serve with green beans, either hot, or cold as a salad.

Green Bean Salad

Cook some prepared French or runner beans. Drain them well and, while still warm, marinade them in a French dressing made from equal parts of oil and vinegar. Add some chopped chives or onion and stand for 1 hour.

Serve on a bed of lettuce.

Angel in the Snow—the egg is separated and the white beaten before grilling—is an excellent dish for an invalid

Cheese and Onion Pie

> 6 oz. pastry
> 2 large onions
> 2 eggs
> 1 cupful milk
> 1 oz. vegetarian
>   margarine
> 3 oz. grated cheese
> Salt and pepper

Make some pastry, using 6 oz. wholewheat flour, etc., and line a 9-in. pie plate with it. Slice the onions into thin rings and cook gently in margarine. Do not let them brown. Boil milk, beat in the eggs and most of the cheese and season to taste. Put the onions in the pastry case, pour over the milk mixture and sprinkle cheese on top. Bake in a slow oven for 40–45 minutes.

Serve with thin slices of onion and cucumber marinaded for 1 hour in a French dressing.

Haricot, Leek and Mushroom Pie

> ½ lb. mushrooms
> 2 cupfuls pulped
>   baked haricot
>   beans (good-quality
>   canned baked beans
>   are suitable)
> 6 plump leeks
> 1 cupful breadcrumbs
> 1 egg
> 1 oz. fat
> 1 oz. flour
> Pepper and salt

Clean and cut leeks into 1-in. lengths, cover with water, simmer for 30 minutes. Meanwhile, prepare and slice mushrooms, simmer in another saucepan with water to cover for 20 minutes. Make thick sauce of the fat, flour and leek and mushroom cooking waters. Mix cooked leeks and mushrooms and put into a well-greased pie dish. Pour in the sauce. Cover with a "crust" made by mixing the bean pulp, beaten egg, breadcrumbs and seasoning. Dot with fat. Bake for ½ hour in moderately hot oven.

Leeks and Fruit with Curry Sauce

> 4 large leeks
> ¼ pint curry sauce
> 4 dried bananas (or
>   prunes or dried
>   figs)

Wash leeks and cut in half lengthwise. Cook in a little water until tender, then drain well, keeping the water to make the curry sauce. Grease a fireproof casserole, put in a layer of leeks, another of bananas (or other fruit) cut lengthwise, topping with one of the leeks. Make curry sauce (see p. 249) and pour over leeks. Cover with lid and put in oven for 30 minutes. Serve with mashed potatoes and hard-boiled eggs.

Brown Gravy

> 1 teaspoonful Yeastrel
>   or Marmite
> 1 oz. wholemeal flour
> 1 oz. margarine
> ½ pint stock
> Seasoning

Brown margarine in saucepan, add Yeastrel or Marmite, flour, and mix well. Gradually stir in stock, stirring until it boils, season and simmer for 5 minutes.

Nut Roast with Chestnut Stuffing

> ¾ lb. hazel nuts or
>   cashews
> 6 oz. wholemeal
>   breadcrumbs
> 2 onions
> 1 oz. vegetarian mar-
>   garine
> Seasoning
> Gravy

Mill nuts, mix with breadcrumbs and seasoning. Cut onion finely, fry to a golden brown. Place onion on top of mixture, pour over about 6 tablespoonfuls gravy, mix into a stiff dough. Form into roll, cut through centre lengthwise, place chestnut stuffing on inner side, replace top half of roast, smooth with knife. Bake in hot oven for 30 minutes.

Chestnut Stuffing

¼ lb. chestnuts   2 oz. breadcrumbs
1 onion   Seasoning

Place chestnuts in a saucepan with cold water, bring to the boil, peel. Cook chestnuts in ½ pint water, strain, mash, add fried onion, breadcrumbs and seasoning, so that the mixture becomes stiff.

Nut Roast

¼ lb. slightly roasted ground cashew or hazel nuts   1 lb. boiled, mashed potatoes
1 teacupful vegetable stock, milk or water   1 small grated onion
    2 dessertspoonfuls fat
1 egg   1 teaspoonful Yeastrel
    Salt to taste
Grated cheese

Beat the egg, pour over the mashed potatoes, mix well with the onion and fat. Dissolve the Yeastrel in the liquid, mix with all the other ingredients, put into a buttered fireproof dish. Sprinkle with grated cheese, put dots of fat on top, bake in a moderate oven for 30 minutes, until golden brown.

Serve with Brown Gravy (see previous page for recipe).

Onions stuffed with Nuttolene

2 large Spanish onions   1½ teaspoonfuls curry powder
1 small can Nuttolene   Salt to taste
Fat for frying

Boil onions until tender. Allow to cool and drain, then scoop out centres.

Mash Nuttolene with a fork on a wooden board, then fry in a little fat to bring out the flavour. Mix in a bowl with the scooped-out onion chopped up small, the curry powder and salt. If the mixture appears dry, add a little milk or water. Stuff the onions with the mixture and place in a greased fireproof dish; if any mixture is left over, place round the onions. A dessert-spoonful of grated cheese will improve the flavour. Place in hot oven and lower the heat. Bake in a moderate oven for ½ hour, and serve with mashed potatoes.

Never use fat with mashed potatoes if you want them to be light; use milk only and beat well.

Red Cabbage with Chestnuts

1 medium-sized red cabbage   2 tablespoonfuls sugar
2 large apples   1½ lemons
1 oz. cooking fat   ½ lb. chestnuts
¼ stick of cinnamon   A little salt
2 cloves   1 pint vegetable liquid
2 small onions   1 oz. margarine

Wash the cabbage in warm water and cut very fine with a knife or vegetable shredder. Wash and dry apples and cut into quarters. Melt cooking fat in a saucepan and add to it prepared cabbage and apples. Cook for about 5–10 minutes. Add cinnamon, sugar and juice of the lemons, one whole onion and cloves, and stew for another 20 minutes. The cabbage should be soft but not sticky when cooked. If a little more liquid is required, use vegetable stock.

Wash chestnuts and cut a cross in each one, bake until half cooked, then peel quickly. Put chestnuts, margarine and one cut-up onion into saucepan and cook for 5 minutes. Add liquid and salt and simmer slowly until chestnuts start to fall to pieces. If a little milk is added at the end, it gives a creamy flavour. Chestnuts are served with the red cabbage, and can also be served as a separate vegetable with salad, but not with potatoes.

Roast Nutmeat

4 oz. mixed milled nuts   1 cupful well-boiled rice
4 oz. milled peanuts   1 cupful brown breadcrumbs
1 egg
1 large cupful fried chopped onion   ½ teaspoonful dried thyme
1 clove garlic, finely minced   ¼ pint vegetable cooking water
Pepper and salt

Mix all the ingredients thoroughly. Pack into well-greased baking dish. Bake in a moderate oven for 45 minutes.

NOTE: See that the onions are finely chopped and fry them slowly until well browned before adding to the mixture. Serve with stuffed tomatoes, peas, gravy.

Stuffed Tomatoes

Cut a slice from the top of each tomato, carefully remove a little of the pulp so as to leave firm cases. Mix the pulp with an equal amount of grated cheese, breadcrumbs and beaten egg; season with pepper and salt and add a grate of nutmeg. Fill the cases with the mixture. Bake in hot oven for 15 minutes, using a well-greased earthenware dish.

NOTE: Roll surplus stuffing into tiny balls.

Gravy

Drain the fat from the pan in which onions are fried, pour ½ pint of vegetable cooking water into pan, simmer for 5 minutes, stir in a coffeespoonful of extract and a few drops of gravy browning. Serve hot, seasoned to taste.

Savoury Egg Pastry

Short pastry to line
 six patty dishes
3 eggs
1 tablespoonful flour
1 tomato
½ cupful of milk
½ onion
Parsley and chives or
 sage
A little salt

Mix the eggs gradually into the flour, add the milk and stir well. Add the peeled, chopped onion, finely cut tomato, chopped herbs and salt. Line patty dishes with pastry, pour in egg mixture and bake in a slow oven for about 20 minutes. The pastry will be ready when the top is light golden brown.

Savoy and Apple Savoury with Curry Sauce

Savoy cabbage
Curry sauce
2 apples
3 medium-sized leeks

Choose a firm savoy and quarter it after washing. (Do not soak vegetables in water but wash them quickly.) Steam the savoy for about 20 minutes, then cool and cut into thick slices. Place in a greased fireproof casserole, then add a layer of thin slices of apple and a layer of leeks, washed and cut lengthwise in four. Cover again with savoy, pour on curry sauce and cook in a moderate oven for 30 minutes.

Curry Sauce

1 level dessertspoon-
 ful fat
2 round dessertspoon-
 fuls wholemeal
 flour
1 heaped teaspoonful
 curry powder
2 heaped teaspoonfuls
 sugar
1 level teaspoonful
 salt
½ pint vegetable stock
 or water

Melt fat, add flour and curry, cook gently, stirring, till yellowish. Add liquid, boil, put in sugar and salt, simmer for 10 minutes.

Lentil cutlets can be made into a variety of shapes and served with potatoes and peas or carrots and spaghetti

Spaghetti Rondelles

4 oz. long, unbroken spaghetti	1 small onion
2 oz. grated cheese	1 oz. margarine
½ cupful tomato pulp	Seasoning
	1 egg

Boil the spaghetti in plenty of water, slightly salted, for 25 minutes. Drain thoroughly, and turn into a fresh saucepan containing the melted margarine. Cook over gentle heat, stirring with a wooden spoon for 3 or 4 minutes. Stir in the grated onion, the cheese, tomato pulp, beaten egg and seasoning. Cook gently for a few minutes, then stand in a cool place for ½ hour. Deposit little bun-shaped rondelles of the spaghetti upon a well-greased baking tin. Bake in a hot oven for 20 minutes. Serve hot with sprouts and butter mint sauce.

Butter Mint Sauce

1 oz. flour	1 tablespoonful chopped fresh mint
1 oz. margarine	
½ pint milk	1 teaspoonful butter
Seasoning	

Melt margarine in a saucepan, stir in flour, gradually add milk, simmer for 5 minutes, season to taste, stir in mint and butter just before serving.

Spinach and Mushroom

1 lb. spinach	½ pint white sauce, made with wholemeal flour
¼ lb. mushroom stalks	
Salt to taste	

Wash and steam spinach; chop up finely. Chop mushroom stalks. Pour a little water into a saucepan, barely covering the bottom, and add a dessertspoonful of oil. (Fats are more easily digested when treated in this way.) Add the mushroom stalks and leave over a small flame until tender. Make white sauce, add the spinach and mushroom to it and simmer for another 10 minutes.

Garnish with fried wholemeal bread and hard-boiled egg; or make a hole in the centre and fill this with scrambled egg. (An economical method is to add a little flour and milk before scrambling in a frying pan.) Sprinkle with cheese or grated nuts.

Stuffed Steamed Cabbage (for 4)

1 cabbage	1 egg, beaten
2 large onions	2 oz. vegetarian margarine
6 oz. wholemeal breadcrumbs	Salt and pepper

Remove the outside leaves from the cabbage and wash them well. Chop the centre part, wash and drain it thoroughly, melt the margarine and cook the cabbage gently in it for a few minutes. Mince the onion and mix together the cabbage, onion and breadcrumbs. Season with salt and pepper, and bind with the beaten egg.

Place a pudding cloth in a basin, then arrange the outside leaves and fill with the mixture. Cover and steam for 1 hour.

Serve with a good brown sauce flavoured with nutmeg, and baked potatoes.

Tomato and Mushroom Patties

Enough puff or short pastry to make six patties

For the filling

3 large tomatoes	1 oz. cooking fat or margarine
½ lb. mushrooms	
1 small onion	Salt or herbs to taste

Wash and dry the tomatoes and mushrooms and cut into slices. Peel onion and cut into small cubes. Melt the cooking fat in a saucepan and fry onions light brown. Add mushrooms and stew for about 10 minutes. After that, add tomatoes and stew for about 5 more minutes. Add a little salt or chopped herbs to taste.

Drain off all liquid which can be used for the gravy. Roll out pastry and cut out large round pieces. Put the mixture on one side of the round pastry piece and cover with the other side of the pastry, thus making a half-circle. Press sides of the pastry together. Brush with egg or water and bake for 20 minutes in moderate oven.

Tomato Sauce

½ lb. tomatoes	1 oz. flour
1 onion	¾ pint stock
1 oz. margarine	½ teaspoonful sage
Seasoning	

Finely chop onion, fry golden brown in the margarine, add tomatoes, sage and seasoning. Sift in flour, add stock, stirring all the time. Put through strainer and re-boil.

Vegetable Medley with Brown Sauce

1 lb. potatoes	3 oz. swedes
6 oz. carrots	4 oz. onions
Frying fat	

Dice the carrot and swede, cover with water, boil until tender. Meanwhile, slice and slowly fry the onions until coloured. Cut the prepared potatoes into Brazil-nut sections. Place the *cooked* carrot and swede, fried onions, and the cut *raw*

Stuffed potatoes for cold-weather meals. If small, slice top and use as lid

potatoes, seasoned, in a well-greased casserole, cover and bake (or simmer on asbestos mat) for 1 hour or until the potatoes are quite done.

NOTE: For an exotic dish, add 6 or 7 soaked prunes, a tablespoonful of nut fat and a teaspoonful of brown sugar prior to final cooking. Serve with Brown Sauce.

Brown Sauce

1 oz. fat	1 small teaspoonful
1 oz. flour	Marmite
¾ pint vegetable	Few drops gravy
cooking water	browning
	Pepper and salt

Melt the fat in a saucepan, stir in the flour and cook gently for 3 minutes. Gradually add half the liquid, stir in the browning and Marmite, add rest of liquid, season to taste, simmer for 2 minutes.

Vegetable Roast

½ lb. lentils	4 oz. mashed potato
½ lb. onions	1 tablespoonful
3 oz. wholemeal	chopped parsley
breadcrumbs	Salt and pepper

Soak the lentils, drain them and cook in 2 pints water with the onions chopped finely. Pour off any surplus liquor and mix in the breadcrumbs, potato and parsley. Season with pepper and salt to taste, and place the mixture in a well-greased

baking dish. Put a few flakes of margarine on top and bake in a moderate oven for 30 minutes until golden brown.

Serve with baked jacket potatoes, spinach, apple sauce and a good brown gravy made from the reserved liquor and some Marmite.

Vegetable Sausage Rolls

Enough puff or short pastry to make six sausage rolls

For the filling

1 carrot	2 potatoes
1 parsnip	Marjoram
1 leek	Thyme
1 onion	A little salt
A few cabbage leaves	1 tablespoonful oats
Frying fat	Marmite (optional)

Clean, peel and cook all the vegetables with a little water, put through the mincer. Mix with the chopped thyme and marjoram and salt, add the oats. If a little

Marmite is added, it improves the taste. Make small sausages out of this mixture and fry, then put away to cool. Roll out the pastry and make squares big enough to cover the fried sausages. Brush tops of the rolls with egg or water and bake for about 20 minutes in moderate oven.

Walnut Roast with Parsley Stuffing

¼ lb. milled walnuts	2 oz. vegetarian mar-
½ lb. wholemeal	garine
breadcrumbs	¼ teaspoonful pow-
(fresh)	dered sage
1 large onion	Seasoning

Make exactly as Nut Roast with Chestnut Stuffing (see p. 247), but stuff with Parsley Stuffing.

Parsley Stuffing

4 oz. fresh wholemeal	½ teaspoonful thyme
breadcrumbs	2 tablespoonfuls
2 oz. grated or melted	chopped parsley
margarine	Grated rind of ½
Seasoning	lemon

Mix all ingredients together and bind with thick gravy.

SAVOURY EGG DISHES

In addition to the following recipes, see also the chapter on Egg Dishes for all the well-known recipes enjoyed equally by vegetarians and non-vegetarians.

Angels in the Snow

4 slices wholewheat	4 large eggs
bread	Pepper and nutmeg
Butter or vegetarian	¼ teaspoonful salt
margarine	

Toast four slices of wholewheat bread, leaving one side more lightly browned than the other, and butter this side.

Separate the eggs, putting each yolk by itself in a cup. Put the whites together in a basin, add the salt and a pinch each of pepper and nutmeg, and beat until stiff but not dry. Spread the beaten egg-whites over the four pieces of toast, taking care to touch the sides, and drop a yolk exactly in the centre of each.

Brown lightly under the grill and serve. The egg-white may be scattered with grated cheese if liked.

This is an excellent dish for an invalid.

Eggs in Onion Sauce

4–8 eggs	Watercress
1 large onion	1 tablespoonful
1 teaspoonful salt	wholewheat flour
Mashed potatoes	¼ teaspoonful pepper
	½ pint milk

Chop the onion and cook it in the milk with the pepper and salt until soft. Blend the flour with ½ cupful cold water and use this to thicken the sauce. Bring to the boil again and simmer for 5–8 minutes until cooked. Meanwhile, poach the egg lightly until the whites are just set. When the eggs are ready, make a border of mashed potatoes on an oval dish, arrange the eggs in the centre and pour the onion sauce over the top. Trim with the best part of the watercress and serve.

Savoury Rice with Eggs

4 oz. rice	¼ pint milk
1 large onion	4–8 eggs
2 oz. fat for frying	4 large tomatoes
2 teaspoonfuls horse-	3 oz. grated dry
radish cream	cheese
1 tablespoonful	Salt
wholewheat flour	

Chop the onion and fry it in the fat until brown. Add the rice and stir until the grains are opaque. Put the rice-onion mixture into a pan with ¾ pint boiling water and 1 teaspoonful salt, bring to the boil, then simmer gently until soft and the water is absorbed. Add more water during cooking if it becomes too dry.

Meanwhile, hard-boil or poach the eggs and keep them warm. Boil the milk, pour it on to the flour mixed with a little water, and return it to the pan. Stir in the grated cheese, horseradish and 1 teaspoonful salt and cook for 5–6 minutes. Cut the eggs into quarters, and halve and grill the tomatoes. Put a ring of rice on an oval dish, pile the eggs in the centre. Pour the cheese sauce over the eggs and surround the mound with grilled tomatoes. A few chopped stuffed olives may be added to the rice if liked.

Vegetarian Scotch Eggs

4 hard-boiled eggs	¼ teaspoonful pepper
2 uncooked eggs	2 oz. mushrooms
2 teaspoonfuls	5 oz. wholewheat
chopped parsley	breadcrumbs
2 oz. butter or vege-	1 large onion
tarian margarine	1 teaspoonful salt

Shell and dry the hard-boiled eggs, chop the onion finely and beat the two uncooked eggs. Skin and chop the mushrooms into small pieces. Melt the butter or margarine in a pan and cook the chopped onion in it until soft, but not brown. Add the mushrooms and cook gently until they are done.

Then remove the pan from the heat, mix in 2 oz. of the breadcrumbs and the parsley, season with pepper and salt, and bind with some of the beaten egg. Divide the mixture into four parts and use it to coat the hard-boiled eggs. It will not stick unless the eggs are quite dry. Stand for a few minutes and then coat with egg and breadcrumbs. Fry in deep fat and serve cold with horseradish cream. Green bean salad is excellent with this dish,

DISHES MADE FROM PULSES

Bean Roast with Tomatoes

½ lb. butter beans or haricots	1 teaspoonful mixed herbs
1 onion	1 tablespoonful chopped parsley
¼ lb. margarine	
2 eggs	1 lb. small ripe tomatoes
¼ lb. breadcrumbs	
Seasoning	

Soak beans overnight, then cook in slightly salted water together with the onion, peeled and sliced, until beans are soft.

Mash and put beans and onion in basin, then add 2 oz. of the margarine, the well-beaten eggs, breadcrumbs, herbs and seasoning. Mix well together. Turn on to a floured board, shape into a neat block and dredge with flour. Place on well-greased baking tin with remainder of margarine in small lumps on top. Place tomatoes round the savoury (whole).

Bake for about ½ hour in a medium oven, basting occasionally. When nicely browned, serve with a brown gravy (see p. 247) and apple sauce (see chapter on Sauces). If preferred, this roast can be eaten cold with salad.

Croquettes

1 pint haricot or butter beans or red lentils	Powdered sage or thyme
2 oz. margarine	1 dessertspoonful lemon juice
Seasoning	

Soak the beans or lentils overnight, then cook in slightly salted water until easy to mash. Dry well and sieve. Melt the margarine in a saucepan, add bean or lentil purée, powdered sage or thyme, lemon juice (if desired) and a seasoning of salt and pepper to taste. Mix well together, heat for a few minutes carefully, then set aside to cool. Shape into croquettes, brush with egg and roll in breadcrumbs; fry to a golden brown in deep fat. Drain and serve hot, garnished with parsley.

NOTE: The flavour of the above may be varied by the addition of 2 oz. chopped, fried peanuts.

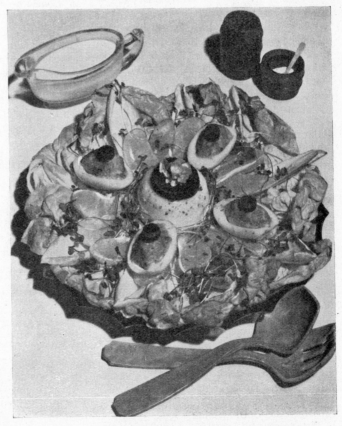

Stuffed eggs, orange segments and lettuce, are the main ingredients of this salad, with cress for decoration

Cutlets

¾ lb. cooked, sieved
lentils, beans or
split peas
1 teaspoonful
chopped sage or
thyme

½ lb. mashed potatoes
Salt and pepper to
taste
2 medium-sized
onions

Mix the purée with the mashed potatoes and add the onions (either chopped and fried or boiled, drained and chopped) together with herbs and seasoning as desired. Moisten the mixture, if necessary, with a little stock used in cooking the pulses. Shape as desired, either flour or dip in egg and breadcrumbs, and fry a golden brown in hot fat.

Family Hot-pot

Potatoes (peeled)
Carrots (cleaned and
sliced)
Celery (cleaned and
cut)
Onions (peeled and
sliced)
Grated cheese

Baked beans in
tomato sauce
¼ lb. mushrooms (if
desired)
Marmite gravy
Herbs and seasoning,
as required
Margarine for frying

Cook onion rings until lightly browned in margarine. Into a fair-sized baking-tin slice a layer of potatoes, then a layer of onions and other vegetables, followed by a layer of baked beans. Season as required. Cover again with a layer of sliced potatoes, add Marmite gravy on top of vegetables, and scatter grated cheese over the top. Bake in fairly hot oven until vegetables are well cooked—about 2 hours. Serve very hot, with a green vegetable.

If preferred, canned peas can be used in place of baked beans. Sliced tomatoes can also be added.

Lentil Soufflés

½ pint lentils
1 oz. margarine
½ small onion
(chopped)

1 oz. flour
¾ pint vegetable stock
or Marmite gravy
2 egg-whites

Prepare lentils by washing and cooking until soft in slightly salted water. Drain and, when dry, put through a sieve.

Melt margarine in saucepan, add onion and cook until tender; then add flour, cook slightly (stirring) before adding stock or gravy. Boil and cook for a few moments, then add to lentils, mixing all together. Whisk egg-whites until stiff and fold carefully into the lentil mixture.

Three-parts fill small, greased, fireproof dishes with the mixture, and bake for about

15 minutes in a fairly hot oven. Serve immediately they are ready. Very nice with chipped potatoes and spinach.

Peasant Lentil Dish

½ pint red lentils
2 oz. margarine or
nut fat

1 peeled and chopped
onion
1 tablespoonful flour
Salt and pepper

Cook lentils until easy to mash, dry and put through a sieve. Melt fat in saucepan, add chopped onion, and fry until slightly browned; then add flour, cooking for a minute or two before adding gradually about ½ pint of water. Boil up, stirring all the time, and cook for 15 minutes or longer. Add lentil purée and seasoning, and continue to cook for a further 15 minutes. Serve very hot with any vegetables.

Savoury Bean Roll

2 breakfastcupfuls
canned beans in
tomato sauce

½ lb. grated cheese
Breadcrumbs (prefer-
ably wholemeal)

Mash the beans, add the grated cheese, together with sufficient breadcrumbs to make a fairly stiff mixture. Shape into a loaf or roll, place in a baking tin and bake in a moderate oven for about ½ hour; baste occasionally with Nutter or Suenut melted in a little water. Serve with vegetables and brown gravy or with tomato sauce.

MEATLESS STEAK DISHES

Meatless Steaks, attractively packed in large or small cans, ready for us, do not contain nuts, but are made from gluten of wheat which has a protein value twice as high as nuts. Apart from their high food value, they look and taste good.

Curried Meatless Steaks

1 large can Meatless
Steaks
2 large onions
2 oz. margarine
3 teaspoonfuls Vesop

1 dessertspoonful or
more curry powder
2 tomatoes
1 sweet apple
1 dessertspoonful
sultanas

Chop onions. Fry in margarine. Add curry powder and continue cooking for several minutes till blended. Add tomatoes, Vesop and fruit. Cook till onions are tender. Add steaks with liquid from can and simmer for 15 minutes.

Serve with plain boiled rice or Pulao (see

Radish roses and watercress are used to decorate a salad of diced mixed vegetables and macaroni

next page) and sweet mango chutney. It is essential to use as little liquid as possible in curries and to rely on fruit and vegetables for thickening. Flour should never be used.

Hungarian Goulash

1 *large can Meatless Steaks*	1½ *oz. margarine*
1 *tablespoonful tomato purée*	*Small pinch caraway seeds*
1 *medium onion*	2 *teaspoonfuls Vesop*
12 *small new potatoes*	1½ *pints water*
1 *teaspoonful paprika*	1 *dessertspoonful flour*

Slice onion thinly. Fry in saucepan, then add paprika, tomato purée, caraway seeds, Vesop and flour blended in liquid from can and water. Simmer for 10 minutes. Add steaks and new potatoes, cooked in their jackets and skinned. Simmer again gently for 15 minutes. Serve with tiny wholemeal dumplings.

Meatless Steak and Mushroom Pudding

6 *oz. wholemeal pastry*	1 *medium-sized onion*
1 *small can Meatless Steaks*	2 *teaspoonfuls Vesop*
	2 *teaspoonfuls flour*
4 *oz. mushrooms*	1 *oz. margarine*
	½ *pint stock or water*

Chop onion and fry in saucepan. Wipe and slice mushrooms and stems. Add to onion and cook for 5 minutes. Blend in flour, Vesop and liquid from steaks made up to ½ pint with stock or water. Allow to cool. Line greased basin with thin pastry. Cut steaks into medium-sized pieces and arrange in the pastry-lined basin. Pour over sauce. Cover with pastry, loosely tie and steam for 1 hour.

The same ingredients arranged in pie-dish, covered with pastry and baked, make a very good pie.

Meatless Steaks Jardinière

1 *can Meatless Steaks*	2 *teaspoonfuls Vesop*
12 *tiny onions*	¾ *pint stock or water*
1 *oz. margarine*	*Mixed cooked vegetables*
1 *dessertspoonful flour*	

Skin onions and fry without breaking until well browned. Carefully remove from fat. Stir flour into remaining fat. Add liquid from can, Vesop and stock. Cook for about 5 minutes until sauce is smooth and thick. Add steaks and onions. Simmer very gently for 10 minutes. Serve with border of diced mixed vegetables with carrots and peas to add colour.

Pulao

1 medium-sized onion
1 large cupful well-washed rice
2 oz. butter or margarine
3 cardamom seeds and cloves
1 bay leaf
Salt

Cut onion finely and fry till brown. Add rice, herbs and seasoning. Cook till rice is pale brown colour. Add water to cover 1 in. above rice level. Cover and cook over gentle heat till all moisture is absorbed and rice grains separate. Shake pan from time to time but do not stir.

Savoury Pasties

12 oz. wholemeal pastry
1 small can Meatless steaks
1 oz. margarine
1 large parboiled potato
1 medium-sized onion
2 teaspoonfuls Vesop

Chop and fry onion. Add cut-up steaks, liquid from can, Vesop and 3 tablespoonfuls water. Simmer gently for 5 minutes. Add potato cut into small dice and leave mixture to cool. Roll pastry thinly and cut into four even-sized pieces. Place steak mixture on pastry and form into pasties. Bake in brisk oven for about 20 minutes till pastry is crisp and well browned.

POTATO DISHES

Potatoes are an important part of vegetarian diet. During the winter they are even more important than during warm weather; their high calorific value—375 calories per lb.—as well as their vitamin C content help to maintain fitness. To get the best value out of them, bake in their skins, a method with many variations.

Bircher Potatoes

2 lb. of potatoes
A little salt
A little caraway seed
Oil or margarine

Scrub potatoes until absolutely clean, dry with a towel. Grease a baking tin with either liquid margarine or oil, sprinkle with salt and caraway seeds and bake till tender. If you do not care for caraway seed, use salt only. The potatoes taste quite different from ordinary baked potatoes and are very nourishing.

Potato Delights

This makes a very good main dish eaten with vegetables. Boil 2 lb. potatoes in their skins. When cold, cut them into thick slices and put a piece of Cheddar cheese on each slice. Put on a greased baking sheet and bake in a hot oven until the cheese melts.

Potatoes in Béchamel

2 lb. potatoes
2 oz. grated cheese
½ pint milk
1 oz. margarine
1 tablespoonful flour
1 egg
Pinch of grated nutmeg
A little margarine for the top

Parboil the potatoes in their skins. Cut them into thick slices and put them into a greased fireproof dish.

Make the sauce as follows: melt the margarine and add flour and milk. Bring to boil and stir well until it is thick and smooth, which takes about 1–2 minutes. Let it stand covered until cool. Add cheese, nutmeg, egg-yolk and stiffly beaten egg-white. If the sauce is too thick, add a little water or milk. Pour it over the potatoes, put a few dabs of margarine on top and bake for about 40 minutes. Serve with a salad.

Potatoes with Cream Cheese

2 lb. potatoes
¼ lb. cream cheese (preferably home-made)
Parsley or chives
Fat for greasing dish
Pinch of salt

Parboil the potatoes and cut into slices. Grease a fireproof dish and put into it alternate layers of potatoes and cream cheese mixed with parsley or chives finely chopped. Salt the potatoes slightly. Finish off with a layer of potatoes. Bake for 20 minutes.

Stuffed Potatoes

Scrub the potatoes and, if large, cut them into halves. If they are small, cut only a piece off like a lid. It can be put over the stuffing. Make a hollow in each potato and fill it with the following mixture:

For the stuffing

1 oz. margarine
1 oz. grated cheese
Brown breadcrumbs
Finely chopped parsley, or dried herbs reconstituted with hot water

Cream the margarine and add the other ingredients. Stuff the potatoes and bake for about ¾ hour.

UNCOOKED MEALS

In a balanced diet one should have at least 50 per cent. of the day's food raw, either a whole uncooked meal or half a lunch or supper uncooked and the other half cooked. But uncooked salad does not mean shredded carrots one day and tomato salad with lettuce the next, or the usual variety (cooked beetroot, two slices of cucumber and four slices of tomatoes). This is, of course, insufficient. An adequate uncooked meal consists of a fruit or vegetable cocktail, a salad consisting of a fruit, root and leaf vegetable; and a small sweet uncooked or unbaked.

Tomatoes, cucumbers and marrows are considered fruit vegetables. During winter time, when tomatoes and cucumbers are very expensive and marrows unobtainable, ordinary fruit can be used in salads. Cabbage, celery, leeks and spinach are leaf vegetables.

Spring onions or ordinary onions finely chopped, parsley, mint, chives, sage, thyme, etc., make excellent dressings when mixed with home-made mayonnaise or lemon and olive oil. For something very appetising, mix raw, grated horseradish roots with a little lemon juice and mayonnaise, and pour this dressing over grated, raw beetroots or red cabbage.

Here are recipes for an uncooked meal. All ingredients are for 6 people.

Tomato Cocktail

Wash raw tomatoes, cut into small pieces, put through a strainer and mix the juice with a little lemon juice and, if liked, a little brown sugar.

Grapefruit Salad

2 *medium-sized grapefruit*	3 *oranges*
4 *apples (Bramleys or any other not-too-sweet kind)*	1 *large tablespoonful whipped cream* 2 *glacé or other cherries*

Peel the grapefruit and oranges and cut into segments, wash the apples (do *not* peel), dry and cut into segments, mix fruit together, top with cream and decorate with cut-up cherries.

Summer salad with sliced hard-boiled egg, cucumber and tomato contains plenty of nourishment

Shredded Beetroots with Herb Sauce

2 *large beetroots*	1 *teaspoonful*
2 *tablespoonfuls*	*chopped herbs (any*
olive oil	*kind) mixed with a*
½ *lemon*	*tablespoonful of*
	home-made mayon-
	naise

Wash the beetroots and soak in cold water for a few hours, grate on Bircher Grater, mix with lemon and olive oil. Pour the mixed herbs and mayonnaise (see Salads chapter) over beetroots.

Green Cabbage Salad with Roasted Cashew Nuts

½ *head of medium-*	½ *lemon*
sized cabbage	2 *tablespoonfuls of*
¼ *lb. roasted cashew*	*home-made mayon-*
nuts	*naise (see Salads)*

Wash and soak cabbage in cold water. Cut cabbage very fine with knife or grate on a coarse grater. Grind cashew nuts finely and mix with grated cabbage, add lemon juice and mayonnaise. Mix well.

Decorate the salads with lettuce and cress. Great care should be taken to make them look as attractive as possible. A good colour scheme which pleases the eye makes a meal much more attractive than the knowledge that it is rightly balanced.

Fruit Medleys

About 1½ *cupfuls of*	1 *teaspoonful lemon*
mixed fruit (raisins,	*juice*
sultanas, prunes,	1 *tablespoonful of*
figs, dates)	*thin cream (top of*
¼ *lb. grated almonds*	*the milk or milk is*
or other nuts •	*sufficient)*
2 *teaspoonfuls brown*	
sugar	

Wash the fruit in warm water, put through mincer, mix all ingredients together into a fairly stiff mixture, form little balls and roll them in grated nuts.

Bircher Pudding

2 *or* 3 carrots	2 *oz. ground almonds*
2 *tablespoonfuls*	*A few drops of lemon*
brown sugar	*juice*
2 *tablespoonfuls of*	1 *cupful of cornflakes*
cream (or top of	*or any other flakes*
the milk)	1 *large apple*

Peel and soak the carrots for a few hours in cold water, grate on a very fine grater. Wash and dry apple, grate finely. Mix grated carrots and apple with almonds, sugar, lemon juice, cream and cornflakes. Press into little pudding basins and put in a cold place for 30 minutes. Turn out on a plate and either top with cream or pour milk over the pudding.

The uncooked meal can be supplemented by cooked or baked potatoes in their skins or by Bircher Potatoes (see p 256).

SALAD IDEAS
by IVAN BAKER

A leading authority on vegetarian cookery and catering and the author of many books on the subject, Mr. Baker also contributed the recipes for Almond and Potato Croquettes; Haricot, Leek and Mushroom Pie; Roast Nutmeat; Stuffed Tomatoes; Spaghetti Rondelles; Butter Mint Sauce, and Vegetable Medley with Brown Sauce.

Tomato, minced onion or capers, olive oil and lemon.

Watercress, diced orange, oil and lemon garnish with little heaps of diced beet.

Finely shredded raw cabbage, small dice of preserved cucumber, a little chopped onion, oil and lemon. Toss well. Chill Serve.

Sliced celery heart, diced apple, walnut halves, sour cream dressing (see below).

Core a large pear, fill with cream cheese previously moistened with mayonnaise. Chill, peel, slice, serve on endive.

Freshly grated raw carrot centre, thin outer ring of finely grated swede flavoured with onion juice. Mustard and cress garnish.

Potato salad made with diced, freshly boiled jacket potatoes, dressed with lemon then oil, while warm, then tossed carefully with a little chopped onion and seasoning.

Russian salad made by mixing: 1 cupful canned peas, 1 cupful small diced cooked carrot, 1 cupful small diced cooked potato, ½ cupful diced cooked swede, oil and lemon, then mayonnaise dressing.

Sliced hard-boiled egg, diced tomato sliced preserved cucumber, diced cooked beet, oil and lemon. Garnish with cress and diced grapefruit or orange.

Sliced chicory, cleaned, soaked sultanas arranged on prepared endive. Garnish with black and green olives and cress sprigs.

Sour Cream Dressing. Stir 2 tablespoonfuls lemon juice into 5 tablespoonfuls unsweetened evaporated milk.

(See also the main Salads chapter for many recipes suitable also for Vegetarians.

INVALID COOKERY

To tempt flagging appetites, food must look specially inviting

Photo: Electrolux

A perfect tray for the sick-room—piping hot beef tea is followed by ice-cold jellied chicken and a cream sweet, all attractively served

THE appearance of food is nearly as important as its flavour and never more so than when it is prepared for the sick-room. Invalids' appetites need tempting, and a daintily arranged tray will often mean that the meal is eaten with relish instead of merely being picked at. As far as is possible, all food intended for the sick-room should be prepared the day it is to be eaten. Most foods look far more appetising served in individual dishes, glasses, etc. A golden rule is never to overload an invalid's plate or tray. Nothing is more likely to discourage a capricious appetite, so make the portions small and attractive to look at and you may be rewarded with a request for a second helping.

Be sparing with seasoning and fats; grill, steam or bake rather than fry, and serve hot food really hot and cold food really cold.

SOUPS FOR INVALIDS

Beef Tea (now used chiefly to promote appetite)

1 lb. lean shin of beef   1 pint lukewarm
Pinch of salt   water

Cut the meat into very small pieces, removing all fat, and put it, with the water and salt, into a double saucepan over boiling water. Cover and simmer for at least 2 hours. If to be used at once, strain and take off the fat with a piece of soft paper. Otherwise, stand in a cool place uncovered and remove the fat when cold.

Beef and Sago Broth

1 lb. gravy beef   1 quart water
1 oz. sago   1 egg-yolk
       Salt to taste

Cut up the meat finely and stew it very slowly in the water for 3 hours. Meanwhile, soak the sago in ¼ pint water for 30 minutes and cook in the top of a double boiler until clear. Strain off the beef tea, return to saucepan and add salt and sago. Cook gently for 30 minutes. Remove from the heat. Beat the egg-yolk in a basin, add a little of the broth, stir well and then pour into the broth. Reheat but do not allow to boil.

Chicken Broth

Use the liquor from a boiled fowl, and the chicken bones and bring to the boil, then simmer for 2 or 3 hours. Strain through a sieve, remove all fat and season to taste. If liked, add a very little cooked rice. To make the broth more nourishing, add a beaten egg-yolk and a tablespoonful of cream to ½ pint of the strained liquor and reheat without boiling.

Soups made from good stock, if not greasy or too highly flavoured, and milk soups are also suitable for invalids, but those containing much vegetable should be

259

Junket is an ideal sweet for an invalid—nourishing and easy to eat

avoided as possibly indigestible. (See Soup chapter for Consommé, Kidney Soup, Tomato Soup, Barley Cream Soup and Rabbit Broth.)

FISH

Avoid the strongly flavoured varieties. Most suitable are sole, plaice, whiting, cod, fresh haddock, halibut and turbot. All fish for invalids should be steamed, poached, baked or grilled, but *not* fried.

Steamed Fillet of Fish (sole, plaice or other white fish)

Wash the fish, lay it on a well-buttered plate, lightly peppered and salted, with another plate on top. Steam for 20–30 minutes over a pan of boiling water. Decorate with a little chopped parsley and serve hot.

Poached Fish

A whole sole on the bone or fillets of sole, plaice or other white fish may be placed in a frying pan, completely covered with fish stock or milk and water, very lightly seasoned with salt and pepper, and gently simmered until tender. It should take about 10 minutes per lb.

Fish Cream (2 helpings)

4 oz. fresh haddock	½ oz. butter
1 tablespoonful milk	1 egg
½ oz. breadcrumbs	Squeeze of lemon
Salt and pepper	juice
½ gill cream	

Wipe the fish and shred it finely, removing bones and skin. Melt the butter in a saucepan, add the egg-yolk, milk and breadcrumbs. Cook until thick, without boiling, add to the fish, mix well together and rub through a fine sieve. Add seasoning, lemon juice, cream and egg-white, stiffly beaten. Turn into a greased basin, cover with greased paper and steam very gently for about 40 minutes. Turn out carefully and serve at once.

Fish in Custard (1–2 helpings)

2 fillets of sole or plaice	1 gill milk
	1 small egg
Pepper and salt	Water biscuit

Beat up the egg with the milk and the biscuit crushed to powder, then add seasoning to taste. Put the fillets one on top of the other in a greased fireproof dish, season and heat in a hot oven. When the fillets are hot, add the custard mixture and continue cooking until the fish is done and the custard set, then lift the fillets carefully from the dish and put on a hot plate with the flakes of custard on top.

Soufflé Pudding

About 1 lb. cod fillet	2 or 3 egg-whites
1 teacupful milk or evaporated milk	Salt, pepper and a squeeze of lemon
2 tablespoonfuls soft breadcrumbs	juice
	Parsley

Skin the cod and chop as finely as possible. Mix with the breadcrumbs, milk and seasonings, including the lemon juice. Fold in the stiffly beaten egg-whites and pour carefully into a greased soufflé dish or casserole. Either steam for about 1¼ hours, then put under a hot grill for a few minutes to brown the top, or bake for 1 hour in the centre of a very moderate oven. Garnish with sprigs of parsley.

OTHER MAIN DISHES

Chicken, rabbit, eggs and various kinds of offal, such as brains and sweetbreads, are more digestible than meat and therefore more suitable for invalids.

Brain Scallop (1 helping)

Set of brains (calf's or sheep's)	1 gill white sauce
1 teaspoonful chopped parsley	Few drops of lemon juice
	½ oz. butter
Breadcrumbs	

Wash the brains several times in salted water, then carefully remove the skin. Plunge into boiling water for 2–3 minutes to blanch, then drain carefully. Simmer in the white sauce for 20 minutes, add the parsley and lemon juice, and put into a greased scallop shell. Sprinkle with breadcrumbs, put the butter in tiny pieces on top and brown either under a hot grill or in a quick oven.

Chicken Panada

Take a lean chicken, wash well and boil gently until the bones can be removed, then return the flesh to the liquor and cook gently until tender. Strain off the liquor. Put the meat twice through the mincer, add a little of the liquor to thin it, and serve either hot or cold, according to taste.

Egg Dishes (see separate chapter, pp. 174–179)

Invalid's Chop (1 helping)

Mutton or lamb chop	2 tablespoonfuls stock
½ oz. breadcrumbs	or water
Buttered toast	Pepper and salt

Shred the meat off the bone and put into a saucepan with the breadcrumbs, stock or water and seasoning. Simmer gently for 10 minutes, then serve on hot buttered toast.

Rabbit Cream (1 helping)

2 oz. raw rabbit
¼ oz. breadcrumbs
½ egg-white
Pepper and salt
¼ oz. butter
¼ gill milk
¼ gill cream

Put the milk, butter and breadcrumbs into a saucepan and heat until the butter melts and the breadcrumbs

swell. Put the rabbit four times through the mincer, then add to the milk, etc. Beat the egg-white to a stiff froth and fold lightly into the mixture. Add the cream and seasoning. Three-parts fill little dariole moulds with the mixture, cover with greased paper and stand in a saucepan with boiling water half-way up the sides. Put on the lid of the pan and steam gently for 40 minutes, then turn out and serve.

SWEETS

Arrowroot Pudding (1–2 helpings)

1 tablespoonful arrowroot	Brandy to taste
1 teaspoonful castor sugar	½ pint milk
	Small egg

Mix the arrowroot to a smooth paste with a little of the milk, boil the rest with the sugar and pour on to the arrowroot, stir well, return to the pan and cook for 5 minutes, stirring continuously. Take off the heat, add the well-beaten egg and brandy, pour into a small, warm, greased pie dish and put into a quick oven for a few minutes to brown the surface.

Bread and Milk (1 helping)

1 slice of bread	Pepper and salt
½ pint milk	or sugar

Remove crust and cut the bread into squares. Boil the milk, pour over the bread, cover and leave for a minute or two. Add a dash of salt and pepper or sugar, according to taste, and serve at once.

NOTE: If liked, half a teaspoonful of meat extract or Marmite can be dissolved

Brains or sweetbreads
are more digestible than
meat and may be served
in cream sauce

in the boiling milk before it is poured over the bread.

Caudle (1 helping)

½ pint gruel	Glass of brandy
1 egg-white	Grated lemon rind
Scrape of nutmeg	Sugar to taste.

To make the gruel, mix together 1 oz. medium oatmeal and ½ pint water, stand for 1 hour, then stir and strain into a saucepan. Stir over the fire until boiling, then simmer gently for 15 minutes, with the brandy, nutmeg, lemon rind and sugar to taste. Let the mixture cool, then fold in the stiffly beaten egg-white.

Cornflour Soufflé (1–2 helpings)

½ pint milk	1 egg
Grated rind of	½ oz. cornflour
¼ lemon	½ oz. castor sugar

Mix the cornflour to a smooth paste with a little of the milk, boil the rest and pour on to the paste, stirring at the same time. Return to the pan and cook for 5 minutes, stirring all the time. Let it cool a little, then add the sugar, lemon rind and beaten egg-yolk and stir well. Whip the egg-white stiffly and fold into the mixture as lightly as possible. Turn into a greased pie dish and bake in a fairly slow oven until a pale brown. Serve at once.

Egg Jelly (3–4 helpings)

½ pint water	1½ oz. castor sugar
Rind and juice of a	¼ oz. powdered gela-
lemon	tine
2 eggs	Sherry to taste.

Heat the water, lemon rind, sugar and gelatine without boiling until the gelatine is dissolved and the flavour of the lemon rind extracted. Strain, then add the lemon juice and the beaten eggs and heat, carefully stirring all the time without boiling. When the mixture is thick and creamy, add the sherry and pour into a wetted mould to set.

Junket

½ pint fresh milk	Vanilla essence, or
1 tablespoonful sugar	dessertspoonful
1 teaspoonful rennet	black coffee to
Nutmeg	flavour

Follow instructions on the packet or bottle containing the rennet (or junket powder) for exact quantity to use, but remember more rennet is needed with pasteurised milk.

Stir in the rennet when the milk has been heated just to blood temperature—tested with your finger—and then remove from heat. Add flavouring and sugar and stand in glasses to cool. Serve cold with a little nutmeg grated on top.

Milk Jelly (3–4 helpings)

1 pint milk	½ oz. powdered gela-
Rind of half lemon	tine
1½ oz. castor sugar	

Put the ingredients into a saucepan and stir over a low heat for 10 minutes or so until the sugar and gelatine have dissolved. Do not let the mixture boil. Take out the lemon rind. Pour the mixture into a basin, stirring now and again until it is the consistency of thick cream. Then pour into small wetted moulds and leave to set.

INVALID DRINKS

Barley Water

1½ pints boiling water	2 oz. pearl barley
Rind of a lemon	1 oz. loaf sugar

Wash the barley in cold water and put into a saucepan, cover with cold water and bring to the boil. Then strain and put the barley back into the pan and add the sugar. Peel the lemon thinly so that none of the white pith is removed, put the peel with the barley and sugar and add 1½ pints of boiling water, then simmer gently for about 15 minutes. Strain into a jug and serve cold.

NOTE: If liked, the juice of the lemon can be added when the barley water is cold.

Black Currant Tea

1 teaspoonful lemon	½ pint boiling water
juice	1 dessertspoonful
1 teaspoonful castor	black currant jam
sugar	or purée

Put the jam or purée, sugar and lemon juice into a jug, pour on the boiling water and stir well. Cover with a plate and stand on the hot-plate for 15–20 minutes, then strain.

Serve hot to relieve colds.

Egg Flip (for 1)

½ pint milk	1 oz. castor sugar
1 egg	Sherry or brandy

Dissolve the sugar in the milk. Beat the egg well and stir the milk on to it, add sherry or brandy and pour into a glass.

COOKING BY TIMER CONTROL

*You set the dials—at the appointed time,
your electric cooker switches itself on, cooks
the meal, and switches off again*

by JOAN WHITGIFT,
author of "Leave it to Cook"

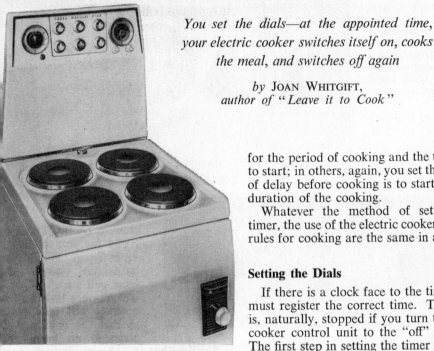

There is an alarm clock as well as timer
control on the Creda Mercury Four, a
four-hotplate cooker with extra large
grill conveniently placed in the roof of
the oven

ELECTRIC cooking by timer control is
today one of the greatest helps to the
busy housewife. Nowadays, most modern
cookers have a timer incorporated in them
and it is nearly always fitted on the splash
plate at the back, but, for those people who
have a manually operated cooker, it is still
possible to buy a timer separately. This
can be fitted on the wall, usually adjacent
to the main cooker control switch, and
so connected that it time-controls the
oven.

Timers are also incorporated in some of
the more modern gas cookers.

There are several types of timers on the
market, and it is advisable to study the
manufacturers' instructions because the
method of setting varies slightly in each
case. In some instances, you set the controls for the period of cooking and for the
time it is to finish; in others, you set them

for the period of cooking and the time it is
to start; in others, again, you set the period
of delay before cooking is to start and the
duration of the cooking.

Whatever the method of setting the
timer, the use of the electric cooker and the
rules for cooking are the same in all cases.

Setting the Dials

If there is a clock face to the timer, this
must register the correct time. The clock
is, naturally, stopped if you turn the main
cooker control unit to the "off" position.
The first step in setting the timer is, therefore, to switch on the cooker control unit
and set the hands of the clock to the correct
time. Set the hands by turning the knob
in the centre of the clock face. Where no
clock face is fitted to the timer this, of
course, does not apply, but it is still important to remember to turn on the cooker
control unit.

Next choose the hour at which you want
to dish up the cooked food and set the
timer accordingly.

Then decide how long the food will take
to cook. In each kind of timer, you set the
dial for the number of hours or part of
hours of cooking.

Finally, turn on the thermostat dial for
the oven, setting it at a temperature suitable for cooking the particular food and, if
there is one, turn the dial on the timer control that sets the mechanism. Nothing will
happen until the set time for cooking to
start. The oven will not heat until the preselected time.

Suppose you want to cook a chicken.
Weigh the bird and decide how long it will
take to cook and what time you want to
eat it. We will suppose it needs 1 hour's

Two Creda cookers made for timer control cookery— (right) the Carefree, and (below) an out-size model with four quick plates called the Mercury Four

cooking, that dinner is at 7 p.m and that it is now 11 a.m.

Put the bird in the meat pan, prepared in the usual way with fat bacon or a little good dripping across the breast, and place it in the correct position for meat in your oven. This will be either on the floor or the bottom runner, according to the manufacturer's instructions. Turn on the main cooker control unit. Glance at the clock if there is one, and make sure it is running at the correct time.

Switches Itself On

Now set the timers. Either set the one dial for the time when cooking is to *start* (that is 6 p.m.), or at the time at which it should *stop* (7 p.m.). Set the second dial for the length of the cooking period, in this case, 1 hour. Then turn the knob which sets the mechanism.

Finally, turn the thermostat control dial. A good temperature for roasting a bird would be 400°, so set the dial at 400° F.

By now it is probably 11.5 a.m., and you can leave the kitchen for the day. At 6 p.m. the oven will switch on and the chicken will

start to cook. It will be ready for you to dish it up at 7 p.m. Should you be delayed, however, the oven will switch off at 7 o'clock, very little further cooking will take place so that the chicken will come to no harm and will still be hot at 7.15 p.m. Indeed, there is no reason why it should not be left to get quite cold in the oven for serving with a salad the following day.

When you do finally return, it is advisable to make a habit of (1) turning the thermostat dial to the off position and (2) setting all knobs at manual control.

Cooking "From Cold"

After a very little experiment this setting of the timer will be found to be quite simple, and it is an enormous help for the housewife to be able to put the evening meal in the oven after breakfast, set the timer, and leave the kitchen until she is ready to dish up at night.

Very often the timer also controls the cooker's heated warming drawer. You can therefore put the necessary plates and serving dishes in, turn the appropriate switch and they will be hot when you are ready to serve the meal.

Housewives are often surprised to learn that nearly all food will be perfect if it is put in a cold oven and allowed to start cooking as the oven heats. This is one of the main principles of cooking by the timer, and it is important that you have complete confidence that the food will cook "from cold" with every bit as good results as if it were put in a hot oven. Unless you have this confidence you are unlikely to get the maximum benefit from the timer, and it is recommended that you make one or two simple experiments. For example, make a Yorkshire batter, pour it into a very well greased tin, put it in the oven and then switch to 450° F. In 30–40 minutes the pudding will be beautifully cooked. Since it was always said that a batter must be poured into boiling fat and put into a very hot oven, this should prove that quite unexpected food will successfully cook from cold.

The second use of a timer is cooking *to* cold. An example is a cake. The oven is possibly heating while you mix the cake, which is then put in at the correct temperature. Set the timers to switch off the oven at the appropriate time. The cake can safely be left to cool off in the oven and you can return several hours later to find it cooked, cold and ready to put on the tea-table. Provided you do not open the door, the cake will cool perfectly in the oven. In fact, because there is less danger of sudden draughts, there is less likelihood of the cake being heavy.

Finally, it is sometimes helpful to cook both to and from cold at once. You can, for example, load an oven overnight with the raw food ready for a hot breakfast and a cold lunch. After the breakfast is served, the oven continues to cook, say, a veal and ham pie, or baked fish or a leg of lamb. At the correct cooking time the oven switches off, the food cools in the oven and is ready to serve with a salad for lunch or dinner.

PREPARING THE FOOD

Some special preparation is required when cooking by timer. This is for three reasons. Firstly, some food, such as peeled potatoes or apples, will discolour if they are left waiting to cook in the oven. Secondly, as you will not be present when cooking is in progress, it is essential that food will neither burn, boil dry, nor boil over. And thirdly, the full value of the timer is only appreciated by cooking a *complete* meal. It is no use to the housewife to have a joint roasting unattended if she has to hurry back to put on the vegetables. It is no help to cook a first course which takes $1\frac{1}{2}$ hours, if she cannot plan a dessert that will take the same length of time in the oven.

Roast Meat needs no more attention than it does when put into a hot oven. Basting has never been necessary with an electric oven, and the meat should merely be put in a lightly greased meat pan with a nut of dripping or lard on the top. Allow the same cooking times as you normally

No need to put a batter into a very hot oven—this beautifully light Toad in the Hole was left in a cold oven for hours and then cooked by timer control

would and put it in the position recommended for meat in your cooker—either standing on the bottom runner or on the floor of the oven. Cook at any temperature between 375° and 425° F.

Boiled Meat can also be cooked in the oven as part of a complete meal. There are two methods. A piece of ham or bacon, a tongue or silverside, is put in cold water and brought to simmering point; a leg of lamb is plunged into boiling water that is immediately reduced to a simmer.

For the first method, soak the meat for several hours to remove excess salt, and then drain off the water. Put the meat in a fireproof dish and add sufficient cold water nearly to cover. Avoid too small a dish or it may boil over during cooking. Add seasoning, a few prepared vegetables or pulses, and cover the dish very closely with aluminium foil or several sheets of greaseproof paper. Put it anywhere convenient in the bottom half of the oven, where it can safely wait for cooking by the timer later in the day. (If you are told not to put the meat pan on the floor, do not put this dish there either or it will overcook.) Allow ½ hour longer than you would if you were cooking on a boiling plate and cook at any temperature between 300° and 350° F. to suit the remainder of the meal.

If the meat is to be boiled by the second method, put it in a fireproof dish and cover with boiling water. Add seasoning, vegetables, etc., and cover with aluminium foil or greaseproof paper as above. It is now quite safe for it to wait in the cold oven ready to cook by the timer control later in the day. Allow ½ hour longer than the usual cooking time, position it anywhere in the bottom half of the oven and cook at any temperature between 300° and 350° F. to suit the remainder of the meal.

Stewed Meat

Meat stewed in the oven is familiar to most housewives in the form of casserole cooking. The method of cooking by timer control is best illustrated by the following example:

Haricot Mutton (for 4)

4 *good-sized mutton chops or* 1¼–1½ *lb. scrag end*	2 *onions*
	1 *carrot*
	1 *turnip*
6 *oz. haricot beans soaked overnight*	1½ *pints of white stock or water*
4 *tomatoes*	*Salt and pepper*

Divide the meat into pieces and remove all the fat. Drain the haricot beans and put them in a deep fireproof dish. Cut the tomatoes in half and put them on top. Then add the peeled and sliced onions, and the diced carrot and turnip. Lay the meat on top, season, add sufficient stock or water to cover. Cover the dish with aluminium foil and put it on the bottom runner in the oven. Set the timer for it to switch to 300° F. later in the day and to cook for 3 hours.

Vegetables

All vegetables can be prepared and left in the oven to cook by the timer, but green vegetables should not cook for too long. Many people will therefore prefer to cook them in a small quantity of water on the boiling plate, as they take only 7–10 minutes. The loss of food value is, however, very little during the waiting period, and they are cooked to perfection in 40–60 minutes at any temperature between 375° and 425° F. If the remainder of the meal is only taking that time, put the prepared vegetables in a fireproof dish with a very little water (half a gill is plenty), add seasoning and seal the top of the dish with aluminium foil or several sheets of greaseproof paper. Place them near the centre of the oven at a convenient position above the main dish.

Potatoes, Boiled.—Peel or scrape and dry the potatoes. Toss in melted margarine until they are thoroughly coated, then put in a fireproof dish. Add ½ in. of cold water, a little salt, and cover the dish with aluminium foil. Place in a convenient position in the oven. Cook at any temperature between 375° and 425° F. to suit the remainder of the meal. They will take a minimum of 60 minutes and will come to no harm if cooked for as long as 1¾ hours.

Potatoes, Roast.—Peel the potatoes and dip twice in melted fat so that they are well coated. Place with the meat in the meat pan. Put the potatoes close to the sides of the oven unless the meat will be taking longer than 1½ hours to cook, in which case bring the potatoes close to the meat as near the middle of the pan as possible.

Carrots, Turnips and Swedes.—Prepare and cook as for boiled potatoes above.

Parsnips can be roasted in the same way as potatoes.

Leeks, Carrots, Celery, Peas.—Prepare

A variety of foods cooked together for 1 hour by timer control—steamed jam pudding, baked stuffed sole, roast loin of mutton and onion sauce, carrots, peas and sprouts

vegetables, place in a fireproof dish, and add a very small quantity of water (substitute milk when cooking leeks, and use the liquor to make a coating sauce). Add pepper, salt and a knob of butter or margarine, and cover the dish with aluminium foil. Cook for 60–90 minutes to suit the remainder of the meal, at any convenient temperature between 375° and 425° F.

Fruit, Stewed

Prepare the fruit, put in a fireproof dish with sugar to taste and about 1 in. of water. Apples and pears, which may discolour, have a better appearance if a dessertspoonful of red jam is added to give them a pink tinge. Be careful that the dish is not too full or it may boil over during cooking. (To ensure that you do not return to a dirty oven, stand it on a baking tray.) Cover the

dish with aluminium foil and cook for 45–75 minutes at any temperature between 375° and 400° F. to suit the remainder of the meal.

Dessert

Pastry comes to no harm if it is left standing in the cold oven and will cook perfectly from cold. If placed at the top of the oven at 400° or 425° F., it will cook in 45 minutes. If brought down in the oven so that it is immediately above the meat, it will take 60–75 minutes, according to size.

Puddings can be steamed in the oven, and the mixture, if cold and placed in a cold oven, can wait till cooking starts later in the day without coming to any harm. Mix in the usual way and turn into a greased pudding basin. Seal with aluminium foil. Stand the basin on a grid or pastry cutter in a second basin. Then add

A complete Sunday dinner put into the oven at breakfast time and left to cook while you are at church. Roast beef and roast potatoes, Yorkshire pudding, peas and apple pie took 1¼ hours at 400° F. and the plates warmed at the same time in the drawer

Breakfast

Bacon and Eggs.—Grease a shallow fireproof dish. Crack the required number of eggs and put them in the dish. Lay a rasher of bacon across each egg. Leave in the oven overnight and set the timers to cook for 45 minutes at 350° F.

Porridge.—Make with rolled oats. Put the correct quantity in a fireproof basin and add the required amount of *boiling* water. Stir thoroughly before covering the dish with aluminium foil. Leave in the oven overnight and set the timers to cook for 45 minutes at 350° F.

Complete Meals

When planning a complete meal to be cooked by the timer, meat is the main consideration because it cold water to half-fill the larger basin and seal it also with aluminium foil. Put it in a convenient place in the oven (probably immediately above the meat) and set the timers at a temperature of 375°–400° F. A small (1 pint) pudding will take a minimum of 1 hour, but a steamed pudding cannot cook for too long and you can safely leave it until the remainder of the meal is cooked. If you are cooking a pudding that will take 2 hours or longer, ensure that the basin containing the water is large enough not to boil dry, as, despite the aluminium foil seal, there is, of course, a certain loss of steam.

cannot be hurried very much. Whether in a fast or a moderate oven, the time required depends on the type of meat, the weight and the thickness. The remaining dishes must therefore be planned to cook for the same time as the meat.

Having arrived at the correct cooking time for the meat and with the knowledge that it requires a temperature of approximately 400° F. (it will cook at any temperature between 375° and 425° F. and can be varied to suit the remainder of the meal), one has a guide for the remaining dishes.

Supposing you want to serve roast beef, roast potatoes, Yorkshire pudding and an apple pie. If the meat takes 1 hour, put the well-coated potatoes at the edge of the lightly greased meat pan, and the Yorkshire pudding and the pie near the top of the oven. If the joint will take 1½ hours, put the potatoes close to the meat and the Yorkshire pudding and pie on a runner immediately above, as conveniently near to the meat pan as possible.

Menu 1

Roast shoulder of lamb (4 lb.)
Buttered carrots   Onion sauce
Roast potatoes
Steamed sultana pudding

Position — Put the lamb and potatoes (very well coated in melted fat) in the meat pan in the correct position for meat in your cooker. Prepare the carrots as on page 266 (when cooked, drain and toss them in a little butter and sprinkle with chopped parsley). Place them immediately above the meat.

Make a sultana pudding, following the general instructions already given for oven steaming, and place on same shelf as carrots.

Put the plates and serving dishes in warming drawer.

Chop 1 large onion and put with ½ pint milk into a pudding basin, add pepper and salt and 3 cloves, and leave to infuse in the warming drawer.

Directions — Set the timer to cook for 1¾

For early risers, what better than a hot breakfast prepared overnight? Here baked grapefruit, porridge, kidneys and bacon, hot rolls, coffee and milk all went into the oven the night before—and cooked themselves in the morning

hours at 400° F. Set the warming drawer to switch on at the same time as the oven.

When you are serving the meal, strain the milk from the onion into a saucepan, add 1 oz. of plain flour blended in a little cold milk and bring to the boil, stirring all the time. Season, and serve hot, returning the chopped onion to the sauce if liked.

Menu 2

Roast beef (3 lb. roll)
Roast potatoes   Peas
Yorkshire pudding
Apple pie

Position.—Put the beef and potatoes

(dipped twice in melted dripping) in the lightly greased meat pan in the correct position for meat in your oven. Put the apple pie and the Yorkshire pudding immediately above the meat and the peas at the top.

Directions.—Set the timer to cook for $1\frac{1}{4}$ hours at 400° F.

Menu 3

Glasgow stew   Dundee pudding

Stew (for 4)

1 *lb. flank beef*	*Bouquet garni*
3 *oz. pearl barley*	*Potatoes*
(*soaked overnight*)	*Pepper and salt*
2 *sticks of celery and*	2 *sliced carrots*
1 *turnip, diced*	2 *sliced onions*
Stock or water	

Cut the beef into inch cubes and remove all fat. Then put all ingredients together in a fireproof dish, cover with whole peeled potatoes and add sufficient stock or water just to cover. Add pepper and a teaspoonful salt. Seal the dish tightly with aluminium foil.

Dundee Pudding (for 4)

$\frac{1}{2}$ *lb. mincemeat*	1 *oz. sugar*
1 *egg*	$1\frac{1}{2}$ *oz. grated suet*
1 *oz. flour*	*A few chopped*
$\frac{1}{2}$ *oz. breadcrumbs*	*almonds*
Pinch of mixed spice	

Mix all together and turn into a well greased small pie dish. Cover with greaseproof paper.

Position.—Place both dishes about $1\frac{1}{2}$–2 in. from bottom of oven.

Directions.—Set the timer to cook for $2\frac{1}{2}$ hours at 325° F. Put the plates in the warming drawer and set the timer to switch on at the same time as the oven.

Menu 4

Baked hake
Duchess potatoes (see Vegetable chapter)
Peas   Apple pie

Place the hake in a greased baking dish. Sprinkle with seasoned flour, dot with tiny pieces of butter. Add a few button mushrooms dipped in melted margarine. Make your favourite apple or other fruit pie. Prepare the peas, as previously described, and make some duchess potatoes, piping or forking them into small heaps on a greased baking tray.

Position.—Put the fish in the position for meat in your oven, either on the floor or on the bottom runner, the vegetables in the centre and the pie towards the top.

Directions.—Set the timers to cook for $\frac{3}{4}$ hour at 425° F.

Menu 5

Roast duck
Duchess potatoes (see Vegetable chapter)
Peas   Sprouts
Apple sauce
Cherry tart

Put the duck in the meat pan, the peas and sprouts in fireproof dishes with salt, a knob of margarine and $\frac{1}{4}$–$\frac{1}{2}$ in. of water, and seal the dishes with aluminium foil; peel, core and cut into chunks two large cooking apples and put them in a basin with a little water and 1 oz. of castor sugar, sealing with aluminium foil. Prepare some duchess potatoes and form them into a flan case on a baking sheet. Make a cherry tart on a plate.

Position.—Put the duck in the position for meat in your oven, the vegetables and the plate tart immediately above, and the duchess flan and apple sauce towards the top.

Directions.—Set the timers to cook for $1\frac{1}{4}$ hours at 400° F. Put the plates and serving dishes in the warming drawer to heat while the oven is on.

When cooked, drain excess liquid from the apples and beat to a pulp. Slide the duchess flan carefully on to a plate, drain the peas and put in the centre.

Menu 6—Breakfast

Baked grapefruit   Porridge
Kidneys with bacon   Hot rolls
Coffee   Milk

Cut the grapefruit in half, loosen from the skin, remove centre, etc., and sprinkle with plenty of brown sugar. Place cut side upwards in a baking tray.

Clean the kidneys, remove the core and split in half. Wrap each half in a rasher of fat bacon and place in a baking tray. Prepare the porridge as on page 268. Make coffee and pour into a fireproof jug. Wrap the rolls in a well damped cloth and stand on a plate. Put the milk ready in a jug.

Position.—Kidneys, porridge, grapefruit and coffee pot just below the centre of the oven. Rolls and milk in warming drawer with serving plates.

Directions. — Set the timer to switch on both oven and warming drawer for 45 minutes. Set the oven at 350° F.

Menu 7—Supper for 4

Scallops
Creamed potatoes
Jam tart

Remove four scallops from their shells, wash and dry. Wrap each one in a piece of fat bacon and put them on baking tray. Prepare some potatoes for boiling in the oven as instructed at the beginning of this chapter.

Make an open jam tart.

Position. — Scallops and potatoes centre of oven. Jam tart standing on a baking tray (in case it should boil over) on bottom runner.

Directions. — Set the timer to switch on for 45 minutes at 425° F. When cooked, cream the potatoes with butter or margarine and serve hot.

No need to waste hours waiting to take a cake out of the oven. All three tiers of this beautiful wedding cake were cooked by timer control—which switched off automatically. All foods in this chapter specially made and photographed in the Creda kitchens

Menu 8—Supper for 3 or 4

Cheese and potato pudding
Baked apples

Line a 1-pint fireproof dish well coated with margarine with mashed and creamed potatoes. Beat together 2 eggs, ½ pint milk, 4 oz. grated cheese, 1 heaped tablespoonful of white breadcrumbs, pepper and salt, a little made mustard and, if liked, about 2 in. of a stick of celery well grated. (If you like garlic, rub a cut clove round the inside of the basin before mixing.) Turn this mixture into the dish and scatter a little more grated cheese on the top.

Wash and core 3 or 4 good cooking apples and cut a slit in the skin right round about 1 in. from the top. Stand in a dish and fill the centre of each apple with raspberry jam and a few chopped almonds or walnuts.

Position.—Put the apples on the bottom runner and the cheese pudding in the centre.

Directions.—Cook for 1 hour at 350° F.

Cake Making

The same principles apply. It is not necessary to remove a cake from the oven immediately it is cooked and to cool it at room temperature on a wire grid. You will get just as good results if it cools in the oven after switching off.

PRESSURE COOKERY

*This modern method saves time and fuel and
preserves the vitamins and flavour in your food*

PRESSURE cookery, which is growing steadily in popularity, has so many advantages that it is surprising any housewife can still lack the courage to try it for herself. At first, however, it does seem a trifle alarming to have to deal with a pan that whistles or hisses and has to be cooled under the cold tap before you can take off the lid. But the reward is a tremendous saving in time, fuel, space and food values. Once you take to a pressure cooker, you will hate the idea of being without one.

But first let us consider the advantages of pressure cookers. These, briefly, are:
(1) The full natural flavour and colour of the food are retained.
(2) Because cooking is quick, at a great heat, and the food is not in direct contact with the water, the all-important minerals and vitamins are preserved.
(3) Time saved averages between ½ hour and 1 hour per main meal, a great consideration for modern housewives, particularly those with outside jobs. For example, a steak and kidney pudding, which would take between 4 and 5 hours in the ordinary way, can be cooked in a pressure cooker in 60 minutes.

NOTE: Cooking time saved is also an economy in fuel. Generally speaking, any dish can be pressure cooked in from one-fifth to one-third the usual time.
(4) Where kitchen space is limited to one gas ring or hotplate, a whole meal can be cooked in one utensil.
(5) Different kinds of foods, even those as highly flavoured as onions, can be cooked in the same cooker at the same time as a pudding or fruit without the slightest danger of contamination.

On the other hand, there is no room for slap-dash guesswork cookery. With a pressure cooker you *must*:
(1) Obey the instructions to the letter and master the perfectly simple principles before you start.

(2) Time each dish exactly and resist the temptation to allow "a minute or two extra" because you can't believe it could possibly be done in the time the book says. Do that, and the bones in an Irish stew would, in a few minutes, turn out quite porous so that you could scrunch them up like sugar, while Brussels sprouts or cabbage would be reduced to a wet mush.
(3) Not expect the impossible. Obviously a pressure cooker will not actually bake, fry or roast, but it *will* do practically anything else, including making the toughest and cheapest cuts of meat deliciously tender in a surprisingly short time. And you can always pop the meat into a very hot oven or under a hot grill for a few minutes to "crisp" the outside like a genuine roast.

Not a New Idea

The idea of pressure cooking is not a new one, and the principles are known to have been applied in the days of the first Queen Elizabeth. John Evelyn, writing in 1682 in his famous Diary, describes a wonderful supper he ate cooked in what he calls "Monsieur Papin's digestors," and from what he says these must have been the ancestors of our present-day pressure cookers.

Since that time enormous progress has been made. The principle of pressure cooking is, nevertheless, a very simple one. At 15-lb. pressure, which is used for everyday cooking, the temperature inside the cooker rises to 250° F., whereas the highest temperature you can obtain in an open saucepan is boiling point, 212° F. Furthermore, all the steam is confined inside the cooker instead of evaporating into the air.

There are various different makes and sizes of pressure cooker on the market, but, generally speaking, the working principle is the same. If you decide to buy one, your best plan is to go to some big store, which is certain to have the latest models, and

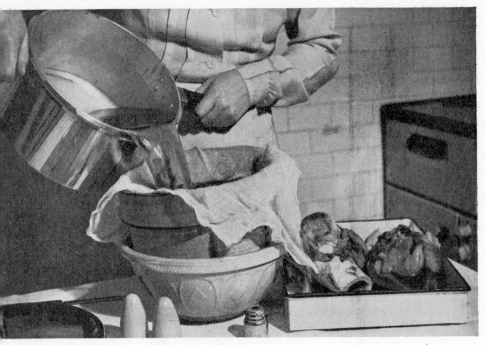

With a pressure cooker stock-making is easy, even from a small quantity of bones.
After cooking, strain the stock in the usual way

inspect them for yourself. What size you choose must, of course, be largely governed by the number of people for whom you cook. The smaller types of cooker are designed to give a pressure of 15 lb. a square inch, or about 250° F. Many of these are so designed that they can be taken straight to table once pressure has been reduced. In some types a spare lid is supplied for this purpose. The larger cookers, suitable for very large numbers, or for bottling fruit and vegetables, have a pressure gauge which registers pressure from 5 to 40 lb.

A family of four can get constant use from a 6-quart and a 7-pint pressure cooker, and a larger family would get the same service from 8-quart and 7-pint sizes. With two pressure cookers for a large family, or a large-sized cooker for a small family, a whole meal can be prepared in less than half the normal cooking time, thus cutting the fuel costs drastically.

30-minute Dinner

Here is a full dinner menu cooked in half an hour:

Fricassee of Veal
Potatoes
Carrots
Apple Charlotte

Fricassee of Veal

1 lb. fillet veal	½ tablespoonful
1 small onion	lemon juice
4 small mushrooms	Dried herbs to taste
6 peppercorns	(blade of mace,
1 oz. margarine	bay leaf, thyme,
1 oz. flour	parsley, marjoram)

½ pint stock or water

Cut veal in small cubes. Place in cooker with mushrooms and sliced onion. Add stock or water, lemon juice and herbs tied in a muslin bag.

Prepare **Apple Charlotte** by mixing together 3 oz. breadcrumbs, 2 oz. sugar, ¼ teaspoonful cinnamon and the grated rind of a lemon. Flavour 3 sliced apples with lemon juice. Put alternate layers of crumb mixture and fruit in a well-greased bowl. Pour 2 oz. margarine over the mixture and cover with two thicknesses of greased white paper. Tie securely. Stand the pudding bowl on the rack in the cooker with the veal. Bring to 15-lb. pressure (according to the manufacturer's specific instructions) and cook for 10 minutes.

Meanwhile, scrape and wash medium-sized new potatoes and new carrots.

After 10 minutes' cooking time, reduce pressure by cooling cooker. Open cooker and add salted vegetables. Close cooker and again bring to 15-lb. pressure. Cook for 5 minutes. Reduce pressure, remove lid and dish up vegetables and pudding. Add prepared thickening (margarine and flour) to veal, and cook for 5 minutes without replacing cooker cover. A little milk may also be stirred in.

Alternatively, if you have two cookers, use the larger one for the veal and apple charlotte, the second for the vegetables alone.

By pressure cooking this meal, a busy woman saves at least an hour's cooking time. Normal cooking methods take 80–90 minutes. She has cut her fuel bill by a third, and all the vitamins in the food remain, for none have been lost by evaporation or dilution in water.

Important points to remember are:

(1) **Safety.** You are enlisting the aid of a powerful force which should be treated with respect and intelligence, but every cooker is fitted with a safety device which operates automatically if too much pressure is building up, and releases it. In the smaller cookers these small safety-plugs are quite easy to replace.

(2) **Loading.** Never fill your cooker more than two-thirds full of food. In the case of liquids, such as soups, do not more than half fill. Allow for swelling in the case of such foods as rice, or pulse vegetables. On no account should food ever be allowed to touch the lid of the pressure cooker. A pudding basin used inside the cooker should never be more than two-thirds full, so that the pudding can rise; for milk puddings, only half full or the milk may boil over into the surrounding water. Cover steamed puddings with two thicknesses of greased paper. Use the rack supplied with your cooker when cooking green vegetables by themselves; when making stews, on the other hand, you do not need it.

(3) **Liquids.** The amount of liquid necessary for pressure cookery depends on the length of the cooking time, not on the quantity of food to be cooked. The amount given may seem very inadequate to the beginner, but it should never be exceeded. The small amount is due to the fact that in pressure cookery there is little or no evaporation.

The amount of liquid varies with the kind of pressure cooker, so it is important to follow the manufacturer's instructions carefully on this point. One general rule, however, applies to all models—for steamed puddings, use 2–2½ pints of water to allow for the pre-steaming period before the pressure control is adjusted, which is required to enable the pudding to rise. When making soups, stews or other dishes containing liquid, only the amount to be actually served with the finished dish should be put into the cooker—provided this is not less than the minimum required for the type of cooker.

NOTE: For milk puddings, allow 3 oz. grain to 1 pint liquid, instead of the usual 2 oz.

(4) **Seasoning.** Be sparing with seasoning. The speed of pressure cookery means that the natural mineral content of the food is retained and less seasoning is therefore needed. It is advisable for this reason, generally speaking, to add seasoning after cooking is finished. Alternatively, salt may be sprinkled on the prepared, washed and drained vegetables before putting them in the cooker.

(5) **Thickening and Gravies.** When gravy or stock is to be thickened, as for example when braising meat, the flour, mixed to a smooth paste with water or stock, should be added at the end of the pressure cooking and cooked in the open pan. If thickened beforehand it might, during the rapid cooking process, stick to the bottom of the pan.

(6) **Bringing to Pressure.** Fix the lid of your cooker firmly into position and put on a high heat until a steady flow of steam comes out of the vent pipe. This means that the water inside the cooker is boiling, turning into steam and has driven out all the air.

(7) **Controlling Pressure.** When the steady flow of steam comes from the vent pipe, adjust the pressure control and leave on high heat until the required pressure is reached. You will know this has happened when there is a continual slight hiss of steam from the vent pipe, or on some models it is recorded on a gauge. Then reduce the heat to "low"—just enough to

Braised Steak and Vegetables, a dish that takes a long time to cook in the oven, will take 20 minutes at the very most in a pressure cooker—and taste delicious. Prepare the ingredients in the usual way (left), brown them in the open cooker first, then bring to pressure

maintain the pressure—and *start timing.* On an electric hotplate, the heat may be switched right off if the cooking time is less than 10 minutes; if longer, it should be turned down to "low." When using electricity, it is sometimes necessary to pull the pressure cooker partly off the hotplate to control the pressure.

(8) **Reducing Pressure.** The cooker cannot be opened while it still contains pressure, owing to the force exerted against the pan and the lid. So never attempt to force off the lid; if it does not come off easily, that means there is still pressure inside and it requires further cooling.

There are two ways of cooling, depending on what is being cooked. Quick cooling, when cold water is run over the sides of the cooker for about 30 seconds, or the cooker is plunged into a basin of cold water, is the best for vegetables. It does not make the food cold, as it only reduces the temperature to boiling point.

Gradual cooling, by moving the cooker from the stove and leaving it in a cool place for between 5 and 20 minutes (according to the contents), is best for meat, poultry, puddings, soups, stews, or when bottling or sterilising fruit in glass jars. Steamed puddings will collapse if the pressure is reduced too quickly, meat may become dry and glass jars are liable to crack.

(9) **Cooking Several Things Together.** To cook together foods requiring differing

times, you can either (*a*) part-cook those with the longest cooking times, (*b*) cut them up smaller, or (*c*) put in the other foods later on in the cooking time. For instance, to cook halved potatoes (8 minutes) with green peas (2–3 minutes), put in the potatoes, add water, pressure-cook for 6 minutes, then cool quickly, open and add peas, close cooker again, bring back to pressure and cook for another 2 minutes. Cool and serve.

"Steamed" Cakes

If you do not want to have your oven on for cake baking, there are certain types of cakes, such as "boiled" fruit cake and gingerbread, which can be steamed in the cooker. It is advisable to put the cake, once you have taken it out of the cooker, under a fairly hot grill for a few minutes to dry off the top. Never fill your cake tin more than two-thirds full, and cover the top of the tin with a double piece of greaseproof paper.

Adapting Favourite Recipes for Pressure Cooking

One of the most exciting aspects of pressure cooking is learning how to adapt famous and exotic recipes—or your own favourites—to the new time- and fuel-saving method. It is surprisingly easy and, though it may take a little experimenting at first, it is well worth it. Once you have the timing correct, the dish will turn out exactly the same over and over again, and in a fraction of the time required by the old method. Soups and casseroles, and such long-cooking, one-dish meals, are an excellent way to start.

There are a few things to remember when working out recipes for pressure-cooking methods:

Time.—In experimenting with cooking time, it is better to err on the side of under cooking rather than over cooking. If, when you open the cooker, the food is a little underdone, it is easy to process for a few minutes more. Roughly speaking, the cooking time should be cut by 66–75 per cent.

Liquid.—Reduce the amount of liquid in the recipe, starting with only a little more than you want in the finished dish. If you used the normal amount of liquid, you would probably end up with a soup instead of a stew. You need to allow $\frac{1}{4}$ pint for every 15 minutes' cooking time in all cookers except the Presto, from which there is absolutely no loss by evaporation.

Seasoning.—As you use less liquid, there will be less to dilute the seasoning, so use less until you have tried out the recipe.

Fat.—Reduce the quantity of fat for browning meat, poultry and game by about one-half.

If you are at all familiar with pressure cooking you will find that, though you may be testing a recipe for the first time, you will have plenty of clues. You may never have cooked Bœuf Bourguignon, for instance, but you will certainly be familiar with the timing for beef stew. Thus you will know that the timing for cooking cubed beef must be the same in both recipes, and though they taste quite different, the difference lies in the use of wine and herbs in the one and not in the way they are cooked.

Here's our conversion for:

Beef Stew (Ordinary cooking)

1½ lb. steak	3 stalks celery
2 oz. fat	2 oz. dried peas
1½ pints stock	1 oz. flour
1 large onion	Salt and pepper

Soak peas overnight. Cube meat, slice onion, dice celery. Brown ingredients in casserole, add stock, bring to boil and sim-

mer gently for at least 1 hour. Season and thicken gravy with flour.

Beef Stew (Pressure cooking)

1½ lb. steak	3 stalks celery
1 oz. fat	2 oz. dried peas
¾ pint stock	1 oz. flour
1 large onion	Salt and pepper

Soak peas overnight. Cube meat, slice onion, dice celery. Preheat pressure cooker, add fat. Brown meat in it. Add vegetables, stock and seasoning. Close and bring to 15-lb. pressure. Cook for 15–20 minutes. Open cooker and thicken. Cook for 3 minutes in open cooker.

Bœuf Bourguignon (French recipe adapted to pressure cooking)

1½ lb. steak	8 small onions
1 oz. fat	Parsley, bay leaf,
¾ pint liquid (¼ pint	thyme, clove of
stock + ½ pint	garlic all in muslin
burgundy)	bag
Salt, pepper and flour	

Cube meat. Dust with seasoned flour. Preheat pressure cooker, add fat. Brown meat. Add onions, liquid and herbs. Close and bring to 15-lb. pressure. Cook for 15–20 minutes. Open cooker and remove muslin herb bag.

STOCK

The speed of pressure cookery makes it well worth while to make stock with quite a small quantity of bones. Here is a recipe using only 2 lb.

Bone Stock

2 lb. bones—marrow	1 quart of water
if possible	1 turnip
2 onions	1 small stick of celery
1 carrot	1 or 2 cloves
Seasoning	

Wash the bones and break up if large. Put into the cooker with the rest of the ingredients and bring slowly to the boil. Skim, then put on the lid and bring to pressure. Reduce the heat and pressure-cook for 45 minutes. When cold, lift off any fat on the top.

MEAT

A joint that has been pressure cooked can be given the authentic crisp appearance of a roast if you place it in a hot oven or under the grill for a few minutes just before serving.

The following table gives a guide to cooking times for meat, as used in stews, casseroles or braises:

Beef, lamb or mutton, veal: cut 1 in. thick, 10–15 minutes.
Pork: cut 1 in. thick, 15–20 minutes.
Beef, lamb or mutton: cut 2 in. thick, 20–25 minutes.
Veal: cut 2 in. thick, 18–20 minutes.
Pork: cut 2 in. thick, 25–30 minutes.

Average times for joints of meat are as follows:

Beef: 8–10 minutes per lb.
Lamb or mutton: 10–12 minutes per lb.
Pork and veal: 12–15 minutes per lb.

MAIN DISHES

Boiled Beef with Dumplings

2–2½ lb. silverside	2 onions, sliced
2 carrots, sliced	Salt and pepper
1 turnip, sliced	1 pint water

Prepare meat and place in pressure cooker with sliced vegetables, seasoning and water. Cook at 15-lb. pressure for 20–25 minutes. Let cooker cool slowly. Drop small dumplings (see Pastry chapter) into the hot liquid and cook for 10 minutes in open pressure cooker.

Braised Pheasant

1 pheasant	½ oz. bacon
1 oz. fat	1 carrot
1 stick celery	1 turnip
1 onion	Herbs
Stock	Salt and pepper

For the stuffing

1 sliced onion	1 shredded apple
1 cut celery stalk	Salt and pepper

Wash and dry bird well. Stuff with a mixture of celery, onion and apple, mixed with salt and pepper to taste. Skewer bird firmly. Preheat open pressure cooker, add fat and brown bird lightly on all sides. Remove bird from pan. Now fry the bacon lightly in the fat and add the thickly sliced vegetables. Fry lightly. Season and add herbs. Just cover with stock (taking care to add at least the minimum quantity of liquid needed for your pressure cooker). Lay the bird on top of the bed of vegetables and close cooker. Bring to 15-lb. pressure and cook for 18–20 minutes. Let cooker cool of its own accord.

Calf's Liver with Herbs

2 lb. liver, cut ½ in. thick	1 teaspoonful chopped parsley
1½ oz. fat	1 teaspoonful chopped chives
¼ pint white wine or stock	Juice of half a lemon
Salt, pepper and flour	

Dredge liver in sifted flour, season to taste with salt and pepper. Preheat open pressure cooker and melt fat in it. Brown liver on all sides. Add wine or stock. Close cooker, bring to pressure and cook at 15-lb. pressure for 8 minutes. Cool Remove liver to warmed dish. Add herbs and lemon juice to liquid in cooker and boil for a few minutes in open cooker. Pour over liver and serve.

Carrots in a Blanket

2 lb. veal cut ½ in. thick (beef may be used instead of veal)	4 or 5 medium-sized potatoes
	2 tablespoonfuls flour
	1 teaspoonful paprika
6 carrots	2 tablespoonfuls fat
2 teaspoonfuls salt	¼ teaspoonful pepper
¼ pint water	

Cut meat in thin strips the width of a bacon rasher. Quarter carrots. Wrap a strip of meat round each carrot segment and fasten with a skewer. Season with salt and pepper and roll in combined flour and paprika. Preheat cooker, melt fat in it, brown

To clear strained stock for clear soups, add the white and shell of an egg, then bring to the boil and whisk well

rolls on all sides. Place potatoes round and on top of rolls. Add ¼ pint water. Close cooker. Cook at 15-lb. pressure for 8–10 minutes. Let cooker cool.

Devilled Neck of Lamb

2 lb. neck of lamb	*1 teaspoonful dry mustard*
1 oz. fat	*2 teaspoonfuls salt*
1 onion, sliced	*¼ teaspoonful pepper*
2 stalks celery, chopped	*¼ pint vinegar*

¼ pint stock

Preheat pressure cooker, add fat. Brown meat well on all sides. Add vegetables and brown lightly. Mix mustard and seasoning with vinegar and add to meat and vegetables. Bring to 15-lb. pressure and cook for 15 minutes. Cool cooker slowly.

Fricassee of Rabbit

1 rabbit	*½ tablespoonful lemon juice*
1 onion, sliced	*Bouquet garni*
4 small mushrooms	*6 peppercorns*
1 oz. fat	*Salt*
¼ pint milk	*1 oz. flour*
½ pint stock or water	

Soak, wash, dry and joint rabbit. Place in cooker with mushrooms and onion and gently fry in the fat. Add stock, bouquet garni, lemon juice and seasonings. Cook at 15-lb. pressure for 15 minutes. Let cooker cool. Thicken with flour and milk and cook for 3–4 minutes without replacing cover.

Hungarian Beef Goulash

2 lb. stewing steak	*1 teaspoonful Tarragon vinegar*
1 oz. flour	*1 teaspoonful marjoram*
1 oz. fat	*1 teaspoonful chopped capers*
2 bay leaves	
1 lb. onions, shredded	
1 teaspoonful paprika	
¼ pint dry sherry }	*or ½ pint stock*
¼ pint stock or water }	

Parsley

Cut beef in 1-in. cubes and dredge with flour. Preheat pressure cooker, add fat. Brown meat well on all sides. Add onion and seasonings. Blend well, add liquid. Cook at 15-lb. pressure for 15 minutes. Let cooker cool. Open cooker, remove parsley and bay leaves. If an extra bright red colour is required, heat a nut of butter and add 1 teaspoonful paprika and 2 tablespoonfuls wine. Bring quickly to boiling point and pour over goulash when served. Traditionally, goulash should be served with noodles (3–4 minutes at 15-lb. pressure)

Jugged Hare

1 hare	*1 tablespoonful red currant jelly*
1 rasher of bacon	*Pepper and salt*
1 oz. fat	*Bouquet garni*
1 sliced carrot	*1½ oz. flour*
1 onion stuck with cloves	*¼ pint red wine*

¾ pint stock

Skin, paunch and joint hare (see Poultry and Game chapter), retaining blood, liver, heart and kidney. Preheat cooker, add fat, and brown hare and bacon in it. Add stock, seasoning, herbs and prepared vegetables. Close cooker, bring to 15-lb. pressure and cook for 30 minutes. Meanwhile, prepare and fry forcemeat balls, using cooked minced liver and kidney of hare. Cool cooker when cooking time is up, remove bouquet garni and stir in blended flour to thicken stock. Bring to boil and cook in open cooker for 3–4 minutes. Now remove onion, stir in strained blood, wine and jelly. Reheat gently. Serve with forcemeat balls (see Poultry chapter).

Porcupine Meatballs

1 lb. minced raw beef	*3 stalks celery, chopped*
3 oz. rice, uncooked	*1 green pepper, sliced*
1 teaspoonful salt	*1 tablespoonful sugar*
1 teaspoonful pepper	*¼ teaspoonful dry mustard*
1 tin tomato soup	*1 gill hot water*
1 oz. fat	*1 teaspoonful salt*
1 onion, sliced in rings	

Mix beef, rice, salt, pepper and a quarter of the tomato soup. Form into eight balls. Preheat open cooker, melt fat in it. Brown meatballs well. Dissolve the salt, dry mustard and sugar in the hot water and the remainder of the soup. Pour over meatballs. Add prepared onion, celery and green pepper. Close cooker and cook at 15-lb. pressure for 20 minutes. Cool cooker. Serve meatballs in sauce.

Salmi of Grouse

2 grouse	*Seasoning*
2 oz. mushroom stalks	*¼ pint cider*
1 oz. fat	*¼ pint stock or water*
1 onion, sliced	*Bouquet garni*
	½ oz. flour

Joint grouse. Preheat open cooker, melt fat. Brown joints all over. Add onion, chopped mushrooms, bouquet garni, seasoning and stock. Add broken-up carcases and giblets if available. Cook at 15-lb. pressure for 10 minutes. Strain off stock. Blend flour with stock and cider, and bring to boil. When cooked, lay joints of grouse in the thin sauce, discard vegetables and carcases. Cook for further 10 minutes at 15-lb. pressure. Cool.

Shrimp Creole

1 oz. fat	½ teaspoonful sugar
3 stalks celery, chopped	4 oz. shrimps
	2 oz. rice
1 onion, sliced	½ teaspoonful chilli
½ pint tomato juice	powder
½ tablespoonful vinegar	Salt

Preheat cooker and melt fat in it. Lightly brown onion and celery, add salt, chilli powder, tomato juice, vinegar, sugar and rice. Stir well to mix. Close cooker and bring to 15-lb. pressure. Cook for 10 minutes. Cool cooker. Open and add shrimps. Stir in open cooker till heated through.

Shrimp-stuffed Cucumber

4 small, stubby cucumbers	¼ pint thick white sauce (see Sauces)
3 oz. chopped shrimps	¼ pint water

Peel cucumbers, cut in half lengthwise and scrape out seeds, thus forming boat-shaped segments. Combine shrimps with white sauce and fill "boats" with the mixture. Place on rack in cooker with ¼ pint water. Close cooker. Cook at 15-lb. pressure for 3 minutes. Cool. Serve with wholemeal bread.

Spanish Rice

6 slices bacon, minced	2 teaspoonfuls paprika
2 onions, sliced	
1 clove garlic (optional)	2 oz. rice
1 green pepper (sliced)	½ lb. tomatoes and ½ pint stock or water (or tin of tomatoes)
2 teaspoonfuls salt	

Preheat open cooker, add bacon. Slightly brown onion, garlic, green pepper. Add washed rice and fry till just coloured. Add tomatoes, stock and seasoning. Cook at 15-lb. pressure for 10 minutes. Cool cooker, stir well and serve.

Spiced Pot Roast

2 lb. brisket beef	¼ teaspoonful cinnamon
2 onions, sliced	
2 carrots, sliced	Salt, pepper, 2 cloves
¼ lb. tomatoes, peeled	1 oz. fat
½ pint vinegar	

Preheat cooker, add fat and brown meat. Add halved tomatoes, sliced vegetables, seasonings and vinegar. Cook at 15-lb.

Vegetable marrow, filled with a savoury stuffing, is a delicious supper dish that lends itself particularly well to quick preparation in a pressure cooker

pressure for 25 minutes. Let cooker cool. Remove meat and crisp in oven. (If your pressure cooker has an indicator weight from which no steam escapes during cooking time, use only 4 tablespoonfuls vinegar.)

Steak and Kidney Pudding (Pressure-cooking time: 60 minutes)

For the pastry

6 oz. flour	2½ oz. shredded suet
1 teaspoonful baking powder	½ teaspoonful salt
	Water to mix

For the filling

1 lb. stewing beef	¼ lb. kidney
1 onion	Salt and pepper
¼ pint stock or water	½ oz. fat
2½ pints water in cooker	

Cube meat and slice onion. Preheat open cooker and melt fat in it. Brown meat thoroughly, then brown onion lightly. Add stock or water and seasoning. Cook at 15-lb. pressure for 15 minutes. Let cooker cool.

Prepare suet crust (see Pastry) and line a pudding basin which fits easily into the cooker. Fill pastry-lined basin with the meat and gravy already cooked. Cover with a top of suet crust. Cover basin with two thicknesses of greased paper or aluminium foil. Place basin on rack in cooker with 2½ pints water. Allow steam to flow gently from vent pipe for 15 minutes. Then bring to 15-lb. pressure and cook for a further 30 minutes. Let cooker cool.

Stuffed Marrow (Pressure-cooking time, including preparation: 20 minutes)

1 marrow	1 oz. melted fat
4 oz. cooked meat, minced	4 mushrooms
	2 sprigs parsley
1 chopped onion	1 oz. breadcrumbs
Salt and pepper	1 beaten egg
¼ pint water	

Peel and cut marrow into 6-in. slices, scooping out all the seeds. Make stuffing by mixing all the ingredients together. Fill each slice of marrow with stuffing. Pour ¼ pint water into a 7-pint size pressure cooker (or ½ pint water for larger cookers), place marrow slices on rack, close cooker, bring to 15-lb. pressure and pressure-cook for 5 minutes. Quick-cool the cooker and serve.

Stuffed Peppers or Capsicums

1 lb. peppers	Cooked Spanish Rice
¼ pint water	(see previous page)

Slice off the top of each pepper and re-move seeds. Place in pressure cooker on rack with ¼ pint water. Cook at 15-lb. pressure for 5 minutes. Cool cooker. Stuff each pepper with prepared rice. Place peppers in a flat dish, add a little fat, and brown in a hot oven or under the grill.

Tuna Fish Casserole

1 can tuna fish	1 teaspoonful salt
1 cupful peas	¼ teaspoonful pepper
2 tablespoonfuls margarine	1 onion, sliced
	Toasted breadcrumbs
3 tablespoonfuls flour	Paprika
½ pint milk	¼ pint water in cooker

Make white sauce by melting margarine and blending in flour, adding milk and stirring until at boiling point. Season. Grease a dish or ring mould which fits easily into the cooker. Flake tuna fish and fill the mould with alternate layers of fish, onion, peas, crumbs and sauce. Repeat layers. Sprinkle top with paprika. Cover with two thicknesses of greased paper, securely tied. Place on rack in cooker with water. Cook at 15-lb. pressure for 10 minutes. Cool. This dish can be crisped and browned under the grill after cooking, if desired.

Vegetable Chop-Suey

1½ oz. fat	¼ pint stock
1 onion, sliced	1 teaspoonful salt
6 stalks celery, cut up, with leaves	4 hard-boiled eggs, chopped
1 green pepper, sliced	2 oz. mushrooms
Soy or Chinese sauce	

Preheat open cooker and melt fat in it. Fry onion. Add stock, vegetables and seasoning. Close cooker and cook for 3 minutes at 15-lb. pressure. Cool cooker. Stir in eggs and sauce. Serve over rice (cooked 8–10 minutes at 15-lb. pressure) or noodles (3–4 minutes at 15-lb. pressure).

QUICK ONE-DISH MEALS

These will save time in preparing, in cooking, in serving and in dish washing. All can be cooked without the help of a pressure cooker, but they will then take much longer.

Porridge

3 heaped tablespoonfuls oatmeal or quick porridge oats	¾ pint water
	½ teaspoonful salt

Bring water to boil in open cooker, add salt, then stir in oatmeal, continue stirring

Because it cooks at such intense heat and the water never touches the food, you can cook a custard pudding, sprouts, carrots—and even onions—all at once without fear of contamination

until quite smooth. Cover and *bring slowly to pressure over low heat*. Pressure cook as follows:

Quick porridge oats: 3 minutes.
Fine oatmeal: 10 minutes.
Medium oatmeal: 15 minutes.
Coarse oatmeal: 20 minutes.

Reduce pressure with cold water and stir before serving.

NOTE: The pressure cooker must never be more than half full when porridge is being cooked.

Surprise Casserole

1½ *lb. pork sausages*	*Medium can of*
3 *onions, sliced*	*creamed corn*
6 *potatoes, sliced*	2 *teaspoonfuls salt*
1 *dessertspoonful fat*	¼ *teaspoonful pepper*
¼ *pint tomato juice*	

Preheat pressure cooker, add fat and brown sausages. Pour off excess fat. In bottom of cooker place alternate layers of potato, onion and corn. Season each layer. Place sausages on top and pour tomato juice over. Cook at 15-lb. pressure for 5 minutes. Cool quickly and serve.

Six-layer Dinner

1 *lb. potatoes, sliced*	1 *lb. tomatoes,*
½ *head celery,*	*skinned*
chopped	2 *teaspoonfuls salt*
½ *lb. minced beef*	¼ *teaspoonful pepper*
2 *onions, chopped*	1 *dessertspoonful fat*
1 *green pepper, sliced*	½ *pint water or stock*

Preheat pressure cooker and melt fat. Add layers of ingredients in order as above. Season each layer. Pressure cook at 15-lb. pressure for 7 minutes. Cool cooker and serve.

Pork and Bean Dinner

6 *oz. dried beans*	1 *medium onion,*
½ *lb. diced pork*	*sliced*
1 *oz. brown sugar*	2 *tablespoonfuls*
1 *teaspoonful salt*	*mushroom ketchup*
½ *teaspoonful mustard*	½ *pint tomato juice*
¼ *pint water*	

Soak beans overnight, then drain. Preheat pressure cooker and brown diced pork. Add beans, sugar, salt, mustard, onion, ketchup, tomato juice and water (enough to cover beans). Close cooker, bring to 15-lb. pressure and cook for 10–20 minutes, depending on type of bean. Let cooker cool slowly.

COOKING VEGETABLES

Fresh, frozen or dried vegetables can all be cooked with excellent results in a pressure cooker.

Fresh Vegetables should be prepared in the normal way, roots being diced, greens and cabbage shredded and cauliflower, for example, divided into flowerets. Several different vegetables can be cooked simultaneously, each retaining its individual flavour. Where there is a difference in the cooking times of vegetables to be cooked together (for instance, potatoes which take 8 minutes and sliced cabbage which only requires 2–3 minutes), those requiring longer cooking can be cut in smaller pieces or pressure cooked for a short time before the others are added.

Always use $\frac{1}{2}$ pint of water in the cooker when cooking fresh vegetables and put it in the cooker first. Place the vegetables on the trivet or in the separators and sprinkle $\frac{1}{2}$ flat teaspoonful of salt over them. Reduce pressure by the quick method of running cold water over the outside or standing the cooker in a bowl of cold water.

Be sure to keep the liquid in which vegetables have been pressure cooked. It is a valuable basis for soups, sauces and gravies.

The following guide gives the approximate times needed to cook various vegetables after pressure has been reached:

Artichokes (Jerusalem) cut in halves or quarters, according to size: 3–4 minutes.
Beans, Broad: 2–4 minutes.
Beans, Green: 2–4 minutes.
Beetroot (small): 15 minutes. (Larger beetroot require up to 1 pint of water and 40 minutes cooking time.)
Broccoli, Sprouting: 2–3 minutes.
Brussels Sprouts (whole): 2–4 minutes.
Cabbage (sliced): 2–3 minutes.
Carrots (diced): 3–4 minutes.
Carrots (new—whole): 5–6 minutes.
Cauliflower (in flowerets): 2–3 minutes.
Celery (sliced): 3–5 minutes.
Leeks: 3–5 minutes.
Onions (quartered or sliced): 3–4 minutes.
Onions (whole): 10 minutes.
Parsnips (sliced): 3–4 minutes.
Peas: 1–3 minutes.
Potatoes (medium-sized whole): 8 minutes.
Potatoes (new): 6–8 minutes.
Swedes (cubed): 3–5 minutes.
Spinach: 1 minute.
Tomatoes (whole): 2–3 minutes.
Turnips (cubed): 3–5 minutes.
Vegetable Marrow (sliced, with skin left on if young and tender): 3–4 minutes.

Frozen Vegetables should be partly thawed or, if still frozen, broken up, then cooked in $\frac{1}{4}$ *pint boiling water only*, either on the trivet or in the separators and with salt to taste.

Approximate cooking time for frozen vegetables after pressure has been reached are as follows:

Asparagus: $3\frac{1}{2}$ minutes.
Brussels Sprouts: 3 minutes.
Cauliflower: $3\frac{1}{2}$ minutes.
Mixed Vegetables: 5 minutes.
Peas: 3 minutes.
Runner or French Beans: 2 minutes.
Spinach: 2 minutes.

Dried Vegetables and Pulses, such as lentils and haricot beans (both a valuable source of proteins), should first be soaked in boiling water, with $\frac{1}{2}$ teaspoonful of salt to every $\frac{1}{2}$ pint of water, for 2 hours. *Then cook in 2 pints of water to every pound* of dried vegetables or pulses, pouring the appropriate amount of water into the cooker first and taking care that, with the vegetables in, the pan is not more than half full. *Bring to pressure slowly over a low heat* instead of the usual high heat; after cooking, reduce pressure the slow way, at room temperature for 5–10 minutes, then run cold water over the cooker for a few seconds before raising the lever.

Here are approximate cooking times after pressure has been reached for the chief dried vegetables and pulses:

Butter Beans, small Haricot Beans: 15–20 minutes.
Lentils: 10–20 minutes.
Peas: 15 minutes.
Pearl Barley: 20 minutes.
Rice: 10–15 minutes.
Split Peas: 10–15 minutes.

Celery with Cheese

Place sticks of washed celery on the rack in pressure cooker with $\frac{1}{4}$ pint water. Cook for 3 minutes at 15-lb. pressure. Meanwhile, make a thick cheese sauce. Pour over the cooked celery and serve with wholemeal bread.

Alternatively, arrange cooked celery stalks on grill plate. Fill each stalk with grated cheese and a few raisins. Cover with a little butter and cook for 1 minute under the grill.

Cauliflower or Leeks and Cheese

All vegetables have greater flavour and

food value when cooked by pressure because none of the vitamins or mineral salts are lost in the cooking liquid. Try cauliflower (5 minutes at 15-lb. pressure) or leeks (3 minutes) with a similar cheese sauce.

PUDDINGS

Ordinary recipes for steamed puddings can be used when cooking puddings in your pressure cooker, but it is generally advisable when using the smaller cookers to steam the mixture in the normal way for at least 20 minutes of the whole boiling time. This can be done quite simply, because, until the lid is fixed in position and the pan sealed, you can treat your pressure cooker just like an ordinary saucepan. This preliminary cooking means that the pudding rises well before it is subjected to pressure. Fill your basin not more than three-quarters full, and cover with a piece of greased paper and a pudding cloth. Stand in the cooker on the rack and pour in sufficient *boiling* water to come half way up the basin, put on the lid and steam normally for 20 minutes, then bring to pressure and cook for the necessary length of time. Time needed for the whole process is one-third of what you would allow if steaming the pudding in the normal way.

Christmas Pudding

4 oz. sultanas	1 teaspoonful mixed
4 oz. raisins	spice
2 oz. currants	½ teaspoonful ground
2 oz. mixed peel	cinnamon
1 oz. chopped nuts	½ wineglassful brandy
1 lemon	(optional)
3 oz. shredded suet	½ gill milk
1 oz. flour	2 eggs
4 oz. soft breadcrumbs	4 oz. soft brown sugar
½ teaspoonful grated	2½ pints water in
nutmeg	cooker
Pinch of salt	

Prepare fruit. Add to sifted dry ingredients, which should be well mixed together. Add grated rind of the lemon and sugar. Mix thoroughly. Mix with beaten eggs, brandy (if used) and milk. Turn into a well-greased pudding basin and cover with two thicknesses of greased paper, tied in position. Put basin on rack in cooker, in which 2½ pints water have been heated. Close cooker; let steam flow gently through vent pipe for 20 minutes before adding pressure control. Bring to 15-lb. pressure and cook for 1½ hours. Let pressure reduce of its own accord.

To reheat home-made or shop-bought

Sponge puddings and suet mixtures are best pressure cooked in small individual moulds covered with greased paper or aluminium foil and securely tied

Christmas pudding, place the pudding, in its mould, on the rack with 1 pint boiling water. Bring to 15-lb. pressure and cook for 15–20 minutes. That will save a lot of time on the day.

If, however, you have a favourite Christmas pudding recipe which you want to adapt to pressure cooking, just cut the cooking time by 75 per cent. Also pre-steam the pudding for 20 minutes before bringing to pressure, then cook at 15-lb. pressure.

"Baked" Custard

2 eggs
¾ pint milk
2 tablespoonfuls sugar

Vanilla or almond flavouring or grated orange or lemon peel
½ pint of water for cooking

Beat eggs and sugar, scald milk, add flavouring and mix with the eggs. Pour into a greased pint-sized mould, cover with one layer of greaseproof paper, stand on trivet in cooker, add water. Cover and bring to pressure and pressure cook for 5 minutes. Reduce pressure at room temperature, turn out custard and either serve hot with jam or caramel sauce, or cold with thick cream and fresh or stewed fruit.

If desired, custard can be made in individual moulds, and will then only need to cook for 2½ minutes.

JAMS, JELLIES AND MARMALADES

For jams and jellies, a pressure cooker provides a short-cut on the pre-cooking of the fruit. Because this part of the process is done in the steam-tight pressure cooker, there is no evaporation or loss of flavour. All your favourite recipes can be adapted, and the recipes given here merely serve to show the general procedure. There are two important points to remember.

(1) **Do not fill your cooker more than half-full.**

(2) **Always cook jam in an open cooker once you have added the sugar.**

Gooseberry Jam

2 lb. gooseberries   2 lb. sugar
¼ pint water

Wash, top and tail fruit. Place in cooker with water. Close cooker, bring to 15-lb. pressure and cool at once. Open cooker, stir in sugar until dissolved and boil for 10 minutes *without replacing lid*. Pot into warm jars and seal at once. Yield: 4 lb. jam.

Times for pre-cooking fruits for jam-making

Apricots: 3 minutes at 15-lb. pressure. Cool at once.

Black Currants: 3 minutes at 15-lb. pressure. Cool at once.

Cherries: 5 minutes at 15-lb. pressure. Cool at once.

Damsons: 5–10 minutes at 15-lb. pressure, depending on type, size, ripeness. Cool at once.

Plums: 5 minutes at 15-lb. pressure. Cool at once.

Raspberries: Bring to 10-lb. pressure. Cool at once.

Rhubarb: Bring to 10-lb. pressure. Cool at once.

Strawberries: Bring to 10-lb. pressure. Cool at once.

Blackberry and Apple Jelly

2 lb. blackberries
Juice of 1 lemon
2 large cooking apples

¼ pint water
1 lb. sugar to each pint of juice

Pick over and wash blackberries. Slice apples, but do not peel or core. Place fruit in cooker with juice and water. Process at 10-lb. pressure for 3 minutes. Cool. Turn contents into jelly bag and strain overnight. Measure juice and place in cooker, adding 1 lb. sugar to each pint juice. Bring to boil in open cooker, stirring all the time, and boil rapidly until jelly sets when tested. Pot and seal at once.

Seville Orange Marmalade

2 lb. Seville oranges   4 lb. sugar
1 lemon   1 pint water

Wash and shred the fruit. Tie pips and some of the pith in muslin and place in pressure cooker with fruit and water. Close cooker, bring to 15-lb. pressure and cook for 15 minutes. Let cooker cool. Open cooker, add sugar and stir until dissolved. Boil in open pressure cooker until a set is obtained.

Any citrus fruit, or combination of fruits, may be used for marmalade. Far less water is needed when you make your marmalade in a pressure cooker, because you do not lose liquid by evaporation.

For **Chunky Marmalade** the recipe above should be used, but the fruit should be sliced thickly, and the fruit and sugar boiled in the open pressure cooker until dark.

After 10 minutes pre-steaming and 10 minutes at pressure, out come these perfect cherry sponge puddings (right)

In a medium or large pressure cooker, you can safely do two layers of pudding moulds at a time (below), provided there is space between the top ones and the lid

water and process for 10 minutes at 15-lb. pressure. Let cooker cool. Remove muslin bag, add sugar and boil quickly until a set is obtained (about 10 minutes).

Sweet Orange Marmalade

1 lb. oranges
1 lemon
3 lb. sugar
1½ pints water

Wash fruit. Slice thinly, tie pips in muslin and place in cooker with water. Bring to 15-lb. pressure and cook for 10 minutes. Let cooker cool. Open cooker, add sugar and stir until dissolved. Boil fast in open cooker until a set is obtained.

Spiced Bramble Jelly

3 lb. blackberries   1 teaspoonful mixed
½ pint water   nutmeg, cinnamon
1 lb. sugar to each   and mace
   pint of juice

Wash fruit and place on rack in pressure cooker with water and spices. Close cooker, bring to 10-lb. pressure and cook for 2 minutes. Cool. Strain overnight in a jelly bag. Next day, measure juice and place in cooker with appropriate amount of sugar. Boil in open pressure cooker until jelly sets when tested.

In true country fashion, the pulp in the jelly bag is not wasted. Make it into:

Lemon Marmalade

2 lb. lemons   5 lb. sugar
          1½ pints water

Wash and peel the lemons very finely. Shred the peel, remove pith from fruit and tie with the pips in muslin. Cut up the flesh and place with muslin bag and contents in the cooker with water. Close cooker, bring to 15-lb. pressure and cook for 10 minutes. Let cooker cool. Open cooker, stir in the sugar until dissolved and boil in open cooker until a set is obtained.

Grapefruit and Lemon Marmalade

4 lemons   3 lb. sugar
2 grapefruit   1 pint water

Shred the peel of the fruit. Remove most of the grapefruit pith and tie with all the pips in muslin. Put in pressure cooker with

285

The time-saving way of bottling fruit in a pressure cooker—first pack the jars with fruit leaving ½ in. headspace, then pour on hot syrup or water and close

Spiced Bramble Cheese

Rub the fruit pulp through a wire sieve, and to each pound of pulp add ¾ lb. sugar. Leave to soak for some hours. Add the juice and grated rind of 1 lemon. Boil together, stirring constantly, and pot and seal while still hot.

Apple and Plum Cheese

3 lb. apples (windfalls will do)
1 lb. plums
¼ pint water
¾ lb. sugar to each pint of pulp

Slice apples, do not peel or core. Place with plums on rack in pressure cooker with water. Cook at 15-lb. pressure for 1 minute. Cool. Sieve fruit and measure pulp. Add sugar in proportion to the pulp and boil in open pressure cooker until a set is obtained. Pot and seal.

Sloe and Apple Cheese is made in the same way, adding a little extra sugar if the sloes are very tart.

Hips and haws are the delight of every country child—and a valuable source of vitamin C. These recipes show how to make full use of them.

Haw Sauce

1½ lb. haws
½ pint vinegar
4 oz. sugar
1 oz. salt and 1 teaspoonful pepper

Wash haws and place on rack in pressure cooker with vinegar. Pressure cook for 10 minutes at 15-lb. pressure. Cool. Sieve haws and return to cooker with sugar and seasonings. Boil in open cooker for 10 minutes, then pot and seal.

Haw Jelly

1 lb. sugar and juice of 1 lemon to each pint of juice
3 lb. haws
1 pint water

Wash haws and place on rack in pressure cooker with water. Cook for 10 minutes at 15-lb. pressure. Cool. Pour into jelly bag and leave to strain. Next day, measure juice and add proportionate amounts of lemon juice and sugar. Bring to boil in open cooker and boil until jelly sets when tested. Pot and seal at once.

Haw sauce and haw jelly are excellent with all meats.

Hip and Apple Jam

1 *lb. rose hips*	¼ *pint water*
1 *lb. apples*	¾ *lb. sugar*

Place hips in cooker with ½ pint water, cook at 15-lb. pressure for 15 minutes. Cool. Strain through jelly bag. Next day, place the sliced apples in cooker with ¼ pint water and bring to 10-lb. pressure. Cool at once. Mash apples to a pulp, add hip juice and sugar, and boil rapidly until a set is obtained.

Pear Catsup

2 *lb. pears*	½ *teaspoonful each of*
4 *oz. sugar*	*pepper, cinnamon*
¼ *pint vinegar*	*and ground cloves*
1 *teaspoonful salt*	

Place pears in cooker with vinegar and process at 15-lb. pressure for 3–5 minutes, depending on type of pear. Rub through sieve. Add remaining ingredients and boil gently in open pressure cooker until thickened. Pot and seal.

FRUIT BOTTLING

Particular delight of the thrifty housewife is a stock of home bottled fruit on her pantry shelves, ready for the winter months. Here's the way the pressure-cooking method of home bottling works out step by step.

(1) Use only jars in perfect condition, rejecting any that are chipped or cracked. Wash in soapy water, rinse in hot water and leave in clean hot water until ready for use.

(2) Select fresh, young and tender fruit, firm but ripe. Grade to size. Clean and prepare as necessary.

(3) Fill jars with fruit, leaving ½-in. head space.

(4) Cover with hot syrup or water. Barely cover fruits which make a lot of their own juice when cooking.

Thin syrup—8 oz. sugar—1½ pints liquid ⎤ water
Medium syrup—8 oz. sugar—1 pint liquid ⎬ or
Thick syrup—8 oz. sugar—½ pint liquid ⎦ juice

(5) Work out air bubbles with a clean knife, or by tapping jars on board. Wipe all seeds or pulp from top of jars.

(6) Adjust closures on jars. If using screw-top jars, screw up band tightly, then release a quarter-turn.

(7) Turn rack upside down in cooker and put in 2 pints hot water.

After anything from 3 to 7 minutes (according to the fruit being bottled) at 5-lb. pressure, you leave to cool, then remove jars to a wooden board and tighten lids. The cooker is the Presto 706B

(8) Stand jars on rack, but do not allow them to touch each other. Pack with newspaper if necessary, or run up a rubber band on each jar.

(9) Stand cooker on high heat. Fix lid. Allow steam to flow through vent pipe for 1 minute.

(10) Fix indicator weight or pressure-control weight. Bring to 5-lb. pressure. Start counting processing time. Do not let pressure fluctuate, as this may cause liquid to be forced from the jars.

(11) When processing time is up, remove cooker from heat. Allow pressure to reduce at room temperature. Do not cool by either of the quick-cooling cold-water methods, as this will cause glass jars to crack.

(12) When all pressure is reduced, open cooker. Remove jars to wooden board or cloth surface, away from draughts. Tighten screw bands. (If jars are still bubbling, wait till all movement ceases before lifting out of cooker.)
Leave for 24 hours. Test seal, wipe jars clean, label and date. Store in cool, dry place.

All fruit bottling should be done at 5-lb. pressure. The following table gives processing time in minutes for different fruits after 5-lb. pressure has been reached.

Apples	4	Cherries	5
Apricots	7	Currants	3
Blackberries	4	Damsons	5
Gooseberries	3	Plums	4
Loganberries	3	Raspberries	3
Peaches	7	Rhubarb	3
Pears	7	Strawberries [1]	3
Pineapple (slices)	4		

[1] Strawberries should be hulled, brought to simmering point n enough medium syrup barely to cover. Leave overnight to soak. Next day, reheat. Pack into jars. Cover with syrup. Process in usual way at 5-lb. pressure.

VEGETABLE PRESERVING

Vegetables cannot be bottled safely and easily like fruits. Certain bacteria, which in fruit are killed by the combination of moderate heat and natural fruit acids, cannot be destroyed in vegetables except at very high temperatures. These organisms may be present in bottled vegetables which look and smell perfectly fresh. There is no way of detecting them, but they are quite capable of causing acute food poisoning.

The *only* way to bottle vegetables with a reasonable degree of safety is by using a pressure cooker with a reliable pressure gauge which will maintain a pressure of at least 10 lb. and a temperature of 240° F. Smaller models without a pressure gauge are *not* to be recommended for this purpose.

CAKES

Basic Cake Recipe

4 oz. margarine or	6 oz. flour
butter	1 teaspoonful baking
4 oz. sugar	powder
2 eggs	2 tablespoonfuls milk

1½ pints boiling water

Flavouring

2 heaped tablespoonfuls cocoa, or
3 oz. glacé cherries, or
Grated rind of 1 lemon or orange, etc.

Cream margarine and sugar, beat eggs, then add them gradually to mixture alternately with the sifted flour and baking powder (and cocoa if making chocolate cake). Stir in milk and fruit (if used), then put mixture into well-greased cake tin and cover with two thicknesses of greaseproof paper. Put tin on trivet in cooker with boiling water. Put lid on cooker and, with pressure control lever up, steam on low heat for 15 minutes. Then put pressure control lever down and pressure cook for 40 minutes. Reduce pressure gradually at room temperature, take out cake and put it under a hot grill for 2 or 3 minutes to crisp and brown the top.

SPECIAL BABY FOODS

Strained and puréed vegetables and fruits can be prepared in the pressure cooker.

Strained Spinach

Wash thoroughly and remove stalks, etc., from spinach. With trivet in cooker, put in spinach, add ¼ pint water, cover, bring to pressure and pressure cook for 2 minutes. Reduce pressure with cold water, dish up and sieve spinach.

Vegetable Purée

Dice the vegetables (either carrots alone or mixed carrot, potato, tomato, etc.) and put them into the cooker containing the trivet. Add ¼ pint water. Cover and bring to pressure and pressure cook for 5 minutes. Reduce pressure with cold water. Dish up and sieve the vegetables, diluting with stock from the pressure cooker.

PARTY SNACKS AND SANDWICHES

For the cocktail, sherry or tea party, food should be dainty and good to look at as well as to eat

THERE is no easier way of returning hospitality than with a cocktail, sherry or after-noon tea party. The success of such enter-taining depends very largely on the array of attractive-looking "eats" provided. (See a l s o Chapters on Entertain-ing and Cocktails, Cups and Punches.) Cocktail or sherry party snacks can include tiny cooked sausages (each with a little stick so that it can be eaten in the fingers), small cooked new pota-toes and minute saus-age rolls, as well as the ever popular olives, po-tato crisps, gherkins, little onions and salted almonds.

Plain biscuits can be spread with caviare, an-chovy, sardines, shrimps or prawns, and there are many suggestions for canapés in the chapter on Hors d'œuvres. Literally, a canapé is a slice of bread fried in butter, but often crisp pastry diamonds and squares are used instead. You can give your canapés a professional touch by brushing them over lightly with aspic jelly, then add-ing the savoury mixture (flaked cooked haddock, sliced gherkin and sliced tomato is one suggestion) and finally spooning a small quantity of the jelly on top.

A tasty platter for a party contains thin slices of Pumpernickel and Gruyère cheese, with curls of butter

Savoury Suggestions

Open savoury tarts are also excellent for cocktail parties. Various mixtures can be used for the filling, but here is one worth trying (the quantities given are sufficient for about nine or ten tartlets). You will need a cupful of cold, flaked haddock, cod or other white fish. Make $\frac{1}{2}$ pint well sea-soned white sauce, using $\frac{3}{4}$ oz. flour, $\frac{3}{4}$ oz. butter and the liquor in which the fish was cooked, and, while it is still hot, stir in a teaspoonful of gelatine dissolved in cold water. Mix in the fish carefully, line the tartlets with strips of skinned tomato and, when the fish mixture is cool to the jellying point, place generous spoonfuls in the tart-lets. Dust with paprika and garnish with either parsley, a slice of tomato topped with pimento-stuffed olive, or chopped caper and a little parsley, or sprinkle with fennel.

Another idea is to serve very tiny fish croquettes—either round ones or cork-shaped—impaled on cocktail sticks.

Cheese Straws

4 oz. plain or self-raising flour	1 egg-yolk
Pinch of salt	2 oz. Cheddar cheese (or 1 oz. Cheddar and 1 oz. Parmesan)
Dash of Cayenne pepper	
2 oz. vegetable fat shortening	1 tablespoonful water

To make the cheese pastry, sieve the flour, salt and Cayenne pepper together, then rub in the vegetable fat shortening until the mixture resembles breadcrumbs. Stir in the finely grated cheese and bind with the egg-yolk and water. Knead lightly and roll out to a square $\frac{1}{4}$ in. thick. Trim the edges with a knife and cut into strips 3 in. wide, then into straws $\frac{1}{4}$ in. wide. Gather the scraps together, roll out and cut into rounds with a 3-in. cutter. Cut out the centres with a smaller cutter to make rings. Place rings and straws on a baking sheet and bake near the top of a hot oven for 7–10 minutes. Cool on a cake rack. Place the straws in the rings for serving. (Makes 70–80 straws.)

Photos on this page taken at the Spry Cookery Centre

Those with a sweet tooth will like these crisp Poinsettias as a change from savouries

Poinsettias

4 oz. flaky pastry	A little icing sugar
2 oz. finely chopped almonds	A few glacé cherries

Roll out the flaky pastry (see Pastry chapter) to $\frac{1}{2}$ in. thickness. Cut into $2\frac{1}{2}$-in. squares. Place the squares on a baking sheet and cut 1 in. in from each corner towards the centre. Fold alternate corners into the centre in pinwheel fashion. Press gently in the centre. Decorate with small pieces of glacé cherry and a few almonds. Bake near the top of a hot oven for 10–15 minutes. Dust with icing sugar and serve as a biscuit with cocktails, sherry, fruit or fruit fools. (Makes approximately 14 Poinsettias.)

Cheese Straws, in neat little bundles slipped through pastry rings, make delicious cocktail savoury snacks

SANDWICHES

Ribbon Sandwiches

Cut three or more slices of bread about $\frac{1}{4}$ in. thick. Alternate layers of brown and

Cocktail sausages and tiny sausage rolls, ribbon sandwiches, miniature vol-au-vents and an assortment of canapés and open tarts, specially made in the Creda kitchens

white bread can be used, if liked. Fill them, using creamed butter, wrap in a damp cloth and put a weight on them. Cut, just before serving, to the size required.

Fillings for Ribbon Sandwiches

(1) Alternate layers of tongue and grated Gruyère cheese.

(2) Alternate layers of chopped cucumber and anchovy essence, with a little cream to mix, and salmon mixed with cream and chopped white of egg.

(3) Alternate layers of chicken and ham, and lettuce.

Rolled Sandwiches

Use fairly new bread, cut in thin slices, remove crusts, spread with creamed butter and any filling liked. Roll up the slices and fasten with cocktail sticks. These are good for wrapping round little sausages or, particularly if brown bread is used, round sticks of canned asparagus.

Suggested Fillings for Sandwiches

Savoury:

Anchovy essence mixed with creamed butter, a very little grated horseradish and a squeeze of lemon juice.

Chicken.

Cream cheese and watercress.

Cucumber moistened with mayonnaise.

Foie gras purée.

Grated cheese.

Grated Gruyère cheese with chopped nuts, Cayenne and salt.

Ham.

Cold scrambled eggs (much easier to spread and so less wasteful than hard-boiled), anchovy paste, a few drops of vinegar and a pinch of mustard, mixed with creamed butter.

Cold scrambled eggs and pickles chopped finely.

Cold scrambled eggs and sliced tomato.

Lettuce and tomato.

Sardines (skinned, boned and mashed),

sieved hard-boiled egg-yolks, a pinch of Cayenne and salt, a squeeze of lemon juice and olive oil to bind.

Tomato and cucumber.

Tongue.

Sweet:

Dates and nuts chopped finely.

Figs and nuts chopped finely.

· Chopped nuts and honey.

Banana and marmalade.

Dates with orange juice.

Cream cheese and strawberry jam.

Sliced banana with raspberry jam.

Crispbread Sandwiches

Butter two pieces of crispbread. Chop some stoned raisins and dates and sandwich them together with this.

Cucumber and Chive Sandwiches

2 *tablespoonfuls salad oil*	$\frac{1}{8}$ *teaspoonful pepper*
	1 *cucumber*
1 *tablespoonful vinegar or lemon juice*	1 *teaspoonful chives, chopped*
$\frac{1}{4}$ *tablespoonful salt*	6 *tablespoonfuls butter*
$\frac{1}{4}$ *teaspoonful dry mustard*	1$\frac{1}{2}$ *teaspoonfuls paprika*
10 *thin slices bread*	

Combine salad oil, vinegar or lemon juice, salt, mustard and pepper. Blend well. Peel cucumber, slice thinly and marinate in the French dressing for $\frac{1}{2}$ hour Add chopped chives. Blend butter and paprika together. Spread on slices of bread. Spread 5 slices with layer of cucumber and cover with remaining slices. Cut into desired shape.

Devilled Sandwiches

2 *oz. almonds*	1 *dessertspoonful*
A little cream cheese	*cream*
1 *tablespoonful chopped pickle*	*Pinch of salt and Cayenne*
Butter	

Blanch the almonds, shred them, and fry in a little butter until pale brown, stirring all the time. Mix together the other ingredients, except the cream cheese, and pour the mixture over the nuts. Cook for 2 minutes, stirring well. Leave to cool. Beat the cream cheese until soft, then season. Spread it on water biscuits, sprinkle the nuts, etc., on top and cover with more biscuits spread with cream cheese.

Savoury Sandwiches

1 *tablespoonful cream*	*Cream cheese*
	1 *tablespoonful*
1 *tablespoonful apple chutney*	*chopped nuts*
	Brown bread
Butter	

Watercress and cream cheese is an excellent mixture for sandwich filling—both tasty and nutritious. It is invariably a favourite with adults and children alike

The simplest sandwiches go up in the world if you use fancy cutters and a dash of imagination. Here you see "wheel" shapes and mushrooms, made from white bread cut thin and a dark-coloured filling for contrast

Put the cream cheese, cream, chutney and chopped nuts into a basin and mix them well together, working in the cheese. Butter some brown bread, spread some of the mixture on it, and put another piece of buttered bread on top. Cut into any shape required.

Open Sandwiches

Top a thin slice or round of wholemeal bread or toast with halibut, cod or haddock creamed with a thick white wine or cider sauce, place on a crisp inner leaf of lettuce and garnish with two twisted anchovy fillets and a dusting of parsley.

A layer of watercress, three thin slices of tomato in oil and vinegar dressing, a dessertspoonful of curried white fish garnished with chopped banana or finely chopped sweet apple.

Halve hard-boiled eggs lengthwise, mash the yolks with a teaspoonful of vinegar, a tablespoonful of oil and a dash of Worcester sauce (to each two eggs). Work in a dessertspoonful of cold flaked fish and season well with chutney, pepper and curry powder. Heap in the egg-whites, grill lightly and serve on rounds of toast.

Jellied Open Sandwiches

For open sandwiches glazed with aspic jelly, the bread should be cut into different shapes, then fried, toasted or lightly buttered and the savoury mixture put on top. To make the glaze, use 1 oz. aspic jelly crystals per pint of water or canned vegetable liquor. Pour it on when it is just setting. Here are some suggestions:

Sliced canned luncheon meat, hard-boiled egg, peas and carrots.

A small roll of ham, carrots cut into shapes, peas, capers, etc.

Slice of canned cheese, tomato, anchovy fillets, peas, etc.

Sliced Vienna sausages, stuffed olives, capers.

Brislings or sild, carrots, peas, hard-boiled eggs, etc.

More ideas for open sandwiches will be found in the chapters on Sweden and Denmark in the "Cookery at Home and Abroad" section.

Turkish coffee is the only kind that should be boiled. Serve it, thick and rich, from a long-handled jug (above)

Right, a streamlined model that makes filter coffee by the infusion method

MAKING GOOD COFFEE

There is no secret, no mystery, only common sense in the very simple art of—

A WORLD of pleasant associations surrounds coffee: lingering over an after-dinner coffee with friends, pausing in one's work for a stimulating cup, having coffee and watching the passers-by at a table outside a Continental café, catching the delicious aroma wafted from a shop when coffee is being roasted—what could be more agreeable? Coffee goes with good humour, hospitality and civilised living.

It is worth making coffee well. In the U.K. the popularity of coffee has increased enormously since the middle of the century. Yet one still hears people sigh that they wish they "could make good coffee like So-and so" or talk longingly about the coffee they had on their holiday abroad—as though coffee making were an innate gift on the Continent but a mystery hidden from most on the other side of the Channel. Yet it is not a difficult art, and there is an infinite variety of efficient and beautiful coffee making equipment on the market.

Coffee is said to have been discovered in Arabia about 1,200 years ago —when a goat-herd was startled to observe the liveliness of his goats after they had eaten the berries of a certain bush. To-day, the beans from these berries invigorate and cheer the heart all over the globe.

Choice of Coffee

East Africa, the West Indies, India, the Belgian Congo and Brazil are the main coffee-growing areas. As coffee acquires different characteristics, according to the climate and soil in which it is grown, choice is a matter of experiment and taste. Some cling to, say, Costa Rica, Kenya, Brazil or Mocha. But a blend of two or more varieties may be preferred. If you buy from a skilled blender, local conditions—climate and type of water—will have been taken into consideration in relation to flavour. It is best to consult reliable coffee suppliers and try out the varieties.

Many households run two or more coffees at the same time—perhaps a mild coffee for breakfast, a pungent, invigorating one at midday, a smooth, full coffee after dinner.

Degree of Roasting

The raw green coffee beans are roasted to drive off moisture and to break down the cells so that the oils which provide the aroma and flavour can be released. In medium roasting, the oils are not fully released, so that, before grinding, medium-roast coffee remains fresher for longer than high roast. The degree of roasting naturally affects the colour and flavour. A lightly roasted, lightly coloured bean will be mild-flavoured; a medium one stronger; and a highly roasted bean will give a dark-coloured, more aromatic and pungent, even bitter, coffee.

Grinding

Nothing c a n b e a t coffee ground just before use. Air is the enemy. It absorbs the oils from the ground coffee, replacing them with moisture, so that freshness is lost. The shorter the time between grinding and brewing, the better the coffee will be. The advantages of grinding at home are obvious.

Vast and fearsome were the grinding machines of our forebears. To-day, coffee mills for the home kitchen are neat and elegant. The *"Mokkaffee"* and *"Peugeot"* box mills, for example, adjustable to the grind required, are useful for the small household. The *"Mokkaffee"* wall mill, for attachment to larder door or dresser, and similarly adjustable, has a practically airtight buff porcelain glass coffee catcher. Even the traveller is catered for—with a handy, small, round, metal-box type mill. An electric grinder produces fresh coffee in a few seconds at the press of a switch.

The mesh size of the filter you use may decide whether you need a coarse, medium or fine grind. Finely ground coffee is more economical. A fine ground is essential for use with Espresso machines.

If your supplier is grinding the beans for you, indicate the grind required. Ask for "Espresso grind" for that type of machine. For Turkish coffee, the beans should be pulverised.

Storing

As exposure to air means loss of strength, it is best to buy in small quantities. In a screw-topped container with a rubber ring, coffee can be kept reasonably fresh for the following periods:

Good coffee deserves a lovely service. Thistle design on Flemish green by Spode-Copeland is perfect on a silver tray in a Regency room

Medium roasted beans .	.	12–14 days
High roasted beans .	.	7–10 days
Medium roasted ground .	.	5 days
High roasted ground .	.	3–4 days
Turkish or pulverised .	.	1 day

Chicory

Although the addition of chicory to coffee is not much favoured by connoisseurs, many people add it because they like the flavour it imparts, or for reasons of economy. It makes the resultant brew darker. Chicory can be bought by the pound, roasted and ground all ready, and added in the proportion of a teaspoonful of chicory to a dessertspoonful of ground coffee.

Packed Brands

Although there is more real satisfaction in choosing one's coffee and grinding shortly before use, one can by-pass the process by buying coffee, roasted and

295

The Russell Hobbs electric coffee pot (with matching basin and jug) makes coffee to your personal taste by means of a time-control selector

ground, in tins, preferably vacuum-packed. Here the air is extracted and replaced by the natural gas of coffee to keep its freshness. Once the tin has been opened, the coffee should be used up in less than ten days, or the flavour and aroma will be lost.

The "instant" coffees in tins, which consist of pulverised coffee to be dissolved in boiling water, are useful for quick cups or for picnics.

BREWING THE COFFEE

General Principles

Use four heaped dessertspoonfuls of ground coffee for each pint of water. Less coffee than this is needed in the Espresso method, and more for Turkish coffee.

Use freshly boiled water, starting from freshly drawn cold water. Do not use water that has been heated before.

Do not let the coffee itself boil, as this spoils the flavour. Turkish coffee is the only exception here.

Serve the coffee as soon as possible after it is ready. Do not let it stand on the grounds for any length of time, or it will become bitter. If it must be kept for a time, strain it into a pot from which it can be served and keep it hot—without letting it boil.

Coffee can be reheated, but with loss of flavour. Again, do not let it boil.

If you are using milk with the coffee, serve it hot or cold, but, when heating it, do not allow it to form a skin or boil. Boiled milk will spoil the flavour of the coffee.

Wash the equipment after each use and rinse with clear hot water. Do not use soda.

There are four main methods of making coffee: by infusion, percolation, pressure and suction.

Infusion

Under this heading comes coffee made in a jug, pot or saucepan.

Measure the coffee into a warmed china jug. Pour on fresh boiling water, stir well, and let it stand for one minute. Draw a spoon over the surface to skim off the coffee grounds standing on top. Let it stand for another four minutes, and then pour it through a strainer into another warmed china jug and serve quickly.

In the *"Melior"* coffee pot, the coffee is infused in the pot and then a metal rod, which comes through the lid and holds a filter inside, is pressed down, so that the grounds are trapped while the coffee is served.

The saucepan method is to put a measured quantity of coffee and water in a saucepan and place on heat. Stir it well and bring just to boiling point and no more—it must not boil. Remove from heat, stir again, cover tightly and let it stand in a warm place for five minutes. Then strain into a warmed jug or pot.

Percolation

This covers coffee made by the great variety of filter or drip methods and in percolators.

The French *café filtre* consists of an earthenware pot with a lower chamber, from which the coffee is served, and an upper chamber with a lid and a fine filter at its base. A perforated disc or filter paper is sometimes fitted over this.

Put the required amount of coffee into the upper section, spreading it evenly over the filter disc or paper (if this is used). Pour boiling water to the required amount over it, cover and let it stand in a warm place until dripping is completed. Then remove the upper section and serve the coffee.

A French way is to stand the pot in a pan of water which is kept hot. The coffee in the upper section is first damped with boiling water and allowed to stand for five minutes. Then boiling water is poured on in small quantities every two or three minutes for about a quarter of an hour.

The one-cup filters, a familiar sight in French cafés, have their own charm. You just sit at table and wait for the coffee in the filter chamber to drip through into the cup in front of you.

The Italian "Napolitana" is a modern and ingenious coffee pot which produces excellent filter coffee and has the added delight of having to be turned completely upside-down. Made of thick aluminium with copper top and bottom, it is one complete unit—i.e. the water is boiled in it. It is in three separate sections. Water is put into the straight-handled section, which is placed on the heat. The ground coffee is placed in the container at one end of the middle section; the perforated cap is fitted on to it and clipped down. The other end of this section is open. It is then lowered gently into the first section (it slides in), the container being uppermost. The third section (from which the coffee will be served) is inverted over the top. When the water boils, the machine is removed from the heat and the whole turned upside-down. It then stands for a time until the water has percolated through the coffee into the "jug" section.

Percolators with a central pipe and a glass top are familiar coffee-making machines. Put the required amount of fresh cold water into the percolator and bring to the boil. Then remove from the heat and place the required amount of coffee into the strainer in the upper part of the pot. Cover, return to the heat and allow the water to bubble up through the tube and percolate gently through the coffee for six to eight minutes. Then remove strainer and serve.

Percolators, however, have a great disadvantage in that the coffee gets boiled in the container, and if the process is continued too long very bad coffee results. An electric percolator is, however, a very quick and easy method for busy people.

The Russell Hobbs electric coffee pot, with its good-looking ceramic body, is equipped with a time-control selector and a special "keep hot" device.

Pressure

In the Italian *Espresso*, coffee is "expressed" under pressure. Cold water is placed in the boiler section of the machine, which is heated. Just before boiling point, the water expands and wets the finely ground coffee in a cage, forming an obstacle to the water which, at boiling point, forces its way through the coffee. The coffee resulting is collected in a pot underneath or

One-cup filters, coffee cup (left), or breakfast cup size (right), work on the infusion method. You just sit and wait till your cup is full

297

in an upper chamber or direct into a cup. The process is quick—taking about four to seven minutes from start to finish. It is also economical. Very finely ground or pulverised coffee is used in the proportion of 1 teaspoonful of coffee to each cup of water, or $\frac{1}{2}$ oz. of coffee to just a little over $\frac{1}{2}$ pint of water (for six demi-tasses).

The machines on the market are admirable in design and finish, and made of an alloy which does not affect flavour or colour. They have the advantage of being unbreakable. Most makes can be obtained either fitted for electric heating or non-electric—in which case the machine is placed directly on the heat.

The *Espresso* method gives an intensely strong brew, especially good for after-dinner black coffee.

Some details are given below of several machines of this type available. The list is, however, not comprehensive.

In the attractive *"Columbia,"* cold water is placed in the machine's lower chamber. Into this is fitted the funnel filter, in which the ground coffee is placed. Over this goes a filter disc, and the collector or top chamber is screwed on to the boiler. The machine is then placed on the heat, and in due course the coffee gushes from the aperture at the upper end of the small pipe standing in the collector. It is retained here, and served.

In the *"Vesuviana"* and *"Trimel"* makes, the expanding water travels over a bridge and is forced through the coffee in a cage. The coffee resulting is collected in a pot underneath. The *"Trimel"* is non-electric only.

The *"Aquilas"* is very suitable for a quick brew direct into glass or cup. It is electric or non-electric; the latter design is for heating by liquid or solid methylated spirit, and is useful for camping conditions.

Suction or Vacuum

This is the principle of coffee-making apparatus, such as *"Cona," "S.L.R.," "Silex"* and *"Whitecross."*

The all-glass vacuum coffee maker is familiar and long-established. To sit at table and watch the proceedings inside the glass bowl is a leisurely after-dinner pleasure in itself. Admirable coffee results, as the water is boiling when it comes in contact with the ground coffee, but the brew itself does not boil.

In the *"Cona,"* the lower bowl containing cold water is placed over the heat at the base. Then the filter and the measured amount of coffee (6 dessert spoonfuls of medium ground to $1\frac{1}{2}$ pints of water) are put in the upper bowl, which is inserted in a vacuum-maker with a vented stem. When the coffee has risen into the upper bowl (except for a small quantity which must remain below), the coffee is allowed to infuse for about two minutes. The infused coffee drains into the lower bowl and, when all has passed through, the upper bowl is removed and the coffee served.

The *"Cona" Rex* is a modern streamlined version of the equipment, which can be carried in one hand. There is a wide variety of attractive models in the Cona range. Some are efficiently heated by means of a tiny spirit lamp and others are powered by electricity.

Turkish Coffee is in a class by itself, as this is the only instance in which boiling the coffee is correct procedure. There are special cooking pots available for its making. Pulverised coffee must be used—about a tablespoonful for each demi-tasse.

Put the coffee and an equal amount of granulated sugar into the pot, add cold water and bring to the boil.

With a coffee mill you can grind your own beans just how and when you want them—and be sure your coffee is absolutely fresh

298

A cup of strong black coffee and a liqueur—the perfect end to a wonderful meal, graciously served.   The Irish linen dinner mats are navy and pale blue embroidered with a wheat design

Stir it gently, take it from the heat, stir again, and replace on heat. Do this several times in succession, until the coffee is thick and foamy. Add a few drops of aromatic water, such as rosewater, and serve at once without milk or cream. As this is very strong coffee, the smallest cups are used.

SERVING THE COFFEE

Black Coffee is usually served after dinner. It should be strong, freshly made and in small cups. Sugar is added according to taste. The French like to add a liqueur-glass of brandy to each cup.

Café au lait

With a pot of coffee in one hand and a pot of hot milk in the other, pour an equal amount of coffee and milk into each cup. It is a breakfast drink, served in large cups or bowls.

Vienna Coffee

Drop whipped cream on strong black coffee in the cup—the result is delicious. It is often served with small cakes.

Iced Coffee

Serve strong coffee, cooled, with cracked ice in tall glasses, and top with whipped cream or ice-cream.

COFFEE FOR FLAVOURING IN COOKING

Make coffee in the usual way, but with less water, as the brew should be as intense as possible.

We are indebted to the Algerian Coffee Stores, Ltd., Old Compton Street, London, W.1, for much useful information regarding coffee making and for all photographs of equipment (except the *Atomic*). They are the sole retailers of the "*Columbia*" and "*Trimel*" machines.

A GOOD CUP OF TEA

*It revives the weary, soothes the nervy and is a joy
to most people on all occasions and at all times*

THROUGHOUT the U.K.—and in many other Eastern and Western countries—tea-drinking is almost a ritual. There is magic in a cup of tea. It revives the weary, soothes the nervy and is in demand on all occasions and at all times. This world-wide fame and much of the satisfaction derived from a good cup of tea is due to the untiring, conscientious work of British tea firms.

A housewife can go to almost any large or small grocer in any part of the U.K. and buy a known brand of tea, at a reasonable price, from which she can be certain to obtain a good brew, provided she and the grocer observe the rules.

Tea firms spend much time, thought and money in producing the right teas, and the right blends, to suit individual palates and varying water supplies. The big national tea firms produce and supply different blends of tea for the hard- and soft-water districts, and the right kind is automatically supplied by the grocers.

Family grocers who blend their own teas take the quality of the local water supply into consideration. Small leaf tea infuses more quickly than large leaf, and is most suitable for use with hard water, which gives a slower infusion. Large leaf can be used satisfactorily in any medium- or soft-water district.

Sometimes no fewer than twenty different teas are used to make up one blend. The quality and flavour of that blend must be constant over the years, and it is, to a great extent, the job of the tea taster to keep it so. When the stock of one tea which is included in a blend runs out, it must be replaced by another which gives exactly the same result. This is not easy, because the buds and leaves gathered from one plantation at different times vary considerably. Samples are sent to the buyers so that the tea can be tasted and judged before it is auctioned in Mincing Lane.

Tea tasting methods are strictly controlled and are the same throughout the trade. First, a sample of each tea is weighed in a highly sensitive scale, using a piece of metal equal in weight to a silver sixpence. The tea is then brewed with carefully measured boiling water, and infused for 6 minutes, strained and tasted warm. Anyone with a normally sensitive palate can become a tea taster, but so far

Tea at breakfast time tastes better from a fine cup. This Spode Stone China service is "Gloucester" patterned in blue on a delicate grey and shaped after a traditional Chinese design

One of the simplest, yet most delightful forms of entertaining is over the tea cups—but the tea you serve must be really good

very few women have taken up this career. After this stage, the blending, cutting of the leaf where necessary, weighing, packaging and labelling are done by machinery.

Treatment of the Dry Leaf.—Tea, particularly in the dry state in which it is imported, is very easily contaminated by other flavours. Up to the time when it leaves the tea firms, it is carefully isolated in wooden boxes lined with tinfoil. When it reaches the grocer, and later the housewife, it should continue to be isolated from anything with a strong smell or flavour. Take note of the way the tea packets are treated at the grocers. If they are stored next to soap, cheese, chocolate, etc., go elsewhere to buy your tea.

When it arrives home, undo the package and tip the leaves into a tin with a close-fitting lid. Most well-made, labelled kitchen canisters are satisfactory. Before using a new tin, store some old dry leaves in it for several days to remove the metallic smell. When the empty tin smells of tea, it is ready for use. Never put new leaves on to old, and never mix different brands

or types. Paper may affect the flavour of tea after a time, so it should not be stored in the packet. More important still, sealed or opened packets must never be left among other foods on larder shelves or in the kitchen, even for a few hours.

Temperature for storage is not important, and tea can keep in good condition in an airtight, moisture-proof canister hanging on the kitchen wall. Provided conditions are right, tea can be stored satisfactorily in the home for as long as six months or more.

The Kettle.—The kind of kettle used for boiling the water is important. Enamel or tin-lined metal is best. Aluminium alloy is not as good until it has become furred, so that the water does not come into contact with the metal. A new aluminium kettle should be seasoned by steam treatment for 1 hour, or by boiling water in it for 2 hours. This seasoning can be destroyed by scouring. Rinse the kettle with cold water, but do not scour.

The Water.—Fill the kettle with freshly-drawn cold water. Heat it till boiling—

that is until steam pours from the spout and the surface of the water is covered with bubbles. Pour immediately on to the tea leaves. A perfect infusion is not obtained with water below boiling point, nor with water that has either stood cold or been warmed slowly, nor water that has been kept boiling even for a few minutes.

Hard and Soft Water.—Infusion of the leaves takes longer in hard than in soft water, and the right blend should be chosen to suit the water. Medium water that is neither very hard nor very soft is the best for tea-making. Tea experts do not recommend the use of artificial softeners, such as bicarbonate of soda, or water-softening plant. Softened water produces a darker-coloured brew, but destroys a great deal of the flavour. Time the infusion and be patient when using hard water—for instance, in London 6 minutes' infusing may be needed, in Manchester 3 minutes, to produce the same result with the same tea.

The Teapot.—Pottery or china is the best material for teapots. Silver or silver-plate come second. Other metals can be used if they are tin or enamel-lined, or well-seasoned as described for the kettle. Teapots should be washed and dried after use.

The "T.T." teapot, invented by Dr. John Tutin and Dr. J. Lockwood Taylor, and on the market since 1954, is designed to economise in the amount of tea used.

The teapot departs from traditional design by having a built-in detachable "hot-water jug." A 1-pint cylindrically-shaped container with a tube fitted to the base is placed in a 2-pint earthenware teapot of orthodox appearance, suspended from a ridge just below the rim. A space remains between the bottom of the tube and the inside of the base of the teapot.

To make tea, you take out the container and warm the teapot, place one scoop of tea in the pot, replace the container, fill the pot with boiling water and allow the usual time for brewing. Infusion takes place in the space between the container and the walls of the pot. As the tea is poured, it is automatically replaced by hot water from the container, which re-infuses the tea. Six good-strength cups of tea can be obtained before refilling with more hot water.

Making the Tea.—Make the pot really hot with plenty of boiling water. Tip out the water. Measure in the tea, allowing 1 *level* caddy spoon per person, and 1 extra (a caddy spoon is slightly larger than a teaspoon). Take the pot to the kettle and pour on the *boiling* water. The amount of water needed varies according to the tea used, and to personal taste.

To obtain the full flavour of the tea it must be made strong enough, but strength of flavour has nothing to do with colour. Cover the pot with a cosy or some kind of insulating jacket, and leave to infuse for about 5 minutes. The full value will be extracted from the leaves in that time. Longer infusing simply produces a darker colour and extracts more tannin, which gives a bitter flavour. The ideal way is to remove the leaves after 5 or 6 minutes, and for this method the specially prepared tea-bags, sold by many grocers, are convenient.

It is better to add the maximum quantity of boiling water to the leaves all at once than to add half or three-quarters of the amount needed, and the rest later.

Pouring the Tea.—There is no golden rule about the addition of milk to tea. Pouring it into the tea usually gives an appearance of strength. Most tea experts favour putting milk in the cup first, and then pouring in the tea slowly. This gives more even mixing and is unlikely to separate the milk. Boiled milk affects the flavour.

It's nice to get up in the morning—when the Hawkins "Tiffee" makes your tea, switches off, then rings the bell to wake you up

COCKTAILS, CUPS AND PUNCHES

Showing you how to mix your drinks the right way

Juleps and cobblers are popular summer evening drinks—served ice cold in frosted glasses with fruit, cherries, olives or sprigs of mint on top

IT is said that in early Roman times a physician invented a mixed drink of wine, lemon juice and a few pinches of dried adders, which was regarded as a splendid apéritif. This recipe may not appeal to all now—but it gives the modern cocktail a history.

The cocktail is a short mixed drink, drunk as an appetiser before lunch or dinner. Popularised at first in America, it became familiar between the two world wars. Before that there were the apéritifs and the long mixed drinks—the wine cup and punch—which are still as popular as ever, with all their modern variations — cobblers, slings, highballs, etc.

The "cup" is not an appetiser, but an alternative to wine, drunk sometimes with the meal, or convivially at leisure during the evening, perhaps in the garden. As the purpose of the cocktail is to whet the appetite, it should not be too sweet (though some are), and should be cold, preferably iced. The cup, on the other hand, is usually sweet, often with plenty of fruit in it, and may be ice cold or piping hot.

The cocktail should be mixed just before it is served and (except for the effervescent and a few other kinds) have a short, sharp shaking. It should not be allowed to stand long—this is detrimental to its quality. It belongs to the age of speed. The cup, on the other hand, goes back to an age of leisure. Its concoction is slow and deliberate; it may need to stand for a while; and, far from being violently shaken, it is comfortably stirred.

There is wide scope for imagination and originality in the making of every kind of mixed drink. Although there is a vast range of accepted recipes, there is pleasure to be had in experimentation and in concocting one's own. Variety is all.

303

APÉRITIFS

To whet the appetite before a meal the well-known French trade-named apéritifs, already mixed, are often served iced, without further addition (except soda water, if desired), e.g. *Amer Picon* (a "bitter"), *Byrrh* (red wine basis), *Dubonnet* (red wine basis), *Lillet* (white wine basis), *St. Raphaël* (white wine basis), *Pernod* (aniseed basis).

Sherry and French and Italian vermouth are also served neat as apéritifs.

COCKTAILS

The cocktail is a mixture of any kind of wine or spirit with any other wine or spirit or liqueur or fruit juice, usually shaken in a special shaker with crushed ice. There are over 5,000 kinds of named cocktails. Most of the recipes given here are for the more familiar and popular ones. The professional cocktail mixer has a great range of bottles on which to draw, but the amateur at home can in fact make good cocktails with very limited resources. As a minimum: from a bottle of French vermouth, a bottle of Italian vermouth, a bottle of gin and a bottle of fruit juice or fruit syrup, one could produce ten varieties.

A cherry can be added most appropriately to a sweetish cocktail (e.g. one made with Italian vermouth), not to a dry one (e.g. made with French vermouth), with which an olive goes well.

For cocktail mixing at home the following items are desirable: two cocktail shakers (one for highly flavoured mixtures and one for milder kinds), a mixing glass (for cocktails needing to be stirred, not shaken, e.g. dry martinis, Manhattans), a corkscrew and bottle opener, spirit measures, bottles of bitters (a few drops of Angostura bitters will do wonders), a strainer, bar spoons and a fruit knife, cherry sticks and drinking straws, a supply of clean, clear ice, and cocktail glasses (which hold 2 or 3 liquid ounces). Also cherries, olives, orange and lemon slices and cut-up peel.

The success of a cocktail depends on a balance of flavours, without one unduly overshadowing the rest. It is advisable, therefore, to use a spirit measure in following a recipe. Fill your shaker no more than four-fifths full of ice and ingredients, and shake it shortly and sharply. Strain your cocktails into chilled glasses if possible.

(If you prefer to have a professional cocktail bartender at your private party, the services of one can be supplied through the United Kingdom Bartenders' Guild, 3 Great Windmill Street, London, W.1.)

Alexander. (An old and well-known cocktail. Iced, it is served before dinner; without ice it is an after-dinner drink.) One-third brandy, one-third crème de caçao, one-third fresh cream. Shake and strain.

Bronx. One-half dry gin, one-sixth each of French vermouth, Italian vermouth and orange juice. Shake and strain.

Dubonnet. One-half Dubonnet, one-half dry gin. Stir and strain. Place a pared piece of lemon rind on top.

Manhattan. Two-thirds rye whisky, one-third Italian vermouth and a dash of Angostura bitters. Stir and strain; add a cherry to each cocktail.

Martini (Dry). (The best known and most popular cocktail of all. A good appetiser; very potent.) One-half French vermouth, one-half gin.

There are variations, e.g. two-thirds gin, one-third French vermouth, a dash of orange bitters; a twist of lemon peel added.

Martini (Sweet). One-half Italian vermouth, one-half gin. Again there are variations depending on taste.

Old Fashioned. (This is served in the tumbler known as the "Old Fashioned" glass.) A glass of whisky (Bourbon, Rye or Scotch), a lump of sugar saturated with Angostura bitters and enough water to dissolve it. A lump of ice. Decorate with orange or lemon slice and a cherry, and serve it with a spoon for stirring.

Orange Cocktail. Half a cocktail glass of Raphaël, half of orange juice, one large spoonful of curaçao, dash of Angostura bitters. Shake and strain. Serve with slice of orange.

Sidecar. (Very popular.) One-third brandy, one-third Cointreau, one-third lemon juice. Shake and strain. (Or, one-half brandy and one-quarter each of Cointreau and lemon juice.)

White Lady. Similar to *Sidecar*, but with gin instead of brandy.

For a festive occasion—a wine or fruit cup in a sparkling green glass bowl shaped like a giant goblet. The ladle has a lip that prevents spilling, and the matching glasses complete the set, from Liberty, London

Speciality Cocktails

Peter, famous cocktail barman at l'Apéritif Grill, London, recommends experimenting in cocktail mixing. The following are among his own prize-winning recipes with which he has won silver cups in European and world international cocktail-mixing competitions.

First Lady. One-third lemon gin, one-third peach brandy, one-third pineapple juice, two dashes of maraschino. Serve with a cherry.

Rye Lane. One-third rye whisky, one-third curaçao, one-third orange juice, two dashes Crème de Noyau (or almond essence).

Torino. One-quarter lemon gin, one-quarter mandarin liqueur, one-quarter Italian vermouth, one-quarter passionfruit juice.

COBBLERS

These are warm weather drinks, American in origin.

Whisky Cobbler. Fill a goblet with cracked ice. Add 2 oz. whisky, one teaspoonful sugar, four dashes curaçao. Stir and decorate with a slice of lemon and any other fruit; also a sprig of mint if desired. Serve with straws.

Rum, brandy or gin can be used instead of whisky.

Wine Cobbler (any wine). Fill 7 oz. wineglass with cracked ice. Add 3 oz. wine, a teaspoonful of sugar and four dashes curaçao. Stir and decorate with fruit and sprig of mint. Serve with straws.

Sherry Cobbler. Thinly slice two oranges and a lemon and place in bowl with pieces of pineapple in layers with a cupful each of fine sugar and shaved ice. Add two cupfuls of cold water and one cupful of sherry; also other fruit for decoration. Stir and serve in goblets with some fruit in each.

COLLINS, COOLERS, SLINGS, HIGHBALLS

These are also long, warm weather drinks. There are many variations of each, but these are standard recipes.

Tom Collins. A famous drink, served in tall glasses and well iced. Place cracked ice in glass, add 2 oz. gin, a teaspoonful of sugar and juice of half a lemon. Stir and fill to the top with water or soda water. Decorate with a slice of lemon. Rum, brandy or whisky can be used instead of gin.

Rum Cooler. 2 oz. rum, juice of half a lemon or one lime, four dashes of grenadine. Shake well with a lump of ice and strain into a tall glass; fill with soda water.

Highball. 1½ oz. brandy, gin, rum or whisky in a tumbler with a lump of ice. Fill with soda water or dry ginger ale and squeeze lemon rind on top.

Gin Sling. (Slings are served in tumblers topped with a slice of lemon.) 2 oz. gin, a teaspoonful of sugar dissolved in water or grenadine, a lump of ice. Fill up with water and stir. This is the basic recipe. Cherry brandy, benedictine, lemon juice are sometimes used in making slings, and brandy, rum or whisky used in place of gin.

CUPS

The "Wine Cup" is generally a summer drink, mixed in a large bowl and served from a glass jug. The main ingredient is usually wine, with the addition of spirits, liqueurs, varied fruits, soda water and ice. A cup should look attractive and interesting—there is plenty of room here for one's own initiative, especially in the choice of fruit, as almost any kind can be used.

Gin, rum, lager beer or cider can provide the basis of a "cup" instead of wine, Or an apéritif can be used.

Whatever the ingredients, the "cup" should be well chilled, but not allowed to become over diluted with melting ice. When soda water is used it should be added at the last moment.

Strain it into the glasses to avoid pips, etc., and place pieces of fruit in the glasses —or not—as desired.

Apricot-quina Cup. Cut six ripe apricots into cubes and steep in sugar with half a wineglass of St. Raphaël for 12 hours in a jug. Then add half a bottle of St. Raphaël and serve with ice and soda water.

Celebration Toast (*Claret Cup*). Ingredients sufficient for 14 glasses: one bottle claret, one bottle soda water, one glass sherry, sugar to taste. Fruit, mint, lemon rind, grated nutmeg.

Pare rind of lemon and place in bowl. Add a little sugar and pour on one wineglassful of sherry. Add the claret. Decorate with fruit and mint and add more sugar if necessary. Add the nutmeg. Allow to stand for an hour. Strain and ice. Serve with soda water (or dry champagne).

Champagne Cup. (1) (Quantities to provide 40 glasses.) Place four lumps of sugar saturated with Angostura bitters in a large bowl with two sliced oranges and a wineglassful of brandy. Add four bottles of champagne. Let it stand for 20 minutes. Serve with an ice cube floating in each glass and add soda water.

(2) (For four persons.) To a quart of champagne add a wineglassful of brandy, a liqueurglassful each of maraschino and Grand Marnier and two liqueurglassfuls of curaçao, with a tablespoonful of fine sugar. Add cracked ice and slices of orange, lemon and pineapple; decorate with sprigs of mint.

Cider Cup. (For four persons.) To a quart of cider add a liqueurglassful each of maraschino, curaçao and brandy (*or* a sherryglassful of sherry, half that quantity of brandy and juice of half a lemon, with sugar to taste). Add any fruits desired, and a couple of sprigs of mint or borage or a sprig of verbena—and cracked ice. Strain.

Cool Sunshine. (Quantities to provide 15 glasses.) To a bottle of white burgundy (Macon Blanc) add pears, oranges and apples, peeled but not cut too small. Allow to stand for 2 hours. Immediately before serving add a wineglassful of brandy and one-third of a wine bottle full of soda water. Serve well iced.

Cooli. (Quantities to provide 12 glasses.) Stir together a bottle of Graves, Clos du Rey, and a liqueurglassful of orange curaçao with a sliced peeled apple. Let it stand for about 2 hours. Add half a wine bottle full of soda water just before serving, and serve well iced.

Coronet. (Quantities to provide 14 glasses.) Place pears, apples or peaches, peeled and cut up, in a bowl with two wineglassfuls of port. Leave in a cool place for 3 hours; then add one bottle of red burgundy (Beaujolais), half a pint of still lemon squash (diluted with water and

Cocktails for two or for a party call for this Martini Mixer, elegant glass stirring rod and long-stemmed glasses, from Liberty, London

sliced crystallised ginger and a cupful of sliced pineapple. Stir in also half a sliced orange and half a sliced lemon. Add a sprig of bruised mint and let stand for 1 or 2 hours. Just before serving add two large bottles of aerated lemonade. Serve with cracked ice.

Rhine Maiden. (Quantities to provide 10 glasses.) Pour a bottle of hock on peeled grapes in a bowl and allow to stand for 2 hours. Then add soda water; ice and serve immediately, leaving fruit in the bowl.

Rose Belle Cup. (Quantities to provide 10 glasses.) Stir well together a bottle of vin rosé, one-third of a wine bottle full of soda water or lemonade and sugar to taste. Serve well iced.

Pride of Oporto. (Quantities to provide 30 glasses.) Squeeze into a bowl the juice of one lemon. Add half a gill of orange curaçao and a bottle of dry tawny port. Decorate with thin slices of lemon and leave for 20 minutes. Top each glass when serving with cold soda water.

Lager Beer Cup. To the juice of four lemons and the pared rind of two in a bowl add a cupful of water, two sherry glasses of sherry and two bottles of lager. Add sugar to taste and a grating of nutmeg.

(For wine cup (hot) see *Mulled Wine* and *Punches* on next page.)

not too sweet). Do not add orange or lemon.

Golden Rod. (Quantities to provide 14 glasses.) Pour a bottle of Alsatian wine into a bowl of peeled grapes, sliced melon and other fruits; leave for half an hour. Add sugar to taste and serve well iced with fizzy lemonade.

Midsummer Revel. (Quantities to provide 8 glasses.) Pour a bottle of white burgundy on to cut-up melon and halved peeled peaches (fresh or tinned) in a bowl and leave for 3 hours. Add a liqueurglassful of maraschino and serve iced.

My Cup. (Quantities to provide 36 glasses.) Stir four bottles of red Algerian wine (Belorah) and one bottle tawny port with a quarter cupful of sugar in a large bowl. Add a cupful of lemon or orange juice or squash, half a cupful of finely

MINT JULEP

This is a very old drink. Crush together in a large tumbler four to six sprigs of fresh mint and half a tablespoonful of fine sugar, with one tablespoonful of water, until the sugar is dissolved and the flavour extracted from the mint. Add 2 oz. of whisky and fill the tumbler with crushed ice. Stir well. When the outside of the glass is frosted, decorate with mint and serve with straws.

A julep is also made using iced champagne instead of whisky, with less mint and sugar and a slice of orange and a cherry added.

MULLED WINE

This hot, spiced drink calls for a cold winter's night as its setting. The less-expensive wines can be used effectively.

Boil to a syrup in half pint water 3 oz. of sugar with a pinch each of cinnamon, ginger and powdered cloves (or nutmeg and cinnamon). Add this to a pint of wine (port, claret, Algerian) and heat to just below boiling point, stirring slowly. Serve while hot, with a twist of pared orange peel in each glass. Or bring the wine almost to boiling point and then add the spices, sugar and boiling water.

PICK-ME-UPS AND SUSTAINING DRINKS

Cold

Brandy Flip. Shake well together one egg, one teaspoonful of sugar and 2 oz. brandy. Strain into a 5-oz. wineglass and grate nutmeg on top.

Rum, whisky, sherry, claret or port can be used instead of brandy.

Pick-me-up Cocktail. Shake well together a cocktail glass of brandy and one of milk, one teaspoonful of sugar with a dash of Angostura bitters. Strain into a tumbler and add soda water.

Prairie Oyster. (A famous non-alcoholic pick-me-up.) Put a teaspoonful each of Worcester sauce and tomato catsup into a wineglass and drop in the yolk of an egg, without breaking it. Add two dashes of vinegar and a sprinkle of pepper.

Hot

Blue Blazer. (A stimulating spectacle as well as drink.) Put 2 oz. Scotch whisky into a metal mug with a teaspoonful of powdered sugar, and a similar quantity of boiling water into another metal mug. Put a lighted match to the whisky, and when it blazes up pour it quickly into the boiling water; then pour it all back and to and fro five or six times—rapidly—so that the blaze is continuous. When it dies down, serve the drink in a small tumbler with a twist of pared lemon peel on top.

Grog. (The old universal remedy.) Place 2 oz. rum in a tumbler with a lump of sugar, the juice of half a lemon, two cloves and a small stick of cinnamon. Fill the glass with boiling water.

Hot Egg Nogg. Beat an egg with a teaspoonful of sugar and pour into a tumbler with 1 oz. brandy and 1 oz. rum. Fill up with hot milk and grate nutmeg on top. (The milk could be cold, and sherry or other wine used instead of spirits.)

Hot Toddy. To 1½ oz. gin, rum or whisky, add one teaspoonful of sugar, two cloves, a small stick of cinnamon and a slice of lemon. Add boiling water. Serve in a small tumbler or an "old-fashioned" glass.

PUNCHES

Rum is the traditional basic ingredient of punch. The punchbowl, in which the host mixed the drink at table before his expectant guests, was a feature particularly of eighteenth-century England. Punch was made hot or cold. For cold punch lime juice was preferred to lemon juice.

Hot

Ale Punch. Bring almost to boiling point in a large pan: a quart of old ale, quarter pint each of gin, rum and whisky, one sliced lemon, a pinch each of ground cinnamon, cloves and nutmeg, adding a pint of boiling water and sugar to taste. Strain for serving into a bowl and decorate with a few more thin lemon slices.

Buckingham Palace Punch (recipe by Monsieur René Poussin, former Buckingham Palace Chef)

1 *bottle dark*	*Juice and grated rind*
Jamaica rum	*of 3 lemons*
1 *bottle brandy*	*Pinch of cinnamon*
2½ *bottles water*	*Pinch of cloves*
2½ *oz. lump sugar*	*Bare ½ grated nutmeg*

Put lemon, spices, sugar and water in saucepan and boil for 5 minutes. Add rum and brandy. As soon as hot, strain through muslin and serve.

M. Poussin uses an old Victorian silver wine-cooler for a punch bowl. You could also use a large fruit bowl, a soup tureen or a jug.

Guy Fawkes' Grog

1 *bottle red wine*	1 *pint water*
½ *pint Jamaica rum*	*Juice and rind of 1*
1 *glassful brandy*	*lemon*
	1 *stick of cinnamon*

Place all ingredients in a large saucepan and heat slowly. Strain and serve very hot with slices of lemon.

Jamaica Fizzer

Juice of ½ lemon	2 *measures Jamaica*
1 *teaspoonful sugar*	*rum*
	1 *measure brandy*

Dissolve sugar in a little boiling water. Add lemon juice, brandy and Jamaica rum and top with boiling water.

Portwine Punch (Negus). Rub a quarter pound of loaf sugar on lemon rind until yellow and place in a large jug; add juice of one lemon, a grating of nutmeg, a pint of port (one of the less expensive kinds would do well) and a quart of boiling water. Stir, let it stand, covered, and serve.

The Rum Banger. Dissolve $\frac{1}{4}$ lb. sugar in a pint of milk. Add the yolks of 2 eggs beaten together. Add a pint of Jamaica rum. Serve very hot but do not boil.

Rum Punch. Heat a quarter pint of rum with a quart of beer, spices, sugar, lemon slices and hot water. (See *Ale Punch.*)

Cold

Brandy Punch (per goblet). Pour 2 oz. brandy and four dashes of curaçao on to shaved ice. Add fruit and mint and stir well, then finish with ginger ale.

Planter's Punch. (1) The traditional recipe is: one of sour (lime), two of sweet (sugar), three of strong (rum), four of weak (water and ice).

(2) (Per tumbler.) Stir together a single measure of rum, one teaspoonful of grenadine, juice of half a lemon. Add lemon and orange slices and soda water.

Non-alcoholic

Fruit Punch. (1) Thinly slice three peeled oranges and place in a bowl with two sliced bananas, a handful of green grapes and a handful of stoned cherries. Pour over a syrup made by boiling 1 lb. sugar and one quart water together for 5 minutes. Add the juice of three lemons and three oranges and let it stand for an hour in a cool place. Then add a pint of ginger ale, half pint of cold tea, a quart of soda water and cracked ice.

(2) Rub quarter pound sugar over lemon and orange peel until yellow and add to a cupful of pineapple pulp with juice, half cupful of orange juice, quarter cupful of lemon juice and one pint of grape juice. Add a small pinch of salt, a grating of nutmeg and a few sprigs of mint. Stir and let it stand, covered, for an hour in a cool place. Strain over cracked ice and add soda water.

A special Christmas Punch Set by Spode-Copeland for convivial entertaining. The 10-in. wide bowl, six cups and a ladle are decorated with Christmas trees, holly and mistletoe

HOME-MADE DRINKS

Home-made drinks are always popular and, incidentally, are very wholesome. Black currant syrup or raspberry vinegar, taken in hot water last thing at night, helps to soothe a cold. Summer drinks, such as lemonade or orangeade, should, whenever possible, have ice cubes added just before serving. Iced tea and coffee are also delicious hot weather drinks.

Black Currant Syrup

6 lb. black currants	12 bruised cloves (in
6 lb. Demerara sugar	muslin bag)

Prepare the black currants. Put cloves in a large jar and fill up with alternate layers of sugar and currants. Cover tightly to exclude all air. Leave for 6 weeks, then draw off liquid and bottle. Keep corked until the syrup is needed.

Ginger Beer

2 lemons	½ oz. cream of tartar
1 oz. bruised ginger	1 lb. sugar
1 gallon cold water	½ oz. yeast on toast

Put the rinds of the lemons into a large saucepan with the ginger, cream of tartar and sugar. Pour the cold water over them and bring to the boil, then leave until lukewarm. Spread the yeast on the toast and let it float on top of the liquid. Cover with a cloth and leave for 24 hours, then strain and bottle. Store in a cool place. It will be ready for use in 2 or 3 days.

Iced Russian Tea

Allow three teaspoonfuls of China tea containing a good proportion of Orange Pekoe for every pint required, infuse with rapidly-boiling fresh water, stand for 10 minutes, strain very clear, then put in the fridge or on ice until very cold. Half a gill of Jamaica rum is enough for a half-pint glass, and the sugar (if liked) should be melted first. Put plenty of ice in the glass, add a slice of lemon stuck with one clove, then pour in the cold tea. For a minty flavour, dust a good supply of fresh sprigs with sugar, place them on top of the lemon slice, and pour the tea through them. This beverage can be prepared in a big glass jug, but it is not advisable to keep the tea too long in the refrigerator.

Lemonade

Rinds of 2 lemons	Juice of 4 lemons and
Rind of 1 orange	2 oranges
1 quart boiling water	Sugar to taste

Put the fruit rinds and juice into a jug and pour the boiling water on top. Add sugar and water, or soda water, to taste.

Lemon or Orange Squash

To every glassful of cold water, or soda water, allow the juice of half a lemon or orange and a dessertspoonful of castor sugar. Stir well.

Orangeade

4 or 5 oranges	1 oz. citric acid dis-
4 lb. loaf sugar	solved in a cupful
2½ pints cold, boiled	of hot water
water	

Rub the sugar against the rind of the oranges, being careful that no pith or juice gets mixed in. (The lumps will turn orange colour.) Pour the cold, boiled water over the sugar, add the dissolved acid (cold) and leave for 2 or 3 days for the sugar to dissolve, stirring occasionally. When the sugar has dissolved, strain the orangeade through a muslin and bottle it. Wax the corks with sealing wax.

Raspberry Vinegar

3 lb. raspberries	1 quart white wine
Sugar	vinegar

Remove stalks from raspberries and put 1 lb. into a china bowl. Pour vinegar over them and leave overnight. Next day, strain off liquor, pour it on to 1 lb. fresh raspberries, and leave overnight. Next day, strain again and pour liquor on to last pound of fresh raspberries. Leave overnight, then strain through a cloth damped with vinegar. Allow 1 lb. of loaf sugar to every pint of juice, put in a preserving pan, heat, and stir until the sugar has dissolved; then simmer very gently for 20 minutes, skimming at the end. Bottle when cold. When using, allow 1 or 2 tablespoonfuls of the vinegar to a glass of water.

NOTE: Strawberry, red currant or black currant vinegar can be made in the same way.

Sloe Gin

3 pints sloes	⅛ oz. bitter almonds
1 lb. castor sugar	2 quarts gin

Wipe the sloes, remove stalks and prick them here and there with a needle. Put into a stone jar with the gin and sugar and the blanched almonds, cork tightly and shake well. Continue to shake well twice a week. Strain through muslin and bottle in a stone jar, corking securely.

THE BEGINNER'S GUIDE TO WINE

Some practical pointers for the inexperienced on the choice of wines at reasonable prices and how to serve them

compiled by the wine buyer, ROBERT JACKSON LTD., *Piccadilly*

THE inexperienced housewife who knows little about wine—except that she has perhaps enjoyed it in a restaurant or at someone else's house—should start her own wine buying by asking the advice of a *reputable* and experienced wine merchant. These are easier to find than might be imagined, and it is simple enough to recognise those who really know their job. The wine merchant who does not take a real interest in his customer's problems (probably because he has not the knowledge or experience to advise her) should be left strictly alone. In such circumstances the best plan is to write direct to one of the old-established wine merchants for help and advice, explaining exactly what the wines are wanted for (for instance, a dance, wedding reception, special dinner party, or just for ordinary consumption at home) and giving some indication of what she is prepared to pay.

There is no reason why wine should be an expensive luxury. You can get a very pleasant bottle of any kind except champagne for under 10s. Since about six good glasses can be got out of one bottle, this should be enough for dinner for four people. Serve two different wines (a white wine with the fish or the sweet and a red wine with the meat), and for an outlay of under £1 you can turn an ordinary meal into a truly festive occasion.

Wines and Foods that Go Together

Now to consider the wines to choose. The general principle is simple enough: with delicately flavoured dishes, serve delicate (white) wines; with more robust food, the full-blooded red wines. In other words, white wines go with white meats (shellfish, fish, veal, poultry, etc.) and sweets; red wines with meat and game; while poultry can be accompanied either by red or white, according to taste. The white wines that go best with fish, cold poultry, etc., are the dry ones, such as Hock, Moselle, White Burgundy or Graves. Sweet white wines, such as Sauternes, should be served with the sweet course.

UNDERSTANDING THE WINE LIST

You will find on a wine list that the various types of wine are grouped together under the name of the district from which they come.

Bordeaux, for example, includes not only wines sold as Red Bordeaux and White Bordeaux, but an amazing variety bearing the names of the Châteaux and the sub-districts of the region.

The wines of Margaux and St. Julien are of a light character, while the wines of Pauillac, St. Estephe and St. Emilion are more full and fruity. For example, in the wine merchant's list you will see:

Red Bordeaux (or Claret)
Château Talbot St. Julien.
Château Lafite, Pauillac.

White Bordeaux
Graves (medium dry and dry).
Cerons (dry).
Sauternes (sweet).
Barsac (sweet).
Lupiac (medium sweet).
St. Croix du Mont (medium sweet).

Burgundy is another wonderful province of France from which come:

Red Burgundies
Beaujolais Mâcon.
Beaune, Corton, Savigny, Pommard.
Chambertin, Nuits Saint-Georges,
   Romaneé, Volnay.

White Burgundies
Meursault, Montrachet, Pouilly-Fuisse.
Chablis.

Alsace
The wines of *Alsace* are of the Hock and Moselle type. Most are named after the grape from which they are produced. Among the best-known are:

Sylvaner (dry).
Riesling (dry).
Gewurstraminer and Traminer.

The wines of Alsace should be served cool or chilled. They may be taken as an apéritif, served most successfully with hors d'œuvre, fish, etc.

Champagne From the Champagne countryside comes the wine for celebrations, a wine to be drunk at any time, with or without food, preferably slightly chilled.

France, the greatest wine-growing and wine-drinking country in the world, produces many other delightful wines, but for the beginner these are enough to be going on with. With the wines of Bordeaux, Burgundy, Alsace and Champagne—plus

Chianti (white or red) and Vermouth from Italy; Sherry from Spain; Hock and Moselle from Germany, and Port from Portugal—to choose from, there is no limit to your possible fame as a hostess.

Though there is no need whatever for the ordinary wine-drinker to set up as an authority on vintages, it is important to know something about them, if only because they cause such apparent diversity in price. The following chart, which has been prepared by the Wine and Food Society, should be used as guidance when considering the choice of wines, but not as a hard-and-fast rule. Remember only the connoisseurs amongst your friends are likely to appreciate a 1928 champagne or a 1945 burgundy. Most of them would be just as happy with a less distinguished and much less expensive wine. On the other hand, an intelligent interest in vintages will repay the enthusiastic amateur. With the help of a good wine merchant you should be able to buy, for no more than about 10s. a bottle, a wine of a good vintage and can let it mature for a few years.

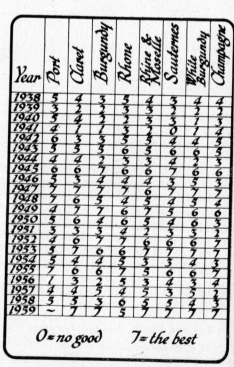

Year	Port	Claret	Burgundy	Rhone	Rhine & Moselle	Sauternes	White Burgundy	Champagne
1938	5	4	3	5	4	3	4	4
1939	3	2	2	3	3	3	2	2
1940	5	4	2	2	3	3	4	3
1941	4	1	1	3	3	0	1	3
1942	6	3	3	5	5	4	4	4
1943	5	5	5	6	5	6	6	5
1944	4	4	2	3	3	2	2	3
1945	6	6	7	6	6	7	6	6
1946	5	3	4	4	4	3	5	3
1947	7	7	7	7	6	7	7	7
1948	7	6	5	4	5	4	5	4
1949	4	7	7	6	7	5	6	6
1950	5	6	4	6	5	4	6	3
1951	3	3	3	4	2	3	3	2
1952	4	6	7	7	6	6	6	7
1953	5	7	6	6	7	7	7	7
1954	5	4	4	5	3	3	4	3
1955	7	6	6	7	5	6	6	7
1956	1	3	2	5	3	4	3	4
1957	4	4	5	4	5	3	5	2
1958	5	5	3	6	5	5	4	3
1959	~	7	7	5	7	7	7	7

0 = no good   7 = the best

Vintage Chart for the years 1938 to 1959, prepared by the Wine and Food Society and reproduced here by their permission

HOW TO SERVE THE DRINKS

Cocktails

Mix just before serving, give a short, sharp shaking with crushed ice, do not stand for long. Serve before a meal, very cold. Pour into small, shallow glasses from the shaker. Add (if liked) a cherry if sweet; an olive if dry. For recipes see chapter beginning on page 303.

Sherry

Decant and serve at room temperature in small deep glasses either before a meal, with the soup, or as a between-meals drink. If served in the all-purpose glass approved by the Wine and Food Society and shown on page 314, serve only one-third full.

Table Wines

RED go with meat and game. Open the bottle two or three hours before the meal and stand in the dining-room so that it is at room temperature. Serve in a rounded bulb-shaped glass, never more than two-thirds full.

WHITE accompany fish, poultry, white meats and sweets. Serve from the bottle, chilled but not frozen. Glasses the same or slightly smaller than those for Red wines.

Champagne

The wine for celebrations, champagne may be drunk at any time, with or without food. Serve chilled, the bottle standing in a bucket of ice. Open when required, wrap the bottle in a napkin and pour into thin saucer-shaped glasses or champagne goblets.

Brandy

Serve at the end of the meal, with coffee, pouring a *very* little into the bottom of a large, preferably warmed, balloon glass, which should be cradled in the palms of the hands to warm the brandy.

Liqueurs

Serve in miniature glasses in small quantities with coffee at the end of dinner. Alternatively, Port may be served at the end of the meal—in a glass much the same shape as a sherry glass but slightly larger.

The etiquette of entertaining is not really formidable, but the rules are well worth following and based on practical common sense

Full-sized white table napkins are essential for a formal lunch or dinner-party. Easiest fancy shape is the Mitre, above. Just fold the napkin in half twice, then fold it diagonally, bring the base points of the triangle together and slip one inside the other.

Prepare grapefruit by first slicing in half crossways, then cutting with a curved knife round the edge where the pith joins the fruit. Use a straight knife to loosen the sections. Top each half with a glacé cherry.

Cutlery is always arranged so that one works from the outside inwards. The place setting, left is laid with fish-eaters for hors d'œuvres on the outside, then a spoon for soup, a small knife for butter and a knife and fork for the main course. Dessert spoon and fork are laid across the top. Right, another style provides for soup, fish, main course, dessert and cheese.

SERVED"

S EATING the guests can be quite a problem. Host and hostess sit at opposite ends of the table and, when numbers permit, the two sexes are placed alternately, husbands and wives being separated whenever possible, and the chief male guest sitting at the hostess's right, the chief woman guest on the host's right. In the case of a party of eight, this obviously is impossible. The hostess's end of the table then remains as it should and adaptations are made at the host's end, as shown below.

C HIEF duties of the host are pouring out the wine and carving. Many couples carve in the kitchen and bring the food in on a hotplate. But if the host carves at table, the hostess or a helper passes round the plates, serving the ladies first, handing vegetables and sauces at the guests' left for them to help themselves.

THE WINE-PRODUCING DISTRICTS OF FRANCE

From each region come wines named   *after the local châteaux and sub-districts*

CHAMPAGNE

- Reims
- Epernay
- Metz
- Nancy
- Strasbourg

PARIS •

ALSACE

Colmar

CHABLIS

VAL-DE-LOIRE

BOURGOGNE

Auxerre

- Orléans
- Tours
- Blois
- Vouvray
- Pouilly-sur-Loire
- Sancerre

Angers • ANJOU
Nantes • Saumur
TOURAINE

MUSCADET

Dijon
CÔTE DE NUITS
CÔTE DE BEAUNE
CÔTE CHALONNAISE

CÔTES DU JURA

COGNAC

Cognac

MÂCONNAIS

Mâcon

BEAUJOLAIS

Lyon

CÔTE ROTIE

BORDEAUX

MÉDOC
Bordeaux

CÔTES du RHÔNE

• Grenoble

HERMITAGE

• Valence

GRAVES   MONBAZILLAC
ST EMILION
SAUTERNES   GAILLAC
BARSAC

CHÂTEAUNEUF
DU PAPE

Avignon

ARMAGNAC   LANGUEDOC

Nîmes

Montpellier

CÔTES de PROVENCE

• Auch

MINERVOIS   Frontignan
Carcassonne • Béziers

Marseille •
Toulon •

Pau •
JURANÇON

Narbonne •

ROUSSILLON

CORBIÈRES
RIVESALTES
Perpignan •
Banyuls •

FRANCE, the greatest wine-growing and wine-drinking country in the world, produces a wonderful variety of wines. You will find on a wine list, either at your wine merchant's or in a restaurant, that the various types are grouped together under the name of their district of origin—Bordeaux, Champagne, Alsace, Languedoc, etc.

Under the general heading of Bordeaux, for example, come many wines bearing the names of the châteaux and the sub-districts of the region of Bordeaux, such as Graves, Médoc and St. Emilion. The wines of Alsace, on the other hand, are mostly named after the grapes from which they are made.

Commonwealth Wines

With the exception of Moselle, Champagne, Chianti, and a few others, practically all types of wine are now produced in the countries of the Commonwealth, notably South Africa and Australia. They are considerably cheaper and often quite as good as their European counterparts, but the only way to discover the ones *you* like is by the old method of trial and error. However, you certainly need not feel ashamed of serving a South African sherry or an Australian burgundy simply because of their origin.

Beautiful glass adds beauty to the dinner table. Above, comport, champagne and goblet in intaglio design in Stuart crystal

Christmas Dinner

Since most families start serious wine-buying at Christmas time, here is a suggested menu, showing a choice of the right wines to serve with various courses.

Apéritif: Dry Sherry, Alsatian Riesling, Champagne or young Moselle.

A lovely example of cut decoration in Stuart crystal—a goblet, cocktail glass and claret glass

With the Turkey: Claret or Champagne.
If *Goose* or *Duck:* Claret or Burgundy.
With the Christmas Pudding: Champagne or Advocat (as sauce).
With Cheese (if served): Burgundy or Port.

Boxing Day Buffet Supper

With Cold Chicken, Turkey, etc.: Moselle or Alsatian wine.

Casual Christmas Entertaining

For a friendly drink at 11 a.m. or a small informal party just before lunch, with cocktail savouries and biscuits, serve dry sherry instead of cocktails.

Dinner Party Menu

Smoked Salmon with White Burgundy
(Pouilly or Chablis)
Steak with Burgundy or Claret
Cheese and Coffee with Cognac

Here is a basic list of the wines and foods that go well together. Like the Vintage Chart, it is to be treated as guidance only—and certainly not as a menu for an outsize feast!

Hors d'Œuvres: Pale Dry Sherry, Vodka or Akvavit.
Oysters: Chablis, Champagne, Moselle.
Soup: Madeira, Sherry, Marsala.

313

Fish: Hock, Moselle, White Burgundy.
Entrée: Chianti, Claret.
Roast: Burgundy.
Poultry: Claret, Champagne.
Sweet: Sauternes, Barsac.
Cheese: Port, Old Brown Sherry. Burgundy also goes well with certain cheeses, notably Port Salut and Brie.
Coffee: Cognac. Liqueurs.
After Dinner with Nuts: Port.

Party Planning

When ordering champagne for a wedding reception, dance or dinner party, quantities should be calculated on this basis:

At a wedding reception, allow 1 bottle for every 3 people. At a dance, allow 1 bottle for every 2 people. For drinking toasts, allow 15 bottles for 100 people.

Table wines should be delivered two or three days before use, but your wine merchant will advise according to vintage and type of wine.

Approved by the Wine and Food Society as the perfect all-purpose wine glass, it is equally suitable for champagne, claret or sherry. Made by Elfverson; obtainable from Heal's, London

The general storage rule is that wines should lie down and spirits stand up; that all wines should be kept in an even temperature of about 58° to 60° Fahrenheit. Red wine should be opened two or three hours before serving and left in the dining-room, so that it is served at room temperature. Do *not* heat it up in hot water or in front of the fire. White wines should be served chilled but not frozen.

When drawing the cork from a wine bottle, first remove capsule, wipe the neck of the bottle clean, and put the corkscrew into the cork *straight*. If a red wine, cover mouth of bottle with a piece of muslin to prevent dirt entering while it is standing to come to room temperature.

Wine Glasses

Rows of elegant wine glasses of all sizes from liqueur to champagne look beautiful on a well-laid dinner table. But for the small family of limited means who want to experiment with wines, it is good to know that a glass has been designed from which everything, with the exception of liqueurs, can be drunk. You simply vary the quantities—serving it only one-third full of sherry, for instance. Sherry, white and red wines, champagne, even brandy can be served in this beautifully shaped all-purpose wineglass.

And here, as a grand finale, are a couple of good recipes for party punches:

Spiced Rum Punch

> 1 *bottle rum*
> ⅙ *bottle orange squash*
> ⅙ *bottle sherry*
> *Pinch grated nutmeg*
> ⅙ *bottle brandy*
> ⅓ *pint strong cold tea*
> *Stick of cinnamon*
> 4 *cloves*

Heat all the ingredients slowly and thoroughly without boiling.

Hot Spiced Burgundy

Place in a saucepan a bottle of Burgundy (reasonable price). Heat slowly but do not boil. Add 10 cloves, ¼ lb. brown sugar, pinch of cinnamon. Serve hot with grated nutmeg.

OPEN-AIR EATING

All food tastes better out of doors, but a good picnic takes planning

PICNIC—all over the world and despite English summers—the word holds a thrill. Most people are quite prepared to risk a dull day for the pleasure of eating out of doors, since fresh air seasoning turns even plain fare into something almost classic.

What Sort of Picnic?

There are several ways of going on an outing that includes lunch and/or tea in the open.

The picnic by car can be fairly elaborate if wished; transport of food and equipment is easy and can even include the pressure cooker.

A most inviting picnic lunch—raised pork pies, baby sausages on sticks, Scotch eggs, followed by cherry tarts and jelly

The walker, cyclist and motor-cyclist must necessarily plan picnic meals that are both light to carry and non-bulky.

A picnic meal in the garden can be prepared beforehand and carried out at the time, or it can be cooked out, barbecue-fashion. The following are victuals and drink suggestions suitable for all categories of picnic.

FOOD FOR LUNCHES

Savouries

Sandwiches are ever popular, and many helpful ideas for fillings have been given in a previous chapter. Here are some suggestions for alternative food:

Stuffed Rolls.—The small, crisp dinner rolls from the baker make a pleasant change from sandwiches. They should be split two-thirds open, some of the soft bread scooped out and the rolls buttered.

then stuffed. Try: (1) finely chopped hard-boiled egg and chopped celery bound with mayonnaise; (2) Gouda or Edam cheese grated and bound with tomato ketchup; (3) cold, cooked fish, flaked, mixed with finely chopped celery or chives, a squeeze of lemon juice and bound with mushroom or tomato ketchup. Garnish with a few sprigs of watercress.

Sausage or Sardine Rolls.—Small succulent rolls of this type, home-made, are sure favourites. Plain shortcrust pastry is preferable to a richer paste, and the sausage meat can be seasoned with a good pinch of mace as well as salt and pepper. Tail the sardines and drain thoroughly on kitchen paper before rolling in pastry.

Savoury Bread Rolls, the long kind, can have a variety of fillings. Split and butter, then fill with: (1) a cooked sausage spread with mustard; (2) long, thick sticks of cheese with a dash of salad cream or sweet

315

chutney; (3) lengths of tender grilled steak or ham with mustard seasoning.

Scotch Eggs and Hard-boiled Eggs are easily eaten in the fingers and as tasty cold as hot. (For Scotch Eggs recipe see chapter on Egg Dishes.)

Cheese and Bacon Savouries are good—roll rashers of cooked bacon round sticks of cheese and fasten with cocktail sticks or wrap in lettuce leaves.

Ham Horseshoes

8 oz. plain flour	5–6 tablespoonfuls
Pinch of salt	water
5 oz. vegetable fat	½ lb. sliced cooked
shortening	ham

Sieve the flour and salt. Divide the shortening into four portions and rub one portion into the flour. Add the water and mix to a smooth non-sticky dough. If any flour is unabsorbed add another teaspoonful of water until the dough is smooth. Sprinkle with flour, form into an oblong shape with the fingers, and turn on to a floured board. Cover with a damp cloth and leave to rest for 30 minutes. Roll out to an oblong 11 × 6 in. Dab small pieces of the second portion of shortening evenly over the top two-thirds of the dough, leaving a margin of ½ in. all round. Fold the bottom third of the pastry upwards, and the top third down to cover it. Brush off surplus flour, seal the open edges with a rolling pin, and turn the pastry half-way round to the left. Roll out again to a strip 11 × 6 in. Add the third portion of shortening, fold the pastry in three, seal, give a half turn and roll again. Repeat once again with the remaining portion of shortening. Roll out, fold and seal for the fourth time without any shortening. Leave covered for 30 minutes in a cool place. Finally, roll out to an oblong 15 × 10 in. with the edges trimmed. Divide into six squares of equal size. Cut across each square to form triangles. Place a piece of ham on each triangle and, working from the longest edge towards a point, roll up the pastry with the ham inside. Damp the corner and secure. Shape gently into horseshoes, place on a baking sheet. Brush with beaten egg or milk and bake in a very hot oven for 15–20 minutes. (Makes 12 horseshoes.)

Aspic Savouries.—A variety of delicacies can be prepared in individual moulds or ramekins and travel well. Packeted aspi jelly saves time in preparation. Shrimp prawns, cubes of chicken, beef, veal o pork, sliced egg are some suggestions fo setting in the jelly, and the well-draine contents of a tin of macedoine of vegetable can also be added for extra interest an flavour.

Accessories for Savouries.—Plain brea and butter sandwiches go well with asp savouries.

Tomatoes combine with almost an savoury, but should be firm so that the can be eaten like apples.

Chunks of peeled or unpeeled cucumbe and sticks of celery stand travel and ar cool and juicy. For perfect transit, pac tomatoes in a tin box and cucumber an celery in tall jars with screw caps.

Lettuce included in sandwiches and rol is liable to arrive limp and faded-lookin; but keeps crisp if packed into a vacuur jar.

Sweets

These need not be limited to a tinful o small cakes or a large cake, which in an case are best kept for tea.

Fruit Jellies can be made in dario moulds or individual waxed cases, sets o which can be bought at good stationer Choose a refreshing jelly, such as lime o lemon, and combine with tinned orang slices, apricots cut in convenient pieces, o fruit salad. For something a little mor subtle, combine fresh grapes, halved an pipped, with strawberry jelly, or put fres grapefruit in pineapple jelly.

Plate Tarts.—If these are replaced i their baking tins after cooling and packe in a round cake tin for travelling, they wi do so without damage. Firm fillings shoul be chosen—bakewell, syrup or jam, o firm fruit such as apple, peach or pear, o pineapple finished with a light glaze (se Pastry chapter).

Table-creams, Jelly-creams. — Packe varieties made with milk come in attractiv flavourings, can be made in individua cases, or set in a coloured basin (if you hav a car for transport) and served from it.

Mousse and Meringue.—One enterpris ing hostess filled small oblong waxed case with chocolate mousse and topped eac with half a coffee meringue; packed firml in a 4-lb. biscuit tin, they emerged un uffled at the picnic and were a great success.

Ice Cream is perfectly possible if you invest in a vacuum jar. Buy the ice as near starting time as possible, or en route, and press it well down into the jar, out of its wrappings.

Thirst Quenchers

Juicy oranges are perhaps the simplest way of carrying liquid refreshment, and if the skins are prepared beforehand by quartering with a sharp knife, they peel easily when needed. Juicy plums are light to carry and refreshing for the odd corners in a one-person lunch box, and transport by car allows for a melon or pineapple to be carried for thirst quenching.

Fruit drinks and milk in parchment cartons are lighter and less bulky than bottled drinks and can be taken through straws. Iced coffee or tea can be carried in vacuum flasks.

FOOD FOR TEAS

As a change from sandwiches and in addition to cake, some of the following suggestions may appeal:

Small cheese scones, split and buttered beforehand; plain scones made with finely chopped walnuts; or brown scones spread with watercress butter.

Sweet scone suggestions: buttered currant and sultana scones; brown scones spread with butter and crystallised honey; home-made plain, sweet buns split, lightly buttered and filled with sliced bananas. A little red jam could be added for extra flavour.

A tinful of small iced cakes in paper cups is more interesting than a whole cake. If a firm icing is used, they travel well. And a tinful of crisp, home-made biscuits is a good finish for a tea-time meal.

Have plenty of tea in flasks, and milk and fruit drinks in cartons if there are children who don't take tea.

NOTE: Much of the "flavour" of vacuum flask tea can be avoided if the tea is poured into the flasks through a fine strainer so that no tea leaves enter, and corks should be covered with greaseproof paper

before use. Milk should always be carried separately and added to the tea when it is poured out. With iced tea serve a slice of lemon instead of milk.

COOKING OUT

Cooking in the backyard is gaining favour: fun for the family weekends, when the weather calls for picnic meals, and grand for entertaining when a summer evening picnic party in your garden can make you a name as a good hostess.

Build the oven firmly of bricks or stones, a back and two sides of a square, and place a grill on top—a discarded rack from the oven is good for this purpose. The open front should face the prevailing wind; the height of the oven should be about four bricks. For fuelling, in general use soft woods for quick cooking—boiling and frying; hard woods for longer processes—roasting, steaming and baking.

Sausages, ribs, chops, kabobs and steaks can be cooked on the grill; hamburger or rissoles, ham or bacon and eggs in a frying pan; potatoes, plain or stuffed, baked in the hot ashes.

The Pressure Cooker

This is an intriguing way of producing a hot meal with the minimum of effort if you travel by car and can carry cooker (with or without a primus stove). Here is a

Ham Horseshoes make a tasty main dish for a lunch out of doors, served with an ice-cold drink

317

tested idea from the Pressure Cooking Advice Bureau:

Macaroni with Meat Balls

1 *lb. minced beef*	2 *tins tomatoes (or*
1 *chopped onion*	1 *lb. fresh tomatoes*
8 *oz. packet of*	*and* 1 *pint water)*
macaroni	*Salt and pepper to*
	taste

Home preparations.—Season beef and form into small balls. Preheat the pressure cooker, add a little fat and brown the meat. Now add onion, tinned tomatoes (or fresh skinned tomatoes and water) and seasoning. Pack the macaroni separately.

When you are ready for your picnic meal, mix the macaroni in with the other ingredients. Bring to the boil, stirring occasionally. Now close the cooker, exhaust all air and bring to 15 lb. pressure. Cook for 12 minutes. Let the cooker cool gradually.

Alternatively, the meal can be cooked at home and will stay hot in the cooker for a maximum of 4 hours, after which reheating will be necessary. In the latter case, the pressure cooker should not be quick-cooled and should not be opened before the food is served.

Wrap the cooker in several newspapers to insulate it.

No creamed foods or chicken dishes should be precooked and left before being used. But there are many other good dishes (such as a beef stew) that can be cooked at home and kept hot for the picnic.

PACKING AND EQUIPMENT

Picnics should be great fun; but they can be an awful bore if their preparation means first scrimmaging round for suitable tins, enough old cups and mugs for drinks, and a vacuum flask that has been used through the winter for holding turps—yes, we have two men friends guilty of this crime! It's well worth collecting adequate equipment and *keeping it for picnic purposes only,* so that it is always ready and in good condition.

A fitted basket or case is an excellent foundation providing, usually, four cups, two flasks, sugar and milk containers, and a light metal sandwich box. It's useful, too, to invest in a small, light fibre suitcase to hold extra equipment and food.

Ideas for further equipment are: plastic spoons for sweets and small plastic plates for savouries; extra sandwich tins for other foods; travelling salt and pepper pots; extra polythene bottles for milk (those supplied in picnic sets are not usually big enough). If you are going to produce anything like a raised pie or galantine, calling for knives and forks and large plates, look around in sports shops and camp equipment departments of large stores for folding sets of knife and fork. These are quite reasonable, much less bulky than household cutlery—and it doesn't matter so much if they get lost. Sets of various sized cardboard plates can be bought at good stationers and can be used several times if greaseproof paper is put under the food. Cardboard cups or beakers are good for cold drinks, but tend to give a characteristic flavour to hot tea or coffee.

Further aids to comfort and convenience: a vacuum flask of warm water and a plastic envelope holding one or more face flannels and guest towels—a boon for dealing with sticky fingers and young mouths after eating. And carry a simple first-aid kit against insect bites, burns (if you are cooking out) and children's tumbles at play.

So much for equipment. Now here are one or two packing tips: damped greaseproof paper or large lettuce leaves, washed and shaken nearly dry, make excellent wrappers for keeping sandwiches fresh in their tins.

Use newspaper in preference to other paper for packing round cakes or individual sweets, as it holds firmly without being hard. It will also keep an ice cream brick cold for up to two hours.

Sets of polythene bags are hygienic, useful for holding such items as shelled hardboiled eggs and Scotch eggs as they are water- and greaseproof, and one can be used finally for the collection of all leftovers and used paper.

Vacuum containers are made now in great variety and can be used to transport hot or cold drinks, hot soup, ice cream or ice cubes for cocktails. Expenditure on several of these items is not therefore an extravagance.

Happy eating-out days to you all.

CAMP COOKERY

*The secret of preparing out of doors three good meals a
day that are substantial enough for lusty holiday appetites*

by W. L. AUSTIN, *Chairman, Camping Club of Great Britain and Ireland*

CAMPING has grown greatly in popularity in recent years. Every summer
thousands spend their holidays and week-
ends enjoying sunshine and fresh air amid
natural surroundings, free from the routine
of their normal daily lives.

Food is an ever-present necessity, however, in camp as elsewhere. To provide
good meals without devoting too much time
to the process, it is essential to find out beforehand something about the most suitable equipment and the different techniques
required.

This chapter is intended primarily for
those intending to camp in tents, really the
most satisfactory form of camping, and so
greatly loved by children. Caravanning,
which is in any case dealt with in a separate
chapter, does not usually present the same
problems, as most caravans are equipped
with a miniature kitchen, including a
cooker powered by compressed gas sold in
cylinders. Cooking therefore becomes a
question of merely turning on taps and pro-
ceeding as at home.

In camp cookery the primary necessity
is to provide heat.

Choosing a Stove

Those whose experience of cooking in
the open is confined to boiling a kettle over
a methylated spirit stove on a windy day,
or over a fitful blaze of damp twigs, may
regard the preparation of complete meals
as an operation far beyond their capabilities. Though this is quite a mistaken idea,
you must have the proper equipment. For
serious cooking, spirit stoves of any de-
scription are not suitable on account of
their slowness, susceptibility to draughts
and the amount of fuel consumed. On the
other hand, wood fires will give good heat
if you know how to make and use them
properly, but have many obvious disadvantages, and for the small family unit have
long been superseded by one of the many

319

types of portable stove burning either paraffin or petrol.

To digress a moment, there is nothing quite like a wood fire in camp for warmth and sociability, especially when twilight falls and the air begins to cool. But it is best kept for that purpose, and then only when sufficient dead wood can be found (no breaking down of living trees). The camp-site owner's permission to light a fire must first be obtained and a suitable place agreed. Owing to fire danger or for other reasons, wood fires are not permitted on some camp sites.

Pressure Stoves

Both paraffin and petrol pressure stoves originated in Sweden, and several reliable types, of Swedish and British manufacture, are available. The air-pressure type, which burns paraffin, is probably the most popular. There are several different pattern burners, but the principle of operation in all paraffin pressure stoves is the same: the burner must be preheated beforehand in order to vaporise the rising paraffin before the stove will burn properly.

This is achieved by burning a small quantity of methylated spirit poured into a small circular cup at the base of the burner or, better still, by using two or three small pieces of broken-up solid-fuel tablet as sold for use with some picnic stoves. The solid fuel is safer and has the added advantages that it is more compact, will not spill and a week's supply may easily be carried in a small tin.

The tank of the stove is fitted with a filler cap, in the centre or side of which is the air-valve screw, a pump for forcing air into the tank and a burner or, in upright collapsible types, a hole into which the burner is screwed, which is closed by a screw plug when the stove is dismantled.

A metal draught shield is usually supplied to confine the heat of the priming fuel around the burner during the preheating process. The air-valve screw must be open while this is taking place, but is screwed down just before the priming fuel becomes exhausted. You then push the pump lightly once or twice, light the burner and the stove should burn with a blue flame and slight hissing sound. When the stove is burning properly, without spitting, a few more strokes of the pump will bring the

flame and the heat up to full power, and may be repeated as necessary.

For camp use, "roarer" pattern burners are best as they are less susceptible to draughts than the "silent" pattern.

If the stove fails to light properly the first time, and, instead of the blue hissing flame, paraffin begins to rise and, possibly, becomes ignited by the remains of the priming fuel, the air-valve screw must be released immediately and the preheating procedure repeated. The ignited paraffin must not be allowed to burn on in the false hope that it may make the stove burn correctly, particularly if the stove is near the tent or other inflammable material.

Provided the burner nipple hole is not blocked, failure to light properly is usually caused by either too little priming fuel, closure of the air valve and pumping too soon, or cool draughts. As a protection against draughts, a windshield in one form or another is essential and consists of three sides of material to fit around the stove, with the central, closed side at the back facing the direction of the prevailing wind. Best for mobile camping is a length of cotton material divided into three sections by metal rods or canes which can be stuck in the turf around the stove. Such windshields can be purchased or made at home.

If these operations sound somewhat complicated to the uninitiated, in practice the knack is quickly acquired, even by children, provided they are old enough to be trusted with matches.

When the stove is alight, the size and heat of the flame may be controlled by judicious use of the air-release screw. By simply unscrewing this and leaving it open, the stove may be extinguished.

Cooking by Petrol

The other types of stove most widely used for camp cookery burn petrol. They have increased greatly in popularity in recent years, particularly among motorists with their ready-to-hand fuel supply. Care must be taken, however, to ensure that the type of stove purchased will burn *all kinds* of petrol, including leaded petrol as generally used in private motor vehicles. Some petrol stoves, mostly small sizes, but including *all* those designed for either paraffin *or* petrol, will only work efficiently with unleaded petrol, which has to be obtained specially from a garage.

Although petrol stoves in themselves are perfectly safe —most are fitted with a safety valve—the usual caution in handling petrol must be observed when refilling.

Petrol stoves differ from paraffin ones in these essentials:

(1) Petrol stoves are not fitted with a pressure release valve screw, for the obvious reason that undoing the screw to extinguish the stove would release petrol vapour, which is extremely inflammable and highly dangerous. (This is the chief reason why petrol should never be used in a stove designed only for paraffin.) In place of the screw valve, a positive on-and-off tap is always fitted, which can also be used for controlling the size and heat of the flame.

(2) No preheating is required except in the smaller sizes, and then only a little, easily applied with a match or two, or a small piece of solid fuel.

With all types of vapour stoves the tiny hole from which the igniting gas escapes must be kept clear of dirt and obstruction. Some stoves are fitted with self-pricking burners, but the majority are not and a supply of prickers (the correct size for the stove) should always be kept at hand. Since the nipple hole is liable to become enlarged with constant use and so impair the efficiency of the stove, it is wise to carry spare nipples and a nipple key.

Stoves of each type are supplied in various sizes, ranging from $\frac{1}{3}$-pint petrol and $\frac{1}{2}$-pint paraffin to about 2 pints in either (quantities refer to tank capacity). Single- and double-burner types are available, the latter mostly in compact folding ranges which are immediately ready for use when opened.

The smaller sizes (up to 1 pint) are suitable for a single camper; the 1-pint alone or 1-pint plus $\frac{1}{2}$-pint for two people. For

Most suitable methods for camp cookery are frying and boiling, whether over a wood fire or on a special stove

three or more, two stoves of at least 1-pint capacity, or a double-burner stove, are really necessary.

Cooking Equipment

For use with camping stoves, special aluminium saucepans have been designed without fixed handles but with a slot to take a detachable handle which fits all sizes.

NOTE: Always remove the handle when a pan has been placed on or lifted from the stove. With it on, it is so easy to tip the pan over.

These saucepans are made in about eight sizes, ranging from approximately 1-pint to 4$\frac{1}{2}$-pints capacity. Each size "nests" in the next larger. Frying pans, also, without handles, are available in different sizes and can be matched to the largest saucepan, and so will act as a cover to the set of pans for ease in carriage. Separate light lids,

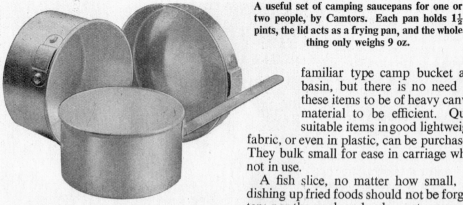

A useful set of camping saucepans for one or two people, by Camtors. Each pan holds 1½ pints, the lid acts as a frying pan, and the whole thing only weighs 9 oz.

with lifting rings, are also obtainable for all pans.

Aluminium plates are most suitable for camp use, as they are light, unbreakable, easily cleaned and carried. Several types of screw-top containers, in aluminium and polythene (unbreakable), can be obtained for carrying different kinds of food and condiments—tea, sugar, jam, etc. For butter and fats, glass or plastic-lined screw-top aluminium containers are best.

The transparent food bags sold for sandwich lunches and storing food in the refrigerator are ideal for all kinds of eatables that do not require a tin. Excluding air, they really do keep the food fresh.

Cups and saucers in unbreakable polythene are best for camp use. Aluminium cups should be avoided; they burn the lips if used for hot liquids.

Large aluminium cans with lids and handles are useful for water and milk, but the wide-necked polythene jars, with screw-tops, are probably better for milk. Water, of course, may also be fetched in the familiar type camp bucket and basin, but there is no need for these items to be of heavy canvas material to be efficient. Quite suitable items in good lightweight fabric, or even in plastic, can be purchased. They bulk small for ease in carriage when not in use.

A fish slice, no matter how small, for dishing up fried foods should not be forgotten; nor the swab and nylon pot scourer or brush for the inevitable washing up. Soap powder should be carried in a screw-top tin; cardboard easily gets damp and soggy in the open.

Although most meals cooked in camp will no doubt consist of boiled, stewed or fried foods in their many varieties, a small oven for camp use is on the market. One type measures 11 by 11 by 9 in. high and is suitable for most stoves.

Steamers are also obtainable, and for those who like toast for breakfast, there is a round, flat, gauze toaster specially for use with camp stoves which is quite efficient. If there are three or more people to cook for, a pressure cooker is invaluable (see chapter on Pressure Cookery).

Planning Meals

When meals are planned, the limiting factors are the capacity of stove or stoves and the size and number of saucepans available. It is, however, quite easy to cook a meal of two courses on one stove; a third

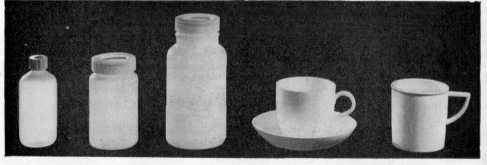

For carrying milk and other liquids, also for cups and beakers, the best material is 'Polythene,' which is unbreakable, tasteless, stainless and can be sterilised in boiling water. (Camtors)

Photo by the Camping Club of Great Britain and Ireland

A windshield, consisting of three sides of material, is essential to protect the stove from draughts. Equipment shown above includes (right), a lightweight camp bucket for water, also aluminium cooking and eating utensils, the saucepans with detachable handles

may be added by the ambitious—by simply changing the pans about and keeping one hot on top of another. For example, when preparing breakfast, the water for tea should first be heated and covered with a plate. The porridge can then be cooked and placed on top of the saucepan containing the hot water, close to the stove, while the bacon and/or eggs are fried. When that is done, the porridge can be warmed for a few seconds and, while it is being eaten, the water for the tea brought to the boil, with the bacon, etc., covered by a plate, keeping warm on top. The same procedure can be followed for other meals. The important thing to remember is that dishes which will not spoil by being reheated, or partly cooked first and finished later, should always be cooked first and put back for reheating just before serving the meal. If two stoves are in operation, it is, of course, much easier, but even then it is advisable to heat a pan of hot water first. It is always necessary in camp cookery to time the operations so that the courses are ready to be served hot as they are wanted.

Tea can be made quite successfully in a saucepan and strained into the cups, though a light aluminium teapot really is an improvement if it can be carried. Another very desirable extra is a tea cosy. A pan of tea that has cooled off will not spoil if it is warmed up on the stove, provided it does not simmer or boil.

Choice of Equipment

When buying equipment, it is advisable to consult one of the firms specialising in lightweight camping equipment, most of which issue very comprehensive catalogues.

For more information about camping in general or to meet other campers, enquiry should be made to The Camping Club of Great Britain and Ireland, 35 Old Kent Road, London, S.E.1, who cater for all forms of camping and caravanning, issue a list of camp sites to members, supply specialist information, and arrange camping fixtures in Great Britain and camping tours abroad.

ONE-ROOM CHEF

*Living alone in limited space, with the minimum of cooking
facilities, is no excuse for not having proper meals*

ONE-ROOMERS of all ages and both sexes can and should eat well by their own hand.

At the outset, limited space and inadequate equipment tend to cast a deep depression over the whole idea, but that can be altered, and a boiled egg and a "cuppa" need not be the sole repertoire for an evening meal.

The elderly and not-so-active need light, nourishing meals; men and women, after work, need equally nourishing but more substantial meals and, above all, those that are quickly cooked.

The right equipment and a small but adequate store cupboard are essentials; so, too, is a collection of quickly cooked recipes to start with.

Equipment

The most important item, naturally, is the cooker.

Personal experience of bed-sitters is of one miniature gas-ring, wobbly, situated in the hearth by the gas-fire and in close proximity to the wooden surround of the mantelpiece. This sort of arrangement does dampen one's zest for home cooking, but no landlord will mind something better being installed, if it is not at his expense, and it really is well worth drawing on savings to get that something better. What you don't spend on meals out will soon close the savings gap.

Bed-sitterites are well catered for by gas and electric appliance manufacturers. You can choose the Big Baby Belling electric cooker, which stands only 36 in. high (42 in. to the top of the splash plate), is 21 in. wide and 16 in. deep. It won't take up much space, but will enable you to cook a full scale dinner for five or six people in its roomy oven, with combined grill-boiler, on which you can cook on top while you grill or toast underneath. It can stand on a table or be supplied with a stand and it boasts a plate-warming cupboard that could do double duty in emergencies as an airer!

Much smaller and costing a lot less ar the various gas hotplates, most of whic have two boiling burners, a grill and spillage tray. It's amazing what a variet of hot dishes can be prepared on these.

Then there are the rapidly growing num ber of electric "cook on the table" appli ances—frypans, skillets, combined cooker fryers and pressure cookers. These ar smart and streamlined, usually with oven glass lids, though the Morphy-Richard Electric Skillet boasts a lovely copper tinted anodised lid.

Three Presto automatic cooking appli ances can all be operated by one electri control unit. So you can buy, say, the fry pan and control master unit first, then ad the pressure cooker, and finally the cooker fryer (which boils, stews, steams, braises deep-fries and comes with its own chi basket).

Apart from the cooker, dual-purpos utensils are worth considering. The three section saucepan or frypan can perforn wonders in cooking a whole meal fo one.

Steamers and double saucepans are goo friends to small-space cooks, and so is th self-basting roasting tin. A Dutch oven i invaluable, and this, by the way, provide the genuine means of roasting—*in front o* a hot fire. For this purpose, a gas fir capable of fierce heat is best.

Two strong enamel plates, dinner size are most useful for cooking over a pa of hot water. And oven-glass ramekin should not be forgotten, nor a clearl marked oven-glass measuring jug, showin cups as well as fluid ounces.

The pressure cooker, of course, is boon and the chapter on Pressure Cooker may be consulted for further information

The Store Cupboard

It is at last possible to buy small size of a good variety of canned foods.

Suggestions for your store cupboard are small-size steak and kidney pudding (ample for one, enough for two); por luncheon meat loaf (Dutch brands are delicious hot or cold, as are good brands of ham and beef loaf); small cans of macaroni cheese; filled ravioli paste; the small size of *pink* salmon makes a tasty meal and is not prohibitive, compared with red salmon. Tuna fish, too, is delicious, and keep in hand a can or two and some packets and cubes of interesting soup. (See also chapter on Emergency Meals.)

Some vegetables, particularly peas, baked beans and macédoine of vegetables, come in handy small cans and so do a variety of fruits, evaporated milk and cream. Small canned steamed puddings and creamed rice are also available.

Frozen foods come to the rescue in many emergencies. When you are right out of ideas for dinner and can investigate the contents of one of those great refrigerator cabinets in good grocers and fishmongers, you might choose fish fingers or chops and peas with a mousse for the sweet course. Eating this way is apt to be expensive, but can be a blessing when, in the mood for entertaining, you want some, say, out-of-season vegetable or fruit to lift your meal out of the ordinary.

Delicatessen shops are another useful source of ideas for preparing quick meals. Various ingredients for all kinds of salads can usually be bought, and save much preparation. If you have a small oven, packets of ready-mixed puff or short pastry may be bought, needing only to be rolled out at home and made up into sweet or savoury dishes. Unfilled, cooked vol-au-vent cases can be filled at home and gently heated for a savoury supper, and a wide variety of cooked meats gives you a base on which to build a satisfying meal.

The Argyll Gas Hotplate is small enough for the tiniest one-room flatlet but has two highly efficient boiling burners and a high-speed grill. Note the push-in safety taps. (Stoves Ltd.)

COLLECTED RECIPES

Light Savouries

Quick Cod.—About ½ lb. cod fillet. Wash, dry and place on enamel plate over a pan of boiling water. Pour a little milk over fish, add a nut of butter and pepper and salt to taste. Cover with another plate or the saucepan lid, and cook for about 15 minutes or until fish is cooked right through. Drain off the liquor and use to make white sauce (see Sauces chapter), or flavour the sauce with finely chopped parsley, sprinkle the fish with a little grated cheese and put under the grill long enough to melt and brown the cheese.

Masked Egg and Spinach.—Prepare about ¼ pint white sauce in the top half of a double saucepan, using the heat from the boiling water in the bottom half of the pan; flavour lightly with tomato ketchup or grated cheese. Cook spinach separately in the water that clings to the leaves after washing. A few minutes before it is ready, put an egg to soft-boil in the bottom half of the double saucepan. Drain and season the spinach, place on a warmed dinner plate. Shell the egg when cooked, place on the spinach and mask both with the sauce.

Savoury Scramble.—Boil water in bottom pan of double saucepan. Dice a slice of luncheon meat or cold, boiled ham, and put into inner pan with 2 tablespoonfuls milk and a knob of butter or margarine.

The Big Baby Belling electric cooker
stands on a table or its own stand.
Combined grill-boiler gives maximum
efficiency—and clothes can be aired
in the plate-warming cupboard!

Heat gently until fat is melted. Remove
pan and stir in a well-beaten egg seasoned
to taste. Return to outer pan and cook
until mixture "scrambles." Turn on to
crisp, buttered toast.

Cheese Custard.—Mix a small, lightly
beaten egg with $\frac{1}{2}$ cupful warm milk. Mix
separately in small basin or soufflé dish $1\frac{1}{2}$
tablespoonfuls each of grated cheese and
breadcrumbs, season to taste and sprinkle
over the custard. Cover securely with
greaseproof paper, place in pan of cold
water to come half-way up basin and bring
gradually to the boil, lid on pan, to set
custard. Boil for about 20 minutes. If you
have a small oven, bake in moderate heat
to set egg.

Stuffed Onion.—Choose a large onion,
Spanish if possible, peel, cross-cut the root
end lightly and cook in boiling salted water
until tender but still firm. Set the pan aside
for the moment. Remove some of the
centre of the onion and chop up with a
little left-over meat, peas, beans or tomato;
season and bind with a little tomato or
mushroom ketchup. Pile into centre of
onion, put onion into small basin, top with
piece of butter or margarine, and put back

over pan, lid off, and bring to boil until
onion is thoroughly heated through. O
serve stuffed onion (or stuffed baked apple
with a hot curry sauce.

Variation.—A quicker onion dish is to
boil the onion, drain, place on a warmed
dinner plate, top with a piece of butter and
plenty of grated cheese and eat with brown
bread or toast.

More Substantial Savouries

One-man Grill.—Toast a large slice of
bread on one side only. On the untoasted
side put $\frac{1}{4}$ lb. raw, minced beef, season with
salt and pepper—and mixed herbs o
chopped parsley and onion, if liked—add
knob of margarine and put under grill
Cook gently until meat changes colour and
loses raw appearance and feels tender
when speared with a fork. Now top with
sliced tomatoes (or mushrooms if you are
feeling extravagant) and grill again for a
minute or two until these are cooked. A
delicious dish, and all the gravy is caught in
the toast.

Mixed Grill.—According to appetite, fry
or grill one or more sausages, bacon
rashers, halved tomatoes, and any left-over
mince. Arrange all on a warmed plate and
add watercress, if liked, add snippets of dry
toast.

Meat Fritters.—Make a simple batter
(see Puddings chapter). Cut thickish slices
of pork luncheon meat loaf, dip in batter
and roll in crumbs, fry in smoking hot fa
to cover. Drain on kitchen paper before
serving.

NOTE: Rolls of kitchen paper towelling
can be bought at good stationers and are
most useful for cooking and other purposes. Drums of ready-prepared brown
crumbs can also be bought and last well.

Main Course Soup.—Open a can of concentrated soup—tomato, celery, mushroom, pea, for instance—dilute with a
canful of half milk, half water, and heat
through. Pour off a helping and the rest will
keep for a day or two for another meal
Reinforce the soup with diced left-overs
of meat and vegetables, and, if you feel
luxurious—and in funds—stir in a spoonful of fresh cream just before eating.

Savoury Pasty (for those with an oven)
—Buy $\frac{1}{4}$ lb. ready-made pastry. Roll out
$\frac{1}{4}$ in. thick and cut out two rounds, using a
small saucer. Milk the edges and fill one

round with cooked meat, fish or chicken, bound with a little egg or well-seasoned thick white sauce. Place second round on top, pinch edges together, brush with beaten egg or milk and cut two air slits on top. Bake in a hot oven until nicely brown.

Kedgeree.—If you have enjoyed Finnan haddock for dinner one night and have about $\frac{1}{2}$ lb. left, use up as follows: put 2 tablespoonfuls rice in boiling salted water and hard-boil a shell egg. Flake fish, remove bones, and heat in a separate pan (on top of double boiler) with 1 oz. butter or margarine. When rice is cooked and drained, add to fish and season. Pile on a dish and decorate with hard-boiled egg rings and chopped parsley.

Mock Kedgeree.—An excellent emergency meal when the larder is low. Wash and cook 2 tablespoonfuls rice in boiling salted water until tender. Drain and, while still hot, work in a teaspoonful of butter or margarine, two skinned and mashed tomatoes, and 1 tablespoonful or more of grated cheese, also curry powder to taste and a few raisins if liked. Stir well, reheat if necessary, and eat with lightly buttered crisp brown toast.

Dutch Oven Cookery

This is a grand appliance if you have no grill; after a little practice you can produce succulent grilled chops and grilled steaks and sausages nicely chippy outside and soft inside. You will also be able to do:

Kebabs. — These are skewerfuls of mouth-sized bites—for example, cubes of grilling steak or lamb, squares of bacon, button mushrooms and thick slices of tomato, threaded alternately on one skewer per person. Season with pepper and salt, brush with oil. Turn up the fire so that the inside of the oven is very hot and grill the kebabs for 10–20 minutes, turning once. If

nothing suitable is available, you may have to invest in an iron trivet on which to stand the oven in front of the fire, or an upturned large biscuit tin or box will sometimes do.

Vegetables

Serve yourself a vegetable with your evening meal, for health as well as variety; canned and frozen are excellent and quick to serve, and here are some tips on fresh vegetables:

Special Brussels Sprouts.—To make more digestible, soak for 5 minutes in cold water after preparing, put in a pan with a little milk and cook gently until tender. When possible, plan to have this vegetable with a main dish needing a sauce and use the milk from the sprouts for the sauce.

Five-minute Carrots.—To have these hot and reduce cooking time, wash, scrape

Portable—you can plug it in to any 13-amp. socket—yet on this electric cooker you can prepare a full-sized family meal. (Power Point Model by Jackson)

327

Smart enough to adorn any dinner table, with its copper-toned lid, the thermostatically heat-controlled Morphy-Richards Electric Skillet (right) stews, fries, roasts and bakes equally well

The Presto Cooker-Fryer (below) is another multiple-use appliance and it runs off the same control unit as the Presto Fry Pan and Pressure Cooker

and then grate finely. Put in a small pan with a good piece of butter or margarine, season, and stir over low heat until fat is melted and the vegetable is hot right through—literally a matter of about 5 minutes.

Potatoes.—If you are making a dish over a pan of hot water, potatoes can be cooked in the water, and to save trouble and give the best flavour and nourishment, scrub and boil in their jackets: as a change, finish them off in the Dutch oven if you acquire one.

Light Sweets

A useful item to have as part of your equipment is a vacuum jar. In this you can collect ice cream—on your way home, per-haps—or a mousse, and keep it until your meal is ready.

If you are entertaining, an individual block of strawberry or coffee ice put between the carefully separated halves of a confectioner's meringue makes a festive and delicious sweet course.

Another simple and pleasant idea is to make up half a pint of packet custard, line the bottom of a small dish with, say, chopped apple, sliced banana and a sprinkle of raisins, and pour over the custard. Leave to get cold. And another fruity idea:

Grapefruit Salad.—Cut top off a small grapefruit and take out most of the inside. Fill the space with any fruit you may have —peeled and pipped grapes, pieces of the grapefruit and pieces of pear, a small can of mixed fruit salad, chopped bananas.

A quick, nourishing sweet is made as follows:

Baked Cup Custard.—Lightly beat an egg in a large, strong breakfast cup. Add milk to about 1½ in. from the top, and sugar to taste. Cover cup with a tight-fitting lid and place in a saucepan of water to come half-way up the cup. Bring to the boil and boil gently for 15–20 minutes.

You cannot improve on fresh fruit in

season for the last course if you feel disinclined to prepare a sweet.

More Substantial Sweets

Canned puddings need only to be heated as directed and a sweet white sauce made if you feel like it; or, for a change, run some Golden Syrup over the top instead.

Here is a recipe for an uncooked cake that makes a good after-dinner sweet:

Biscuit Cake.—¼ lb. margarine; ¼ lb. block chocolate; 3 tablespoonfuls sugar; 1 egg; ½ lb. biscuits of the oval rich tea or petit beurre type.

Break biscuits in small neat pieces and put into a fairly large basin. Break an egg into a small basin or cup and beat well until smooth. Now melt margarine, sugar and chocolate in a double saucepan until sugar is dissolved, chocolate melted and all are smoothly blended. Add beaten egg and continue cooking, stirring all the time, for about 7–10 minutes. The mixture must not boil. When cooked, pour mixture over biscuits and stir carefully to coat them thoroughly. Grease an oblong bread tin, press mixture into this and leave to get cold. Turn out and slice as required.

Sweet Rice.—Wash and cook 1 or 2 tablespoonfuls rice in boiling salted water. Drain and eat hot with moist brown sugar, honey or Golden Syrup, and butter.

A good sweet to make at week-ends when there is more time for preparation:

Tapioca Apples.—Take 1½ tablespoonfuls of large tapioca and ½-pint milk together with a sliver of lemon rind for flavouring. Place in double saucepan and cook for about 1½ hours. Meanwhile, peel and core three medium-sized cooking apples, cut these in quarters and stew gently in a little water, with sugar added. When apples and tapioca are ready, put half the tapioca in a fireproof glass dish, add half the apples, remaining tapioca, and lastly, the remaining apples. Cover with a layer of apricot jam, and pop under grill or in oven, if you have one, before serving.

Batter Sweets.—Pancakes (see Puddings chapter) are always popular and can be eaten with sugar and lemon juice, or folded over jam or fruit.

Bananas, split lengthwise, apple rings and orange rings are delicious dipped in batter, fried and rolled in sugar before eating.

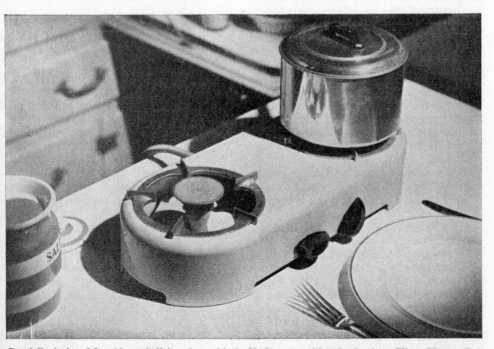

Specially designed for old people living alone, this double-burner cooking ring by Ascot Water Heaters Ltd. is fitted with a device to prevent gas escaping once the tap has been turned on, until the small pilot light is lit

JAMS, JELLIES, MARMALADE, PICKLES AND CHUTNEY

There is nothing quite so satisfying as a well-stocked store cupboard,
full of good things you have made—and maybe also grown—yourself

JAM MAKING

JAM MAKING is not difficult, provided certain rules are carefully followed, and does not take an unduly long time. For anyone who grows fruit in the garden, there is the special joy of "all my own work." Even those who have to buy the fruit will find it worth while and a saving to make jam when seasonable fruits are cheap.

Weighing and measuring must be absolutely accurate, and the jam must be boiled until a good set is secured. A common failing of home-made jam is that it is too runny, and preparations are on the market to make it set. But jams and jellies containing nothing but fruit, sugar and water should set perfectly. Certain fruits—such as strawberries, cherries and marrow, for example—are deficient in pectin (the acid which makes jams set), but it is easy to counteract this by adding the juice of fruit rich in pectin, such as lemon, gooseberry or redcurrant. The juice of the two latter can be extracted by boiling them with a little water until tender and then straining the juice.

The best sort of preserving pan to use is a strong aluminium one. Failing this, a copper pan can be used, but never in any circumstances use a galvanised container. Never fill the pan too full or the jam may boil over.

Either loaf or granulated sugar can be used for jam and jelly. For good results, 1 lb. of sugar should be used for every 1 lb. of fruit.

Here are a few special points which should be carefully noted:

(1) Always use firm, undamaged fruit, not too ripe, freshly picked (on a fine day, if possible). Wash the harder fruits. Go through the fruit carefully and remove bad ones or blemishes.

(2) Tough fruit should be simmered in a little water until tender before the sugar is added. Tender fruit can have the sugar added at once. Care must be taken that it does not burn before the juice comes out of the fruit.

(3) Jam must always be stirred once the sugar is in, and the sugar should be warmed first. Do not let the mixture boil until all the sugar has dissolved.

(4) When the sugar is dissolved, boil the jam rapidly. A large amount of scum will come to the surface. Wait until the jam is nearly done before removing it, as a large part of it will boil back into the jam; the rest can easily be removed with a fish slice or shallow spoon. A good way of using up jam skimmings is to make a Queen's Pudding with them (see Puddings chapter).

(5) As the jam thickens and the fruit becomes clear, test the juice, to see if it will set, by dropping a very little on to a china plate and putting it by the window for a minute. Touch the drops lightly with one finger. If the surface crinkles the jam is done.

(6) In some jam the fruit is apt to rise to the surface, leaving only syrup at the bottom of the jars. To prevent this, let the jam cool in the pan and give it a stir before pouring it out.

(7) The jars should be scrupulously clean, absolutely dry, and heated a little in the oven, otherwise they may crack.

(8) Fill the jars very full because jam sinks as it cools. Use a sauceboat or small jug and, if necessary, wipe the tops and sides of the jars while still hot. A jam funnel put in the neck of the jars will keep the top and sides quite clean.

(9) There are two schools of thought about when to cover jam, some people doing it when still hot, others leaving it to cool. The former method is probably preferable as the sooner the jam is covered the less likely are mould spores to enter. The difficulty about covering jam while hot is that

it sinks during cooling so that an inner paper put on at once either goes down with the jam or sticks to the sides of the jar, leaving a space between it and the jam. Cellophane covers applied dry the moment the jam is potted, and secured with rubber bands or strings, keep the jam in excellent condition. (There are one or two jams, such as strawberry, which it is advisable to leave for a time before potting, as otherwise the fruit tends to rise to the top of the jars.)

(10) Jam should keep perfectly for a year if stored in a cool, dry place.

Apricot Jam (Dried Fruit)

3 lb. dried apricots
9 pints water
9 lb. sugar
2 oz. almonds

Wash the apricots, cut in pieces and stand them in the water for 24 hours. Blanch the almonds and cut them to resemble kernels. Boil the apricots and water until the fruit is tender—40–50 minutes. Add the sugar, let it dissolve, and boil rapidly until the juice will nearly set. Add the almonds and boil until the juice will set, skimming if necessary. Pour into warm, dry jars and tie down at once.

Apricot Jam (Fresh Fruit)

| 4 lb. fresh apricots | 4 lb. sugar |
| ¾ pint water | Juice of a lemon |

Wash fruit, halve and remove stones. Crack a few stones and blanch the kernels. Put fruit, water, lemon juice and kernels into the pan and bring to the boil. Cook gently until fruit is tender, then add sugar, stir till boiling. Boil hard until a set is obtained.

Jam and jelly making is not at all difficult but, for success, the ingredients must be accurately weighed and measured. A strong aluminium or copper pan should be used

Blackberry and Apple Jam

| 8 lb. blackberries | 3 lb. apples |
| Sugar | 1 pint water |

Remove stalks and put the blackberries in a pan with a gill of water. Simmer until tender, then put through a sieve. Peel, core and slice the apples coarsely, put with the rest of the water into the pan and cook until soft, then mash up with a fork, add the blackberry juice and weigh, allowing an equal weight of sugar. Heat slowly

331

while the sugar dissolves, then increase the heat and boil briskly until it will set when tested. Skim, if necessary, pour into warm, dry jars and tie down at once.

Blackcurrant Jam

6 lb. blackcurrants   7½ lb. sugar
4 pints water

Remove the stalks and larger snuffs from the currants, place with the water in the preserving pan, and boil gently until the fruit is quite tender and the mixture considerably reduced. Add the sugar and let it dissolve. Boil until the jam will set when tested. Skim towards the end, if necessary. Pour the jam into warm, dry jars and cover at once.

Cherry Jam

12 lb. black cherries   Sugar
1 lb. redcurrants   Water

Stone and weigh the cherries. To every 1 lb. of stoned cherries allow 1 lb. of sugar. Boil the currants, adding a little water. When they have boiled for ½ hour, strain through a jelly bag and add the juice to the cherries. Boil the cherries with the juice for about ½ hour until soft. Add the sugar and bring slowly to the boil, allowing the sugar to melt before it boils. Boil quickly until the juice is thick and not too runny, skimming if necessary, then pour into warm, dry jars and cover at once.

Gooseberry Jam

6 lb. gooseberries   1½ pints water
7½ lb. sugar

Wash, top and tail the gooseberries and place them in the preserving pan with the water. Simmer until the fruit is mashed and tender and the contents of the pan considerably reduced. Add the sugar and let it dissolve. Boil until the jam will set when tested, skimming if necessary. Pour it into warm, dry jars and tie down at once.

Marrow Jam

6 lb. marrow   3 lemons
6 lb. sugar   1½ oz. root ginger

The marrows must be quite ripe and almost woody, or they will boil pulpy. Peel them, remove all the soft parts and seeds, and cut into cubes of about 1 in. Put the marrow and sugar into a preserving pan with the juice and very finely cut rind of the lemons. Mix all together and let it stand for 24 hours. Then add the ginger, bruising it well and putting it into a muslin bag. Cook until the cubes of marrow are transparent and the juice is sticky but not runny. Remove the ginger. Skim, if necessary. Let the jam stand until nearly cold before pouring into the jars. Cover at once.

Nectarine Jam (Dried Fruit)

This can be made in exactly the same way as peach jam, substituting dried nectarines for the dried peaches.

Peach Jam (Dried Fruit)

3 lb. dried peaches   9 lb. sugar
9 pints water   Juice of 2 lemons

Wash the peaches and cut into pieces. Stand them in the water for 24 hours. Add the lemon juice and boil slowly until the fruit is tender. Add the sugar, let it dissolve, and then boil rapidly until the juice will set when tested, skimming if necessary. Pour into warm, dry jars and cover at once.

Peach and Raspberry Jam

2 lb. fresh peaches   3 lb. sugar
(stoned)   2 lb. raspberries
¼ pint water

Skin the peaches and cut them into pieces. Crack the stones, take out kernels and blanch. Put the fruit, water and kernels into the preserving pan and cook gently until tender. Add the sugar and stir until it has dissolved, boil for 15 minutes, then test for set.

Pineapple Jam

1 large ripe pineapple   Juice of a lemon
Sugar

Peel the pineapple and cut out the woody parts. Chop up the rest into neat cubes. Weigh it and place in a pan with an equal weight of sugar. Let it stand all night. Next day, add the lemon juice and boil until the cubes are transparent and the syrup thick. Skim, if necessary. Let it stand until nearly cold and then pour into warm, dry jars and cover at once.

Plum Jam

6 lb. plums   7½ lb. sugar
2½ pints water

Wash the plums and cook them in the water until quite tender and until the contents of the pan are considerably reduced.

(Remove any stones that come away easily —the rest can be removed after the sugar has been added, when they will come to the top.) Add the sugar, dissolve slowly over a low heat, then bring to the boil and boil quickly until the jam will set when tested. Skim, if necessary. Pour into warm, dry jars and tie down at once.

Raspberry Jam

Take freshly picked raspberries, look them over carefully and weigh them. Allow 1½ lb. sugar to every 1 lb. raspberries. Put the sugar and fruit into a preserving pan and heat until the sugar is dissolved, stirring well. Then bring to the boil and boil hard for exactly 3 minutes, skimming if necessary. Pour into warm, dry jars and cover at once.

Redcurrant Jam

To every 1 lb. of fruit put 1 lb. of sugar. Remove the stalks from the fruit. Bruise the currants first. Add the sugar to the currants, let the sugar dissolve slowly, stirring all the time, and then boil gently until clear and sufficiently stiff, skimming if necessary. Pour into warm, dry jars and tie down.

Redcurrant and Raspberry Jam

6 lb. redcurrants	*8 lb. sugar*
2 lb. raspberries	*A very little water*

Remove the stalks from the currants and put them with the raspberries in a very little water. Simmer the fruit until the currants are tender and cooked. Then add the sugar and let it dissolve, stirring all the time. Boil until the jam will set when tested, skimming towards the end if necessary. Pour into warm, dry jars and cover at once.

Rhubarb Jam

3 lb. rhubarb (cut up)	*1½ oz. root ginger*
3 lb. sugar	*2 small lemons*

Cut the rhubarb into small pieces and put into a preserving pan with the sugar. Heat slowly until the sugar is dissolved, stirring all the time. Add the lemon juice and finely grated lemon rind; bruise the ginger, tie it in a muslin bag and add. Boil until the mixture sets when tested, skimming if necessary. Remove the ginger and pour the jam into warm, dry jars. Cover at once.

Strawberry Jam

5 lb. hulled straw- *berries*	*1 gill gooseberry* *juice, or juice of 2*
5 lb. sugar	*lemons*

Place all the ingredients in preserving

Blackberry and Apple is one of the most delicious fruit mixtures for home-made jam—and you can usually pick the blackberries in the hedgerows for nothing

pan and heat until the sugar is quite dissolved. Boil until the jam will set when tested. Skim towards the end, if necessary. Let the jam stand until almost cold and then pour it into the jars. Cover at once.

Strawberry Jam (Quick method)

2 lb. small straw- berries	½ teaspoonful tartaric acid, or juice of 1
3 lb. sugar	lemon, or red- currant juice

Butter the preserving pan thoroughly, put in strawberries and mash them slightly. Add sugar and acid (or lemon or redcurrant juice), stir until the sugar melts, then bring to boil and boil hard for 3 minutes. Remove from heat and *stir for 5 minutes*—this is absolutely necessary— skimming as required. (Yield: 5 lb. jam.)

Tomato Jam

9 lb. ripe tomatoes	6 lb. sugar
A little lemon juice	

Pour boiling water over the tomatoes and remove the skins. Put the fruit, sugar and lemon juice in a preserving pan and bring it to the boil slowly, allowing the sugar to dissolve. Boil until the fruit is transparent and the syrup thick. Skim towards the end, if necessary. Let the jam stand until cold, then pour into the jars and cover at once.

JELLY MAKING

The prime essential is a good jelly bag. Various kinds can be bought, but it is quite easy to make one's own. Use strong butter muslin and make the bag wide at the top, tapering to a point. Sew on loops. A broom handle threaded through the loops can be balanced on two tables, or the backs of two kitchen chairs, over the basin.

Always scald jelly bags before using them.

Here are a few points to bear in mind when making jelly:

(1) The fruit, which need not have stalks or husks removed, should be put in the preserving pan with water and simmered until tender.
(2) The whole contents of the pan should then be put into the jelly bag. Let it drip all night into a basin. *Never* squeeze the bag or try to hurry up the dripping process. If you do, the jelly will be cloudy instead of clear.

(3) The next day, measure the juice and add the sugar, usually 1 lb. of sugar to each pint of juice. Let the sugar dissolve; then boil rapidly until the jelly will set, stirring all the time. Skim towards the end, if necessary.
(4) Test as for jam, but the drops should keep their shape, as well as crinkling on the surface.
(5) Pour jelly into jars as soon as it is done. Do not stir after it leaves the fire, or it will be full of bubbles.

Apple Jelly

Quarter the apples and cut away any bad parts. Put in the preserving pan with enough water to float them, and boil until they are soft but not pulpy. Put the mixture into a jelly bag and leave to drip through all night. Measure the juice and allow 1 lb. of sugar to every pint. Put juice and sugar into the pan and let the sugar dissolve before the mixture boils. Stir all the time. Then boil until it will set when tested, skimming if necessary. Pour into warm, dry jars and tie down.

Blackcurrant Jelly

6 lb. blackcurrants	Sugar
2 pints water	

Put the fruit (which need not be stalked) and water into a pan and simmer until tender. Mash well and pour into a jelly bag. Leave to drip all night, then measure the juice and add 1 lb. of sugar to every pint of juice. Put the sugar and juice in a preserving pan and heat slowly until the sugar is dissolved, stirring all the time. Then bring it to the boil and continue boiling until the jelly will set when tested, skimming if necessary. Pour into warm, dry jars and tie down.

Bramble Jelly

6 lb. blackberries	Sugar
1 pint water	

Pick the blackberries on a fine day. Remove the stalks, put with the water in the preserving pan and boil gently for about 20 minutes, until the fruit is tender. Mash well, then pour the pulp into a jelly bag and leave to drip all night. Measure the juice and add 1 lb. of sugar to every pint of juice. Put the sugar and juice into the preserving pan and let the sugar dissolve before it boils, stirring all the time. Boil quickly until it will set in a good jelly, skimming if necessary.

NOTE: Blackberries gathered early in the season make the best jelly.

Crab Apple Jelly

Make in the same way as apple jelly (see opposite), but instead of cutting up the apples put them in the preserving pan whole, just as they are. Do not on any account let them get mashed or the jelly will be too acid.

Gooseberry Jelly

Wash the gooseberries but do not top and tail them. Place them in a preserving pan with just enough water to cover and simmer until they turn to a pulp. Pour the mixture into a jelly bag and leave to drip all night. Remove the pulp, place in the preserving pan, cover with water and simmer for about 1 hour, stirring occasionally. Strain again through the jelly bag and mix both lots of juice. Weigh the juice and allow 1 lb. of sugar to every pint of juice. Let the sugar dissolve slowly, then bring the mixture to the boil and boil briskly until it sets. Skim, if necessary. Pour into warm, dry jars and cover at once.

Grape Jelly

6 lb. grapes
Juice of 2 lemons
1 quart water
Loaf sugar

Stalk and wash the grapes, put into the preserving pan with the water and bring slowly to the boil. Simmer until the fruit is a soft pulp, then turn into a hair sieve over a large bowl and allow the juice to drip through, stirring without squeezing. When dripping stops, add the juice of two lemons (for tartness) and for each pint of liquid allow ¾ lb. sugar. Put the juice in the preserving pan and boil quietly for 15 minutes. Add the sugar, stir until it dis-

solves and continue boiling until the liquid sets on testing. Pour into warm, dry jars, cover and store in the ordinary way.

Excellent as an alternative to Redcurrant or Crab Apple Jelly, or to "mask" an open fruit tart.

Loganberry Jelly

6 lb. loganberries　　1½ pints water
Sugar

Make in exactly the same way as blackcurrent jelly (see opposite page).

Quince Jelly

Make in the same way as apple jelly (see opposite), but remove the cores and pips before boiling the fruit.

Redcurrant Jelly

Make in exactly the same way as blackcurrant jelly (see opposite page).

MISCELLANEOUS RECIPES

Damson Cheese

Place the damsons in an earthenware pan. Sprinkle them with sugar to bring out the juice. Put them in the oven until quite soft, then rub through a hair sieve while still warm. Measure the pulp and add 1 lb. of sugar to every pint of pulp. Put the sugar and the pulp in a preserving pan and boil gently until it will set when tested. Pour into jars and cover when cold.

Lemon Curd

6 lemons
6 eggs
6 oz. butter
12 oz. castor sugar

Place the butter in a 7-lb. stone jam jar and stand it on the fire in a saucepan a quarter full of boiling water. Sieve the sugar on to a piece of paper. Grate the yellow part of the lemon rind on to a plate. Squeeze the lemon juice into a small basin. Beat the eggs together in another basin. When the butter is melted, add the sugar,

FOND OF WELSH RAREBIT?

Here's a tip to make the cheese go further, and taste creamier too, from the experimental kitchen of Brown & Polson Ltd.

Melt 1 oz. butter, stir in 1 teaspoonful cornflour, add ½ teacupful milk, grated cheese and seasoning. Stir over gentle heat till smooth and thick.

then the lemon juice and rind and, finally, the eggs. Stir continuously over the boiling water until the mixture becomes thick (20–30 minutes). Pour into jars and tie down as soon as it is cold.

Orange Curd

This is made in exactly the same way as lemon curd, using 4 sweet oranges and 2 lemons or Seville oranges. If made with sweet oranges alone, it is apt to be rather sickly.

Mincemeat

1 lb. suet	1 lb. castor sugar
1 lb. raisins	4 oz. candied peel
1 lb. sultanas	1 lemon
1 lb. currants	1 teaspoonful salt
1 lb. apples (peeled	Cinnamon
and cored)	Nutmeg
1 gill rum or brandy	

Chop the suet very finely and put in a basin. Stone the raisins, chop them finely with the apples, sultanas, currants and peel, and add them, with the sugar, to the suet. Add the grated lemon rind and strain in half the juice. Lastly, add the brandy, salt and spices and stir the whole mixture thoroughly. Tie a piece of greaseproof paper over the basin and put it away for a few days. Then give the mincemeat another good stir and put it into jam jars, tie down the covers and store in a cool, dry place.

MARMALADE MAKING

Marmalade can be made very successfully and economically at home. Seville oranges can be bought in the U.K. from the beginning of January until the beginning of March. February is the best month to make marmalade, as the fruit is then at its best and cheapest.

For those who find the cutting up by hand too laborious, a special cutter is obtainable, but with practice one can do it very quickly by hand. The secret is to have a very sharp knife to begin with and to sharpen it from time to time.

Grapefruit Marmalade

3 grapefruit	1 sweet orange
3 lemons	6 lb. sugar
6½ pints water	

Boil the grapefruit whole for 2 hours in 6 pints of water, take out and allow to cool. Cut the lemons and orange in half and scoop out the insides. Break them up well and put to soak in the water the grapefruit was boiled in. Put the pips to soak separately in ½ pint of water. Peel the grapefruit and slice the peel very finely. Break up the insides and put in a separate basin from the other fruit, keeping out the pips, which are added to the lemon and orange pips.

Next day, add the grapefruit, and the water the pips were soaked in, to the other fruit and water. Bring to the boil and boil sharply for 10 minutes. Then add the sugar, heat gently until the sugar is dissolved, stirring all the time, then boil quickly until the juice will set in a jelly when tested. Skim if necessary, pour into warm, dry jars and tie down at once.

Ginger Marmalade

2 lb. crystallised	4 lb. sugar
ginger	1 teaspoonful ground
3 pints water	ginger

Chop the ginger up into small pieces. Boil sugar and water to syrup, add ground and crystallised ginger, and boil until it will set when tested. Put into warmed pots and cover at once.

Lemon Marmalade

Use equal weights of lemons and sugar. Wash and cut lemons in half, squeezing the juice and putting it on one side. Put pips in a little cold water. Peel lemons and cover the peel in the preserving pan with cold water. Cook until peel is tender, remove from heat, cut off the pith and slice the peel thinly. Put sugar, juice and water in which the pips have soaked into the pan and boil to a syrup. Add lemon peel and boil until it will set to a jelly when tested. Leave to cool and then cover.

Orange Marmalade (1)

Slice Seville oranges very thinly, taking out only the pips. To each 1 lb. of sliced fruit add 3 pints of cold water, and let this stand for 24 hours.

Then boil until the peel is quite tender and allow to stand until the next day. Weigh, and to every 1 lb. of fruit add 1 lb. sugar. Boil the whole until it is clear, skimming if necessary. Let it stand for a little while before pouring it into warm, dry jars. Tie down at once.

The ever popular Piccalilli is particularly tasty when home-made from your own garden produce—or you can pickle the various vegetables separately

Orange Marmalade (2)

12 *Seville oranges*	12 *pints cold water*
2 *lemons*	12 *lb. sugar*

Peel the oranges and lemons; break up the insides into a large basin, taking out the pips and putting them into a small basin. Slice the peel as finely as possible and add to the large basin. Next, add the water, keeping back ½ pint which is poured over the pips. Let all stand for 24 hours. Strain the water from the pips through muslin and add it to the fruit. Boil the fruit for about 2½ hours until the peel is quite tender. Then add the sugar and let it dissolve, stirring all the time. Boil quickly until the juice is clear and will set into a good jelly. Skim, if necessary. Pour into warm, dry jars and tie down at once.

NOTE: To make a more bitter marmalade, put the pips in a muslin bag, bruise them well with a hammer and boil them with the fruit until the sugar is added. The peel should be cut rather more coarsely than for ordinary marmalade.

Orange Marmalade (3) (Quick Method)

5 *Seville oranges*	1 *lemon*
5 *pints boiling water*	6 *lb. sugar*

Cut oranges and lemon up small, removing pips and putting them into a muslin bag, and cover with the boiling water. Tie the bag containing the pips with string and put into the pan with the fruit. Boil hard until fruit is thoroughly tender. Remove pan from heat, take out pips, and add sugar. Bring to the boil and cook steadily until a little of the marmalade tested on a cold plate sets—probably about 1½ hours, according to how much the fruit was cooked first and how fast it has been boiling.

Tangerine Marmalade

12 *tangerines*	*Sugar*
3 *lemons*	*Water*

Remove the lemon rinds and slice up the insides. Pare the tangerines and shred the peel, then slice the insides and put them into a basin with the shredded peel and the insides of the lemons. Cover the fruit with cold water, allowing 2½ pints to every 1 lb. of fruit, and let it soak for 24 hours. Put all the pips in a separate basin with a little water. The next day, strain them and add the liquid to the fruit and water. Boil the mixture for ½ hour and let it stand again for 24 hours. Then add the sugar, allowing ¾ lb. to every pint of pulp. Dissolve the sugar slowly, stirring well, and then boil quickly until the juice will set into a jelly when tested. Skim and pour into warm, dry jars. Tie down at once.

PICKLES AND CHUTNEY

These are very easy to make at home. Jars with screw tops, such as are used for bottling fruit, are excellent for storing pickles and chutney, but ordinary jam jars can, of course, be used.

Apple Chutney

6 lb. peeled and cored apples	3 oz. mustard seeds
3 lb. sultanas	3 lb. shallots
4½ lb. Demerara sugar	1 tablespoonful salt
	¾ oz. Cayenne pepper
4½ pints vinegar	

Chop the apples and shallots. Place all the ingredients in a pan together and boil until thick, about 2 hours. Pour the mixture into warm, dry jars and fix down the tops at once.

Green Gooseberry Chutney

2 pints gooseberries	2 pints vinegar
3 medium-sized onions	8 oz. brown sugar
12 oz. raisins	2 tablespoonfuls ground ginger
1 saltspoonful red pepper	A little salt
	A little mustard seed

Top and tail and chop the gooseberries; also chop onions and raisins, and place in a pan with all the dry ingredients. Mix well together. Add the vinegar and simmer for about 1 hour. Pour into warm, dry jars and screw the tops down immediately.

Green Tomato Chutney

3 lb. tomatoes	1 lb. sultanas
4 oz. mustard	2 tablespoonfuls salt
3 lb. apples	1 teaspoonful Cayenne pepper
1½ lb. moist sugar	
2 quarts vinegar	2 teaspoonfuls white pepper
3 lb. onions	

Skin the tomatoes and peel and core the apples, and chop them up finely with the onions. Place in a preserving pan with the sultanas and 1½ quarts of vinegar and boil until quite soft. Then mix the mustard with the rest of the vinegar and add it to the tomatoes, etc., with the sugar, salt and pepper. Boil until the mixture will set like jam. Pour into warm, dry jars and screw down the tops at once.

NOTE: To skin tomatoes easily, plunge them into boiling water for 2 or 3 minutes then peel with a sharp knife.

Marrow Chutney

8 lb. ripe marrow	2 oz. turmeric
2 quarts vinegar	A little ground ginger
8 chillies	2 oz. mustard
12 shallots	12 oz. loaf sugar
Salt	

Peel and cut the marrow into small cubes. Cover with salt and leave overnight. Boil the vinegar, sugar, turmeric, chillies and shallots for ¼ hour. Add the marrow, first draining off the salt, and boil until very soft. Add the ground ginger and, finally, the mustard mixed with a little cold vinegar. Put into warm, dry jars and fasten down.

Tomato Chutney

3 lb. ripe tomatoes	2 lb. small onions
3 lb. peeled and cored apples	2 teaspoonfuls Cayenne pepper
1½ lb. sultanas	4 teaspoonfuls salt
1½ lb. raisins	24 cloves
2 lb. brown sugar	16 chillies
4 pints vinegar	

Place the tomatoes in hot water and remove the skins. Chop up finely the tomatoes, apples, raisins and onions. Put all the ingredients, except the vinegar, into a pan and simmer for ½ hour. Add the vinegar and simmer for 3 hours. Pour the mixture into warm, dry jars and cover at once.

Piccalilli

Cauliflower		1 oz. flour
Cucumber	4 lb.	1 quart vinegar
Button onions		1 oz. turmeric
French beans		1 oz. mustard
4 chillies		2 oz. loaf sugar
A little ground ginger		Salt

Prepare 4 lb. of vegetables. The cauliflower should be broken up into small branches, using only the flower. Choose small beans and string them only. Peel the onions but leave them whole. Peel the cucumber and cut it into good-sized pieces. Spread all the vegetables out on a large dish, sprinkle with salt and stand for 24 hours. Drain well and leave to dry. Mix the mustard and flour to a smooth paste with a little of the vinegar. Put the rest of the vinegar on to boil with the turmeric, chillies, sugar and ground ginger. Then add the mustard paste, stirring it well. When it boils, put in all the vegetables and boil gently for about 5 minutes. When cool, bottle the piccalilli, and tie down when cold.

Pickled Beetroot

Cook the beetroots and, when cold, cut them into thin, round slices. Place in jars and pour over them spiced vinegar.

For the spiced vinegar, allow $\frac{1}{4}$ oz. each of cinnamon, cloves, mace and allspice, and a few peppercorns to a quart of vinegar.

Pickled Cauliflowers

Cauliflowers   *Mace*
Vinegar   *Peppercorns*

Break the cauliflowers into sprigs and put into a pan of strongly salted water. Leave to soak all night. The next day, boil them in the salted water for 5–10 minutes. Drain, and put aside to cool. When cold, place in the jars.

Boil the vinegar, mace and peppercorns together, allowing $\frac{1}{4}$ oz. mace and $\frac{1}{4}$ oz. peppercorns to every quart of vinegar. Strain the liquid and pour it over the cauliflowers. When quite cold, screw down the tops of the jars.

Pickled Cherries

3 *quarts cherries*
    (whole, firm, tart
    cherries, not stoned)
1½ *pints vinegar*
½ *cupful brown sugar*
1 *tablespoonful whole*
    cloves
4 *blades of mace*

Stir the sugar, cloves and mace into the vinegar and bring it to the boil. Boil for 5 minutes and leave to cool. Place the washed cherries in the jars. Strain the vinegar, etc., when cold, and pour it over the cherries, filling the jars to the brim. Screw down the tops of the jars.

Pickled Mushrooms

Use small button mushrooms. Rub each mushroom with salt, and put in a jar. Boil sufficient vinegar, with a little pickling spice, to cover the mushrooms. Let it cool, then strain it and pour over the mushrooms. Cover the jar and let it stand for a fortnight, when the mushrooms will be ready to eat.

Pickled Red Cabbage

1 *large red cabbage*   1 *oz. whole black*
Salt   *peppercorns*
2½ *quarts vinegar*   *Saltspoonful Cayenne*
½ *oz. whole ginger*   *pepper*
    (bruised)

Take off the outer leaves of the cabbage, cut it into four, remove the thick stalks, cut into thin slices and spread on a large dish. Sprinkle with salt, cover with another dish and leave for 24 hours.

Drain in a colander and pack the cabbage into screw-top jars.

Boil the vinegar with the spices and pepper, and strain it. Let it cool. When cold, pour over the cabbage. Screw up the jars. Let it stand for at least a fortnight before it is used.

NOTE: If kept too long, the cabbage becomes discoloured and soft.

PUDDINGS TAKE WINGS...

Baked and steamed sponges are extra light if you replace I tablespoonful of the flour in the recipe with I tablespoonful cornflour. The same goes for cakes and biscuits if you want them to have a lovely, light, melt-in-the-mouth texture. Tested at the experimental kitchen of Brown & Polson Ltd.

Pickled Walnuts

Use green walnuts and test each one with a needle, removing any that have begun to form shells. Put into brine, made with $\frac{3}{4}$ lb. salt to every quart of water, for 9 days, changing the brine every third day. Drain, place on a dish and put into the sun until they turn black, then put into dry jars.

To every quart of vinegar allow 2 oz. peppercorns, 1 oz. allspice and bruised ginger. Simmer together for 10 minutes, strain, then pour hot over the walnuts. Tie down.

FRUIT BOTTLING

A simple, easy way to enjoy summer fruits in the depth of winter—and to take full advantage of your own garden crops

THE bottling or "sterilising" of fruit for the store cupboard is a simple process provided certain rules are followed. There are three main types of container suitable for the purpose:

(1) Vacuum jars with rubber rings, glass lids and metal screw caps.

(2) Vacuum jars with metal tops, rubber bands and clips.

(3) Ordinary jam jars sealed by metal snap closures, fitted with rubber bands, with clips to keep the closures in place; or by plastic skin which is available to fit any sized jar.

Fruit can be sterilised either in the oven or on the hot-plate. In either process the following points should be borne in mind:

(1) Use only perfectly clean, sound bottles —chipped or cracked ones should be discarded.

(2) Rubber bands should be pliable and fit tightly; if very stiff, put them in warm water for 15 minutes to soften. Never use bands that have been stretched and are beginning to perish and lose their shape.

(3) Metal screw tops or lids must not be rusty.

(4) Use only sound, just-ripe fruit picked when dry and pack it as tightly as possible into the bottles without bruising it. It shrinks in cooking, so have a spare jar from which to fill up the others. Hard fruit should be washed in cold water and then drained. Soft fruit should be handled carefully; put it into a colander and hold it under the cold tap with just a trickle of water flowing over it. Large fruit (pears and plums) may be cut in half.

(5) Fruit can be bottled either in plain water or sugar syrup. Sugar syrup undoubtedly gives more flavour and preserves the colour better. *To make the syrup.*—Bring 1 lb. sugar and 1 quart of water to the boil, cook for a few minutes, then skim. Use either hot or cold as directed.

(6) Never put hot bottles down on a cold

surface or they may crack and even break.

7) Leave the bottles undisturbed for 24 hours, then test to make sure the vacuum is perfect. Remove the screw or clip and lift the bottle by the glass lid only. If it holds, the jar is sealed; if the lid comes away, the jar must either be re-sterilised or the fruit eaten quickly.

8) Before storing your bottled fruit away in a cool, dry place, remove the screw caps, if used, and smear the insides lightly with Vaseline, then put back loosely.

The Hot-plate Method

For this you need a deep vessel, preferably with a lid of some kind and a false bottom on which to stand the bottles so that they do not come into direct contact with the heat. Thin pieces of wood nailed together do very well, or you can use a thick layer of old rags or an old blanket. Be careful to see that the bottles do not touch each other.

Fill your bottles with the fruit, then add the covering liquid *cold*, filling to the brim. Put on the rubber rings, lids and screw caps or clips. If screw caps are used tighten them, then give them a half-turn back. Otherwise, when the glass expands during the heating process, it may crack.

Stand the bottles on the false bottom, fill the vessel with cold water to cover them

For the hot-plate method, stand the bottles in a large deep vessel with a false bottom and cover the fruit with cold water or syrup

completely, put on the lid and bring the water very slowly to the required temperature (see next page). If you have no thermometer, bring the water up very slowly to a gentle simmer—it should on no account boil—and keep at that temperature for the time given in the table on the next page.

Remove the bottles one by one—it is best to bale out some of the water first as it is easier then to get hold of the bottles—and if screw caps are used tighten them at once.

Soft fruits need gentle handling to avoid damage. Remove red or black currants from their stalks with a fork

Apples, apricots, blackberries, damsons, gooseberries, loganberries, raspberries, rhubarb:

Bring the temperature up slowly to 165° F. in 1½ hours and maintain at this temperature for 10 minutes.

Black or red currants, cherries, plums, peaches:

Bring the temperature up slowly to 180° F. in 1½ hours and maintain at this temperature for 15 minutes.

Pears, quinces, tomatoes:

Bring the temperature up slowly to 190° F. in 1½ hours and maintain at this temperature for 30 minutes.

The Oven Method

The oven temperature should be round about 200–220° F. Fill the bottles with the fruit, but do not add any liquid. Cover them with their own lids or patty pans to prevent the fruit on the top from discolouring, then stand them on a piece of stiff cardboard in the oven. Do not let them touch each other.

When the fruit shrinks and the juice begins to flow, it is cooked sufficiently. Rhubarb, gooseberries, raspberries, logan berries, etc., will take about 45 minutes; plums, tomatoes, pears and quinces as long as 1½ hours or more; cherries, apricots, currants, peaches, damsons, etc., about 1–1½ hours.

Have ready the covering liquid (either water or sugar syrup) brought to boiling point and maintained at this temperature while you remove the bottles from the oven. Take out one at a time, remove the lid, add extra fruit from spare bottle if necessary, and fill to overflowing with the boiling liquid. Put on the rubber ring, lid and screw cap or clip. Be as quick as you can in filling and covering the bottles so as to make sure you get a vacuum.

Bottling with Preserving Tablets

This is a particularly suitable method for fruits that are peeled before bottling, such as apples and pears. The fruit is covered with cold water, the instructions on the packet should be carefully followed and, when the fruit is opened, it should be put, with the liquid, into an uncovered saucepan and boiled hard for a few minutes to remove the chemical.

Fruit Bottling in a Pressure Cooker

This is a very quick and easy way. (See Pressure Cookery chapter.)

Bottling Tomatoes

Tomatoes can be bottled most successfully in the same way as other fruit, but to get the full flavour, no liquid at all should be added. If liked, the tomatoes can first be skinned, after being well washed (plunging them into boiling water for a minute will loosen the skins). Sprinkle between the layers ¼ oz. salt to each 2 lb. tomatoes and, if liked, a teaspoonful of sugar. Press the tomatoes well down with the handle of a wooden spoon, then put on the rubber bands, etc., and proceed as for the hotplate method. Bring the water round the bottles up to 190° F. in 1½ hours and keep at this temperature for 30 minutes.

Watch for Fermentation

Watch for fermentation, a sign that some form of bacteria is active. The signs of this are discoloration of the fruit, small bubbles and a distinctive taste rather like vinegar; the liquid will probably have begun to ooze from the bottle. The reason for fermentation is insufficient sterilising, so make a point never to try to hasten the process. It is advisable not to eat fermented fruit even if the vinegary taste is only very slight.

If you should find traces of mould on the top of bottled fruit, it is an indication that spores from the air have somehow found their way in while the fruit was cooling. To prevent this, see that the bottles are sealed quickly. Usually the mould can be removed easily and the contents are not affected, provided it is detected early.

Vegetable Bottling

The bottling of vegetables is a more difficult process than that of fruit, on account of the difference in their chemical composition. The acid contained in fruit actually helps the sterilising process, while in vegetables there is little or no acid present. Also, vegetables contain soil bacteria which are very resistant to heat, so that even if heated to boiling point and maintained at that temperature for 2 hours the spores may not be killed and, if the vegetables are stored for some time, may cause decomposition. So it is safer not to bottle vegetables.

USING UP LEFT-OVERS

*"Waste not, want not" is sound advice, but how to make the odd
scraps in the larder really appetising . . . ? Here are some ideas*

EVERY larder has its
left-overs, and every
cook her headache
thinking up ways of
using them. Here are
some ideas: others will
be found in the chapter
on Cold Meat and
Made-up Dishes.

MEAT

Savoury Mince

Remove the remains
of the joint from its
bone and put through
mincer. Season well,
moisten with gravy and
add any, or all of the following: piece of bacon,
chopped; one or two
slices of tinned luncheon
meat cut in cubes; one
medium or two small
tomatoes, peeled and
chopped (or canned to-
mato or sauce or purée); one small, diced
onion and a pinch of powdered mace.

Cook slowly for about 30 minutes,
preferably in a covered casserole in the
oven or on top of a double boiler. Serve in
a ring of mashed potato or boiled rice.

Macaroni Mince

8 oz. minced cooked	Salt, pepper
meat	2 oz. grated cheese
½ pint stock	1 tablespoonful
8 oz. cooked	tomato purée
macaroni	

Put the macaroni and meat in a greased
pie dish. Sprinkle with grated cheese. Mix
stock, tomato purée, salt and pepper, and
pour over the meat and macaroni. Cook
for 15 minutes in a hot oven.

A Quick Supper Dish

½ lb. chopped cooked	1 small can peas
meat	6 oz. quick-cooking
1 onion	macaroni
1 apple	1 dessertspoonful
Salt, pepper	Tarragon vinegar
Fat for frying	

Diced cold meat takes on a new lease of life set in aspic
jelly with a few peas and egg slices for colour

Cook the macaroni and drain well.
Slice onion and apple, and fry in the fat
for 5 minutes. Add peas, vinegar, salt,
pepper, meat and macaroni. Simmer for
10–15 minutes.

Jellied Meat

Cut up meat into cubes and place in
shallow dish. Make up packet aspic jelly
according to instructions, pour over meat
and set in moulds. When cold, turn them
out and serve on a bed of salad. Sliced,
hard-boiled egg and/or left-over cooked
vegetables may be added to meat before
setting in jelly. A few green peas or a
sliced tomato add colour as well as flavour.

Meat in Batter

To make slices of a left-over joint go
farther, dip in batter, drop into boiling fat
and fry quickly on both sides. Drain,
season and serve with a freshly cooked
green vegetable or green salad.

343

Meat on Toast

A little left-over meat goes a long way if diced and stirred into a good thick, white sauce, well seasoned (see Sauces chapter). Serve on rounds of toast with grilled tomatoes or mushrooms as a supper dish.

VEGETABLES

Bubble and Squeak

Mix together equal quantities of cold, cooked, mashed potatoes and cold, cooked, chopped cabbage. Add salt and pepper. Heat a little bacon fat, put the mixture into it, smooth down and cook gently. When the underneath is brown, turn carefully and brown the other side. Be sure it is heated right through.

You will never have left-over mashed potato if you cook it as follows:

Baked Potato Puff (for 6)

6 medium-sized potatoes	1 teaspoonful baking powder
3 tablespoonfuls butter	1 shallot, finely minced
1 egg	2 tablespoonfuls fresh parsley, finely minced
3 tablespoonfuls milk	
½ teaspoonful salt	

Boil potatoes, preferably unpeeled, in enough water to cover. Drain and dry thoroughly. Peel and mash potatoes. Add remaining ingredients and beat until creamy. Pile into a well-buttered baking dish. Bake 30 minutes in a moderate oven or until puffy and brown. Serve while hot.

Curried Vegetables

1 apple	½ oz. rice flour
1 onion	Curry powder to taste
A squeeze of lemon juice	Salt
1 teaspoonful chopped chutney	Cold potatoes, carrots, turnips, green peas, parsnips, etc., cut up small if necessary
½ pint vegetable stock	
1 oz. butter	

Fry the onion and the apple, sliced, in the hot butter until brown. Add the rice flour, curry powder and salt, stirring well, and cook for 5 minutes. Stir in the stock, and bring to the boil. Put the cold vegetables in, add the chopped chutney and re-heat. Remove from the fire and add a squeeze of lemon juice last thing.

NOTE: If uncooked vegetables are used, cook them all together first and use the vegetable water instead of stock to make the curry. Then add the vegetables as already described above.

Macédoine of Vegetables makes a tasty savoury served on toast. Mask any cold cooked vegetables in velouté sauce and top with parsley

Serve Baked Potato Puff piping hot and straight from the oven in its baking dish—it's a sure family favourite

Macédoine of Vegetables

*Cold carrots, green
    peas, turnips,
    parsnips, cut into
    small pieces
½ pint velouté sauce
    (see Sauces chapter)
    or mayonnaise
    sauce (see Salads
    chapter)*

Make a thin velouté sauce and warm the vegetables in it, or serve cold in mayonnaise sauce.

Parsnip or Artichoke Balls

Mash cold boiled parsnips or artichokes, season with salt and pepper, moisten with a little milk. Make into small round cakes, roll in flour and fry in a little butter until brown.

Parsnips (Fried)

Cut cold, boiled young parsnips into slices lengthways. Fry in a little butter until light brown, and sprinkle with pepper and salt.

Roman Pie (for 3)

*4 oz. short pastry
½–1 oz. cooked
    macaroni
1 chopped tomato
½ gill cheese sauce
    (see Sauces chapter)*

*6 oz. mixed vege-
    tables
1 chopped mushroom
1 dessertspoonful
    grated onion
Brown breadcrumbs*

As an alternative to Bubble and Squeak, fry up cold potatoes with a little chopped parsley for a change

Line with the pastry a 5-in. cake tin which has been greased and coated with brown breadcrumbs, saving enough pastry to make a lid. Fill with layers of vegetables, sauce and macaroni, and cover with the lid. Bake in moderate oven for 40–45 minutes.

PUDDINGS

Using Up Cold Sweets

Enough for several helpings can be made out of the remains of baked custard puddings, plain jellies, blancmange and trifle by adding fruit. Use fruits such as dates, stoned and chopped, sliced banana, raisins and cooked prunes, stoned and chopped. Carefully break up the pudding and mix in the fruit, fill into individual glasses and top with whipped cream or evaporated milk.

Oddments of stewed or canned fruit, if fairly firm, can be used up in a freshly made steamed sponge pudding. The fruit should be *well* drained of syrup to make it as dry as possible, and cut into small uniform pieces.

If the fruit is on the mushy side, press through a hair sieve and set in a plain fruit jelly or use for a mousse.

The oddment of rice pudding could be incorporated into a similar pudding on the lines of the following recipe, reducing the amount of macaroni proportionately and using a little less sugar. Break up the cold rice pudding finely, moistening with a little milk if stiff, and mix with the macaroni or beat it up with the eggs.

Macaroni Custard Pudding

4 oz. cooked macaroni 2 eggs
Grated rind of ½ 1 tablespoonful
  lemon sugar
  1 pint of milk

Put macaroni in greased pie dish, beat eggs, and add sugar and milk. Scatter the lemon rind on the macaroni, pour over the milk and bake in moderate oven until top browns and custard has set.

Using Up Boiled Puddings

Sponge puddings and Christmas or other fruit puddings can be made fit to appear at another meal, as follows: Break up pudding in a basin, moisten with a little milk and mix well with a fork. If the pudding was first baked with a jam, syrup or other topping, see that this is well mixed through to distribute the flavour, add a handful of raisins and/or currants, if liked. Grease individual moulds or tiny basins, fill with the pudding, tie down with paper and steam for about 1 hour.

Suet pudding left-overs are good used up in this way: Slice pudding ¼ in. thick in small rounds or other shapes with pastry cutters, and fry in butter or good margarine. Drain and sprinkle with sugar before serving.

CAKES

Stale fruit or ginger cakes can be turned into individual fruit puddings if prepared in the same way as for left-over sponge puddings described above. No extra fruit should be necessary, but some finely chopped almonds or walnuts might be added to give extra flavour. To a ginger cake, add a little Golden Syrup or treacle.

Pieces of sandwich cake, filled or unfilled, and remnants of sponge cake make an even more delicious trifle than the more usual sponge fingers from a confectioner. Cut cake into thin fingers and stick any unjammed pieces together with fresh jam.

Lay in a glass dish, and if you have one or two stale macaroon biscuits, crumble and scatter over cake, or sprinkle over a little ground almond if you can spare it. Moisten with sherry, if possible, and pour over custard. A more elaborate trifle should be topped with whipped cream and include ratafia biscuits.

EGG-WHITES AND YOLKS

When a recipe calls for egg-whites or yolks only, the remainder sometimes presents a problem. The following suggestions provide ideas for using them up.

Whites, Sweetened

Meringues.—The obvious answer is: make meringues! These are handy as well as delicious, because they can be stored in an airtight tin. Put waxed paper between each layer and use with whipped cream or individual blocks of ice cream between the halves. For success, cook in a *really* slow oven, 200° F. or gas setting at ¼, for about 1½ hours. (See Puddings, page 138.)

Apple Snow.—One pound of cooking apples are washed, roughly cut up but not peeled or cored (just the damaged or bruised parts being removed), and cooked to a pulp with no more than about a tablespoonful of water. When soft enough, rub through a sieve. Stir in one stiffly whipped egg-white and Golden Syrup or sugar and lemon juice, as liked. (NOTE: Only very sour apples need sugar when cooked this way.)

Coconut Pyramids.—Fold approximately 2 oz. desiccated coconut and castor sugar (according to how much egg is sweetened) to each egg-white. Place small peaked heaps on rice paper in a baking tin and bake in a moderate oven for 10 minutes.

Supper Dish.—Beat together 1 egg-white, 1 grated sour apple and 3 oz. castor sugar. Use just as it is, uncooked, on crackers or other plain biscuits, or spread on thin pre-cooked pastry fingers and cook gently in the oven for about 10 minutes.

You can add a party touch to an open jam tart, fruit flan or baked custard pudding by using the egg-whites, beaten, to cover the top. Gently brown under the grill or in the oven.

Whites, Unsweetened

Cheese Puffs.—Season stiffly beaten egg-white with salt and pepper, fold in two tablespoonfuls finely grated hard cheese. Bake as for Coconut Pyramids; alternatively, drop dessertspoonfuls into smoking hot fat and fry until golden. Drain well and eat warm.

Yolks

Yolks only are needed for egg-and-breadcrumbing, and if 2 teaspoonfuls oil are added to each yolk, well beaten in, to mix thoroughly, the coating that results is light and fluffy.

An egg-yolk can very well be added to every $\frac{1}{2}$ lb. flour when making shortcrust pastry. If using plain flour, add $\frac{1}{4}$ teaspoonful baking powder for each yolk.

An egg-yolk can also be worked into mashed potato, making it rather richer but extremely good.

Zabaglione.—This Italian sweet takes care of egg-yolks nicely. Allow $\frac{1}{2}$ oz. castor sugar and just over 2 tablespoonfuls Marsala wine or Madeira to each egg-yolk. Put yolks and sugar in a basin and beat until almost white and very light. Add wine and mix thoroughly. Pour into saucepan, put over quick heat and beat incessantly without boiling or thickening. The moment it rises, remove pan, pour into warmed glasses and serve *immediately*.

NOTE: **Yolks** keep in good condition for several days if beaten up with 1 teaspoonful cold water to each yolk. **Whites,** for all purposes, must be beaten to a stiff froth to give successful results. Use an egg whisk rather than a rotary beater. Start slowly and steadily until whites become a loose globular mass, then a little quicker until globules close up, then as quickly as possible, but always steadily, until the consistency looks like whipped cream, and a mass comes away with the beater without a drop falling.

One or two egg-whites left over? Make some meringues and fill them with whipped or ice cream for a tea-time treat. If there are any left, they keep well in a tin

STALE BREAD

After parties, Christmas, any time of extra catering, bread is a frequent left-over, and sometimes bread and butter.

Breadcrumbs

Now is the time to cut off the crusts, dry and brown them in the oven, roll them fine with a rolling pin and store in an airtight tin for breadcrumbing. A mixture of brown and white bread crusts makes a good breadcrumb.

Plan a meal starting with soup and use some of the bread for fried croûtons to go with it.

A soup that will help use up the remains of a loaf is:

Onion Soup, French Style (for 6–8)

1 lb. chopped onions	2 oz. butter or margarine
1 teaspoonful curry powder	2 pints hot water
1 tablespoonful meat extract	6–8 slices buttered bread
3–4 oz. grated cheese	Salt and pepper

Cook onions and curry gently in margarine with the lid on till soft (about 15–20 minutes). Add hot water and meat extract. Simmer 5 minutes or till onion is quite tender. Season. Sprinkle cheese on bread, brown under the grill. Cut and put three or four small pieces in each serving of soup.

Supper Dish

Grease a pie dish, fill with alternate layers of breadcrumbs, grated cheese and sliced tomato, seasoning each layer. Moisten carefully with milk but do not make the mixture wet. Top with grated cheese and browned crumbs, add dots of butter or margarine, and cook for half an hour in a medium oven.

Hot or Cold Sweet (also uses up egg-yolks)

Soak 2 teacupfuls breadcrumbs in 1½ pints boiling milk, add 2 oz. castor sugar, grated rind and juice of half a lemon or orange. Mix lightly, adding egg-yolk if available, and bake in a gentle oven for about 30 minutes.

Left-over bread and butter makes a delicious crispy topping on a baked custard pudding, and can also be used up in an apple charlotte. For the former, place carefully on top of liquid, butter side up, and scatter with sugar before baking. For the charlotte, line dish with the pieces, butter side down, follow with alternate layers of apple and bread and butter, finishing with a topping of bread and butter. Sprinkle sugar, grated lemon rind or nutmeg, and dots of butter between layers.

And of course there is always that delightful sweet, Bread and Butter Pudding (see Puddings chapter), which uses up milk and an egg as well. If made with stale bun loaf, no sultanas are needed.

There is no difficulty in eating up left-over sandwiches if they are put under the grill, toasted on both sides and eaten hot. Watercress is good with these.

MILK

Too much milk in the larder can be introduced into some soups, substituting milk for part of the quantity of water. When using canned soup, thin the contents of each can with a further canful of milk. And here are two unusual milk recipes:

Cream of Corn Soup

Put 5 cupfuls fresh or canned corn in a double boiler with a peeled onion and 2½ cupfuls milk. Cook until both are soft, then put all through a sieve. Heat 2 tablespoonfuls butter and stir in the same amount of flour and 2½ cupfuls milk, less 2 tablespoonfuls. Season with pepper and salt, stir until boiling. Cook for 5 minutes, add corn purée and bring to boil. Draw to side of stove, add 2 egg-yolks beaten in the 2 tablespoonfuls of milk, whisk well and serve very hot.

Almond Milk Soup

Put 2 pints milk in a saucepan with 2 oz. ground sweet almonds and 1 teaspoonful ground bitter almonds, 1 tablespoonful sugar and a pinch of salt. Bring to boil and simmer gently until well blended. Mix 1 tablespoonful flour to a smooth paste with a little cold milk and gradually stir in boiled milk. Return to saucepan and bring to boil, stirring all the time. Boil gently for a few minutes longer and serve.

To encourage the drinking of left-over milk, give it a fillip, such as 1 teaspoonful Virol or Marmite to ½ pint warm milk. A drop or two of flavouring essence, vanilla, almond, banana, coconut, etc., to ½ pint, well whisked with a rotary beater, a little

Quick and easy to make and an excellent way of using up an egg-white left over from some
other recipe—Coconut Pyramids are popular tea-time favourites

sugar added if necessary, makes a milk shake that pleases children.

Sour milk, of course, helps to make excellent scones, and a very good home-made cream cheese. To do this, place a piece of fine linen in a basin, pour in the milk, pick up the corners of the linen and tie round with string, finishing the string off in a loop. Hang the milk directly over the basin and leave to drip until the next day. Season the resulting curds with pepper and salt and chopped chives, if liked, and pat into a neat shape.

PASTRY

Those oddments of paste left over from tart and flan-making can be finished up as follows: press together and roll out into as large a sheet as possible. Spread butter over one half and sprinkle thickly either with brown sugar or grated cheese. Fold over other half and pinch edges together neatly. Milk or egg the top and mark into thin finger-lengths before baking. Six, eight or more sweet or savoury fingers can be made for nibbling this way. The left-overs are also useful if rolled out and cut into plain fingers and small shapes, baked and stored in a tin: pleasant to eat with

cheese or as a basis for cocktail snacks. They may be warmed in the oven and allowed to cool, to crisp them before use if this is necessary.

NOTE: Uncooked pastry will keep for a week or more wrapped in a polythene bag in a refrigerator, ready for use when wanted

JAMS

A spoonful or two of jam left in each of several jars is the sort of left-over that never seems to be finished up. One sure way is to blend them together and fill into individual pastry tartlet cases. Orange marmalade can be included—it adds interest to the flavour—and any large pieces of peel can be chopped into small bits first. Bitter marmalade is not recommended, but oddments of jelly marmalade and other fruit jellies are all usable in this way.

Oddments of jams and jellies may be added to 1 pint water, brought to the boil and boiled gently until dissolved by stirring. The liquid should be strained through a hair sieve or fine linen, and can then be used as a basis for fruit drinks, adding bottled lemon, lime or orange juice or barley water, and soda water if liked.

DICTIONARY OF
COOKERY TERMS

A brief guide to some of the commoner words
and phrases in the language of the culinary
art (see also chapter on Restaurant French)

ASPIC: Meat glaze or jelly.

AU GRATIN: Topping of breadcrumbs (*not* necessarily with cheese).

BAIN-MARIE: A pan of hot water in which a saucepan is stood to keep its contents nearly boiling.

BAKING: Cook in an oven. Meat and poultry usually at high temperature for 10–15 minutes to seal in juices; thereafter at reduced temperature with frequent basting.

BARDING: The process of covering the breast of poultry or game with strips of fat bacon, tied in position, to add flavour and juiciness. Bacon is removed about 10 minutes before serving and the flesh frequently basted to brown.

BASTING: When roasting foods, particularly meat or poultry, keep them moist by frequently spooning over them the juice from the pan.

BÉCHAMEL: The famous white sauce with foundation of milk or cream; the foundation of other sauces (see Sauces).

BINDING: To add sufficient liquid (usually eggs, milk or water) to make a mixture hold together.

BLANCHING: A method used to improve colour or reduce strong flavour of foodstuffs, facilitate cooking generally or as a help in cleansing or preparing vegetables. As a general rule, foodstuffs other than vegetables are placed in cold water and brought to the boil, then removed; vegetables are plunged into fast boiling salted water.

BLANQUETTE: A white stew, due to the white or pale-coloured flesh and sauce.

BOILING: A method of cooking food in liquid. Some foods are put into cold water and brought to the boil therein; others plunged into the water when it is boiling.

BOUILLON: Beef, veal or chicken stock.

BOUQUET GARNI: Herbs used for flavouring and removed before serving; either tied in a bunch or put in muslin bag. Where selection of herbs is not indicated, thyme, parsley and a bay leaf make a popular choice.

BRAISING: A method of stewing over a slow heat or in a slow oven in a vessel with close-fitting lid. Best results come from using the minimum of liquid in a utensil that holds the contents closely. Originally braising was done in iron pots on an open fire with hot coals piled on the lid to provide heat all round the pot. Hence modern braising is best done in an oven.

BROCHETTE: A savoury made by threading blended titbits (e.g. mushrooms and bacon) on a skewer and frying in butter.

BROILING: See Grilling.

CARAMELISE: To melt sugar slowly till it turns dark brown.

CASSEROLE: Glazed earthenware or ovenproof glass vessel. To cook in a casserole.

CLARIFYING: (1) *Butter*—put in small saucepan and warm over very low heat until froth rises and sinks, solidified, to bottom. Strain clear liquid butter through a thin cloth and it is ready for use. The object of this treatment is to remove impurities that might otherwise burn in cooking and appear as black specks. (2) *Other Fats*—bring to the boil with water, leave to cool, and remove fat and sediment. (3) *Soups*—when cold, put two egg-whites in a saucepan, beat lightly but not to a froth, add the crushed egg-shells and stock. Bring very slowly to boil, stirring and beating all the time. All scum rises to the surface on the boil and this should continue for about 15 minutes without stirring. Remove and strain soup into a basin through a jelly-bag.

CREAM: To work a mixture with a spoon or knife until it is smooth and creamy.

CROQUETTES: A method of serving minced, cooked meats or fish bound with sauce and formed into shapes, rolled in egg and breadcrumbs, and fried crisp.

CROÛTES, CROÛTADES: Large pieces of fried bread as a base on which to serve minced or other meats.

CROÛTONS: Small dice of bread fried and used to garnish or in soup.

DARIOLE: Minced meat entrée shaped in a mould—the name of such a mould; also small pastries.

DREDGE: To sift flour, etc., evenly over food.

ESPAGNOLE: The foundation brown sauce (Spanish) used as a base for other sauces; made with brown stock, vegetables and herbs, and white wine (see Sauces chapter).

FINES-HERBES: A mixture of finely chopped herbs.

FOLDING: Gently stirring in an ingredient without allowing the air to escape from the mixture. Cut downwards through the mixture with the spoon, run it across bottom of bowl, then up again so that part of the surface is folded under.

FRICASSÉE: A white stew of chicken or veal.

FRYING: There are two kinds: (1) deep frying, in which the food is completely covered with fat; (2) shallow frying (sauté), in which only a small quantity of fat is used. In either case, fat must be very hot, giving off a thin bluish smoke.

GALANTINE: A roll of cooked meat or boned poultry with a covering of its own jelly.

GLAZING: A garnish for a preparation such as galantine, or the sugar coating on cakes or buns. Meat glaze is made by reducing brown stock to the consistency of syrup and bottling in a glazing jar while still hot.

GNOCCHI: Small choux paste shapes flavoured with cheese and poached in boiling salted water.

GRILLING: A method, like roasting, of cooking food at a high temperature at first to seal, the time taken for cooking depending on the thickness of the meat, fish, etc. The grill should be pre-heated.

KNEADING: To work a dough by pressing it firmly with the hands.

LARDING: A method of adding flavour and juiciness to meat and poultry by "stitching" short, narrow strips of fat bacon through flesh in vertical rows, using a larding needle.

MACÉDOINE: A mixture of fruits or vegetables cut up in small dice.

MARINADE: See Marinating.

MARINATING: A method of preserving, flavouring or tenderising meat, in which it stands in a mixture of finely chopped flavouring vegetables, with wine and/or vinegar and oil. Meats for grilling are sometimes marinated for a short time by sprinkling with salt and pepper and moistening with oil and lemon juice.

MARMITE: A stew pot.

MASKING: A rich sauce covering meat, of which Béchamel is the base with grated Gruyère and Parmesan cheese added; or mayonnaise.

MULL: To warm ale or wine with spices and flavourings.

PANADA: A mixture of bread, flour or rice with milk, water or stock, boiled until thick and used with stuffing.

PARBOIL: To cook in boiling water until partially but not completely cooked.

POACHING: Cooking in hot liquid so as to keep shape.

POUND: To pulverise by beating.

PURÉE: Finely ground vegetables, fruit or other foodstuffs; obtained by pressing through a hair sieve with a wooden pestle made for the purpose.

RAGOÛT: A rich stew.

RAMEKINS: Small moulds for savouries.

RASP: To grate stale bread crusts.

RÉCHAUFFÉ: Indicates any dish reheated.

REDUCING: Evaporating moisture by fast boiling.

RENDERING: Fat is purified by slow heating so that it melts.

RISOTTO: A savoury rice dish served plain with grated cheese or with various additions, such as chicken giblets, mushrooms, etc.

ROASTING: Originally a method of cooking meat and poultry over or in front of a clear hot fire, on a spit or in a Dutch oven; close to the fire to begin with to form a thin crust quickly and seal in the juices, then drawn farther from heat for remainder of cooking: superseded by baking in the oven.

ROUX: Butter-and-flour thickening for sauces; may be termed (*a*) brown, (*b*) blond (or (*c*) white, the colour depending on the length of time the butter and flour are cooked and the type of sauce for which it is to be used.

SALMI: A stew of game.

SAUTÉ: See Frying.

SEASON: To add salt, pepper and other seasonings.

SEPARATE: To separate the white from the yolk of an egg.

SHORTENING: Fat, butter, margarine, vegetable fat, lard.

SHRED: Cut into thin strips.

SIMMERING: Often wrongly interpreted as slow boiling. Simmering liquid should show no more than a faint movement or ripple.

SOUSE: To cover with vinegar and spices.

STEAMING: For best results a steamer should be used, or, failing that, a double boiler. Specially recommended for invalid diet.

STEWING: See Braising.

STOCK: The base of many soups, sauces and stews. Stock in which meat for a main dish has been cooked or stock prepared primarily for soup-making is not necessarily gelatinous enough for sauces and aspic jellies, and for good results a separate stock is usually prepared for these items.

SWEAT: To heat very gently to get the full flavour.

TERRINE: A small earthenware pot used for potting meats.

TIMBALE: A mould; a pie baked in it.

VOL-au-VENT: Round puff pastry crust holding a savoury filling bound with sauce.

WEIGHTS AND MEASURES

THE inexperienced cook is wise to rely on accurate scales for good results. However, there comes a time when everyone may need an alternative to scales, and the following tables will be useful though only approximate.

Measurements by Cup

Liquid Measures

1 breakfast cup equals ½ pint or 2 gills.
1 tea cup equals ¼ pint or 1 gill.
1 wine glass equals ½ gill.

Solid Measures

1 breakfast cup, heaped, moist brown sugar equals ½ lb.
1 breakfast cup, rounded, granulated sugar equals ½ lb.
1 breakfast cup, level, castor sugar equals ½ lb.
1 breakfast cup, heaped, icing sugar equals ½ lb.
1 breakfast cup, level, rice equals ½ lb.

1 breakfast cup, heaped, lard, butter or fat equals ½ lb.

1 breakfast cup, heaped, chopped suet equals ¼ lb.

1 breakfast cup, level, stale breadcrumbs equals ¼ lb.

1 breakfast cup, heaped, sago, semolina, tapioca equals ½ lb.

1 breakfast cup, heaped, flour or cornflour equals ¼ lb.

1 breakfast cup, heaped, raisins or currants, equals ½ lb.

1 breakfast cup minced beef, pressed tightly, equals ½ lb.

Measurements by Spoon
Liquid Measures

1 teaspoonful equals 55 drops.

4 teaspoonfuls equals 1 tablespoonful.

3 tablespoonfuls equals 1 wine glass or ½ gill.

6 tablespoonfuls equals 1 tea cup or ¼ pint.

Solid Measures

1 tablespoonful, heaped, finely chopped suet equals 1 oz.

1 tablespoonful, heaped, flour or cornflour equals 1 oz.

2 tablespoonfuls, level, flour or cornflour equals 1 oz.

1 tablespoonful, heaped, moist brown sugar equals 1 oz.

1 tablespoonful, rounded, granulated sugar equals 1 oz.

1 tablespoonful, level, castor sugar equals 1 oz.

1 tablespoonful, heaped icing sugar equals 1 oz.

1 tablespoonful, level, rice equals 1 oz.

1 tablespoonful, heaped, sago, semolina, tapioca equals 1 oz.

1 tablespoonful, heaped, raisins, currants equals 1 oz.

1 tablespoonful, heaped, coffee equals ½ oz.

1 tablespoonful syrup or jam equals 2 oz.

2 tablespoonfuls melted butter equals 1 oz.

1 tablespoonful solid butter equals 1 oz.

Smaller Quantities of the Above

1 heaped teaspoonful equals ¼ oz.

1 heaped dessertspoonful equals ½ oz.

Measurements by Weight of Coins

These will be a guide if you have scales but find some of the smaller weights missing.

1 halfpenny weighs slightly under ¼ oz.

1 penny and 1 halfpenny, or 1 half-crown equals ½ oz.

3 pennies, or 5 halfpennies equals 1 oz.

6 pennies equals 2 oz.

Fluid Measurements

3 tablespoonfuls equals 2½ fluid oz.

1 breakfast cup equals 10 fluid oz.

6 tablespoonfuls equals 5 fluid oz or 1 gill.

4 gills equals 1 pint.

2 pints equals 1 quart.

4 quarts equals 1 gallon.

Conversion of Fluid Measure to Dry

1 pint equals 1 lb.

Miscellaneous Measurements

9 afternoon tea cubes of sugar equals 1 oz.

5 average size eggs equals ½ lb.

2 eggs and their weight in butter, flour and sugar make an excellent basic recipe for a sandwich cake.

When you use cups and spoons for measuring, take care not to use different kinds for the ingredients of your recipe. For example, if you have one of those sets of measuring spoons, ranging from 1 tablespoon to ¼ teaspoon, use them for measuring *all* the ingredients. If you use these for some of the ingredients and, say, a tablespoon out of the cooking drawer for other ingredients, you may get a discrepancy in weight that might spoil your dish. When buying a set of measuring spoons, be sure it is one approved by the British Standards Institution and bears their mark.

If you need a level spoonful or cupful of some dry ingredient, first fill it to overflowing, then slide the back of a knife across the top of the measure to remove the surplus.

For greater accuracy, sift such items as flour, castor and icing sugar, and free salt, etc., from lumps, before weighing. Pack butter and fats solidly, so that no weight is lost through air pockets.

If you can, without offending your milkman, hang on to one half-pint and one pint milk bottle and keep as emergency measures; also the one-ounce drums in which pepper and spices are packed can be used as approximate measures. If they are thoroughly wiped and left to air, any spicy smell soon goes off.

5,000 YEARS OF KITCHEN IMPROVEMENTS

by JOAN E. WALLEY, *Head of the Department of Household Science,*
Queen Elizabeth College, University of London

IT is the ambition of every woman to have a home of which she can be truly proud, and many to-day consider the kitchen, which is the workshop of the house and the place where she will spend a great part of her working day, to be the most important area of the home.

Although in primitive times, the cooking area was considered to be first in importance, there have been periods of history when it was relegated to a very inferior position. The elegance of the exterior and the layout of the gardens, the balanced proportions of spacious rooms and the noble sweep of wide stairways were considered in great detail, while the premises for the preparation and cooking of food were pushed away out of sight, very frequently into a basement where lighting and ventilation were unsatisfactory.

Other Nations Lead

To-day in the United Kingdom our heritage of beautiful houses from the past is outstanding, but is not matched by a legacy of fine kitchens. In this field we are indeed outstripped by Sweden, New Zealand, Australia and the United States of America.

In many British homes the kitchen is still not as convenient as it could be for the work to be done there. The housewife may blame the architects and builders of the past, and even of the present, for these deficiencies, but in the long run it is all too true that she gets what she deserves. If she

From prehistoric times, through the days when cooking was done in a cauldron or on a spit, to the most up-to-date scientific kitchen planning

knows what she wants and voices her requests in the course of time notice will be taken of her demands and the final outcome will be a convenient kitchen. It is the responsibility of the housewife, then, to study the problem and learn all she can about it whenever possible and from all aspects, thus ensuring that the kitchens of to-morrow will be far in advance of those of yesterday.

Prehistoric Cooking

Before going on to discuss the basic principle of planning, it is interesting to review briefly the history of the kitchen and to trace its evolution from prehistoric times. It is some five or six thousand years since cooking in its simplest form was first practised, following closely on the discovery of fire. It is thought that sparks for igniting the fire were produced by striking together flint and iron pyrites. As those early people dwelt in caves and had, of course, no culinary vessels, the only possible method of cooking the meat and fish obtained through hunting and fishing was to roast it in front of, or grill it over, a glowing fire.

They may also have boiled some of their food, but not as we do to-day because the only containers they had would be of wood or leather. To boil in these they adopted a rather ingenious method. The container with the meat and liquid was put in a hole in the ground and boiled by continuously dropping into it stones which had been

354

Small boys were employed to
turn the spit (left) on which
meat, fish and birds were
roasted whole

A cauldron suspended over a wood
fire—and no chimney to take off the
smoke (below)—a common kitchen
sight in the early days of cookery

How different is this clean L-shaped kitchen by
Easiwork. Note the eye-level cupboards with
sliding glass doors and continuous working surfaces
with storage space underneath

This English Electric model kitchen has its preparation and cookery sections divided by the
stainless steel sink unit from the laundry section

heated in the fire, the stones being known as pot-boilers.

With the Stone Age came the cultivation of grain. This was ground into meal and used to make a simple form of bread by moistening with water, forming a flat cake and cooking on a bakestone heated by the fire. The result was an ember cake or bannock.

The next important development was the use of bronze and iron for hunting, fishing and cooking equipment. Bronze, an alloy of copper and tin, was used first in about 1800 B.C. and made into knives, flesh hooks, beakers and—less frequently because they took more metal—into cauldrons. These were valuable items of cooking equipment because they made boiling over the fire a practical possibility, thus superseding the arduous process requiring pot-boilers. In about 500 B.C. iron followed bronze and, because of its greater toughness and flexibility, was quickly adopted for all types of equipment.

Baking is another cooking process practised to some extent in these early days, but again not as we understand it in the home to-day, although this pioneer method is still sometimes used by campers. A hole lined with stones is made in the ground and a fire burned in it until the stones become very hot. The fire is then raked out and the food, well wrapped in leaves, put in and the hole covered with a stone and a layer of turf.

Roman Pottery

The Roman occupation of Britain from A.D. 43 to about A.D. 410 is the next important period in the history of the kitchen in Britain. Until this time a special area had been set aside in the dwelling for cooking purposes, but it was not until the advent of the Roman villa that the well-equipped kitchen (*culina*, hence the word culinary) became a definite part of the house. The cooking was done on a raised structure, the fire being held by metal supports, known as fire-dogs, situated in the middle of the room. Wood and charcoal were burned, the latter in braziers suitable for grilling food. Peat and coal were also common in some districts, but not all over the country. A considerable variety of cooking utensils is known to have been in common use, such as saucepans, frying pans,

globular stewing pans, strainers, jugs and ladles, as well as gridirons, tripods and pot-hangers for suspending pots over the fire. The art of pottery developed considerably about this time, and various utensils, either moulded or thrown on a potter's wheel, were available for use in the kitchen and on the table. Spoons, knives and other table and cooking equipment were also made from pewter, silver, bone and iron.

Early Community Feeding

Thus the general scheme of the kitchen was laid, and subsequent examples of Anglo-Saxon and Norman times followed the earlier pattern quite closely. One feature of the feeding arrangements from about the eighth to the fourteenth century was the large hall in the Anglo-Saxon dwellings and Norman castles where the community all ate together. Large quantities of food were required at a time. Sometimes the cooking was done in the kitchen; sometimes out of doors, as, for example, when a whole ox was roasted, a practice still recalled to-day in the American barbecue. Apart from this communal feeding, the main developments from now on are in the design and use of equipment and in the greater variety of dishes on the menu; the two, of course, being interrelated.

The arrangement of the fire itself went through many stages before the coal range emerged at the end of the eighteenth century. First of all it was situated in the middle of the room and later, in about the seventeenth century, moved over to the wall, but it was not until still later that a chimney was built on to the outside wall to take away the smoke. It may seem strange to us that chimneys were not adopted earlier, but as long as wood was used as a fuel, the smoke which filled the rooms, although troublesome, was not nearly so offensive as that from coal.

Cauldron and Spit

The fire was used for all types of cooking; the cauldron being suspended over it or stood on it. Several dishes were cooked together in the one container by the skilful use of separators (cloth bags for puddings and jars to hold other foods). Meat, fish and birds were roasted on the spit and there were many inventions for

356

Kitchens can be *too* big! Little over 100 years ago they were huge and spacious, like the one above, from an old painting of the artist's own kitchen in London—but nobody thought of the work they made

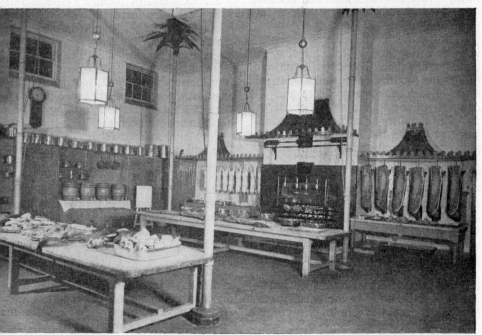

Brighton Corporation photograph

The Duke of Wellington had his initials—"D.W.L." (the L for London, as opposed to his country house)—on every piece of kitchen equipment. They were also numbered with a corresponding number on the appropriate shelf. The "batterie de cuisine" is now at the Royal Pavilion, Brighton

People took their bread, meat and pies to the bakeshop to be
cooked, then carried them home to eat

keeping the food in continuous rotation as it cooked in front of the fire. Silas Marner hung a "bit of roast pork on his door key" suspended by a length of twisted string which slowly unwound itself and rewound in the opposite direction for quite an appreciable time.

Motive power in the form of a weather-vane or a dog in a wheel was also employed at one time. The screen or reflector behind the food being roasted also passed through various stages. There was the damped straw ring like an archery target, and then the three-sided metal box which, while protecting the food from draughts, also acted as a reflector for the heat.

The Salamander

The fire was also frequently used to heat the Salamander, a metal ball or plate of some 12 in. diameter attached to a long rod. When the ball was red hot it was held above the surface of such foods as pies and tarts to give them a brown exterior.

The oven, though used in quite early times, was not, of course, in such general use as it is to-day. In the country most farmhouses would have a brick oven built into the wall beside the fireplace but heated quite independently by a wood fire inside which was raked out before the bread or other foods to be cooked were inserted. Many of these ovens still exist in old houses, sometimes being used as cupboards.

In towns, and particularly in London, the people relied on the bakeshop and the cook-shop for their bread and other baked goods such as meat and pies. Little, if any, cooking was done in many homes, the only hot meal of the day being taken at midday and eaten in the cook-shop or the food carried back and eaten at home. The other two meals of the day, breakfast and supper, consisted of bread, ale and cheese or cold meat or pickled fish. This practice of getting the baker to roast the joint has persisted until quite recent times.

"A very Genteel Dinner"

Menus gradually became longer and the variety of dishes increased. In 1662 Pepys tells us "we had a fricasee of rabbits, and chickens, a leg of mutton boiled, three carps in a dish, a great dish of a side of lamb, a dish of roasted pigeons, a dish of four lobsters, three tarts, a lamprey pie, a roast hare pie, a dish of anchovies, good wine of several sorts and all things mightly noble to my great content."

Parson Woodford relates in 1784 how "we had a very genteel Dinner, Soals and Lobster Sauce, Spring Chicken boiled and a Tongue, a Piece of rost Beef, Soup, a Fillet of Veal rosted with Morells and Trufles and Pigeon Pye for the first course —Sweetbreads, a green Goose and Peas, Apricot Pye, Cheesecakes, Stewed Mushrooms and Trifle." Clearly the kitchen to produce such noble repasts had developed considerably from the very simple one of earlier days, but it is in the Victorian times that the beginnings of the modern kitchen were first seen and made possible the elaborate recipes beloved of Mrs. Beeton.

The kitchen range, with its oven and boiling-top heated first by coal and later by gas and electricity, was a tremendous contribution to the art of cooking. When

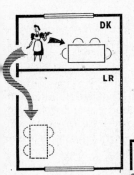

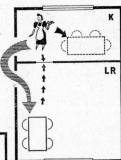

Four typical meal arrangements studied by the Council of Scientific Management in the Home show: (left), dining kitchen with passage access to living room; (right) working kitchen with hatch and passage access; (below left) working kitchen with passage access only; (below right) working kitchen with direct door access

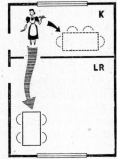

the two public ser-vices — water and drainage—followed, all the essentials for the creation of a modern k i t c h e n were achieved.

The kitchen prem-ises of a middle-class family living in a town house were exten-sive: they consisted of the kitchen proper, together with a number of ancillary rooms including the larder, scullery, washhouse and, because all these were situated at some distance from the dining room and fre-quently in the basement, a butler's pantry near the dining room. The equipment was usually adequate for cooking, but was de-signed neither for ease in use nor in clean-ing, and the kitchen layout was not arranged for convenience. This was mainly because there was then in the United King-dom a ready supply of cheap kitchen labour available. In English-speaking countries abroad, however, where the supply of labour has always been at a premium, labour - saving kit-chens came into existence much sooner.

Motion Study

To-day when few housewives have help with the cooking or with the cleaning of the house, and many of them in addition do a full-time paid job outside the home, it is essential that domestic work should be done with the minimum expenditure of time and energy. Consequently much thought has been given in recent years to the design and layout of the modern labour-saving kitchen. Such thought has been focused on two main topics: motion study and the design of equipment and materials.

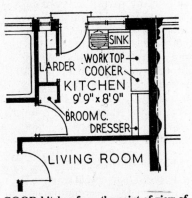

GOOD kitchen from the point of view of work sequence, with working surfaces and storage conveniently placed

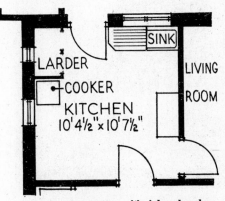

BAD work sequence, with sink and cooker far apart in corners, and no adequate continuous working surfaces

Diagrams by the Council of Scientific Management in the Home

A considerable amount of research has been done in Sweden, the United States, and latterly in the United Kingdom into the housewife's pattern in the kitchen. The distances covered by the housewife herself and by the goods and utensils she uses have been carefully measured. The survey method has also been used, and in 1955 the Council of Scientific Management in the Home issued a report based on a questionnaire completed by 700 British housewives about their kitchens in council houses built during the preceding five years. The report summarises the findings and publishes drawings of some of the plans examined. Its recommendations on the relationship between various pieces of equipment and fittings in the kitchen are useful, not only to architects and builders, but also to the housewife wishing to improve the layout of her own kitchen.

Considerable progress has also been made in making kitchen equipment easier to clean and to use. This applies not only to large items, like the cooker and sink, but also to small pieces such as, for example, a grater or a stainless-steel vegetable knife. Existing items have been improved in design and new ones invented to minimise effort and save time in domestic work. Foremost among these are the electric

Built-in door shelves for milk, eggs and fats are a feature of this roomy but inexpensive Thermcold Gas refrigerator by Main Refrigeration Ltd.

washing machine and dryer, the vacuum cleaner, and the electric mixing machine which, in addition to beating and mixing, will perform a number of other operations such as grinding, grating and sieving. Materials for floor and working surfaces have also received considerable attention, with consequent improvement in design, and there is now no need for the housewife to use her energy in scrubbing either floors or tables which can be kept clean with a damp cloth or a mop.

Planning a Kitchen

Before considering the actual planning of a kitchen it is useful to examine in some detail the work which is to be done there and the equipment which will be required. The main function of the kitchen is the provision of meals, but it is also frequently used for the washing and ironing of clothes and for the cleaning of shoes and of various metal utensils made of silver, copper, brass and pewter. The work concerned with meals falls under three main headings: (1) preparation, cooking and serving; (2) pastry- and cake-making; (3) washing up. A part of the kitchen must be suitably equipped for each; thus we have the cooking centre, the mix centre and the sink centre.

The essential equipment of the cooking centre consists of the stove, an adjoining working bench and shelves, cupboards and drawers for the storage of equipment used in the preparation and cooking of meals. The serving of meals is so intimately related to the cooking that provision for this is usually made part of the cooking centre. Thus, if a working bench is provided on both sides of the stove and also cupboards to hold the dishes required for service, the cooking centre will be adequate for all the operations in meal production.

The mix centre consists of a working bench and of suitable cupboards and drawers for the storage of all equipment and utensils used in pastry- and cake-making. In a small kitchen the mix centre and cooking centre are frequently combined, but where they can be separated it is clearly more convenient to have them so. In addition to the washing-up unit in the third centre, storage provision for detergents and other cleaning materials and receptacles to hold refuse is required. It

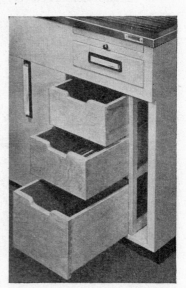

A pedal-controlled refuse container (left) is built into the sink unit at a convenient height, by Nevastane

Drawers specially designed to fit their contents (right), by Nevastane, provide economical use of space and convenient storage

A sectional cutlery drawer (below) has a space specially constructed for every item, so whatever is wanted is always ready at hand—a great time saver when cooking

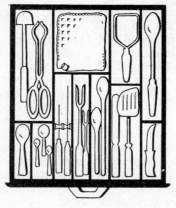

may also be convenient to store vegetables here, because they will then be close to the place where they are prepared. The washing-up unit consists of one, two or three sinks with a draining board on one side and a bench for stacking used dishes on the other. The stacking bench is often also a draining board, but this is not necessary and it is of more use as an ordinary working bench, in which case it need not be grooved.

Basic requirements for the washing and ironing of clothes are simple: a suitable sink, an adequate supply of hot water and a table for ironing. To-day there are also a number of items of labour-saving equipment, including the electric washing machine, the electric dryer and the rotary or table ironer. If these are to be used in the kitchen, a considerable amount of space will be needed to house them. It is sometimes held that because of the extra space required, it is preferable to house and use them in a separate utility room, provided one is available.

The other activity of the kitchen—cleaning—does not necessitate extensive fitted apparatus. All that is needed is a cupboard where cloths, brushes and materials can be kept, and a table or wall bench where the work can be done. It is usually quite easy to fit this in with the other work in the kitchen.

A Bright Outlook

When a new house or flat is designed, there are a number of points about the kitchen to be considered at an early stage. One of these is its location in relation to the other rooms, and particularly the dining room; also to the entrance for the delivery of goods by tradesmen. The aspect of the windows is also of importance. Though there is no doubt that good work is difficult in an overheated kitchen, there is really little justification in the English climate for excluding all sunshine by giving the kitchen a northerly aspect. It is both pleasant and stimulating for the housewife to have a bright kitchen.

The second point to be considered is the size and shape of the kitchen. This will, of course, vary according to the use to which it is put, a greater area obviously being allowed where it is required also for dining than when for cooking only. A bigger kitchen is needed also where a considerable amount of laundry work is done, requiring bulky equipment. Further, the size of the

A bar electric heater with a rail fitment above dries kitchen cloths quickly—an idea from the experimental kitchen of Brown & Polson

household influences the amount of kitchen space required. But bearing all these factors in mind, 100 sq. ft. is a good average figure for a working kitchen, and 135 sq. ft. for a dining kitchen for a family of 4–6 persons. The shape of the kitchen is of importance, and a rectangular kitchen of 12 by 8 ft. will give a more convenient layout than a square one 10 by 10 ft.

Doors and Windows

The position of the doors and windows also affects the planning. There are usually two entrances to a kitchen in a house, and often only one to a kitchen in a flat, which makes the latter easier to plan. If in the house kitchen the doors are at opposite ends, the kitchen is converted into a passage way which children will constantly use, causing inconvenience to the housewife and perhaps some risk to themselves when utensils holding hot liquid are being carried about. The main problem created by windows is that they interfere with the placing of wall cupboards over working surfaces, a matter to be considered later under the storage of equipment.

The third point for consideration relates to personal comfort, as it is influenced by lighting, ventilation and heating. The three are, of course, interrelated. Windows that provide natural light also assist in ventilation, while the inconvenience of steam and condensation can be reduced by ensuring that the kitchen is never too cold. Effective lighting, both natural and artificial, is important on all working surfaces and on the

sink, 7–10 foot-candles being accepted as a good standard for artificial lighting. Natural ventilation by doors and windows is quite satisfactory in the majority of kitchens, provided this is not obtained at the expense of the rest of the house. It is not pleasant to have smells of cooking carried to other rooms, particularly to bedrooms. This can usually be avoided by careful placing of the stove, and in the event of difficulty an extractor fan can be installed over it.

Turning now to the layout of the kitchen, the problem can be divided into two parts: one concerned with the placing of the equipment in each work centre and the relationship of each centre to the remainder and to the dining area; the other with the storage of utensils and apparatus. The first is comparatively simple, but the second requires considerable thought and time if satisfactory relationship between all items of apparatus is to be achieved.

Time spent at the Sink

In arranging the layout of the work centres, the results of recent research are valuable. These show that the housewife spends more time at the sink than in any other area of the kitchen. The next area used most frequently is that around the cooking stove. The cooker should therefore not be very far from the sink. A convenient layout can be achieved with the sink between the cooker and mix centre. In the past it was common practice for all the work of preparation for meals and for baking to be done on the kitchen table in the middle of the kitchen. In many kitchens to-day this work is done on a wall bench adjoining the cooker. A disadvantage of the centrally placed table is the obstruction it causes to cross-kitchen traffic, the housewife having to walk round the table instead of directly across the room. Thus, modern designs for kitchens incorporate a run of bench surface at the same height as the cooker and sink tops along the kitchen wall. If a table is considered necessary, it is not placed centrally but with one end to a wall. In this position it can be used for dining and any other suitable work, but is not intended for the main work of meal preparation. One advantage of the table is its height for, whereas the wall bench is usually fixed at a height of 36 in., the table is only 30 in., and it is useful to have a working area at a lower height, particularly for jobs which can be done sitting.

U and L shapes are two common designs for convenient kitchen layouts; others include the "straight run," where all the equipment is along one wall, and the "corridor," where it is on two opposite walls, the distance between them being not more than 6–7 ft.

The Larder

Practically all old kitchens in the United Kingdom have larders, whereas the majority of modern kitchens in the United States are designed without, a refrigerator and possibly a deep-freeze cabinet being provided instead. The explanation is no doubt due to inside temperature differences

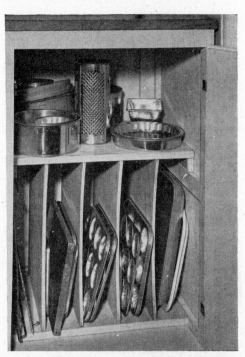

Vertical storage, the most practical for cake tins, baking sheets, trays, etc., is a novel feature of the English Electric kitchen, and well worth copying

between the two countries. Not only do many American housewives have to contend with hotter weather in summer for much longer periods, but in winter American houses are run at a higher temperature than British. As the common method is central heating, a temperature usually in the region of 70° F. is maintained.

The larder is intended for the day-to-day storage of foods which should be kept cool but which do not necessarily require the low temperature of a refrigerator. Moreover, foods kept in a refrigerator need tightly covering to prevent drying, which does not occur in a larder. In the United Kingdom, such foods as pies, tarts, meat and cheese can be kept very well in a larder for several days. In many houses the larder is also used for the storage of most of the ingredients used in cooking, as well as for canned and bottled foods and even for utensils and small equipment. If, however, adequate storage facilities were available in more convenient places, it would not be necessary for the larder to be

This revolving corner cupboard in English Electric's Queen's House kitchen makes clever use of an otherwise awkward space

Under-sink cupboards by Nevastane have shelves exactly the right size for the packets, etc., they are to contain. No fumbling for what you want

used as a general store. Moreover, many of the goods could be stored under more suitable physical conditions elsewhere. Canned goods, for instance, will rust if kept in a damp place, and preserves are best kept at an even temperature, so a larder is not really suitable for either.

List Your Stores

The question of storage arrangements for all utensils and equipment housed in the kitchen is of great importance and one to which considerable thought should be given if really satisfactory conditions are to be achieved. In the first place it is necessary to make a list of exactly what is to be stored. Categories of goods include food in packages, tins and jars of various shapes and sizes, ranging from large packets of breakfast cereals to small containers of

pepper; utensils, cutlery and equipment for cooking; china, glass and cutlery for service; linen for kitchen and table use; cleaning equipment and reagents; washing-up and laundry equipment, trays, trolleys, flower vases and occasional equipment, such as preserving pans.

The next question is where and how should all these things be stored. The answer is simple to state but complicated to work out: at the point of first usage. Thus the tea- and coffee-pots and the canisters holding tea and coffee should be kept beside the cooking stove, perhaps on a shelf above or adjoining; the dinner service should also be nearby, a convenient place being a bench cupboard adjoining the cooker or a wall cupboard close at hand. Cups, saucers, plates and table cutlery should be near enough to the dining table to be lifted straight off the shelves on to the table.

Of course, difficulties will arise in putting into practice generally the precept of storing at the point of first usage. For instance, some ingredients, such as flour and salt, are needed at both the cooking and the mix centre, and the answer lies in duplication. In general, however, although compromise may sometimes be necessary, the rule can be followed.

When considering how to store all the various goods, there are several conditions to be borne in mind. Firstly, they should

Single-row storage saves space and makes for efficiency. Nothing is tucked away at the back of these narrow tiered shelves in the Brown & Polson kitchen, so everything is clearly visible and easy to reach

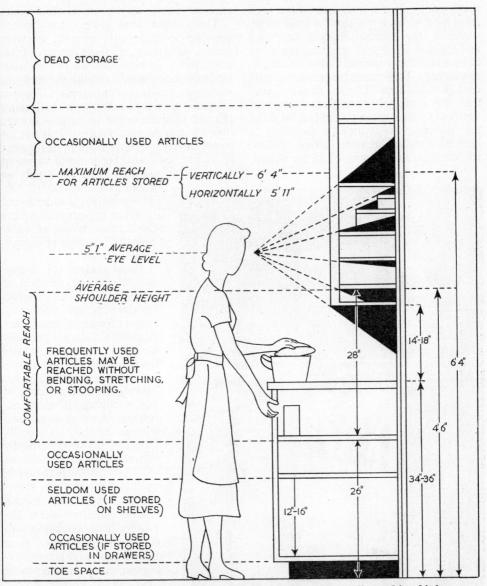

DEAD STORAGE

OCCASIONALLY USED ARTICLES

MAXIMUM REACH
FOR ARTICLES STORED ── { VERTICALLY ── 6' 4"
HORIZONTALLY 5' 11"

5"1" AVERAGE
EYE LEVEL

AVERAGE
SHOULDER HEIGHT

COMFORTABLE REACH

FREQUENTLY USED
ARTICLES MAY BE
REACHED WITHOUT
BENDING, STRETCHING,
OR STOOPING.

OCCASIONALLY
USED ARTICLES

SELDOM USED
ARTICLES (IF STORED
ON SHELVES)

OCCASIONALLY USED
ARTICLES (IF STORED
IN DRAWERS)

TOE SPACE

14"-18"   6' 4"

28"

4' 6"

34"-36"

26"

12"-16"

Diagram shows the most convenient storage heights for the various supplies used in a kitchen by a housewife 5 feet 4 inches tall—also the correct height for her working surface so that she stands comfortably upright

be easily accessible and visible. One has only to examine a few kitchen cupboards to realise how rarely this is so. Take, for example, the bottom shelf of a bench cupboard of 21-in. depth. In order to see and take out what is at the back, it is necessary to get down on the hands and knees, peer into the gloom and remove everything from the front. The diagram above shows the convenient heights for shelves

for a woman of average stature; anything above or below these limits should be occupied by only occasionally used items, or devices should be adopted to make the goods more accessible.

Single-row Storage

Secondly, it is obviously economical to use the complete cubic capacity of a cupboard, and this means that goods should occupy not only the total area of the shelf from front to back but also the total height —that is, the distance between one shelf and the next. The only way to achieve this is to adopt the principle known as single-row storage. This means that a shelf is wide enough to accommodate one item only and that the distance between each pair of shelves is a little greater than the height of the package. As it may be necessary to alter the distance between shelves to allow for changes in the sort of items stored,

shelves should all be made adjustable.

The conventional system for kitchen shelving in cupboards consists of wide shelves of 18–24 in. fixed about 18 in. apart. This method does not provide particularly convenient conditions and is, moreover, wasteful of cubic space. The two illustrations on p. 364 show how much more efficient in space is the single-row storage than the conventional method. It is not, of course, always possible to adopt this system in its simplest form, but a useful variation consists of narrow racks on doors as shown on p. 360. This principle is to be found in many refrigerators, where the maximum use of cubic capacity is always of importance.

Fixed shelves, of course, are not the only method of storing goods; sliding shelves or drawers are very convenient for many items, particularly if they are specially designed to accommodate their contents. Sliding shelves are a device very suitable for making the storage space of bench cupboards more accessible. Another convenient storage method is to fix sheets of plywood vertically between shelves at distances of 2–3 in. This is particularly useful for storing trays, pastry boards and baking sheets. Another useful device for both bench and wall cupboards is known as a Lazy Susan, and is a revolving cupboard intended to be used as a corner fitting, thereby making it possible to use all the available space for readily accessible storage.

A problem which always faces planners of kitchen fitments and particularly of wall cupboards over working benches is the design of doors which will not be inconvenient when opened above a working bench. Sliding doors offer one solution,

Another fine example from the Brown & Polson kitchen of storage space specially designed for its contents—this pull-out cabinet has a slotted fitment to hold kitchen knives on one side, metal holders for spoons on the other; below, trays and baking sheets stand upright

but even if they always run quite smoothly these somewhat impede easy access to the cupboard. Another alternative is to make each door in two halves hinged together vertically and folding back. Yet another way is to fix blinds or roll-top shutters which can be pushed up completely out of sight when the cupboard is in use.

Replanning a Bad Kitchen

Such a modern kitchen is attractive and labour-saving and the dream of every housewife today. But only a few can build new houses and many must continue to live in those designed years ago when ideas on kitchen planning were very different. Kitchens in existing houses can, however, usually be improved considerably by judicious replanning, bearing in mind the general principles already stated. The best way to set about it is, first of all to examine the kitchen critically and discover its inconveniences. This may prove quite unexpectedly difficult because one grows so used to overcoming difficulties that one ceases to realise they exist. Any thoughtful and practical friend would quickly be able to see them and point them out.

Then calculate the area of the kitchen and compare this with the recommended standard. If it is less, ingenuity will be needed to overcome deficiencies; if it is more, only part of the whole area should be used for the main work of the kitchen. The next point to examine is the distance walked in doing specific and frequently occurring operations, such as clearing the table, washing up and putting away. Professional kitchen planners would plot such traffic routes on a plan and, after carefully recorded observations, would show the most frequently used routes by heavier lines.

The next point to examine is the amount and position of working bench space. Deficiencies in this respect make for inconvenience, but it is usually quite a simple matter to provide working bench space

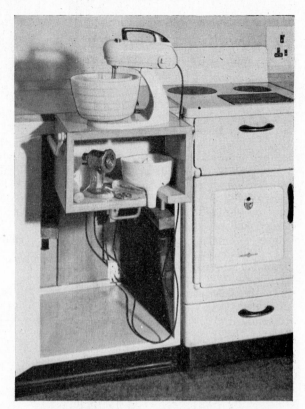

The English Electric food mixer has its own built-in cupboard just where it is needed, between cooker and working surface

alongside a cooker where it does not already exist. Now consider the relationship between the work centres and particularly between the cooker and the sink. If these two items are at opposite ends of the room, the only solution is to move one or the other. Usually the cooker is more easily moved than the sink because only one service is involved, whereas the sink is connected with both hot and cold water and drainage.

What has already been said about suitable fitments is equally applicable to new or adapted premises, but this can be one of the most important factors in the improvement of a kitchen. Special attention should be paid to the heights of working benches and of the sink. If either is too low or too high, work will be much more tiring than it need be. Although it may be expensive to raise the level of a sink, a wood block of the correct height under each leg is usually all that is required for a table.

When all the above points in a kitchen have been examined, the time has arrived for replanning. In the example illustrated here, the original kitchen was only 63 sq. ft., and therefore an extension was necessary. The main defects were the very limited amount of working bench, the position of the cooker and of the stove water heater, which could only be cleaned and re-fuelled when the table which was hinged to the wall was lowered. The cooker was much too near to the door for safety, and the paint on the door had in fact become blistered through over-heating. Moreover, the cooker was in such a position that the smells of cooking immediately penetrated into the hall and up the adjoining staircase to the bedrooms.

In the new arrangement these defects were corrected. It will be noticed that, as in all adaptations, perfection is not usually possible, and the main defect in this one is the distance

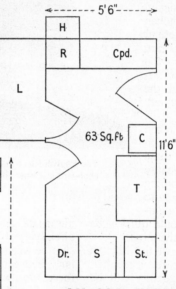

from the servery to the cooker and sink. But although in this case, extension of the area was necessary, this is not always so.

Very often kitchens inherited from Victorian and Edwardian days are much too large for present-day requirements. The one in the house where I grew up was about 12 by 18 ft. and had five doorways—to the hall, back stairs, a large cupboard, the larder and the scullery—and either the larder or the scullery would be large enough for the kitchens we should plan to-day. To replan my childhood kitchen, the solution would probably be to discard it altogether and make either the scullery or the larder into a modern kitchen.

Each adaptation has its own particular problems, and no two solutions are the same. The essential thing is to provide suitable fitments in the most convenient position for the work to be done, bearing in mind the needs of the particular family. Even if perfection is not attainable, improvements are readily possible. Such improvements will pay big dividends in the saving of time and energy and in the wear and tear on the nerves of the housewife, thus contributing to a happier life for all.

AN OLD KITCHEN MODERNISED

THE plan above shows the kitchen as it was; on the left, and in colour opposite, after modernisation.

It was first extended by building on an L-shaped piece 6 × 7 ft. A small opening 2 × 1¼ ft. in the new short wall was fitted with a door for the withdrawal of a rectangular waste bin kept under the draining board. The hinged flap (W) is raised and waste material dropped into the bin. The new larder (L) was made from a brick coal bunker on the wall by the back door by removing part of the kitchen wall and fitting a roll shutter. The former larder was converted into a cupboard (Cpd.) to house the ironing board and cleaning equipment. The large hatch (H) in the new kitchen was made from the cupboard backing on to the dining room by removing part of the wall. Double doors painted white were fitted in the dining room and a roll top shutter in the kitchen. This hatch is also used for the permanent storage of china, cutlery, condiments, etc., in current use.

Abbreviations : B=Bench; C=Cooker; Cpd.=Cupboard; Dr.=Draining Board; H=Hatch; L=Larder; R=Refrigerator; S=Sink; St.=Stove; T=Table; W=Waste.

KITCHEN WITH IDEAS

Ingredient cupboard immediately over pastry working bench shows single-row storage

The larder has a roll-top shutter; beside the sink unit is a small table with a tray for clean dishes

Left, water heater and electric cooker, with cupboard for dinner service and drawers for kitchen tools, cloths and paper. Above, the hatch, refrigerator and cupboard with trolley and trays stored neatly underneath

COLOURFUL KITCHEN

Too small for violent colours, this compact kitchen gains a feeling of space from its pale, clear tones and gentle contrasts.   The coolness of sky-blue woodwork and the deeper blue of floor and curtains is balanced by the glow of peach-tinted walls and the deep pink of the wall-rack, stool top, etc.   Equipped by Froy of Hammersmith

TYPE OF FOOD	CENTRE OVEN TEMP. °F	THERMO-STAT SETTING	HEAT OF OVEN
Fruit Bottling	240°	$\frac{1}{4}$	Very Cool
Stews	260°	$\frac{1}{2}$	Very Cool
Custard and Egg Dishes Milk Puddings	280°	1	Cool
Rich Fruit Cake	300°	2	Cool
	320°		Warm
Slow Roasting Shortbread	340°	3	Warm
Plain Fruit Cake, Madeira Cake, Biscuits	360°	4	Moderate
Queen Cakes, Sponges	380°	5	Fairly Hot
Plain Buns, Plate Tarts, Short Pastry	400°	6	Fairly Hot
Scones Roasting	420°	7	Hot
Puff and Flaky Pastry	440°	8	Hot
	460°	9	Very Hot
	480°		Very Hot

TURNING ON THE HEAT

Nothing is more vital to successful cooking
than the right temperature for the job

ABOVE is a handy and comprehensive guide to the right oven temperature at which to cook various foods, prepared by the North Thames Gas Board.

WHEN a recipe says "bake in a hot oven," you have only to turn to this chart to see that this will mean 420° F. on an electric cooker, Thermostat Setting 7 if you use gas. But do be sure also to follow the instructions provided by the makers of your cooker as to the best place in the oven in which to cook different things.

CHOOSING THE COOKER FOR YOU

Whether it is powered by gas,
electricity or solid fuel, it can be
a streamlined, labour-saving piece
of modern equipment

CHOOSING your cooking stove is a momentous event, second only to choosing your life partner. For you and the cooker you finally select from to-day's dazzling array will doubtless have to work together in harmony for many years to come. Whether you choose gas, electricity or solid fuel—or the decision is made for you by circumstances—standards of efficiency vary very little these days, and all leading manufacturers produce a first-rate article. The choice is therefore largely a matter of personal preference.

GAS COOKERS

The gas cooker has what many women consider a definite advantage over all others in that it is the only means of cooking which gives a visible flame with instantaneous control. This means that it can be adjusted at once to ensure exactly the necessary heat for whatever is cooking on the hot-plates or in the oven, with, in many cases, a corresponding economy in gas consumption.

In step with the general trend among manufacturers of cooking appliances, the makers of gas cookers have carried out extensive research to effect (1) the utmost economy in the use of gas; (2) streamlined, easy to clean models with a pleasing, modern appearance; (3) high-grade efficiency in operation.

Modern gas cookers have four boiling burners and a grill. Ovens have been sub-

stantially enlarged, many being big enough to take a 28-lb. turkey.

All gas cookers, in common with other domestic appliances sold in gas showrooms, bear the Gas Council's Seal of Approval—a visible guarantee that they have been thoroughly tested and approved.

All are fitted with safety pattern taps, each clearly marked for each burner and hot-plates have smooth, glide-over tops giving stability and enabling heavy saucepans to be slid over the surface into position without lifting. One cooker has a sealed hot-plate, which will take any spillage, and the burner heads, which are removable for easy cleaning, fit flush into the hot-plate surface.

Automatic ignition to hot-plate burners (and sometimes to the oven as well) is a feature of all new gas cookers and, where automatic ignition to the oven is not provided, a gas taper or torch is fitted to the side of the oven for easy lighting and there is usually a convenient lighting port in the centre front of the oven base.

All ovens are fitted

Designed as two independent units—hot-plate and grill with a separate oven—the Radiation New World 72 gas cooker can be built in just where you want it. The oven has a drop down door

A built-in, high level, fold-away barbecue grill for spit-roasting is a feature of this Cannon gas cooker, with its large sealed type of hot-plate and drop-head burners for easy removal

And now a hot-plate controlled by a thermostat, just like the oven! You set the Magitrol dial for the required heat and the special sensitive element in the burner adjusts the flame accordingly. Parkinson Cowan's Renown Seven gas cooker, right

with thermostat control and some cookers are designed with removable oven ceilings and base for easy cleaning. Storage drawers or compartments are fitted beneath the oven, some being separately heated, others heated when the oven is in use. They will take plates and dishes for warming, or food that is to be kept hot without drying up and they also provide valuable storage space for cooking utensils.

The most important current development in gas cooker design is the trend towards greater flexibility of cooking components. Instead of a cooker all in one piece, you can now build into your kitchen units a separate oven and hot-plate, which may be placed side by side or on opposite sides of the kitchen, according to the shape and design of your working surfaces.

This means that the hot-plate and grill are put in at exactly the right height to suit the individual user's convenience and comfort and the oven fitted at body level, to

avoid stooping. With this arrangement, the drop-down oven door is particularly useful, because it provides a convenient resting place for dishes being moved in and out of the oven or for basting.

For the first time a British cooker has been fitted with a thermostatically controlled burner. It works very much like the familiar oven thermostat, a numbered dial being inset into the splashback of the cooker. This gives precision cooking and all that is required is to turn on the gas and set the dial to the number for the food being cooked. When the contents of the pan reach the required temperature, the

flame adjusts itself automatically. On this burner, milk cannot boil over and omelette-making, stews, deep or dry fat frying operations are all perfectly controlled. No special kind of pan is required, provided it is of good quality.

Another new development is a combined barbecue-grill for spit-roasting poultry and joints on an automatic revolving spit. The grill is at high level on the splashback of the cooker and, when required for ordinary grilling purposes, the spit attachment is quite easily removed.

The position of the grill on the modern gas cooker is very largely a matter of personal preference. Some are situated on the splashback or at hot-plate level, some are of fold-away type, all enabling the food to be watched conveniently from any position in the kitchen. Strip lighting on the splashback is another improvement, giving clear visibility into the contents of the saucepans on the hot-plates.

Automatic control devices are fitted to some of the new cookers. This means that a meal can be put in the oven before the housewife goes out for the day, a simple setting of a time control dial and the gas turns itself on at a pre-set time and off again when cooking is complete. The meal is ready for serving at the time required when she returns.

Your own particular needs must be fully considered when buying any type of cooker. Gas cookers, for example, include a large number of "family" models, ranging from those costing about £25 to luxury types considerably more expensive. There are also small-scale portable cookers for the person living in a small flat or bed-sitting-room.

What about cleaning? With earlier models this was a disagreeable and tedious business, which has now largely been overcome by interchangeable oven burners and pan supports, vitreous enamel finish, both inside and out, and new type racks which do not rust and are easily kept spotlessly clean. Hot-plate tops, now of vitreous enamelled sheet steel, can be removed as a whole or in two sections, wiped over and replaced within a matter of minutes.

ELECTRIC COOKERS

Electricity now rivals gas for cooking, and the chief reasons for its growing popularity are briefly:

(1) Efficiency.
(2) Cleanliness.
(3) Wide variety of choice in designs and prices.
(4) Time and trouble-saving devices incorporated in the latest models.

Running costs are reasonable. There is no need to fit a canopy, vent or exhaust fan with an electric cooker; cooking odours are reduced to a minimum, and can easily be prevented from spreading into other rooms in the home.

One of the principal advantages of the electric cooker is that there is no product of combustion in operation; absence of fumes means that oven interiors are readily maintained in a perfectly clean condition, and no deposit is caused on surrounding walls and ceiling. Vitreous enamel surfaces, both inside and out, need only to be wiped over with a damp cloth immediately after use.

Cooking on a modern electric appliance is quick, the average time for an oven to heat up being from 12 to 15 minutes, while quick-boiling rings bring liquids very rapidly to boiling point.

The design and construction of the solid

A reasonably priced luxury gas cooker, the New World Rangette by Radiation, has a comfort-level grill in the middle of the splashback that can be folded out of sight, a large oven, warming chamber storage compartment

type of hot-plate has been vastly improved in recent years and some will boil a pint of water in four minutes. But some housewives prefer one of the hot-plates to be of the radiant type, which certainly has the advantage that it glows red, is faster and more quickly controlled for simmering and can be used with any type of saucepan, whereas with the solid plates ground-base pans are needed.

The hot-plates of most up-to-date cookers now have multi-heat and variable heat controls, with five or more marked settings. By this means, the heat can be controlled as accurately as in any other means of cooking. No matter how small the quantity of liquid in the pan, for instance, you can, with a multi-heat switch, obtain perfect simmering. A new development on one radiant ring maintains a sauce at a preselected temperature or keeps a pan of milk hot all day without danger of it boiling over.

The grill, one of the most constantly used parts of the cooker, since electric grilling is second to none, may be combined with one of the boiling rings, sited below the hob, at eye-level or in the top of the oven. Wherever it is, the electric grill has one inestimable advantage—it is self-cleaning, spots of fat simply burning off the element.

The oven is thermostatically controlled and a light on the switch goes out when the selected temperature is reached. The tendency is towards larger ovens and grills, the ovens in many of the bigger cookers being capable of taking a 35-lb. turkey and all the trimmings without trouble. Where the grill is at the top of the oven, it may be used to boost the heating-up speed of the oven and wherever the grill has been taken away from the hob, the space saved is invariably used for plate-warming. Some ovens have flap-down doors, others inner glass doors and the new non-tilt rod shelves are made of rust-proofed metal, while hobs and hot-plates are quickly removable for cleaning.

Auto-timers, enabling a meal to be left to cook by itself, are the newest development in electric cookery, but the automatic control panel carrying the ringer and oven timer, can be fitted to existing cookers at a later date and at quite moderate cost. (For more details about Timer Control cookers and cookery, see page 263.)

The Tricity Built-in electric cooker consists of two separate units—oven with hot cupboard and grill; surface unit with four radiant hot-plates. The oven has an inside light and inner glass door

The modern trend in electric, as well as gas cooking, is towards the built-in unit— the oven and the surface unit being both specially designed for easy installation anywhere in the kitchen to suit the owner's personal taste. A Canadian manufacturer is making these "built-ins" with an oven whose racks can be adjusted to the desired height by turning a knob on the control panel and without even opening the door; an electric meat thermometer that rings the buzzer when the roast is done rare, medium or well, according to setting on the dial; and an automatic, clock-controlled, self-basting Rotiss-o-mat for charcoal-type barbecuing. The hot-plates, with seven-heat selection and fingertip control, can be turned full or partly on, according to the size of the utensil being used, an ingenious way of saving fuel.

Designers and manufacturers are constantly improving electric cookers, and the latest models are attractive in appearance, economical in operation, and safe to run. Oven elements are shock-proof, each heating element being separately earthed. Servicing can be done without removing the cooker from its position.

To use an electric cooker to its fullest advantage it is necessary to invest in the heavier-type pots and pans sold for the purpose and which are initially rather more expensive. This is a point to be borne in mind, although over a period of time the heavier steamers, saucepans, etc., give longer service and so prove no more expensive.

Finally, there are the Infra Red Grills which cook chops, steaks, fish, chicken and similar dishes at great heat and fantastic speeds. Grills cooked by infra red radiation are more tender and juicy because the pores of the meat are sealed instantaneously, so that none of the juices or the flavour escape. There is automatic control to prevent the food from burning and both sides are cooked at the same time. Sausages can be grilled in 90 seconds, a chop in 3 minutes, bacon in 20 seconds. Some models are equipped with a revolving spit, enabling the hostess to roast a chicken or joint on the dinner table in full view of her guests.

SOLID FUEL COOKERS

Solid fuel cookers fall into four main classes: (1) heat storage, (2) thermostatically controlled free standing, (3) free standing, and (4) combination grates, which combine an open fire with an oven at the side, over or at the back of the fire.

The cookers are designed to burn continuously and can "idle" for at least ten hours without attention, providing cooking facilities at all times. Ovens are evenly heated and usually have a heat indicator and there are hot-plates for boiling and simmering. Some cookers have a second oven for slow cooking or a hot cupboard for keeping food hot or warming plates.

When choosing a cooker, be sure it is going to be large enough for your requirements and has a boiler big enough to provide adequate hot water for your needs; it is more economical to run a fire slowly than race it to provide adequate heat. Have your cooker installed, according to the manufacturer's instructions, by a competent builder and insulate the hot water cylinder.

As the name implies, with the Heat Storage Cooker, heat is stored up and released to oven and hot-plate. This is achieved by means of a "heat storage" unit—a thick metal casting placed next to the fire, which has the power to absorb and retain heat for long periods. The whole cooker is heavily and thoroughly insulated, and the hot-plate has a thick insulated cover which is kept down when the cooker is not in use.

Heat storage cookers of this type are more expensive than other kinds of solid fuel cookers, but over a period of years the initial cost is redeemed by saving in fuel.

Weekly consumption of fuel should be about $1\frac{1}{4}$ cwt. of anthracite, or $1\frac{1}{2}$ cwt. of coke.

Rate of burning can be adjusted by thermostatic control, and stoking is normally only necessary twice in every 24 hours.

A boiler is incorporated with a number of cookers of this kind, and there are often two ovens, which are constantly maintained at different temperatures.

Smokeless fuels—coke, phurnacite or anthracite—are used for most solid fuel heat storage cookers, but one model has now been adapted to burn coal as well. To obtain the best results, flues should be cleaned about once a month.

A thermostatically controlled free standing cooker, with numbered thermostat for controlling the oven heat, can also have a boiler and, under average conditions, fuel consumption is $1\frac{1}{2}$ to $1\frac{3}{4}$ cwt. per week, though faulty operation increases this consumption.

All these cookers are more efficient and convenient if burnt continuously and the manufacturer's instructions for operation should be followed carefully.

The free standing cooker, which may have an open or closed fire, can also have a boiler and many have a left- or right-hand oven heated by hot air circulating inside or round the oven or by flue gases passing round the oven. With correct operation, which varies with different makes, this type of cooker uses between $1\frac{1}{4}$ and 2 cwt. of fuel a week.

The modern combination grate is a very suitable appliance for a living-room

CHOOSING THE COOKER FOR YOU

All the switches and the timing dial are at eye level on the splashback of the Revomatic electric cooker (left) that switches on and off at selected times—and there's a strip light on the switch panel too

From Canada come Moffat electric "built-in" ovens and surface units (right) with all the latest devices, seen here in a show house at Weymouth. You can move the oven racks without opening the oven door and the thermometer sounds the buzzer when the joint is cooked as you like it!

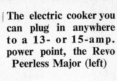

The raised oven of this English Electric cooker (above) has a glass port in the door —the grill's in the oven too. Fitted with automatic timer control, it has a roomy storage cupboard below

The electric cooker you can plug in anywhere to a 13- or 15-amp. power point, the Revo Peerless Major (left)

High-line grill, automatic cooking, boiling plates with 6-heat control, oven with glass door, hot cupboard with big withdrawable wire basket— these are features of the Jackson Highline electric cooker (right)

kitchen, with its cheerful open fire and a fire-box which can be controlled for continuous burning. All such grates can also have boilers.

Some models have the oven over the fire, some at the back, but in a normal family house the side oven combination grate is usually the most satisfactory. As the heat is taken round the oven in the form of flue gases, good results are obtained by using coal, but smokeless fuels can also be used and with correct operation, fuel consumption will be 1½ to 2½ cwt. a week.

Briefly, the advantages of the solid fuel cookers can be summed up as follows: ·

(1) The majority are designed to provide hot water as well as cooking facilities, doing away with the necessity for a separate domestic boiler.

> *They will provide up to 350 gallons per week, if the hot water system is compact and is well "lagged."*

(2) Continuous burning supplies a regular, steady warmth to the room in which the cooker is installed, and does away with the need for any other heating appliances.

(3) Hot-plate and oven are both fully heated by the one fire, so that no extra cost is involved when full use is made of both of them.

(4) As a heat storage cooker is storing up heat all the time, it is always ready for full use.

While many households will find the advantages of the solid fuel cooker far outweigh its disadvantages, others will need to bear in mind the following points:

(a) the need for fuel storage space;

(b) the fact that freshly boiling water is not so quickly available first thing in the morning;

(c) the solid fuel cooker cannot be so finely and immediately regulated as the cooker operated by tap or switch;

(d) neither is toast so quickly made nor so crisp;

(e) the kitchen, which will be kept pleasantly warm in winter, may become a trifle over-heated for comfort in the event of real summer weather.

(f) there must always be a certain amount of dust and dirt where a fire has to be made up with solid fuel and ashes removed.

The Rayburn Yorkmaster is a thermostatically controlled free standing cooker with a thermostat for controlling oven heat and can also have a boiler

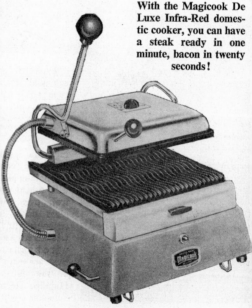

With the Magicook De Luxe Infra-Red domestic cooker, you can have a steak ready in one minute, bacon in twenty seconds!

MAKING THE BEST OF WHAT YOU HAVE

Many people have to make the best of the cooker already installed, even when moving into new premises. If, for instance, it also provides domestic hot water and central heating and is quite effective for cooking, it would obviously be an unjustifiable expense to replace it, simply because of a preference for one kind of cooking over another.

The most practical alternative under such circumstances is to learn to get the best out of the existing cooker and supplement it with one of the new electric "cook at the table" portable appliances.

A continuous burning heat storage cooker provides excellent cooking facilities at all times. Above is the Aga CB De Luxe Model

Solid fuel cookers will roast or bake at all temperatures and the hot-plates provide graded heats. Below is a Rayburn Royal freestanding cooker

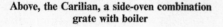

Above, the Carilian, a side-oven combination grate with boiler

There are frypan/cookers, cooker/boilers, griddle/hot plates, pressure cookers, all made of heavy aluminium and quite smart enough to come to the dinner table.

Cooking is simplified to positively mathematical precision, there being a thermostatic setting and time for every dish. Best of all, the hostess has only to prepare the raw materials for the meal beforehand and the guests sit round the table and watch the food cook. There is even a portable Rotisserie for spit-roasting, the fat-free method of cookery that really does preserve all the flavour.

KEEPING FOOD FRESH

*For absolute safety, particularly in summer, many foods must be
stored at low temperatures, and that means some form of refrigeration*

The cheapest fridge on the
market, the 2 cubic feet
capacity Gascold is ideal for
the tiny kitchen. Absolutely silent, it's white, lined
turquoise green

THE safe storage tem-
perature for most
perishable foods is below
45° F. Uncooked meat
and poultry require a still
lower temperature, a few
degrees above freezing
point. This means that,
however good the larder
accommodation, all
homes should, ideally,
have a refrigerator to ensure safe food storage
during summer months.

REFRIGERATORS

Apart from the safety
angle, a refrigerator is a
most useful piece of
household equipment. It

The New World 200 gas refrigerator
can be installed as a wall fitting.
Its cabinet is made of plastic all in
one piece and won't chip

saves food spoilage, thus reducing
costs; cuts out the need for very frequent shopping and makes it possible
to use left-overs appetisingly. It also
permits an increased repertoire of interesting dishes without adding to
catering costs, enables frozen foods to
be stored for two or three days and ice
cream for several hours, and provides
ice for drinks.

Domestic refrigerators are of both
the absorption and motor compressor
type. The former can be operated by
mains (gas or electricity) or bottled
gas or paraffin as well as by electricity.
Motor compressor types are electrically driven.

In appearance the two types are
practically indistinguishable, though
each make differs slightly in styling
and detail. A five-year
guarantee of the unit (absorption or compressor)
and one-year of the cab-
inet is usual. Neither
kind should cause radio
or television interference.

Absorption Refrigerators

Absorption refrigera-
tors have the advantage
of being permanently si-
lent and free from vibra-
tion. Due to the absence
of any moving parts,
mechanical wear is non-
existent and the potential
life of the cooling unit
long. Also electric models
can be operated on D.C.
as well as A.C., and vol-
tage changes can be easily
and inexpensively carried
out. Conversion from
one system (paraffin, gas
or electricity) to another
can also be effected quite
inexpensively. An ab-

of every inch of storage space (most important in today's small kitchens) and their adaptability. Many of the small and medium size models can be installed either in a free standing position, built under existing work surfaces, or placed chest high in a line with kitchen units.

There are doors to open within the width of the cabinet which can be provided with either right- or left-hand opening, so that the refrigerator can, if kitchen space is limited, be pushed up tight against other units. One wall-

You can choose the Hotpoint Iced Diamond with a door that opens left or right, have it built under a working surface or placed chest high. There's an inside light

Prestcold's "New Big Four," with gay coloured table top, has concealed wheels for easy moving, lots of storage space and a large salad "crispator"

sorption unit can be made as small as desired and therefore refrigerators of $1\frac{1}{2}$ to $2\frac{1}{2}$ cu. feet at low prices are available.

Motor Compressor Refrigerators

Star features of compressor refrigerators are high freezing speeds and specially low running costs. Modern units are enclosed and hermetically sealed, which cuts down running noise considerably and minimises wear.

Full Use of Space

Most outstanding features in modern refrigerator design are the skilful arrangement of interior fittings to make full use

mounted refrigerator has the handle at the bottom of the door.

For ease of movement when cleaning, one is mounted on rollers, another equipped with two wheels which brake automatically.

Inside there is a place for everything. Plastic or polythene is much used for shelf coverings, thus making the shelves smooth and quiet in use. Adjustable shelves help to increase storage space. The adjustable shelves of one four-cubic-foot model give a choice of twenty basic arrangements. Frozen food compartments are larger,

The English Rose Heat Pump provides 5·4 cubic feet of refrigeration, hot water for bathroom, sink and basins and cool air for the kitchen in summer

In colour, white and cream are still top favourites and cool cleanliness is reflected inside by fittings in pale and crystal shades —turquoise, ice-blue, beige, pearl grey and pale green.

Portable Model

There is even a portable refrigerator compact enough to fit into a car boot, yet with a storage capacity of 1·25 cubic feet, which can be run from a mains or low voltage supply and is therefore suitable for use on boats, in beach huts and caravans. It has a top-opening lid, a food rack that lifts right out and is quite safe at any angle—an important consideration in a boat or caravan.

Prices

Styling and detail do affect price a little, but generally speaking, it is usually commensurate with capacity, irrespective of type. Smallest and cheapest model costs £29 inclusive of tax.

Care and Servicing

Beyond keeping scrupulously clean, remembering always to close the doors firmly and to defrost periodically, refrigerators need little attention from the housewife. Any spilt liquids should be wiped up immediately and the interior washed regularly with warm water in which a little bicarbonate of soda is dissolved. Soap or detergent is not recommended. Detailed instructions for defrosting are supplied with each machine. There is now a compact little unit, the Smiths-Waldy Defromatic, as easily wired as an ordinary plug-top, that will automatically de-frost any electric refrigerator during the night. Instructions as to loading the cabinet to best advantage and to regulation of temperatures are also given. Electric and gas models are thermostatically controlled. Any make of machine is liable to need expert servicing periodically and most manufacturers send

colder and often wider; for example, the freezer of one model will store nearly 7 lb. of frozen foods and contains a separate compartment for ice cubes.

One refrigerator is made from plastic throughout. The cabinet is in one piece, without cracks or crevices to collect dirt. It cannot chip, rust or discolour. Many of the table-top models are heat-proof and colourful, providing a handy tray as well as a useful working surface. Special features include door space to keep butter at "spreading temperature," an egg rack and room for bottles, large and small; chill trays for fish and meat, and an easy-close, no-slam lock on the door.

out their own service engineers.

FRIDGE-HEATERS

A very interesting alternative to a refrigerator for those building or converting a house is a unit that, while heating all the domestic hot water, simultaneously cools a kitchen and also provides an ice-box.

This unit works on the heat pump principle, utilising warmth from the air. Electricity is required to provide the motive power, and running costs (on average national rate) are estimated at about 10s. per week for 500 gallons of hot water at 140° Fahrenheit or 6s. 6d. a week for 250 gallons, including refrigeration at a temperature of 38° Fahrenheit in the cabinet and 15° Fahrenheit in the evaporator, and cooling air to the kitchen when required in hot weather.

Deep freeze has come to stay. The "Presto-freeze" has a capacity of 5 cubic feet at a temperature of 0° Fahrenheit, easy running castors, four wire baskets

The Sivia Model 31 portable has three wire shelves that lift right out, runs from a mains or low voltage supply—ideal for boats and caravans

When the outside temperature drops below 40° Fahrenheit, the efficiency of the Heat Pump is maintained by an automatic booster, which can also be brought into operation when abnormal demands are made on the supply of hot water.

HOME FREEZERS

Home freezers are a form of cold store operating at much lower temperatures than the ordinary domestic refrigerator. They have a dual purpose: first, to freeze specially prepared fresh food and secondly to store the food at a very low temperature for periods of months. Summer fruits and vegetables can be frozen as they ripen and kept, ready to serve in fresh condition in the depth of winter. The same applies to poultry, meat, game and fresh-caught fish.

All food frozen and stored in a home freezer has to be correctly prepared. Vegetables require blanching and fruit sugaring, or putting into syrup. Poultry must be drawn and cleaned. Packing in special boxes, cartons or bag containers with heat sealing, sealing with special tape or with a bag fastener is advisable. Home freeze cabinets are more expensive than the largest size domestic refrigerators, but for those with substantial quantities of home-grown produce, they soon pay back their cost.

Dairy produce may also be frozen and stored at 0° F., and baked or unbaked cakes, bread and pastry can also be cooled, packaged and kept in the freezer until required.

381

PRACTICAL FOOD STORAGE

Perishables, dry goods, even cans and jars only remain
at their best if kept under the proper conditions

Defrost your refrigerator regularly. Stains will come off easily if shelves are wiped with a mild sudsing cleanser and a damp cloth. Specially photographed at the Hedley Home & Beauty Information Service)

WITH A REFRIGERATOR

STORING food the right way when you get it home is just as important as buying it wisely and economically. Even perishable goods like fish, vegetables, fruit and meat generally have to wait for a few hours between being bought and cooked. Groceries, butter and canned articles, on the other hand, are usually purchased at weekly or monthly intervals and used only as required. So everything has to be stored either for long or short periods, and it is therefore important to know the exact conditions under which different types of food keep best.

A refrigerator does, of course, solve more than half the problem. The next best thing—and still valuable even if you have a "fridge"—is a good airy storage cupboard in a cool, dry place, preferably facing north, where it will not be subjected to drastic changes of temperature. Instead of having the cupboard in the kitchen, which gets hot whenever you bake, then cools down suddenly when you open the window to let out the cooking smells, it is far better to choose a spot just outside where the temperature will remain constant. Otherwise the condensation will produce damp, dry goods will go lumpy, packets get limp and soggy, and canned foods be in danger from rust, which is quite capable of eating its way into even the best of lacquered food cans after a time.

Choose a lot of shallow shelves in preference to a few deep ones, fix up a good light so that you can see what you are looking for without fumbling, label everything clearly—and also write the date of purchase on all tins, jars, packets, etc., as well as the date on which jams were made or fruits bottled. This will help you to use up the older ones first and also remind you when things have been in store a long time and ought to be used, before they begin to deteriorate.

At least four times a year—more often if you have the time—a food cupboard should be turned out, thoroughly cleaned and the contents inspected. In view of the need to keep out damp, do be sure to dry the shelves thoroughly after washing them. Dry goods need very careful watching because of the various forms of tiny mites that sometimes flourish in them. Anything contaminated by these should be thrown away before it infects the other contents of the cupboard. Canned goods need wiping with a dry cloth and should be watched for the appearance of pinpoints of rust. It is advisable to open and use the contents of a can beginning to rust rather than risk further damage. Tins of fruit, fruit juice, milk, cream and other liquids should be turned upside down when the cupboard is cleaned, so that the liquid runs to the other end of the can.

A food can with an inward dent in it need not worry you; the chances are that it has been dropped in the shop or factory and no harm will come to the contents. But an outward bulge indicates the presence of air and is a serious danger sign. Such a can and its contents should be thrown away forthwith and no attempt made to taste or experiment with the food inside. This condition is, however, a very rare occurrence nowadays, and canned foods are as safe as fresh ones (sometimes safer).

Some foods like extreme cold, others keep better at a more moderate temperature. Here is a guide, starting with those requiring very low temperatures.

Store in the coldest part of the refrigerator, or in the coolest available spot:

Uncooked Fish—no need to cover it, and it will not contaminate other foods if stored in the tray just below the freezing unit, the coldest part of the refrigerator.

Milk is at its best at a temperature of 50° F. Keep it high up in the refrigerator, but remember always to cover milk, in or out of the fridge and even when standing on the table for more than a few seconds, because it is so susceptible to flies and dust. You can either replace the dairy's bottle top or cover bottle or jug with a washable plastic cover. These can be bought in assorted sizes to fit anything from a milk bottle to a mixing bowl—and some have elastic round the base to make them fit tightly.

Butter, Margarine, Cooking Fats and Cream require the same conditions as milk. They tend to absorb the taste of stronger flavoured foods with which they come in contact, so should always be well wrapped in greaseproof paper.

Uncooked Meat and Poultry need dry cold, as close to freezing as possible. May be uncovered in a refrigerator, but need protection from flies elsewhere.

Quick Frozen Foods.—Keep in a cold area for up to 24 hours and thaw out at room temperature one hour before cooking.

Store lower down the refrigerator, in the cool but not freezing:

Cooked Meat, Fish, Left-overs, Soups and Stock can all go, uncovered, into the

If all the bottles, jars and cans in your store cupboard are dated when you buy them, you can be sure of using up the oldest first and not keeping anything too long

refrigerator, but must be covered if kept in a cupboard. Cold meat can be wrapped in greaseproof paper to prevent hardening on the outside due to the cold in the fridge.

Eggs need a good current of cool air and should be put into a bowl or basket and kept low down in the refrigerator.

Raw Vegetables, such as cauliflower, asparagus, new carrots, tomatoes and radishes, keep best, uncovered, at the bottom of a refrigerator or in a cool place. Vegetables and fruits want a cool, moist atmosphere to keep them fresh and crisp.

Salads—lettuce and other salad greens should be washed and dried, then stored low down in the refrigerator in covered containers or plastic bags so that they retain their moisture.

Soft Fruits, both cooked and raw, may be kept in the refrigerator. Low temperatures prevent them from ripening too soon.

Bacon, so long as it is well wrapped in greaseproof paper to prevent it becoming hard, may be kept in the refrigerator or any cool place.

Do not store these foods in the refrigerator:

Cheese gets hard on the outside in intense cold and also tends to contaminate other foods. Cheeses, particularly the strong kinds, keep best if they are wrapped in muslin steeped in vinegar and water and put in a cool place.

Bananas, Pineapple and Melon have a habit of contaminating everything else in a refrigerator with their own flavour, so keep them out.

Cucumber can be chilled for a short time, but will not keep if stored in the refrigerator

A good free circulation of air, both inside a refrigerator and in a cupboard, is essential if food is to be kept fresh and good. It is therefore unwise to pack too many things in on top of one another. If the refrigerator gets overcrowded, you will find that plastic food bags, being soft and pliable, take up less space than solid containers.

Bread, of course, comes into a category of its own from the storage point of view. It likes a ventilated bread bin, preferably on a ledge or shelf in a cool spot where there is a good current of air. Lacking these conditions, it may go mouldy.

Canned Goods

Remember, too, that even canned goods, those standbys of the emergency cupboard, have a life span which should not be exceeded and which varies between 6 months and 5 years. That is why it is so important to write the date of purchase on cans. Then you can be sure to eat up:

Canned Fish in Oil and *Canned Meat* before it is more than 5 *years old.*

Canned Jam and *Honey* within 3 *years.*

Canned Vegetables in under 2 *years.*

Canned Fruits and *Milk* and *Canned Fish in Tomato Sauce* within 12 *months* at the very most.

Condensed Milk in 6 *months.*

Dry Goods

Amongst the dry goods in your store cupboard, you will find that cornflour lasts almost indefinitely, provided you keep it screwed up and in a dry place; barley, peas and beans keep for about 6 months before

A portable bell-shaped safe like this one can be hung up in a good draught to keep its contents cool and fresh

POTS AND PANS GO GAY TOO

Cooking utensils, like everything else in the well-planned modern home, are now decorative and colourful as well as
practical and labour-saving.   From the Mirroware range, with their gay red and white handles, come the selection
shown here—top, the saucepan available in three sizes; centre, the Tallboy Dial-o-matic pressure cooker; right, the
Mirromagic "can't boil over" milk pan with its unusual shape; and below, the fish fryer with basket and lid.

OVENWARE COMES TO TABLE

It's smart enough for any occasion—
and keeps the food really hot, too

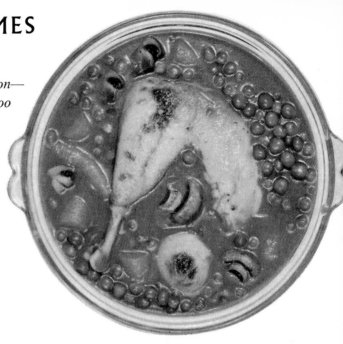

Decorative ovenware has brought a new interest to the twin arts of cooking and entertaining. Nowadays you prepare the food for the table, arranging it with an eye to shape, colour contrast and general appearance, when you get it ready for the oven. At the appointed time, cooking completed, out it comes ready, after the slightest attention, for transport to table.

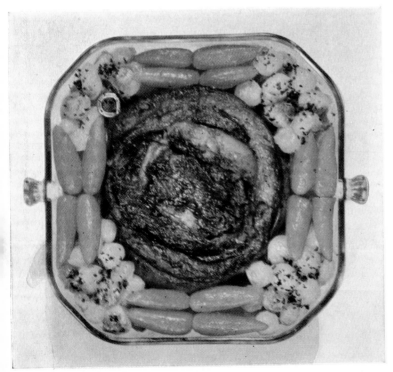

There is a variety of shapes—and colours, too—obtainable in oven-glass. Two from the Phoenix Gourmet range are seen on this page with their lids removed. The round one (above) contains chicken cooked with mushrooms and green peas in a rich sauce; the square one (left) a round of beef roast with new potatoes and baby carrots.

Top left, a delicious breakfast menu of chipolata sausages and fried eggs served in Rorstrand Gratina ovenware from Sweden, with its ruby-red exterior and soft bluish-green inside.

Remember: even the best ovenware doesn't like being exposed to sudden drastic changes of temperature—from oven to sink, for instance!

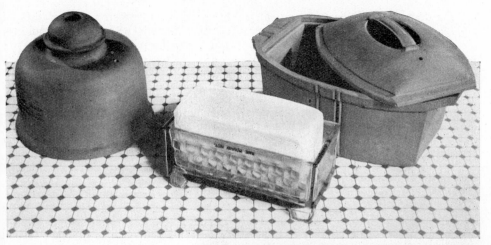

When you can't keep dairy produce on ice, keep it in the coldest possible conditions—standing in a little cold water in these covered coolers, for instance

This simple food safe is fly- and dust-proof when the door is pulled down, but gets a good current of air through wire mesh sides

becoming hard; custard powder stays good for at least 1 year, cocoa for 6 months, flour for 3 months, oatmeal for 2 months and dried fruits for 6–12 months. Coffee and all ground spices (except pepper, which lasts indefinitely) lose their strength quickly and should always be bought in small quantities and used promptly. Even if kept in an airtight container, coffee loses its flavour within a day or two of grinding. It is therefore much more economical to invest in a grinder and buy coffee beans for grinding at home as required.

WITHOUT A REFRIGERATOR

Compiled by the National Institute of Houseworkers

Making a Larder

IT is essential to have a larder, a ventilated food cupboard or a food safe to store perishable foods in the absence of a refrigerator. Food will go bad quickly if it is shut up in a cupboard without any air, but it should not be left about, as it will encourage mice and flies.

If there is nowhere suitable for food storage in your house it is quite simple to make a food safe if you are handy with hammer and tacks. Take a strong wooden box (an apple box with a division in the centre which can act as a shelf is excellent).

make a door, using a sheet of wire gauze and the wood from the lid to form a frame. Fix on with hinges and fasten with a turn button. Place this safe in an airy place and use for the storage of all perishable foods.

A shelf with a cool surface is a great asset in a larder or food cupboard. A marble top from an old washstand, a piece of slate or plate glass, or even a couple of butcher's trays, are excellent for the storage of perishable goods.

Care of the Food Safe

Put food left over after a meal on clean dishes. Never put steaming hot food into the larder or food safe as it may turn the existing contents bad. Every day see what food is left over and use it up. Wipe up any food that has been spilt. Once a week scrub out with a good soap; if bothered with flies, spray the inside of the larder or safe with a D.D.T. atomiser, first making sure that there is no food about. Keep food covered, using pieces of clean muslin, talc or wire covers, Cellophane or metal foil paper. Wash these covers once a week.

Some foods need special care if they are to be kept in good condition, especially in warm and thundery weather.

Meat.—Wipe raw meat with a cloth wrung out in vinegar and water. Place on a grid over a clean plate and keep covered. If any portion of a piece of meat gets contaminated by flies, that piece must be cut off. Cooked meats or the remains of the joint can be wrapped in greaseproof paper. Keep bacon in clean greaseproof paper, and use rashers where a bone has been removed first, as these go bad quickly.

Raw Fish is not a good food to keep, so buy and use up as soon as possible. If it has to be kept, place on a clean dish and sprinkle liberally with salt. A whole fish will always keep better than fillets.

Milk.—Never leave milk standing on the doorstep for any length of time; it may well be in the blazing sun, where dogs and cats can lick round the bottles and birds often remove the caps and drink the cream. If you are out when the milk is delivered arrange with the milkman to leave it in some shady safe place. If there is no alternative, leave a covered tin on the doorstep for the milk to be put in.

Milk keeps best in bottles. Special milk coolers are available, which have to be soaked in cold water and then put over the bottles; alternatively the bottles can be stood in a vessel containing salt and water (2 teaspoonfuls to the pint) and covered with a piece of muslin, the ends of which must dip down into the water so that the muslin always keeps wet.

Never mix the previous day's milk with the new supply, as the old milk may turn the new milk sour very quickly, and do not use dirty milk jugs for fresh milk. If, despite all your efforts, milk goes sour, use it for mixing scones, cakes or puddings.

In hot weather it may be necessary to scald milk to keep it fresh. To do this, bring the milk to the boil quickly, pour it into a jug and stand it in a basin of cold water to cool quickly.

Fats must be kept on the cool shelf in your safe or larder. They can also be treated like milk—that is, placed under a cooler or in a bowl which stands in another with salt and water in it and covered with muslin.

Lettuce and Green Vegetables.—Keep in a dark place, wrap in newspaper or keep in an old saucepan with the lid on.

Apples and Root Vegetables.—Look over and use first any that are bruised. A damaged apple or vegetable will cause others to decay unless removed.

Soft Fruit.—Look over, remove stalks and place in a basin with sugar.

Butter and fats will not turn to oil in hot weather if kept in a cooler soaked first in cold water

HOME PRECAUTIONS AGAINST FOOD POISONING

*For the protection of your family, watch for the
unsuspected dangers that lurk in your kitchen*

by A. H. WALTERS, F.I.M.L.T., M.R.SAN.I.

"THE standard of food hygiene in this country must be raised." That statement has been voiced in the press, on the radio, in Parliament, even on the village green, with increasing frequency during the past few years. And rightly so, for it concerns us all. But it is the housewife particularly who has it in her power to see that the standard *is* raised.

She can start off by boycotting shops that are obviously dirty; ones where food is handled unnecessarily by assistants who do not appear to be clean in their personal habits, who blow in paper bags to open them or lick their fingers to get a better hold on a piece of greaseproof paper and, in between whiles, dangle a cigarette from their lips.

Having made sure that she has bought her foodstuffs from the cleanest possible source, it is up to the housewife to practise what she preaches in her own home. And this includes setting a high standard of hygiene for the rest of the family to follow.

The word hygiene, often thought of as being synonymous with "extra" cleanliness, is, in fact, open to the widest possible interpretation. Some people consider food-handling hygiene almost as a religion, while others regard it as rather a fad. However, since hygiene is a system of rules for promotion of health and the prevention of disease, it naturally follows that food-handling hygiene is a system of rules for the promotion of health by the prevention of food poisoning; and as most food poisoning is infectious, it must be preventable.

"Food poisoning" is the term used to describe any illness caused by eating or drinking anything unfit for human consumption. There are two principal causes of food poisoning, namely: chemical and bacteriological.

Direct Chemical Causes

Food poisoning due to contamination of food with metals is occasionally reported. Antimony poisoning can arise from food cooked in cheap grey-enamelled pots; cadmium poisoning has been reported when acid fluids such as wine, fruit drinks and jellies have been stored in cadmium-lined containers; and zinc poisoning when acid fruits, such as apples, have been cooked in a galvanised iron kettle. Barium carbonate and sodium fluoride have been mistaken for flour or baking powder and put into pastry and tarts.

Certain mushrooms and toadstools have well-known toxic properties, and occasionally rhubarb leaves, eaten as greens, have caused oxalic acid poisoning. Rye meal or fungus-infected rye bread can cause ergot poisoning. Certain mussels may contain an excess of complex alkaloids which can be toxic. Most fish food poisoning, however, is the result of microbic infection.

Indirect Chemical Causes

If certain bacteria infect food they will grow rapidly in it, especially if warm, moist conditions prevail, and as these germs multiply they excrete a poison which can be toxic to man when the food is eaten.

Here are two examples:

(1) Botulism (botulus, a sausage) is caused by the toxin produced in food by the anærobic soil bacterium, clostridium botulinum. This infection is found principally in canned foods, such as sausage, fish, meat and vegetables, and arises where heat treatment at the canning factory has been insufficient. Ordinary warming does not destroy the toxin, but thorough boiling does. Owing to excellent canning factory control, botulism is very rare indeed in the U.K. to-day.

387

(2) Staphylococcal food poisoning is caused by a toxin produced in food by the microbes known as staphylococci. Foods that may be affected include meat pies, cakes, sandwiches, meats, pastries, gravies, trifles, bread puddings, fish cakes, tarts, brawn, salad cream and synthetic cream. Unlike those affected with Cl. botulinum, foodstuffs affected with staphylococcal enterotoxin in amounts sufficient to cause food poisoning very rarely have any untoward odour or taste. Only prolonged boiling will break down this toxin. Many food poisoning cases are due to staphylococci, and these germs are frequently found in the noses, throats and hands of food handlers, and in skin infections such as boils and pimples.

Infection

Certain food poisoning bacteria other than staphylococci can infect food and grow in it without detectable taste or smell. Then, when the food is eaten, these germs gain access to the gut of the consumer, multiply there and cause a typical gastro-enteric form of poisoning.

An example of this type of infection is that caused by the Salmonella group of bacteria. These germs are normally carried in the gut by pigs, poultry, cows, bullocks, sheep, domestic animals and rodents, and, to a lesser extent, human beings. Eggs (especially duck), egg powder and milk can also be affected.

These three examples briefly outline the main chemical and microbic causes of food poisoning.

The hygiene hazards in the kitchen run by the housewife with a comparatively small turnover of meals and utensils will, of course, be generally far less than those in large kitchens with a huge turnover and attendant staff problems. But there can be very real problems in the home, and the first of these concerns personal hygiene.

For the housewife this not only affects herself but also everyone else in the home, since she is the common link between them all. Obviously she will be aware of the risks of transferring any possible infection from her own person into food through handling, hair and clothing; and there is also the possible transmission of infection

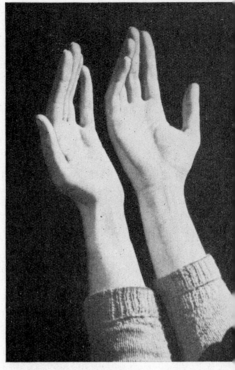

Always wash the hands in hot water with soap after going to the toilet and before preparing food

via similar sources from other members of the household. Undoubtedly, the most important vehicles for carrying infection to food in the home are the hands.

Hands

Staphylococcal food poisoning can start from infected hands. Hands in contact with food must be free of any septic spots, cuts or rashes. Sodden or dirty linen bandages do not provide adequate protection and if someone with a hand or finger lesion has to go on handling food, waterproof dressings must be used.

After using the lavatory, hands must always be carefully washed in hot water with soap. After handling and preparing vegetables, which are often soiled with manured earth, the hands should be washed (see also next chapter).

The Kitchen

Obviously the better planned and equipped a kitchen is, the easier work becomes and the simpler it is to keep clean

It does not follow, however, that good hygiene cannot be achieved in an old-fashioned kitchen or that eye-appeal modernity will automatically ensure good hygiene. The questions most housewives will want answered are these:

How much scrubbing down is necessary in a kitchen?

Do tea towels need boiling every day?

Do food utensils actually hold any contamination?

To the bacteriologist all these questions centre on cleaning and the answer is: All surfaces with which raw food has been in contact require thorough cleaning and so do all utensils which have been used for the preparation and cooking of food.

Dishcloths

Before cooking, meat is freely handled and placed upon or cut up on surfaces. Cooking sterilises, but what of the cook's hands, and the cloth which may have been used to wipe over the meat and also to mop over any surfaces with which the meat came into contact? Here, obviously, are ways of spreading infection.

Vegetables are often soiled with mud and manure, yet they are introduced right into the kitchen, often on to a table or draining board. After they have been prepared, the surface on which they have been may get a quick wipe with the dishcloth—again a possible means of spreading infection.

On some days the pots and pans may get particularly sticky and require a lot of rubbing around during cleaning. The hot water supply may not be all that one might desire, so the dishcloth will pick up food residues. Then, possibly, flies from the dustbin outside alight on the dishcloth left on the side of the sink—it can happen. Suddenly a basin is wanted quickly in which to make a custard, or artificial cream. Perhaps this particular basin has not been used for some time and is dusty. The dishcloth is rapidly wiped round the inside of the basin, and then warm custard or synthetic cream is put into it. This may happen in the morning and the custard or cream will not be eaten until evening. So, any infection which may have been transferred from the dishcloth to the basin now has a good medium in which to grow for perhaps as long as eight hours.

Under such conditions, disease germs can flourish and food poisoning may be the result. Also, sometimes cutlery is hastily wiped over with a dishcloth that may not be too clean—another way of transferring disease germs.

The dishcloth should always look white and clean, never greasy and stained, for in that condition it is certain to carry infection. To keep dishcloths in a satisfactory

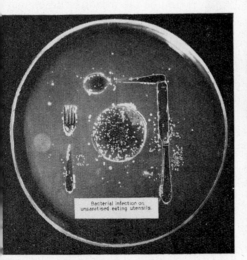

Cutlery washed up under insanitary conditions reveals extensive bacterial infection and could very easily cause illness

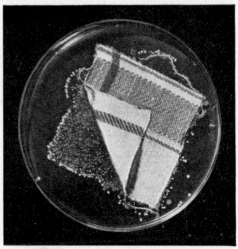

That stained, greasy dishcloth that lives on the edge of the sink and is used for all sorts of jobs is a source of extensive bacterial infection

condition, they can be boiled in soda water, or, better still, soaked in a hypochlorite solution which will free them from infection, deodorise them and keep them white.

Airborne Infections

Apart from infections that can be brought into the kitchen by the food itself and spread by careless washing and handling, there is the possibility of airborne infections. These may be caused by coughing and sneezing, dust

Dirty sinks and dishcloths (above) and greasy washing-up water always harbour infection. Plates washed like that are dangerous to all who eat from them

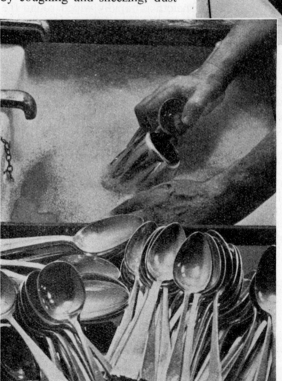

A clean grease-free sink and plenty of hot water softened with soap or detergent (above) spell good hygiene in the kitchen

alight on cold meat or custards or creams, can grow and cause food poisoning.

Some housewives are not too particular when sweeping up in a kitchen, shaking mats or dusting. Raising clouds of dust in these ways may have an effect similar to that of coughing and sneezing and be the means of disseminating disease germs in a kitchen. Reasonable care is all that is necessary, coupled with damp dusting—if dusting is required.

One of the things which strikes an American housewife on entering the average kitchen in the U.K. is the almost universal lack of wire screening over windows and doors to keep out flies. Curiously enough, at the turn of the twentieth century, wire screening of pantries was common in Britain but is rarely seen to-day, perhaps because of the growth of refrigeration and the good supply of fly-sprays now available. Flies usually breed outside in rubbish, garbage and dung, and then gain entrance into the house as adult winged specimens; they are a disease menace which must be seriously considered when discussing food hygiene.

and flies. It is obvious that if a person has a bad cold, the way to spread the infection around is to sneeze and cough about the place. In this way, many thousands of droplets are expelled from the nose and throat. These carry potential disease germs, not only of the common cold, but, in certain circumstances, also certain types of staphylococcus germs which, if they

The Human Hazard

It sometimes happens, as is well known, that a perfectly healthy person can carry disease germs in the gut, nose and even on the skin without being aware of it. Those who have recently suffered such diseases as dysentery can carry the germs for several months after recovering completely from the original infection. Indeed, a famous case was that of "Typhoid Mary," an American cook, a typhoid carrier, who was paid a pension by the U.S. Government for nearly fifty years in order to keep her away from the kitchen. She was, of course, an exceptional case.

Any such hazard from a housewife would best be met by her own fastidiousness in the matter of handwashing and personal hygiene. For good kitchen habits add up to good food hygiene, and this is especially important in the training of children.

In the home kitchen a good housewife can maintain a high standard with elbow grease, sufficient hot water and her own homely methods properly done. Experience and common sense prove this every day. On the other hand, a filthy, soaking tea towel is obviously wrong. So is a dirty brown, greasy dishcloth or a stained sink. All these things speak for themselves—and are not seen in any decent household. But if there is contagious illness in the home, there is an added hazard present which demands added precautions. Food utensils,

linen, thermometers, everything used by the sick person should be disinfected after washing.

In the country, or when travelling abroad, there may be the hazard of infection in the water supply through lack of chlorination. This risk can be easily overcome by the use of a chlorine compound such as Milton, which can also be used for sickroom disinfection.

Washing-up

Is there any proof that dishes which have been washed and air-dried are less contaminated than those which have been dried with cloths?

This is a question often asked of the bacteriologist concerned with food hygiene. It all depends on the state of the dishwater, the surface of the dishes and the conditions of the drying cloth. In a well-run home kitchen, either rack-drying or cloth-drying is satisfactory. In a communal meal kitchen there is usually less contamination after air-drying utensils because cloths get wet over and over again.

Food covers present another problem. Though the type of cover used is entirely a matter of taste, badly designed ones covered with nooks and crannies should be avoided, also metal covers which go rusty. Food covers should be thoroughly washed in very hot water, or given a sterilising chemical rinse, the best method for plastic,

To sum up, the climate of opinion on the subject of food-handling hygiene swings violently from fadism on the one hand to *laissez faire* on the other. Between these two extremes, common sense and experience must operate. And to-day, with the aid of science, simple rules of hygiene can be drawn up and systematically applied:

(1) Scrupulous cleanliness required for: sinks, draining boards, chopping boards, table tops, dishcloths, tea towels, mincers, cream bags, crockery, cutlery, basins, pots and pans.

(2) Protect all food from dust, flies and unnecessary handling.

(3) Especially in hot weather, use all perishable foods on the day they are prepared; or use a refrigerator.

(4) Keep hands and nails in good trim. Wash thoroughly after toilet or housework and before handling food.

(5) Do not sneeze or cough over food.

The common house fly is a menace to health. He lives outside on dung or refuse, then, if you let him, comes into the house and walks all over uncovered food

HANDLE WITH CARE

These foods may be a source of danger

by A. H. WALTERS, F.I.M.L.T., M.R.SAN.I.

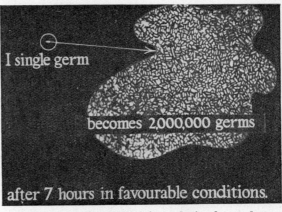

I single germ

becomes 2,000,000 germs

after 7 hours in favourable conditions.

Suppose a single germ gets into a basin of custard at 10 a.m.—by teatime there are 2,000,000 germs to set up acute food poisoning

THE efforts of the Public Health Authorities to improve food hygiene are aimed at reducing the high number of cases of food poisoning which occur every year. Quite apart from the mass outbreaks after outings or parties, or in schools or resident institutions, odd food poisoning cases occur every day in our homes. Often they are the result of some mistake in food handling in the household kitchen. It may be no more than just the occasional case of diarrhœa and possibly vomiting among the children. Nevertheless, the risks of such infections are avoidable; and my purpose is to describe the possible causes and outline methods of prevention with regard to particular foodstuffs.

Meat

Most women hate the thought of an abattoir. Such places are necessary but not pleasant. In them, blood and fæces of animals are splashed about and, although hygiene conditions are improving, the slaughtermen, as a rule, do not pay much heed to such niceties as the sterilisation of their knives or wiping-down cloths. Then follows the journey the carcases must make in the (sometimes not too clean) meat lorry, after which they are humped on the back of a meat porter into the butcher's shop. The butcher usually displays and finally handles the meat while cutting and serving it to his customer, who leaves the shop with the purchase quite possibly wrapped rather inadequately. So, from the time the living beast passes into the abattoir, until it reaches the kitchen table as meat, its surface, at least, is exposed to a number of infection hazards.

The degree of surface infection varies, but the risk is always there. When the meat reaches the kitchen, it will either be used straight away or stored. As soon as possible after reaching the kitchen, the meat should be carefully inspected for fly ova deposits. Joints should be quickly washed under the cold running tap and any discoloured portions cut away. If a refrigerator is available, cold storage will not permit any surface infection to increase. If stored at atmospheric temperature in the kitchen or larder, then infection can multiply on the meat surface according to season, humidity and length of time before cooking.

Such hazards have been recognised for centuries by cooks and housewives, and all over the world different methods of meat preservation are to be found, such as sprinkling with salt and soaking in brine or vinegar. To-day, particularly in hot weather, many housewives wipe over meat with a clean cloth previously wrung out in a solution of electrolytic sodium hypochlorite (such as Milton) for the purpose of destroying surface infection.

Cooked Meat

The act of cooking meat is, in most cases, equivalent to sterilising it. Indeed, some historians believe that cooking was evolved as a primitive method of keeping meat. In the oven, in the pan or on the grill, the meat is heated at a sufficiently high temperature for long enough to kill any growing germs which might be present on or in it. But it does not follow that once meat or meat products have been cooked they are safe from contamination. This applies particularly to stock, gravies, soup and meat jellies, which may be allowed to stand about from one day to the next in a hot kitchen. Such foods can pick up infection from dust and utensils (as explained in the previous chapter) and food poisoning bacteria can grow rapidly in them. Reheating is not usually sufficient to kill any infection or toxin which may have been generated. Food poisoning therefore can and does arise.

The housewife may wonder why it is she needs to be so particular to prevent infection in most meats, but is encouraged to allow certain feathered game, hare and venison to hang before cooking until it gets high. The reason is that the birds and animals concerned are killed out of doors and in the wild state. The kinds of bacteria peculiar to high meats are similar in one respect to those which produce cheeses like Stilton, Blue, Gorgonzola and Camembert, in that they do not produce toxins injurious to man. Further, the conditions under which these peculiar types of germs grow do not normally permit disease germs to multiply. In any case, cooking renders all high meats quite safe. Nevertheless, if any meats, high or otherwise, are left about too long after cooking, especially if remaining in their own gravy or jelly, then food poisoning germs may grow in them.

Meat Products

All meat products, brisket, brawn, pies, mince and sausage, which may be bought pre-cooked may be open occasionally to some food poisoning risks during manufacture and transport. Against such risks the housewife is powerless unless the meat or meat product shows some obvious sign, such as greening, or has a detectable smell or unpleasant taste. However, she usually knows the origin of such foodstuffs and will take all reasonable precautions at the time of purchase. But once these meats or meat products are in her kitchen, the same hygiene rules apply to them as to any other meat. Briefly, all meat products should be kept cool and free from dust and flies; if not refrigerated, they should be eaten as soon after purchase as is reasonably possible.

Vegetables

Vegetables intended for cooking carry only one risk: they bring soil and perhaps particles of manure into the kitchen. After suitable preparation and cooking, vegetables are rendered both palatable and safe. So it only behoves the housewife to be careful in cleaning all surfaces or utensils with which the raw vegetables have been in contact.

But vegetables to be eaten raw in salads are different. Apart from washing, they pass direct to the eater from the ground, or, in the case of watercress, from bed or river which may carry sewage contamination. Anyone who has lived in the tropics knows well the risk of contracting enteric diseases after eating uncooked salads. Formerly, in hot countries, such salad vegetables were disinfected by soaking them in Condy's fluid, but recent research has proved even this to be unsafe and hypochlorite has taken its place. In temperate zones there is nothing like so great a danger arising from salad vegetables, but there are on record outbreaks of enteritis traced from this source in England, France, Germany, the United States, Scandinavia and other countries. The poliomyelitis virus is passed in human excreta and will live in water for several weeks. It is thought by some research workers that the virus may be passed on via sewage-contaminated vegetables, particularly, in some places, watercress and celery.

The disinfection of salad vegetables of both bacteria and viruses has been carefully studied and a very simple method evolved. All that is necessary is to immerse the washed vegetables for 15 minutes in a dilute hypochlorite solution (2 tablespoonfuls Milton to 2 quarts water). No taste or discoloration results from this treatment, which makes the vegetables perfectly safe to eat. Fruit, if desired, can be similarly treated but, broadly speaking, the food poisoning hazards with fruit do not loom large.

Eggs

Any egg, either fresh or preserved, which is considered suitable for eating should, when opened, have a pleasant smell, a yellow yolk free from spots, surrounded by a clear "white." Normally the contents of an egg are sterile, but just occasionally a diseased bird lays infected eggs. Some eggs are produced under dirty conditions and may thereby become infected. Hence the housewife should be suspicious of dirty eggs unless she knows where they came from. Ducks, if not kept under close supervision, often wander into all kinds of excreta and garbage and pick up infection which cannot be detected by the ordinary tests of sight and smell.

So, for safety, all duck eggs should be hard-boiled for 10–15 minutes. Before the war, in Germany, all duck eggs were labelled with such an instruction. Mayonnaise made from raw eggs, and also whipped raw-egg dressing, have been the cause of outbreaks of food poisoning. Both dried egg powder and frozen liquid egg

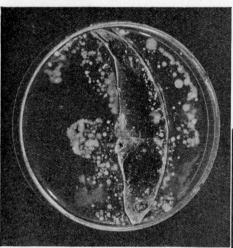

Invisible to the human eye, unfortunately, but just look at the bacterial infection on the uncooked fish (above)

have been shown to be potential carriers of food poisoning germs. For that reason, they should be used only for dishes or cakes which are to be cooked at a high temperature.

Generally speaking, in the home it is unwise to use egg powder or liquid egg for anything to be served uncooked or lightly heated. These products are used on a large scale, however, in industry, where they are under close supervision.

Fish

Fresh, cured, pickled or smoked fish sold in the fishmonger's is remarkably safe from food poisoning. Every housewife knows by smell and appearance if the fish is good, and very rarely indeed is it otherwise. But once it reaches the kitchen, the food hygiene rules already described apply, whether or not the fish has been cooked. So often fish heads and tails are put outside for the cat, and it is forgotten that what the cat leaves makes excellent breeding rubbish for flies.

Shell-fish such as crabs, lobsters, crayfish, prawns and shrimps, if not fresh, usually tell their own tale. The following characteristics indicate staleness: limpness, faded appearance, wet or sticky claws, offensive smell under shell, and a limp tail which, if pulled back, fails to spring forward again. In shell-fish such as oysters, mussels, cockles, scallops, periwinkles and whelks, other signs must be looked for. In former times, oysters were often responsible for food poisoning because they were grown in sewage-polluted water. Now,

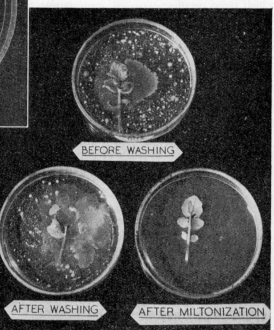

BEFORE WASHING

AFTER WASHING   AFTER MILTONIZATION

Watercress comes direct from bed or river which may carry sewage contamination. Ordinary washing is not enough. For absolute safety, immerse in a Milton solution for 15 minutes

however, they are carefully cleansed in chlorinated water and have become very safe indeed. One point, however, needs attention. When a housewife asks the fishmonger to open oysters for her, he should do this under the slow-running tap and not in a bowl of static water which may be infected with fæcal bacteria.

Mussels, cockles, scallops, periwinkles and whelks are all cooked before being eaten and very rarely cause any trouble, provided they are fresh. Occasionally, cockles which have been badly handled before reaching the fishmonger have caused food poisoning, but this is quite rare.

Sometimes, when on holiday, children gather mussels and cockles and like to cook them for home consumption. Such shell-fish should be inspected before cooking for gaping shells or offensive smell, which will indicate that they are unsound.

Fish cakes are usually made mainly from cooked fish and potatoes, and should contain at least 35 per cent. of fish by weight. These should be cooked and eaten as soon as possible and not stored at room temperature.

Canned fish should be turned out of the can when opened, but otherwise can be treated like any other foodstuff. Fish pastes are made from cooked fish, fat and cereal fillings, plus seasoning, flavours and colourings. The whole is crushed to a paste and packed into jars which are sealed and sterilised. Such pastes must contain at least 70 per cent. of fish. They are so manufactured that they keep well, especially if refrigerated, and when opened, if kept with the lid on when not in use, rarely, if ever, become infected except with harmless moulds. These, however, usually indicate to the housewife that it is time to throw the pot away.

Cream

Fresh cream is usually pasteurised before being offered for sale and so, when purchased, is safe from food poisoning germs. If stored in a refrigerator, pasteurised cream will remain fresh for several months. The practice still persists in some places of selling unpasteurised cream direct from an uncovered bowl on the dairy counter. Unless the producers and the retailers are scrupulously clean, such cream is wide open to infection from several points,

especially as preservatives are forbidden by law. The methods by which clotted creams are produced usually ensure a safe product, but contamination may occur during packing. So, if clotted cream is received by post, especially during very hot weather, it should be carefully examined before eating. If it is incorporated into whipped decorations for fruit salad and so on, cream should never be left exposed to dust. Even so, by the ordinary tests of sight and smell, it may not be possible to detect infection. However, if the cream was packed under unsatisfactory conditions it will probably show some signs of souring, which will put the housewife on her guard. Canned cream is quite safe and should be treated like any other canned food, but should be used soon after being turned out of the tin.

For decorating and filling pastries, artificial or "synthetic" cream is widely used in the catering and baking industries, but relatively little in the home. Such artificial creams have frequently been associated with outbreaks of food poisoning and should be used only strictly according to the maker's instructions.

Ice Cream

Ice cream is looked upon as a modern product. As an item of food it is, but as a rare luxury it has been eaten at least since the seventeenth century. At the everyday consumer level, ice cream was introduced in the United Kingdom by an Italian called Gatti about 1860. Until relatively recent times ice cream had been frequently associated with food poisoning, but better methods of manufacture and control have made it safe during production, except for rare accidents. However, the manner in which, after manufacture, it may be served is still often open to question. Wafers and cornets are dispensed with unsterile utensils taken from a milky and possibly infected jar of water, and the server may be handling wafers and cones with anything but clean hands. The housewife should watch these points before allowing her children to purchase ice creams. She would be wise to insist on buying only from vendors with a clean hygiene service. There are cases, however, where ice cream, badly handled, has become infected in the home. It has been placed on infected surfaces or cut with infected knives. Some people think that

After piping cream from savoy bags, the bags must always be boiled. Mock cream should only be used in accordance with maker's instructions and not kept too long

the low temperature of ice cream kills germs, but it does not.

Water ices, or iced lollies, so much favoured by children, have little or no nutritive value, and therefore cannot truly be said to be responsible for food poisoning. These products are not processed—only frozen—and no outbreak of food poisoning has been traced to them. Some criticism has been directed against them because minute traces of metal from the moulds have been found in them, but no marked untoward results have been reported.

Milk

There is little comment to pass on milk, provided it is pasteurised and properly stored. In raw milk, however, disease germs of several kinds, as well as those of food poisoning, can be passed to the drinker. Everything depends on the conditions under which the milk is collected, distributed and stored. Considering the possible hazards, there is no doubt that pasteurised milk is safest, but considerable quantities of raw milk are still consumed daily.

The growth of the T.T. herds, the use of abortus vaccines and the help given by the National Agricultural Advisory Service represent great strides in making raw milk safer, but housewives still need to be careful about using it and really ought to know the conditions under which it is produced. Special care needs to be exercised in the case of babies, and naturally the doctor, midwife and health visitor will advise on infant feeding. For bottle-fed babies it is wise to use a regular routine of sterilisation of the bottles and teats such as the well-known Milton method (see chapter on Having a Baby).

Home Care

In a comparatively short space it is impossible to mention all the points about prevention of food poisoning. But this is intended merely as guidance for the housewife, whose standby must be common sense and experience. The fact remains, however, that in the United Kingdom to-day there is still far too high an incidence of food poisoning, a certain percentage of which arises in the home. These cases could be almost completely eliminated if the simple points described were generally understood and the food hygiene rules followed by all.

The tummy upset is too common to be ignored—its prevention starts in the rules of the kitchen.

EQUIPPING A KITCHEN

How to choose the domestic utensils which really are essential for cooking

Compiled by the National
Institute of Houseworkers

A set of food storage containers is a "must." Those above are in
clear polystyrene with red, ivory or green lids. Bex

Right, the Prestige wall type can opener is magnetised so that the
lid does not fall into the can as it comes off

CHOOSE the equipment for your kitchen with care and forethought. Kitchen utensils get used more than anything
else in the house and there will be many
an occasion to be grateful for the article
that pleases you and saves labour, while
ill-chosen or badly made equipment will
often cause annoyance.

A young married couple should choose
a gas or electric cooker that will allow for
an increase in the size of the family. The
extra cost is not great when spread over the
years in hire purchase, but if you should
want to change a stove in a few years time
you will find that little is allowed for a
second-hand cooker.

Easily Cleaned Surfaces

See that the working surface in the kitchen is covered with some easily cleaned
material rather than wood that needs scrubbing. There are some wonderful new
laminated plastic table coverings obtainable in sheet form that will withstand very
hard wear. If new linoleum is going down
on the floor, you can order an extra piece
for the table, as oilcloth is sold by the yard.

Good saucepans are expensive but they
last for years and save fuel. The best
saucepans are the heavy aluminium ones,
and special ones with cast bases are required for electric stoves. There is no need
to buy a lot of saucepans. It is usually
better to buy individual ones rather than
sets, as you then obtain the sizes you really
need for the requirements of your family.

Saucepans

The following should meet the basic
needs of a small family:

Two medium-sized saucepans for potatoes and a second vegetable.

A large pan that will take a steamer and
will also do for making soup or boiling a
piece of bacon. A steamer to fit this saucepan.

A small pan for custard or sauce.

A milk saucepan. Those with a slightly
turned-over edge all round are much better
for pouring than those with lips.

A cheap enamel saucepan for boiling
eggs.

A frying pan. Before buying a frying
pan, see that it will stand level, as so often

the handles are too heavy. Choose a fairly heavy frying pan because thin ones burn and buckle so easily.

A kettle. If you only have one, make it a good-sized one, say to hold 6 pints, and only half fill it when making tea for two or three. There is a good whistling kettle on the market, and the strong enamel ones last well.

Additional pans can be added as circumstances permit and according to the amount of cooking you do.

For the Oven

A roasting tin is usually provided with the cooker, but it is wise to buy a smaller one for cooking a small piece of meat or making Yorkshire pudding.

Flat baking tins are also often provided with the cooker. These are useful for scones, biscuits, etc., or for placing under a fruit tart that may boil over. If none are available, a couple of swiss-roll tins will answer the purpose. For making cakes or jam tarts, two sets of bun tins are required, and for a large cake a 7-in. cake tin with a removable bottom. Two sandwich tins are very useful for making jam sponges and for tarts or flans.

Cooking Bowls and Casseroles

You will need a large bowl for mixing pastry, puddings or cakes—either oven-glass or pottery—and one or two pudding basins of varying sizes, one large enough for a family-sized steamed pudding.

At least one casserole is an indispensable kitchen item. Have one big enough for a stew and vegetables for the family. An oven-glass one, the lid of which also serves as a dish, is a good investment. A collection of varying sized casseroles is a great asset to any kitchen.

A glass pieplate is a good buy: it can be used for making pies, for baking tomatoes or apples and for re-heating food. An oven-glass pie dish is also useful, as it will do duty for a fruit dish as well as for pies or milk puddings.

Wooden Articles

If there is a good cool working surface in the kitchen, there is no need to have a pastry board, but a small chopping board is very necessary. Choose the simplest rolling-pin available—just a cylindrical piece of wood without handles does the job best.

Kitchen Tools

The following are essential:

A tablespoon, dessertspoon and teaspoon kept for cooking.

A wooden spoon.

A sharp vegetable knife; a sharp steel, fair-sized knife.

A palette knife or large flexible round-ended knife.

A cutlery tray (above) in green, white or blue, with an extra long compartment for carvers, bread knives, etc.

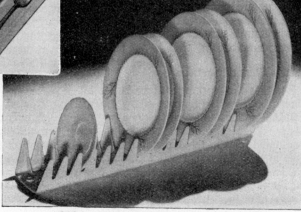

The dish dryer (right) in polystyrene—ivory, green or red—takes up little room but holds 16 large plates. Both are from the Bex range of household equipment

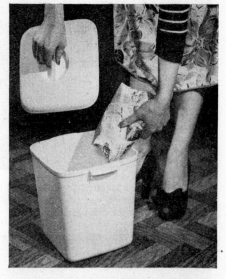

Everything for baking in the "Ovenex" Carry-Home Pack (above). It contains 20 tins, each one labelled to explain its purpose to the inexperienced

You can use the Bex toughened polystyrene bin (right) for damp refuse without danger of corrosion or rust

A potato peeler. A tin opener. A master key for sardines, etc.

A fish slice.

A wire or rotary whisk.

Miscellaneous Articles

A plastic or enamel bowl for washing up and cleaning vegetables.

A plate rack for draining plates after washing up.

A colander for straining vegetables.

Some jars for storing dry goods.

In addition, these items are practically indispensable:

A round strainer to serve as strainer or sieve.

A pint measure for measuring all types of liquids.

A cheese grater.

A pair of kitchen scissors to cut rind off bacon, chop parsley, etc.

A mincer.

A wire cake rack.

Three useful accessories (above) in various colours — Hi-Speed chromium plated beater, potato peeler with finger rest, and Tap-master rubber fitments for taps

Invaluable for lifting hot and easily broken foods are the Nutbrown food tongs (below)

Care of Equipment

Saucepans. — Soak all pans immediately they are empty; greasy ones in hot water and those that have been used for starchy foods, such as custard or porridge, in cold

There is a Prestige Colour-Glo Singing Kettle for every kitchen colour scheme — Capri blue, cherry, old gold or evergreen

The Swedish cook's knife (above) is angled for an easy rocking action when chopping vegetables. From the Prestige range

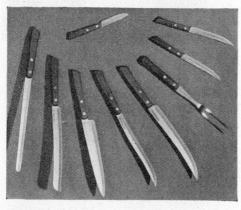

Hollow-ground cutlery with stainless-steel blades and rosewood handles for all carving and culinary purposes. Prestige

On the wall rack hang a spatula, bowl ladle, 3-prong fork, potato masher, straining spoon and fish slice. Skyline, in stainless steel

water. It is best not to use soda for aluminium pans. Use steel wool or a nylon scourer to clean and dry well before putting away.

Or bring a little water and detergent powder to the boil in the pan and leave to soak for a few minutes to remove obstinate marks and stains.

One exception to the soaking rule is the omelet pan. Many people have very strong views on its treatment and only wipe it clean with kitchen paper after using never washing it or allowing water to come into contact with it at all. Wipe the pan while it is still hot after use and it will come quite clean without difficulty.

Tins.—After making gravy in a roasting tin, place a lump of soda in the tin, fill with water, put back on the stove, and bring to the boil, clean with steel wool or saucepan cleaner, rinse, dry, and then place in the oven, which will still be warm, to dry off. Cake tins can be rubbed clean with newspaper or a dry cloth while still hot; if washed, dry completely in a warm oven.

Casseroles.—After using a casserole or pie dish, it is best to leave it soaking for a little while and then clean with steel wool or a nylon scourer that will remove the brown marks. Rinse and dry.

Wooden Utensils.—Pastry and chopping boards, rolling pins, etc., should be scrubbed well with soap and warm water, rinsed and dried, then stood in a current of air until quite dry.

A piece of pumice stone is a good thing to keep by the sink for rubbing the kitchen knives that are not stainless. It will keep them bright.

Kitchen Cloths

Choose linen teacloths if possible; they dry up better, last well and do not leave fluff on the dishes. Keep these for drying dishes only, and have an oven cloth or oven gloves for taking things from the oven and a dry dishcloth for drying pans. Wash all kitchen cloths frequently and spread the dishcloth out between washing-ups to become dry—it will be much sweeter than if left wet.

If you look after your pots, pans and other kitchen equipment, they will last for years and serve you well.

GETTING INTO
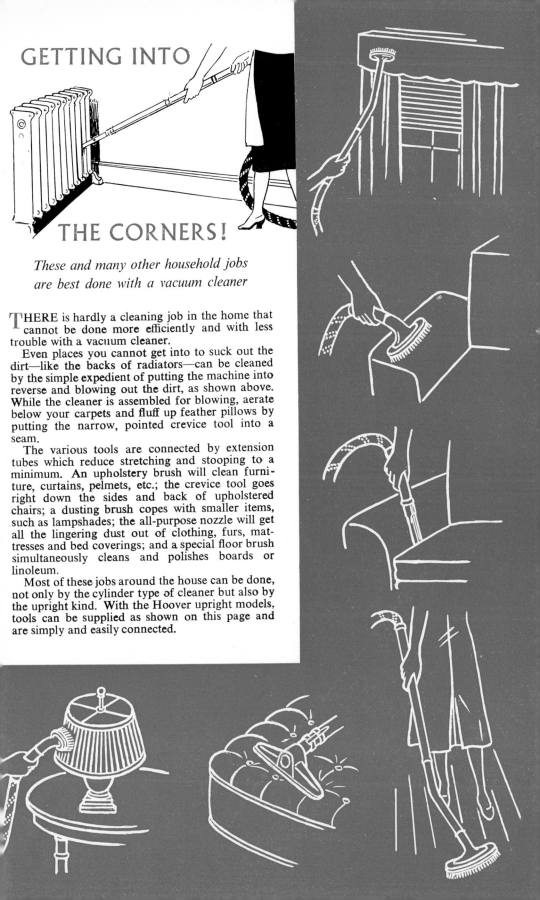

THE CORNERS!

*These and many other household jobs
are best done with a vacuum cleaner*

THERE is hardly a cleaning job in the home that cannot be done more efficiently and with less trouble with a vacuum cleaner.

Even places you cannot get into to suck out the dirt—like the backs of radiators—can be cleaned by the simple expedient of putting the machine into reverse and blowing out the dirt, as shown above. While the cleaner is assembled for blowing, aerate below your carpets and fluff up feather pillows by putting the narrow, pointed crevice tool into a seam.

The various tools are connected by extension tubes which reduce stretching and stooping to a minimum. An upholstery brush will clean furniture, curtains, pelmets, etc.; the crevice tool goes right down the sides and back of upholstered chairs; a dusting brush copes with smaller items, such as lampshades; the all-purpose nozzle will get all the lingering dust out of clothing, furs, mattresses and bed coverings; and a special floor brush simultaneously cleans and polishes boards or linoleum.

Most of these jobs around the house can be done, not only by the cylinder type of cleaner but also by the upright kind. With the Hoover upright models, tools can be supplied as shown on this page and are simply and easily connected.

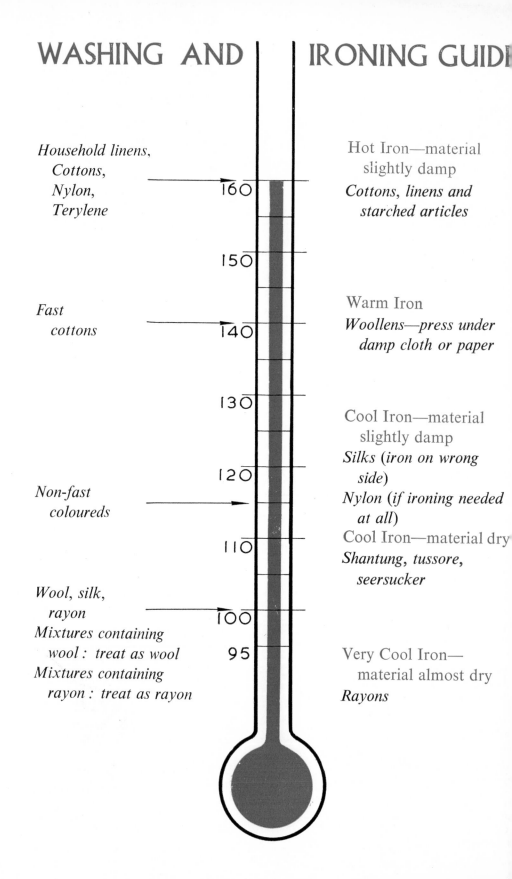

WASHING AND IRONING GUIDE

Household linens,
  Cottons,
  Nylon,
  Terylene

160

150

Fast
  cottons

140

130

Non-fast
  coloureds

120

110

Wool, silk,
  rayon
Mixtures containing
  wool : treat as wool
Mixtures containing
  rayon : treat as rayon

100

95

Hot Iron—material
  slightly damp
*Cottons, linens and
  starched articles*

Warm Iron
*Woollens—press under
  damp cloth or paper*

Cool Iron—material
  slightly damp
*Silks (iron on wrong
  side)*
*Nylon (if ironing needed
  at all)*
Cool Iron—material dry
*Shantung, tussore,
  seersucker*

Very Cool Iron—
  material almost dry
Rayons

THE WEEKLY WASH

There are three guiding principles: know your fabrics, choose your own soap or detergent, regulate the heat of the water

1. THE METHOD

IF you are setting up house and facing the miscellany of a weekly wash for the first time, it may easily seem something of a task. Add to your own things a husband's laundry, together with household goods, and no one would be anything but sympathetic if you felt a little daunted at first.

The greatest help is to know the kind of fabrics that you have to launder. Then it is an easy matter to learn how each should be treated. When you buy a fabric, make full enquiries as to what it is: apart from pure wool, silk and cotton materials, there are many synthetic mixtures—Rayons, Nylon, Orlon, "Terylene," on their own or blended—and other fabrics again, containing "Ardil" and "Fibrolane" synthetic fibres. The best way to resolve your wash-day problems is to plan the job in advance.

Soaps and Detergents

First of all, we must consider what to use for the weekly wash—"old-fashioned" soaps or the newer detergents. Soap is made from natural fats in cake form, flakes or powder; a detergent is a synthetic cleansing agent in liquid or powder form. We recognise the soaps in such well-known names as Puritan, Sunlight, Lux, Sylvan, Persil and so on; detergents, in liquid form, as Stergene, Quix, etc., and in powder form as Dreft, Tide, Daz and others.

Soaps and detergents are both excellent for lifting grease and dirt from fabric. In hard water soap forms scum, and thorough rinsing is essential to remove it. A water softener, such as ammonia, should be combined with soap to obviate this, using ammonia in the quantity advised on the bottle. Detergents create no scum in hard water.

One point that cannot be stressed too much is: both soaps and detergents *must* be used in the quantities advised by the manufacturers. The tendency is to use too much, and it does not get clothes any cleaner or wash them faster. It is not only wasteful and uneconomic, but there is the risk that too much detergent may be detrimental to sewage systems and therefore to public health (not to mention your poor hands).

Water Temperatures

The right temperatures for washing different fabrics have been most carefully worked out by exhaustive tests, and for first-class results the home laundress is wise if she takes advantage of these results of research:

Hand-hot water is advised for washing and rinsing: Cotton and cotton net; linen; nylon; Orlon; "Terylene."

Warm water for: Chiffon; georgette; organza; shantung; tussore.

Lukewarm water for: Broderie anglaise; coloured and printed fabrics; cottons with embossed, lacquered or other special finish; elastic (foundation garments); embroidered materials; lace; leather (washable gloves).
Rayons: crêpes, doeskins, jersey, plush, sharkskin, taffeta.
Velvet, velveteen, corduroy (washable).
Wool and wool mixtures, including "Ardil" and "Fibrolane."

NOTE: *Coloureds*
(1) Unless you are already sure of colour fastness, test all garments before washing. Wet a small piece of the garment in cold water and press with a hot iron between two pieces of dry white cloth.
(2) If the colour holds fast and does not come off on the white cloth during this test, wash the garment as you would anything delicate. Using a fine-fabric detergent such as Dreft, knead the garment quickly and gently through the suds.
(3) Rinse thoroughly until the water is crystal clear—a most important step for keeping colours pure and bright.

(4) Squeeze out excess moisture or roll the garment in a towel; dry away from strong light, either flat or hung carefully over your line or rack.

If your test shows that the colour dye is at all unstable—and don't forget that dark colours are usually the least stable of all—then remember:

(5) Never soak the garment before washing.

(6) Always wash any such garment by itself and never wash with whites.

(7) The less time your clothes linger in the water, the less time they will have to streak and run, so wash your coloureds often, before they need soaking or long, hard washing to remove the dirt.

(8) A tablespoonful of vinegar to a gallon of water in the final rinse will have a stabilising effect on some dyes.

(9) Dry striped garments with the stripes hanging downward, patterned garments flat, so that there'll be less chance of streaking and running after washing.

(10) Iron while still slightly damp with a warm, not hot, iron.

WASHING ROUTINE

Like any job, laundrywork done to a set order is more manageable and takes less time in the end. These are the stages into which to divide it:

Sorting and Preparation

Divide the wash into piles of like material:

(1) White and colour-fast linens and cottons, household and personal.
(2) Garments, etc., that may not be colour-fast.
(3) Fine fabrics and lingerie.
(4) Woollens, separating whites and coloureds.

Close lightning fasteners. Empty pockets and detach any pins, clips, brooches. Remove from frocks belts, unless washable, shoulder pads and covered buttons (rust tends to come through them during washing). Run a tack line down double thickness of ties to hold interlining in place.

Check everything for stains and repairs.

Deal with stains before washing (see page 405), and carry out necessary mending or the weight of water may enlarge holes and tears.

Soaking

Much research has proved that the long overnight soak is inefficient. Soaking loosens dirt and it floats free, but unless the articles are soon removed and the water squeezed off, dirt settles back again and any stains become set; therefore the short soak of 20–30 minutes is advised. It is not necessary to soak everything It is helpful in the following cases:

Dust-laden Goods (such as curtains).—Soak in lukewarm water.

Handkerchiefs (especially after colds).—It is a good idea to keep special containers for used handkerchiefs only and train the family to use them, thus saving the search through pockets and all over the house for missing ones on wash-day. Soak in cool water, allowing 3 tablespoonfuls salt to each quart of water. Rinse in cool clear water before washing.

Discoloured Whites.—Soak in bleach, used according to directions. Rinse thoroughly before washing.

Greasy Articles.—Soak in warm water and detergent. Rinse before washing.

NOTE: Never soak any kind of woollen garment or material.

Boiling

White goods need not be boiled as a matter of course. If grey or yellowish, then boil after soaking, starting in cold water and bringing up to boiling point. Keep at a brisk rolling boil for 10 minutes. Follow the maker's instructions for the amount of soap or detergent to use. The use of blue detergent powder makes a blueing rinse unnecessary.

NOTE: Confine boiling to cotton and linen only.

Washing

While the boil progresses, start the wash. Work through the items needing hot water, doing the heavy ones first and fine things on their own; follow with the warm-water items and, finally, those needing lukewarm water.

Method.—In the main, wash by means

of squeezing. This forces suds through the fabric, bringing soil with them. Shoulder straps may need gently rubbing with the fingers. To remove the crease line on collars, rub a little dry soap or detergent in with the finger-tips—or better still with a nylon pot scourer—then squeeze in the suds. Firm, strong fabrics such as household linens and cottons may have soiled areas rubbed together, or scrubbed with a soft nailbrush.

Wool, silks, nylon and other synthetics, lace, silk nets, special-finish cottons and all such delicate fabrics should never be rubbed, only gently squeezed. Nylon stockings and undies are best washed after every wear for, if dirt ingrains, it is almost impossible to remove. Treated this way, broken fibres and unnecessary creasing are avoided.

Foundation garments may be lightly rubbed or scrubbed with a soft brush on soiled areas.

Rayons are very stretchable when wet, and should be well supported and kept as compact as possible until excess moisture is removed.

Velvet, velveteen and corduroy, if washable, should be handled as little as possible. Wash by swirling around with the finger-tips.

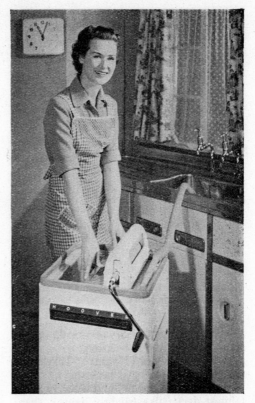

The electrically operated Hoover Mark II washing machine has a hand wringer and pump for emptying

Rinsing

This must be thorough, in one or more clear waters until no trace of suds remains. If blueing is necessary, add to the final rinse.

Starching

Cotton and linen shorts, shirts, blouses, frocks and slacks and table wear look trim and resist dirt better if starched. Use a good brand and follow the instructions for the type of garment to be starched; alternatively, use a plastic starch that lasts through several washes before another application is required.

Drying

All fabrics that may be squeezed in washing may be gently squeezed after rinsing to remove excess moisture, otherwise roll in a towel and pat out water. Strong, heavy fabrics may be wrung by hand or put through a loose wringer.

The velvet group must be hung up straight out of the rinsing water and dripped dry. Hang pile downwards.

Hang up all articles immediately, out of doors whenever possible. White goods may catch the sunlight as it helps to bleach. Coloured goods should be dried in the shade to avoid fade.

Dry *blouses and shirts* on hangers; peg *frocks* at the waist and peg up the hem of a full *skirt* to prevent dropping; peg *socks and stockings* by the toe tips; dry *foundation garments* by threading on to the line. Gently pat and pull woollies into shape and dry flat, or roll in a thick towel. *Ties* also should be dried flat. *Gloves*, dry on wire or plastic "hands." Peg *trousers, slacks* and *skirts* by the waist.

IRONING

If your iron is not heat-controlled for different fabrics, these are the main points to remember.

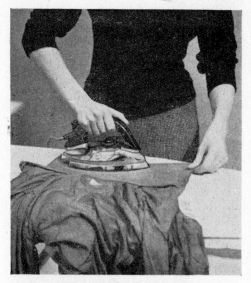

TO IRON A BLOUSE: First press seams and thick parts, then stretch collar into shape with left hand

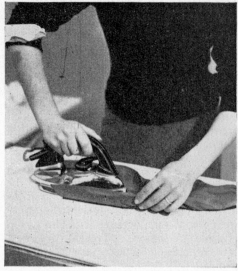

Start sleeves by going over shoulder seams and cuffs, then round cuffs and press main part of sleeves

The right stage of dryness or dampness for ironing is given in brackets:

COOL IRON for Nylon; "Terylene"; Orlon (dry if ironing is necessary).

WARM IRON for wool and wool mixtures (almost dry); silks (slightly damp); shantung and tussore (dry); special-finish cottons (slightly damp); matt rayons, sharkskins, crêpes and other rayons except spun (almost dry); lace (slightly damp); foundation garments, non-elastic parts (slightly damp).

MODERATELY HOT IRON for linen; plain, glazed and polished cotton, cotton net (slightly damp); spun rayons (slightly damp); folkweave, candlewick (slightly damp).

NOTE: With the exception of finishing linen, iron all fabrics on the wrong side.

When ironing handkerchiefs, go all round the hems first to keep them on the square.

Tips about Certain Fabrics

When you iron *linen*, iron until dry and finish on the right side to bring up the sheen. Fabrics in the *velvet group* are never ironed. They should be lightly shaken at intervals during drying and the pile smoothed downwards with a soft cloth. Iron *rayons* the moment they are dry enough; if some areas are damper than others, the fabric will have a blotched effect when ironed. Crinkly rayons and those that shrink up should be ironed carefully across and up and down to ease back into shape.

The Order of Ironing

To get a good finish follow this order: (1) collars; (2) shoulder pads, when not removable; (3) sleeves, from cuff upwards; (4) bodice front (of frock), left and right fronts (of blouse), front (of shirt). Iron up to seams, but not over them or they will mark the right side. Iron facings last and work the point of the iron between buttons, not over them.

Shirt.—Iron double thickness of yoke and buttonhole strip first, then the rest of the front; (5) back of frock bodice, blouse or shirt; (6) skirt, starting at hem and working up to waist. Press pleats into place last; iron a bias-cut skirt on the straight of the material; never iron along a hem or it may flute. (7) Turn garment right side out and press any frills, pocket flaps or revers. Finally, give a last press to collar and shoulder line.

Press trousers on the wrong side, working up from the turn-ups.

Washday Snags

Despite great care, even the most experienced housewife sometimes has a laundry

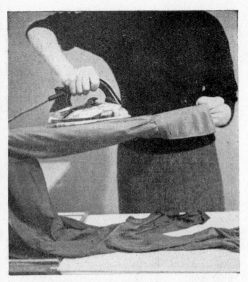

Cuff gathers need a sleeve board. Use point of iron and stretch material well with left hand, then press back

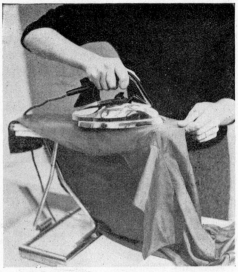

Iron front nearest you first, flat on board. Press pockets and seams, finish shoulder gathers on sleeve board

failure, but there is usually a way of preventing this. These are the commonest snags and how to overcome them:

Felted wool may be due to using too hot water, too much soap or cleanser, wringing or rubbing.

Small holes may result from twisting or rubbing fine fibres and breaking them, using too hot an iron or ironing over buttons.

Shine is usually due to too hot an iron or pressing or ironing on the right side of the fabric.

Blotches appear on some rayons and are due to uneven dampness.

Yellowness on white silk and wool comes from too much heat, either water or drying atmosphere, or too hot an iron.

Stains

If a spill can be washed immediately or quickly diluted with warm water, there

Finally, hang blouse up to air on well covered hanger, shoulder seams lying straight to keep collar in shape

is every chance that no stain will result. When it does, there are several remedies that are easy enough to keep in stock:

(1) A liquid dry-cleaner such as carbon-tetrachloride—for greasy marks, tar and oil.
(2) Turpentine—for paint.
(3) Glycerine—for fruit, tea, coffee and cocoa.
(4) Salt or milk—for ink.
(5) Methylated spirits—for ball-point pen ink.

Apply any of these stain removers to the outside of the mark first, using a piece of clean rag, and work inwards to the centre of the stain in a circular movement.

After any stain treatment, wash the fabric according to the rules for that particular kind; if a stain is not removable by home methods, let a professional dry-cleaner undertake the job, but be sure to state the nature of the stain and the home remedies already applied so that correct treatment can be given by the professional.

Baby Clothes

Special care is needed in the laundering of baby's things. *Nappies* should be soaked in cold water for half an hour or more, washed in pure soap, rinsed in several changes of clean water, then dried, if possible in the open air. Boil regularly to keep white. But not every time they are washed —once every 3 or 4 times is enough.

Woollies should be laundered like other woollens, washing in warm (not hot) water and soap or detergent. Rinse well, pat out moisture in a clean towel and dry flat. No ironing is needed for woollies or nappies, but they must be well aired.

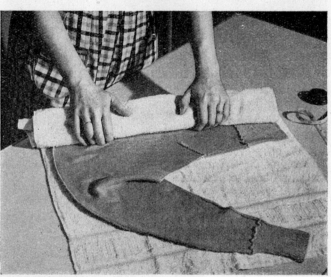

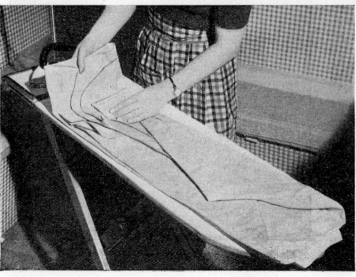

To dry knitwear: Place on a towel on a flat surface, measure and ease into shape, then roll up in a bath towel (above)

To fold a man's shirt: Turn sleeves to the back, then fold tails over cuffs, and finally double in half

Photos taken at the Tide Washing Clinic

EQUIPMENT

PROBABLY the most popular piece of labour-saving home equipment to-day is the electrically driven washing machine. It cuts out all the hard work of rubbing clothes and greatly reduces the time necessary for home laundry work.

WASHING MACHINES

A large number of different models, several all electric and others with electric agitators or pulsators to swirl the water through the clothes but gas water heaters, are now on the market. A good many are closely similar, or differ mainly in design details or in having this or that refinement. All come into three broad classes, according to whether they have hand or electric wringers or spin-extract the water.

Cheapest and usually the smallest capacity machines are those with hand wringers. The spin-extractor ones are considerably more labour-saving even than the power-wringer kind, as practically all the handling of wet clothes is eliminated. Washing, rinsing and spin drying may be separate operations, each switch-controlled; or there may be a completely automatic action.

The Dean twin-heat gas wash boiler, with fold-away wringer, fits under a draining board. Temperature control by foot switch. Four minutes—and Philips Spin Drier (left) will have wet washing ready for the iron

Incorporated Water Heaters

Several models have twin tubs. While one washes, the other rinses and then spin dries, while the wash-tub washes another load, thus doubling the quantity done in the time. In one model, the suds spun out of the clothes in the rinsing tub are automatically returned to the washing-tub for re-use, thus saving on soap or detergent. Another has a built-in heater that can be controlled to boil or simmer. Many are equipped with dials which only need to be set for the appropriate temperature for washing different fabrics. Arguments against an integral water heater are put forward by some domestic science experts as well as manufacturers. They say that clothes boiling is unnecessary and deleterious, and that water may be heated more economically by other means. Machines with a water heater cost, without tax, a few pounds more than closely similar models without a heater.

Automatic Pumps

An accessory that makes an appreciable contribution to wash-day ease is an automatic pump for emptying the water from the machine. Most power-wringer types have one fitted, but not all the hand-wringer kind do.

Capacity of Machines

This can be measured in two ways. (1) The dry weight or "load" of clothes that can be dealt with at one time. Smallest capacity machines take $3\frac{1}{2}$ lb.; largest $10\frac{1}{2}$ lb.

height (around 36 in.), but some of the bigger machines stand appreciably higher. Mobility is an important feature and most up-to-date washing machines are mounted on castors so they can be stored in a convenient spot and wheeled to the sink when required.

Safety aspects, too, have been considered by the manufacturers and one fully automatic machine has a removable handle, to prevent children from opening the door while the machine is operating.

Washing Techniques

A question frequently posed by those considering the purchase of a machine is whether it will get the clothes really clean. As

Set two simple dial-the-fabric controls and the mobile English Electric Liberator (left) will carry out any of six different washing cycles automatically. The Bendix " Dialamatic," below, has a gas heater and the famous tumble action washing. Load it and you don't touch the clothes again until the job is complete

(2) The amount of water required for the operation. Some machines require less water for washing a given weight of clothes than others. If water has to be used with care, as in some country districts, this may well affect choice. It also governs to some extent the cost of water heating, if this has to be taken into account, and the amount of soap or detergent used. The completely automatic, spin-extractor machine requires most water, the full cycle of washing and triple rinsing taking about the same as for a good hot bath—26 gallons. Other types of machine require from 6–11 gallons for washing only, according to size and design.

Overall Size and Mobility

The majority of machines are square, "cabinet shaped." The wringer usually folds down inside or at the back of the cabinet or is detachable and stowed in the bottom of the cabinet. Small capacity and some medium-size types are designed to stand under a kitchen draining board. Both medium and large capacity models come in the average "working surface"

with hand washing, it is usually recommended that extra dirty parts (i.e. neckbands) should be rubbed with dry soap powder or detergent before immersion. Similarly, heavily soiled things, such as mechanics' greasy overalls, need longer in the machine, boiling, or treatment with a bleach. On the whole, it is fair to say that a reliable machine will give as good or better results than hand washing. For very fragile articles such as nylon stockings and fine woollies, hand washing is generally safer.

Modern appliances have, however, been designed with the *whole* family wash very much in mind. Plastic agitators, tumble action washing, a pulsator that creates a "boiling action," "no tangle" action—all these methods are gentle enough for even the finest fabrics, as well as highly efficient. Much thought has also been given to thorough rinsing and gentle drying by tumble action or spinning.

The automatic timer has taken the guesswork out of the weekly wash and saves the housewife hours of valuable time.

Running Costs

These are extremely low. Apart from any water heating, consumption of $\frac{1}{2}-\frac{3}{4}$ unit of electricity per hour is average.

WASH BOILERS

Costing little more than half the price of a small, simple washing machine are gas and electric wash boilers. They heat the water to the required temperature and provide a good, deep wash tub. The most labour-saving types are square "cabinets" with table tops to supply an additional working surface when the boiler is not in use, and a fitted hand wringer that folds away at the back or inside the tub. With some designs a separate agitator lid attach-

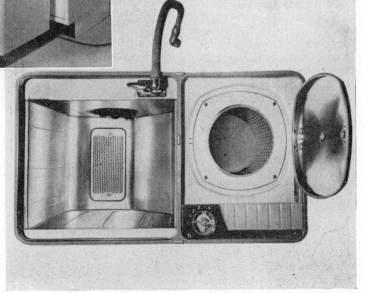

The Hotpoint Countess is a small-size machine with a power wringer high enough to wring clothes into the sink— and " no tangle " washing action

Wash by " boiling action " in one tub, rinse in the other, while suds are returned to the first for re-use, then spin-dry all in the Hoovermatic

ness of the material being wrung. Smaller, less expensive models do not permit of manual adjustment, but the rubber rollers will cope, within reason, with different thicknesses. Both kinds can be obtained to fix on special wood or tubular metal stands or to clamp directly on to the side of an ordinary glazed earthenware sink. The latter, which are usually small enough to stow away in an under-sink cupboard, are invaluable in a flat or anywhere where space is restricted.

Cabinet and table wringers are designed as permanent pieces of kitchen furniture. Initially they cost a little more than a wringer on stand, but they provide a useful working surface and also keep the wringer dust-free and ready for the next washday.

Clothes "Cradles"

A labour-saving alternative to the traditional wicker clothes basket is a folding canvas "cradle," with a pocket for pegs, on a strong but light metal frame. Its height

A compact gas washboiler for a large family wash, the Morley 59 has a fold-down Acme wringer, rubber-tyred wheels, easy heat control

The Ada-matic, right, washes, rinses and spins dry automatically, heats the water and empties by auto pump too

ment, which turns the boiler into a hand washing machine, can be supplied at a small extra charge.

A gas or electric power point is needed. Both kinds of gas and electric boiler are portable.

WRINGERS

Any "machineless" wash, unless only a very few things are done at a time, will be much less strenuous with the aid of a good wringer. "Big wash" types have special top screws to adjust the pressure according to the thick-

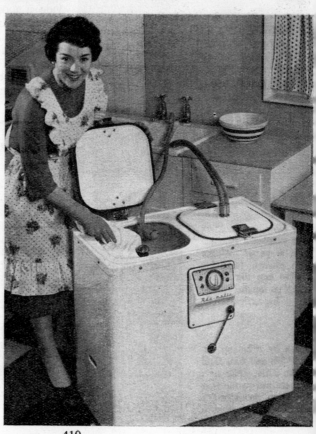

You can drip-dry in or out of doors with a Bisley's Bathorse in wood strung with 32 feet of strong nylon line. Lay it flat over the bath to dry woollies

obviates the tiring stooping-and-rising associated with pegging out the clothes, and it is easily carried to the garden and back. A further point in its favour is that it stands at a convenient height by sink or ironing table.

Outdoor Clothes Dryers

Clothes lines that mark the washing can cause much unnecessary work. Most satisfactory, because smooth and easy to keep clean, is a strong, plastic-covered line. These are available both for outdoor and indoor use, and range from a 25-ft. indoor line. A 36-ft. outdoor line has a special eyelet end.

Various types of wooden or light metal telescopic dryer, easily portable, are good for the small back garden where space is restricted. With more room available, and a bigger wash to cope with, the rotary clothes hoist is efficient. Made from strong galvanised alloy, this resembles the frame of an umbrella and provides ample clothes lines in a compact space. All pegging out can be done without moving from one spot. The most labour-saving models can be raised or lowered by the turn of a handle. Even in a slight breeze, the lines circulate so that drying is speeded up.

Indoor Clothes Dryers and Airers

There is a wide choice of both wooden and light-weight tubular metal folding dryers and airers. Some metal ones have rustproof finishes; slightly more expensive ones are anodised or plastic covered. Lack of space is no obstacle, and there are models for wall fixing that fold flat, others to place across the bath or even to hang from the back of a chair.

Heated Dryers

Enclosed drying cabinets into which the washing is put straight from the

The Acme small wringer (left) clamps on any straight sided sink that is not more than two inches thick

Outdoor clothes drying is simple with the Hills Hoist rotary dryer—it turns in the breeze. The trolley is a Laundri-Jinka

The Inferation indoor dryer hangs on the wall, doubles as heater and hot towel rail, consists of four open-out panels

wringer, there to be dried by air heated by gas or electricity, are available in considerable variety. In one kind the wet clothes are arranged on swing-out rails and an enclosed heater, thermostatically controlled, heats the air sufficiently to dry them in from 1–2 hours, according to fabric and power of the heater.

Family-wash models, usually about 6 ft. tall and about 2 ft. wide, resemble narrow wardrobes and do not take up much floor space. Loading is usually $2\frac{1}{2}$–3 Kw. with electric types and a similar power in gas-heated ones. There are smaller "junior" cabinets, sometimes tall and narrow but more often about 4 ft. high, with a lower loading. Folding ones, opening out to take the washing which is then covered by a plastic curtain, are still less expensive and need less room. The smaller types are naturally much less powerful.

"Tumbler" and "Forced Draught" Dryers

In the former the clothes are "tumbled" gently round until dry enough to iron or bone dry, as required. This method, it is claimed, makes bath towels and blankets beautifully fluffy and is very quick and trouble-saving. With the rather less expensive forced draught drying machine, heating is by means of a propeller rotor in a miniature wind tunnel. You can have medium or slow heat by special control, and garments—or crockery—may be dried flat. The cabinet is easily movable on its castors and is standard working surface height (36 in.).

"Spin" Dryers, much smaller and less powerful (100–350 as against 2,000 watt loadings) are designed largely to take the place of a wringer, though they extract more water in less time. A small size model will take 22 lb. of *wet* washing and damp-dry it *ready for ironing* in as little as 4 minutes. Rather larger ones will take an average washing-machine load. All the spin dryers are small and compact (around 2 ft. high and 17 in. diameter) and are ideal for a flat or where space is a consideration. They really do telescope the job of washing and ironing by bridging the time gap for drying.

TWO LABOUR-SAVERS

Two small pieces of equipment, each costing a few shillings only, and equally

412

useful with a washing machine or a wash boiler, are a sink hose and a pair of wooden washing tongs for handling the damp clothes. The hose is invaluable for filling machine or boiler and also obviates the need for lifting heavy buckets to the sink.

Rather more expensive (around 30s.), but a still bigger labour-saver, is a special type of hose which both fills and empties a washboiler or a washing machine that is not fitted with its own pump.

IRONING EQUIPMENT

Hand Irons

Most irons are self-heating, the overwhelming majority by electricity, though mains and bottled gas types are useful alternatives where electricity is not available.

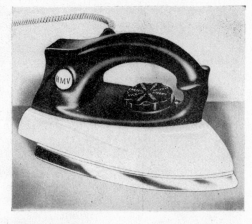

A streamlined iron, one of the H.M.V. Household Appliances, with a dial showing correct heat for different kinds of fabric

One of the most tiring of domestic jobs, ironing can be done sitting down in comfort, with the Sit-at ironing table

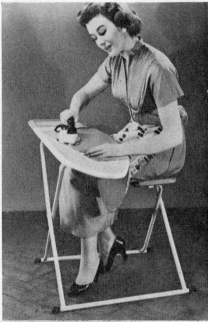

Where to put a hot iron in safety? The Metal-Maid iron tidy screws easily to the wall, takes the iron while it cools. One model for electric, one for a steam iron

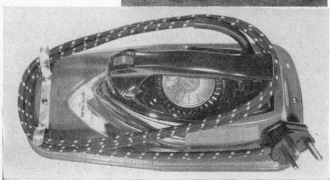

A heavy iron with polished sole-plate covers is also made for heating on the hot-plate of a continuous-burning solid-fuel stove. This last does not, of course, have the refinements of the self-heating iron and is more fatiguing to work with.

Thermostatically controlled electric irons, which by a flick of the switch give the correct temperature for different types of fabric, make ironing less tiring as well as safer and more foolproof. A heavy iron is no longer necessary, and 4 lb. weight is a good average for a heat-controlled iron. Reliable makes are fitted with radio and T.V. interference suppressors, and there is a special safety tip-up model.

The steam - and - dry iron, thermostatically controlled for dry ironing, does away with the need for damping down, thus saving trouble, and is also excellent for pressing woollen suits, etc. Drawback is that in hard-water

You can do the week's ironing sitting down, with the foot-controlled Morphy Richards Rotary Ironer—and have two hands free to guide the clothes over the roller

No damping down is needed with the Hoover Steam-or-Dry Iron (below). Switch the dial, and water turns to steam drop by drop

districts the steam outlets tend to fur up. To overcome this, one popular-priced iron is sold complete with de-scaling fluid for home use. A separate steam-plate adaptor, designed to fit most standard-sized electric irons, is also now available.

Ironing Tables

Fatigue is lessened when a correctly shaped ironing table of the right height is used. Metal ones, with tubular supports and perforated tops for coolness, cost more than the conventional wooden folding tables, but have many advantages. Best types are firm, have a larger surface, a useful pointed end, a detachable sleeveboard, tailored cover and are adaptable to various heights. Some can be adjusted so that sitting down to work becomes a practical proposition.

One good model is actually a combined ironing table and seat. Made of plastic-painted tubular steel, the padded, leather-cloth covered seat and table fold together in a moment for easy storage. It is said to be equally comfortable for women of differing heights.

Ironing Machines

Being able to sit down comfortably to the job with an ironing surface ten times that of a hand iron, and not having frequently to raise and press down the iron,

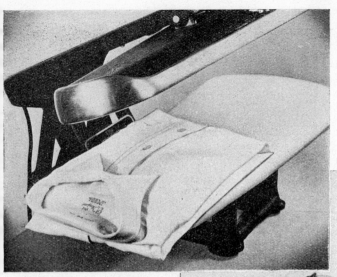

The correct way to iron a shirt collar, below, on the Rotalux Rotary Ironer. You can operate the control by hand or elbow

A man's shirt can be ironed perfectly in a few minutes in the Parnall Ezy-Press (above). You just pull the garment between the plates

are advantages of an ironing machine. On a number of washing machines, the power wringer can be interchanged with a rotary ironer. This takes a matter of minutes only, though an extra power outlet, or a two-way plug, is necessary, as the ironer must be both mechanically driven and heated.

Self - contained independent versions of the rotary ironer can also be bought. Though rather more expensive, there are many points in their favour. They can be used on any convenient table from any suitable power point. A less expensive, similar alternative is the flat-press ironer. These, too, have automatic temperature control, a large ironing surface, and the operator can sit down to the job. Both rotary and flat-press machines give very good results once the necessary technique is mastered. Flat articles such as sheets are quite straightforward, but a shirt or frilly blouse calls for practice. A private lesson on the machine can always be ar-ranged for at the time of purchase, and is advisable.

Damp-It-Down Laundry Bag

A very inexpensive ironing labour-saver, for those not possessing a steam iron, is a polythene bag which automatically "damps down" the wash. Dry laundry is piled loosely in the bag and a couple of cups of water added. The top is then fastened, and within two or three hours the clothes are evenly damped ready for the iron. They will remain in this condition for several days.

The general trend in modern wash-day equipment is to make it do double — or even treble duty—and for everything to be as easily portable as possible. Safety is another prime consideration and an excellent idea is a metal "iron tidy" that screws flat to the wall. You slip the hot iron into it and it cools off there in perfect safety.

A portable clothes dryer (above), the **Dryette** folds up as small as a briefcase (right) for easy storage in small homes; can be had in pink, blue or green

An average week's wash will dry on the tubular rails inside the **Flavel** gas-heated drying cabinet (left). Mesh guard over the burner prevents scorching

PLANNING THE HOUSEHOLD ROUTINE

Some practical hints on how to organise your housework
by K. G. WHAPHAM, *the National Institute of Houseworkers*

MOST people will agree that some sort of plan is essential in running a home, but let it first be made clear that household routine is a very individual matter, and it is impossible to lay down hard and fast rules. However, as all homemakers have to struggle with the problem, let us see if some useful guidance can be given which will help every household to work out its own salvation.

A home may consist of anything from one room to a mansion, and the inhabitants thereof from a lone dweller to a large family of three generations, so the first step in planning a routine is to consider the home and the people in it. People are more important than things, and the routine must fit in with the members of the household and not vice versa. The king-pin of the household is the housewife herself, and the routine must suit her temperament, capabilities and tastes. Many a young, inexperienced housekeeper has come to grief because she tried to follow the plan of a quicker and more experienced worker. The age and occupation of the various members of the household is important too.

All Should Help

We all know how the arrival of the first baby alters the running of the home, while the addition of an elderly relative to the family circle may make as big a difference. Planning may be particularly difficult in households where the mother is doing part- or full-time work outside the home, or where some of the family are on shift work. It is important for the housewife to get the co-operation of the whole household in her plan, and to enlist their help with some of the chores. It is excellent training for both boys and girls to do their share in running the home, and they enjoy it if they feel that they are being really helpful and that their efforts are appreciated, even if the results are not always perfect. The old folk, too, like to be useful, and can make a real contribution by undertaking some of the lighter jobs.

The position of the home and the area in which it is situated will affect the amount of time and effort which must be spent. In an outlying country district shopping may be the chief problem, while in an industrial town the cleaning often constitutes the worst difficulty. The facilities available must be considered also: Do tradesmen deliver goods? Are gas and electricity laid on? Is domestic help available? Another factor is the layout of

Stains quickly come off a Formica-topped kitchen table—just wipe with a mild powder cleanser and damp cloth

the house and the size and number of the rooms it contains.

Be Economical

In planning a routine be economical, not only with money but with time and effort as well. The three are closely linked, though the word economy is thought of only too often in terms of money alone, and many housewives waste time and effort doing unnecessary chores which could be avoided by careful planning.

What has to be Done

The next step is to decide what has to be done to keep the household happy, healthy and comfortable.

The first essential is good feeding, and this is a task needing knowledge, skill and ingenuity. It includes planning, shopping and the preparation of interesting, well-balanced meals, plus serving, washing-up and clearing away day after day for seven days a week.

Next to feeding comes clothing, for if the supply of clean, tidy clothes runs out, the members of the family will find themselves in dire straits indeed. Household linen and soft furnishings must be included in this too and, whether the laundry is done at home or sent out, time must be allowed for care and attention to clothing, and making, mending and renovation.

Third on the list is the care and cleaning of the home, from daily attention and thorough cleaning to special cleaning in all parts of the home, decoration, renovation and repairs.

Last, but by no means least, the housewife must find time for her own relaxation and recreation, and to take an understanding interest in the life and pursuits of her family. The routine must be adaptable, or family difficulties will arise because the mother has worn herself out trying to keep to a strict plan and has no energy left to deal with personal problems or to devote to entertaining.

We now have to fit all this into a workable plan. Begin by arranging the home for easy running. It is helpful to try and look at your home as though you have never seen it before, and see whether the space is being used to the best advantage and whether furniture and fittings are placed as conveniently as possible.

Have you ever counted the number of steps you take while setting a tea tray and making a pot of tea? Perhaps you could save time and effort in this simple everyday job by keeping tea caddy, china, cutlery and tray near the cooking stove instead of having them at opposite ends of the kitchen. Do you have to carry trays through awkward doorways from kitchen to dining room? It might be possible to have a hatch made in the wall between the two rooms, or it might help to use a trolley instead of a tray. Do you have to scrub a whitewood kitchen table every day when, with a small outlay of money and time, you could cover it with easily cleaned laminated plastic? These are only small examples of time and effort saving, but multiplied many times throughout the home, such adjustments can help to make the routine easier. Another great help, if you are a hoarder, is to "clear the decks" and get rid of odds and ends which you hope will "come in" useful some day.

The Daily Work

The easiest way to plan the daily work is to divide it into three parts. The first is the daily tidying up and quick cleaning, including airing and putting straight all rooms and parts of the house in daily use, removing surface dirt and dust, bed-making, attention to fires, central heating apparatus and water heaters if any, and sanitary fittings such as bath, hand basin and lavatory pan. The time required for this work will vary greatly according to the type of home and family, but it will be less troublesome if such jobs as airing and straightening of living rooms, emptying ash-trays and putting away books and papers are done overnight.

The second daily job is the preparation, serving and clearing away of meals. Careful planning is of great help here, so that the time and effort spent in shopping is minimised and the amount of cooking done is not excessive.

The Weekly Turn-out

The third job is the weekly or thorough turn-out of some part of the house. This may sound a contradiction in terms, but every day except perhaps Saturday and Sunday, part of the home in turn must be thoroughly cleaned, though not necessarily

WHEN YOU TURN OUT A ROOM . . .

Whether it's the annual spring clean or a more frequent occurrence, a point-by-point plan will save time and wasted energy

TO turn out and clean a room really thoroughly, you must first clear the decks. So put on your working gloves to protect your hands, tie up your hair and away we go. . . .

Take down pelmets and curtains so that you can really get at the windows and surrounding paint.

Remove loose covers from armchairs and sofas—and go carefully down the sides with your hand—you will probably discover all kinds of lost property secreted down there. Clean upholstery, carpets and rugs with vacuum cleaner attachments.

Having taken down mirrors, pictures, ornaments, etc., stack large furniture in the middle of the room, cover with dust sheets — and then pause for "elevenses" so that you don't get too tired.

Curtains and pelmets should be cleaned with vacuum, sent to cleaners or laundry or washed before hanging again in a freshly cleaned room

Tackle ceiling, walls and paintwork, removing surface dust with a clean, brush or mop with a clean cloth tied ove

Continuing our point-by-point plan for turning out a room with maximum efficiency, minimum effort

4. *With plenty of warm water, soapless detergent and a soft sponge, wash down walls (provided they are covered with a washable enamel paint) and paintwork. Rinse thoroughly in clean water and polish with a dry cloth.*

5. *Scrub floor and tackle dirt patches on carpet—either with soapless detergent or a cake of special carpet soap. It won't do any harm, provided you rinse well and don't make the carpet too wet.*

6. *To give mirrors a professional shine, first remove surface dust, then clean thoroughly with a proprietary glass cleaner, following the instructions given. Or sponge with a chamois leather wrung out of warm water and a little vinegar and polish with newspaper.*

7. *Next comes polishing—plenty of elbow grease for furniture and a good wash for all ornaments, glass picture frames, etc., before they go back in place.*

8. *Put on clean loose covers, hang fresh curtains and pelmets—and be ready to greet the spring, the sunshine or to welcome a guest.*

every part *every* week. Rooms not regularly used may only need turning out occasionally, others perhaps every two or three weeks, though bathroom, lavatory and kitchen are among the three weekly "musts." If this regular cleaning is done conscientiously, the occasional or "spring" cleans will be less formidable, and may not be necessary at all except when redecoration is required. It helps to do at least one "special" piece of cleaning each week, too, such as washing the paintwork in one room, turning out a cupboard or cleaning a carpet.

Bedding lasts longer if well and regularly cared for. Brush and air your mattresses well on both sides once a week. Put pillows on the window ledge to air or, in winter, into an airing cupboard every day

and money in the various branches of home-making.

Planning meals well ahead is the greatest help. Shopping can be done economically, meals dovetailed to save time, materials and fuel, and the food made varied and really nourishing. It is all too easy to have sufficient bulk without enough body-building and protective foods in a family diet. The housewife should learn all she can about food values and cooking methods and keep up to date with food news.

In addition to these items, time must be allowed for the inevitable odd jobs that crop up in any household, such as answering the door and telephone, dealing with tradesmen, and for the personal care of the family and of the housewife herself.

Economical Hints to Remember when Planning

It may be helpful to set down some simple hints for economy of time, effort

Sensible Shopping

Shopping is most important, but it can take a great deal of time and effort. Keep a pad and pencil in the kitchen and jot down requirements as you think of them, so that you have a list ready when you go

Plan one special cleaning job each week, such as washing paintwork. A loofah and mild detergent suds in warm water are excellent for this

shopping. Choose shops which sell clean, fresh food, and which are as near each other as possible; it is a great time waster if the butcher is at one end of the town and the greengrocer at the other. Do as much shopping as you can at one time, particularly when buying dry stores. If you have a cool larder or a refrigerator, you may also be able to get enough perishable foods to last two or three days, always remembering the importance of serving food as fresh as possible.

Try and avoid week-end shopping, when prices are often higher and it takes longer to get served. It is wise to select food personally, but take advantage of any delivery services available. If you do have to take your own purchases home, choose a basket that is light, strong and easy to carry, or use a basket or box on wheels. Be careful to get the right quantities for the meals you have planned, and if you are tempted to buy heavily during a glut, make sure you can use the extra quantity before it deteriorates.

Keep a store of foods which can be used for emergency meals in case visitors call unexpectedly, or you have sickness in the house and cannot get to the shops. Correct storing of different foods is important, and if you have enough space it is usually more economical to buy larger quantities of dry stores than to buy them in "penny numbers." Arrange your store cupboards so that everything can be easily seen, and have everything clearly labelled.

Cooking

To streamline the preparation and cooking of meals, plan the kitchen for easy working, with simple, accessible equipment, good lighting and working surfaces the right height for you. Remember it is often possible to save fuel and work by cooking a stew in a saucepan and steaming potatoes and a pudding over it. When the oven is on, use it to capacity, so that the heat is not wasted. Fireproof dishes in which food can be cooked and served are time- and work-savers, and so are pressure cookers. Use as few utensils as possible, clearing up as you go along, so that you are not faced with a pile of washing-up when you have finished. Avoid unnecessary fussing with food—it tastes and looks better if it is not handled too much.

Washing-up

Serving and clearing away meals need not be laborious and time-wasting if you plan sensibly. However simply laid, a table will look attractive if everything is clean, neat and sparkling. Have table linen that is easily laundered, china and glass that is easy to clean, and store it conveniently for table laying. Good preparation takes the worst of the drudgery out of washing-up, and a few minutes spent collecting and sorting, stacking and soaking is well worthwhile. Scrape off scraps and wipe very greasy things with newspaper before washing. This takes only a moment, but it saves hot water and water softener and provides a cheap firelighter. A good hot-water supply is a great help, and the right amount of soda for the water in your district softens the water cheaply and does not hurt your hands. Though a plate rack is useful, do nevertheless rinse crockery before putting it in the rack, so that it dries free from streaks. Silver needs only occasional cleaning if it is washed as soon as possible after use, rinsed at once and rubbed with a chamois leather before being put away.

Care of Clothes

When buying new clothes, household linen or soft furnishings, choose materials that are crease-resisting, pre-shrunk, fast coloured and easy to launder. Avoid articles, however attractive, which may prove difficult to wash or clean, or which are badly made and finished and will soon need repairing. When buying or making children's clothes allow for growth, as well as for wear and tear. Try always to have enough of everything to meet emergencies, so that if the laundry fails to deliver or you are ill and cannot do the washing, the family will not run out of essentials.

All clothes, and particularly shoes, wear better if they have regular "rests," so it pays to have enough to wear on alternate days only. Make time for a regular check of clothes and household linen, so that necessary mending can be done at once, and keep your work-box tidy, with some needles threaded for emergency repairs. Start the care of clothes as soon as they are bought by attending to such things as sewing on loose buttons and strengthening toes and heels of socks. Sponging, removal of spots as soon as they appear, brushing immediately after wear and regular use of coat-hangers, hat stands and shoe-trees, all help to save major overhauls, while regular shaking or suction cleaning of blankets, curtains, loose covers, heavy coats and suits saves frequent cleaning.

Find out the different types of service offered by your local laundries and dry cleaners, and use the ones most suitable to your needs, remembering to mark and list everything clearly and to "rough mend" any tears before sending. Items of modern equipment such as washing machines, drying cabinets and heat-controlled irons are all a great help

in home laundering, but choose those most suitable in size and design to your household. Find out from experiment and personal experience the soap, washing powder or detergent which suits you best, and use it economically, following carefully the directions given by the maker. Care in hanging to dry and in folding means less work in ironing. You will save time and temper if you find out at once which materials need little or no ironing, which need ironing very wet and which nearly dry.

House-cleaning

Before beginning any kind of cleaning of the home, collect the equipment and cleaning materials you require for the job, carrying the small items round with you in a box or basket so as to keep them to hand. Work with method from the top down, so that nothing is missed, and take care to remove all dust and dirt before beginning to polish. Find out the simplest way of cleaning each surface, so that you do not waste time and effort for little result. Use cleaning materials sparingly, remembering that the more polish you put on the harder it is to rub off, and that it is regular attention which gives that "well-cared-for" look.

Choose simple, well-made equipment, light to handle, easy to keep clean, and suitable to your particular

The secret of efficient cooking is never to let the oven get really dirty. Cleaning it is no longer a painful chore. Just rub with Oven Stick, and wipe clean with a damp cloth. Before you start, be sure to turn off gas or electricity

421

needs. Learn to use equipment efficiently (this applies particularly to suction cleaners), and take care of it, remembering that dirty dusters, mops, brushes and brooms make dirt instead of removing it, that suction cleaners and carpet sweepers need emptying regularly, and that electrical equipment wants oiling and servicing occasionally. When you have cleaned a room, look round before you leave it to see that everything is in order and that furniture, books and papers are where they should be, so that the family do not have to hunt for misplaced articles.

Lastly, try to avoid getting overtired by finding the easiest and quickest way of doing every task. Have a stool of a suitable height for the kitchen working surface and sit down to do jobs such as peeling vegetables, which are only tiring if you stand to do them.

Special Problems

Although no two household routines will be alike and each home has its own diffi-

Jot down the items as you run out of them, then make up a detailed shopping list before you set out

culties, there are some circumstances which make planning particularly tricky.

Take the case of a family where both parents are in full-time work. Early rising is essential if the mother is to give the family breakfast, air and tidy the rooms and make the beds before she leaves for work. She must plan the day so that when she comes home she has time for a short rest before getting the evening meal, putting the children to bed, doing the special job for the day, seeing that everything is ready for the morning and having a little leisure and relaxation herself. The husband and children must do their share so as to lessen the strain on the housewife, and Saturdays and Sundays must not become overburdened.

The family where one or more members work unusual hours or are doing shift work may also be a difficult one to organise. It is important not to disturb those who have to sleep during the day, and some of the work normally done in the morning has to be done in the afternoon or evening. If the working hours vary from week to week, the housewife must use all her ingenuity to keep everything running smoothly. The planning of meals is particularly important, so that the worker has as much freshly cooked food as possible and does not have to put up with a diet of reheated meals.

The arrival of the first baby in a family will upset the routine considerably, and the young housewife may find it difficult to adjust herself to this, especially if she is not feeling quite fit. It is best to start the adjustment well before the baby arrives, by thinking out ways of cutting down work, re-arranging the home if necessary, and deciding what activities must be curtailed for the time being. Mealtimes will have to be altered, and probably some of the cleaning cut out to allow time for the extra washing. The early feed means early rising, and a good deal of work must be fitted in between this and the next feed and bath time, so a mid-morning break and a

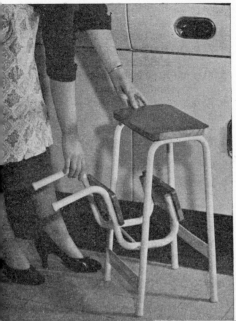

pace. Patience and understanding may be needed to arrange this. If they are well enough they can take the responsibility for definite jobs, but only those things which do not involve mounting a chair or step-ladder, and the housewife must be prepared to take over on days when they do not feel up to the mark. If there is an infirm elderly person in the household, time must be allowed daily for the necessary care and attention and for some social life and companionship. Fittings and furniture should be arranged to ensure as much comfort as possible, and to avoid the risk of accidents.

In spite of all the hard work, housekeeping is a fascinating and rewarding job. The time and trouble you spend in making and carrying out a smooth-running routine will be amply repaid by the happiness and contentment of your family.

Every kitchen should have a stool—to encourage you to do as much work as you can sitting. This Sky-line Step-Stool serves a double purpose, is also a step-ladder

Plastic materials are work-savers in the kitchen. Right, curtains at windows and under the sink, apron and protective cuffs are all made of Velbex

rest after lunch are essential. Time has also to be made for a walk with the baby, and the routine planned so that the mother can go to bed soon after the last feed.

The household containing one or more elderly people also has its special problems. The old folk should be encouraged to help, as this keeps them mobile and gives them the feeling that they are making a useful contribution to the home, but they must work in their own way and at their own

Here are suggested daily routines for three quite different families.

Family 1. *Woman with husband at work and three children at school (No help)*

FAMILY: The husband (clerical worker) with regular office hours.

Three children at school, age 7, 10, 12.

Wife at home all day, and has no paid help.

(Children have a midday meal at school and husband has a light lunch.)

DWELLING: Semi - detached 2 - storey house in a small country town. It comprises 4 bedrooms, bathroom, lavatory, landing, staircase and hall, dining room, living room, kitchen, downstairs cloakroom with lavatory.

7.00 a.m. Rise, open bed, air room, attend to boiler. Prepare breakfast. Husband supervises children washing and dressing themselves and airing and making their own beds.

7.45 a.m. Breakfast.

8.15 a.m. Husband leaves for work.

8.30 a.m. Children leave for school. Clear away and wash up.

9.00 a.m. Give daily attention to bedrooms, bathroom, lavatories, hall, stairs, landing, entrances, dining room, living room (omitting any part that will have a special clean on this day).

10,00 a.m. Begin special work (see next column for details).

10.45 a.m. Break for coffee.

11.00 a.m. Continue special work. Prepare light lunch for self and do some preparation for high tea and evening meal if necessary, and do daily work in the kitchen.

12.45 p.m. Lunch and rest, change and tidy self.

1.45 p.m. Walk, shopping, gardening and mending.

4.00 p.m. Prepare high tea for children and begin preparation of evening meal for self and husband.

4.30 p.m. Have cup of tea and snack with children.

5.00 p.m. Prepare substantial high tea and lay table.

6.00 p.m. Have high tea with husband and children. Clear away and wash up.

7.00 p.m. Put youngest child to bed. Recreation. Supervise older children going to bed.

9.30 p.m. Drink and snack for self and husband.

Special Weekly Work

MONDAY. Washing, by hand and using washing machine. Some ironing if possible.

TUESDAY. Weekly work in living room and dining room (alternate weeks). Finish ironing.

WEDNESDAY. Weekly work in bedrooms (2 on alternate weeks).

THURSDAY. Weekly work in bathroom, lavatory, hall, stairs, landing and entrances.

FRIDAY. Weekly work in kitchen and larder. Extra shopping for week-end.

SATURDAY. Extra baking for week-end.

SUNDAY. Do the bare minimum.

Family 2. *A young wife with young baby*

FAMILY: The husband is a local tradesman and comes home to a midday meal. He has a half day off on Thursday and works all day on Saturday. There is a young baby being breast fed at 6 and 10 a.m. and 2, 6 and 10 p.m. Wife is at home. Feeding times should be kept as accurate as possible, but the other timing must depend on baby's behaviour, as he comes first.

DWELLING: A council house in a London suburb comprising 3 small bedrooms, bathroom and lavatory combined, dining room, sitting room, hall, stairs and landing and kitchen.

6.00 a.m. Rise, feed baby and put him back to sleep.

6.30 a.m. Attend to boiler. Air rooms. Prepare breakfast.

7.15 a.m. Have breakfast.

7.45 a.m. Husband leaves for work. Clear away and wash up. Do daily work of house.

9.30 a.m. Wash, dress and feed baby. Put to sleep in pram. Do baby's washing.

11.00 a.m. Break for rest and refreshment.

11.15 a.m. Do special clean (see below) and prepare dinner.

1.15 p.m. Have dinner with husband, who helps wash up.

2.00 p.m. Change and feed baby. Rest with feet up. Take baby out. Do necessary shopping.

4.30 p.m. Have tea. Odd jobs such as sewing, mending and ironing.

6.00 p.m. Feed and attend to baby, and put to sleep.

6.30 p.m. Prepare supper. Have supper with husband. Clear away and wash up. Recreation.

10.00 p.m. Feed baby.
Get to bed as soon as possible.

Special Weekly Work

MONDAY. Family washing in washing machine. Some ironing.

TUESDAY. Weekly work in living room and dining room (on alternate weeks). Finish ironing.

WEDNESDAY. Weekly work in bedroom and baby's room on alternate weeks.

THURSDAY. Weekly work in bathroom, and alternate weeks landing and stairs or hall and entrance.

FRIDAY. Extra shopping and cooking for week-end.

SATURDAY. Weekly work in kitchen and larder.

SUNDAY. Do the bare minimum.

Family 3. *Working wife who must do chores before leaving for office or factory*

FAMILY: The husband works in a factory from 8 a.m. till 6 p.m. and has a good midday meal at the canteen. There are no children. The wife is a shorthand typist working from 9 a.m. till 5 p.m. and having a midday meal at a canteen. She does not work on Saturdays, and the husband works every other Saturday.

DWELLING: Top-floor flat in an old converted house in a large industrial city, comprising 2 bedrooms, living room, kitchen with dining recess, bathroom and lavatory combined and a small hall.

6.30 a.m. Rise. Open bed and air the room. Prepare breakfast.

7.10 a.m. Breakfast.

7.30 a.m. Husband leaves for work. Clear away and wash up. Make bed. Give daily attention to bedroom, living room (including fireplace) and bathroom.

8.20 a.m. Leave for work.
Shopping in lunch hour.

5.45 p.m. Return home, light fire if required. Prepare evening meal and do special work (see below).

6.30 p.m. Husband returns, has cup of tea and lays table.

8.00 p.m. Evening meal. Clear away and wash up. Leisure.

Special Weekly Work

MONDAY. Washing (heavy washing sent to laundry, sometimes done at launderette).

TUESDAY. Ironing.

WEDNESDAY. Leisure.

THURSDAY. Weekly work in bathroom and hall, and in spare bedroom as necessary.

FRIDAY. Weekly clean bedroom and living room alternately. (Husband at night school.)

SATURDAY. Shopping. Weekly clean kitchen. Cooking for weekend. Take soiled laundry and collect clean.

SUNDAY. Do the bare minimum.

SPRING CLEANING

The pros and cons of this old-established domestic practice discussed

by BARBARA HAMMOND, *Senior Lecturer in Housecraft,*
Battersea Training College of Domestic Science

WHAT do we mean by spring cleaning? In Victorian times, by all accounts, in most households it meant a time of hardship and discomfort for every member of the family, when household routine was disorganised, the cleaners themselves were over-tired and short-tempered, and the excessive cleanliness of the house became more important than the happiness of its inhabitants.

Nowadays, with cleaner methods of lighting, room warming and cooking, with more simply furnished rooms and with the use of electric suction cleaners, spring cleaning is of much less importance. Doubts are even expressed as to the need for it at all. There are, however, many reasons for continuing the practice and for doing it in the spring rather than at any other time of the year.

Late spring is the time when clothes moths prepare to lay their eggs in woollen materials and furniture beetles in well-seasoned wood, and these two destructive little insects are reason enough for a large part of spring cleaning.

Guarding against Moth

First for the clothes moth. The most favoured place for the moth to lay her eggs is soiled woollen material stored in a closed cupboard or drawer. The eggs laid in such conditions will hatch into grubs, which then feed on the fabric, causing the familiar and dreaded moth holes. The simplest and most effective preventive is cleanliness. Therefore, before the weather gets really warm, woollen clothing, blankets, carpets and upholstery should be washed, dry cleaned or shampooed.

Woollen garments that are not washable may be treated with a moth preventive, in addition to the usual cleaning, by most firms of dry cleaners. The washing of blankets is easily done at home if outdoor drying space is available. For washing, soapless washers make rinsing easier and remove the dirt most effectively. Mechanical aids such as a good wringer, a washing machine or the commercially run "launderettes," of course, lighten the work, which is best spread over several weeks. As well as blankets, all bedspreads, curtains and loose covers are usually laundered or dry cleaned in the spring. The heavier materials will, of course, be dry cleaned, but for lighter materials home or commercial laundering is cheaper and usually more suitable.

Cleaning Carpets

Carpets, for their moth-proofing treatment, should be completely freed of dust by vacuum cleaning, on both sides if possible, or by beating out of doors. They

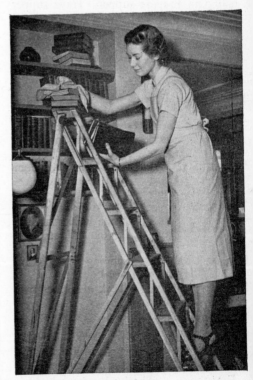

The annual spring clean is the time to dust and sort out the books on the top shelves

Washing down walls is a comparatively easy task with a long-handled sponge squeezee that will reach almost to the ceiling and warm detergent suds

Carpets can be shampooed at home in the foam from a soapless detergent solution, then wiped with a soft cloth. Use a soft brush for bad stains.

This and photos on pages 417, 428, 430, 435 and 437 specially taken by the Hedley House and Beauty Service in Selfridges Household Dept.

When wringing a blanket, hold it over your arm to take the weight and help it through without dragging on the wringer

may then easily be shampooed at home, using a small spray gun supplied with some makes of vacuum cleaner and following the directions supplied. In the absence of such a device, they may be sponged or brushed with tepid water and either carpet soap or a soapless washer, working the way of the pile and sponging off the lather with a cloth wrung out in clean tepid water. Similar treatment may be given to woollen upholstery, taking great care to use very little water.

Clothing, blankets and hangings, once cleaned, are often put away for the summer months, and they should, in this case, be packed with a moth preventive. Specially prepared paper bags that have been chemically treated may be bought for this purpose, but a good substitute is clean newspaper used as a wrapping, with "Selo-tape" to seal the edges. Inside the parcels or loose in the drawer or cupboard, for further safeguard, a patent moth preventive may be added. These are mostly strong-smelling and nowadays contain D.D.T. For those who dislike the characteristic mothball smell, there are on the market various mixtures of cedarwood chips and aromatic herbs which have pleasanter smells.

Safe Storage

The cleanliness of woollen articles may be useless against moths unless the place of storage is also clean. For this reason, as well as for preventing attack by the furniture beetle, all chests of drawers, wardrobes and hanging cupboards should be cleaned thoroughly inside. The unpolished part of the wood should be dusted, brushed or vacuum cleaned, wiped with paraffin and aired. This applies to the backs, undersides and inner framework of cupboards and chests as well as to the insides of drawers, as it is in these hidden and unpolished parts of the wood that the furniture beetle is likely to lay her eggs. Paraffin is recommended because, unpleasant as its smell is, it is an excellent repellent of most insects. In any case the smell quite soon wears off.

If worm holes actually do appear in wood, it is wisest to remove the affected piece of furniture from the room and treat it with a commercial preparation specially made to kill this pest. As a further precaution, treat other furniture in the room.

The cleaning and turning out of cupboards and wardrobes is an excellent starting point for sorting the contents and discarding useless or outworn articles.

Chimney Sweeping

Another necessary preliminary to spring cleaning is the sweeping of chimneys when the need for fires is presumably over. If the vacuum method of sweeping is used, the sweep should be asked to scrape the chimney as well if smoky coal or wood has been burnt.

These different kinds of work form a large part of spring cleaning. The final stage is the removal of dust from every accessible and inaccessible surface, ledge and corner, and the suitable washing, cleaning, scouring and polishing of every surface, both fixed and movable, in the room.

It is this final stage in the campaign that is most debatable. It may be argued that this kind of cleaning is better done bit by bit throughout the year. This is largely a matter of opinion; to many women the feeling of achievement when spring cleaning has been completed is enjoyable and stimulating.

HOW TO CLEAN DIFFERENT KINDS OF FLOORING

There is a special method for almost every type of floor surface

by BARBARA HAMMOND, *Senior Lecturer in Housecraft,*
Battersea Training College of Domestic Science

THE cleaning of floors is undoubtedly hard work, but it is a most rewarding task; the floor forms such a large and obvious part of any room that its appearance makes or mars the well-kept look of that room and of the house as a whole.

The first stage is, of course, getting rid of dust and grit, which, if left, collect in corners and are trodden in to spoil any but the hardest surface. The golden rule here is to remove without scattering the dust. Other cleaning methods vary according to the kind of floor surface. Some must never be washed; others will withstand even scouring. Some may be polished or oiled, while others are ruined by wax or oil. Very hard surfaces are often made dangerously slippery if they are polished. Rooms where food is prepared and stored must be kept scrupulously clean, and so should lavatories and cloakrooms; the floors in these rooms should therefore be washed frequently. Where there are little children or old people in the house it is unwise to have highly polished floors.

WASHABLE FLOORS

Let us consider first floors that may be washed; this class includes stone, concrete, tiles, some jointless flooring, rubber and linoleum.

Concrete and stone of all kinds are hard and may be given harsh treatment. They may be washed with very hot water and soda; scouring powders will not harm them, and they may be scrubbed vigorously. The cleaning agents to be avoided are acid, which roughens any stone surface; soap and polishes which would make the surface dangerously slippery. To avoid undue slipperiness after washing, stone floors should be dried with a tightly wrung floorcloth or mop. A concrete floor that has been left rough by the builders can be improved by treating with one of the patent "fillers" or "dressings" now on the market.

Tiled floors of all kinds are also washable, but soda should be avoided, as it may remove some of the colour and in time roughen the surface. Soap may be used and the red clay tiles may be given a most attractive gloss with ordinary wax and turpentine floor polish. It is not wise to polish the harder vitreous tiles which are generally used in patterns of black and white and dark colours. This kind is far too slippery if polished.

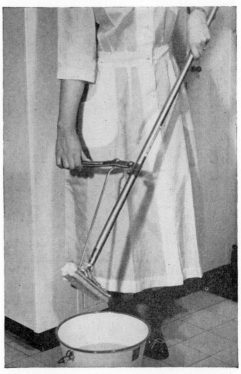

No effort required to wash a floor with the Prestige Minit Mop. You can wring, rinse and clean the sponge head without stooping or even wetting your hands

429

A composition tile floor can perfectly safely be scrubbed when desired with a hard brush, a mild green household soap and only a little water

Linoleum may also be washed; again, soda and scouring powders should be avoided and linoleum should not be scrubbed. Such treatment roughens the surface so that it gets dirty more quickly. Linoleum should be washed with warm water and soap, rinsed and dried and may, when dry, be polished with either a wax or a non-slip cream polish. To make linoleum more dirt-resistant and easier to clean, it may be treated with a linoleum dressing, and when this is dry, with polish in the ordinary way. As an alternative to washing, linoleum may occasionally be cleaned with a very little paraffin and then repolished.

Rubber floor covering, whether laid in sheet or tile form, may be washed, using very little water and soap. Only if a rubber floor has been specially treated by the makers and if the polish has been recommended by them should rubber be polished; it may be treated with a dressing as for linoleum to make it more resistant to dirt; subsequently it may be washed in the usual way.

Modern jointless or composition floors are a little more confusing, as some may be washed while for others washing is not recommended. They are of two main types: those containing asphalt and those termed "magnesite." The asphalt type may be washed with warm water and soap, but should be polished only with a cream or "water-emulsion" wax polish. "Magnesite" floors are really better if not washed, but may be rubbed with a very little linseed oil when new and thereafter polished in the same way as linoleum. If it seems absolutely necessary to wash a "magnesite" floor, very little water and soap should be used, and never soda or scouring powder for either type. If the kind of jointless floor is not known, the safest method of treatment is very little washing and polishing with a cream polish.

Softwood board, the one other washable floor, is now so out of fashion that it is nearly always hidden under linoleum or rubber or disguised with stain and polish.

NON-WASHABLE FLOORS

All other timber floors are non-washable.

Wood block, hardwood parquet, hardwood strip flooring and the newer **plywood squares** are set in some form of adhesive or cement and, if made wet, will swell and rise unevenly from their bedding. They should all be kept well polished, as this not only improves their appearance, but protects the surface from wear. The secret is, of course, very little wax or cream

polish, which if possible should be left to dry for about half an hour and then rubbed hard with a weighted polisher or a brick wrapped in felt or flannel, or, where available, with an electric polisher. Just occasionally, for instance at spring or autumn cleaning, the old polish may be removed with turpentine or paraffin or the surface may be cleaned with fine, dry steel wool. In each case the floor must be repolished before it is much used again and it will take several repolishings to restore its highest polish.

Cork floor coverings require treatment similar to that of wood floors. Cork carpet, which is laid in sheets like linoleum, although soft and warm, is difficult to keep clean because of its rough surface. It is best cleaned with very little cream polish or a wax polish thinned with turpentine. The use of a dressing as for linoleum will make subsequent cleaning easier.

Cork carpet may be washed, but if no polish is used, washing will need to be repeated frequently. Cork tiles or squares should be given a surface dressing by the skilled workmen who lay them. If properly surfaced, they are easy to keep in good condition with a thin polish sparingly applied. They should never be washed for, like parquet flooring, they will rise from their adhesive bedding if they are made wet.

★　　★　　★　　★　　★　　★　　★

TO SUM UP THE RECOMMENDED TREATMENTS:

Stone.—Wash with soda.

Concrete.—Wash with soda; apply "dressing" or "filling" to make dirt-resistant.

Tiles.—Wash with soap.

Linoleum.—Wash with soap; clean with paraffin or turpentine; polish with wax or cream; apply "dressing" or "filling" to make dirt-resistant.

Rubber.—Wash with soap; polish only with a special polish recommended by the makers; apply "dressing or "filling" to make dirt-resistant.

Asphalt Jointless Flooring.—Wash with very little soap and water; polish with a water-emulsion wax polish.

Magnesite Jointless Flooring.—Oil and polish.

Wood.—Clean with paraffin or turpentine; polish with wax or cream.

Cork.—Polish with wax or cream; apply "dressing" or "filling" to make dirt-resistant.

431

TAKE CARE OF YOUR HOUSEHOLD EQUIPMENT

Good and regular maintenance will lengthen the life of your domestic tools and ensure their efficiency

compiled by the National Institute of Houseworkers

WHATEVER the job to be done, it pays to buy tools and equipment of good quality—and to take the trouble to give them proper care.

Brushes

The Sweeping Brush.—Never let a brush rest on its bristles, as this flattens and wears them down. Hang brushes up when not in use or stand them on their handles. Never sweep a wet floor; always mop up any moisture before starting to sweep. After use, remove all fluff from the bristles and wash when necessary. Do not let a brush get too dirty or it is very difficult to get it clean.

Wash mops and brushes frequently in warm soapy water and hang them up to dry. Never put away damp

To Wash a Brush.—Use some hot soapy lather (water from the boiler after the clothes have been boiled would be excellent). Wash the brush by bobbing it up and down in the soapy water, and scrub the handle. Rinse well and shake as dry as possible. Hang up to dry (most brushes have a hole in the handle through which a piece of string may be threaded so that they can be hung on the line). Do not use until quite dry.

Scrubbing Brushes.—Rinse well after use and shake as dry as possible. Hang the brush up or put on its side to dry in an airy place. A scrubbing brush that is left wet gets smelly and rotten and then the bristles fall out.

Mops

Dry Mops.—These should be used only for removing dust from polished floors or linoleum. When used as a polisher, tie a duster over the mop head. (Special polishing mops can be obtained.) Always remove any moisture from the floor before using the mop. Shake well after use and remove any threads. Wash frequently and never allow to become very dirty. If the mop head is removable, take it off and wash as for a duster; if fixed, wash in the same way as a sweeping brush.

Wet Mops.—Rinse after use in several waters and hang up to dry. Mops left wet in buckets always smell. Wash and dry frequently.

The Carpet Sweeper

Empty after use and remove any threads from the brushes. Occasionally remove the brushes and wash them, remove all threads and dirt from the inside of the sweeper and replace the brushes when dry. Oil at places indicated and wipe the varnished parts with a clean damp duster. Store the carpet sweeper in a dry place.

Dusters and leathers should be washed before they get really dirty or the necessary scrubbing will wear them out

The "Suzy" Floor Shiner (above) is equally useful for polishing stairs, panelled walls, doors, skirtings, picture rails, etc. In anodised aluminium, it is light to carry

An all-round dust-absorbing impregnated polisher (left) picks up the dust and revives the polish on the furniture at the same time. "Straight Jane" Dazzle Duster

The Vacuum Cleaner

Keep all parts of the vacuum cleaner together in a safe dry place. Empty the bag frequently and remove threads from brushes, if any. When using, be careful not to pull on the flex or to knock the cleaner against anything. Always carry by the correct method and never drag the cleaner. Arrange to have the machine overhauled regularly. Dust with a clean damp duster. Use a wall plug rather than electric light fitment.

The Wringer

After the wringer has been used, loosen the tension and leave loose until it is required again. Clean the rollers with a little paraffin on a rag or a little scouring powder, rinse and dry. Dry all the surrounding parts. Never force too-thick articles through the wringer. If it is difficult to turn the handle, loosen the tension or refold the article.

The Boiler

Turn off the gas or electricity as soon as the clothes have been boiled for the necessary time. Then remove the clothes. Empty the water out and use this for washing the floor or brushes. Before the water has all drained away, wash round the boiler, thus removing any scum from the sides. Remove every drop of water and then dry the inside and outside of the boiler.

Dusters, Leathers and Floorcloths

Never allow dusters or leathers to get too dirty, because they will then need very hard washing or scrubbing and this wears them out. Do not use dusters for cleaning brass or polishing floors; it is better to use rags. Keep clean dusters on a shelf or in a drawer and do not mix the dusters in use with the clean ones. Wash leathers frequently in a warm soapy lather and rinse in another soapy lather. This helps to keep the leather soft. Dry slowly, and rub well when nearly dry to restore the softness of the leather. Wash out floorcloths after use and hang up to dry.

NOTE: Never wash leathers in detergents of any kind; use only soap or they will go into holes.

CARE OF GLASS, CHINA AND COOKING EQUIPMENT

The basic rules both for routine washing and special cleaning
by N. F. CUDDY, *the National Institute of Houseworkers*

WASHING-UP

WASHING-UP is a necessary evil, so make it as quick and easy as possible by having a definite method and routine.

First collect all the dishes on a tray or trolley and stack them on the draining board, according to kind, first scraping off scraps of food from plates and dishes and wiping very greasy ones with a piece of paper.

Remember that glasses should *not* be stacked one inside the other. If two or more glasses do stick in this way, stand them in warm water for a few minutes. The outside glass will then expand slightly, and the inner glasses may be gently removed.

What you Need

If you have to boil your water in kettles, heat sufficient to add to the washing-up water as it cools. If the water in your district is hard, the addition of a very little soda or one of the many detergents on the market will make your work easier and prevent the unpleasant scum which forms with hard water.

Plastic materials are a boon in the kitchen. Plastic washing-up bowls now available at quite reasonable prices are a great improvement on old enamel ones. They are easy to clean, almost noiseless and unbreakable, and there is less risk, when washing-up, of breaking delicate china and glass.

Having prepared the hot water, detergent, a mop or dishcloth, an abrasive and steel wool or a pot scourer, you are ready to face the worst.

Just a word about drying-up cloths. It really is worthwhile having two "on the go," one for glass and silver and the other for china. They ought, of course, to be absorbent but not fluffy. Linen or a mixture of linen and cotton is best. You can get them with the gayest designs that almost make drying-up a pleasure.

The actual washing-up should be done in this order:

(1) Glasses.
(2) Silver and cutlery.
(3) Cleanest crockery—i.e. cups, saucers, etc.
(4) Greasy crockery.
(5) Kitchen utensils.

Jugs, saucepans, glasses, etc., which have been used for milk should be filled with cold water immediately after use, then washed in very hot water.

Teapots should be emptied into the sink tidy, or the tea leaves may be wrapped in newspaper and put in the bin. If a teapot gets very stained from tannin in the tea, fill it with hot soda water and leave for several hours. Rinse *very* well before using it again.

NOTE: Soda should never be used in an aluminium teapot—instead, scour well with very hot water and steel wool or a pot scourer, using an abrasive if necessary. Clean the spout with a brush which is specially made for the purpose and can be bought for a few pence.

Be sure to add hot water or to change the washing-up water as soon as it gets cool or dirty. If a plate rack is used, rinse the plates before putting them in the rack or they will dry smeary.

Production-line Methods

When washing-up for a large number of people, you will find it a good idea to put all the knives together in an old jug or jar of hot water, taking care not to get the handles of the knives in the water or they will discolour. The spoons and forks can be put into another receptacle.

Many modern kitchens have two sinks and two draining boards which simplifies and considerably lightens the work. In

Washing-up is easy if you organise it, stacking the dirties neatly on one side, using plenty of hot water softened with detergent and a nylon pot scourer and/or brush

Right, the best way to get a cut-glass bowl clean without risk of damage is to use a soft brush and a mild soapless detergent

this case, stack all the dirty things on one board, wash them, rinse them in the other sink, and put them on the second draining board to dry, working from right to left or vice versa, whichever is easier for you.

Dry glass and silver while still hot, rubbing briskly to give a good polish.

After draining the crockery, dry well and put away.

When the washing-up is finished, wipe down the draining board, wipe out the sink tidy and clean the sink. Rinse out the mop or dishcloth, squeeze or wring well and put it to dry.

Flush the sink first if possible with hot water, then with cold water. Hang tea-cloths to dry. Wash them out when they get grubby and boil them occasionally. Putting them in the open air helps to keep them fresh and a good colour.

CUT GLASS AND DELICATE CHINA

Old china, glass and porcelain require special care in handling to preserve their beauty and to prevent damage. Great care must be taken not to have the water too hot or very thin glass and china may crack. Special care is needed when old and valuable china has been mended with glue or china cement.

As for ordinary washing-up, collect the pieces to be washed on a tray and stack them neatly. It is a wise precaution to put

435

To remove a fixed stopper from a decanter,
pour a little oil down the neck

a folded tea towel or several sheets of newspaper in the sink or to use a pulp or plastic bowl. Use plenty of fairly hot water and a good detergent or soap flakes. A small soft nailbrush or old toothbrush is excellent for cleaning the crevices in cut glass; also for getting into the crevices or round the handles of cups, jugs and decorated china such as Dresden figures.

Avoid abrasives which may scratch glass and even remove gilding, and soda which may discolour delicate china.

To give an extra polish to glass, rinse it in warm water and just enough vinegar to colour it faintly.

Dry glass while it is still warm, and polish with a lintless cloth; old damask table napkins are excellent for this purpose.

Wine glasses with stems need great care in both washing and drying, as it is so easy to twist the base from the stem.

To remove a Fixed Stopper from a Decanter

(1) Put a little sweet oil round the junction of the stopper and the neck of the decanter; or

(2) Tap carefully all round the neck of the decanter; or

(3) Warm the neck of the decanter by placing a warm cloth round it or by running hot water over it. This causes the outer glass of the neck to expand, thus releasing the stopper.

To remove Stains from Glass

Fill vases with salt and vinegar (2 tablespoonfuls salt to $\frac{1}{2}$ pint vinegar) or with well-washed tea leaves and water. Leave for a few hours, then wash in the usual way.

Stains on water jugs and tooth glasses are due to the deposits of chalk from the water contained in them, and can be removed by soaking in vinegar and water.

CARE OF CUTLERY

To keep cutlery, forks and spoons in good condition, store them in a drawer or box lined with baize to prevent them getting scratched. If little used, wrap in tissue paper, then in baize, and put away in a box or drawer.

Regular Cleaning.—Wash in very hot water, keeping the handles of the knives out of the water, or they will get discoloured. Wipe and rub briskly while still hot to preserve a polish.

When washing table silver, keep spoons and forks separate so that the forks do not scratch the spoons.

Special Cleaning.—There are several ways of cleaning silver and electro-plate.

(1) Mix plate powder to a thin paste with (*a*) water, or (*b*) ammonia, or (*c*) methylated spirit. Using a soft rag, rub the silver briskly with the paste and allow to dry. Rub off with a second soft cloth and finish with a chamois leather. For engraved parts and between the prongs of forks use a silver polishing brush.

(2) Impregnated cloths need no other polish. Simply rub the silver and finish with a clean soft cloth or chamois leather. Impregnated silver cloths can be simply and cheaply made at home by soaking a piece of flannelette or similar material in a solution of whiting, jeweller's rouge and ammonia. When dry, the material is thoroughly impregnated with the whiting and jeweller's rouge. The cloths should not be washed.

(3) *Polishing Liquids.*—There are several on the market, designed to save the busy housewife's time. The silver is dipped straight into the liquid, then rinsed in cold water and finished with a soft cloth or leather.

THE CARE OF COOKING UTENSILS

Cooking utensils must be kept scrupulously clean. Dirty ones are a breeding place for germs and a source of danger to those eating food which has been cooked in them. They also spoil the flavour of the food and wear out more quickly. Put all utensils to soak as soon as you have finished with them. Those which have been used for milk, egg or starchy mixtures (e.g. cakes and pastry, sauces, etc.) should be soaked in cold water. Hot water hardens these foods and makes them difficult to remove. Utensils used for fish should also be soaked in cold water.

If food sticks or burns, soak the pans well before attempting to clean them. A little detergent in the water is a great help. Try to avoid scratching saucepans during cleaning. Do not use a harsh abrasive or pot scourer. Steel wool or a saucepan brush or nylon pot scourer should be sufficient. This also applies to casseroles and glass ovenware. Salt is excellent for re-

A stiff nylon brush and sudsy powder cleanser will clean without scratching your favourite frying pan. By the way, an omelet pan should not be washed at all, but wiped clean after each use with paper only

moving obstinate stains where an ordinary abrasive may be harmful.

Do not pour cold liquid into a hot pan; this makes even the stoutest saucepan buckle in time. Similarly, do not pour very cold liquids into a hot casserole or glass ovenware dish; and never put hot dishes on to a cold or wet surface.

Leave wooden articles (rolling pins, sieves, pastry boards, etc.) to dry thoroughly before putting them away.

Always thoroughly dry enamel and aluminium saucepans after use.

Never use commercial polishes on metal cooking utensils.

Aluminium.—Never use soda to clean an aluminium saucepan. It will react on the metal and discolour it.

Soak in very hot water if greasy; otherwise in cold water. For stains, use steel wool. Rinse well and dry.

Special Clean. — A badly stained aluminium saucepan should be filled with water to which has been added some lemon peel, apple peelings or a rhubarb leaf. Rinse well and dry.

Chromium.—As for aluminium.

Special Clean.—Wash in hot soapy water, dry, and polish with a soft cloth.

Obstinate stains can be removed from a metal teapot with powder cleanser and a nylon pot scourer

Enamelware.—Great care must be taken not to scratch or chip the enamel. Soak the saucepan in very hot water unless it has been used for milky, starchy or egg mixtures, when it should be soaked in cold water, then washed in hot water. Rinse and dry very thoroughly before putting away.
Special Clean.—Wash a stained saucepan well in hot water, using a mild abrasive and a saucepan brush or nylon pot scourer. Rinse very well and dry thoroughly.

Stainless Steel.—Clean as for aluminium. As soda does not react on stainless steel, it may be used for very greasy pans.
Special Clean.—As for aluminium.

Staybright Metals.—As for chromium.

Tin.—If very dirty, soak in hot soda water. Use a mild abrasive or steel wool; rinse well and dry very thoroughly to prevent rust.
Special Clean.—As above. A special polish may be given to tin kettles, etc., by rubbing with a little dry whiting and polishing with a soft dry cloth.

Baking Tins, Frying Pans and Grilling Pans.—As these generally get very greasy, wipe them well first with some paper (newspaper or any soft kitchen paper will do), which may then be burnt. Then clean according to the kind of metal.

Cake Tins should be washed as little as possible. This prevents cakes sticking. Wipe them with soft clean paper immediately after use, while they are still warm.

Mincers and Graters.—Soak in very hot water, adding soda if necessary, and wash in the usual way.

Earthenware and Glass Ovenware.—Wash in very hot water, adding soda if the dishes are very greasy. Rinse well and dry.
Special Clean.—If the dishes have been used for milky foods or if food has been burnt on, soak them well in cold water, remembering not to put in cold water while the dishes are still hot. Then wash in the usual way.

Wood (pastry boards, chopping boards, rolling pins, sieves, etc.).—Scrape off any pastry, etc., adhering to the wood with the back of a knife. With fairly hot water and a little soap, scrub the way of the grain to keep the wood smooth. Rinse well in cold water and put in a current of air to dry before putting away. Use a brush for hair or wire sieves and rinse under the tap.
Special Clean.—Vegetable or blood stains on chopping boards can be removed by scrubbing with salt or a mild abrasive. Wash as before.

IT WILL MEASURE ANYTHING!

This unbreakable polythene measuring jug will withstand boiling water, is impervious to acids and most chemicals, and remains firm even when filled to the brim. It is marked with cups, half-pints, fluid ounces, litres, cubic centimetres and angled pouring levels. From the Bex range made by Halex

SILICONES IN THE HOME

*They have become a household word, making
light of polishing and repelling water*

THE first introduction that many thousands of people in the U.K. had to silicones was during the Motor Show at Earl's Court a few years ago. Here a manufacturer of a silicone car polish demonstrated the unique properties of the product by carrying out a series of experiments to show that silicones, applied to a motorcar in the form of a silicone polish, raised a shine that lasted for many months without repolishing, gave a water-repellent surface, protected the finish from all weathers, provided a surface to which nothing would stick, and took only minutes to apply.

The silicone car polish was the first of an extraordinary assortment of silicone products. Development became faster in America, where a large silicone industry was soon built up.

Special silicone preparations have revolutionised the baking industry, where thousands of man hours were wasted every day. Greasing machines, applying grease to pans so that the bread would not stick, and scrubbing down walls and ceilings to remove smoke stains used to be a major headache for commercial bakers. Now, using silicones, there is no smoke, no charred residue to remove from the tins and no grease to scrub from floors, walls and ceilings. What is more—one application of silicones to a baking tin means that hundreds of loaves can be baked in it before re-greasing is necessary. This application shows a silicone product used as an abhesive (opposite to adhesive) so that nothing will stick to it.

Milk will not boil over

Silicones are used in industry as anti-foam agents. Some processes involve high fire risk due to foam boiling over and catching alight. The production of varnish is an example of this kind. In other processes foam is just a nuisance, and it helps considerably if it can be eliminated. For example, it is a strange fact that brewers do not like foam in the manufacturing stage and use silicones to cut it out. To bring this application to the home would be fairly simple. For example, milk would not boil over if a mere spot of silicone fluid were dropped into it.

Silicones are so versatile that a form can

To polish antique furniture, apply Topps silicone furniture cream with
a soft cloth, leave a few seconds to dry, then wipe with a light touch

be produced to perform almost exactly as it is required to do. It is this versatility that makes silicone products pop up everywhere with amazing properties. Sun-tan lotions that are still effective after swimming, materials so fine that you can see through them, and blow smoke from a cigarette through them yet they will not let water through. This treatment can be applied to almost any material and demonstrates the water repellency of silicones. The material still "breathes" in the normal manner, yet you can laugh at rain if caught without a coat. Rain just rolls off without wetting the material and stains simply slide off leaving no mark.

New applications of silicones in the U.K. are constantly appearing, but readily available are furniture and floor polishes which are based on silicones. Of course, for a start there is no hard rubbing, but there are other differences too.

The adoption of silicones as an ingredient for polishes meant an entire change in the actual technique of polishing. In the old days it was common to apply a thick coating of wax or similar substance and then to "buff" this coating down until a shine was achieved, and, indeed, very often the amount of shine one obtained on a piece of furniture was in exact proportion to the amount of elbow grease one applied.

Again, one coating was applied over the other until obviously the dirt, which was sealed in, gradually tended to darken the furniture until, although a reasonable finish could be obtained, the colour of the furniture was noticeably different from its colour when new.

No scrubbing needed

Silicones change all that. Silicone polishes are merely applied with a soft cloth and allowed to dry, which only takes a few seconds, and then the haze is simply removed with another soft cloth with the lightest possible touch, no rubbing at all being necessary.

Silicone polishes clean at the same time as they polish, so that you do not get the continual building up of dirt layers, and in this way the silicone polish preserves the original finish and colour of the furniture.

Silicones are quite inert and non-toxic: in other words, they are not poisonous and they don't react in any way to anything else. The tins that your bread is baked in in many bakeries are, as you know, coated with silicones to enable the bread to be removed without difficulty, for nothing will stick to a silicone surface. This means, again, that once furniture is polished with a silicone polish it does not show fingermarks, the finish will not water-stain and certainly there will be none of the "bloom" which was the bane of so much furniture until now. One application of a silicone polish lasts for many months, and it is only necessary to dust the surface at intervals in order to restore the really amazing finish that is easily obtained.

Silicones are being adopted by the building trade for the treatment of masonry and brickwork. Surfaces so treated are rendered water repellent whilst at the same time the passage of air is not impeded. A silicone treatment in such cases prolongs the life of masonry and prevents the destructive qualities of moisture normally absorbed by entry to bricks—it is not generally known that a brick can absorb up to its own weight in water.

Other Silicone Applications

It once seemed fantastic to suggest such an absorbent material as suède could be made waterproof, but, in fact, once suède shoes have been treated with silicones, water literally bounces off when you walk in the rain.

Other silicone applications include siliconised wallpaper that can be wiped down, frying pans that need no cooking fats, sealed silicone-lubricated bearings in electric motors for washing machines, clocks, fans. Once sealed, the bearing requires no further lubrication throughout its life.

Paints are able to withstand temperatures that would blister and burn if they were not siliconised. Velvet hats do not spot.

Are there no disadvantages to silicone products? With silicone paints, the paint must be stripped before repainting—but that is quite a usual practice anyway. With a silicone car polish, the car cannot be resprayed unless the silicones have first been removed by rubbing down. But here again this should be done in any case—however little it may appeal to lazy garage boys.

SILICONES IN THE HOME

Left, water runs off the section of a wall treated with silicone water-repellent, while the untreated sections either side are drenched

Water droplets (below) on shoe leather treated with silicone water repellent, which also makes the leather softer, more flexible and resistant to oil, grease, etc.

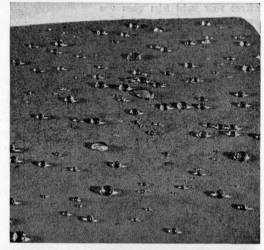

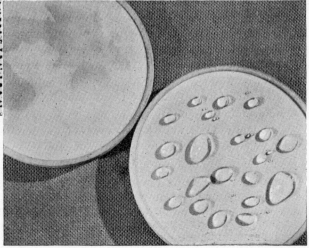

Not a drop of water will pass through the netting, above, because it is silicone treated—but cigarette smoke will

Right, two samples of cloth—the silicone treated one repels water, the other does not

Photographs by Midland Silicones Ltd. and I.C.I.

HOUSEWORK FOR THE FIGURE

Eileen Fowler, the B.B.C.'s Television "Keep Fit" expert, shows how she makes a daily beauty treatment out of her domestic chores

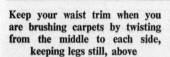

Keep your waist trim when you are brushing carpets by twisting from the middle to each side, keeping legs still, above

When you dust or polish, stretch as far as you can with the right arm, raising the left leg, then repeat with left arm and right leg

Tighten up your thigh muscles when dusting chairs by bending from the knees with your back straight as you hold the chair, left

I have exercised all my life and I am convinced that if the muscles all over the body—which are put there by nature to form a natural corset, bra and general support—are kept toned and supple as in youth, they will retain their elasticity and keep the figure young.

I don't set aside certain hours for my exercises—they are always with me. The few moments waiting for the kettle to boil or the bath to run—that's when I stretch, relax, bend and swing. There is no time to overdo it, but these gentle day-in, day-out movements are enough to keep the muscles strong and happy.

As we get older, the pull of gravity seems stronger. We don't feel so tall, our head droops, and the lines of our faces run downwards. Upward movements are young, so stretch and stretch, reaching

I AM a housewife. I know just how tiring and thankless housework can be. I know that the daily chores leave little time for looking after one's face and figure.

But there does come a time when neglect begins to show, when you find you have to take a size larger than the last time you bought a new dress, when your muscles seem to be set.

442

nd, looking up, pull your bust away from your hips and leave the midriff neat and slim.

When you are tensed up, relax your whole body by crumping right over to the floor. Stand up and swing round as far as you can, twisting the waist as far as it will go. Move the trunk in all directions as you polish and, when you pick up things, bend your knees to save backache later on.

We don't need violent exercise every day, but these basic movements are essential. Domestic duties involve a great deal of movement and, by merging them with easy exercises, you can help your figure.

You need only one piece of equipment for these exercises— will-power. If you really *want* a good figure they won't be tedious.

To strengthen tummy muscles, try this exercise to the count of 6; sit on the floor, hugging your knees, with your hands clasped; then bend your head well over (right)

Now stretch your legs out and upward, feet pointed, and spread your arms out (below). Relax to knee-hug again and repeat

To a count of 8, touch your left foot in front with right hand (above left), then right foot with left hand. Next, touch left foot behind you (above), then right. Repeat

Improve your posture as you walk upstairs by ignoring the rail—keep your back straight. Slim your legs by walking on the ball of the foot

ROTATION EXERCISE FOR A FIRMER BUSTLINE

1. Right: Seated, fists closed gently and elbows at your sides, place both hands on shoulders

Tighten up tummy muscles when dusting high ledges by stretching up as far as you can from tiptoes

2. Left: Moving one elbow forward, rotate arm from shoulder in two fully-described circles

3. Left: Repeat this movement with other arm, so that you can feel the pull on your chest muscles

4. Right: Both arms together, describe four circles to count of 3 each

444

1. Above: Kneel with your arms flung back behind you, your back straight, head up and eyes looking straight ahead

2. Above: Drop forward until your forehead touches the floor, and then rise again to the original position

SWALLOW DIVE FOR TUMMY AND WAISTLINE MUSCLES

4. Above: Rise again and repeat this movement to the left side; then regain upright position as at the start

5. Above: Finally, stretch arms above head, counting from 1–8 for each swallow action and as you stretch

3. Left: Turning to the right, bend from the waist until your head comes down to rest close to your knees

445

HOUSEHOLD PESTS

*Their haunts, breeding places, habits, season and damage
done—and how to outwit them in your home*

compiled by the National Institute of Houseworkers

PESTS can be divided into four classes:
(1) True household pests which breed and live indoors, e.g. cockroaches and silverfish.

(2) Garden-living pests which may invade the house at times, e.g. ants, wasps, earwigs, etc.

(3) Body pests such as bed-bugs, which may live and breed in houses but need humans or animals on which to feed.

(4) Pests which may live and breed inside or outside the house, e.g. flies, mice, etc.

No pest is likely to become a menace to health or to cause serious damage to property unless it has the chance to breed undisturbed and reach such great numbers as to be dangerous. Therefore, the first and finest defence against all household pests is *cleanliness*.

If the house is cleaned regularly and cupboards and drawers turned out at reasonable intervals, any signs of infestation will be discovered before it has time to become serious. The habit of extra thorough cleaning throughout the house in late spring or early summer has much to commend it, as most pests breed faster in warm weather, and any over-wintering adults can be destroyed before they have time to breed. Quick disposal of rubbish, by burning if possible, discourages pests and checks breeding.

Ants

Haunts.—Will sometimes enter the house in summer in search of any uncovered food, particularly sweet things.

Breeding Places.—In cracks between paving stones or crazypaving. A hole can be seen with a mound of fine sandy soil thrown up from it and ants will be seen entering.

Season.—Late spring and summer.

Damage Done.—May ruin sugar, jam and other sweet things.

Prevention. — Keep all sweetstuffs covered in larder. Paint paraffin or turps or sprinkle borax around the outside edges of the larder windows and along the front door threshold.

Control.—If nest can be found, pour into it some paraffin or D.D.T. spray with a paraffin base. This will destroy the grubs and eggs. Spray ants in the house with D.D.T. spray.

Black Beetles (see Cockroaches)

Bluebottles or Blowflies

Haunts.—Dustbins, rubbish and manure heaps, any filth or decaying matter.

Breeding Places.—Tries to lay its shiny white eggs on raw or cooked meat or fish left uncovered. Lays near the bone or in cracks in the meat. Eggs hatch and the grubs eat the meat.

Season.—All the year in mild weather, but most active in summer.

Damage Done.—Carries dirt and germs from rubbish on its sticky feet to food and anything on which it may settle. If eggs are laid on meat or fish the food is rendered unfit for human consumption.

Prevention.—Keep larder fly-proof and all food covered. See that dustbin lids fit tightly.

Control.—Kill any bluebottles seen in the house with a flyswatter or spray with D.D.T. Clean dustbins with disinfectant when they are emptied. Keep rubbish and compost heaps as far from the house as possible.

Bed-bugs

Haunts.—Behind wallpaper and in cracks in walls and woodwork, chiefly in bedrooms. Can move from house to house and remain in an empty house without food for a year.

Breeding Places.—In cracks in plaster or woodwork, mostly in old houses or those in bad repair.

Season.—Summer months, except in centrally heated houses or flats, where they may be active all the year.

Damage Done.—Bites human beings during the night to feed on their blood, causing inflammation and swelling.

Prevention. — Cleanliness and good maintenance of houses so that no breeding places are provided.

Control.—Spray likely places with D.D.T. spray. It is not necessary for the liquid to hit the insects. The spray remains on the surface. If the infestation is very bad, inform the Sanitary Inspector and arange for bedding to be moved.

Cockroaches or Black Beetles

Haunts.—Warm places such as kitchens, bakeries, boiler-houses and near radiators and hot pipes.

Breeding Places. — As above, and in cracks in walls near hot pipes.

Season.—All the year round.

Damage Done.—These pests do not actually eat much human food, but anything on which they walk is made inedible because of the foul smell which remains, and which is not removed by cooking. If other food is not available cockroaches will eat whitewash, hair and books.

Prevention.—Cleanliness round and under radiators and continuous-burning cookers. Filling in of all cracks around hot pipes. Food should be covered and stored in metal or glass containers instead of sacks and cartons.

Control.—A mixture of sodium fluoride and pyrethrum powder can be put down where cockroaches are known to run. D.D.T. powder can also be used. Both these powders should be kept away from children and pets.

Daddy-long-legs

These occasionally stray in from the

The housewife's best weapon against moth and other pests is a spray gun of D.D.T. used generously and often

garden or parks. Kill any seen with a fly swatter. They are harmless indoors but a major garden pest, as the grub stage is the leatherjacket, which eats the roots of grass and food plants.

Earwigs

Another garden visitor during the summer months. Destroyed by D.D.T. spray. It is helpful to brush household spray containing D.D.T. along thresholds of outside doors and along the outside ledges of larder windows.

Flies (a major pest)

Haunts.—Rubbish and compost heaps, badly kept dustbins, any decaying or putrid matter. Manure and animal droppings.

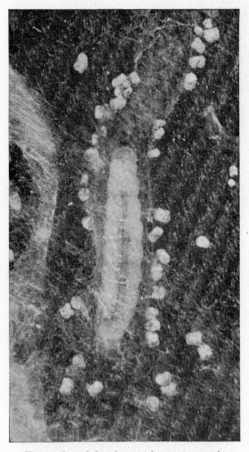

The moth grub hatches out in a cosy spot in a woollen garment, spinning itself a thin silken tube from the fibres of the fabric

Breeding Places.—As above.

Season—Mainly in warmer months.

Damage Done.—One of the worst disease carriers known. Walks with sticky feet on filth, then flies on to human food and household utensils or settles on the skin and thus transfers germs and bacteria. It also regurgitates its food on to any surface on which it may be resting, making "fly spots"—a good breeding ground for germs.

Prevention.—Scrupulous cleanliness in handling, storing and using all foodstuffs. Larders should be rendered fly-proof with fine-mesh covers to the windows or air-bricks. All food should be kept covered, and fruit and vegetables washed before using. Thorough cleaning out of all corners or crevices where flies might hide over the winter months is strongly recommended. Disinfection of drains and dustbins at frequent intervals is advisable.

Control.—Swatting of individual flies where feasible. It is helpful to spray the kitchen at night after all food has been put away, with a household D.D.T. spray in a spray gun or with the aerosol type of sprayer. Other rooms which seem to attract flies should be treated in the same way. Special impregnated papers in fancy shapes can be hung where flies are seen to congregate. The flies pick up the poison through their feet. Special rings are sold which can be put over electric light bulbs. These will diffuse a poisonous vapour when the light is on (quite safe for human beings).

Furniture Beetle or Woodworm

Haunts.—The beetle is rarely seen. Presence is recognised by small holes in unpolished wood, usually in the hidden parts, such as behind desks, sideboards, underparts of tables, and in rafters and other wood in the loft. When the worm is active, it throws up a fine wood dust from the holes.

Breeding Places.—As above, mostly in deal, pine, beech and oak.

Season.—Egg-laying in May, worms start boring in June.

Damage Done.—Large numbers can make furniture unusable, and can cause it to collapse by weakening the wood with boring. The holes can be very deep.

Prevention.—Periodical examination of likely breeding places. It is wise to polish the hidden parts of all furniture occasionally.

Control.—Special fluids are obtainable in tins with fine nozzles, through which the liquid can be injected into the holes. Treatment of the surface is useless; the worm is at the bottom of the hole and laying is done at the farthest end. Very badly infected pieces should be burnt, as floors and neighbouring furniture are quickly affected. After treatment, watch carefully during the following May and June to see whether worms are still active.

Mice

Haunts.—Behind skirtings and under floorboards.

Breeding Places—As above.

Heat is the worst enemy of the moth. Treat an affected carpet by ironing with a damp cloth

Season—All the year.

Damage Done.—They eat and taint many kinds of human and animal food, particularly fats, cheese and cereals. Will leave little black "mouse dirts" over the food and shelves where they have fed as well as a mousy smell.

Prevention. — Careful watch should be kept for signs of holes near the floor, which should be filled at once or have a metal cover nailed over them. All food in larders should be covered, and dry stores put into glass, metal or plastic containers.

Control.—A good cat will keep a house free of mice. Traps can be set where mice are known to run. Poisonous bait can be laid if it can be kept away from pets and children. If the trouble is persistent, consult the Pests Officer or Sanitary Inspector.

Moths

Haunts.—Clothing cupboards and trunks used for storing bedding or winter clothes.

Breeding Places.—Any article made of animal fibre (e.g. wool, hair, fur, feathers), upholstered furniture, clothing and carpets.

Season.—Summer and early autumn.

Damage Done.—Eggs are laid on woollen and similar garments, usually in a fold. Grubs hatch and eat holes in the fabric. A few moth grubs can ruin a garment quickly.

Prevention. — Moths prefer soiled material for their egg-laying, and will choose places such as the underarm of frocks, and the part of a carpet under furniture where dust may collect. Disturbance of breeding places is the

To keep a good mattress free of the moth and in perfect condition, vacuum clean it once a week without fail, going well into the crevices

best preventive. All garments or bedding to be stored away should be washed or dry-cleaned first. Clothes in the wardrobe in the summer should be taken out and beaten in the sunshine from time to time. Moth-proof bags are available for storing valuable furs and coats. Cold storage can be arranged with most big furriers and stores.

Control.—Heat will kill all stages of moths, eggs, grubs and flying insects. Sunshine or a hot iron can be used. Trunks or parcels of clothes for storage should contain paradichlorbenzene crystals (ask the chemist for P.D.B.). D.D.T.-impregnated papers can be hung in wardrobes, but must be renewed after three months.

Mosquitoes

Haunts.—Seen in the house mostly at night when the lights are lit.
Breeding Places.—Breeds under water in water butts, pools and any stagnant water.
Season.—Summer months.
Damage Done.—Bites human beings and causes considerable swelling and irritation. Can carry malarial infection.
Prevention. — Keep any ornamental ponds as far from the house as possible.
Control.—Spray any water butts or pools with an oily based D.D.T. liquid. Kill any mosquitoes seen in the house.

Rats

Haunts.—Rubbish heaps where food refuse is thrown. Storerooms where cereals are kept.
Breeding Places.—Nests built in and under sheds and outbuildings. In very old houses may tunnel under the floor.
Season.—All the year.
Damage Done.—Eats great quantities of human and animal food, mainly in farms and warehouses. If it can get into the domestic larder, will eat any uncovered food.
Prevention.—Fill any cracks in walls, skirtings and floors. Cover all food and store goods in solid containers.
Control.—There are rat poisons on the market, but they must only be laid where children and pets cannot get them. If rats are suspected it is advisable to inform the Sanitary Inspector.

Silver Fish

Haunts.—Dark, warm and preferably slightly damp places near hot pipes or continuously burning fires or cookers.
Breeding Places.—As above.
Season.—All the year.
Damage Done.—Feeds on paper and glue or paste, such as books, wallpaper or cartons. May attack clothing made of cotton and rayon.
Prevention. — Regular sweeping and cleaning of cupboards and surroundings of cookers and pipes.
Control. — Sprinkle D.D.T. powder where silver fish have been seen.

Spiders

These are not really a pest; in fact they do good by killing flies, but if they are present in large numbers they can be a nuisance. Superstition calls it unlucky to kill a spider. Large ones can be lifted in a duster and put outside.

Wasps

Haunts.—Rubbish and compost heaps, garden fruit when ripening. Will enter the house to find sweet foods.
Breeding Places.—Complex nest is built underground, usually under hedges or in grassy banks.
Season.—Late summer.
Damage Done.—Can cause painful stings and swelling, eat or spoil much fruit. Will eat jam, sugar, sweet drinks and beer left uncovered.
Prevention.—Cover all sweet foods, especially jam and stewed fruit. Cover all larder windows with muslin or wire mesh.
Control.—Swatting of all wasps found in the house. If the nest can be found it should be destroyed. After nightfall pour a cupful of petrol down the entrance and then block up with a brick or stone. Spray the kitchen and larder with aerosol or other D.D.T. liquid. Primitive traps of syrup or beer in a jam-jar are useful when jam-making. If infestation is very bad and the nests cannot be found, this is another case when it pays to ask the help of the Sanitary Inspector.

Woodworm (see Furniture Beetle)

STAIN REMOVAL

First aid treatment for accidents of all kinds to carpets, clothes, furnishings, bed linen and furniture

SPOTTING the stain in time is a good maxim for everyone, and the quick application of an antidote is an even better one. Clothes, furniture and soft furnishings are all subject to accidents now and then, however careful we are; fortunately there are few results of these mishaps that cannot be remedied completely, or at least with reasonable success, by home methods. When faint marks still remain, a good firm of dry cleaners can usually complete the removal. But they should have the article immediately, together with notes on the nature of the stain and the home treatment already applied.

CLEANING AIDS

The following are useful home helps which it is always good to have at hand, and are the main ones referred to under the following *Treatments*:

Carbon tetrachloride (grease solvent).
Detergent, liquid (Quix, Octim, Stergene).
Glycerine.
Hypo (photographic).
Milk.
Oxalic acid (poison).
Salt and starch.
Turpentine.

Carbon tetrachloride, hypo and oxalic acid should be bought from a chemist. Have the last two made up in solution for cleaning purposes and keep safely stored out of reach when not in use. The liquid detergents are recommended for on-the-spot stain removal, as powder detergents may leave a white mark in cases where thorough rinsing is difficult. Other cleaning agents which are useful for emergencies are methylated spirits and ammonia. Care must be taken with all inflammable liquids, and cleaning should never be done near a naked flame or while smoking a cigarette.

To clear the grease mark from the inside of a collar and freshen up the material, sponge with ammonia solution

Grass stains often occur on children's frocks. Sponge them gently with methylated spirits or cream of tartar

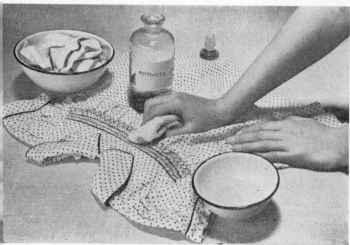

Photo : Irish Linen Guild

Tea, coffee or fruit juice will quickly come out of table linen if you stretch it over a bowl and pour on boiling water from a height

THE TREATMENT

The Stain

ALCOHOL (wines, beer, spirits).—*On clothes:* Mop up excess liquid at once. If article is washable, launder; otherwise sponge with warm liquid detergent solution mixed according to directions. Rinse with clear water.

On carpet, upholstery: Rub with a clean cloth wrung out of detergent solution; rinse in the same way with clear water. Rub lightly from the outside of stain inwards with a circular motion.

On white linen and cotton: Soak in household bleach diluted according to directions. Rinse and launder, or boil if necessary.

BLOOD.—Can very often be removed by soaking for 10 minutes or so in cold water. Make a thick paste of starch and water. Cover mark and leave until paste dries, then brush off with a soft brush; safe for all fine and coloured fabrics and should completely remove stain. If slight discoloration remains and fabric

is washable, launder or sponge in detergent solution and rinse; alternatively have dry cleaned.

On white cotton and linen: Steep area in basin of cold salt water, 1 tablespoonful to 1 pint, and leave for 20–30 minutes. Rinse; boil if necessary.

COCOA.—As for *Alcohol.*

COFFEE.—Swab immediately with plain water to dilute as much as possible. Mop up excess moisture and treat as for *Alcohol.*

DISTEMPER.—*On clothes:* If still liquid, swab off with a wet cloth and rub as dry as possible. If dried, rub gently between fingers to loosen and brush off. Dissolve remaining particles by swabbing with warm water. If discoloration remains, treat with glycerine, and if washable, launder; alternatively, have dry cleaned.

On floors: Try to mop up with a wet rag as splashes occur. Any that harden should be chipped off with the edge of a penny and the rest scrubbed off with hot soapy water.

DYE.—Colour that has run from one fabric on to another should be rubbed with a mixture of 3 or 4 drops household ammonia in 1 teaspoonful methylated spirit, working from the outside of the stain inwards.

On white cotton or linen: Steep in household bleach according to directions. Rinse; boil if necessary.

EGG.—Soak in cold water.

FRUIT.—Pour boiling water through; or moisten with lemon juice and bleach in sunlight.

GRASS STAINS.—Make stains fairly damp and rub gently with cream of tartar or methylated spirits on a damp cloth. Alternatively, cover with glycerine, leave for an hour and then wash.

GREASE.—*On fabric:* If colour is fast, hold over a deep basin and pour through water just off the boil. If washable, launder in rich detergent suds, rinse well; alternatively, dry after water treatment and dissolve any remaining grease with carbon tetrachloride rubbed over the mark from outer edges inwards.

On carpets and upholstery: Mop or blot or scrape off as much as possible with a spoon or back of a knife and apply a dry cleaning solvent, then sponge with hand-hot detergent solution; rinse by sponging with clear water.

On wallpaper: Not easy to remove but a paste of Fuller's earth mixed with water should be applied as quickly as possible, or a warm iron over blotting paper. The stain can also be swabbed carefully with the grease solvent as a final measure.

INKS and IODINE.—*Red and writing ink (excluding ball-point) and iodine:* Swab immediately with water or milk to dilute. If milk is used, rinse in warm water, then soak article for a few minutes in solution of hypo, rinse and launder.

On carpets and upholstery: Sponge with warm detergent solution, rinse with clear water. Repeat if necessary.

Ball-point ink: Sponge with methylated spirit and white vinegar. Blot quickly to avoid spreading. Wash with detergent solution.

On wood: Apply a little warm oxalic acid solution on to the stain itself, using a fine brush. Rinse thoroughly, after a couple of minutes, with warm water.

On walls: Try swabbing with milk.

IRONMOULD.—*On white linen and cotton:* Soak in household bleach according to directions. Boil if necessary.

On coloured goods: Sponge repeatedly with tomato juice; finally wash in detergent suds.

LIPSTICK.—Loosen stain with vaseline or glycerine. Wash in warm soap flake solution. If necessary, bleach with peroxide of hydrogen solution.

On coloured goods: Soak in detergent suds for 10 minutes; rinse. Wash in fresh suds, rubbing gently, or squeezing if wool, and finally rinse.

MILK.—Swab with hot water to dilute and dissolve fat particles. Mop up moisture, sponge with detergent suds and rinse in clear water.

MUD.—*On clothes and upholstery:* Allow to dry, then beat off with a fine cane, and finish with a brush. Any remaining marks should be sponged with detergent suds and rinsed in clear water.

NAIL VARNISH.—Apply acetone or varnish remover but not to rayon fabrics, then brush lightly to remove the dissolved polish.

OIL.—Apply glycerine from outside of stain inwards. Leave for an hour, then sponge with warm detergent solution and rinse with clear water. If any mark remains, apply carbon tetrachloride.

PAINT.—*On clothes:* If still wet, remove with turpentine on a clean rag. Hang garment in air to dry out, then sponge or wash in detergent suds and rinse well.

If paint has dried, carefully break the blobs between the finger-nails and dissolve by repeated dabbing with turpentine. Finally sponge or wash in detergent and rinse well.

On wood: Liquid paint will yield to turpentine. Prick the surface of hardened blobs with a skewer and soak with turps. It may be possible to chip off a certain amount with the edge of a penny. If coloured paint, and any dye remains on the wood, treat with oxalic acid as described under *Ink on Wood.*

On glass: Chip off with a penny and dissolve any that remains with turps. Clean glass finally with chamois leather damped with methylated spirit and polish with a piece of silk.

PERFUME.—Sponge with methylated spirit

Soot marks need not disfigure your carpet; rub in some kitchen salt on a damp cloth, then brush up as soon as possible; finish by sponging or washing in detergent solution if necessary.

PERSPIRATION.—Soak stained area for 10–15 minutes in cold water. Squeeze and rub with a juicy piece of lemon. Leave for a minute or two, rinse and launder.

POLISHES (shoe and furniture).—Scrape off as much as possible. Sponge with detergent solution, rinse and mop up. If any sign of stain remains, sponge with methylated spirit and repeat detergent treatment.

RUST (on carpets from castors).—Sponge with detergent solution, rinse and mop up excess moisture. Apply warm oxalic acid solution with brush, leave about one minute, then rinse off thoroughly. Mop off and smooth carpet the way of the pile.

SALT-WATER MARKS.—Sponge or wash in detergent solution, adding white vinegar in the proportion of one eggcupful to each pint of detergent. Rinse well.

SCORCH.—Treat immediately by squeezing gently under running water; rub over carefully with a piece of household soap and rinse again; or sun bleach.

SOFT DRINKS.—Treat as for *Alcohol*.

SOOT.—*On clothes:* Shake or blow off as much as possible. Treat any smears with carbon tetrachloride and wash or sponge with detergent if necessary.

On carpets and upholstery: Take up with vacuum cleaner if possible; otherwise carefully brush up into dustpan with a soft brush, using a lifting, flicking movement. Treat smears with carbon tetrachloride or rub with salt on a damp cloth, finally brushing up salt into dustpan.

TAR.—Apply glycerine and leave. Wash or sponge with detergent solution and rinse well. If any stain remains, apply the grease solvent.

TARNISH.—*On gold and silver thread fabrics:* Rub gently with a cloth damped with liquid ammonia; alternatively, pound a small quantity of rock ammonia to a fine powder and rub tarnished threads with the powder. A chemist will supply rock ammonia.

On silver cutlery and ornaments: In the absence of a proprietary tarnish remover, remove with bicarbonate of soda on a dry cloth and finish with a good brand of silver polish.

If you have to store silver articles, pack them with camphor to avoid tarnish.

TEA.—Treat as for *Alcohol*.

WAX.—Carefully chip off as much as possible with a finger-nail. Melt the residue by holding a hot iron a few inches above the mark and scrape off with the back of a knife. Finally, apply carbon tetrachloride.

MISCELLANEOUS

Here are a few further stain removal agents, with notes on their uses for various household stains.

A lemon: Handy to have around, apart from cooking, for stains on ivory, and fruit, vegetable and nicotine stains on fingers. Rub over the area with a juicy piece of the fruit, rinse and dry; gently bleaches skin, and ivory, as well as cleaning.

Linseed oil and turpentine mixed in equal quantities is one of the surest removal agents for white rings on furniture left by wet glasses.

Paraffin: Removes surface rust from metals and certain yellow stains from baths. Yellow stains that still persist should be rubbed with warm oxalic acid solution, and this must be thoroughly rinsed away.

Salt and salad oil: Mix salt to a paste with the oil and spread over hot dish marks on polished wood. Leave at least one hour, remove and polish wood normally.

Silver foil off blocks of chocolate, if crumpled in a ball and rubbed over chromium, will remove surface rust and marks and impart a brilliant polish.

Steel wool, fine grade, is the best medium for removing oil and marks from wooden tableware, bowls, platters, breadboards, and so on.

Steel wool and paraffin: Fine-grade steel wool dipped in paraffin may be used to remove cigarette burns and obstinate stains on linoleum.

Steel wool and turpentine: Soiled and stained hardwood floors can be cleaned and freshened by rubbing with medium-grade steel wool dipped in turpentine. Rub the way of the grain.

HOW TO HAVE A
WELL-DRESSED FAMILY

*A little home maintenance will
keep clothes looking smart—
and make them last longer too*

Suits don't develop a tell-tale shine if they are damp pressed
regularly. Do the shoulders on a sleeve board or a rolled
Turkish towel and take care with the trouser creases

A HUSBAND'S sartorial standard depends largely on his wife, even if *he*
thinks it's all in the way he wears his suit
and knots his tie. To aim high, she needs
a watchful eye on:

Jackets and Trousers

Maxim here: often worn, often pressed,
to discourage shine and bagged knees and
to keep trouser creases knife-edged. Press
jacket collar and revers out flat so that you
don't put a sharp edge on the roll-back. A
sleeve board is the quickest and most efficient aid to pressing shoulders and sleeves.

Waistcoats

De-spot with cleaning fluid and press
weekly when constantly worn. Pay special
attention to the points, pressing extra well
to prevent curling. (See chapter on Stain
Removal for more details on this important
point.)

Suits need well hanging when not in use.
Choose the type of hanger designed to take
the shape and weight of men's suits and
coats. They can be
bought from good
haberdashers c o m-
plete with trouser
grip, or the latter can
be bought as a separ-
ate unit.

Overcoats, light or
heavy, need the same
care, and it is prac-
tical to have suits
and coats profession-
ally moth-proofed by
a dry-cleaner when
new, and periodically
afterwards. Outer garments should be
well shaken or brushed and hung on their
right hangers when taken off.

Ties

These accessories are perhaps the
trickiest to deal with, although they can be
washed carefully and dried flat after patting
back into shape. You can tackle the job
with ease and no worry if you use a tie
valet. This is an arrangement of two tie-
shaped pieces of aluminium to be slipped
into the tie. Wash and rinse and stand up
to dry all on the valet and there's no need
to iron. The price is around 9s. 6d. and
haberdashery counters the source of
supply.

Shirts

The ones made of nylon, Orlon or Terylene are the most labour-saving of all. Expensive to buy, but they last a long time,
dry quickly and need no ironing. Failing
them, shirts with detachable collars look
freshest a second day when worn with the
spare collar. Ironing will be eased if he

455

His hat will keep its shape and colour if it has a daily brush—from left to right, the way the nap lies. Keep the hatband fresh with cleaning fluid

chooses the open-out-flat shape. Prolong the shirt's smartness by turning the cuffs on the first hint of fray.

Give shirts their own drawer space and fold like this: Do up buttons, lay shirt front down, pick up side seams and fold over towards centre; fold sleeves back and lay flat over side folds to form a straight edge from shoulder to hem; pick up bottom of shirt and sleeve ends firmly and fold up to collar.

Socks

See that he has enough for a fresh pair daily and some in reserve. Daily laundering saves much darning. Socks made of nylon, Orlon and Terylene, or these fibres combined with silk, wool or cotton, are hard-wearing, easier to wash and dry quickly. You may hand-knit his socks and you can buy sock wool incorporating the synthetic fibres. The spiral type of sock has distinct advantages. Its tubular appearance may look odd but assures a perfect fit, and the wear is distributed all round instead of being always in one place. Most wool shops have instruction leaflets for this type of sock.

Shoes

Shoe cleaning is definitely a job for the man himself; if he had a spell of Service life he should know how! Keep a well-

equipped shoe-cleaning kit in a handy place. Include a tin of leather soap for an occasional spring-clean and dirt and stain removal. Even with gleaming toes, rundown heels will run the man down too. So take the offending shoes to the cobbler promptly.

NOTE: A wise wife leaves her own shoes handy when her husband is attending to his own—it's a task for men.

Space savers for his wardrobe: pegs to take hats; ties hung on expanding wire or elastic inside doors; clip-on trouser hangers to keep in the creases; and special racks for shoes, which should be on trees when not being worn

Hats

Men's felt hats are liable to absorb grease from hair and forehead which, if it seeps through to the outside, makes ugly marks that cannot be removed by home methods. Avoid the trouble by slipping a strip of thin plastic fabric between the grease band and the hat on the inside. Then, as one of your maintenance jobs, wash and thoroughly dry the plastic in hats that have been in use.

Apply a medium-soft brush daily and use a light, quick, sweeping movement. Cushion the brim in one hand while you brush it with the other to preserve its shape. Never touch a wet hat, but leave it on a stand or table in a warm room until dry. Don't put it near a fire or on a radiator, or its shape and texture will suffer. Men's hats don't usually rain-spot, but if one does dry and look spotted, run the steam from a boiling kettle all over it evenly, then gently brush the whole in one direction only.

Gloves

If he likes the chamois leather kind he'll need at least two pairs to wear alternately. You can wash them on your own hands in lukewarm pure soap suds. Rinse in soap suds to keep the leather supple. Squeeze gently, pull into shape and blow into them also, to restore shape, and dry in the open (on a window sill will do), but not in heat. If they are a little stiff when dry, roll briskly between the hands to soften. Other leather gloves need regular dry-cleaning to keep them good-looking.

Umbrella and Briefcase

Dust the inside of his case, lightly polish the outside and rub up any metal. A brief-

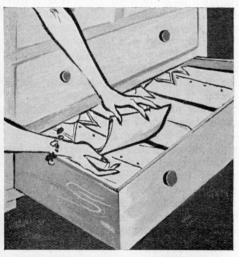

The best way to store his shirts is to give them a drawer or shelf to themselves and put them carefully on top of one another to avoid creasing. Socks, underwear and handkerchiefs need special spaces

case out in all weathers would be a good subject for a fortnightly application of Kiwi waterproofing polish.

As for the umbrella, if this is carried daily but not often used, it gets dingy with dust and metal parts tarnish. Every now and then unfurl it, shake and rub up metal.

Open it up too, and inspect for defects or holes—it's a bad show if a well-groomed man opens up his brolly and a naked spoke protrudes. A small hole can be effectively mended with a piece of iron-on adhesive mending tape; when the cover comes adrift from a spoke, the repair may need professional attention. Dry a wet umbrella open, if space permits; it is quicker and better for frame and fabric.

Dinner and Evening Clothes may figure in his wardrobe but seldom outside it. If he is to look well-turned-out at short notice, his evening togs must have a very regular shake, brush and a good airing, out of doors if possible. And keep them hung up rather than packed away, for the sake both of preservation and moth discouragement. Have these, of all clothes, moth-proofed, because the fine cloth is a prime favourite with the moth.

Evening shirts should be stored free of starch and rough dried. Roll them in blue tissue paper to lessen the risk of yellowing when they are not often in use. (See chapter on The Weekly Wash for information on discoloured whites.)

Odds and Bobs in your job of making the immaculate man:

Well-made hangers preserve the cut of a jacket. Brush suits well before putting them away, to keep free of fluff and staleness. A suit should be rested a day between wearings if possible—and that goes for shoes too

(1) If possible, hang his things as shown on previous pages; it is temper-saving when he's in a hurry, time-saving for you when you valet.

(2) Gently discourage him from stuffing pockets and spoiling the shape of his garments.

(3) If he carries a formidable battery of pens and pencils in a breast pocket, stitch a thin plastic lining into the pocket, to preserve its shape and prevent damage from pen and pencil points and ball-point ink.

(4) Keep a very watchful eye on *all* buttons, most important in a man's dress, and remember that the weight of their jackets and overcoats calls for an inside reinforcing button when you have to renew outer buttons. Raise these buttons away from the cloth to allow for the thickness of the other side when buttoned over. It is helpful to stitch on the outer buttons over a matchstick, remove the stick and take several turns of thread round the threads connecting button to cloth before finishing off.

(5) Men, too, suffer from "B.O." and spoil clothes with underarm stains, so encourage him to be as fastidious as you are yourself and to use a deodorant regularly. There is now on the market a variety of suitably perfumed toileteries, which are acceptable to the most masculine taste. Modern deodorants dry quickly, leaving no trace of stickiness or cloying perfume.

VALETING THE REST OF THE FAMILY

To be a good lady's maid and valet to oneself and the family pays big dividends. Clothes and accessories that are well cared for look better, wear longer and in the end cost less. It's good, too, for everyone's morale to know that their clothes cannot court criticism for lack of care.

This does not mean that a busy wife and mother should do it all herself. On the contrary, it's good for children to be trained to treat clothes tidily. Men, too, should be encouraged to do some of their own valeting—particularly shoe-cleaning.

Good Habits

Nothing is so deflating to a garment's looks as spots and stains; and the quicker stains are dealt with, the less likely they are to leave marks. Urge your family to make a habit of bringing the trouble to you as soon as possible. Children will do so if they understand it to be a co-operative effort and not the signal for a scolding. Urge the menfolk to draw your attention to accidents to their clothes when they come home in the evening.

Train everyone to use a clothes brush morning and night on outer garments of all but the finest fabrics, and help the drill by keeping good brushes at all strategic points.

Provide plenty of coat, skirt, blouse and trouser hangers and foster the habit of hanging up all garments after use, to keep their shape and avoid creases.

General Care

It is a good plan to allow time once a fortnight to go over all non-washable garments and accessories for anything that needs attention. Set aside those ready for dry-cleaning and give the rest a thorough brushing. Pay special attention to the undersides of collars, revers and pocket flaps, the insides of turn-ups and seam allowances. It is quite startling sometimes to find how much fluff and dust collects in these places if not brushed regularly. Keep on hand a bottle of carbon tetrachloride and a bottle or tube of a proprietary dry-cleaning agent. Use on necklines if there is any indication of grease or powder marks.

Check for loose buttons, press and lightning fasteners, holes in pocket linings, splits in seams and hems coming undone. Take time out to do these small repairs on the spot; not only for the sake of good grooming, but because it saves time in the end—and possible embarrassment.

Check for any indication of "shine." It can be successfully treated with a solution of one teaspoonful ammonia in one pint of warm water. The mixture should be brushed into the fabric with a medium soft nailbrush and excess moisture wiped off with a clean, dry cloth. Press on the wrong side until dry, using a warm iron over an evenly damp pressing-cloth. The latter should be firm linen or cotton, free from starch and dressing.

Press pleats and "seat" of skirts. Have a thick pad handy when pressing and lightly beat out the steam when the damp cloth is removed, working from top of garment to bottom. This is a precaution against shrinking the material, and for the same reason the iron should not be too hot nor the pressing-cloth over-damp.

While you attend to these jobs, air clothes not in constant use. Shake and lightly beat furs. On a fine day, hang in the open, keeping light-coloured garments in the shade; otherwise, place in a current of air indoors. This will deter moth and dust from settling in and will keep the clothes looking and feeling fresh.

Accessories

Women's straw hats collect a surprising amount of dust in the small crevices of the weave. Blow hard or brush clear with an artist's springy paint brush. All felts should be lightly brushed. Tired - looking velvet hats

Adequate storage is essential for clothes maintenance. This big cupboard, papered with different designs in Crown wallpapers, was made from three old wardrobes and some additional wood

can be freshened by letting steam from a boiling kettle blow right through from the wrong side. Hang in a warm atmosphere, shaking frequently and smoothing the way of the pile with a soft, dry cloth until quite dry. Petersham and other fabric and fur fabric hats may be bought as washable; if not, it is safer to have them dry-cleaned.

Renew inside ribbon bands from time to time, and as an anti-grease measure rub over the inner bands with cleaning fluid every fortnight.

Handbags.—Turn out once a fortnight. Brush out the inside. Wipe over the outside with a clean cloth, paying attention to gussets where dust accumulates. Rub up any metal parts. Leather should be very lightly polished with a good white furniture cream to keep the skin supple. Plastic handbags can be sponged evenly all over with a cloth wrung out of warm suds,

rinsed in the same way with clear water and rubbed briskly until dry.

Carry cosmetics in a plastic make-up holder because drifting powder gives a handbag lining a dusty, greasy look and lipstick smears are almost impossible to remove. But if any of these misfortunes do occur, apply cleaning fluid and leave handbag empty and open until any odour has disappeared.

Shoes.—New pairs that are rubber-soled and heeled at once last wonderfully well. Shoes should be put on to well-shaped trees as soon as they are taken off. When the rubber shows wear, leather heels begin to run over or leather soles show a thin spot, have them repaired. Every fourteen days is a good time to apply a wet-proofing polish made by Kiwi, as this is the time limit claimed for the efficacy of each application and it is certainly a safeguard to

It's never too early to teach them care of their clothes. Boys take fairly kindly to shoe-cleaning

the life of shoes. Shoe polish may be applied later if a brighter shine is needed.

Special Mending

Apart from the more usual mends already mentioned, there are one or two, rather more complicated, to be considered:

Dragged Pocket Corners.—This trouble arises, of course, from putting too much weight into thinly lined pockets or digging one's hands down into them. A neat mend can be made with threads drawn from an inside part of the garment. To do this, choose the longest stretch of material on the straight, lift up a thread on a needle and snip it free. Lift up the same thread about 12 in. away, if possible, and snip it free. Continue to lift the thread from the weave with the needle until long enough to hold, then gently draw out. If this is difficult, use a matching mercerised thread.

Undo any lining to free the back of the pocket and darn the tear as neatly and closely as possible, on the wrong side. Finish by adding a small piece of the iron-on type of adhesive mending tape to strengthen. If the repair is too visible, try outlining the pocket with decorative dressmaker braid, twisting it into a flat scroll at each corner to hide the mend.

Pulled Pleat Heads.—The point where the stitching ends above an inverted pleat is a likely place for fray or a small hole to appear. It may be possible to neaten it with drawn threads; the best policy is to have a professional repair with the addition of machine-embroidered arrow-heads to strengthen.

Bound Buttonholes.—These are apt to pull away from the binding and spoil the look of a garment; the most satisfactory treatment is carefully to unpick the binding and remove. Place a piece of tailor's canvas (from a draper) over the slit on the wrong side. Run a sewing thread round the slit as close to the edge as possible, catching in all fabric threads and sewing through the canvas. Slit the canvas to match the fabric slit, then buttonhole closely and neatly, using matching buttonhole twist on woollen cloth, a lighter silk on silk and finer fabrics.

Mackintoshes.—Tears behind buttons and in other parts can be effectively mended with the iron-on tape already mentioned. This comes in a useful variety of shades from haberdashery counters.

Frayed Cuffs and Elbows.—For cuffs, unpick sleeve lining round cuff and unpick hem of cuff. Press out creases both on sleeve and lining. "Fill" and strengthen the frayed part of the cuff by darning across the threads with matching mercerised thread. Turn under again so that frayed part comes just inside the sleeve, press and slip-stitch the hem in place. Replace the lining, adjusting length as necessary, and give a final press.

It may be possible to deal successfully with elbow thinness and small holes by darning with drawn threads as already described, or the repair may need professional attention. It is a great help to provide men's sports jackets, when new, with ready-cut leather elbow patches and cuff bindings. Sets can be bought from haberdashery counters.

Knitwear.—When dealing with holes in hand- and machine-knitteds, tack a small piece of dress net over the hole on the wrong side, matching, if possible, or a dark colour under dark wool, and so on. If the garment is knitted in stocking-stitch, fill the hole with lines of chain-stitch embroidered over the net with wool left over from a hand-knitted, or use matching

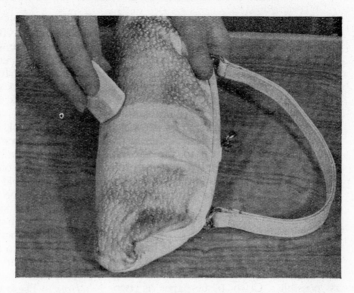

A really dirty white leather handbag comes clean when it is rubbed gently with a Persuede cleaning block

strands from a skein of mixed colours bought from a draper. Another possible method of mending is to catch up each loop of the knitting at the base of the hole on a crochet hook and work the broken threads up to the top of the hole in chain-stitch. Fasten off all ends very firmly.

Shoe Renovation

Suède shoes with the suède worn right off in places can be rejuvenated and made to look like leather instead of suède. Brush off any mud and dust. Rub in black Kiwi shoe polish evenly and fairly liberally until pile is flattened, then polish. Leave for several hours, when the whole process should be repeated and a pair of black leather shoes will emerge.

Anything made of suède, reversed calf, buckskin or nappa (like most light-coloured shoes and handbags) can be kept free of dirty marks with Persuede. It is a cleaning block, obtainable in most colours, and is clean to apply too.

Dry-cleaning

The importance of this service to personal smartness and the well-being of clothes is undoubted. The number of times a garment is cleaned depends on the wear and tear it gets and the atmosphere in which it is worn. In grubby districts it may need cleaning every ten days; every two or three weeks in clean air. Judge by the state of the garment and never let it get too soiled.

It pays to go to a firm of high repute. Not only will they do a good job, but they will not undertake work that may be unsatisfactory without advising you, and they have many services to offer—retexturing, fur-cleaning, de-shining, repairs and renovations, even, in some cases, unshrinking.

Cleaning firms have many problems with some of the new fabrics; embossed, lacquered and gold-printed materials are some that may not dry-clean, so make sure about this at the time you buy.

Dyeing also is rarely satisfactory if the garment has faded or discoloured patchily. The chances are that it will dye patchily.

Storage

Putting away winter things for the summer, and vice versa, is quite a big job, but, if you have been systematic with general

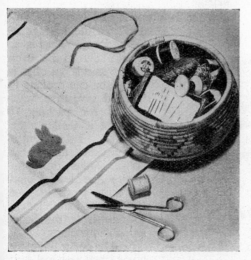

A rabbit marks the spot—where a little girl made a hole in her pinny. A clever idea for disguising the damage

maintenance, not a long one. Naturally, everything must be freshly laundered or cleaned, perfectly dry and moth-proof. This applies equally to clothes and to the storage cupboard or container. Moth-proofing measures are described in detail elsewhere; but remember, moths are allergic to newsprint, so pack garments between layers of newspaper, as an extra precaution, putting the heaviest clothes at the bottom and working up to the lightest. Arrange for professional storage of furs whenever possible, making enquiries for local facilities at the shop where the fur was purchased.

Folding

If you take good care of clothes, you will want to know how to fold properly so that they travel—or store—as creaselessly as possible. Crisp tissue-paper is two-thirds of the answer, the remaining third, practice. You need plenty of space, and an old sheet spread over the floor is a good answer if a large-enough table or a double bed is not available.

Coats and Jackets.—Do up buttons and remove belts. Lay front down on sheet, pull straight, with hemline even. Place double thickness of tissue-paper down centre. Grip side seam under armhole and below waist and fold over on to back of garment for about 4 in. Grasp cuff of sleeve and armhole seam and lay sleeve over fold. Repeat with other side and sleeve; fold bottom of jacket up to collar.

Fold the skirt of a coat from hem to waist and then up to collar.

Skirts.—One with all-round pleating can be rolled and encased in an old footless stocking kept for the purpose (seal cut threads of stocking with colourless nail varnish). Pack by laying round sides of case to avoid folding. All other pleats should be tacked down (or fastened in place with paper clips), the skirt laid front downwards and the sides folded over tissue-paper. Fold in three.

Frocks.—Fold as for coats. A very full skirt should be spread out, the bottom corner of one side taken over to centre until an almost straight line down the side is reached, then the corner should be brought back to the side again in a second fold, with plenty of tissue between folds. Repeat with other corner.

Hats.—These travel best crown downwards packed round with soft garments to hold them firmly and provide a "rest" for the brim. Fill crowns with crumpled newspaper.

Pack a suitcase as for storage, with heavy garments at the bottom and the lightest at the top, and cover all with several layers of tissue-paper before closing the lid. If possible, pack separately the hard items, such as shoes, cosmetic boxes and bottles, hair and clothes brushes, and so on.

Luggage

All the family neat and happy? Well, don't let the luggage let them down. This is an item likely to be overlooked as it is not often in use. You can prolong its life and save time, when needed for packing, if you give it regular attention also. Take it out of storage, dust and lightly polish leather or damp-sponge the leather-cloth and fibre types of case. Polish metal and take a soft brush to the inside lining and pockets.

Shabby paper lining can be renewed very well with left-over wallpaper and a good adhesive.

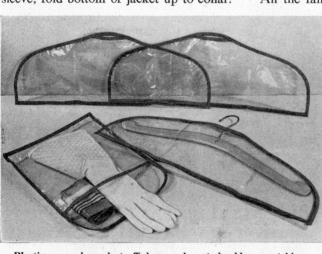

Plastic covers keep dust off dress and coat shoulders, matching plastic envelopes take gloves and scarves

VACUUM CLEANERS, POLISHERS, CARPET SWEEPERS & SHAMPOOERS

*There is equipment, hand-operated or electric, for every need,
the choice depending largely on what kind of home you have*

VACUUM cleaners and carpet sweepers, electric and non-electric, have revolutionised home cleaning. They are designed for maximum efficiency in cleaning with the minimum of labour. They are also hygienic in performance. Dust and grit are collected and can be disposed of without the housewife coming into contact with them. The machines are simple to operate and should last for years. In addition, they are attractive in appearance—streamlined and colourful, with gleaming metal and plastic finishes. It is a pleasure to guide one of these beautiful machines about the

No need to touch—or even see—the dirt collected by the Hoover vacuum cleaner. Simply take out and throw away the "Disposall" bag without touching the contents

floor and see it doing the hard work so effectively.

An electric cleaner or polisher is a large and valuable piece of equipment to buy. It is therefore worth choosing carefully from among the various makes available. If you have a number of the newest models demonstrated in action in the shop, you can compare how they work, and how they feel to you when you handle them; and consider which is the type and size best suited to your particular requirements. Improvements are constantly being made and new models produced, so that it pays to investigate what is currently available before making a choice. A guaranteed quality product will serve you reliably for many years.

VACUUM CLEANERS

Vacuum cleaners draw up dust, etc., by suction and collect it in a bag from where it can be easily emptied. An electrically driven motor creates suction and operates

The Hoover Cylinder model cleans upholstery, carpets and linoleum equally well. The dust is collected in a paper bag inside the dustbag

both the revolving brushes and beaters (where these are included). Great ingenuity has gone into their design since the days when the first vacuum cleaners made their appearance. That was in 1901, when the firm which now makes the Goblin vacuum cleaners produced a machine worked by a hand pump, which was driven about the streets on wheels. The operators cleaned private homes by thrusting hoses and other appliances through the windows. People used to give parties so that their friends could watch this novel method of cleaning. Now, with electricity in almost every house to supply the power, the vacuum cleaner may have lost its value as a novelty—but gained in prestige as a well-nigh indispensable piece of household equipment.

Does a Vacuum wear out the Carpet?

Does the powerful action of a vacuum cleaner wear out a carpet? This query is sometimes raised. The answer is that a carpet can hold more than its own weight in dirt, and minute particles of grit grinding into the pile are more likely to damage it than the action of a vacuum cleaner, which can remove the particles effectively. Used normally, say, two or three times a week, a vacuum cleaner should add to the wearing qualities of your carpet by preserving it from the ravages of dirt.

The cleaning of carpets and rugs is generally the first use of a vacuum cleaner, but most makes have a wide range of accessory tools which can be fitted to the apparatus, so that its usefulness is greatly extended and all kinds of cleaning can be tackled.

Long-handled machines are buffered in rubber and the various tools shaped for their particular purposes and sometimes covered in soft plastic, so that damage to walls and furniture is avoided. The cleaners are fully insulated for safety and fitted with a device for suppressing interference with radio or television. Care is also taken to keep the motor as quiet in action as possible.

There are types and sizes to cater for differing needs—for dealing with wide stretches of carpet in big rooms, or for cleaning carpets or rugs in small rooms where there has to be much manœuvring and where there are many corners. Your choice of cleaner will depend largely on what kind of a house or flat you have.

When you buy, you can arrange at the same time for the cleaner to be serviced by the manufacturer's specialist at regular intervals of, say, six months, according to the amount of use it will have. It is worth giving your expensive, precision machine this attention. It may go on working for years without being inspected, but it may not be giving its full value.

Two Types of Electric Cleaners

The electric cleaners fall into two main categories: the cylinder type and the upright type .

A cylinder model rests on runners and can be pulled along the floor by its flexible hose. The dust, etc., is extracted by its powerful suction and carried into its internal dustbag. The air drawn in, freed from the dust, is blown out forcibly from the end of the machine and can be utilised by accessory tools for various purposes.

Tools include a nozzle which glides over carpets; a swivel brush for floors, walls and ceilings; a small nozzle for reaching the corners in upholstery or on stairs; a dusting brush for picture rails; a crevice nozzle for reaching very narrow spaces— such as radiators and bookshelves; sometimes a sprayer to spray carpet shampoo, distemper, insecticides, disinfectants, etc.

The modern tendency, however, is to combine these into two main tools, like the Electrolux combination floor tool which consists of a carpet nozzle and floor brush operated by a toe switch, and a combination dusting tool consisting of a small nozzle and a dusting brush.

Some models have dustbags fitted with an air purification pad impregnated with an antiseptic medium, so that the air which sucks up the dust is filtered and cleaned before passing back into the room.

An upright model is guided along the floor by its long handle. It incorporates a brush and beater mechanism to loosen the dirt, which is then removed by suction and collected in a dustbag suspended on the handle. With most kinds, a hose and accessory tools for attachment to the front or side of the machine and dependent on the suction alone can be supplied also.

Both types—the "suck and blow" cylinder models and the "beat and suck" upright models—have their advantages and

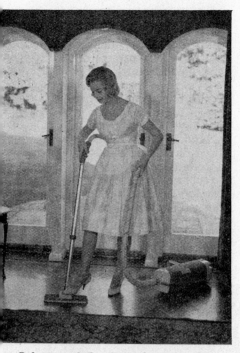

Only two tools for all the cleaning with an Electrolux. The floor tool switches with a tap of the toe from carpet nozzle to floor brush (above)

The Electrolux combination dusting tool has a nozzle for soft furnishings: reverse it to bring the dusting brush into action. There are also a crevice nozzle and a sprayer

The Straight Jane Carpet Shampooer has a roller that spreads the shampoo foam evenly while its brushes remove dirt and grit. No rinsing; just leave to dry

t is often difficult to choose between them. The advocates of the cylinder models maintain that using suction alone means little wear and tear on the carpets, and point to their manoeuvrability and the usefulness of the blowing end. Those who prefer the upright types maintain that the beating action loosens the dirt as nothing else can and that the strain on the carpet is not excessive—unless the cleaner is used too often. (Naturally, if a cleaner is accidentally left standing in one spot for a long period with the current on, the carpet may show signs of its ordeal.) It may be that if you have carpets in large rooms, an upright model will be your choice. If you have small rooms and a good deal of furniture on the carpets, a cylinder model may suit you better. Some of the vacuum cleaner manufacturers produce both kinds. Both are efficient.

In most models the dust is carried into a strong paper bag inside the dustbag, which is easily removed. It can be discarded immediately and replaced, or emptied and used many times.

PORTABLE ELECTRIC DUSTING MACHINES

These are small machines, fitted with a nozzle, a dustbag and a carrying handle, designed to remove dust from the smallest corners by suction. Their small size and handiness make them particularly useful in flats or where storage space is limited.

ELECTRIC POLISHERS

These long-handled machines are designed to take the grind out of polishing floors of wood—parquet or stained—linoleum, tile and other surfaces. The polishing is done by electrically driven rotating circular brushes as the machine is guided without effort over the floor. The work is done far more quickly than by hand, and the result is good. Liquid or wax polish is placed directly on the floor or sometimes on the brushes.

The machines are fully insulated and built to stand up to hard use for many years. They are rubber-buffered to protect furniture and walls, and many of them have special pads for furniture polishing. One, with the addition of scrubbing brushes, becomes an electric scrubber, fel

Sling the smart and very light Hoover Dustette over your shoulder (above) and your hands are free to use the attachments. The throw-away paper bag (right) for hygienic emptying fits inside the zip-fastening dustbag

One of these has a throw-away paper bag for hygienic emptying, which fits into the dustbag. A strap is provided so that it can be slung over the shoulder, thus making it easier for the user to guide the cleaning tools.

CARPET SHAMPOOERS

These comparatively new but highly practical appliances clean the carpets with foam, which never makes them really wet and so eliminates the danger of rotting. Most of them operate by means of rollers which distribute the foam evenly. In some, the special liquid shampoo (which *must* be used) is poured into the tank; with other models, the shampoo is put into a dip tin and the shampooer rolled in it like a paint roller.

polishing pads and lamb's-wool pads snapping over the polishing brushes. The special scrubbing brushes are easily fixed.

NON-ELECTRIC POLISHERS AND SWEEPERS

There are useful tools available, simple in design, but with devices to make the work lighter and more effective. For instance, a polisher that consists of a pad hinged on a long handle, to which a duster is attached; a soft triangular mop impregnated with special oil, which slips on to a metal frame to which the long handle is hinged and can be slipped off to be washed and re-impregnated.

There is also a Rotary Polisher which has two circular polishing brushes attached to a long handle which rotate when pushed to and fro on the floor.

VACUUM CLEANERS AND CARPET SWEEPERS

Non-electric carpet sweepers are a great help, as they remove day-to-day dust and litter on the floor swiftly and easily. Their general principle is to sweep the dust into inner metal containers by means of a brush or brushes rotated by the friction from the wheels as the machine is pushed.

By means of a press button or lever on top of the machine, the containers open to drop the contents straight into the dustbin. The machines have an automatic device for cleaning the brushes. Sweepers are buffered in rubber and the wheels rubber-tyred. Handles are adjustable to enable sweepers to go under low furniture.

The two rotating brushes of the non-electric "Polywhirl" polish floors without leaving a smear and with so little effort that a child can quite easily use it

Shampooing carpets is now a simple, regular, "done at home" job by the foam method. The Bex-Bissell Shampoo Master (right) has a tank into which goes special shampoo and water. You can regulate the flow of foam as you go along

Rubber flooring, linoleum, parquet, tiles and furniture, all respond to the Hoover Electric Polisher (above) with its two brushes rotating in opposite directions at speed

ELECTRIC MIXERS

*The cook's most up-to-date aid to good cake making and
to innumerable other kitchen tasks*

AS the electric vacuum cleaner is probably the biggest labour- and fatigue-
saver in the work of house cleaning, so is
the electric mixer the cook's best aid in
cake making and many kindred tasks.

The term **"electric mixer"** is used rather
loosely to describe machines that differ
in the jobs they do as well as in their
appearance.

DIFFERENT MACHINES

Food Mixers proper, consists essentially
of motor-driven beaters of one type or another. Some rely on one all-purpose design
of beater. Others have several interchangeable implements—for example, flat
beaters, whisks and dough hooks, for
pastry and bread making, as well as whipping eggs, beating icing, etc.

In addition, a number of this kind of
electric mixer have attachments, usually
sold as optional extras, which enable juice
extracting, mincing and other culinary processes to be carried out.

Liquidisers and Blenders, also sometimes called electric mixers, take the form
of a glass goblet, with lid, inside which
motor-driven knives cut and pulverise.
These can be used for a variety of chopping and grinding jobs, and also for making
purées, whips and so on.

Simplest and least expensive is the **portable mixer**, which is held in the operator's
hand and controlled by a finger button. It
has a minute consumption of current,
but whisks whole eggs and whites as
stiffly as required by any recipe, whips
cream, creams fats and sugar, and mashes
potatoes with high efficiency. Light to
hold, it quite eliminates the hard work of
cake making. Use of the mixer speeds up
the job as well as banishing effort, though
it does not cut time to the same extent as do
the full-size machines.

Portable mixers are not supplied with
special bowls. A small stand, or, more
accurately, a rest, for
when the beaters are
not working, is obtain-
able for the miniature
mixer.

With **variable-speed
medium-size mixers,**
both bowl and stand are
an integral part of the
design. All-purpose

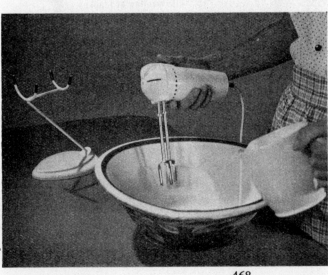

The Valmix electric food
mixer in cream plastic
whips cream in seconds,
beats eggs, mashes
potatoes to a cream and
makes batters, sauces and
beverages of a fine smooth
texture. Can be used
with one or two beaters

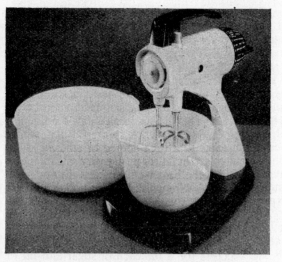

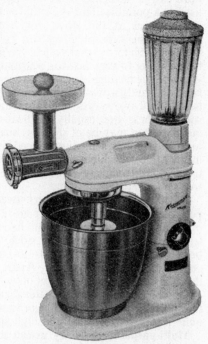

The Sunbeam Mixmaster is a full-size mixer (see photo above) that can also be used as a portable (see photo below right) when mixing at the stove is necessary. There are twelve speeds on the Mixfinder dial and the beaters fit the contours of the bowl and revolve it automatically. It has two heat-resistant bowls of different sizes for large and small quantities

The Kenwood Major, above, has a mincer, a liquidiser, whisk, dough hook and the stainless steel mixing bowl is big enough for 12 lb. of dry mixture. Additional attachments include a coffee mill, slicer and shredder, potato peeler, can opener, sausage filler and juice extractor

beaters are fitted. If required, the mixer head can be detached from the stand and used as a portable. This is useful for mashing potatoes at the stove, for instance. Speed of this type of mixer can be regulated by a finger-tip dial switch, from slow for blending to very fast for whipping and white-of-egg beating. Included are a mixer head on stand, two detachable stainless-steel beaters and two bowls, one large and one small. These are usually of heat-resisting glass, but may be of stainless steel. A juice extractor is a medium-priced attachment. Mincers, which necessitate an additional power unit, are rather more expensive optional extras.

Advantages of these mixers over the portables is that they are rather more automatic and quicker, and that the hands are left free. Scraping down the sides of the bowl where the mixture tends to congregate is required fairly often. Apart from this, the cook is left free to get on with another job. Speed is rather greater than with the portables. Noise and vibration are quite noticeable, especially at high speeds.

Multi-purpose, planetary action mixers are still larger and more powerful. They are remarkably efficient. Bowl and stand are an integral part of the design. The mixer head cannot be detached. This type of mixer has a special action by which the beaters both revolve on their own axis and travel on an axis inside the surface of the

bowl. This ensures extra thorough mixing and also largely does away with the necessity for constant scraping down of the mixture. Owing both to the action and the power, this kind of mixer needs relatively lower speeds than the medium-size type. This means less noise and vibration, making the mixer very comfortable to work with. The various implements are fitted in a few seconds. A powerful flat beater creams to a high degree of efficiency, but also rubs in fat for pastry very satisfactorily, which the beater-only mixers do not do so well. A wire whisk "brings up" cream and egg-whites with great speed, and a dough hook deals with all kinds of yeast dough. One bowl only is supplied but, owing to the machine's design, it can be used with equal success for 2 oz. each of sugar and fat or 6 lb. of stiff cake mixture.

In addition to the snap-in cake-making implements, a large variety of optional attachments to speed up other food preparation jobs are obtainable. As well as juice extractors and mincers, there are graters and shredders, colanders and sieves, oil drippers, coffee mills, potato peelers and liquidisers, though not all attachments are available with every make.

LIQUIDISERS

The Liquidiser (or liquefier), whether bought as an attachment for one of the higher-powered mixers or as a separate unit, does both dry and wet chopping, grinding and pulverising without any manual work other than putting the ingredients in the goblet and switching on. No job takes more than a minute or two. This almost magical aid chops parsley and mint, makes breadcrumbs, chops nuts, pulverises sugar, grinds coffee. It also purées vegetables and fruits (raw or part cooked), makes mayonnaise, "shakes," etc.

The Built-in Unit. This is a single 6-speed power unit, which can be fitted into the top of a kitchen cabinet. The actual power unit is so small that it can be installed on the top of a cupboard without affecting the storage space of the shelves. When not in use, it is unobtrusive, consisting of a flat sheet of metal set into the top of a working surface. When required, the appropriate appliance is simply and easily plugged into position.

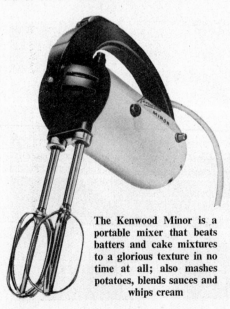

The Kenwood Minor is a portable mixer that beats batters and cake mixtures to a glorious texture in no time at all; also mashes potatoes, blends sauces and whips cream

The latest idea in mixers is the Cannon NuTone Multi-purpose Power-Maid, a single 6-speed power unit built into the top of a kitchen cabinet and operating all sorts of appliances. Here the triangular-shaped Blender is seen in position

Among the exciting variety of different appliances that can be operated with the Cannon built-in Power-Maid unit is a highly efficient Knife Sharpener that sharpens both sides of the blade at once

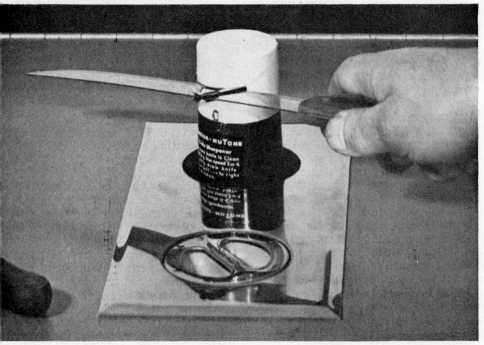

These include a Mixer with a power-driven bowl revolving in the opposite direction to the beater, and with a special "pouring" rim, while the beaters can be operated in any of six different positions. Then there is a powerful Blender, which will purée, blend, grate, beat, liquefy or whip; being triangular, it is easy to grip, and the high-speed stainless steel blades are sealed away in the container's bottom for safety. Coffee Mill also chops nuts and pulverises sugar in seconds.

HOW TO HAVE A NICE WARM BED

One sure way to keep out the chill of winter is to treat yourself to the luxury of an electric bedwarmer

The Hurseal electric bed-sheet keeps you warm all over and you can regulate the heat – or have separate controls on the double-bed size. You can even wash it safely

IN terms of cost measured in pence per week it is claimed that the electric bed warmer provides comfort more cheaply than any other appliance. Doctors recommend their use, and in cold weather they can certainly make all the difference to a night's sleep.

The reason lies in the fact that bedclothes, even in a room not itself damp, may contain several pints of moisture. This is partly absorbed from the atmosphere and partly from body perspiration. It cannot evaporate at winter temperatures but is trapped in the bed, thus causing the chilly feeling which piling on the bedclothes so often fails to dissipate. The only real remedy is to get into a bed that is properly warmed and aired. The old copper warming pan did this job to some extent, and now the electric bed warmer does it much more thoroughly and efficiently.

How Electric Bed Warmers Work

Although there are a good many differences in construction and finish, all electrically heated blankets, sheets and pads, which comprise the great majority of bedwarming devices, work in roughly the same

way. The heating source is of comparatively low temperature (for the technically minded, the resistor runs at a temperature well below black heat) but, in a closed-in bed, the heat is given off as fast as it is created. Thus a comfortable temperature is soon reached.

Hang up the blanket in free air and no warmth would be perceptible. On the other hand, if it were rolled up inside an eiderdown, while still switched on, the heat would build up so that eventually it might burst into flames.

Safeguards against Overheating

The heater must not be allowed to get too hot, yet at the same time it must generate enough energy to do its job reasonably quickly. In the simplest, least expensive type, the current input is so restricted that even if it is left switched on, the heat will not rise to a dangerous degree during ordinary use. This means that rather a long time will be needed for heating up to working temperature.

To overcome this, some models use rather higher loadings controlled by thermostats. The latter, by applying an automatic off-switch, prevent overheating and also maintain the appliance at the desired temperature. In single-heat blankets, duplicate thermostats are usually fitted as a safety check. With the more expensive variable or three-heat types, there are four thermostats.

With the variable heat blanket, heated by two resistors of different resistance, the temperature can be altered as wished by a selector switch. The most luxurious double bed models even have *two* selector switches, so that each occupant can adjust the temperature on one side as required.

Another kind of warmer employs an alternative to thermostat control known as a temperature-sensitive resistance in the

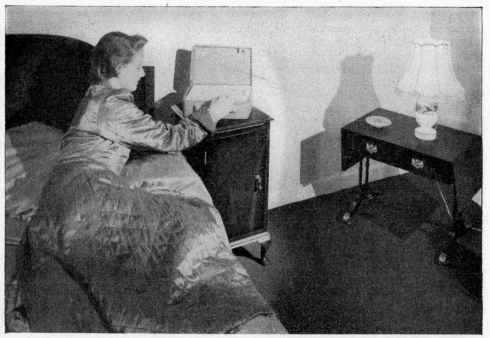

All the bedside comforts of electricity – you relax in a bed warmed by an electric blanket, with a radio at your side, a shaded lamp and electric fire nearby

circuit. This resistance varies according to the heat and so regulates the temperature.

Guarding against the possibility of Shock

All these devices are designed to guard against overheating and the consequent possibility of local scorching. But with electric equipment, precautions against shock must also be taken. This is usually done by spacing the resistor wires in such a way that the full mains current is at opposite sides of the appliance. As a damp-safeguard, most resistors are asbestos-covered, while some have a plastic insulation said to be even more effective.

One or two brands of blanket are claimed to be washable. In all other cases a moisture-resistant cover is an advisable precaution if there is any likelihood of the blanket getting really damp or wet, as in illness or with small children. Most makers supply such covers as an optional extra.

Some makes of bed warmer operate with a transformer stepping down the usual mains voltage to a low one of 12–24 volts. In the unlikely event of a shock occurring, it would be so slight as to be harmless. The advantage of this kind of blanket is

that it can, if preferred, be left switched on all night. Most other bed warmers should be switched off before the occupant gets into bed, or removed from the bed altogether.

Various Types of Warmer

Different kinds vary in the way they should be used. In general, those described by the makers simply as electric bed warmers are designed to be used as an under blanket, **under** the bottom sheet. Others advertised as blankets are slipped **between** the sheets, while a third group, usually made from pure wool, take the place of an ordinary blanket **on top** of the bed. These are often big enough to tuck in, though only the part that rests flat on the bed will be heated. Almost all models, whatever the type, can be supplied with ordinary washable covers for a moderate extra cost. It is wise to use each kind in the way prescribed by the manufacturer.

Prices of the different types, and of individual models, vary quite considerably. Those with variable heat switches, thermostats or other refinements cost more than the simple, most straightforward designs

The material of which the bed warmer is made also governs price, as does the size. The latter needs to be checked carefully when comparing values, for some firms' idea of a large double bed size is scarcely bigger than other single models. Lengths may be 40, 48, 50, 52, 60, 62, 70 or 72 in., while widths range from 30 to 56 in. with almost as many in-between variations. The larger the heating surface in relation to the size of the bed, the better the result. Price range is roughly from £5 upwards, inclusive of tax. A luxury double bed version with two switches will cost around £20. Running costs, in all cases, are truly infinitesimal; less than one unit a week is a usual estimate.

An electrically heated blanket fitted with switch and 9 feet flexible lead has a fleecy woollen cover in white, blue or pink fabric. H. J. Baldwin

Heating Pads

These resemble a small blanket in appearance, but they are not just small-size versions. They are expressly designed to give a gentle sustained pain-alleviating warmth to sufferers from localised rheumatism or kindred complaints. As they can be used at any time, in or out of bed, many have a higher proportionate loading than the electric blanket. Some are definitely not recommended as bed warmers.

Most blankets and pads can be used without fear of television interference.

Non-blanket Types of Bed Warmer

Two additional kinds of bed warmer operate on different principles from the blanket-type ones. One is a circular metal container, rather like the old-fashioned warming pan but a good deal larger and, of course, with no handle, and the heat source is a 40-watt lamp. It uses only about 1 unit of electricity per week to warm and air the bed daily, and is cheaper to buy than any blanket-style bed warmer. It is obtainable in pink, blue or primrose.

An inexpensive (around £1) bed warmer consists of an openwork frame ($24 \times 12 \times 7\frac{1}{2}$ in.) in the centre of which is an ordinary light bulb (60 or 100 watt) protected by a stove-enamelled mesh guard. It is said to air and warm a bed in 15 minutes.

When buying an electric bed warmer, you will want, above all, to be certain of its safety. The one sure way to satisfy yourself on this point is to choose one which carries the kite mark. This means that it is made to British Standard 2612 and that the British Standards Institution certifies this, after elaborate tests, factory inspections, market check purchases and careful supervision of manufacturers' methods of quality control.

The DP Three Heat electrically heated bed-warming pad with a detachable quilted floral sateen cover is waterproofed within

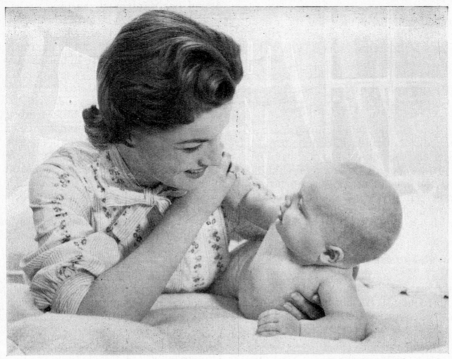

Photo: Johnson & Johnson Ltd.

HAVING A BABY

How to keep well and happy while planning and
preparing for the happiest event of your life

MODERN science has done more for mothers and babies than for any other section of the community. As a result, pregnancy and childbirth have fallen into their right perspective—as perfectly natural functions in no way connected with illness.

Modern expectant mothers—and fathers, for that matter—discuss their hopes and start advance planning for the event almost from the beginning. This is a thoroughly sound attitude, and very necessary in these overcrowded times when hospital beds and arrangements with midwives have to be booked months ahead.

The time for a woman to consult her doctor for the first time is when she is reasonably sure that she is pregnant—i.e. immediately after the second missed period and certainly not later than after the third; earlier, if she is troubled with morning sickness or other symptoms. The doctor will then be able to confirm the pregnancy and will help with arrangements for having the baby.

These are the alternatives to be considered:

1. Hospital

To go into hospital for the confinement and attend the hospital's ante-natal clinics beforehand. This is the usual course for a first confinement; for subsequent confinements, owing to the shortage of beds in most hospitals, it is only possible if special care is needed from a medical or obstetric point of view (if, for instance, the last confinement was not straightforward, or the mother suffers from diabetes or heart trouble).

2. Home Confinement

Delivery by a State midwife who also attends during pregnancy and for a month after the birth, under the care of the patient's own doctor. The doctor will *not* be at the confinement unless the midwife sends for him; if a specialist is needed, the doctor can call one free. This is the usual course for second and subsequent confinements.

NOTE: If the midwife considers the home unsuitable for a confinement, the patient may be admitted to hospital.

Costs.—There is no charge for the doctor's or midwife's care or at hospital. The Maternity Grant for home confinements is higher than for hospital ones, and there is an allowance to cover home expenses.

3. Private Nursing Home

Fees vary considerably. A National Health patient is entitled to the doctor's and (if required) specialist's treatment free, but if she wishes to be delivered by a specialist and her case is perfectly normal, there will be a charge for this.

4. Home Confinement attended by a Private Midwife

Midwife's and doctor's fees (if attending as a private patient) to be paid. These are not fixed; they vary enormously and are usually high.

ANALGESIA

Gas and air analgesia, by Minnit's apparatus operated by the mother herself, is available to anyone who wants it, free of charge.

Details will be explained by the doctor or at the ante-natal clinic.

ANTE-NATAL CARE

Date of Birth

The date of delivery is estimated as follows: Take the first day of the last period (say, August 10); go back three months (to May 10); add 7 days—May 17 is therefore the date of the baby's expected arrival.

Medical Examinations

At her first visit to her doctor (immediately after the second and not later than after the third missed period), the mother-to-be will either arrange for the doctor to attend her throughout the time or be referred to a clinic. Her own or the clinic doctor will give a thorough physical examination, probably including heart, chest, abdomen, blood pressure and urine. Blood samples are usually sent for tests, the result of which will help in treatment during pregnancy and at delivery. A visit to her own dentist is usually advised: teeth tend to suffer because the mother's calcium supply is diverted to bone-building during pregnancy. Unless she has already been inoculated against Polio, she should have this done now.

After that, there are regular attendances at the clinic, or visits to the doctor, at four- to six-weekly intervals, until the seventh month; and then fortnightly and, in the last month, often weekly visits. This constant medical supervision is of the utmost importance for the health and safety of both mother and baby, and appointments should on no account be broken, even by an expectant mother who feels perfectly well. By attending regularly, when told to do so, she is guarding against difficulties at the confinement, and making it possible for symptoms to be treated in the early stages.

Diet

It is now realised that diet is an essential part of ante-natal care, for putting on too much weight is a danger signal of as great significance as a rise in blood pressure, for it may be the beginning of a toxæmia of pregnancy. A rule-of-thumb guide is not to put on *more* than 1 lb. a week, preferably less.

The doctor taking care of her during pregnancy, will watch the expectant mother's weight most carefully and will tell her if the gain is excessive. *The items to restrict are:*

Carbohydrates.—i.e., bread, cakes, suet and pastry puddings, biscuits, cereals, sweets, sugar, jams, potatoes, etc. Bread should be limited to three slices a day.

Fluids.—Not more than 2 pints of fluid of *every* kind should be taken in each 24 hours, preferably ½ pint milk, plus 1½ pints of other fluids.

Salt.—The body can retain fluids and therefore put on weight, only if there is enough salt to form the saline solution. It therefore helps to prevent fluid retention in the body to take no salt on the plate and, if possible, no salt in cooking. There will still be natural salts in vegetables.

Do not eat seasoned foods. Cut down on fried foods, cheese, bacon and ham, cured fish, tinned foods, sausages, meat extracts, bicarbonate of soda, fats.

The following foods may be eaten freely: lean meat, liver, kidneys and offal; steamed or boiled (but not cured or tinned) fish; eggs, fruit, vegetables (except potatoes, artichokes, peas and baked beans).

Remember, most people cannot lose weight without going hungry. When the pangs of hunger become worrying, fruit and vegetables can be eaten. Saxin should be used for sweetening tea and coffee. One vitamin pill should be taken twice a day.

Relaxation

Many clinics now run courses of Relaxation Exercises, which are a great help in giving confidence when the time of labour comes. These can be practised at the beginning of the afternoon rest, lying on the back on a wide couch or fairly hard bed, with a small bolster under the head and shoulders and a small pillow or cushion under the knees. Arms by the sides, elbows half bent, hands half closed, knees slightly separated, i.e. all joints as far as possible in semi-flexion.

Relax in this order:

Shoulders, by thinking of them "opening outwards."

Arms, by imagining them falling out of shoulder girdle, as though they did not belong.

Back, by imagining the body sinking through the couch on to the floor.

Legs, knees and feet, letting them fall outwards by their own weight.

Head, making a dent in the pillow.

Eyelids, half closing by their own weight.

Face, as though hanging from the cheek bones.

Jaw, hanging loose.

About two minutes should be allowed for each part of the body and the exercise should be taken in the same order each time.

Breathing.—Let the chest wall collapse with its own weight on expiration and pause for two seconds (or until wanting a new breath) at the end of expiration. To get a feeling of general relaxation, let all the joints give a little more with each outgoing breath. This should be done six times.

Note the sequence of sensations to the limbs: usually heaviness, followed by lightness or "floating"; faint transient pins and needles in the hands, feeling of warmth passing up from the extremities. A pleasant torpid, day-dreaming state generally follows, as in sunbathing, and thinking should be deliberately directed into day-dreaming. Sleep is not aimed at. After half to one hour, get up slowly and stretch.

Rest

Eight hours' sleep a night are a minimum requirement, plus an hour's proper rest on the bed each afternoon during the last three months. Light but warm bedclothes, plenty of fresh air from an open window and a hot milk drink last thing will all help towards a good night's rest. A couple of pillows in the hollow of the back may be needed in the last month or so.

Heartburn

Different people benefit from different treatments, so the only way is to experiment. It often helps to eat little and often —every two hours if necessary. Greasy, rich, highly seasoned and fried foods should be avoided. Antacid or peppermint tablets may also help.

Constipation

Strong laxatives must not be taken; the most suitable are senna tea or emulsion of liquid paraffin and agar.

To make Senna Tea.—Put 6 to 12 senna pods (regulate the quantity in the light of experience) in half a tumbler of cold water and leave to stand overnight. Take first thing in the morning, followed by a hot drink. "Senokot" granules or tablets are a proprietary form of senna, which are pleasant to take. The dose can easily be regulated according to individual needs.

Constipation may best be avoided by eating plenty of green vegetables, salads and fresh fruit.

Morning Sickness

Not by any means everybody suffers from morning sickness, but those who do, generally have it in the first four months. One of the seasickness cures is now frequently prescribed by doctors and clinics. It also helps considerably to get up and dress in really leisurely style and to eat a plain dry biscuit before getting out of bed.

Care of the Breasts

All they require is to be washed daily with soap and water, rubbed dry with a rough towel, the nipples being drawn out with finger and thumb and gently massaged with Vaseline. This should keep them supple and prevent any danger of their cracking later on.

A brassière that fits really well, provides comfortable uplift and does not squash the breasts, is an absolute necessity. It must be replaced by a larger size the moment it begins to feel even a trifle tight and should not be bought without first being tried on.

Varicose Veins

This is a condition which often occurs during pregnancy, particularly as a result of standing for long stretches during the early months. Rest with the feet raised is all-important. Elastic stockings should be worn but *must* always be put on in bed *before* putting the feet to the ground.

Clothes

Maternity belts must always be fitted by experts. Advice as to whether one is required should be obtained from the doctor or ante-natal clinic. Women who do not normally wear belts of any kind may not need one at all during pregnancy. All garments should be loose-fitting and hang from the shoulders. Garters and high-heeled shoes should be avoided during pregnancy; garters because they can so easily cause varicose veins and high heels because they are bound to be most uncomfortable owing to the shift in the body's balance.

Marital Relations are not advisable in the last three months.

Other Symptoms

Though the modern attitude is to regard pregnancy as perfectly natural and not to think of it as an illness, certain symptoms do act as a warning. If, for example, there is bleeding, however slight, at any time after the second missed period, the expectant mother should go straight to bed and stay there until the doctor comes.

Medical advice should also be sought about persistent vomiting, headaches, abdominal pains, troubles with the sight, attacks of giddiness or fainting, swelling of the legs, feet or hands, discharge of any kind, or trouble in passing water (abnormally increased frequency, pain or burning sensation, though a certain amount of increased frequency is perfectly normal in the first months and also towards the end).

LABOUR

The first signs of the onset of labour are usually a blood-stained discharge known as "the show"; backache moving round towards the front and becoming more regular, from intervals of 20–30 minutes at first; the breaking of the waters.

Hospital, midwife or doctor should be called when the pains become regular.

CLOTHES FOR MOTHER AND BABY

What to have ready for Mother

When a mother makes her arrangements for the confinement with a hospital, nursing home or midwife, she is invariably issued with a printed list of items to take with her or advised as to what to prepare.

A typical list of requirements when being admitted to hospital is:

Two face flannels, 2 tablets toilet soap, hair brush and comb, nightdress, 2 bath towels, toothbrush, bedroom slippers, dressing gown, sanitary belt, safety pins, 3 dozen large sanitary pads, one 3-in. crêpe bandage.

For a home delivery a light airy room without too much furniture should be chosen. The necessities in the way of furniture are:

A single bed with a firm mattress.
A cot for the baby.

478

A kitchen table and one other table or dressing table.
2 chairs.

Everything else, including carpets and rugs, should be removed from the room, which should be thoroughly cleaned, warmed and aired a few days before the expected date.

The Layette

Here is a practical minimum layette, which can, of course be increased, *ad lib.*, according to the generosity of friends and relations and their skill at knitting and sewing.

4 gowns made from Clydella and preferably shaped to button at the bottom and keep the feet in. These will be in constant wear, day and night, for the first six months and can usually

For smart babies to wear both summer and winter—an attractive pair (above) hand-smocked consist of frock and matinée coat. Another little jacket (left) can be chosen to match baby's dresses. All are from the Clydella layette range of easily washed long-wearing baby fashions

the first size as they are grown out of so quickly and tend to shrink from constant washing.
2 to 3 pairs mittens.
3 to 4 pairs socks.
2 shawls, preferably a smart new one for going out, plus an old one (or two) to wrap round the baby and make it feel cosy at home, but which will not harm from a wetting.

Knitting instructions for all the knitted garments suggested are to be found in the pages that follow. Turn to colour page facing page 497 for diagrams and making-up directions for the Clydella nightgowns. There is also a large variety of ready-made baby fashions to choose from in the Clydella layette range.

be worn as nighties for at least another year.
4 vests—shaped to cross over at the front, not to pull over the head.
2 dozen Harrington squares (gauze): there are endless additional uses for these, as bibs, etc., as time goes on.
2 dozen Turkish towelling squares—a smaller quantity is a false economy because of the difficulty of drying and airing.
4 matinée coats—this is quite enough of

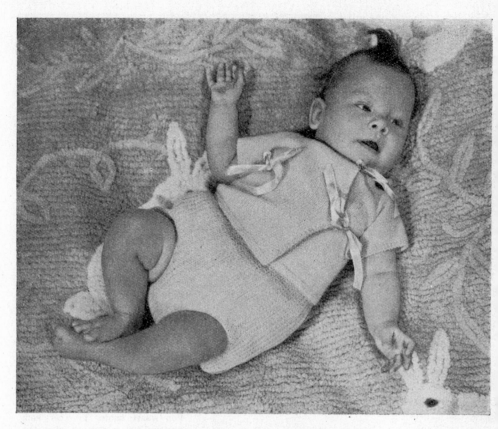

BABY'S LAYETTE

Shawl, matinée coat, cross-over vest, and pilch (photographed above), bootees and mittens—all that the new-born baby requires

SQUARE SHAWL

Materials.—7 oz. Patons Beehive Fingering 2-ply, Patonised. A pair No. 8 "Beehive" needles.

Measurements.—Approx. 45 × 45 in.

Tension.—7 sts. and 9 rows to an inch on No. 8 needles measured over stocking-stitch.

Abbreviations.—Inc., increase; k., knit; p., purl; p.s.s.o., pass slipped stitch over; sl., slip; st., stitch; tog., together; t.b.l, through back of loops; wl. fwd., wool forward.

Centre

Cast on 128 sts. Work in garter-stitch, i.e. every row knit, for 19 in. Cast off loosely.

Border

Knit up 128 sts. along one edge of centre. Next row: k. 1, p. to last st., k. 1. Continue in lace pattern as follows:

1st row: inc. in 1st st., * wl. fwd., slip 1, k. 2 tog., pass slipped stitch over, wl. fwd., k. 3; rep. from * to last st., inc. in last st.

2nd and alternate rows: k. 1, p. to last st., k. 1. **3rd row:** inc. in 1st st., k. 1, * k. 3, wl. fwd., sl. 1, k. 2 tog., p.s.s.o., wl. fwd.; rep. from * to last 2 sts., k. 1, inc. in last st.

5th row: inc. in 1st st., k. 2, * wl. fwd., sl. 1, k. 2 tog., p.s.s.o., wl. fwd., k. 3; rep. from * to last 3 sts., wl. fwd., k. 2 tog., inc. in last st. **6th row:** k. 1, p. to last st., k. 1.

Work rows 1–6 inclusive 15 times more, then rows 1–4 inclusive once. Cast off loosely.

480

THE ORDER OF ABY'S BATH

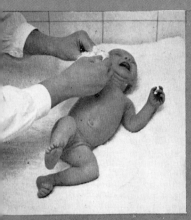

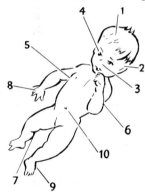

Here is the right way to bath baby: *Top left*, soap her gently all over lying on a towel and don't worry if she cries. *Left*, lather the folds in neck, arms and legs thoroughly. *Below*, plunge her gently up to the armpits into the nice warm water. *Below right*, dry and powder as she lies comfortably on a warm towel

These are important points to remember:

1. Soap and water head daily to prevent dandruff.

2, 3 and 4. Wipe ears, nose and eyes with cotton wool dipped in boiled tepid water, but don't probe too deeply.

5, 6 and 7. Wash creases at armpits, elbows, knees and neck well, dry and powder thoroughly.

8 and 9. Soap, rinse and dry well between fingers and toes.

10. Wash, dry and powder navel liberally.

*is exciting for
other—and father
-to be home with
new baby, but the
ily bath may be
alarming at first*

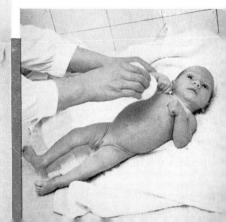

FOR SAFE BOTTLE FEEDING

When a baby cannot be breast fed, the greatest care must be taken to keep his bottle absolutely clean

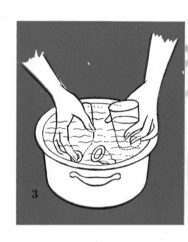

YOU NEED: A jug to hold 1 quart of water; a plastic tablespoon; a small tumbler **or** meat-paste jar to cover and protect the teat; a bottle of Milton.

YOU DO: Make up Milton solution only once in 24 hours. Add 1 tablespoonful Milton to 2 pints cold water in jug.

1. After feeding baby, rinse outside of teat and bottle under cold tap, before taking off teat (below)

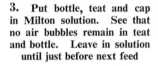

3. Put bottle, teat and cap in Milton solution. See that no air bubbles remain in teat and bottle. Leave in solution until just before next feed

4. At next feed, first wash hands, then remove bottle, teat and cap from Milton solution. Put feed in bottle, put on teat and place cap over teat until ready to feed baby (below). Rinsing is not necessary

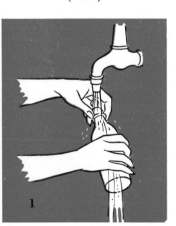

2. Remove teat, rinse inside of teat and bottle under cold tap. Brush out bottle with detergent and rinse again. Turn teat inside out, clean thoroughly, rub with salt and rinse

Start with a clean bottle, rinse under cold tap and immerse in 1 tablespoonful Milton to 1 quart cold water till first feed.

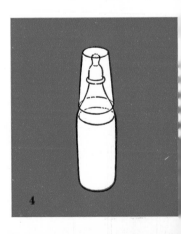

Complete remaining three sides in same way.

Lace Edging

Cast on 8 sts. ** **1st row:** k. 2, wl fwd., k. 2 tog., k. 2, wl. fwd., k. 2. **2nd and alternate rows:** wl. fwd, k. 2 tog., k. to end. **3rd row:** k. 2, wl. fwd., k. 2 tog., k. 3, wl. fwd., k. 2. **5th row:** k. 2, wl. fwd., k. 2 tog., k. 4, wl. fwd., k. 2. **7th row:** k. 2, wl. fwd., k. 2 tog., k. 5, wl. fwd., k. 2. **9th row:** k. 2, wl. fwd., k. 2 tog., k. 6, wl. fwd., k. 2. **11th row:** k. 2, wl. fwd., k. 2 tog., k. 5, wl. fwd., k. 3 tog., k. 1.

13th row: k. 2, wl. fwd., k. 2 tog., k. 4, wl. fwd., k. 3 tog., k. 1. **15th row:** k. 2, wl. fwd., k. 2 tog., k. 3, wl. fwd., k. 3 tog., k. 1. **17th row:** k. 2, wl. fwd. k. 2 tog., k. 2, wl. fwd., k. 3 tog., k. 1. **19th row:** k. 2, wl. fwd., k. 2 tog., k. 1, wl. fwd., k. 3 tog., k. 1. **20th row:** wl. fwd., k. 2 tog., k. to end.

Work these 20 rows 18 times more. Mitre corner as follows: **1st row:** k. 2, wl. fwd., k. 2 tog., k. 2, wl fwd., k. 2. **2nd and alternate rows:** wl. fwd., k. 2 tog., k. 6, turn. **3rd row:** k. 1, wl. fwd., k. 2 tog., k. 3, wl. fwd., k. 2. **5th, 7th and 9th rows:** k. 6, wl. fwd., k. 2. **11th, 13th, 15th, 17th and 19th rows:** k. 4, wl. fwd., k. 3 tog., k. 1. **20th row:** wl. fwd., k. 2 tog., k. 6 (8 sts. on needle). ** Work from ** to ** 3 times more. Cast off loosely.

Two first-size matinée coats like this will see baby through for chilly days indoors and for summer pram wear out of doors as well

To Make Up

Join four corners of border. Join cast on and cast off edges of edging. Stitch into position. Roll shawl in a damp cloth and leave for several hours, then pin out to given measurements and leave to dry.

MATINÉE COAT

Materials.—2 oz. Patons Beehive Baby Wool, Patonised. A pair No. 10 "Beehive" needles. One button. Length of ribbon.

Measurements.—To fit 19-in. chest. Length from top of shoulder, 10 in. Sleeve seam, 5 in.

Tension .—7½ sts. and 9½ rows to one inch on No. 10 needles measured over stocking-stitch.

Ridge and Lace Border

1st–4th rows: k. **5th row:** k. **6th, 8th, 10th, 12th and 14th rows:** p. **7th row:** k. 1, k. 2 tog., wl. fwd., * k. 3, wl. fwd., slip 1, k. 2 tog., pass slipped stitch over, wl. fwd.; rep. from * to last 6 sts., k. 3, wl. fwd., k. 2 tog. through back of loops, k. 1. **9th row:** as 7th. **11th row:** * k. 3, wl. fwd., sl. 1, k. 2 tog., p.s.s.o., wl. fwd.; rep. from * to last 3 sts., k. 3. **13th row:** as 11th. **15th–18th row:** k. These 18 rows form the lace border.

Eyelet Stitch

1st row: k. **2nd and alternate rows:** p. **3rd row:** k. 1, * wl. fwd., k. 2 tog., k. 4 rep. from * to last 2 sts., wl. fwd., k. 2 tog. **5th row:** k. **7th row:** * k. 4, wl. fwd., k. 2 tog.; rep. from * to last 3 sts., k. 3. **8th row:** p. These 8 rows form the pattern.

Back

Cast on 105 sts. Work rows 1–18 inclusive of ridge and lace border. Work rows 1–8 inclusive of eyelet stitch. Continue in eyelet stitch until work measures 6½ in. from beg., finishing at end of a p. row.

Shape armholes by casting off 3 sts. at beg. of next 2 rows. Dec. 1 st. at each end of every row until 89 sts. remain. Work 3 rows. Next row: k. 7, (k. 2 tog.) 38 times, k. 6 (51 sts.). K. 5 rows.

Continue in eyelet stitch until work measures 3½ in. from beg. of armhole shaping. Shape shoulders by casting off 8 sts. at beg. of next 4 rows. Cast off.

Right Front

Cast on 62 sts. Knitting 5 sts. at front edge on every row and working remaining 57 sts. in ridge and lace border, work rows 1–18 inclusive of ridge and lace border.

Still knitting 5 sts. at front edge and working remaining sts. in eyelet stitch, work rows 5–8 inclusive of eyelet stitch, then continue working rows 1–8 inclusive until work measures same as back up to armhole shaping, finishing at side edge.

Shape armhole by casting off 3 sts. at beg. of next row. Dec. 1 st. at armhole edge on every row until 54 sts. remain. ** Work 3 rows. **Next row:** k. 5 * (k. 2 tog.) 4 times, k. 1; rep. from * to last 4 sts., (k. 2 tog.) twice (32 sts.). K. 2 rows. **Next row:** k. to last 4 sts., k. 2 tog., wl. fwd., k. 2 (for buttonhole). K. 2 rows.

*** Still knitting 5 sts. at front edge and working remaining 27 sts. in eyelet stitch, starting with a 5th row, continue until work measures 2½ in. from beg. of armhole shaping, finishing at front edge.

Shape neck by casting off 10 sts. at beg. of next row. Dec. 1 st. at neck edge on every row until 16 sts. remain. Continue on these sts. until work measures same as back up to shoulder shaping, finishing at armhole edge.

Shape shoulder by casting off 8 sts. at beg. of next and alternate rows.

Left Front

Work as right front until ** is reached. Work 2 rows. **Next row:** (k. 2 tog.) twice, * k. 1, (k. 2 tog.) 4 times; rep. from * to last 5 sts., k. 5 (32 sts.). K. 5 rows. Complete to match right front working from *** to end.

Sleeves

Cast on 33 sts. Work rows 1–18 inclusive of ridge and lace border. **Next row:** * inc. in next st., k. 1 (inc. in next st., k. 2) 3 times; rep. from * to end (45 sts.). **Next row:** p. Work rows 3–8 inclusive of eyelet stitch.

Continue in eyelet stitch, inc. 1 st. at each end of next and following 16th row (49 sts.). Continue on these sts. until work measures 5 in. from beg.

Shape top by casting off 1 st. at beg. of

every row until 33 sts. remain; 2 sts. until 21 sts. remain. Cast off working 2 tog. all across row to last st., cast off last st.

Neckband

Join shoulders of back and fronts. With right side facing, starting 2 sts. in from right front edge knit up 57 sts. round neck, finishing 2 sts. from left front edge. K. 1 row. **Next row:** (k. 2, wl. fwd., k. 2 tog.) 14 times, k. 1. K. 2 rows. Cast off.

To Make Up

Press work lightly on wrong side with a warm iron and damp cloth, taking care not to stretch yoke. Join side and sleeve seams; insert sleeves. Thread ribbon through neckband. Sew on button. Press seams.

CROSS-OVER VEST

Matching bootees and mittens to keep tiny hands and feet warm—you can knit a pair in an evening

Materials.—2 oz. Patons Beehive Baby Wool, Patonised. A pair of No. 10 "Beehive" needles. Length of ribbon.
Measurements.—To fit 16 (18) in. chest. Length from top of shoulder, 9 (10) in. Sleeve seam, 2 in.
Tension.—$7\frac{1}{2}$ sts. and $9\frac{1}{2}$ rows to an inch.
NOTE: Second size in brackets thus ( ).

Right Front

Cast on 43 (48) sts. **1st–4th rows:** k. **5th row:** k. **6th row:** p. to last 3 sts., k. 3. Rep. last 2 rows 19 (23) times.

Make slot as follows: **Next row:** k. 28 (30), cast off 2, k. to end. **Next row:** p. 13 (16), cast on 2, p. to last 3 sts., k. 3.

** Continue in stocking-stitch as before until work measures $5\frac{1}{2}$ ($6\frac{1}{4}$) in. from beg., finishing at end of a p. row. Shape sleeve by inc. at sleeve edge on next 3 rows, then cast on 11 sts. at sleeve edge on next row: 57 (62) sts.

Knitting 3 sts. at each end of needle on every row, continue on these sts. until work measures 8 ($8\frac{3}{4}$) in. from beg., finishing at neck edge. Shape neck by casting off 21 (23) sts. at beg. of next row. Dec. 1 st. at neck edge on every row until 33 (35) sts. remain. Continue on these sts. until work

measures 9 (10) in. from beg., finishing at neck edge. ** Slip sts. on to a length of wool and leave.

Left Front

Cast on 43 (48) sts. **1st–4th rows:** k. **5th row:** k. **6th row:** k. 3, p. to end. Work as for right front from ** to **.

Cast on 22 (26) sts. for back of neck, slip sts. from right front on to left-hand needle, with right side of work facing, k. across these sts. (88 (96) sts.)

Knitting 3 sts. at each end of every row and working remaining sts. in stocking-stitch, continue until work measures 3 ($3\frac{1}{2}$) in. from 22 (26) cast-on sts.

Shape sleeves by casting off 11 (11) sts. at beg. of next 2 rows. Dec. 1 st. at each end of every row until 60 (68) sts. remain. Continue for back, until work measures $8\frac{1}{2}$ ($9\frac{1}{2}$) in. from 22 (26) cast-on sts., finishing at end of a k. row. K. 4 rows. Cast off.

Neckband

With right side facing, starting at corner of right front knit up 85 (93) sts. round neck, finishing at corner of left front. **1st row:** k. **2nd row:** k. 1, * wl. fwd., k. 2 tog.; rep. from * to end. Cast off.

To Make Up

Press lightly. Join side and sleeve seams. Thread length of ribbon through holes at neck. Attach ribbon to side edges of right and left fronts and to corresponding position on garment. Press all seams.

RIBBED PILCH

Materials.—1 oz. Patons Beehive Baby Wool, Patonised. A pair No. 10 "Beehive" needles. Length of elastic.
Measurement.—Length at centre front, 8½ in.
Tension.—7½ sts. and 9½ rows to an inch.

Starting at front, cast on 77 sts. **1st row:** k. 2, * p. 1, k. 1; rep. from * to last st., k. 1. **2nd row:** * k. 1, p. 1; rep. from * to last st., k. 1. **3rd and 4th rows:** as 1st and 2nd. **5th row:** k. 2, * wl. fwd., k. 2 tog., p. 1, k. 1; rep. from * to last 3 sts., wl. fwd., k. 2 tog., k. 1. Work 5 rows in rib. **Next row:** * k. 1, p. 1; rep. from * to last st., k. 1. **Next row:** p.

Rep. last 2 rows until work measures 5½ in. from beg., finishing at end of a p. row. Divide work as follows:

Next row: k. 1, (p. 1, k. 1) 12 times, k. 2 tog., k. 1, turn. Continue on these 27 sts. as follows: **1st row:** k. 1, k. 2 tog., p. to end. **2nd row:** work to last 3 sts., k. 2 tog., k. 1. Work 1st and 2nd rows 5 times more, then 1st row once (14 sts.). **Next row:** work to last 2 sts., inc. in next st., k. 1. **Next row:** inc. in 1st st. knitways, p. to end.

Work last 2 rows 6 times more (28 sts.). **Next row:** in pattern. Break wool.

Rejoin wool to sts. on needle and continue on centre group of sts. as follows: **1st row:** k. 2, (k. 1, p. 1) 8 times, k. 3, turn. **2nd row:** k. 2, p. 17, k. 2. Work these 2 rows 12 times more, then 1st row once. Break wool.

Rejoin wool to group of 28 sts. **1st row:** k. 1, k. 2 tog. through back of loops, work to end. **2nd row:** p. to last 3 sts., k. 2 tog. t.b.l., k. 1. Work these 2 rows 6 times more. **Next row:** inc. in 1st st., work to end. **Next row:** p. to last 2 sts., inc. in next st. knitways, k. 1. Work last 2 rows 6 times more (28 sts.). Work 1 row.

Continue on all sts. until work measures 16 in. from beg., finishing at end of a p. row. Shape back as follows: **1st and 2nd rows:** work to last 4 sts., turn. **3rd and 4th rows:** work to last 8 sts., turn.

Continue working 4 sts. less on every row until the 2 rows "work to last 28 sts., turn" have been worked. **Next row:** work to end. Starting with a 2nd row, work 5 rows in rib as at start. **Next row:** as 5th. Work 3 rows rib; cast off in rib.

To Make Up

Omitting ribbing at waist, with wrong side facing, press work lightly. Join side seams. Press seams. Thread elastic through holes at waist.

DIAMOND PATTERN BOOTEES AND MITTENS

Materials.—1 oz. Patons Beehive Baby Wool 3-ply, Patonised. A pair of No. 10 "Beehive" needles. Scraps of coloured silk for embroidery.
Tension.—7½ sts. and 9½ rows to an inch.

Bootees

Cast on 37 sts. **1st row:** p. 1, * k. 1, p. 1; rep. from * to end. Repeat this row 4 times more. **6th row:** * p. 1, k. 5; rep. from * to last st., p. 1. **7th row:** p. 1, k. 1, * p. 3, k. 1, p. 1, k. 1; rep. from * to last 5 sts., p. 3, k. 1, p. 1. **8th row:** k. 2, * p. 1, k. 1, p. 1, k. 3; rep. from * to last 5 sts., p. 1, k. 1, p. 1, k. 2. **9th row:** p. 3, * k. 1, p. 5; rep. from * to last 4 sts., k. 1, p. 3. **10th row:** as 8th. **11th row:** as 7th.

Repeat 6th–11th rows inclusive 4 times more, then 6th row again. Now make holes for ribbon. **Next row:** * p. 1, wool round needle, p. 2 tog.; rep. from * to last st., p. 1.

Here divide for instep. **Next row:** (p. 1, k. 1) 6 times, slip these sts. on a safety pin, p. 1, k. 5, p. 1, k. 5, p. 1, turn, slip remaining 12 sts. on a second pin. Continue on instep sts. as follows:

1st row: p. 1, k. 1, p. 3, k. 1, p. 1, k. 1, p. 3, k. 1, p. 1. **2nd row:** k. 2, p. 1, k. 1, p. 1, k. 3, p. 1, k. 1, p. 1, k. 2. **3rd row:** p. 3, k. 1, p. 5, k. 1, p. 3. **4th row:** as 2nd. **5th row:** as 1st. **6th row:** p. 1, k. 5, p. 1, k. 5, p. 1. Rep. these 6 rows 3 times more. Break wool.

With right side facing, rejoin wool to sts. on second pin and k. 1, p. 1 to end. **Next row:** moss 12, pick up and k. 12 sts. along side of instep, moss 13 instep sts., pick up and k. 12 sts. along other side of instep, moss 12. Work 6 rows moss-st. over all sts.

Next row: moss 12, turn and moss back. **Next row:** moss over all sts. **Next row:** moss 12, turn and moss back. **Next row:** moss over all sts. Now work 4 rows moss, dec. 1 st. at each end of needle and each side of centre 13 sts. on every row. Cast off.

Join foot and leg seams. Embroider small flowers in the top row of diamonds. Thread ribbon through holes. Press.

Mittens

Cast on 37 sts. Work pattern rows 1–11 inclusive as given for bootees, then rows 6–11 inclusive, then rows 6–8 inclusive. Now make holes for ribbon. **Next row:** p. 1, * p. 2 tog.; rep. from * to end. **Next row:** * k. 1, wl. fwd., k. 2 tog.; rep. from * to last st., k. 1. **Next row:** p. 1 (p. twice in each st.) all along.

Work pattern rows 6–11 inclusive twice, then rows 6–9 inclusive once. Shape top as follows: **1st row:** k. 1, k. 2 tog., k. 1, p. 1, k. 3, p. 1, k. 1, p. 1, k. 3, p. 1, k. 1, k. 2 tog., k. 1, k. 2 tog., k. 1, p. 1, k. 3, p. 1, k. 1, p. 1, k. 3, p. 1, k. 1, k. 2 tog., k. 1. **2nd row:** p. 4, k. 1, p. 1, k. 1, p. 3, k. 1, p. 1, k. 1, p. 7, k. 1, p. 1, k. 1, p. 3, k. 1, p. 1, k. 1, p. 4.

3rd row: k. 1, k. 2. tog., k. 2, p. 1, k. 5, p. 1, k. 2, k. 2 tog., k. 1, k. 2 tog., k. 2, p. 1, k. 5, p. 1, k. 2, k. 2 tog., k. 1. **4th row:** p. 3, k. 1, p. 1, k. 1, p. 3, k. 1, p. 1, k. 1, p. 5, k. 1, p. 1, k. 1, p. 3, k. 1, p. 1, k. 1, p. 3.

5th row: k. 1, k. 2 tog., k. 3, p. 1, k. 1, p. 1, k. 3, k. 2 tog., k. 1, k. 2 tog., k. 3, p. 1, k. 1, p. 1, k. 3, k. 2 tog., k. 1.

6th row: p. 6, k. 1, p. 11, k. 1, p. 6. **7th row:** k. 1, k. 2 tog., k. 2, p. 1, k. 1, p. 1, k. 2, k. 2 tog., k. 1, k. 2 tog., k. 2, p. 1, k. 1, p. 1, k. 2, k. 2 tog., k. 1. **8th row:** p. 3, k. 1, p. 3, k. 1, p. 5, k. 1, p. 3, k. 1, p. 3. Cast off.

Fold mitten over, join top and side seam. Thread ribbon through holes at wrist. Embroider small flowers in top row of diamonds, as on bootees.

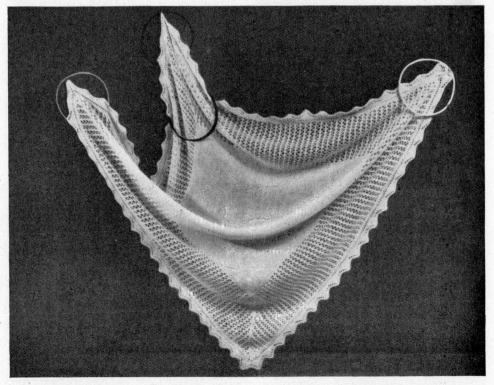

This beautiful shawl has a fascinating border and lace edging—a lovely gift for a new baby from a proud relative or devoted friend

PLANNING THE NURSERY

*Whether it is just a corner of your bedroom or a real
nursery, baby needs special equipment*

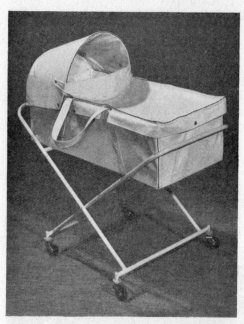

Most useful bed is a carry-cot, like this one
in cream, pink or blue American cloth, with
tubular steel stand

EVERYTHING depends, of course,
upon the amount of space available. A
corner of the parents' bedroom may have
to be converted into a miniature nursery,
but the ideal is a fairly large room, preferably facing south-east (*not* west or the
afternoon sun will make it hot and keep
baby awake in the summer evenings). The
great thing to aim at is a comfortably warm
room. Whatever the floor covering, it must
be warm—so that the baby can safely be
put down on a rug and, as a toddler later
on, run around barefoot. A good old carpet
often serves this purpose well and can be
vacuum-cleaned and sponged regularly to
keep it clean. Ventilation is important in a
nursery but draughts must be avoided.
Curtains may be as bright and gay and
colourful as you like, with all the nursery
figures and flowers, but it is well worth
while giving them thick, dark linings to keep

out the light on summer evenings and early
mornings.

Here are the most important items to
look for when furnishing a nursery:

A screen—invaluable in shielding the cot
or bath from draughts.

A table—a good solid, strong one of the
kitchen variety. Some mothers, no
doubt, are naturally adept at managing
their babies on their laps, but it is not
easy for everyone. It is much simpler to
have a big table, spread a blanket on it,
put the baby on the blanket and there
change nappies and do all the other
dressing and toilet jobs.

A basket for toilet accessories (powder,
pins, etc.). Some lovely baby baskets
can be bought in the shops. Or you can
find a good-sized wooden box, preferably with sloping sides (wider at the top)
about 1 foot × 2 feet and cover it inside
and out with pretty material—and there
is a nursery basket for a few shillings.

Bed.—The best all-purpose buy is a carry-
cot, in which the baby can sleep and in
which he can be moved about, in the
house and garden, by car or train. It
can be stood on a drop-sided toddlers'
cot until the baby outgrows it and transfers to the bigger one—or put on a box
or sofa.

Bedding:

(1) A hair mattress.
(2) Waterproof sheet.
(3) Wool blankets—one for underneath,
two on top.
(4) Winceyette blankets—six if possible,
so that there will be replacements
when they get wet.
(5) Pram pillow—for use in the pram
only, to raise baby to look round, not
in the cot, when he should lie flat.
At about one year a baby may need
a cot pillow, which is larger than a
pram one—but not before.
(6) Pillow slips; as many as possible.
(7) A warm, light eiderdown.

486

A nursery to last from baby-hood to schooldays, with cream, pink or blue enamelled furniture and a gay rug, at Treasure Cot

For easy bath times—the Enna bath in enamelled aluminium or papier mâché, with a metal stand, plain and quilted rubber bath mat

The correct way to make a baby's bed or drop-sided cot is in this order, working from below upwards: Mattress, wool blanket, waterproof, winceyette blanket, baby. Then on top, wool blankets and, if needed, eiderdown.

THE BATH

If there is a large lavatory basin and the bathroom is warm, baby may safely be bathed in this for the first 6 months, when he will be promoted to the bath. Otherwise, the best thing is a papier mâché bath large enough for him to stretch in, which should be placed on a low table or stand in a warm, sheltered corner of the nursery, protected, if necessary, by the nursery screen. Other bath time requirements are a warm apron (made of towelling or flannel) for Mother, pure *baby* soap, two face cloths, clean towels and baby talcum powder.

THE PRAM

A young baby spends a great deal of time in the pram, so it is important to buy a good one from a well-known manufacturer. Points to watch for when choosing a pram are these:

(1) The inside must be soft and smooth with nothing that could scratch or hurt baby.

(2) Hood and apron should give protection against the weather.

(3) The pram should be firm, with an efficient brake and incapable of being tipped over by an active child.

(4) There must be a strong strap to hold the baby in.

(5) It should be light and easy to push, with a handle that is a convenient height.

Later on, a harness will be required to keep baby safe when he pulls himself up.

The pram's bodywork may be sponged out as necessary with warm water, then polished with furniture polish; the chromium parts require only an occasional rub with a damp leather, and the hood can be kept in good condition if it is always left up until thoroughly dried after rain and brushed with a clothes brush. Even the least handy of husbands will undertake the simple task of oiling the wheel hubs.

REGISTERING THE BIRTH

As soon as possible, usually within two or three days, the birth must be registered with the local Registrar of Births, Marriages and Deaths, giving the full names of both parents. Two kinds of birth certificate are obtainable:

(1) A full copy of the record in the register, costing 3s. 9d.

(2) A shortened form, giving only the child's name, sex, date and place of birth. This costs 9d.

Christening

Application should be made to the Vicar or minister, who will make the necessary arrangements. There is no fee for the ceremony.

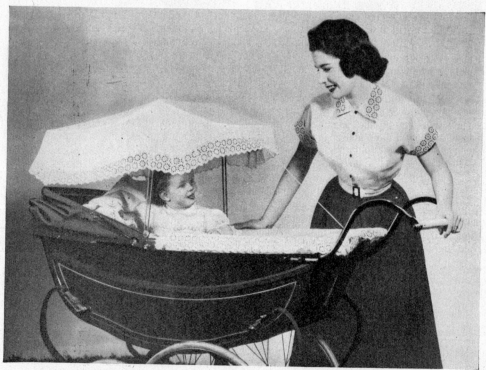

For summer a pram canopy is needed to protect baby from the sun. This attractive one by Morlands of Glastonbury, with white broderie anglaise edging, has a restful green lining and a matching pram apron

BABY CARE

Guiding principles to help the new mother through some of the problems of the first year

EVERY baby, from the moment of birth, is a person, an individual in his own right and not necessarily like anybody else. Rules for his care and upbringing are excellent as a general guide, but the wise mother will adapt her routine to suit the baby—never, as does sometimes happen, try to mould her child to fit into a set of rules.

For this reason alone, the information given here must be regarded as general guidance only. Individual problems affecting both mother and baby should be referred to the local Maternity and Child Welfare Clinic, where help and advice can be obtained.

Bath time should be one of the happiest times of the day for baby. Bath him at night and it will send him off to sleep quickly and contentedly

FEEDING

For the first few months of life, the most important—and probably the only—really vital things in a baby's life are food, sleep and warmth.

The perfect food is, of course, the one provided for the purpose by Nature—mother's milk, which is completely safe, easy to digest and contains everything necessary to give a baby the best possible start in life and to protect him from the infections which are a danger in infancy.

Breast Feeding

Breast feeding should therefore go on as long as possible. The quality can be relied upon, even if the quantity varies, though that can be increased. The best way of doing so is to drink at least 1 pint of milk a day, plus 4 or 5 pints of other fluids. There are also milk-forming tablets which can be obtained from the clinic. Rest is another important factor in maintaining a good milk supply, and no heavy work or shopping should be attempted.

Suckling increases the quantity of milk, so at each feed baby should be put to both breasts, if only for a few minutes. Generally, ten minutes each side will be required at each feed.

Difficulties, such as sore or cracked nipples or insufficient milk, should, of course, be reported promptly to the clinic. But if baby is obviously still very hungry *after* breast feeding and you cannot immediately get advice, he should be given a bottle (2 to 3 oz.). Use half-cream powdered milk for a baby up to 10 lb. in weight; full-cream powdered milk if over 10 lb. If powdered milk is not available, use as an alternative 2 oz. boiled cow's milk, 1 oz. boiled water and 1 teaspoonful sugar, cooled to blood heat. Be sure to get the advice of doctor or clinic as soon as possible.

Bottle Feeding

The Bottle.—It is advisable to buy a feeding bottle and teats (those with medium-sized holes are best to start with) when getting ready for the baby's arrival. You will then be prepared for emergencies, though it is always possible to use a medicine bottle, provided it is first thoroughly cleaned.

First boil the bottle and teats for 10 minutes, starting with cold water and bringing it to the boil. Keep both bottle and teats covered with boiled water when not in use.

Milk

Though breast feeding is infinitely better than any form of artificial feeding, there are many instances where the mother's milk supply fails completely or must be supplemented. In such cases there are a number of alternatives to choose from:

(1) Cow's milk (in the proportion of 2 oz. to 1 oz. boiled water and 1 teaspoonful sugar).
(2) Powdered milk: (*a*) humanised, which is made as much like human milk as possible; (*b*) half-cream cow's milk for young babies; (*c*) full-cream cow's milk.

National Dried Milk is the cheapest and may be obtained with a special coupon (obtainable from the National Insurance Office) from clinics and certain shops. Obtain advice from the clinic or doctor before deciding which type of milk to use. Remember, too, that frequent changes of diet upset a baby's digestion, and that whichever kind you choose it should be given a fair trial over a reasonable period of time.

Feeding Times

Baby requires a feed every 3 or 4 hours, but will generally go for 6 or 8 hours at night after the first few weeks. There is no need to wake him from a sound sleep for a feed; when he is hungry he will wake of his own accord. If on the other hand he wakes half an hour before feeding time, it is far better to give him his feed right away than have him lying there hungry and fretful. A young baby's habits vary a little each day, but quite soon he will establish a reasonably regular rhythm of feeds. A healthy baby usually requires feeding every 4 hours—at 6 a.m., 10 a.m., 2 p.m., 6 p.m. and 10 p.m.

Quantities of Food

A baby needs $2\frac{1}{2}$ oz. of milk every 24 hours for every 1 lb. of body weight. Thus an 8-lb. baby gets five 4-oz. feeds a day.

Vitamins

Vitamins A and D (contained in cod liver oil) and vitamin C (in orange juice, rose hip syrup or black currant juice) are good for all babies and essential for artificially fed ones. Start giving one drop each of cod liver oil and of one of the fruit juices or syrups containing vitamin C at about 6 weeks; gradually increase to 1 teaspoonful of each.

Preparing the Feed

Before handling any of baby's feeding utensils, the hands must be thoroughly washed. Instructions for making the feed should be read carefully and followed exactly, only enough for one feed being made at a time. Only freshly boiled water must be used.

The following utensils should be kept together on a large tray ready for use:

Three feeding bottles with teats and valves.
At least three extra teats.
Brush for cleaning bottles.
Measuring jug.
Milk saucepan.
Tablespoon and teaspoon.
Cup and enamel bowl.

Bringing up the wind

Feeding should not take longer than between 10 and 15 minutes or the contents of the bottle will get cold and may cause colic, as well as being unappetising. Always nurse baby while feeding him; it will make him happier and more contented, and enable you to get rid of his wind by lifting him up to your shoulder and gently patting his back two or three times during the feed. A baby fed in a cot or pram tends to swallow the wind, while the teat may slip right out of his mouth and the feed get cold before he has nearly finished

Cleaning the Feeding Bottles

(*a*) *Daily cleaning:* Feeding bottles and teats must be sterilised once every day. Put them into the enamel bowl in cold ater and bring to the boil. Remove teats nd valves just after boiling or the rubber ay stretch. Boil the bottles for 10 minutes, en leave in the water to cool. When old, immerse them in cooled, freshly oiled water and cover with muslin ready or the next feed.

(b) *After feeds:* One of the simplest and afest ways of cleaning bottles, teats and alves after feeds, and which is practised in ost maternity and children's hospitals, is e Milton Method shown on the colour age facing page 481.

After each feed, flush the inside and out-de of the bottle, teat and valve with plenty f cold water. Then make a solution of filton and cold water—3 teaspoonfuls of filton to 2 pints of water—in the enamel owl. Immerse bottle, teat and valve com-letely until the next feed but, before using em again, wash thor-ughly under the cold tap.

Iotions

A breast fed baby gener-lly has a motion every one r two days, but can go with-ut for up to a week and ome to no harm. The stool mustard coloured, soft in onsistency and has a pecu-ar sweet smell.

An artificially fed baby as a paler-coloured but soft ool, and should have at ast one motion daily. If is does not happen, give oiled water with a little gar between feeds and lso slightly increase the mount of sugar in each ottle. Remember, however, at too much sugar in a aby's diet will result in fre-uent frothy motions.

WEANING

Solid foods should be in-oduced gradually at about months, or when baby is bout 16 lb. in weight. Be-in with a cereal before the reast or bottle feed at 10 .m. Always give the solid od from a spoon, *before*

his breast or bottle feed when he is hungry and therefore prepared to accept something new. About half a teaspoonful will be enough to start with. Mix it with a little of the bottle feed or, for a breast fed baby, with two-thirds cow's milk and one-third water, both boiled. Gradually in-crease the quantity of cereal to 1 table-spoonful at a time and, after a week or two, introduce cereal into the 6 p.m. feed also.

At 5 to 6 months it is time to start on bone and vegetable broth, either home-made or bought in a bottle or can. Begin in the same way as with the cereal, with half a teaspoonful before the milk feed, in-creasing gradually to a reasonable helping. Now is the time to start introducing other flavours, such as beef or tongue broth, strained vegetables, eggs.

Between 9 and 10 months baby will give up sitting— and start crawling everywhere at steadily increasing speed and with great enthusiasm

491

But it is essential to allow each child to develop in his own way and at his own speed. Most infants take to mixed feeding with alacrity and thoroughly enjoy everything except when they are off colour, when they invariably revert to a milk diet for a few days. A baby who does not get on well with the transition to a mixed diet is probably going too fast. The best plan is to go back to breast or bottle for 5 or 6 days and then start again more gradually with the weaning process.

Diet at Five Months

6 *a.m.*—Breast or bottle, 6½–7 oz.

10 *a.m.*—½ teaspoonful egg-yolk, gradually increased to 2 teaspoonfuls; 2 oz. cereal and milk; milk mixture, 5 oz.

2 *p.m.*—1 or 2 tablespoonfuls homogenised carrots, bone and vegetable broth or liver soup; milk mixture, 5 oz.

6 *p.m.*—2 oz. cereal with milk; 5 oz. milk mixture.

10 *p.m.*—Breast or milk mixture, 6 oz.

NOTE: 1 teaspoonful cod liver oil and 2 teaspoonfuls fruit juice (orange, rose hip or black currant) are essential daily.

Diet at Six Months

From six months onwards, a baby begins to need something hard to exercise his jaws and help his teeth.

6 *a.m.*—Breast or bottle mixture, 6–7 oz.

10 *a.m.*—Hard crust or rusk 10 minutes before, then 2–3 oz. cereal with milk; ½ teaspoonful lightly boiled egg-yolk, gradually increasing to 2 teaspoonfuls; 5 oz. breast or milk food.

2 *p.m.*—Bone and vegetable broth or homogenised carrots, or 2 teaspoonfuls creamed potatoes; breast or bottle mixture, 5–6 oz.

6 *p.m.*—Crust or rusk spread with a little dripping or butter; breast or bottle mixture, 6–7 oz.

10 *p.m.*—Breast or bottle mixture, 6–7 oz.

NOTE: Cup and spoon feeding should be started now, with cow's milk or bottle mixture or fruit juice in the cup. In this way, baby gradually learns to take less milk feed and more of the mixed diet.

From now on a well balanced diet is needed, containing the right quantities of proteins, fats, carbohydrates, mineral salts and vitamins, plus enough hard things for teeth and jaws and sufficient solids to develop the digestion.

Diet at Seven Months

6 *a.m.*—Breast or bottle mixture, 6–7 oz.

10 *a.m.*—Crust or rusk 10 minutes before, then 2–3 oz. oatmeal porridge with milk; half a lightly boiled egg-yolk two or three times a week; breast or bottle mixture, 5 oz.

2 *p.m.*—Homogenised bone and vegetable or meat broth with creamed potato and homogenised carrots; oat jelly served with homogenised apple or egg custard or semolina pudding; breast or bottle mixture, 5 oz.

6 *p.m.*—1 teaspoonful Marmite with breadcrumbs; cereal; breast or bottle mixture, 5 oz.

10 *p.m.*—Breast or milk mixture, 6–7 oz.

Diet at Eight Months

6 *a.m.*—Breast or bottle mixture, 6–7 oz.

10 *a.m.*—Buttered crust or rusk 10 minutes before feed, then 3 oz. cereal with milk; half a lightly boiled egg three times a week; breast or bottle mixture, 5 oz.

2 *p.m.*—Steamed fish (plaice or sole) with vegetable marrow and 2 teaspoonfuls mashed potato; stewed apple and a little custard, semolina or cornflour pudding; milk to drink.

6 *p.m.*—Buttered rusk 10 minutes before, then breast or bottle mixture, 6–7 oz.

10 *p.m.*—Breast or bottle mixture, 6–7 oz.

NOTE: A baby of 8 to 9 months needs every day 1½ teaspoonfuls cod liver oil and 2 to 3 teaspoonfuls orange, rose hip or black currant juice.

Diet at Nine Months

6 *a.m.*—Orange juice diluted with water.

10 *a.m.*—Rusk 10 minutes before, then 3 oz. porridge, cornflakes or bread and milk; half an egg-yolk three times a week with fried bread; milk mixture, 5 oz.

2 *p.m.*—Bone or meat and vegetable broth, or minced beef or gravy with mashed potato or steamed fish, rabbit or liver with carrots and creamed potatoes; milk or sponge pudding; milk to drink.

6 *p.m.*—Buttered rusk 10 minutes before, then cereal with milk.

10 *p.m.*—Small quantity of milk feed.

At 9 months most babies are completely weaned from breast or bottle and are on

"Wasn't it fun in the bath to-night? The hot's so hot and the cold's so cold!" . . . And even the soap suds taste delicious, apparently

iet of proper meals—breakfast, lunch, tea nd supper or high tea. They often wean ιemselves from the 10 p.m. feed, but this an in any case be gradually discontinued. 'he important thing now is to ensure regu-ιr meal times and no tit-bits in between, xcept for cold (boiled) water to drink.

Diet at Ten Months

reakfast on waking (*about* 8 *a.m.*).—Bread fried in bacon fat or buttered crust or rusk; half a lightly boiled egg-yolk three times a week; cereal with milk mixture.

Lunch (*noon*).—Minced meat with pota-toes or carrots, or bone or meat and vegetable broth, or egg with potatoes and vegetable marrow, or steamed fish (her-ring); milk pudding, baked apple or apple purée with custard; water to drink.

Tea (4–5 *p.m.*).—Buttered crust or bread and butter with jam or honey or Mar-mite sandwich; plain cake; milk to drink.

Supper (*at bedtime*).—Small quantity of milk mixture or fresh boiled cow's milk.

Diet at Twelve Months

Breakfast (8–9 *a.m.*). — Orange juice diluted with water or apple purée with black currant juice; 2 oz. cereal with milk; toast with butter or half a lightly boiled egg or half a rasher of bacon; 4 oz. milk to drink.

Dinner (12–1).—Broth, soup, gravy with homogenised carrots, spinach or peas; or mashed potato or fish with vegetable marrow, cauliflower; or egg with mashed potatoes and carrots or salad (lettuce, mustard and cress with grated cheese and potato); milk pudding or custard with baked or stewed apple.

Tea (4–5 *p.m.*).—Marmite, grated cheese, chopped mustard and cress, jam or honey sandwiches; plain cake and milk to drink.

NOTE: At 12 months a baby should have every day 2 teaspoonfuls cod liver oil and 2–3 teaspoonfuls orange, rose hip or black currant juice.

SLEEP

The average baby spends most of his time asleep and can be expected to sleep as follows:

Birth to 2 months: 21 hours in 24.

2–4 months: 19 hours in 24.

4–6 months: 18 hours in 24.

6–12 months: 16–17 hours in 24.

He will sleep well and peacefully provided:

(1) He is properly fed.
(2) His wind is brought up. To do this, hold the baby up to your shoulder and rub his back upwards. This should be done in the middle of the feed and immediately afterwards. Gripe water may also help, but should be used sparingly. Quite often a little boiled water proves just as effective. If a baby is badly troubled with wind the doctor may prescribe a mixture.
(3) His nappy is dry.
(4) He is warm but not too hot.

Fresh air is a great aid to sound sleep. The nursery must therefore be well ventilated (but not draughty) at night. During the day, a baby should sleep out of doors for as long as possible. In pouring rain, the pram must obviously be put under cover and care should be taken, too, in very cold weather, particularly when there is snow or a bitter wind.

A light should not be kept on in the nursery at night, and baby should be left alone, lying on his side. If he cries persistently, make sure that it is not due to a wet napkin, tight clothing or because he is thirsty. A drink of water often sends a baby quickly back to sleep, and so does a minute or two of cuddling and reassurance.

EXERCISE AND PLAY

From 3½ months, a baby begins to need quite a lot of exercise. Kicking and stretching both help him to grow and develop healthy limbs. It is a good plan to allow 10 minutes for kicking exercise before each feed and to loosen his napkin so that he can move freely. A little later he should take his exercise on a warm, good thick blanket in a play-pen.

Playtime is an essential part of every happy baby's day and should be fitted in, however busy mother is, just before bedtime. This will send him to sleep tired and contented.

DAILY ROUTINE

It is useful to have a timetable, particularly to guide the inexperienced mother, but this must never be regarded a a set of cast-iron rules or a schedule whic cannot under any circumstances b broken. Many babies establish their ow routine, which often proves just as satis factory as those in the textbooks. So d treat all plans and charts for baby's day a entirely flexible and, if you can fit in you way of life with your baby's individua habits, so much the better.

Here is a typical daily routine on whic to base yours:

6 a.m.—Feed and change napkin; the sleep.

9 a.m.—Wash, toilet, etc.

NOTE: Be sure to have everything yo want ready before you start.

10 a.m.—Feed; sleep in garden.

2 p.m.—Feed, change napkin; sleep i garden or walk.

6 p.m.—Feed; bath; playtime; then bed

10 p.m.—Feed and change napkin.

Bathing Baby

The best time for the daily bath is i the evening, when it will make baby sleep Get everything ready before fetching baby from his pram:

(1) His enamel or papier mâché baby bath, which he will use for the first (months, with a napkin in the bottom to prevent him slipping.
(2) Two face cloths, one for baby's face one for the body.
(3) Two clean dry towels.
(4) Super-fatted soap.
(5) Cotton wool and saline or boracic lotion.
(6) Talcum powder.
(7) Plenty of hot water, which you wil test with your elbow to make sure it is not too hot.

Choose a warm part of the nursery out of the draught, or screen a corner off for the bath. Put on your thick Turkish towelling apron, lay baby on his back on a blanket on the nursery table, undress and wash him thoroughly with well-soaped hands, cleanse eyes, ears and nostrils carefully with twists of cotton wool. Then lower him gently into the bath, rinse all over and let him kick and splash for a few minutes. Take him out, dry him thoroughly, and lay him face downwards on

he table again or on your lap to be powered (particularly in all the creases) with
alc. Then put on a clean napkin and dress
im for bed.

Two or three times a week his hair
hould be well lathered with soap and
hen thoroughly rinsed, making certain
hat no soap is left behind.

At 9 months, baby should be promoted
rom his own baby bath to the big one in
he bathroom.

Changing Napkins

Baby's napkin should be changed after
each feed. This is the best time to do it as
most infants soil their napkins during or
after feeding. At other times, a wet napkin should always be changed if it is causing the baby discomfort.

There are a number of methods of putting on napkins. You may fold a thin napkin into a triangle and fix it in three-
cornered style, then wrap a thicker one
round the baby's body like a skirt; or fold
a thin napkin and a thick one both in half
with their corners pinned to baby's vest.
Some mothers favour a pad of cotton wool
between baby's legs, with a napkin
fastened on in triangular style to hold it in
place.

When changing napkins, cotton wool (if
used) must be destroyed and soiled napkins dropped immediately into a bucket of
cold water and left to soak before washing.
There is no need to boil them every time,
but they must be washed in Lux, rinsed
in three or four waters and should be boiled
at about every third or fourth washing.

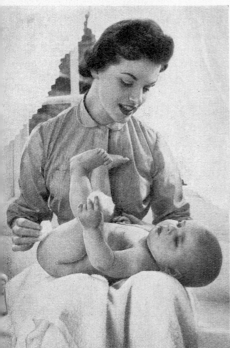

Photos: Johnson & Johnson

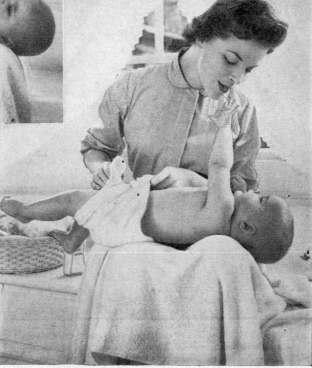

**His bath over, baby must
be thoroughly dried in a
thick warm bath towel,
then well powdered (above),
especially in the folds and
creases. Then put on a
clean napkin (right). If
there is any sign of napkin
rash, powder him after every
napkin change as well as
after his bath**

Whenever possible they should be dried in the fresh air.

THE FIRST YEAR

During the first 12 months a baby makes greater progress than in any other year of life. This fascinating development, both mental and physical, can be watched from the first few days after birth, when he only opens his eyes in semi-darkness, to the appearance of teeth and the discovery of words. In one short year a baby learns to use his hands, to smile, to sit up, to crawl, walk—and a hundred other things.

Naturally enough, every stage in his progress is excitedly—and sometimes anxiously—watched by the parents, who tend to become quite fiercely competitive about their offspring's achievements. This attitude can, however, lead to unnecessary anxiety, because all babies do *not* progress at exactly the same speed. Though useful guidance can be given as to what can reasonably be expected, it must be remembered that, even in the same family, one child will be slower than the rest learning to talk or walk, but will often catch up in the end. Here then is a general guide to progress:

The Early Milestones

1 *month*.—Baby lifts his head, purses his mouth, wrinkles his forehead; his eyes will follow a moving light and he will grasp a finger tightly. His first real smile can be expected at about 6 weeks.

2 *months*. — Smiles, coos, gurgles, sheds real tears, turns his head towards a noise and blinks.

3 *months*. — Now able to roll and wriggle and grasp a rattle.

4 *months*.—Head ceases to wobble and can usually hold it up, this being considered the first sign of will power. Muscles are much stronger and he kicks vigorously, reaches for things and wants to play at feeding time.

5 *months*. — Recognises familiar faces and may be shy with strangers. He is now beginning to reason and to be apprehensive.

6–11 *months*.—The second half of the first year is a period of tremendous progress. Baby laughs, chuckles aloud, loves to make as much noise as possible and to bang everything within reach, plays with his hands and feet. Time of cutting teeth varies tremendously, but first teeth usually appear between 6 and 9 months. From sitting erect at

Made in two sizes, Viyella and Clydella baby gowns are warm, hard-wearing, well-made and will stand up to any amount of washing and ironing

GETTING YOUR FIGURE BACK
TO NORMAL

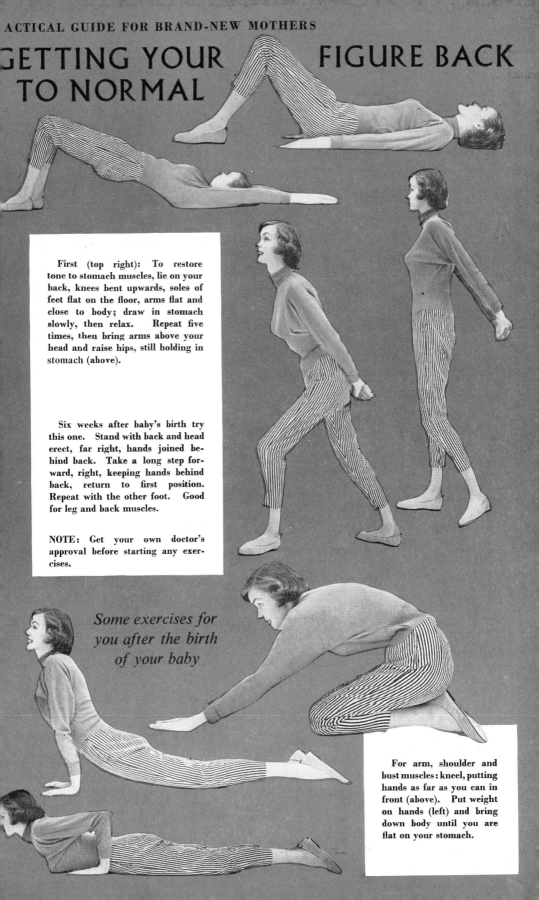

First (top right): To restore tone to stomach muscles, lie on your back, knees bent upwards, soles of feet flat on the floor, arms flat and close to body; draw in stomach slowly, then relax. Repeat five times, then bring arms above your head and raise hips, still holding in stomach (above).

Six weeks after baby's birth try this one. Stand with back and head erect, far right, hands joined behind back. Take a long step forward, right, keeping hands behind back, return to first position. Repeat with the other foot. Good for leg and back muscles.

NOTE: Get your own doctor's approval before starting any exercises.

Some exercises for you after the birth of your baby

For arm, shoulder and bust muscles: kneel, putting hands as far as you can in front (above). Put weight on hands (left) and bring down body until you are flat on your stomach.

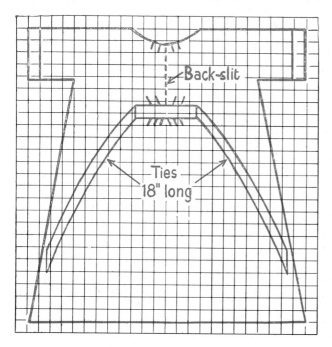

Back-slit

Ties
18" long

FIRST GARMENT
TO MAKE

Nightdress and sleeping bag
to cut out from diagrams

THE nightdress requires 1½ yd. 27
or 36 in. Clydella and the sleep.
bag, which has a deep flap to butt
over baby's feet, can be cut from
yd. of 54-in. width blanket cloth
velour cloth.

To make the Nightdress. Cut p
tern from diagram (top left), in wh
each square equals 1 in. Then f
material, as shown in cutting-
diagram at foot of page, the spare 4
being used to make the two ties a
the facings. Allow ½ in. seams. Sco
out neck (lower in front), make slit
back (about 5 in.), hem sleeve and f
neck edges, make slots in cuffs and
neck for drawstrings, put in gathers wh
marked, sew on waist ties across gathers a
assemble garment.

Sleeping Bag. The two diagrams, left, sh
how to cut patterns, one square equalling 2
Back is 6 in. deeper for flap to button o
front. Place patterns on folded 54-in. materi
as shown below. The mitts are attached to ba
of sleeve and flap over sleeve front, covering
hand. Make button holes along bottom of ba
to correspond with buttons sewn about 6 in.
from bottom of front.

Above, how to cut the
pattern for the night-
dress. Each square
represents one inch.
Cut on paper folded
double, the fold coming
along shoulders.

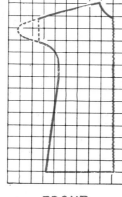

FRONT

Above, the front of the
Sleeping Bag—one
square equals 2 in.;
zig-zag line shows where
a zip fastener goes in.
Left, the back is 6 in.
longer than the front to
provide a flap that
buttons over

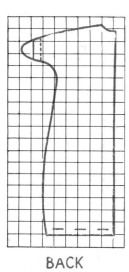

BACK

Selvedges 54in. material

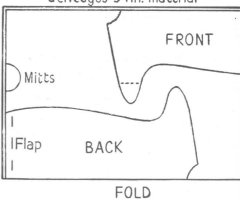

Mitts

FRONT

Flap

BACK

FOLD

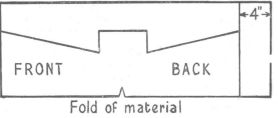

FRONT   BACK

Fold of material

←4"→

Above, how to cut out the Sleeping Bag from 1½
yards of 54 in. material, placing centre of back
pattern on fold and cutting two small pieces
(4 in. across and 4 in. long) for the mitts. Left,
how to cut out the nightdress from 1½ yards 36 in.
Clydella, ties and facings from the odd 4 in.

Whatever acrobatics baby gets up to, he can't get his toes cold in the "Niteysac," a practical little garment which buttons up at the hem. From the Clydella layette range, it will stay in use until baby is two or three

months he will probably start to crawl between 9 and 10 months. He recognises his name and can hold and drink from a cup.

12 *months.*—Most children can say a few words, have 6 to 8 teeth and can stand without assistance.

15 *months.*—He starts to walk alone.

18 *months.*—By now the fontanelle or soft spot on baby's head, which begins to close in at birth, should be completely closed.

$2\frac{1}{2}$ *years.*—The first set of 20 teeth is usually complete and the child talking well, though many perfectly normal children are late starters both in cutting teeth and talking.

PREVENTION OF ILLNESS

Vaccination should be done when about 4 months old. At this stage a baby is

little disturbed by it and very few complications arise. If it is left until later—when it may have to be done for the first time in the 'teens—vaccination may cause much more discomfort. Some doctors vaccinate on the sole of the foot, but most prefer the arm; the thigh is not generally advisable because it is so difficult to keep it dry.

B.C.G. Vaccination (against tuberculosis) may be done on a doctor's recommendation where a baby is likely to come into contact with T.B. infection or there is a family history of the disease.

Immunisation against—

(1) *Diphtheria* is most important. Diphtheria is a killing disease. It used to be very prevalent in the U.K., and has been practically wiped out since this highly efficient inoculation was introduced. It should be done when about 6 months old, consists of two injections

at 1 month's interval and causes very little disturbance.

(2) *Whooping Cough* is now much more successful than it was at first, causes little disturbance and generally prevents the disease. It consists of three inoculations at intervals of 1 month.

(3) *Tetanus* is usually given at the same time as diphtheria and whooping cough immunisation, rarely alone, and it also causes little disturbance.

All three inoculations can now be given together. Some doctors, however, prefer to do each series separately.

(4) *Polio* is now available from the age of 6 months to 40 years and can be done either by the family doctor or at the clinic. There are two injections a month apart and a third 7 months later.

Health Problems

Constipation.—A breast fed baby may go as long as a week with no motion, and this can be quite normal. A bottle fed baby needs a motion each day. This can be regulated by ensuring adequate quantities of fluids and sugars (see Motions, p. 491).

Napkin Rash.—To cure, the following action should be taken:

(1) Be sure baby is properly fed and having normal motions.

(2) Keep him clean and dry. Change his nappy immediately he is dirty and as soon as possible after he is wet. Wash buttocks frequently, dry carefully in the folds and creases, then powder.

(3) Apply zinc and castor oil ointment to protect buttocks at each nappy change.

(4) Put napkins to soak in cold water immediately they are removed. Wash them in hot Lux suds and rinse quite clean. Then put them in cold water, bring to the boil and boil for 5 to 10 minutes. Rinse and dry in fresh air.

When baby has a napkin rash the napkins should be boiled daily; otherwise once every 3–4 days is ample.

Scurf (or Cradle Cap) is a very common complaint. The best treatment is to rub the scalp with liquid paraffin. In districts where the water is hard, baby's head should not be washed with soap.

Thrush or White Mouth is usually due to dirty teats. It is quickly cured by applying to the mouth a 1 per cent. aqueous solution of gentian violet, which your doctor or clinic will supply.

Sticky Eye.—Promptly see the doctor, who will provide drops. Meanwhile, be sure baby lies with the bad eye near the pillow, and does not infect the good eye.

Sticky Navel.—The doctor should be consulted at once. Clean with surgical spirit and be careful baby's napkin does not rub the navel.

Catarrh is very prevalent among babies in some parts of the U.K. It can prevent a baby from feeding, as he can only suck if he can breathe through his nose. It may also wake him and disturb his sleep. If necessary, the doctor will prescribe nasal drops.

Teething can be a very painful process, especially if the gums are swollen and blistered. A bone ring or hard rusk to bite on will prove a comfort. During teething a baby may get bronchitis, diarrhœa, spots or napkin rash; he may go off his food and suffer from sleeplessness. If any of these symptoms occur, consult the doctor.

Circumcision is not now considered medically necessary unless baby is unable to pass urine. The necessary stretching should take place of its own accord, and frequent baths will maintain cleanliness. Parents wishing to have their baby circumcised for religious or other reasons should have it done in the first few weeks of life.

Protruding Umbilicus.—Unless this is very pronounced, it generally rights itself within a year or two

Nævi (Birth Marks).—Many small ones disappear within the first 2 years of life. They should be watched by the doctor if they are very large or protuberant, when plastic surgery may be advisable later on.

Congenital Abnormalities.—These vary from a tongue tie or extra toe to severe deformities like hare lips, malformations of the lip and congenital hearts. Every baby should be seen by a doctor as soon as possible after birth to determine that he is all right and, if not, for treatment.

Infectious Diseases only very rarely occur before 3 months of age and hardly ever when a baby is being breast fed. It is important, nevertheless, not to let a baby come in contact with infectious diseases which can make him very ill indeed.

THE TODDLER

Growing out of the baby stage into a self-possessed young person is an exciting experience for child and parents alike

" More please! " The easiest way to feed a toddler is in his own high chair—and preferably from his own pretty china

FROM 1 to 2½ years, the first half of the toddling stage, is a period of learning to grow up— mastering the arts of walking, eating by one's self, talking and behaving like a grown-up. It is a tremendously exciting time for both child and parents, but it also has its frustrations.

By 2½ years old your child will nearly have grown out of the baby stage and will have turned into quite a grown-up, self-possessed and reasonable little person. But don't be lulled into a sense of false security by this. He needs as much care and protection as he did in infancy—in some ways, more—but now he must be allowed to feel independent and to find things out for himself. It is up to you to help him to learn by experience without hurting himself, for this is the age when accidents so easily happen, both in the home and out in the streets.

1. *Patience.*—You will have to be *very* patient and also firm, but without exerting your authority by showing just how strong and all-powerful a grown-up can be. To do that only frustrates and upsets a child, who will gradually become more and more reasonable.

When a child is keen to do something obviously impossible, the best thing is to divert his attention. Dangerous things should be kept out of his way. But a parent who has reached the stage of being unable to remain patient any longer should say so. "I really cannot put up with this any more, so you will just *have* to do so and so," often makes a child see he will have to give in. That is far better than getting angry. Remember always that anger can transform the face of a loved

parent and be quite terrifying to a small child. It is therefore an emotion to which a parent must not give way under any circumstances in front of a child.

2. *Routine* can be broken occasionally, but certain broad principles should always be kept to:

(*a*) *Bedtime* should never be later than between 5 or 6 p.m., according to how tired the child is and what fits in with your household routine. It should always be a special time in a child's day—with a bath, probably supper, then some quiet games, or a story read aloud. Up to 5, a child needs at least 12 hours' sleep every night.

(*b*) *Daytime Rest.*—Some children get tired by 11 a.m. or noon and need their rest then; others can have it after lunch. The ideal solution is often for the toddler to have lunch at 12.30, then go to sleep while the rest of the family lunch in peace.

(*c*) *Meal Times* for toddlers can be fitted

499

in with the family. Eight o'clock breakfast, 1 p.m. lunch and 5 p.m. tea is often a satisfactory programme, with a drink for the child on waking, elevenses and a drink before bed. Here is another meal-time plan which fits in well with many households:

8 *a.m.*—*Breakfast:* Porridge; egg or kipper or bacon or sausage, toast and milk.

11 *a.m.*—Fruit juice and biscuits.

12.30.—*Lunch:* Meat and vegetables; pudding, fruit, etc; fruit juice to drink.

4 *p.m.*—*Tea:* Milk or fruit juice; biscuits or cake.

6 *p.m.*—*Supper* (in the nursery after a bath): Jelly or custard, etc., banana, milk, biscuits or cake or scone and butter.

New foods should be gradually introduced until, by the age of 5, the child is having a normal well-balanced diet, *plus at least* 1 *pint of milk per day.*

(*d*) *Exercise.*—The toddler takes exercise at every available opportunity; the problem is not to provide it but to keep the child *off* his feet occasionally. Usually the only time a toddler really sits is while eating a meal. To keep him off his feet, he should go out in the push-chair during the afternoon and have a chair of his own to make sitting more attractive.

(*e*) *Fresh Air.*—At least an hour out of doors every day should be the aim. The midday sleep can be taken out of doors in the pram, under cover if it is raining or snowing, otherwise with the baby just wrapped up against the cold. When it is fine, a child should, if possible, be out for part of the morning and all the afternoon, but *not running about alone.*

Sleeplessness

Nearly all toddlers seem to wake occasionally at night and take quite a long time to go back to sleep. The cause is generally cutting teeth. The best way to deal with the situation is to change the nappy, give a drink or a biscuit and reassure with a good cuddle, after which a child will often go back into the cot with a favourite teddy bear in his arms.

If a child is very wakeful and parents growing desperate, sedatives may be prescribed, but the sleeplessness generally clears up when the teeth are cut. A light may help children who do not like the dark, and it is good policy not to leave a child alone against his will for longer than, say, 10 minutes.

Talking and Walking

Most children learn to walk and talk without very much outside help and should not be forced to develop faster than their natural speed. A little encouragement to take the first steps is permissible; so is a certain amount of guidance in the pronunciation of words.

Clean Habits

This, like walking and talking, is something that should be allowed to develop gradually and at the child's own natural rate of progress. The following points must be borne in mind:

(1) Toddlers are often rather apprehensive of the pot.

(2) Napkins have had one use all the child's life, and he naturally sees no reason to stop soiling them so long as he is wearing them.

(3) It takes time to learn to control the bladder and bowels.

The pot should be introduced very early—provided baby takes to it calmly—and used regularly after each feed

mean—and the weather is warm enough—it is best to abandon nappies in the daytime as far as possible and have a pot always ready for use. Cleanliness of habits usually comes quite suddenly, in about 2 weeks somewhere about the age of 18 months to $2\frac{1}{2}$ years, generally 2 years.

Teeth Cleaning

It is important to teach a toddler to clean his own teeth. Get him a small soft toothbrush, dip it in Milk of Magnesia and encourage him to do as his parents do. He

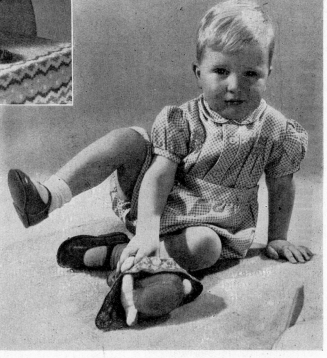

Cleaning your own teeth is great fun. Remember it should always be done last thing at night—*after* the last sweet has been chewed

The ideal outfit for active toddlers—the Clydella Buster Romper, with elasticated legs and blouse that buttons to knickers, is in checks of red, yellow, green and blue

The best solution is probably to introduce the pot at the very beginning, holding baby out regularly whenever changing his napkin and after each feed—provided he takes it placidly. If he rebels, then it should be stopped and tried again later.

It should be made clear to the child that his parents use the pot. He should be allowed to see them do so and should be encouraged to tell you when he has passed urine or had a motion, when of course his napkin should promptly be changed.

As soon as a baby can walk and is old enough really to understand what you

will find it great fun. Remember to do this last thing at night.

Holidays

Some small children love going away to stay, but the majority dislike a strange bedroom and any kind of change from their normal nightly routine. Daytime outings are, however, universally popular, and the best plan seems to be to avoid as much as possible any long periods away from home. If they are necessary, it is surprising how quickly a child adapts himself to different conditions.

Clothes

These should be as simple as possible, but there must be plenty of clothes to allow for frequent changes.

For play in winter a child should wear a woollen vest, a bodice or blouse, a jersey and dungarees, with either woollen pants or towelling pants or nappy and waterproof pants, wool socks and well-fitting shoes.

Shoes should last about 3 months for size, and it is absolutely essential that they should be properly fitted and bought from a shop where the child's feet can be X-rayed. A soft yet firm model should be chosen. (Jumping Jacks are excellent.) If a child turns his toes in, it may be necessary to buy shoes with a heel by the age of 2 years. It is in any case as well to get a doctor's advice if he does not walk properly by the age of 2 years. Be sure to discard shrunken socks; when they are too short they are as uncomfortable and as bad for growing feet as tight shoes.

For best wear: For girls a petticoat and dress and cardigan; for boys a Viyella or Clydella suit or cardigan.

For out of doors: Coat and leggings; hat or bonnet and gloves; a scarf adds cosiness. In cold weather use the pram, *not* a push-chair. Wellingtons, strong walking shoes and a raincoat for playing in the garden and walking in wet weather.

Night clothes: The great requirement is that they should be warm and easily washed. Sleeping suits with feet are excellent when the child is big enough to get out of bed; until then the baby nightgowns can usually still be worn, with a cardigan or sleeping bag in cold weather.

When the Toddler is Ill

When a toddler is ill, he is generally too miserable to be very much trouble. He sleeps in his cot or is only too anxious to be cuddled and comforted, but is fretful and in need of constant attention. When a child shows these symptoms, it is wise to call the doctor and take his advice. Give the child plenty to drink and only what he fancies to eat (unless forbidden by the doctor) and do not try to force food on him. The great thing to remember is that he does not know what it is all about and why he should feel as he does. Give him plenty of reassurance. Try to find toys and books that are interesting when he begins to cheer up. If you cannot keep him in bed, at least confine him to one room and avoid draughts (see chapter on Nursing a Sick Child).

Playing with Others

If there are older brothers and sisters in the family, the toddler will try to do everything they do and will learn a lot from them. An only child will not naturally play with other children, unless he is in their company habitually.

Where there is a younger baby, the toddler invariably has his nose put out of joint to start with. Some mind more than others and may even return to the bottle, try to suckle the breast or go back to nappies after having learned clean habits. These, however, are exceptional cases. The normal slight jealousy usually dies down of its own accord if Mother is fair to both. Excessive attention to either the new baby or the toddler is disastrous.

Education

At this age everything is an education. The child is learning every waking moment —from new impressions and discoveries made, from people and things he sees, and the things he is told. The only direct teaching that is either necessary or desirable is to answer his endless questions and allow the child to copy grown-up activities as much as possible.

(*a*) *"Helping Mummy."*—Boys and girls alike love to try their hands at making beds, cooking, sweeping, dusting, washing-up, digging in the garden, watering the flowers—almost anything they see their parents doing. This should be encouraged, and the child allowed to trot round the house, "helping" Mummy with the chores, or assisting Daddy in the garden, preferably using their own miniature brushes, brooms, watering cans, dusters, etc.

(*b*) *Animals, birds and flowers* are of the most absorbing interest to a child, who will learn far more by direct contact with them than by reading about them in books or hearing of them at second hand. From family pets he will learn to be kind and gentle and at the same time not to be afraid

A room of his own (above), charmingly furnished by Treasure Cot in miniature, but just like his parents', with fitted wardrobe and chest. Note the bed from which it's hard for a child to fall out

of animals. But do remember that at this age a child cannot be expected to look after his own puppy, kitten, chicken, hamster, tortoise or whatever it is. He will learn from his pet and love it dearly—but that won't prevent him forgetting to feed it.

(c) *Noise and Mess.*—Making a glorious mess and a deafening noise is also an essential part of a child's normal development, and so must not be prevented. Far better provide the wherewithal, then retire to a safe distance, leaving your child to enjoy himself in this perfectly natural way. Sand and water—either in the garden or at the seaside—are ideal; so are those constructional toys with pegs to be hammered into holes; and so are toy drums that a child can bang to his heart's content. Provide these for use in the garden or nursery and your furniture (and nerves) will be spared a good deal in the long run.

(d) *Reading.*—The first attempts to "read a book" are another form of copying what the grown-ups do. But if you let it take its normal course—starting with all-picture books, then reading stories aloud, and finally introducing simple books with

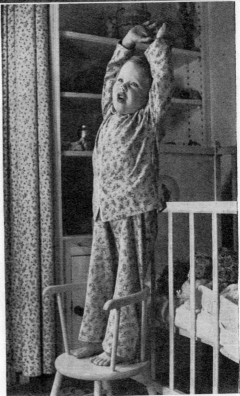

Tough enough to withstand all sorts of childish pranks, these trimly tailored pyjamas are made of Clydella for long wear, easy washing and ironing and cosy warmth

503

words and pictures—a bright child may be able to read quite well by the time he is 5 years. But those who cannot are not in the least backward and should not on any account be forced.

(*e*) *Lessons*.—Set lessons of any kind should certainly not begin for any child before the age of 5 years. Though school starts then, most of the first two years, from 5 to 7, is largely spent in play and other kindergarten activities, with the minimum of real classes. Serious school lessons do not therefore begin until the child is 7, which is quite soon enough.

However, soon after they are 2½ years, children seek out other children to play with, start copying one another and learning to share their toys and co-operate in their activities. By the time they are 4 years, they are craving for some kind of organised occupation. At this stage, a child may derive great benefit from going to a kindergarten or nursery school in the morn-ings, where the time will be spent with others of the same age, playing singing games, listening to stories, drawing, painting, dancing, etc.

Dancing lessons, if there are suitable classes near by, are excellent for children as young as 3 years. They improve deportment and teach a child to be light of foot—just at an age when the natural tendency is to be about as graceful as a young elephant. Swimming, too, may well start between 3 and 4 years, particularly if one of the parents is a keen swimmer and the child is already used to the water and not afraid of it.

Guarding against Accidents

All kinds of fires and electrical apparatus of every sort (wall plugs, lamps, switches, irons as well as heaters) *must* be guarded adequately in any house where there are children. The safest kind of fireguard is a strong wire-mesh one that fastens to the wall on both sides and completely covers the whole fireplace, preferably including gas taps or electric plugs.

Upstairs nursery w i n d o w s should also be barred to prevent the youngster attempting a dangerous voyage of discovery which might end in disaster. You can buy narrow painted steel bars—or make wooden ones—and fasten them across the window; or there are decorative enamelled steel window guards with coloured animal characters made in three sizes to fit various types of window.

Staircases and open street doors are other sources of possible danger. A portable safety gate—you can get them made of metal or strong string, adjustable to different widths—can be fitted quickly, at head or foot of stairs or across a doorway, as required.

It is never too early to instil into a child the need for constant care and watchfulness in the street. Teach him to hold your hand and to look both ways before crossing. Impress on him that he must never play in the street.

A practical protection—the Braddell Fireguard has spring clips at the top for attaching to the fireplace and a hinged door. Keeping warm in front is a musical teddy bear

SCHOOLDAYS AND ADOLESCENCE

For them it's an exciting adventure;
for their parents this is a testing time

WHEN a child starts at school, it is the parents who have the greater re-adjustment to make. They must accustom themselves to their child's new interests, his growing independence and the friends he makes outside the family circle.

They have to reorganise their evenings to allow for homework and their outings so that there shall be no late nights during the week. (Far too many parents fail in this respect, largely, no doubt, through sheer lack of thought.) Then there are examinations, school functions and difficulties over lessons to contend with, all of which can make the school years quite a problem for conscientious parents.

But not an insurmountable one, provided they face the fact from the start that school is going to play an increasingly large part in the child's life and that that is as it should be if he is to get the full benefit and enjoyment from his education. Whether you look back on your own schooldays with pleasure or not, most modern children thoroughly enjoy their schooling, and everything should be done at home to help them to do so.

Earn their Confidence

The sure way to lose a child's confidence is to criticise his new friends and refuse to accept them in your home, to interfere unnecessarily in his outside activities, or go to the other extreme and take no interest in them.

Suppose your child strikes up a friendship with a youngster of whom you disapprove? Don't on any account make a fuss about it; that will only stir up his sense of loyalty and his determination to be independent. Far better encourage him to bring the child home to tea, knowing that childhood friendships blow hot and cold with amazing rapidity, and the chances are

that by next week they will have forgotten all about one another.

Then, again, it may be something of a strain for mother to remember the football team's fixtures or all the details of the end-of-term play. But she will be amply rewarded for the effort by the trust and confidence of her children. Never fail to attend a school function (it is terrible to be the only child whose parents don't turn up), get to know the teachers and take an active part in the parent-teacher association at your child's school. Then if minor difficulties ever arise, you can so easily put them right by a tactful word to a teacher you know personally—which is so much better than letting some childish problem go unsolved, or writing an official letter to the Head.

Homework

This is a subject about which you will have to be sympathetic—but firm. Arrange for it to be done under proper conditions, in a warm room in winter with adequate lighting, away from noise and distractions. See that the right amount of time (no more, no less) is given, *not* late at night. If a child is really in difficulties with homework, the wise parent tries to help and explain—but does not on any account do it for him.

505

During term-time, evening outings to cinemas and parties and late television programmes should be restricted to weekends, however inconvenient this may be for the rest of the family. Remember, a child under 10 years old should be in bed between 6 and 7 p.m. every night, and over 10 should not be up later than 8 p.m. except on special occasions. Sleep starvation is every bit as bad as under-nourishment and much more prevalent among growing children these days.

Exams, now an established part of the educational system, must be taken in the child's—and the parents'—stride. Encourage the child to work hard for them, but do not allow them to become the cause of an emotional crisis. A child must never be allowed to feel that he has let his parents down if, after a reasonable effort, he does not pass an exam or win a coveted scholarship.

Permanent Teeth

During school years, between the ages of 6 and 12, a child gets his permanent teeth, all except the wisdom teeth, which usually come through between 17 and 25. Wisdom teeth sometimes cause trouble, but the rest of our 32 permanent teeth, unlike their predecessors, normally appear without pain or difficulty.

Adolescence

If early schooldays throw a strain on to parents, it is at the time of adolescence—from age 12 to 18—that they can do most to help their children by their tact, understanding and affection. Physical and emotional changes due to the action of developing hormones are taking place, transforming the child into an adult man or woman—and the process, as we all know if we care to think back, is a difficult one.

The physical signs are well known. A boy's voice breaks, hair begins to grow on face, chest, etc.; a girl starts her periods, her figure fills out and becomes more feminine, her breasts develop. Both sexes may be troubled with acne and obesity at this time, due to hormonal causes.

But an even greater strain is imposed by the emotional changes. These manifest themselves in a dawning interest in sex, in early love affairs or romantic "pashes" or people of the same sex, usually teachers or prefects at school. To make matters worse, all this occurs at a time when young people are busy taking important exams, going for interviews that may affect their future

Parents must be sympathetic but firm about homework—and never do it for their children

Display boards on the wall are a novel feature of the room (left) in pale grey with accents of cherry and blue. One Vantona counterpane in blue with nursery figures, is on the bed, two more make matching curtains

Dream room for the schoolboy (below)— tiered bunks save space, and space ships in colour adorn the wallpaper, which is from the Crown range

THEY WILL WANT TO COME HOME TO THESE ROOMS

BOYS and girls *want* to spend their leisure at home as they grow up, if they have attractive rooms of their own from the beginning, where they can entertain their friends and pursue their own hobbies. Besides, space permitting, it gives the rest of the family much more peace

Younger children will love a huge blackboard and one of the lovely nursery wallpapers from the Crown range, with designs for them to copy

careers, leaving school and starting in jobs —and longing to launch out on their own as adults before they are physically and emotionally quite ready.

At this transition stage, a boy or girl needs all the love, understanding and wise guidance that parents can possibly provide. More than that, they need to be prepared for these changes, both physical and mental, before they happen.

When and how do good parents tell their children what used to be known as " the facts of life"? It is, of course, quite impossible to lay down hard and fast rules for so intensely personal and individual a matter. The great thing, surely, is not to leave it too late or the child will have gained his own sketchy information from less reliable sources; nor to try and force knowledge on an infant far too young to understand it. Neither should parents shelve the duty, on the grounds that such subjects are now dealt with in school classes.

The best practical compromise is never to try and keep a child in ignorance, however young; to answer his questions honestly and truthfully and to talk perfectly frankly in front of him from the start. In that way, and by letting him see both parents without clothes on, you gradually build up a background of sex knowledge until, at the age of 10 or 11, a boy or girl should be in full possession of the facts and quite prepared for the personal application of adolescence.

At this time of adolescence parents must exercise all their powers of persuasion to prevent a son or daughter from becoming overtired and overwrought. Boys tend to get moody, silent and irritable; girls to burst into sudden tears or develop a convenient headache to get out of schoolwork. Both will come home in the evenings too worn out to help mother or even talk politely, but quite prepared to go dancing into the small hours or to play strenuous games with their friends.

The old bedtime rules cannot, obviously, be enforced with 'teenage girls and boys, nor evening dates prohibited, yet they badly need 8 to 10 hours' sleep a night. The best a parent can do is persuade a son or daughter to cut down on late nights to one or two a week —preferably at the week-end—and to concentrate on making the home surroundings so attractive that they like to be there and to bring their friends home.

A mother who takes a helpful and practical interest in her daughter's clothes and make-up will gain her lifelong trust and affection, as well as helping her over a difficult period of adjustment. A girl will stay in and get a good rest if she is given a pretty, essentially feminine bed-sitting room of her own; and a boy, if nobody minds his playing his favourite gramophone records all the evening.

Watching their Health

It is important, too, at this stage that they get a good balanced diet, with plenty of fresh fruit and vegetables, supplemented by vitamins A, D and C in tablet form to build up resistance to infection and provide calcium for bone-building and good strong teeth.

Exercise, fresh air and enough rest are the real essentials. Lack of sufficient exercise is usually the direct cause of dysmenorrhœa (or painful periods) from which so many adolescent girls suffer. The cure is not to stay in bed with a hot water bottle, but a more spartan one—to go for a good brisk walk or play an interesting game. If the pain prevents a girl from sleeping, a couple of aspirins may be taken at bedtime and, of course, if the trouble persists despite reasonable exercise, she should see her doctor.

CHILDREN'S MEALS

*Some clever disguises are sometimes needed to persuade
youngsters to eat what's good for them*

IN planning suitable meals for children of
all ages, the important thing to remember
is that the object of their food is to *build*
as well as to *sustain*. Youthful bodies are
growing all the time. Whether this progress
goes on apace depends entirely upon us.
For, as Walter de la Mare puts it,

> "It's a very odd thing—
> As odd as can be—
> That whatever Miss T. eats
> Turns into Miss T."

A WELL-BALANCED DIET

The chief constituents of a well-balanced
diet are: proteins for growth and repair;
carbohydrates (sugar and starch) for heat
and energy; fats for heat, tissue-building,
nerve-protecting, and, in the case of butter, egg-yolk, cod-liver oil, cream and other
animal fats, for certain very valuable vitamins which prevent rickets. Add to these the
vitamins that are found in fresh fruit and
vegetables, which provide protection
against infection, etc., and we have all the

ingredients of a really well-chosen diet for
any growing child.

How to balance these ingredients so that
a small son or daughter does not get too
much of one kind of food or too little of
another is often a puzzle. A great many
children, for instance, eat too much carbohydrate and not enough protein; others are
overfed with fats, and their worried parents
wonder why they haven't more appetite; a
few children are given too much protein and
suffer from over-taxed digestive organs.

A well-balanced diet is perfectly possible without any suspicion of the "faddi-
ness" which makes school life difficult for
a child. However, the wise mother must be
ready to study and respect little variations
in appetite even in infancy, and to help her
children to look upon their meals as a
pleasure rather than a duty. Despite this,
she must not lose sight of the importance
of milk in a child's diet and should make
sure that, whether as a drink or in puddings, soups or egg or fish dishes, an average of 1 to $1\frac{1}{2}$ pints is taken every day.

The Toddler's Breakfast

When the toddler is about 1 year old his breakfast should contain some protein and not be confined to carbohydrates only. Most children can have eggs three times a week quite safely—either coddled, poached or scrambled. If a child really dislikes eggs or they cause biliousness, a little fish or crisp bacon can be given instead. Cereal should be omitted entirely or very much reduced in quantity when the child is having egg, bacon or fish for breakfast; if not, there is always a danger that he will eat a large amount and leave no room for the protein dish that follows.

The most suitable kinds of fish for small children are whiting, plaice, sole (lemon or witch are lighter than Dover soles, as well as cheaper), fresh haddock, Devon hake. Cod is heavy, halibut rather too close in texture. Small quantities of kipper or bloater can be spread on toast for the toddler and are very nourishing. Sardines, also spread on toast or in sandwiches between brown bread and butter, are excellent and usually very popular; the bones and skin should be removed.

Cheese—one of the most highly concentrated protein foods there is—is recommended by doctors and clinics for children from 9 months onwards because it is rich in calcium, which is essential for forming strong healthy teeth and bones. At 9 months a child should have his cheese grated and sprinkled on bread and butter at tea-time. From 18 months onwards, it is quite safe to give a finger of cheese to chew, provided he chews it well.

Some children prefer savoury to sweet dishes, and here a cheese-flavoured white sauce often transforms an otherwise unpopular meal into a favourite; it is also a good way of getting more milk into the meals.

Food unsuitable for Children under 5

Pork, veal, tea, coffee, over-ripe or under-ripe fruit, fruits with seeds or pips, cakes containing currants, and fried foods generally are unsuitable for small children.

Some cannot take bananas, pears or plums; sweet oranges and ripe grapes are the safest fruits for little people; even apples (in most cases so wholesome) sometimes prove indigestible. It is most important to peel oranges and other fruits before letting children handle them; the peel is very unlikely to be free from dust and germs, and cases of thread-worm trouble (and possibly worse infections) are often due to children holding unwashed and unpeeled oranges, bananas, apples, etc., and then sucking their fingers. Ripe bananas are excellent.

Those who do not like Milk

Children aged 2 to 5 are growing very fast and plenty of "growth" foods are needed. It is rather a temptation to let them "fill up" with lots of bread and butter, but unless proteins are also given they will lack muscle and stamina. Those who do not care for milk as a drink will often take it at their tea-supper meal in the form of junket (coloured pink with a cherry on the top for preference), or milk jelly or blancmange in an attractive colour and turned out of a pretty mould. Some of the nicest moulds in which to make puddings can now be bought with animals, fish, flowers, etc., on top. One of these has two rabbits on the top: you make a little chocolate-coloured custard or blancmange (just enough to fill in the shapes of the rabbits), then fill up the rest of the mould with another coloured pudding. When you turn it out, there are two brown bunnies sitting on top, just inviting a child to eat his pudding.

A Week's Sample Dinners for a 5-year-old and over

Sunday: Roast beef or mutton, potatoes and vegetables. Stewed fruit and custard. If the adults are having fruit tart, a small portion of pastry, but not too much.

Monday: Vegetable soup (lentil, pea, artichoke, tomato), with sippets of toast or light suet dumpling, according to time of year. Baked apple and custard.

Tuesday: Fish baked in oven with a little milk and buttered paper over it, with potatoes and/or cauliflower. Stewed prunes and sponge fingers.

Wednesday: Irish stew (neck of mutton, onions, carrots, potatoes, rice or pearl barley). Junket and jelly.

Thursday: Steamed chicken, rabbit or tripe, with potatoes and vegetables (onions, in the case of tripe, but remember to bring them to the boil and throw away the first water after five minutes:

this makes the onions more digestible and less likely to spoil the colour of the tripe). Sponge pudding (steamed) with jam.

Friday: Fish, steamed or made into a fish pudding, with brown bread and butter as a change from potatoes. Apple charlotte.

Saturday: Fresh minced beef (cooked in a double saucepan for 1½ hours and the gravy thickened slightly before serving), with potatoes and green vegetables. Treacle pudding.

In planning dinners it is important that the first and second courses should supplement and not echo one another. For instance, a steamed pudding should not be given after a meat course containing suet or starch; and custard should not be given after a first course containing eggs or milk.

Milk puddings may be served with fruit instead of custard; taken alone they are apt to be constipating.

SPECIAL DIETS

Children who tend to constipation need careful feeding. They should have very little white bread, solid cake, pudding, rice, etc. They need plenty of wholemeal bread, fruit, honey, black treacle, green vegetables, onions, leeks and fats such as butter and dripping. Very often they do better on diluted than on whole milk. Plenty of water should be drunk between meals and everything must be thoroughly chewed.

The bilious child should be kept off all fatty and greasy foods (such as dumplings, pastry, suet puddings and rich iced cakes) and should take a little barley sugar after meals.

Ideal for children, this PVC "embroidered" plastic mat will sponge easily, won't stretch or break, comes in cream, pastel blue or green in the Bex range of household equipment

The child who is subject to diarrhœa should never be given food containing "roughage," such as husks, seeds, pips or currants. His diet should be as bland and as unirritating as possible. But the mere appearance of certain foods (such as spinach or carrot) in a child's motions does not mean that it disagrees with him; so long as the motions are otherwise healthy-looking, it only means that this particular food has helped to carry off waste products of the bowel, as it was meant to do.

CHILDREN'S RECIPES

Most of the simpler dishes for which recipes are to be found in the Basic Cookery chapters of this book are perfectly suitable for children, but here are a few very simple "nursery specials" which may be helpful.

Oat Jelly is very useful for babies when first introduced to cereals. Mix 2 level tablespoonfuls of Robinson's Patent Groats to a smooth paste with cold water, add a pinch of salt, make up to ½ pint by stirring in boiling water. Boil gently for ½ hour or cook in double saucepan for 1 hour. Serve warm with a little milk poured over it.

Barley Jelly.—Make in the same way, using Robinson's Patent Barley instead of Groats. This can be given alternately with Oat Jelly, and in summer weather is rather less heating.

Raw Beef Juice (useful as a pick-me-up

The smiling pastry faces on these Jack o' Lanterns just invite young people to taste and see what's inside—a nourishing vegetable and cheese mixture

in children's ailments or for delicate or anæmic babies and toddlers).—Cut ¼ lb. steak into small pieces, place in a cup, just cover with cold water and leave for an hour. Then squeeze out the juice through a piece of clean boiled muslin, add salt and serve warm. If made hot, the albumen in the beef coagulates, and the appearance as well as the value of the raw beef juice will be spoilt.

Steamed Custard.—Heat ½ pint milk and beat it up with 1 egg and a dessertspoonful sugar. Pour into a deep soup-plate and stand over a saucepan of boiling water until just set. Don't shake or stir it while it is setting. This is a good dish to make while boiling potatoes or vegetables, as it can cook over the saucepan.

Chicken (Steamed).—Pour a breakfast-cupful of water into a saucepan, add chopped carrot and onion and a little salt. Bring to the boil, then gently lay the chicken on top of the vegetables, cover closely and simmer for about 1½ hours for a small chicken or until the breast begins to split. Care must be taken that the liquid

does not boil too quickly or the pan may burn dry; the juices of the chicken and vegetables should combine with the small quantity of water to make a nourishing broth and the chicken itself, cooked in the minimum of water, will have a special flavour and food value.

Jack o' Lanterns.—This is an attractive way of presenting vegetables and cheese to children:

4 oz. flour	½ lb. mixed cooked
Pinch of baking	vegetables
powder	Cheese sauce (see
1 oz. margarine	Sauces chapter)
1 oz. lard	

Make the flour, baking powder and fats into pastry (see Pastry chapter). Mix the vegetables with the cheese sauce, season well and place in individual fireproof dishes. Roll out the pastry and cut into circles the size of the dishes, then make them into faces with holes for eyes, nose and mouth. Put the pastry faces on top of the vegetable mixture, brush lightly with milk or egg, and bake in a moderate oven until pastry is crisp and golden.

Banana Chocolate Pudding combines two of most children's favourite flavours and looks as good as it tastes

Wholemeal Cheese Biscuits (20–30 biscuits)

2 oz. wholemeal flour
Good pinch of salt
Pinch of Cayenne
   pepper
½ oz. margarine

4 oz. finely grated
   Cheddar cheese
Approximately 1
   tablespoonful cold
   water

Sieve the flour and seasonings into a bowl and rub in the margarine. Add the Cheddar cheese and mix well. Add sufficient cold water to bind, and knead the dough firmly. Roll out to ⅛-in. thick on a lightly floured board, prick with a fork and cut into fancy shapes. Place on a lightly greased baking sheet and bake towards the top of a hot oven for 6–8 minutes until a golden brown. Cool on a wire tray. These biscuits will keep well in an airtight tin.

Banana Chocolate Pudding (for 4–6)

2 oz. self-raising flour
1 oz. cocoa
½ teaspoonful golden
   raising powder
2 oz. castor sugar
1½ oz. One-Minute
   Quaker Oats

1¾ oz. shredded suet
4 bananas
1 egg
3 teaspoonfuls coffee
   powder
¾ tablespoonful milk

Try Wholemeal Cheese Biscuits with milk for nursery supper and see how quickly they disappear

Sift flour, cocoa and raising powder. Stir in sugar, Quaker oats and suet. Mash 2 bananas and mix with the coffee powder. When blended, beat in the egg and the milk. Stir into the dry ingredients.

Put the mixture into a greased basin and cover with a piece of greased paper and a pudding cloth. Put basin into a saucepan with boiling water, cover and boil for 3 hours. Turn out on to a hot dish and use the two remaining bananas for decoration.

FOOD PREJUDICES

Most children have a strong prejudice against fat and greens. Even those who eat them up without complaint at home will start leaving them on their plates when they have meals at school and see other children doing it. In contrast, most youngsters like anything crisp.

It therefore pays, when planning nursery meals, to try to disguise the unpopular foods and make everything as crisp as possible, so that it will be eaten and enjoyed. A pastry crust makes meat much more attractive to children, and steak pie is therefore a popular dish. A crumbly top has the same effect in making the less-favoured types of stewed fruit acceptable. Fat will often be eaten with gusto in the form of dripping spread on hot toast or when used to fry bread.

TEMPTING A SICK CHILD

A single flower in an egg-cup or glass makes a bedtime tray more interesting. Always see that the cloth is speckless, even if it involves frequent washing. Many plastic cloths are now available. Small children appreciate attractive china with familiar nursery figures on it. To reach the picture at the bottom of a plate a child will often eat everything on it, even if he is not hungry.

Many ordinary dishes are more attractive if disguised thus:

Egg Flip (a raw egg beaten up in a glass of milk with sugar) can be served with straws to help it down. Given a special name, such as Creamade, its contents can be disguised.

Scrambled Egg is easier to eat served on thin bread and butter instead of toast.

White Fish is more interesting if pressed into a small mould and steamed lightly, served with white sauce or butter.

Potatoes should be mashed, rather than plain boiled, unless new, with butter.

Jellies dissolved in a little boiling water and then made up to round quantity with whipped evaporated milk are nourishing and different. Fruit juice may be added in the case of such flavours as orange and lemon.

Black Currant Purée whipped up with white of egg and served on a little sponge cake in the bottom of a small glass dish is light and easy to eat.

Soups can be made more nourishing by the addition of milk.

Vegetables.—Sieved vegetables are far easier to digest when a patient is ill. If there is no time to sieve fresh ones, excellent varieties can be bought ready in small tins.

Helpings.—Never serve too much on a plate at a time. There is nothing more calculated to put a patient off eating anything at all. Second helpings can always be provided if they are wanted.

A sick child will eat his meals if you serve them daintily and make them look and taste exciting and unusual

AMUSING SICK CHILDREN

Some suggestions for games to be played
during convalescence without getting out of bed

WHEN a child is really ill, it is not difficult to keep him in bed, but once recovery begins, the trouble starts for mother. Many parents are reluctant to allow anything that makes a mess of the bed, in case the doctor or a visitor arrives. This difficulty can easily be overcome by putting a really large dust-sheet over the bed; it can be picked up by its four corners and the bed will be free of "bits."

Pop in to see the child very frequently. He will play happily by himself as long as he knows you are quite near.

Plasticine, Glitter-wax, etc. —A small quantity will keep a child happy for a long time. A protective covering for the bed is advisable! Suggest that he or she makes models of members of the family, or of the house, or some known object.

Jig-saw and other puzzles provide hours of entertainment, provided the child has a large tray or bedtable to spread them on. This can be lifted off the bed if the doctor comes unexpectedly

Cutting-out. —Quite small children may be given a pair of blunt scissors and old magazines or papers to cut up. Cutting-out books, too, are quite inexpensive. For older children, allow paste or gum and suggest that they make a scrap-book, either for themselves or for some local hospital. Paste and gum are now available in tubes.

Knitting. —Many small children love to try and knit as their mother does. Spend a little time in showing them how to do this —with large needles to begin with, and thick wool—and you will be well rewarded.

Patience. —Older children will amuse themselves for hours with games of patience. Many adults have pet patience games, which should be carefully stored against a day when your child is in bed.

Postcard Books. —Keep all the picture postcards you receive, then when your child is in bed, buy a postcard book and let him put them in. Thereafter, you will

find that any future day in bed is partly spent in reorganising the order of the cards.

Book-making. —Suggest that an older child should write a story for you, illustrating it at the same time. An exercise book or old paper block is ideal for the purpose. A pleasant occupation and good for composition, too.

Picture Cards. —Although you can buy these ready to work, you can also make them. Take an ordinary plain card or piece of very thin cardboard. Draw or trace a bold picture of a house, dog, cat or other familiar object. Make small holes with a thick pin or needle at regular intervals round the outline. Supply a blunt needle and coloured cotton or silk. Let the child work the outline, going in and out of the holes.

Weaving. —Cut equal numbers of strips $\frac{1}{4}$ in. wide and 12 in. long in two different coloured papers, which should be shiny and fairly substantial. Fasten one end of

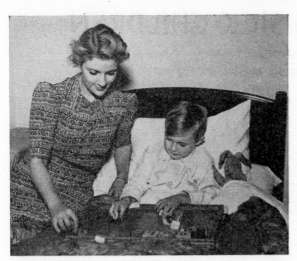

The great thing is that mummy should be close at hand and willing to stop for a minute every so often

half the strips, alternate colours, to a board or tray with adhesive sticky paper and let the child weave a mat by putting in the other strips alternately. Ultimately the ends can be bound with adhesive sticky paper.

Raffia Work.—An older child can do simple raffia work by plaiting equal numbers of strands, say six in each of three groups, joining on lengths until the whole is big enough to make a mat. Then coil, catching every $\frac{1}{8}$ in. or so. In this way, pretty table mats can be made which the child will be glad to give as Christmas or birthday presents.

Ball-making. — Keep all your odd scraps of wool. Make two rings of cardboard, an inch or two inches in width with a centre hole about two inches in diameter. Holding the circles together, start with the first ball of wool and wind in and out over the circles, covering

Being read to is one of the unforgettable pleasures of being ill when you are a child, but small people usually like their stories short or in brief instalments

them equally. When the first ball is exhausted, start on the next, until the ring is quite full and no more will go in. Holding firmly, cut through the wool and push the rings gently downwards but not right off. Tie right round the middle of the wool and fasten off firmly. The rings can then be removed and the ball fluffed out to the right shape.

Drawing. — Coloured chalks never fail to keep a child amused for quite a time. Newspaper and magazine advertisements provide admirable pictures for colouring without the expense of buying books for the purpose. A large book of plain paper on which to scribble is always appreciated.

Reading.—Most children like to be read to or, if they are able, to read. They also appreciate stories made up by the grown-ups and told to them. Better still, start such a story, then leave them to think up an instalment by the time you next come into the sickroom. You then add some more to the story, which turns into a serial full of surprises.

Box puzzles, requiring a steady hand and considerable dexterity, are also popular.

Put away some of the child's Christmas and birthday presents—especially books, jig-saws and other games and toys suitable for use in bed—and bring them out during convalescence.

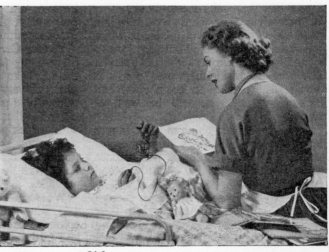

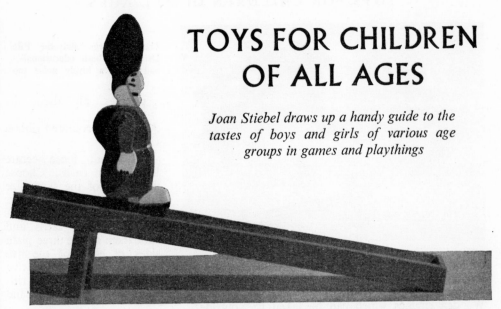

TOYS FOR CHILDREN OF ALL AGES

Joan Stiebel draws up a handy guide to the tastes of boys and girls of various age groups in games and playthings

The Walking Soldier needs no winding up but marches down the slope on his own. Made by disabled workers and obtainable, with many other lovely toys, from Homebound Craftsmen

TOYS have a fascinating habit of reflecting current tastes, interests and social customs. Victorian children played with elegantly dressed dolls or bowled their hoops in the park. In contrast, modern little girls like nothing better than to help in the house, cooking on miniature stoves, sweeping, cleaning and ironing with scale-model equipment, while their brothers are occupied chiefly with aircraft, tanks and equipment for conquering outer space.

Educational toys, made on highly scientific lines and designed to develop the child's faculties, simultaneously teach and amuse the very young. For older children, the constructional kit provides interest and mental stimulation.

But for many parents—and certainly for proud uncles, aunts and godparents—it is often a problem to choose the right kind of toy for the correct age group.

The following is a general guide. Often toys are suitable for more than one age. In these cases it is suggested for the youngest age group when it is likely to be appreciated, though it may well be suitable for an older child.

UNDER 1 YEAR

A child of this age is not interested in toys as such, but these are suitable gifts:

Rattles. Small birds, bunches of bells, etc., to hang on pram. Small soft toys.

An easy toy to make is:

Pram String

You will require:

¾ yd. hat elastic
20 coloured beads 1 in. from end to end. Plastic beads are best. If wooden, be sure that the paint will not lick off

Turn in 3½ in. at either end of elastic and sew firmly in place. Make a large knot at the top of one loop and thread beads along elastic. Make a second large knot at the top of the other loop. The string can now be fastened across a pram and will provide a great deal of amusement for the 9-month to 1-year-old child.

AGES 1–3 YEARS

This is when educational toys are first appreciated and they will last for several years. When choosing soft toys, stick to small ones, because children of this age love to carry their toys about but cannot lift a huge one.

Soft Toys.—Small animals and soft unbreakable dolls.

Books.—Small sized with brightly

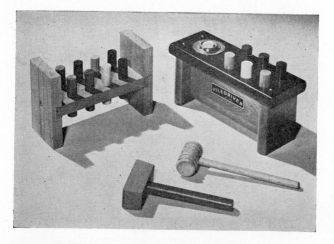

Hammer Pegs and the Pile Driver are both educational— and make a lovely noise too

coloured pictures, easy for child to hold. Rag books.

Educational and Constructional Toys.— Wooden engines which can be taken to pieces. Pyramid of coloured shapes. Building beakers, barrels and baby boxes, all of which fit together or into each other. Brick trolley containing coloured bricks (this can be pulled—an added attraction). Screw toy, consisting of wooden nuts which go on and off a rod. Screwboard (pegs screw into holes). Stepped abacus; large coloured beads which thread on to stout pegs. Hammer pegs, coloured pegs with mallet to knock them into a board (making a noise is such fun!).

General.—Small horses, trucks and cars to push or pull. Rubber or plastic animals to float in the bath. A most attractive duck is available, which quacks when squeezed without plug and floats when the plug is inserted. Sand tray (this is a large toy and is really only suitable where there is either a garden or nursery). Sand tools, rubber buckets and scoops. Pedal car. Nursery rocker. Miniature telephone. Rubber or plastic balls. Moving toys—i.e. those which move without being wound up. Homebound Craftsmen of 25a Holland Street, London, W.8, make a most attractive Walking Soldier, and all their merchandise is made by disabled workers.

Toys to make

Christmas Card Book

You will need:

20 old Christmas cards with bright, gay pictures, all about the same size.

A length of coloured ribbon

Gum

Take out loose centre leaves from cards. Choose five cards of the same size for the leaves of the book. Cut the pictures from the remaining fifteen cards and stick them on the three plain sides of each of the five cards. Make two holes in fold of the five cards, insert inside one another. Put ribbon through holes and tie firmly on the outside.

Reel Stick

You will require:

1 flat cork about $1\frac{1}{2}$–2 in. in diameter and $\frac{1}{4}$–$\frac{1}{2}$ in. in depth

A pointed stick, such as a wooden meat skewer, but thin enough to go through the centre of a cotton reel

4 or 5 empty cotton reels

Paint suitable for children's toys

Strong glue

Drive the stick into the cork. Pull out again, cover thinly with glue and reinsert. Leave till dry. Meanwhile, paint in different colours as many cotton reels as will go on to the stick. Leave until dry. Then put on stick (which may also be painted if liked). A child will get hours of amusement from taking the reels off and putting them back.

AGES 3–5 YEARS

At this age a child needs games and books to stimulate his imagination. He also begins to enjoy being read to and will quickly repeat familiar stories and verses. He will begin to learn numbers, and at about four, his alphabet.

Soft Toys.—Dolls, particularly soft ones in uniforms or fancy dress. There is a good and very inexpensive make which is unbreakable and small enough for a little child to handle; another which is soft, feels rather like human skin and can be bathed. Leather and felt animals, particularly the more unusual types such as those seen at a zoo. Small glove puppets which the child can work himself (Homebound Craftsmen have a good variety).

Books.—Small, with stories or verses suitable for reading aloud, with bright illustrations. Nursery rhyme books. Alphabet books with big letters and pretty pictures of objects beginning with each letter.

Educational and Constructional Toys.— Posting box with different shapes to post in the appropriate holes. Large bricks made of plain wood and obtainable in big canvas bags—not cheap, but they will be used by children for several years to come. Multibuilder and connector, from both of which various lorries, trucks, cars and boats can be made and supplementary sets are available. Screw bench which has wooden pegs to screw in and wooden implements. Minibrix rubber bricks which press-stud together; there are various sets, and this again is a toy which can be supplemented. Constructional clock made of wood with numbers to peg into its face. Wooden numbers. Nursery symbols—pictures of everyday objects and toys. Plasticine or one of the other modelling materials. Puzzle numerals, consisting of two pieces, one having numbers on it, the other the appropriate number of pieces; they are jig-saw cut and fit together. Cutout alphabets and numbers. Picture blocks. Percussion instruments, such as cymbals, Indian bells, tambourine, etc. Cards to embroider. Paper weaving. Baby jig-saw puzzles which are very thick and have few pieces.

General. — Simple painting books with crayons to colour. Children's brushes, carpet - sweeper, vacuum cleaner. Clothes for dolls.

Any youngster with a garden—or a window box—would love these miniature garden tools and packets of seeds

Doll's cot and pram. Doll's house and furniture. Cooking stove and pans. Grocery or other shop. Balls of all sorts. Small cars and clockwork trains. "Hopping" toys worked by squeezing a bulb. Junior driver, a miniature driving wheel which fixes by suction to any flat surface. Postman's outfit. Tricycle. Playhouse. Small wheelbarrow and garden tools (if the child has any garden in which to play). Small wooden or pottery animals—a collection for a child's room is a fascinating hobby. Small wooden merry-go-round, rocking cradles and jumping animals.

Toys to make

Sewing Cards

You will need:

6 pieces of thin card approximately 7 in. long by 5 in. wide.

A stiletto or other sharp instrument to make holes

Six bold designs of animal, flower, house, etc., about 1 in. smaller than the card all round

Embroidery silks

A crewel needle

Place each design in centre of a card. Prick through to card with stiletto at intervals of about $\frac{1}{8}$ in., making sure you go right through the card. When you have done the whole design, remove and draw a line lightly from hole to hole to make complete outline. Pack in nice box, with silks and needles in separate compartment

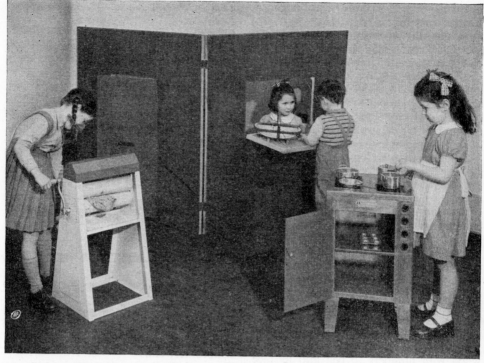

Scale models of domestic equipment are always favourites. The wringer and electric stove shown above, and the toys on the opposite page are from Paul and Marjorie Abbatt

(made by putting in small pieces of cardboard as divisions). Boys as well as girls enjoy this work.

Paper Weaving

You will need:

6 sheets of shiny coloured paper—different colours

6 squares of thick white paper or card 6–8 in. square

Reel of Sellotape, either clear or in one of the colours of the paper

Cut the coloured paper into strips $\frac{1}{4}$ in. wide. Pack strips, white paper and Sellotape into box.

To make mats, the child takes a square of paper, lays alternate strips on it until it is covered, secures tops of strips with length of Sellotape and then weaves alternate colours in and out across, finishing each mat with a strip of Sellotape at the sides and bottom.

Picture Dominoes

You will need:

8 copies of each of seven small pictures approximately the same size (advertisements, grocery packets, etc., provide suitable pictures)

28 pieces of cardboard big enough to take two pictures each

Gum

Make your dominoes in the same way as an ordinary set. On one card stick two of the same picture (for the double) in each group and then one with each of the other pictures. Stick firmly. Pack in a small box, sticking two spare pictures—if you have them—on the outside. The game is played exactly as dominoes.

AGES 5–8 YEARS

During this time, the child goes from nursery to school, and his interests develop accordingly. At first, he will want whatever toy happens to be popular amongst his school friends: then he will start reading easy books, providing they are sufficiently interesting. Boys will develop an interest in sport; girls start sewing and other handicrafts. Educational toys are replaced by ordinary schooling, but hobbies are very much to the fore. At seven, collecting probably starts in earnest, and stamps, wild flowers, coins, autographs, cigarette cards and photographs will all have their place.

Soft Toys.—Larger animals. Dolls.

Books.—Easy stories and books with scenic panoramas. Large print is important as, at about six, the child should start reading himself. More advanced books for reading to the younger ones such as the "Thomas the Tank Engine" series, many of Enid Blyton's and Beatrix Potter's books; Alison Uttley's "Little Grey Rabbit" series and other similar authors. Annuals—there are many suitable for young children. A subscription to one of the better "Comics" or other children's papers. From about seven, books on the child's particular interest—for the stamp collector plenty of books are available, and a well-illustrated book on wild flowers would delight the would-be naturalist. Cutting-out books of models, such as farmyards.

Constructional Toys.—Wooden outfits for model making. Meccano or Trix. Paint box with brushes and book of blank paper. Painting books (an inexpensive box of paints is far better than a very good one at this age). Gummed shapes to make pictures. Jig-saw puzzles. Raffia sets. Bead-threading outfits.

Games.—Card games such as Happy Families, Patience cards, Snakes and Ladders, race games, Tiddlywinks, Ludo, Wordmaking and Wordtaking, Pik-a-Styk, Questions and Answers—there are many versions of this game—Dominoes, Chess, Halma, Draughts, Table Football, Table Croquet, Cricket Bat, Tennis Racquet,

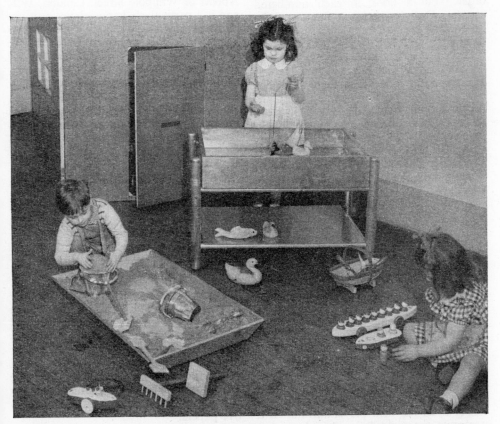

Where there is a garden or a playroom big enough, a sand tray for making castles or a bath for sailing boats will provide hours of pleasure

Football, Diabolo. Compendium of various games.

General.—Album for stamps or autographs. Kite, skipping rope, cut-out models to make. Blunt scissors. Outfits for dressing-up. Model boats, aeroplanes, farmyard with animals, cars and garage, Noah's ark. Indoor fireworks. Doll's tea set. Puppets. Model theatre. Model railway.

Toys to make

Number Board

You will need:

A pastry or other similar board
12 hooks that screw in
Black paint or Indian ink
Rubber rings

Divide the board into twelve squares by drawing or painting thick black lines. Number each square *not* in consecutive order. Put a hook in each numbered square. Drill two holes at the top of the board and put in strong cord or wire to hang it.

Each player has three rings and, standing 6–9 ft. away (according to age), throws. The score is totalled each time, and whoever reaches 100 or any other agreed number first wins. To make it a little more difficult, the numbers can be scored only in order—i.e. 1, 2, 3, etc.—and whoever gets a ring on to No. 12 first wins.

Another alternative is to omit the hooks when making the board and play the game with darts.

"Get-it-in"

You will need:

One ½-dozen size egg-box (the cardboard container kind with six holes)
1 ping-pong ball
Paint

Paint the outside of the box. Number each of the holes with bold figures.

To play the game, the players take turns, standing about 6–9 ft. from the box (according to age). The ball has to be thrown into each of the holes in turn from 1 to 6. If it does not go in, or goes into the wrong hole, the next player throws. If it goes into the right hole, the player has another turn, and so on until he misses. The first player to get the ball into all six holes wins.

AGES 8–10 YEARS

Although in recent years there has been a tendency for girls to share their brothers' toys, at this age the sexes begin to develop individual tastes.

Books.—On hobbies, natural history, sport, adventure, family and school stories.

Constructional Toys.—*For girls:* Equipment for sewing, knitting, weaving and easy handicrafts. Toy sewing-machine which works—beware of those which do chain stitch, as this comes undone at once. Basket-making. Workbasket. Toy-making kit. *For boys:* All kinds of model-making kit and fretwork outfits. Carpentry tools. Box of oddments for carpentry, which, in common with many other items mentioned here, is available from Paul & Marjorie Abbatt of Wimpole Street, London, W.1, and is a particularly happy choice as it has all manner of odd pieces of wood, etc., to keep a young carpenter happy. Multiple hammer (handle contains other tools). *For both boys and girls:* Toy typewriter. Printing outfits. Interlocking and other puzzles. Passe-partout and chemistry sets.

Games.—Almost all games mentioned for previous age group, plus Mah Jongg, Bagatelle, Miniature Billiards, Contact Quiz, Solitaire, Kan-u-Go, Jokari, Stilts, Roller skates.

General.—Model railways and aircraft. Jet-propelled toys. Space gun and ship. Working models, such as mechanical cranes, electrically driven cars, washing machines, tilting lorries. Pocket compass.

AGES 10–13 YEARS

Toys are now very largely replaced by definite hobbies and special interests. An additional truck for a model railway will be far more acceptable than, say, a book—but remember make and gauge are of paramount importance. A Boy Scout or Girl Guide will appreciate equipment for Scouting or Guiding or a subscription to their respective papers.

Suggestions.—*Books* depend very much on the individual child. In addition to the

Dolls reflect current fashions. These two are very up to date, one in duffle coat and drainpipe trousers, the other wearing a dungaree suit. Both are Violet Potter dolls, obtainable from Heals and Peter Jones, London

suggestions for the two previous groups, the classics must be considered. These can be bought in excellent inexpensive editions and added to on anniversaries. Choose the most easily read ones first. One or two of Sir Walter Scott's novels are suitable. A subscription to a library with a good children's section is a welcome gift.

Constructional Toys.—For girls: Flower-making sets. Colour-foil outfits to make pictures on glass. Sculptocraft from which ornaments can be made. *For boys:* More advanced construction kits, such as those for *Bounty* galleon, Barbary pirate and *Cutty Sark.* Xacto tool set, consisting of knives and assorted blades for all types of woodcraft. Electro-plating or electrical set.

Games, Sports, etc.—All games previously mentioned. Canasta and Samba Sets, Monopoly, Cludo, Scrabble (excel-

lent for improving everyone's spelling, this one).

General.—As for previous groups and, in addition, Dan Dare Walkie Talkie Apparatus, projector and films, miniature autographed cricket bats.

Girls at this age are often passionately fond of amateur dramatics and "dressing up." They will therefore get a lot of pleasure out of a collection of old fancy dress costumes or evening dresses, or a simple play for small numbers.

Young people of over 13 are not interested in ordinary toys, but model railways often persist into second-childhood. Carpentry implements, constructional outfits which are really difficult and so forth are usually suitable. Books are excellent presents, but a Book Token gives the recipient the pleasure of choosing his own.

LET'S MAKE  A TOY

by Peggy Tearle, author of
"Circus Toys," "Felt Glove
Puppets," etc.

MAKING a toy
is a small work
of craftsmanship
that is within the
scope of most of us
—and one that
brings a great deal
of fun and interest
with it.

Even a first attempt can be a character, like
this Bambi, made and designed by a girl of
twelve from the instructions in this chapter

Among the ad-
vantages of toymak-
ing as a hobby are
(*a*) the fact that little
or no outlay is needed for equipment, (*b*)
all sorts of odd scraps can be pressed into
use, and (*c*) many of the processes are
familiar to anyone able to sew; yet this is a
craft with endless possibilities, full of interest right from the start, and giving immense scope for imagination.

With practice, moreover, as the technique becomes familiar, experiments in
design and pattern cutting can be carried
out—and from this point the work will
steadily increase in interest.

EQUIPMENT

A pair of cutting pliers.

An assortment of wooden stuffing sticks,
such as old knitting pins, skewers and
orange sticks, all of which should be
blunted and smoothed at the tips

Sewing materials.

Felt

This is quite the most satisfactory
material for toymaking, since it is nonfraying, easy to sew and beautifully strong
and pliable. Felt is obtainable in a great
array of colours.

Leather

Good-quality gloving leather is excellent
also, but less easy to work, more expensive
and, of course, rather more sober as to
colour.

American Cloth

Good for glossy boots
and hats and for sponge-
able toys; not very easy
to model.

Baize

For Teddies and all
cuddly toys. Baize needs
careful cutting as the
stroke of the pile must be
matched.

Velvet

A most effective mat-
erial, but not recom-
mended for the inexperi-
enced. The stroke of the pile must be
matched, as for baize.

Stockinet

Very good for dolls' bodies, but inclined
to be floppy unless the toy is wired.

Scraps

Useful for dolls' clothes and for trappings, harness, etc. Old belts, stockings,
hats, handbags and pieces of fabric left
over from dressmaking should be saved for
this purpose. Small animals made of fabric
look most attractive with striped or spotted
hides.

Decoration

Decorative oddments should also be collected—odd bits of braid, fringe, fur and
feather, and belt studs, buttons, beads and
sequins are of great value to the toymaker
in providing small-scale ornament.

Cotton Flock

The easiest and cleanest material to use
for stuffing.

Galvanised Wire

Lampshade or toymaker's wire is used
to make frames for toys.

Adhesive Plaster

Half-inch adhesive plaster is useful for
covering sharp ends of wire which might

otherwise pierce the outer covering of the toy.

PATTERNS AND CUTTING OUT

A good pattern is the first essential, and it should be studied well before cutting out. Having made sure you understand how the pieces go together, lay the material, right side down, on a flat surface, and arrange the pattern pieces with all economy, remembering—if a woven material is used—that all pieces, as far as possible, should be cut on the bias. If leather is used, stretch the skin both ways, before cutting, by drawing it backwards and forwards over the edge of a table.

For felt or fabric toys, pin the pattern to the material, inserting pins at right angles to edges; for other materials, hold the pattern in position with weights and mark all round with a sharp pencil—not forgetting to mark in guide letters, features, etc. When using material with a right and wrong side, pattern pieces that are used twice (such as body sides and ears) must be turned over for the second cutting. Baize and velvet should have the direction in which the pile strokes marked on the back of the material with arrows, and the finished toy should stroke across and down— roughly from the ear to the hind foot.

Great care should be taken when drawing and cutting patterns, as this is the foundation on which a toy is built, and no amount of "cheating" afterwards can hide a poor line.

MAKING UP

Hand-sewing is undoubtedly the best, but the main seams of fabric toys can be machined, and, of course, dolls' clothes. Nonfraying materials can be made up on the right side, which method is strongly recommended for the beginner.

The important point to remember about making up

is that all seams must be strong, sewn (unless by machine) $\frac{1}{12}$-in. from the edge with a tight tension, and the thread very firmly secured at each end—otherwise there is a danger of the seams gaping or even splitting when the toy is stuffed. Always pin or tack first, matching guide letters and noting which portions of the toy are to be left open for stuffing; when stitching the seams, hold the material flat between forefinger and thumb, to avoid easing one side.

Saddlestitching (Diagram 1A), oversewing and double-oversewing (Diagram 1B) are good toymaking stitches; the latter forms a decoration in itself and looks effective in a colour contrast to that of the toy.

STUFFING

Toys should be stuffed from the extremities inwards—feet first, then head, neck, shoulders, arms (if any) and body.

Fluff the flock between the fingers and remove any hard pieces; then, using small amounts at a time, push into place with a stick and pack firmly. It is important that toys should be firmly and evenly filled, as weak patches and any empty crevices will always show up with wear. Danger points are the extremities, seam lines, sharp angles, and (on an animal) the top of the leg and the area just above it, which should be well filled out to look realistic. The top of the inside leg is another point to watch—here there should be a small fold to define the change of angle between leg and underbody. If wires are used, they should be kept absolutely central and be well embedded in flock.

When stuffing, turn the work constantly and, at intervals, view it from a distance or through a mirror to ensure a good shape all round. At this stage, photographs of the animal concerned are a great help,

A lifelike penguin in black, white and orange felt, by the author for Marshall & Snelgrove Ltd.

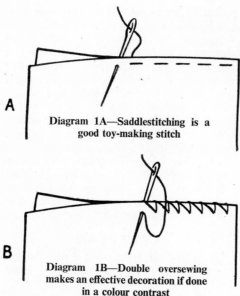

Diagram 1A—Saddlestitching is a good toy-making stitch

Diagram 1B—Double oversewing makes an effective decoration if done in a colour contrast

FINISHING

It is at this stage, when the toy comes to life, that the work gets really exciting; the set of the eyes and the ears, the detail and ornament of harness, trappings or costume can make or mar a toy, and it is worth while spending some little time in trying out the trappings and placing the features, in order to get the effect you want. All features, so far as possible, should be made first, then pinned on and considered in relation to each other, when it will be found that the smallest alteration in position or angle can change the whole character.

Eyes

Beads, buttons, sequins or felt can be used for eyes, and glass eyes can be bought at craft shops; the latter are on a wire which should be cut short and shaped into a shank with pliers. When setting in this type of eye, make a slit in the felt to take the shank, so that the eye can be drawn well into the head. All eyes other than felt should be sewn on with a strong darning needle and a double strand of button thread.

Diagram 3 shows the method for an animal with eyes in the side of the head—the needle is taken right through the head from side to side, both eyes joined on, the thread drawn up as tightly as possible and secured by knotting behind one eye. For animals with eyes in the front of the head, a similar method is used, but the eyes are attached separately and the thread taken from the eye to the back of the ear (Diagram 4). Pliers are useful for pulling the needle through awkward places.

Ears

Animals' ears should first be folded, then attached in a curve not unlike the shape of a human ear (see Elephant pattern, page 530). Having sewn on both ears, take a few stitches right through the head, from ear to ear, before

or, better still, a live specimen to study.

If felt or fabric is used for the toy, small imperfections in the stuffing can be smoothed out with a strong needle used through the material from the outside; in this way the flock just under the surface can be moved a little, lumps dispersed and modelling accentuated.

As the final seam of a toy closes, and space becomes restricted, stitch no more than $\frac{1}{2}$ in. of the seam at a time and work in very small pieces of flock with an orange stick. This takes patience, but it will achieve a neat and shapely finish.

WIRE FRAMES

Wiring adds considerably to the life and strength of a toy, and frames for the legs are not difficult to make; the required length of wire is bent into an arch with the ends turned forward at right angles for feet; ends are then bound with adhesive plaster (Diagram 2). A symmetrical arch with foot angle nicely adjusted should stand on its own. The frames are slipped inside the toy before stuffing and tacked to the soles.

Diagram 2—Wire leg frames have ends turned forward for feet and bound with adhesive plaster

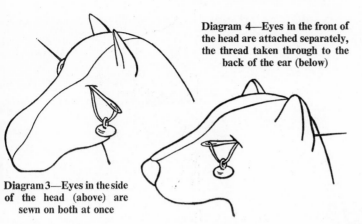

Diagram 4—Eyes in the front of the head are attached separately, the thread taken through to the back of the ear (below)

Diagram 3—Eyes in the side of the head (above) are sewn on both at once

needle and draw right through the nose, leaving a suitable length projecting one side; take a small backstitch to secure, then draw the whisker right through the nose again and trim; continue thus from alternate sides of nose.

ending off, and note the alteration in expression as the thread is tightened or loosened; a fairly tight thread pricks the ears and makes the animal look intelligent.

Manes and Tails

The simplest way to make horses' manes and tails is to fringe a strip of felt for the mane and a square for the tail; the pieces can then be inserted as the toy is sewn up —the tail first having been rolled up tightly and stitched; fringe or ostrich feathers can be used for more glamorous horses. For long-tailed furry animals, such as monkeys, the tail can be made separately and sewn on; for other animals, it is best to cut the tail in one with the body (see Elephant pattern, page 529).

Noses, Mouths and Whiskers

Noses and mouths are usually worked in mercerised cotton, but a very effective nose can be made from a semicircle of felt or leather folded at the "corners" and fitted on the toy.

Black and white whiskers can be bought from the craft shops and should be attached as follows: thread whisker through a

DESIGNING AND PATTERN CUTTING

Having gained some experience in the actual making of toys, and thereby some knowledge of toy patterns, the next step is to try your hand at designing. This is not such a formidable task as it may sound, since no great skill in drawing is needed and pattern cutting for a simple felt toy, as described below, is not difficult. Delightful miniature toys have, in fact, been made by children from their own designs.

First make a profile drawing of a standing animal (with only one fore and one hind leg), keeping the legs fairly straight. Do not concern yourself too much about anatomical correctness—aim rather for a slight caricature of the animal concerned, exaggerating such points as the length of a foal's legs or the plumpness of a pig. Photographs and picture books are a great help and may provide a suitable

The author's Lion and Unicorn in golden brown and white peccary, trimmed gold kid, with silver gilt crown and coronet

MATERIALS FOR MAKING THIS ELEPHANT

Felt:
Half a yard 36-in. grey for body. Scraps of white for tusks, toenails and eye-backings. Scraps of black for eyes. 3¼ by 3 and 2¼ by 7 in. for saddlecloth. Brightly coloured pieces for head mat and girth.

Also:
Two 14-in. lengths thick wire for legs. Cotton flock for stuffing. Adhesive plaster. Braid or cord to decorate trappings. Cardboard for insoles.

picture for tracing, should drawing be out of the question.

The completed profile drawing can be turned into a simple pattern as follows:
(1) Rule a straight line (A—B) level with the soles of the feet.
(2) Rule a line (C—D) parallel with A—B from tail to chest.
(3) Thicken legs, head and the neck down to the level of C—D (this because these portions will have no gusset).
(4) Trace one complete body side and cut out.
(5) Trace one body side from soles to C—D, marking in the line C—D. Fold tracing paper along C—D and cut out through double thickness of paper. This is the gusset.

If soles are made, remember it is the

length of the curved edge (not the length of a straight line) from centre front to centre back that must tally with the length of the foot (see sole on Elephant pattern). Allow extra width on the ear for folding.

Cut out two body sides and one gusset, then sew gusset to sides, starting at the legs; join up the remaining seam, leaving the neck and back open, and stuff the toy as described for the Elephant.

MAKING THE ELEPHANT

Draw the pattern on 1-in. squared paper, following the scale diagram. For a larger or smaller elephant, work on ¾-in. or 1¼-in. squared paper. Trace all the pattern pieces, not forgetting to mark in guide letters and position of features, and cut

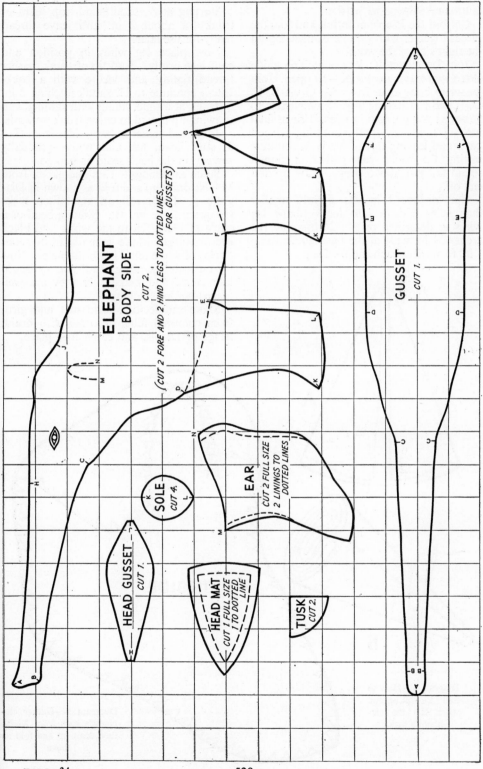

ELEPHANT
BODY SIDE
CUT 2.

(CUT 2 FORE AND 2 HIND LEGS TO DOTTED LINES, FOR GUSSETS)

GUSSET
CUT 1.

EAR
CUT 2 FULL SIZE
2 LININGS TO
DOTTED LINES

SOLE
CUT 4.

HEAD GUSSET
CUT 1.

HEAD MAT
CUT 1 FULL SIZE
1 TO DOTTED LINE

TUSK
CUT 2.

out to make the paper pattern.

Cut out the Elephant in felt and join the pieces together with double oversewing on the right side of the work.

Join leg gussets to legs, matching guide letters and leaving soles (K—L) open. Join gusset to body sides from A—G via B, C, D, E and F, stitching tops of leg gussets to gusset as you go; join in soles. Fringe final inch of tail, then stitch, omitting fringed part, and leaving thread ready to continue sewing up back; run gathering thread round tail just above fringe, draw up and end off.

Cut cardboard insoles slightly smaller than soles and fit into feet. Shape leg wires as described on p. 526, making the arches $3\frac{1}{2}$ in. wide at the base and turning 1 in. forward at each end for feet.

Starting at A, saddlestitch top seam of trunk for about 2 in. and leave thread ready for use later.

Now place leg wires in position and stuff legs firmly. Stuff tip of trunk, gather thread tightly and secure with a back-stitch; continue to H, saddlestitching 2 in. of trunk at a time, filling with stuffing, and drawing up thread to curve trunk upwards

Join head gusset to body sides from H—J; stuff head, tail and body—gradually sewing up the back seam as you go.

Stitch ear-linings to ears and gather from M—N; draw up and fold as shown in Diagram 5. Fold, roll up and stitch tusks (Diagram 6, A and B). Stitch a bead or a circle of black felt to the white and black eye-backings. Make toenails from semi-circles of white felt $\frac{3}{8}$ in. in diameter. Now try on features, using small pins driven in like tacks, and make sure they are well placed before stitching.

Make saddlecloth, head mat and girth from coloured felts, decorate with braid, fringe or tassels, and catch into place.

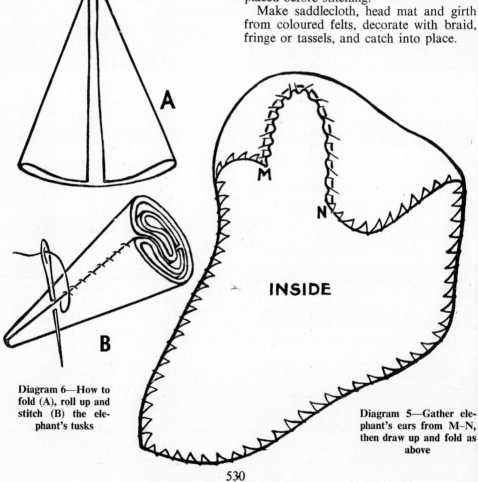

Diagram 6—How to fold (A), roll up and stitch (B) the elephant's tusks

Diagram 5—Gather elephant's ears from M–N, then draw up and fold as above

CHILDREN'S PARTIES

Festive fare to delight the young—games to keep them amused and ideas for entertaining boys and girls of all ages

by JOAN STIEBEL

A SUCCESSFUL children's party depends, not on the amount of money it has cost, but on the ingenuity and thought that have gone into its preparation.

Whether you decide on a film show, conjurer or well organised games, the first item to be considered is, obviously, party fare. For the very young this will have to be a sit-down tea, but for the 8–12 age-group, try a 5.30 to 8.30 evening party, with a help-yourself buffet meal.

Tastes seem to have changed and modern children of all ages often prefer savouries to too many cakes and sweet dishes. Cold drinks are much more popular than hot ones and you cannot go wrong if you offer a choice of orangeade (with ice cubes chinking in the jug if possible), Coca-cola, milk or tea. Drinking straws should be provided and much of the danger of breakages is eliminated if drinks are served either in plastic washable beakers or cardboard picnic cups that can be thrown away after use.

Sandwiches should be varied, made with thinly sliced bread, preferably with the crusts cut off, and be labelled with flags describing the fillings. If there is an amateur artist in the family, little drawings of a chicken, an egg and so on, on the sandwich flags, will add to the fun.

SANDWICH FILLINGS

The old favourites—egg, sardine, chicken paste, cheese grated and mashed with butter—are still popular. And here, in addition, are some other ideas for fillings:

Peanut Butter—a great favourite with some children.

Bacon—small thin rashers grilled and put, when cold, into brown bread.

Cream Cheese and Pineapple—Mix well

531

together a small cream cheese and a small can of pineapple cubes chopped small.

Tomato and Egg—Skin the tomatoes by placing them for a moment in boiling water. Mash with hard-boiled eggs and beat with a wooden spoon to a soft paste.

Mashed Banana, either by itself or on buttered bread on one side only, the other half of the sandwich being spread with strawberry jam or clotted cream.

A bumper sandwich can be made like this: Remove the crusts from a sandwich loaf. Slice lengthwise in six. Butter each slice. Spread two slices with mashed banana, two with strawberry jam and two with clotted cream. Sandwich together alternately. Slice in the normal way fairly thickly and serve.

This method can also be used with savoury fillings: Sardine, egg and tomato. Lettuce, cheese and tomato. Marmite, lettuce and cheese. Sandwich spread, tomato and egg.

For very small children, cut the sandwiches into animal shapes, etc., with a sharp cutter. Small bridge rolls make an attractive alternative to bread.

Open Sandwiches are much too difficult for small children to manage, but they make a pleasant novelty for older ones. French bread, a round loaf or fingers of toast may be topped with: Lettuce, cheese, egg and tomato. Lettuce, banana and cheese. Thinly sliced cheese, beetroot and tomato. Sardine, egg and tomato. Grilled bacon (cold), egg and cheese. Finely chopped celery and Dutch Edam cheese spread lightly with salad dressing. Scrambled egg topped with a few fragments of flaked, cooked kipper. Gouda cheese and split date. Chopped hard-boiled egg on slices of tomato. Ham and tomato. Date and banana or date and raw eating apple

Small sausages, heated and speared on cocktail sticks; potato crisps and cheese croquettes piping hot from the oven, and savoury (salt or cheese-flavoured) biscuits all introduce a very grown-up air to a children's party and are all the more popular for that.

Along with your cakes, give them some petits-fours and dates stuffed with chocolate truffle.

Chocolate Truffle

Whip $\frac{1}{4}$ pint evaporated milk till it doubles its quantity. Stir in 3 oz. melted chocolate, $\frac{1}{4}$ teaspoonful vanilla essence, $\frac{1}{4}$ teaspoonful strong coffee or coffee essence. Make into a creamy paste by adding icing sugar gradually—probably about 3 tablespoonfuls. Stuff dates with the paste.

For a **Fruit Salad** it is surprising how far a sliced fresh peach or two or even a small fresh pineapple will go, with sliced fresh apricots, pears or plums, bananas, grapes, orange segments, all steeped in castor sugar to make a syrupy juice.

CAKES

Cakes depend for their success upon novelty of appearance rather than richness, so it pays to devote a little extra time and thought to the icing and decoration.

Named Cup Cakes

2 oz. self-raising flour	Pinch of salt
1 small dessertspoon-ful cocoa	2 oz. margarine
	2 oz. sugar
1 egg	Vanilla essence
Little liquid to mix	

Arrange a dozen cake cases on a baking tray. Cream the margarine and sugar until light and fluffy. Beat in the egg gradually, then fold in the sieved flour, cocoa and salt. Add vanilla essence and then liquid as necessary to make a soft dropping consistency. Place spoonfuls in cake cases so that they are not more than two-thirds full. Bake in moderately hot oven for 10–15 minutes. Ice some with chocolate icing, others with icing in different colours, and write the names of the small guests in contrasting icing on the tops of the cakes (see Icings chapter).

Cactus Cakes

2 oz. self-raising flour	2 oz. sugar
1 small dessertspoon-ful cocoa	1 egg
2 oz. margarine	Pinch of salt
	Vanilla essence
Liquid to mix	

Chocolate butter cream

2 oz. margarine	3 oz. icing sugar
1 tablespoonful cocoa	

For the Cactus (Almond Paste)

2 oz. ground almonds	A few drops green
2 oz. castor sugar	colouring
Little egg to mix	

Make as Named Cup Cakes (above)

Bananas are favourites with most children. Serve them sliced on peanut butter; mixed with chopped ham, celery and onion; spread sliced on chopped raisins and mayonnaise

and then, when cool, spread with chocolate butter cream made by beating the ingredients together.

For Cactus, mix almonds and sugar and bind with egg. Add a very little colouring. Making sure paste is not too soft, mould into various c a c t u s shapes and place on top of butter cream.

Here is a wonderful individual party cake that will thrill every boy or girl from 6 to 16.

Banana Candlestick Cake

Plain sponge cake *Orange slices cut in*
Lemon butter icing *half*
Bananas

Cut cake in ½-in. slices—one for each child—and then in 3-in. rounds with biscuit cutter or large glass. Cover each round with lemon butter icing made by creaming 2 oz. butter with ½ lb. icing sugar, the grated peel of ½ lemon and enough lemon juice to make icing spread easily. Place iced rounds on plates for individual service. Slice oranges across and put half a slice against each round of cake to form candlestick handles. Immediately before serving, peel bananas, one for each two servings, cut across and place each half, cut side down, in centre of round to represent candles. For very small children, place candied cherry on top of banana to look like flame. For older children, put small candle in top of banana, light and serve.

Cook's tip.—Cake trimmings can be used for fruit trifle or, as crumbs, they make an excellent base for fruit flan.

The one cake that never loses its appeal to children is Chocolate. The following cakes will keep fresh for at least a week.

The quantities given are ample for 20 children.

Chocolate Cake

1 lb. flour	1 teaspoonful
8 oz. butter or mar-	bicarbonate of soda
garine	¼ teaspoonful salt
14 oz. castor sugar	½ pint milk
4 eggs	1 teaspoonful coffee
8 oz. grated chocolate	essence

Chocolate icing and coffee butter icing
(see next page)

Grease three 9-in. (or four 7-in.) sandwich tins and line with greased paper. Warm the grated chocolate in the milk until it has dissolved and leave on one side to cool. Cream the butter or margarine with the sugar and beat until it is white and very soft. Sieve the flour with the bicarbonate of soda and salt. Beat the eggs, one at a time, into the butter and sugar, adding a little of the flour if it shows signs of curdling. Then stir in the remainder of the sieved ingredients, alternately with the milk and chocolate. Add the coffee essence. Divide between the tins and bake in a moderately hot oven for 30 minutes or until cooked.

When the cakes are cooked, cool on a cake rack and sandwich together with coffee butter icing. Coat top with chocolate icing and sides with coffee butter icing Decorate in any way.

Suggestions.—Divide cake into equal portions with piped line of coffee butter icing and write name of one child on each piece. Make a bunch of violets or mimosa, with crystallised violets or mimosa balls and angelica cut into strips. Pipe any design with the coffee butter icing.

Coffee Butter Icing

8 oz. butter or mar-garine	Coffee essence as required
12 oz. icing sugar	

Cream the butter and sugar, and beat until creamy. Add the coffee essence.

Chocolate Icing

8 oz. icing sugar	2 tablespoonfuls
Vanilla essence	cocoa
Hot water as required	

Sieve together the icing sugar and cocoa. Add vanilla essence and enough hot water to give a smooth coating consistency. Use immediately.

Another popular cake:

Rainbow Gâteau

9 oz. butter or mar-garine	Milk to mix
	Cochineal
9 oz. sugar	Cocoa
4–5 eggs (depending on size)	Saffron or other yellow colouring
13 oz. flour	Vanilla glacé icing
1½ teaspoonfuls baking powder	(see chapter on Icings and Fillings)

For vanilla butter cream icing

6 oz. butter or mar-garine	12 oz. icing sugar
	Vanilla essence

Grease and flour four 7-in. sandwich tins. Sieve together the flour and baking powder. Cream the butter or margarine and sugar together until white and creamy. Beat in the eggs, one at a time, adding a little of the flour if there is any sign of curdling. Add the sieved ingredients and mix with a little milk to a soft dropping consistency.

Put a quarter of the mixture into a sandwich tin. Colour one quarter with a few drops of cochineal, one quarter with the yellow colouring and the other chocolate colour with a little cocoa. Bake in a moderate oven for 25 minutes or until done. Cool on a cake rack.

To make butter cream icing, cream fat until soft and beat in the sieved sugar slowly. Add the vanilla essence. Use this to put the cakes together when cold.

Coat cake with vanilla glacé icing, leaving a little to which add a drop of cochineal. Drop this from a spoon on to the top of the cake whilst the white icing is still soft, and spread with a palette knife so that it forms a marbled effect on top.

Another favourite cake is—

Sponge Sandwich

4 oz. flour	4 eggs
	4 oz. castor sugar

Prepare two 7-in. sandwich tins by greasing and flouring. Sieve the flour. Break the eggs into a basin and whisk. Add sugar, and whisk over pan of hot water on low flame until the mixture is thick and creamy and will retain the impression of the egg-whisk. Remove from heat. Beat for a few minutes until cool. Fold in flour quickly and put into sandwich tins.

Bake in quick oven for 10 minutes or until cooked. To test, press gently with finger. If impression remains, the cake is not ready.

Suggested Fillings

Coffee butter cream and raspberry jam.—Spread one cake with thick layer of raspberry jam and the other with coffee butter cream (made as vanilla butter cream in Rainbow Gâteau recipe above).

Orange and cream.—Whip small-size carton of double cream. Add grated rind of 1 orange. Spread half on each cake and sandwich together.

Chocolate and cream.—Whip small-size carton of double cream. Add 2 oz. grated chocolate. Spread half on each cake and sandwich together.

Orange and lemon cream.—Make butter cream as for vanilla butter cream icing (see Rainbow Gâteau recipe), but substitute grated rind of ½ lemon and ½ orange instead of vanilla essence. Spread and sandwich cakes together.

A plain fruit cake which can be iced or not, according to taste, is a good stand-by and may be popular with older children.

Sultana Cake

12 oz. flour	¼ teaspoonful salt
1 teaspoonful baking powder	8 oz. sultanas
	6 oz. sugar
6 oz. butter or mar-garine	2 eggs
	Milk to mix

Prepare a 6-in. cake tin by greasing and

flouring. Clean sultanas by rubbing in a floured cloth.

Sieve flour, salt and baking powder into a basin. Rub in the butter or margarine until the mixture is of the consistency of breadcrumbs. Add the sugar and sultanas, and mix well.

Beat the eggs thoroughly: make a well in the centre of the dry mixture and stir in the eggs with enough milk to make the mixture moist and of a dropping consistency. Pour into the prepared tin. Bake in moderate oven for 20 minutes. Then reduce heat slightly and cook until the cake is done—approximately 40 to 50 minutes.

Dominoes

For the chocolate sponge

2 *eggs*	2 *oz. plain flour*
2 *oz. sugar*	1 *oz. cocoa*
	Pinch of salt

For the white sponge

2 *eggs*	3 *oz. plain flour*
2 *oz. sugar*	*Vanilla essence*
	Pinch of salt

Line and grease two Swiss roll tins. Make each sponge separately by whisking the eggs and sugar together until thick and foamy, then lightly folding in other ingredients. Pour into prepared tins, spread evenly and bake in a hot oven for 7 minutes. Cool. Ice chocolate sponge with white icing and white sponge with chocolate icing (see chapter on Icings and Fillings). When cold, cut into slices. Pipe domino numbers in contrasting colours.

Chocolate Biscuit Characters

All you need is a packet of chocolate biscuits in various shapes, a tube of ready-made icing (available in various colours) or some made yourself (see chapter on Icings), a few almonds, glacé cherries and angelica. You just "ice" the features on, using round biscuits for the faces. Cut hats out of rice-paper and stick them on with a dab of icing. Incidentally, a pin stuck in the back will hold the biscuits together while the icing sets—but don't forget to remove the pins before serving!

"Poached Eggs"

Cut as many squares of sponge cake as there are guests. Put a teaspoonful of straw-

These quaint party characters are made from Cadbury's chocolate biscuits in various shapes, the faces "made up" with coloured icing, cherries and angelica—the hats are rice-paper

berry jam in the centre of each square. Place half a tinned peach on top, the stone cavity over the jam. Mask with whipped cream.

Fruit and Sponge Delight

Line a mould with sponge fingers. Make packet jelly in any fruit flavour according to directions on packet. Pour one quarter into mould and leave until cool but not set. Put in prepared grapes, tangerine sections, pear or any other fruit and add remainder of jelly, which should be kept just warm over hot water. Leave to set. Turn out and serve with border of fruit.

Jelly Soufflé

Boil a tin of evaporated milk and leave in cold place (preferably refrigerator) overnight. Put orange or lemon jelly in a basin and melt in a very little boiling water. Leave to cool. Whisk evaporated milk until it has greatly increased in bulk and is so thick that it will retain the impression of an egg whisk. Add juice and grated rind of 1 lemon and 1 orange to jelly. When cool but not setting, add to milk and mix thoroughly. Pour into glass dish and leave until set. This mixture sets very quickly and can be used within an hour or so.

Bon-bon Jelly

Make strawberry or raspberry jelly as directed on packet. Pour one quarter into mould rinsed in cold water and leave until almost set, keeping the remainder of the jelly tepid over hot water. Press fondants and other soft sweets top downwards into jelly and add remaining jelly. Leave until set and turn out.

Meringues are another popular favourite. See chapter on Puddings and Sweets.

Trifle

Cut 16 sponge cakes in half and spread with strawberry or other jam. Sandwich together and cut in half. Line a large glass bowl with the pieces, fitting them together and adding layer after layer until all are used. Pour over $\frac{1}{2}$ pint of fruit juice. The syrup from canned fruit is suitable, diluted black-currant purée, or juice from any stewed fruit. Make $1\frac{1}{2}$ pints custard. Cool for a few moments, pour over and leave trifle overnight. Decorate next day

with whipped cream, glacé cherries, almonds—these should be omitted where the party is for very young children—and glacé fruits or crystallised violets and rose leaves.

Ice cream can generally be purchased locally. The neapolitan variety is a great favourite. Wafers should be provided, preferably a very pretty variety shaped like fans. If you have a refrigerator, you can also make those top favourites—iced lollies. Freezing containers the right shape can be bought in most shops and you only need to make a good strong fruit drink and freeze it (see also Chapter on Ices).

PARTY GAMES

On the children's arrival, here is a game that will break the ice.

Letter Post

Preparation beforehand — four large cards, about 15 in. by 12 in., on which are boldly printed eight or more place names; also a quantity of small cards each bearing *one* of the place names—there can be more than one card for each place. These cards should be put ready in an open box.

To play, choose four guests to be post offices and give to each one of the big cards and a handful of dried beans or peas. Send them off to different parts of the house. Put the box of small cards on a table in the party room and give the signal to start. All who are not post offices are postmen and they dive for the box of small cards, pick one each and race away to find the post office bearing that name. The post office checks that the name handed in appears on his card, and if so awards the postman two beans. The postman dashes back to the party room, hands in one bean, keeps the other and picks another card from the box. Allow so much time for play, then give the post offices a turn at being postmen. When all have been post offices, beans should be counted and the one with the most wins.

Find Your Other Half

Make small slips, one for each guest, bearing the name of one of a pair of characters such as Jack and Jill, Laurel and Hardy, Harlequin and Columbine, or objects such as Egg and Bacon, Brush and Comb, Bucket and Spade. Pin one on to

EAT YOUR
EASTER BONNET

Specially photographed in the Brown & Polson kitchens

No little girl will be able to resist these coloured biscuits that look like hats

TO MAKE THE HATS:

6 oz. plain flour
2 oz. cornflour
I level teaspoonful baking powder
Marshmallows
3 oz. butter
3 oz. sugar
I egg

Sift flour, cornflour and baking powder together. Cream the butter and sugar, add flour mixture and beaten egg alternately, kneading the mixture lightly with the hand and making a smooth firm dough. Roll out thinly and cut into rounds with a 3-in. plain or fluted cutter. Bake some on a lightly greased baking tin and some in shallow patty tins—to make flat and curved brims. When cold, put half a marshmallow in the centre of each biscuit for the crown of hat, and cover the whole with glacé icing in different colours. Decorate the hats by piping with a contrasting coloured icing or with tiny feathers or hat pins made rom cocktail sticks.

To make the icing: Sift I level teaspoonful flavoured cornflour with 4 tablespoonfuls icing sugar and add enough milk or water to make a stiff icing. Flavoured cornflour is obtainable in six flavours—banana, raspberry, caramel, strawberry, pineapple and chocolate—and has the added advantage of providing icing of different colours as well as taste!

When made and decorated, the tiny hats can either be arranged on a plate for the tea table, perched on miniature glass vases as in a milliner's shop window for the centre piece of the table—or one can be placed at each girl's place.

the back of each child and let them discover their identity by asking questions which can only be answered "Yes" or "No." When they discover who they are, they must find their partners. A small prize can be given to the first pair who report to the judge.

Donkey

Draw a donkey on thin cardboard and then draw 100 small circles all over its back. Number these 1–100. 100 must be the spot for the donkey's tail. Cut out a tail in thick cardboard. Either hang the donkey up if you have a suitable wall, or lay it flat on a table. Blindfold each player in turn. Lead them a few yards away from the donkey. Give them the tail, with a drawing-pin inserted. They must walk to the donkey and pin the tail on the spot where it should be. Whoever gets it nearest to the 100 wins the game.

Blowing the Feather

Place one saucer for each child at the end of a fairly large room. (If there is not sufficient space for all players together, the game can be arranged in heats and the winners of each heat can then play against each other.) Each child kneels at the far end of the room. Give each one a fairly large feather. When the starter says "Ready, Steady, Go!" they put their feathers down in front of them and blow them down the room, the object being to get the feathers on to the saucers. The first player to get his feather on to the saucer is the winner.

Balloon Blowing

A string is stretched across the room. The players are divided into two teams. Each team stands on one side of the string. The object is to keep the balloon, which is thrown in by the starter, going backwards and forwards across the string. It must be blown and must not be touched by hand. Anyone touching it is out. Any member of a team failing to blow it across or failing to blow it back is out. Players will therefore gradually drop out. The winning team is that which has the last player(s) in.

Treasure Hunt

Ten or twelve clues should be provided, depending on the space available. It is more amusing to think up original clues, but the following is a suitable set:

Clue 1 (handed to players at the start)
"I don't grow, but the things in me do.
Look around me and you'll soon find a clue."

Clue 2 (hidden near a flower-pot)
"Growing, you said, well you grow when you sleep,
I'm up the stairs and quite near a heap."

Clue 3 (hidden beside a pile of cushions or pillows on a bed)
"Wake up, young hunter, a long way you must go.
Cross mountains and oceans, the road they will show."

Clue 4 (hidden, just showing, in an atlas)
"Back to old England and into the fray,
So pretty my home is, all festive and gay."

Clue 5 (hidden in or near decorations)
"The floors are all covered and so is the hearth.
I think I'll consider just having a bath."

Clue 6 (hidden under floor covering in bathroom, or under bath mat)
"Tidy, by nature, when I am turned out.
You can be quite certain the dustman's about."

Clue 7 (hidden in wastepaper basket)
"Welcome, young stranger, when you cross me you're in.
I know all your soles be they clumsy or thin."

Clue 8 (hidden under door-mat)
"When you come to a party, you surely intend
To sample our sweetness before it does end."

Clue 9 (hidden beside sweet dish, bag or box)
"Steep is the way, bend knee after knee;
When lifting your foot, this clue you may see."

Clue 10 (hidden under stair-carpet)
"A rest you would like, well, perhaps so, but still,
You rest on my top and not under my frill."

Clue 11 (hidden under armchair with frill)
"Once you have found me, you've got the whole lot.

CHOCOLATE GOLLIWOGS

1 orange jelly
2 bananas
2 level tablespoonfuls custard powder
1 level tablespoonful cocoa
1 pint milk
¼ pint coffee
3 oz. sugar
A little whipped cream

Make up the jelly to just under 1 pint, and set in individual dishes with two-thirds of the bananas, cut into slices. Allow to set. Mix the custard powder, cocoa and sugar together and blend with a little cold milk. Mix the rest of the milk and coffee together, bring to the boil, pour on to the blended custard, return to saucepan and boil 1 minute. Allow to become almost cold, then pour on to the set jelly. Set aside until quite cold.

Cut the rest of the bananas into slices to form eyes, pipe cream on top and place a currant in the centre to complete eye. Use the rest of the cream to make the nose and mouth. Serve quite cold.

Photograph by Alfred Bird

When I'm discovered, you may feel warm or perhaps hot."
Clue 12 (hidden near a lamp bulb, fire or similar appliance)

NOTE: One slip must be made out for each player, and a complete set brought to the judge. The first player to do so wins the Hunt.

Advertisements

Cut out the pictures, and/or slogans of 15 or 20 well-known advertisements, omitting names of products. Paste them on several sheets of cardboard and display round the room. Give each player a sheet of paper and pencil. Allow 20 minutes for them to discover the names of the products advertised. For smaller children, the *type* of product can be taken as sufficient, i.e. "Tyres" instead of the name of the particular brand of tyre.

Remembrance Test

Place 24 articles on a tray, such as a pin, an ash tray, a rubber, a cork, a spoon, a sock, a book, a needle, a penholder, a piece of coal, a sweet, a cigarette, a brooch, a hairpin, a comb, a piece of ribbon, a nail, a bead, a toothbrush, a piece of candle, a reel of cotton, a handkerchief, a china ornament, a glass. Let the players look at the tray for 3 or 5 minutes. Take it away. Give each player paper and pencil, and allow 15 minutes for them to list as many objects as they can remember. The player with the largest number of accurate answers is the winner.

Smelling Game

Prepare 12 receptacles with such things as ginger, curry powder, lavender, scent, dried mint, dried sage, coffee essence, lemon, orange, peppermint, thyme, nutmeg. Cover over so that the contents cannot be seen. Each dish is numbered. The players smell the dishes in turn, writing down against the corresponding numbers on the papers provided what they think the contents are. Fourteen minutes should be allowed. The winner is the player who has the largest number of correct answers.

Fruit Salad

Prepare a set of cards, one for each player, beforehand, taking the names of twelve fruits and mixing up the letters, i.e. GROANE (ORANGE), PALPE (APPLE), PPPENALEI (PINEAPPLE), PRAGE (GRAPE), NAAANB (BANANA), BCLAKUNTRRCA (BLACKCUR- RANT), WASBRTRYRE (STRAW- BERRY), GRINTNAEE (TANGER- INE), CAPRITO (APRICOT), CHEAP (PEACH), GOBNARYLRE (LOGAN- BERRY), MULP (PLUM). More can be added if it is desired to lengthen the game. Print each mixed name on one line and leave a space beside it for the correct an- swer. Allow 10 minutes for older children, 15 for younger. The winner is the player with most correct answers.

Statues

A gramophone or piano is needed for this. The music starts and the players move round the room in any way they like. Im- mediately it stops, they must stop, too, in whatever position they may be. Anyone moving after the music has stopped is eliminated. This is repeated until only one player is left.

Stool of Repentance

One player is the Recorder. One goes out of the room. The others each make some remark about the absent player which the Recorder notes. Naturally, the more un- likely the remark made, the less chance the Guesser has of finding out who made it. The player is then recalled and sits on a chair in the middle of the circle, or in front of the other players. The Recorder reads out the remarks and when the player guesses who has made a remark, that player goes out and the game proceeds as before.

Step Carefully

Everyone goes out of the room. Several cushions or other objects are put on the floor and the first player is told that he is going to be blindfolded and must then cross these objects without touching them. Im- mediately he is blindfolded, the objects are quietly taken away and when he reaches the other side of the room and removes the bandage, he sees that he has been stepping over—NOTHING. The next player comes in, and the first player will enjoy watching his efforts to overcome the non-existent ob- stacles.

Party Presents

A small gift for each child at the end of the party may be made more interesting by wrapping it up and attaching a very long string to it. The strings are then tangled and wound all over the house.

SPECIAL PARTIES

Where the family consists of a boy and girl, try having two parties.

For the girl, or girls

A games party, with perhaps a conjurer. Tea with sandwiches and cakes.

For the boy, or boys

A visit to a local cinema, ice hockey or circus, with a substantial and very mascu- line tea-supper when they return. Sausages and mash, fish and chips, substantial sand- wiches, trifle, jellies and ice cream.

For the older age-groups

For girls aged 8–12, break the ice with a treasure hunt for thimbles, bath cubes, hair ribbons and inexpensive brooches and necklaces. Boys of the same age would enjoy round games to start off with, fol- lowed perhaps later by a turn each at show- ing off conjuring or chemical tricks, card games and perhaps even a well-controlled boxing match. They should, of course, be spared the ordeal of dressing up. Girls love it.

Mixed Parties

Dancing is gaining in popularity even amongst the boys, particularly if variety is introduced with novelty numbers.

"Excuse Me."—One boy is given a favour. He decides which girl he wants to dance with and hands the favour to her partner.

Poses.—When the music stops, everyone stops and anyone moving is eliminated.

Quiz Dance.—When the music stops, the M.C. says:

"Everyone wearing a pink ribbon off the floor," or something similar. The more amusing the items, the greater the fun.

Supper should be served in the middle of the evening and, if it is a winter party, hot soup before the guests depart or, in sum- mer, a cold drink, ice cream, fruit salad, etc.

A YOUNG LINE FOR MOTHERS

Trim your figure as you work, with T.V.'s "Keep Fit" expert, Eileen Fowler

Wrong: Above, you strain muscles by lifting baby (or anything heavy) from the hips only

Correct: Left, save your back by squatting down, then pushing up with your legs and thighs as you rise from the ground

The washing, drying, ironing, airing, pushing baby in his pram—these can all take on a different aspect if done with figure consciousness.

Relax to the basket and stretch to the line, to keep a flat diaphragm.

Good posture is so important that it is essential to bear it in mind when lifting, carrying and pushing heavy objects. Head in line with the spine, feel tall and very straight and think about your carriage—and don't wilt over the handle of baby's pram.

Even if you are relaxing, there are different ways of doing it to renew your energy fully. For example, I always keep a small stool under the kitchen table and have made a habit of reaching for it when I sit down, and putting my feet up.

To start you thinking about your figure in relation to the daily chores, try the simple movements illustrated here and then see also "Getting Your Figure Back to Normal."

But remember "new" mothers in need of special post-natal exercises should consult their medical adviser

YOUNG or old, young mother or bride-to-be, we all want to keep that youthful line from shoulder to hip. Cycling, tennis, walking, swimming and other sports can help, but when there's no time or opportunity for this, you can get the exercise you need in your everyday activities about the house.

541

TRIM YOUR LINE TO THE RHYTHM

Stretch to the ceiling . . .

relax to the floor . . .

swing to the window . . .

swing to the door . . .

bend by the table . . .

foot on the chair . . .

head to your knees . . .

stretch in the air

SETTING A GOOD TABLE

*How to serve all kinds of meals, from family breakfast to a formal
dinner or dainty afternoon tea*

Wedgwood's Persephone dinner service in fine earthenware,
yellow or blue, looks lovely in a modern setting. The same
pattern in fine bone china, Golden Persephone, was chosen for the
Foreign Secretary's Coronation Banquet

A LARGE part of "setting a good
table," as the old housewifely phrase
has it, naturally depends on the food provided All the same, service of the food and
the way the table is set out play a big part
in the enjoyment of meals and so in their
nutritional values. Convention, which is
largely based on common sense, and
fashion, determined by more immediately
topical considerations, lay down certain
rules for different meals and occasions.
These need not be followed slavishly, but
a general observance of them is the sign of
good manners and social "know-how."

GENERAL PRINCIPLES OF
TABLE SETTINGS

Suitability is the key to good table setting. In these days, when most households
are "help-less," a simple
table, with the mini-
mum of cutlery and
china necessary for
actual use, is obviously
sensible and therefore
correct. So long as the
cloth or mats and table-
ware are fresh and clean
and each person has
adequate "instruments"
for each course, nothing
more is essential except
serving spoons, forks,
etc.

If guests join the
family and more of an
occasion is made of a
meal, rather more
formality is fitting. The
coloured check table-
cloth that seems so
agreeably homely when
breakfast or lunch is
taken in the kitchen,
will look rather out of
place on a polished
table in the dining-
room. Then with serv-
ing dishes on the sideboard or table, more
in the way of mats, implements, etc., will
be called for. An extra, or more decorative cruet, a sugar caster instead of a bowl
and spoon, and special butter and cheese
knives are the sort of details that make the
difference.

It is also pleasant to vary the table settings according to the meal and the time of
day. At breakfast, colour and freshness
matter most. The importance of the main
meal, whether taken at midday or in the
evening, should be marked by a more
elaborate setting. This may involve using
a different cloth, or linen mats instead of
coloured plastic ones, or perhaps a "best"
set of china. For afternoon tea, both
napery and china should be lighter and
daintier than for other meals.

Balance between china, cutlery and table

HOW TO BE A PERFECT HOSTESS

Prepare in advance, set the scene with care and enjoy yourself, too

GOOD teamwork between host and hostess makes for smooth entertaining and ensures that you also enjoy the party. When the guests arrive, the host should dispense sherry or cocktails, leaving the hostess free to deal with coats and wraps—and to keep an unobtrusive eye on what's going on in the kitchen. Plan the seating arrangements together beforehand. A good division of labour is for the food to be the hostess's responsibility and the drinks the host's.

When the host brings the guests into the dining room, the candles should be burning, plates ready (on a hot plate if for hot dishes) and the first course—a cold one leaves the hostess free—already on the table. Note the charming low flower arrangement—tall flowers make conversation across the table impossible—and the place-mats and napkins in three colours.

When the invitation says:

"REQUESTING THE PLEASURE OF YOUR COMPANY"

Above, a modern dining room with a warm welcome. Stylecraft tableware in Arden pattern, with a leaf motif and shaded grey, hand-decorated band, goes charmingly with a contemporary setting. Scarlet placemats are a gay colour contrast in a cool green scheme

To grace your tea table, Wedgwood's Wakefield (right) has a spray of windblown autumn leaves in rich subdued colouring. It is fine bone china which, despite its fragile, translucent appearance, is actually stronger than earthenware. Note the new coupe-shaped plates —concave and rimless— very popular in the U.S.A. and on the Continent

linen also contributes largely to the "rightness" of a setting. A seersucker or gingham cloth and vivid straw mats go perfectly with thick stone or earthenware pottery, plain coloured glasses, wooden cruets and wooden, horn or cane-handled cutlery. In contrast, snowy, well-starched damask or hand-worked, lace-enriched linen mats demand real china or at least semi-porcelain, sparkling clear glass, gleaming silver and cutlery in time-honoured designs. In between the two extremes comes napery of plain linen in solid colours or fresh-looking patterns, with which semi-porcelain or pottery of a not-too-heavy type looks well. Patterns may be traditional or contemporary, so long as the individual items go well together. This type of setting is the most versatile and practical for the average home as it can easily be dressed up, or down, as occasion demands.

For complete correctness, general surroundings, table settings and menu will all be in harmony. In practice, the clever home-maker chooses her tableware so that it has the same general "feeling" as her room. For instance, with strictly contemporary furnishings, all-steel cutlery, functional shapes and geometric patterns in the tableware, and dark or strong-coloured napery seem right. Yet, however good they were in themselves, these items would strike a jarring note against an ornate Regency décor. But generally speaking, personal taste can be followed, bearing in mind one guiding principle: that sturdy oak or cottagey furnishings demand simple accessories, while the sophistication of polished woods is best shown off by more elegant trimmings.

BREAKFAST

Gay colour and informality are the key-notes.

Napery

Cloths can be smaller than the table and put cornerwise, or individual oblong mats, one to a place, used instead. As freshness has a special psychological value first thing in the morning, easily washed fabrics that need no ironing and make frequent change practical are the best choice. Seersucker is excellent, so are ginghams and crash. Plastic material can be used too, especially of the opaque type. For mats, it looks especially well when quilted and

The breakfast table may be informal but must be fresh and colourful. Breakfast service is Butterfly in blue on white earthenware by Rorstrand. Note the easily copied raffia egg cosies

For high tea, a boldly checked cotton cloth, earthenware plates with a snowy white glaze, deep plain glass cups and saucers, colourful ovenware, all by Rorstrand of Sweden

left on bread board, and buttered individually as required.

Decorations

A simple bowl or vase of flowers or a bowl of raw fruit.

If a breakfast tray is taken to the bedroom, it should contain miniatures of all the accessories that would be set on the table. A tea- or coffee-pot cosy should also be included.

LUNCH OR SUPPER

When the family is alone, the table can be set as for breakfast, though a little more formality is pleasant. Choose linen mats over heat-resisting ones or a plain cloth to cover the table completely. On a polished table, decorative heat-resisting mats are a practical alternative. Simple medium-size napkins to match or tone with cloth or mats are ideal, but *plain, dinner-size* paper ones will save laundry.

Tableware

Pottery or semi-porcelain. Dinner plates for the main course, except for children, for whom dessert-size ones are often better. Side plates need not be laid unless bread with butter or cheese is taken. For the sweet, dessert plates or small glass or china bowls, perhaps with the pudding served from a matching dish or bowl. Glasses for actual use only should be laid. Any simple white or coloured glass is correct, with a glass jug for water.

Place Setting

Small knife, if butter or cheese is being taken; knife and fork and/or fish-eaters, soup spoon if soup is served. Dessert or pudding spoon and fork across top of place setting, spoon with handle to right, fork to left. Glass at top right. Napkin on small plate or in centre between knife and fork.

If preferred, the restaurant style of setting with dessert spoon and fork laid *first*,

padded. Napkins (never correctly called "serviettes"), which need to be only 8 in. square, should preferably match, in colour if not in fabric.

Tableware

If tea is served, breakfast-size cups in not-too-thick earthenware or semi-porcelain; for coffee, rather thicker cups in earthen- or stoneware are permissible. Dessert (or pudding)-sized plates for bacon and egg or other cooked dish, and bowls or soup plates for cereal or stewed fruit will, if possible, match the cups. Simple wooden or pottery salt and pepper pots and egg cups. For fruit juice, an inexpensive thin coloured glass looks pretty. Tea or coffee pot of brown earthen- or stoneware is perfectly correct.

Place Setting

Small knife, knife and fork if cooked dish is served, cereal spoon to the right of knives. Napkin in space between knives and fork or on small plate.

Accessories

Spoon for marmalade or other preserve; butter serving knife. Toast, if placed on table, can be in rack or, if liked soft and hot, laid inside a folded napkin on a plate. If bread is served instead of toast, it is cut in medium thick slices, placed in basket or

Above, the Little Mermaid's Supper Party in Wedgwood Queensware —white plates in traditional shell shapes, Dolphin candlesticks and a huge conch shell called a Nautilus Centre, with jasper-blue linen

Specially designed by Spode-Copeland for the Royal tour of Australia, the Flemish Green ware (right) has sprays of mimosa or wattle

to the right and left respectively of centre, inside the knife and fork, can be followed. In this case the small knife, if used, can be placed across the small plate to the left. The rule to follow when setting the places for lunch, supper and dinner is that one works from the outside inwards. Thus the soup spoon goes on the extreme right (or a small fork if hors d'œuvres is being served instead), then fish eaters, meat knife and fork, dessert spoon and fork and cheese knife.

When salad is served on a separate plate, a small fork can be laid across the plate. Lay the fork alongside an individual crescent-shaped salad plate, which should be placed to the top left of each place setting, so as not to conflict with the small bread plate. Never lay more cutlery than is re-

quired for the actual dishes to be served. If fresh fruit takes the place of a sweet, or follows it, a dessert knife or fork should be brought on with the plate after the table has been cleared.

Accessories

Bread is placed uncut on a breadboard on the table or a side table. A roll can be placed on the side plate or arranged with the napkin. Alternatively, rolls and cut bread, in thickish pieces, are often put on the table in a raffia or other bread basket. A three-piece cruet or separate salt cellars and pepper pots can be used. If a salad dressing is to be mixed at table, oil and vinegar in little glass decanters, mustard and soft sugar will be laid. When entertaining, remember one salt cellar between each two saves frequent passing. Serving spoons and forks are laid on the table or on a side table, whichever is more convenient.

Decorations

Flowers are a matter of taste, but if there is a simple floral arrangement it should be kept low and not take up too much space. Raw fruit can look well, but with some colour in the tableware or linen, anything extra is not strictly necessary.

DINNER

Whether served in the evening or midday, the appointments are similar to those for lunch, except that, as the main meal of the day, everything can be rather more formal and elaborate. This, of course, applies mainly when entertaining or for special occasions. These are the times when the best china, glass and linen are enjoyed, and when silverware adds lustre,

One of the most important aids to good meal service is an efficient trolley. The Compactom Chatsworth, above, is a neat three-shelf affair with trays covered in washable Vynide

figuratively and literally, to the feast. For the "company dinner," a white starched damask cloth used to be almost obligatory. It certainly makes a wonderful foil for decorated china and sparkling glass. But white or écru linen mats, or a cloth with some self-colour embroidery or other decoration are equally conventional and look most attractive.

Coloured napery can be used, too, and there are alternatives to linen. Some smart hostesses like fine organdie through which the wood can be seen, but whatever is chosen should have character. Napkins should always be provided. Matching damask or linen ones are to be preferred, but if paper has to be used, the largest size thick white paper ones, sold as *dinner* napkins, are recommended.

Place Setting

As already described for lunch. Glasses are placed at the top right of each setting, the first to be used closest to the cutlery.

Glasses for wine destined to be served at dessert (port, brown sherry or madeira, brandy or liqueur) are not laid before the meal but brought on with the dessert after the table has been cleared. Port, sherry, madeira and also claret may be decanted if liked. This should be done some hours ahead and the decanters left in the dining room so that any sediment may settle and the wine take the temperature of the room (chambré). Coffee is more often taken later in the sitting room.

Accessories are as described for lunch, though finger bowls, half filled with warm water, should be added at a formal party if there is occasion for them. This will be if asparagus or globe artichokes, which are eaten with the fingers, feature on the menu or if dessert is served. In the former case, they can either be set on the table at the beginning of the meal, or, better still, handed from the sideboard after the vegetables have been eaten. Otherwise they are brought on with the dessert.

AFTERNOON TEA

Taken in the sitting room, settings for this light meal should be as pretty and delicate as possible. A lace or lace-trimmed or embroidered smallish linen cloth, put cornerwise on an occasional table, is usual, but coloured organdie is sometimes preferred. Small, 6–8-in. napkins should match or tone, though plain or printed paper ones may be used. China should be as thin and fine as possible, real china, in contrast to pottery or semi-porcelain, being the ideal. To-day it is not considered essential that cups, saucers and plates should

Fine bone china, delicate and graceful, makes all the difference to the tea table. Above, "Devon Sprays," a charming design from Wedgwood

are usually placed on the pouring-out table or on portable cakestands.

A cold supper dish, chocolate with pears, is daintily served in coloured ovenproof glass dishes to blend with tea and coffee cups and a checked cloth
Photographed at Brown & Polson's experimental kitchen

match exactly. Some hostesses prefer a harlequin set (a different colour but same design for each person). If antique china is used, each cup and saucer may be quite different, linked together only by the fact that every piece is lovely in its way. Teapot, milk jug and sugar basin may be of china, real silver or silver plate. Naturally they should harmonise in style with the tableware.

A single plate is handed for each person. A small afternoon tea knife and pastry fork, if there are creamy cakes, are optional, but everything should be small enough to eat with the fingers. Enough little tables to put down cups and plates should be provided. Plates of thin bread and butter, sandwiches, scones and cakes

FAMILY OR DINING ROOM TEA

This popular alternative to drawing room tea is served like any other meal at the dining table. Settings, tableware and so forth should be just as attractive and dainty as for afternoon tea, though a larger and perhaps plainer cloth will be used. As it is easier to eat sitting at table, a slightly more substantial repast is likely to be served, so a knife and pastry fork for creamy cakes should be laid with a plate and tea napkin for each person. If hot scones or fish paste are served, a second set of plates, hot or cold as appropriate, should be to hand. Large plates of bread and butter, cakes, etc., are put on the table, together with jam or other preserves in decorative containers, each with a large special jam spoon.

HIGH TEA

This early evening meal, a cross between tea and supper, should reflect some of the characteristics of both. The same cloth and china can be used as for family tea, though rather more substantial appointments are often preferred. If liked, breakfast china and a supper cloth can be laid. Napkins should be bigger and plainer than afternoon tea ones. Cutlery will depend on what is being served, but individual settings should be laid on similar lines to those used for breakfast.

SOME QUERIES ANSWERED

Mats or Tablecloths?

The inexperienced home-maker may wonder which is smarter or in better taste —dinner mats or tablecloths—or if there are any rules to be followed. Individual taste and circumstances are the best guides. The advantage of mats is that they ease laundry. After a single use it may not be necessary to launder all the mats, while a cloth would have to be washed and ironed before being used again for guests. On the other hand, mats demand a table in good condition with a well-polished top. A tablecloth can be a useful camouflage. In practice it pays to have a selection of sets of mats and cloths of different sizes and types. For informal meals, the single oblong "place setting" mat is gaining in popularity. Otherwise, the conventional round or square mat for the plate with a smaller one for the glass is correct.

For breakfast, a no-iron brightly coloured cloth will prove economical as well as gay, while a similar type of cloth, in a larger size, is practical for a family lunch. For entertaining at lunch or dinner, mats usually save work in the long run and are easier to keep in first-class condition. At afternoon tea there is no substitute for a pretty cloth. Dining-room tea, too, usually looks nicer when laid with an appropriate cloth, but there is no hard and fast rule about this.

White or Colour?

Colour has a very definite place in table settings. White, to be attractive, must be immaculate. Nothing looks worse than a soiled or not quite fresh white cloth, and starched white damask, in particular, needs infinitely more care and time in laundering. Colour also has a psychological value. During the war, when coloured china was unobtainable, people craved for brilliant napery. A bright colourful table, especially

first thing in the morning, is normally more likely to promote good appetite.

The home-maker, when choosing both linen and china, should not only balance one with the other, so that the total effect is pleasing, but also select them with some regard to the general colour scheme of the rooms in which they will be used. On the whole, the vivid geometric patterns spell informality and should be reserved for in-the-kitchen and similar family meals. Plain coloured damasks and delicate floral designs make a good foil to the finer china which is appropriate to tea time and to formal dining room lunches and dinners.

Should Napkins be Folded?

In the past a formal dinner table would be thought to be unfinished if the napkins were not folded in one of a variety of prescribed ways. To-day, the single-handed hostess has little time for such niceties and so the fashion is for simplicity. It is correct to lay the napkin, ironed square, just as it is in the centre of each place or on the small plate, to fold it in half or to make a simple holder for a roll with it. This is done by folding the square diagonally and then folding back each corner to the middle, tucking one into the other, so that the napkin will stand up. Anything more elaborate than this requires a firmly starched napkin and is not to be recommended. Napkins are sometimes pleated into fan shapes and stood in a glass, but though this would be quite suitable for a festive table or a children's party, with brightly printed paper napkins, it is not quite in tune with contemporary taste for lunch or dinner.

PARTY SETTINGS

Christmas and other festive occasions provide an opportunity for more originality. For instance, for a Christmas dinner, large-size, holly-patterned paper doyleys make gay substitutes for place mats (tiny ones can be used for glass mats) and mean much less work for the hostess. With patterned mats, plain white large paper dinner napkins look best. Instead of flowers, a centre garland of holly and berries, with extra colour introduced by tinsel ribbon bows, lends gaiety, especially if small red candles in green wire holders

The Knole trolley from Compactom is an invaluable aid to the busy hostess, extending at both ends to a maximum width of 5 ft. 5 in. Obtainable in oak, mahogany and walnut

are placed at intervals. Scarlet Cellophane can be folded into colourful little holders for roll and napkin, and place settings marked by miniature fir trees. If a cloth is used, a plain white or pastel green one (and either might be of paper) would fit in with the scheme. Two small-sized cloths may be banded together with long red satin or tinsel ribbons or broad strips of Cellophane trimmed with flat bows and will look most effective.

Settings for children's parties, anniversaries and so forth can be improvised on similar lines. Choose a bold and simple colour scheme, which should be carried right through, and select some fitting emblem around which to base the decorations. Examples are a key for a twenty-first birthday, white heather for a send-off party, a rabbit for small children, and so on.

The Buffet Table

When more than a few people are being entertained, something in the nature of a help-yourself or buffet table proves most practical and successful. Cold "party" food looks attractive and colourful and, with sparkling glasses arranged in groups,

the gleam of rows of spoons, forks and other silver, very little extraneous decoration is required. Trails of smilax, the Edwardian favourite greenery for table use, take a lot of beating. Ordinary garden ivy also looks well, so does virginia creeper or, indeed, any long green or tinted trails that can be laid flat on the buffet. One or two important flower pieces, according to the length of the buffet table, will give the necessary contrast. These can be composed of mixed flowers and colourings, or in one tone only to echo the dominant note of the china. A bold effect should be the aim.

Alternatives to Floral Decorations

Dessert fruit, with or without sprays of leaves and berries, massed in a bowl or soup tureen or piled on a large pottery or wooden platter or silver salver, can look quite lovely. Well-washed young summer vegetables can be used in a rather similar treatment, provided the general atmosphere is deliberately countrified and informal. Checked cottons, peasant pottery, wood-handled knives, with food and drink to match, are the thing.

Candles make a fashionable form of table decoration. Many specially designed ones come from Scandinavia. There are big flat candles like rosettes that will float in a bowl with a few flowers, and tall, slender, taper-like ones, also to put among the flowers, as well as a big choice of more ordinary shapes. The flower-lights can be used for a centre-piece alone or with tall, conventional-shaped candles to give the sole illumination to the table.

Dining by Candlelight

The soft light of candles has undoubted glamour, but they need using with care. Branched candelabra on the sideboard and candelabra at intervals on the table provide enough illumination for more than six persons. For a smaller party a single candelabra on the table will suffice. A more modest substitute are tall candlesticks, preferably of silver, wrought iron or decorated china, furnished with tall, slow-burning wax candles. If smaller candles or improvised holders are used—say, for a Christmas table—it is prudent to stand them in a small saucer or ashtray so that wax does not drip upon the table. An efficient pair of snuffers should be close at hand, though many candles now on the market do not drip at all.

Electric Lighting for the Dining Table

The right kind of light is of immense importance. It should be strong enough, but not harsh. A high-up central fitting means a dull, flat, all-over light that is becoming neither to diners nor decorations. One posed above the table that can, by means of a counterweight, be pulled down to within a couple of feet of the diners' heads will give a soft, yet sufficiently powerful, suffused light to make everything and everybody look much more attractive. In a large room, indirect general lighting, by means of wall fixtures or cornice lights, and a low-powered, adaptable centre pendant over the table, should prove excellent.

Aids to Table Service

Hot food should be really hot, and cold food ice cold, though the latter is rarely as difficult to achieve as the former. Unless food is eaten "right off the stove," some form of hotplate in the dining room is called for. In many ways the most trouble-free is the electric table hotplate, with polished steel, chromium or silver-plated top. The loading is just powerful enough to keep food at the temperature at which it comes from the oven or stove and to heat plates from cold. Owing to the need for a length of flex, it is better placed on the sideboard than on the dining table. A nearby lighting point to take a 5-amp plug is necessary.

The old methylated spirit hotplate had the advantage of being completely portable, but it did involve a certain amount of work. An inexpensive contemporary adaptation is the plastic hotplate "powered" by nightlights. This is surprisingly efficient for just keeping food from cooling. A home-made version can be evolved by putting a couple of nightlights in a shallow fireproof or oven-glass dish and placing a wire rack or meat grid, topped by an asbestos mat, over the top.

For bringing food and dishes to the table to and from the kitchen, an easily running trolley cannot be surpassed. If the shelves are covered with a laminated heat - resisting plastic, it will prove even more labour-saving.

For those who do double duty as cook and hostess, the English Electric Plate Warmer solves many problems. Pilot light shows when the current is on

CHOOSING POTTERY

*Household tableware, which is in constant use in every home, should
be both decorative and practical*

FEW household possessions are in more
constant use than our tableware. Several
times a day our cups, saucers and plates
make their appearance, are used, washed
and put away again. Not only are they
utilitarian; they are decorative too—the
results of teamwork between artists and
craftsmen—and the shapes and colours we
choose from all the variety available are
an expression of our own taste. It is a
recurrent pleasure in itself to have such
common objects pleasing to the eye. Moreover, the meals served with them gain in
value; a good dinner is enhanced—even a
mediocre one improved—by being served
on attractive plates.

A well-stocked shop presents a great
choice. There are sets of fine china and
(the greater part) of fine earthenware or, as
it is often described, semi-porcelain. In
both there will be many kinds of shape and
decoration—some traditional, some contemporary. There will also be hand-
made pottery pieces, often of red earthenware.

Most of the services to be seen will be
English, as their manufacture is one of
Britain's major industries. Some of the
ware will be stamped with names like Coal-
port, Minton, Royal Crown Derby, Royal
Doulton, Royal Worcester, Spode and
Wedgwood—the productions of historic
firms who have maintained their high standards of quality and craftsmanship through
the years. But there are over 200 potteries
in the U.K., and their productions have a
world-wide reputation.

Tableware is usually sold in complete
sets or half sets for 12 or 6 persons. A
complete dinner service is composed of 12
soup, dinner, side and sweet plates, 3 meat
dishes of different sizes, 2 vegetable dishes
with covers and 2 sauceboats with stands.
A half set has 6 of each of the plates and
the same number as the full set of the serving dishes. A complete tea set has 12 cups,
saucers and plates, 2 bread and butter
plates, a slop or sugar basin and a cream
jug. A half tea set has 6 cups, saucers and

Delightful Rorstrand ovenware in feldspar
china with white and blue glaze by the
Swedish designer, Hertha Bengtson

plates, one bread and butter plate, a basin
and a cream jug.

Open stock patterns are generally carried through the whole range of requirements, including coffee sets, breakfast sets,
salad sets, fruit dishes, porridge bowls,
hors d'œuvre dishes, etc. An advantage of
buying the products of well-known manufacturers is that extra pieces in a set or replacements of the same pattern are usually
easily obtainable. Stock patterns continue
to be available for years, and pieces can
be bought separately.

Many people, when buying china, focus
on a dinner service, adding pieces to make
up other sets (the side plates, for instance,
can be used as tea plates). One of the best
ideas is the "starter set" composed of 4
cups, saucers, tea plates, dinner plates and

Tea service, right, with a gilt band, can be bought by the piece. Colclough "Stardust" by Ridgway Potteries

The charming modern teapot, below, comes in white, black or brown, shiny or dull surfaced, from Finnish Designs Ltd.

cereal dishes, to which further pieces of the same pattern can be added according to individual needs. Or as the family and the bank balance increase.

Continental ware has great charm and you could bring variety to your table with, say, a coffee service in one of the admirable contemporary designs from the potteries of Denmark, Sweden or Germany; thick, wide breakfast cups or drinking bowls with peasant patterns from France; pottery jugs, plates, cruets, etc., in the traditional blue, white and yellow ware of Spain, or decorated with the vivid and intricate designs of Italy, each characteristic of its own region. Much Continental ware is now available in the U.K.; if it is brought back as a memento of a holiday abroad it has, of course, a special charm.

The regional ware of Britain, too, can provide many treasured pieces — for example, hand-made pots and dishes from the small-scale potteries of Devon and Cornwall.

Kitchenware, once strictly utilitarian, has more attention paid to its looks in this age. Colour has come into the kitchen with gay storage jars, rolling pins, two-colour mixing bowls and oven dishes of stoneware and heat-resistant porcelain. There are many gay and attractive designs from Italy and much thought for efficiency has gone into their design. Clearly, storage jars, however glamorous, should have well-fitting lids and ovenware should be easy to hold.

CHINA AND EARTHENWARE

Although the word "china" is often used loosely to cover all forms of pottery, china is, in fact, porcelain and should be distinguished sharply from earthenware, of which the greater part of the tableware in general use is made. Sometimes it is not easy to distinguish them at first glance, as types of shape and design are common to both and the manufacturing processes are similar. China, however, has an unsurpassable quality and beauty as well as

some practical advantages. A china service will cost about two and a half times as much as an earthenware one, because of the greater individual care and craftsmanship involved in its manufacture.

China is harder and more durable than earthenware, therefore thin cups, etc., of great delicacy of appearance yet, in fact, surprisingly strong, can be made of it. It can be recognised by its characteristic translucency; hold your hand behind a china plate and you can see

Casseroles in all shapes, sizes and colours, including green, blue and brown, come in the Denby range, above

Right, a lovely example of the regional ware of Britain—a selection of Winchcombe pottery from Heal's

Below, Wedgwood's "Summer Sky" in pale blue and cream fine earthenware

"Grey Mayfield" by
Wedgwood has flowers of
ruby-red and green, with
handles and rims of plates
in a soft silver-grey

are opaque when held up to the light, and it is less cold to the touch than china. As it is not so hard as china, it is more liable to chip and crack and, as it is porous, a stain on a broken surface will spread under the g l a z e. Earthenware dishes, etc., are made in many varying degrees of thickness. Some are almost as thin as china and have a quality of shape and design in the best traditions of the industry. Some of the famous manufacturers of fine china—Doulton, Josiah Wedgwood and Spode-Copeland—also produce earthenware services.

Manufacture

The processes are essentially the same for china and earthenware, though the production of china makes greater demands on craftsmanship and time.

The ingredients are first mixed with water and passed through screens and over magnets to remove impurities. Excess moisture is then removed. To make plates, a portion of the clayey dough is thrown upon a revolving mould—the modern form of the potter's wheel—and is flattened by the potter's hands, while a kind of mould is used to standardise the form. Hollow ware is shaped by pouring semi-liquid clay into porous moulds. When sufficient clay has dried around the inside edge of the mould, the surplus is poured off. The shape is then baked at a high temperature for days. The resulting hard body, known as the "biscuit," is dipped in liquid glaze and then fired again for many hours.

Decoration can be applied direct on the biscuit before glazing or else on the glaze. China ware (as the body is very hard) is almost always decorated on the glaze, greater delicacy of pattern and a wider range of possible colours being obtained by this method. With earthenware (as the

the shadow through it. China gives out a clear ring when tapped, and is cold to the touch. It does not chip or crack easily, and when it does, the broken surface remains in a clean condition because china is non-porous and so does not absorb stains. Also china can be decorated in a wider range of colours—both more delicate and brighter—than earthenware.

Its raw materials are white china clay or kaolin, which gives plasticity, china stone, felspar and bone ash. The use of a high proportion of ground calcined bones is a characteristic of British manufacture. Almost all "bone china" is made in the U.K., where its production was first developed by Josiah Spode at the end of the eighteenth century, to replace the earlier imitations of Oriental china. This celebrated product plays an important rôle in British export trade. It is considered finer and more beautiful in texture than all other forms of china, as well as more durable than the Continental felspar china. It is pearly white in colour; felspar china is bluish-grey.

"Stone china" is midway in quality between china and earthenware. It is a blue-grey earthenware and so not translucent, but it will take colour decorations impossible with ordinary earthenware and is fine in texture and harder. There is only a limited amount on the market. It is made at the Spode potteries, where it originated.

Earthenware is composed of ball clay, felspar, china clay and flint. There are many variations in the ingredients and the resulting colour. Dishes made of it

Lustrous white bone china, with a classic design in grey and platinum — Royal Doulton's "Debut," above, has coupe-shaped, rimless plates

Top right, a charming modern design by Doulton called "Bamboo," in shades of brown and beige

Cool blues and greys bring a clean-cut freshness to this lovely design, Ice Rose, by Robert Minkin, by Wedgwood in fine bone china with coupe plates

This Rorstrand design for ovenware by Marianne Westman, called "Picknick," is modern in style and very colourful

Gold wreath on white bone china—Royal Doulton's "Rondo" was the design chosen by the citizens of Blackpool to present to Sir Winston and Lady Churchill

body is slightly porous) under-glaze decoration is largely used. Though the colour effects are more restricted with under-glaze decoration, the pattern has the advantage of being protected by the glaze and so is not easily damaged in use.

The decoration may be entirely by hand, or the pattern in outline transferred on to the glaze or the biscuit, and the colour filled in by hand. Or, in the cheaper types of ware, the entire design may be lithographed or transferred. The piece is again fired after decoration.

Gold, silver and platinum decoration is always applied on the glaze, and means yet another firing as it cannot take so high a temperature as the other decorations. In the best ware pure gold is used, gold dust being put on in a paste, and then hand-burnished—a slow and exacting process. The less costly "liquid gold" is used on cheaper ware. This is bright in appearance but not so lasting as burnished gold. Silver decoration is mixed with platinum, as silver on its own would tarnish.

Shape and Design

There is a clear distinction here between the traditional and the contemporary.

Which you choose depends largely on your personal taste and on suitability to your general type of furnishing. The delicate and intricate forms and patterns of traditional china are at home with old-style furniture. The flowing curves and more functional aspect of contemporary ware harmonise with the streamlined effects of modern décor. There is also a great deal of tableware produced which successfully combines the old and new and will not look out of place in any setting.

Traditional.—The graceful traditional shapes often owe their inspiration to the great potters of the eighteenth and early nineteenth centuries. The elaborately curved and indented edges and the fluting sometimes derive from silver models of the period.

Early designs—generally floral, and often using a great deal of gold ornament—are still used, though somewhat modified. For instance, Spode-Copeland's "Gold Arundel" design is a simplified version of one of Josiah Spode I's patterns, and their "Turquoise Florentine," of fine bone china, shows the outline print filled in by hand with ceramic colour in the old manner. Wedgwood's "Green Leaf" has a recent design of traditional inspiration on the "Queen's" shape—a shape Josiah Wedgwood was commissioned to create by Queen Charlotte in 1776.

Designs like Wedgwood's "Santa Clara," with the grapevine motif, Doulton's "Rondo" design, with its formal gold wreath of stylised plumes, and their

Dinner, tea and coffee services can be had in Wedgwood's beautiful "Turquoise Florentine"

Right, a simplified version of one of Josiah Spode's first patterns—Copeland-Spode's "Gold Arundel" with hand-painted sprays in pastel shades

Wedgwood's "Hathaway Rose," above, shows the sprays treated in a new way by designer Peter Hall, in warm pinks; greens and other colours

Avocado, left, a design by Wedgwood's Art Director, Victor Skellern, in the famous "Queen's" shape, the brown print hand-enamelled in yellow and black

Bright and striking, Midwinter's "Red Domino," below, blends attractively into a contemporary setting or provides gay contrast in a traditional one

"Debut," with a design of classic elegance in grey and platinum, are linked with the past, but have been produced to harmonise with the décor of any period.

Contemporary.—The tableware of the present period is characterised by its simplicity of line and decoration. The smooth unornamented curves of the best shapes are pleasant and graceful. The decoration is often bold—bands and splashes of colour, geometrical and abstract forms being used. On the other hand, small, delicate patterns with fine lines are increasing in favour. Floral patterns have become very popular —a particularly beautiful example is Doulton's "Sweetheart Rose"— and for those who dislike pattern in the centre of the plate there is Wedgwood's "Summer Garland."

The use of solid colour—(i.e. all-over colour, the clay itself having been stained in manufacture)—is a feature of both English and Continental contemporary tableware.

In shape, a recent and popular innovation is the "coupe" shape, in which the plates have no rims. The wide, shallow curved plate gives a wider "eating surface"

—and also an unbroken field for the design. Wedgwood's "Wild Oats" all-over design in grey, hand-painted in platinum on fine bone china, shows effective use of the coupe shape.

In most dinner services, bowls have taken the place of soup plates. When the rim is retained it is usually narrow, as in Wedgwood's "Grey Mayfield," which is an outstandingly good example of the modern treatment of a floral pattern.

The modern functional shapes appear throughout contemporary tableware. The pieces are designed to hold maximum capacity while occupying the minimum of space on the table or tray or in the cupboard—they are often square or oval. Handles are simple and shaped for comfortable and safe holding. Tea pots are "chunky" with short, strong spouts. The shapes generally are robust, low in height and with rounded edges, which cut down the danger of breakages and make for easy cleaning.

These characteristic forms can be seen in Midwinter's "Primavera" design, the abstract "Festival" design and in the use of solid colour in the black-and-white "Nature Study."

Doulton's coupe-shaped "Desert Star" and "April Showers," too, have cups turquoise outside and beige inside, with a delicate pattern on the beige.

Preserving Your China

The glaze and colours of tableware will last indefinitely if care is taken.

Plates should be warmed slowly and evenly—not exposed direct to fierce heat, or they will crackle and break through too rapid and uneven expansion. Warm them in a rack above the stove, or, if they are to be warmed on the stove, a wire cake rack on short feet is recommended on which to place them, to prevent direct contact with the hot metal.

When washing china, avoid pouring boiling water suddenly over it, or the glaze may be damaged. Do not let it stand long in water or soap and water. Dishes on which there are food acids—e.g. vinegar or lemon juice—should be washed as soon as possible, as these may cause damage, particularly to the on-glaze decoration of fine china. Wash the dishes in hot water with soap flakes or a mild detergent—do not be too lavish with the detergent.

A non-sud detergent is recommended for use with washing-up machines. Harsh abrasives should be avoided.

Have only a few things in the bowl at the same time—they can then be washed more efficiently and will not be so liable to get chipped.

The most precious pieces are best washed separately with a folded cloth placed in the bottom of the bowl for protection.

Rinse in clear water, dry thoroughly and polish with a soft cloth.

When putting them away, be careful not to scratch the glaze when stacking plates. Cups can easily be damaged if they are stacked one inside the other; it is preferable to hang them on hooks.

A sprinkling of desert flowers in turquoise to match cups and jugs— Royal Doulton's "April Showers" in fine earthenware, above

Left, "Nature Study" in Midwinter's Stylecraft range, has flowing lines, unusual modern shapes, the dinner plates coupeshaped and with maximum eating surface

THE STORY BEHIND TWO LOVELY DESIGNS

Designer Terence Conran took the familiar ingredients of a salad as his theme and drew them in vivid colours. Result—amusing modern china, Midwinter's "Salad Ware" (above) in exciting new shapes. Note the boomerang dish and unusual bowls.

Here the inspiration comes from the ancients—Copeland Spode's "Moondrop" dinner service (below) has a design on Celtic lines, the flowers symbolising Trinity and the scrolls Eternity, the name a reminder that, to the Celts, the moon was the symbol of purity

THE JOY OF
"DOING
THE FLOWERS"

In the leisured days of long ago, when servants did all the real work, it was Madam's privilege and duty to "do the flowers." In these two charming arrangements a modern floral artist, Constance Spry, puts roses in a deep bowl, carnations in a jardinière. Both containers are Spode-Copeland's Fortuna Ware in pale green and ivory

HOW FAIR IS THE ROSE!

"You may break, you may shatter the vase, if you will,
But the scent of the roses will hang round it still"

SO wrote Thomas Moore. Like all poets, the sight and scent of roses translated him to romantic mood.

Loveliest of flowers, no garden anywhere is complete without them; and such is the sturdy nature of their growth, that roses will flourish in almost any garden.

They prefer clay to sandy soil, and in spite of their beauty they are very greedy. Decayed vegetable matter well forked in, if you cannot obtain cow manure, should be mixed and used also on the surface as a mulch.

Weather permitting, roses can be planted any time between November and March, but the ground must be dry; never plant them in sodden or frozen soil.

Pruning must begin severely in the spring to encourage new growth, and this should be done with very sharp secateurs unless you are an expert with the pruning knife.

Do not hoe around the roots too deeply; they are very near the surface. Also in warm weather they want constant drenching with water.

Watch out all the time for the rose's main enemies—caterpillar and greenfly. The former attacks both the leaves and the buds, and the pest should be either removed by hand, or—if you don't like this —by preparations sold for the purpose everywhere. Greenfly can be recognised in clusters on new shoots, and they must be discovered early and sprayed.

Before ordering your roses, go, if possible, to see them growing in the nurseryman's garden. Then you can plan their transfer, draw up colour schemes, or ask advice about soils.

LOVE LETTERS MADE OF FLOWERS

"An exquisite invention this,
Worthy of love's most honeyed kiss,
This art of writing billets-doux
In buds, and odours, and bright hues!
In saying all one feels and thinks—
In clever daffodils and pinks"

wrote Leigh Hunt in a charming poem called "Love Letters Made of Flowers," which mainly concerned the carnation. And how right he was is proved by the number of bridal bouquets made of carnations.

Any garden can grow them in a sunny border, or with other flowers in a herbaceous border. Carnation growing is not an expensive hobby. In July each year you can propagate your own by layering, which means selecting strong shoots, stripping off the leaves to about the fourth pair from the tip of the shoot, then making a cut halfway through a joint below to produce a tongue to be pressed into sandy soil on the surface.

It is kept in position by a hairpin or wooden peg, and, if watered often, the layers will root in about six weeks. You can then sever, lift and replant—but in cold districts keep in a frame for the winter.

If carnations are planted too deeply, they die of stem rot, so the safest way to winter them is in $2\frac{1}{2}$-in. pots in a greenhouse.

Disbudding is important, as carnation stems carry a number of buds, none of which will be of good quality unless the numbers are reduced.

It is always the topmost bud that will develop into the finest flower, so remove the side buds by pinching them out.

Most precious of all scents, when they release their fragrance on a summer evening, carnations generously reward their grower.

MAKING A GARDEN FROM SCRATCH

*How to set about turning a plot of neglected
land into that lovesome thing, a garden*

WHATEVER the size of a new garden,
consider first the prospect from your
house. Look long and earnestly from the
windows of the rooms which will be most
used. Ask yourself the question: What do
I want to *see* when this garden has been
made?

So many alternatives suggest themselves.
A lawn and a lily pond, against a background of rambler roses tumbling opulently over arches and pergolas.

Or—if the builders have left behind a
litter of bricks and rubble which must be
moved anyway—a rock garden blazing
with colour and bright, sweet-scented
camomile paths.

Or again—an old-fashioned cottage garden to produce fresh fruit and vegetables,
and to fill the store cupboards with bottled
produce for the winter.

A Fascinating Hobby

Or perhaps, to save labour, just a garden
of flowering shrubs to give a nice show of
colour even in mid-winter. A fascinating
hobby this, and inexpensive, because
others with similar gardens are always
generous with their cuttings.

The choice is wide. Perhaps you'd like
a garden just to potter in—a miniature
rock garden here, a plot of vegetables
there, and roses where the sun shines most.

Well, it's *your* garden, and starting from
scratch you can make it what you like.
You can take your time about it and walk
before you run, providing always that first
you provide yourself with something to
walk *on*.

Clean, dry paths are a first essential; they
are the veins of every garden, and indeed
two of them might be called arteries—one
leading to the line where washing is hung
out, and the other to the compost heap—
a strong path, this, to withstand heavy two-way barrow traffic. Neither need be permanent at first, but they must be provided.
Afterwards the pattern may well shape it-

self. Paths can be broad or narrow, straight
or winding, they can be "crazy," or merely
stepping stones laid flush with the lawn to
avoid interference with the mowing. They
can be of grass, or concrete, or of gravel.

The Choice of Paths

Before making final plans, study the
pros and cons. Nothing is more beautiful
in a garden than a broad grass path running between mixed flower borders; and
the older it gets, if well mown and tended,
the lovelier it becomes. *But* will a grass
path stand up to barrow traffic in wet
weather? The answer, regretfully, is—no.

A *concrete* walk, on the other hand,
bordered by flowers to soften the effect, is
very serviceable. In fact, it has every advantage except one—it may be too permanent. Once it is down you cannot shift it
easily, and later on it may not conform to
the unfolding design of the garden.

Crazy paving is not so rigid. It can be
used as a compromise between the formal
and the informal, and when curved can
produce a most artistic effect, softened
later by green moss.

But crazy paving produces problems of
its own. Weeds grow as well as moss, or
better. The crevices are soon inhabited
by groundsel, dandelions, docks and
nettles, and these involve an annual charge
on the estate in the purchase of chemicals
with which to eliminate them. When this
happens the moss dies too.

Why not Stepping Stones?

A *gravel* path has many advantages, and
it is economical to make if you have on
the premises plenty of broken brick and
hard stones or clinker with which to drain
it. All these must be rammed home before
the gravel is put on. The surface must
then be rolled, after which the path can
stand up to normal traffic. What it will
not stand up to, however, and this must be
faced, is prolonged rain. Thunderstorms

Clean, dry paths are the first essential, particularly one leading to the washing line and another to the compost heap

play havoc with a gravel path. They may even shift most of the gravel from the surface into the flower beds at either side.

Return, therefore, to the window with a pencil and a pad. Why not compromise for a while by laying *stepping stones* which can be lifted or twisted, curved or laid straight? Use large rectangular slabs of stone placed at even distances and spaced for comfortable strides. Maybe in the end you will stick to this idea.

Enclosing the Boundaries

Now take a walk round the boundary, for fruit trees and flowering shrubs in other gardens become part of *your* picture from the windows. There may be none, of course, just as there may be neither fencing nor hedges. A simple wooden fence permits the maximum of light and air to the garden, but unless the posts are embedded in concrete they will rot in the ground and have to be replaced. The same applies to screens or a closely boarded fence, but the expense is worth it if you want privacy. This may depend on location; a town garden calls for more privacy

than a country garden. Screens make an excellent background for mixed flower borders, or you can train fruit bushes or trees against them and harvest profitable crops.

Hedges might be more suitable for your boundaries, and to divide the vegetable garden from the lawn, if so desired. They take up a lot of space, but starting from scratch they are economical in comparison with fencing and screens of wood. For quick growth there is nothing to touch the sometimes despised privet, if it is planted in November and cut down from the start. The same applies to Cupressus Macrocarpa, which is cheap and quick-growing and maintains a fresh colour all the year round. Holly, too, makes a grand hedge, but it is slow-growing; box and yew are slower still.

Sweet briar and Rosa rugosa make lovely hedges, providing both flowers and scent, and both are very hardy. But they are difficult to keep clean at the base, and are so prickly that thick gloves are needed for the pruning. Laurel forms a stately hedge, but it needs a lot of room. And pruning requires secateurs rather than shears or the hedge will become stunted.

Quince makes a good utility hedge, especially if the soil is damp and heavy. Young bushes can be intertwined as they grow, and they make an effective barrier, while the fruit is valuable for jellies or for flavourings.

Preparing the Soil

If, from the window, decisions about paths and boundaries have been made, what is the next step in starting a garden from scratch? The answer is—to get the soil into some sort of condition in which plants will grow.

First make a heap of old bricks, stones and rubble. Another heap of weeds, brambles, thistles, couch grass, plantain and buttercup—for burning. During this preliminary work, you will get a rough idea of the first layout, and when it is done peg out a scheme (it will be changed many times as work progresses) of paths, lawn areas and beds.

The task may seem rather hopeless if the soil has been under a heavy covering of weeds and grass, but the point to keep in mind is that *there is no such thing as bad soil*. Every variety of soil has some virtue, and it can be prepared to produce something good. For this reason, whatever it may look like, the arduous work of digging can be cheerfully begun.

Cut the top growth down with a sickle or a hook. Then remove the turves, but do not dig them into the top layer of soil. The odds are that the turves are still full of perennial weeds, so start your compost heap with them in a corner, dusting each layer with lime or sulphate of ammonia.

Now dig to a spade's depth (or "spit"), turning each spadeful over and chopping up the lumps as you go. At once the problem arises—shall I trench the soil to three spits deep and thus ensure good drainage from the very beginning?

On this subject the opinion of experts varies greatly. But the type of soil you have should dictate. If it is naturally well-drained, deep trenching might well do far more harm than good. But if the plot is of stiff clay, making it wet and boggy, there can be no doubt that deep digging pays, though the labour is heavy and tedious and apt to be discouraging.

Why not compromise once again? Everyone with a new garden is eager to see something growing, so if the season is right for their sowing a start can be made with potatoes. Dig therefore to one "spit's" depth and sow potatoes.

The reason this plan is advocated is that potatoes will grow almost anywhere; when they appear above the surface they must be earthed-up and hoed at frequent intervals, which improves the top soil. And when they are harvested finally, you have dug the ground. By that time not only will you have learned a great deal about your soil and its needs, but you will have had some return from it as well.

Perhaps you will never grow a potato again after that first crop, but always you will be grateful to that wonderful pioneer tuber, the cultivation of which teaches so much. Your lawns, roses and flower beds can follow potatoes, always to their advantage, provided the tubers have been properly dug out, leaving none behind in the soil.

The Lawn

A garden with a lawn is by far the most popular. It provides an outdoor playroom for the children, a deck-chair haven for week-ends and holidays, exercise with the mower for parents; it is a place in the sun when it shines. Besides, making and tending a lawn is a fascinating pursuit.

Autumn is the best time to start work digging, levelling and rolling the soil; and if the surface is sloping, it can be drained quite easily by laying pipes in herringbone fashion. The main drain needs a pipe of larger diameter, and for the best results fill the trenches with clinkers or stones. For a small lawn on the level clinker drains are enough, at intervals of about 20 ft.; and these will deal with pools of water after heavy rain.

After the final rolling, let the soil lie for a few weeks; then rake and roll the surface until it is smooth and even. For the seed sowing in April use an empty coffee tin with a hole punched in the lid, and to ensure that the seed is sown evenly, mark off the ground in strips a yard wide with the garden line. After this marking off, get a measuring stick 3 ft. long, and mark off square yard by placing it at right angles to the line. For each square yard thus marked

2 oz. of grass seed will be required, so that if every strip is sown in this manner the total quantity of seed required will be easily estimated.

Rake the seed in after sowing, and if leaving the job temporarily, erect a good scarecrow. A pole and crossbar on which to hang old clothes is the best method to scare away the innumerable birds that love to feed on grass seed.

An alternative and quicker method of making a lawn is to lay turf, which is usually sold in strips 3 ft. by 1 ft., but this is expensive. In either case, much attention will be needed during the first year with fertilisers and constant weeding. Deep-rooted weeds such as docks or dandelion must be extracted immediately they appear, whereas daisies and plantains can be burned off by applying sulphate of ammonia to the leaves. This will leave patches of bare earth which can be dealt with by adding sifted soil and sowing more seed.

The first mowing of a lawn is an important operation, for the grass must not be allowed to get too thick and long before it is cut. The mowing machine should be sharpened and well oiled and the blades set high. On no account should a new lawn be mown when the weather is wet. The same applies to rolling, which clogs the soil so that surplus water cannot drain away. Even without rolling, the lawn may need to be aerated by pressing a digging fork at intervals deeply all over the surface.

During the summer the edges have to be trimmed, and if they are curved edges to conform with wavy paths, this must be done frequently or the lawn will soon start wandering.

Garden Adornments

Adornments such as pergolas and rustic arches can now be considered, though again it is advisable to return to the windows and survey the scene before erecting anything permanent. Too much "furniture" in a garden gives the same impression of overcrowding as it does in a room, and if you are growing rambler roses over it they, too, require a lot of space. So first

Rock gardens, often begun from the bricks and rubble left by the builders, are the answer to desert plots, but they need a strong core of stone

draw a plan on paper to see how it fits in with the garden design.

What does greatly improve a small garden with a lawn is a lily pool, at the back of which you can erect a trellis arbour containing a seat. The *Dorothy Perkins* rambler will grow quickly over the arbour, and give masses of lovely pink colour; or you can mix other varieties with it, such as *Excelsa* (crimson), *François Juranville* (salmon), or *Alberic Barbier* (creamy white).

To make a lily pool, first peg out the design to the dimensions most suitable, then drive the pegs in deeply and dig to a depth of 18–24 in. Nail 3-in. sawn timber against the pegs, then after trimming and levelling, pour in the concrete composed of three parts sand and one part cement to a depth of $1\frac{1}{2}$ in. over the bottom and sides.

Remove the timber when the concrete has set, and surface the pond surround, including the floor of the arbour, with a mixture of sand and cement.

But of course this suggested design is only one of dozens that may be applied to a small garden with a lawn, and many owners are understandably shy about introducing cement, which is so permanent. They prefer to try out ideas which can be changed until the right design is discovered. How wise they are!

The Rock Garden

Rock gardens can be either a small part of the general design (often begun from the bricks and rubble left behind by the builders), or with winding paths they can occupy the whole space. In the latter case, the owners are usually confirmed rock gardeners who make a study of the large variety of plants which are available for this delightful hobby.

Beginners often take it up through sheer heartbreak caused by very poor soil in which it is impossible to grow anything on the flat. For example, in a new housing estate which was built on an old brickfield, ample space was provided for gardens but as there was no soil of any kind left, nothing would grow.

Then one enterprising tenant turned his desert plot into a rock garden, and all his neighbours followed suit. Between them they produced original designs of great beauty, although at first they made avoidable mistakes. It is essential to have a strong core of stone to prevent sinking. On this a plentiful supply of old bricks, set tightly together, using clay as mortar, can be built into slopes and mounds. Soil must be imported and riddled into the crevices before anything is planted, but the expense of this should not be great.

Rock gardeners, even on a small scale, soon become internationally minded. They can grow peonies from the Balearic Islands, stemless geraniums from the Andes, or gentians from the Alps.

Cottage Gardens

The *old-fashioned cottage garden* demands good soil, unceasing cultivation and loyalty to the first principle that the weight of compost or manure dug in annually must be at least equal to the weight of the crops harvested. Knowing this, the cottage gardener never wastes a thing. His kitchen refuse, bonfire ashes, weeds, potato haulms, all are composted to be returned to the soil. And in return he sets out to provide himself and his family with vegetables, fruit, smokes and wines, all of which may be harvested annually from a small-sized plot.

Knowledge is required for this and much labour, but the rewards are manifold. A cottage garden is a visible income producer; it can eliminate greengrocery bills from the budget.

There is no reason why it should not be beautiful as well as economical. If there is a strip between the gate and the front door, this should be filled with a jumble of all sorts of flowers—Canterbury bells, sweet williams, pansies, stocks—in addition to crocus and daffodils in the spring.

No nice country cottage is without this type of front strip, which is usually the special pride of the housewife; but the real business of supplying the kitchen from the garden goes on at the back, in the male partner's province. It has become a skilful art with many amateurs who have studied country technique. They have learned how to till their plots for crops to follow each other in quick succession to fill the store cupboards.

Starting from scratch in the knowledge that the garden's productive powers will be taxed to the utmost, the digging must be thoroughly completed. When breaking

Daffodils were first brought to London by a confirmed garden "potterer," who
grew them behind his chemist's shop off Holborn in 1600

up new grass land in preparation for vegetable crops, the top soil must be removed while the subsoil is broken up, and then the turves thrown in grass side downwards to be chopped up before the top soil is replaced. This provides humus and drainage below the first spit, and though it may produce weeds later on, they can be tackled on the surface as they come up.

Rotation of Crops

At this point we come to the second principle which must be obeyed—*the rotation of crops*. Briefly, this is the ordering of a succession in such a manner that the crops will tax the mineral elements in a different manner.

Here is a simple plan for dividing the space into three plots so as to have a rotation on each covering three years:

Plot	1st Year	2nd Year	3rd Year
A	Cabbages	Peas	Turnips
B	Leeks	Carrots	Seakale
C	Brussels sprouts	Onions	Celery

This can be greatly varied. The owner of a small garden can get as much produce from his plot as one with twice the area by *intercropping*. Different vegetable crops vary in the time they take to reach maturity, so the ground between the slow-moving plants can be used. For instance, shallots can be planted 1 ft. apart each way in January. In March you can sow two broad bean rows between the shallots, and these will be 3 ft. apart when the shallots are pulled in June. Now the unoccupied ground can be planted with (say) broccoli or cabbage.

In this manner the cultivator stirs up the soil, and is continually exposing fresh surfaces to the atmosphere. Remember that *the very air that plants breathe is a powerful manure*. It affords them much of their food, but they will fail from exhaustion if organic manure or compost is not dug in for every new crop as well. Parsnips and carrots are perhaps an exception. They push down so much deeper than the brassicas to obtain their mineral food, and the roots are apt to become distorted by manure. The parsnip is a splendid root to grow on poor land. Its ashes contain potash, lime, phosphate of iron and common salt, and for this reason parsnips make excellent wine.

Other vegetable crops leave behind them valuable minerals on which certain successors will thrive without the addition of humus. For example, peas sown where celery has been grown will thrive without any further preparation beyond the levelling of the ground and the drawing of the necessary drills.

If space permits, a plot can be profitably devoted to *permanent* crops that will occupy their quarters for many years. Asparagus, mint, rhubarb, seakale and herbs all come under this heading, though the herbs which are in everyday use in the kitchen, such as parsley, chives, thyme and tarragon, should be as near the back door as possible in case they are urgently needed on a wet day.

Asparagus has ceased to be an aristocrat in the vegetable world; it grows as readily in a new garden as it does in a walled enclosure. From seed the crop takes 208 weeks to reach maturity, which is the reason why three-year or four-year-old crowns (which produce crops the same year as planted) are so expensive. But if you have the patience and space, sow asparagus seed and wait for it. Once the beds are in bearing, they go on indefinitely with very little trouble beyond constant hoeing.

Permanent Crops

Ground for the permanent crops must be deeply dug and enriched beforehand. The Persian word for manure is "rishwa," meaning bribery, which tells its own story in a nutshell. Volumes have been written about the making of composts and the rival claims of farmyard manures and artificials, but the truth is that you can *bribe* your cottage garden with almost anything, and if by chance the gardener has a surplus of vegetables he cannot use, or the stalks and outer leaves of cabbages and Brussels sprouts left behind, he can chop them up and return them to the soil again. The grower should try to understand the housewife's viewpoint. One who keeps her household happy with fruit and vegetables all the year round entirely from a cottage garden tended by her husband asked me to guess what was her most profitable crop.

My guess was onions, because at home we eat a lot of them, sometimes pickled and often cooked in stews and soups. But in her view onions came only third in value; celery was first and leeks were second. She said that in her kitchen, celery won easily because not a scrap of it was wasted. The outside leaves and stalks made soup and wine, while the remainder (when the tender white centre had been extracted for eating raw) could be cooked as a main dish in a variety of ways.

Why did leeks take second place in this estimate? Simply because of that "Hungry Gap" (April–June) which is a nightmare for housewives. The common leek is then indispensable because, with celery, it helps to fill that gap when only the most expensive vegetables (generally imported) can be had in the shops.

As a matter of interest, cauliflower came fourth in this list because it can be used so often as a separate dish, especially with the cheese left-overs. This common-sense domestic review has been of the greatest assistance to our planning.

Using Cloches

The "Hungry Gap" can be eliminated altogether by the introduction of *cloches*, a development that has enriched cottage gardeners beyond measure. The portable glass can be used for warming the soil before sowing, for protecting early crops against frost and birds, for keeping superfluous wet out, and for hurrying everything along. For example, one year we enjoyed on May 25th our first dish of green peas from a dwarf variety sown in November, and new potatoes, started under cloches, on June 6th.

Cottage gardeners are finding out new ways of using cloches every year, and there are some ingenious designs on the market which are like outdoor greenhouses. You can grow cucumbers and melons or even grapes under cloches, and crops such as these add a new interest and sophistication to the routine. We cut our melons with a length of stem attached, put them in jars filled with blackberry wine (the cheapest French red wines will do as well) so that the melons draw the wine through their stems and all their flesh becomes suffused with it—a delicious and delightful experiment which can be recommended.

August is a good month to start with cloches; the plan being to keep them busy all the year round. The moment they come off one crop, down they go on another strip which has been made ready and sown with lettuces, peas, carrots or radishes (see chapter on The Small Cloche Garden).

Always in the cottage garden there must be room for *fruit*. A blackberry bush can be trained on a fence, and is a valuable asset because it will produce heavy crops for jams, jellies, pies, bottling or wine.

Find Room for Fruit

Similarly, a row of raspberry canes can be tucked away alongside a fence to be trained cordon fashion. Strawberries in a cottage garden need not be trained as permanencies; they can follow early potatoes to yield for one year only. Then they are grubbed up to make way for something else.

Gooseberry bushes or black currants are in a different category, as they are permanent and take up a lot of room; but if you look over the fence of almost any country cottage garden you will find they usually occupy an honoured place amongst the vegetables here and there. And, because the ground is turned over so frequently around them, they can supply a bumper harvest for the winter. You may even see an apple tree, though in making a garden from scratch this is not advised unless there is plenty of room.

But if an apple tree is introduced, make sure that it is not a variety such as Cox, which cannot fruit without another apple tree to act as a polinator. It is better to plant a moderate spreading variety for general purposes, such as the *Grenadier*. This hardy tree produces a useful early cooker; and when ripe in August or September the fruit can be used for dessert as well.

A plum tree is not recommended. It might get the dreaded "silver leaf" disease from which there is little chance of recovery, while in terms of value it will probably only fruit when there is a glut of plums and they are very cheap to buy. The same remarks apply to damsons, which are extremely temperamental.

Tomato Cultivation

Home-grown tomatoes are always a gamble with the weather unless they are cultivated in a greenhouse, but they make such a difference to our salad bowls during the summer that most gardeners take a chance. They can be grown out of doors to yield good crops at least two years out of three, but at any time it is fatal to plant them out too early in the season when the soil has not been warmed up by sunshine and there is still a danger of frost. The best time in the south of England is the end of May, and in the north mid-June.

The plot *must* be sunny and warm and sheltered from wind.

For outdoor tomatoes both light and heavy soils need organic material before planting, and the plot should be enriched with a balanced fertiliser containing hop manure. Tomatoes require nitrogen, phosphate and potash to ensure healthy

Magnolia, with its splendid white flowers, is one of the most popular of the flowering shrubs. But it does not like east or north positions

growth, so work the hop manure into the top nine inches of soil and do not bury it in the bottom of a trench.

There are so many varieties, all of them good, that the nurseryman should be consulted before purchase. He will advise which do best *locally*—an important point.

Growing routine is quite simple. The plants are placed 18 in. apart, in rows 30 in. apart. Dig a generous hole for the root ball, and then firm in the plant with the fingers slightly below the level of the ground. This gives a hollow round each plant to retain water and moisture.

Tomato plants need regular feeding when the first truss is set, and for this there are many reliable fertilisers sold with all the necessary instructions, but a point to remember is that the application should be made in circles round the plant, otherwise scorching will occur; and always *water after feeding*.

This treatment should be repeated at intervals of about 10 days; it is the secret of successful tomato growing, and only by this method (plus, of course, the necessary sunshine) can heavy crops be ensured.

Tomatoes for store purposes and for bottling should be picked as soon as they begin to colour. They will gradually ripen in a dark room or in straw over a much longer period than those which are left on the plants.

Marrows and Cucumbers

Marrows are accommodating and will flourish in any odd corner, but there is a strange reluctance in the U.K. to try new varieties. It is worth while hunting through the seed catalogues for originality in marrows. For example, "Banana Squash" is not a fruit drink; it is a marrow you can eat like a melon, uncooked. If it is cut with a long stem and placed in a jar containing a little red wine, it will absorb this and be delicious to eat.

Young marrow plants are raised in pots in a cold greenhouse, and planted out when they have three or four leaves. They require plenty of compost or manure underneath in a large, deep hole, but the spread of the plant becomes great as they grow and they need a lot of surface room.

Much the same cultivation routine applies to outdoor Cucumbers, known as "Ridge" cucumbers. These can be grown on 4-ft. beds by taking out the soil to a depth of 15 in., spreading about that depth of compost to which leaves or litter may be added, and covering with a foot depth of soil. The seeds may be sown direct in May. Put the plants at 30 in. apart right along the bed and, when growing freely, nip out the points once only when five or six leaves have developed.

Outdoor cucumbers make a slow beginning if the weather is cold, so it is a good plan to provide them with shelter by growing one or two rows of runner beans on the windward side of the ridge. Once the cucumbers begin to thrive they are brisk in their movements if they have a good bed. They have prickly backs and are not so handsome as the greenhouse varieties, but in flavour they are quite equal to them. And if the crop should be enormous, as sometimes happens, they can be put to excellent use for making lotions.

A first-class recipe for beauty treatment (or, for men, after-shaving lotion) is to cut six ripe cucumbers into slices about $\frac{1}{2}$ in. thick. Steam till soft enough to pass through a colander, then press through a piece of butter muslin. Measure the pulp, and for every 3 oz. allow $\frac{1}{2}$ pint of distilled rose water, $\frac{1}{4}$ drachm of powdered borax, and 25 drops of tincture of benzoin. Dissolve the borax in the rose water, add the benzoin drop by drop, shaking the bottle at intervals. Lastly, add the rose water to the pulp and shake up again.

Clean, dry paths are essential to the *Garden of Flowering Shrubs*, otherwise the pleasure of enjoying a walk after rain is denied, and shrubs are always at their best after a downpour.

Flowering Shrub Garden

The choice of plants is wide. You can have climbing and wall shrubs, dwarf shrubs or tall; or shrubs suitable for windy and bleak aspects which bring gaiety with them.

If shrubs for covering walls are chosen for the garden from scratch, there are many which will soon transform dreary spaces. Ivy lovers should be careful however; it is a good servant and a very bad master. Ivy is best grown over a low edging of stones on which it can creep and be kept under control. Choose several different varieties for a good show.

What more delightful than a border of herbs, with its delicious fragrance and decorative foliage?

Clematis, too, when allowed to grow wild, has destroyed many a strong veranda, but when kept within limits and properly trained to cover a wall, the flowers repay all trouble.

The honeysuckles provide lovely covering, but they must have their heads in the sun and their roots in cool soil. Seedling plants discovered in the woods do well when transplanted in gardens, and there is no scent comparable with that of wild woodbine. For the sophisticated houseowner the nurserymen grow many varieties of honeysuckle, notably the "Scarlet Trumpet," which makes a fine show of golden-scarlet flowers throughout the summer. They have also autumn flowering honeysuckles which will bloom until Christmas.

Jasmine is a sun-lover and will provide a lovely hanging curtain over an ugly space. There are winter varieties which are very hardy. All wall shrubs are subject to dryness however, especially when they are trained on south or west walls, and they need a good mulching to keep them fresh.

For bordering the paths at little outlay, dwarf or "carpeting" shrubs are useful, such as conifers, rhododendrons, and daphnes, and they mix very well with a show of spring bulbs. The rhododendron family is one of the largest in the world, and for this reason some of their admirers cultivate nothing else. The Royal Horticultural Society's handbook on the subject contains the names of 2,500 different species, and room can be found for quite a number of these even in a comparatively small garden.

The bush rhododendrons, if allowed, will grow to a great height if their roots are kept cool and well mulched. There are many modern hybrids such as the crimson Pink Pearl and Hugh Koster; while a delightful carmine is the John Waterer.

Magnolias are also a big family, and the easiest to grow is M. soulangeana, the white flowers of which are stained with purple on the reverse. These shrubs require a deep well-manured soil, and they do not like exposed east or northerly positions.

The Berberis family is attractive, and can be had in tall or dwarf forms. Their

The Rotogardener (left) takes the backache out of gardening. It digs, hoes, levels, weeds, cuts long grass, hauls a trailer, ridges uncultivated land and furrows

Mowing the lawn is as light a job as pushing the pram with the Rotoscythe (below)

flowering periods can be spread over half the year by planting Berberis Japonica Bealei for masses of yellow flowers in February; Berberis Darwinii for orange flowers in April; or Berberis Wilsonæ for a striking mass of colour in the autumn. Thinning and pruning is not a difficult matter if heavy gloves are worn to protect the hands from sharp spikes.

Beginners are advised to make a start with only a few shrubs, to be sure that they are planted in the right places. Grouping plans prevent mistakes; from the windows of the house it is good to be able to see an effect of (say) winter cherry blooms from November till February, as a background to the rhododendrons, which will come into full flower later. Or if hydrangeas are introduced for late summer blooming, they in turn must not be masked by the rhododendrons. Each shrub, in fact, should be treated as an individual and not as in the Victorian idea of a "shrubbery," where they were all massed together and none grew well. The aim nowadays is to grow shrubs rather like herbaceous borders, in depth.

Shrubs cost practically nothing in upkeep. They require little labour and maintenance; very often the stock can be acquired from friends who are only too pleased to present cuttings.

A development of the shrub garden which has become very popular is the heath garden. Heaths are products of the moors, and when transplanted to gardens they take care of themselves. But they do not like lime or waterlogged soil.

Heath Gardens

Once again a modest start is recommended, because heaths take pleasure in extending themselves and single plants soon become dozens. Even a small collection will provide flowers all the year round, demanding only the most trifling attention.

In preparing the soil for heaths, work in plenty of decayed vegetable matter and some moss peat which can be bought from any nursery. In planting, the same principle should be applied as for the shrubs, the dwarf heaths in front and the taller ones in the rear. After that, arrange the plants in groups to supply the best colour schemes.

You can have triangles of reds and deep purples, or whites and blues; and if you think you can improve on the original plan, heaths can be moved about without harm.

Paths of the kind needed in other types of garden are unnecessary for a heath garden as the plants themselves have a habit of carpeting over them, but stepping stones are recommended if only to keep feet dry after rain.

Gardens for Potterers

The garden to potter in is the dream of many on retirement. It is the garden which may have begun from scratch some time previously with the object of leisure in view. The span of life is about 20 years longer than it was in 1900; and a garden to potter in is the answer to the problem of what a man shall do with those extra 20 years.

It should contain a greenhouse, no matter how small, if only to afford an alternative to the house on a wet morning. Dull days can be most enjoyable in a greenhouse, where so much young stock for the outside garden can be raised from seeds or cuttings. There are many designs of portable greenhouses on the market, and the cost is not great if you think of the saving in supplying stock.

It can be a hobby, too, for flower lovers. As an example, Schizanthus (the Butterfly Flower) can be sown in September to produce lovely blooms at Christmas; and even the smallest greenhouse will help to raise fuchsias, hydrangeas and chrysanthemums.

The lean-to greenhouse is the most popular type, but the site should be carefully chosen, facing south if possible. Interior heating can be added, but it is expensive in any form, and beginners are advised to learn first from experience the science of greenhouse management. This is a fascinating hobby.

Rose growers are said to be perfectionists, and why not? Roses bloom the first year after planting, and the more you cut them the better they thrive; above all, they display themselves best in small beds cut out in grass.

Rose beds must contain plenty of humus prior to planting; in fact it is a good plan

You may start with a mountain of rubble or a desert waste, but you can end up with a garden like this, its beds of tulips ablaze in the spring

to turn over the top spit and break up the subsoil to a depth of 18 in., mixing it with leaves, grass cuttings, etc., before replacing the top soil. Finish off by adding 4 oz. of bone meal to every square yard on top.

A rose bed 5 ft. wide will take three rows, the plants at 2 ft. apart, and of course there is a wide choice of varieties among standards, weeping standards, bush roses, dwarf and climbing roses. The rose grower soon finds himself immersed in such technical affairs as budding, pruning and grafting, all of which are simple enough when tackled in the manner laid down in the official R.H.S. handbooks.

Sweet Peas

Sweet peas also have an appeal in this type of garden. By careful study, the grower can produce an amazing diversity of colours, enlargement of size and number of flowers on each stem. Trenching the soil beforehand is important, for the roots of sweet peas run to a considerable depth, and here again it is a good plan first to dig in all available green refuse and compost for the plants to feed on.

The cordon system of growing sweet peas is very popular for shows or house decoration. The plants are put out in double rows 1 ft. apart, and spaced a foot apart in lines. Each plant carries two shoots only, each provided with a rod about 10 ft. high. The rods are placed 6 in. apart in the rows, with a stout pole at the end of each row to which a substantial cross-piece is fixed. From these cross-pieces wires, to which the rods are tied, are stretched tightly. As growth develops, the plants must be disbudded, the laterals and tendrils are removed, and each cordon is tied to its supporting rod with raffia. Results justify all this "pottering," and the culture of sweet peas becomes a joy.

Bulb culture is another hobby for the potterer. The merit of bulbs is the ease with which they can be forced into flower, especially at a period of the year when bright blossoms are precious. The daffodil was first brought to London by a real "potterer" in 1600. He was an apothecary called John Parkinson, who cultivated his daffodils in a small garden sloping from his shop to the cobbled pavements of Holborn. He taught himself how to hybridise from specimens of wild daffodils he found in St. John's Wood—then in the country.

A garden to potter in may always be the setting for adventure. Mushrooms can be grown beneath the greenhouse shelves, rhubarb may be forced for the making of wine, orchids can be raised. Such a garden often contains a fruit cage, but this is *not* recommended to the beginner starting from scratch, though it was fashionable not so very long ago.

Fruit growers avoid fruit cages now because the ground inside is difficult to keep clean, and weeds flourish along the wire borders where they cannot be got at. Also, in time the wire becomes rusty and the roof sags.

Admittedly the temperature inside is several degrees warmer and the fruit therefore ripens earlier, which is a great advantage with red fruits such as red currants, gooseberries, raspberries and strawberries; and these are also protected from the ravages of birds. But in the long run the weeds in a fruit cage win. They grow not only through the wires but through the gooseberries; they twine themselves round the raspberries and choke the currants, until the scene is one of desolation because the owner cannot use his hoe and is constantly bumping his head on sagging wire.

Let the "potterer" spend the time he saves by denying himself a fruit cage on growing his fruit in the open, the bushes spaced at the correct intervals, so that he can use his tools, prune and mulch without the nagging presence of wire—and he will be much happier. If he also possesses a beehive, the insects will assure polination. They will provide him, too, with honey for the brewing of mead—the finest of all rewards at the end of a day's work for the adventurer in gardening.

In the days when farm labourers were poorly paid, their gardens helped to restore the balance, and this can be done with new gardens to-day. People who are buying their own properties through building societies, banks or mortgages can look to their gardens to provide the rent. They need not worry about making mistakes at first; they will learn the craft as they go along. And the best way to start is to tackle every job as it comes, whether you know how or not. No garden is the same as another therefore the technique or cultivating it must be the owner's own discovery.

When starting a fresh garden job, pack all the tools you will need into the barrow and wheel it to the spot. Small hand tools are best kept together in a trug

TOOLS FOR THE GARDEN

Choosing the essentials and learning how to
use them without undue fatigue

GARDEN tools are like golf clubs; you can have a lot or only a few indispensables—and the fewer the better in the beginning. It is better for tyros to learn how to use a spade or hoe properly before increasing the stock, and good-quality tools improve with use.

The **digging spade** comes first on the list of indispensables. Sizes are standardised and numbered to suit the build of their owners, an important factor, particularly for housewives who cultivate their own gardens without help. A spade which is too heavy increases labour; worse, it encourages indifferent technique. It is the only tool which will turn over the soil and chop up hard lumps. For proper digging the left hand should be placed palm downwards to grip lightly, while the right hand is used as a lever and pushes downwards when the laden spade is lifted.

Fatigue associated with spade work is caused by rushing at the job. Professional gardeners work slowly and steadily, "leaning" on their spades every now and then to avoid overstraining muscles. They insert the spade into the soil at an angle which makes it almost perpendicular before pressing with the foot, and this ensures the proper size of "spit."

Stainless steel spades are labour-saving

and easy to keep clean, but they are expensive.

Forks, like spades, come in a variety of standardised sizes. The **garden fork**, however, was never designed for digging like a spade. It is an implement for loosening and breaking up soil. It can be used for shifting piles of weeds to a barrow, or for spreading manure or compost, or for turning over soil which has already been dug. If you try, however, to dig new ground with a fork, the prongs will soon get sprung.

Next comes the **rake**, a delicate instrument for light use in top soil only, prior to seed sowing. This iron (not steel) tool should not be used to pull out weeds or rubbish, or indeed for any kind of rough work. Its purpose is to create that lovely, even top tilth in which the seeds will flourish.

Hoes vary in design as well as size, because each is used for a different purpose. The Dutch hoe is a cutting instrument shaped rather like a horseshoe with a sharp-edged base. It must be used flatly and propelled by pushing, the idea being to sever the roots of weeds from their tops. A draw hoe, on the other hand, is a goose-necked perpendicular hoe, which is used in exactly the opposite manner for drawing earth towards the worker. It is valuable for drawing lines for seed-sowing, for earthing-up garden potatoes, and for levelling.

The five-pronged cultivator can be added to the list of hoes, and it is like a clutching hand. The steel prongs are finely sprung and they can be used for weeding delicately between plants, or more roughly for breaking up surface soil or levelling. It is the most popular of garden tools, and beginners always enjoy working with it, possibly because results seem quicker, and the springy prongs convey a pleasant rhythm.

All the tools so far mentioned are essential to a garden if it is to be profitably cultivated. They should be of good quality, because good work is impossible with poor tools. After use, each tool must be cleaned and dried. A final rub with an oily rag gives that extra touch of pleasure and ensures that the tool is always ready for the next job.

Garden tools are best stored in some shed or building where they can be hung on the walls. A good plan is to whitewash the walls, and then draw the shape of each implement round it with a pencil. Thus, if a spade or fork is missing, you immediately notice the vacant spot and can make a prompt search.

The stock increases with time. For corners where rough grass and nettles accumulate, a **sickle** is the best. But it can be a dangerous weapon if wielded too vigorously and a short stick should be used in the left hand to counter possible blows. This stick also acts as a rake to take away the rubbish as cut.

A **mattock** or **pick-axe** is helpful for breaking up hard subsoil, and it will greatly reduce spade work. This is one tool that may usefully be "borrowed" or "lent," though interchange of other garden tools is not recommended. Spades and garden forks can be returned sprung by careless borrowers who have pressed too heavily against the handles in heavy soil. A scythe should never be lent or borrowed, because it becomes as personal to its user as a violin to a professional musician.

Finally the **wheelbarrow**, which if not a tool is certainly an indispensable. Ask yourself what sort of paths you have before acquiring a barrow. A pneumatic-tyred wheel is the best for grass paths or wheeling over soft soil because it does not tend to sink too much. But if your paths are concrete, the old-fashioned wooden wheel is just as good.

Do not try to wheel loads that are too heavy. Small metal barrows with rubber wheels are on the market and are designed to save backaches.

Finally, before starting a new job in the garden, treat the wheelbarrow as a portable workshop. Assemble *all* the tools you will require in the barrow, and wheel them to the starting point. This will save much walking to and fro.

Small hand tools usually consist of a trowel and hand-fork—and both of these are indispensable for rock-gardens, greenhouses, for inserting bulbs, etc.

Because they are small they are easily lost in long grass, so a good plan is to keep them always in a trug or gardening basket, which can also be used for collecting weeds. There are innumerable other hand tools for various purposes on the market, but most of them would come under the heading of "gadgets."

DO IT YOURSELF IN THE GARDEN

You can make these ornaments as well as grow your own plants

BIRD BATH

WELL-PLACED garden ornaments heighten the beauty of their surroundings, and a bird bath introduces that "Open-air Theatre" atmosphere; it should be situated in view of the principal living-room window.

Make it yourself, as follows: Three separate wooden moulds are required—one for the base, one for the pillar and another for the bath top. Level the base soil first, and place the first mould in position with a spirit-level to make sure. It is simply a hollow box in which you now nail the pillar mould, about 3 ft. high, with pieces of iron rod to give strength. Now fill up with a mixture of 1 part cement to 3 parts sand, and ram this down. Finally, nail on the top mould with an old kettle in the middle to form the bath, and then fill around this with cement. When the cement has set, the wooden sides of the mould can be knocked off. A few finishing touches with the trowel will be enough.

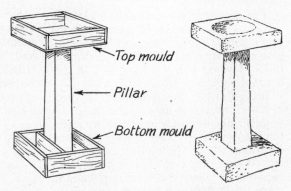

Top mould

Pillar

Bottom mould

Three wooden moulds are needed for the Bird Bath—one each for the base, pillar and top. When the cement sets, knock off the wooden sides and finish with a trowel

SUNDIAL

In a sunny spot, especially when crazy pavement leads up to it, a sundial creates an old-world atmosphere.

Vary the procedure here with bricks and tiles. Twenty-four bricks, and fifteen 4-in., four 5-in., and some roofing tiles, are needed, the latter about ¾ in. thick.

Make a rough wooden tray 18 in. square and 1 in. deep, and in it spread a three-to-one mixture of sand and cement to form a foundation. On top of this lay eight bricks to form a square, and on these place the second course composed of four bricks forming a hollow square, and set with the sides running diagonally across the corners of the first course.

Allow the cement to set before beginning on the column proper, then remove the wooden tray and place the base on its permanent site. Now proceed to lay two courses of two bricks each, and afterwards make a course of the thin roofing tiles. On the layer of tiles lay three more courses of bricks and the column is ready for its ornamental top.

The top is composed of five courses of tiles, which must be soaked in water before being used, and the final course forms the dial platform. Ready-made dials are quite cheap to buy.

A LILY POND WITH ARBOUR

Start a lily pond by pegging out the design to the required dimensions. Drive the pegs in deeply and dig to a depth of 18 to 24 in. Now nail 3-in. sawn timber against the pegs. After trimming and levelling, pour in concrete composed of 3 parts sand and 1 part cement, to a depth of 1½ in. over the bottom and sides.

Remove the timber when the concrete has set, and surface the pond around with a mixture of sand and cement.

Now dig out the holes for the four corner posts of the arbour, and join these up with horizontal beams. Next place the roof or short horizontal beams in position and screw them down.

This arbour will be strong enough to take the weight of climbing roses or other creepers; and under it a seat can be placed for watching the lilies and the goldfish in the pool.

CRAZY PAVING

The essentials are cement and distance pieces—i.e. 2-in. strips of sheet metal cut into pieces 18–30 in. long, and fastened together in pairs by nailing or screwing a block of wood 1 in. by 1 in. by 2 in. between the strips.

Being flexible, the pieces can be bent, and they are laid in an irregular design. It is rather like a jig-saw puzzle at this stage, but the centres are filled in with a mixture consisting of two spadefuls of cement to a barrow-load of gravel. This is poured into the spaces between the distance pieces and made level afterwards with the tops of the metal strips.

All the distance pieces are removed when the cement has set in the first sector, then they are placed in position again for the next one. While the second sector is setting, the crevices between the paving of the first can be filled in with soil in which to grow moss. Dwarf-growing thymes and campanulas can also be sown, but weeds such as dandelion and thistle are apt to introduce themselves (see chapter on "Making a Garden from Scratch").

A ROCK GARDEN

The site chosen should be sunny, as most of the alpines are sun lovers.

It is better to have a few rocks and many plants, but if the site is level, an irregular outline must be achieved by building mounds here and there. A winding path should divide the site. Other paths can be introduced if space permits.

Soil taken from the path-making can be used to create mounds and "cliffs," and sandstone or weathered limestone is the best "rock" material. If these are unobtainable, or too expensive, the "rocks" can be home-made from cement.

First of all, mark out the area with pegs, which will indicate the extent of the proposed rockery at the base. If the soil is heavy, it will be necessary to dig out the area to a depth of 12 in. and fill in with rough stones, for drainage purposes. If the soil is light or sandy, no preparation is required.

The "core" of the rockery can now be built up with rough stones or broken bricks, and should be 6 in. deep near the edge, rising to 18 in. in the centre. On this "core," place your garden soil to the depth of about 3 ft. Tread this down to prevent sinking when the stones are added.

When placing the rocks, arrange them so that the grains are all running in the same direction. Use the largest stones at the base, and bed each stone so that it is half buried and tilts slightly backwards. This directs rain water to the soil and the plant roots.

Build upwards in tiers irregular in size; and always allow a few weeks to elapse before planting.

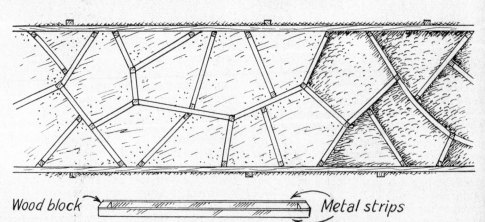

Wood block — Metal strips

Crazy Paving is like a jig-saw puzzle. Mark out with flexible strips of sheet metal fastened together in pairs with a wood block in between

MARKING OUT FLOWER BEDS

To make a circular bed, a peg should be driven in to mark the axis of the circle, and one end of a piece of cord tied round it in a loop. Tie another peg to the other end of the cord and, after making sure that the cord is the required length, keep the line taut to form a circle.

TO BUILD A PERGOLA

Decide first whether it is to be arched or square. Select the timber from larch, fir or oak poles, strip off the bark and creosote the ends.

Pergolas of squared wood look more formal, and may consist of uprights 4 in. square, placed about 7 ft. apart in line on either side of the path. The width should be not less than 5 ft., to avoid shower baths when passing through after rain.

Pergolas need not be massive in construction, as they are only designed to support roses, vines and climbing plants. But for stability in stormy weather, a concrete foundation is recommended for the pillars.

Train the climbing plants as they grow, with *loose* ties. Rambler roses, for example, are rampant and must be disciplined from the start. Every winter they must be overhauled and the old wood cut out, using new ties for the new wood. Also watch out for pests, such as caterpillar and green-fly.

For stability in stormy weather, the pillars of a pergola should have a concrete foundation

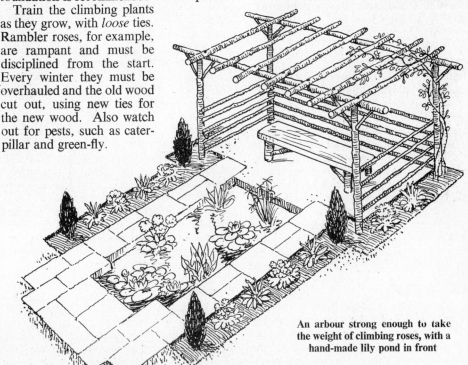

An arbour strong enough to take the weight of climbing roses, with a hand-made lily pond in front

GROW YOUR OWN FRUIT

A miniature orchard is one of the most profitable
outdoor hobbies—and helps keep the doctor away

AMATEUR fruit-growers who shape their gardens into miniature orchards enjoy the most profitable of hobbies. The dividends are exceptional. Fruit cultivation ensures healthful, open-air recreation without undue physical strain. With each crop harvested comes the delight which only fresh, glowing fruit can bring to the table; its consumption undoubtedly *does* keep the doctor away. In addition, fruit-growers have the unique satisfaction of filling their store cupboards with jams, bottled produce and home-made wines. Nothing is wasted in a fruit garden; even the prunings from the trees and bushes provide excellent firewood, after being kept to dry for a space, and the aroma is like incense.

The suggestion grow your own fruit, then, is not a counsel of perfection. It can be done in remarkably small spaces *to perfection,* as a visit to any local produce show will prove.

How much Space?

But there are still thousands of gardens in the country which could be planted with fruit, and are not. The owners would like to grow it, but are scared of making the attempt in case of failure. Admittedly there is a scientific and highly technical side of the subject which can sound quite terrifying in the company of professionals, but to the householder this does not apply.

He can plant his miniature orchard and reap its fruits at small expense, by complying with very simple rules. He will make mistakes, but these need not be costly. He can let his trees and bushes do most of the work, and then discover that this, above all things, is what they want to do.

How they are going to do it is the business of the owner-gardener, and in this you may be governed by the space at your disposal. From the very beginning you become an architect who can shape the destiny of your trees. Maybe you would like double cordon pear trees, trained so

that they will make edgings to your paths; you can train them almost parallel to the ground and only about a foot from it, so that no harmful shade is cast, say, on the strawberries enclosed.

Apples, too, you can grow as cordons from a single stem either trained upright or, to gain more sunlight, at an angle of 45 degrees, on wires. The stems are only 3 ft. apart, so by this method dozens of apple trees can be planted in a very small space.

Or you can have fan-shaped trees, trained against a wall or fence; this method suits luxurious growths like peaches, figs, nectarines, cherries, apricots and plums.

Or again—espaliers for pears and apples, which consist of training five or six tiers of horizontal branches growing at 1-ft. intervals, and at right angles to the main stem.

All these methods have been tried *together* in small gardens, with the utmost success. With many, the results in produce have been outstanding. The beginner can obtain, from a nurseryman, young stock already trained to the shape required. After planting you will learn much by watching growth intently, and helping the produce to maintain its shape.

When space is available, bushes are less trouble, but they too need much attention, because the branches should be trained in goblet shape to admit the maximum of sun and air. Half-standards are much taller, and are very popular with growers of apples, pears and plums. Standards are the orchard tree, with branches spreading 30 ft. or more. You see them sometimes in small gardens, but little else; it is amazing how much room a standard plum or apple tree requires.

Planting

To watch an experienced grower planting a fruit tree is highly exhilarating, but the technique is quite simple and easily acquired. A tree is placed in the site prepared for it, on a little mound in the centre of the hole, but it usually comes out again

Even in a small garden, standard fruit trees are possible for those who really want them, though they leave little room for anything else

with a gesture of impatience when the planter has had a good look at it. There follows some fuss, like a dentist taking wax models of the palate; the tree goes in again, to be studied intently while some helper holds up the branches.

The tree may have to come out again, sometimes five or six times, but when it remains in an approved position you feel instinctively (as a watcher) that the tree is where it wants to be, not for a season, not for a year or two—but for life. The secret, of course, is that the roots have been spread out correctly, and a planter with "green fingers" will handle the fernlike roots as if he were combing the hair of a beautiful woman in front of her own looking glass, while she nods smiling approval.

Not all of us are born with "green fingers," but that need not debar us from planting fruit trees in the proper manner,

or from completing the job by thumping in the soil firmly with a stump of timber, which is better than treading it in with our feet. Each tree or bush will need a stake at this stage, to give it strength in a storm.

In a small garden, every inch of space is invaluable. There should be a planned space for everything, according to its size and shape. Trained trees like the espaliers, or fan-shapes for the walls, should be four years old; cordons, only two years; half-standards three; and standards about four. The question of "stocks" arises too, i.e. the root system on which the variety is grafted. These are classified as "very dwarfing," "semi-dwarfing," "vigorous," etc., and for the miniature orchard they are important. On dwarfing stocks, the trees never grow large.

When the trees arrive from the nursery, they will be packed in straw; they should be unpacked at once and "heeled in." This means digging out a shallow trench in which the roots may be covered temporarily to keep them damp and healthy.

The planting season is from November to March, but autumn planting secures better growth and earlier fruiting. Top fruits are not pruned until the spring of the following year, but bush fruits, like raspberries and blackcurrants, should be cut down at once to within 9 in. of the ground level.

Crops in Succession

Before stocking a small orchard, the owner-gardener should consult the family as to what kinds of fruit they want grown, a choice that may well be governed by household requirements. When space is limited, the fruits grown must give crops in succession. The order of ripening is important. For example, strawberries come along first, closely followed by cherries, gooseberries, blackcurrants, redcurrants and raspberries. After the soft fruits comes a gap, then—plums, apples and pears, according to the variety planted.

In making a small orchard, therefore, remember that most of the stock will be permanent, so much time will be saved if it is in the right place to begin with. Aspect is not a major consideration, for all owner-gardeners have to accept their plots according to the situation of the house and plan the garden afterwards. The quality of soil is also a gamble, but it is comforting to note that all soils will grow fruit if the principles of cultivation are followed.

These include constant mulches of manures, fertilisers, compost and fallen leaves on the surface, and all this in time regenerates even the poorest of soils. But in your plan it is advisable to have the bushes or trees on the outer edge of the plot, with the soft fruits in the centre, if this is possible. And the situation of the paths is of the utmost importance. The cordon trees can be trained to fit in with them and produce fruit in places which would otherwise be unproductive.

STRAWBERRIES

Strawberries come first in the order of ripening. Their leaves occupied a proud position in the Great Turk's crown, and now adorn the coronets of dukes, earls, marquesses and viscounts, so they deserve pride of place in every orchard.

As a contrast, strawberries are extremely vulgar in their growing habits. They revel in bad company; they will clasp to their bosoms dandelions, chickweed, groundsel and thistles with dissolute abandon. To grow strawberries is easy, but always they are a responsibility; they have to be watched.

Almost any soil is suitable for strawberries, but the varieties chosen should be right for your particular soil. For heavy soils, choose Sir Joseph Paxton (an old time Victorian favourite); on light soil, grow Royal Sovereign (the large, sweet, juicy type that the Ascot ladies like in June). If the soil happens to be peaty, there is Tardive de Leopold (a late strawberry, with a strong, hardy habit of growth).

Before planting, mix in a good dressing —one good barrow load to 8 yd. of well-rotted compost together with some meat and bone meal, and fork this into the top 6 in. of the soil at least three or four weeks ahead of planting dates.

Maidens—i.e. plants a few months old obtained from the nursery—should be put in the ground in the autumn, though this may be delayed as late as March or early April. They are trowel-planted, and the hole made must give plenty of room for the roots to spread out. If they get bunched-up, they never straighten out afterwards. Conditions should not be too wet, or, for that matter, too dry, when this planting is done.

Before the runners are planted, make certain they are free from pests, by covering the roots in warm water (temperature 110° F.) for about twenty minutes, to kill red spiders, aphides and eelworm.

The usual distances for planting are 15 in. apart in the rows, and 30 in. between rows. Experience has proved that it is not advisable to retain the plants after the third season of fruiting, but this need not discourage a beginner. Strawberries propagate themselves in the most prolific manner, by means of "runners" from the parent plant. These are maiden plants attached to long, thin stems, and the method is to peg the latter down to the ground beside 3-in. pots to which the new plants are transferred.

The soil in the pots must be regularly watered.

June or early July is the best time for this layering process, which is a pleasurable occupation. Later on, the plantlets are severed by cutting the stem, and they will be found growing briskly in the pots by themselves. If enough are taken each year to form a new plot, the household will never be short of fruit.

Strawberries are surface-rooting, so the hoe must be kept going on the surface until the time comes to put the straw in position. It must be clean and dry, for soon the weight of the trusses will bear down on it and, in turn, the crop is kept clean and dry. Mildew may appear, but this is soon remedied by a dusting of flowers of sulphur in the early morning when the dew is still on the plants.

When all the crop has been gathered, the straw should be removed and burnt; if it is left too long, the new "runners" will get mixed up with it and will be very hard to separate.

Nets are more necessary for strawberries than for any other fruit. Blackbirds and thrushes are the worst offenders, but almost any bird will sell his soul for straw-berries, so the fine cotton netting which is available for the purpose of defeat-ing them is a good invest-ment. A philosopher called Boteler said of strawberries, "Doubtless God could have made a better berry, but doubt-less God never did," and with this summing-up the birds—and most human beings—are in agreement.

CHERRIES

Nearly forty different varieties of cherries grow in the U.K., so the be-ginner has a wide choice, though for the small or-chard he would be well advised to plant only bush trees or fan-shaped, and plant them at a minimum of 12 ft. apart.

The cherry is a problem tree because the sweet varieties are self-sterile. Cross pol-lination is obtained by purposely introduc-ing another variety, but there are only certain types which will "marry." Charts giving the necessary information can be obtained from the nurserymen.

For the miniature orchard, a variety like Waterloo (dark red to black fruit with a delicious flavour) is suitable to grow against fences or garden walls. The time to pick is June, so for a pollinator, choose a later fruiting variety, such as Florence (a golden yellow) which ripens at the end of July, and thus the enjoyment can be extended. Beware of overplanting cherries, however, as their growth is extremely vigorous. Other successful combinations are Early Rivers and Governor Wood; or Waterloo with Emperor Francis.

The second problem is birds again, for unless cherries can be netted you have no hope of getting any, unless you protect your trees with a gun from dawn till dusk. In the large commercial cherry orchards, men are hired for this purpose; otherwise

Apple trees must be sprayed at least twice a year, in spring and winter to kill various pests

the fruit would never reach the markets. Birds do not wait for cherries to ripen; they pick them green.

Problem number three is to keep the growth of cherry bushes, and those trained for walls, within bounds. They are so vigorous in growth that root-pruning is often necessary in addition to branch pruning, especially if the soil is light and well drained.

From the household point of view the Morello, a sour cherry, is useful for bottling and culinary purposes. The fruit is large and beautiful to look at, but impossible to eat raw. However, the Morello has one inestimable advantage—it will grow in a bleak northern site, where nothing else will grow, and thus provide shelter for other stock.

GOOSEBERRIES

Gooseberries are a thrifty crop; they seldom let the grower down. Often, in a bad season when other fruits have suffered severely through late frosts or wet spring, the gooseberry bush is the brightest spot, producing bumper crops.

Neither is there any waste with gooseberries. When the berries are large enough to be thinned, the "thinnings" can be used for bottling and for pies; and this process continues till the main crop ripens for dessert.

For the miniature orchard, it is no good planting gooseberry bushes all over the place, because some varieties become very large and bushy indeed. It is advisable to buy them as forked cordons, with either single, double or treble stems. In this form they are usually sold as two-year-olds, and they can be planted as edgings for paths and take up very little space. They can also be trained against wires like a fan. At least 5 ft. between the plants is required.

The best time to plant is in October or November; the roots must be moist and all bruised portions cut off before planting. Put them in 4 in. deep, and tread the soil around firmly.

Wear gloves when pruning gooseberries, and the first step in this important operation is to shorten laterals to within 1 in. of their base. This forms spurs; but, in addition, all exhausted wood (it is easily discernible by its sear look) should be cut away from the main branches. Leading shoots can be tipped, with beneficial results.

Bird attacks on gooseberries are best dealt with by winding black cotton freely over the bushes. Birds cannot see this obstacle, and they hate getting tangled with it. The job should be performed early, when the fruit buds are forming.

Thirty varieties, at least, the planter has to choose from. In growth, some of these droop and some spread. Droopers include Careless (an early, smooth, very big, creamy white); Leveller (one of the largest, egg-shaped, yellow, sweet, juicy, dessert); and London (biggest of all, round, oblong, red. Cooks well before ripe, and a rich dessert fruit later). Droopers must be pruned to keep branches off the ground.

Upright growers include Lancashire Lad (large red, prolific cropper for mid-season); Laxton's Green Gem (good for all purposes, green-yellow); and the ever-popular Golden Drop (medium yellow dessert, hairy).

Gooseberries need plenty of manure or compost, and if neither is available, a heavy dressing of basic slag should be applied. About 3 oz. per square yard.

BLACKCURRANTS

Blackcurrants are often described as "greedy," the term applied to all fruit trees or bushes which provide us each year with heavy crops.

Every time the gardener harvests a crop, he takes away with it part of the soil's nitrogen, phosphorus and potassium; and to replace these elements fertilisers must be provided. There are many kinds of fertilisers. They can be classified as organic, which means they are derived from animal or vegetable remains; or as inorganic, which denotes that they are mineral in origin; but it is important to realise why these three elements matter so much to all fruit trees, large or small.

Nitrogen is the food for leaf and stem growth, phosphorus for root development, while potassium supplies food for sugar and starch production in the plant, i.e. general health and vigour. In a small orchard, therefore, from which heavy crops are taken, there is seldom enough manure

HOW TO LAY OUT
A HERBACEOUS BORDER

Choose your plants by size and flowering season

The art lies in combining plants of different flowering seasons for a continuous show. Choice of plants must be made in sizes. Herbaceous plants up to 2 ft. high may include : Aster Amellus, (*Aug.-Sept.*), Campanula carpatica (*June-July*), Geranium (*June*), Geum (*June-Oct.*), Helenium (*June-Oct.*), Iris (*April-May*), Phlox (*July-Sept.*), Salvia (*July-Aug.*), Veronica (*May-June*).

Herbaceous plants up to 4 ft. high include: Anemone japonica (*Aug.-Oct.*), Michaelmas Daisy (*Sept.-Oct.*), Campanula (*June-July*), Chrysanthemum maximum (*Aug.*), Delphinium Belladonna (*June-July*), Helenium (*July-Sept.*), Lupin (*May-June*), Peonia (*May-June*), Scabiosa (*July-Oct.*), Veronica (*June-Aug.*).

Herbaceous plants up to 6 ft. high include—Campanula latifolia (*June-July*), Bronze Helenium (*Aug.-Sept.*), Hollyhocks, white, yellow and crimson (*July-Aug.*), Yellow Verbascum, (*June-Aug.*).

Having made the choice, and worked out a plan on paper, the next step is to transfer the whole scheme to the border. But first this must be well dug and manured. Later on, when the plants are growing, they should be fed with dressings of artificials. Early in the growing season, apply sulphate of ammonia (1 oz. per square yard) and follow this up in May with a general fertiliser.

1. Veronica. 2. Geranium. 3. Salvia. 4. Campanula. 5. Blue Veronica. 6. Aster Amellus. 7. Helenium. 8. Aster. 9. Aster (Little Pink Lady). 10. Geum. 11. Lupin, Goodwood. 12. Chrysanthemum. 13. Peony. 14. Phlox, M. von Hoboken. 15. Lupin, saxe blue. 16. Scabiosa. 17. Aster, Blue Eyes. 18. Michaelmas Daisies. 19. Delphiniums. 20. Aster, Barr's Pink. 21. Anchusa, Morning Glory. 22. Hollyhocks. 23. Delphinium, Mrs. Paul Nelke. 24. Yellow Verbascum.

To hide ugly stems the cloud-like and prolific Gypsophila paniculata can be arranged as a screen.

MAKING THE MOST OF YOUR SPACE

Four plans for four quite different sizes and types of garden

AN EASILY KEPT GARDEN (above)

A simple plan demanding the minimum of labour. The beds on the left of the path are ideal for annuals, or plants with lots of colour, such as sweet peas, geraniums, outdoor chrysanthemums. They shout "welcome" to visitors, while on the right of the path there are always some of the flowering shrubs in bloom. The strip of turf and the herbaceous borders delight the eye from the windows and create a very pleasant atmosphere of privacy.

TINY CITY PLOT (below)

This is a small-size garden in which essential features only are shown. But it can become a blaze of colour in spring and summer, with the addition of tubs and hanging baskets. If the small hedges on either side are of lavender, a perfect setting is provided for, say, pinks and stocks planted in tubs on either side of the door. The effect and fragrance would be heightened by hanging baskets over the small windows. These would also supply mixed flowers for indoors.

COUNTRY COTTAGE GARDEN (below)

Here we have the cottager's dream garden, from which he can keep his kitchen going with fresh fruit and vegetables; and use the surplus for bottling, jams, chutneys, etc., for the store cupboard.

Note how the herbs are placed near the house so that they can be in daily use, and how the flower bed greets the eye with colour.

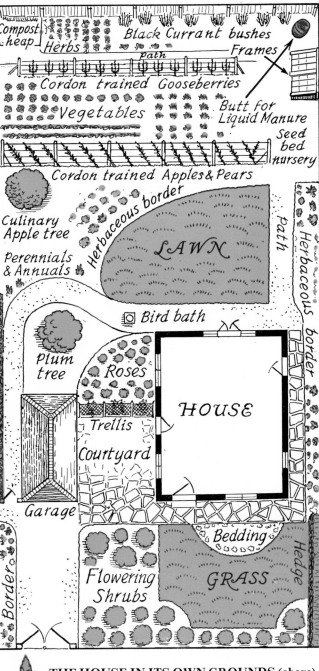

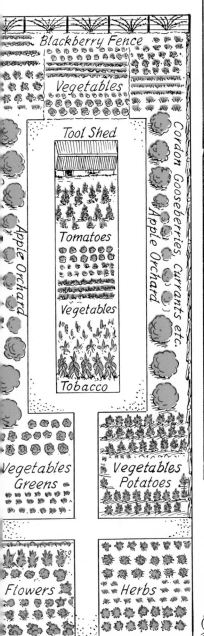

THE HOUSE IN ITS OWN GROUNDS (above)

Lawns in this garden give the atmosphere of leisure. Either of them can be used for children's playgrounds, or for the family to enjoy with deck chairs and portable garden furniture. Everywhere a visitor may look he will see flowers, but also this is a practical garden which will produce useful quantities of both soft and top fruits. The site we chose for the bird bath could be equally well occupied by a sundial if the house is facing south.

FLOWERS ALL THE YEAR ROUND

JANUARY. *Winter Jasmin*
Yellow flowers on smooth stems before the leaves appear. Brightens the dullest time of year.

FEBRUARY. *Snowdrops*
First harbinger of spring. Grow best in cool, shady spots, or are quite happy in the open.

MARCH. *The Crocus*
Everyone's favourite—in beds, borders or grass. Grows quite happily in any type of soil.

APRIL. *Tulips*
They range in size from dwarf to giant. Early Single, Early Double and Parrot are always popular.

MAY. *Bearded or "Flag" Iris*
Loves lime, so add $\frac{1}{2}$ lb. crushed mortar-rubble to each plant. Use hand fork with care.

JUNE. *Roses*
Even the smallest garden can make a great display of roses, which last from June to November.

JULY. *Geraniums*
Always fresh and vivid, with leaves as beautiful as the flowers. Should be treated as an annual.

AUGUST. *Gladioli*
A fine show for little attention. But do push in stakes to keep them safe in windy weather.

SEPTEMBER. *Lupins*
Lovely both for garden decoration and for supplying the home with cut blooms indoors.

OCTOBER. *Michaelmas Daisies*
Outstanding for outdoor show. A hardy perennial, very easily raised from seed.

NOVEMBER. *Chrysanthemums*
Plant in large clumps or sheltered corners. Treat like hardy annuals till Christmas.

DECEMBER. *Daphne*
Purple-rose flowers, followed by red berries—a display that radiates happiness.

or compost available for cultivation, so reinforcement in the form of a good, balanced compound fertiliser is required. This can be obtained from any dealer, with full instructions as to use.

The blackcurrant is therefore only "greedy" because of its handsome and generous crop production. Its contribution to children's health during the years when orange juice was not available was miraculous, and to-day many families have continued to use blackcurrant jam in preference to any other.

For planting, two-year-old bushes are best, and the branches should be cut down to the ground so as to ensure plenty of strong growth the following year. Sometimes it is hard to bring oneself to do this, because the plants look so good when they arrive from the nursery. Later on, the succession is maintained by means of cuttings 9 in. long, which can be taken from the current year's growth.

If space is restricted, the blackcurrant can also be grown as a fan-trained tree against east or north fences. Pruning is simple, as the bushes only require to have the old and exhausted wood cut away each season.

There are twenty varieties, but for the owner-gardener Seabrook's Black is recommended. It is immune from the "big bud" disease, has a neat, strong growth, and is an excellent cropper.

RASPBERRIES

Raspberries can be placed in a more shady position than most of the soft fruits; and when the canes arrive and have been planted, they also must be cut down to the ground. They should be about 15 in. apart, and it is just as well to provide the necessary supports at the beginning. The usual method is to place stout posts about 4 ft. high, at intervals of 20 ft., and to these nail on T-pieces to which wires are attached. Another method is to have higher posts at about the same interval, but with three taut wires stretched to form a frame to which the canes are tied when they attain maturity. This means, however, that pruning becomes intricate, as the old canes have to be untied before the new wood can be tied in.

One of the most prolific raspberries is the

Picking a bumper crop of currants, one of the most useful of the soft fruits

Norfolk Giant, but this is better for jam-making than for dessert. For the table, the most delicious varieties are Lloyd George and Pyne's Royal. The latter comes from Devonshire, where it is a great favourite. The berries are large, conical, deep red with firm flesh, but there are at least thirty other varieties which grow freely in the U.K.

APPLES

The apple-grower's problem is that he either has too many or too few.

Grow the variety of apple you and your family like best, but if the vote happens to be for Cox's Orange Pippin, remember that there are only certain parts of the U.K. in which it will grow. It likes sandy, well-drained soils and early sunshine.

There are hundreds of varieties besides Cox, but do not introduce more than half a dozen in a small orchard, and amongst these include at least one good culinary apple for the kitchen. Lane's Prince Albert is a small, spreading tree which serves this purpose well. Another moderate grower which can be relied on to produce fine cooking apples is Grenadier.

Dessert apples are, of course, more interesting, but as the grower will be confined to those that can be bought with dwarf stocks, the range of choice becomes narrower. The most popular "eaters" are Worcester Pearmain, Ellison's Orange, Laxton's Superb and James Grieve, all of which can be planted to act as pollinators to Cox's Orange Pippin, which is self-sterile—always provided that the latter will grow in your district.

Cordon and bush trees should be planted at two years old, and espaliers at four; or you may start with a one-year-old "maiden," and rear it to grow where and how you would like. Beware of letting it fruit too soon or it will overtax its strength; heart-rending though this may be, the blossom should be pinched out for the first year.

Organic manure is not essential for apples grown on dwarf stocks, so artificial fertilisers of the same balanced type previously described are all that is necessary for their welfare at the root end. But pruning apples at the top end is an art which beginners fear because it seems so intricate. Bear in mind that the main object of pruning is to let air and sunshine into every branch of the tree. Only when treated thus will an apple produce good fruit spurs. Pruning also maintains vigour and, if it is neglected, the trees may be subject to all sorts of diseases.

Look at the tree carefully before pruning, and it will often dictate its own needs, but beforehand ask your local librarian for one of the many classic volumes on the subject, preferably one with diagrams showing the various steps.

Spraying is another subject too wide to deal with in detail here. But some idea of its importance may be gained from the knowledge that most of the big commercial apple-growers spray their trees as many as fourteen times during the year.

This can be reduced in the small garden to perhaps these essentials: winter, petroleum oil to kill the capsid bug and red spider; spring, lime sulphur and nico-tine sprays applied at various stages to control scab, sawfly, and other pests.

The grower, either small or large, must work hard to obtain first-class apples, but one never hears complaints that the effort was not worth it.

PEARS

Pears are more susceptible to climatic conditions than are apples, and the varieties for cordon culture are all grafted on quince stock. There are many of them, but, before purchase, the nurseryman should be consulted as to suitability for the locality. Some are more dependent on warmth and sunshine than others, which are hardy enough to grow anywhere.

Perfection in the life of a pear is said to be reached for one day only; and the grower's problem is to avoid missing that day. Knowing this, the big growers go in for the varieties which they can gather green and ripen in store, and the home-producer might well copy this example.

In the garden the varieties Conference, Dr. Jules, Marie Louise and Williams Bon Cretien are all self-fertile, and this is important, as many others need pollen from another tree and the flowering periods do not always coincide. This accounts for much of the grumbling one hears about non-fruiting pears which look healthy enough otherwise.

The general requirements of pears are the same as for apples. Pruning, in the main, is very similar, the aim being to thin out the laterals and tip the leaders. During the first few years, pears should only be pruned lightly until you have trained the main branches into a suitable shape and position. Later on there may be occasions when the pruning saw has to be used on biggish boughs—their growth is so strong and vigorous once they have settled down to fruit.

PLUMS

Perhaps more difficult to fit into the small orchard, plums are purchased normally as half-standards and require a lot of room. Research and experiment at the famous East Malling establishment has produced a stock called "common mussel" on which plum trees may be grafted. This is used for bush trees, and has now been extended to fan-shaped plums for fences or trellises. Even so, they should be planted at least 15 ft. apart.

Farmyard manure is by far the best fertiliser for both plums and damsons, as they are grosser feeders than apples or pears. When this is not available, bone meal is the best substitute.

Pruning plums is a delicate matter because of the danger of silver-leaf disease. Expert growers leave the pruning as late as possible in spring, as the spores of silver-leaf are more active in the winter. As an additional precaution, they also paint over all cuts with thick white-lead paint to avoid bleeding.

Many varieties are self-sterile, so for walls or fences choose Rivers Early Prolific, Czar, Victoria, or Oullin's Golden Gage. Sometimes the crops of these are so heavy that additional support for the branches must be supplied in the form of props or wires. On the other hand, there are seasons when you will have no plums at all.

Choose not more than half a dozen varieties of apple for a miniature orchard and include one good cooker

BRAMBLE FRUITS

In the order of ripening, the blackberry comes next, but this valuable fruit, so useful for jams, jellies and home wine-making, is discussed at length in the chapter entitled "Grow Your Own Drinks." The cultivated blackberry is one of the great joys of a small garden, but he is only one of a large family, which includes loganberries, dewberries, veitchberries and other bramble fruits.

The latter are all very useful, especially the loganberry, which many housewives prefer to raspberries for bottling. The fruit is said to be a cross between the blackberry and the raspberry, but it is so individual in its growth and maintains itself so persistently year after year, that this is doubtful. One bush is worth inclusion in the miniature orchard.

The dewberry is not so acid as the loganberry, and the fruit is jet black in colour. It is a very strong, good cropper, and the flavour is highly esteemed by home-made wine growers. Veitchberries are a direct cross between the raspberry and common blackberry, but they are not recommended for the small garden, unless there is room for one bush to provide fruit for the bottling department.

NUTS

Last on our list come cob nuts and filberts, which deserve far more attention than they get. Because, like blackberries, they grow wild in the hedgerows, many do not consider them worthy of attention. Both cob nuts and filberts will grow well on almost any soil, the trees do well on

587

their own roots and, with careful pruning and cultivation, they will give valuable crops.

No more vigorous tree exists in the U.K. than the hazel, so, when introduced to the garden, its growth must be kept under rigid control. Bush form is the best, and it should be kept pruned into an open cup-shaped form. Otherwise the general operations of the year fit in with apples and pears.

The Kentish Cob crops heavily and is so widely popular that other varieties of nut are not known at all. The nut is large, light brown in colour, and rather flat.

Cosford, on the other hand, is a thin-shelled nut, large, round, and said to be the sweetest flavoured of all the family.

For size, Red Filbert or Webb's Prize filbert are splendid varieties. The husks are smooth and longer than the nut; they keep well and the flavour is very good.

The study of nut growing is delightful for the amateur horticulturist, because the male blossoms are borne in the form of catkins, or drooping tassels, and they appear very early in the autumn. The female flowers do not appear till February and are small, crimson and thread-like. To ensure nuts forming, therefore, it is essential not to prune away the catkins until it is seen that the female flowers have been fertilised, and constant movement of the branches helps.

APRICOTS, PEACHES, NECTARINES, GRAPES, FIGS

Apricots, peaches and nectarines have been purposely omitted from this chapter, though many small gardens grow them successfully. But it always must be a gamble except inside the greenhouse, as also is the vine, though grapes are now being produced in vineyards under cloches.

It is claimed that the apricot will grow out of doors south of the Thames, but this statement must also be qualified. It blossoms very early in April when the weather favours, and the bloom is quickly cut down by late frost.

Peaches and nectarines also will do well enough up to a point, and again that point is frost, that spring enemy which no garden can escape. The Fig has been excluded too, not only as a frost victim, but also because of its vigorous growth.

See also chapter on "The Small Cloche Garden" for further information about how to make the strawberry season last from early May until early June. Raspberries, blackberries, loganberries and grapes can also be grown under cloches and trained along low wires, and melons also thrive.

In conclusion, it may be claimed that fruit growers enjoy a hobby that has no end to it. So enthusiastic do they become that they are often inclined to over-plant, if only for the joy of seeing something new in their miniature orchards. Surplus bushes or trees, however, can be readily eliminated.

Grapes are always a gamble but are now being grown under cloches

Photos: "Smallholder"

LETTUCE ALL THE YEAR ROUND

*Grow it yourself for health, beauty and pleasure, eat it raw
or cooked as a vegetable that's different*

LETTUCES should be treated with re-spect; they are the wonder of the vege-able world. They have been cultivated everywhere for so many centuries that no one can trace their origin. Our Saxon ancestors called them "Lactuce," and rubbed the foreheads of those "sicke and weake wanting sleepe" with the juice of lettuce mixed with oil of roses. The Chinese also use them as a cure for sleeplessness; in India, they are eaten as a remedy for cholera; in Southern Europe and in the Far East, to keep scurvy away.

The Right Treatment

We know, too, that lettuces contain an alkaloid which is capable of brightening the eye and purifying the skin, and this is why they are so popular with young women on slimming diets. The rest of us are inclined to keep them in a refrigerator to go with cold meats. But when we treat them thus, we are eating something that is *dead*.

Real lettuce lovers are fussy people. They dash out a few minutes before lunch or dinner, and gather a lettuce that has been *quickly* grown and with a nice fat heart. They wash it in salted water (some claim that to wash a lettuce properly takes a dozen changes of water), and then, to dry it, they *swing* it in a dry, clean muslin cloth so that all the life in it is unimpaired. They never try to pat it dry with an ordinary cloth, because such treatment ruins the flavour.

Ordinary folk may have little time for formalities of this nature, but—try it some time and you will taste the difference. Moreover, you will take more interest in the crop, for it is possible in the U.K. to grow lettuce in a small garden *all the year round*.

A Sun Lover

The plant is not deep rooting and the soil must be neither too heavy nor too dry. It should be deeply dug, and then manure or compost introduced to the top spit, otherwise the roots of the plant will not reach it. Keep weeds down by constantly using the hoe. Remember—lettuce loves sunlight.

Mark out the rows about 8 in. apart by running the garden line from end to end of the row. Draw the drill along the line, only about ¼-in. deep, and repeat for each row. Then sow the seed very thinly by mixing it with sand and taking a pinch between the fingers for every few inches.

This method may sound tedious, but many people sow lettuce far too thick; when that happens, they come up in clumps and have to be heavily thinned afterwards. This is sheer waste.

After sowing, cover the seed by drawing the rake, upside down, lightly over each drill. Then use the back of the rake again to firm over the seed so that it comes in contact with moist soil.

This easy routine may be undertaken by anybody, but the secret of growing lettuce all the year round is to choose varieties that will mature at different seasons. Some do well in the early part of the year when the days are short, others thrive in the summer, and a few varieties are at their best in the shortening days of the autumn. It is possible also, with the aid of cloches, to enjoy lettuces from December till March, even with snow on the ground.

The rule, therefore, is—choose the correct varieties, sow them at the correct time and grow them under the right conditions.

If the garden is sunny and sheltered, it is possible to produce four out of the six crops which are sown during the year in the open without any cloches at all. The late Eleanour Sinclair Rohde, who was a great expert in the growing of lettuce, did this with unfailing success. After the turn of the year, when the cold weather set in, she used the stems of Michaelmas daisies to stick along the rows of lettuce seedlings as a protection against frost. She believed that this was an improvement on cloches, as the soil beneath them is apt to get caked and cause the young plants suffering. So she kept the soil aerated with a hand fork, and relied on the side branches of the Michaelmas daisy stems to do the rest.

Cloches Essential

But most gardens in the U.K. are not sheltered, though they may be sunny. Cloches for certain sowings are therefore essential, and if they seem expensive to begin with, they pay for themselves in a very short time. My own cloches have been in continuous use for growing lettuces for over sixteen years. They recovered their cost in the first six months.

You can start with a few cloches of any size. Designs on the market are numerous, but the familiar "tent" cloche, either large or small, is as good as any and is so simple that handy people can make their own at home. Something of the kind must be used for the first sowing in December.

Provided the soil is in a nice workable condition, lettuce seed sown up to the first week in January will have germinated and produced strong seedlings by the middle of March, if the varieties chosen were either *May King, May Queen, Feltham King* or *Market Favourite.* One ounce of seed will sow a row about 200 ft. long, so moderate the order accordingly, and do not buy too much, for it is a mistake to keep lettuce seed for future occasions.

When the sowing is completed the cloches are set over the seed rows, placed closely together, and the ends sealed from draughts with odd sheets of glass held in position by wooden sticks. The whole is then made secure by threading a stout piece of string through the handle of the first cloche and tying both ends to a stick. Seedlings must be thinned in March, but in the case of this first sowing they need not be wasted. They can be transplanted and

Lettuce likes sunlight. Weeds should be kept down by constant hoeing

covered with other cloches or, better still, put into a cold frame; and will provide good heads for cutting in the early part of May. But the main crop may well be in advance of this if the weather is sunny and fine. In fact, it may be necessary to open up the cloches in the daytime to give additional ventilation, by removing the ends and perhaps a few cloches as well. They must be replaced in position (and the ends) in case of frost at night.

Second Sowing

The next sowing should take place in the third or fourth week of March, under cloches as described above, but here there is a big difference because protection may not be needed after the middle of May.

The low-barn cloche (above) is one of the most popular types for lettuce

The simplest form of cloche is the easily movable Chase tent seen on the left

For this sowing we have a choice of varieties, such as *Continuity* or *Webb's Wonderful*, though the latter, with its curly, dark - green leaves, may grow too large for some households. It can reach the size of a cabbage sometimes, so Continuity is recommended in preference. Its leaves are tinged with brown, but this is quite natural and has nothing to do with scorch.

Again the seedlings have to be thinned, but in this case transplanting the surplus is not recommended for, unlike the very early seedlings, they dislike disturbance and will "bolt" into useless foliage if moved.

Third Stage—In the Open

A third sowing period occurs about the middle of May, when the seed may be sown in the open on the site in which it is to mature after being thinned as described. Varieties *Market Favourite, All the Year Round* and *Continuity* again are suitable. The soil is apt to be dry at this period, so soak it well to about 4 in. beneath the surface before sowing. Also work in some wet peat moss with the rake as a precaution against possible drought.

This third stage is the time to sow *Cos*. Its long, fat growth makes it unsuitable for cloches; and to enjoy it at its best it should have been bound up with tape or string while still growing, so that the inside leaves become blanched. All lettuces require a rich soil with plenty of humus on the top, as we have described, but the Cos is even more particular about moisture. The variety *Bath Winter* is a thirsty Cos, and will imbibe water like a sponge.

The Cos is a great favourite with lettuce connoisseurs. They like anointing the leaves with oil and vinegar at table, and then ramming a whole leaf, no matter how large, into the mouth until sometimes oil gushes over the chin. What one must never do, however, is to cut up a Cos leaf with a knife. For some reason this is simply "not done," though I fear I have been guilty of the misdemeanour on many occasions.

Not all the Cos varieties need "corseting" during their growth. There are many types which are self-folding, and they have a lovely white heart with a pretty touch of pink in the centre.

August Sowing

The fourth sowing of the year is in August, and although this may be made in the open as in the third stage, the rows should be spaced to allow cloches to be placed over them in September, to protect the seedlings against early frost.

The heads are due for cutting in October and November, and the best varieties to choose are *Market Favourite, Sutton's Imperial*, and our old friends again, *Feltham King* and *May King*. But none of these will thrive if the soil is allowed to become dry.

August-sown lettuce will come in very useful about Christmas, when there is an enormous demand in the shops for something fresh and green to go with cold turkey and cold goose.

Spring Lettuce Again

The fifth sowing is regarded by many as the most important of the year, for from this the grower hopes to have fine, firm heads about April or May.

But the race against weather is on, and the soil may have to be pre-warmed by placing the cloches in position well before the sowing date, which must not be later than October 15th. A variety known as *Victor* is good for this sowing, but *May King* or *May Queen* will once more fill the gap, and the seedlings should be thinned to about 4 in. apart because the winter growth is painful and slow. The surplus *can* be transplanted under protection, and will come away in good time for use. They may, indeed, forestall the need for the sixth sowing.

This one is mostly performed by commercial growers, who sow again in November under cloches, to provide the shops with good heads in May.

At this point the question may be asked —who wants lettuce all the year round? Salads, with hard-boiled egg and dressings are all very nice in the summer, but the average household might not rejoice at them in the winter.

The answer is, of course, that lettuce can and should be eaten cooked as often as raw, and the only reason it isn't is that it is usually so very expensive.

Lettuce Soup is a delicacy to be much enjoyed when there are plenty of heads at hand in the garden. You cut two lettuces and a handful of spinach into strips, and cook them in butter with a handful of parsley (chopped small) until they are soft. Add hot water, salt and pepper, bring to the boil and simmer for about three-quarters of an hour. Before serving, add the beaten yolk of an egg—and you have a nourishing soup.

Braised Lettuce

Waste leaves can be added to almost any soup, but the *Cos* connoisseurs have a useful recipe for braised lettuce. Take off the stump and the outside coarse leaves, and blanch the head in boiling water for about six minutes, then take it out and plunge it into cold water, pressing the water away with the fingers before bending over the tops and tying them.

Now line a stew pan with rashers of bacon, and on these put some slices of carrot and onion. Put the lettuces on top and the pan on the stove, then pour over enough hot stock to cover the lettuces, and bring it to the boil. They must now be braised in a moderate oven for about an hour, then drained and served hot.

Peas and Lettuce

The French have a splendid recipe for cooking peas with lettuce, in a brown casserole with a tight-fitting lid. To two pints of shelled peas add the heart of a lettuce and a small piece of sliced onion, sugar, salt, pepper and a large knob of butter.

Then add two tablespoonfuls of water, put the lid on the top, and the pot on the stove on an asbestos mat, and let it simmer for about half an hour.

Stuffed Lettuce

Lettuce stuffed with sausage meat and tied up with a piece of cotton so that the meat does not fall out, is also a familiar dish in France, but rarely seen in the U.K.

Way back in the sixteenth century, people regarded lettuce as a medicine to be taken thrice daily *after* meals. We can do better and combine the pursuit of health and beauty with the pleasure of eating the most wholesome vegetable of them all.

KNOW YOUR ONIONS

How to plant, harvest, store and pickle these invaluable edible bulbs

ONION growers start in the autumn by making the ground ready for next year's crop—a long-term policy which becomes a habit with those gardeners who prefer home-grown produce. They get to know their onions and eat them all the year round.

Any kind of soil will do, provided it is first deeply dug and then left fallow during the winter to await sowing time. In this interval the onion plot may become a dump for fireside ashes and even waste matter from the bins—unsightly perhaps, but invaluable, for it is dug in with the compost well before the moment of sowing arrives.

Planting onion seedlings in pots

Onions are greedy feeders and their appetite must be curtailed. If you give them rich stable manure they become large and misshapen, and are not tasty like the "mediums," which should weigh about five or six to the pound. Before sowing, a top-dressing of lime and soot is beneficial; it helps growth and prevents maggot disease, to which all onion crops are prone.

Owners of new gardens may plan their onion bed as a *permanent* site, as it is helpful to grow this produce on the same ground year after year. The process ensures continuous improvement of the soil. As skill in production improves with experience, those who grow their own onions discover that this amazing bulb in its handsome satin wrappings imparts life to half the things they eat.

Patience Needed

But to know your onions, much patience is required. Sowing and raising them is slow in the initial stages. The work of sowing must be done with care, and the beds should first be marked off in breadths of 4 ft., with 1-ft. alleys in between.

Sowing onion seed is the needlework of the garden. The rows are only 9–12 in. apart, and the drills should be drawn across the bed at right angles to the alleys to help in the hoeing later on.

March and April are the usual months for spring sowing, and the seed should

Frequent hoeing between the rows is vitally important as soon as the crop appears

593

The onion harvest can be stored in the greenhouse or, in mild districts, under the house eaves, facing south. Hung from the rafters, they are always available for use

be only just covered with fine earth. Then gently pat in with the back of the spade before touching it over with the rake again, for onions make weak "grass" at first and they cannot easily push their way through earth that is heavy or caked over it.

Now we arrive at a major problem. Weeds grow between the rows much faster than the onions, so as soon as the new crop is visible on the ground the hoe comes into use at once. If not, the seedling onions will be choked to death in their very early stages.

Battle with Weeds

With the help of the hoe the rows become defined, but the battle with weeds continues, and it must be fought to a finish or there will be no onions at all. This is the stage when thinning the seedlings begins, a process which adds much-needed strength to the remainder.

The first thinning may

be made with a penknife and it may seem to be rather tedious; but reward soon comes because growth is fast, and soon the thinnings will be very suitable for salads.

When onions are growing well, they lift themselves up and sit on the earth because they need light and air for the bulbs. Keep the hoe at work continuously or this privilege will be denied to them. If the weeds spread among the bulbs they will be robbed of light and air, but when hoeing it is important not to draw loose earth towards the bulbs, because really fine onions are never produced in loose ground.

For the stringing process, three pieces of string are attached to a nail at convenient height

Photos: "Smallholder"

Some of this preliminary toil can be avoided by sowing the seed in boxes in a greenhouse, instead of in the open: and then planting out the seedlings at a stronger stage, when they are better able to enter the battle with the weeds. But they still have to be watched very carefully with the hoe always in hand.

The harvesting of an onion crop requires care too; if all goes well they will ripen naturally, but before storage they must be drawn and dried on the ground for a few days, *with their roots looking southwards*. This is not a gipsy myth, but because the bulbs must have the maximum of sunshine to attain perfection. The yellowing off of the foliage is the signal that all is well for storage.

Storage

Stringing for storage is a pleasurable occupation, but again it requires patience and time. Three pieces of string are needed, and these are tied together in a knot at one end—and then hung from a hook at a comfortable height for working.

The onions are placed in position one by one, and the strings wound round their necks like plaiting a maiden's hair. In this way much space is saved, as these delightful festoons can be hung from rafters and are always available for use. In mild districts the onions can be hung under the shelter of the eaves facing south. Light frosts do the crop no harm, and the walls keep the bulbs warm and dry.

Pickling

For pickling purposes, onions may be sown from the quick-growing varieties, as late as July or August. This crop will provide an abundant supply of saladings and will also produce the small bulbs which can be put in brine (1 lb. of salt to 1 gallon of water), and left standing for 12 hours.

Peel these pickling onions and soak again in fresh brine for 36 hours before packing loosely in jars. Then they should be covered with cold, spiced vinegar and kept for at least 6 months, though twice that time would be better. Some say a pickled onion does not reach its best for 18 months, but the main point is that the jars must be topped up with new vinegar at intervals, as it soon evaporates.

One superstition about onions, which is firmly held amongst country people, is that a boiled onion with white sauce (and nothing else) is a certain cure for a cold if eaten before bedtime; so perhaps all the trouble required in growing the bulbs is worth while.

In very dry weather it is of the utmost importance to soak the young onion bulbs really thoroughly from a watering can at regular intervals

SWEET CORN IN THE GARDEN

If you enjoy eating this delicious North American favourite,
try the adventure of growing your own

SEED-MERCHANTS are conscientious tradesmen and, considering their vast annual output, complaints about quality are very few. Some of our leading firms have been in the business for centuries, and their name on a packet of seeds is a hallmark of its worth. If conditions are right for the seed, germination may be considered as certain.

That is why sweet corn is excluded from so many of the catalogues. The seed is wrinkled and quite distinguishable from maize, but it sometimes throws back and on occasion will refuse to germinate at all. Those firms who do advertise it prefer to stick to two varieties which are now becoming more dependable. These are "John Innes Hybrid," which, as its name implies, is the result of many trials and breeding experiments at the famous Horticultural Institution; and "Golden Bantam," the ever-popular Canadian sweet corn, which can be imported from the West.

Yet in spite of these uncertainties, those who enjoy *eating sweet corn* should never forgo the adventure of growing it in their gardens, for the reward is extremely handsome when the preliminaries go well. It is a table delicacy containing a high percentage of sugar, a blessing from the Western world, where it is so esteemed that folks think nothing of eating twelve cobs at a sitting. If you had nothing else to eat, you could live on sweet corn.

Beware of Frost

If the plants are nursed through their early stages, they grow as easily as potatoes and give no trouble. But the seedlings are delicate and, until the end of May, frost is an enemy and certain killer if the seed has been sown in the open. Growers who want an early crop and sow in mid-May must therefore cover the seed with cloches, or sow in large "60" pots in a greenhouse. After that the plants can be "hardened off" and transplanted at the end of May. Many nurserymen sell them at this stage, which is ideal for the beginner.

As an alternative, of course, you can risk the climate and sow your own seed in the open in the first week in June. This will pay if the summer is hot and dry, but otherwise the plants may not be able to catch up or the cobs ripen in time.

Rows are usually 2 ft. apart. and groups of two or three seeds are dibbled in at intervals of about 18 in. The soil should not be heavily manured beforehand, as this is likely to produce too much green foliage. A moderate dressing of a general fertiliser is enough, and the plants do not require much water. Sweet corn needs full sunshine, and shade should be avoided.

Hitting the Roof

Growth is so rapid in the early stages that, when the seed is sown under cloches, the young shoots are apt to hit the roof before the danger of frost is over. This is the main period of anxiety, because too early de-cloching would mean disaster. It is safer, therefore, to keep the glass on at the risk of deformed plants. Experience has proved that they shake themselves out quickly after their "growing pains."

Once away the young plants flourish, though storms can be a menace to their well-being. Staking each plant is a tedious business, but it is well worth while. In addition to the added strength to withstand wind, staking keeps the male flower-spikes, which are situated on the top of each plant, in their proper position for pollinating the females. These grow lower down on the stem, and end in long bunches of "silks" or silky hair, which catch the pollen, and the cobs form themselves beneath.

After fertilisation the grains pass through several stages known as "watery," "milk" and "dough," and this is where sweet corn differs from the common maize —*it is a hybrid*.

This hybrid breeding increases the vigour of the plants and their ability to resist both wind and drought. But you cannot save the seed from year to year. The "John Innes Hybrid" produces cobs

To prepare corn on the cob for cooking, remove the "silk," which is dry when quite ripe, and take the cob out of the green outer leaves

which are thick and creamy, and is usually earlier than "Golden Bantam." But neither is pulled before the "silks" become *dry*. This point is stressed because some people pinch the grains to see if they are ready for pulling, and this can lead to trouble.

Supposing the cob is *not* ready and you leave it? You have pierced its outer armour and left it defenceless against earwigs and birds. The thumbnail test is therefore a bad one—the only test of ripeness is to look for dryness in the "silks." In the West, even the "silks" are not wasted. Many people roll them in cigarette papers and enjoy a free smoke.

There is a method of pulling corn when the "silks" are dry. You hold the cane in the left hand while you break off each cob with a sharp jerk.

At almost any stage of its growth, sweet corn is the victim of birds, who ignore the minor forms of scarecrow such as balls of paper on string or old electric bulbs. Nothing but the old-fashioned hat-and-coat scarecrow is of any value, and this must be shifted frequently to keep the birds away.

Cooking is quick and simple. You strip off the husks and plunge the cobs into boiling water with salt, as you would new potatoes; but there has been much argument between chefs as to how long they should be kept there. Personal experience has dictated 20 minutes rather than the 10 minutes usually recommended. There is nothing more indigestible than a half-cooked cob.

Eat without Ceremony

When cooked, pour off the water and serve hot with a generous smear of butter, and eat without ceremony as if you were playing a mouth-organ.

There are many more polite methods of using sweet corn, though none so enjoyable. You can strip the grain from the cob after boiling, or leave it to cool off for use in a salad; or you can give the cobs 5 minutes in the pressure cooker, and then beat the grains up with egg, salt and pepper and half a cupful of flour to make a delicious sauce which goes well with fish.

Sweet corn should not be kept long after picking; it should be used as soon as possible.

BEANFEASTS FROM THE GARDEN

More nutritious than wheat, beans provide health and exuberance
in plenty—hence the phrase "full of beans"

BEANS contain 24 per cent. of nitrogenous matter; they are more nutritious than wheat; they provide the maximum of physical health and exuberance—hence the term "full of beans." The bean king at a beanfeast was the man who had the good fortune to get a slice of cake in which there was a bean. "If the pale beans bubble for you in a red earthenware pot, you can decline the dinners of sumptuous hosts," wrote Martial, a great Roman who lived about A.D. 80. He refused to cross a field of beans and thus damage the crop, even when enemies were pursuing him.

Wise gardeners, therefore, grow their own beanfeasts. The bean family is large; all its members are hardy and very accommodating as to soil.

The **Broad Bean** is perhaps the most popular because it arrives early, is tender, full of flavour and looks so appetising when served steaming hot. It is easy to grow, and sowings for early crops may be made in warm situations or under cloches in November. One pint of seed will sow a row 40 ft., and there is a wide variety of highly productive seed to choose from. A very early and hardy variety suitable for autumn sowing is Mazagan; for spring sowing Giant Broad Windsor is recommended, or a good all-round heavy cropper called Leviathan Long Pod.

When broad beans blossom, pinch out the tops (they can be used as a green vegetable) to avoid almost certain attack by the black dolphin fly, an airborne wingless insect which arrives like a parachute in the night. It likes the tender tops; and if a grower is taken unawares, the plants should be sprayed at once with soft soap melted in tepid water.

Broad beans are brittle in their growth and easily wrecked in high winds. They should be supported by stakes at about 4-ft. intervals at each side of the row, and then boxed in with twine to keep them upright.

The **Dwarf French Bean,** or "Legionnaire," is adored by good cooks in its native country, where it is the basis of innumerable savoury dishes. According to the French, the dwarf bean should not be cut up and shredded, but when young, just nipped at the tip and stalk ends, or when old, opened for the seeds inside to be cooked as "flageolets," unpeeled and prepared exactly like green peas.

Unlike the broad bean, the dwarf French

Dwarf French Beans dislike overcrowding and should be gathered daily to ensure continuous supply

Photos: " Amateur Gardening "

Runner Beans are handsome and accommodating. One pint will sow a 60-ft. row, and whatever
type of scaffolding is used it must be stable

plant is sub-tropical, susceptible to frost, and should not be sown till May. After then it will flourish if the soil has been well dug, and successional sowings can be made right through the summer if the plants are thinned out to about 6 in. in the rows. They dislike overcrowding, and the beans should be gathered daily, whether they are wanted or not, to ensure continuous supply. Otherwise they will become coarse and can only be used as "flageolets," which for some reason are not popular in the U.K., perhaps because of the difficulty in judging just the right moment to shell the semi-ripe pods.

One pint of dwarf French beans will sow a row of 80 ft. Excellent varieties are Canadian Wonder, Masterpiece, the Prince and The Wonder, all of which are long-podded, finely flavoured and prolific.

The **Haricot Bean** is not a purely American product, in spite of the fame it has acquired as a canned food. "Haricot" is a generic title covering self-coloured beans such as white, green or brown; all are suitable for drying.

The seeds should be allowed to ripen in the pods, which must not be removed from the plants but hung up with the haulm in a dry place where they can remain until there is time to harvest the beans into jars or tins for winter supply.

For use, the beans should be soaked overnight and then boiled with just sufficient water to cover them in the saucepan. A popular dish, and very useful because it can be served hot, cold or warmed up, is:

Bacon and Beans

½ lb. haricot beans	1½ tablespoonfuls
½ lb. fat pork or	vinegar
streaky bacon	1 teaspoonful dry
1 tablespoonful black	mustard
treacle	½ teaspoonful salt
	¼ teaspoonful pepper

After the beans have been boiled as described, the liquid is strained into a bowl and mixed with the treacle, vinegar, salt and pepper. The bacon (or pork) is cut into chunks and rolled in the dry mustard. Then alternate layers of beans and pork are put into an earthenware pot with lid. Cook in a slow oven for 5–6 hours.

This recipe comes from Canada, where it is a staple dish, inexpensive, convenient and a real beanfeast.

Runner Beans are the handsomest and most accommodating of all garden vegetables. They twine in a contrary direction to the movement of the sun and were originally imported for the beauty of their flowers rather than their food value.

Generous cultivation of the soil is required before sowing (1 pint to 60 ft. this time), and the rows should be trenched with compost or manure, as the roots are greedy and extensive. Good varieties are Bijou, a semi-dwarf but heavy cropper, which grows to about 4 ft; Empress, very ornamental with red and white flowers; Prizewinner, the pods of which grow to a foot in length; or, if size for exhibition purposes is wanted, Streamline, which attains 20 in. in length.

The scaffolding required for runner beans always excites controversy amongst countrymen, for its architecture varies in different counties, and each belittles everyone else's designs. At least there is unanimity on one point: the structure must be sound and capable of bearing immense weight in a storm. (The ruins of a 30-ft. row overthrown by a gale are more than two strong men can lift, and restoration to the perpendicular is a complicated task.) Stability from the start is essential, whether you cross the poles like an Indian wigwam or insert them deeply in a straight line and then hang strings for each plant from horizontal poles wired to the tops.

Alternatively, they can be trained against a wall to reach such astonishing heights that the "Jack and the Beanstalk" story seems quite credible.

Preserving Beans

Runner beans are so prolific that there is often much wastage in their harvesting. This can be avoided by preserving them for use during the winter months. It is very little trouble and ensures fresh, green and delicious runner beans all the year round.

Pick the beans young, wash them well, slice and then tie in a bundle with butter muslin.

Plunge the bundle into boiling water and keep it there for one minute only.

Strain and dry off the beans. Now place a layer of salt in the bottom of an earthenware crock, then put in a layer of beans. Continue alternating a layer of beans and a layer of salt throughout the picking season, covering each crock closely when it is full.

Climbing Beans can be preserved in the same way and have the additional advantage of being stringless when young.

Poles as scaffolding are not required for climbing beans, which are more delicate in their growth than the runners. Pea sticks (one for each plant) are necessary, however, and these should be inserted perpendicularly in the soil. If the plant grows taller than its support, the top can be pinched out.

Varieties: Tender and True produces a long, straight pod of delicate flavour; St. Fiacre is a later cropper, and the pods can be relied upon to be stringless.

For drying purposes the Waxpod, or *Butter Bean*, is excellent value for, after soaking, the pods can be cooked whole and are always an appetising standby.

The seed is allowed to ripen in the pods, as described for the haricot, and then hung up with the haulm to dry before harvesting into bottles or tins, which must be kept in a dry place.

On Twelfth Night the Bean King concluded a short reign of twelve days only, but his last official duty was to predict the weather for twelve *months* ahead.

Some records prove that his forecasts were nearly always right.

ALL THE YEAR ROUND
IN THE GARDEN

*Planning your working programme—and making some
practical suggestions for each of the twelve months*

Dump manure for later use

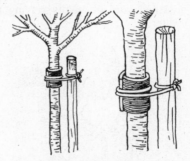

Old inner tubes for staking trees

JANUARY

IF the soil is frostbound, wheel the manure and compost and dump it in heaps for use later on. If the weather is dry, continue digging.

When ordering potato seed, change the varieties from what you had last year, even if they did well.

An early crop of radishes is always welcome; and if the weather defeats it, the loss is small. Try sowing in a dry border and keeping a heap of dry litter nearby to cover the seedlings in case of frost. The small, round varieties are most likely to succeed, but they must be thinned as they grow.

Everyone gets a diary of some sort as a Christmas gift. Keep it for jotting down notes about garden tasks completed; seeds, for instance, sometimes fail to come up, and you wonder when they were sown.

Your lawn may look very weedy at this time of year. Try a soluble form of 2·4 dichlorophenoxyacetic (the chemist knows all about it), which is slow acting and *does* kill buttercup, daisy, dandelion and clover. One teaspoonful to two gallons of water is enough.

Seed orders should be got off, including your choice of potato seed. Don't overdo quantities, but be careful about using surplus seed from last year, as deterioration through damp may have set in.

FEBRUARY

Local garages will be glad to get rid of old inner tubes. Cut them up into 4-in. sections for staking young fruit trees. This eliminates the friction caused by wind.

Search for uncommon vegetable seeds. Celeriac is neglected because the leaf stalks become a root, but if boiled and served with cheese, these roots make a delicious dish. Sweet peppers can be stuffed with mince, and they are very good. Include some pumpkin seeds in your list. Pumpkin pie makes a nice change and is a national dish in America (for recipe, see Cookery in the U.S.A.).

A bush of common elder planted near the kitchen window will keep away flies. The leaves are coarse but beautiful, and the flower has a pungent honey scent which flies dislike. All the old cottages and farmhouses have elder bushes outside their kitchens; the new ones have flies.

Do you keep a diary of garden work? Begin by making entries of work completed each day. This leads to proper planning for to-morrow. Soon you will be working to a programme.

Carrot juice is called "carotene" by the medical profession. It is sometimes prescribed for people suffering from skin troubles or falling hair. It helps girls to

601

enjoy a good complexion, and balding men to grow more hair; so plan to sow carrot seed in succession—and eat plenty.

Newly-broken ground *always* requires a surface dressing of lime. Buy this unslaked in lumps, then place it in heaps over the plot where it will absorb moisture and break itself down into powder. This is economical because lime absorbs 40 per cent. of its weight in moisture, and if you buy it slaked you are really buying that much water.

Chives grow almost anywhere

This is the month for scarecrows

MARCH

Spread old soot and ashes to prepare a good seed-bed. This will produce a fine tilth if the garden rake is used to complete the task.

Sow a quantity of potatoes for early use, mixing the soil with the charrings of hedge clippings or any other light rubbish. The potatoes will flourish if the trenches are filled with burnt chips and sticks.

Expert sweet-pea growers affirm that the rows should run north and south. Sow them in clumps if the ground is exposed.

Mulch more and hoe less. Use lawn mowings, leaf mould and garden compost in the rows between the crops. When they are cleared, the compost is there ready to be dug in.

This is the month to think of scarecrows. The best of all is an old coat and trousers stuffed with straw and then hung up on a framework of sticks. Tuck a thick stick under one arm of the scarecrow to look like a gun.

Another good scarecrow: Use elastic from old golf balls. This not only hums in the breeze, but the click when touched makes an effective bird-scare An old golf ball contains 400 yards of elastic.

APRIL

Plant a few clumps of chives for use in salads later on. They grow well almost anywhere and the fine leaves from the clumps should be cut whether for use or not.

A dressing of bonfire ash prior to breaking down the soil will help to provide a good tilth for the maincrop carrots. Sow the seed very thinly and start hoeing as soon as the rows of carrots are visible. Then give a dusting of old soot to ward off the carrot fly.

For hand weeding, which so often has to be done on damp ground, use two pieces of board, each about 12×5 in., and two old sacks as kneeling pads tied round the knees. By moving the boards you can cover the ground without rising (kneel on one board and move the other to the next position); this will also keep you dry.

If you suffer from sore feet when digging, a geranium leaf inside the soles of the stockings will give relief at once; and if you suffer from backache, boil a handful of groundsel for 20 minutes in a quart of water. Drink a tumblerful in the mornings. The above remedies have been proved for centuries by country labourers.

A new use for old nylons—when lifting bulbs, tie them up in the stockings and hang up on a nail in a dry shed. The air circulates through and dries out the bulbs, and when the time comes to plant again they are ready for use. Don't forget the labels.

Any spare beans in the packet may be sown at the end of the rows, and later transplanted to fill up the gaps. This is better than keeping them in an envelope and forgetting all about them until next year.

Peg main stems of marrows with
small twigs

Feathers stuck into a potato scare
the birds off strawberries

MAY

Test all flower-pots for dryness by tapping them with a wooden stick. The ring will indicate the condition of the soil.

In some recent housekeeping reviews celery was acclaimed as the most valuable vegetable. Leeks came second. Cauliflowers and onions dead-heated for third place. Beans were fourth.

Nasturtiums flower in great profusion. The seeds make a delicious sauce with cold meat and pickles.

As plants pass out of flower, all dead blooms should be removed, especially azaleas and rhododendrons. If these are allowed to seed, they will make poor growth next year.

The growth of marrows is very rapid. Peg the main stems down with small twigs and they will root at the joints and maintain the vigour of the plants. Another marrow tip is to plant them at the end of your rows of early potatoes, which will be dug up soon, leaving plenty of room.

When spinach leaves are ready for gathering, they should be removed, whether wanted or not. Sow spinach beet now; it is *perpetual* and does not bolt. When picking spinach, allow half a pound of leaves for each person.

Treat your hoes like golf clubs, each for a different purpose. Use the Dutch hoe for shallow cultivation, and sharpen its edge with a file. Use the swan-necked hoe for opening-up seed drills and earthing-up potatoes. A draw hoe and a soil scarifier complete the set.

An easy way to trap wireworms is to bury pieces of potato at intervals, and mark the spots. Dig up these "traps" every few days—and kill off the visitors attached.

JUNE

Don't *breed* vegetables. Eat them, as the French do, when they are youngest and sweetest, especially beans and peas.

To keep birds off the strawberries, get a potato, three feathers, a long stick and a piece of string. Stick the feathers into the potato and hang it from the stick like a fishing-rod over the bed to be protected. It takes a brave bird to face this jumping redskin's headgear. He thinks there is a concealed tomahawk somewhere, and goes off to the next garden.

Your garden can grow its own anti-pest powder. Plant two or three tobacco seedlings and, when they grow up, dry the leaves and grind them into powder. Sprinkle this round all newly planted seedlings, and these will be left alone by all the crawling brigade, including wireworms. But do not smoke the stuff yourself or your family will leave the house.

Growth of runner beans can be curtailed at 4 ft. above the ground by "pinching" out the tops. Many market growers do this to save high staking. The yield is quite as heavy and the plants not exposed to winds.

When using your compost heap, chop it downwards with a sharp spade. This conserves moisture; also, it is like cutting a cake; you can see what is inside.

Night-scented stocks (*M. tristis*) are weedy and drab in appearance, but if planted inconspicuously amongst other flowers in a window box, the reward comes on a summer's evening. From the open window they fill the room with delicious scent.

Fading sweet peas should be removed before seeding, or the pods will steal the energy that goes to make continued blooming. Sweet peas also like shower baths.

Time to clip evergreen hedges

Plant bulbs in window boxes

JULY

Enjoying your garden peas? Well, don't throw away the pods; let them simmer for 30 minutes in a saucepan with a small onion and some outside lettuce leaves. Push through a sieve, thicken with flour and milk—result, a soup fit for the gods.

Derris is a powerful insecticide. Buy it in small tins like pepper pots and carry one about in the pocket. If you see black fly or green fly, you can deal with them at once, instead of having to go back and fetch a spray.

Evergreen hedges should now receive a clipping. Use laths set at intervals along the hedge to provide levelling lines. This keeps a beautiful symmetry; better than guesswork.

Copy the squirrels and harvest something all the time. As this month advances, the early crops will be finishing and their space becomes vacant. Sow seeds of quick-growing vegetables and salads, and the cropping capacity of the garden is widely extended. A friend made some window boxes with her own fair hands. She collected knobbly bits of stone for rock-garden effects, and planted a Dresden-china picture with pansies, violas, pink double daisies and aubretias. Into the middle of this she put a bowl containing goldfish. The effect is enchanting.

Lawn troubles often come now. Sulphate of ammonia ($1\frac{1}{2}$ oz. per square yard) destroys clover and daisies; it also stimulates the grass to overcome weeds. But docks and dandelions must be uprooted even if they leave bare patches. These can be covered with sifted soil and sown again with grass seed.

AUGUST

Garden culture is primeval. Our ancestors dug without hurry; habitually they paused and rested on their spades. To-day the over-zealous often find themselves in bed with strains and backaches through trying to do too much all at once.

When window boxes are filled with sad-looking wallflowers that cannot help shrivelling up in cold winds, the winter seems long. Plant bulbs instead, such as coloured Italian hyacinths with winter aconites for companionship. Or you can plan a gorgeous show of anemones to fill the eye later in the spring.

"Even the flowers have nodding to do," joked a radio comedian, but if *your* bedding plants are nodding in August they need watering and hoeing.

Twist the tops off beetroot

SEPTEMBER

Loosen the soil round beetroot before pulling it out. The tops, after lifting, should be twisted off, *not cut*, about 2 in. above the root. This avoids "bleeding."

Why not a *decorative* vegetable garden next spring? One that attracted much attention in a front garden had a centre bed in which there was a pyramid of scarlet runners. Round this there was sweet corn, fennel, tomatoes and kale; and finally a massed border of herbs. In stone vases on each side of the door marrows trailed instead of geraniums.

Time to plant out cabbages

OCTOBER

Forestall the "Hungry Gap" when vegetables are in very short supply (April, May and June). Plant out a good bed of cabbage now; plant them firmly, and later in the month draw some soil up to the stems for protection against strong winds.

Now is the time to plant new hedges and renew old ones. After planting, *all* hedging plants must be cut down to half their original height. This ruthless pruning may seem sad at the time, but if neglected the bottom of the hedge will be thin and the top never stiff enough to be worth calling a hedge.

Make a bonfire with bricks

NOVEMBER

The children always want something to burn with the Guy on November 5th. Offer them hedge clippings and all the rubbish you don't want for composting. Or make a bonfire yourself with single layers of bricks to provide air holes. Start the fire with coals and sticks, then add damp rubbish such as tomato haulms. This will burn for days and make little smoke to annoy neighbours.

This is the perfect planting month. Try making a *little* hedge of berberises and cotoneasters to take away the garden's flat look and curtain off the vegetables.

Try just *one* gooseberry bush if the garden is small. The gooseberry likes to be alone, and a single bush will produce twice as much fruit as it would in a row.

Bean poles covered with yellow decaying foliage are a depressing sight at this time of year, so dismantle them before a gale does it for you. Then tie up the poles in bundles of twelve, and store them away till wanted next year. This is one of the autumn jobs that everyone hates, but it saves a lot of expense when spring arrives suddenly, and the poles are wanted again.

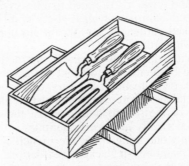

Garden tools as a gift for Christmas

DECEMBER

Watch the sweep; he'll get away with *your* soot if he can. He'll say, "It's too fresh for the garden, the sulphur in it will burn up everything; you've got to keep it in a dry place for 6 months." Show him a "dry place" to put it.

For Christmas give your life partner a stainless steel trowel and hand-fork wrapped up in fancy paper. That should start the urge to use them right away. Mixing potting soil indoors in frosty weather is a good beginning.

When poring over the seed catalogues, note varieties with county or local names—the cabbage family in particular. Leeds Market grows best in Yorkshire; Early Kent prefers its own county.

THE SMALL CLOCHE GARDEN

Melons grow under cloches released from runner beans or sweet corn

It will provide vegetables and fruit in continuous succession without a heated greenhouse

THE word "cloche" is French for bell, and it was also applied to a heavy, bell-shaped covering of glass used by French market gardeners for the protection of growing crops.

With this they achieved international fame by producing, without the assistance of heated greenhouses, very early tender vegetables. Moreover, by intensive cultivation of the soil to hold cloches, they obtained greatly increased quantities.

Only one thing about the French cloche was wanting—it lacked ventilation. To overcome this handicap, the heavy glass domes had to be propped up with pegs on one side. This was a tedious job which our commercial growers avoided. But when new designs appeared on the market with top ventilation, and British inventors started vying with each other, small growers as well as the professionals took them up. Quickly it was proved that, even when space is severely restricted, cloches can be used anywhere with profit.

Ventilation problems were not the only ones our inventors tackled. They produced designs to provide *continuous* covering for rows of seedlings, and this was a great advance on the old-fashioned bell which could only work in small "islands." In addition, they devised continuous cloches, mostly portable, which can be moved quickly for the normal operations of hoeing and weeding.

A vast selection of designs is now available, some the size of jam jars, others like portable greenhouses, so that they come within the reach of all pockets. They can be fitted to any requirement, and capital outlay may be spread over the years merely by adding at convenient times.

Continuous Cloches

For soil to be covered with continuous cloches, it is only necessary to cultivate to a depth of 9 in. if it is also correctly manured. Strawy animal manure is the best perhaps, if this is buried at the rate of a barrow load to every 10 yd.; but it is difficult to obtain. When dung is not available, composted vegetable refuse will often serve the same purpose, or hop manure, seaweed or peat-moss. All of these provide humus to release the plant foods that are already in the soil, but if the small gardener uses the household refuse, such as potato peelings, tea leaves, pea pods, turnip tops, carrot tops, pea and bean haulms, and rots these down on the heap, they answer just as well.

Once the ground is prepared for sowing, the value of continuous cloches becomes immediately apparent. They can be used for 14 days beforehand for warming up the ground.

In the U.K. this is of vital importance, because the gardener's chief enemy is damp. Plants suffer far more from damp than they do from frost. By using cloches the ground can be dried before sowing, and rapid germination of the seed will result. Moreover, by sowing the seed very thinly, a great economy is effected from the very beginning.

For small seeds the drills should be shallow, and even for the larger ones, like peas or beans, they need be only 2-3 in. deep.

One of the biggest advantages of continuous cloches in the private garden is that they give a succession of vegetables. We have dealt in a separate chapter with lettuces all the year round, but as you decloche your lettuces by degrees, the cloches can be moved to cover strawberries. This will give a succession of strawberries so that the picking season will last from early May until early June, when you can start picking from unprotected plants. In the same way with peas and beans, the cloches can be transferred from the "earlies" to the "second earlies" when the former have been picked.

All the Year Round

A suitable routine for private gardens designed to supply the kitchen regularly with fresh vegetables is, say, to cover carrots from November to the middle of February, then move the same cloches to cover a row of onions till the end of April. Move them again to cover a row of potatoes which are showing, to protect them against late frost. At the end of May the cloches may be used to cover a row of tomatoes until July; and start the winter campaign again in early September by covering spring cabbage.

But this is only one example. Easily grown flowers such as nigella, godetia, larkspur, mignonette and virginian stocks, when sown under cloches, can be induced to flower four weeks before the normal time. Clarkia and sweet peas sown in March will have excellent blooms ready for cutting by mid-June. Anemone corms

Ripe strawberries grown under Chase cloches being picked in early May

covered with cloches in the early autumn, before the first frosts appear, will be as safe as if they were in a heated greenhouse.

No hard-and-fast rules need be laid down. High adventure with melons and cucumbers may follow with cloches released from runner beans or sweet corn.

The chart which follows is a handy one for providing a luxurious supply of early vegetables for the home, and in every seedsman's catalogue will be found the varieties most suitable.

Vegetable	Time to sow	Ready for use	Covering during months
Beet	End of Feb.	Early June	March, April, May
Broad Beans	3rd week Jan.	Early June	Feb., March, April
Runner Beans	3rd week April	2nd week July	April, May
Carrots	3rd week Jan.	Early May	Feb., March, April
Peas	3rd week Jan.	Mid-May	Feb., March, April
(Next crop)	2nd week Feb.	Early June	Feb., March, April, May
Potatoes	2nd week Feb.	Mid-May	Jan., Feb., March, April
Cabbage	3rd week Oct.	April	Oct.–April
Cauliflower	1st week Nov.	Mid-May	Nov.–April
Marrow	3rd week April	June	April, May
Lettuce	See Chapter on "Lettuce all the Year Round"		
Sweet Corn	1st week March	July	March, April, May
Cucumbers	3rd week April	August	April, May, June
Tomatoes	3rd week April	July	April, May, June

Raspberries, blackberries, loganberries and even grapes have also been grown with success under cloches and trained along low wires. The small cloche garden offers much scope for originality and adventure.

GROW YOUR OWN DRINKS

A collection of old country recipes for home-made wines from home-grown crops that are both healthful and delicious

SUGAR is the secret of home-made wines. When it was not available for making them during two world wars, many of the old country recipes were lost. Those that follow are the result of talks with elderly people who had always grown their own drinks from cottage gardens.

Blackberry is a Favourite

By far the most popular was **Blackberry Wine,** for several very good reasons. It was easy to make, it could be drunk at once, or it could be kept until it assumed a remarkable resemblance to old vintage port.

All you have to do is to place alternate layers of *ripe* blackberries and sugar—at intervals during the blackberry season—in wide-mouthed jars; and when there are no more blackberries to pick, leave the fruit and sugar standing for three weeks. Then it can be stirred up with a wooden spoon, and the liquor strained through a muslin jelly bag direct into bottles. All that remains is to add two or three raisins to each bottle, corking lightly at first, but tightly in about a week.

This wine can be made from wild blackberries, but if room can be found in the garden for a bush of *Himalayan Giant*, this can be cultivated to produce an enormous crop of large berries. It has rampant growth and can be trained to make a thick hedge. Each year the old wood must be cut right out (a somewhat formidable task without thick gloves), and the roots should be dressed with plenty of manure, compost or bonfire ash—all three if possible, for blackberries are very greedy feeders.

Trained and fed in this manner, the crop from one full-grown bush will supply enough fruit, not only for wine, but for bottling, jam, jelly, puddings and pies. It is a very profitable addition to any small garden.

Boysenberries and Laxtonberries serve exactly the same purpose, and have (in the wine) a rather more delicate flavour. They are not quite so rampant in growth as the *Himalayan Giant*, but their method of cultivation is exactly the same.

An alternative which costs nothing is to dig up roots of the wild blackberry for garden cultivation. If fed and trained in the same way, the size and quality of the fruit improve at once.

Next in popularity, again because of its simplicity to make, was **Parsnip Wine,** which has a remarkable resemblance to champagne.

Take 3 lb. of parsnips to each gallon of water, cut them into pieces about $\frac{1}{2}$ in. thick, with two lemons and one orange also cut up into small pieces, including the skins.

Boil this mixture until the parsnips are soft, then strain and pour the liquor over 3 lb. of white sugar.

Keep stirring until this is dissolved, and bottle while warm, only adding to each bottle a small piece of yeast about the size of a shilling in circumference. All that remains is to keep the bottles full while fermentation is in process; and when the hissing noise has ceased, cork very firmly or the cork will blow out in the cupboard.

Like Champagne

Before using, wrap a napkin round the bottle and remove the cork slowly over a glass, otherwise much of the wine may be wasted. It should be clear, sparkling, and very sweet, as parsnips contain a lot of sugar.

Many gardeners refuse to grow parsnips because they dislike them as a vegetable, so for wine-makers a few instructions may be useful.

The ground must be prepared by deep-digging where preferably top crops such as peas, beans or cabbage have grown before. The seed is then sown in March in drills about 1 in. deep and 18 inches apart, dropping the seeds from the hand in twos and threes about 6 in. apart. Cover these over at once with a rake. When the seedlings appear, ply the hoe regularly to keep down weeds; later thin out the crop to prevent overcrowding. They make rapid growth, and are ready for use in November. Many follow the country custom of lifting them then, but leaving them on the ground lightly covered with earth, because frost adds to the flavour. If parsnips are left in the soil during hard frosts, the ground becomes iron-bound and it is impossible to get at them.

Nettles have their Uses

Nettles, alas, grow in every garden, and at certain times the main preoccupation is to be rid of them. But they have their uses, and **Nettle Beer** is one of them. It is a refreshing drink on a hot day, and many claim it to be a good tonic and blood purifier.

Ingredients required for Nettle Beer are: 20 lb. *young* nettle tops, $\frac{1}{2}$ oz. root ginger, 4 lb. malt, 1 oz. yeast, 2 oz. hops, 4 oz. sarsaparilla, 2 gallons water and $1\frac{1}{2}$ lb. castor sugar.

Wash the *young* nettles (their youth is emphasised because old seedy tops are of no use at all). Put them into a saucepan with water, the ginger, malt, hops and sarsaparilla, and bring the lot to boil for 15 minutes.

Next, put the sugar into a large pan, and strain the nettle liquor on to it, stirring until the sugar is quite dissolved. Beat the yeast into a cream before adding, and soon the mixture will begin to ferment. Again, when this process stops, pour into bottles and cork tightly in case of accidents.

Nettle beer keeps, but it is better used at once as a spring and summer drink.

On the other hand, **Nettle Syrup** will keep indefinitely, and it has wonderful health-giving properties.

Take the tops of *young* nettles, wash them well, and to every pound of tops add about 1 quart of water.

Boil for 1 hour, then strain, and to every pint of the liquor add 1 lb. of sugar. Boil again for 30 minutes, and bottle up when cold.

Nettle syrup should be used like lime juice, either with water or soda-water, and drunk from a tumbler.

Tonic Stout is also made from nettles, but the ingredients are more complicated and some are not everywhere available. They are: 1 oz. dried stinging nettles, $\frac{1}{4}$ oz. black liquorice, 1 oz. hops, 8 oz. burnt malt, 2 large potatoes, 2 oz. brown sugar, 1 oz. yeast and 10 pints water.

Boil the water, and add the nettles, malt, hops, liquorice. The potatoes need not be peeled, but should be well washed and stabbed with a fork. Drop them in at boiling point.

Simmer this mixture for 1 hour in a large pan. Dissolve the yeast and then stir it in with the sugar. Cool off, and allow to stand for 24 hours.

Before bottling, skim off the "top," then pour the liquor into the bottles and leave without corking for 2 days. It can be used at once and, when opening, tilt both bottle and the glass, for the "stout" has a creamy top.

Dandelion wine is a popular country drink cheaply made from weeds

Another tonic drink is *balm wine*. Balm is a perennial herb, which can be propagated from cuttings or grown as an annual from seed. The leaves are full of oil, and the old-fashioned use they were put to was for making *tea* when dried. It was said to be valuable for reducing temperatures during chills or fevers.

Fit for a King

Balm Wine is made as follows: Take 4 gallons water, 8 lb. loaf sugar, the juice of 6 lemons, 4 egg-whites, 20 lb. balm leaves, and a piece of yeast the size of a marble.

The egg-whites should be well beaten, and then boiled in the water with the sugar and lemons for 1 hour. Skim this mixture before putting the balm leaves in a large pan with some thin peelings of the lemons. Pour the boiling liquor over the balm leaves and keep stirring until cold.

Now float the yeast on top, on a piece of toast, and let the liquor work for 3 days before straining off. Squeeze the balm leaves through a cloth, and keep the jars open until all hissing noises have ceased. Then cover very tightly.

Bottle at the end of 3 months, and a drink fit for a king (with properties guaranteed to keep him fit) can be enjoyed.

Potato Wine is rather potent and therefore should be enjoyed only in small quantities at a time. Warmed up it is good for chills; and it is simple to make.

Take 5 lb. of small potatoes, cut them in half after a good washing, and put them in a pan with 1 gallon of cold water and 3 pieces of ginger. Bring slowly to the boil, and keep boiling for 10 minutes. In another pan have 3 lb. of sugar (granulated), ready with 2 sliced lemons and 2 sliced oranges. Strain the potato water on to the sugar, and boil again for about 30 minutes. Bottle when cold.

This wine requires no yeast; it will ferment though, so do not bottle until it has stopped "working." Can be used at once, but improves with keeping.

Rhubarb Wine, on the other hand, should be used at once. It is an excellent drink for children in warm weather.

Cut up 2 lb. of rhubarb, and mix with ½ lb. of balm leaves before putting into a pan with 4 quarts of water. Bring slowly to the boil, and then boil for ½ hour. Strain, then add ½ oz. yeast, ½ oz. citric acid, and about 2 lb. of Demerara sugar.

Let the liquor work for about 24 hours, then skim off the top and bottle. It is not intoxicating.

Apart from wine making, no garden should be without its patch of rhubarb. This should never be situated under trees. The easiest way to establish a small plantation is to purchase the roots and then plant them in one long row about 3 ft. apart. Spring is the best time to start a rhubarb bed, but if

Serve your choicest home-brewed wines from old Chianti bottles, which make colourful containers

610

owers appear they hould be cut off at nce. Pulling should be one in moderation, for very leaf pulled veakens the plant.

Well treated with ood dressings of man- re or compost, and fre- uently hoed between he plants, rhubarb can e looked upon as a ermanent crop which vill go on for years. 'rofessional growers re- ard it as a fruit rather han a vegetable.

Blackcurrant Wine is n established remedy or coughs and colds in he winter, but it is also . most palatable bever- ge.

Blackberry wine is easy to make and can be drunk at once or kept until it closely resembles vintage port

The currants must be ipe and free from twigs. Take 10 lb. lackcurrants, 6 lb. sugar to 2 gallons vater, and the method of our ancestors vas to make the wine as follows: First the urrants were put in a large earthen jar vith a cover to it. Then the sugar was oiled in the water, skimmed and poured, till boiling, on the currants. This liquor vas left to stand for 48 hours, and then strained through muslin into another re- eptacle before returning it to the jar.

After that, tightly covered, the wine was eft to stand for a fortnight before bottling.

Long Fermentation

Amateur wine-makers may be dis- couraged by the number of receptacles re- quired. With the exception of *balm wine*, however, the wines so far described can all be bottled almost at once from the ordinary earthenware bowls. The recipes which follow do require large earthenware jars which can be tightly corked for periods of between 3 and 6 months before bottling.

In the old days casks were used for that stage, but they are too expensive now and the jars must take their place. They soon pay for themselves if the proper wine- making technique is observed.

Unlike soft drinks, wine is *alive*. During the early process it must be able to breathe

until the bottling stage is reached. This ap- plies to another popular country drink made from weeds—**Dandelion Wine.** The recipe which follows is probably pre-1066, and all that.

Take 3 quarts of dandelion flowers, pick them off their stalks and put them in a large bowl. Now bring 1 gallon of water to the boil and pour this over the flowers. Leave for 3 days under cover, but open up and stir each day.

Now add 3 lb. of sugar and the rinds of 2 lemons and 1 orange, and boil the lot to- gether for 1 hour. Put back again in the bowl and add the *pulp* of the lemons and orange. When cool, add 1 oz. of yeast.

Another interval of 3 days, and the liquor is ready to strain into jars, at which stage 1 lb. of raisins is added. Fermentation con- tinues for quite a time, so if *dandelion wine* is made, say, in June, it should not be bottled until October, for use at Christmas and after.

No need to explain how to *grow* dande- lions, but a point to remember is that the flowers are at their best for wine-making purposes in May and June.

Crab-apples are cheap, and **Crab-apple Wine** is really delicious, and the longer it can be kept the better it tastes. The recipe which follows can also be made from any kind of eating apples, but the crab-apple imparts a peculiar flavour which is quite distinctive.

Take 5 lb. of sliced crab-apples and put them into 1 gallon of water to soak for a fortnight. Now strain through a muslin bag. Add 3 lb. of Demerara sugar to each gallon of the liquor, stir frequently, and fermentation will at once begin. When all hissing noises have ceased, leave the wine for 3 days and then pour it into jars. Bottle *after* 3 months.

If large apples, other than crab, are used, they should be sliced small, but they need not be peeled or cored. No yeast is required for this wine, yet if it can be kept for a year or more it becomes quite potent, though without any harmful effects.

Two from the Hedgerows

The elderberry supplies us with two wines claimed to be good for sleeplessness.

Elderberry Wine can be started with 7 lb. of the *berries* and 2 gallons of water. To each gallon of the liquid, add 3 lb. loaf sugar, 1 lb. raisins, ½ oz. ground ginger, ½ oz. bruised whole ginger, 6 cloves, ¼ stick cinnamon and 1 lemon.

Pick the berries off their stalks and pour boiling water over them. Let this stand for 2 days, then bruise the berries with a wooden spoon and strain the mixture through muslin into an earthenware bowl. Now add the sugar and the lemon cut in slices, but keep out a little of the liquid in which to boil the cloves, ginger, raisins and cinnamon; strain this mixture and add it to the bowl.

Allow this to stand for about a week, then skim and strain again into jars, leaving top open until fermentation ceases. Then cork tightly, and bottle up in 6 *months'* time.

Elderflower Wine is an entirely different drink. For this you must dissolve 3 lb. of sugar in 1 gallon of water, then stir in the beaten white of 1 egg.

Put about 1 pint of the elderflowers into an earthenware bowl, with 1 lb. of raisins and the juice of a lemon. Pour in the sugar-egg water, and when cool add about 1 oz. of yeast.

Keep this standing for 10 days, stirring frequently, then put it into an earthenware jar, and cork tightly but not till it stops working. The time required before bottling is again 6 months.

Elderflowers and berries are not normally grown in gardens for the purpose of wine-making, but they are to be found in hedges and woods almost everywhere. Children love gathering both with the prospect of delicious drinks in sight.

Wine from the Garden

One wine that does grow in the garden under the most careful cultivation is—*celery wine*.

Celery Wine is made from the *outside* pieces, and to each pound of stalks measure 1 quart of water. Boil until the celery is tender, then strain the liquor off, and to each gallon allow 3 lb. of Demerara sugar. Then pour into jars and add about ½ oz. of yeast. Wait once again until fermentation (i.e. the hissing noise) ceases before closing.

Celery wine requires patience, for it should be kept for 12 months before bottling. It is highly prized by sufferers from rheumatism.

The cultivation of celery demands a strict routine, from the sowing of seed in March, to the transplanting, or planting out time, right through the season to the earthing-up period until use, but how worth while that is when there is so little else to eat during the later winter.

Beginners, getting their new gardens into shape, need not be deterred by the sight of gigantic celery which is often seen at shows. The moderate-size celery can be grown by anyone.

There are dozens of wines, of course, which can be made from broom, burnet, clover, cowslip, coltsfoot and gorse; and damson wine has been purposely omitted because the tree is not common to every garden. Also, it is a wine for keeping, and 2 years or more is too much to expect for storage in normal households.

But growing your own drinks (or finding them in the woods and hedges) is great fun and can be made into a very profitable hobby. Keep a "log" to remind you of the dates when fermentation is due to cease and for final bottling. And label each bottle, not only with the name of the wine but with the date of bottling to ensure that it may be drunk at the proper time. Good health!

GROW YOUR OWN SMOKES

*And blend your own tobacco
to suit your personal taste*

FROM seed sown in March, or from young plants obtained in May or June, amateur gardeners can grow sufficient tobacco to provide them with cigarettes, pipe tobacco or even cigars, up to a limit of 25 lb. per person in the household.

This generous concession was made by the Excise in 1948, when there was a world tobacco shortage. It applies only to gardener-smokers, and the tobacco may not be sold in any form. Penalties are severe for default, but there have been few cases of misuse, and charity has benefited indirectly through the efforts of a clergyman called Hugh Cuthbertson of Tilty in Essex, who founded the National Amateur Tobacco Growers Association. Membership costs only 5s. per annum, and profits are devoted to the rebuilding of an abbey.

Little Attention Needed

The tobacco plant is easy to grow. It is not particular about the type of soil, nor is it discouraged by lack of sunshine or heavy rain. It is a weed, not a tropical plant, and it grows well with the minimum of attention. Before planting out, the earth should be dug and broken up to a fine tilth, with a small quantity of organic manure added, but not dug in deeply. Horse, cow, pig, chicken, or compost manure are equally satisfactory, provided the ground encircling each plant is kept aerated by hoeing. This must be done lightly, as the roots do not penetrate very far.

When they are put out in May, the plants are only about 4 in. in height, but ten weeks later they will have grown to 5 ft. or more, almost an inch per day. The leaves are more than 2 ft. in length and up to 15 in. in breadth, while the main stem develops into a tree-like girth about 4 in. in diameter at soil level. A good Havana plant bears a dozen large leaves, and will weigh, with its stalk, between 4 and 5 lb. Cultivation consists of continual hoeing and watering with a weak solution of

Tobacco plants grow to a great size. This leaf is 34 in. long and 14 in. wide and weighed 4½ oz. before drying

liquid manure at intervals. The plants are not affected by late frosts, but the roots are so near the surface that they may become dry in warm weather. The remedy for this is a mulch of lawn mowings, which can be watered to hold moisture.

Beware of Storms

Maturity of tobacco plants is reached at a time when weather should normally be good, and if the leaves can be dried in sunshine, the grower can rely on a second crop of leaves later from the same plants. Storms are perhaps the worst enemy. The roots are so shallow that the heavy plants can be blown over in high winds unless anchored to stakes. Heeling-in by pressing the earth firmly round the stem is helpful.

Other enemies are slugs, snails and wireworm, which are all fond of the young shoots. To guard against this, proprietary slug-baits are obtainable from chemists.

When the plants are about a foot high, the first forming leaves at the bottom should be removed. This is known amongst professional tobacco-growers as "priming," and causes the plants to grow more rapidly and the air to circulate freely below the first main leaves.

Earthing up the tobacco plants one month
after planting out

From this it will be seen that the cultivation of tobacco is easy, indeed far easier than that of, say, tomatoes; but there are certain technicalities which the beginner must study before starting. He must think ahead regarding the type of tobacco he likes best to smoke, and *nominate* each plant.

The secret lies in blending. Instead of growing only one variety with space enough to develop large leaves and thick mid-ribs, British experts now advise a mixture of varieties and crowd the plants into a smaller patch. Twenty inches apart has been proved to be quite enough (either way), and in this little forest a small leaf of finer texture is produced, which can be blended into a milder tobacco than was grown at first in Britain.

There are about forty different types of guaranteed seed, and before ordering either seed or plants, advice can be obtained either from Mr. Cuthbertson at Tilty (it is near Dunmow), or from the British Pioneer Tobacco Growers' Association, at Redfields, Crookham, Hants—both of whom undertake the curing, fermenting and maturing of the tobacco at a later stage.

But there are some popular varieties with which it is impossible to go wrong. Havana, Virginian Gold Leaf, Monte Calme, Rustica, Balkan, Burley, Harrow Velvet can all be obtained for 1*s*. 6*d*. per packet of seed; or the average price of plants works out at about 7*s*. a dozen.

All these provide a crop of smaller leaf and finer texture, with thinner mid-ribs; and the result has proved to be a very much milder tobacco. The only drawback is that there are a larger number of small leaves to handle instead of a few big ones, though this does not cause much extra work.

Flowering heads should be nipped out, and by August the first crop will be ready for picking. Only the lower leaves are gathered, but so amazing is the growth of the tobacco plant that the weight from each should be about 2 lb. Later, near the end of September, a further harvest may be taken, averaging in weight well over 1 lb. per plant.

Harvesting must be done on a dry day when the dew is off. There are three stages. The leaf must be yellowed and dried, then fermented or matured, and lastly, cut up, but for the average home grower the simplest method is to join a Curing Centre or Association, in

Tobacco harvest. The leaves are hung up to dry before being
fermented or matured

which case he can pack and label his leaf after drying and send it off to be fermented and processed on a communal basis.

At either Tilty or Crookham only 25 lb. can be accepted from each member. The advantage lies in the fact that the leaf is properly treated for a nominal charge of about 3d. per ounce. Growers receive in return an excellent quality of cigarette or pipe tobacco, which only needs shredding at home to be ready for immediate smoking. The cost of a shredding machine, which enables an ounce of tobacco to be shredded in a few minutes (or several pounds in the course of an evening), is less than the tax on 1 lb. of tobacco purchased in a shop.

£60 Saved

Indeed, the estimated annual saving on the full permitted 25 lb. of tobacco works out at about £60.

All the leaf sent in for processing is kept by the Associations in separate bundles, so that each member receives back his own leaf. It is returned in from 2 to 3 months. Alternatively, those who have the leisure to do everything for themselves can cure their own at home by using a 25-watt electric globe plugged into the circuit, and here again advice regarding the entire procedure before the shredding period is reached can be obtained from the Curing Stations.

Much useful and practical literature on the subject of tobacco-growing in the garden has been published. The following pamphlets are recommended:

From the Tilty Abbey Publications, Dunmow: *Home Tobacco Craft*, illustrated, price 2s. 3d., post paid. Also *Varieties of Tobacco*, in which various tested types are described, price 1s. 2d., post paid.

From the British Pioneer Tobacco Growers' Association: *The Cultivation of Home-grown Tobacco from Seed or from the Young Plant*, price 2s. 6d., by Mr. Eric Troward, F.R.H.S.

The beginner may argue, "But I don't like continental types of tobacco. What about the American varieties that are so popular in British shops?"

The answer is that in our shop-bought "Virginia" there is not more than 10 per cent. of American Virginia tobacco, the rest being a blend of Rhodesian, Balkan and other types. In fact, pure "Virginian" would be unpalatable; so beginners are advised to make their own personal experiments. There is plenty of room for many tastes. The British are no strangers to the art of growing tobacco, for back in the seventeenth century the plant was grown in thirty-one counties of England and Scotland.

From beginning to end growing your own smokes is great fun. As one enthusiast put it: "It's like working in a chocolate factory where you can eat as many as you like without cost," but I noticed that he was so busy with his shredding and blending, that he forgot to smoke.

His wife left him to get on with his pipe tobacco while she was busy making cigarettes for herself, and excellent in quality they were. The pair seemed very happy in the knowledge that they could not afford to smoke at all except by growing their own tobacco.

Tobacco seedlings (White Burley) ready for pricking out into boxes. After putting out they grow fast

GROWING WITHOUT SOIL . . . .

Bigger crops from smaller space, without back-breaking toil

PLANTS can be grown without soil by feeding them on chemical solutions. In the Darjeeling district of India, and in waterless areas like Aden, this method has been practised for many years. Scientists claim that the superiority of hydroponics over ordinary soil culture will become universally recognised, if only because bigger yields can be produced from smaller space, valuable time can be saved, and there is no back-breaking toil involved.

Plants grown by hydroponic methods can be planted much closer together than soil-grown plants because the elements essential for their nutrition are provided by mixtures of fertiliser salts in water, or by synthetic resins. The grower has complete control over his crops, and the uncertainty of normal soil crops is eliminated. The yields of crops have been increased to as much as four times the normal.

Lettuce or Flowers

Under such conditions lettuce is an obvious choice, but flowers such as carnations, chrysanthemums, dahlias and roses give excellent results. An expert in Manchester who practises the method claims to be able to alter the colour of flowers as well as greatly increasing their size.

The plants are grown in beds or troughs made of wood, bricks or mortar, and the best width is 1 yd. These receptacles are then filled to a depth of 8 in. with coarse gravel, broken bricks and two parts sand, and this medium is kept continually moist.

Nutrient mixtures can be obtained, ready prepared, from chemists or agricultural suppliers. They contain the elements normally found in fertilisers, such as nitrogen, potassium, phosphorous, calcium, etc., all of which are necessary for plant development and fruiting. These chemicals are literally fed to the plants in dry form, and at the rate of between 1 and 2 oz. to each square yard. Afterwards they are watered in, this being necessary once every week or 10 days. Recent developments have reduced this "feeding" to tablet form, and there is also a "sludge powder" which is quite odourless and can be quickly absorbed by the plants. Beginners should, however, first study some of the books obtainable from horticultural institutes.

No digging or weeding is required of the soil-less culturist. The technique of hydroponics is now practised by many because it reduces labour costs. Once the troughs have been installed, the beds will last for 20 years, and experts claim that the capital outlay can be recovered within the first 6 months. It offers a great opportunity for the handy-man opportunist who can do things for himself—and enjoy doing them.

Newly planted carnations are fed with nutrient piped down the centre of the bed

AND WITH ARTIFICIAL SUNLIGHT

Plant irradiation encourages winter growth, competes with hot-house culture

ALL growth depends on sun and light, which cannot, unfortunately, be switched on and off at will. Artificial illumination can, however, be used to control the growth of many plants. Producing the effects of sunlight, plant irradiation, as this technique is called, encourages growth even during the winter months when natural growth is normally dormant.

Already it has become a competitor of hot-house growing, and cucumbers, tomatoes and strawberries are treated for early yields. Tomatoes are especially suitable, and early crops have been increased up to 100 per cent., so that the capital outlay of the equipment is quickly recovered. Among the flowering plants, tulips and chrysanthemums have been commercially successful —the former producing full blooms at Christmas, and the latter having their blooms held back by continuous irradiation at night.

One Sieray lamp on a simple pulley operates the entire length of a greenhouse

The latter process is not recommended to push "earliness" to extremes; the plants mostly want a "rest" period when they can absorb the extra carbohydrates produced by the treatment. But growth can be encouraged right through the winter months.

Glasshouses are less suited than any other kind of building for the mounting of heavy equipment, and at first when experiments were being made in the art of plant irradiation the gear required was both costly and unwieldy.

Now within the reach of all

After ten years' research, however, the difficulties were overcome by the combined efforts of the horticultural institutes, the growers and the Siemens Laboratories. In perfecting the Sieray Plant Irradiation Unit, they brought an original form of cultivation within the reach of all.

The unit consists of a low intensity lamp, parabolic in shape, with an internal silvered reflector. This combines two totally different light sources in one bulb, i.e. the red and blue ends of the spectrum are so balanced that they produce simulated natural sunlight, and plants so irradiated do not show any weakness caused by the normal greenhouse "forcing" routine.

Units are suspended about 2 ft. above the soil level, and each is effective for an area of 4 sq. ft. These can now be introduced into any greenhouse without endangering its structure. Moreover, the reaction of the plants is twofold. First, their breathing or respiration rate increases, and secondly, the plants absorb carbon dioxide and convert it into carbohydrates which they use for food.

Wiring the greenhouse is extremely simple, but it should be done by a qualified electrician. The porcelain lamp-holder is provided with shrouded cable entry and exit.

A number of professional growers have had up to two years' experience of plant irradiation techniques, and the figures of their financial returns are quite impressive. It may well be that amateurs, even with only small lean-to glasshouses, will find that irradiation is the answer to many of their problems.

"Smallholder"

Khaki Campbells have produced unbelievable results in the number and quality
of their eggs, which are pearly white and delicious

DUCK-KEEPING FOR PROFIT

They lay well, are less trouble—and
more affectionate—than hens!

COMPARED with most livestock the duck requires little attention; all it asks for is a handful of grain each morning and one good feed of wet mash each evening. If you have a garden, it is profitable to keep a few ducks; they lay 98 per cent. of their eggs before 9 a.m., and one good layer will produce an egg for breakfast every morning for nine months of the year.

Why, then, doesn't everyone who can, keep ducks? They are less trouble than hens, they are beautiful and have brains, they respond to kindness and, in turn, display affection.

Prejudice against Duck Eggs

The answer to this question is—there exists a universal prejudice about duck eggs. This bias is persistent, although its foundation has long disappeared; it was caused by farmers' wives raking the pond for ducks' eggs before they went to market. The large, green eggs obtained in this way were sold regardless of age, and this was unfair to both the public—and the ducks.

A new-laid duck's egg should be white and delicious to eat, whereas a stale, green duck's egg is addled and obnoxious. It is the keeper's fault if the egg is sold in bad condition. Domestic duck owners never suffer, because they pick up the eggs daily in the run and consume them in the home. Many prefer duck eggs for omelets and scrambles; they go much farther.

Water Essential

The beginner has only one simple lesson to learn—ducks must have water. They can be kept on dry land with success only so long as they are given a plentiful supply of clean water in suitable containers. They are clumsy with their feet (though only in confinement), and they will knock over and foul basins or bowls. Proper water containers for ducks are cheap and easily obtained, but the rule for success is to keep them well filled.

This applies to all ducks, including the *Indian Runners*, which are sometimes called "land ducks." They are the best variety to keep in a small space because they can live quite happily without swimming water. On free range, or if loose in the garden during the dormant season, they will pick up much of their own living in the form of insects.

The Runner duck looks like a penguin; he has an upright carriage and waddling

The Indian Runner, which has an upright carriage, can live without swimming water (right)

The Buff Orpington (below) is a heavy bird, and slow of movement.

"Smallholder"

"Smallholder"

movement which is attractive. He is a native of Malaya and China, countries in which the very poorest of the populace cultivate and appreciate ducks for their food value in meat and eggs. But the Runner thrives in the U.K., and the number of eggs per annum which can be obtained from a small pen of, say, five ducks and a drake, can average 250 per bird per annum.

This quantity can be excelled only by the *Khaki Campbell*. This wonderful breed has produced unbelievable results in the number and quality of eggs, which are of a pearly white colour and light and delicate to taste. The birds are good to eat, too, and were originally of wild duck stock.

Mrs. Campbell, the originator of this breed, wished to produce an active, moderate-sized, good-looking duck, capable of laying a large number of eggs—and she succeeded. As the dual name implies, they are khaki in colour, which is an asset when they are confined in small quarters, because they do not show dirt on their feathers when, in rainy weather, the run becomes muddy. After a bath they are extremely handsome, and

The Muscovy grazes on grass, and should not be kept in close confinement because it likes to fly about—an ideal bird in a rough garden

also most intelligent.

Buff Orpington is a breed of duck as well as a breed of hen, and they have much the same characteristics, in that they are both heavy and slow of movement. From the table point of view, these ducks are more plump and full-breasted than the Khaki Campbell, but though very good layers, they do not compete in quantity of eggs with either the Khaki Campbell or the Runner. They are ideal in confinement because they become very tame and children can make pets of them.

The *Aylesbury* is the large, white duck —the best of all table breeds. The breed originated in and around Aylesbury, and vast flocks of these ducks are kept to supply the London market with ducklings for banquets and festive occasions.

But the Aylesbury is also a good layer and will average 100 eggs per annum when the birds are kept in confinement. They show dirt, however, unless they have plenty of bath water—then their pure white colour proves them to be very handsome.

Other lesser-known breeds include the *Rouen*, a lovely duck with golden plumage; the *Crested Duck*, rather like the Orpington, except for a beautiful crest on his head; the *Magpie*, an attractive black and white, which is popular with those who like something out of the ordinary about the house; and the *Pekin*, a large white duck with an orange bill like the Aylesbury, very popular with breeders for table purposes.

The *Muscovy* duck, however, is different because he is more like a goose and grazes on grass in the same way—a very useful bird to keep in a rough uncultivated garden.

As Tame as Kittens

Muscovies should not be kept in close confinement because they like to fly like pigeons, though they always come home if fed at regular times. In fact, they become so tame that they will weave their way through the keeper's legs like kittens.

This breed is increasing in popularity in Britain, not so much for its eggs as its table qualities. The ducks are also wonderful mothers, and will brood for 36 days on a nest which contains as many as 15 eggs— and hatch them all out unaided. They are, indeed, independent creatures, who look after themselves almost from hatching, going their own ways in a manner which is delightful to watch; and if a strange dog should make a rush at them, they sensibly fly out of his way.

Accommodation and Feeding

Ducks do not roost like hens, so a duck-house needs no perches. What it does need is $\frac{1}{4}$-in. wire-netting on the floor to keep out rats. Or if wooden flooring is used, it is an advantage to have the floor just off the ground to give air space.

Many breeders keep ducks in compounds, which can be quite small for a few birds. If you have an old poultry house without a floor, the ducks will use this for shelter, and if attacked by rats in the night, they can move about so long as the door is kept open—or low shelters can be fixed up with a straw-thatched roof.

Ducks like bibbling for grain in water, rather than shovelling it up off the ground, so throw it into a bowl of clean water, about a handful to each bird.

For mash feeding, galvanised iron troughs are easy to clean. Each evening a feed of 3–4 oz. of wet mash should be given. If food is left over, take it away (rats again), but ducks are usually good "doers" and clean up everything in about fifteen minutes. They like greenstuff cut up and added to the mash.

The best of all table birds—the handsome and famous white Aylesbury

The W.B.C. hive is the most suitable for the English climate

MONEY IN HONEY

First steps in the fascinating business of beekeeping

HONEY is a sterling product. It improves with saving, and you can release it when it is most required. There is money in honey.

There is also good health. No one tastes the heady wine of spring like a beekeeper standing amongst his hives on a May day. The air is charged with the tiny creatures; the flow of early nectar has made them ecstatic. They flash, they dance, thousands of moving wings make continuous and lovely music.

The occupants of a beehive are one Queen, 300 to 400 drones and up to 40,000 workers. The Queen is larger and has a more elongated body than the rest; she spends her life in laying eggs to ensure the existence of the colony.

Drones are the next largest type, and are the males. They take no part in the ordinary work in the hive and they live on the food gathered by the workers. Their one duty is to provide from out of their number a mate for the Queen, and when this function is fulfilled and the honey flow is

over, they are killed off by the workers—a harsh ending to a life of luxury.

Workers form the main body of the colony. They perform all the work in the hive, each has an allotted task and no shirkers are tolerated. Some gather pollen, others fan their wings outside and inside the hive to maintain a required temperature. They guard the entrance against possible marauders. Others are the "Maids of Honour," in constant attendance on the Queen. More workers still look after the "nursery," and act as "nannies" to the embryo bees.

A Perfect Organisation

Thus the beekeeper introduces himself to a perfect organisation with a complete subdivision of duties. The Queen and the drones are concerned with the propagation of the race. The workers, deprived by nature of all sexual desires, minister to the daily wants of the colony, and perform the routine duties. They look after the feeding and cleanliness of the society as a whole. So perfect does it seem, this world of insects, that a beginner in beekeeping may well ask himself—where do I come in?

To this question the bees themselves provide the answer. They know that summers are short and winters are long. They get to know their owners, much as dogs do. They will allow him (or her) to lay his hand across the entrance when they are most busy, they will race to and fro over his hand without stinging it. He is the only "extra" they require, for his duty is to feed them and keep the hives warm during the hard months of the year.

First Lesson

This is the first lesson the beginner beekeeper has to learn. Bees must be *fed* when their store of natural honey is insufficient for the life of the colony. It is of no use for him to acquire a hive, place it in his garden, and then expect the bees to provide the household with a regular supply of honey. Some people do this, but their bees die during the winter and often starve to death during a wet, cold summer.

Bees must be fed at all times when their own store of natural food (honey) becomes insufficient for their needs. Sugar is supplied to them not only to be eaten, but also to be translated into honey.

Lots and lots of sugar, at least 15 lb. per hive per annum. This is used in three ways and at different times: in the autumn as a concentrated solution of sugar and water; in the spring, when the honey-flow begins, as a dilute solution of sugar and water; and, almost any time if conditions are bad, as a safeguard, a prepared candy made of sugar.

Starting the Hive

Bees are delivered either in a skep or a travelling box, and the most suitable time for hiving is after the sun has gone down. The hive having been placed in position, preferably facing south-west with no trees or hedges in front, the roof and outer casing is removed so that only the brood chamber remains on the floor-board. The tops of the frames are then covered with a cloth, and a board about 2 feet wide is placed from the alighting board to the ground, and this again covered with a sheet.

On to this platform the bees are shaken from the skep, and having a natural inclination to walk uphill, the swarm immediately proceeds to travel into the hive, a process which takes only about fifteen minutes, but which will

be watched goggle-eyed by the novice as an unforgettable experience.

The huge mass formation guarding the Queen looks like a review of trained soldiers on a ceremonial inspection, except that it is far too busy to bother about salutes. It just moves until it is housed, and the new owner is left gasping, for there is something quite inexorable about bee business.

The outer parts of the hive are now replaced, but at once feeding comes into operation. Into the feeder you pour, for a week or ten days, a mixture consisting of three-quarters of a pint of water to every pound of sugar, brought to the boil and then allowed to cool before feeding to the bees.

Bees, like humans, dislike occupying a new house in which there is no food in the pantry, so the purpose of this first feed is obvious—it is a "housewarming." And the feast should continue every day until they have settled in.

Equipment

The best kind of hive to purchase is called the W.B.C., which has been adopted as the most suitable for the English climate, while the size of the frames is standardised.

This is important, as there are many

Keep always to one pattern of hive so that lifts and frames are interchangeable

types of hives on the market which vary considerably in quality and size. Keep always to one pattern is the rule, so that lifts and frames are interchangeable if the stock is increased later on. The hive should be given three coats of white paint.

But before its future inhabitants take possession, the new beekeeper is advised to make himself acquainted with the "furniture." It consists first of a floor-board, to which the legs are attached (good circulation of air underneath is essential), and then there are the outer case, two lifts and a roof to complete the external parts.

Inside, resting on the floor-board, is the brood chamber, containing ten frames, as well as a division board to conserve heat.

The frames are spaced at equal distances apart by metal ends, and over this brood chamber there is a box of shallow frames which, except in size, are the same as those in the brood chamber, and are used for extracted honey.

Between the brood chamber and the shallow frames a piece of flat open-work zinc known as the "Queen Excluder" is placed. This will allow the worker bees to go up into the shallow frames, but will not allow the Queen to move up, the size of the slots being so cut that she, being considerably larger, cannot get through. Poor lady, she must be allowed no diversions! Her job is to get on with depositing 2,000 eggs a day in the cells made by her workers for that purpose.

Protective clothing for the beekeeper

Handling Bees

The aim of the beekeeper when handling bees should be slow movement and confidence. A veil should always be worn; also gloves with gauntlets.

During the middle of the day, when the majority of the bees are out foraging, is the best time to approach the hive from the rear. The roof is lifted carefully, then one corner of the quilt of felt, before blowing in a few puffs of smoke by means of the smoker. This causes the bees inside to cling to the frames and start filling themselves with honey. A few puffs gently administered is all that is required; they should never be smoked until they become quite senseless.

A popular idea that bees are difficult or dangerous to handle will be found quite erroneous by those who follow the above simple rules. No attempt should ever be made to open hives on a rainy, thundery or windy day. Bees hate wind above all things.

The Honey-flow

When to "super"—i.e. add extra storing room to the hive—is always a problem. The bees should be storing in the tenth comb before any supering is begun. It is only a matter of adding an extra lift, and in the English climate this is not necessary at all in some years.

In other years, when the season is good, you may get wild excitements which are almost embarrassing. For instance, the year 1933 was the most wonderful honey year on record. In some districts, notably Norfolk, 400 lb. of honey were obtained from a single colony. One lady in that county took from her six hives a total of 1,289 lb., an average of 215 lb. per hive.

Similar bumper seasons happened in 1916 and 1921, but there was no previous indication of the miracles. A beekeeper's luck cannot be forecast, and, alas, he may be up against the worst, such as happened in 1954, when in some places the bees had to be fed continuously during the wet, stormy, sunless season—and there was very little honey at all. Yet my own bees, for some strange reason known only to themselves (or possibly because they had been carefully nursed through the previous winter and spring), averaged 40 lb. per hive in 1954, which has been about their yearly average for several years.

The harvest is therefore quite unpredictable, even when you grow borage, mustard and sweet herbs, as we do, almost at the entrances to the hives to conserve the bees' energy.

But there is nothing quite so interesting as removing the section racks, and this should be done in the evening to avoid all chances of robbing. The smell of honey is a great attraction to passing bees, who will sometimes make a dead set on the hive that has been opened up, and a terrible battle ensues.

However much you may grow to love your bees, they remain wild creatures in certain circumstances; you may tame a Bengal tiger, but you can never *tame* a bee. It is better, therefore, during harvest time, to work quickly and to store away your honey in a dark, dry cupboard out of all reach. If the frames are left about, the bees are sure to discover them, and take the honey back to their hives. They become very angry indeed, and will sting at sight.

Listen to Your Bees

For the same reason, extracting should be done in a bee-proof shed. This is done in a machine, which may be borrowed from another beekeeper for a day or two if you only have one or two hives. People who keep bees are usually helpful, generous folk who are only too anxious to assist beginners. Many beekeepers talk to their bees, and all listen to what the bees have to say when they are on the air. In this way they learn from experience, which is by far the best way.

One book written in Latin about 1637 by a clergyman called Charles Butler can still be consulted for wisdom. He says the bees should be kept in sight of the house because of the chance of "fighting, swarming or sudden hap," and that is excellent advice to-day. Also he gives recipes for various ways of using honey, and a special one for the mead which was the only ration King Harold's armies had when they beat the Danes at Senlac, and marched 200 miles to do it without undue fatigue.

In our home we eat toast and honey for breakfast all the year round, and sometimes drink honey in a glass of hot milk, which is ambrosia, at bedtime. And from our six hives there is usually a considerable surplus to sell, proving beyond dispute that there is money in honey, not to mention—good health!

A scientist named Tsitsin asserts that, in addition, there is "long life," and that beekeepers in Russia who have little to eat except their own honey, live to be more than a hundred. This may be true—we have not proved it yet and much prefer a short life and a merry one on mead.

A veil is necessary when handling the bees

EGGS AT TRIFLING COST

*With six or a dozen fowls in your backyard, you
can be sure of 200 eggs per bird in the year*

Many small poultry-keepers dislike cross-bred chickens and favour the beauty of
thoroughbreds like these Light Sussex

A SMALL family with six chickens, or a
large one with twelve, will be assured
of its egg supply all the year round at a
trifling cost—always provided that someone
in the home takes good care of the birds,
which are home-loving creatures of unfailing industry.

A hen has so much to do in a short life
that she hasn't a moment to spare. As a
chick she kicks herself out of her own shell.
She arrives in the world bright-eyed, self-
contained and eager; if need be, quite
capable of travelling long distances in a
cardboard box as a " day-old."

As a growing chick she is never idle for a
moment, and scarcely has she attained full
plumage than she starts laying eggs. Two
hundred of these per bird is a normal ex-
pectation for the household, but with extra
care the total can be much more.

How many Pullets?

Investment in between six or twelve
pullets is therefore certain to produce good
dividends, but why are these two figures so
important? The answer is the result of
wide experience. *There is no half-way
house between the small poultry-keeper
who feeds his birds mainly on kitchen
waste, and the big commercial producer
who can buy his feeding stuffs wholesale.*
Both are economic propositions. It is the
middle way of 50–500 birds, for whom
grain and meal have to be bought at high
prices, that is a dangerous path to tread.

Housing the Birds

The traditional method is to keep
chickens in the garden or backyard pen.
So domesticated have the birds become,
that there is no cruelty whatsoever in their
confinement. Their health and well-being
are assured, always provided that certain
simple rules are observed.

A dry, draught-proof house is a first
essential, and there are many designs on
the market which are sold in sections easy
to erect, though a handyman in the house

might well prefer to build his own. Either way, ⅝-in. boarding is necessary for the sides, and ¾-in. for the floors. The most popular design has a compartment on the right-hand side of the door, for the birds to roost; and a wired-in run on the left.

Nest boxes are in front, or at one side, and they should be fixed for comparative darkness and privacy. Hens fortunately do not all lay at the same time, so you don't want a nest box for each, but as they like to be alone during the process, a proportion of three nest boxes for six hens is about right. If each has a shutter so that the eggs can be extracted without disturbance, so much the better.

Different breeds of poultry vary greatly in size, so it is wise to start with a house of twice the apparently adequate dimensions. The rule is to allow about 12 cu. ft. per bird, though it is far more important that the roost should be well lighted and ventilated. There should be inlet and outlet ventilation holes above the heads of the birds as they perch, the air being controlled during severe weather by covering the apertures with perforated zinc.

There should be a door in the house for the owner to enter for cleaning work, and, of course, a pop-hole for the bird, with a sliding shutter controlled by string from the outside. If poultry are not shut up at night, foxes soon get to work.

Importance of Cleanliness

Cleanliness is essential, so at the back of the roost there must be a drop-board several feet wide, and a foot above this a removable perch slipping into sockets. Each morning the drop-board should be scraped and a little sand or dry earth scattered on it; this saves the floor from becoming fouled, which is most important.

A wooden floor is necessary, so that a good depth of scratching litter can be kept in dry condition. This normal procedure should not be confused with what is now known as the "deep litter method" of keeping chickens. This has been widely adopted by the big commercial producers, who keep their poultry indoors in large sheds and barns, and feed them exclusively on grain, which the birds scratch for on the floor.

This method can be applied to any henhouse, but the householder with his six or twelve birds should be more concerned

with using up the kitchen waste, which costs nothing. Moreover, the mash method of feeding keeps the layers just as busy with production.

Economical Feeding

But first of all, what is meant by the term "kitchen waste"? Scraps of bread, meat, bacon-rind, boiled potato peelings, cabbage left-overs, should be put daily in the bucket. When the time comes for feeding, all this waste is chumped up and then dried off with the addition of what the grain-merchants call "Layers' Mash." Blended in this way the food feels crumbly in the hand and is extremely palatable. This constitutes the principal meal of the day, and it should be served in a metal hopper which the birds cannot easily turn over.

Many designs, most of them good, are on the market; so are drinking vessels, which should be large enough to contain a goodly supply of water and have covered tops to prevent fouling. Water must be renewed each day.

The time to serve the principal meal of the day will vary to suit the convenience of the householder, but the birds will adapt themselves. This is a useful routine for people who are at home most of the day—

Breakfast.—About 1 oz. per bird of grain, thrown into the litter for scratching purposes.

Midday.—Some raw green food, hung up away from the litter just high enough to jump at.

Tea (while there is still plenty of daylight). Roughly 2½ oz. of mash per bird.

Many household poultry-keepers give the mash at breakfast time or midday and the grain at night before shutting up. Be sure to remove any surplus food that the birds may have left behind in the feeding trough. Sparrows are a nuisance, but far worse are rats. At all costs, vermin must be kept away, not only from the hens, but from the home.

The labour, certainly, is considerable, but consider the profit side for a moment. While the big commercial producer reckons 180 eggs per bird per annum, the backyarder, with his six or twelve fowls, can be sure of 200 eggs per bird; and the retail price is frequently 5s. a dozen for produce which is mainly imported, and cannot always be relied on. A new-laid egg from your own henhouse is worth a lot of trouble, quite apart from the saving of money.

But there is another argument in favour. Hens are quaint things, with interesting habits; and keeping them may well become a delightful hobby. It is only when you raise a few chicks for yourself that their full qualities are discovered.

Raising Your Own Stock

For this reason, when possible, it is advisable each year to buy settings of fertile eggs and put down a "broody" or two. Better still, start that way—and raise your own stock.

The best chicks are produced between February and April, and it is sometimes possible to borrow or hire a broody hen from a neighbour during that period (if you have not got one yourself). You set the bird in a roomy box, 15 in. square or larger, and cover the bottom with 1-in. wire netting to keep out rats.

This nest box should be placed in a quiet corner of the yard or garden, well away from the poultry house so that the broody has privacy. Over the wire-netting floor should be a newly dug piece of turf, put in grass-side down and made saucer-shape with the hands. This holds the eggs and keeps them from rolling out. Pack up hollows and corners with straw.

For the first day or two use only dummy eggs in the nest, to allow the broody time to settle down. Replace these by the full setting (thirteen eggs), when she seems content to sit.

Now starts another daily routine—food and water must be given regularly to the broody, and a handful of maize once daily. Some hens refuse to leave the nest, and these must be lifted off very gently, and kept away from the nest for at least 15 minutes, during which time they will evacuate and not soil the eggs.

The chipping of shells begins on the nineteenth day of sitting. The broody should then be left quite undisturbed until the twenty-second day, when she will have completed her task of hatching. The turf

Cleanliness is essential in the hen house. Each morning drop-boards need scraping to save the floor from getting fouled

should now be withdrawn so that the chicks have a flat surface on which to move round the broody's feathers.

Another method of raising chickens to save initial costs is to purchase day-olds and introduce these to a broody hen in the hope that she will take to them at once. This is more likely to be successful if the bird has been sitting on dummies for a week or so beforehand, and the chicks are introduced very quietly in the dusk of an evening. This method saves time and has one inestimable advantage over the egg-setting method; you can rely on the chicks being 100 per cent. pullets.

For obvious reasons, the small poultry-keeper must avoid cockerels. Apart from the fact that they are noisy creatures and soon start crowing and annoying the neighbours, their only value is for food, and to feed them to the stage when they are heavy enough for the pot is very expensive.

"Sex-linkage"

Guaranteed day-old pullets, on the other hand, can be obtained from all the commercial producers who hatch them in incubators by the thousand, and send them anywhere (even by 'plane to foreign countries sometimes) to arrive punctually on an agreed date. These dealers separate all their hatchings into male and female by a process known as "sex-linkage." The colour of the down on the newly hatched chick is linked with its sex, and every beginner should know something about how this is achieved.

If a coloured cock, such as a Rhode Island Red or a Buff Leghorn, is mated with a silver hen—say, a Light Sussex or a White Wyandotte—the resulting progeny will have golden-brown down (the females), and others a creamy-white down (the males). So scientific has the method become, that the "professionals" can now do without the help of the Japanese sex-linkers who were employed before the war.

Yet another method of raising pullets from day-olds is useful to know about when, as often happens, a broody hen is entirely unobtainable. Chicks do not need any food at all until they are forty-eight hours old, and even then they eat very little at first. During this time, they can be introduced to a foster-mother in the shape of a home-made "Brooder," in the centre of which there is a lamp to provide the necessary warmth for the chicks—about 90 degrees.

Factory-made "brooders" can be purchased complete from any dealer, but the principle is so simple that many beginners improvise the equipment in the home, provided there is someone around who can check up on the temperatures.

Six feeds daily are given to chicks once they begin to get hungry, and each should be cleared away after 10 minutes. They consist of chick-feed and chick-mash. The former contains dried milk and cod-liver oil; it is moistened with water and fed into troughs protected by wire netting so that the chicks do not walk on their food. Chick-mash can be mixed with a very little greenstuff such as cabbage. Quantities should be increased daily, for in one month the birds will eat three times the quantity with which they started. After about six weeks they will be strong enough to take the same food as the adult hens.

From then onwards the main thing to remember is—plenty of fresh water daily for both chicks and adults, a box full of grit available at all times and, for nature's cleansing of feathers and body, a dust box. This may be filled with ash from the house grates, and if a little sulphur powder is added the birds will keep themselves fresh and clean.

Choosing a Thoroughbred

Many small poultry-keepers dislike cross-bred chickens, for the simple reason that they never attain the dignity and magnificence of feather of a thoroughbred. For them it is a matter of selecting one of the many breeds, and domestic poultry is of two quite distinct types—heavy and light.

Light breeds, especially the Leghorns, came to us originally from the Mediterranean countries where temperatures in the summer are so consistent that eggs laid in a nest will hatch themselves without the help of a sitting hen. The consequence of this is that the light breeds have lost the virtue of broodiness, and are now regarded simply as egg-laying machines. So light in weight are they that they are practically useless for table purposes, the carcases being all skin and bone.

The light breeds lay only white-shelled

eggs, a disadvantage since brown-shelled eggs are far more popular.

Against this, however, the light breeds are a great deal more active than the heavies, and this accounts for the popularity of White and Black Leghorns, Anconas, Minorcas and Buff Rocks.

Dark or Light?

But here another aspect of the subject presents itself. Dark-plumaged birds are far more suited to town and city runs, where the white ones always look dirty. In choosing therefore, the silky Black Leghorn, whose feathers shine in almost any conditions, is preferable to his pure white brother. Or, if you prefer a brighter and more colourful compromise, there is the Old English Pheasant or the Silkie.

Heavy breeds include the three most popular varieties in the world—the Rhode Island Red, the Sussex and the Wyandotte. All have reputations for large eggs and a big output, and have proved their worth for general utility purposes. And when you must kill your chickens as three-year-olds, their intensive laying life being over, why not have something that will provide a good meal when it comes to table?

Bantams

Fun for the children can be combined with bantam-keeping for eggs, though the latter are small in comparison with those of the heavy breed hen. However, some of the records are surprising in view of the difference in size: 100 eggs in the winter months from a Partridge Wyandotte, while a White Wyandotte bantam laid 202 eggs in twelve months.

Bantams do not need large houses and runs, nor do they eat very much, so those

Keeping chickens soon becomes a fascinating hobby, shared enthusiastically by the children

with small space should consider keeping them from the investment point of view. Children can be trained to look after them, and are very quick to realise the value of the eggs, so it soon becomes a self-supporting hobby that pays dividends in pocket money.

Feeding is the same as for larger birds, but in smaller quantities. The main appeal of bantams, however, is their superb self-confidence, beauty and cheekiness. Moreover, they love being handled and made a fuss of and—an endearing feature this—their curiosity about the family is unbounded.

KEEPING A DOMESTIC GOAT

Once you have tried this creamy milk in the home, you will never want to give it up—and it's perfectly safe for babies too, says Gilbert Harris, M.R.S.

PRODUCING your own household milk can be profitable, health-giving and also an interesting occupation. If you have about a third of an acre of spare land, or wide grass verges, common land, or waste ground nearby, then all you need is a dairy goat.

The milk of the goat is one of the finest milks that nature provides. It has more cream than cows' milk, is richer in valuable minerals and is naturally free from tubercular infection. This means that there is no need for the milk to be pasteurised to make it safe for human consumption and it takes only about twenty minutes to digest as against four hours for cows' milk. It is therefore an excellent milk for babies.

The goat is a lovable and intelligent animal, and makes a grand pet who pays handsomely for her keep. Contrary to popular belief, the nanny goat does not smell. It is only the male goat that smells during the mating season. You can reasonably expect to get from five to eight pints of milk a day, and the cost of a suitable animal for household purposes ranges from £5 to £15.

When buying a goat, look for a sleek one with a shiny coat, a long, slender neck and a fine-featured, feminine head. The body should be narrow and shallow at the front legs, and deep and broad at the rear. Do not buy a fat goat; she will turn her food into flesh instead of milk. One that has kidded only once will be between one and a half and two and a half years old and should give you plenty of milk for eight to ten years. A reasonably good one will need mating only every other year. In the U.K. a National Stud Scheme enables you to obtain the services of a top-grade male for as little as 7s. 6d.

A goat needs very simple accommodation. The house can be as small as 4 ft. square, so long as it is dry and draught-proof. A draughty house will reduce the milk yield considerably. It should have a brick, concrete or wooden floor, and a small hay rack fixed to one wall with the base about 3 ft. 6 in. from the floor. Straw, dried bracken or heather make excellent bedding. This will need renewing once or twice a week. Heap the used bedding in a corner of your garden for compost.

During the spring and summer, your goat will find most of its own food. It has a wonderful digestive system and will thoroughly enjoy such things as docks, thistles, nettles, gorse and heather, as well as ordinary grasses. It is the goat's ability to handle this wide variety of herbage that enables it to produce such excellent milk.

How to Feed Her

There are, however, some things that are poisonous to the goat. The deadly ones are Box, Yew, Laburnum, Rhododendron and Nightshade. Others that should be avoided are Laurel, Privet and Convolvulus. On the other hand, she will enjoy your rose-tree clippings; fruit-tree prunings; cabbage leaves and stalks; onion, carrot, beet, celery, radish and parsnip tops and any surplus roots; pea haulms and pods; bean stalks and pods; windfall apples and pears; freshly cut lawn mowings and any vegetable thinnings. Do not feed potato tops or rhubarb.

From your household waste she will eat all vegetable parings and pea and bean pods. Potato peelings are good food, but they need drying in a warm oven first. Waste bread, cakes and pastry will be treated as a luxury.

In the winter, when there is not much browsing, a ration of hay will be necessary. Three to five pounds daily is about the average need, depending on how much household waste is available. Two feeds a day of concentrates should be given. A suitable mixture is two parts of bran with one part of flaked maize and a handful or so of dairy nuts. Oats or barley can be substituted for the maize for a change. It is difficult to estimate exactly how much an individual goat will need, but £6 a year should meet your concentrates bill.

The goat should be encouraged to drink

as much as possible. Do not leave a bucket of water in the stall. Rain water is usually preferred to tap water, and a little salt added will often induce her to drink more. In the winter she will appreciate water with the chill taken off it. Get a salt-lick and leave it in her stall.

The goat takes kindly to tethering. A very light chain can be used, for preference 18 ft. of No. 8 best white, waxed sashcord, which stands the weather well and will not cause damage if the goat gets it tangled round her legs. If possible, move her at least once every day. In hot weather, make sure that she has shade.

A goat can go out in most weathers, but it is advisable to keep her in if there is a very cold wind or cold, heavy rain. If she is really unhappy, she will stand with her back humped up, tail tucked in and head down. Bring her in if you see her looking like this. Leave her in every night and you will get more milk.

Milking should be done twice a day and as nearly as possible at twelve-hourly intervals, for the goat is a creature of habit.

Milking is Easy

The goat has only two teats and milking is quite simple. A teat should be held firmly but not tightly in each hand, with the end attached to the udder resting in the crook of the first finger and thumb. To draw the milk, first press your first finger and thumb together to close the entrance of the teat to the udder; then, keeping the teat closed at the top, squeeze the milk out of the other end into the milking pail. This is best done by applying pressure with the second, third and fourth fingers, in that order, until you have the teat more or less pressed flat and all the milk expressed. Release the pressure of all fingers to allow the teat to fill up again and repeat the procedure until there is no milk left in the udder. It is essential to see that all milk is drawn to the last drop at every milking or your milk yield will slowly drop. It is not necessary to pull the teat as in milking a cow; just squeeze. Milking can be done with the goat standing on the floor, but if you want to prevent backache, build a little bench, about 14 in. high, for her to stand on, she will quickly learn to jump up on to it and it will be comfortable for both.

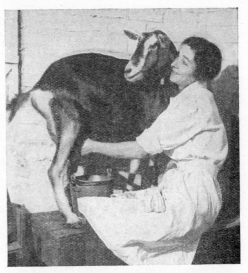

A goat will quickly learn to jump up on to a bench about 14 in. high, which makes milking more comfortable for both

After the milk has been drawn, it should be cooled quickly to preserve its flavour, by standing the pail in plenty of cold water or in a refrigerator. It should also be strained through a piece of butter muslin and covered until you are ready to use it.

Once you have had coffee, milk puddings and egg custards made from this lovely creamy milk, you will never want to go back to the milk your milkman brings. From any surplus you have, you can skim the cream. Put the milk into a large shallow pan and let it stand in a cool place for thirty-six hours, when a thick layer of cream can be taken off the top. Excellent cheese can also be made from goats' milk.

There is no better milk—other than the human variety, of course—for feeding babies. It can be fed to a newborn babe without fear. Do not add water to it and do not boil it; merely bring it up to body heat. Boiling will destroy much of its value and make it less easily digestible. When goats' milk is substituted for cows', a baby only needs four-fifths of the recommended quantity because of its higher feeding value.

As to the economics of domestic goat-keeping, your annual expenditure at a maximum should not be £12. If you only average five pints a day, this would cost you more than £50 from your milkman.

IT is as important to use a needle of the correct size as it is to choose a pattern that fits. A needle which is either too thick or too thin for the fabric will be awkward in use and may ruin the finished appearance of the garment. In the following chart a selection of fabrics has been divided into groups according to weight and type, with corresponding thread, machine needle and hand needle sizes. Note that the method of numbering machine needles differs from that of hand needles. In the former case, the higher numbers denote the thicker needles; in the latter case the smaller numbers denote the thicker needles.

When using the sewing machine, always adjust it to have the correct number of stitches to the inch. Too many stitches to the inch makes the fabric liable to tear at the seam.

FABRICS	THREAD SIZE No.	MACHINE NEEDLE No.	MILWARDS HAND NEEDLE No.	STITCHES TO INCH
Heavy overall fabrics, heavy curtains, rugs, canvas, etc.	Coats Six-Cord No. 10	23–21	3	10
Heavy furnishings, heavy velvets, heavy coatings, heavy suitings, heavy tweeds	Coats Six-Cord No. 24 or Coats Satinised No. 24	19–18	5 or 6	12 to 14, depending on thickness of fabric
Serge, heavy cottons and linen	Coats Six-Cord No. 30 or No. 36, or Coats Satinised No. 40	18–17	5 or 6	12 to 14, depending on thickness of fabric
Dress cottons, household linens, light weight woollens, suitings and tweeds, winceyette, flannel, gaberdine, fine corduroy, dress velvet, medium curtain fabrics	Coats Six-Cord No. 40 or Coats Satinised No. 40	16	6 or 7	14
Fine cottons, gingham, cambric and heavy silks, piqué, poplin, tussore, dress crêpe	Coats Six-Cord No. 50 or No. 60, or Coats Satinised No. 60	14–13	6 or 7	14
All fine and delicate fabrics. Lawns, voiles, chiffons, muslins, organdie, georgette, fine silks	Coats Six-Cord No. 80 or Coats Satinised No. 60	12–9	8 or 9	14 to 16, depending on thickness of fabric
Nylon, Terylene and other synthetic fabrics	Coats Gossamer	14–9, depending on thickness of fabric	8 or 9	16 to 18 fine fabric, 14 to 16 medium or heavy fabric

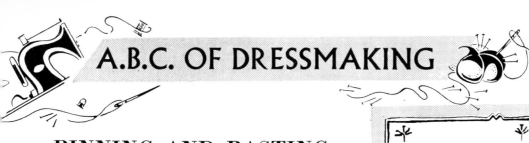

PINNING AND BASTING

PINNING

HOW TO PIN . . . Use fine pins and place them at right angles to the basting or stitching line, as shown right. If placed otherwise, the pins will prick the hand while hand basting or will catch under the presser foot of the machine when machine stitching.

In pinning, pick up the least possible amount of fabric. Insert first pins at points indicated by chalk marks, tailor's tacks or other markings; match notches. Pin intervening spaces, inserting pin at centre point of each space until sufficient pins are in position to hold the fabric securely.

An experienced sewer may machine stitch her garment directly after pinning, but basting by hand or machine is necessary where fitting is required.

WHEN TO REMOVE PINS . . . When **hand basting,** remove the pins as you work over them so that the thread will not tangle.

When **machine stitching,** if using a jointed presser foot machine, leave pins in until the stitching is completed.

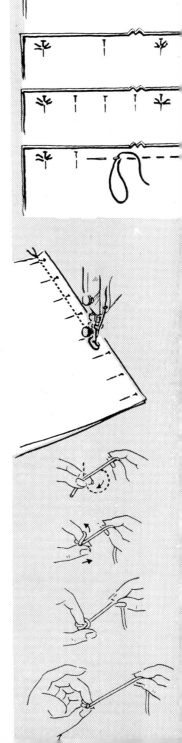

BASTING

Basting serves two purposes:

1. To mark lines on single layers of fabric, such as centre front and centre back, grain lines, etc.
2. To hold two or more pieces of fabric firmly in position for fitting or stitching.

Basting stitches are temporary stitches to be removed once a garment is permanently finished. To make removal easy, the basting thread should always be in a colour contrasting with the fabric.

Length of thread should never be more than the arm of the sewer (see left); longer threads are more difficult to handle.

Cut . . . never break the thread from the spool, so that the end will be sharp and easy to thread into the needle. Draw quarter of the length through the needle.

Make a knot at other end of thread by twisting it around forefinger, as shown right.

If thread twists and snarls in sewing, try placing the knot on opposite end of thread. If snarling still persists, watch handling of needle. Twisting the needle in sewing will affect the natural twist of the thread.

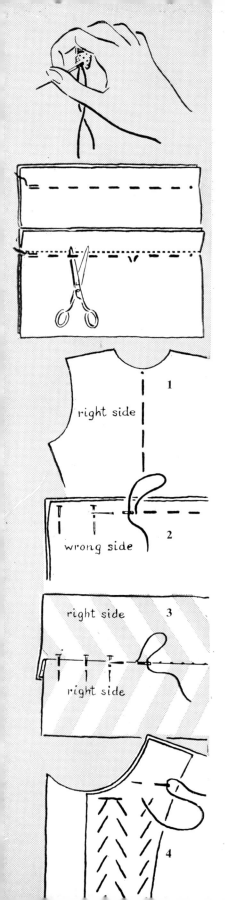

A THIMBLE IS A NECESSITY IN HAND SEWING . . . Place the thimble on the middle finger of the hand you use for sewing. The thumb and forefinger hold and guide the needle, but the middle finger, protected by the thimble, should be used to push the needle through the fabric, as shown left.

START BASTING with the knot in full view, where it is easy to remove.

FINISH BASTING with two small stitches taken close together (see left).

TO REMOVE BASTING, clip thread every few stitches, as shown left; pull out, starting with knot. Removing long basting threads without clipping may wrinkle the fabric.

BASTING STITCHES

Each basting stitch has a special purpose

BASTING BY HAND

1. UNEVEN BASTING is only used for marking on one layer of fabric. It is large and loose so that the fabric gives naturally. Stitches may be 1 in. long. There are many variations: all long stitches; one long and one short; one long and two short, etc.

2. EVEN BASTING is used for holding two pieces of fabric together. The stitches should be short, not over $\frac{1}{4}$ in. in length, so that the fabric is held almost as firmly as with permanent stitching.

3. SLIP-BASTING is often called right-side basting, because you work on the right side of the fabric. It is used for matching seams in a patterned material.

Turn under the seam allowance on one section and lay the folded edge in position on the right side of the other section, matching seam lines exactly. As you pin, match the design (see below, left). Run the threaded needle through the fold of the upper section, taking a stitch $\frac{1}{4}$ in. in length. Then take a $\frac{1}{4}$ in. stitch in the under piece of fabric, making certain that the needle enters the fabric exactly opposite the point where the thread comes from the fold. This makes a plain seam with even basting.

4. TAILOR BASTING, sometimes called **DIAGONAL BASTING,** is used to hold two or more surfaces together. The stitches are about 1 in. in length, and are executed as shown, bottom left. Sometimes this is worked horizontally.

BASTING BY MACHINE

MACHINE-BASTING is a quick and generally satisfactory way to do even basting, though it is obviously impossible to do Uneven Basting by machine. Use the largest stitch size and loosen the top tension slightly so the bobbin thread can be removed easily.

Do not use machine-basting on fabrics that mark easily, such as taffeta, satin, bengaline, etc.

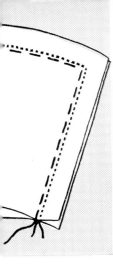

NOTES ON MACHINE STITCHING

The correct position for machine stitching is just "outside" the basting (see diagram left), so that the garment will not be tighter than when fitted.

THE BULK OF THE FABRIC should generally be placed at the left as you stitch.

THE DIRECTION OF STITCHING is important, since it may affect the position of the grain. Generally, stitch from the wide to the narrow part . . . on a skirt, stitch the seams from hem to waistline. Working in the other direction is apt to fray the edges and cause ripples in the seam. Stitch side seams of bodice from underarm to waistline (see left below).

EDGE STITCHING is easy to do if the folded edge is placed at your left. This enables you to place stitching very close to the edge.

STITCHING ON JERSEY. A seam in jersey sometimes appears either tight or stretched. Try the following suggestions to find the one which best helps to prevent this:

1. Stitch over tissue paper which is easily torn away after stitching.
2. Use both hands, one in front and one at the back to feed the two layers of fabric through machine at the same rate.
3. Lengthen the stitch.

STITCHING ON NYLON often results in puckering. The following suggestions should help to overcome this:

1. Use nylon thread on nylon fabrics, since the thread and the fabric have the same characteristics.
2. Use a fine needle and not too small a stitch . . . 10 to 12 stitches to the inch.
3. Be sure the tension is balanced.
4. Stitch over tissue paper and remove. Tear it away afterwards.

STITCHING ON PLASTIC should be done with mercerised thread, not nylon. Use a large stitch and a fine needle, since plastic has a tendency to tear when perforations made by the machine needle are close together. If the plastic sticks, brush lightly with talcum powder along edges to be stitched.

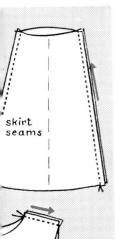

skirt seams

bodice seams

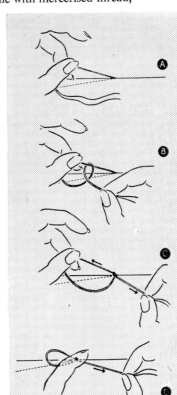

TO FASTEN MACHINE STITCHING

No fastening is necessary if another row of machine stitching is to be sewn across the one just completed. However, threads must be fastened where there is no crossing seam, as at end of pleat, dart, etc. This may be done by hand or by machine.

FASTENING BY HAND, as shown right . . . Draw both thread ends to one side of the fabric. A. Hold threads taut. B. Form a loop on the taut threads. C. Draw loop to end of machine stitching. D. Place forefinger on loop and draw knot tight.

FASTENING BY MACHINE . . . Stitching may be fastened before it is removed from the machine by taking several stitches in the same position. When stitching is completed, raise presser foot slightly with one hand, hold fabric firmly in position with the other hand, and take several stitches in the one position.

STITCH AND PRESS

Press as you sew should be your slogan. For a professional appearance, press each seam, dart, etc., before crossing it by another seam. Don't press over basting, since you may find it difficult to remove the thread marks

PRESSING

IRON

Pressing should be distinguished from ironing. Pressing is placing the iron firmly on the fabric. The iron must be lifted each time it is moved. In **ironing,** the iron is moved without being lifted. Always iron with the grain of the fabric.

Press all fabrics on the wrong side.

Most fabrics require dampness in pressing. Dampen lightweight pressing cloths by wetting one half, wringing it out, folding the wet over the dry section and wringing both together. Damp heavy pressing cloths with a wet sponge. The pressing cloths should contain enough moisture to press a fabric without wetting it.

Consider the fibre, texture and finish of the fabric to determine the correct temperature and moisture needed (see chapter on "The Weekly Wash").

The diagram below will be a guide to the degree of heat each fibre will stand.

Before pressing any part of the garment, try pressing a scrap of the fabric.

SPECIAL NOTES ON FABRICS

RAYONS . . . to prevent marking, place one or more sheets of tissue paper under the damp cloth when pressing.

VELVETS . . . Pile fabrics should be pressed over a velvet board or steamed over a standing iron with a damp turkish towel draped round it. Handle fabric carefully to avoid finger marks.

Lowest Heat				Greatest Heat
Rayon Nylon	Silk	Wool	Cotton	Linen

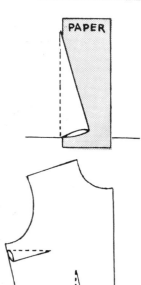

PAPER

PRESS AS YOU SEW

Use brown paper strips (left) under seam edges or darts to avoid impression on the right side.

Seams . . . Press plain seams open.

Darts and Tucks . . . Waistline and shoulder darts and tucks are pressed towards centre of garment.

Underarm darts and elbow darts are generally pressed downward. On heavy fabric—darts may be slashed through centre and pressed open, great care being taken to prevent fraying.

Hems . . . Always **press** on a well-padded surface to avoid an impression on the right side.

Shrinking a part of the garment is sometimes necessary in the process of sewing; for instance, on sleeve cap or around a hem.

SLEEVE ROLL . . . If you do not have a **sleeve board,** make a sleeve roll as follows: Roll a magazine tightly to make a 2 in. roll, fasten with gummed paper and cover with cloth.

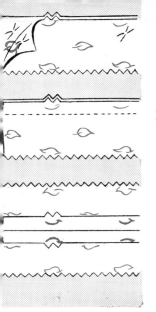

SEAMS AND SEAM FINISHES

*Choose the right seam to suit the
fabric, design and purpose
of the garment*

THE PLAIN SEAM

WHEN TO USE :—Where two straight edges are to be joined together, and in some cases where shaped edges are being joined. Since made with only one row of stitching, it should not be used where great strain will be exerted on the seam. Use on dresses, suits, etc. Raw edges of seam allowance must be finished satisfactorily.

TO MAKE A PLAIN SEAM (diagrams, above left)

1. Place fabric edges together with right sides facing.
2. Pin and stitch on seam line.
3. Press seam open.
4. Finish the raw edges of the seam allowance.

PINKING (top right)

WHEN TO USE :—When fabric is firm and edge will not ravel with wear.

HOW TO DO :—Pinked edge is made with pinking shears.

STITCHING AND PINKING (right, 2nd from top)

WHEN TO USE :—When fabric is fairly firm but may ravel slightly.

HOW TO DO :—Stitch close to edge of seam allowance before pinking.

OVERCASTING (3rd diagram, right)

WHEN TO USE :—To prevent ravelling. Edge may be pinked before being overcast.

HOW TO DO :—Holding raw edge in horizontal position, overcast from left to right with matching thread.

EDGE STITCHING (4th diagram, right)

WHEN TO USE :—On light-weight fabrics only, in place of overcasting when the inside of the garment is to be seen, e.g. an unlined jacket.

HOW TO DO :—Turn in edge of seam allowance $\frac{1}{4}$ in. and machine stitch close to the edge. Trim off excess fabric.

BINDING WITH SEAM BINDING (5th, 6th and 7th diagrams right)

WHEN TO USE :—On medium weight or heavy fabrics when the inside of the garment is to be seen.

HOW TO DO :—Shrink binding by wetting in warm water. Press. Fold and press binding so that one side is slightly narrower than other side. Baste in position on trimmed edge of seam allowance so that wide part of binding is on under part of seam allowance. Stitch at edge of narrow part, catching wide part of binding underneath. Press.

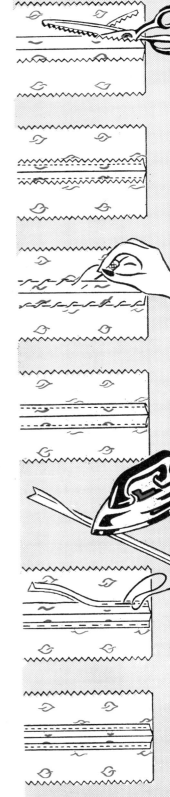

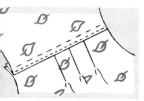

THE LAPPED SEAM

WHEN TO USE:—When applying a shaped piece to a plain or shaped piece, e.g. a pocket to a garment or a shaped yoke to a shaped edge. It is often used on straight seams when one edge of seam is very full, since with both seam allowances facing in one direction, the seam will have a flat finish.

TO MAKE A LAPPED SEAM

1. Turn under seam allowance of top section at seam line and baste in position (top left).
2. Pin top section to lower section, matching seam line to seam line. Baste if seam is bulky.
3. Machine stitch from right side of garment through folded edge of lapped seam. Stitching should be close to the fold (second left).
4. Remove bastings and press. **5.** Finish seam allowance.

A double-stitched lapped seam (left), which gives extra strength, may be made by first stitching a plain seam. Press seam open as a plain seam, then press both seam allowances towards side where lap is to be formed. Stitch from right side of garment close to seam line, stitching through both seam allowances.

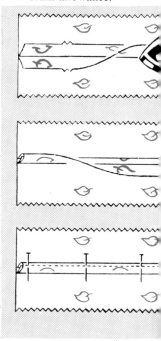

This seam is often used on lingerie, where a double-stitched seam is advantageous, since it can be made more quickly than the flat felled or French seams.

THE FLAT FELLED SEAM

WHEN TO USE:—Where double stitching is needed for extra strength and a flat finish for comfort. Since the raw edges of the seam allowance are enclosed, this is a suitable seam for garments which will be laundered frequently. In babies' clothes and sleeping garments, the seam is made inside out, so that the smoother side will be on the inside of the garment.

TO MAKE A FLAT FELLED SEAM

1. Place fabric edges together with right sides facing.
2. Pin and stitch on seam line. **3.** Press seam open.
4. Press again, pressing both seam allowances in the desired direction (top right). (Side seams are pressed towards back; shoulder yoke seam towards waistline.)

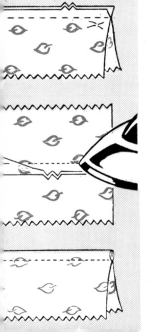

5. Trim off seam allowance on the under side to about $\frac{1}{8}$ in. ($\frac{1}{4}$ in. if fabric ravels easily).
6. Trim top seam allowance double the width the finished seam is to be.
7. Fold top seam allowance in half (2nd diagram, right) over narrow part, and baste flat to the garment.
8. Edge stitch the fold, stitching the seam flat to the garment (third right).
9. Press.

THE FRENCH SEAM

WHEN TO USE:—Where double stitching is needed for extra strength, but a flat finish is not necessary. A good seam for fabrics which ravel and for garments requiring frequent laundering.

TO MAKE A FRENCH SEAM (diagrams, left)

1. Place fabric edges together with wrong sides facing.
2. Pin and stitch the desired width of seam "outside" the seam line.
3. Press as a plain seam.
4. Press seam allowances to one side (second left).
5. Trim to $\frac{1}{8}$ in. from stitching.
6. Fold fabric at stitching line so that right sides of fabric are brought together.
7. Pin and stitch on seam line. **8.** Press.

DOUBLE-STITCHED SEAM

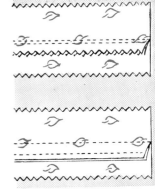

Where a seam requires the strength of a double-stitched seam but the work must be done quickly to save time, a plain seam may be stitched twice, pressed so that the two seam allowances face in one direction, and the two edges finished by pinking, as shown top right.

When the extra strength is not needed in the seam, the stitching may be placed ¼ in. "outside" the first stitching and the seam allowances trimmed almost to the stitching (right). This makes a quick method for seam finishing both seam allowances together and is quite satisfactory for some fabrics. It is especially good for the armhole seam.

FACINGS

A facing is a piece of fabric stitched to a raw edge for the purpose of finishing the edge.

TO FACE A STRAIGHT EDGE:—The facing should be on the same grain as the edge being faced.

1. Pin the facing on the edge to be faced, right side of facing to right side of fabric.
2. Stitch along seam line (see top left).
3. Press open as plain seam.
4. Press again, pressing both seam allowances in one direction (2nd left).
5. Trim seam allowances evenly to a little less than ¼ in. (3rd left). If fabric is heavy, trim one seam allowance slightly less than the other, to taper the bulk.
6. Turn facing to inside (4th left).
7. Baste close to the edge so that the stitched line is at the edge of the fold. (Use a small basting stitch and a fine sewing thread for basting in this case.)
8. Press lightly while basting threads are in place.
9. Without disturbing fabric, clip basting and remove in small sections (5th left).
10. Finish pressing (bottom left).

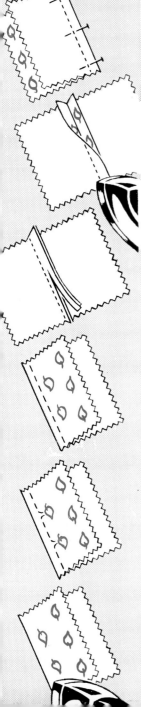

TYPES OF FACINGS

The **fitted facing** is shaped the same as the edge and is on the same grain.

The **bias facing** is made of narrow bias, usually applied to a curve.

The **shaped facing** is shaped on the inside edge for decorative purposes. It is often finished on the right side as part of the design of the garment.

The **double facing** is usually of bias fabric applied double and finished on the right side. After being turned on the seam line, it is usually edge stitched on the outside close to the seam line.

Note: Where it is not possible to press the seam open and closed, omit.

FACING FINISHES

Any of the seam finishes may be used on the raw edge of the **straight** or **fitted facings**.

The **bias facing** is finished by turning ¼ in. in on the raw edge and hemming.

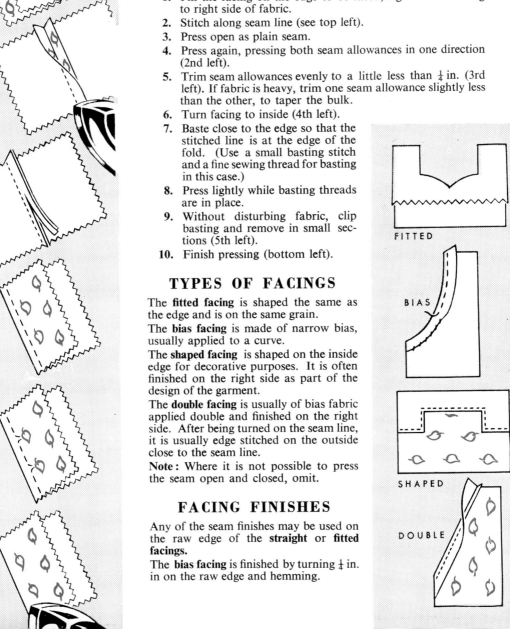

FITTED

BIAS

SHAPED

DOUBLE

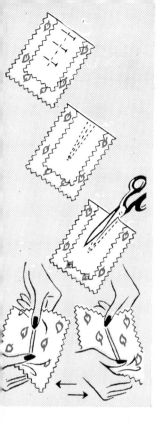

SIMPLE FACED OPENING

The simplest faced opening is the slit which may be held closed with buttons and loops, a tie, a concealed hook and eye, or a zipper.

WHEN TO USE :—At the neckline, front or back; at the wrist, etc.

NOTE: DO NOT SLIT FABRIC UNTIL OPENING IS STITCHED.

HOW TO DO:—

1. Pin and baste facing in position on line where opening is to be, right side of facing to right side of garment (top left).
2. Stitch in narrow V $\frac{1}{4}$ in. to $\frac{3}{8}$ in. wide at top (2nd left). To make the turning easier, take an extra stitch at point of the V.
3. Remove basting and slash to point (3rd left).
4. Turn facing. Holding stitched point between thumb and fore-finger, pull faced section from side to side to remove any puckering from the point (below left).
5. Baste and press as items 7 and 10, "To Face a Straight Edge."

A piece of silk binding or organdie, placed on the bias on the wrong side of the fabric, will reinforce the point of the opening. The whole can be reinforced by stitching on the right side close to the edge.

DARTS AND TUCKS

DARTS are used to shape flat pieces of fabric into garments that fit the curved surface of the body.

It is easier to stitch a dart from the wide end to the point, although it is sometimes necessary to stitch in the opposite direction. Generally, darts are stitched on the inside. Stitching on most darts is ruler straight.

TO STITCH A DART

Pin dart markings to-gether exactly on the stitching line (right).

1. Begin stitching at the wide end.
2. Stitch ruler straight to within $\frac{1}{16}$ in. from the point of the dart. A folded paper (right) beside the stitching line will help.
3. To prevent puckering, taper to a fine point by curving the stitching ever so slightly and making 3 or 4 stitches on the edge of the fold.
4. Fasten thread ends.
5. Press in the correct direction to give the garment its proper shape.

If the fabric is heavy, the dart may be slit down the fold and pressed open, the small point being pressed the same way.

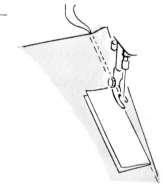

TUCKS are used to remove fullness from parts of the garment, but may be decorative as well. Unlike darts, tucks are even in width.

When stitching tucks (diagrams, right), first pin the tuck markings together exactly on the stitching line and baste if the tuck is long. Since the tuck must be even in width, some type of guide should be used by even the most experienced sewers.

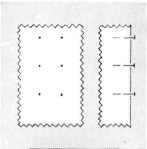

A. A folded piece of paper may be sufficient if the tuck is short.

B. For longer tucks, masking tape may be laid an even distance from the fold (below right) beside the line to be stitched and removed from the fabric after stitching. Before using masking tape, test the tape on a scrap of your fabric to make certain the fabric will not be marked.

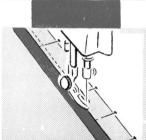

C. A gauge may also be used. A tuck inside may be stitched from either end, but the threads must be fastened to prevent ripping if the tuck ends within the pattern piece.

CURVE AND CORNER FINISHES

CURVES are not difficult to stitch but, even when stitched perfectly, may be ruined by poor finishing.

THE FACED CURVE

The facing, which is usually cut from a pattern, should be on the same grain as the curved section. Following the stitching, trim the seam allowance.

For a smooth outward curve, cut small V's from the seam allowance. When reversed, the V's come together and the curve will be flat and smooth.

For a flat inward curve, clip the seam allowance almost to the stitching. When reversed, the seam allowance spreads and lies flat.

The amount of notching or clipping depends on the curve.

For finishing instructions, see "To Face a Straight Edge," items 7 to 10.

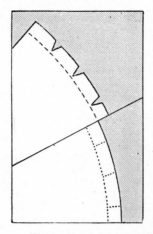
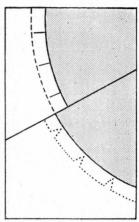

For an outward curve, cut small V's from the seam allowance (left). For a flat inward curve (right), clip seam allowance almost to stitching; when reversed, it will spread and lie flat

1. From the underarm down to the waistline.
2. From the hem up to the waistline.

If you try to press the whole seam at once, the shape of the curve may be lost.

Curved lapped seams should have the seam allowance clipped when the lap is turned, so that the seam will be flat for the final stitching.

FACED SCALLOPS

To be sure scallops will be perfectly shaped, the edge to be scalloped and the facing should be cut straight, stitched according to the pattern, then cut as shown left.

To finish, clip the seam allowance to the point of the scallop and follow instructions given above for a faced curve.

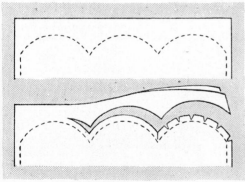

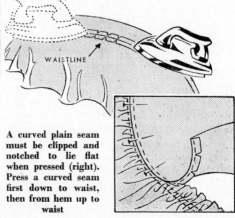

WAISTLINE

CURVED SEAMS

Curved plain seams should be clipped and notched so that they lie flat when pressed. For the seam which curves as it crosses the waistline (e.g. in a princess style dress), the seam allowance must be clipped at the waistline and again $\frac{1}{2}$ in. above and below. Press in two steps:

A curved plain seam must be clipped and notched to lie flat when pressed (right). Press a curved seam first down to waist, then from hem up to waist

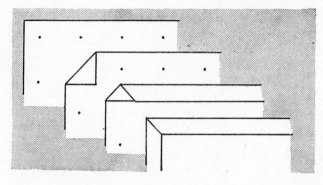

Diagram (left) shows how to mitre a corner in four stages. Below that, how to cut part of a heavy fabric away when folding on bias

By opening up the corner and turning to wrong side, stitch from point of corner to hem line, then stitch at right angles as shown. Trim to within $\frac{1}{8}$ in. of stitching, fold back into position and press well.

CORNERS

may be reinforced by stitching just inside the seam allowance before clipping and turning on the seam line. The stitching should be turned so that it will not show from the right side.

A small piece of silk binding placed on the wrong side of the fabric and on an angle to the grain will reinforce a corner.

When a corner is mitred, there is no chance of the raw edge showing at the seam line. This is specially important when preparing a patch pocket.

TO MITRE A CORNER

1. Crease fabric on seam line (see top of page).
2. Fold fabric on bias exactly at point of corner.
3. Fold on seam line.
4. Press.

If the fabric is heavy, part of the fabric may be cut away at Step 2.

If the corner is to be finished so that both sides may be shown (e.g. in making a place mat), fold to mitre and also turn in the seam allowance on the wrong side to form a hem. Press well.

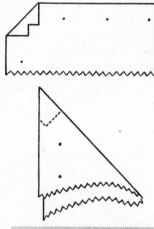

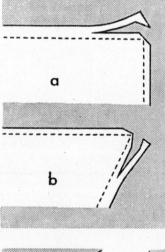

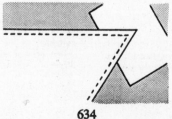

Excess fabric at a corner (e.g. corner of a collar) should be trimmed away so that the point will not be lumpy.

If the point is a right angle, clip straight across, close to stitching as shown (a).

If the point is less than a right angle, the seam allowance at both sides should also be trimmed slightly (b).

When **edge stitching around a point,** the point often catches on the feed under the presser foot. This will not happen if a piece of tissue paper is placed under the point being stitched. When the stitching is finished, the tissue can be torn away.

Centre: (a) shows how to cut straight across when point is a right angle; (b) when point is less than a right angle, trim both sides. Left: put tissue paper under point when edge stitching

Time-saving Hint

When one measurement is used many times, a gauge to help you measure accurately and quickly may be made from cardboard or a folded piece of paper.

1. Mark measurements needed on folded edge of paper or cardboard.
2. Cut notches with one straight side so that the straight side is always the line used for measuring.

BIAS

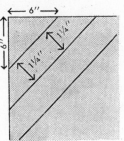

A true bias is the diagonal of any square of fabric.

TO CUT STRIPS OF TRUE BIAS

1. Straighten a piece of fabric.
2. Measure from one corner an equal distance in both directions and chalk mark a line joining these points. This line is on the true bias (see diagram right).
3. Measure width of bias (rarely less than $1\frac{1}{4}$ in.) from the true bias line to mark bias strip. Several strips may be marked at the same time.
4. Cut strips of true bias as required.

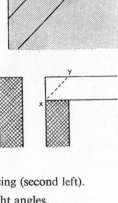

TO JOIN STRIPS OF BIAS

1. Be sure ends of bias strips are on straight grain by drawing a thread from the ends of the strips (left).

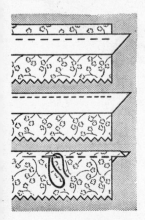

2. Lay two strips together, right sides facing (second left).
3. Move top strip to place the two at right angles.
4. Stitch from x to y (third left).
5. Press seam open and trim ends.

Some may find it easier to join bias strips if the ends are cut square (second from top right). At the third step, the right angle is formed and the strips are stitched from x to y.

TO JOIN BIAS APPLIED TO A CIRCULAR OPENING

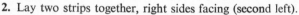

1. Be sure ends of bias are on straight grain.
2. Turn up one end $\frac{1}{4}$ in. to wrong side (right).
3. Place other strip on top, as shown, making sure that the straight edges are parallel (right).
4. Pin in place and baste to folded edge.
5. Slip stitch fold from right side.

NOTE.—Always consider that bias being applied to an edge has only $\frac{1}{4}$-in. seam allowance. If a wider seam allowance is permitted, you may have considerable difficulty stitching the bias to the fabric on a sharp curve or corner.

TO BIND AN EDGE WITH SINGLE BIAS

1. Place bias in position, right side to right side of garment.
2. Pin, baste and stitch on seam line.
3. Trim seam allowance evenly to desired width—usually about $\frac{1}{8}$ in. or slightly wider (right).

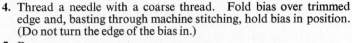

4. Thread a needle with a coarse thread. Fold bias over trimmed edge and, basting through machine stitching, hold bias in position. (Do not turn the edge of the bias in.)
5. Press.
6. Remove basting. Basting marks should show on back section of bias.
7. Trim bias about $\frac{1}{8}$ in. outside of basting marks.
8. Turn bias on basting marks; pin and hem into machine stitching.

When applying bias to a corner or curve, ease the bias on an outside curve and stretch it slightly on an inside curve.

TO BIND AN EDGE WITH DOUBLE BIAS

Use double bias for binding on lightweight fabrics. Some beginners find it easier to apply the double bias, since the turning of a hem on the single bias is eliminated.
1. Cut the bias twice the required width (top left).
2. Fold lengthwise, right side out, and press.
3. Stitch the cut edges to seam line on right side of garment (2nd left). Trim the seam allowance.
4. Fold bias over trimmed edge (3rd left).
5. The folded edge may be hemmed in position or, provided fold reaches below stitching line, machine stitched in position by stitching from right side of garment on first stitching line (4th left).

Single or double bias may be used for facing an edge.

PREPARED BIAS BINDING

Prepared bias binding, in many colours, is sold in most needle-work departments. It is satisfactory for binding cottons. The best bindings are made of mercerised nainsook and are colour fast.

This prepared bias can be easily applied by using the special sewing machine attachment for the purpose.

FALSE BIAS BOUND HEM (see left)

This is a quick method for finishing a raw edge, particularly the hem of a full skirt.
1. Trim the fabric 1 in. below the desired seam line.
2. Turn fabric up on right side of garment about 1 in. and machine stitch an $\frac{1}{8}$ in. tuck.
3. Press tuck towards hemline.
4. Turn $\frac{1}{4}$ in. at edge of fabric and, binding over tuck, pin in position so that stitched tuck is well covered.
5. Machine stitch from right side on tuck stitching, catching hem on wrong side.

PIPING · CORDING · ROULEAU BUTTON LOOPS

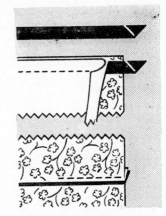

PIPING

A **piping** is a narrow fold of fabric, or a specially prepared edging, inserted in a seam to give it a decorative finish. Fabric piping is usually made from bias strips.

TO PIPE A PLAIN SEAM

1. Prepare piping from a strip of bias by folding lengthwise, right side out, and pressing (top right).
2. Place between the two pieces of fabric to be used for the plain seam so that the fold faces away from the raw edge and extends about ⅛ in. past the seam line (2nd right).
3. Pin and stitch on seam line.
4. This seam is rarely pressed open as a plain seam. It is more often pressed to look like a lapped seam with the seam allowances all facing in one direction. It may be stitched again close to the piping, so that it looks exactly like a lapped seam. When the seam is at the edge of a garment, it may be left without additional stitching or it may be reinforced by stitching close to the piping through both pieces of fabric after the facing has been turned.

CORDING

Cording is piping with a cord inserted in the fold to give a round appearance.

TO MAKE CORDING

1. Fold bias, right side out, over a cord or soft string (left). Pin and baste to hold cord in place.
2. Using cording or zipper foot in place of the presser foot on the sewing machine, stitch as close to cord as possible, drawing the bias tightly around the cord.
3. Use like a piping but do the final stitching of the seam with the cording foot to bring the stitching close. The first row of stitching should not show on the finished seam.

ROULEAU

Rouleau is a fabric cord made from a strip of bias and used for button loops and decorative finishes.

Since rouleau is made from bias, it stretches easily. Part of this stretch should be removed before stitching by pulling the bias strip lengthwise several times.

Bias being made into rouleau should be kept in a stretched position while it is being stitched. Otherwise the thread may break when the rouleau is stretched in use.

TO STITCH ROULEAU

1. Fold a strip of bias wrong side out and pin or baste to hold in position.
2. Begin stitching by making a funnel at the end (see next page) to bring stitching about ⅛ in. from fold.
3. Stitch an even width from fold. Bias should be pulled gently from both in front of and behind the presser foot to keep it stretched while it is being stitched (see right).
4. Stitch another funnel at end of strip.
5. Trim seam allowance to approximately ⅛ in.
6. Cut funnel ends to shape (shown on next page).

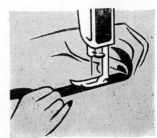

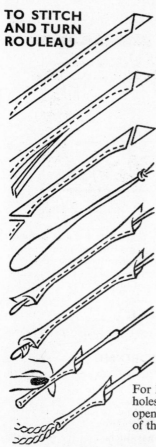

TO STITCH AND TURN ROULEAU

TO TURN ROULEAU

1. Make a wire loop by doubling about 18 in. of very fine uncovered wire. Knot and anchor the ends firmly on a nail or hook (see fourth left).
2. Slip the rouleau on to the wire loop (see fifth left).
3. Draw the point of the funnel at the end of the rouleau through the wire loop and sew securely to the wire.
4. Pinch the wire loop closed and, drawing the fabric over the loop, turn the rouleau right side out.

Rouleau, as above, without filling is called tubing or spaghetti, while rouleau filled with cord is corded rouleau.

TO FILL ROULEAU

1. Prepare rouleau for turning (see 3 above).
2. Before pinching the wire loop closed, slip a soft cord through the loop so that the cord is doubled.
3. Turn the rouleau, drawing it over the cord at the same time.

If the fabric from which the rouleau is being made is very soft, the seam allowance may be left on to be used as a filler.

BUTTON LOOPS

Rouleau or corded rouleau may be used for button loops.

For ladies' clothes, loops and button-holes should be on the right side of the opening, whether on the front or back of the blouse or dress.

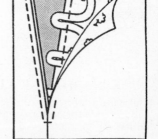

TO MAKE BUTTON LOOPS

1. Pin and stitch loops in position on the right side of the fabric, facing the loops away from the opening (see right).
2. Stitch facing over loops and finish as a faced opening.

Mark position for buttons on left side of opening and sew them in position.

Continuous lines of button loops are usually shaped as shown (below right), but single loops may be shaped in different ways, since they are often a part of the design.

WORKED BUTTON HOLES

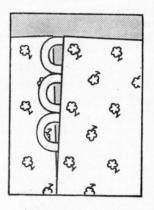

On ladies' garments, buttons are always placed on the left of the opening, whether on the front or back of the garment, and button-holes on the right; men's clothes button in the opposite direction. Buttonholes may be worked by hand or by machine, so that the raw edge of the slit is protected by thread. Since buttonholes are subject to heavy wear, hand-worked buttonholes on coats and suits should be made with a heavy six-cord thread or button-hole twist, although a fine thread may be satisfactory for garments of lightweight fabrics. This is the only type of buttonhole used on men's garments and is quite frequently used on ladies' clothes, particularly on shirtwaist blouses, tailored suits and cotton garments. For ladies' clothes the bound, or French, buttonhole is more frequently used, but it should not be made on sheer fabrics where the patch, used in construction, shows through the fabric.

POSITION OF THE BUTTONHOLE

Buttonholes may be at right angles to the edge or parallel to it but, where there is much strain on the buttonhole, it should be at right angles to the edge. If the buttonholes are in a fly front where space is limited, they will have to be parallel to the edge.

For a centre front opening, buttons should be sewn to the centre front line and the holes made so that, when fastened, the point where the button will sit is on the centre front line.

When the buttonhole is fastened, there should always be a pleasing space between the edge of the button and the edge of the fold. This may be wide or narrow, according to the design of the garment, but in no case should the button cross the folded edge of the opening.

LENGTH OF THE BUTTONHOLE

The length of the buttonhole is determined by the size of the button. It should be $\frac{1}{16}$ in. longer than the diameter of the button plus a slight extra amount for height where specially thick or ball buttons are used. In case of doubt as to correct size, cut a sample large enough for the button to pass through easily and measure it.

In cutting a slit of this type, fold the fabric at the centre, snip the fold, lay the fabric flat and cut from the centre to both ends of the buttonhole.

MARKING THE BUTTONHOLE

Buttonholes are marked in many ways, depending on the type of buttonhole being made and the fabric used. Machine buttonholes require only a thread mark designating one end of the buttonhole, but handworked or bound buttonholes require two lines, in correct position, showing the length the button-

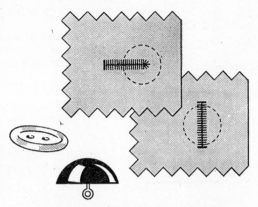

Where there is much strain on a buttonhole it should be at right angles to the edge (above left) rather than parallel (right). Remember to allow for button's height and diameter

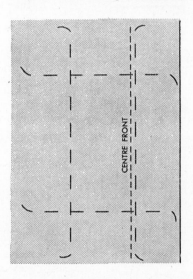

hole is to be made and one line showing the position. These may be marked by hand basting, machine basting or dressmaker's chalk.

THE WORKED BUTTONHOLE

Buttonholes made at right angles to the opening have a fan at the end into which the shank of the button will fit and a bar at the end farthest from the opening.

If the buttonhole is parallel to the edge of the opening, it is made with a bar at both ends.

All buttonholes should be worked through at least two thicknesses of fabric.

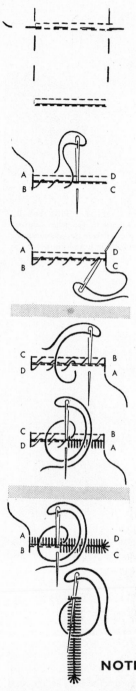

TO MAKE A WORKED BUTTONHOLE

1. Machine stitch on both sides of the buttonhole marking so that the stitching is only one stitch apart (top left). Do not stitch across the fan end.

2. Remove marking thread and cut the buttonhole.

3. Begin work at the bar end. Using a single thread without a knot, take two stitches the width of the buttonhole (A, B), leaving the thread end loose.

4. Overcast the lower edge from B to C, catching the machine stitching (second left).

5. At the fan end, take two stitches (D, C) to match those at the bar end.

6. Put needle in slash and bring it out at D. Turn buttonhole around and overcast from D to A.

7. Take two bar stitches (B, A), bringing needle out at A.

8. Begin the buttonhole stitch and work from A to D.

9. Take stitches in fan shape at the end between D and C.

10. Buttonhole stitch the other side from C to B.

11. When the last stitch is completed, insert the needle into the purl of the first buttonhole stitch and bring it out at B. (This will help to prevent the spreading of the buttonhole.)

12. Take one or two more stitches from A to B and clip the loose end of thread left from the beginning stitch. All of the stitches in this position form the foundation for the bar.

13. Blanket stitch the bar. The blanket stitches should be made over the bar only; they may catch the fabric slightly, but they should not show on the underside.

14. To finish, stab the needle to the underside at A and run under the stitches for about $\frac{1}{4}$ in. before clipping the thread.

BUTTONHOLE STITCH

BLANKET STITCH

NOTES ON BUTTONHOLE AND BLANKET STITCHES

Buttonhole stitches are worked from right to left; blanket stitches from left to right. Buttonhole stitches should be the width of the thread apart; blanket stitches may be any distance apart, according to the design. For the buttonhole stitch, draw the thread away from you; for the blanket stitch draw the thread towards you.

EASING · GATHERING · SHIRRING

Easing, gathering and **shirring** are three ways of controlling fullness. Since all three techniques are usually a part of a seam, the fullness is drawn up on rows of stitching to fit in the seam. These rows of stitching, or construction threads, may be put in by hand or machine. For lightweight fabrics, the machine stitch should be lengthened slightly while the longest machine stitch will be required for heavy fabrics. If the top thread tension is loosened slightly, gathering or shirring will be easier. Always stitch from the right side of the garment.

Easing, which consists of one row, often occurs in a shoulder seam. Gathering, which consists of two rows, is often used to gather a full skirt into a waistband. Shirring consists of three or more rows, and the threads become part of the design.

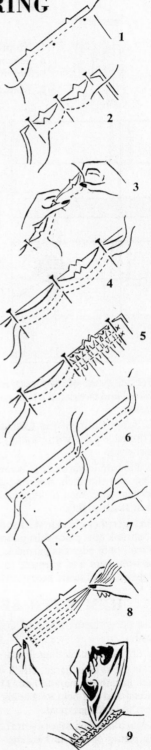

HOW TO EASE *(See diagrams 1, 2 and 3, right)*

1. Adjust the machine to give a slightly larger stitch than normal.
2. Place one row of machine stitching just "outside" the seam line, leaving thread ends 3 in. long.
3. Matching notches, pin the seam at known points.
4. Quite frequently, the machine stitching draws up the fabric sufficiently. If additional easing is necessary, hold one end of bobbin thread, ease the fabric along the thread and work the fullness between thumb and forefinger. Repeat, holding other end of bobbin thread.
5. Pin remainder of seam. Clip thread ends.
6. Stitch with full side up.   7. Press on a padded board.

HOW TO GATHER *(See diagrams 4, 5, 6 and 7, right)*

1. Adjust the machine to give a larger stitch (about 6 to 10 stitches to the inch, depending on weight of fabric).
2. Loosen the top thread tension slightly.
3. Place two rows of machine stitching $\frac{1}{4}$ in. apart; one row $\frac{1}{8}$ in. above and the other row $\frac{1}{8}$ in. below the seam line. Leave 3 in. ends of threads.
4. Match notches and pin the seam at known points.
5. Holding both bobbin threads at one end, gather half of fabric to correct size and fasten threads. Repeat at other end.
6. Pin remainder of seam. Clip thread ends.
7. Stitch with full side up.
8. Remove gathering thread which shows on right side.
9. Press into the gathers with the point of the iron.

If the edge to be gathered is long (as for the top of a skirt), gather in separate sections.

For short lengths of lightweight fabrics, use a continuous gathering thread and gather from one end only.

HOW TO SHIRR *(See diagrams 8 and 9, right)*

1. Adjust the machine for gathering.
2. Place one row of stitching just "outside" the seam line, leaving 3 in. thread ends; the second row in the seam allowance, about $\frac{1}{4}$ in. from first, and remaining rows an equal distance apart. Since these threads will not be removed, the stitching must be straight and parallel.
3. Fasten one end of all machine threads.
4. Holding all free bobbin threads, draw shirring up.
5. Fasten each row of machine stitching separately.
6. Match notches, pin and stitch seam.
7. Press seam line only with point of iron.

HEMS

PREPARING A HEM

1. To prevent a bias skirt from sagging, fasten it to a hanger and let it hang for forty-eight hours before marking the hemline.

2. Marking the hemline . . . Decide upon the length for skirt, measure distance of hemline from floor. Have someone mark this distance all around with a yardstick or hem marker, with pins placed close together parallel to floor (right).

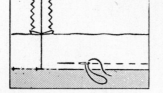

Note: If lower edge of skirt is cut on the straight grain, as in a dirndl, mark distance from floor once; remove garment and measure same width from cut edge all around.

3. Turning up the hem . . . Fold fabric on marked line, turning hem to inside. Keep folded edge in even line around hem. Baste close to fold (left), removing pins as you go along, and press lightly.

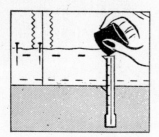

4. Marking width of hem . . . From 2″ to 3″ is a satisfactory width for a hem except on a circular skirt, where it should not exceed 1″. Start measuring at narrowest part of hem allowance, set gauge to desired measurement and mark that width all around, with chalk or pins, through one thickness of fabric only (left).

TAILOR'S HEM

For all types of garments in wool or wool-like fabrics. Gored and circular skirts in any fabric which does not ravel easily.

1. Stitch through one thickness of hem on marked line. Trim edge to $\frac{1}{4}$″ with pinking shears. If fabric ravels, overcast edge.

2. Pin hem to garment $\frac{1}{4}$″ below stitching. Turn back pinked edge and slipstitch, inserting needle into machine stitching on hem edge, then picking up a thread of the garment with each stitch (right).

On a gored or circular skirt some fullness in the hem should be shrunk out: place skirt on ironing board, pull up machine thread until edge fits garment. Place a piece of heavy paper between hem and garment to avoid an impression on the right side, and steam hem until it is as flat as possible (below).

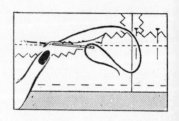

HEM WITH SEAM BINDING

Use on garments made of lightweight fabrics which ravel easily.

1. Shrink seam binding. Press.

2. If the skirt is flared, stitch through one thickness of the hem just above marked line. This stitching acts as an easing thread and will help in shaping the turned up section of the hem to fit the garment.

3. Machine stitch edge of seam binding on marking line, allowing plenty of ease in binding.

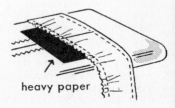

heavy paper

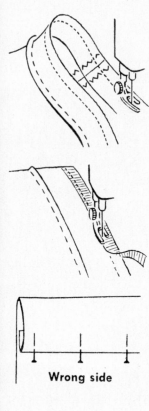

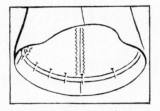

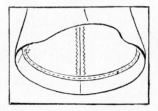

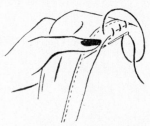

4. Trim fabric under seam binding to within ¼″ from stitching.

5. Place a piece of heavy paper between hem and garment and press with a damp cloth to shrink in excess fullness.

6. Pin hem to garment at seams, centre front and back, then at intervening spaces. (See top right.) Baste.

7. Hem loosely, by hand, using matching thread. As the hemming stitch is taken into the body of the garment, it should catch only a few threads of the fabric. If the thread is left quite loose at each stitch (right), the line of the hem will not show from the right side.

8. As an aid to preventing hem ripping, take two stitches in the same position over edge of seam binding every two inches.

MACHINE HEM

A quick and easy method of making a hem on dirndl skirts, children's clothes, aprons, curtains, or any straight hem on cottons.

On the right side it looks like a hand finished hem but it is made by machine, using a regular presser foot. The first turn is stitched at the same time as the hem is caught in place.

To get the knack of this method, try it first on a sample of your fabric. (See diagrams at left.)

1. Turn in raw edge of hem ¼″. Turn hem the desired width. Press a sharp crease. Pin to hold in place.

2. Fold back against right side with hem extending about $\frac{1}{16}$″ beyond the fold.

3. Set the machine to 10–12 stitches to the inch. Stitch on extending edge of hem for 5 stitches. With machine needle in the fabric and by raising presser foot slightly, pivot fabric and allow needle to take a stitch into body part of the garment. Before raising needle from this stitch, pivot fabric again into original position and continue in this way:

5 stitches in edge of hem. 1 stitch in body part of garment.

Remove pins as you go along. **4.** Unfold hem.

Wrong side

Wrong Side

Wrong Side

ROLLED HEM

This is a narrow finish for fine sheer fabrics. Trim hem allowance to ¼″. Fold raw edge in ⅛″. Slip the needle in the fold so that the knot will be hidden. Catch a thread below the raw edge, then slip the needle through the fold as shown, spacing stitches ¼″ apart. Draw thread tight to form roll after every few stitches (right).

ALWAYS PRESS A HEM TO GIVE IT A PROFESSIONAL FINISH

FITTING

Do not overfit. Home sewers requently make this mistake. If you have made the necessary alterations in the pattern, very little fitting should be required.

Do not fit portions of a garment

At the time of the first fitting, the only parts of the garment which are not sewn and pressed are the side seams, the waistline seam and the armhole seams. These are basted.

REMEMBER THESE PRELIMINARIES

Do have someone to help you. Even with a full length mirror, it is difficult to make adjustments on yourself.

Always fit your dress over the under-garments to be worn. Wear shoes with heels the height you intend to wear with the dress.

Put dress on, right side out. If shoulder pads are to be worn in the finished garment, they should be pinned in place.

Pin closings together and put on belt if there is to be one.

Look at the garment in a mirror; does it need any alterations? Close-fitting garments emphasise figure faults and may not look as attractive when you are walking as when you are standing still. Follow the lines of the pattern in order to keep the style of the garment and allow for plenty of ease.

SLEEVE

BUSTLINE

center guide basting

WAISTLINE

HIPLINE

CHECK THE FOLLOWING POINTS

The average home sewer should pin for fitting **at basted seams** only. Keep **centre lines in position** throughout the fitting.

Check the sleeves . . . A properly fitted sleeve will show the guide-basting as in the illustration, left, where the lengthwise grain-line falls ever so slightly forward on the arm.

A sleeve may be moved slightly in the armhole to bring the grain into position.

Check the waistline . . . It may have to be raised or lowered slightly, since all fabrics do not drape in the same way.

Check the side seams . . . Generally speaking, the same alterations should be made on both sides of a garment, but it is possible that alterations on one side may differ slightly from the other in order to keep centre lines in position.

The **bustline** should be kept easy to avoid a tight or pinched look.

The **waistline** should be fitted snugly but without strain.

From **waist to hip** a skirt should lie smoothly without wrinkles or strain.

At the **hipline** the garment should have enough ease to allow the skirt to hang freely.

PREPARE TO FINISH THE GARMENT

After the fitting, unpin openings and remove dress. Since the garment has been fitted on the right side, transfer markings to the inside.

Re-pin two layers of fabric together and baste new seam lines.

Put on again to check alterations.

Sew corrected seams permanently.

TAKE CARE OF YOUR SEWING MACHINE

It can do all sorts of exciting stitches, but it needs to be understood and kept in order

This is the Singer 201—streamlined, lightweight, and a range of fashion aids helps every sewing job

Y OUR sewing machine may be a family heirloom, a second-hand bargain, a modern straight-sewing machine or the newest zig-zag type. It may be operated by hand, foot treadle or electricity. Whichever method is used and whatever its age, the sewing machine is an appliance of the greatest value in every home and as such should be given the care it deserves.

A well-made model, however old, will go on giving good service indefinitely if it has the care that any machine needs.

Regular Care

(1) Have your machine regularly serviced. There are always small jobs that can only be done properly by the trained expert.

(2) When not in use, keep the machine covered. Fine dust and fluff will clog the delicate moving parts, causing uneven stitching.

(3) Keep the machine away from open windows, where it will get dusty and perhaps damp, and away from radiators or fires, where excess heat will dry out the oil.

(4) Keep the machine and its attachments handy. When put away in an inconvenient cupboard, they will not get the use or give the service required. Remember a patch put on by machine will probably take a fifth of the time needed for hand-sewing. A workroom, where the machine is always ready, and where work need not be continually cleared away, is, of course, ideal where space permits.

(5) Keep the machine clean. Fluff accumulates very quickly under the needle plate. Broken ends of threads tie themselves round moving parts. Use a small stiff brush to remove all fluff, dust and cotton ends. If this is not done regularly and thoroughly the machine may not work at all, through no fault of its own.

(6) Oil the machine when necessary, using the oil recommended by the makers, but avoid over-oiling, and wipe away any spills thoroughly.

Using Your Machine

The first step to successful sewing is to study the instruction book supplied with the machine. This should tell you exactly how to look after and use it and its attachments. Having read the instructions carefully, study them step by step, carrying them out on the machine, until you are

645

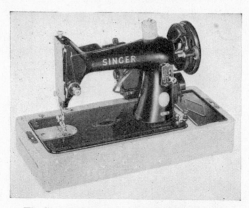

The Singer 99 is equipped to do backwards and forwards stitching, and has a tension indicator and numbered stitch regulator. Both hand and electric portable models are available

(2) Check size of needle and thickness of thread best suited to fabric.

Some instruction books supplied by sewing-machine manufacturers give charts showing tensions and needle and thread sizes for various types of material. These charts are of great value but, even so, it is wise to check on your own material before starting work.

On many modern machines the tension is clearly marked with numbers, which makes setting easy. On old machines adjustment must be made by trial and error methods on trimmings of the material. Size of needle and thread must be checked at the same time on trimmings of the material used double. Only when the stitching is perfectly satisfactory should the actual sewing be started.

Before starting the work, have ready everything that is needed, such as threads, trimmings, fastenings, etc. Keep your work and yourself neat. Untidiness in either is not conducive to good results.

Have a comfortable chair at the right height, plenty of room round the machine and plenty of space for the work. Good lighting, both day and artificial, is essential. If all these points are observed, and they are not difficult ones, successful sewing should be assured. If not, difficulties, disappointments and serious mistakes are almost inevitable.

Buying a Sewing Machine

The choice of sewing machines to-day is very wide, varying from small hand machines costing about £29 to the newest zig-zag machines costing £100 or more. The latter are quite fascinating, as not only

thoroughly conversant with each direction. Failure to do this can cause trouble with the machine, disappointments in sewing and very limited use of the machine, particularly with the new zig-zag types. Study the attachments and practise with them on odd pieces of material until there is no hesitation in fitting and using them successfully. Knowledge of the attachments greatly adds to the interest of sewing and to the usefulness of the machine.

If you have recently acquired a new or a second-hand machine, make enquiries about lessons. It is usually possible to have a free course of lessons on a new machine, either at the maker's showrooms or in your own home. Some makers also give lessons on old machines, either free or at a small charge. These practical lessons are of great value; many people find it far easier to follow a practical demonstration than written instructions. But remember that practice between and after the lessons is essential, particularly in the use of the attachments and in working the wide variety of stitches and patterns possible with the zig-zag machines.

Preparations for Sewing

No matter how experienced you are, the following preparations should always be made:

(1) Check tensions, according to the type and thickness of material to be used.

The Alfa " Streamline " incorporates all the newest features of far more expensive models. It allows you to sew from one thickness on to several—without stopping !

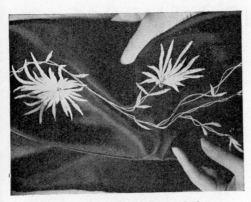

Embroidery in metal thread worked on a Necchi machine, which can be used for free or automatic embroidery

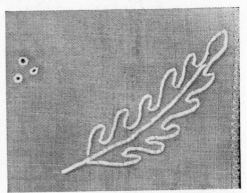

Also worked on the Necchi, a charmingly decorative leaf and eyelet design is easily carried out on plain dress linen

can all the stitches worked by an ordinary straight-sewing machine be carried out, but also all kinds of embroidery stitches, sewing on buttons, making button-holes and darning socks.

Possibilities with these machines are virtually unlimited, being restricted only by the ability of the operator. *Petit point, broderie anglaise* or simpler embroidery can be worked to look almost like skilled hand-work. Summer dresses can be embroidered with simple or elaborate designs. Hems or seams can be fixed with decorative stitching in a matter of minutes. Attractive table mats can be scallop edged in single or double coloured satin stitch in less time than it takes to hand hem the edge. Heavy furnishing fabrics and the most delicate dress materials can be embroidered equally well.

All machines of this type are fitted with a double as well as single needles. The double needle can be used with two different coloured threads to work two rows of embroidery simultaneously. All can be used at normal speeds, or with a special control to give automatic slow speed for intricate work.

The question of the wisest choice of machine can only be answered by the purchaser herself, for features vary from model to model. If you want to use your machine for darning and household mending, choose one with a free arm. Do you expect to be able to do delicate, intricate work on it? If so, look for a machine with a choice of speeds.

The fully automatic, with all its possibilities, may be wasted on the woman who does only straightforward dress-making, simple curtains and pelmets and household mending. But it may start an entirely new interest and create a reformation scene in the home.

Most of the new models can be bought in pastel colours. This is an advantage if you wear glasses or suffer from eye strain in doing close work.

Just touch a knob and the needle of this Necchi machine is threaded automatically. A magnifying lens enables you to read the pattern - regulating scale without eye-strain

MAKING AND MENDING

Practical hints on stocking the workbox and on simple repairs and sewing

Compiled by the National Institute of Houseworkers

Essentials for the Housewife's Workbox

1 pair medium-sized sharp scissors.

Mixed sewing (4–8 sharps) and darning needles.

Pins and pin cushion.

Tape measure.

Thimble.

White cotton, No. 40 and No. 60.

Black cotton, either No. 24 or No. 40.

Wools to match the family socks.

Nylon and cotton darning threads in assorted colours.

Spools of machine twist in colours suitable for the family's shirts, pyjamas and underclothes. Peach, pale blue and grey will almost certainly be needed.

Bodkin.

The two usual types of mending with which the housewife has to deal are darning and patching.

Hints on Darning

(1) Darn before the hole gets too large or, even better, when there is only a thin place.

(2) Use a thread or wool to match in thickness as well as in colour the garment being mended, i.e. linen on linen, wool on wool. One advantage of home-knitted things is that there is usually some of the wool left for mending.

(3) Unless the hole has been caused by a cut, be sure to spread the darn well beyond the hole itself, so that not only is the hole filled up but the weak, worn part round about is strengthened. Keep the darn irregular in shape, to lessen the strain on the old threads. Leave loops of wool at the end of each row of stitches, as the new wool or thread may shrink in the wash and pucker badly if this is not allowed for.

(4) To strengthen a thin piece in a woollen garment, such as an elbow or underarm of a jersey, darn lightly on the wrong side; if hand-knitted, picking up the actual loops of the knitting, using matching wool. This will be practically invisible on the right side and the garment will have an extra lease of useful life.

(5) If you have to darn heavy socks which get very hard wear in gumboots, use a thread of wool and two threads of stranded cotton together to give extra strength. This is a tip, too, for hand-knitted socks; use a ball of fine crochet cotton or stranded cotton with the wool when knitting the heel.

Patching

(1) Save work by patching thin places before they become holes.

(2) If it can be avoided, never patch with new, unlaundered material. For patches on bed linen, use the good parts of an old sheet or pillow case. A patch of new material will tend to pull away from the older stuff.

(3) Be sure the patch is big enough to cover the hole and extend over the worn fabric surrounding it. When mending pyjamas, shirts or blouses which have split near a seam, undo the seam and put the edge of the patch into it; this will be much neater and stronger than stitching over or close to the seam.

(4) Use hidden parts of the garment for patches that will be visible, i.e. the tail of a shirt to patch the collar or fronts, and replace with another material.

(5) It is wise to put protective patches on some children's clothes before they are worn at all. Reinforce the seats of pants, if not already done by the maker. For the knees of dungarees and elbows of lumber jackets one can use a contrasting colour, and make a decoration of it, putting the patch on the outside; otherwise patch inside.

Dressmaking

At one time or another nearly every woman gets the urge to make a frock or underclothes for herself or her children. It can be great fun, and at the same time stretch a dress allowance. Full details are given in the chapter, A.B.C. of Dressmaking, but here are some basic rules for beginners:

(1) Choose a reliable paper pattern by a good maker.

(2) Don't be too ambitious to start with. It is better to make a real success of a simple garment than a muddle of an elaborate one. Many people have been put off further efforts by trying something too difficult the first time. Most good pattern-makers label some of their designs "simple" or "easy." These are just as smart as the harder ones.

(3) Buy the pattern first and see exactly how much material you will need.

(4) Do not buy anything too cheap or flimsy for a first attempt; it will only fray and be difficult to handle. A good material to begin with is a firm cotton print that will not pull out of shape.

(5) Choose a material with a small all-over pattern which conceals, instead of showing up, small irregularities in making and stitching. A fabric with a large design will be difficult to match at the joins, and a plain one will show every tiny fault.

(6) Get a friend to try the pieces of the pattern against you, or try them against a frock that fits you. Even if the bust and hip measurements are correct, it may be necessary to alter the length of the sleeve or the length from shoulder to waist. It is easier to do this before cutting than afterwards.

(7) Be very careful how you lay out the pieces on the material. It is most important that the instructions should be followed, otherwise the frock will not hang correctly when finished.

(8) To pin the pattern to the material, use, if possible, fine steel pins. Brass pins make holes and sometimes dirty marks as well.

(9) Mark carefully all perforations and notches on the material with tacking stitches. Do not cut the notches, as this wastes material you may need for fitting.

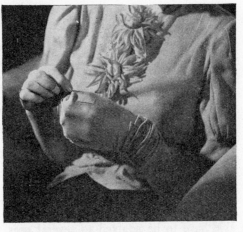

Always darn before the hole gets too large or, better still, when there is only a thin place

(10) All joins should first be pinned together, then tacked, and the garment fitted on and any adjustments made. Stitch by machine or hand, following directions carefully.

(11) Choose a sewing thread to match the predominant colour in the design. For cottons, use No. 40 or No. 60 cotton, or a mercerised machine twist. For rayons use a mercerised twist; for silk, real silk if possible; and for nylons, use nylon thread. There is now an exceptionally evenly spun mercerised machine twist in three thicknesses: No. 24 for heavy work such as curtains and furnishings; No. 40 for dresses and children's wear, and No. 60 for lingerie. This is worth buying and the range of colours is very good. The usual machine twist is equivalent to a No. 40 cotton.

(12) Follow the step-by-step instructions given with the pattern for making up. Press each seam as it is stitched and try on frequently.

(13) Choose buttons, belts, ribbons, etc., for the garment as carefully as you did the material and pattern. They have a lot to do with the finished effect.

(14) Do not forget when making underclothes, dresses or blouses of nylon, Terylene and other man-made fibres, to get nylon ribbon, elastic and sewing threads, or your "home-mades" will not dry as quickly as they should.

THE LINEN CUPBOARD–ITS CONTENTS AND MAINTENANCE

All you need to know about how much to buy per person—and the best
way of storing all sorts of household linen, compiled by the National
Institute of Houseworkers

THERE are not many housewives to-day who can choose the ideal house; fewer still can claim to have the perfect arrangement of cupboards. In most houses, flats and bed-sitting-rooms the cupboards available have to be adapted to several uses, but one of the most important needs is a suitable place for the storage of household linen.

In the larger homes of the last generation it was usual to find a linen room fitted with shelves and drawers and containing a table and sewing machine for repairs. Nowadays it would cost a small fortune to stock our homes with the large numbers of sheets, towels, pillowcases and tablecloths which our grandmothers had; consequently the storage and care of these articles is a much simpler matter.

Shelves are Best

Very often in modern houses the linen cupboard and airing cupboard are the same, but this is not a good plan. The airing of household linen is very necessary for the health of the family, but if linen is kept constantly in a warm temperature the fibres become weakened and the life of the fabric is seriously reduced. It is wise, therefore, to have a cool ventilated cupboard for the storage of linen and to use a heated cupboard only for airing after the weekly wash. If only one cupboard is available, it is a good plan to fit a simple bar heater at the bottom of the cupboard and to switch it on and off when warmth is needed. It can be fixed very easily, and the consumption of current is small.

Except for small articles, shelves are much better than drawers for the storage of linen. Several sheets can be very heavy, and are not easy to remove from a drawer. If the shelves of the linen cupboard are slated, it will be easier for air to circulate. Never pack the linen cupboard too full or place articles against the sides and back. If the cupboard is a high one, the blankets and bedcovers not in use should be put at the top, out of the way. If blankets are to be stored for a time, they should be packed with moth preventative and may be wrapped in newspaper, which moths dislike, and the parcel then sealed with gummed paper.

Household linen should be placed in convenient piles and, if various members of the family use the cupboard, the shelves could be labelled. It is very aggravating to have a neat pile of sheets or towels upset because someone else was looking for a pillowcase in a hurry. Every linen cupboard will have some sheets or towels which are badly worn and are waiting to be "sides to middled" or to be re-hemmed or cut down for other purposes. Keep all these separately, so that they are not brought out in mistake for good ones. If bedmaking is one of the jobs you dislike and you are very busy, it can be most upsetting to put a clean sheet on the bed, only to notice when you spread it out that it is too thin to stand another week's wear.

Unless you prefer to keep them in a separate drawer, tablecloths are best kept rolled and tied with tape.

Keep all the linen cupboard shelves free from dust by covering with dust sheets. A useful tip is to fasten two cup hooks to the shelf above, at the back, and to hang a piece of muslin or clean old sheeting from these over the shelf below.

Linen for a Family

The amount of linen necessary for each household depends very largely on the amount of money available and whether or not the washing is done at home. If one sheet per bed is changed every week and washed at home, then it is possible to make do with only three sheets per bed. This must only be regarded as the absolute minimum, and does not allow for illness, emergencies, frequent visitors or for a reserve. The usual quantity of linen to allow for a family of moderate means is at least:

2 pairs of sheets per bed
4 pillowcases per bed
1 bedspread per bed
2 face towels per person
2 bath towels per person
Extra guest towels
3–6 tablecloths
2–3 afternoon cloths
12 table napkins
1–2 sets table mats
3 dishcloths
2 floorcloths
4 hand towels
½–1 doz. tea towels
2 oven cloths
6 dusters
1 cover for ironing board
2 dust sheets
2 lavatory towels

Drying-up the dishes is no longer a dreary chore when cloths are so gay. Choose from clowns in a circus or colourful cookery hints printed on Irish linen glass cloths

There is a party theme here—and a riot of brilliant colours—a selection of Irish linen printed glass cloths gay with cocktail glasses, balloons and streamers

It is always wise to buy the best possible quality and to buy from a reliable firm. There are so many materials with different finishes that it is not easy to judge quality.

Remember that hemstitched sheets and pillowcases are inclined to go at the stitching after wear: corded or plain hems are more practical for hard wear.

For bed and table linen it is much better to choose a good mixture of cotton and linen than a poor quality linen.

A closer woven fabric will give much better wear than a loose weave. When buying Turkish towels, hold them up to the light. If they are firm enough for satisfactory use, it should only be possible to see tiny pin-holes of light.

If you are lucky enough to have a very generous supply of linen in your cupboard, try to use it all in rotation. Sheets which have been in store for a long time do not wear so well and will not be such a good colour as new ones. Never store starched linen for long periods.

CHILDREN AND CLOTHES CAN GROW TOGETHER

Some of the best makes allow for this—others need fairly drastic alteration

by L. K. DONAT

IN families with many children, clothes can be handed down from one to another, but, where there is an only child, or a pigeon pair, the same clothes have to be worn for a longer time. At Daniel Neal's London showrooms some of the best ideas can be seen.

The Kamella pure wool sleeping-bag is convertible into a dressing-gown once the child has outgrown the sleeping-bag phase. It is zipped down the front and, once the flap is unpicked, the dressing-gown is ready.

For boys from 5–8 there are coats with such really generous turnings at sleeves and hems that two let-downs are quite possible. Any boy's coat made by a reputable firm has a 3-in. hem and a 2½-in. turn-in at the sleeves. The same applies to girls' frocks.

The Judy, two-size frock, for girls from 3–15, is made by Judy Fabrics and can be bought at many stores. Nothing is easier than altering these frocks to the next size. There are three rows to unpick. The first where the bodice joins the skirt (the new seam is ready inside); another one, a French seam, at the bottom; a third one, from shoulder to hip, will give the right width to a dress now one size larger than it was before. The dresses are made both in cotton for the summer and in woollen material for the winter.

When there's No Room to Grow

If children's clothes have no more seams to let down or, as in the case of snow-suits, the manufacturer has not provided for growing, there is a lot you can do yourself to give them a new lease of life. To lengthen a **snow-suit**, take out the zip fastener in front. Then take the child's measurements: (1) from shoulder to waist, down the front; (2) from armpit down to the waist; (3) from the small of the back to the waist in front; (4) pass the tape measure between the legs of the child and let it sit down. By doing this, you will provide for a comfortable fit. Write down these measurements on a piece of paper. Now measure the snow-suit and compare the measurements. Let us assume that there is a difference of 2 in. (Forget about the sleeves and legs for the moment.) We now have to insert a 2-in. wide piece plus an allowance for seams.

Carefully mark all round where you want to cut through at the waist line. Cut and tack in your strip of material. Try it on the child before sewing it in permanently. If you have been unable to buy the right kind of material, you can lengthen the suit just as efficiently by inserting a piece of knitting.

Sew on the zip fastener, beginning at the top. It will now be 2 in. too short, so that you have to sew up the last 2 in.

To make *wrist* and *ankle bands*: measure how much longer the sleeves and trouser-legs ought to be. Take out the elastic (if the garment has been finished that way). With two No. 11 or 12 knitting needles, and 3- or 4-ply wool, knit four pieces in rib, knit 2, purl 2. Sew the wrist and ankle bands in place.

Wind-cheaters are comparatively expensive, and so they, too, deserve to be lengthened and widened. The easiest way to lengthen one is to put on a knitted welt and wrist bands, as described for the snow-suit, but, if it has become too tight, we must widen it as well. Remove zip fastener or buttons. Take the child's measurement around the chest and see how much wider the wind-cheater has to be. You will need about ¼ yd. of material, similar in quality, but either patterned or of a contrasting colour.

We shall now make two new front pieces. Say you want the wind-cheater to be 3 in. wider: make a paper pattern of your front half, allowing 1½ in. plus allowance for seams. Cut out the material and tack it into place. Try it on and see if it fits well.

Three ways to lengthen a girl's dress: (1) with contrast band at waist and matching collar; (2) make a knitted yoke and sleeves; (3) with embroidered strips.

If the wind-cheater does not need more than this, sew the new front into place and put back the zip fastener, or make button-holes and sew on buttons. If, however, it is also tight at the back, cut away the old front pieces and insert a strip made of these pieces in the centre of the back. Make a knitted welt and wrist bands, as described for the snow-suit.

To Lengthen a Girl's Dress

Use a piece of material contrasting in colour or pattern, i.e. for a plain dress use patterned material, and vice versa. Insert a wide piece of material between bodice and skirt. (See Diagram 1.) Make a collar or bind the neck to match. For a woollen dress, the insertion can be made in ribbed knitting, using 3-ply wool the same colour as the dress and No. 12 needles.

Another way of lengthening a dress, especially suitable for woollen or jersey, is to make a knitted yoke and sleeves.

Make a paper pattern for the yoke and sleeves, modelling it on the dress, but allowing for the increase in length. (See Diagram 2.) You will need one or two parts for the front, according to the style of the dress, and one part for the back of the yoke, as well as the pattern for the new sleeves, should you wish to make these as well. Although it might at first sound difficult, there is nothing easier than working to a paper pattern, once you have tried it out.

Moss stitch is suggested for the yoke and sleeves. This is just knit 1, purl 1, changed over in the next row.

Another good way of lengthening and widening a dress, which looks charming done in two bright colours, is the following.

Buy $\frac{1}{4}$ or $\frac{1}{2}$ yd. (according to width) of material in a contrasting colour. For a green dress, for instance, use pink; for a blue one, yellow, etc. Unpick the shoulder seams and the waist. Following Diagram 3 insert 1-in.-wide bands on both sides. Insert a similar piece at the waist and another in the skirt. You will now have lengthened and widened the dress by 2 in. If you have been using pink strips on a green dress, embroider those strips with either lazy daisy or large cross-stitches. If there are pockets, decorate them in the same way.

"HERE'S A
PRETTY THING...

1. *Three miniature
jam jars*

3. *A pair of
cocoa tins*

2. *A pickle jar and paste pot*

3. If you can find a couple of cocoa or sweet tins, you can dress them up to look smart on a shelf or for guest-room biscuits. Sandpaper the surface, then cover with a suitable glue. Cut bright decorative wall- or wrapping-paper to size and stick on quickly. Or cover with two coats of enamel paint, then add dots of sealing wax and paper stars

1. This charmingly original three-in-one table centre is made from miniature jam jars. With a steel crochet hook and raffia, crochet 5 chain. Close into a ring, then work in double crochet until the raffia cover is big enough to take a jar. Change to a contrasting colour, work 4 double crochet into last round and 3 chain. Make single crochet into first chain. Complete edge. Cover the other jars in the same way, attach to base and fill with cigarettes, matches and a flower.

2. Two for the dressing table—a decorated pickle jar makes a good container for cotton wool if you get a hole cut in the centre of the lid by your local ironmonger, then paint the jar in whatever pattern you like. A large relish or paste jar— stripped of all its labels—has been decorated with a Zodiac sign—you can buy transfers at local stores—and then varnished

A very pretty thing"—and all these decorative containers are made from discarded boxes, jars, tins

5. *Cigar box*

4. *Talcum powder box*

4. You want an evening bag to match your new dress? Make one from a talcum powder box. Cut material to fit lower part of box, a strip to go round the lid and two circles for the top and bottom. Seam the sides and sew the top and base to the sides, covering the seams with matching or contrasting braid. Paint the inside of the box. Glue the covers to the top and base. Make a handle of braid and sew it on

6. *Powder box*

5. An old cigar box takes on a new—and decorative—lease of life if covered with felt. Cut the felt to go right round the box, with a separate piece for the lid. Then cut out small circles in lighter coloured felt (say white or red on black) to look like the spots on dice and sew into place. Stick felt to box and lid, using a roller to press it quite flat and smooth. Smart as an oddments box

6. A talcum powder box makes a cute little dressing-table tidy and the lid a pin cushion. Pad the lid with kapok or cotton wool and stretch fabric across top. Glue down and cover with velvet. The striped covers are made in exactly the same way as the evening bag described in number 4. Glazed cotton or plastic material would look pretty in the bedroom or bathroom

GIFT NOTIONS TO MAKE

A pretty feather spray for evening, a flower posy for a party and an original table cloth for the card-player

The feather spray (above) can be worn on the shoulder or in the hair; the flower posy (right) brightens a dark frock

Feather Spray

FOR six flowers you will need: 18 small feathers about 2 in. long, 12 feathers about 3 in. long, 6 pearl stamens (from handicraft shop), 72 small green beads, 6 small red beads, 36 gold bugle beads, fine wire, white crêpe paper, cotton wool, glue, red nail varnish and acetone.

Cut one end off pearl stamens and thread stem with 12 green beads. Cut six lengths of wire 8 in. long; on to each thread one red bead to middle, bend wire and pass it double through 6 gold beads. Bind together. Use long piece of thread, attach it to the stamen below last bead and bind stamens on one by one, then bind on the feathers—two 3-in. and three 2-in. to each flower. Twist the wire ends together and twist a wispy layer of cotton wool over wire, bind round with thread; cover with crêpe paper ½ in. wide, glue one end under flower and bind stalk. Bind end of stalks together; draw feathers over a knife blade; paint with dots of varnish and tips with reddened acetone.

Flower Posy

You will need two packets of 2-in. wide bias binding in light and dark yellow, 4 yd. of ½-in. green binding. Yellow sewing silk.

Be very careful to use cotton bias binding for the posy; the silk or cambric type is much too fine for making the flowers and leaves. The posy consists of 14 flowers —7 pale yellow, 7 dark, with pale green leaves and stems.

To make one flower, cut 5 in. of green binding for stalk, fold to third of its width and press. Cut two strips of wide binding, each 2 in. long; fold in half lengthways (without creasing), then round off cut ends, unfold, then twist in centre, fold in half and pleat folded edge, secure with a few stitches. Stitch stalk to flower just made. Fold and cut a second piece of wide binding, then fold round the first flower and stalk and stitch.

Turn over the petals at top. Make altogether seven light and seven dark. Cut strips of bias binding for leaves, shaping the top of each to a point. Bunch flowers together, placing leaves at back; bind with bias binding.

Card-table Cloth

You will need 1 yd. of green and ⅓ yd. of white felt 36 in. wide, and small pieces of red and black felt.

Cut four strips of white felt, each 2 in. wide and 36 in. long for border. Mitre corners, stitch together and put round edge of green felt. Make twelve "playing cards" about 2½ in. by 1½ in. Cut out hearts, spades, diamonds and clubs from black and red felt, and sew on to "cards." Put three "cards" in each corner and sew on with running stitches.

POTATO PRINTS

by Lilian K. Donat

This is a grand way of keeping the children amused printing their own party invitations, greeting cards and wrapping papers

Here are some simple ideas to start them off—including some gay candles, a two-colour ball and various geometrical figures. Turn the page for more suggestions, then let the children design their own patterns

MAKING potato prints is a wonderful occupation for children. Afternoons pass only too quickly, and there is a real sense of achievement when invitations to parties, Christmas or Easter cards, wrapping paper, etc., have been decorated. It is also an ideal pastime for a sick child, provided that an old towel or sheet is first spread over the blankets. A bread board or tray will then do in place of a table.

Simple Requirements

For the printing you will need: one or two large potatoes, unpeeled and cut across; saucers for mixing the paint; pencil, paintbrush, a sharp kitchen or pen knife, poster colour or Indian ink and, most important, plenty of old newspapers to cover the working surface.

A simple design is worked out on paper first. This is then cut out on the surface of a halved potato so that a raised pattern is formed which will act as a die. For very small children a square or oblong will be the easiest to manage. Then a

Some more suggestions for potato print designs . . .

Above, an all-over pattern that would print a large sheet of wrapping paper most effectively in two strongly contrasting colours

Above, a selection of small motifs with lots of possibilities—use one to decorate the corners of paper table napkins, another for a colourful card or party invitation

Left, another attractive all-over design with a contemporary flavour; would look equally good in brown and blue or yellow and black

little poster colour is thinned with water to a creamy mixture, or Indian ink is poured on to a saucer. The paint is then transferred to the potato with the help of the brush. The potato is now firmly held down for a moment on the object to be printed, then carefully lifted up.

The printing should be done when the potatoes are freshly cut. If several colours are wanted for one pattern, several halves of potatoes have to be used, one for each colour, and each must be printed only when the previous colour is thoroughly dry.

SMOCKING

It looks complicated as well as dainty, but is really very simple work to do

THERE are many uses for smocking, such as gathering for skirt waists, obviating the necessity for elastic, and this is most effective on children's dresses, blouses, smocks and lingerie.

Although it looks very complicated, smocking is quite simple work and most lightweight materials are suitable.

Preparing Work

Sheets of transfer dots can be bought to ensure even gathers. These vary in width, and the transfer used will depend on the work to be undertaken. The transfer should always be ironed off on the *wrong* side of the material or the dots will show when the article is finished.

Gathering is the next step in the preparation. This, too, is done on the wrong side, using a long thread. Lift each dot on the needle, taking care to keep stitches even,

This enchanting party frock for a little girl in pale pink nylon can be smocked from instructions overleaf

or the effect of the smocking is spoilt. Continue lines of gathering in this way until you have the required depth for the pattern. Then pull up threads so that the material forms into pleats. The wider the dots, the more material is required.

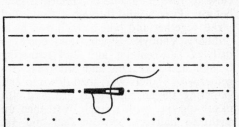

Gather by picking up dots ironed off a transfer

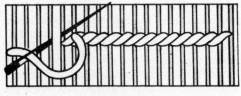

Outline Stitch

STITCHES

Outline Stitch.—The needle should be held diagonally for this stitch and thread kept above needle, each stitch taking up one pleat or fold. Thread kept below the needle will alter the angle of the stitch.

Cable Stitch.—For this stitch, the needle is kept level with dots and thread goes alternately above and below needle. Two rows of this are often worked together.

Wave Stitch.—Take thread across the 1st pleat with thread above needle. Keeping stitch level, insert needle in 2nd pleat slightly lower, repeat with 2nd and 4th pleats. Now work upwards. Keeping thread below needle, work in this way till row is finished. Two or three rows can be repeated as required.

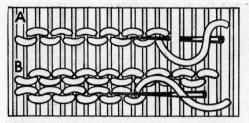

Cable Stitch (A) and Double Cable Stitch (B)

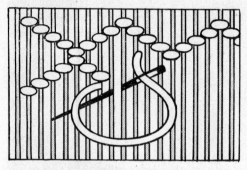

Trellis Stitch

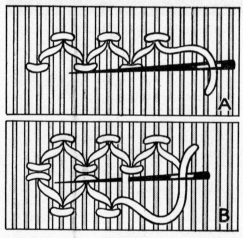

Diamond Stitch—the first half (A), the other half (B)

Trellis Stitch.—This is worked in the same way as Wave Stitch, but the 2nd row is worked to form a diamond.

Diamond Stitch.—Working from left to right, bring needle through at 1st pleat, take needle through level on 2nd pleat with thread below needle. Take next stitch slightly above in the 3rd pleat with thread below, and another in 4th pleat with thread above. Next stitch down level with 1st with thread above and next stitch beside with

thread below. Continue in this way, taking 1 stitch in every pleat. To form the diamond, another row is started immediately below the 1st stitches and arranged as shown in diagram.

Crossed Diamond Stitch.—Work in the same way as for Diamond Stitch. Then work a 2nd row on the same line over the 1st row, but take together the 2 pleats which were missed on the 1st row. For instance, if the 1st and 2nd pleats were taken together in 1st row on level of 1st gathering thread, these will be taken on level of 2nd gathering thread.

Vandyke Stitch.—Bring needle up on 1st pleat on right side of material, halfway between 1st and 2nd gathering threads, pass needle through 1st two pleats together and take another stitch over; then come down to 2nd gathering thread, and take 2nd and 3rd pleats together with another stitch over, then up halfway between 2nd and 1st gathering thread take 3rd and 4th pleats together with another stitch over, and so on to end of line. This stitch should always start halfway between two gathering threads and be worked down to the line. A space of half the distance between two gathering threads should always be left after every line.

Double Vandyke Stitch.—This is used to finish off a pattern and requires to be headed by a row of outline or single cable. Start thread on 2nd pleat, bringing needle up in 1st pleat on right side of material close to row of outline or cable that goes before. Pass needle through 1st and 2nd pleats together and take a stitch over as in ordinary Vandyke Stitch; then come to halfway between 1st and 2nd gathering threads and take 2nd and 3rd pleats together with a stitch over; then down to 2nd gathering thread and take 3rd and 4th pleats together with a stitch over; then up again to halfway between 2nd and 1st gathering thread, taking 4th and 5th pleats together with a stitch over; and then up to 1st gathering thread and take 5th and 6th pleats together with a stitch over, and so on to end of line. The second half of stitch is worked in a similar way. Start thread at 3rd gathering thread, taking 1st and 2nd pleats together with a stitch over; and then up to halfway between 3rd and 2nd gathering thread and take 2nd and 3rd pleats together with a stitch over; then up to 2nd gathering threads and close to stitch of line above, take 3rd and 4th pleats together with a stitch over, and so on to end of the line.

Honeycomb Stitch.—This is a more elastic stitch than any of the other smocking stitches. Begin in 1st pleat. Take a stitch through top of 2nd and 1st pleats together, catch them together with a 2nd stitch, but taking needle down back of 2nd pleat until 2nd gathering thread is reached. Then bring out. Catch 3rd and 2nd pleats together with a stitch, make a 2nd stitch over this and take needle up back of 3rd pleat and out at 1st gathering thread. Continue up and down in this way until row is complete. Work a 2nd row on 3rd and 4th gathering threads and consecutive rows if required.

Surface Honeycomb Stitch.—Bring up needle on left side of 2nd pleat from right: make a stitch over these 2 pleats and take needle down on right side of 2nd pleat and pass it through 2nd and 3rd pleats halfway between 1st and 2nd gathering threads. Continue up and down as in Vandyke Stitch, advancing one pleat with every stitch. Work a 2nd row of stitches from halfway between 1st and 2nd gathering threads to 2nd gathering thread. Arrange stitches as shown in diagram.

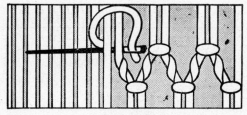

Vandyke Stitch

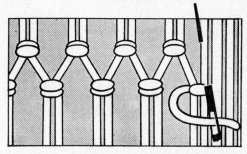

Honeycomb Stitch

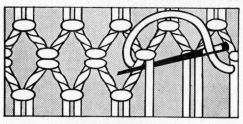

Surface Honeycomb Stitch

Pattern for the Party Frock photographed

This pattern can be repeated as often as required, according to length of bodice, and is both simple and effective.

1st row: Outline stitch.
Leave $\frac{1}{4}$ in. space.
2nd and 3rd rows: Honeycomb stitch.
4th row: Outline stitch.

Alternative Pattern for a Child's Dress

(Across at sleeve level)
1st row: Cable stitch.
2nd row: Cable stitch worked very close to 1st row. Leave $\frac{1}{2}$ in. space.
3rd, 4th and 5th rows: Large Vandyke stitch.
6th row: Vandyke stitch worked to form diamond shape.
7th row: Outline worked to come close to point of diamonds.
8th row: As 6th row, taking care points correspond.

9th, 10th and 11th rows: Large Vandyke stitch.
12th row: Cable stitch.

(At waist level)
1st row: Outline stitch.
2nd and 3rd rows: Wave stitch.
4th row: Cable stitch.
5th, 6th, 7th and 8th rows: Wave stitch arranged to form large diamonds.
9th row: Cable stitch.
10th and 11th rows: Wave stitch.
12th row: Outline stitch.

FINISHING

Before removing gathering threads, press work. Place work wrong side up on ironing board or table. Cover with damp cloth. Press *very* lightly till cloth is dry. Remove cloth. Hold iron over material till steam has dried. Remove gathering threads. Make up.

Diagrams reprinted from "Smocking by Penelope," by permission of Wm. Briggs & Co Ltd.

FABRIC	Clark's Anchor Embroidery Threads	Thickness	Milwards Needle Sizes	Remarks
Organdie, muslin, voile, georgette, fine linen, lawn or sheer silk	Stranded Cotton	1, 2 or 3 strands	Sharp Pointed Crewel Needles No. strands	These fabrics, threads and needles are for working designs traced or transferred on to the fabric.
Medium weight linen, rayon, silk, etc.	Stranded Cotton	2, 3 or 4 strands	8 — 1 7 — 2	The number of strands may be varied on any article according to the
Heavy linen, crash, furnishing fabric, etc.	Stranded Cotton	6 strands	6 — 3 & 4 5 — 6	requirements of the design.
Very fine mesh canvas, fine even weave linen or other fabric	Stranded Cotton	1 or 2 strands	Blunt Rounded Points Tapestry Needles No. strands	For working over counted threads of canvas or fabric. Mainly used for cross stitch, tent stitch, gobelin stitch.
Medium mesh canvas and medium weight even weave linen and fabric	Stranded Cotton	3 or 4 strands	25 — 1 24 — 2	
Heavy mesh canvas and coarser weight even weave linen and fabric	Stranded Cotton	6 strands	23 — 3 & 4 21 — 6	
Heavy linen, crash, furnishing fabric, etc.	Soft Embroidery or Flox No. 10	—	Sharp Pointed Chenille Needle No. 19	For traced or transferred design.
Canvas, heavy even weave linen and fabric	Soft Embroidery or Flox No. 10	—	Blunt Rounded Points Tapestry Needle No. 19	For working over counted threads of fabric in cross stitch, etc.

THE threads mentioned in the chart are from the range of Clark's Anchor Embroidery Threads. Anchor Stranded Cotton, easily separated into different thicknesses, is suitable for all types of embroidery. Anchor Soft Embroidery, a matt-finish thread, and Anchor Flox, a loosely twisted thread with a fine lustre, are used for larger designs on heavier fabrics.

A.B.C. OF EMBROIDERY

Here, for the novice, are the basic stitches needed for most kinds of simple embroidery, with the correct method of working clearly explained and shown in diagrams. The experienced embroidress will also find some stitches that are new to her, as well as many which she already knows. Try out some of the less well-known ones and you will find a fresh and absorbing interest in embroidery.

It is the effective combination of fabric, thread, design and stitch, all carefully chosen for their suitability in relation to one another, that produces work of real beauty. You will find on the opposite page a chart to help you make your choice and showing the correct type and size of needle required for each purpose

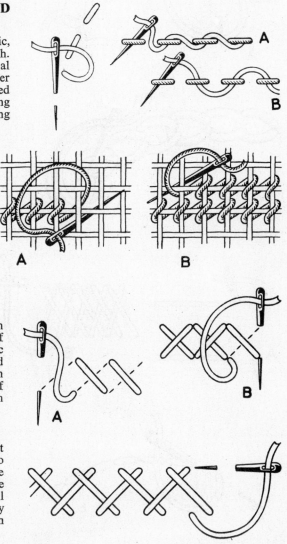

1 and 2. RUNNING AND LACED RUNNING STITCHES

Pass needle over and under fabric, making upper stitches of equal length. Under stitches should also be of equal length, but half the size or less of upper stitches. Running Stitch can be whipped (A) or laced (B) with a contrasting colour. Use a blunt needle for whipping or lacing and pick up no fabric.

3. TENT STITCH

Worked on single thread canvas. 1st row: bring thread through at left side on top part of first stitch (A), pass needle down over crossed canvas threads, then under two canvas threads (A); 2nd row: work from right to left, the needle passing the crossed canvas threads up and over, then under two canvas threads (B).

4. CROSS STITCH

Bring needle through on bottom right line of cross and insert at top of same line, taking a stitch through fabric to bottom left line (A); continue to end of row in this manner and in the return journey complete the other half of cross (B). The upper half of stitch must lie in one direction.

5. HERRINGBONE STITCH

Bring needle out on lower line at left side and insert on upper line a little to the right, taking a small stitch to the left. Next, insert needle on lower line a little to the right and take a small stitch to the left. The stitches lifted by the needle and the spaces between stitches should be of equal size.

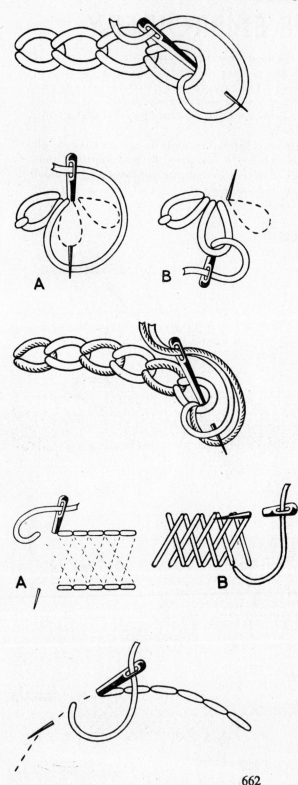

6. CHAIN STITCH

Bring thread out at top of line and hold down with left thumb. Insert the needle where it last emerged and bring the point out a short distance away. Pull through, keeping the working thread below needle.

6a. DAISY STITCH

Also known as Detached Chain Stitch. Work in same way as Chain Stitch (A), but fasten each loop at bottom with a small stitch (B). This stitch can be worked singly or in groups to form flower petals.

7. CHEQUERED CHAIN STITCH

Worked in the same way as Chain Stitch, but having two contrasting threads in the needle at the same time. When making loops, pass one colour under needle and let the other colour lie on top; pull through both threads. Work next loop with the other colour under the needle.

8. DOUBLE BACK STITCH

This stitch is used as Shadow Work on fine transparent fabric and can be worked on the right side of fabric as in (A)—a small back stitch worked alternately on each side of traced double lines; the dotted lines on diagram show the formation of thread at back. This shows the colour delicately through fabric. (B) shows the stitch worked on the wrong side of fabric and is worked as a Closed Herringbone Stitch with no spaces left between stitches.

9. BACK STITCH

Bring thread through on stitch line, then take a small backward stitch through the fabric. Bring needle through again a little in front of first stitch, take another backward stitch, pushing needle in at point where it first came through.

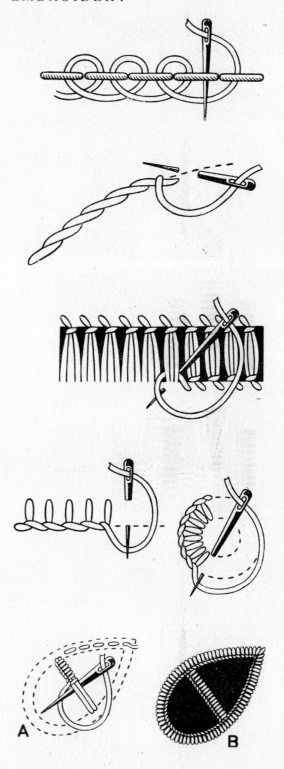

10. PEKINESE STITCH

Work Back Stitch in usual way, then interlace with thread to tone or of different colour. The stitch is shown open in diagram, but loops should be pulled slightly when working. This stitch can be used as a filling or outline.

11. STEM STITCH

Work from left to right, taking regular, slightly slanting stitches along line of design. The thread always emerges on left side of previous stitch. This stitch is used for flower stems, outlines, etc. It can also be used as a filling, rows of close Stem Stitch being worked round shape until it is filled in completely.

12. HEMSTITCH

Draw threads from fabric for required width. Fasten thread near drawn threads at right side, pass needle behind 3 loose threads (the number of threads taken together may be varied to suit fabric), then pass needle behind the same 3 threads, this time bringing needle point through fabric ready for next stitch (folded hem of the article is turned to edge of drawn threads and secured with this stitch). Diagram shows Hemstitch worked along both sides of drawn threads; this is called Ladder Hemstitch.

13. BLANKET STITCH AND BUTTONHOLE STITCH

These stitches are worked in the same way, the stitches being closer together in Buttonhole Stitch. Bring thread out on the lower line, insert needle in position on upper line, taking a downward stitch with the thread under the needle point. Pull up stitch to form loop and repeat.

13a. BUTTONHOLE STITCH BARS

Used in Cut-Work and Richelieu Work. Work a running stitch between double lines of design as padding for Buttonhole Stitch. When a bar occurs, take thread across and back, securing with a small stitch and Buttonhole Stitch closely over the loose threads without picking up any of the fabric (A). Buttonhole Stitch round shape, keeping looped edges of stitch to the inside, then cut away the material from behind bar and round inside of shape.

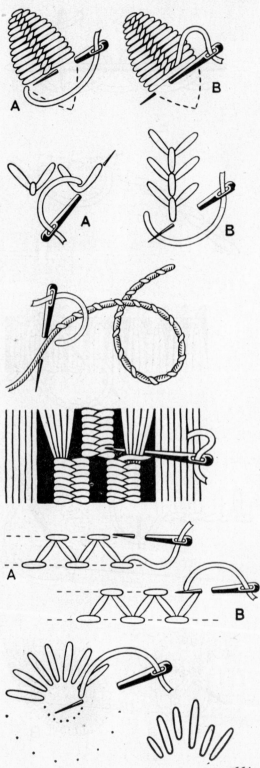

14. ROUMANIAN STITCH

Bring thread through at top left of space, carry thread across and lift a stitch on right side of space, thread below needle (A). Take a stitch at left side, thread above needle (B). Keep stitches close together. The size of the centre crossing stitch can be varied.

15. FLY STITCH

Bring needle out at top left, hold thread down with left thumb, insert to the right on same level a small distance from where it emerged and take a small stitch downwards to centre. With thread below needle, pull through and insert needle again below at centre (A) and emerge in position for next stitch. This stitch can be worked singly or in horizontal rows (A) or vertically (B).

16. COUCHING

Lay a thread along line of design and with another thread tie down at even intervals with a small stitch into the fabric. The tying stitch can be of contrasting colour to the laid thread if desired.

17. NEEDLEWEAVING

Withdraw number of threads required for pattern and weave over and under groups of threads alternately. Diagram shows how a narrow border of 2 rows of groups can be worked, passing on from first row to second row in alternate groups. If using a thick embroidery thread and fairly heavy fabric, one row (back and forward) is usually sufficient to replace one drawn thread. Withdraw only the threads required.

18. CHEVRON STITCH

Bring thread through on lower line on left side, insert needle a little to the right on same line and take a small stitch to the left, emerging halfway between stitch being made. Now insert needle on upper line a little to the right and take a small stitch to the left (A). Insert needle again on same line a little to the right and take small stitch to the left, emerging at centre (B). Work in this way alternately on upper and lower lines.

19. STRAIGHT STITCH

Also known as Single Satin Stitch. Single spaced stitches worked either in regular or irregular manner and sometimes with stitches of varying size. Stitches should be neither long nor loose.

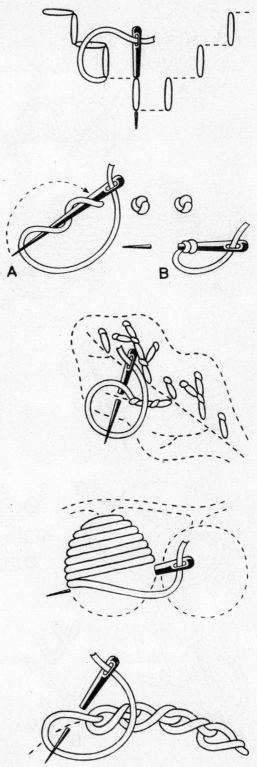

20. HOLBEIN STITCH

Work first row of this stitch from right to left, similar to Running Stitch, but with all stitches of equal length. On return journey, work in same way from left to right, filling in the spaces left by first row. This stitch is used sometimes as an outline to Cross Stitch designs, but a design can be worked throughout in Holbein Stitch.

21. FRENCH KNOTS

Bring needle out at required position. Hold thread taut with left thumb and encircle thread twice with the needle (A). Still holding thread firmly, twist needle back to starting point and insert close to where it first emerged (see arrow). Pull through to back and secure for single French Knot or pass on to next position (B).

22. CORAL STITCH

Bring thread out at right end of line, lay thread along line of design and hold down with left thumb. Take a small stitch under line and thread and pull through, bringing the needle over lower thread, as in diagram.

23. SATIN STITCH

Proceed with Straight Stitches across shape as shown in diagram. If desired, Chain Stitch or Running Stitch may be worked first to form a padding underneath to give a raised effect. Care must be taken to keep a good edge. Do not make the stitches too long, as they are liable to be pulled out of position.

24. TWISTED CHAIN STITCH

Start as for ordinary Chain Stitch, but instead of inserting the needle into the place from where it emerged, insert close to last loop and take a slanting stitch coming out on line of design and pull thread through. The loops of this stitch should be worked closely together to give the correct effect.

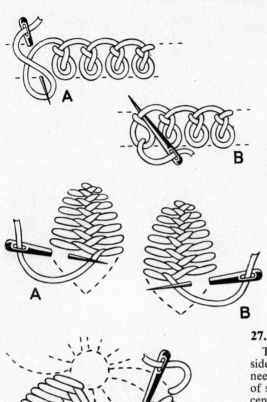

25. ROSETTE CHAIN STITCH

Bring needle through at right end of upper line, pass thread across to left side and hold down with left thumb. Insert needle into upper line a short distance from where thread emerges and bring out just above bottom line. Pass thread round under needle point (A), draw needle through loop and then pass under top thread (B) without picking up any fabric. Use for small flowers or borders.

26. CRETAN STITCH

Bring needle through at top centre and take a small stitch on right side. Take a stitch on left side, needle pointing inwards and with thread under needle point (A), take a stitch on right side in same way (B), continue from side to side until space is filled. For open Cretan Stitch, allow more space between.

27. FLAT STITCH

Take a small stitch alternately on each side of space to be filled with the point of the needle, always emerging on the outside line of shape. Two lines can be drawn down the centre of shape as a guide for size of stitch. Stitches should be close together and fold into one another.

28. BULLION STITCH

Pick up a Back Stitch the size of Bullion required, bringing needle out where it first emerged. Twist thread over needle to equal space of stitch. Hold left thumb on the coiled thread, and pull needle through, turn needle back to where it was inserted (see arrow) and insert in same place (A). Pull thread through. Use a needle with a small eye to allow thread to pass through the twists easily.

29. FEATHER STITCH

Bring needle out at top centre, hold thread down with left thumb, insert needle a little to the right on same level and take a small stitch down to centre, keeping thread below needle point. Next, insert needle a little to the left on same level and take a stitch to centre (A), keeping thread under needle point. Work these two movements alternately. Diagram (B) shows double Feather Stitch in which two stitches are taken to the right and two to the left alternately.

—AND NOW A FLOWER MOTIF FOR YOU TO EMBROIDER

**This fascinating floral design can be traced off and embroidered into
a charming tea cloth. For details and instructions, please turn over.**

THE FLOWERS THAT BLOOM...

*Embroider them yourself on the corners of your tea-
cloth and have the joy of saying "all my own work"*

fabric. Follow Diagram 1, opposite, and key below for the embroidery details. All parts shown similar to numbered parts on the diagram are worked in the same colour and stitch.

Diagram 2 at the foot of this page shows the method of working Closed Buttonhole Stitch: The stitches are made in pairs, forming triangles. Bring the thread through at A, insert the needle at B, and, with the thread under the needle, bring it through at C. Insert the needle again at B and bring it through at D.

Instructions for the other stitches used are to be found in the preceding pages.

Press the finished embroidery well on wrong side. Turn back ¾ in. hem to wrong side and slipstitch invisibly.

KEY TO DIAGRAM
(Opposite)

Stem Stitch: 1–877; 2–821; 3–669; 4–972; 5–407; 6–411; 7–Black.

Satin Stitch: 8–946; 9–669; 10–972.

Chain Stitch: 11–411; 12–946; 13–463; 14–821; 15–407.

Twisted Chain Stitch: 16–877; 17–821; 18–972.

Back Stitch: 19–877; 20–972; 21–Black.

French Knots: 22–946; 23–Black.

Running Stitch: 24–Black.

Herringbone Stitch: 25–411; 26–407.

Fly Stitch: 27–Black.

Feather Stitch: 28–Black.

Daisy Stitch: 29–Black.

Blanket Stitch: 30–407.

Closed Buttonhole Stitch: 31–407.

MATERIALS REQUIRED

CLARK'S Anchor Stranded Cotton: 2 skeins each 946 (Chartreuse), 877 (Turquoise), 407 (Gobelin Green) and Black; 1 skein each 463 (Parrot Green), 669 (Flame), 821 (Beige), 972 (Linen) and 411 (Violet). Use 2 strands for Black, 3 strands for rest of embroidery. 1 yd. square Old Bleach embroidery linen E.L. 45 (White); 1 Milwards "Gold Seal" crewel needle No. 6.

Fold the fabric across each way from corner to corner diagonally, creasing slightly. Transfer one motif centrally on each diagonal fold 8 in. from each corner point of

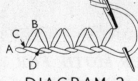

DIAGRAM 2.

668

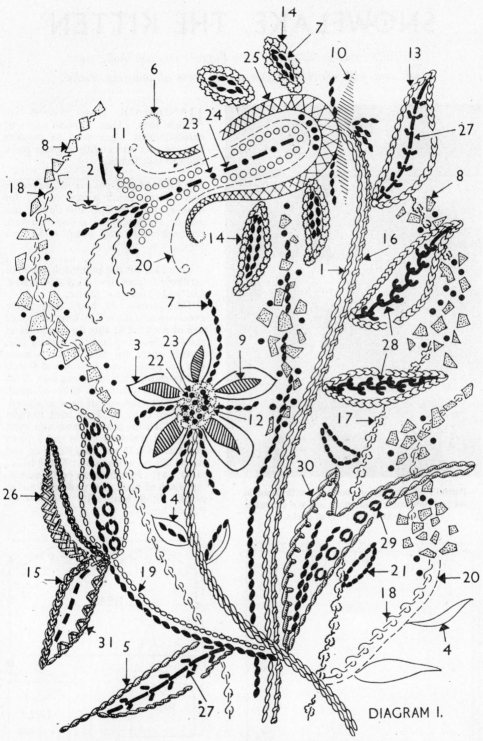

The key opposite shows the stitches corresponding to the numbers shown above. All parts similar to numbered ones are worked in the same colour and stitch

SNOWFLAKE, THE KITTEN

No child could resist these Glove Puppets you can make your-self and with which you can do all sorts of amusing tricks

Perch the finished toy on your hand, with thumb in one paw, first finger in the other, and you can make Snowflake do all sorts of tricks

HAND-MADE glove puppets are ideal toys. They provide hours of entertainment when used as puppets and are soft and cuddly enough for a child to take to bed.

MATERIALS: $\frac{1}{4}$ *yd. fur fabric makes two kittens; small scraps of felt for nose, eyes and mouth; stiff thread; cat-gut or similar material for whiskers, cotton-wool to stuff head; ribbon for bow.*

To make, cut out pattern in paper or cardboard from the diagrams below. Cut body from fur fabric.

Take centre of body and make evenly-spaced darts 2 in. long to reduce size of neck. Cut slits for armholes as shown. Seam up back on wrong side, leaving space for tail. Hem bottom. Cut out head. Join A to A and B to B and seam together on wrong side. This seam forms centre of back of head. Make dart each side of head as shown. Sew from C to D. Turn back to right side. Stitch on mouth, nose and eyes, and insert whiskers. Cut out 2 paws and fold each in half and stitch up and round top on wrong side. Make tail in same way. Join head to body, adjusting width of neck. Sew paws and tail in place. Stuff head with cotton-wool. Put on bow.

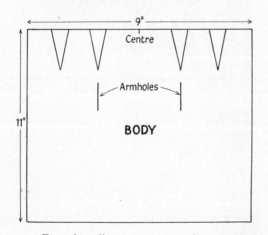

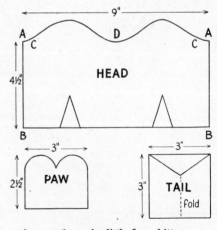

From these diagrams you can make your pattern for cutting out the perky little furry kitten

HETTY, THE HEN

What nicer gift to greet a youngster on Easter morning than this gay old bird?

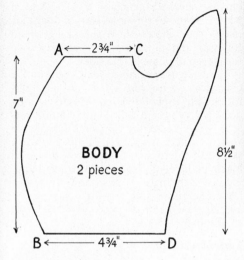

A ← 2¾" → C

7"

8½"

BODY
2 pieces

B ← 4¾" → D

Make her peck and crow realistically and you will delight any small child

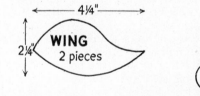

← 4¼" →

2¼"

WING
2 pieces

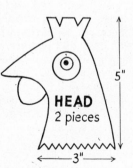

5"

HEAD
2 pieces

← 3" →

2 EYES

2"

COMB
Fold along

WATTLE
2 pieces

Dart

BEAK

1"

← 3" →

MATERIALS: *For body, ¼ yd. of hairy fabric or two 9-in. square pieces of felt. Shoulder pad for stuffing. For head and wing, one 9 in. square of felt. For eyes, beak, wattle and comb, felt or leather scraps. Small amount of stuffing.*

USING the diagram on the left as a guide, draw and cut out paper patterns of the various pieces. Pin the patterns on to the materials and cut out.

If hairy fabric is being used for the body, seam it on the wrong side, and then turn right side out. If felt is used, seam it on the right side, using saddle stitch. Next make the wing, and stuff lightly.

Sew one eye and one wattle piece on to each half of the head. Fold the comb piece in half, as indicated in the diagram on the left, and place it in position between the two head pieces. Seam the head pieces together with saddle stitch. Make a dart on the beak to form a curve on the tip, and stitch the beak in place. Sew on the wing, and then join the body to the head. Finally, the shoulder pad should be sewn inside to fill out the breast.

COSTUMES FOR A FANCY DRESS PARTY

ALL children—and many adults as well —love dressing up, which explains the assured success of a fancy dress party. To buy or hire a costume is expensive and quite unnecessary, if mother is willing to devote some time and inventive genius (plus raw materials) to making one.

There is no need to be an expert dressmaker. It does not matter how roughly you sew a fancy dress, provided it stays intact until the party is over. Many a prize has been won with a costume made up of borrowed household goods and family finery. A pretty tray cloth might provide your small daughter with a dainty apron for a Dutch girl or Little Red Riding Hood; a large white table napkin makes the perfect headdress for a nurse and a deep white paper pie dish frill is an excellent Elizabethan (or clown's) ruff.

The secret of dressing-up is improvisation and the larger selection of outgrown clothes, beads, trimmings, bits of fur, old hats, feathers and jewellery, you have to draw upon, the easier it is. When material has to be bought, choose the cheapest you can find to give the necessary effect, bearing in mind that the costume is not likely to be worn more than two or three times, its success being largely dependent upon its surprise value.

Mother's Evening Dress

Kings and Queens, national characters (Dutch or Chinese, etc.), pirates, fairies, Red Indians and spacemen are always popular; so are the well-known characters out of the nursery rhymes. An old evening dress will often form the basis of a very regal-looking costume, which must always be of a rich fabric in sumptuous colourings. A girl might wear it long and flowing, caught in at the waist with a gold belt or cord, the extra length being tacked up into a deep hem in front and allowed to form a train at the back. A boy king might wear a brocade tunic cut from an old evening coat or dress. Both would need crowns, which can be made from gold paper cut into the appropriate shape and size, glued firmly on to buckram and pinned round the head.

Make the crowns really sparkle with a generous application of sequins or jewel-bright buttons.

The basis of a Dutch girl outfit is really only a checked gingham frock. Add a white organdie apron, a pair of long fair plaits (see chapter on Wig Making which follows) and a little white organdie cap turned up in points at the sides.

You can transform a small boy into a Chinaman in no time at all. Over a tight-fitting pair of plain pyjama trousers he only needs a loose tunic of brilliant Oriental pattern, Chinese coolie slippers (obtainable very cheaply nowadays), a black sateen skull cap to cover his hair and with a long black plait (made from black wool) hanging down the back. Finish him off with a bowl and chopsticks or a little clay pipe— and do teach him to walk with the right shuffling short steps.

Tinsel for a Fairy

Spacemen and women can wear almost anything, preferably made from shiny plastic and (if you have them) with underwater swimming goggles and flippers just to make the whole effect a little more "out of this world."

You can dress a little girl as a fairy in about half an hour. All you need is sufficient white or pale pink net (nylon or Proban-treated to avoid danger from fire) for a very full, short skirt and to cover the bodice part of a petticoat, plus plenty of tinsel. Crown her with a large silver star (made from silver paper stuck on to buckram) liberally scattered with tinsel and sequins.

For cowboy or Red Indian costumes one of the best materials is hessian. It is strong, easy to sew and it fringes well. As it is usually natural in colour, introduce a note of brilliance in the feather headdress and with furnishing braid or fringe in reds and greens. Another useful material is felt, which comes in wonderful colours and which you can get in small squares for about a shilling or by the yard in all widths. Use it in green to make a hat for a young Robin Hood and for many other touches of colour.

ANCY
RESS
O MAKE

Five charming costumes to be made from Leach-Way patterns — or to suggest ideas for you to adapt yourself

Each adult pattern costs 2s. 6d. post free and each child's pattern is 2s., up to 10 years of age ; 2s. 3d. over 10 years. To order, send postal order with your own name and address in BLOCK LETTERS, stating the number of the pattern required, and the size, to The Pattern Shop, "Home Management," 136/7, Long Acre, London, W.C.2.

No. 13081

No. 13066

QUEEN OF HEARTS, a pretty costume for a girl in her teens, consists of a long full white skirt, a fitted red or orange bodice and sleeves trimmed with hearts and a crown of hearts. The pattern is No. 13081 and is cut in bust sizes 30, 32, 34, 36 and 38 inches.

JESTER'S PARTNER is a gay two-colour costume with a short, very full skirt of tarlatan, the points on collar, skirt and cap all trimmed with little silver bells. It should be worn with long net ballet stockings and ballet shoes. The pattern is No. 13066 and is cut in bust sizes 30, 32, 34, 36 and 38 inches.

FANCY DRESS TO MAKE

INDIAN SQUAW consists of a fringed skirt and tunic, which could well be made in hessian trimmed with red and green wool fringe, and a stiffened headdress with 23 brilliantly coloured graduated feathers mounted on it. Pattern No. 12720 is cut for ages 6–8, 8–10 and 10–12 years.

No. 13085

No. 12720

RED RIDING HOO includes a dress, but y might prefer to ma the hood and apr only. Pattern No. 130 is made for ages 4– 6–8 and 8–10 years.

No. 13086

LITTLE BO PEEP is a charmer for a pretty, small girl, with its puff sleeves, dainty lace-edged scalloped skirt and little flower-trimmed hat tied under the chin. Make in a flower print. Pattern No. 13086 is made for ages 4–6, 6–8 and 8–10 years.

MAKING WIGS

The right hair makes all the difference to a fancy dress

WIGS are expensive to buy or hire, and hot and heavy to wear. Fashioned at home from ordinary knitting wool, they are cheap and exceedingly light and comfortable. Coloured "hair" is extremely effective. Generally speaking, most of the pastel shades and some bright colours are becoming to girls, while for men orange, crimson and bottle-green are amusing. Sprinkle the hair or wig of a queen or fairy with some of the iridescent stardust obtained from chemists.

Sew to a Shingle-Cap.

For a foundation, use a well-fitting net shingle-cap. Even easier to sew the wool on to, provided it is in sound condition and fits down well over the ears, is an old hat lining. For the wig itself you will want, according to the style, from two to four 1-oz. hanks of 4-ply knitting wool. Wool ready wound into balls is useless for this purpose.

To make a girl's wig in any style, open out two hanks of wool, without cutting them and loop them over a small table. Spread out the part lying on the table-top smoothly to form a thin, even layer, and then put in the parting with a long embroidery thread in flesh colour.

To do this, start at the end of the hank farthest away. Slip half the thread under the first half-dozen strands of wool. Bring it up and tie it once to the half on the top. Go on knotting and tying each little group of strands together, working towards you, till all the wool is " parted."

Fasten your net-cap firmly round some kind of head-block (a saucepan does very nicely), padding out the flat bottom of the pan with a little tissue paper, so that the cap is kept taut. Then lay the "parted" hanks of wool over the front part of the cap, with the parting at centre front or side.

Working from the parting down to where the ear will be, lightly sew the wool, in thickness of about a dozen strands at a time, down to the cap. Use rather sketchy tacking stitches. They will sink into the wool and be lost. If the wig is for a girl, push the wool, as you stitch, into waves with your fingers.

Put the wig on the wearer to judge where the hanks should be cut. On the left side leave the wool long enough to twist into a small "ear-phone." On the right side cut it much longer, so that the strands, when plaited later, will be long enough to go across the back of the head. Plaiting shortens the wool, so allow for this when cutting.

From the wool cut off, lay aside enough for the right-side ear-phone. Use the rest to fill in the back part of the wig. Do this with loops about twenty strands thick, placing each loop inside the previous one until the space is all filled up. Plait the long end of wool that was allowed for the purpose on the left-hand side, and bring it across the back of the cap, just above the neck, so that it covers the cut ends of the loops.

Plaits, Curls and Buns

If long plaits are wanted, use another hank of wool for each plait, and sew one end in place under each ear-phone, which should be kept as small and flat as possible.

Curls can be fixed in the same way, twisting shorter lengths of wool into spirals and holding them with paste or spirit gum.

A "bun" or a Greek knot are both easily twisted up from a length of wool and sewn or hair-pinned into place.

For a man's wig proceed as described, but lay the wool straight instead of with waves and cut off at the correct length all round.

QUICK QUILTING

*Three charming and original furnishing ideas for which you can quilt
your own fabrics—and a simple way to bedroom cosiness*

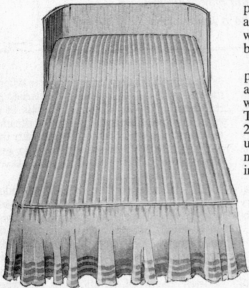

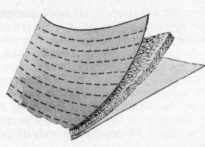

As warm as an eiderdown, the bedcover is
quilted on top only, interlined with wadding
and backed with sheeting

THE charm of quilting lies in its versatility—and the fact that it also provides
warmth, the thick padding giving " body "
to soft furnishings, such as bedcovers. On
these two pages four simple yet different
kinds of quilting stitches are introduced.
Try them all—and then think up some
adaptations of your own.

The Bedcover, which is quilted on the
top only, is interlined with wadding
and backed with sheeting or any suitable
cotton material. The top is made from
warm coating velour, as the purpose of this

particular bedcover it to take the place of
an eiderdown. For a double-bed size, begin
with the top at least 12 in. wider than the
bed, because the quilting takes it up.

Spread your three layers of material in
position on a large table and strongly tack
a line lengthways up the centre of the
work, taking up the three thicknesses.
Tack another line parallel to the first, but
2 in. to the left of it. Continue in this way
until you reach the outer edge of the
material. Tack similar lines at regular 2-in.
intervals on the right of the centre.

Stitch along these lines, either by
machine (using a special quilting foot)
or by hand in stem-stitch or back-stitch.
Trim off top to required size, measuring
over the made-up bed, and allowing for
turnings. Join on gathered or pleated
flounce, which can be in a matching or
contrasting material.

The Chair Cover is interlined in the
same way as the bedcover with wadding,

Little crosses about an inch apart (as seen in
the fabric sample above) are worked on the
material for the chair cover

674

and need only be backed with something very light like butter muslin. Cut out the cover pieces as for an ordinary loose cover, but rather on the large side, then cut the other two layers to match exactly, and tack together with quick all-over tacking. With embroidery thread, work little crosses about 1 in. to 1½ in. apart all over each piece. Then make up cover in usual way.

The Bed Jacket can be cut out from any simple pattern, preferably in silk. Tack together the silk and wadding only and work French knots in an all-over pattern as for the chair. Make up the lining separately, join together the quilted pieces of the bed jacket and hem in the lining.

The Bedroom Stool is made from alternate stripes of plain material and "patch" work. Tack together the patches, using any pretty bits from your workbag, then tack them on to the plain strips. Be careful

This pretty bed jacket is warmly quilted and decorated with French knots in an all-over pattern

Re-cover a bedroom stool in modern patchwork stripes, using up all the colourful scraps from your work basket

to choose material of the same type for your patches — all cotton would be ideal. The important thing is not to mix cottons, silks, rayons and wools. If you do, your cover will not wash and wear so well, as different fabrics require different washing treatments and what suits one might make another run or shrink. Tack the whole to the wadding and back with muslin. Work round all the patches with feather-stitch or cross-stitch and attach to the stool.

HOW TO BE A GOOD KNITTER

Presenting some ideas and hints to help you achieve
the professional touch

KNITTING is an almost essential accomplishment for the housewife with a family to clothe. If you become really expert, you can knit without looking, which makes it the ideal occupation while watching television.

This chapter only aims to present basic ideas and hints to help you achieve the professional touch. It is not intended to teach those who have never knitted before. The easiest way to learn to knit is to get someone to show you how it is done. Then practice will soon make perfect, and perhaps the following pages will add to the pleasure you get out of your new achievement.

Abbreviations

Throughout the patterns in this chapter, the following abbreviations appear:

K.—knit; p.—purl; st.—stitch; sts.—stitches; tog.—together; beg.—begin or beginning; rep.—repeat; sl.—slip; m.—make (this is done by putting the wool over the needle); inc.—increase (by knitting or purling twice into one stitch); dec.—decrease (by knitting or purling two together); p.s.s.o.—pass slipped stitch over; st.st.—stocking stitch, which is knit 1 row, purl 1 row; wl. fwd.—wool forward; wl. bk.—wool back; w.r.n.—wool round needle; w.o.n.—wool over needle; in.—inch.

DESIGNING YOUR OWN JUMPER OR CARDIGAN

Don't be afraid to try your skill at designing your own jumper or cardigan. It's fun and not too difficult if you take a little trouble over it.

The following are basic designs for plain stocking-stitch garments. By using the table of tensions for various wools and needles, you can alter them to suit your own needs. Moreover, you can forsake stocking stitch and branch out into fancy patterns, cables, ribs or a combination of several.

The one essential in all knitting is to get your tension right. You must knit a sample of whatever pattern you have chosen on, say, 20 stitches with the wool and needles which you will be using. Press, then pin this small piece of material flat and measure it both across and up and down. Check the number of stitches you are putting on and see if the tension is right. If it is too tight, use a size larger needles; if too loose, a size smaller. Different wools of the same ply vary and no hard and fast rule can be given. The following is a rough guide:

Crossways Tension

Needles	2-ply wool stitches to in.	3-ply wool stitches to in.	4-ply wool stitches to in.
7	6½	6	5½
8	7	6½	6
9	7½	7	6½
10	8	7½	7
11	8½	8	7½
12	9	8½	8
13	9½	9	8½
14	10	9½	9

The number of rows to the inch depends greatly on both pattern and wool used, and must be measured for each garment made.

To work out the number of stitches needed at the widest point of the garment, divide the total measurement by two. In the case of a 34-in. bust measurement, this would be 17 in. Multiply this by the

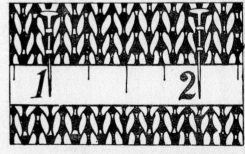

Correct tension is essential. Knit up a sample of your pattern with the wool and needles to be used, press and then measure it carefully

676

Pretty June Thorburn wears a classic hand-knitted twin set in a lovely shade of coral pink. You can knit such a set for yourself, either plain or in a fancy design, simply by adapting our basic pattern

number of stitches indicated on the tension chart for the ply wool and size needles to be used for the main part of the work. For instance, if you use size 10 needles and 2-ply wool, the number would be 136. If, however, you are making a ribbed welt, cast on 20 or 30 stitches less than the number needed for the widest part, namely, 116 or 106.

BASIC JUMPER PATTERN

The following instructions are for a classic jumper, round neck, short sleeves, in stocking stitch. You can make a similar jumper in any stitch, but, before starting, check your tension. It can be knitted in 2-, 3- or 4-ply wool by varying size of needles as indicated. Instructions are in

2-ply wool for 32-in. bust measurement. Changes for 34-, 36-, 38- and 40-in. bust are given in brackets. For other wools, use needles as indicated.

Materials.—2-ply wool—4 (5, 5, 6, 6) oz. 1 pair of needles size 12, 1 pair size 10.

3-ply wool—6 (7, 7, 8, 8) oz.; 1 pair of needles size 13, 1 pair size 11.

4-ply wool—8 (9, 9, 10, 10) oz.; 1 pair of needles size 14, 1 pair size 12.

3 small buttons.

2-ply Tension.—8 sts. to 1 in. over st.st.

Stitches.—Welts, cuffs and neck edgings are in k. 1, p. 1 rib. Remainder of work is in st.st. (k. 1 row, p. 1 row).

Back

With size 12 needles, cast on 112 (120, 128, 136, 144) sts. Work $3\frac{1}{2}$ ($3\frac{1}{2}$, $3\frac{1}{2}$, 4, 4) in. in k. 1, p. 1 rib. Change to size 10 needles and st.st. Work 4 rows. Inc. 1 st. each end of next and every 6th row until there are 132 (140, 148, 156, 164) sts. Continue in st.st. until the jumper measures $12\frac{1}{2}$ (13, $13\frac{1}{2}$, 14, $14\frac{1}{2}$) in. or desired length to armholes. *Shape armholes:* Cast off 5 (6, 7, 8, 9) sts. at beg. of next 2 rows. Dec. 1 each end of every alternate row until there are 104 (108, 112, 116, 120) sts. Continue until armholes measure 5 ($5\frac{1}{4}$, $5\frac{1}{2}$, $5\frac{3}{4}$, 6) in. on the straight. End with p. row. Divide work for back opening. Continue as follows: K. 48 (50, 52, 54, 56) (p. 1, k. 1) 4 times. Turn. Finish this side first. **Next row:** (P. 1, k. 1) 4 times, p. to end. Work 18 rows, keeping the inside edge stitches in k. 1, p. 1 rib. *Shape shoulder:* **Next row** (armhole edge): Cast off 8 (9, 7, 8, 9) sts., work to end of row, keeping last 8 sts. in k. 1, p. 1 rib. Continue work, casting off 8 (8, 9, 9, 9) sts. in alternate rows at armhole edge 3 times. Leave remaining 24 (25, 26, 27, 28) sts. on holder for neck. Join wool to edge of remaining sts. and cast on 8 sts. for underflap of neck opening. (K. 1, p. 1) 4 times, k. to end. Work 20 rows. *Shape shoulder:* Cast off at armhole edge 8 (9, 7, 8, 9) sts. once and 8 (8, 9, 9, 9) sts. 3 times. Leave remaining 24 (25, 26, 27. 28) sts. on holder for neck.

Front

Cast on and work as for back until armhole measures $4\frac{3}{4}$ (5, $5\frac{1}{4}$, $5\frac{1}{2}$, $5\frac{3}{4}$) in. measured on the straight. End with p. row. *Shape neck:* K. 44 (45, 46, 47, 48). Turn.

Finish this side first. * Cast off at this edge 2 sts. 3 times. Then dec. 1 at same edge every alternate row until 32 (33, 34, 35, 36) sts. remain. Work 4 rows. *Shape shoulder:* Cast off 8 (9, 7, 8, 9) sts. at armhole edge once and 8 (8, 9, 9, 9) sts. 3 times. Sl. centre 16 (18, 20, 22, 24) sts. on to holder, or large safety-pin or piece of wool. Join wool to neck edge of remaining sts. K. to end of row. **Next row:** P. Then work other side as from *.

Sleeves

With size 12 needles, cast on 88 (92, 96, 100, 104) sts. Work 1 in. in k. 1, p. 1 rib. Change to size 10 needles and st.st. Work 4 rows. Inc. 1 st. each end of next and every 4th row until there are 98 (102, 106, 110, 114) sts. Work until sleeve measures 4 ($4\frac{1}{2}$, 5, 5, 5) in. or desired seam length. *Shape top:* Cast off 5 (6, 7, 8, 9) sts. at beg. of next 2 rows. Dec. 1 each end of every k. row until there are 40 sts. Cast off 3 at beg. of next 6 rows. Cast off.

Neckband

Sew shoulder seams together. With the right side of work towards you and size 12 needles, k. up sts. round neck; 24 (25, 26, 27, 28) from holder at left back, 32 down left side, 16 (18, 20, 22, 24) from holder at centre front, 32 up right side and 24 (25, 26, 27, 28) from remaining holder. This will give you 128 (132, 136, 140, 144) sts. in all. Work in k. 1, p. 1 rib for 6 rows. Cast off in rib.

To Make Up

Press st.st. lightly on wrong side under damp cloth, making certain that you do not stretch or shrink it. Using oversewing for rib and back stitch for rest of work, set in sleeves. Sew side and sleeve seams. Sew down underlap. Crochet, or embroider three small loops. Sew on buttons opposite. Press seams.

BASIC CARDIGAN PATTERN

The following, like the jumper pattern, is a basic pattern made in k. 1, p. 1 rib and st.st. It can be varied in the same way as the jumper, and materials can be changed by changing the size of the needles. Instructions are for 2-ply wool, bust size 32 in., with changes for sizes 34-, 36-, 38- and 40-in. in brackets.

Materials.—2-ply wool—6 (7, 7, 8, 8) oz.; 1 pair of needles size 12, 1 pair size 10.

3-ply wool—8 (9, 9, 10, 10) oz.; 1 pair needles size 13, 1 pair size 11.

4-ply wool—10 (11, 11, 12, 12) oz.; 1 pair needles size 12, 1 pair size 14.

1-in. wide ribbon for facing fronts.

9 buttons.

2-ply Tension.—8 sts. to 1 in. over st.st.

Stitches.—Welts, cuffs and neck edgings are in k. 1, p. 1 rib. Remainder of work is in st.st. (k. 1 row, p. 1 row).

Back

With size 12 needles, cast on 112 (120, 128, 136, 144) sts. Work 3½ in. in k. 1, p. 1 rib. Change to size 10 needles and st.st. Work 4 rows. Inc. 1 each end of next and every 6th row until there are 134 (142, 150, 158, 164) sts. Work until back measures 13 (13½, 14, 14½, 15) in. or desired length to armholes. *Shape armholes:* Cast off 5 (6, 7, 8, 9) sts. at beg. of next 2 rows. Dec. 1 each end of next 3 rows, then every alternate row until 106 (110, 114, 118, 122) sts. remain. Work until armholes are 7¼ (7½, 7¾, 8, 8¼) in. measured on straight. *Shape shoulders:* Cast off at beg. of next and following rows 9 (7, 8, 9, 10) sts. twice and 8 (9, 9, 9, 9) sts. 6 times. Sl. remaining 40 (42, 44, 46, 48) sts. on to holder for neck.

Left Front

With size 12 needles, cast on 60 (64, 68, 72, 76) sts. Work 3½ in. in k. 1, p. 1 rib. Change to size 10 needles and st.st. Work 4 rows. Inc. 1 st. at beg. of next and every 6th row until there are 72 (76, 80, 84, 88) sts. Work until front measures same as back up to the armholes, ending at side edge. *Shape armholes:* Cast off 6 (7, 8, 9, 10) sts. at beg. of next row. Dec. 1 at same edge every row 4 times, then every alternate row until 59 (61, 63, 65, 67) sts. remain. Work until armhole is 5 (5¼, 5½, 5¾, 6) in. measured on the straight, ending with a k. row. *Shape neck:* Cast off at this edge 12 (13, 14, 15, 16) sts. once, 3 once and 2 three times. Dec. 1 at same edge,

CASTING OFF TWO NEEDLES TOGETHER

Place the two needles side by side and treat as one left-hand needle. Place point of right-hand needle under 1st stitch on both left-hand needles, knit the two stitches as one. Repeat on next two stitches, draw the second stitch on right-hand needle over the first as in ordinary casting-off

every alternate row until 33 (34, 35, 36, 37) sts. remain. Work 4 rows. *Shape shoulder:* Cast off at armhole edge 9 (7, 8, 9, 10) sts. once and 8 (9, 9, 9, 9) sts. 3 times.

Right Front

Work as for left front, reversing shapings and remembering to make buttonholes. Make first buttonhole at centre front when work measures 1½ (¼, 1, 1¾, ½) in., as follows: Work 4, cast off 3, continue to end of row. In next row, cast on 3 above cast-off sts. of preceding row. Work 8 more buttonholes 2 (2¼, 2¼, 2¼, 2½) in. apart.

Sleeves

With size 12 needles, cast on 56 (60, 64, 68, 72) sts. Work 3 in. in k. 1, p. 1 rib. **Next row:** P. 5 (7, 9, 9, 11) sts. * Inc. in next st., p. 8 (8, 8, 9, 9) sts., rep. from * to last 6 (8, 10, 9, 11) sts. Inc. in next st. P. to end. There should now be 62 (66, 70, 74, 78) sts. on needle. Change to size 10 needles and st.st. Work 8 rows. Inc 1 at each end of next and every 8th row, until there are 100 (104, 108, 112, 116) sts. Work until the sleeve measures 18½ in. or desired seam length. *Shape top:* Cast off 5 (6, 7, 8, 9) sts. at beg. of next 2 rows. Dec. 1 at each end of every k. row until 40 sts. remain. Cast off 3 at beg. of next 6 rows. Cast off.

Neckband

Sew up shoulder seams. With right side of work towards you and size 12 needles, k. up 42 (43, 44, 45, 46) sts. from right side of neck, 40 (42, 44, 46, 48) sts. across back and 42 (43, 44, 45, 46) down left side. There should now be 124 (128, 132, 136, 140) sts. on needle. Work in k. 1, p. 1 rib for 8 rows. Cast off in rib.

To Make Up

Press st.st. lightly on wrong side under damp cloth, making certain that you do not stretch or shrink it. Using oversewing for rib, and back stitch for rest of work, set in sleeves. Sew side and sleeve seams. Face centre front edges with ribbon. Cut buttonholes in facing and buttonhole stitch ribbon and knitting together. Press seams. Sew on buttons.

Front Bands

These are always better knitted in one with the garment and not sewn on afterwards. They should be finer than the rest of the work, so use needles two sizes smaller for the front band stitches only. When finished, always face the front bands with ribbon of the same width. Cut buttonholes through facing and buttonhole stitch through wool and facing round the buttonholes.

Picking Up

Always pick up through the double cast-off edge, or you will have an untidy line. Do not cast off stitches at neck when work-ing main part of garment if these are afterwards to be knitted up. Leave on stitch-holder, safety-pin, spare needle or piece of wool.

Casting On

If a firm edge is required, cast on as follows: Make a loop and slip on to left-hand needle. K. into this loop and sl. st. thus made on to left-hand needle. Then k. between sts., slipping each st. on to left-hand needle until you have sufficient sts. If a loose edge is required, cast on by k. into each preceding st. and slipping on to left-hand needle.

Casting Off

Always cast off in the st. you are using, i.e. k. for plain knitting or k. row of st.st.; p. for purl or purl row of st.st.; rib when working ribbing.

Knitting Sleeves

The knitting of sleeves, particularly long ones, is most knitters' bugbear. It is far more satisfactory to knit the two sleeves at the same time, as the increases are then exactly the same. It is also far less tedious. Cast on two separate sets of stitches on one pair of needles, using two balls of wool and then proceed in accordance with your pattern, knitting each sleeve in turn.

Seaming Knitted Garments

The finishing off of knitted jumpers, dresses, etc., is all-important. If badly done, it can ruin beautiful work. An

CASTING ON WITH TWO NEEDLES

| Make loop, place it on left-hand needle, place point of right-hand needle through loop | Passing wool from ball over first finger of right hand, wrap round point of right-hand needle | Draw loop on point of right-hand needle through stitch on left-hand needle | Place stitch from right-hand needle on to left-hand needle. Repeat as required |

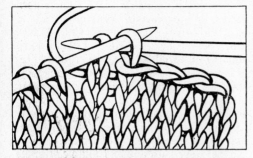

To cast off, knit 2 stitches, place point of left-hand needle in second stitch and draw this over first stitch. Knit next stitch and repeat until one stitch remains, draw loop through this

ordinary back-stitch seam is the most satisfactory method, but ribbing should always be overcast, care being taken to keep it absolutely even so that the right side of the seam maintains the rib.

Neck and Sleeve Edgings

The most usual form of edging is, of course, rib. This is generally either k. 1, p. 1, or k. 2, p. 2. There are, however, other methods of finishing necks and sleeves, and the picot edge is one of the most popular.

Picot Edging

Work the required depth of neck or sleeve band in st.st. For picot row (knitted on an even number of sts.), * m. 1, k. 2 tog. Rep. from * to end of row. Then work another strip of st.st. the same depth as the neck or sleeve band. Cast off loosely. Fold over on picot line and sl. st. loosely.

Hems

In some patterns,

hems are substituted for welts and cuffs. This idea is worth trying if you are designing your own jumper, dress or cardigan. Knitting the hem up is far more satisfactory than merely sewing. Work the required depth for the hem. Mark the next row by carrying a thread through it which can be pulled out afterwards. Work the same depth as that already done and turn the hem up at the

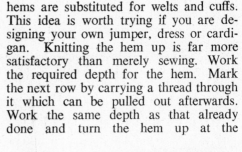

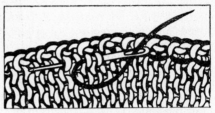

To make up with a Back Stitch Seam, place the two pieces together (left), right side. to right side, and pin. Make a small stitch, then insert needle ¼ in. along pinned seam, draw through; * insert into end of last stitch and bring out ¼ in. along. Repeat from *. Press seam open

marked row. Hold the cast-on edge together with the needle holding the sts. and proceed as follows: * Put the needle into the 1 st. on left-hand needle, then into the corresponding st. of the cast-on edge and k. the two sts. together. Repeat from * to end. When the hem is made, you proceed as usual with the work.

Pressing

Unless the pattern indicates to the contrary, all work should be lightly pressed before being sewn up, except for rib, which

To knit a hem, work required depth, then hold cast-on edge together with needle holding sts., put needle into 1st st. on left-hand needle and of cast-on edge and k. 2 sts. together

should never be pressed. Iron on the wrong side under a damp cloth. If the garment has to be stretched to a certain size, pin out wrong side up on your board or table to required measurements. Place a damp cloth over and press lightly. Leave pinned until the pieces are dry.

"COURTURIER" KNITTING

Have you ever longed to knit a blouse or dress like those you see in pictures of Paris collections? It is not nearly so difficult as it sounds and, with practice, you will probably become quite daring.

Choose **an ordinary** blouse paper pattern, such as you would use for cotton or silk, sticking to something very simple at first. Then decide in what pattern you will knit it. Measure the back and front of the blouse from the top of the shoulder to the bottom of the pattern and across at the widest point. Do the same with the sleeve pattern. Then, using the tension measurements given on p. 676 as a guide, cast on sufficient stitches to make a strip as wide as the widest point in your garment. Knit an absolutely straight strip in pattern until it is the same length as the front measurement. Cast off loosely. Repeat for the back. Make two strips for sleeves in the same way.

Press the four strips lightly under a damp cloth, unless you are working in rib, when no pressing is necessary. Lay your pattern pieces on the various knitted strips and tack very firmly in place with small stitches. Machine through the edge of the pattern and the material all the way round. Repeat, so that you have two rows of machine stitching. Pull pattern away. Using sharp scissors, cut all round outside stitching. When this is done, your garment is ready to make up in the ordinary way. Edges may be hemmed or, if you prefer, stitches can be picked up and, if suitable, ribbing welts, neckbands and cuffs added. This method ensures a really good fit. It is impossible to give exact quantities of wool, but, providing the pattern from which the blouse is cut is simple, it will take about 1 oz. more than the amount given in any ordinary knitting pattern for similar garment. If you are skilled enough to work in a fancy stitch without a pattern, or are using plain stocking stitch, garter stitch, etc., a blouse will take about:

5–6 oz. for short sleeves, 7–8 oz. for long sleeves in 2-ply wool; 7–8 oz. for short sleeves; 9–10 oz. for long sleeves in 3-ply wool; 9–10 oz. for short sleeves, 11–12 oz. for long sleeves in 4-ply wool.

Some Patterns to Try

The following is a small selection of patterns you may like to try, using either the basic jumper or cardigan pattern, or for your first attempt at "couturier" knitting.

BACK CABLE STITCH

CABLE

Cable pattern is a firm favourite in its various forms, but, for some reason, inexperienced knitters hesitate to undertake it. Actually, it is little harder than an ordinary rib.

Fundamentally, cable pattern is always the same. It consists of a basic rib of whatever width is desired, the stitches being "twisted" at regular intervals. It is advisable to have a *short* spare double-pointed needle in the same size as the pair you are using. Cable may be "twisted" in front or behind the work, the effect being slightly different. Some patterns alternate the two for an interesting effect.

Left, Fisherman's Knit, and above, showing how to purl into stitch one row below, at same time slipping off stitch above

The original was done in 4-ply wool on size 10 needles.

FRONT CABLE

Cast on a number of sts. divisible by 11. Then cast on 1 extra st.

1st row: * K.. 1, p. 2, k. 6, p. 2. Rep. from * across row, ending k. 1.

2nd row: * P. 1, k. 2, p. 6, k. 2. Rep. from * across row, ending p. 1.

3rd row: As 1st.

4th row: As 2nd.

5th row: * K. 1, p. 2, sl. the next 3 sts. to spare needle, and drop to front of work, k. 3, bring back sts. on spare needle and k. 3, p. 2. Rep. from * across row, ending k. 1.

6th row: As 2nd.

BACK CABLE

Cast on a number of sts. divisible by 15. Then cast on 12 more.

1st row: P. 1, * k. 10, p. 2, k. 1, p. 2. Rep. from *, ending k. 10, p. 1.

2nd row: K. 1, * p. 10, k. 2, p. 1, k. 2. Rep. from *, ending p. 10, k. 1.

Work these 2 rows 4 times more.

11th row: P. 1, * sl. next 5 sts. on to spare needle and leave at back of work, k. 5. Bring forward sts. on spare needle and k. 5, p. 2, k. 1, p. 2. Rep. from *, ending p. 1.

12th row: As 2nd.

DUAL CABLE STITCH

Cast on a number of sts. divisible by 14. Add 1 more.

1st row: * K. 1, p. 2, k. 4, p. 1, k. 4, p. 2. Rep. from * across row, ending k. 1.

2nd row: * P. 1, k. 2, p. 4, k. 1, p. 4, k. 2. Rep. from * across row, ending p. 1.

Rep. these 2 rows twice more.

7th row: * K. 1, p. 2, sl. next 2 sts. to spare needle and drop to back of work, k. 2, bring forward sts. on spare needle and k. 2, p. 1, sl. next 2 sts. to spare needle and drop to front of work, k. 2, bring back sts. on spare needle and k. 2, p. 2. Rep. from * across row, ending k. 1.

8th row: As 2nd.

FISHERMAN'S KNIT

Cardigans or sweaters knitted in this stitch in double knitting wool are both warm and smart. The wool being so thick, they are quick to do. The original of the photograph was knitted in double knitting wool on size 8 needles. The pattern consists of only one row.

Cast on an even number of sts.

If you are not working a garment which has a welt, k. 1 row before beginning pattern.

Pattern row: Sl. 1 knitwise. * K. into back of next st., p. into following st. but through the loop of the row below, *at* *same time* slipping off st. above. Rep. from * to last st., k. 1.

Repeat this row throughout.

When testing tension for above, cast on 11 sts. Work in st.st. (1 row k., 1 row p.) for 15 rows. Cast off. Press. The piece should be 2 in. square. If it is more, use a size smaller needles: if it is less, use a size larger needles.

BLACKBERRY STITCH

BLACKBERRY STITCH

Cast on a number of sts. divisible by 4.

1st row: P.

2nd row: * (K. 1, p. 1, k. 1) all into 1 st., p. 3 tog. Rep. from * to end.

3rd row: P.

4th row: * P. 3 tog. (k. 1, p. 1, k. 1) all into 1 st. Rep. from * to end.

These 4 rows form the pattern.

The original of the photograph was knitted in 4-ply wool on size 7 needles.

OPENWORK STRIPE

Cast on a number of sts. divisible by 6. Then cast on 4 more.

1st row: K. 3, * (k. 2 tog., m. 1) twice, k. 2. Rep. from * to last st., k. 1.

2nd row: P. 3, * (p. 2 tog., m. 1) twice, p. 2. Rep. from * to last st., p. 1.

The original of the photograph was knitted in 2-ply wool on size 10 needles.

OPENWORK STRIPE

BASKET WEAVE

Cast on a number of sts. divisible by 16.

1st row: * K. 8, (k. 1, p. 1) 4 times. Rep. from * to end of row.

Repeat this row 7 times.

9th row: * (K. 1, p. 1) 4 times, k. 8. Rep. from * to end of row. Repeat this row 7 times.

These 16 rows make up the pattern.

The original was knitted in 2-ply wool on size 10 needles.

DIAMOND CENTRE

Cast on a number of sts. divisible by 6. Then cast on 2 extra sts.

BASKET WEAVE

1st row: K. 2, * m. 1, sl. 1, k. 1, p.s.s.o, k. 1, k. 2 tog., m. 1, k. 1. Rep. from * across the row.

2nd row: P.

3rd row: K. 3, * m. 1, sl. 1, k. 2 tog., p.s.s.o, m. 1, k. 3. Repeat from * across the row, ending k. 2.

4th row: P.

These 4 rows make up the pattern and would look well combined with alternate blocks of, say, 16 rows st.st., 8 rows pattern.

The original of the photograph was knitted in 1-ply wool on size 10 needles. 2- or 3-ply wool would also be suitable.

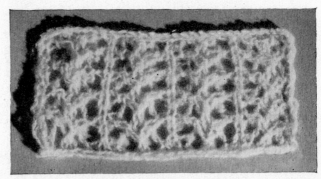

DIAMOND CENTRE

LATTICE WORK

Cast on a number of sts. divisible by 7.

1st row: * P. 1, w.o.n., sl. 1, k. 1, p.s.s.o., k. 1, k. 2 tog., w.r.n., p. 1. Rep. from * to end.

2nd row: * K. 1, p. 5, k. 1. Rep. from * to end.

3rd row: * P. 1, k. 1, wl. fwd., sl. 1, k. 2 tog., p.s.s.o., wl. fwd., k. 1, p. 1. Rep. from * to end.

LATTICE WORK

4th row: * K. 1, p. 5, k. 1. Rep. from * to end.

The picture is of material knitted in 3-ply wool on size 8 needles.

FEATHER STITCH

Cast on a number of sts. divisible by 12. Then cast on 6 extra sts.

1st row: K.   **2nd row:** K.

3rd row: K. 1, (k. 2 tog.) twice, * (wl. fwd. k. 1) 4 times, (k. 2 tog.) 4 times; repeat from * to last 9 sts. (wl. fwd. k. 1) 4 times, (k. 2 tog.) twice, k. 1.

4th row: P.

The original of the photograph was knitted in 1-ply wool on size 10 needles.

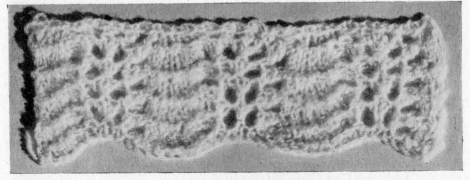

FEATHER STITCH

All diagrams in this chapter specially prepared by Patons & Baldwins

KNITTING MACHINES FOR THE HOME

All you need to know about choosing and using these gadgets, invaluable for making knitted garments at speed

by LILIAN K. DONAT

DURING the last fifteen years a new gadget has been introduced into many homes: the hand-knitting machine. Though, strangely enough, the first knitting machine was invented in 1589 by a certain Reverend W. Lee, it was only in the nineteenth century that the first industrial knitting machines were introduced. To-day's hand-knitting machines, derived from their much more complicated industrial predecessors, are a comparatively simple though efficient equivalent of hand knitting.

There is no more need to be mechanically minded to use a hand-knitting machine than to use a sewing machine, and they are invaluable in households where there is a demand for knitted garments, such as underwear, pullovers, jackets, socks, etc.

This does not mean that an equal quality of work will be achieved by everyone using the same type of machine. After all, those who use the same sewing machine and the same pattern do not produce garments of the same quality. But modern machines have simplified working considerably and, after a few hours' practice, the knitter becomes remarkably expert.

By a flick of a dial any type of wool or yarn may be used, from baby wool to twine, from the lightest to the heaviest, the finest to the coarsest.

Fitting and Finishing

Many manufacturers issue knitting designs, but most magazine and hand-knitting leaflet patterns can be worked by machine, provided the correct wool is used. Changing the ply is a common fault which can produce most unfortunate results. Another mistaken idea is that tailored garments must be sewn up by hand, the seams being done with the knitting wool. This often spoils a really tailored look.

If a sewing machine is available, it should be used for sewing the seams of all knitted garments—the result is a much firmer finish and straighter seams. Naturally nobody would machine babies' garments or articles knitted in very fine wools, but for heavier items it is preferable. A hand- or hand-machine-knitted garment should always be tacked and fitted like any other garment. Though measurements may be the same superficially, there are no two people with exactly the same figure, and it is worth while taking the little extra trouble. After all, your knitted fabric is an expensive piece of material, counting the price of wool and labour involved—so why not treat it as such?

Machine Knitting Speeds

The working speed of hand machine knitting varies with the operator. On fast machines fifty rows can be knitted in a minute by the experienced knitter, but even the slower types of machine are about ten times as fast as hand knitting.

Most modern machines have automatic row counters and tension adjusters. On some machines ribbing can be done automatically; for others a separate ribbing adjustment can be bought. Most machines are fitted with rubber pads, so that they can be used on any flat surface. There are two types of machine available to the home knitter. Before deciding which one to buy, it is advisable to see several in use, as what suits one person may not suit another.

Types Available

The **single-bed machine,** which is the cheapest and most popular, is certainly the easiest for the beginner. This machine has needles with a latched hook on the knitting end. The carriage, travelling from one side to the other, knits one row of stitches with each movement.

KNITTING MACHINES FOR THE HOME

The only snag is that it cannot be used for ribbing, but a ribbing attachment can be bought separately.

The working is very simple, as there are no combs or other attachments, and each row is knitted by the simple, one-handed, one-stroke movement of the arm.

These machines have as a rule about 168 needles and it is possible to knit two pieces of the garment at one and the same time if they are not too wide; for instance, two sleeves can be worked, row by row, in the same operation.

Increasing and decreasing are done by adjustment of the needles, which takes only a moment.

Many patterns, based on stocking stitch, can be produced at great speed. Though tuition is given free with all types of machine at the time of purchase, the use of the machine can be learned from the book of instruction given free with each machine.

The **double-bed machines,** based on the same principle as the single-bed machines, can do automatic ribbing, cir-

The Knitmaster "Super-Plus" 7500 is truly one-hand automatic knitting. It has 203 needles and knits over 10,000 stitches a minute

cular knitting and a kind of weaving stitch, suitable for various purposes. They claim to be able to knit up to 15,000 stitches per minute. The tension can be very fine, but most thicknesses of wool can be used. The knitting looks more like the work of an industrial machine and cannot be mistaken for hand knitting. To learn the technique is a little more difficult than for the other machine, but six lessons are usually sufficient.

The Knitmaster "Ambassador" is entirely British made and the cheapest on the market—a knitting machine within the reach of all

Details of the three leading machines sold in this country are given below.

The KNITMASTER is a British machine of wide range. The AMBASSADOR model is the cheapest on the market. A RIBMASTER attachment to fit this machine makes it into the equivalent of a double-bed machine. This can be bought separately at any time and is a useful addition when the beginner has become really proficient.

For the more ambitious, there is the KNITMASTER "SUPER-PLUS" 6500 with 169 needles, working 50 rows and more than 8,000 stitches per minute.

Also the KNITMASTER "SUPER-PLUS" 7500 with 203 needles, working 50 rows and more than 10,000 stitches per minute. Ribmaster attachments are available to suit both these machines.

There are no combs, weights or clamps, and the machines are fully guaranteed for twelve months. All-metal, unbreakable needle-bed and an automatic wool dispenser are two important features and it is claimed that the result given is as good as perfect hand knitting.

The PASSAP AUTOMATIC is a Swiss machine with 201 needles, and their close setting—seven needles to the inch—ensures a soft, firm fabric. Its Automatic Lock incorporates a fool-proof wool feed, ensuring perfect automatic knitting of 201 stitches in one movement. The row counter not only counts forward, it can also set back row by row, or reset at zero by moving a lever. It has a tool tray which fits in any one of three positions, so that your tools are always where you want them, and feather combs ensure that end stitches are perfectly knitted. A ribbing attachment to fit this machine is obtainable.

A more expensive model—the PASSAP DUOMATIC, has an automatic patterning mechanism and, the makers claim, thinks for you!

The GIROTEX MULTIMATIC is a double-bed machine of German manufacture, and is available with an electric motor as an optional extra. The six-position racking lever, which is pre-set, enables the knitter to produce an infinite range of fully automatic patterns. There is no limit to the variety of stitches which can be knitted, and because of its versatility many of these are produced automatically.

It can be swiftly and easily converted to enable a row of up to 401 stitches to be knitted in one movement, thus covering an immense range of extra-wide fabrics, such as rugs and blankets, to be knitted.

Most of these machines knit an ounce of wool in one minute—it is clear that though the knitting machine will not oust hand knitting, it is a welcome newcomer.

A few of the wide range of stitches done by the Passap Automatic, a machine of Swiss manufacture

DESIGNS FOR MACHINE KNITTING

A selection of garments for men, women and children and
a pretty table mat, to enable you to practise your new skill

Abbreviations used throughout: K. = knit.
Beg. = beginning. Dec. = decrease. Rep. =
repeat.

MATINÉE COAT

For 4-10 months

THIS little Raglan coat has a small yoke
with picot edging along all the borders
and a tiny upright collar.

Materials: 3 balls Wendy Baby Wool 3-
ply. ¾ yd. 1 in. wide silk ribbon to tie a
bow in front (not shown in the photograph).

Measurements: Chest 24 in. (this is a loose-
fitting coat), length 10 in., sleeve seams 7
in.

Tension: On Record Handknitting
Machine Screw Type first short line, on
Lever Type No. 2. 8 stitches and 12 rows
to 1 in. The jacket is worked on the stocking stitch comb.

Back: Cast on 120 stitches. K. 8 rows.
9th row: Put 2nd stitch on to the 3rd, 4th
on the 5th and so on to the end of the row.
K. 8 rows. Turn up hem and k. across and
back.

Start **Pattern:** *1st row:*
* Skip 5 stitches. Put
the 6th and 8th stitch
on to the 7th. * Rep.
from * to * to the end of
the row. K. across and
back.

3rd row: Put 6th on
5th and 8th on 9th,
again shifting the holes
to left and right, away
from the centre. K.
across and back.

5th row: Put the left
hole-stitch to the left
and the right to the
right. Repeat to the end
of the row. K. across
and back.

7th row: Work as for the 3rd row. Shift
sts. again and in the 9th row you will
have 5 stitches between 2 holes and 3
stitches together on 1 needle as in the 1st
row, but the pattern has shifted to the left.
Rep. pattern twice, beg. with the 3rd row,
to the next centre point (3 stitches on 1
needle) (see 9th row).

Work in stocking stitch for 46 rows.

Shape Armholes: At the beg. of the next
8 rows cast off 2 stitches. Knit 2 rows.
At the beg. of the next 40 rows dec. 1
stitch, but after the 20th decrease work as
follows: Remove work from the machine
on to a spare knitting needle and put it back
in the following way to make **Yoke:** The
first 8 stitches on 8 needles,* 2 stitches on
to the needle.* Rep. from * to * until
only 8 stitches are left. Put the last 8
stitches on to 1 needle each. Continue to
work until the 40 decs. are finished. Put
the remaining stitches on to a stitchholder.

Fronts: Both can be worked at the same
time, using 2 balls of wool. Instructions
are given for one side only, and the other

A dainty little matinée coat
for boy or girl, with stand-
up collar and fancy border

side is worked in reverse. Cast on 60 stitches. K. 8 rows. Continue as for back, keeping 4 stitches for front edge, until the whole pattern has been finished as for back. Then pattern is worked across 24 stitches only. When work measures the same as back, shape **Armhole:** At the beg. of every other row cast off 2 stitches twice and 1 stitch 22 times. After the 12th decrease take off 30 stitches (beg. at the armhole), and put them on to a spare needle. Put them back 3 stitches on to each needle. In the same row start shaping the **Neck** while continuing to decrease at the armhole. For neck cast off at the beg. of every alternate row as follows: 5 stitches once, 3 stitches once, 2 stitches once and 1 stitch until the 20 decreases at armhole are finished. Cast off.

Sleeves: Cast on 48 stitches. Work as for the back until lace pattern is finished; then continue in stocking stitch. Increase 1 stitch at the beg. and end of every 6th row until there are 60 stitches altogether. Work straight until sleeve measures 7 in. **Shape Top:** At the beg. of the next 18 rows cast off 2 stitches. At the beg. of the next and following rows cast off 1 stitch. When only 3 stitches are left, cast off.

Neck: Pick up 19 stitches along neck of left front, the stitches of the back from the stitchholder, and 19 stitches along right front. K. 8 rows. 9th row: As 9th row at the beg. of back. K. 8 rows. Cast off loosely.

Front Border: From neck to bottom edge of coat pick up 68 stitches. K. 2 rows. 3rd row: As 9th row back. K. 6 rows. Cast off. Work border on other front in the same way. **Making Up:** Fold over the neck border along the line with holes and sew on inside. Do the same with front borders. Sew up sleeve seams and insert Raglan sleeves. Sew on ribbon for bow.

Made in crochet cotton, this elegant table mat can be used on tray or trolley or as a place mat for the dinner table

TABLE MAT
In cotton and lace stitch

Materials: 1 ball Coats Crochet Cotton No. 10.

Measurements: 18 in. × 13 in.

Tension: On Record Hand Knitting Machine Screw Type 2nd short line, on Lever Type No. 5. The mat is worked on the garter stitch comb. Cast on 81 stitches. K. 10 rows. 11th row: Mark centre stitch (41st stitch) and shift stitches as follows: Towards the left: 40th on 39th, 38th on 37th, 34th on 33rd, 32nd on 31st, 18th on 19th, 16th on 17th, 12th on 13th, and 10th on 11th. Do the same towards the right. Knit across pattern row. 12th row: Garter stitch. 13th row: All the stitches to the left of the hole-stitch which have been shifted to the left in the previous pattern row are to be shifted again to the left. Those shifted to the right are shifted again to the right. 14th row: Garter stitch. Rep. rows 13 and 14 until 3 stitches meet on 1 needle in 2 places of the 23rd row. 24th row: Garter stitch. 25th row: Reverse pattern; this means that all the stitches which have been shifted to the left must now be shifted to the right and vice versa until the centre pattern is closed again (see row 23). Continue in the same way until 4 complete centre patterns have been worked. Make 10 rows in garter sitch. Cast off. Using the hand tool, work all around the mat with double crochet, making 1 double crochet for each stitch, 2 double crochet at the corner. Close the round by working 1 slip stitch into the first double crochet. Make 1 chain.

2nd row: * Make 1 treble into third double crochet of previous row; 1 chain; make a second treble into the same double crochet. Make 4 chain, slip stitch into the top of the treble to make a picot. Make 1 treble, 1 chain, 1 treble, 1 chain into the same double crochet as before, miss 2 double crochet, make 1 double crochet into the next. Make 4 chain, 1 slip stitch on top of the double crochet to form a picot.*

Rep. from * to * all round the mat. Break off cotton.

THE MAYFAIR
Man's embroidered pullover

THIS pullover is very simple to make, as only the horizontal lines are knitted in and the vertical ones are embroidered in Swiss stocking stitch when all parts are finished.

Materials: 15 oz. Emu Scotch 4-ply fingering in yellow, ½ oz. each brown and green, 1 set No. 12 knitting needles, 1 pair No. 11 knitting needles.

Measurements: Length: 23 in., sleeve (under arm) 19½ in., chest 40 in.

The horizontal lines of the Mayfair pullover (right) are knitted in, the vertical ones embroidered on afterwards in Swiss stocking stitch, as shown in the diagrams below

Tension: For the rib No. 3½, for the other part of the work No. 4 on some machines. 8 stitches and 11 rows to 1 in.

Maximum number of stitches: 168.

Front: With yellow wool cast on 139 stitches. Work in rib, k. 2, p. 2, for 30 rows. Put work on No. 11 knitting needles. Work the next two rows by hand as follows: K. 6, increase 1 stitch into the next.* K. 13, increase 1 stitch into the next.* Rep. from * to * 8 times, k. 6. *Next row:* P. Put the work on to the machine and set at main tension. *3rd row:* K. 1 yellow, k. 1 green. Rep. this to the end of the row. Break off green. K. 3 rows yellow. Increase 1 stitch at the beg. and end of next row. K. 5 rows. *13th row:* Increase 1 stitch at beg. and end of row. *14th row:* K. across. *15th row:* K. 1 yellow, 1 brown. Be careful that the brown stitches in this row are exactly above the green stitches in the former pattern row. Rep. this pattern to the end of the row. Continue the increases at beg. and end of every 6th row and work next pattern

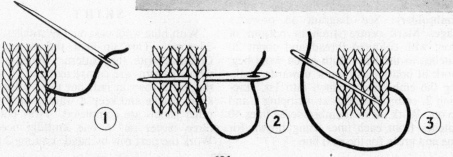

with the green on the 33rd row, counting from brown pattern. Work brown-yellow row 12 rows after this. These colour rows are repeated throughout the whole pullover and sleeves.

When you have 168 stitches altogether, continue to work straight until the front measures 14½ in. **Shape Armholes:** At the beg. of the next and every following row cast off: 6 stitches twice, 4 stitches twice, 2 stitches 4 times, and 1 stitch continuously until there are 130 stitches left. When the work measures 16½ in., divide in half. Work both sides separately, using a second ball of wool for the left-hand side, then increase 1 stitch in the 8th row at the **Armhole.** Rep. increase 6 times. At the same time decrease at neck 1 stitch every other row 20 times. Then decrease 1 stitch every 3rd row 8 times. Work neck straight to the end. After 7th increase at the armhole, k. 10 rows straight. **Shape Shoulders:** For each shoulder cast off at the beg. of every other row 8 stitches 5 times. Cast off the remaining stitches.

Back: Work in the same way as the front without shaping of neck. For shaping shoulders cast off at the beg. of every row as follows: 8 stitches 10 times, 4 stitches twice. Cast off the remaining stitches.

Sleeves: Cast on 70 stitches. Work in k. 2, p. 2 rib for 30 rows. Change to main tension. Start pattern in the 3rd row after ribbing. Increase 1 stitch at beg. and end of every 6th row until there are 122 stitches altogether. Work straight until sleeve measures 19½ in. **Shape Top of Sleeve:** At the beg. of every row cast off as follows: 6 stitches twice, 4 stitches twice, 2 stitches twice, 1 stitch 6 times. Work 6 rows straight. Cast off 1 stitch at the beg. of the next 30 rows. Cast off 2 stitches at the beg. of next 20 rows. Cast off 3 stitches at the beginning of the next 2 rows. Cast off remaining stitches.

Make second sleeve in the same way.

Embroidery: See diagram on previous page. Mark centre stitch at bottom of front with coloured thread and count 20 stitches to the left. With green wool beg. work at bottom and work upwards, making the embroidered stitch into 1st, skipping 2, embroidering next, skipping 2 and so on. Work the next embroidered lines 40 stitches from each line, using brown for one and green for the next line.

Mark the centre stitch of sleeve and embroider 1st line along this in green and 40 stitches to each side in brown.

Making Up: Block and press every part. Sew up shoulders. *Neck Band:* With No. 12 needles pick up 62 stitches along the front on one side, 62 stitches along the other side and 56 stitches along the back. Work in k. 2, p. 2 rib as follows: Decrease 1 stitch each side of centre front in every other round. Work 12 rounds altogether. Cast off loosely. Sew up side and sleeve seams. Sew sleeves into place.

GIRL'S PULLOVER AND SKIRT

Age 6-7 years

THIS charming outfit can be worn several ways—with a blouse underneath, tied with a bow, or with an open neck, according to taste. The skirt can also be worn separately. The vertical lines are embroidered in chain stitch.

Materials: Wakefield's Springtime 3-ply fingering in the following colours: 8 oz. navy blue, 2 oz. green, and 1 oz. each red, grey and white. A pair No. 10 knitting needles. 20 in. elastic for the waist.

Measurements: Length of pullover 13½ in. Length of sleeve 14 in. Chest 28 in. Length of skirt 14 in. Waist 20 in.

Maximum number of stitches: 139.

Tension: 7½ stitches and 11 rows per in. No. 2 on Record Screw Type Hand Knitting Machine (first *short* line) and No. 3 on Lever Type. The whole outfit is worked on the same tension.

Skirt Pattern: 12 rows blue, 2 rows grey, 12 rows blue, 1 row white, 12 rows green, 6 rows red, 2 rows white, 2 rows green, 2 rows red. Stocking stitch is used for the whole garment. The skirt consists of three equal panels.

SKIRT

With blue wool cast on 139 stitches. K. 23 rows. Turn up hem, then k. across. Continue with the pattern. When three whole patterns are completed, ending with the last 2 rows in red, put the work on a spare needle and keep it waiting until two other panels are completed. Now put all three pieces on to one knitting needle Work the next row by hand, knitting 2 tog

This attractive two-piece outfit can be worn as separates or with a blouse under the pullover. The horizontal lines are knitted in, the vertical ones embroidered afterwards in chain stitch

to the end of the row. Work 3 rows in rib, k. 2, p. 2. Cast off.

Waistband: This is done with green wool. Cast on 24 stitches. K. until the strip is 22 in. long. Cast off.

Before beginning the embroidery, which makes it a tartan instead of a striped skirt, join the three panels. Beginning at the

hem, work a row of chain stitch with white wool to cover the seams. Each stitch covers 2 stitches of the knitting. Fold each panel in half so that the white chain of one seam lies on the one at the next seam. Mark centre at the bottom of the skirt and work another white line. Repeat with the other panels. Fold up again so that white line lies on the next white line and mark centre. Work a line with grey wool. Repeat with other panels. Mark the 6th stitch from each white line and work a line in red. Repeat all over the skirt. Mark the 6th stitch from each grey line and work a line in green. Repeat all over. This will complete the embroidery. Gather the top to 22 in. width. Join the two short sides of the waistband, put right side of waistband on to right side of skirt and sew it on. Have elastic sewn together to form circle. Fold waistband over it and sew it on inside skirt.

PULLOVER

Back: With blue wool cast on 100 stitches. Work 23 rows. Turn up hem and k. across. **Border:** 25th *row:* Use red wool. Break off. 26th *row:* Use white wool. Break off. With blue wool, increase 1 stitch at beginning and end of next and every 12th row. Repeat this 4 times. Work straight until the back measures 9 in. from the beginning. Shape **Armholes** as follows. At the beginning of the next and following rows cast off: 5 stitches twice, 3 stitches twice, 2 stitches 4 times, 1 stitch 6 times. Continue to work straight until the back is 13½ in. long. At the beginning of next and following rows cast off: 6 stitches 8 times, 5 stitches twice. Cast off.

Front: Work in the same way as the back until after the shaping of the armholes. Divide the work by putting the last 40 stitches on a stitch holder. Work the first half as follows. K. 2 rows. Start shaping the **Neck:** * Decrease 1 stitch at the end of the row (neck end). K. 3 rows.* Repeat from * to * until 24 stitches remain. Work straight until the front is 13½ in. long. At the beginning of every other row cast off for the shoulder 6 stitches 4 times. Break off. Put the last 40 stitches back on the machine and work the other half of the front, decreasing at the beginning of the row for the neck.

Sleeves: With blue wool cast on 52 stitches. Work 23 rows. Turn up hem. Knit across. Work 1 row in red and 1 in white as for Border (see Back). Continue work with blue wool. Increase 1 stitch at the beginning and end of every 8th row until there are 72 stitches altogether. Work straight until Sleeve measures 10½ in. **Shape the Sleeve Top:** At the beginning of the next and following rows cast off as follows: 2 stitches 4 times, 1 stitch 28 times, 2 stitches 8 times, 3 stitches 4 times. Cast off altogether. Work the other Sleeve in the same way.

The Collar is worked in the same pattern as the Skirt.

Collar: With blue wool cast on 20 stitches. Knit across. * Cast on 3 stitches. K. across.* Repeat 3 times from * to *. * Cast on 2 stitches. K. across.* Repeat 9 times from * to *. Increase 1 stitch at the beg. of the next 24 rows. When you have worked the pattern including 12 rows green, continue as follows. Keeping the first 29 stitches on the machine, put the rest of the stitches on to a stitch holder. You are now working the right-hand side of the collar. Continue in pattern, working straight for the next 6 rows. Then decrease 1 stitch at the end of every other row (neck end) working the outer edge of the collar straight. When only 4 stitches remain, cast off. Break off wool. Put the work back on the machine. Cast off the centre stitches, leaving 29 stitches on the machine. Work as for the other side, decreasing 1 stitch at the beg. (neck end) of the row. When this side is finished and the collar taken off the machine, mark its centre. Pick up 76 stitches from centre to point of collar along the outer edge. Put work back on to the machine and work 1 row red, 1 row white. Repeat this once more. Cast off very loosely. Work the edge of the other half in the same way.

Making Up: Turn over the edge of the collar and sew it on inside so that 2 rows are outside and 2 rows inside. Work in chain stitch with white wool as for the skirt, beginning at the 8th stitch counting from the outer edge of the collar. Do the same on the other side. Work a red line along the 6th stitch from the white line. Mark the centre of the collar and work a grey line 3 stitches to the left and a green line 3 stitches to the right. Block and press all parts of the garment. Join side and shoulder seams. With the wrong side facing you, mark centre of the back and centre of collar. Put the collar with its right side on to the wrong side of the pullover and pin it into place. The corners meet in the V of the neck. Sew on, joining the corners with a few stitches. Sew up sleeve seams. Tack on sleeves and sew them in.

PARTY PULLOVER

An unusual design with contrast chiffon trimming

THIS unusual pullover is very simple to make and will certainly catch many an eye.

Materials: 6 oz. 3-ply Wendy Nylonette; No. 11 crochet hook; 1 yd. of chiffon cut into half and joined to form a 2-yd. strip. No. 12 knitting needles for casting off shoulders.

Measurements: It will fit a 34–36-in. bust. Measurements for 36–38-in. bust in brackets. Length from shoulder to edge, 21 in.

Tension: 8 stitches and 12 rows to 1 in.

Maximum Number of Stitches: 138.

Pattern: Stocking stitch.

Back: Cast on 120 stitches. Work 36 rows.

Then begin the decrease for the **Waist:**

37th row: Cast off the first 2 stitches. Work across.

38th row: Cast off the first 2 stitches. Work across.

Repeat these two rows twice. You have now decreased 12 stitches. For the larger size do not decrease any more until you come to the 51st row, but for the smaller size work 5 rows without decrease and 4 rows with the decrease.

51st row: Work across. Increase 1 stitch at the end. Repeat this row once, then work 2 rows without increase. Repeat the last 4 rows 11 times so that you have increased 24 stitches. There are now 124 (132) stitches altogether. Work straight until there are 124 rows.

125th row: Work across. Increase 1 stitch at the end.

126th row: As 125th.

Repeat these 2 rows once (twice). Work without increase until there are 160 rows.

161st row: Now begin shaping for the **Neck:** K. 67 (71), k. 2 tog., turn. Put the rest of the stitches on the stitch holder.

Work 2 rows straight.

A delightfully unusual evening jumper with contrasting chiffon threaded through loops across the front and round the edge

164th row: K. tog. the first 2 stitches. Work across. Work 2 rows straight.

167th row: K. tog. the last 2 stitches. Work across.

168th row: Work back.

169th row: As 167th.

170th row: As 164th.

Continue with this decrease at the neck side in the following rows: 173, 176, 179, 180, 182, 185, 188, 190, 191, 194, 197, 199, 200, 203, 206, 209, 210, 212, 215, 218, 220, 221, 224, 227. All the other rows are worked straight. Work 228th row and put the rest of the stitches on to a spare knitting needle. Work the other side in reverse.

Front: As the equivalent of the first 30 rows is done in crochet, the Front begins with row 31. Cast on 120 stitches and work in the same way as the Back. Put the shoulder stitches on spare needles.

Making Up:

Facings: Using 2 balls of wool, cast on both facings at the same time and work 2 strips, each 10 stitches wide and 160 rows long. Cast off.

Join the shoulders in the following way: put right side on right side and with a third needle pick up alternate stitches from each needle. Cast them off in the next row, 2 at a time. Put facings, right side on right side, along the armholes, pin and sew them on. Turn inside and sew on invisibly. With the crochet hook work one round in single crochet around the neck. Press the work under a damp cloth and then join the side seams. Now work the crochet border which takes the place of the first 30 rows along the front.

Border: Work 11 single crochet down to the edge along side. Work back 11 single crochet and a 3rd row of this downwards. Make 6 chain. Wind wool 8 times over hook, pick up a stitch at the edge of the Front less than 1 in. from the side seam, work through it in single crochet and repeat this through every loop on the hook. *Make 6 chain, wind wool 8 times over the hook, pick up a stitch less than 1 in. from the first one, work through this and every loop on the hook in single crochet.* Repeat from * to * until you reach the other side. Work 3 rows of single crochet along side in the same way as at the beginning, but finishing up with the row connecting the border with the side seam. Break off wool. Turn in ½ in. along the back and sew up a hem.

Loops along the Front: Put tape measure from left shoulder to right bottom edge. With pins mark every 1½ in. Mark slantwise 1 in. from each pin so that each loop will be 1 in. wide. Using wool double, and beginning at the lower mark, pick up the stitch with your crochet hook, make 6 chain, pick up the stitch at the higher mark and pull through. Thread needle with the 2 threads, go through to the wrong side of the work and make 2 stitches to anchor the loop firmly. Work all the other loops in the same way.

Press once more. Fold chiffon strip in half, using it double from shoulder to edge and, dividing it in two, slot those two ends through the border and tie into a bow.

HAT AND MITTENS, HANDBAG AND SCARF
All made to match

Tension: 6½ stitches and 8 rows to 1 in., 4½ and every other needle on Latch Needle machines.

HAT

Materials: 2 oz. turquoise and ½ oz. white Copley's Double Knitting Wool. A scrap of material for lining and either Vilene or thin stiffening for interlining.

With turquoise wool, cast on 100 stitches. K. 5 rows. *6th row:* Push up in Holding Position some of the needles. This is done at random; for instance: Push up 6, leave 10, push up 15, leave 4, push up 4 and leave the remaining stitches. Lift the right knob, k. across with white wool and bring the cambox back to the right. Push down the knob.

Pattern: The whole pattern consists of these 6 rows, changing the white stitches at random. At the beginning and end of next and every 4th row, decrease 1 stitch five times. At the beginning and end of next and every alternate row, cast off 1 stitch twelve times. At the beginning and end of next and every alternate row, cast off 2 stitches five times. At the beginning of next 2 rows, cast off 3 stitches. At the beginning of next 2 rows, cast off 4 stitches. Cast off.

Pattern on Record Handknitting Machine Screw Type 2nd long line and on **Lever Type** No 5. Pattern is always worked with white wool. Push knob to the right so that pulling pins push through between the comb pins. With white wool: Skip first 5 stitches, wind wool around next 10 stitches in the same way as done by the machine. Pass wool behind next 6 stitches and wind around following 4 stitches. Continue at random throughout the row. Using the hand tool, lift the blue stitches of the previous row over the white stitches, leaving the other stitches untouched. Lift comb, pull down work. With blue wool, k. 5 rows.

Border: Cast on 20 stitches. K. 1 row in

blue and 1 in white alternately. Repeat these 2 rows until there are 180 rows. Cast off. Press both pieces. Cut out lining and interlining for main part. Fold in half along the casting-on line and sew it up. Do the same with lining and interlining. Insert interlining and lining and tack them on around the edge. Sew up the two short ends of the border. This corresponds with the seam at the back of hat. Put right side of border on to right side of hat and sew it on tightly, holding in the edges. Using the legs of an old pair of stockings to form a roll, fold border over it and sew up inside.

With four blue and white threads of wool make two separate cords and twist them together. Sew on cord along front. Fold back the point of the hat and stitch it on about 3 in. lower. Make a bow with cord and stitch it on to the point of the hat.

MITTENS

Materials: 2 oz. turquoise and ½ oz.

Scarf and capacious yet smart handbag are made in the same pattern to match the cap and mittens

white Copley's Double Knitting Wool.

With blue wool, cast on 50 stitches. At the beginning of next and every alternate row, increase 1 stitch five times. K. 5 rows straight. At the beginning of next and every alternate row, decrease 1 stitch five times. Starting with the 8th stitch counting from the *end* of the row, cast off 18 stitches for thumb opening. *Next row:* With white wool, cast on 18 stitches where you cast them off in the previous row. Continue knitting 1 row blue, 1 row white, working the increase and decrease as for the first part of the glove. After the 19th

The little pixie hat and matching mittens would be perfect for a 'teen-ager to wear on a winter's day

row (white), make 2 rows blue, then continue in stripe as before. (26 rows for inside and the same for outside of mitten.) Work other mitten in the same way but starting with the stripes.

Thumbs (both alike). With blue wool, cast on 8 stitches. Increase 1 stitch at the beginning and 3 stitches at the end of every alternate row four times. Increase 3 stitches at the end of next row. K. 1 row. Repeat the last 2 rows once. K. 2 rows. From now onwards, decrease in the same way as you increased before, until 8 stitches remain. Cast off. Make another thumb.

Making Up: Sew up thumbs and sew them into place. Sew up mittens, leaving 1-in. long opening at the wrist. Work 1 round of double crochet along wrists.

HANDBAG

Materials: 4 oz. turquoise and 2 oz. white Copley's Double Knitting Wool; ½ yd. lining (sufficient for scarf also); ¼ yd. Vilene for stiffening, 4 small white rings; stiff cardboard the size of the bottom and a strip 2 in. high to fit around the four sides of the bottom.

Measurements: 12 in. wide and 9 in. deep.

Sides: Using blue wool, cast on 70 stitches. These plain rows will come underneath the border. K. 20 rows. Start pattern, as for hat. When work is 11 in. long, cast off. Work other side in the same way.

Bottom: With blue wool cast on 50 stitches. K. 22 rows. Cast off.

Border: Pattern: 1 row blue, 1 row white. Cast on 20 stitches. K. 1 row blue. By doing this, you have now the blue wool on the left-hand side. K. 1 row white (white wool is now on right-hand side). Bring the blue wool *behind* the needles to the right-hand side, put in front and k. across. Take white wool to the left-hand side and k. across. By working this way, you will have the loose wool at the back of your work, ready to be cut in fringes of

even length. K. 150 rows in this way. Cast off.

Making Up: Press all parts under a damp cloth. Cut out stiffening the size of the two sides of the bag. Cut out lining ¼ in. larger all round and one piece the size of the bottom. Cover the bottom with cardboard and then with lining, and sew them together. Take strip of cardboard, put around the four sides, and bend at the corners so that it will fit exactly. Join seams of interlining and lining separately. Sew bottom of bag on to sides.

Fold border in half so that wool at the back hangs down one side; join the two short ends. Sew border on along lower part of bag, 2 in. from the bottom. Cut through fringes. Turn in 15 rows at the top. Sew on lining. Sew on 2 rings each side of bag, 2½ in. from top edge and 2½ in. from side seam. With 3 threads of white wool, make cord. Do the same with blue wool and twist them into single cord. Slot through rings and tie at the end. Fold corners of bag inside to give it the tent shape.

SCARF

Materials: 5 oz. turquoise and 2 oz. white Copley's Double Knitting Wool.

Same pattern as handbag. With blue wool, cast on 56 stitches. K. 5 rows.

6th row: Work in pattern. Continue to work until scarf is 36 in. long. Cast off.

Border: Work in 1 row blue, 1 row white, as for border of bag. Cast on 24 stitches. K. 66 rows. Cast off. Work another piece in the same way. Cut wool at the back and knot the fringes to hang down one side of each piece.

Making Up: Press pieces under a damp cloth. Sew on borders each end of scarf. Turn in ¼ in. along the long sides. Cut out lining to fit inside scarf, shaping it slightly at both ends so that the border part comes about ½ in. narrower than the main part on each side. Sew in lining and press once more.

☆ ☆ ☆ **FOR USERS OF EVERY TYPE OF KNITTING MACHINE** ☆ ☆ ☆

☆ Keep your machine in good working order by covering it when not in use, by
☆ removing dust and fluff with a soft brush and by oiling it regularly with sewing-machine oil. How often this is necessary depends on how much the machine is
☆ used. On the average, oil once a month, but if the machine is used all the time,
☆ it may be necessary to oil more often. Remember: only well-kept tools can
☆ produce satisfactory work.

☆ ☆

HOW TO CROCHET

*Whether you are a knitter or not, crochet work is
quick and easy to learn; here are all the stitches*

Abbreviations.—St. = stitch; ch. = chain;
s.c. = single crochet; d.c. = double crochet;
h. tr. = half treble; tr. = treble; l. tr. = long
treble; w.o.h. = wool over hook.

Holding Wool and Hook

Holding hook between first finger and
thumb of right hand and letting second
finger rest near point of hook, make a slip
loop and pass it on to hook.   Holding
work, as it is formed, between first finger
and thumb of left hand, pass wool from
ball over first and second fingers, under
third and round little finger.

Chain Stitch (*basis of all crochet work*)

Holding wool and hook as described
above and making a slip loop to begin
with, * pass hook from left to right under
wool (held in left hand), draw this thread
through loop already on hook and rep.
from * for length required.

Single Crochet (or "slip stitch")

Make required length of chain.
1st row: Miss end ch. (near hook), * pass
hook through next ch., draw wool through
both sts. on hook, rep. from * to end of ch.,
turn.
2nd row: 1 ch. (1 *ch. at beginning of row
always forms last st. of next row*), * inserting hook in second s.c., draw wool through
both sts. on hook, rep. from * to end of
row, turn. Rep. 2nd row for length required.

Double Crochet

Make required length of chain.
1st row: Miss 2 ch., * draw a loop through
next ch., then draw a loop through both
sts. on hook, rep. from * to end of row,
turn.
2nd row: 2 ch. (2 *ch. at beginning of row
form last st. of next row*), * draw a loop
through next d.c., draw a loop through
both sts. on hook, rep. from * to end of
row, turn. Rep. 2nd row for length required.

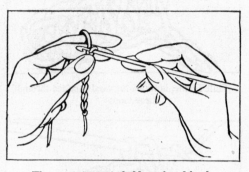

The correct way to hold wool and hook

Making a Chain Stitch, basis of all crochet work

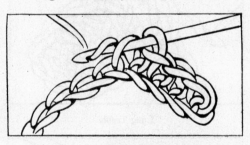

Single Crochet or Slip Stitch is used for joins
and in fancy patterns

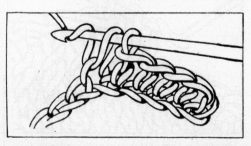

Double Crochet is usually worked firmly, evenly

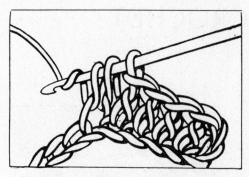

Half Treble, in which the wool is pulled through three loops

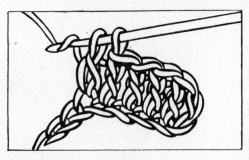

Treble Stitch

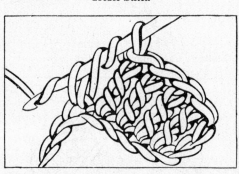

Long Treble

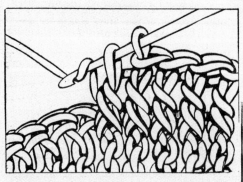

Treble round Treble produces a good fabric for blankets

Two different effects can be produced:

1st: Flat surface, produced (for each new st.) by inserting hook *through two threads,* forming a chain along top edge of previous row.

2nd: Ridged surface, produced (for each new st.) by inserting hook *through back threads* of sts., that lie along top edge of previous row.

Half Treble

Make required length of chain.

1st row: Miss 3 ch., * pass wool round hook, draw a loop through next ch., draw a loop through all 3 sts. on hook, rep. from * to end of row, turn.

2nd row: 3 ch. (*3 ch. at beginning of row form the last st. of next row*), * pass wool round hook, draw a loop through next h. tr., draw a loop through all 3 sts. on hook, rep. from *. Rep. 2nd row for length required.

Treble Stitch

Make required length of chain.

1st row: Miss 3 ch., * pass wool round hook, draw a loop through next ch. to height st. is required to be when finished, draw a loop through first 2 loops on hook, then draw another loop through 2 remaining loops, rep. from * to end of row, turn.

Take care to draw up first loop to its full height. Do not finish off top of st. too loosely, or a ragged effect will be produced.

2nd row: 3 ch. (*3 ch. at beginning of row form last st. in next row*), work 1 tr. on each tr to end of row, turn. Rep. 2nd row for length required.

Long Treble

Make required length of chain.

1st row: Miss 4 ch., * wool twice round needle, draw a loop through next ch., draw a loop through first 2 loops on hook, draw a loop through next 2 loops, then another through last 2 loops (thereby completing one long treble st.), rep. from * to end of row, turn.

2nd row: 4 ch. (*4 ch. at beginning of row form last st. of next row*), work 1 l. tr. on each l. tr. to end of row, turn. Rep. 2nd row for length required.

Treble round Treble

(This st., used frequently in modern

crochet designs, produces a very suitable fabric for blankets, etc.)

Instead of working treble into top of st. in usual way, it is actually worked round treble as illustrated.

Joining Wool

When only a few inches are left, take end from new ball of wool and complete last st. with this. Continue working over both ends of wool for several sts., afterwards continuing with new thread.

Increasing

In plain fabric, work 2 sts. into one. In fancy st., work 2 pattern groups into one; detailed instructions are usually given.

Decreasing

In plain fabric, usual method is to miss a st., or, * wool over hook, draw a loop through next st., wool over hook, draw through two loops, wool over hook, draw a loop through next st., wool over hook, draw through three loops, wool over hook, draw through two loops *, rep. from * to * as many times as required.

In a fancy pattern detailed instructions are always given for decreasing.

Linking Up

Working in trebles and holding second colour behind first colour, draw second colour through last two loops of last treble of first colour, then passing first colour upwards, over top of second colour, continue using second colour along row in usual manner.

Two-colour Pattern

When working in trebles and in pattern, colour to be used next is drawn through last two loops just worked, and colour in use is then worked over colour not in use.

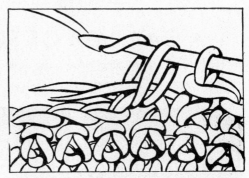

Joining wool, working over both ends for several stitches

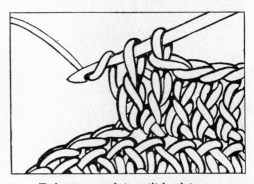

To increase, work two stitches into one

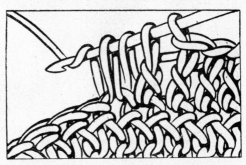

Decreasing: usual method is to miss a stitch

How to do a two-colour pattern

Linking up two colours

Diagrams by Patons & Baldwins

A GAY PAIR OF SUMMER SANDALS

*In their two-colour scheme they would look cool
and gay on the beach or around the house*

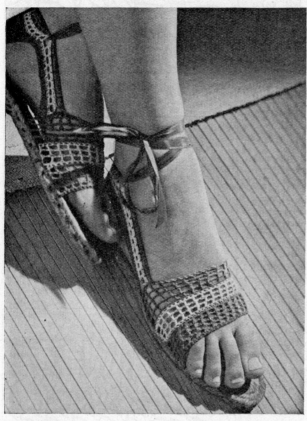

**Being crocheted in shirring elastic, they will fit any size
and you can have them done in no time at all**

Materials: Rope or other soles; 2 spools shirring elastic in white and 3 in red; $2\frac{1}{2}$ yd. narrow red ribbon; steel crochet hook No. 1.

Abbreviations: Ch., chain; d.c., double crochet; tr., treble; r., red; wh., white; patt., pattern.

Pattern consists of 3 ch. at beginning of each row (they stand for first tr.), * 1 ch., 1 tr., * into 3rd stitch, therefore leaving out 1 stitch from previous row. Continue from * to * to end of row.

Wide Strap: With r. elastic, make 35 ch. Turn. **1st row:** Leaving out 1st ch., make d.c. into each of following ch. to end of row. **2nd row:** 3 ch., 1 tr. into 3rd stitch. Continue in patt. Repeat second row 3 times, always making tr. into tr. of previous row.

6th row: Work in d.c. into each stitch. Break off. **7th row:** Using wh. elastic, work row in d.c. **8th, 9th and 10th rows** are worked in patt. Break off. **11th row:** Using r. elastic, work in d.c. Next four rows are worked in patt. **16th row:** D.c. to end of row. Break off.

Long Strap: With r. elastic, make 55 ch. Turn. **1st row:** Leaving out 1st ch., make d.c. into each of following ch. to end of row. **2nd row:** Work in patt. Break off.

3rd row: Using wh. elastic, work in d.c. **4th row:** Work in patt. **5th row:** Work in d.c. Break off. **6th row:** Using r. elastic, work in patt. **7th row:** Work in d.c. Break off.

Short Strap: Using r. elastic, make 12 ch. Turn. **1st row:** Work in d.c. **2nd row:** Work in patt. **3rd row:** As 2nd. **4th row:** As first. Break off.

Make another strip in the same way.

To Make Up: Sew short sides of wide strap on to sole. Stitch one end of long strap across last 4 patt. of wide strap, and do same with other end.

Two short straps have to be adjusted, one on each side of long strap at heel. Slot ribbon through long strap.

Make second sandal in same way.

Having made one pair, you will want to make them for the rest of the family. That's the joy of shirring elastic, you can use the same pattern to make sandals for men, women and children.

AND A SMART TOWN HAT

This neat, head-hugging little tailored model is quickly crocheted and trimmed with bells

Materials.—4 oz. Patons Moorlands Double Knitting; small ball of contrast for medallions. A No. 7 and No. 8 crochet hook.

Measurement.—To fit an average head.

Tension.—3 double trebles and 1 row of double trebles measure just under 1 in.

Abbreviations. — Tr., treble; dbl. tr., double treble; d.c., double crochet; s.s., slip stitch; ch., chain.

Start at centre of crown. With No. 7 hook and wool used treble, make 6 ch., join into a ring with a s.s. **1st round:** 8 d.c. through centre of ring, join with a s.s. **2nd round:** 3 ch. (this 3 ch. at beginning of every round counts as 1 stitch), * 2 trs. in 1 d.c.; rep. from * to end, s.s. into 3rd of 3 ch. (16 trs.).

3rd round: 3 ch., * (2 trs. in 1 tr.) 3 times, 1 tr. in 1 tr.; rep. from * to end, s.s. into 3rd of 3 ch. (28 trs.). **4th round:** 4 ch. (counts as 1 stitch), * 3 dbl. trs. in 3 trs., 2 dbl. trs. in 1 tr.; rep. from * to end, s.s. into 4th of 4 ch. (35 dbl. trs.).

5th round: as 4th, but work sts. over after last increase in plain dbl. trs. (43 dbl. trs.). **6th round:** as 4th (53 dbl. trs.). **7th round:** 4 ch., * 4 dbl. trs. in 4 dbl. trs., 2 dbl. trs. in 1 dbl. tr.; rep. from * to end, s.s. into 4th of 4 ch. (63 dbl. trs.). Break off one thread.

Next round: 2 ch. (counts as 1 st.), * 1 d.c. in 1 dbl. tr.; rep. from * to end, s.s. into 2nd of 2 ch. Repeat last round 3 times more. Join in 3rd thread again and continue for brim on No. 8 hook thus. **Next round:** 3 ch., * 4 trs. in 4 d.c., 2 trs. in 1 d.c.; rep. from * to end, s.s. into 3rd of 3 ch. (75 trs.).

You can make it just like this, with the tiny turned-down brim or, if you prefer, give it a deeper brim to turn up at the front or back—instructions are given for both

Next round: 3 ch., * 5 trs. in 5 trs., 2 trs. in 1 tr.; rep. from * to end, s.s. into 3rd of 3 ch. (87 trs.). This completes small brim for cap model worn down all round.

For a deeper brim to turn up at the front or back, work another round of plain trs. Finish off with a round of s.s. for both models; fasten off.

Medallions.—With No. 8 hook and single contrast wool, make 4 ch., join into a ring with a s.s., 6 d.c. through centre of ring. **1st round:** * 2 d.c. in 1 d.c.; rep. from * to end. Mark the start of each new round with coloured thread to check increasings.

2nd round: * 2 d.c. in 1 d.c., 1 d.c. in 1 d.c.; rep. from * to end. **3rd round:** * 6 d.c. in 6 d.c., 2 d.c. in 1 d.c.; rep. from * to end. **4th round:** * 1 d.c. in 1 d.c.; rep. from * to end; fasten off. Make 4 more in the same way.

Darn in all ends. Sew on bells or medallions as shown in photograph. Press brim under a damp cloth.

703

MADE FROM THE ODDMENTS BOX

Practical ways of using up those different wools we all have left over

Make these neat cosies to brighten the breakfast tray

TEA COSY

Cast on 90 sts. with dk. wool. K. 3 rows.

4th row: Begin ptn. With dk., k. 9 sts.; with lt., k. 9 sts.; rep. to end (right side).

5th row: Work dk. on dk., lt. on lt., keeping wool not used in front of work. Rep. these 2 rows 3 times. Now alternate the colours for the next 8 rows, using dk. on lt. and lt. on dk. By changing the colours every 8 rows you get a chessboard effect. When 59 rows have been worked (including first 3 rows), cast off. Make another piece in the same way. Draw together at top, then sew up sides, leaving openings for spout and handle. For the loop, cast on 16 sts. and work 4 in. in garter-st. Sew up lengthwise and stitch to top.

EGG COSY

Cast on 42 sts. and k. 3 rows. Now work as for tea cosy, working 7 sts. in each colour until 27 rows have been worked. Cast off. Make another piece. Join sides, draw up top. For loop, cast on 8 sts. and k. 1½ in. Sew up lengthwise and stitch to top.

CHECKED JUMPER

Materials: 5 oz. of Emu Zephyr 3-ply Botany in light grey; 1 oz. of the same wool in dark grey and black. A pair each of Nos. 10 and 12 "Aero" knitting needles. A set of No. 12 "Aero" needles with points both ends.

Measurements: Length, 20 (20, 21) in. To fit 34 (36, 38) in. bust. Sleeve, 5 (5, 5½) in.

Tension: 7½ sts. to 1 in.

Additional Abbreviations: L.G., light grey; D.G., dark grey; B., black.

The Back

Using No. 12 needles and L.G., cast on

SOONER or later, everyone who does any knitting accumulates an oddments box, full of balls and half-balls of different coloured wools. Here are instructions for tea and egg cosies, a checked jumper, and striped socks for a man, all made from small quantities of wool.

Abbreviations: K., knit; p., purl; st.(s.), stitch(es); st.st., stocking stitch; beg., begin(ning); cont., continue; rem., remain-(ing); inc., increase; dec., decrease; in., inch(es); sl., slip; rep., repeat; ptn., pattern; foll., following; tog., together; t.b.l., through back of loops.

The cosies are worked in garter-st. (every row k.). The pattern consists of 9 sts. in dark (dk.) and 9 sts. in light (lt.). The wool which is *not* used is put behind the needle on the right side and in front of work on the wrong side. It is important to keep the wool which is not used above the thread which is used, to avoid entangling it. The first st. in every row is worked with both threads to get an even pull at the back.

Materials: About 4 oz. of remnants of Sirdar Double Knitting Wool in various colours. A pair of No. 10 knitting needles.

116 (124, 132) sts. and work in a k. 1, p. 1 rib for 2 (2, 2½) in. Change to No. 10 needles and work in st.st., inc. 1 st. at each end of 3rd and every foll. 10th row until there are 128 (136, 144) sts. Cont. straight until work measures 12½ (12½, 13) in.

Shape Armholes: Cast off 9 (10, 11) sts. at beg. of next 2 rows, then dec. 1 st. at beg. of every row until 98 (104, 110) sts. rem. Cont. straight until work measures 20 (20, 21) in.

Shape Shoulders: Cast off for 1st size 8 sts. at beg. of next 8 rows. For 2nd size: 11 sts. at beg. of next 4 rows, then 12 sts. at beg. of foll. 2 rows. For 3rd size: 7 sts. at beg. of next 8 rows, then 8 sts. at beg. of foll. 2 rows. Put rem. 34 (36, 38) sts. on a st. holder.

The Front

Work as given for back to end of rib, then work in foll. check ptn., but at the same time inc. both ends of 3rd and every foll. 10th row until there are 128 (136, 144) sts., keeping extra sts. in 1st and last colour block. Twist wools when changing colour; use a new ball for each block.

1st row: K. 14 (18, 22) L.G., 22 D.G., 22 B., 22 L.G., 22 D.G., 14 (18, 22) B.

2nd row: P. in colour order. Cont. in check ptn., inc. as above, until 24 rows have been completed. Break off wools, leaving long enough ends to sew in.

2nd block of checks: Work as follows: D.G. above L.G.; B. above D.G.; L.G. above B. for 24 rows.

3rd block of checks: Work as follows: B. above D.G.; L.G. above B.; D.G. above L.G. for 24 rows.

4th block of checks: Work thus: D.G. above B.; B. above L.G.; L.G. above D.G. for 24 rows.

5th and 6th block of checks: Work as given for the 1st and 2nd blocks, but when work measures 12½ (12½, 13) in., shape armholes as for the back.

7th block of checks: Work as given for 3rd block until work measures 18 (18, 19) in.

Shape Neck: Work across 37 (40, 41)

Gay contrasting checks on a trimly tailored jumper

sts., place 24 (24, 28) centre sts. on to a st. holder. Join in new balls of wool, work across rem. 37 (40, 41) sts. Working on both sides at once, dec. 1 st. at neck edge in each side on every alternate row until 32 (33, 35) sts. rem. each side. Cont. without further shaping until the 24 rows of ptn. are completed.

8th block of checks: Work as follows: L.G. above B.; B. above L.G.; L.G. above D.G. until work measures 20 (20, 21) in.

Shape Shoulders: Cast off at each armhole 8 (11, 7) sts. 4 (3, 5) times.

The Sleeves

Using No. 12 needles and L.G., cast on 76 (80, 82) sts. Work in a k. 1, p. 1 rib for 12 rows. Change to No. 10 needles and cont. in st.-st., inc. 1 st. both ends of every foll. 4th row until there are 88 (92, 96) sts. Cont. without shaping until sleeve measures 5 (5, 5½) in. from beg.

Shape Top: Cast off 8 (9, 10) sts. at beg. of next 2 rows, then dec. 1 st. at beg. of every row until 32 (32, 34) sts. rem. Now cast off 2 sts. at beg. of next 6 rows on each size. Cast off.

The Neckband

Press work with a hot iron and damp cloth. Sew up shoulder seams. Using the set of No. 12 needles and L.G. and with right side of work towards you, k. across sts. of back neck, pick up and k. 31 (31, 32) sts. down side of neck, k. across sts. of centre front, then pick up and k. 31 (31, 32) sts. up other side of neck. Divide sts. on to 3 needles and work in a k. 1, p. 1 rib for 12 rounds. Cast off loosely in rib.

To Make Up

Darn in all ends neatly. Sew sleeves into armholes, sew up seams. Press seams.

MAN'S SOCKS

Materials: 2 oz. Copley's "Excelsior" Super Fingering 3-ply in grey; $\frac{3}{4}$ oz. in navy; $\frac{1}{2}$ oz. in blue. Set of 4 No. 12 knitting needles.
Measurements: Length to bottom of heel, $13\frac{1}{2}$ in. Foot from back of heel, 11 in.
Tension: $8\frac{1}{2}$ sts. to 1 in.
Using grey wool, cast on 72 sts. (24 on

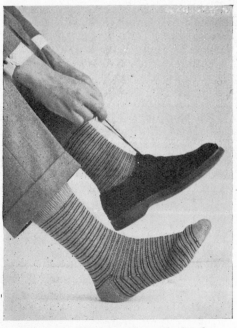

Any man will welcome these striped socks

each of 3 needles) and work 4 in. in k. 1, p. 1 rib.

Change to striped ptn. and, working every round k., work thus: * Work 3 rounds grey, 1 round navy, 1 round blue, 1 round navy *. Rep. from * to *, dec. at beg. of 1st and end of 3rd needle on 20th round and every foll. 12th round until 64 sts. rem. Cont. straight until 13 ptns. worked. Break off blue and navy wools.

Work Heel: K. 16, sl. last 4 sts. on to 2nd needle, turn and p. 16, then p. 16 from 3rd needle. Now divide rem. 32 sts. on to 2 needles and leave for instep. Working backwards and forwards on the 32 heel sts., make a double heel piece thus:

1st and 3rd rows: K.
2nd row: (Sl. 1, p. 1) to end.
4th row: (P. 1, sl. 1) to end.

Rep. last 4 rows until heel piece measures 3 in., then turn heel thus: K. 20, k. 2 tog., turn, sl. 1, p. 8, p. 2 tog., turn, sl. 1, k. 9, k. 2 tog., turn, sl. 1, p. 10, p. 2 tog., turn, sl. 1, k. 11, k. 2 tog., turn.

Cont. in this way, working 1 more st. before dec. and turning on every row until there are 20 sts. on one row again. Sl. the 32 instep sts. on one needle (this will be 2nd needle of round), k. 10 sts. of heel sts. on another needle (3rd needle). Shape instep thus:

1st round: 1st needle: K. 10, pick up and k. 17 sts. down side of heel piece. 2nd needle: K. across instep sts. 3rd needle: Pick up and k. 17 sts. up other side of heel piece, k. 10. Cont. in ptn., beg. with 2nd round of grey.

2nd round: 1st needle: K. to last 3 sts., k. 2 tog., k. 1. 2nd needle: K. without shaping. 3rd needle: K. 1, k. 2 tog. t.b.l., k. to end.

3rd round: K.

Rep. last 2 rounds until 64 sts. rem., then cont. straight until foot measures 9 in. from back of heel (or 2 in. less than length required). Cont. in grey. Shape toe thus:

1st round: 1st needle: K. to last 3 sts., k. 2 tog., k. 1. 2nd needle: K. 1, k. 2 tog., t.b.l., k. to last 3 sts., k. 2 tog., k. 1. 3rd needle: K. 1, k. 2 tog., t.b.l., k. to end.

2nd round: K.

Rep. last 2 rounds until 24 sts. rem., break wool, leaving a long end, arrange sts. on 2 needles and graft.

SMART SET IN STRAW

Here's a tonic for a tired frock—a collar and cuff set that will give it new life

These charming trimmings are made from millinery straw and would look delightful in any pastel colour

THIS collar and cuff set, that's guaranteed to transform your outfit, is simplicity itself to make and the necessary materials are so very inexpensive.

It wouldn't be difficult to think of variations, either.

Materials.—2 yd. millinery straw, approximately $1\frac{3}{4}$ in. wide; 1 yd. narrow bead elastic (colour to match the straw); hook and eye; 9 in. black velvet ribbon $\frac{1}{2}$ in. wide.

COLLAR

Cut off a 20-in. length of the straw and run the fine bead elastic through one edge of it. Draw it up to fit your neck measurement and secure in place.

Weave back 1 in. of the straw at each end. Now cut off a 28-in. length of straw and sew it to the lower edge of the first piece, easing in the fullness. Stitch on the hook and eye to fasten, tie the black velvet ribbon into a trim bow and sew neatly to one edge.

CUFFS

Divide remaining straw in two (giving two 12-in. pieces). Weave back loose ends of each piece. Thread one edge of each piece with bead elastic, draw up to wrist measurement, gathering straw slightly. Sew ends of elastic together. For wearing on short sleeves, make cuffs a little larger.

707

GETTING MARRIED

The essential formalities and the etiquette to be observed

"Who giveth this woman to be married to this man?" In a quiet country church a young couple are joined together in holy matrimony

Immediately after the ceremony, the happy bride signs her maiden name for the last time (right)—in the marriage register while the groom looks on with pride

ANY couple contemplating marriage in England or Wales must abide by (*a*) the rites of the Church of England; (*b*) the rites of other religious denominations; or (*c*) have a civil ceremony in a Register Office.

For those who wish to be married in the Church of England there are four different forms of procedure:

(*a*) Marriage by Banns;

(*b*) Marriage by Common Licence;

(*c*) Marriage by Special Licence;

(*d*) Marriage by Superintendent Registrar's Certificate.

The preliminary formalities of the first three as well as the ceremony are, of course, carried out by the Church. In the fourth instance the preliminaries are in the hands of the State and only the ceremony is conducted by the Church.

Marriage by Banns.—This is the usual procedure and the clergyman concerned must be given at least three clear weeks' notice of the marriage. This delay is neces-

sary, since the banns must be duly published by being read out in church on three successive Sundays. If the parties live in different parishes, the banns must be read in both. During the three-week period the parties must remain resident in their parish or parishes. Temporary absence, i.e. for business reasons, is allowed.

The necessity for the three-week waiting period and the publication of the banns is two-fold: to inform the public of an intended marriage, and to give anyone entitled to object an opportunity of doing so.

Banns remain valid for three months. After that time, if the marriage has not been solemnised, they must be republished.

Fees.—Publication of banns, 7*s*. (14*s*. if published in two parishes).
Certificate of publication of banns, 3*s*. 6*d*.
Marriage fee approx., £1 2*s*.
Certificate, 3*s*. 9*d*.

Marriage by Common Licence.—This eliminates the three-week delay, as no banns have to be published. One of the parties, however, must have lived within the parish where the marriage is to take place for at least fifteen days immediately preceding the application, and one clear day's notice must be given for the licence, applications for which should be made to the Diocesan Registrar, or any Surrogate for granting Marriage Licences in the Diocese, or from the Faculty Office, 1 The Sanctuary, Westminster, London, S.W.1, and is valid for marriage anywhere in England and Wales.

After their marriage actress Janette Scott and singer Jackie Rae wave to well-wishers

At the reception the bridegroom helps his bride to cut the cake

Personal application for the licence must be made by one of the parties and a declaration filled in giving such particulars as names, addresses, nationality, age, condition and relationship (if any). If the parties are over 21, the words "of full age" are sufficient.

Fees.—Marriage fee, £1 10s.
Licence, £2 15s.

Marriage by Special Licence.—This form of marriage is rare. The licence is obtainable only by permission of the Archbishop of Canterbury and application must be made to the Faculty Office (see address above). It allows a couple to be married at any convenient place or time. Neither party need have any residential qualifications and the ceremony can be held in church, private house or hospital (though in the last two cases, reasons must be stated when making application), and can take place immediately after the issue of the licence at any hour whatsoever. It is not always possible to get a Special Licence. When it is granted, however, some time will elapse between the application and the issue.

Fees.—Licence, approx. £20.
Marriage fee differs and is usually left to the discretion of the clergyman.

Marriage by Superintendent Registrar's Certificate.—This certificate must be obtained for marriages other than in the Church of England. It can also be issued to members of the Church of England.

At least two witnesses must be present, apart from the minister and the couple to be married, and the only other legal requirement is that the church doors must be left open to the general public during the ceremony.

Fees.—Registrar's certificate and church fees, if both parties live in the same district, £1 13s.

If parties live in different districts, £1 16s.

Certificate, 3s. 9d.

Marriage in accordance with the Rites of Other Religious Denominations

A Superintendent Registrar may issue certificates for marriage to:

(a) *Nonconformists* and *Roman Catholics*, in their respective places of worship if certified as such and registered for marriage.

(b) Members of the *Society of Friends* (Quakers) in a meeting-house of their own choice.

(c) *Jews,* in a place of their own choice.

The certificate may be issued with or without licence. Without a licence it involves a delay of at least twenty-one days after notice of the proposed marriage has been given to the Registrar. Each party must have resided in the district during the seven days immediately preceding the giving of the notice. Where they live in different districts, notice must be given to Registrars in both districts.

Marriage with Licence avoids delay, as the certificate can be granted one day after the entry of notice of marriage. In order to qualify for this certificate, the man or woman must have resided in the Registrar's district for at least fifteen days. Notice may be given by either party.

Fees.—Superintendent Registrar's fee, £3 3s.

In the case of a marriage in church further fees are payable to the minister and will be named by him.

Certificate, 3s. 9d.

The applicant for a certificate is required to make a declaration that there is, as far as he knows, no impediment to the marriage, that the residential qualifications have been complied with and that, if either of the parties is a minor, the necessary consent has been obtained.

After the issue of the certificate, the marriage ceremony must take place in one of the districts in which notice has been given, with the following exceptions:

(a) If the usual place of worship of one or both of the parties is a registered build-ing within two miles outside the district or one of the districts where notice has been given, the parties may marry in that place of worship.

(b) Parties who belong to a Christian denomination which has no place of worship in the registration district may marry in the nearest registered building outside the district or one of the districts.

(c) Jewish marriages may be celebrated anywhere.

(d) The marriage of parties wishing to conform to the rites of the Society of Friends may take place in any meeting-house they choose.

Rules governing Certain Faiths

Roman Catholics may not, according to the laws of their Church, marry non-Catholics except by special dispensation from the Church authorities, when certain undertakings have to be given. The parish priest should be consulted.

The rules of the *Society of Friends* do not require that either party need necessarily be a member of the Society, provided they have received permission from it to marry in a meeting-house. No hours are prescribed for the wedding and the doors need not be open to the public.

The *Jewish* faith requires that both parties shall be members in order to contract a Jewish marriage. The ceremony can take place anywhere—synagogue or private house—at any time. Consult the Rabbi of the nearest Synagogue.

Marriage by Civil Ceremony in a Register Office

This type of marriage is open to all members of the public, regardless of their religious beliefs. The necessary preliminaries (issuing of a Superintendent Registrar's certificate) have already been described in detail.

The ceremony, which must not include a religious service, requires the presence of two witnesses and the doors must be open to the public. Both parties must declare that they know of no lawful impediment to their marriage and state that they take each other as lawful wedded wife (or husband).

Legal Times for Marriages.—With the exceptions already named, all marriages must take place between the hours of 8 a.m. and 6 p.m.

Marriage by civil ceremony in a Register Office requires the presence of two witnesses, the doors must be open to the public, and both parties must declare they know of no impediment to their marriage

General

As will be seen, it is important to realise that one cannot get married anywhere at a moment's notice, and that before fixing a date for a wedding, if it is to take place in church, it is wise and courteous to consult the Minister first, in case the day chosen may not be convenient or possible for him.

Residence.—For the purposes of the law, a room at one's own home normally kept vacant for one, counts as "residence."

Legal Freedom to Marry.—When giving notice to marry, whether in church or before a Registrar, a declaration that no obstacle exists to the marriage is required.

Where either or both of the parties have been married before, evidence must be provided of (a) death of former partner; or (b) legal divorce. In the case of (a), any proof is acceptable—e.g. death certificate, certificate of probate, newspaper publication or other evidence agreeable to the Minister or Registrar eligible to perform the ceremony. In the case of (b), the Decree Absolute, or other evidence acceptable to the Registrar, must be produced. The words: "Previous marriage dissolved" will be entered in the register.

The Church of England, like the Roman Catholic Church, does not recognise divorce and therefore will not remarry a divorced person. Many ministers, however, are willing to give the couple the Church's blessing following a civil ceremony. Nonconformist churches are not so adamant and it is left to the minister's discretion. A Nonconformist divorced person wishing to remarry in church should contact the minister and ask his feelings in the matter.

Where either or both of the parties are under age (21), a document ("Consent to the Marriage of a Minor"), obtainable from the Registrar, signed by parent or legal guardian, must be produced, and in the case of Wards of Court, the consent of the High Court must be obtained.

The *latest* time for producing this evidence is just before the ceremony.

Marriage of Aliens.—Visiting or resident nationals of other countries, who have not become naturalised British subjects, will be asked to show passport or other identification papers, but in all other respects, provided residential qualifications are satisfied, they can be married according to rules applying to citizens of Britain.

Scotland, Ireland and Commonwealth Countries

As the procedure varies in these countries, if either party resides there, he or she should seek advice from Church or civil authorities in plenty of time. If both parties reside in Scotland, since the marriage laws there differ in many respects, they should consult a Scottish Minister or the Registrar, who will explain all formalities.

WEDDING PLANS

These are adjusted according to taste and circumstances, but there are certain points of etiquette to be observed.

Wedding Invitations

Invitations should all be sent on the same day three weeks before the wedding, by the bride's mother. The bridegroom's parents make a list of his relations and friends to be invited and these invitations should also be dispatched by the bride's mother. Final decisions on the number of guests are left to the bride's parents, who bear the brunt of the expense. In the case of a small wedding, or following a death in the family, formal invitations may be replaced by a short personal note from the bride's mother. If a bride has no parents, she can get her closest relative to send the invitations or write to her friends herself.

A combined invitation for ceremony and reception is generally used. Invitations should be engraved in plain script (often in silver but sometimes in black) on a double sheet of cream or white paper 7 by $4\frac{1}{2}$ in. and be drafted in the third person. Any good stationer will have samples in stock, but here is a specimen:

Mr. and Mrs. John Rogers
request the pleasure of

....

company on the occasion of
the marriage of their daughter
VERONICA JASMINE
to
Mr. ARTHUR BROWN
at St. Mary's Church, Waddington,
on Saturday, March 19th,
at 11.30 a.m.
and afterwards at The Crown Hotel,
Waddington.
R.S.V.P.
100 Mountview Terrace,
Waddington, Bucks.

If the wedding takes place in the country, it is customary to send with the card of invitation, one on which are listed the times of the trains to and from the nearest station. Cars should be there to meet these trains and all details of such an arrangement should be mentioned on the card. Facilities for getting guests to their home-going trains may also be provided when possible.

Replies to the invitation are also made in the third person:

"Mrs. C. R. Marlow has much pleasure in accepting Mr. and Mrs. John Rogers's kind invitation to the marriage of their daughter, Veronica Jasmine, to Mr. Arthur Brown at St. Mary's Church, Waddington, on Saturday, March 19th, and afterwards at The Crown Hotel, Waddington."

If the invitation has to be declined, say: "Mrs. Marlow much regrets that she is unable to accept . . ." etc., but make no reference to time and place of ceremony.

Wedding Gifts

Everyone should reciprocate the courtesy of an invitation by sending a gift, however small, when accepting or declining the invitation to the wedding. The bride, no matter how busy she is at this time, should acknowledge all gifts immediately. When in doubt as to what to send, it is now quite customary to consult the bride and bridegroom—or, better still, the bride's mother, so that there will still be an element of surprise but no unnecessary duplication. To avoid this, there is a growing custom for couples to provide friends with lists of gifts they would like to receive.

Bride's Mother

She is usually responsible for the decoration of the church, the selection of the music (in consultation, of course, with her daughter), the catering at the reception and all the social details. She may sometimes hold an informal dinner-party for relatives and close friends on the eve of the wedding.

Bride's Father

It is his duty and privilege to give his daughter away. (If the bride's father is not living, her brother or some other male relative or friend of the family may perform this function.) To him falls the responsibility of paying for the invitations, the reception, the floral decorations, music and choir, his daughter's trousseau, the awning at the church (if any), printing of service leaflets, cars to take the bride, family and house guests to and from the church, and cars to fetch guests from the station when necessary. He may propose the health of the bridal couple at the reception, or this may be done by another male relative or friend, according to choice.

Bride

She drives with her father to church, where her bridesmaids are waiting. The bride takes the right arm of her father and passes up the aisle.

The bridegroom, with the best man, awaits them on the right of the chancel entrance. The bride takes her place at the bridegroom's left side, with her father, or

WEDDING FLOWERS

In the church, remember that the flowers must be placed high or they will be concealed by people standing—a fact sometimes forgotten when seeing the church empty beforehand. Above is a green, white and yellow group —green leek heads and arum leaves, yellow and white lilies, white eremuri and yellow carnations. Arrange in position rather than attempt to move such a heavy vase

For the reception, a group of mixed colours (left) with a spreading background of hedge parsley (Queen Anne's lace): white and yellow arum lilies, pink and red peonies, pink, red and yellow carnations, cornflowers, roses and yellow kingcups

whoever is giving her away, on her left.

After the service the bridegroom gives his bride his left arm and they follow the clergy into the vestry to sign the register, where they are joined by the bride's and groom's parents and the attendants. After this, the couple walk slowly arm-in-arm down the aisle to the porch. The wedding photographs are sometimes taken here as well as, or instead of, at the reception.

Bridegroom

His financial responsibility includes the clergyman, the marriage licence, wedding ring and bouquets for bride and bridesmaid(s). He should also give the bridesmaids a small gift, generally jewellery. He provides the buttonholes for himself, the best man, ushers, etc., the car to take himself and his best man to and from church and the car that takes the bride and himself from the church to the reception. He pays for the honeymoon and the furnishings of the new home, though nowadays, when girls often earn as much as their fiancés, many brides contribute substantially towards the home, and relatives also help.

Bridesmaids

They are chosen from the unmarried relatives of bride and groom or are close friends of the bride. If a young married woman is chosen, she is known as the Matron of Honour. Numbers vary, but four to six is usual at big weddings. Bridesmaids to-day usually pay for their own dresses and choose them in consultation with the bride. A sister of the bride is often chief bridesmaid. She has many duties and acts as the bride's right hand, helping the bride to dress for her wedding, and later to change into her going-away outfit after the reception.

The chief bridesmaid proceeds to church ahead of the bride and awaits her at the church door with the other bridesmaids. She goes up the aisle behind the bride and her father. When the minister says "Who giveth this woman to be married?", the bridesmaid takes the bridal bouquet. After the signing of the register, the chief bridesmaid, on the arm of the best man, follows bride and groom down the aisle and out of the church.

Best Man

The best man, generally but not necessarily a bachelor, must be the perfect *chargé d'affaires*. Much responsibility rests on his shoulders.

Before the wedding he makes all the arrangements with the vestry clerk about the type of service required—after consulting the bride—makes plane, ship or train reservations for the honeymoon, attends to the luggage and sees that the bridegroom's travelling clothes are sent to the place of reception, to be there when he is ready to change into them.

On the wedding day the best man goes to the church with the groom half an hour before the ceremony. Both await the bride's entrance at the front of the church on the right-hand side, and the best man takes charge of the ring. During the service he stands at the groom's right, slightly behind him. After the service, accompanying the chief bridesmaid, he follows the couple to the vestry, where the bridal pair and their parents all sign the register.

After walking down the aisle with the chief bridesmaid, he sees bride and groom off in their car and makes sure that all the family and guests drive off in suitable sequence. He pays the clergyman, choirmaster, organist and bellringer (discreetly in envelopes), and then leaves for the reception himself, where in due time he replies to the toast to the bridesmaids, and reads aloud the telegrams. These are afterwards handed to the bride for acknowledgment.

As the best man's duties involve some monetary outlay, the bridegroom should make an adequate advance to him to cover necessary expenses. This applies, too, to the bride's father in connection with payments to the organist, etc.

Ushers

These are usually relatives or close male friends of the bride and bridegroom. They assist at the church before and after the ceremony, and should be at the church an hour before the service. As each guest arrives, the usher asks if he or she is a "friend of the bride or of the groom." Friends of the bride are shown to the left-hand pews and friends of the groom to the right. The ushers also hand out printed sheets of the service if these have been prepared.

LOVE AND MARRIAGE

*Every normal man and woman tries to find the true
mate and wants to make a success of marriage*

MEN and women are complementary to each other and, in the consummation of love, expand their personalities and every aspect of their lives. Fortunate, indeed, are those who, by intuition, good judgment or even good fortune, find and are united to a love mate who is true and constant. For them the opportunities for joyous companionship, reciprocal passion, happy family life, health of mind and body, and, indeed, success in all walks of life.

These are simple truths which are generally accepted but not always understood. Marriage in these days has come to be regarded as a difficult relationship, where failure is all too frequent. Yet every normal man and woman tries to find the true mate and, at heart, wants to make a success of marriage.

Unfortunately, there are many factors in our contemporary social life which tend to undermine marriage. Most significant of these is a lack of unity and cohesion in the family group. The structure of the family is much looser than it was: the ties and loyalties have become devalued. Broken families are common, and so there has grown up a generation who are suspicious, if not actually cynical, of marriage.

Sex Education

Children from unhappy homes seldom make happy marriages when they become men and women. They have had no chance to form a high ideal of love or marriage and often repeat the pattern of their parents' marriage. To be born into a happy family is therefore the best safeguard to a happy marriage. Unfortunately, that is not within our choice; yet in so far as we possess intelligence and character, we can make a success of our marriage if we are alive to the pitfalls and study our responsibilities. After all, the great majority of men and women *do* get married, and the great majority *do* maintain their marriages throughout the natural term of their lives.

It should be part of our education to

When we fall in love, we are responding to a
basic drive from our whole being, physical,
mental and spiritual

understand the true meaning of our sexual life. Many of the tragedies of sex are the outcome of ignorance, and many young men and women approach marriage with distorted knowledge and tainted experience. Children are interested in sex as they are interested in all other things, and their curiosity should be satisfied according to their level of maturity.

It is usually when the parents treat sex as a forbidden subject that children develop an abnormal interest. If there is no atmosphere of tension in the parents when children seek sex knowledge, a wholesome and dispassionate attitude will be implanted. On the other hand, if the atmosphere is one of secrecy, shame and taboo, children are sure to acquire information in an underground way and come to regard sex as something unpleasant and wrong. No human instinct is more liable to distortion in early life than the sexual instinct.

Of great importance is the adolescent phase of sexual development. Ripening of mind and body are taking place and the youth of both sexes are becoming conscious of the sexual drive within them. Wise, sympathetic and tolerant guidance on the part of parents and teachers is essential. Much will depend upon the love atmosphere of the home and the example set. Parents who are unhappy in their own love lives will find it difficult to talk freely and frankly, but they should face this responsibility with courage and insight. Adolescents should be taught that sexual desire is normal, that no harm can come from continence, and that it is advisable to engage actively in recreational pastimes, while trying to avoid consciously thinking about sex. It should be explained that energy directed along the channel of sex can be redirected into constructive channels until marriage takes place. It cannot be over-emphasised that many of the sex difficulties in marriage are due to the faulty pattern of sex laid down in childhood.

The Right Partner in Life

Most damaging to the future love life is a smothering love and over-protectiveness on the part of a parent. Too often this is merely a form of parental selfishness. The parents, usually from dissatisfaction with their own love life, fear to see their children grow up, and satisfy their own frustrated love needs by excessive demands for affection from their children. As a result, the emotional and sexual development of the child is stunted. Such children remain immature, and immaturity is probably the greatest single cause of marriage difficulties. Men and women who are mother or father fixated (to use the technical phrase) have difficulty in finding the right mate; they are still at the self-love stage and they look for a mother or father in their marriage rather than a wife or husband.

When we fall in love, we are responding to a basic drive from our whole being, physical, mental and spiritual. While the primary object of marriage may be the continuation of human life, the sexual relationship is intertwined with the highest and subtlest human emotions and activities: it is a harmonising and liberating influence giving wholesome balance to the whole organism.

Havelock Ellis wrote: "Apart from any sexual craving, the complete spiritual contact of two persons who love each other can only be attained through some act of rare intimacy. No act can be quite so intimate as the sexual embrace. In its accomplishment, for all who have reached a reasonable human degree of development, the communion of bodies becomes the communion of souls." We should therefore approach love and marriage with high idealism.

In the search for a life partner, much depends upon the dictates of our emotional and intellectual make-up and needs. External appearance and bodily charm play a part and in some are the dominating factor, but mere physical attraction or sensuality alone is a poor basis for marriage. There is always a danger, especially in the immature person, for the projection of his ideal upon the woman of his choice: he endows her with the qualities which he desires and is blind to her real personality. Disillusionment must inevitably arise.

Then there are men who seek a mate whose personality most nearly coincides with their own. This is dangerous, for it indicates a morbid self-love and implies that they want their mate to be merely an expansion of themselves: in time, the woman will revolt, for she will feel that she has no separate identity.

The Danger of Immaturity

While it is possible for an immature man to marry a mature woman and to be helped towards maturity by his marriage, there is much peril when an immature man, who needs mothering, marries an immature woman who is seeking the protection and security which she had in childhood. This is a common enough situation, making for tension and frustration, unless both can learn the art of growing-up.

Men and women to avoid are the selfish and vain who do not understand that happiness can be achieved only by giving as well as taking. Then there are those with debased ideals who regard the love relationship only as an opportunity for crude sexual gratification, and those who, conscious of their sexual attractiveness, abuse their power and are unfaithful by nature.

People find themselves in romantic circumstances and the consequent exhilaration causes them to imagine themselves deeply in love

"Love at first sight" may be unwise but by no means always so. There are men and women who are powerfully intuitive but who are nevertheless remarkably sound in their judgments when these concern the major issues of their lives. Experience should teach us whether or not we can trust our intuitions; in general, we should beware of sudden infatuations.

People find themselves in adventurous and romantic circumstances, and the consequent exhilaration causes them to imagine themselves deeply in love. In such cases, there may well be an aftermath of unhappiness. Again there are those who are for ever deceiving themselves in a quite genuine way: they dramatise every situation and fail to realise they are play-acting. Beware of the romanticists: their affections are often short-lived.

Men and women who have suffered some serious disappointment in love are very apt to plunge quickly into a new love, popularly called "the rebound." Needless to say, it is a situation fraught with risks and one to be avoided. Too often, it is a spite reaction, a mode of registering hate against the former love, a poor attempt at restoring the injured pride. After an unfortunate love affair the personality may be seriously disturbed, and to attempt to make a vital decision in this state is perilous. One should wait till the wounds are fully healed before beginning the search for a new mate.

In deciding on marriage we should remember that we are making what should be a lifetime decision upon which our future well-being and happiness depend. Much havoc can result if we make the wrong decision—not only for ourselves, but also for the children we may bring into the world.

One final piece of advice: sex continence before marriage is both possible and desirable without sex repression. Creative work in any form can provide a suitable means of expression for sex-energy. In the courting period before marriage, sexual chastity, apart from moral reasons, is desirable on psychological grounds. Failure to achieve it may lead to subsequent regret, to guilt and to anxiety. It will deprive the marriage of its joy and adventure, and it cannot become the really great moment in life that it should be. Sexual purity before marriage is a strongly rooted social sentiment and represents a standard of personal conduct to be aimed at and realised.

Early Days of Marriage

It is in the first years of marriage that the really sound foundations of the union should be established. Strains may come later, but they are never likely to reach breaking point if there have developed ties of physical, intellectual and spiritual intimacy. In the growth of a true marriage, men and women absorb something of each other's being and this creates a bond not easily broken.

Therefore, although the early phase of a marriage may sometimes be difficult, the partners should strive towards a happy adjustment and, if need be, should not be too proud to seek help from a doctor or the Marriage Guidance Council.

Everyone entering marriage should do so feeling that the marriage *is* going to last. It may seem superfluous to state this, but if people begin their marriage with a background idea that, if all does not go well immediately, there is always divorce or separation to solve the problem, an insecurity will ensue which of itself may lead to a broken marriage. In this respect, parental example is significant. It is well-known that the divorce rate is higher among those whose parents have been divorced than in those who come from families where divorce is unknown.

In every marriage there are "growing pains." In the day-to-day activities occasional frictions must arise. The adjustment of two personalities, even when there is great love between them, must take time, but temperamental difficulties should be tackled early in marriage. It is not that husband and wife should try to dull their individuality. They should really try to understand each other and appreciate the need for individual self-expression. To live with someone who has become a pale reflection of one's own personality is deadening to a true and stimulating love relationship. Mutual respect there must be and an ability to be sensibly tolerant of each other's imperfections. Indeed, it sometimes happens that little weaknesses add charm to the personality, while perfection can be very irritating. That is human nature.

A successful marriage demands a lively imagination, the capacity to make the relationship interesting and varied, to foster the growth of the personalities by full and energetic living. Marriage should never be a retreat from life: it should be an active, adventurous partnership always reaching forth into life. There is no place for selfishness or being wrapped up in

In marriage there must be mutual respect and sensible tolerance of each other's imperfections

The birth of the first child is the beginning of a new era of responsibility in married life, and a father can no longer expect the undivided attention of his wife

oneself, for that will slowly but effectively destroy affection. Common aims and objectives make for unity of purpose and afford a common motive to inspire the marriage.

Parenthood

If a marriage is steering towards success, the parental instinct will manifest itself and become insistent. The maturing of love brings with it the desire for children. This is most desirable, for children are a binding link which gives security to the marriage.

Postponing parenthood for economic reasons may be sometimes justifiable, but husband and wife should be quite sure they are not making this an excuse for selfishness. Establishing a family has a maturing effect upon love and marriage. It

is well to remember, too, that it is unfair to a child to have no brothers or sisters. Therefore aim to have more than *one* child.

The birth of the first child is the beginning of a new era of responsibility in married life. Fathers must be prepared to accept that they cannot now expect the undivided attention of their wives. Should a feeling of jealousy arise, and this does happen in the immature type of man, it must be resisted and a feeling of protection developed towards mother and child.

It requires to be emphasised that if there is to be a good relationship between parents and child, the primary emotional needs of the child are its need to be loved and its need to have its own love accepted as good. The failure to satisfy either of those needs leads to a basic insecurity which disturbs the personality development of the child in a way which may mar the happiness of the marriage. It is the unconscious emotional atmosphere engendered by the parents which, enfolding the child, influences its behaviour to a profound extent. Some parents, because of disharmony in their own minds, have not the ability to be emotionally natural, and this is bound to make for insecurity in the child.

As parents, we must aim at complete sincerity in our attitude to our children. It is virtually impossible to deceive the strong intuitions of the child. If our children are difficult, we must ask ourselves if we are difficult parents. Children brought up in a free and considerate atmosphere, where there is love and trust between the father and mother, will grow up to hold their parents in respect and affection, will themselves develop into happy individuals, and will add joy and security to the marriage.

Avoiding Marriage Failure

Failure to have children when they are truly desired may give rise to intense disappointment. This may result from an abnormality in the husband or the wife. Medical advice should be obtained, for some of the causes of infertility can be remedied. Should a husband and wife remain childless, they must face the situation squarely and with courage, and should consider carefully the question of adoption. This may be a difficult decision to make, but it can be said that, for many husbands and wives who are deprived of children, adoption will often prove a great blessing and be a potent factor in maintaining happiness in marriage.

The causes of marriage failures are as complicated and varied as the problems of human life itself. Consciously, most men and women want their marriages to be happy and successful, but unfortunately there are often unconscious drives in the opposite direction. Conscious problems can be sorted out and usually dealt with on a rational basis: unconscious problems, which are submerged deeply in the mind, can play havoc with marital happiness because the nature of the hidden conflict is not understood. If held in the grip of hidden emotional troubles, a man and his wife can flounder from one mishap to another until disaster is inevitable, in spite of the best intentions on the part of both.

In the close emotional relationship of marriage, it is not easy to be objective about oneself or one's partner. Distorting emotions set up by inner mental conflict destroy the capacity for clear thinking. Moreover, disturbed emotions in one partner can engender distorted emotions in the other. Tension and anxiety are set up and the difficulties are intensified, for no one is capable of wisdom in thought, word or act unless there is peace and security of mind.

Thus a vicious cycle is set up from which escape may be impossible without expert psychological help. It is not the marriages in which there are frequent conscious clashes of personality that fail irreparably. The real disasters in marriage, leading to divorce, occur when two personalities have aroused in each other deep emotional conflicts with which their conscious minds cannot grapple. These tragedies are all the greater because they are tragedies of frustrated love.

Physically, on the sexual plane, such victims of deep conflict may be satisfied; it is on the higher and wider aspects of their love life that they cannot find harmony and fulfilment. In these cases, sometimes a period of separation, mutually agreed, will permit inner adjustment of mind to take place and so save the marriage. Certainly no marriage should be allowed to disrupt finally without expert investigation (and treatment) such as may be afforded through the services of a Marriage Guidance Council. This is imperative where there are children of the marriage. It should be remembered that in the breaking up of a marriage, it is the children who suffer most.

Tolerance Essential

A common cause of marital disharmony is the seeking for something in the partner to fulfil an inner need, and the failure to find that something. Many people enter marriage with ideals into which husband and wife expect each other to fit. They expect too much from each other and must in time suffer some degree of disappointment which may be followed by indifference or even bitterness.

It cannot be over-emphasised that husbands and wives must be realists in the acceptance of each others' personalities, taking the good with the less good, the faults with the virtues. Wise tolerance, a sense of human perspective and, not least, a sense of humour, are the very necessary qualities for success in marriage.

Actual sexual difficulties are, of course, a frequent cause of marriage troubles. It must be realised that a happy and satisfied sex life is the bedrock of marriage. Where there is complete fulfilment of the sex and love life in its widest implications, a marriage is not likely to come to grief. Sexual adjustment is not easy for many people at the beginning of marriage. But if the young married people will confide frankly to each other and understand that the fullness of sexual experience develops with the marriage, many initial troubles will be overcome and there will be no failure in confidence. However, if sexual difficulties persist, the doctor should be consulted. Many such difficulties are quickly remediable.

Seeking consolation from a third party is not really the cause of a broken marriage but the symptom of a marriage disorder. If husbands and wives would only recognise the incipient and warning signs, and realise that marriage ills, like bodily ills, can be diagnosed, treated and often cured, marriage failures would be much less frequent than they are.

Apportioning the blame from the moral aspect in an unhappy marriage, except where there is gross cruelty on one side, is difficult, probably unwise and generally unhelpful. It is much more important to find the psychological origins of the disharmony and seek by psychological methods of treatment to put them right.

Fundamentally, in any broken marriage there must have been defects or weaknesses in the personalities of the man and woman—faults attributable to inheritance and early upbringing. But there must have been also a failure in the sentiment of love in the fullest sense, a failure to establish true friendship and companionship. We must be alive to the perils of marriage if we are to know and sustain its joys.

Seeking consolation from a third party is not really the cause of a broken marriage, but the symptom of a marriage disorder

PRACTICAL PSYCHOLOGY

*To help you develop your own personality and understand
the effect early influences can have on your children*

SELF-EXPRESSION

FOR successful living, we must know how to express ourselves to our own satisfaction as well as to the satisfaction of others. One of the arts of life is the art of self-expression. Many people have much to give to life but fail because they are frustrated in their capacity for self-expression. Of course, we express ourselves in everything we do, even in the most trivial acts, but it is our ability to express the creative spirit within us to others that really matters.

You may have interesting ideas and fine thoughts, but these will remain sterile and profitless if you cannot give them form and so be able to communicate them to your fellow creatures. To have something worth while to say and to know how to say it affords an intimate satisfaction which enhances our personalities, not only for ourselves but for other people.

Adequate self-expression is a means to a happy and successful social life. The man or woman who can converse in a bright and interesting fashion is always sure of a welcome in any society. The power of words is not to be despised. True, it can be abused, but this will not arise if behind the words there is rightness and clarity of thought, and sincerity.

Learn to Think Clearly

Now, sound thinking depends in part upon knowledge. Therefore, we must constantly seek for new facts and new ideas. To be a good conversationalist, you must be knowledgeable, and to-day, with newspapers, journals, periodicals, the radio and television, many opportunities are afforded to acquire information easily. But a mind merely full of bits and pieces of knowledge is of little value. Knowledge must be integrated and built up into our total mental structure, and when we are able to add values to the digested knowledge, we may become truly cultured.

Then, to express ourselves, we must learn to think clearly. Confused thinking leads to confused talking, loss of self-confidence and embarrassment. For clarity of thought, there is nothing so helpful as the exercise of expressing your thoughts on paper. Writing requires concentrated effort and implies the logical assembly of your ideas. By such effort you may not become a brilliant stylist in writing, though you may discover you have talent, but you will certainly improve your capacity for lucid and direct thinking, which in turn will give you confidence to express yourself in the spoken word. One of the most enjoyable ways of practising the written word is by letter-writing. Master this technique and you will find your capacity for conversation much improved.

Judged by What We Say

It is by what we say that we are judged as personalities, more than by any other form of self-expression. Speech is the main method of contact with our fellow creatures. In every aspect of our lives we need to speak well to achieve success. It is often said that to-day conversation is a decayed art. That is because so much of our leisure tends to be taken up by passive entertainments. Radio, television and the cinema are certainly competitors to conversation, but whenever intelligent people forgather there will be good talk. People who cannot talk well are greatly handicapped socially and occupationally. Remember, however, that conversation, like all arts, requires to be practised: hence the value of social group activities, study circles, societies and clubs where people of like interests can assemble for the interchange of thoughts and views. We should all apply ourselves with seriousness to learning the art of conversation.

There are, of course, many other forms of self-expression. Most of us have something in us that is worthy of expression, not only for our own good but for the good of others. Self-expression in the best sense is self-giving. Colourful personalities are expressive personalities, but we must beware of over-dominating our environment with aggressive self-expression. We must temper our self-expression with tact, sympathy and consideration for others. People who constantly express their views in an over-assertive way are never popular and sooner or later will find themselves cold-shouldered. Self-expression is a gentle art which helps us to maintain good relations all round.

Hindrances to self-expression may arise from conflict and anxiety within the personality. A mind preyed upon by anxiety can never give of its best. On the other hand, controlled emotion, composure and a reasonable belief in oneself lead to a mental attitude which makes possible the expression of one's individuality in a graceful and efficient manner.

Apart from speech and writing, there are a host of artistic forms of self-expression —painting, drawing, playing a musical instrument, photography, dressmaking, gardening and crafts of all varieties. We can express ourselves in the furnishing of our homes, in collecting, and not least in our job, whether it is inside or outside the home.

We should endeavour to place the stamp of our personalities upon everything we do

Master the technique of letter-writing and you will find your capacity for conversation much improved

in a creative way. That may require much experiment, but most of us will discover something that we are good at and we should practise to become expert at it. We can all leave behind us some footprints in the sands of time which will have made our lives worth while. The chronically dissatisfied people are those who have never found ways and means of creative self-expression. They feel unhappy and frustrated, always finding fault with things external to themselves. Their attitude to life is negative. They cannot receive because they do not know how to give. Let such people discover a hobby, a recreation, a cultural pursuit, an altruistic social activity, and their lives and outlook will be transformed.

One of the great problems of to-day is the proper use of leisure. With a general shortening of working hours, most of us have time to

Many people have much to give to life but fail because they are frustrated in their capacity for self-expression

spare, but this can be squandered on passive, merely distracting entertainment, or wasted in boredom. We must educate ourselves to use our leisure so that it will add substance to our lives and contribute to our greater satisfaction. Not that we do not all need some relaxation. We cannot exercise our intellects all the time, but we should so plan our lives that a part of our leisure is directed to a worthy and constructive objective. That way lies happiness and contentment.

THE BALANCED PERSONALITY

To achieve harmony within the self, to develop a balanced personality, these are the time-honoured ideals which give a real purpose to human life. Whether we are conscious of this aim or not, we are all striving, often blindly, for its realisation. Happiness will elude us if our minds are riven by conflict and if we try to face the realities of life with our personalities lacking in unity.

For unity or integration implies self-control, with the deep desires of our natures synthetised and regulated in accordance with worth-while standards and moral values. Unfortunately, to-day there are many who regard the holding and pursuit of ideals, personal and social, as old-fashioned and sentimental. Such people are merely trying to find an excuse for their own selfishness and immaturity: they may find pleasures in life but will never discover the true meaning of happiness.

The balanced personality comes from a gradual process of self-development from childhood onwards. We should adopt the attitude that there is always something fresh to learn from life, no matter what our age in years may be. We should always be eager to continue our experiences of living and should never allow our sense of curiosity to grow dull. We must strive to maintain lively interests, so broadening the mind and adding to our vitality.

It is well to remember that much of the satisfaction in life comes not so much from achievement as from the process of achieving. Thus we should not rest upon our accomplishments but should continue to seek fresh records. A man's reach should exceed his grasp.

A balanced personality gives us the way to a balanced life. It means that we can express ourselves by the *whole* of our personality, so permitting healthy adjustment to reality. It means that we can face life's problems squarely, confident that our responses will be in harmony with our real selves: it means that our actions will be controlled according to principles founded on right ideals. It does *not* mean a narrow self-complacency.

The possessors of a balanced personality will be able to drink deeply of the joys of human life. They will enjoy happy relationships with their fellow beings; above all, they will be able to *give* much happiness and be a positive and constructive force in this conflicting world. We should all keep on discovering fresh reasons and worthy objectives for living, and, with that thought ever in our minds, we shall surely achieve that rich measure of success and happiness which we all desire.

OVERCOMING INFERIORITY

There are many people who go through life with an ever-present sense of inferiority in relation to other people. They are over-weighted with a feeling that they are inadequate and they are given to self-disparagement: they underrate their abilities and believe they are not as good as the next person. They constantly feel embarrassed under certain circumstances, perhaps with a member of the opposite sex, or even with their parents; maybe with their employers, and often when they have to meet a stranger. They experience a most uncomfortable feeling which may render them almost inarticulate in extreme cases, and certainly affects their efficiency in self-expression: frequently they blush and behave awkwardly.

Now, most of us at some time in our lives and in certain circumstances feel such "inferiority," particularly when we are young. In the adolescent phase, we often find ourselves in situations which demand more from us than we have to give and which make us conscious of some of our weaknesses. None of us can hope to escape such occasions. They may be humiliating and painful, yet they are part of our training for life. Without an awareness of our limitations, be they of knowledge, of experience or of the vulnerable aspects of our personality, we cannot hope to improve and to mature ourselves. But we must not let ourselves be for ever dominated by a sense of inferiority. If we do, we shall never realise the full potentialities of our minds, nor can we be really happy and successful.

Origins of Inferiority

From the time of our birth there is within all of us a constant struggle for power and for the satisfaction of our desires, and arrayed against us are opposing forces which have to be met with and controlled. We have within us a need to master our environment and, clearly, without this urge the development of man and civilisation could not take place.

Infants and young children are relatively weak and helpless in relation to their parents and other adults. Their equipment is inferior, but they are constantly trying to overcome this and their efforts in this direction instigate their growing-up. As always, when it comes to personal human destiny, it is the attitude of the parents which determines how the child will manipulate its drive for power. Oversheltering and over-protection may dull the impulse so that the child always wants to be cushioned: rejection and domination may lead to insecurity and revolt. Parents must strike a reasonable balance in their attitudes: reasonable protection without making life too easy, love with sincerity and constructive criticism which should never be harsh and hurtful.

A child's soul is a delicate thing, and wounds inflicted, especially by persons they love, may

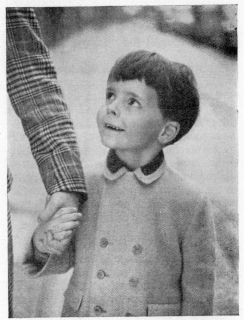

Every child needs and deserves to have complete confidence in its parents who should provide reasonable protection without making life too easy

Love from its mother is all-important to a child; if she gives it freely, she helps her children to grow up happy and well balanced

remain with the child all its life. A child's conception of itself is easily undermined, often through the thoughtlessness of parents.

Above all, the child needs love from its mother. If there is rejection, conscious or unconscious, the child turns the fault upon itself. "Mother is good and kind: if she does not love me, it is because I am bad." So argues the child intuitively, and this may be the starting-point of an inferiority complex. Non-responsiveness on the part of the mother leads to anxiety and aggression in the child and a quest for power, which cannot be achieved and which only further intensifies the sense of inferiority.

Physical Defects

Of great significance in the genesis of inferiority is the existence of any physical incapacity or weakness which makes the child feel different from other children and which, from time to time, may be adversely commented upon by those to whom the child wants to feel worth while. It may be a simple matter; the child is unusually fat or thin, tall or small; it may have flat feet, a freckled complexion, or a squint. Or there may be some serious deformity such as a club-foot or a paralysed limb, or there may be some measure of deprivation, such as deafness or short-sight.

If the child is made painfully aware of these defects by unthinking criticism, by teasing or ridicule, much harm is done to the child's conception of itself, and the foundations may be laid for an inferiority complex which seriously impairs development and may lead to undesirable compensatory character traits. And yet it should be realised that the existence of these physical inferiorities can and often does lead to noble effort and achievement. We all know of people who have suffered from grievous handicaps and who have risen above them by sheer force of moral character, sometimes doing more for themselves and other people than they would have done if they had been normal. Inferiority properly handled can be a spur to creative effort in all spheres of life, given courage, persistence and the right ideals. In the mind of the victim of inferiority, this thought should be ever present.

A temporary inferiority feeling may arise acutely even in a robust and well-balanced personality under severe stress. A person may have built up a reasonable security in life, meeting responsibilities satisfactorily and happily, when he is assailed by some external event which shakes the personality and undermines his confidence. Maybe some childhood inferiorities are revived and the person feels that his world is not the safe place that it was and that he no longer is master over it.

From being assured in his social and occupational relationships, he becomes anxious, fearful of the future and sensitive of failure. Temporary set-backs of this nature are not infrequent, having regard to the hazards of life, but they should be recognised as *temporary* and strenuous efforts should be made to get hold of the situation, get on top of it, reshape life if need be, and achieve once more the former worth-while feeling. But let us remember that even a temporary inferiority feeling may become a habit. That is a danger to be fought vigorously and persistently.

Effects of Inferiority

Persons who suffer from a sense of inferiority never feel really happy or at ease, either with themselves or with other people. Feeling life difficult, they are prone to evade its serious demands. Conscious that they are different, they are always afraid of what other people are thinking of them. They want to be valued, but feel they are always undervalued. They want to be loved, but are doubtful of love extended to them. Their embarrassment in social life may lead them to a lonely existence which only accentuates the inferiority feeling. Unable to stand comparison with other people, they seek isolation.

This moving away from the stream of life has secondary repercussions upon the personality. The associated loss of interest increases the loneliness. All effort, especially that involving social contact, becomes progressively more difficult. In a defensive way, the person may become suspicious, resentful and even hostile to those towards whom he would naturally be affectionate. Personality distortion becomes progressive, and the worst construction is put upon any mishap, however trivial or accidental it may be. More and more, refuge may be taken in fantasy, and the more fantasy the less action. It is easy, though dangerous, to realise one's ambitions in dreams. In time these faults may well stretch the personality to near breaking point and may result in such a failure to meet life's requirements that a "nervous breakdown" ensues. No lonely or socially isolated person can ever be really happy.

In some people there may be an unconscious or near conscious drive to overcome a sense of inferiority by some exaggerated adjustment of the personality, by some over-emphasis in the opposite direction. A timid and oversensitive person may cultivate aggressiveness and harshness, or even cruelty, in his attitudes to others.

Over-compensation

Sexually fearful and inadequate types may constantly seek "conquests" for no other reason than to make themselves feel superior. This attitude is often seen in adolescents who are sexually insecure: youths will smoke and even drink excessively, or dress in exaggerated styles, and girls may caricature themselves with "make-up" just to prove to themselves that they are sexually potent men and women. In slight degree, this may be regarded as almost normal during this phase of life, but its persistence is a sure sign of the inadequacy of the personality and of sexual insecurity. The Don Juans of both sexes in adult life are over-compensating for an inherent fault in their sexual development. They are the essentially immature, vainly protesting their maturity.

We often see similar over-compensations in the morbid pursuit of wealth and power. Tyrants are often basically weak characters—vain, conceited and labouring under a sense of grievance. Ruthless "strong men" are often those who are putting up a façade to cover secret weaknesses which they cannot accept to themselves and rectify. Bullies are usually cowards; the excessively amorous are sometimes impotent. The obsessional money-grabber, whose life is dictated by the search for wealth for its own sake, is often striving to

People with a sense of inferiority seek isolation because they are unable to stand comparison with others

over-compensate for a deep sense of social inferiority.

Needless to say, we all know from our day-to-day experience, how such "over-compensation" unbalances the personalities of such victims, makes them "difficult" and often socially unacceptable. They are sometimes said to have "superiority complexes," but are in reality over-compensated inferiorities which are indicative of unsatisfactory, maybe even pathological, maladjustments of the personality.

Appearing Superior

Over-compensation is not a healthy way of overcoming a sense of inferiority. Indeed, such a remedy may well be worse than the disease, for often it will only intensify the person's relative isolation from ordinary people and increase his loneliness and inner frustration. Setting out to be a "superior person" in any sphere of human life is always dangerous and sometimes tragic.

Too often, "over-compensation" is fostered or dictated by low standards and false values of life. Worship of power without understanding its responsibility, pursuit of material gain, egotism and lack of social conscience, self-gratification irrespective of how it affects others—all these are character weaknesses which in the inferiority personality will colour and shape the over-compensation.

Right Ways to Overcome Inferiority

Given some understanding of the origins and causes of inferiority feeling, it should be apparent that there are right ways and wrong ways of dealing with this personality problem. We have noted the dangers of over-compensation and of permitting the inferiority reaction to become chronic and habitual. We must remember that, during the developmental years, some feelings of inadequacy are bound to be experienced, but that these, acknowledged and understood, can act as a natural stimulus to our advancement.

It is from this sense of weakness, in the face of the perils of existence, that man has developed strength, and that truth is applicable now as it was in the dark days of primitive man. A frank and honest recognition of the inferiority feeling is the first step to its liquidation. A little self-analysis will be necessary. Start from childhood and try to understand clearly and in an unbiased way your relationships to parents and other adults who have played a part in your life.

You may have suffered at their hands, but now is the time to understand and to forgive, to bring to light any concealed bitterness and to erase it from the mind. If parents were thoughtless and unkind, it was most likely because *they* were unhappy, so let no rancour persist. If there have been humiliations in your life, remember that everyone has suffered in this way, and rid your mind of resentment.

Try to develop independence and self-reliance, recollecting that "growing-up" is not easy and often painful. The family is intended to give you security in your growing years, and can be a support in times of trouble, but it is not meant to cushion you and over-protect you from the world for the rest of your life. You must always strive to come to grips with life and not escape its demands. Seek the right experiences, and the more you achieve, the more you *will* achieve.

It is of the very greatest importance that those with feelings of inferiority should shun loneliness and do all that is possible to cultivate social life. It may be difficult at first, but each effort makes the next effort easier. Seek entertainment, recreation and hobbies which will bring you into contact with people. The more varied the personalities you meet, the more you will gain from the association. Every encounter with a really live personality will add something positive to you and will increase your self-confidence. At a social gathering, be interested in the people present: that will help you to forget about yourself, to be less self-conscious.

Prepare Beforehand

If possible, try to discover something about the people you are likely to meet beforehand. Most people are responsive to questions about themselves, their work and their achievements, and the more simple the approach the easier the contact. Social grace is a quality that grows with practice. None of us is wholly self-sufficient. The herd instinct is strong in us. We all need friends, and friendship is not only sustaining to our morale but energising.

One of the difficulties besetting the person with inferiority feeling is *thinking for himself*. He is inclined to think emotionally, to accept ideas uncritically because of the undue influence of wishes or fears. He is often afraid of expressing his own ideas and points of view because of self-depreciation. Such a person must train his mind to reason clearly and directly, influenced only by facts and premises arrived at objectively and dispassionately. Thinking for oneself does not mean thinking differently from everyone else on every occasion. That would merely indicate perversity and an aggressive over-compensation for some inner weakness.

It is a good exercise to take every opportunity—for example, when seeing a play or film, or reading a novel, or visiting an art exhibition—to formulate criticisms in your mind which you are prepared to discuss and to defend in a calm and logical way. Progressively you will gain confidence, and your faculty for clear and reasoned thinking will improve. Training the mind in this way demands persistence of effort: it must be done conscientiously and deliberately, and it will take time: but it will expand your personality and make people interested in you, and that is a comforting feeling which will go a long way towards overcoming a sense of inferiority.

Self-tolerance Necessary

A reasonable degree of self-tolerance is essential for all of us and especially for those who labour under inferiority. Often the timid, shy person is making excessively harsh demands upon himself and setting fantastically high standards. He is incapable of accepting in a balanced way the frailties of human nature in general, and of his own nature in particular. He must learn to know that everyone is subject to desires of the flesh, to impulses to gratify the basic instincts, and he must not allow his mind to be poisoned with feelings of guilt about these matters.

To repress these desires is usually to increase their intensity. What is necessary is to learn how to control and direct them; to realise that mistakes and failures are inevitable in the training process of life. An exaggerated and rigid conscience will distort the smooth growth of personality and may induce a morbid sense of sin with its consequent sense of inferiority.

A realistic assessment of the liabilities and the assets of our personality is highly desirable. We should know our abilities as well as our limitations, and knowing our limitations does not mean a *passive* acceptance of them. It implies their recognition plus a technique to make reasonable adjustments to them. In the case of physical handicaps—for example, a congenital deformity or malformation—it would be pernicious to permit this to cause a perpetual sense of resentment: it must first be accepted and then a continuous effort made to effect a useful and personally satisfactory compensation. As has been indicated previously,

It may be hard at first, but those with feelings of inferiority must seek recreation which brings them into contact with other people

the presence of some physical body defect may bring out the very best in human character.

To sum up: it is obvious that inferiority feeling must be tackled from many aspects if it is to be conquered. The human personality is most complex and there is no single method of remedying its inadequacies. Perhaps the most important factor is the *desire* to change: you must really want to change yourself if you want to overcome inferiority. Without the newer *will* nothing can be achieved. It is imperative to avoid a fatalistic attitude, to be resigned to going through life crippled and handicapped by inferiority. Unfortunately, there are some people who seemingly wish to hold on to their inadequate personalities and, in such cases, the help of a psychotherapist should be sought, for it is likely that there is a deep disturbance of the personality.

Tackle Inferiority Feelings Early

Success and happiness cannot co-exist with inferiority feeling that is ingrained. Therefore tackle this problem early when you are first conscious of it, and, if you have courage, understanding and strength of will, you will assuredly reinforce your personality and be enabled to lead a full and satisfying life.

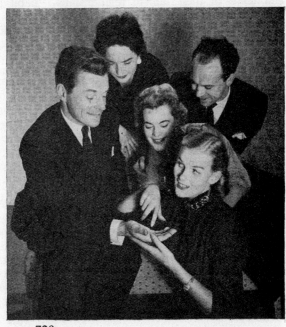

LEARN TO RELAX AND VANQUISH WORRY

*It takes time to master the art,
but it brings relief from tension*

The born worrier makes his own life a misery—and affects all those around him with his constant anxieties

A NOTICEABLE feature of life to-day is the large number of people who experience and suffer mental tension. In all classes of society, in all walks of life, at all ages, we find men and women who are tense in themselves, tense in their work and tense in their human relationships. This tension of mind and body occurs in all degrees, from a mild "tautness of the nerves" to an incapacitating fear or panic. Much personal unhappiness and inefficiency are the inevitable consequences. It is impossible to achieve easiness of mind, balance and poise, and successful day-to-day activities if our nervous energy is squandered on tension and anxiety.

There is alleged to be much in the current mode of social life which leads to tension, but people are always apt to try to find the causes of mind troubles outside of themselves. We must remember that it is we who dictate our lives and that more frustrations arise from within ourselves than are imposed on us by outside influences. It is important to bear this in mind and, when we are subject to tension and anxiety, we should attempt to discover the causes within ourselves. These we can sometimes put right or at least make adjustments to—whereas it is often impossible to obtain a change in our circumstances to suit what are sometimes our special weaknesses.

Mental tension shows itself by an uneasiness or disquietude of mind and feelings. It may be present more or less continuously or may only arise under obvious environmental difficulties. It is accompanied by a tension of the muscles of the body which is quite perceptible and may even be mildly painful. We are all familiar with the furrowed brow, the frown, the rigid and tremulous limbs and the jerky movements of the tense person.

Such muscle tension, spread throughout the body, is apt to be perpetuated as a habit and often, indeed, persists during sleep. It leads to a constant leakage of nervous energy, causing fatigue and, in time, exhaustion. It is a fact that excessively tense people tire quickly, and that they have to make almost violent demands upon themselves to accomplish quite simple tasks. They seem to be putting a great deal into their work and yet achieve little. It is a common fallacy that we do our best when we are "strung up"; actually, it is the opposite: maximum output and best quality are accomplished only under conditions of a calm and untensioned nervous system.

A State of Fear

A tension or anxiety state is really a state of diffuse fear. Occasionally, however, it may be so acute as to assume the proportion of a panic. Simple anxiety can arise, of course, in some situation which is a challenge to the individual—for example, during an examination. One may regard that as a normal transitory reaction. When a person is in a state of more or less constant tension and apprehension, we must look for the cause in some submerged conflict within the mind—to some deep emotional insecurity.

Anxiety is a symptom of some threat to the personality from within the mind. Disturbing emotions are being evoked which repercuss upon the working of all the body organs. Emotions are the great driving forces of human activity, but we must learn, as we travel through life, how to use them properly, and to direct them constructively, not destructively. Emotions can destroy health of mind and body.

The fretful, worrying, tense person is spendthrift of the creative force within him and he is taking great risks with his future organic well-being. Tense people can drive themselves into peptic ulcer and high blood pressure with all its consequences: they impose a great handicap upon their mental efficiency and happiness.

Muscle Tension

Normally, in order to maintain our posture, certain groups of muscles are in a state of "tonus" or mild contraction. We are unaware of this muscle contraction in health, but, in tense, anxious people, unnecessary groups of muscles go into contraction, especially in any situation involving emotional stress. There is a widespread muscular contraction and there is a vague consciousness of muscle tension. Moreover, the involuntary muscles of the heart, blood vessels and gastro-intestinal tract

may be involved if the mental stress be marked. It is a well-recognised phenomenon that under great fear the pupils dilate, the heart beats faster, the stomach and intestinal movements are reduced or cease and the bladder loses its tone.

It is to be noted that voluntary muscles, while controlled by motor nerves from the brain, are also supplied with sensory nerves which pass to the brain. Thus, excessive muscle tension leads to a continuous stream of sensory impulses of a mildly painful kind reacting on a mind that is already over-burdened under emotional stress. Also, it has been shown experimentally that there is no electrical activity in a healthy muscle at rest, but in tense subjects some activity is present even when the subject regards himself as relaxed.

Muscle tension is very marked in the respiration of anxious persons. Investigations have shown that the breathing is more shallow than in the case of normal people and the rate is irregular. This is noticeable even to the casual observer. Nervous people often sigh and yawn and breathe spasmodically.

With the acceptance that mind tension is closely related to muscle tension, it is reasonable to postulate that any methods of releasing the muscle tension will have a beneficial effect upon the mind tension. It may be suggested that mere rest and quiet

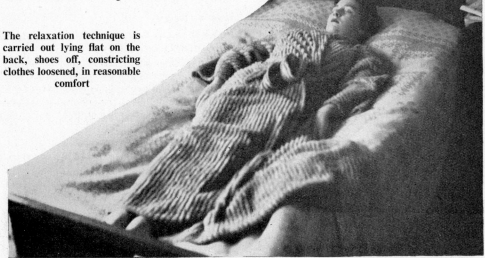

The relaxation technique is carried out lying flat on the back, shoes off, constricting clothes loosened, in reasonable comfort

should have the desired effect, but from observation we know that rest and quiet in a tense person do not necessarily lead to relaxation of tense muscles. Evidence of this is shown by the experience of many anxious people who wake up from sleep acutely aware of the painful or uncomfortable tensions in their muscles.

What is required is a system or procedure which will enable true and complete muscle relaxation to take place, in this way removing both the effect and cause of mental tension. Such a technique of relaxation has been devised and, if practised intelligently and diligently, can help that tense anxious person to a state of relative peace and calm. When a victim of tension learns for the first time that he can control his "nerves" by his own efforts, a wonderful improvement in morale takes place and there develops a new confidence that will enable him to cope successfully with situations which previously provoked stress and anxiety.

SYSTEMATIC RELAXATION

It is necessary for those who would practise relaxation therapy to understand the relationship between mind and muscle tension, and that, though there is nothing essentially difficult in the technique, it demands perseverance and courage. The tense person himself must effect the relief. He has got his muscles into a habit of tension and he himself must learn how to undo that tension.

Position

The relaxation technique is carried out with the person lying flat on his back.

A flat unyielding surface is best. A rug on the bedroom floor will suffice, though some may prefer to be on the bed. Any constricting clothes should be loosened and the shoes removed. A pillow should be placed under the head. The legs should rotate slightly outwards from the hips and the knees should be slightly bent. For greater comfort, a cushion may be placed under each knee. The arms should lie by the side and with the forearms so arranged that the hands lie with the palms touching the front of the thighs. This will cause a slight reflexion at the elbows and wrists, while the fingers will be flexed on the line

of the thighs. It is desirable that the student of relaxation should be reasonably comfortable, and once this position is achieved all wriggling and fidgeting should be deliberately suppressed.

Discovering Tensions

It is first necessary in the relaxation technique for you to be able to recognise muscle tension in the different muscles as opposed to actual muscle contraction. To do this you should first consciously contract the muscle groups of your body in succession, focusing your attention on the sensation which arises.

It is best to start with flexion and extension of the elbows and thence proceed to the other joints of the body. In this way you can learn to isolate the sense of contraction in the different muscle groups. This will require practice—as much as a quarter of an hour twice daily—for several days.

With this appreciation of the sensation of active muscle contraction, you should next endeavour to appreciate tension within these muscle groups without actually contracting the muscles. That is stage number two. Muscle groups are tensed without leading to joint movement until there is a clear recognition of the tense sensation in the separate muscles.

The purpose of all this is to ensure that *tension is recognisable*, for only then will it be possible to recognise the objective of relaxation, which is the *absence of muscle sensation*.

How to Relax

Assuming you have learned to know your muscle tensions, you can now proceed to the actual practice of relaxation. The first session is devoted to practising relaxation of the hands and forearms.

Place yourself in the position as described, then induce yourself to feel that your fingers and forearms are "quite limp," that they "feel heavy," that they are going "quite loose." If this mental attitude is persisted with, a stillness will come over the hands and forearms, and the muscles will feel soft. If you are successful, when someone lifts your forearm and lets it go, it will drop back limply by its own weight. Concentrate and persevere with both your hands and forearms until you are certain you have achieved relaxation. It will require much attention to begin with, but most people will be successful within 10–15 minutes, which should be the average duration of the session.

You then proceed to the other muscle groups, seeking relaxation in exactly the same way. Sessions must be devoted to the upper arm and shoulder girdle, the feet and lower legs, the upper legs (thighs) and hip region. Lastly should come the relaxation of the neck muscles, which may prove a little difficult, and the muscles of the face. Effort should also be made to relax the eyes by a conscious effort to "let them fall back in their sockets."

Practise Breathing

Coincidentally with the relaxation procedure, it is usual to practise breathing exercises. If at the start of your course you carry out deep breathing and observe it closely, you will most probably notice that it is irregular and a little jerky. You must therefore learn to breathe in a relaxed way. You must try to ensure that the air passes in and out of your lungs in a smooth way at a constant velocity, judged by the sound of the air intake and output.

The intensity of inspiration and expiration should be the same. Roughly four seconds should be

Even when sitting in a chair you can, with practice, produce a fair degree of relaxation, as Eileen Fowler, the B.B.C.'s television "Keep Fit" expert, proves here and on the following pages

taken for breathing in and breathing out and there should be no pause between. In this way a smooth rhythm of breathing will arise. It is therefore advised that each session of relaxation should begin and end with these breathing exercises and, in addition, during the session care should be taken to avoid any tendency to shallow, jerky breathing.

The objective of the relaxation technique is reached when you can produce complete generalised relaxation of all your muscles. Most people will do this by the successive steps which, with practice, follow each other rapidly. In other words, if you try to relax "yourself" nothing will happen, but if you relax hands, arms, shoulders, feet, legs and head muscles, one after the other, complete relaxation will arise.

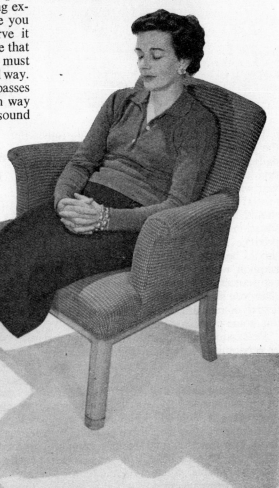

Getting the best out of life, whatever your age

To whittle your waistline: (left) sit forward, feet together, head and spine straight, shoulders back but not tensed. Then (above) swing right arm back and up, twisting from waist. Repeat, then swing left arm twice

It may take several weeks, carrying out the procedure for about 15 minutes twice daily, to be really accomplished in relaxation technique, but success will provide you with a most effective weapon against mental tension. Once you are skilled, you should be able to "turn on" relaxation in situations which you know are likely to produce mental tension. Moreover, you should be able to produce a degree of relaxation which is as complete as the circumstances permit. Even when sitting in a chair you should be able to produce a fair degree of relaxation, though to succeed in this, some practice is necessary.

Relaxation technique also teaches you to be economical in the use of your muscles. If you are carrying out some work which requires only one group of muscles, you will know not to involve other unnecessary groups of muscles, thus saving much nervous energy. You will know not to contract muscles other than those essential for the task in hand. Knowledge of relaxation technique can also be put to your service in employments which necessitate awkward and tiring postures.

WHAT YOU CAN EXPECT FROM RELAXATION THERAPY

As has been indicated, this method of treatment is based on the belief that with generalised relaxation of the muscles of the body no emotion can be experienced, and that the state of relaxation can be achieved by systematic training. Considerable practical experience has amply demonstrated that relaxation can ease most varieties of mental tension and anxiety, provided that the sufferers from tension states conscientiously apply the discipline which has been outlined here. Even in long-standing cases of nerve tension, improvement can be reasonably anticipated. But it is important to realise that success implies intelligent and sustained application of will directed towards the development of a special muscular ability. The victim of tension must understand what he is setting out to do and must be prepared to set aside time for this purpose.

A woman is only as old as her feet

Sitting tall and straight, body well back in a comfortable chair (left), raise legs with toes together, heels out. Then (below) put heels together and toes out. Repeat movements to loosen ankles and tone up thigh muscles

T.V. EXPERT EILEEN FOWLER SHOWS HOW

Those most likely to benefit from relaxation therapy are the tense, obsessional types, the people who set high standards, who drive themselves hard, who are conscientious, energetic, anxious for success and for the high esteem of their fellow creatures. They are the people described as "living on their nerves," and who are tense in all their human relationships. They often suffer from sleeplessness and headaches. Although valuable at all ages of life, relaxation therapy is often most successful with middle-aged people.

What may you expect when you have mastered the technique? It is reasonable to anticipate that you will be able generally to lower the mental tension of your emotional life and that you will have at hand a weapon to defeat an attack of tension precipitated by external events.

Secret of Self-confidence

You will know how to dissipate an acute fear and to maintain poise and self-control in a difficult situation. If your sleeplessness is a result of tension, you can educate yourself to sound sleep without the aid of narcotics. And if you can incorporate the technique into your daily life, you will gain in self-confidence, mental efficiency and happiness. In relaxation we have a key to nervous control, stability and peace of mind.

VANQUISH WORRY

The origin of the word "worry" is from the Middle English "worowen" which means "to strangle." That is a true indication of the meaning of the word, for in the toils of worry a human soul may be virtually strangled. Nothing can be more destructive to peace of mind, to mental efficiency and happiness than worry. None of us can aspire to go through life, with all its hazards, without an occasional worry, but there are many who, by *incessant* worry, make not only their own lives a burden but also those of all with whom they are in intimate contact.

Worrying is to be in a state of anxiety and apprehension concerning some particular problem. It is a form of emotional

Stretch and relax to tone up

Sit forward but straight, with both arms stretched slightly back and hands hanging downwards

Now swing forward and down, head to knees, feet together, and stretch hands as far forward on the floor as you possibly can

thinking and it is generally ineffectual in so far as it never helps to solve the prevailing difficulty. Kraines, an American psychiatrist, provides us with a good definition. "Worry is an emotional phenomenon wherein a problem is evaluated in the light of wishes and fears instead of objectively on the basis of facts as they are." In other words, instead of trying to *reason* out the difficulty, the worrying person thinks about it *emotionally,* thus magnifying the situation through the eyes of fear, distorting the issue and losing all sense of perspective. Even though the problem may sometimes be seen clearly enough, there is fretful over-concern about the solution.

The Worrying Child

Worrying people abound in the world to-day. Insecure personalities have a natural inclination to worry even over trifles. They are in a constant state of emotional distress, pouring out energy to no useful purpose; energy which ought to be used for the rational working out of the provoking situation. It is accepted that any one of us may find ourselves "up against it" when circumstances affect us adversely and we are consequently disturbed, but, in contrast to the chronic

"worrier," if we have stable and mature personalities we quickly overcome our anxiety and apply our energies to a calm and logical sorting-out of the situation.

Worrying easily becomes a habit and is a difficult one to eradicate. It may begin in childhood, sometimes as a result of worrying parents. Children are apt to absorb the emotional atmosphere of the home, and where there is apprehension and the worst is always feared and anticipated, such a pattern may be almost indelibly imprinted upon the children's minds. Such children often have difficulty in school and their educational attainment seldom reaches their intellectual capacity. Their school reports indicate that they "are capable of better work" and their relative failure is a matter of chagrin to both teachers and parents. Moreover, the worrying child is seldom a happy child: he meets troubles half-way and is for ever in a state of tension which makes his human relationships uneasy.

The worrying adult has nearly always been a worrying child, so the conquest of worry should start by prevention in childhood. Parents should realise how intuitive sensitive children are to the emotional background of the home. If they, the

tummy and back muscles

Watching posture carefully, sit up, elbows
bent, fists on shoulders, and pull shoulders
back slightly

Then stretch right up, arms apart, relax completely
and come back to starting position, doing the whole
exercise to count of four

parents, have emotional problems, they should endeavour to solve them by unemotional thinking and thus set a good example to their children. The child who sees its parents tackle a critical or disturbing situation in a calm, balanced and reasonable manner, is likely to adopt this pattern of behaviour for its own problems.

Sense of Insecurity

For the chronic worrier, nearly every event which requires a decision becomes a matter for worry and, when he has no immediate worries of his own, he takes on the troubles of his friends and acquaintances. Basically, in such a person there is a sense of insecurity and inferiority, and this must be overcome before he can learn to approach problems logically. Then the facts of the situation must be ascertained and elucidated as they really are and freed from associated fears. After that should come an analysis of the possible solutions.

Some lines of action may be more de-

sirable than others, but each should be dealt with as unemotionally as possible. The best solution should be decided upon with an understanding of its advantages and disadvantages, and, to avoid worry, this solution should be *accepted* until, if need be, a better one can be worked out.

The fact that a plan of action has been made and a decision arrived at will help to dissipate the feeling of worry and will add to self-confidence and stability. If this technique is practised, there will result a new and unemotional attitude of mind which will make possible a logical and reasoned approach to all difficulties and problems of life.

In the case of problems which do not demand an immediate solution, it is unwise to allow them to be constantly subject to analysis. Continuous thought will lead to "rut-formation" and possible solutions are missed because of an accustomed pattern of thinking. Non-urgent problems, therefore, should be deliberately excluded from the mind of the person inclined to worry until such time as an answer is really necessary.

It is important to remember that the course of action decided upon should be carried through, even though it may be unpleasant and arduous. Accept this attitude without emotion and it may be possible later to effect a happier result. It is always better to do what is planned than to drift aimlessly on a sea of indecision, which must inevitably engender worry. The mere making of a decision will usually lead to a cessation of emotional tension and stress.

Make Your Own Decisions

Most of us have experienced this, although, when we *are* in difficulties, we are apt to lose sight of it. It is also desirable that we should make this decision *ourselves*. It is a great temptation, especially in inadequate persons, to have someone else make up their minds for them. This must be resisted, for it tends to perpetuate

an unhealthy attitude of mind and hinders the cure of worry.

No matter how hard they may be, make your own decisions in life. Dependency on other people weakens the personality and destroys courage. Every decision in our lives that really affects our destiny must come from within ourselves.

Worrying people are always excessively preoccupied with themselves. Even their apparent worrying concern over other people may not be disinterested and indeed may really be a form of selfishness. Parents who constantly worry over the welfare of their children will hamper their children's lives. The deep motive for this may lie in an excessive possessiveness for the children's love.

There is one significant point to be noted concerning worry. It is useless to tell a person *not* to worry. No one consciously wants to worry. It is unpleasant and painful: it takes away the joy of life and results in second-best achievement. The person who worries must try to discover *why* he worries: he must discover the origin of his worrying disposition: he must learn to remove a bad habit by the substitution of a good habit. He must replace emotional thinking by reasoned thinking. He must learn to *accept* a certain amount of trouble in life as inevitable and he must avoid indecision at all costs. He must cultivate a cheerful philosophy, remembering that "the misfortunes hardest to bear are those which never come."

Finally, it should never be lost sight of that worry is lifeshortening. Many physical illnesses originate from worry. High blood pressure, peptic ulcer, spastic colitis, disordered action of the heart and certain skin affections are definitely related to the habit of worry. For the health of our minds and bodies, therefore, we must strive to subdue this insidiously destructive force.

The habit of worrying usually begins in childhood, when an atmosphere of apprehension is easily absorbed

CULTIVATING OUTSIDE INTERESTS WHEREVER YOU LIVE

Gone are the days when living in a remote village meant isolation from books, music or other pursuits

ANYONE who lives in a town, village or remote hamlet, or even in an isolated dwelling some miles from a post office, can always share *some* "outside" interest with other like-minded people.

Communications have expanded to such a degree in recent times that very few need be cut off from some means of access to a cultural centre. There is now so much facility for contact with interests and information through the written word, published or postal, and, of course, by radio and television, that in many cases choice of pursuit or hobby is the only problem.

Yet the readiest means by which people can get in touch with their favourite activities are not always known. This applies particularly to those who have changed their home or way of life, and so have time or desire for pursuits hitherto unknown to them.

"Culture" and "entertainment" are, in derivation and practice, interchangeably linked, and the history of the arts always includes "small beginnings." Outstanding examples of success, enjoyment and initiative can still be found among tiny, even isolated groups, which should prove encouraging to those unable to attach themselves to community enterprises.

The cultural arts, which include many subjects of homely and familiar appeal, can be classified in various ways, but categories must to some extent overlap. So also do the main institutions

which provide facilities for taking part in or enjoying them and which are, to many people, literally household words. None the less, their functions and helpfulness are not always as widely known as they might be, and we therefore summarise their special scope.

CHURCH

The Parish Church of your district, whether village or town, is, traditionally and actually, a centre of information about activities in the district. In a village this would apply in greater detail, and the vicar or rector is accustomed to enquiries from new residents, whether they belong to the established Church or not. Cultural groups —e.g. for Music or Drama connected with the church—are, of course, generally run by and for people who attend the church. This applies also to other denominational

Gramophone records as well as books may be borrowed from many public libraries for enjoyment at home

The library van takes books to outlying village libraries set up for a few hours a week in village halls, schools, etc., even sometimes in shops or private houses

churches, including Roman Catholic and Free Church (Methodist, Baptist and others). Ministers of religion are, however, ready to give information or help where possible to enquirers who wish to be put in touch with various means of pursuing their chosen interests.

LIBRARIES

Books are by far the greatest single factor in everyone's cultural life, and the Public Library provides a remarkable service of supply and also of information about various activities in the district. In a survey published for the British Council after the Second World War, Lionel R. McColvin, Honorary Secretary of the Library Association, said: "British readers probably borrow books much more than those of other countries, and a closer study of our magnificent library system clearly indicates that this tendency has been well catered for and fostered, through great foresight, pioneer work and constant new enterprise."

The story behind this network of libraries is in itself a fascinating one.

Until the eighteenth century all British libraries were associated chiefly with learning. Since then, with the growth of education, many different types of library have come into being, including centres for erudite study and research on highly specialised subjects, as well as flourishing circulating libraries which cater largely for those who want recreational books.

Through the complex trends and traditions has emerged the Public Library. All the functions which this institution performs throughout the U.K. can be summed up in a sentence from the survey mentioned above: "The public library is a universal opportunity, breaking down barriers . . . between any man or woman and the full enjoyment of the benefit of books. . . ."

Premises and stocks will vary from place to place, but a feature of the library system is that, whether you use a County Library (i.e. a Headquarters Library) or a Branch, large or small, the headquarters' supply is ultimately at the disposal of the individual borrower. At a Branch Library the request for a particular book is handed in, on a card provided, to your own local Librarian.

In villages where no permanent library exists, Library Centres have for many years proved a much valued service up and down the country. Books are brought

740

Most public libraries have special children's sections, where youngsters can sit down for a quiet read or borrow books to take home

Library. Notices of current activities are well in evidence in the building. Especially for newcomers to the district, a Library visit brings reassurance of many channels of communication and contact which are to be had, once the initial steps are taken.

If you cannot make a personal call, or want to obtain books before you are likely to have the opportunity of calling, write for information to the County Librarian at your County Library Headquarters (e.g. of your local county town).

For schoolchildren, information about all juvenile library facilities is, of course, obtained through the schools.

by van from the Headquarters Library—supplies being regularly exchanged and renewed—and distributed at the Centre (often the village hall or school) at given times by voluntary workers. This system is now being increasingly replaced by Travelling Libraries, in modern "coaches." The "halts" arranged by these mobile stores of books make it possible for people in hitherto remote villages to keep in personal touch with the bookshelves. A certain excitement and social interest is automatically provided—not unlike the atmosphere associated with the stage-coach—when the modern, streamlined van is due in the district.

How to get the Best from Your Library

Town dwellers, and those who visit town at intervals for shopping, should call in person and consult the Library staff, who are there to help and advise, as well as to "serve out" books.

The personal call gives opportunity for inspection of reading and reference rooms, which are now a normal part of the Public

THE WOMEN'S INSTITUTE

The W.I. has been a stronghold of the country-dwelling woman for many years. Its background and scope usually surprise any newcomer to rural life.

Following a lecture in 1897 by a Canadian farmer's wife on the valuable work being done by countrywomen, the movement came to England in 1915. Two years

One of the many activities of the Women's Institutes —a pottery course is well attended

later there were 137 Institutes, and the programme of development has since then resulted in similar organisations being set up all over the world. At the time of writing there are 8,180 W.I. centres in England, Wales and the Channel Isles alone.

The W.I. has taken in mining villages, small towns and "dormitory" suburbs. New Institutes are only formed in places with a population of 4,000 or under.

The aims of the W.I., though rooted in the needs of agriculture and food production, were soon widened to include all kinds of interests. In fact, these aims, summed up as being *"to improve and develop conditions of rural life,"* imply exactly that for the individual. She can offer and develop skill, not only in the domestic arts through the corporate and competitive activities at her local branch, but also find opportunities for taking part in, or helping to initiate, activities such as handwork, music, folk dancing, drama, and all forms of debate and discussion. Outstanding national events, organised by the National Federation of Women's Institutes with representation from all over the country, illustrate the high standard attained, which is the goal of every branch.

Programmes for each season's activities are planned to keep a balance between members' preferences. Fresh talent and ideas are constantly welcomed.

This "working for the common good" has ensured friendship and companionship for women of all ages, classes, parties, creeds and conditions in country life.

It is unlikely that any woman will fail to find some opportunity for expression or development of talent through the contacts and facilities which membership of the W.I. provides.

The address of the W.I. in any area, or that of the local secretary, can be ascertained from the post office, church or school—and probably from any shop or resident as well.

TOWNSWOMEN'S GUILD

In places where the population is over 4,000, the counterpart of the Women's Institute is the now well-established and enterprising organisation known as the Townswomen's Guild.

The aims of the Guild, with special applications to town life and citizenship, are similar to those of the W.I., and again the range of cultural interests is wide. In 1929 the women who organised the first five guilds for the study of citizenship saw that giving women the right to vote was not an end in itself. Much has been accomplished since then—successful fostering of skill and talent in all the arts is demonstrated by pageants, conferences and exhibitions of arts and crafts on a national scale.

Although the dweller in even a small town has easier access to opportunity for culture and entertainment than has her country friend, it is yet evident that the personal and friendly atmosphere created in all T.G. branches provides the sort of *entrée* particularly valued by the woman whose life and work keeps her largely at home. Membership of the T.G. also flourishes among young unmarried women at many local branches.

The same non-party, non-sectarian basis of membership applies as in the case of the W.I.

Information about headquarters address in a district will almost certainly be supplied through any of the normal channels of enquiry—e.g. post office, parish church, school or telephone directory. Where there is uncertainty about the most convenient Guild centre, as in the case of people intending to take up residence in a new town, enquiries may be sent to the National Union of Townswomen's Guilds, 2, Cromwell Place, South Kensington, London, S.W.7.

THE NATIONAL BOOK LEAGUE

The League, "for all who care for books and the life of the mind," is more than nation-wide, as is the love of a good book. The N.B.L., which dates from 1946, recognised the claim of the *reader*, as distinct from the writer, publisher or bookseller, to an association of prestige. It has many overseas members, and countless publications from abroad are included in its exhibitions.

The League covers a wide field of activity connected with books. There are "children's book weeks," and exhibitions which go to schools, factories and local

There is a longing in many people to express themselves through drama, and the Women's Institutes run play readings and dramatic performances both indoors and out. Above, a course in drama for mixed teams at Denman College

Gardening is a subject many women long to study seriously and, by doing so, they sometimes discover that they have natural "green fingers"

libraries everywhere. Examples of notable men who have given N.B.L. lectures to big audiences at the London Headquarters are the late Archbishop of Canterbury, Dr. William Temple; the Poet Laureate, John Masefield; Bertrand Russell; Viscount Samuel and Somerset Maugham, Discussion groups, too, are well attended.

. Membership is by subscription only, and members visiting London for the day find the League's Headquarters at 7, Albemarle Street, near Piccadilly, a most congenial *rendezvous*. There are reading and writing rooms, a first-class library (of books *about* books), usually an exhibition to view, as well as a restaurant and bar. The Headquarters, in fact, provides the accommodation of a club in the heart of the West End. All members are kept in touch with news of books and authors through the monthly magazine.

ENGLISH-SPEAKING UNION

(Headquarters address: Dartmouth House, Charles Street, Berkeley Square, London, W.1)
and

OVERSEAS LEAGUE

(Over-Seas House, St. James's, London, S.W.1)

Both these organisations, which are widely established throughout the Commonwealth and Empire, have as their broad objective the fostering of friendship and common interests between English-speaking people of the homeland and of Commonwealth countries. Members visiting the U.K. from overseas are given welcome and splendid facilities for entering into the life of the country during their stay.

The Headquarters offices will supply attractive literature, information about subscriptions, terms of membership, etc., and also details about provincial centres which exist in various towns. All branches of the arts, as well as discussion groups in great variety, are actively pursued at the London Headquarters and also at provincial centres according to local facilities and support. Those who are interested in making contact with either of these two institutions, but who are not within reach of a branch or who do not wish to pay the full subscription, may join as Associate members. Full details will be supplied on application to the Secretaries at the London Headquarters addresses given above.

UNIVERSITY

For those living in or near a town which has a University or University College,

A section of one of the many international book exhibitions frequently held at the London headquarters of the National Book League, which caters for "all who care for books"

Technical Colleges provide evening courses of study in all sorts of subjects, for young people and adults working during the daytime. Modern equipment and methods are here seen in a wood-working class at Cardiff Technical College

facilities are available for "Extension" lectures organised outside the academic courses for internal students. These lectures, given by professors and tutors of the University, include "occasional" events, as well as planned series, and subjects may cover the Arts, History and Languages. Full details will be supplied on application to the Registrar's Office at the address of the University.

SCHOOLS

Many schools, both Grammar and Primary, especially in small places, provide opportunities for entertainment and activity to local people other than pupils and parents. This is widely appreciated where a flourishing Grammar School exists in a town of otherwise limited "cultural" opportunities, or where the population has grown rapidly through industry and largely consists of residents who have not the time or experience to organise cultural groups. In any case, Heads or Secretaries of such schools are likely to be well informed on other existing activities or those in neighbouring places.

Through the School also can be obtained

information about local arrangements for Evening Classes.

CORRESPONDENCE COURSES

Details are available in some cases from University or Public Library. Also advertising pages of many magazines and newspapers.

THE ARTS COUNCIL OF GREAT BRITAIN

The Council was set up by the Government in 1946 to develop "a greater knowledge, understanding and practice of the fine arts exclusively, and in particular to increase the accessibility of the fine arts to the public."

The function of this body for the individual enquirer is likely to be that of supplying information or advice about the founding or continuance of local artistic groups. There are many regional offices throughout the country.

The arts, although they are now attracting far bigger audiences than ever before, cannot catch up with present-day rising costs of production. Many of the national institutions for music and drama in the U.K. would have to close down without the public money invested annually by the Arts Council and Local Authorities. There would be no Covent Garden, Sadler's Wells and Old Vic, and the Hallé and London Philharmonic as well as many other outstanding orchestras would all have to disperse if there were no subsidies.

Although theoretically the Council concerns itself with the whole field of fine arts, in practice activity is limited to music, opera, ballet, drama, poetry, painting and sculpture. Working in conjunction with existing bodies to promote the arts, the Council is also prepared to supply a local need, even if no organisation exists. Even a modest music society in a tiny hamlet which receives a grant from the Council is wholly self-governing in its affairs.

Enquiries should be addressed to Arts Council Headquarters, 4, St. James's Square, London, S.W.1.

PICTURE LENDING LIBRARY

Looking at works of art can greatly enrich life.

Visits by individuals or groups to art galleries in London and the provinces are common enough, and group visits can often be arranged, where demand is sufficient, through such organisations as those already described.

Less known is the enterprising plan which now flourishes through the A.I.A. (Artists International Association), whereby pictures by outstanding modern artists can be enjoyed at leisure in one's own home. The private citizen who is interested in pictorial art, and wants to develop taste —and particularly to keep in touch with contemporary developments—can now get first-hand experience of "living with" works of art. The A.I.A. have made it possible to hire pictures from their "Library," a scheme worth following by other groups of artists.

The usual, and best, first step, of course, is to make contact with the A.I.A. Gallery on a personal visit to London, where a permanent exhibition is open to visitors from 11–6 daily, including Saturdays, at 15, Lisle Street, Leicester Square, London, W.C.2.

Three of the modern pictures available on hire through the A.I.A., specially photographed in home settings by John Lockie. Above is a painting by Prunella Clough

A visitor who decides to join the "Library" pays an annual subscription of £1 1s., and is then entitled to "take out" as many pictures as desired for a monthly hiring fee of from 5s. to 7s. 6d. per picture. If, as often happens, the borrower decides finally to buy the picture, hiring fees are deducted from the purchase price.

Reduced rates are made available to schools, hospitals, colleges and institutions. Transport is arranged to any part of the British Isles, and charges for packing and carriage are not likely to exceed 15s. per parcel. More than one picture can sometimes be included in a parcel.

Those who are interested in this service, but are unable to visit the A.I.A. Gallery in London, can send for a list of the artists whose work is available for hire and make arrangements by post. In this case, a borrower may enjoy the element of surprise in choosing a "new" picture.

Travelling Exhibitions are also arranged by the A.I.A. Costs vary according to size of exhibitions, distance, etc. Full details are available from the Gallery. Notice of impending exhibitions in any district is usually posted in the Public Library or Town Hall, or both.

Modern art fits in very happily with period furniture—the painting shown here is by Christopher Hall, from the enterprising A.I.A. loan scheme

Fred Uhlman's fine painting, seen in the home of an art lover who belongs to A.I.A. and hires her pictures for a few shillings a month

HANDY INDEX TO YOUR SPECIAL INTERESTS

and appropriate contacts for local information

Most of these local organisations give information about each other.

The local papers are invaluable sources of general information, both through reported events and advertising columns.

Art (visual) drawing, painting, sculpture:
Town: Public Library, Technical School, Townswomen's Guild.
Village: School, Women's Institute, Post Office.

Books

Town or Village: Public Library, by personal or postal enquiry (see Libraries; National Book League).

Choir

Town or Village: For church choir, Vicar or Minister of your own place of worship (see Music).

Church

For all specifically religious interests, contact clergy or minister of place of worship chosen, or any official of parochial groups or Church Council. (Names are given in the parish magazine in the case of Church of England.)

Dancing

For all types of dancing with cultural or historical interest—
Town: Enquiries through Library, Town Hall (often same building), Townswomen's Guild.
Village: Women's Institute, Library.

Drama

Town: Public Library. In all cases the Public Library is usually the most convenient channel for information about *study* of the subject, as well as about local facilities for active pursuit, by beginners or others.

Education (Adult, Evening Classes, etc.): Enquiries through Public Library, School, University, Technical College.

Entertainment

Town: Local Paper, Public Library, Townswomen's Guild.

Village: Local Paper, Women's Institute.

Friendship

Opportunities of meeting people of similar general interests, without pursuit of particular study or hobby: Enquiries through local church, Women's Institute or Townswomen's Guild.

Gardening

Town: Public Library, Local Paper (news of horticultural shows, etc.), Townswomen's Guild.

Village: Women's Institute, Local Paper.

Handicrafts

Town (Exhibitions and Study): Public Library, Technical School or School of Art, Townswomen's Guild.

Village: School or Women's Institute (see also Needlework).

History

General (see Education)

Local: Enquiries through local vicar or rector of parish church; Local Museum.

Industry

Study of local or general: Public Library, Women's Institute or Townswomen's Guild.

Journalism

For immediate contact: Local Paper. Study: Public Library (see Education).

Languages

Town: Public Library, School or University. Advertised language tuition in papers of high standing.

Village: Library, Women's Institute, private advertisement in Local Papers (tuition), Correspondence Course. Broadcast lessons in (U.K. see *Radio Times*). Linguaphone Language Institute, 209, Regent Street, London, W.1, for information about tuition by gramophone records.

Music

Town: Public Library, Local Paper (especially for private tuition), Arts Council of Great Britain, Townswomen's Guild. (Orchestral, choral or solo—see Church.)

Village: School, Women's Institute, Local Paper (see above; see Church).

Natural History, Nature Study

General or *local:* Public Library, School, Townswomen's Guild or Women's Institute. Also any local Museum (this is often situated at the Public Library building).

Needlework

Exhibition and Study: Public Library. Practical (see Education), also Townswomen's Guild or Women's Institute. Church Needlework groups for embroidery or practical needlework are common (see Handicrafts).

Sport and all forms of Exercise (indoor and out)

For advice and information about local arrangements or for specialised kinds of holidays (sailing, pony trekking or ski-ing, for instance), consult the Central Council of Physical Recreation, 6, Bedford Square, London, W.C.1.

Travel

Study: Public Library (see also Education), Townswomen's Guild or Women's Institute. Contact with Commonwealth countries (see English-speaking Union and Overseas League). See also Sport.

Tuition

In individual subjects, giving or receiving: advertising in Local Papers, and special publications (e.g. Church Magazines, etc.). Also contact through Townswomen's Guild or Women's Institute.

Youth Work

Particularly for older women, or those of any age who are interested in contact with the young, Club Leadership, etc. Enquiries through Townswomen's Guild or Women's Institute, or from Headquarters of National Association of Girls' Clubs and Mixed Clubs, 32, Devonshire Street, London, W.1. Information will be supplied of all clubs affiliated to the Association in the enquirer's district, and also of scope and conditions for formation of others. Cultural activities of all kinds can be taught or pursued through Youth Clubs.

ARRANGEMENTS FOR FUNERALS

*When bereavement comes to a family, it is helpful
to know what procedure must be followed*

BEREAVEMENT comes at some time to every family, and at a time of sorrow practical problems can be avoided if one knows the usual procedure when a death has taken place.

The first person to be contacted is the doctor, who will issue a death certificate and will usually put the family in touch with someone who can lay out the deceased.

The death certificate must be taken or sent at once to the Registrar of Births, Deaths and Marriages *in the district in which the person has died,* together with his/her Medical Card and Old Age Pension Card, if any, which must be surrendered. The Registrar will then issue a Disposal Certificate. This is absolutely essential, as no burial or cremation can take place without it. It is eventually signed by the officiating clergyman or any other person conducting the burial or cremation ceremony. If a claim is being made for a Death Grant under the Ministry of Pensions and National Insurance, the registrar will issue a special Death Certificate free of charge, which must be handed in to the local National Insurance office when application is made.

Functions of the Undertaker

The Disposal Certificate is now handed to the Undertaker, who can be said to be a true friend of the family. From then onwards he will take charge completely and relieve the relatives of those duties which, at a time of sorrow, are irksome and distasteful.

When the undertaker arrives he will, if the doctor has not been able to suggest a person to do the laying-out, arrange for someone to attend, or do it himself. The relatives inform him as to the deceased's religion, the type of coffin and the number of cars needed, whether a memorial or tombstone is required, and other details. He will help them to apply for, and fill in, any National Insurance forms; make the necessary arrangements with the minister or priest as to the time of the funeral and all other relevant matters; will attend to cemetery fees and those payable to the minister, the verger and the grave-diggers. If a choral service is desired, he will, if requested, arrange with organist and choir. Cemetery fees are payable to the local Council, who in turn pay the minister, but the undertaker's account will include them all.

If the deceased is to be buried in another district—say, in a family grave or vault—the undertaker will get in touch with a colleague in that district and make all the necessary arrangements for transport and reception, obtaining permission from the Council (if a cemetery) or the church incumbent (if a churchyard) for a family grave or vault to be opened.

It used to be "law" that anyone dying of an infectious disease had to be buried or removed to the mortuary within forty-eight hours of death, but with the advance of medical science this is no longer considered necessary. However, in these days of small houses and flats, a body is seldom laid out at home, but is more often taken to the undertaker's mortuary chapel to await burial or cremation. Here everything is conducted with the utmost reverence and good taste.

A list of flowers and messages received is made out and handed to the relatives later for acknowledgment and thanks. Flowers after a cremation are often de-wired and sent to a hospital, especially if the deceased died there.

Funeral fees vary, but an average sum for a lined coffin, with brass handles and name-plate, pillow and shroud, hearse and one car, would be about £28. Many undertakers include embalming without extra cost; where this is not so, embalming would add about 5 gns. to the basic cost. These figures, of course, do not include cemetery, minister's, verger's and grave-digger's fees, and memorial costs.

It may happen that someone with no next-of-kin dies in a boarding-house or lodging-house. Even in such a case, the undertaker will help the householder over the difficulty, making the necessary contacts with the Council or other authorities if the person in question has left no instructions for burial. The householder must first get promptly in touch with a doctor.

Burial Services

In the normal way the incumbent of the parish to which the deceased belonged takes the burial service, unless there is a friend or relative of the family in Holy Orders whom they wish to officiate.

The night before a Roman Catholic or Anglo-Catholic burial, the body is taken to the church and received by the parish priest. It lies before the altar on a cata-falque surrounded by lighted candles. The Requiem Mass precedes the burial.

Free Church funerals are conducted according to the rites of the individual Church involved.

For people of Jewish race and faith, the normal procedure at a death would be to contact at once the special Burial Society usually connected with a Synagogue—the Rabbi of a Synagogue is, as a rule, attached to such a society. Essentially similar procedure is followed for the different groups of practising Jews, though the actual ceremony or service may vary to some degree.

In the rare event of a Jew having to be placed in a Christian mortuary chapel, awaiting burial, the Cross or Crucifix is removed from the wall. Women do not attend Jewish burials.

Where the deceased is explicitly said to be of no religion, the undertaker has been known to conduct the burial.

Cremation

To-day, something like three in five people are cremated rather than buried. Roman Catholics, by the laws of their religion, may not be cremated except in times of war or plague, or in other exceptional circumstances, when special permission has to be obtained from the Church authorities.

The Church of England Cremation Service is the same as the burial service, except for the substitution of the words "consigned to the flames." There are also non-denominational forms of cremation service.

The undertaker makes all arrangements for a cremation, as for a burial, in whichever crematorium is chosen. Ashes can be scattered, buried, placed in an urn and housed in a memorial building in the Garden of Remembrance, or retained by the relatives to dispose of as they wish.

Before arrangements for cremation can be made, the death certificate must be signed by two doctors, who do not work in partnership. Where death is the result of an accident *of any kind*, the Coroner's certificate is sufficient and an additional doctor's signature is not required.

Death Grants

The person responsible for meeting funeral costs in the U.K. should apply to the local Ministry of Pensions and National Insurance office. The registrar or undertaker will always help in this respect.

Providing the contribution conditions are satisfied, grants are paid in respect of:

The death certificate issued by the doctor must be taken or sent to the Registrar of Births, Marriages and Deaths. Right, a simple printed card may be sent in acknowledgment of flowers and letters of sympathy received

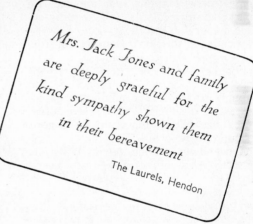

Mrs. Jack Jones and family are deeply grateful for the kind sympathy shown them in their bereavement

The Laurels, Hendon

1 (*a*) A man of eighteen or over (unless born before 5th July, 1893) £25
  (*b*) A woman of eighteen or over (unless born before 5th July, 1898) £25
2 (*a*) A man born between 5th July, 1883, and 5th July, 1893 £12 10*s.*
  (*b*) A woman born between 5th July, 1888 and 5th July, 1898 £12 10*s.*
(No grant is payable for a man born before 5th July, 1883, or a woman born before 5th July, 1888. The reason for this is that they will not have paid in any contributions; in the same way, those classified as 2 (*a*) and (*b*), above, are entitled to a lesser grant because they have not been paying contributions for so long a time.)

Up to the age of eighteen the following grants are payable:

3 Under 3 years £7 10*s.*
   3 to 5 years (inclusive) £12 10*s.*
   6 to 17 years (inclusive) £18 15*s.*

No grant is paid for a still-born baby.

Full details of contribution conditions and procedure can be seen in a leaflet issued by the Ministry of National Insurance, No. N.I.49.

Exhumation

If, for any reason, a disinterment is necessary, permission must first be given by the Home Office. Here again, the undertaker will help to put the right machinery in motion, and conduct the exhumation. When permission has been granted, the body must be exhumed between sunset and sunrise, with the grave decently screened. A coffin, six inches larger all round than the one to be disinterred (the intervening space to be filled with charcoal), must be in readiness to receive the exhumed coffin.

Headstones and Memorials

These can, of course, be ordered independently from the stonemason, but it saves much trouble if the undertaker is asked to arrange for them, under instructions. He has all the necessary contacts and it will cost no more. A fee is due to the local Council for all lettering on tombstones in cemeteries.

Legalities

The laws governing inheritance are so complicated that no layman can hope to deal with them without the help of a lawyer, and the fees payable usually represent money well spent (see also chapter on the Law and Your Home). People with incomes below a certain sum who feel unable to afford regular lawyer's fees can engage the services of a Poor Man's Lawyer. Particulars of this service can be had from any Citizens' Advice Bureau.

For the sake of one's heirs, the importance of making a Will cannot be too strongly stressed. The administration of the estate is simpler and far less costly. When the will is drawn up by a good solicitor, there is little possibility of misunderstandings arising later. Wills are perfectly legal, provided they are signed *at the same time by two witnesses who are not beneficiaries in each other's presence and in the presence of the testator,* but what may appear to him a simple statement of fact can often make endless trouble for his heirs because it is capable of different interpretations; whereas a solicitor knows the correct phraseology and the many pitfalls to be avoided.

A will can be revoked only by

(*a*) destruction;

(*b*) the making of another will revoking the earlier one.

When a person dies having left a properly made will, this must be handed at once to the executor, who should instruct his solicitor to extract a Grant of Probate. If the executor is the next-of-kin, say the widow, the solicitor will want to know about all the deceased's assets, will prepare a statement for the Inland Revenue officials and help her to administer the property.

If the named executor has died since the will was made, the next-of-kin should apply for Letters of Administration, attaching the will to the application, and will be required to take an oath that he/she will administer the estate in accordance with the law.

It is sometimes felt that, to avoid family disagreements after death, it is better when making a will not to name a relative as executor. In this case one can approach the Public Trustee or a bank, who will act impartially in this capacity. The office of the Public Trustee is non-profit-making and the only charges incurred will be costs.

Should a person die intestate, the next-of-kin should apply for letters of administration, as above. If the deceased has children living, the widow (or widower) can claim all personal chattels and up to £5,000, duty and costs paid, with interest at 4 per cent. until the sum is paid over. The children take half the residue and the other half comes to them after the death of the remaining partner.

When there are no children living, widow (or widower) can take up to £20,000, duty and costs paid, and as above.

Where there are collateral and other blood relations, adjustments are made.

Death Duties

Death duties are levied on all estates of £3,000 and over, with a sliding scale of taxation which increases in proportion to the greater sum involved, so that an estate of £1,000,000 would be taxed at the rate of 80 per cent.

A widow who resides for two years after her husband's death in the house left to her will have the property taxed for death duties at a lower rate. In consideration of any housing shortage that may obtain at the time and consequent inflated property prices, for the purposes of taxation an Extra Statutory Concession may be granted, reducing the dutiable value of the house. This also applies to next-of-kin other than widows. Certain adjustments are made at times if the widow or next-of-kin wishes to move to a smaller house, but the solicitor should be consulted about this before definite steps are taken.

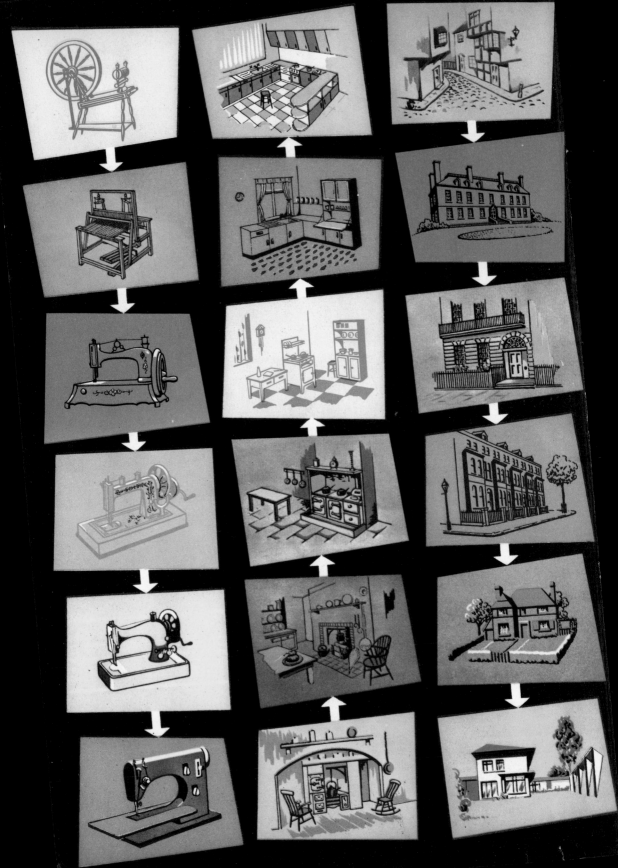